March 19–21, 2018
Tempe, AZ, USA

Association for Computing Machinery

Advancing Computing as a Science & Profession

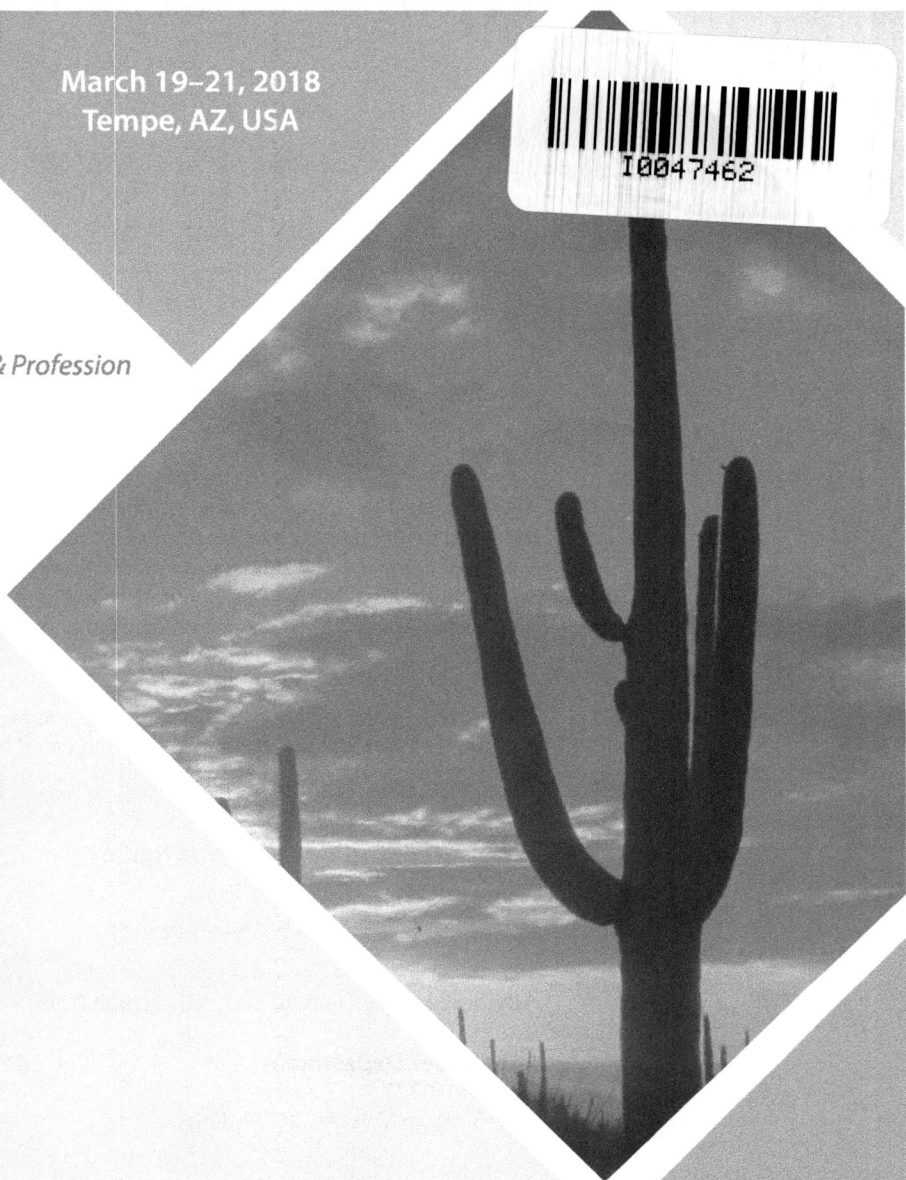

I0047462

CODASPY'18

Proceedings of the Eighth ACM Conference on

Data and Application Security and Privacy

Sponsored by:

ACM SIGSAC

Supported by:

Arizona State University, Cybersecurity & Digital Forensics, PayPal, Samsung, and Allstate

Association for Computing Machinery

The Association for Computing Machinery
2 Penn Plaza, Suite 701
New York, New York 10121-0701

Advancing Computing as a Science & Profession

ISBN: 978-1-4503-5632-9 (Digital)

ISBN: 978-1-4503-5879-8 (Print)

Additional copies may be ordered prepaid from:

ACM Order Department
PO Box 30777
New York, NY 10087-0777, USA

Phone: 1-800-342-6626 (USA and Canada)
+1-212-626-0500 (Global)
Fax: +1-212-944-1318
E-mail: acmhelp@acm.org
Hours of Operation: 8:30 am – 4:30 pm ET

Foreword

It is our great pleasure to welcome you to the eighth edition of the ACM Conference on Data and Application Security and Privacy (CODASPY 2018), which follows the successful seven editions held in February/March 2011-2017. This conference series has been founded to foster novel and exciting research in this arena and to help generate new directions for further research and development. The initial concept was established by the two co-founders, Elisa Bertino and Ravi Sandhu, and sharpened by subsequent discussions with a number of fellow cyber security researchers. Their enthusiastic encouragement persuaded the co-founders to move ahead with the always daunting task of creating a high-quality conference.

Data and applications that manipulate data are crucial assets in today's information age. With the increasing drive towards availability of data and services anytime and anywhere, security and privacy risks have increased. Vast amounts of privacy-sensitive data are being collected today by organizations for a variety of reasons. Unauthorized disclosure, modification, usage or denial of access to these data and corresponding services may result in high human and financial costs. New applications such as social networking and social computing provide value by aggregating input from numerous individual users and the mobile devices they carry. The emerging area of Internet of Things also poses serious privacy and security challenges. To achieve efficiency and effectiveness in traditional domains such as healthcare, there is a drive to make these records electronic and highly available. The need for organizations to share information effectively is underscored by rapid innovations in the business world that require close collaboration across traditional boundaries. Security and privacy in these and other arenas can be meaningfully achieved only in context of the application domain. Data and applications security and privacy has rapidly expanded as a research field with many important challenges to be addressed.

In response to the call for papers of CODASPY 2018, 110 papers were submitted from Africa, Asia, Australia, Europe and North America. The program committee selected 23 full-length research papers (20.9% acceptance rate). These papers cover a variety of topics, including security issues in web, cloud, IoT, and mobile devices, privacy, access control, authentication, malware, code analysis, and hardware and system security. The program committee also selected 12 short papers for presentation. The program includes a poster paper session presenting exciting work in progress. The program is complemented by three keynote speeches by Christian Collberg, Ninghui Li and Brad Wardman. This year's edition also features three workshops: the International Workshop on Security and Privacy Analytics, the ACM International Workshop on Security in Software Defined Networks & Network Function Virtualization, and the ACM Workshop on Attribute-Based Access Control.

The organization of a conference like CODASPY requires the collaboration of many individuals. First of all, we would like to thank the authors for submitting to the conference and the keynote speakers for graciously accepting our invitation. We express our gratitude to the program committee members and external reviewers for their efforts in reviewing the papers, engaging in active online discussion during the selection process and providing valuable feedback to authors. We also would like to thank Yuan Cheng (web and publicity chair), Adam Doupé (workshop chair), Aimee Hill (local arrangement chair), Hongxin Hu (poster chair) and the committee of the poster track, and Carlos Rubio-Medrano (proceedings chair). Finally, we would like to thank our sponsor, ACM SIGSAC, for supporting this conference.

We hope that you will find this program interesting and that the conference will provide you with a valuable opportunity to interact with other researchers and practitioners from institutions around the world. Enjoy!

Ram Krishnan
CODASPY'18 Program Co-Chair
Univ of Texas at San Antonio, USA

Gabriel Ghinita
CODASPY'18 Program Co-Chair
Univ of Massachusetts Boston, USA

Ziming Zhao
CODASPY'18 General Co-Chair
Arizona State University, USA

Gail-Joon Ahn
CODASPY'18 General Co-Chair
Arizona State University, USA
Samsung Research, Korea

Table of Contents

Session: Attacks I (Vulnerability Analysis/Malware)

Session Chair: Hoda Mehrpouyan *(Boise State University)*

Reception and Posters

Session Chair: Hongxin Hu *(Clemson University)*

Keynote Address II

Session Chair: Ziming Zhao *(Arizona State University)*

Session: Access Control and Authentication

Session Chair: Mohamed Nabeel (*Qatar Computing Research Institute*)

Session: Virtualization/System Security

Session Chair: Hongxin Hu (*Clemson University*)

Session: Mobile Security

Session Chair: Anna Cinzia Squicciarini (*Pennsylvania State University*)

Session: Attacks II (Networks)
Session Chair: Xiruo Liu *(Intel Labs)*

Session: Web Security
Session Chair: Luca Allodi *(Eindhoven University of Technology)*

Session: Code Analysis
Session Chair: Samira Briongos *(Universidad Politécnica de Madrid)*

CODASPY 2018 Conference Organization

General Co-Chairs: Ziming Zhao *(Arizona State University, USA)*
Gail-Joon Ahn *(Arizona State University, USA & Samsung Research, Korea)*

Program Co-Chairs: Ram Krishnan *(University of Texas at San Antonio, USA)*
Gabriel Ghinita *(University of Massachusetts Boston, USA)*

Proceedings Chair: Carlos Rubio-Medrano *(Arizona State University, USA)*

Local Arrangements Chair: Aimee Hill *(Arizona State University, USA)*

Publicity and Web Chair: Yuan Cheng *(California State University, Sacramento, USA)*

Poster Chair: Hongxin Hu *(Clemson University, USA)*

Workshop Chair: Adam Doupé *(Arizona State University, USA)*

Steering Committee Co-Chairs: Elisa Bertino *(Purdue University, USA)*
Ravi Sandhu *(University of Texas at San Antonio, USA)*

Steering Committee: Gail-Joon Ahn *(Arizona State University, USA & Samsung Research, Korea)*
Elisa Bertino *(Purdue University, USA)*
Alexander Pretschner *(Technische Universität München, Germany)*
Ravi Sandhu *(University of Texas at San Antonio, USA)*

Program Committee: Gail-Joon Ahn *(Arizona State University, USA & Samsung Research, Korea)*
Vijay Atluri *(Rutgers University, USA)*
Elisa Bertino *(Purdue University, USA)*
Barbara Carminati *(University of Insubria, Italy)*
Lorenzo Cavallaro *(Royal Holloway, University of London, UK)*
Yuan Cheng *(California State University, Sacramento, USA)*
Naranker Dulay *(Imperial College London, UK)*
Manuel Egele *(Boston University, USA)*
Elena Ferrari *(University of Insubria, Italy)*
Philip Fong *(University of Calgary, Canada)*
Debin Gao *(Singapore Management University, Singapore)*
Hannes Hartenstein *(KIT, Germany)*
Hongxin Hu *(Clemson University, USA)*
Christian Jensen *(Technical University of Denmark, Denmark)*
Martin Johns *(SAP Research, Germany)*
Murat Kantarcioglu *(University of Texas at Dallas, USA)*
Alexandros Kapravelos *(North Carolina State University, USA)*

Additional reviewers:

Nazmiye Abay
Mohsen Ahmadvand
Irfan Ahmed
Aisha Ali-Gombe
Imrul Anindya
Aref Asvadishirehjini
Rudraprasad Baksi
Alexandre Bartel
Vibha Belavadi
Dominik Breitenbacher
Thang Bui
Sze Yiu Chau
Pietro Colombo
Changyu Dong
Eyasu Getahun
Giacomo Giorgi
Jan Grashöfer
Juan David Guarnizo
Hasini Gunasinghe
Kyle Haefner
Martin Haerterich
Behnaz Hassanshahi
Médéric Hurier
Sufatrio Syed Hussain
Thomas Hutzelmann
Daoyuan Li
Hongda Li
Li Li
Kui Liu
Shane McCulley
Shagufta Mehnaz

Francesco Mercaldo
Joern Mueller-Quade
Subhojeet Mukherjee
Dieudonne Mulamba
Marius Musch
Saahil Ognawala
Oyindamola Oluwatimi
Yi Qin
Chenxi Qiu
Fang-Yu Rao
Jérémy Robert
Gokhan Sagirlar
Aleieldin Salem
Andrew Santosa
Andrea Saracino
Prateek Saxena
Fahad Shaon
Mina Sheikhalishahi
Oliver Stengele
Lianshan Sun
Yan Sun
Kushagra Tiwary
Flavio Toffalini
Junao Wang
Xueou Wang
Weng-Fai Wong
Zhiju Yang
Dongsheng Zhang
Qingji Zheng
Husheng Zhou

CODASPY 2018 Sponsor & Supporters

Sponsors:

Supporters:

Managing the Crossroads of Academia and Industry

Brad Wardman
PayPal, Inc.
Scottsdale, AZ

ABSTRACT

The transition between academic research and joining the industry workforce is often met with uncertainty, doubt, and changes in perspectives. Things that seem important while taking courses, reading through the literature, or getting captivated in a research topic can quickly change when starting to work in the industry. It takes many recent college graduates more time than expected to acclimate during their transition to the industry. This presentation will provide deeper insights into what to expect during the transition into industry, an overview of attacks the industry battles day-to-day, the importance of collaboration, details around why communication skills are a necessity, and methods for continuing to be a successful researcher as a security practitioner.

In optimal situations, industry and academia partner together to address difficult to solve problems with innovative solutions. However, there is sometimes a disconnect between academia and the industry. Industry often has lofty expectations of joint research projects with academia but often provide poorly defined data sets for those projects. On the other hand, academia can struggle with their industry partners because the industry researchers lack time and struggle to properly scope problems. These differences can often cause projects to not get funded or lose focus and fade away. Despite this, successful collaborations between industry and academia surface every so often in the literature. Such work is often highly successful because of the precision and drive that academic researchers offer being complemented by the industry's real world data sets and the breadth and depth of knowledge around specific issues. The presentation will provide the audience with successful project use cases that PayPal's Information Security team has accomplished through internships and funding university projects.

CCS Concepts/ACM Classifiers

- Security and privacy → Social engineering attacks
- Security and privacy → Systems security
- Computing / technology policy → Computer crime

Author Keywords

Cybercrime investigations, phishing, open source intelligence (OSINT)

BIOGRAPHY

Brad Wardman is the Head of Threat Intelligence at PayPal. Brad sits on the Board of Directors for the Anti-Phishing Working Group (or APWG) and serves as the general chairman of the Symposium on Electronic Crime Research (eCrime). Brad is deeply versed in detecting, tracking, and fighting cybercrime, with a publication record that has pioneered ground-breaking discussions on cybercrime detection and mitigation. Brad is an active inventor and researcher having 9 issued security patents to the US Patent Office, 15 additional patents pending filed an additional 15 patents, and is an author on 18 peer reviewed conference and journal publications. Dr. Wardman completed his PhD in Computer Science from the University of Alabama at Birmingham (UAB) studying in the Computer Forensics Research Lab under mentor Gary Warner.

CODASPY'18, March 19–21, 2018, Tempe, AZ, USA.
© 2018 Copyright is held by the owner/author(s).
ACM ISBN 978-1-4503-5632-9/18/03.
DOI: http://dx.doi.org/10.1145/3176258.3175505

Minimizing Privilege Assignment Errors in Cloud Services

Matthew W Sanders
Colorado School of Mines, Golden, CO
mwsanders@mines.edu

Chuan Yue
Colorado School of Mines, Golden, CO
chuanyue@mines.edu

ABSTRACT

The Principle of Least Privilege is a security objective of granting users only those accesses they need to perform their duties. Creating least privilege policies in the cloud environment with many diverse services, each with unique privilege sets, is significantly more challenging than policy creation previously studied in other environments. Such security policies are always imperfect and must balance between the security risk of granting over-privilege and the effort to correct for under-privilege. In this paper, we formally define the problem of balancing between over-privilege and under-privilege as the Privilege Error Minimization Problem (PEMP) and present a method for quantitatively scoring security policies. We design and compare three algorithms for automatically generating policies: a naive algorithm, an unsupervised learning algorithm, and a supervised learning algorithm. We present the results of evaluating these three policy generation algorithms on a real-world dataset consisting of 5.2 million Amazon Web Service (AWS) audit log entries. The application of these methods can help create policies that balance between an organization's acceptable level of risk and effort to correct under-privilege.

ACM Reference Format:
Matthew W Sanders and Chuan Yue. 2018. Minimizing Privilege Assignment Errors in Cloud Services. In *Proceedings of Eighth ACM Conference on Data and Application Security and Privacy (CODASPY '18)*. ACM, New York, NY, USA, 11 pages. https://doi.org/10.1145/3176258.3176307

1 INTRODUCTION

Cloud computing has revolutionized the information technology industry. Organizations leverage cloud computing to deploy IT infrastructure that is resilient, affordable, and massively scalable with minimal up-front investment. Small startups can rapidly move from an idea to commercial operations and large enterprises can benefit from an elastic infrastructure that scales with unpredictable demand. Because of these benefits, cloud providers have seen significant growth recently with cloud computing industry revenue up 25% in 2016 totaling $148 billion [27]. Despite the wide adoption of cloud computing, there are still significant issues regarding security and usability that must be addressed. Privilege management is one such security and usability issue.

The principle of least privilege requires every privileged entity of a system to operate using the minimal set of privileges necessary to complete its job [19], and is considered a fundamental access control principle in information security [25]. Least privilege policies limit the amount of damage that can be caused by compromised credentials, accidental misuse, and intentional misuse by insider threats. Least privilege is also a requirement of all compliance standards such as the Payment Card Industry Data Security Standard, Health Insurance Portability and Accountability Act, and ISO 17799 Code of Practice for Information Security Management [21].

Despite the importance of implementing least privilege policies, they are not always implemented properly because of the difficulty of creating them and sometimes they are not implemented at all. Previous research on the use of least privilege practices in the context of operating systems revealed that the overwhelming majority of study participants did not utilize least privilege policies [17]. This was due to their partial understanding of the security risks, as well as a lack of motivation to create and enforce such policies. Failing to create least privilege policies in a cloud computing environment is **especially high risk** due to the potentially severe security consequences. However, it is also **significantly more difficult** to achieve least privilege in the cloud computing environment than in other environments due to the large variety of services and actions as detailed in Section 3.

Automatic methods for creating security policies that are highly maintainable have received a significant amount of research in works that address the Role Mining Problem (RMP). However, the maintainability of policies does not directly address how secure or complete a policy is. To directly address the goals of security and completeness in policies, we define the **Privilege Error Minimization Problem (PEMP)** where automatically generated policies for future use are evaluated directly on their security and completeness. The most important metric of a generated security policy should be how secure it is (minimizing over-privilege) and how complete it is (minimizing under-privilege).

We use machine learning methods to address the PEMP which is fundamentally a prediction problem. Audit logs contain the richest source of data from which to derive policies that assign privileges to entities. We mine audit logs of cloud services using one unsupervised and one supervised learning algorithm to address the PEMP along with a naive algorithm for comparison. Note that researchers often take a program analysis approach to find which privileges are needed by specific mobile or other types of applications; we do not take this approach to address PEMP because the privilege errors in PEMP are associated with privileged entities, not an application. The F-Measure is a commonly used metric for scoring in binary classification problems which we adapt to our problem. We show how the β variable of the F-Measure can be used to provide a weighted scoring between under-privilege and over-privilege. We present the results of our algorithms across a range of β values to demonstrate how an organization can determine which approach to use based on its level of acceptable risk.

CODASPY '18, March 19–21, 2018, Tempe, AZ, USA
© 2018 Association for Computing Machinery.
ACM ISBN 978-1-4503-5632-9/18/03...$15.00
https://doi.org/10.1145/3176258.3176307

The main contributions of this paper are: (1) a formal definition of the PEMP which describes the problem of creating complete and secure privilege policies regardless of the access control mechanism, (2) a metric to assess how well the PEMP is solved based on the F-Measure, (3) a methodology of training and validating policy generation algorithms, and (4) one supervised and one unsupervised learning algorithm applied to generating least privilege policies and an analysis of their performance.

Section 2 reviews related works on role mining and automated least privileges. Section 3 presents a comparison of the privilege spaces of various environments and a description of our dataset. Section 4 formally defines the PEMP and a scoring metric for evaluating how well it is solved. Section 5 details specific algorithms and methods used in our approach to addressing the PEMP and Section 6 analyzes the results of these algorithms. Section 7 concludes this work and discusses potential research areas for future work.

2 RELATED WORK

There are two areas of work closely related to ours: role mining and implementing least privilege policies in other environments. Role mining refers to automated approaches to creating Role Based Access Control (RBAC) policies. Role mining can be performed in a top-down manner where organizational information is used or in a bottom-up manner where existing privilege assignments such as access-control lists are used to derive RBAC policies [7]. The problem of discovering an optimal set of roles from existing user permissions is referred to as the Role Mining Problem (RMP) [26].

While we do not directly attempt to solve the RMP or one of its variations, our work has aspects in common with works that do. The authors of [7] defined role mining as being a prediction problem which seeks to create permission assignments that are complete and secure by mining user permission relations. We also employ prediction to mine user permission relations and create policies to balance completeness and security. Our work differs from those that address RMPs in several key ways however. We mine audit log data produced by a system in operation, not existing or manually created user-permission assignments. We do not assume that the given data naturally fits into an RBAC policy that is easy to maintain and secure. Most importantly, instead of evaluating an RBAC configuration based on its maintainability, we focus on evaluating user privilege assignments based on their completeness (minimizing under-privilege) and security (minimizing over-privilege). We view our work as complementary to RMP research as once balanced user permission assignments are generated, existing RMP methods can be used to derive roles which are more compact.

Another area of research closely related to ours is works that use audit log data to achieve least privilege. Privileged entities often already possess the privileges necessary to do their jobs, thus roles can be derived from existing permissions via data mining methods [22]. Methods of automated policy generation have been studied in several environments. Polgen [24] is one of the earliest works in this area which generates policies for programs on SELinux based on patterns in the programs' behavior. Other notable examples of mining audit data to create policies include EASEAndroid [28] for mobile devices, ProgramCutter [29] for desktop applications,

and Passe [2] for web applications. [16] used Latent Dirichlet Allocation (LDA), a machine learning technique to create roles from source code version control usage logs. In [4], the same group used a similar approach to evaluate conformance to least privilege and measured the over-privilege of mined roles in operating systems.

Previous approaches have several shortcomings which are addressed in this paper. Polgen guides policy creation based on logs but does not provide over-privilege or under-privilege metrics. EASEAndroid's goal is to identify malicious programs for a single-user mobile environment, not to create user policies. ProgramCutter and Passe help partition system components to improve least privilege but do not create policies for privileged entities. Only [16], [4] and [20] present metrics on over-privilege and under-privilege by comparing policies to usage. Key issues with these works is that they assume roles are stable, not accounting for change in user behavior over time, and use cross-validation for model evaluation which is not appropriate for environments where temporal relationships should be considered. We address these short comings using the rolling forecasting and sliding simulation methods discussed in Sections 4.3.2 and 5.3, respectively. Finally, our work addresses the trade-off between over- and under-privilege and the selection of different algorithms based on how an organization values over- vs. under-privilege. A metric based on the F-Measure for scoring over-privilege and under-privilege by comparing policies to usage and naive algorithm only for building policies was presented in [20] which we expand upon and use the naive algorithm presented in that work for comparison purposes.

3 DATA DESCRIPTION

The cloud environment is multi-user and multi-service, with **high risk** where errors in privilege assignments can cause significant damage to an organization if exploited. With a large number of services, unique privileges to each service, as well as federated identities and identity delegation, the cloud also presents **more complexity** to security policy administrators than environments previously studied for policy creation such as mobile, desktop, or applications. To quantify the scale of privilege complexity, we consider the size of the privilege spaces for three environments: Android 7, IBM z/OS 1.13, and AWS. Android [8] requires an application's permissions to be specified in a manifest included with the application with 128 possible privileges that can be granted. For IBM z/OS [10], we consider the number of services derived from the different types of system resource classes; there are 213 resource classes and five permission states that can be granted to every class. The privilege space of AWS is much larger however, with over 104 services and 2,823 unique privileges as of August 2017 [1].

Our dataset for training and evaluation consists of 5.2M AWS CloudTrail audit events representing one year of cloud audit data provided by a small Software As A Service (SaaS) company. To better understand how much of the privilege space is used in our dataset, statistics about privileged user behavior are shown in Table 1. This table separates the metrics by the first month, last month, and total for one year of data. *Users* is the number of active users during that time period. *Unique Services Avg.* is the average number of unique services used by active users. *Unique Actions Avg.* is the average number of unique actions exercised by active users, and $\sum$

Action Avg. is the average of the total actions exercised by active users. The standard deviation is also provided for Unique Services, Unique Actions, and $\sum$ Actions metrics to understand the variation between individual users. For example, looking at both the Unique and $\sum$ Actions, we observe that their standard deviation is higher than the average for all time periods, indicating a high degree of variation between how many actions users exercise.

Table 1: One Year Total Usage of our Dataset

Metric	First Month	Last Month	One Year
Users	7	13	18
Unique Services Avg.	5.86	8.08	13.50
Unique Services StdDev.	2.97	5.22	9.04
Unique Actions Avg.	13.71	45.31	88.78
Unique Actions StdDev.	20.21	48.13	91.99
$\sum$ Actions Avg.	91.97	78.38	238.30
$\sum$ Actions StdDev.	299.89	261.95	1271.15

4 PROBLEM SCOPE AND APPROACH

The problem we address is that of automatically creating least privilege access control policies in the cloud environment.

4.1 Problem Definition

We refer to the problem formally as the Privilege Error Minimization Problem (PEMP) and define it using the notation from the NIST definition of RBAC [6].

- *USERS, OPS, and OBS (users, operations, and objects, respectively).*
- $PRMS = 2^{OPS \times OBS}$ *, the set of permissions*
- $UPA \subseteq USERS \times PRMS$*, a many-to-many mapping of user-to-permission assignments.*

Additionally we define the following terms:

- $UPE \subseteq UPA$*, a many-to-many mapping of user-permission relations representing permissions exercised by users during a time period.*
- *OBP observation period, the time-period during which exercised permissions (UPE) are observed and used for creating user-to-permission assignment UPA.*
- *OPP operation period, the time-period during which the user-to-permission assignments UPA is to be considered in operation.*

While both UPE and UPA are user-to-permission relations, UPE represents exercised permissions but UPA represents all assignments. Using the preceding terms, we now define the PEMP.

Definition 1. Privilege Error Minimization Problem (PEMP). *Given a set of users USERS, a set of all possible permissions PRMS, and a set of user-permissions exercised UPE, find the set of user-permissions assignments UPA that minimizes the over-privilege and under-privilege errors for a given operation period OPP.*

The PEMP is fundamentally a prediction problem. Given available information over time-period OBP, we seek to predict the set of permission assignments UPA that will be necessary for privileged entities to complete their tasks during a given operation time-period OPP. This UPA should bound the set of permissions exercised during the operation time-period as tightly as possible to avoid both unused permissions (over-privilege) and missing permissions (under-privilege). We have intentionally left the assessment

metric of how privilege assignment errors are measured out of the problem definition. A problem may have many solutions as well as many metrics for determining if a problem is solved. This separation of the problem and assessment metrics allows for the discussion of metrics separate from the problem itself.

4.2 Algorithm Overview

Now that we have defined the PEMP as being a prediction problem, we adapt existing prediction algorithms to address it. We utilize two machine learning methods in this paper to generate privilege policies from mining audit log data. First, we employ clustering to find privileged entities which use similar permissions, making the problem analogous to that of finding similar documents in a text corpus. After finding similar users, we generate policies that combine the privileges used by clustered entities. The second machine learning method we employ is classification. Using a set of user-to-privilege relations exercised during the observation period, we train a classifier to learn which user-to-privilege relations should be classified as grant and which should be denied. Once trained, we use the classifier to generate policies for an operation period. More details on the application of these algorithms to generate least privilege policies are discussed in Section 5.

4.3 Model Assessment

We borrow techniques and terminology used in machine learning literature for assessing the effectiveness of our algorithms in addressing the PEMP. Using a standard approach for evaluating the effectiveness of a predictive model [11], we take a test dataset for which we know the expected (target) predictions that the model should make, present it to a trained model, record the actual predictions that made, and compare them to the expected predictions. We first present our method for scoring individual predictions, and then our method for splitting up the dataset into multiple partitions.

4.3.1 Scoring individual predictions. Policy generation for a given operation period is a two-class classification problem where every user-to-permission mapping in a generated policy falls into one of two possible classes: grant or deny. By comparing the predicted privileges to the target privileges, we can categorize each prediction into one of four outcomes:

- True Positive (TP): a privilege that was granted in the predicted policy and exercised during the OPP.
- True Negative (TN): a privilege that was denied in the predicted policy and not exercised during the OPP.
- False Positive (FP): a privilege that was granted in the predicted policy but not exercised during the OPP.
- False Negative (FN): a privilege that was denied in the predicted policy but attempted to be exercised during the OPP.

Using the above outcomes we can then calculate **precision**, **recall**, and the F_1 **measure**, a frequently used set of performance metrics in machine learning and information retrieval [11]. Precision and recall are defined as follows[11]:

$$precision = \frac{TP}{(TP + FP)} \quad (1)$$

$$recall = \frac{TP}{(TP + FN)} \quad (2)$$

In terms of this problem domain, precision is the fraction of permissions accurately granted by the predictor (TP) over all permissions granted by the predictor ($TP + FP$). If there were no permissions granted by the predictor that went unused in the OPP, then $precision = 1$. Thus a high precision value is an indicator of low over-privilege. Similarly, recall is the fraction of permissions accurately granted by the predictor (TP) over all permissions exercised in the OPP ($TP + FN$). If there were no permissions denied by the predictor that should have been granted, then $recall = 1$. Thus a high recall value is an indicator of low under-privilege.

Precision and recall can be collapsed into a single performance metric, the F_1 measure, which is the harmonic mean of precision and recall. For predictive assessment, it is often preferable to use a harmonic mean as opposed to an arithmetic mean. Arithmetic means are susceptible to large outliers which can dominate the performance metrics. The harmonic mean however emphasizes the importance of smaller values and thus gives a more realistic measure of model performance[11]. For example, the arithmetic mean when precision=0 and recall=1 is 0.5, however the harmonic mean of those same values is 0.

The F_1 measure is "balanced" because it gives equal weighting to precision and recall. For our assessment we utilize a general form that allows for a variable weighting between recall and precision (or, under-privilege and over-privilege), β. High β values increase the importance of recall, while low β values increase the importance of precision. The weighted measure, F_β is defined in Equation 3.

$$F_\beta = (1 + \beta^2) \cdot \frac{Precision \cdot Recall}{(\beta^2 \cdot Precision) + Recall} \qquad (3)$$

The β weighting is important because it is not reasonable to expect all potential users of a policy generation tool to value over-privilege and under-privilege equally. Molloy et al. identified equal weighting between over- and under-assignments as a problem in several previous works addressing the RMP [15], and preferred to weight more importance to reducing over-privilege. It is also reasonable to expect that some organizations are willing to accept more risk from over-privilege to minimize the cost of privileged entities not being able to perform their duties due to under-privilege.

4.3.2 Scoring multiple predictions. Following the standard approach for evaluating model effectiveness described earlier, we will compare predicted results to expected (target) results. Rather than using a single operation period for our evaluation which may not be representative of the entire dataset, we must partition the dataset into multiple training and test sets using a sampling method. We then aggregate the results of evaluating these partitions to produce a single score for a proposed solution.

For our scenario however, we observe that there is **a temporal aspect to permissions and interdependencies between the exercised actions** which imposes specific restrictions on how we should partition the dataset. For example, a resource such as a virtual machine must be created before it can be used, modified or deleted. Methods such as hold-out sampling and k-fold cross validation which randomly partition a dataset do not account for interdependencies in the data and may not allow for learning algorithms to observe these dependent actions to occur. Thus we use a sampling approach for scenarios like ours which considers a time

dimension with interdependent data referred to as "out-of-time sampling"; it is a form of hold-out sampling which uses data from one time period to build a training set and another period to build a test set[11]. The application of out-of-time sampling to generate and score multiple training and test sets is sometimes known as "rolling forecasting origin", which is similar to cross-validation but the training set consists only of observations that occurred prior to those in the test set [9]. Suppose k observations are required to produce a reliable forecast. Then rolling forecasting origin works as follows [9].

(1) Select the observation at time $k + i$ for the test set, and use the observations at times $1, 2, ..., k + i - 1$ to estimate the forecasting model. Compute the error on the forecast for time $k + i$.
(2) Repeat the above step for $i = 1, 2, ..., T - k$ where T is the total number of observations.
(3) Compute the forecast accuracy measures based on the errors obtained.

Adapting the above method to our domain, we allow the training set/observation period to be comprised of any set of dates before time $k + i$, and the test set/operation period is specifically at time $k + i$. We define the step size i to be of one day, which is an adequate amount of time to complete most tasks using related permissions. Also, when using an automated solution to generate permission policies, it is reasonable to expect that new solutions can be generated on at least daily basis.

The measure of forecast accuracy in our scenario is the F_β score for a given operation period described in Section 4.3.1, where a perfect prediction with no over-privilege and no under-privilege present would score a 1.0. We use a rolling mean to compute the accuracy of a proposed solution across all operation periods. Thus our quality measure used for assessing an automated solution to creating permission policies should maximize the average F_β measure across all operation periods:

$$\frac{1}{T - k} \sum_{i=1}^{T-k} F_\beta(Precision_i, Recall_i) \qquad (4)$$

5 METHODOLOGY

This section describes the algorithms and techniques we design to address the PEMP in the cloud environment. We first present a naive algorithm which will be used to establish a performance baseline for us to compare the performance of our learning based approaches to. While the naive algorithm merely uses a privilege entity's observed privileges to build policies, the learning based approaches also account for the behavior of other users in generating policies. Each of these methods is applied for a single operation period. The evaluation of an algorithm across multiple operation periods is done using the method described in Section 4.3.2.

5.1 Naive Policy Generation

The naive approach shown in Algorithm 1 takes all privileges exercised during the observation period as input and combines them to form a privilege policy to be used during the operation period. This seems a reasonable approach for a policy administrator to take if they needed to implement a least privilege policy in an environment where all privilege entities previously had unrestricted access to all permissions. By examining all previous access logs or only the access logs up to a specific point in the past, they can discover all privileges used by each privileged entity and thus expect this to be the set of privileges required for a privileged entity to perform their duties. Although infrequently used privileges will not be captured if they are outside of the observation period, policy generation algorithms can still achieve good results without knowing the frequency for which these privileges are exercised because infrequently used privileges will have little impact on the F_β score, particularly for low β values which value minimizing over-privilege. Furthermore, in a low β environment it is likely that infrequently used privileges should be denied by default and granted by exception instead of always being granted by a long-term policy.

Algorithm 1: Naive Policy Generator

Input: UPE The set of user-permissions exercised during the observation period OBP.

Output: UPA The mapping of user-to-permission assignments.

1 $UPA \leftarrow \emptyset$;
2 **for** $user, perm \in UPE$ **do**
3     $UPA_{user} \leftarrow roles_{user} \cup perm$;
4 **end**
5 **return** UPA

5.2 Unsupervised Policy Generation

Our unsupervised learning policy generation method (Algorithm 2) uses a clustering algorithm to find clusters of similar privileged entities based on their permissions exercised. By placing each permission exercised by an entity into a separate document and applying clustering to the document corpus (lines 2-5), we have made the problem analogous to finding similar text documents in a corpus. Once similar entities are grouped by clustering, each group is assigned a shared role and granted the combined permissions of all entities in that role (lines 6-14). Entities which do not belong to any cluster are granted only the privileges they used during the observation period just as in the naive method (lines 15-19). It is important to note that using this method of combining similar entities only grants permissions additional to those used during the observation period. This is **useful in environments where minimizing under-privilege is more important than minimizing over-privilege**.

There are several details of our application of clustering worth describing here. Each document is converted to a feature vector for clustering using a Term Frequency-Inverse Document Frequency (TF-IDF) vectorizer. TF-IDF is a common approach for finding similar documents in information retrieval [14]. The TF-IDF weighting has the advantage that it preserves information about how often each permission is exercised by a user. Once vectorization is complete, the specific clustering algorithm we use for finding similar users is the DBSCAN algorithm of the scikit-learn library [18], an implementation of the algorithm originally published in [5]. The DBSCAN algorithm has several advantages for our scenario, primary among them being that we do not need to specify the expected number of clusters ahead of time unlike other popular clustering

---

Algorithm 2: Unsupervised Policy Generator

Input: UPE The set of user-permissions exercised during the observation period OBP.

Output: UPA The mapping of user-to-permission assignments.

1 $UPA, documents \leftarrow \emptyset$;
2 **for** $user, perm \in UPE$ **do**
3     $documents_{user} \leftarrow documents_{user} \cup perm$;
4 **end**
5 $clusters, outliers \leftarrow DBSCAN(documents)$;
6 **for** $cluster \in clusters$ **do**
7     $role \leftarrow \emptyset$;
8   **for** $user, document \in cluster$ **do**
9   **for** $perm \in document$ **do**
10          $role \leftarrow role \cup perm$;
11   **end**
12   **end**
13     $UPA_{user} \leftarrow role$;
14 **end**
15 **for** $user, document \in outliers$ **do**
16   **for** $user, perm \in document$ **do**
17        $UPA_{user} \leftarrow roles_{user} \cup perm$;
18   **end**
19 **end**
20 **return** UPA

---

algorithms such as k-means. The performance of DBSCAN also scales well in regards to the number of samples given when compared to other clustering algorithms [23]. There is one relevant hyper-parameter for DBSCAN which we vary in our policy generation experiments, ϵ, which is the maximum distance between two samples for them to be considered as in the same cluster. We **explore three methods for calculating** ϵ: the mean distance between all points, median distance between all points, and middle point between the minimum and maximum points in the vector space.

5.3 Supervised Policy Generation

For the supervised learning approach, we design a classification algorithm to generate policies as follows (and in Algorithm 3). First we construct a training set of documents from the permissions exercised during the observation period and select a subset of previous data for creating the class labels (line 3). We then train a classifier using the training set for each permutation of the Classifier Algorithm Parameters (CAP) (lines 4-6). These multiple instances of the classifier with different permutations of the CAP are used for hyper-parameter selection using the "sliding simulation" method to be described in Section 5.3.2 . Next we create a set of possible permissions that may be exercised during the operation period based on the Policy Generation Parameters (PGP) (line 9). Each of the possible policy permissions is tested against the classifier which will predict that the permission should be either granted or denied, and the results of this classification are used to create the policy for the next operation period (lines 10-15).

Algorithm 3: Supervised Policy Generator

Input: *UPE* User-Permissions Exercised. The set of user-permissions exercised during the observation period *OBP*.

Input: *PRMS* The set of possible permissions.

Input: *TSP* Training Set Parameters. Mapping of parameters used to build the training set.

Input: *CAP* Classifier Algorithm Parameters. Mapping of parameters used to build the predicted policy from a trained classifier.

Input: *PGP* Policy Generation Parameters. Mapping of parameters used to build the predicted policy from a trained classifier.

Output: *UPA* Mapping storing the roles generated by each of the classifier instances.

1 $UPA \leftarrow \emptyset$;
2 **for** $tParams \in permute(TSP)$ **do**
3      $featureVector, labelSet \leftarrow$
          $createTrainingSet(tParams, UPE)$;
4   **for** $clfParams \in permute(CAP)$ **do**
5          $clf \leftarrow decisionTree(clfParams)$;
6          $clf \leftarrow clf.train(featureVector, labelSet)$;
7   **for** $pParams \in permute(PGP)$ **do**
8              $roles \leftarrow \emptyset$;
9              $possiblePrivs \leftarrow$
                  $createPossiblePrivs(pParams, PRMS)$;
10   **for** $user, perm \in possiblePrivs$ **do**
11   **if** $clf.predict(user, perm) == 'granted'$ **then**
12                     $roles_{user} \leftarrow roles_{user} \cup perm$;
13   **end**
14   **end**
15             $UPA_{tParams, clfParams, pParams} \leftarrow roles$;
16   **end**
17   **end**
18 **end**
19 **return** UPA

5.3.1 Classification Algorithm and Feature Selection. We use a **decision tree (DT)** classification algorithm for supervised learning, also from the scikit-learn library [18]. The algorithm implemented in the library is an optimized version, an implementation of the CART algorithm published in [3]. The advantages of the decision tree algorithm used are speed and the ability to display the set of rules learned during classification. It was also the top performing classification algorithm in our preliminary comparison of 15 different classification algorithms in the scikit-learn library.

We utilize five features available directly from the audit log data for training: the time at which a permission was exercised, the unique identifier of the executing entity, the type of entity (user or delegated role), the service which the action belonged to, and the type of action performed. Instead of using the absolute time of an action, we derive features capturing whether it was exercised on a weekend or weekday, as well as the specific day of the week. These are all bottom-up data attributes available directly from the access logs. Other top-down information such as job role or organization

department was not available with our dataset (nor does it exist in many small organizations), but could easily be integrated with the exercised privilege information if available.

5.3.2 Sliding Simulation for Supervised Parameter Selection. Several hyper-parameters must be selected for our supervised learning approach. These include parameters for the decision tree classifier, the constructions of the training set, the policy construction from the trained classifier. Our method for selecting optimized hyper-parameters uses only out-of-sample data and is an adaptation of the "sliding simulation" method presented in [12].

The sliding simulation method of [12] is based on three premises. First, a model should be selected based on how well it predicts out-of-sample actual data, not on how well it fits historical data. Second, a model is selected from among many candidates run in parallel on the out-of-sample data. Third, models are optimized for each forecast horizon separately, making it possible to use different models and optimize parameters within models. The method operates by running several prediction models in parallel across a sliding window of data, computing the accuracy of each model for a given period and selecting the model(s) with the best score to be used in creating the forecast for the next period. Using this technique, the author in [12] showed that it outperformed the best method of a previous competition in statistical forecasting (the *M*-Competition [13]) by a large margin.

As in the sliding simulation method, we run many permutations of parameters in parallel on out-of-sample data and use the best performing parameters to create a future prediction. Modifications were implemented to adapt sliding simulation to our problem domain. Sliding simulation originally dealt with making numerical predictions and measuring the error between a predicted and actual value. In our scenario a security policy is the prediction and we use the F_β score presented in Section 4.3.1 as our scoring criteria. While [12] used all observation points before the forecast period, the most recent exercised permissions are most relevant to predicting future permissions; training a classifier with older and less relevant permissions had a negative effect on prediction accuracy.

5.4 Model Decomposition

Time series decomposition is a common technique used to improve predictions [9], it identifies patterns in data and decomposes the data into different models based on those patterns. **We applied time series decomposition to our data after recognizing significant differences between the privileges exercised during weekdays and weekends**. While given enough data and the proper features a supervised approach should be able to learn and use these patterns to make predictions, decomposing the data provides several advantages: (1) improves scores for both naive and unsupervised algorithms, (2) less training data is needed for the supervised approach since it does not need to learn the different behavior patterns in weekdays and weekends, and (3) information about weekday or weekend patterns can be used in hyper-parameters that control the creation of the training set for supervised learning.

We use two methods of decomposing the time series data which we term *filter decomposition* and *filler decomposition*. For the filter method, the days which do not fit into the chosen model are filtered out of each observation period in the sliding window evaluation before the data are used by the algorithms. With the filler method, the end date of the sliding window evaluation is used as a starting point and the observation period is created by enlarging the window by moving the start date backward until the observation period is "filled" with only data matching the chosen model. Consider a sliding window evaluation with a window size of 10 days using these two decomposition methods. For the filter method, the number of days fitting the weekday model will vary from 6 to 8, and the number of days fitting the weekend model will vary from 2 to 4. For the filler method, the number of days fitting a model will always be 10 days when the sliding window size is 10 days.

The decomposition method used for evaluation is chosen based on the β value we wish to optimize for. For algorithms seeking to score well for $\beta > 1$, increasing the window size results in better scores, and the filter approach is used where the variations in the observation dataset size are smoothed out across larger windows. For experiments which seek to score well for $\beta < 1$, smaller window sizes score more favorably but the variable number of matching days which fit within a chosen time period can have undesirable effects on the results when using small window sizes. Thus the filler model is used in experiments for $\beta < 1$ which gives a consistent number of days for data points in each window.

6 RESULTS

This section analyzes the performance of our algorithms for generating security policies. We first examine the results using the complete model and then show how decomposition and the use of multiple decomposed models can improve on those results.

6.1 Complete Model Results

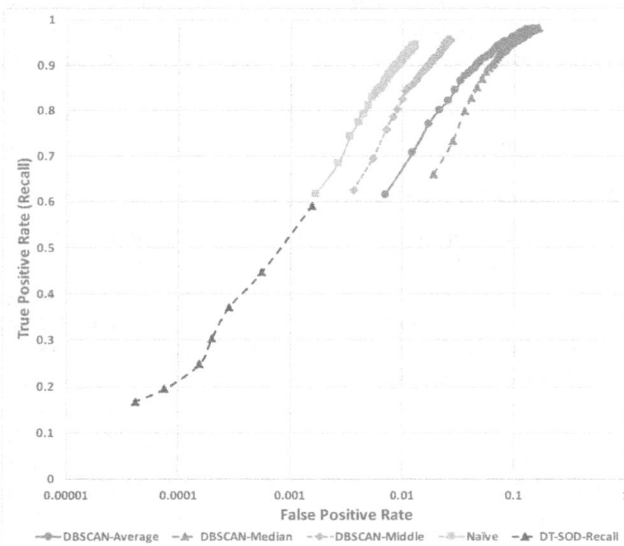

Figure 1: Receiver Operating Characteristic Curves

The Receiver Operating Characteristic (ROC) curve is a graphic commonly used to chart the performance of binary classifiers. It charts the trade-off between the True Positive Rate (TPR, also called recall) and the False Positive Rate (FPR) of a binary classifier, with

the ideal performance having a TPR value of one and FPR of zero. While the ROC illustrates FPR, the rest of the charts in this section use F_β described in Section 4.3.1. The ROC curves for the naive, three unsupervised (DBSCAN) and one supervised (DT) algorithms across multiple observation period lengths are presented in Figure 1. All of the algorithms perform well in terms of minimizing the FPR with the unsupervised methods being able to provide higher recall than the naive approach but at the cost of higher FPR. The supervised approach is not able to score as well as the other algorithms in terms of recall but maintains a lower FPR for all data points. The use of specific observation period sizes for the sliding window method described in Section 4.3 prevents the data points from spanning the entire range of the chart which is typical for ROC curves.

The performance of the naive, three unsupervised, and two supervised algorithms across F_β values for $1/100 <= \beta <= 100$ is presented in Figure 2. Two separate methods are in this section for labeling the training data: substitution/overlapping daytype (SOD) where a day of the same type (weekday or weekend) is used which overlaps with the observation period, and substitution/non-overlapping day of week (SND) where a day on the same day of the week is used which was prior to (non-overlapping) the observation period. Additionally, the performance of the policy that allows all privileges are also shown in this chart for comparison. The scores on this chart represent the best performance of each algorithm regardless of the size of the sliding window used for the observation period. Some important trends are evident from this chart. For β values where $1 < \beta < 50$, the naive approach performs the best with the unsupervised methods scoring slightly better after $\beta > 50$. The policy that allows all privileges comes close to scoring as good as the naive approach at $\beta = 100$, but even for such a high β, the naive and unsupervised algorithms are still favorable over the allow all policy. While the performance of the unsupervised algorithms is not very compelling in this chart, later results using decomposition will show a larger performance gap between the naive and unsupervised methods for high β values. The supervised algorithms score relatively poorly for $\beta > 1$. For β values where $\beta < 1$, the supervised algorithms score significantly better than the naive algorithm as β decreases with the performance gap widening until $\beta < 1/30$, where the scores of the supervised and naive algorithms cease to improve as β decreases. The unsupervised algorithms score relatively poorly for $\beta < 1$.

The trends in these charts highlight the **strengths and weaknesses of each algorithm**. By granting users the privileges used by similar users, the unsupervised algorithms predict privileges a user may use in the future. But there is no mechanism for the unsupervised learning algorithm to learn which possible privilege grants may result in over-privilege and restrict these privileges accordingly. The supervised algorithms attempt to learn any patterns in the past data and use these to predict future privilege assignments. While privileges used previously are likely to be used again and rarely used privileges can be denied with some degree of confidence, it is difficult to predict the usage of a future privilege that has never been used before using only past patterns.

Figures 1 and 2 show the scores of algorithms regardless of the size of the observation period. We next examine the performance of these algorithms for fixed β values as the observation period

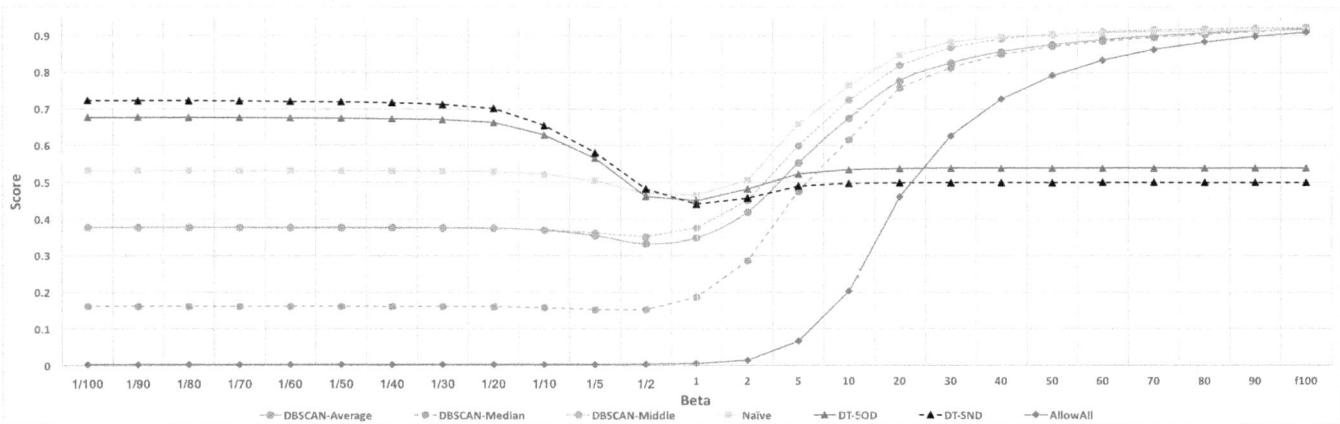

Figure 2: Beta Values Curves

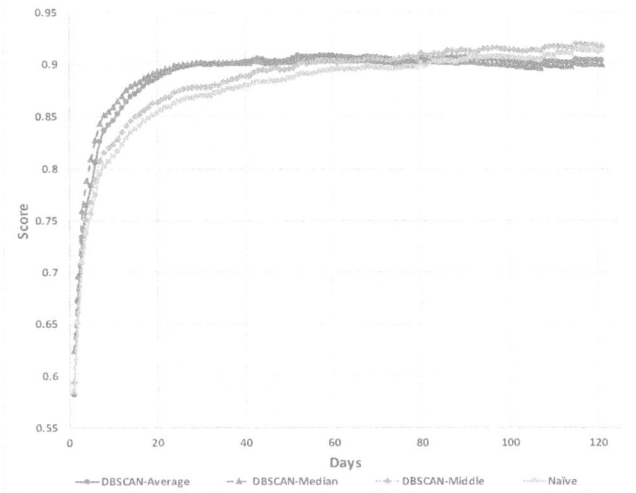

Figure 3: $\beta = 80$

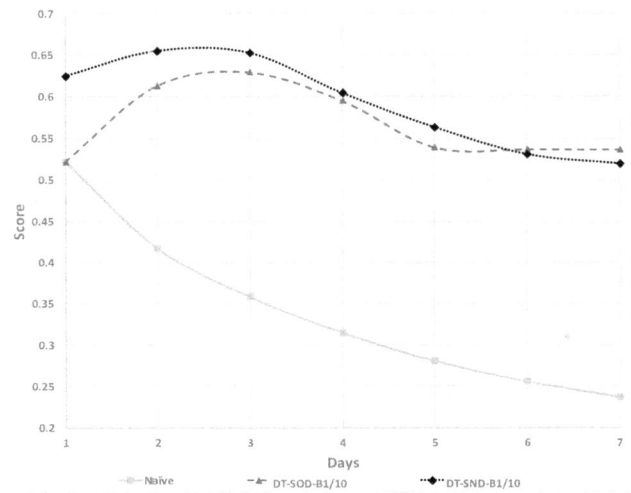

Figure 4: $\beta = 1/10$

size varies. We chose values $\beta = 80$ and $\beta = 1/10$ because these seemed the most interesting in terms of the trade-offs between the various methods. The performance of the unsupervised and naive algorithms for $\beta = 80$ are shown in Figure 3. The choice of ϵ as the threshold for determining which users are alike presents interesting trade-offs between window size and score. In general, using the median for calculating ϵ consistently provides slightly better scores than the naive approach across all window sizes with the scores for both the unsupervised algorithm (with the middle method) and naive algorithm peaking at 115 days. Using the average and middle methods for calculating ϵ both provide better scores for observation periods < 40 days, but their scores level off there and begin to gradually decrease after peaking at 59 days for the average method and 68 days for the median method.

The performance of the supervised and naive algorithms for $\beta = 1/10$ are shown in Figure 4. The naive algorithm achieves its best performance with an observation period of one day and steadily declines after that. The supervised algorithms all achieve their best performance with an observation period size of 2 or 3 days and then decline until leveling off around six and seven days.

Among the supervised methods, the SND approach performs the best for observation periods less than five days but declines more rapidly than the SOD labeling method. Although not charted here, the precision score of the supervised methods constantly increases and the recall score constantly decreases as the observation period increases. The increase in precision is not rapid enough to overcome the decrease in recall after the observation period exceeds 3 days however, which is why the scores for the supervised algorithms decrease or level off after that point. Conversely, the precision score of the naive method constantly decreases and the recall score constantly increases as the observation period increases.

6.2 Decomposed Models Results

In this section we present the results after decomposing the dataset in separate models for weekday and weekend data using the decomposition methods discussed previously in Section 5.4.

The performance of the complete and decomposed models for β values $>= 1$ for both the naive algorithm and the unsupervised algorithm (with the average method for calculating ϵ) are shown in Figure 5. For both algorithms, the weekday model performance

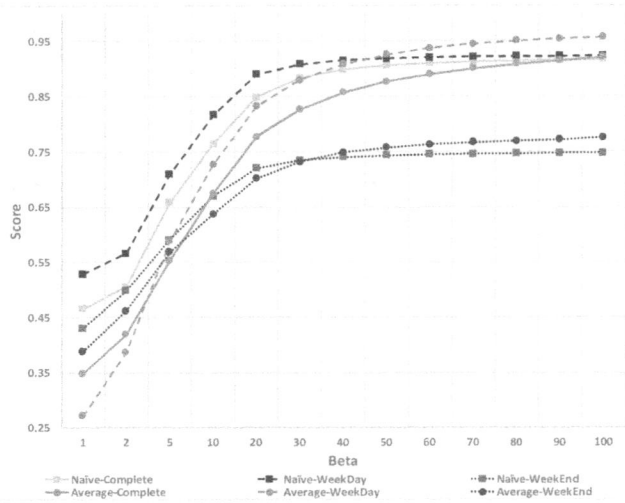

Figure 5: Decomposed Models Unsupervised $\beta >= 1$

is superior to the complete model for β values $>= 1$. The trend previously illustrated in Figure 2 of the unsupervised algorithm under-performing the naive algorithm for low β but eventually outperforming it as β increases is also present in this chart but more pronounced. The performance gap between unsupervised and naive algorithms widens in the decomposed models with the unsupervised algorithm overtaking the naive algorithm at $\beta = 50$ for the weekday model and $\beta = 40$ for the weekend model, where previously the unsupervised algorithm did not outscore the naive algorithm in the complete model until $\beta = 90$. The weekend model performance is generally worse than the complete model performance. There are two primary reasons for this: first, there is less data available to the weekend model, with only 28% of the complete model data; second, the activity of users on the weekends is lower and highly inconsistent, making it harder to find similar entities and less likely that similar users will exercise similar privileges in a cluster if identified.

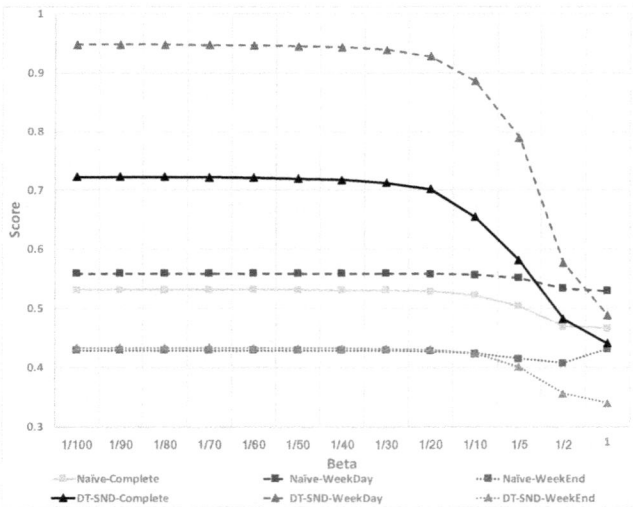

Figure 6: Decomposed Models, Supervised $\beta <= 1$

The performance of the complete and decomposed models for β values $<= 1$ for both the naive algorithm and the supervised algorithm (using the SND labeling method) are shown in Figure 6. As with the unsupervised algorithm and β values $>= 1$, the weekday model outperforms the complete model while the weekend model under-performs the complete model where β values $<= 1$ as well. The performance gap between the weekday and complete models for the supervised algorithm is much larger than in previously examined experiments. With the inconsistent activity of the weekend actions removed, the supervised algorithm is better able to identify and leverage patterns to create security policies. The performance of the supervised algorithm for the weekend model decreased substantially compared to the complete model however. For $\beta = 1/30$, the supervised weekend model scored 39% lower than the complete model, while the naive weekend model scored only 19% lower than its complete model. The reasons for the lower weekend model scores for the supervised algorithm are the same as the lower weekend model scores for the unsupervised algorithm: there is less data to work with and higher variability in that data.

6.3 Recomposed Models Results

Section 6.2 illustrated how decomposition improved scoring for the weekday model, but we are interested in finding the highest possible score across all days in the available dataset. **To improve the overall score, we combine two previously examined models** using one model and algorithm for the weekday policies and another model and algorithm for the weekend policies which we refer to this as a recomposed model. To build the recomposed model, we use policies from the weekday model when evaluating weekdays, but as the previously examined results have shown, the weekend models performed fairly poor so we will instead use policies generated by the complete model when evaluating weekends.

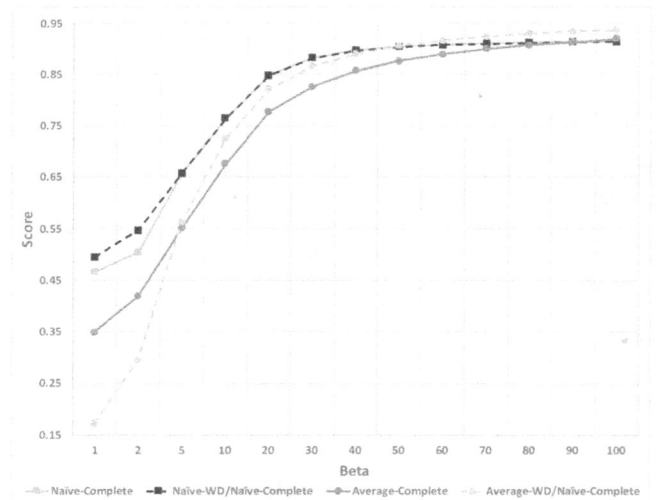

Figure 7: Recomposed Models, $\beta >= 1$

The performance of the complete and recomposed models for β values $>= 1$ for both the naive algorithm and the unsupervised algorithm (with the average method used for calculating ϵ) are shown in Figure 7. For the unsupervised algorithm, the recomposed model outscores the complete model for β values >= 5, and outscores the naive algorithm for both the complete and recomposed models for β >= 50, with the performance gap increasing after that as β increases. For the naive algorithm however, the improved scores of the weekday model are not enough to offset the poorer scores of the complete model for the weekend days, thus the recomposed model using the naive algorithm scores almost the same as the complete model for β > 5. The scores for the highest β value tested are .9379 for the recomposed model with the unsupervised algorithm and .9149 for the recomposed model with the naive algorithm, an improvement of 2.5% over an already fairly high score.

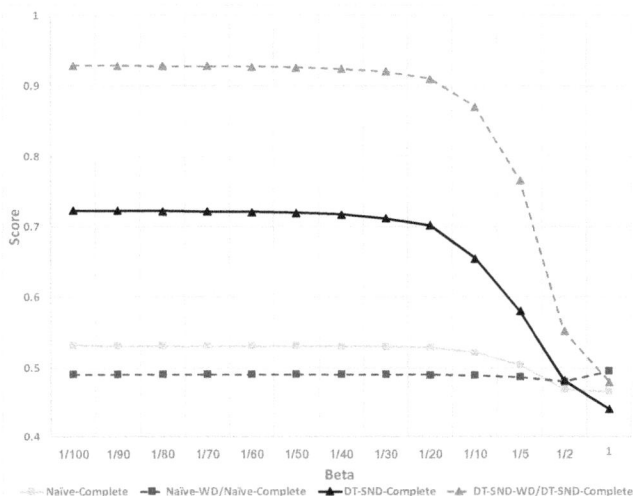

Figure 8: Recomposed Models, β <= 1

The performance of the complete and recomposed models for β values <= 1 for both the naive algorithm and the supervised algorithm (using the SNDT labeling method) are shown in Figure 8. For the recomposed model using the supervised algorithm, the significantly improved scores of the weekdays using the weekday model are combined with the weekends from the complete model to improve the overall scores by 89% compared to the naive complete model at β = 1/100. For the recomposed model using the naive algorithm, the improvement provided by the weekday model was not enough to offset the poor scores of the weekend policies in the complete model, resulting in the recomposed model scoring lower than the complete model for β < 1/2.

6.4 Results Summary

Creating security policies is inherently an optimization problem that must balance between minimizing over-privilege and minimizing under-privilege. How much one values achieving one of these objectives vs. the other can be expressed using the β value as described in Section 4.3. The results of this section demonstrate the **effectiveness algorithms and decomposition methods that can be used to create better security policies** for a cloud environment with "better" being expressed in terms of the F_β score.

We also presented the results of using decomposition methods to decompose the dataset into weekday and weekend models and then use the best aspects of the weekday and complete models for

scoring across the complete dataset time period. Not all audit log datasets will exhibit similar behavior that benefits from such decomposition, but it is reasonable to expect many datasets consisting of audit log events generated by human privileged entities working a five-day work week will. Regardless of the decomposition method used, we find that the **unsupervised algorithm performs more favorably as β increases** due to its ability to use information from similar users to predict the future use of privileges. The unsupervised algorithm does not have a mechanism to deny privileges however, so its scores are relatively low for small β values. Conversely, **the supervised algorithm performs more favorably as β decreases** but poorly for large β values. The supervised algorithm is able to use the recurring patterns in data to score well for restricting privileges, but scores poorly at predicting possible new privileges that privileged entities may use. The naive approach performs well only for values near β = 1, representing its favorability for environments which value balancing over- and under-privilege nearly equally but it is outperformed by the other algorithms as the β value increases or decreases away from β = 1. **The key takeaway from these results is that how an organization values over-privilege vs. under-privilege will determine which algorithm is best suited for generating that organization's security policies; none of the three examined algorithms is clearly superior to the others for all likely scenarios.**

7 CONCLUSION

This paper addressed issues related to automatically creating least privilege policies in the cloud environment. We defined the Privilege Error Minimization Problem (PEMP) to directly address the goals of completeness and security when creating privilege policies, and introduced a weighted scoring mechanism to evaluate a policy against these goals. We adapted techniques from statistical forecasting and machine learning to train and evaluate a supervised and an unsupervised learning algorithm for automated policy generation. The results of our analysis show that the supervised algorithm performed well for reducing over-privilege while the unsupervised algorithm performed well for reducing under-privilege compared to a naive approach. These results demonstrate the potential to apply such automated methods to create more secure roles based on an organization's acceptable level of risk in accepting over-privilege vs. its desire to minimize the effort to correct under-privilege.

This paper suggests many possibilities for future research in automated least privileges approaches. The policy generation approaches described in this paper are based on features directly available in the audit logs such as the service name, user name, and privilege exercised. We would consider additional features for future research such as properties of the requesting entity and the resources being operated on such as a user's job title and organizational unit or the subnet(s) which a virtual resource operates within. Combining the ability of the unsupervised algorithm (to predict the use of future privileges based on clusters of similar users) with the ability of the supervised algorithm (to restrict privileges which are unlikely to be used in the future) may also improve scoring.

ACKNOWLEDGMENT
This research was supported in part by the NSF grant DGE-1619841.

REFERENCES

[1] Amazon Web Services. 2017. IAM Policy Generator Source Code. https://awsiamconsole.s3.amazonaws.com/iam/assets/js/bundles/policies.js. (2017). Accessed: 2017-05-04.

[2] Aaron Blankstein and Michael J Freedman. 2014. Automating isolation and least privilege in web services. In *Security and Privacy (SP), 2014 IEEE Symposium on*. IEEE, 133–148.

[3] Leo Breiman, Jerome Friedman, Charles J Stone, and Richard A Olshen. 1984. *Classification and regression trees*. CRC press.

[4] Suresh Chari, Ian Molloy, Youngja Park, and Wilferid Teiken. 2013. Ensuring continuous compliance through reconciling policy with usage. In *ACM Symposium on Access control models and technologies (SACMAT)*. ACM, 49–60.

[5] Martin Ester, Hans-Peter Kriegel, Jörg Sander, Xiaowei Xu, et al. 1996. A density-based algorithm for discovering clusters in large spatial databases with noise.. In *Knowledge discovery in databases (KDD)*, Vol. 96. AAAI Press, 226–231.

[6] David F Ferraiolo, Ravi Sandhu, Serban Gavrila, D Richard Kuhn, and Ramaswamy Chandramouli. 2001. Proposed NIST standard for role-based access control. *ACM Transactions on Information and System Security (TISSEC)* 4, 3 (2001), 224–274.

[7] Mario Frank, Joachim M Buhmann, and David Basin. 2010. On the definition of role mining. In *ACM Symposium on Access control models and technologies (SACMAT)*. ACM, 35–44.

[8] Google, Inc. 2017. Manifest.permission | Android Developers. https://developer.android.com/reference/android/Manifest.permission.html. (2017). Accessed: 2017-01-10.

[9] Rob J Hyndman and George Athanasopoulos. 2014. *Forecasting: principles and practice*. OTexts.

[10] IBM Corporation. 2012. z/OS Security Server RACF General User's Guide. https://www.ibm.com/support/knowledgecenter/en/SSLTBW_1.13.0/com.ibm.zos.r13.icha100/toc.htm. (2012). Accessed: 2017-05-17.

[11] John D Kelleher, Brian Mac Namee, and Aoife D'Arcy. 2015. Fundamentals of Machine Learning for Predictive Data Analytics. (2015).

[12] Spyros Makridakis. 1990. Sliding Simulation: A New Approach to Time Series Forecasting. *Management Science* 36, 4 (1990), 505–512.

[13] Spyros Makridakis, A Andersen, Robert Carbone, Robert Fildes, Michele Hibon, Rudolf Lewandowski, Joseph Newton, Emanuel Parzen, and Robert Winkler. 1982. The accuracy of extrapolation (time series) methods: Results of a forecasting competition. *Journal of forecasting* 1, 2 (1982), 111–153.

[14] Christopher D. Manning, Prabhakar Raghavan, and Hinrich Schütze. 2008. *Introduction to Information Retrieval*. Cambridge University Press, New York, NY, USA. 117–119 pages.

[15] Ian Molloy, Ninghui Li, Tiancheng Li, Ziqing Mao, Qihua Wang, and Jorge Lobo. 2009. Evaluating role mining algorithms. In *ACM Symposium on Access control models and technologies (SACMAT)*. ACM, 95–104.

[16] Ian Molloy, Youngja Park, and Suresh Chari. 2012. Generative Models for Access Control Policies: Applications to Role Mining over Logs with Attribution. In *ACM Symposium on Access control models and technologies (SACMAT)*. ACM, 45–56.

[17] Sara Motiee, Kirstie Hawkey, and Konstantin Beznosov. 2010. Do windows users follow the principle of least privilege?: investigating user account control practices.. In *Symposium on Usable Privacy and Security (SOUPS)*. ACM.

[18] Pedregosa, F., et al. 2011. Scikit-learn: Machine Learning in Python. *Journal of Machine Learning Research* 12 (2011), 2825–2830.

[19] Jerome H Saltzer and Michael D Schroeder. 1975. The protection of information in computer systems. *Proc. IEEE* 63, 9 (1975), 1278–1308.

[20] Matthew Sanders and Chuan Yue. 2017. Automated Least Privileges in Cloud-Based Web Services. In *Hot Topics in Web Systems and Technologies (HotWeb)*. IEEE.

[21] SANS Institute. 2010. A Compliance Primer for IT Professionals. https://www.sans.org/reading-room/whitepapers/compliance/compliance-primer-professionals-33538. (2010). Accessed: 2017-09-24.

[22] JÃijrgen Schlegelmilch and Ulrike Steffens. 2005. Role mining with ORCA.. In *ACM Symposium on Access control models and technologies (SACMAT)*. ACM, 168–176.

[23] scikit-learn developers. 2016. Overview of clustering methods. http://scikit-learn.org/stable/modules/clustering.html. (2016). Accessed: 2017-09-01.

[24] Brian T. Sniffen, David R. Harris, and John D. Ramsdell. 2006. Guided policy generation for application authors.. In *SELinux Symposium*.

[25] Harold F Tipton and Kevin Henry. 2006. *Official (ISC) 2 guide to the CISSP CBK*. Auerbach Publications.

[26] Jaideep Vaidya, Atluri Vijayalakshmi, and Qi Guo. 2007. The role mining problem: finding a minimal descriptive set of roles.. In *ACM Symposium on Access control models and technologies (SACMAT)*. ACM, 175–184.

[27] Bob Violino. 2017. Cloud Computing Sees Huge Growth Rates Across All Segments. http://www.information-management.com/news/infrastructure/cloud-computing-sees-huge-growth-rates-across-all-segments-10030682-1.html. (2017). Accessed: 2017-09-07.

[28] Ruowen Wang, William Enck, Douglas Reeves, Xinwen Zhang, Peng Ning, Dingbang Xu, Wu Zhou, and Ahmed M. Azab. 2015. EASEAndroid: Automatic Policy Analysis and refinement for security enhanced android via large-scale semi-supervised learning. In *USENIX Security Symposium*. USENIX, 351–366.

[29] Yongzheng Wu, Jun Sun, Yang Liu, and Jin Song Dong. 2013. Automatically partition software into least privilege components using dynamic data dependency analysis.. In *IEEE/ACM International Conference on Automated Software Engineering (ASE)*. IEEE Press, 323–333.

Secure Storage with Replication and Transparent Deduplication

Iraklis Leontiadis*
Ecole Polytechnique Federale de Lausanne (EPFL)
School of Computer and Communication Sciences
Lausanne, Switzerland
iraklis.leontiadis@epfl.ch

Reza Curtmola
New Jersey Institute of Technology (NJIT)
Department of Computer Science
Newark, NJ, USA
crix@njit.edu

ABSTRACT

We seek to answer the following question: *To what extent can we deduplicate replicated storage ?* To answer this question, we design ReDup, a secure storage system that provides users with strong integrity, reliability, and transparency guarantees about data that is outsourced at cloud storage providers. Users store multiple replicas of their data at different storage servers, and the data at each storage server is deduplicated across users. Remote data integrity mechanisms are used to check the integrity of replicas. We consider a strong adversarial model, in which collusions are allowed between storage servers and also between storage servers and dishonest users of the system. A cloud storage provider (CSP) could store less replicas than agreed upon by contract, unbeknownst to honest users. ReDup defends against such adversaries by making replica generation to be time consuming so that a dishonest CSP cannot generate replicas on the fly when challenged by the users.

In addition, ReDup employs transparent deduplication, which means that users get a proof attesting the deduplication level used for their files at each replica server, and thus are able to benefit from the storage savings provided by deduplication. The proof is obtained by aggregating individual proofs from replica servers, and has a constant size regardless of the number of replica servers. Our solution scales better than state of the art and is provably secure under standard assumptions.

CCS CONCEPTS

• **Security and privacy** → **Database and storage security**; *Security protocols*; • **Information systems** → *Deduplication*; *Distributed storage*; • **Computer systems organization** → *Reliability*; *Redundancy*;

KEYWORDS

remote data integrity checking; RDIC; replication; deduplication

ACM Reference Format:
Iraklis Leontiadis and Reza Curtmola. 2018. Secure Storage with Replication and Transparent Deduplication. In *CODASPY '18: Eighth ACM Conference on Data and Application Security and Privacy, March 19–21, 2018, Tempe, AZ,*

---

*This work was done while the author was affiliated with NJIT.

USA. ACM, New York, NY, USA, 11 pages. https://doi.org/10.1145/3176258.3176315

1 INTRODUCTION

Outsourcing storage to cloud storage providers (CSPs) has become a popular and convenient practice. Despite its cost-saving benefits, cloud storage remains rife with security issues [16]. There are reported incidents of lost data or service unavailability due to power outages [15], hardware failure, software bugs [14], external or internal attacks, negligence, or administrator error. Moreover, cloud infrastructures lack transparency and data owners have to fully trust the CSPs. All these factors limit the suitability of cloud platforms for applications that require long-term data integrity and reliability. Of particular concern to data owners is that although storage can be outsourced, the liability in case data is lost, damaged, or stolen cannot be outsourced.

Several approaches can be used to ease these concerns. First, to improve *reliability*, data can be stored redundantly by replicating it across geographically dispersed cloud storage servers. Whenever data is damaged at one replica server (RS), data can be retrieved from healthy replication servers in order to repair the damaged data and restore the desired level of redundancy. Second, the transparency of cloud infrastructures can be improved by using an auditing mechanism such as *remote data integrity checking* (RDIC) [4, 5, 9, 22], which allows data owners to efficiently check the integrity of data stored at untrusted CSPs.

At the same time, a popular trend is that of *data deduplication*, which allows CSPs to reduce their storage costs by exploiting common properties of files stored by different users. When different users upload the same file at a CSP, deduplication ensures that only one copy is stored. Recent studies show that cross-user data deduplication can lead to significant savings in storage costs, ranging from 50% to 95% [20, 21].

Although deduplication across multiple users' files is economically beneficial for CSPs, the individual users whose files get deduplicated do not benefit from these savings. Typically, each user gets charged an amount that is proportional with the amount of data stored and any savings due to deduplication with other users' data are not passed to the end user. Recently, Armknecht et al. [3] introduced *transparent deduplication*, which gives users full transparency on the storage savings achieved through deduplication. This enables a new pricing model which takes into account the level of deduplication of the data: The more users store the same piece of data, the lower each individual user gets charged for storing that piece of data.

We wish to design a system that provides both integrity and reliability (via RDIC and replication) as well as cost-efficient storage via transparent deduplication, when faced with an economically motivated adversary that controls some or all of the storage servers. Adversarial servers will try to "cut corners" and gain an economic advantage as long as it remains undetected. This can be achieved either by using less storage than required to fulfill their contractual obligations for replication, or by charging users according to a deduplication level that is lower than the real one. To achieve this goal, we are faced with two main challenges that were not addressed by previous work:

Challenge 1: *Overcoming the replicate on the fly (ROTF) attack.* Previous work has established that the storage servers should be required to store different and incompressible replicas [10, 12]. Otherwise, if all replicas are identical, an economically motivated set of colluding servers may try to save storage by simply storing only one replica and redirecting all data owner's RDIC challenges to the one server storing the replica. One approach to generate different replicas is by encrypting the original file with different keys. This mitigates the "redirection" attack described earlier: A storage system cannot successfully pass RDIC challenges for the t replicas without actually storing the t replicas.

However, in order to enable deduplication across users, the replicas generated by two users for the same file for the same storage server should be identical. For example, two users must generate identical replicas H_1 for storage server RS_1, identical replicas H_2 for storage server RS_2, etc. To achieve this, users should use the same keys to generate replicas for the same storage server. This introduces the *replicate on the fly (ROTF)* attack, a novel attack unique to this setting: if at least one user shares with the CSP the keys used to generate replicas, then the CSP can recover and store only the original file instead of storing the t replicas. The CSP can then generate on the fly a particular replica to pass an RDIC challenge for that replica. This will hurt the reliability of the storage system, because the CSP does not store t replicas, unbeknownst to the client.

Challenge 2: *Efficient transparent deduplication for multiple replicas.* Transparent deduplication has been investigated only when the data is stored at a single cloud server [3]. When data is replicated at multiple storage servers, the previous solution does not scale well and transparent deduplication becomes more challenging to achieve securely and efficiently.

Contributions: In this work, we propose ReDup, a secure storage solution with Replication and transparent deDuplication. ReDup provides users with strong integrity, reliability, and transparency guarantees about data that is outsourced at cloud storage providers. To the best of our knowledge, ours is the first proposal to provide all these guarantees at the same time. Specifically, ReDup offers:

- *Integrity*: ReDup employs a remote data integrity checking (RDIC) mechanism to allow users to check the integrity of their outsourced data. Each user runs periodically a RDIC protocol to check the health of her data at each replica server. Whenever data damage is detected at a replica, data from healthy replica servers can be used to restore the desired replication level. Such a RDIC mechanism allows users to assess the health of their data by periodically verifying the integrity and replication level of their data.

- *Reliability*: ReDup provides data reliability by replicating a user's data at multiple storage servers that are geographically dispersed. Since different users may have different reliability needs, ReDup offers multiple replication levels and allows users to choose a replication level suitable for their needs. We consider a more realistic adversarial model which includes not only collusions between storage servers, but also between storage servers and users of the system. This introduces a novel attack, the *replicate on the fly (ROTF)* attack, which allows the CSP to store only one copy of the data and generate replicas on the fly to respond to RDIC challenges. To defend against the ROTF attack, we make the replica generation be time consuming and we enhance the standard RDIC challenge-response model to include an additional check regarding the time needed to generate the RDIC proof. In this way, dishonest CSPs that try to generate replicas on the fly will not be able to pass the RDIC challenges. In ReDup, replicas are generated from the original file by applying a novel *shortcut-free time consuming function (SFTCF)*, which we define formally and then instantiate with a butterfly construction.

- *Efficient and transparent deduplication for multiple replicas*: When a user's data is replicated at multiple servers, ReDup provides a proof to the user attesting the deduplication level that occurs at each replica server. The proof is obtained by aggregating individual deduplication level proofs from replica servers, and has a constant size regardless of the number of replica servers. Users are charged inversely proportional to the deduplication level of each of their replicas. ReDup reconciles the seemingly contradictory notions of replication and deduplication: The data of each user is replicated at multiple servers to increase reliability, whereas deduplication is applied independently at each replication server across different users' data to reduce storage costs.

- *Collusion resistance*: These guarantees hold even in the presence of collusion between replica servers or between replica servers and users.

The remainder of the paper is organized as follows: In Section 2 we present background information and related work. We describe the system and adversarial model in Section 3, along with the security guarantees sought by the system. In Section 4 we provide some preliminaries for our basic building blocks. A solution overview of the protocol is depicted in Section 5 and its full description is described in Section 6. Section 7 analyses the security of ReDup and finally we conclude in Section 8.

2 BACKGROUND AND RELATED WORK

Remote data integrity checking for multiple replicas. Remote data integrity checking (RDIC) [4, 17, 22] is a mechanism that allows to check the integrity of data stored at an untrusted cloud storage provider (CSP). A data owner uploads at the CSP their data together with metadata consisting of a set of verification tags, and then periodically challenges the CSP to provide a proof about the health of the data. The CSP is able to create such a proof based on the data and the metadata initially uploaded by the owner.

To ensure data reliability over time, the data owner creates multiple replicas of the data and stores them at multiple storage servers. The data owner then uses RDIC to periodically check the health of each replica, and if a replica is found corrupt, data from the other healthy servers is used to restore the desired redundancy level in the system [10, 12]. Previous work has established that the storage servers should be required to store different and incompressible replicas [10, 12].

Transparent Deduplication. Armknecht *et al.* [3] introduced the notion of *transparency* for deduplicated storage: The cloud provides to users proofs that attest the level of deduplication across users employed by the cloud over their files. This enables a new pricing model which takes into account the level of deduplication of the data, allowing end users to get the benefits of deduplication. Users are protected against a cloud provider that uses a certain deduplication level, but charges users based on a lower level.

The solution lies in a Merkle tree tailored for this application, which allows an honest user to verify a) how many users have also uploaded the same file and b) that information about the user's file has been correctly incorporated in the bill issued by the cloud. Although this solution is efficient when files are stored at a single storage server, when translated to a multiple replica scenario it becomes inefficient as it would require multiple instances of the Merkle tree, one per each replica.

2.1 Other Related Work

Current literature in remote data integrity checking protocols either does not address deduplication in a multiple replica scenario, or does not consider the challenging multi-user scenario with collusions between users and economically-motivated replica servers.

Multi-User with Tags Deduplication. Vasilopoulos *et al.* [24] proposed a combination of existing deduplication schemes with proofs of retrievability to further reduce the storage cost of tags for identical blocks. In their model, there is a single replica storage policy and users do not collude with the cloud provider. Armknecht *et al.* [2] considered the same model, whereby a single replica server stores only once tags coming from different users for the same data block. The solution lies on shared aggregated tags based on BLS signatures [8] incorporating the secret keys of all users and can tolerate collusions between users and a malicious cloud storage provider: Deleting a deduplicated block tag and obtaining the secret key from a malicious user cannot help the cloud to reconstruct the tag without the participation of all the other users. Their model, however, does not consider providing both multiple replica storage and deduplication.

Replicated Storage. Curtmola *et al.* [12] considered a model in which a single user stores replicas of a file at multiple storage servers to tolerate faults. The user relies on an RDIC protocol to verify faithful storage at each replica server. However, this scenario does not consider multiple users nor the deduplication functionality. Armknecht *et al.* [1] considered a multiple replica storage scenario enhanced with proofs of correct replication by the user. This work differs in two fundamental aspects from ours: 1) its focus is towards delegating the replica computation to the CSP, and 2) the tunable puzzles used in the replication scheme rely on the assumption that computation is more expensive than storage, which may not always

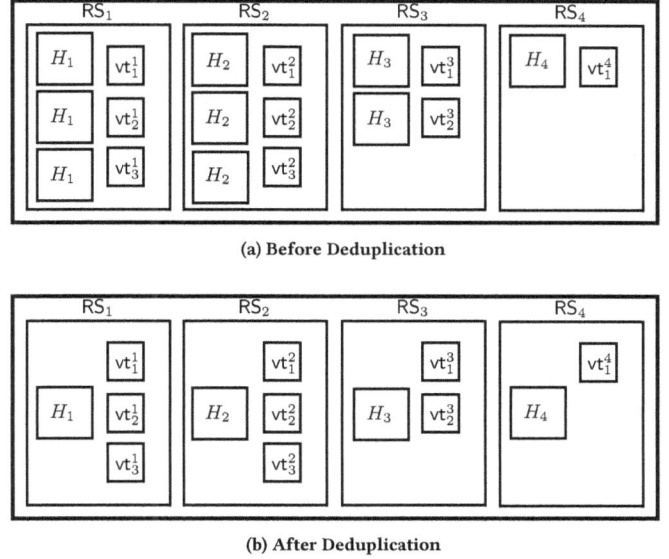

(a) Before Deduplication

(b) After Deduplication

Figure 1: An example of deduplication applied to multiple replicas.

be applicable. Other work [7, 13, 25] seeks to establish the physical location of replicas. Our goal is different.

3 SYSTEM AND ADVERSARIAL MODEL

3.1 System Model

A set of users, $\mathcal{U} = U_1, U_2, U_3, \ldots, U_m$, store their files at a cloud storage provider (CSP). To ensure data reliability and protect against data damage, the CSP exposes an interface that allows users to store multiple replicas of their files at different replication servers. Each user uses remote data integrity checking (RDIC) to check the integrity of their replicas stored at each replica server; in case data damage is detected at a replica server, the user leverages replicas from other healthy replica servers to restore the desired level of redundancy.

Replication level. As users have different budgets and needs, the CSP allows users to choose the desired *replication level* (rl) for their files. Without loss of generality, we assume the CSP offers a fixed number of replication levels (*e.g.*, in practice it may offer three levels, corresponding to high, medium, and low reliability). Fig. 1(a) shows an example with three users choosing different replication levels, $rl_1 = 4, rl_2 = 3, rl_3 = 2$. User U_1, who chose $rl_1 = 4$, will generate four replicas H_1, H_2, H_3, H_4 and the corresponding RDIC verification tags $vt_1^1, vt_1^2, vt_1^3, vt_1^4$, and will store them at replication servers RS_1, RS_2, RS_3 and RS_4. Whereas user U_3, who chose $rl_3 = 2$, will generate two replicas H_1, H_2 and RDIC verification tags vt_3^1, vt_3^2, and store them at servers RS_1, RS_2, respectively.

We assume identical files will result in identical encrypted ciphertexts when stored at the CSP. This assumption is typical in the secure storage deduplication literature and ensures that if two users want to store the same file, the replicas generated for the file will be identical, thus allowing deduplication to be applied at each replica server. The mechanism used to achieve this is outside the scope of the paper, but we enumerate here existing approaches: Users can rely on variants of convergent encryption to derive an encryption key securely with a multiparty computation protocol between users [19]. Or, deduplication can occur with the aid of a semi-trusted server and *message lock encryption* [18].

Deduplication level. Whenever possible, the CSP employs deduplication across different users' files at each replication server: If multiple users store identical files, the CSP keeps only one copy. In the example of Fig. 1(b), servers RS_1, RS_2, RS_3 perform deduplication for the files H_1, H_2, H_3, and the *deduplication level* (dl) is $dl_1 = 3, dl_2 = 3, dl_3 = 2$, respectively. Server RS_4 does not perform deduplication, as it already stores only one copy of file H_4. Notice that deduplication occurs at each replication server independently, meaning that different copies of the same file will be dispersed along replica servers to ensure reliability, but at each replica server deduplication is applied and only one copy of multiple identical files is stored.

Pricing model. The system divides time into epochs (*e.g.*, one epoch is one day) and users get charged at the end of each epoch. A user's bill for each epoch is directly proportional to the chosen replication level and inversely proportional to the deduplication level that occurs at each replica server. This means that if a user is uploading a file at a replica server and that file is already stored by r other users, then each of the $r + 1$ users that store the file will get charged an amount that is $r + 1$ smaller compared to the case when no deduplication occurs.

To prevent a dishonest CSP from charging users more by claiming a lower deduplication level, the system employs transparent deduplication: the CSP provides to each user at the end of each epoch a proof that attests to the deduplication level that occured at each replication server.

System overview. As depicted in Fig. 2, the system consists of four protocols: Setup, Replicate, RDIC, and AttestDedup. Each user U_j, with $1 \le j \le m$, runs these protocols. We give an overview of these protocols next:

Setup($1^\lambda, n, rl_j$): During Setup, each user U_j chooses rl_j, the replication level for her files. Users also generate the secret keys fk, k_j, according to the security parameter λ, that will be used during the other protocols of the system.

Replicate(F, fk, k_j, rl_j): Each user U_j runs the Replicate protocol to generate replicas $H_1, H_2, \cdots, H_{rl_j}$ for file F, using the key fk. Identical files by different users are stored only once at each replica server, but are stored multiple times according to the replication level choice rl_j to ensure reliability. User U_j also uses key k_j to compute the set of RDIC verification tags vt_j^i on top of each replica H_i, with $1 \le i \le rl_j$. Finally, U_j uploads replica H_i and verification tags vt_j^i at server RS_i.

RDIC(F, $< U_j : Q >$, $< RS_i : \sigma_i >$): Each user U_j engages in a remote data integrity checking protocol (RDIC) with replica server RS_i to check faithful storage of the replica file H_i, for $1 \le i \le rl_j$. In the RDIC protocol, the user issues a challenge Q to a replica server, and the server responds with a proof σ_i that attests the integrity of the replica stored at that server (this proof is constructed using the challenged replica file and its corresponding verification tags). The user verifies the correctness of the proof received from the

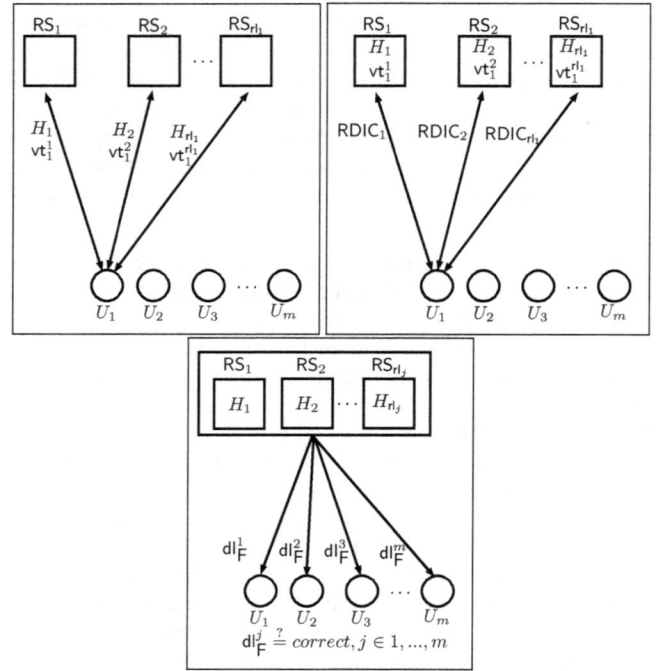

Figure 2: Setup, RDIC, AttestDedup **for a user** U_1 **storing a file** F.

server. Unlike in a standard RDIC protocol, the user performs an additional check in order to prevent the ROTF attack: whether the server's response time is below a threshold T.

AttestDedup(ep, U_j, F): Each user U_j runs the AttestDedup protocol during each epoch ep to verify the CSP's claim about the deduplication level employed for the user's replica files during that epoch. During each time epoch, the CSP issues a bill to each user based on the replication level chosen by the user for her files, and on whether the user's replica files benefited from deduplication. The bill includes a proof that allows the client to verify the deduplication level of its replicas. The AttestDedup protocol prevents dishonest CSPs from claiming a lower deduplication level that the one deployed at its servers in order to charge users a higher bill.

3.2 Adversarial Model

We assume an adversary that controls some or all of the storage servers and is rational and economically motivated. Adversarial servers will try to cheat and "cut corners" as long as cheating remains undetected and it provides an economic benefit. For example, the CSP may use less storage than required to fulfill its contractual obligations for replication, or it may charge users according to a deduplication level that is lower than the real one. An economically motivated adversary captures many practical settings in which malicious servers will not cheat and risk their reputation, unless they can achieve a clear financial gain. Moreover, the communication between users and the CSP is done over an authenticated channel.

The ROTF attack. In addition to controlling storage servers, the adversary may also corrupt users of the system. As such, users may collude with the CSP to share their secret key material. For example, a user may share with the CSP the secret key material used to generate replicas. This allows the CSP to recover the original file and only store that file instead of storing multiple replicas as required by contract. Whenever a user sends an RDIC challenge to check a particular replica, the CSP can generate that replica on the fly based on the original file and on the key material obtained from the colluding user. As described in previous work [10, 11], a storage server that is challenged and does not possess its replica, can either forward the challenge to a server that stores the file (which will generate the needed replica on the fly), or can retrieve the file in order to generate the challenged replica on the fly. By allowing collusions between the CSP and its users, our adversarial model is stronger and more realistic compared to previous work.

We note that users are willing to collaborate in order to benefit from cost reduction due to deduplication. However, we want the system to be resilient to the possibility that some users may be malicious and may collude with the untrusted CSP.

Incorrect deduplication level. A CSP may advertise appealing costs for deduplicated files: Users are charged inversely proportional to the number of times a file has been stored. However, a dishonest CSP may try to claim a lower deduplication level in order to increase its revenue.

3.3 Security Guarantees

Inspired by the aforementioned adversarial model, we define the security guarantees of our system. They protect an honest user U_j from a coalition of malicious replica servers and users who will try not to follow the contractual agreement with respect to **1)** faithful storage of file replicas at rl_j replica servers and **2)** the correct deduplication level used for U_j's files.

3.3.1 Collusion Resistant Replica Integrity. The CSP must prove to a user U_j that it faithfully stores rl_j replicas of the user's files in their entirety. In contrast with multiple replica RDIC protocols designed for single users [1, 12], ReDup seeks to provide data integrity of each replica file when confronted with ROTF attacks that involve collusion between malicious users and dishonest replica servers. More specifically, we say that ReDup provides:

- SG1: *Replica integrity*, if each replica server RS_i can convince a user U_j with high probability that the replica H_i remains intact in its entirety, for $1 \le i \le rl_j$.
- SG2: *Storage Allocation*, if the amount of data stored by a CSP for a file F of size $|F|$ on a replication level rl is at least $rl|F|$.

SG1 protects the users from a CSP that does not store replica files in their entirety. SG2 protects users from a CSP that does not respect its contractual obligations of storing rl_j replicas and tries to reduce its costs by storing less replicas. Together, SG1 and SG2 imply that the CSP faithfully stores all rl_j replica copies of a file F. We capture these two guarantees under the *Collusion Resistant Replicas Integrity* (CR^{2}P) property, formulated with a standard security game between the adversary and the challenger:

In our adversarial model, we assume $\mathcal{A}$ can collude with another user U or another replica server RS. During the game, we allow $\mathcal{A}$ to have access to the oracles, which provide all the secret transcripts.

We denote by $O^{abc}(k, l, m; x, y, z)$ the abc oracle, which takes as inputs the parameters k, l, m and executes its code with local variables x, y, z, which are unknown to the caller–the adversary $\mathcal{A}$. We denote by $\mathbf{a}_i$ a list with i elements. Let $\mathcal{U}'$ be the set of corrupted users and $\mathcal{U} - \mathcal{U}'$ be the set of honest users. We use $\mathcal{RS}'$ to denote the corrupted replica servers and $\mathcal{RS} - \mathcal{RS}'$ the faithful servers. We use $U_i \rightarrow \mathcal{U}$ to denote the insertion of element U_i into the set $\mathcal{U}$. $\mathcal{A}$ has access to the following oracles:

- $\mathcal{U}', \mathcal{RS}' \leftarrow O^{Setup}(\mathbf{uid}_{m-1}, \mathbf{sid}_t; m, rl_j)$: Whenever invoked with parameters a list of users ids $\mathbf{uid}_{m-1}$ and replica servers ids $\mathbf{sid}_t$, the O^{Setup} oracle stores the ids to the appropriate sets $\mathcal{U}', \mathcal{RS}'$, denoting the list of corrupted users and replica servers, respectively.
- $H_i \leftarrow O^{GenReplica}(F, j; fk, i)$: The $O^{GenReplica}$ oracle takes as input a file F and a user id j. It first checks if $U_j \in \mathcal{U}'$. If that user is corrupted then it outputs the replica copy H_i for the replica server RS_i for that user on file F using the key fk. The oracle keeps track of the uploaded files and for similar files it uses the same key in order to simulate the deduplication process. Finally $O^{GenReplica}$ also stores $H_i \rightarrow H$ in the list H and sends H_i to $\mathcal{A}$.
- $vt_j^i \leftarrow C^{TagFile}(H_i, j; k_j)$: The $O^{TagFile}$ oracle on input H_i and j first checks if $U_j \in \mathcal{U}'$ and $H_i \in H$. If both hold, then computes the tags vt_j^i using k_j and forwards them to $\mathcal{A}$.
- $c_F^j \leftarrow O^{Challenge}(F, j; k_j)$: The $O^{Challenge}$ oracle outputs a challenge for file F for the user $U_j \in \mathcal{U} - \mathcal{U}'$.
- $\beta \leftarrow O^{Verify}(proof_F^{j, i}, \tau_i; T)$: The O^{Verify} oracle takes as input a proof $proof_F^{j, i}$ and a response time τ_i. It outputs $\beta = 0$ if either the proof is not valid or $\tau_i > T$, otherwise it sets $\beta = 1$.

During the $\mathsf{Game}_{\mathcal{A}}^{CR^2P}$ game the adversary communicates with the oracles in order to create the environment to be challenged upon as follows:

$\mathsf{Game}_{\mathcal{A}}^{CR^2P}$
1 : $\mathcal{U}', \mathcal{RS}' \leftarrow \mathcal{A}^{O^{Setup}}$ // $\mathcal{A}$ compromises users and servers
2 : **for** $i = 1 \ldots rl_j$ **do**
3 : $\quad H_i \leftarrow \mathcal{A}^{O^{GenReplica}(F,j;fk,i)}$ // $\mathcal{A}$ learns replica copies
4 : $\quad vt_j^i \leftarrow \mathcal{A}^{O^{TagFile}(H_i,j;k_j)}$ // $\mathcal{A}$ asks for verifications tags
5 : $\quad c_F^j \leftarrow \mathcal{A}^{O^{Challenge}(F,j;k_j)}$ // $\mathcal{A}$ is challenged
6 : $\quad proof_F^{j,i}, \tau_i \leftarrow \mathcal{A}(\mathcal{U}', \mathcal{RS}', F, H_i, vt_j^i, c_F^j)$
7 : $\quad \beta_i \leftarrow O^{Verify}(proof_F^{j,i}, \tau_i; T)$
8 : **return** $\beta = \bigwedge \beta_i$ // Experiment is successful if $\beta \stackrel{?}{=} 1$

Finally the game outputs a value $\beta \in \{0, 1\}$. We define the success probabilities of an adversary $\mathcal{A}$ playing the $\mathsf{Game}_{\mathcal{A}}^{CR^2P}$ game as: $\mathsf{Succ}_{\mathcal{A}}^{CR^2P} = \Pr[\mathsf{Game}_{\mathcal{A}}^{CR^2P} = 1]$. The heuristic is that if the output of the experiment equals 1 then $\mathcal{A}$ should posses all replica copies $H_1 \ldots H_{rl_j}$. In order to formulate that heuristic we employ the notion of the extractor $\mathcal{E}$, which can communicate with the adversary and rewind her at different steps in order to extract a file F from all replica copies $H_1 \ldots H_{rl_j}$. We define the success probability of the extractor $\mathcal{E}$ as follows: $\mathsf{Succ}_{\mathcal{A}}^{Extract} = \Pr[F = F_{fh} | F_{fh} \leftarrow \mathcal{E}^{\mathcal{A}}]$.

DEFINITION 1. *(CR^{2}P: Collusion Resistant Replica Possession)* ReDup *system guarantees Collusion Resistant Replica Possession if under any collusions for a set users $|U|$ who have stored the file F in rl_j replica servers* $\text{RS}_1, \text{RS}_2, \text{RS}_3, \cdots, \text{RS}_{\text{rl}_j}$ *and for any PPT adversary $\mathcal{A}$, for any security parameter λ and a negligible quantity $\text{negl}(\lambda)$, it holds that:*

$$\Pr[\text{Succ}_{\mathcal{A}}^{\text{Extract}} \leq \text{negl}(\lambda) \wedge \text{Succ}_{\mathcal{A}}^{\text{CR}^2\text{P}} > \text{negl}(\lambda)$$

$$: \mathcal{E} \xleftarrow{\mathcal{U}', \mathcal{RS}', \text{F}, H_i, \text{vt}_j^i, c_{\text{F}}^j} \mathcal{A} \leftrightarrow \text{Game}_{\mathcal{A}}^{\text{CR}^2\text{P}}] \leq \gamma$$

Intuitively, the CR^{2}P definition establishes an upper bound γ on the event that an adversary $\mathcal{A}$ wins the **Game**$_{\mathcal{A}}^{\text{CR}^2\text{P}}$ game with non-negligible probability and that an extractor $\mathcal{E}$ is not able to extract the file after interacting with $\mathcal{A}$.

3.3.2 Deduplication Correctness. An economically motivated dishonest CSP may employ a certain deduplication level, but may charge users a higher amount by claiming a lower deduplication level. Previous work uses an authenticated data structure (ADS) to accumulate the users' file deduplication levels, and provides to each user a proof of membership in this ADS. To ensure deduplication correctness, it suffices to provide:

- **dc1**: Proofs attesting that each of the user's files has been included in the ADS.
- **dc2**: A proof attesting the correct size of the ADS.

We capture these two guarantees under the *Deduplication Correctness* property:

DEFINITION 2. *(Deduplication Correctness) During an epoch ep, each user U_j stores file replicas at replica servers* $\text{RS}_1, \text{RS}_2, \text{RS}_3, \cdots, \text{RS}_{\text{rl}_j}$ *and the deduplication level for a file F at each replica server RS_i is dl_{F}^i. The system guarantees Deduplication Correctness if, for any epoch ep, an honest user U who runs the* AttestDedup(ep, U, F) *algorithm will detect with high probability if a dishonest CSP claims a deduplication level $\text{dl}_{\text{F}}^{i'} \neq \text{dl}_{\text{F}}^i$ for file F at replica server RS_i.*

4 PRELIMINARIES

In this section, we present building blocks that will be used in our construction.

4.1 Shortcut Free and Time Consuming Function (SFTCF)

We put forward the definition of a Shortcut Free and Time Consuming Function S. S is a symmetric trapdoor function which takes input I with v blocks and outputs H with v blocks. Moreover S should adhere to the shortcut free property which states that the holder of any output H' with $v' < v$ blocks will not help her to recover the remaining $v - v'$ output blocks in time less than a threshold T, even when it knows the trapdoor of S. Finally the running time of S should be considerably greater than the running time of a well known functionality G. The properties of a SFTCF are:

(1) **Shortcut Freeness**: Storing any intermediate state st, which is smaller than the original size v of the input, does not result in evaluation time smaller than the running time of S

on the original input of size v: S cannot be decomposed in $S_1, S_2, \ldots, S_v$, such that $S(v) = S_1() \circ S_2() \circ, \ldots, \circ S_v()$

(2) **G-Detectable Time Consumption**: Evaluation of the function requires computational resources, which results in a considerable detectable time for its evaluation. That is, for another function G whose complexity is $\Omega_G(v)$ we say that S guarantees G-Detectable Time Consumption if $\Omega_S(v) \gg \Omega_G(v)$.

Security. An SFTCF is correct if it allows the recovery of the original input I from the output H. Evaluating S and S^{-1} cannot be done without having the secret key.

DEFINITION 3. *An SFTCF S is secure if it assures shortcut freeness and is G-Detectable Time Consuming for any G with $\Omega_S(v) \gg \Omega_G(v)$.*

For readers familiar with the hourglass function primitive [23], we clarify that our goal in the definition of the SFTCF function is to adapt the security requirements of the hourglass primitive in order to fit the needs of our protocol. The goal of the hourglass function in [23] is to ensure storage of a file in an appropriate format, whereas ReDup's goal is to attest faithful storage of all replicas in case of collusions between users and the CSP.

4.1.1 SFTCF Instantiation. We instantiate the SFTCF S with the butterfly construction proposed by Dijk et al. [23]. Let I and H be the input and output domain consisting of v block files. The output is computed in $d = \log_2 v$ levels. At each level, an atomic operation w takes as input pairs of blocks and outputs another pair, acting as input for the next level. A PRP such as AES can be used for w. More formally $S : I^v \rightarrow H^v$. The input blocks are denoted as $I_1[u]$ and the final output blocks as $H_d[u]$, with $u \in [1, \ldots, v]$. Overall, w is invoked $\frac{v}{2} \log_2 v$ times ($\frac{v}{2}$ times at each level).

Shortcut Freeness: An example of a SFTCF instantiation is shown in Fig. 3, with $v = 8$ blocks and $d = 3$. Each of the blocks on the last level is the result of mixing all of the v input blocks. The SFTCF meets the shortcut freeness requirements because a malicious cloud server that is missing even one block on the last level cannot evaluate S in less time than $O(v)$.

G-Detectability: As shown in [23], the butterfly-based hourglass construction induces considerable computation overhead. More specifically, setting G be the response time of a benign cloud, the running time of G is 0.077 seconds on average according to [23, Table 2] and the corresponding running time for a malicious cloud, who tries to run the butterfly hourglass function, equals 18.065

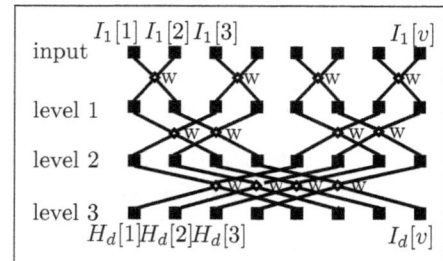

Figure 3: Example of SFTCF based on a butterfly construction, with $v = 8$ input blocks.

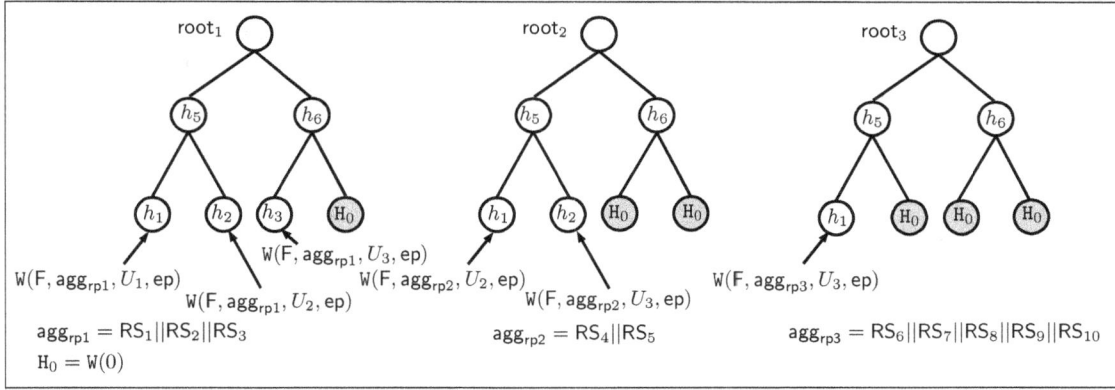

Figure 4: ReDup uses optimized Merkle trees for deduplication level proofs. The CSP offers 3 deduplication levels, $rp_1 = 3$, $rp_2 = 5$, $rp_3 = 10$. Three users U_1, U_2, U_3 choose replication levels $rl_1 = 3$, $rl_2 = 5$ and $rl_3 = 10$, respectively. There will be 3 trees corresponding to 3 replica server groups: $agg_{rp1} = \{RS_1, RS_2, RS_3\}$ for U_1, U_2 and U_3, $agg_{rp2} = \{RS_4, RS_5\}$ for U_2 and U_3, and $agg_{rp3} = \{RS_6, RS_7, RS_8, RS_9, RS_{10}\}$ for U_3. Grey nodes marked H_0 are "zero" leaves obtained by hashing the 0 value. During verification, for example, U_2 receives the following proofs for the file corresponding to the $root_1$ tree: for dc1 h_1, h_6, and for dc2 h_5.

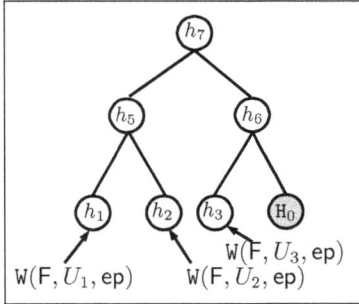

Figure 5: A CARDIAC example with deduplication level 3: leaves h_1, h_2, h_3 correspond to three users U_1, U_2, U_3 who store the same file. The tree contains one "zero" leaf H_0. The deduplication level proof for user U_2 consists of: dc1) the sibling path for h_2, and dc2) the rightmost non-zero leaf h_3 and the sibling path for h_3.

seconds on average for a 2GB file. This experimental evaluation supports the detectability property of our SFTCF.

Alternatively, an SFTCF may be be instantiated with the construction based on tunable puzzles proposed by Armknecht *et al.* [1]. However, the design of their protocol does not explicitly provide provisions against *ROTF* attacks, since the authors make certain assumptions regarding the higher price of computation costs compared with storage costs, which may not hold in all systems and is subject to change over time.

4.2 Merkle Hash Trees

We use a standard Merkle hash tree, which uses a collision resistant hash function $W : \{0,1\}^* \to \{0,1\}^\lambda$ to compute its root with the MHT algorithm. To prove membership for a leaf element, a prover calls ProveMT which computes the corresponding sibling path and the verifier uses CheckPath to verify the membership proof.

5 ReDup OVERVIEW

We give an overview of ReDup, focusing on the challenges addressed by our system:

CH1a (Resiliency against collusions between servers): ReDup encrypts the replicas with different keys. As such, when RS_i does not store its replica copy H_i, it cannot use the replica copy from another server RS_j to answer RDIC challenges on the fly because RS_j stores a different replica copy H_j.

CH1b (Resiliency against collusions between a user and replica servers): Each user U_j generates each replica file by applying the SFTCF function S on the original file F with a different key for each replica. The user then computes verification tags over each replica and uploads the tags and replicas to the replica servers. The user runs an RDIC protocol with each replica server to ensure faithful storage of each replica file by each replica server. In contrast with previous RDIC protocols, ReDup uses an RDIC verification procedure that succeeds only if the time to verify the integrity of each replica copy is below a threshold value T, which is greater than the time to evaluate $S(F)$. As such, U_j can detect malicious behavior of a replica server RS_i that colludes with a dishonest user to answer the RDIC challenges without storing the replica file.

CH2 (Scalable transparent deduplication for multiple replicas): To ensure the correctness of the deduplication level, we adapt the solution based on accumulation Merkle trees used in CARDIAC([3], Section 3.2.1). In CARDIAC, the CSP publishes in each epoch the root of a Merkle tree for each deduplicated file. The Merkle tree has two types of leaves: "non-zero" and "zero" leaves. Each "non-zero" leaf corresponds to a user whose file has been deduplicated, and contains a hash of the user identifier, the file identifier and the epoch. The deduplication level equals the number of non-zero leaves. The rest of the leaves are "zero" leaves, *i.e.*, hashes of the 0 value. The proof of deduplication level correctness for a user consists of two parts: **dc1**) a membership proof, which establishes that this user's file was included in the Merkle tree and **dc2**) a proof attesting the correct number of non-zero leaves, which consists

RS_i	Replica server i, $1 \le i \le n$ (n is the number of replica servers)
U_j	User j, $1 \le j \le m$ (m is the number of users)
f_u	File block u, $1 \le u \le v$ (there are v blocks in the original file F)
S	Shortcut Free and Time Consuming Function (SFTCF)
fk	Secret key used by SFTCF S to generate file replicas
k_j	Secret key used by U_j to compute the tags over her file replicas
W	A hash function $W : \{0,1\}^* \rightarrow \{0,1\}^\lambda$
vt_j^i	Verification tags created by user U_j for her replica stored at RS_i
dl_F^i	Deduplication level of file F at RS_i
rl_j	Replication level for user U_j
fh	Fixed height of the Merkle tree
nz	Index of the rightmost non-zero leaf of a Merkle tree
Z^F	A list of users owning file with id F
$l_{\mathcal{U}}^F$	A list of hashes of each element of the list Z^F
$root^F$	The root of the Merkle tree for file F
h_0^F	The signed root of the Merkle tree for file F
apm_j^F	The authentication path for node h_j of the Merkle tree with root h_0^F
h_{nz}^F	The rightmost non-zero leaf of the Merkle tree with root h_0^F
apc_j^F	Rightmost non-zero leaf authentication path with tree root h_0^F
$\pi_j^{F,ep}$	U_j's proof of deduplication correctness at ep epoch for file F

Table 1: Notation used throughout this section.

of the rightmost non-zero leaf and its sibling path. Fig. 5 shows a CARDIAC accumulation tree example.

Naive solution. A naive adaptation of CARDIAC to a multi-replica scenario does not scale well with different replication level policies per user. Imagine 10 replica servers, one file and three users with three different replication levels: $rl_1 = 3, rl_2 = 5, rl_3 = 10$ for users U_1, U_2, U_3. A CSP following the naive CARDIAC approach has to maintain 10 different trees, one per each replica server. To check the deduplication level, U_3 has to obtain proofs for 10 different trees, which implies a tenfold increase in the communication bandwidth and in the proof computation and verification time.

Optimized solution. Recall that each user U_j chooses her replication level rl_j out of a fixed number of replication levels, *e.g.*, 3 levels corresponding to low, medium, and high reliability. Our solution reduces the number of Merkle trees per file from rl_j to a constant number (*e.g.*, 3), which is the number of different replication levels offered by the CSP. We aggregate different replica server Merkle trees which accumulate the same users and thus have the same structure. In the example provided in Fig. 4, user U_3 who chose a replication level of 10 gets only 3 proofs instead of 10 proofs as in the naive application of CARDIAC.

6 THE ReDup SYSTEM

The full details of the ReDup system are presented in Figures 6 and 7. We start by presenting in Table 1 commonly used notation throughout this section.

A file F consists of file blocks $f_1, f_2, ..., f_v$. The CSP keeps track of two data structures, FL and RL. FL serves as a file log that records which users have stored a specific file. FL is abstracted as a dictionary keyed by the id of a file F. FL[F].append(U_j) denotes the insertion of user U_j under the key F and FL[F] returns a tuple set with the id of all users who have stored the file F. RL is a log dictionary that contains the replication level choice of a user and the files stored by that user: RL[U_j] = (rl : rl_j, f : ()). We describe next the four phases of the protocol, Setup, Replicate, RDIC, AttestDedup.

Setup: Each user U_j runs the Setup algorithm, which outputs RDIC tagging keys k_j (Fig. 6, Setup algorithm, line 1). Users agree

on a key fk to compute the replica copies. Furthermore, each user chooses its replication level rl_j and forwards it to the CSP (line 2), which in turn stores it in the RL dictionary (line 3).

Replicate: Each user runs this algorithm, which outputs the replica copies and the corresponding verification tags to be stored at each replica server RS_i. A key fk_i is derived from fk for each replica server RS_i with the use of a PRF (Fig. 6, Replicate algorithm, line 4). The replica copy H_i for RS_i is then obtained by applying the SFTCF S to the blocks of the original file $f_1, f_2, ..., f_v$ (line 5). To generate the RDIC verification tags, ReDup can use any existing RDIC protocol with private verification [4, 17, 22] (line 6) using secret keys k_j. However, unlike previous RDIC protocols, the TagFile is not applied directly on the file F but on the output H_i of the SFTCF function S.

RDIC: ReDup uses the standard Challenge, Prove and Verify algorithms of an interactive RDIC protocol to check the integrity of the replicas. The user provides as input the challenge Q and the CSP produces a proof σ_i for each replica server. In contrast with the previous RDIC protocols, ReDup uses an RDIC Verify procedure that succeeds only if the time to verify the integrity of each replica copy is below a threshold value $T > \text{Time}(S(F))$, where $\text{Time}(S(F))$ is the running time of $S(F)$. Assuming a computationally-bounded CSP and depending on the client needs, T can be set as $T >> \text{Time}(S(F))$ to detect large corruptions, or as $T \approx \text{Time}(S(F))$ to detect small corruptions.

AttestDedup: The CSP computes the Merkle trees in each epoch with the AttestDedup.P algorithm (Fig. 7, AttestDedup.P algorithm, lines 1-14). In lines 6-9 the correct symmetric replica servers for rp are accumulated in the leaf of each user and finally the leaf Z^F is being hashed with a collision resistant hash function W to output the digest $l_{\mathcal{U}}^F$. For the remaining $2^{fh} - |l_{\mathcal{U}}^F|$ nodes, zero leaves are computed as W(0) to fill in the tree of height fh. Once all the leaves of the tree have been computed, the CSP calls the MHT algorithm, which computes the root of the Merkle tree $root^F$ (line 12) and signs it $h_0^F = \text{Sig}(root^F)$ (line 13).

To compute the proof for a user U_j, the CSP computes the sibling paths apm_j^F for all the trees the user has been included in (line 4), using the standard Merkle tree membership proof (ProveMT algorithm). To establish a correct deduplication level for the file (*i.e*, number of non-zero leaves), the CSP fetches the rightmost non-zero leaf node h_{nz}^F of each tree U_j has been included in and computes its sibling path apc_j^F as well (lines 5-6). Finally, it sends the proof $\pi_j^{F,ep} = (apm_j^F, h_{nz}^F, apc_j^F, fh, |l_{\mathcal{U}}^F|)$ to U_j.

Upon receipt of the proof $\pi_j^{F,ep}$, U_j invokes AttestDedup.V algorithm (cf. Fig. 8) to verify the proof. It first checks whether the claimed deduplication level is consistent with the zero leafs for a tree of height fh (AttestDedup.V algorithm, line 4). For **dc1**, which ensures that the user id was included in the tree(s) of the corresponding files, U_j calls CheckPath to verify the consistency of the returned sibling path apm_j^F (AttestDedup.V algorithm, line 5). For **dc2**, which atests the deduplication level $|l_{\mathcal{U}}^F|$, U_j first verifies the paths of all h_{nz}^F with the CheckPath Merkle tree algorithm (line 6). Afterwards, U_j checks if the CheckPath algorithm on input the $(2^{fh} - 1) - |l_{\mathcal{U}}^F|$ nodes computed as zero leaf nodes, along with

- Setup($1^\lambda, n, \text{rl}_j$): // Run by U_j
  1 : $(k_j, fk) \leftarrow$ KeyGen($1^\lambda, n$)
  2 : U_j sends rl_j to CSP
  3 : CSP sets RL$[U_j].\text{rl} = \text{rl}_j$
  //CSP stores the replication level in the log file RL
- Replicate(F, fk, k_j, rl_j): // Run by U_j
  1 : **for** ($i = 1, i \leq \text{rl}_j, i + +$) **do**
  2 : $H_i \leftarrow$ GenReplica(i, F, fk) :
  3 : **parse** F $as\ f_1, f_2, \ldots, f_v$
  4 : $\text{fk}_i = \text{PRF}_{\text{fk}}(i)$
  //Derive the key for replica to be stored at RS$_i$
  5 : $H_i = S_{\text{fk}_i}(f_1, f_2, \ldots, f_v)$
  //Run the SFTCF S on the original file blocks
  6 : $\text{vt}_j^i \leftarrow$ TagFile(H_i, k_j)
  7 : U_j sends H_i, vt_j^i to RS$_i$
  8 : CSP runs FL$_i$[F].append(U_j)
- RDIC(F, $< U_j : Q >, < \text{RS}_i : \sigma_i >$):
  1 : **for** ($i = 1, i \leq \text{rl}_j, i + +$) **do**
  2 : $Q \leftarrow$ Challenge(l, n)
  3 : $\sigma_i \leftarrow$ Prove(Q, H_i, vt_j^i)
  4 : $\tau_i \leftarrow$ (Time(Verify(σ_i) $\leq T$)) : 1?0
  5 : **if** $\bigwedge \tau_i \stackrel{?}{=} 1$ **return** 1 **else return** 0
- AttestDedup(ep, U_j, F):// Run by U_j and CSP
  1 : **for** ($ep \in \mathcal{T} \wedge F \in FL \wedge U_j \in \mathcal{U}$) **do**
  2 : $\pi_j^{F,ep} \leftarrow$ AttestDedup.P(ep, U_j, F)
  3 : $\{0, 1\} \leftarrow$ AttestDedup.V($\pi_j^{F,ep}$)

Figure 6: The ReDup system.

$\pi_j^{ep} \leftarrow$ AttestDedup.P(ep, U_j, fh): // Run by the CSP
  1 : $pp = 1$
  2 : **foreach** rp **do**
  // For replication levels 3, 5, 10, at every loop rp = 3, 5, 10
  3 : **for** (F $\in$ RL$[U_j].f$) **do**
  // For every file fetch the id thereof from RL
  4 : **for** $\mathcal{U} \in$ FL[F] **do**
  // Retrieve the set of users who stored the file
  5 : $Z^F = \mathcal{U}||ep$
  6 : **for** ($j = pp; j \leq$ rp) **do**
  // Aggregate all the RS of that replication level group
  7 : **if** (RL$[\mathcal{U}].\text{rl} > j$) **continue**
  8 : $Z^F + = ||\text{RS}_j$
  // Aggregate all the replica servers.
  9 : $l_{\mathcal{U}}^F + = W(Z^F)$
  // Using a CRHF W hash the leaf value.
  10 : **for** ($z = 1; z \leq (2^{fh} - 1) - |l_{\mathcal{U}}^F|; z + +$)
  11 : $l_{\mathcal{U}}^F + = W(0)$
  // Pad with 0 leaf nodes
  12 : $\text{root}^F \leftarrow$ MHT($l_{\mathcal{U}}^F$)
  // Build the merkle tree for $l_{\mathcal{U}}^{F,\text{rl}}$
  13 : $h_0^F =$ Sig(root^F)
  // Sign the root
  14 : $pp = $ rp
  1 : **foreach** rp **do**
  // For replication levels 3, 5, 10, at every loop rp = 3, 5, 10
  2 : **if** (RL$[U_j].\text{rl} <$ rp) **continue**
  3 : **for** (F $\in$ RL$[U_j].f$) **do**
  // For every file fetch the id thereof from RL
  4 : $\text{apm}_j^F \leftarrow$ ProveMT($h_j, l_{\mathcal{U}}^F$)
  // Compute the sibling path for U_j's leaf
  5 : $h_{nz}^F \leftarrow$ FetchR(h_0^F)
  // Fetch the rightmost non-zero leaf
  6 : $\text{apc}_j^F \leftarrow$ ProveMT($h_{nz}^F, l_{\mathcal{U}}^F$)
  // Compute its sibling path
  7 : $\pi_j^{F,ep} = (\text{apm}_j^F, h_{nz}^F, \text{apc}_j^F, fh, \text{dl}_F^{\text{rp}})$
  8 : **return** $\pi_j^{F,ep}, \forall F \in$ RL$[U_j].f$

Figure 7: The AttestDedup.P algorithm run by the CSP.

their sibling nodes, verifies correctly the Merkle tree (line 7). If all the checks succeed, AttestDedup.V outputs 1 for successful verification.

Discussion. In ReDup, users encrypt their files before uploading them to the CSP. As such, there is no need for the CSP to encrypt data at rest. We note that, consistent with the secure deduplication literature, the IND-CPA or IND-CCA definitions for privacy cannot be achieved. Thus, we inherit the security guarantee for deduplicated messages: PRIV-CDA (privacy under chosen distribution attacks) [6], which guarantees that encryption of unpredictable messages should be indistinguishable from a random message of the same length. We also note that, if users choose weak keys to encrypt their files, the CSP can apply semantically secure encryption for data at rest independently on top of ReDup.

7 SECURITY ANALYSIS

THEOREM 1. *If S is a Shortcut Free and G-Detectable Time Consuming Function (SFTCF), then ReDup guarantees Collusion Resistant Replicas Possession (CR^{2}P) against a rational and economically motivated CSP and any colluding user.*

PROOF. (Sketch) Let δ_i^u follow a Bernoulli distribution with success probability δ_i^u denoting the probability $\mathcal{A}$ corrupts block f_u at replica server RS$_i$ and failure probability $1 - \delta_i^u$. Let U_{uid} be the user who challenges the CSP. Then all the $vr\text{l}_{\text{uid}}$ blocks have

Figure 8: The verification algorithm for AttestDedup: **The Client** **verifies the proof.**

corruption probability δ_i^u for $u \in [1 \ldots vrl_{uid}]$. The success probability $\text{Succ}_{\mathcal{A}}^{CR^2P}$ for $\mathcal{A}$ to pass a challenge of size l depends on the failure probability $1 - \delta_i^u$ and the success probability δ_i^u to corrupt f_u by outputting the correct challenge on time less than T. We assume S is a secure SFTCF. The probability to correctly guess the challenged blocks equals the probability to randomly guess the output of S for each block of the challenge of size l, and is equal to $\text{Succ}_{\mathcal{A}}^{CR^2P} = \prod_{u=1}^{l} (1 - \delta_i^u + \frac{\delta_i^u \epsilon}{2^v})$, where ϵ is a negligible probability that corresponds to the event of evaluating S in time less than T. From that we conclude that $\text{Succ}_{\mathcal{A}}^{CR^2P} \leq \text{negl}(\lambda)$.

The extractor $\mathcal{E}$ simulates the O^{TagFile} oracle. When $\mathcal{A}$ queries the O^{TagFile} oracle with input (H_i, uid), $\mathcal{E}$ first checks if $uid \in \mathcal{U}'$ and $H_i \in H$. If both hold then it computes the tags vt_{uid}^i and forwards them to $\mathcal{A}$. We assume $\mathcal{A}$ stores only $s < vrl_{uid}$ blocks. By storing we mean both the blocks and the verifications tags. Thus, during the challenge, $\mathcal{A}$ has to correctly guess the blocks and tags of the challenge. Let some $s' < l, s$ blocks of the total l-block challenge be stored by $\mathcal{A}$. We denote by E_1 the event $\mathcal{A}$ correctly guesses the remaining $l - s'$ challenged blocks (which are not stored), E_2 the event $\mathcal{A}$ computes the responses for that challenge correctly and E_3 the event the O^{TagFile} oracle outputs a special malicious output h^*, from which $\mathcal{A}$ can compute the remaining $l - s'$ blocks and the responses on the fly. Accordingly, the probabilities for E_1, E_2, E_3 are p_1, p_2, p_3, respectively.

Clearly, $p_1 = p_2 = \frac{2^{l-s'}}{2^v}, p_3 = \frac{1}{2^q}$, where q is the digest size of the O^{TagFile} response. As such, $\text{Succ}_{\mathcal{A}}^{\text{Extract}} = 1 - (p_1 p_2 + (1 - p_1 p_2) p_3) = 1 - p_3 + p_1 p_2 (p_3 - 1) = 1 - \frac{1}{2^q} + \frac{2^{2(l-s')}}{2^{2v}} (\frac{1}{2^q} - 1)$, meaning that $\text{Succ}_{\mathcal{A}}^{\text{Extract}} > \text{negl}(\lambda)$. As such, $\Pr[\text{Succ}_{\mathcal{A}}^{\text{Extract}} \leq \text{negl}(\lambda) \wedge \text{Succ}_{\mathcal{A}}^{CR^2P} > \text{negl}(\lambda)] \leq \text{negl}(\lambda)$. □

THEOREM 2. *If* W *is a collision-resistant hash function, then* ReDup *guarantees Deduplication Correctness against a rational and economically motivated adversary* $\mathcal{A}$ *who controls all the replica servers* RS_i.

PROOF. (Sketch) Assume the adversary claims an incorrect deduplication level $dl_F^{i'}$. If $dl_F^{i'} < dl_F^i$, an honest user will accept the server's proof with negligible probability $\text{neg}(\lambda) \leq 2^{-\lambda/2}$, where λ is the image length of the collision resistant hash function W. The collision resistance property of W prevents $\mathcal{A}$ of computing a set of leaves $l_{\mathcal{U}'}^{F,rl}$ different than the correct set of leaves $l_{\mathcal{U}}^{F,rl}$ with the same root digest $h_0^{F,rl}$. Otherwise, $\mathcal{A}$ can be used to break W's collision resistance.

An economically motivated adversary will never claim $dl_F^{i'} > dl_F^i$, as this implies a higher deduplication level than the real one, and individual users whose data are deduplicated will be charged less than they should.

□

8 CONCLUSION

We have demonstrated that two seemingly contradictory notions, replication and deduplication, can be reconciled without violating the security guarantees of outsourced storage. Our solution, ReDup, leverages time-consuming replica generation to tolerate collusions between users and a rational CSP that tries to cheat by storing less replicas than agreed upon with its clients. Moreover, ReDup provides transparent deduplication for multiple replicas, thus preventing a malicious CSP from claiming that it deduplicates less files than it actually does. ReDup does this in a scalable manner by presenting to clients a proof that has a constant size regardless of the number of replica servers. This enables a new pricing model which takes into account the level of deduplication of the data: The more users store the same piece of data, the lower each individual user gets charged for storing that piece of data.

ACKNOWLEDGMENTS

This research was supported by the US National Science Foundation (NSF) under Grants No. CNS 1054754, CNS 1409523, and DGE 1565478, and by the Defense Advanced Research Projects Agency (DARPA) and the Air Force Research Laboratory (AFRL) under Contract No. A8650-15- C-7521. Any opinions, findings, and conclusions or recommendations expressed in this material are those of the authors and do not necessarily reflect the views of NSF, DARPA, and AFRL. The United States Government is authorized to reproduce and distribute reprints notwithstanding any copyright notice herein.

REFERENCES

[1] Frederik Armknecht, Ludovic Barman, Jens-Matthias Bohli, and Ghassan O. Karame. 2016. Mirror: Enabling Proofs of Data Replication and Retrievability in the Cloud. In *Proc. of the 25th USENIX Security Symposium (USENIX Security '16)*. 1051–1068.
[2] Frederik Armknecht, Jens-Matthias Bohli, David Froelicher, and Ghassan O. Karame. 2016. SPORT: Sharing Proofs of Retrievability across Tenants. Cryptology ePrint Archive, Report 2016/724. (2016). http://eprint.iacr.org/2016/724.
[3] Frederik Armknecht, Jens-Matthias Bohli, Ghassan O. Karame, and Franck Youssef. 2015. Transparent Data Deduplication in the Cloud. In *Proc. of ACM CCS '15*. ACM, 886–900.

[4] Giuseppe Ateniese, Randal Burns, Reza Curtmola, Joseph Herring, Lea Kissner, Zachary Peterson, and Dawn Song. 2007. Provable data possession at untrusted stores. In *Proc. of ACM CCS 2007*. 598–609.

[5] Giuseppe Ateniese, Randal Burns, Reza Curtmola, Joseph Herring, Lea Kissner, Zachary Peterson, and Dawn Song. 2011. Remote Data Checking Using Provable Data Possession. *Transactions on Information and System Security (TISSEC)* 14, 1 (2011).

[6] Mihir Bellare, Sriram Keelveedhi, and Thomas Ristenpart. 2013. *Message-Locked Encryption and Secure Deduplication*. Springer Berlin Heidelberg, Berlin, Heidelberg.

[7] Karyn Benson, Rafael Dowsley, and Hovav Shacham. 2011. Do You Know Where Your Cloud Files Are?. In *Proc. of ACM Cloud Computing Security Workshop (CCSW '11)*.

[8] Dan Boneh, Ben Lynn, and Hovav Shacham. 2001. Short Signatures from the Weil Pairing. In *Proc. of ASIACRYPT 2001*. Springer Berlin Heidelberg, Berlin, Heidelberg, 514–532.

[9] Kevin D. Bowers, Ari Juels, and Alina Oprea. 2009. Proofs of Retrievability: Theory and Implementation. In *Proc. of ACM Workshop on Cloud Computing Security (CCSW '09)*. 43–54.

[10] Bo Chen and Reza Curtmola. 2013. Towards Self-repairing Replication-based Storage Systems Using Untrusted Clouds. In *Proc. of ACM CODASPY '13*. ACM, 377–388.

[11] Bo Chen and Reza Curtmola. 2017. Remote data integrity checking with server-side repair. *Journal of Computer Security* 25, 6 (2017).

[12] Reza Curtmola, Osama Khan, Randal Burns, and Giuseppe Ateniese. 2008. MR-PDP: Multiple-Replica Provable Data Possession. In *Proc. of ICDCS 2008*. IEEE Computer Society, 411–420.

[13] Mark Gondree and Zachary N. J. Peterson. 2013. Geolocation of Data in the Cloud. In *Proc. of ACM Conference on Data and Application Security and Privacy (CODASPY '13)*.

[14] http://www.computerworld.com/. 2015. OOPS: Google "loses" your cloud data. (2015). https://goo.gl/zXRAdR.

[15] http://www.datacenterknowledge.com/. 2012. Amazon Data Center Loses Power During Storm. (2012). https://goo.gl/anNoI.

[16] http://www.infoworld.com/. 2016. The dirty dozen: 12 cloud security threats. (2016). ttps://goo.gl/i6tAsF.

[17] A. Juels and B. S. Kaliski. 2007. PORs: Proofs of Retrievability for Large Files. In *Proc. of ACM Conference on Computer and Communications Security (CCS '07)*.

[18] Sriram Keelveedhi, Mihir Bellare, and Thomas Ristenpart. 2013. DupLESS: server-aided encryption for deduplicated storage. In *Proc. of USENIX Security '13*. 179–194.

[19] Jian Liu, N Asokan, and Benny Pinkas. 2015. Secure deduplication of encrypted data without additional independent servers. In *Proc. of ACM CCS 2015*. ACM, 874–885.

[20] Dutch T. Meyer and William J. Bolosky. 2011. A Study of Practical Deduplication. In *Proceedings of the 9th USENIX Conference on File and Storage Technologies (FAST '11)*. 1–1.

[21] Dutch T. Meyer and William J. Bolosky. 2012. A Study of Practical Deduplication. *ACM Trans. Storage* 7, 4 (Feb. 2012), 14:1–14:20.

[22] Hovav Shacham and Brent Waters. 2008. Compact Proofs of Retrievability. In *Proc. of ASIACRYPT 2008*. Springer Berlin Heidelberg, 90–107.

[23] Marten van Dijk, Ari Juels, Alina Oprea, Ronald L. Rivest, Emil Stefanov, and Nikos Triandopoulos. 2012. Hourglass Schemes: How to Prove That Cloud Files Are Encrypted. In *Proc. of ACM CCS 2012*. ACM, 265–280.

[24] Dimitrios Vasilopoulos, Melek Önen, Kaoutar Elkhiyaoui, and Refik Molva. 2016. Message-Locked Proofs of Retrievability with Secure Deduplication. In *Proc. of ACM CCSW '16*. 73–83.

[25] Gaven J. Watson, Reihaneh Safavi-Naini, Mohsen Alimomeni, Michael E. Locasto, and Shrivaramakrishnan Narayan. 2012. LoSt: location based storage. In *Proc. of ACM Cloud Computing Security Workshop (CCSW '12)*.

Server-Based Manipulation Attacks
Against Machine Learning Models

Cong Liao
College of Information Sciences and Technology
Pennsylvania State University
cxl491@psu.edu

Sencun Zhu
Department of Computer Science and Engineering
Pennsylvania State University
szhu@cse.psu.edu

Haoti Zhong
Department of Electrical Engineering
Pennsylvania State University
hzz133@psu.edu

Anna Squicciarini
College of Information Sciences and Technology
Pennsylvania State University
acs20@psu.edu

ABSTRACT

Machine learning approaches have been increasingly applied to various applications for data analytics (e.g. spam filtering, image classification). Further, with the growing adoption of cloud computing, various cloud services have provided an efficient way for users to train, store or deploy machine learning algorithms in an easy-to-use manner. However, the models deployed in the cloud may be exposed to potential malicious attacks launched at the server side. Attackers with access to the server can stealthily manipulate a machine learning model so as to enable misclassification or introduce bias. In this work, we study the problem of manipulation attacks as they occur at the server side. We consider not only traditional supervised learning models but also state-of-the-art deep learning models. In particular, a simple but effective gradient descent based approach is presented to exploit Logistic Regression (LR) and Convolutional Neural Networks (CNN)[16] models. We evaluate manipulation attacks against machine learning or deep learning systems using both Enron email text and MINIST image dataset[17]. Experimental results have demonstrated such attacks can manipulate the model that allows malicious samples to evade detection easily without compromising the overall performance of the systems.

CCS CONCEPTS

• **Computing methodologies** → **Neural networks**; • **Security and privacy** → *Domain-specific security and privacy architectures*;

KEYWORDS

Convolutional Neural Networks; Model Manipulation; Adversarial Machine Learning

ACM Reference Format:
Cong Liao, Haoti Zhong, Sencun Zhu, and Anna Squicciarini. 2018. Server-Based Manipulation Attacks Against Machine Learning Models. In *Proceedings of Eighth ACM Conference on Data and Application Security and Privacy (CODASPY '18)*. ACM, New York, NY, USA, 11 pages. https://doi.org/10.1145/3176258.3176321

1 INTRODUCTION

Machine learning approaches have been successfully adopted to address various applications for data analytics on large datasets (e.g. spam filtering, image classification). In parallel, with the growing adoption of cloud computing, cloud services have increasingly offered online services to train, store or deploy machine learning models in a simple-to-use manner. For example, Microsoft Azure provides a full suite of machine learning cloud-based services that enable users to train, test, deploy or even share analytic models for classification tasks [2]. The online application of Azure ML studio [20] can fulfill users' need of building a machine learning model in an iterative cycle of uploading data, refining data, defining features, experimenting a learning algorithm, evaluating the resulting learning model and improving the model by updating the feature selection again. Once a model is finalized, users can directly deploy the model as an online web service that can provide predictive analytic solutions for other applications. Similarly, Google also provides cloud-based tensorflow service [12] that allows users to download/upload or store machine learning models at the server, and even deploy if necessary.

When machine learning models are deployed and used for security sensitive applications such as spam filtering, intrusion detection or malware detection, the robustness of the model is of great importance [3]. However, due to the probabilistic nature of these predictive models, they may be vulnerable to well crafted malicious input in an adversarial environment. Researchers from both security and machine learning communities have investigated the vulnerabilities exposed by various types of attacks, e.g., evasion attack [3] and poisoning attack [4], against machine learning models [25]. These types of attacks usually start with manipulating the input samples by adding certain noises or obfuscating features to baffle the model into misclassifying the malicious samples. Another unique type of attack targets the online machine learning service and is instantiated by querying the service multiple times in order to infer the model and its parameters used by the service [10, 11, 30].

Intuitively, models deployed in the cloud are easy to manipulate through these attacks, as they are beyond the direct control of the service requesters (i.e., the end users). In particular, attacks that directly manipulate the models are more straightforward and efficient as they do not require to modify the input samples as evasion attacks do.

In this paper, we explore a new type of attack under an unexplored adversarial scenario. Instead of crafting a malicious sample in a typical setting of adversarial machine learning, e.g., evasion attack, an intelligent attacker with access to the server can choose to stealthily manipulate a machine learning model, so as to enable misclassification or introduce bias regardless of the test set. This will achieve a similar effect of causing the adversarial sample to evade detection. Here, the adversary is assumed having access to the machine learning model in the cloud, and therefore is capable of manipulating the model directly to cause certain targeted samples to be misclassified. This attack is potentially much more dangerous and effective than classic adversarial models. First, for this attack to be successful we do not need to make assumptions regarding whether the targeted samples are well crafted or not. The proposed manipulation attack directly targets the learning model by modifying the model parameters using a simple but effective gradient descent based approach. Second, the manipulated model adapts to the targeted samples so as to misclassify these samples into the labels specified by the adversary. This attack is demonstrated on two well-known machine learning models, Linear Logistic Regression, and the increasingly popular Convolutional Neural Network models.

We extensively evaluate our suggested attack on two common types of data type - text and image -, representing a binary classification and a multi-class problem, respectively. Our results demonstrate the effectiveness of the proposed attack strategy at the cost of reasonable accuracy loss when the number of target samples is limited. In particular, we show the potential of this attack for convolutional neural networks in the case of multi-class models: manipulation can be successful with no significant impact to the overall model accuracy. Our contributions are summarized as follows.

(1) We introduce a new type of adversarial scenario where machine learning models are subject to potential threats posed by an adversary who has access to the model at the server side, compared to common attacks in the typical setting of adversarial machine learning.

(2) We extensively evaluate the proposed manipulation attack on two representative types of machine learning models, i.e., a linear model Logistic Regression (LR) and a deep learning model Convolutional Neural Networks (CNN), using two general types of dataset, i.e., texts and images.

The rest of the paper is organized as follows. In section 2, we describe our proposed scenario and attack in detail. In section 3, we summarize state-of-the-art attacks against machine learning models, and discuss the similarities and differences compared to ours. In Section 4, we provide the modeling of adversary, and explain the attack strategy against two types of machine learning models

in Section 5 and Section 6 respectively. In Section 7, we conduct experiments to evaluate the proposed attacks, and present our findings in Section 8. Finally, we discuss future works in Section 9.

2 PROBLEM STATEMENT

We consider the scenario of an outsourced machine learning service where a machine learning model is trained and deployed in the cloud as shown in Figure 1. The model is subject to the threats posed by those who have the ability to control how the model is trained and used. This can either come from insiders who have managerial roles or outsiders who gain access privilege by exploiting vulnerabilities at the server side. To make matters worse, it also can be a collusion between the two parties. A manipulated model can fail to capture some target samples for the sake of certain malicious intent, e.g., a spam successfully bypassing a spam filter.

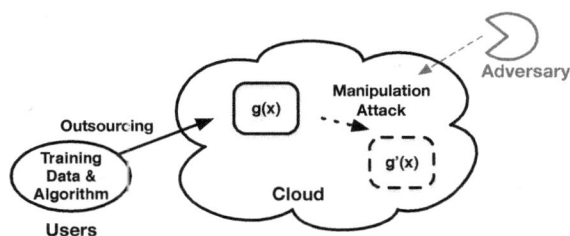

Figure 1: A scenario of outsourced machine learning

Specifically, we investigate how a machine learning model can be stealthily manipulated to intentionally allow certain samples to be misclassified or evade detection. As mentioned, for this attack to be successful, the adversary (e.g. the cloud service performing the model training) must have access to the model stored and deployed at the server. Since model training is outsourced to the server, the adversary should be capable of affecting the training process by tampering the training data or the computational process. For instance, swapping the labels of instances between two different classes is very likely to produce a misleading model. However, this type of tampering carried in a large scale (for a large number of samples) is easily noticeable. Small scale tampering such as flipping the labels of a few instances instead might go unnoticed, but it does not guarantee the effectiveness of the attack, i.e., causing inconsistent influence over the trained model. Therefore, in order to be stealthy, we study the case of a strategic adversary which mainly intends to manipulate the model directly.

This attack strategy is also supported by the observation that although users provide training data for the server to train a machine learning model, it is difficult for the server to influence the training process to accommodate a given spam sample. Hence, it is reasonable to assume that the adversary is interested in directly manipulating the parameters of the model. Additionally, for the attack to be successful, manipulation of the model parameters should be bounded (to avoid drastic degradation of accuracy).

The machine learning model we study mainly refers to classification model in the domain of supervised learning, e.g., Logistic Regression (LR), as well as that in the area of deep learning such as Convolutional Neural Networks (CNN).

3 BACKGROUND AND RELATED WORK

To date, much work has been carried out in the realm of adversarial machine learning. We summarize the main lines of work and our relationship with these efforts in the remaining of this section.

3.1 Attacks

The machine learning systems targeted by the attacks in adversarial settings include both traditional machine learning models, both supervised and unsupervised, as well as state-of-the-art deep learning or neural network systems.

Support vector machine (SVM)[7], a supervised learning algorithm, has been extensively evaluated against both evasion and poisoning attacks, showing some important vulnerabilities of these models. Some recent studies have focused on application specific machine learning systems such as spam filtering, biometric, intrusion detection, face recognition systems that are either based on SVM or other domain specific classification algorithm [8, 9, 23]. There is also an increasing number of studies that investigate attacks that exploit vulnerabilities of deep learning or neural network systems [26], which is loosely related to our approach, as discussed in the next sections. Researchers even explore a more practical black-box attack against a deep neural networks system deployed in real world scenario [25].

Evasion Attack. Evasion attacks attempt to bypass a deployed machine learning model [3] at the test time. Given a learning model, attackers derive a malicious sample that is fed to the model, and observe the outcome to check whether the evasion is successful or not. If unsuccessful, attackers can generate new samples based on the previous result. The process will continue repeatedly until the evasion is achieved.

In such a scenario, the attacker's goal is to craft a sample that can cause the model to misclassify selected samples [14, 18, 21]. Typically, the attacker is assumed to have certain knowledge of the learning algorithm and data including a part of the training data, feature space or feature representation, the model itself and its feedback. Moreover, the attacker is capable of modifying the data sample and features.

Poisoning Attack. Poisoning attacks mainly focus on compromising the training data in order to further influence the final learning result [4, 22, 28]. Regular training data are tainted with data that come from a malicious source by attackers. The poisoned training data are used to train a model which may fail to capture certain malicious samples later.

In the adversarial setting, the attacker's goal is to generate data samples whose addition will affect the performance of the model to be trained. Generally, the attacker is assumed to have knowledge of the training samples, feature representation, the algorithm and its model parameters. In addition, the attacker is able to add data points that will result in modifying the data distribution, and alter the feature values of samples.

Inversion Attack. Inversion attacks target machine-learning-as-a-service systems by querying the online service in order to infer the model (i.e. the model parameters) used by the system [10, 11, 30]. In this case, the attacker is assumed to know the algorithm itself and be able to query the APIs provided by the online machine learning service multiple times, and receive feedback containing the classification scores. With such knowledge, the goal is to infer the parameters of the machine learning model used for the online service. Inversion attacks against online machine learning services have targeted services that are built upon decision trees, logistic regression, SVM.

3.2 Relationship with Adversarial Machine Learning

On the one hand, we bear a similar goal as some of the traditional adversarial machine learning problems, i.e., evading correct classification of selected model samples. On the other hand, we consider a new type of attack, wherein the adversary has a different perspective and insight of the model. In our case, the adversary targets the machine learning model itself. The adversary is assumed to be able to directly manipulate the parameters of the model to achieve the evading effect. Compared to the attacks discussed in the previous section, we differ as follows. In the case of an evasion attack, the training process of a model is assumed intact, but the adversary manipulates individual samples. The attacker crafts a malicious sample by modifying its feature values so that it can evade the detection of a trained model at the test time. With regard to poisoning attack, although similar in the sense that the adversary can influence the training process, our attack method mainly chooses to target the model directly but with the aim of minimally affecting the overall performance of the model. In contrast, traditional poisoning attack methods inevitably affect the model performance by compromising the training data. Finally, unlike the evasion attack, which crafts one malicious sample at a time, we tend to accommodate multiple samples at the same time - by affecting the model parameters, and still achieve a reasonable model performance.

4 ADVERSARY MODEL

In this section, we describe the attacker's goals, knowledge, and strategies.

4.1 Notations

A classification problem can be simply noted as a function $y = f(x)$, i.e., a given sample x is assigned to a particular label y that comes from a collection of predefined classes Y. A sample x is represented in certain feature space $x \in X$. As to Y, the possible labels may be a finite number k. In the simplest case, i.e., binary classification, $Y = \{0, 1\}$. For example, if we consider the typical problem of classifying emails or messages as spam or not, 0 refers to the legitimate class and 1 indicates the spam class.

In general, the assignment of a label y is yielded by comparing the output of model $g(x)$ against a certain threshold. For instance, if we choose a threshold of 0.5 , $y = 0$ if $g(x) = p(f(x) = 0|x) > 0.5$, and otherwise $y = 1$ if $g(x) = p(f(x) = 0|x) < 0.5$.

4.2 Knowledge

In the scenario of an outsourced computation to train a machine learning model, we assume users provide training data and a selected machine learning algorithm for the server to conduct the training process.[1] For instance, when interacting with machine

---

[1] This is the most common setting of current cloud services.

learning services provided by Microsoft Azure, users will be instructed to go through the process of uploading their data, pre-processing, defining features and applying a learning algorithm of user's choice [20]. Hence, the adversary is assumed aware of the training set, feature representation of the training data and specifics of the machine learning algorithm. Once a model is generated after the training process, it can be either stored in the cloud service or downloaded locally. Users can easily upload the model and iterate the same procedure to refine it or deploy the model as a web service directly. Therefore, the adversary also has access to the trained model, i.e., the parameters of the model. However, the server does not have access to the testing data, which is typically kept by users to evaluate the performance of the trained model. We assume that users will not be able to precisely verify the trained model by themselves (for the lack of local resources) or by another service provider (for the short of budget).

4.3 Goal

In general, the adversary's goal is to manipulate a machine learning model in a way that a given sample can evade the classifier or be misclassified. For simplicity, we start with considering the case of spam filtering modeled through a Logistic Regression (LR) algorithm, which could be generalized as an attack towards a linear model. The attacker aims to find a model $g(x)$ similar to the original model $g(x)'$ such that a spam sample x can obtain an estimated posterior probability $p(f(x) = 0|x)$ greater than the threshold 0.5, and therefore be labeled as non-spam. In order to avoid detection, the attacker aims to maintain a satisfactory performance of the model accuracy, such that it is non-trivial to distinguish between $g(x)$ and $g(x)'$. This goal can be expressed in terms of a loss function that the adversary intends to minimize. In this case, the attacker's goal is to produce a new model $g(x)'$ which has similar weights to the original model $g(x)$ that minimizes the loss of $g(x)'$'s prediction given certain samples. This minimization function is further subject to the constraint that model accuracy is preserved within reason, i.e., the two models (original and compromised model) are as close as possible.

5 ATTACK STRATEGY IN THE CASE OF A LINEAR MODEL

A näive attacker strategy could consist of adding the target instances with the desired labels to the training set before the model is trained as expected[2]. However, such a strategy has two limitations, with one being that the server may not know which instances need to be manipulated during the training phase for the attack to succeed. The other issue is that flipping the labels in the training set does not guarantee the model will produce the desired output for two reasons: 1) the training accuracy is not 100%, and 2) the manipulated instances are more likely to be treated as outliers for the model.

Given the above considerations, our proposed attack strategy is to modify the trained model $g(x)$ so as to predict certain target instances with the desired labels, and yet minimize the accuracy loss.

---

[2]This is similar to the poisoning attack, though the attacker's goal in the case of the poisoning attack is different in that it aims to affect performance

We provide the detailed attack strategy toward a LR model. Assume a given LR model, per the following equation.

$$g(\mathbf{x}) = \frac{1}{1 + \exp^{W^T \mathbf{x} + w_0}}, \quad (1)$$

The target function we would like to minimize is presented as follows.

$$loss = -\sum_{\mathbf{x_i} \in D_A} \sum_{c \in C} y_c * log(g(\mathbf{x_i})) + \alpha * ||\mathbf{W_{old}} - \mathbf{W_{new}}||^2, \quad (2)$$

Here, $loss$ represents a linear combination of the model's cross-entropy loss and the quadratic distance between the old and the new model's parameters. Specifically, for the cross-entropy, C is the set of possible classes, and y_c is the indicator function which equals 1 when c is equal to the target class number. D_A is the dataset which contains all the malicious target instances. $\mathbf{x_i}$ is the feature representation of an instance i, $\mathbf{W_{old}}$ is the parameter of the model before manipulation, $\mathbf{W_{new}}$ is the parameter of the current modified model, α is the regularization coefficient which constrains the model's weights from changing too drastically.

5.1 Algorithm

Our goal is to reduce the loss function until the model is able to produce the intended classification outcomes for the target samples. In the case of LR, we use gradient descent to optimize Equation 2. Gradient descent is motivated by the fact that given a differentiable function F and a point p, the value of function F will decrease the fastest along the direction of the negative gradient of the function F at that point. This method is widely applied in finding the minimum of a function. The algorithm takes steps proportional to the negative of the gradient of the loss function at the current weight point to find a local minimum of the function. In our case, the partial gradient of loss function in Equation 2 is:

$$\nabla_{W_{new}} loss = -\sum_{i \in D_A} \frac{y_c}{g(\mathbf{x_i})} \nabla_{W_{new}} g(\mathbf{x_i}) - 2\alpha * (\mathbf{W_{old}} - \mathbf{W_{new}}), \quad (3)$$

We update W_{new} with Algorithm 1 with a relatively small learning rate, denoted as β. Learning rate is used to control how fast the weight is updated. The iterative optimization process stops once the model produces the desired output to all target instances. The process of attacking a LR model is illustrated in Algorithm 1. As shown, in the algorithm, we decrease α, the constraint coefficient if labels are not changed to the target class and 10000 iterations are completed. Note that we decrease α dynamically to slowly relax our main constraint, in case we cannot find a solution for the optimization problem after multiple iterations. Empirically, we relax the constraint coefficient α by a factor of 0.9.

Algorithm 1: Attack to a LR Model

Data: D_A - sample set needed for manipulate
INPUT: W_{old} - weights of the original model, α_{init} - initial value of α, β - learning rate, C - target label
OUTPUT: W_{new} - weights of the manipulated model
$W_{new} = W_{old}$;
$\alpha = \alpha_{init}$;
$iter = 0$;
while $\exists g(x_i) \neq C$ **do**
  $\quad W_{new} = W_{new} - \beta * \nabla_{W_{new}} loss$;
  $\quad iter++$;
  $\quad$ **if** $iter == 10000$ **then**
  $\quad\quad \alpha = \alpha * 0.9$;
  $\quad\quad set\ iter\ to\ 0$;
  $\quad$ **end**
end

---

6 ATTACK TO DEEP LEARNING MODELS

We further investigate the potential of the attacker's success in the context of a deep learning model – Convolutional Neural Networks (CNN) [16]. For clarity of presentation, we start by introducing the concept of multilayer perceptron (MLP) that a CNN is built upon, and then move on to the description of CNN.

6.1 MLP and CNN

MLP can be considered as a neural network that consists of many nodes known as "neurons". Neurons form layers where each neuron is fully connected with the neurons in the adjacent layer. A simple 3-layer MLP is shown in Figure 2

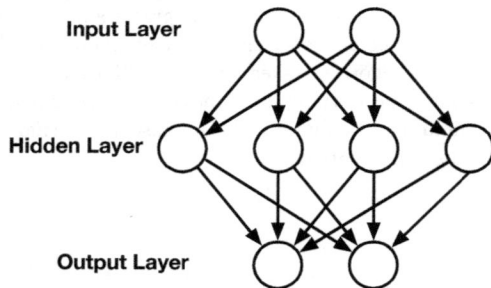

Figure 2: A 3-layer MLP

A CNN has three types of layers, i.e, input layer, hidden layer and output layer. A neuron in a hidden lay represents a computing unit associated with parameter weight w, intercept b and a non-linear activation function f. More formally, a layer can be denoted as:

$$x_i = f_i(W_i * x_{i-1} + b_i) \tag{4}$$

where x_i is the output of ith layer, x_{i-1} is the output of $(i-1)$-th layer, W_i and b_i are the parameters of ith layer. To train a MLP,

the set of parameters $\{W, B\}$ can be learned using stochastic gradient descent with mini batches [5]. The partial derivatives in each iteration that updates the $\{W, B\}$ over a mini batch of the entire training data are computed using the back-propagation algorithm [27].

Deep Learning Networks (DL) refer to architectures which have more than 2 hidden layers (e.g., traditional MLPs). The model we investigate here is the Convolutional Neural Network (CNN)[16], which is the standard benchmark designed for image classification and object detection tasks. One peculiar feature of CNN is that certain layers are not fully connected. Those layers are typically referred to as convolutional layers. Usually, a neuron in a convolutional layer is connected to a small region of neurons in the previous layer. The small region is known as a local receptive field. It acts as a filter that slides across the input with a certain stride size. A convolutional layer can have a certain depth with each corresponding to certain filters used to represent different features in the input. Moreover, another type of layer named pooling layer is periodically inserted between convolutional layers to downsample the spatial size of input as a way to reduce the amount of parameters in CNN. Additionally, a CNN usually consists of a fully connected layer, the same as that in MLP at the end.

6.2 Attack Strategy

Since different layers have their own regularization terms, it is hard to choose proper regularization coefficients for every layer in the network. In our approach, we adapt a transfer learning approach[29], which keeps the weights of the initial layers in the model frozen while retraining only the fully-connected layer using the gradient descent. We further add a constraint on the fully-connected layer. This constraint is presented in Equation 5, and it tries to keep the weights from changing drastically.

$$loss = - \sum_{i \in D_A} \sum_{c \in C} y_c * log(g(\mathbf{x_i})) + \\ \alpha_0 * ||\mathbf{Wo_{old}} - \mathbf{Wo_{new}}||^2 + \alpha_1 * ||\mathbf{Wh_{old}} - \mathbf{Wh_{new}}||^2 \tag{5}$$

In this equation, $\mathbf{Wo_{old}}$ is the parameter of the output layer of the model before modification, $\mathbf{Wo_{new}}$ is the parameter of the output layer of the current modified model, $\mathbf{Wh_{old}}$ is the parameter of the hidden layer of the model before modification, $\mathbf{Wh_{new}}$ is the parameter of the hidden layer of the current modified model, α_0 and α_1 are the regularization coefficients which limit the model's weights from changing too much. Back propagation (shown in Appendix A) is used to update the CNN.

The process of attacking a CNN model is summarized in Algorithm 2. Similar to Algorithm 1, we decrease the constraint coefficient if not all the labels of the target instances are changed and 10000 iterations are completed. Empirically, we choose to relax the constraint coefficient α by a factor of 0.9.

7 EXPERIMENTAL ANALYSIS

In this section, we report experimental results to demonstrate the effectiveness of the proposed manipulation attack against LR and CNN. We first introduce the dataset used for our experiments. Next,

---

Algorithm 2: Attack to a CNN Model

Data: D_A - sample set to be manipulated
INPUT: W_{old} - weights of the original CNN
OUTPUT: W_{new} - weights of the manipulated CNN
freeze all layers' parameters except fully connected layer;
$iter = 0$;
do
| If layer is "output", compute *loss* per Eq. 5 at the output layer;
| Update weights from input layer to hidden layer based on back propagation shown in Appendix A;
| iter++;
| **if** $iter == 10000$ **then**
| | $\alpha = \alpha * 0.9$;
| | $iter = 0$;
| **end**
while *not all target instances are classified as intended*;

---

we describe the basic experimental settings. Finally, we discuss various attack scenarios and report our findings.

7.1 Datasets

For our experiments, we use two datasets, a textual dataset and an image dataset. The text dataset is the well-known Enron Spam Emails dataset [19]. The image dataset is the MNIST Handwritten Digits dataset [17]. The Enron-Spam dataset consists of ham (non-spam) messages from six individual users selected from the Enron Corpus [15], and spam messages drawn from three different sources. In total, the dataset includes over $16,000$ hams and $17,000$ spams. Each email sample is converted into a word vector based on the bag-of-words model, and the feature value uses binary representation, i.e., presence (1) or absence (0).

The MNIST dataset consists of various handwritten digits from 0 to 9. Each image has the size of 28x28 pixels, with each pixel value ranging from 0 (white) to 255 (black). The dataset has a training set of $60,000$ instances and a test set of $10,000$ instances. Each image instance is represented by 784 pixels in total as its features.

7.2 Settings

For the Enron-Spam dataset, we randomly select 80% of emails from both categories as the training set, and the remaining samples are used as the test set. As to the MNIST dataset, we use the default training set and test set. The attack procedures shown in Algorithm 1 and Algorithm 2 are implemented based on Tensorflow [1] library in Python. The configurations used to test the attacks for LR and CNN are presented in Table 1 and Table 2, respectively.

7.3 Results

We describe various scenarios where the attack strategy against LR and CNN are evaluated, and discuss the corresponding experimental results.

7.3.1 A Naïve Approach. A simple approach to carry a manipulation attack consists of the adversary adding target samples in the

Configuration	Value
Learning rate (training)	0.01
Training epoch	25
Batch size	100
Learning rate (attack)	0.001

Table 1: Configuration of tested LR models

Configuration	Value
# of convolutional layers	2
# of max pooling layers	2
# of fully connected layers	1
Input size	784
Class size	10
Batch size	128
Stride	1
Max pooling filter size	2x2
Dropout	0.75
Learning rate (training)	0.001
Training iteration	200000
Learning rate (Attack)	0.000001

Table 2: Configuration of tested CNN models

# of Target Samples	Average Success Rate		
	MNIST CNN	MNIST LR	Enron-Spam LR
1	0%	2%	5%
2	0%	1%	0%
3	0%	0%	0%
4	0%	0%	0%
5	0%	0%	0%

Table 3: Attacker success rate

training set and marking them with the target label, e.g. the adversary could add target spams and label them as non-spam, before the model is trained. The underlying objective is that spams or similar spams will be misclassified by the model, and still avoid detection. We argued in the beginning of Section 5 that such tampering is not effective in attacking a model compared with direct manipulation. Hence, we conduct the following experiment to validate our hypothesis.

To simulate this naïve approach, we randomly select n samples at a time from one class and label them as a different class. For the Enron-Spam dataset, samples are chosen from the spam class and labeled as legitimate. In the case of the MNIST dataset, samples are drawn from a random class and marked as a new class other than the original one. We then train a model (either the LR or CNN) with the modified training data. Lastly, we check whether all the n selected samples are successfully misclassified by the trained model or not. n ranges from 1 to 5. For each n, we repeat such procedure 100 times and measure the average success rate.

As we can see in Table 3, the success rate is 0% in most cases, indicating that this baseline approach would not affect the trained model at all. In other words, tampering the labels of a few target samples is unlikely to lead to successful misclassification of all those samples, and the trained model is robust enough to correct such minor changes in the training data. Therefore, a more strategic attack for manipulating the trained model is necessary.

7.3.2 Manipulation Attack with Enron-Spam. Since CNN is designed specifically for image classification, we evaluate the proposed attack against the LR model solely against the Enron-Spam dataset. In this experiment, an LR model is already trained using the original Enron-Spam dataset. We demonstrate how we can manipulate a trained LR model causing certain number of samples to be misclassified as a different class.

In the experiment, we begin by randomly choosing n samples from the spam class as the target instances. Given the trained model and selected samples, we further apply the attack approach illustrated in Algorithm 1. Lastly, the performance of the newly generated model is evaluated against the test set. n varies from 1 to 5 and such process is repeated 100 times. Each time, we compare the accuracy of the new model with that of the original model, and calculate the difference as the accuracy loss. The average accuracy loss is reported in Figure 3.

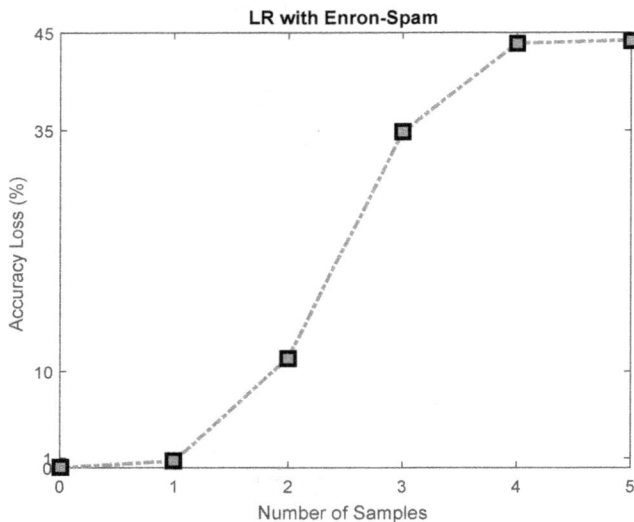

Figure 3: Enron-Spam: LR Accuracy loss with increasing number of target samples

As we can see from Figure 3, the accuracy loss increases drastically as the number of target samples increases. When we have 5 samples to be targeted at the same time, the accuracy loss is near to 45%. In other words, as more samples are being targeted as the same time, LR model becomes less robust in terms of its classification capability. Its overall performance is sacrificed in order to accommodate those target samples. However, when there is only one target sample at a time, the accuracy loss is minimal (only 0.68%), which is hardly noticeable.

7.3.3 Manipulation Attack on MNIST dataset. In this experiment, we evaluate the proposed attack against both LR and CNN on the

MNIST dataset. In each case, a model is already trained using the original dataset. We show how we can manipulate a trained LR or CNN model causing certain number of samples to be treated as a different category.

We begin with selecting n random samples from one of the categories. In contrast to the binary classification case, the handwritten digit dataset has 10 classes in total. Hence, we consider four different settings in terms of chosen samples and attacking labels, i.e.,

(1) Setting 1: each sample is chosen from a random class and it is manipulated into a random class label
(2) Setting 2: each sample is chosen from a random class and it is manipulated into a target class label
(3) Setting 3: each sample is chosen from a target class and it is manipulated into a random class label
(4) Setting 4: each sample is chosen from a target class and it is manipulated into a target class label

As in the previous experiments, we vary n from 1 to 5 and repeat the experiment 100 times. The performance of the manipulated model over the test set is evaluated for both LR and CNN models. Each time, we compare the accuracy of the new model with that of the original model, and calculate the difference as the accuracy loss.

$$\text{Accuracy Loss } (\%) = Accuracy_{g(x)} - Accuracy_{g'(x)}$$

Setting 1 With both CNN and LR models, we randomly select samples regardless of their original labels and initiate the manipulation attack to classify the samples with another random class among the possible ones. This is the most general case where a sample can be randomly manipulated into any class different from the original one. The average accuracy loss is visualized in Figure 4.

As clearly shown, for both LR and CNN, the accuracy decreases as the number of target samples increases. However, the trend of change for CNN is significantly less drastic than that of LR, regardless of the number of samples considered. In particular, when 1 and 2 samples are targeted, the accuracy loss for CNN is negligible, which is 0.35% and 0.39%, respectively. The accuracy loss in case of the attack for the LR model is much more significant, up to 13.5% for 5 labels, and over 10% with only three labels modified.

Setting 2 In these experiments, the samples are also chosen randomly but the target class label is fixed as one of the 10 classes from digit 0 to 9 excluding the original class label. For each of the target digit, we repeat the process of random selection of samples and manipulation attack.

The average accuracy loss is shown in Figure 5. In addition, Figure 6 reports the loss for the same setting with the LR model. As shown, for each target label with CNN and LR, the general trend is a decrease of accuracy as the number of targets grows, which is consistent with our findings from experiments carried out under setting 1. In general, we again note that LR performs worse than CNN in each case. Further, in the case of CNN, we see relatively greater loss on average when samples are attacked into class label 2 or label 8. On the contrary, for LR, target label 4 on average has more accuracy loss compared to other digits. We discuss in Section

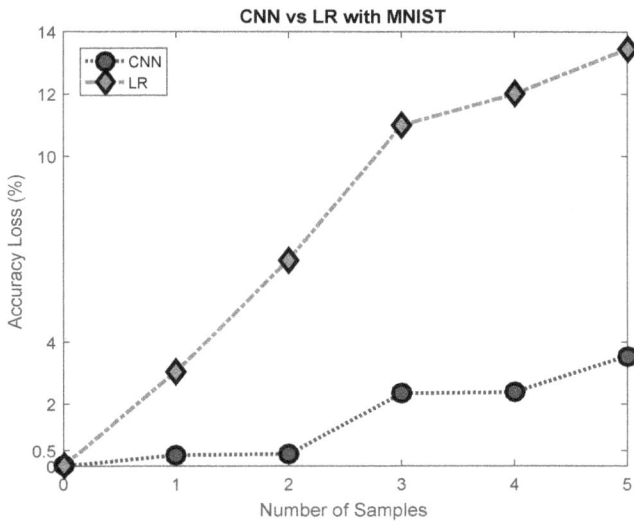

Figure 4: MNIST: CNN and LR Accuracy Loss in Setting 1

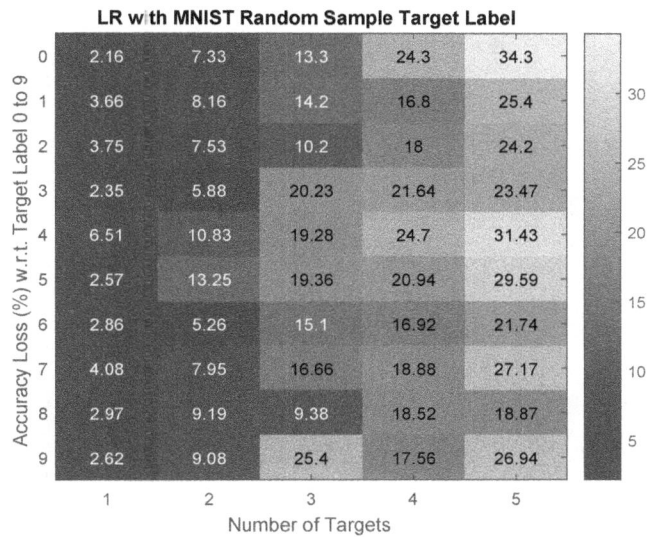

Figure 6: MNIST: LR Accuracy Loss in Setting 2

8 some possible reasons for the differences in their performance over different labels.

6 are harder to attack with LR but easier to attack with CNN. The reasons for this difference in performance may be manifold. We elaborate on this matter in the next section.

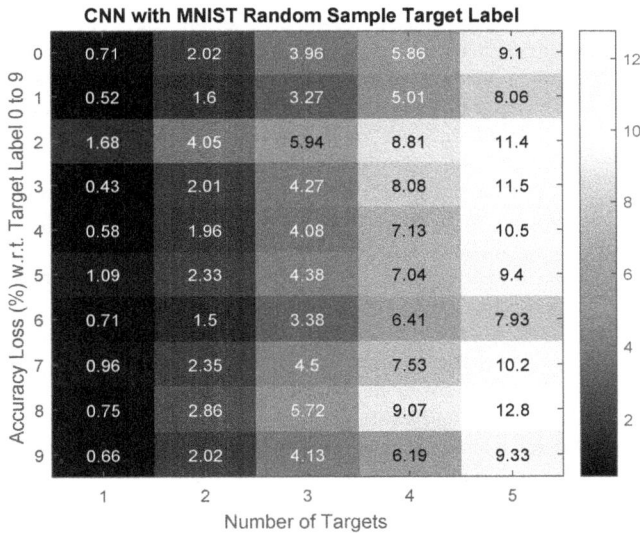

Figure 5: MNIST: CNN Accuracy Loss in Setting 2

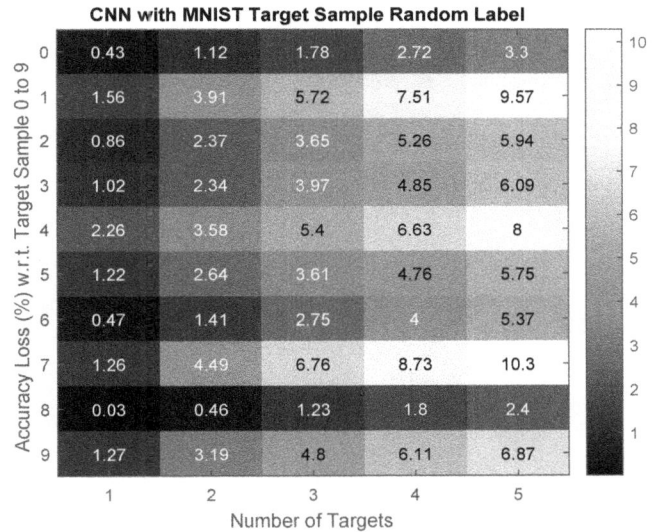

Figure 7: MNIST: CNN Accuracy Loss in Setting 3

Setting 3 Here, samples are selected from an individual digit class, while the target label is randomly assigned except for their original class label. Again, the attack is repeated for each class. The average accuracy loss for CNN model is shown in Figure 7, whereas the performance of the attack for the LR model is shown in Figure 8. As we can see, a similar trend is observed as the trend reported for the experiments under setting 2, in terms of accuracy loss. For CNN, samples from class label 8 are the easiest to attack while samples from class label 7 are much difficult to attack for both CNN and LR. Moreover, we note that samples chosen from class label 3 and

Setting 4 Samples are selected from a designated class and are targeted as a specific label among the 10 digit classes other than the original one. In particular, we choose 2 samples and repeat the attack. While, for setting 4 with LR model, the average accuracy loss is shown in Figure 10. As we can see from the Figure 9, comparatively it is more difficult to attack a sample from class label 4 to another digit class and easier to attack class label 8. Interestingly, we note that certain pair of class labels have similar degree of attack difficulty, such as class 3 and 9. Some pairs have contrasting results,

LR with MNIST Target Sample Random Label

Accuracy Loss (%) w.r.t. Target Sample 0 to 9	1	2	3	4	5
0	2.17	9.59	11.11	9.87	13.96
1	4.31	7.63	12.9	8.79	8.75
2	1.49	6.49	10.6	14.7	12.98
3	7.2	7.85	12.22	9.53	10.83
4	1.23	4.31	8.85	12.86	15.18
5	2.57	5.34	8.79	11.13	11.27
6	6.88	5.33	8.26	10.7	11.7
7	4.65	6.84	9.43	10.54	13.3
8	2.14	9.3	7.14	11.9	8.37
9	2.13	1.61	8.38	7.62	12.8

Number of Targets

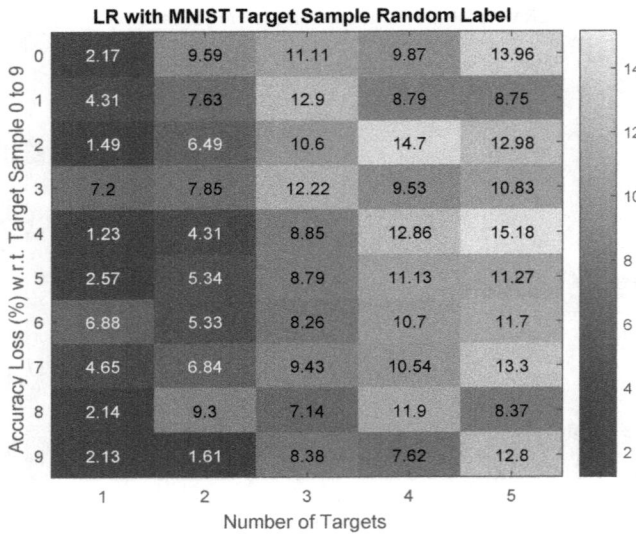

Figure 8: MNIST: LR Accuracy Loss in Setting 3

e.g., for class 8 and class 4 it is much easier to attack a sample of label 8 into label 4 and not the other way around. We have similar observations for the case of LR in Figure 10 as well, where certain pairs have similar degree of attack difficulty.

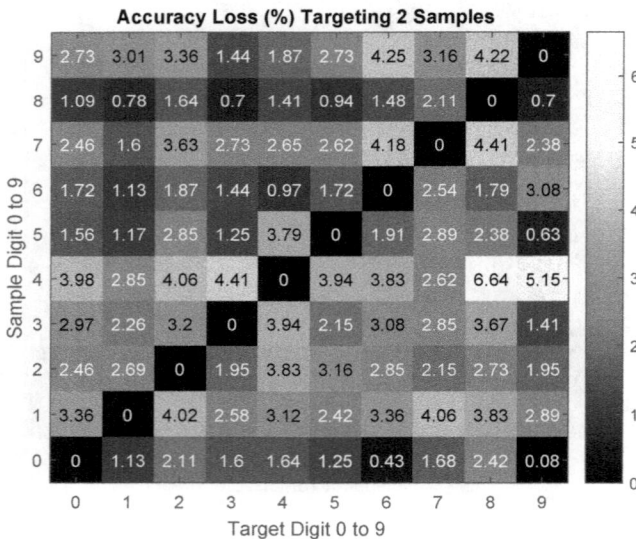

Accuracy Loss (%) Targeting 2 Samples

Sample Digit 0 to 9	0	1	2	3	4	5	6	7	8	9
9	2.73	3.01	3.36	1.44	1.87	2.73	4.25	3.16	4.22	0
8	1.09	0.78	1.64	0.7	1.41	0.94	1.48	2.11	0	0.7
7	2.46	1.6	3.63	2.73	2.65	2.62	4.18	0	4.41	2.38
6	1.72	1.13	1.87	1.44	0.97	1.72	0	2.54	1.79	3.08
5	1.56	1.17	2.85	1.25	3.79	0	1.91	2.89	2.38	0.63
4	3.98	2.85	4.06	4.41	0	3.94	3.83	2.62	6.64	5.15
3	2.97	2.26	3.2	0	3.94	2.15	3.08	2.85	3.67	1.41
2	2.46	2.69	0	1.95	3.83	3.16	2.85	2.15	2.73	1.95
1	3.36	0	4.02	2.58	3.12	2.42	3.36	4.06	3.83	2.89
0	0	1.13	2.11	1.6	1.64	1.25	0.43	1.68	2.42	0.08

Target Digit 0 to 9

Figure 9: MNIST: CNN Accuracy Loss for 2 Target Samples in Setting 4

8 DISCUSSION

Our experiments provide some interesting insights and open questions, as discussed below.

- As noted, increasing the number of target samples consistently results in lowering the overall accuracy, for both LR

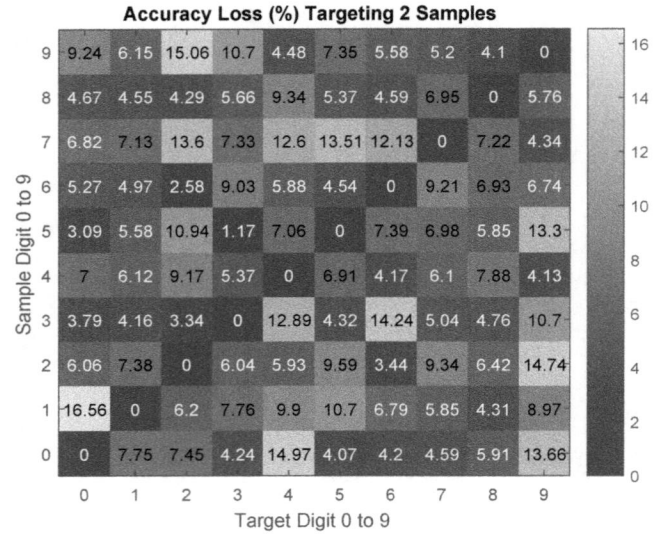

Accuracy Loss (%) Targeting 2 Samples

Sample Digit 0 to 9	0	1	2	3	4	5	6	7	8	9
9	9.24	6.15	15.06	10.7	4.48	7.35	5.58	5.2	4.1	0
8	4.67	4.55	4.29	5.66	9.34	5.37	4.59	6.95	0	5.76
7	6.82	7.13	13.6	7.33	12.6	13.51	12.13	0	7.22	4.34
6	5.27	4.97	2.58	9.03	5.88	4.54	0	9.21	6.93	6.74
5	3.09	5.58	10.94	1.17	7.06	0	7.39	6.98	5.85	13.3
4	7	6.12	9.17	5.37	0	6.91	4.17	6.1	7.88	4.13
3	3.79	4.16	3.34	0	12.89	4.32	14.24	5.04	4.76	10.7
2	6.06	7.38	0	6.04	5.93	9.59	3.44	9.34	6.42	14.74
1	16.56	0	6.2	7.76	9.9	10.7	6.79	5.85	4.31	8.97
0	0	7.75	7.45	4.24	14.97	4.07	4.2	4.59	5.91	13.66

Target Digit 0 to 9

Figure 10: MNIST: LR Accuracy Loss for 2 Target Samples in Setting 4

and CNN, regardless of the dataset used. This is within our expectations, since modifying the weights of the model implies that we have to to adapt the model to every target sample's feature pattern perfectly. Moreover, with more samples being targeted at the same time, the classifier will be "confused", since the target samples may share similar feature patterns with certain instances in the training set with their original (and therefore different) labels. Therefore, the more samples we intend to accommodate at the same time, the harder it is for us to manipulate the machine learning model. Also note that the actual samples chosen for model manipulation may have a significant impact on the success of the attack, as shown in our experiments for Setting 2 and 3. In addition to the influence brought by randomness in selecting samples, we speculate that samples from certain class label have common feature patterns to allow the model to efficiently adapt itself to the target label, and therefore lead to a low accuracy loss. For example, sample digit 8 has the lowest accuracy loss on average when it is attacked into other digits for both CNN and LR in Setting 4. Further investigation is however required to confirm this hypothesis.

We note that this is not a unique limitation of our model as compared to other similar attacks (e.g. poisoning attack). To our knowledge, other attacks in adversarial machine learning settings are relatively simpler, in that they only craft one single attack sample at a time. Importantly, other attack strategies (as discussed in Section 3.1) are not concerned about how the model performs, as long as their crafted sample can evade detection.

- We notice that it is relatively easy to manipulate a CNN model for a few instances, without affecting the overall performance. We speculate that this is because CNN models typically face the problem of overfitting, i.e., they capture noise of the data. In contrast, in the case of LR, even a modest change could lead to an apparent difference in the output of the model, i.e., a drastic accuracy loss and significant drop in terms of model performance. This is mainly because of the inherent characteristic of linear model, which is highly sensitive to changes with respect to model parameters. Intuitively, this means that the attacker could potentially have more leverage in complex CNN models. We plan to test this hypothesis in the near future.

- As to LR, the attack performance is not consistent across the two datasets. As the number of samples to be targeted increases, the model performs worse on the textual dataset than on the MNIST. We believe this is mostly due to the difference in terms of feature representation. We use bag of words with binary weighting for spam (textual) dataset, where each feature word has low correlation with each other. In contrast, in the image dataset, certain pixel features have high correlation among one another, to define the shape of individual digits. Hence, classifying a digit image based on correlated pixels yields better performance than that of spam email represented by word vector.

In common adversarial machine learning settings, the major attack venue comes from the adversarial examples crafted by attackers to either evade or poison the training model. Hence, when it comes to defense strategies, some researchers have tried to make the model more robust by countering the effects of the existing adversarial examples [6], while others focused on finding them [13]. However in our case, the attack was applied directly on the model instead of crafting adversarial samples. Therefore, exploratory efforts are still needed in order to develop new defense mechanism.

9 CONCLUSION

In this paper, we presented a new perspective for attacking a machine learning (computational) process carried out in a remote location. Our approach, applied to two different supervised classification models, shows that - within certain constraints - it is possible to compromise a model without significantly sacrificing model accuracy.

Our results however also highlight some limitations of the proposed attack and pave the way for interesting future work. As shown, the difficulty of manipulating a machine learning model grows with the number of samples to be targeted, especially for a linear model like LR. Since our attack solely focuses on the learning model itself, the sensitivity of the model will have a great impact on the effectiveness of the attack. To overcome this limitation, we will study more sophisticated attacks that also target input sample, similar to evasion attacks. In this regard, an interesting direction is to explore a hybrid approach that not only takes advantage of the input sample but also exploits the model itself. Moreover, with a deeper understanding of the attack surface, we will investigate possible defense strategies.

10 ACKNOWLEDGEMENTS

We would like to thank our anonymous reviewers for their helpful comments. The work from Squicciarini and Zhong was partially supported by NSF 1421776. The work of Zhu was supported through NSF CNS-1618684.

REFERENCES

[1] Martín Abadi, Paul Barham, Jianmin Chen, Zhifeng Chen, Andy Davis, Jeffrey Dean, Matthieu Devin, Sanjay Ghemawat, Geoffrey Irving, Michael Isard, et al. 2016. TensorFlow: A System for Large-Scale Machine Learning.. In OSDI, Vol. 16. 265–283.

[2] Roger Barga and Valentine Fontama. [n. d.]. Predictive analytics with Microsoft Azure machine learning. Springer.

[3] Battista Biggio, Igino Corona, Davide Maiorca, Blaine Nelson, Nedim Šrndić, Pavel Laskov, Giorgio Giacinto, and Fabio Roli. 2013. Evasion attacks against machine learning at test time. In Joint European Conference on Machine Learning and Knowledge Discovery in Databases. Springer, 387–402.

[4] Battista Biggio Blaine Nelson, and Pavel Laskov. 2012. Poisoning attacks against support vector machines. arXiv preprint arXiv:1206.6389 (2012).

[5] Léon Bottou. 2010. Large-scale machine learning with stochastic gradient descent. In Proceedings of COMPSTAT'2010. Springer, 177–186.

[6] Xiaoyu Cao and Neil Zhenqiang Gong. 2017. Mitigating evasion attacks to deep neural networks via region-based classification. In Proceedings of the 33rd Annual Computer Security Applications Conference. ACM, 278–287.

[7] Corinna Cortes and Vladimir Vapnik. 1995. Support-vector networks. Machine learning 20, 3 (1995), 273–297.

[8] Harris Drucker, Donghui Wu, and Vladimir N Vapnik. 1999. Support vector machines for spam categorization. IEEE Transactions on Neural networks 10, 5 (1999), 1048–1054.

[9] Julian Fierrez-Aguilar, Javier Ortega-Garcia, Joaquin Gonzalez-Rodriguez, and Josef Bigun. 2005. Discriminative multimodal biometric authentication based on quality measures. Pattern recognition 38, 5 (2005), 777–779.

[10] Matt Fredrikson, Somesh Jha, and Thomas Ristenpart. 2015. Model inversion attacks that exploit confidence information and basic countermeasures. In Proceedings of the 22nd ACM SIGSAC Conference on Computer and Communications Security. ACM, 1322–1333.

[11] Matthew Fredrikson, Eric Lantz, Somesh Jha, Simon Lin, David Page, and Thomas Ristenpart. [n. d.]. Privacy in Pharmacogenetics: An End-to-End Case Study of Personalized Warfarin Dosing.

[12] Google. [n. d.]. TensorFlow. https://www.tensorflow.org/. ([n. d.]).

[13] Kathrin Grosse, Praveen Manoharan, Nicolas Papernot, Michael Backes, and Patrick McDaniel. 2017. On the (statistical) detection of adversarial examples. arXiv preprint arXiv:1702.06280 (2017).

[14] Uyeong Jang, Xi Wu, and Somesh Jha. 2017. Objective Metrics and Gradient Descent Algorithms for Adversarial Examples in Machine Learning. In Proceedings of the 33rd Annual Computer Security Applications Conference. ACM, 262–277.

[15] Bryan Klimt and Yiming Yang. 2004. Introducing the Enron Corpus.. In CEAS.

[16] Alex Krizhevsky, Ilya Sutskever, and Geoffrey E Hinton. 2012. Imagenet classification with deep convolutional neural networks. In Advances in neural information processing systems. 1097–1105.

[17] Yann LeCun, Corinna Cortes, and Christopher JC Burges. 2010. MNIST handwritten digit database. AT&T Labs [Online]. Available: http://yann. lecun. com/exdb/mnist 2 (2010).

[18] Patrick McDaniel, Nicolas Papernot, and Z Berkay Celik. 2016. Machine learning in adversarial settings. IEEE Security & Privacy 14, 3 (2016), 68–72.

[19] Vangelis Metsis, Ion Androutsopoulos, and Georgios Paliouras. 2006. Spam filtering with naive bayes-which naive bayes?. In CEAS, Vol. 17. 28–69.

[20] Microsoft. [n. d.]. Azure Machine Learning Studio. https://studio.azureml.net/. ([n. d.]).

[21] Seyed Mohsen Moosavi Dezfooli, Alhussein Fawzi, and Pascal Frossard. 2016. Deepfool: a simple and accurate method to fool deep neural networks. In Proceedings of 2016 IEEE Conference on Computer Vision and Pattern Recognition (CVPR).

[22] Mehran Mozaffari-Kermani, Susmita Sur-Kolay, Anand Raghunathan, and Niraj K Jha. 2015. Systematic poisoning attacks on and defenses for machine learning in healthcare. IEEE journal of biomedical and health informatics 19, 6 (2015), 1893–1905.

[23] Srinivas Mukkamala, Guadalupe Janoski, and Andrew Sung. 2002. Intrusion detection using neural networks and support vector machines. In Neural Networks, 2002. IJCNN'02. Proceedings of the 2002 International Joint Conference on, Vol. 2. IEEE, 1702–1707.

[24] Michael A Nielsen. 2015. Neural networks and deep learning. (2015).

[25] Nicolas Papernot, Patrick McDaniel, Ian Goodfellow, Somesh Jha, Z Berkay Celik, and Ananthram Swami. 2017. Practical black-box attacks against machine learning. In Proceedings of the 2017 ACM on Asia Conference on Computer and Communications Security. ACM, 506–519.

[26] Nicolas Papernot, Patrick McDaniel, Somesh Jha, Matt Fredrikson, Z Berkay Celik, and Ananthram Swami. 2016. The limitations of deep learning in adversarial settings. In Security and Privacy (EuroS&P), 2016 IEEE European Symposium on.

IEEE, 372–387.

[27] David E Rumelhart, Geoffrey E Hinton, Ronald J Williams, et al. [n. d.]. Learning representations by back-propagating errors. *Cognitive modeling* 5, 3 ([n. d.]), 1.

[28] Shiqi Shen, Shruti Tople, and Prateek Saxena. 2016. A uror: defending against poisoning attacks in collaborative deep learning systems. In *Proceedings of the 32nd Annual Conference on Computer Security Applications.* ACM, 508–519.

[29] Hoo-Chang Shin, Holger R Roth, Mingchen Gao, Le Lu, Ziyue Xu, Isabella Nogues, Jianhua Yao, Daniel Mollura, and Ronald M Summers. 2016. Deep convolutional neural networks for computer-aided detection: CNN architectures, dataset characteristics and transfer learning. *IEEE transactions on medical imaging* 35, 5 (2016), 1285–1298.

[30] Florian Tramèr, Fan Zhang, Ari Juels, Michael K Reiter, and Thomas Ristenpart. 2016. Stealing Machine Learning Models via Prediction APIs.. In *USENIX Security Symposium.* 601–618.

A BACKPROPAGATION ALGORITHM

Backpropagation algorithm provides a fast way to compute the gradient of a cost function C with respect to the parameters, e.g., weight w and bias b associated with each layer, in the neural networks [24]. We start with the following notations.

w_{jk}^l: the weight of the connection from k^{th} neuron in $(l-1)^{th}$ layer to j^{th} neuron in l^{th} layer

b_j^l: the bias of the jth neuron in l^{th} layer

$\sigma()$: activation function, e.g., a sigmoid function

a_j^l: the activation output of the jth neuron in l^{th} layer

Then, the activation output of the jth neuron in l^{th} layer is computed as

$$a_j^l = \sigma(\sum_k w_{jk}^l a_k^{l-1} + b_j^l). \tag{6}$$

where a_k^{l-1} is the activation output of kth neuron in $(l-1)^{th}$ layer.

Therefore, the activation output of the lth layer can be denoted in a succinct form as

$$a^l = \sigma(w^l a^{l-1} + b^l) \tag{7}$$

If we denote $z^l = w^l a^{l-1} + b^l$, the above equation becomes

$$a^l = \sigma(z^l) \tag{8}$$

Suppose for the neural networks we have a cost function C, which is expressed in terms of the activation output a^l and desired output y of an input x. For instance, for a given input x, its cost function can be defined as $C_x = ||\mathbf{y} - \mathbf{a^L}||^2$. The error produced in the last output layer L can be computed as

$$\delta^L = \nabla_a C \odot \sigma'(z^L) \tag{9}$$

where $\nabla_a C$ denotes the partial derivative of cost function C with respect to activation a^L of output layer L, $\odot$ represents the element-wise product of two vectors, and $\sigma'(z^L)$ denotes the derivative of activation function $\sigma()$ with respect to z^L.

Then, the error computed in the last output layer is backpropagated all the way to the first layer after the input layer. The error in layer l is computed based on the error in the next layer $l+1$ when $l = L, L-1, \ldots, 2$, which is expressed as

$$\delta^l = ((w^{l+1})^\top \delta^{l+1}) \odot \sigma'(z^L) \tag{10}$$

where $(w^{l+1})^\top$ is the transpose of matrix w^{l+1}.

Lastly, for each layer $l = L, L-1, \ldots, 2$, we can compute the gradient based on δ^l to update the parameters w and b of each neuron on each layer accordingly.

$$\frac{\partial C}{\partial w_{jk}^l} = a_k^{l-1} \delta_j^l \tag{11}$$

$$\frac{\partial C}{\partial b_j^i} = \delta_j^l \tag{12}$$

SmartProvenance: A Distributed, Blockchain Based Data Provenance System

Aravind Ramachandran
The University of Texas At Dallas
Richardson, Texas
axr156530@utdallas.edu

Murat Kantarcioglu
The University of Texas At Dallas
Richardson, Texas
muratk@utdallas.edu

ABSTRACT

Blockchain technology has evolved from being an immutable ledger of transactions for cryptocurrencies to a programmable interactive environment for building distributed reliable applications. Although the blockchain technology has been used to address various challenges, to our knowledge none of the previous work focused on using Blockchain to develop a secure and immutable scientific data provenance management framework that automatically verifies the provenance records. In this work, we leverage Blockchain as a platform to facilitate trustworthy data provenance collection, verification, and management. The developed system utilizes smart contracts and open provenance model (OPM) to record immutable data trails. We show that our proposed framework can securely capture and validate provenance data that prevents any malicious modification to the captured data as long as the majority of the participants are honest.

KEYWORDS

Distributed systems, Knowledge Management, Data Provenance, Blockchain platform

ACM Reference Format:
Aravind Ramachandran and Murat Kantarcioglu. 2018. SmartProvenance: A Distributed, Blockchain Based Data Provenance System. In *CODASPY '18: Eighth ACM Conference on Data and Application Security and Privacy, March 19–21, 2018, Tempe, AZ, USA.* ACM, New York, NY, USA, 8 pages. https://doi.org/10.1145/3176258.3176333

1 INTRODUCTION

As the data used for research increases exponentially, ensuring information quality and preventing data manipulation has emerged as an important factor affecting the research results. For example, an audit conducted by the Cancer and Leukemia Group B, one of the multi-center cancer clinical trial groups sponsored by the National Cancer Institute found an incidence of fraud of 0.25 percentage of the trials conducted [11].

To avoid data frauds such as data fabrication, under-reporting and falsifying the results to match research objectives in critical

research, the provenance of the data has to be maintained. In this context, data provenance is a meta-data that describes where the data of interest originated, who owns the data and what were the transformations that were done on the data. Data provenance facilitates the integration of data from diverse sources as well as providing information of these sources. Also, it acts as a yardstick for measuring how far the results of the experiments support the actual objectives of the research. This results in increased transparency and trustworthiness of the research. For example, in [16], authors highlight the increase in transparency and trustworthiness of research results due to data provenance tracking. Therefore, provenance details of the data must be recorded from its generation to the transformations to the productions of results. In section 7, we discuss a real-world setting where the provenance of data is crucial to prevent fraud.

Main challenges for a provenance system are secure collection and storage, verifiability and preserving the privacy of the collected provenance data. Data used in any form of research may come from a myriad of sources and may contain sensitive information such as patient records. A data provenance management system should ensure that the data is protected against unauthorized access and privacy violations.

Due to the importance of collecting provenance information, systems such as Chimera [28] and myGrid [6] have been developed to store and process provenance information. Many of the existing provenance systems are based on a centralized storage model. The downside to the centralized system architecture is that if the central server is compromised, the whole data provenance trails could be compromised. In provenance systems based on distributed architecture, the security of the data provenance information is another area of contention. Any authorized users can corrupt the data stored in the provenance system. To our knowledge, the current provenance systems do not try to validate the changes before they are stored. Our proposed *SmartProvenance* addresses these issues by using Blockchain as a medium for storing provenance information and providing validations for each of the changes before logging the changes using smart contracts. Due to the immutable nature of the Blockchain environment, the approved provenance changes that are logged cannot be modified by any users once they are stored. In *SmartProvenance*, due to the distributed nature of the Blockchain, the data provenance trails are replicated on every node of the blockchain ensuring high availability and fault tolerance.

1.1 Overview of Our Contributions

To address the above-mentioned challenges and requirements, we propose a system, *SmartProvenance*, to securely capture scientific provenance data. *SmartProvenance* provides a platform, built using autonomous programs called smart contracts in the blockchain, for automated generation and verification of provenance data. The proposed system implements techniques such as secure storage of data trails, access control policies, voting mechanism, and penalty payments to ensure that no malicious changes are made to the provenance trails. The *SmartProvenance* system provides customized verification scripts for users to determine whether the submitted changes are valid or not.

We have implemented a *SmartProvenance* system on top of the Ethereum blockchain [5] along with Meteor framework [24] for developing interfaces for the user's client module. We evaluate the system in the real-world scenario of clinical drug trials. The results show that *SmartProvenance* system captures data provenance with fixed cost and moderate overhead.

The paper is structured as follows: Section 2 describes the system model. Section 3 discusses the system architecture and provenance life cycle. In Section 4, we take a detailed look at the various components of the system and their functionalities. Section 5 describes the voting process implemented for verification of data modifications. In Section 6, we analyze the security and privacy parameters of the system. Section 7 details the results obtained by implementing *SmartProvenance* in real-world environments. In Section 8 we compare *SmartProvenance* with other related blockchain based systems. We conclude the paper with Section 9.

2 BACKGROUND

In this section, we discuss some of the tools used by our system and our threat model assumptions.

2.1 Ethereum

SmartProvenance is built on top of the Ethereum [30], a distributed public blockchain. Ethereum is a worldwide network of interconnected computers that execute and validate programs. Ethereum provides a decentralized Turing-complete platform called Ethereum virtual machines to run application codes called *smart contracts*. Smart contracts are codes that reside within the Ethereum blockchain environment that execute when specific conditions are met. Each unique entity (user or smart contract) in the network is identified by a unique public key known as an address. As the smart contracts reside on top of the blockchain, each execution of a smart contract is also recorded in the blockchain. A smart contract has two types of data storage: state storage which stores data of the variables in the smart contract and the event logs. Events are notification mechanisms in the smart contract that allow it to trigger some external functionalities. Event logs are as the name suggests an immutable record of the sequence of events that are emitted by a smart contract. A smart contract is called or triggered through transactions. A transaction can be viewed as a message that is sent between addresses in the network. Transactions may not involve value exchange. Ethereum also provides a currency called *ether* that is used to implement value exchange between parties in the platform. In the Ethereum blockchain platform, each computational step has a cost associated with it called *gas* [30]. To execute each transaction, the initiator of the transaction has to pay the corresponding gas price for each step executed in the transaction. At the time of writing this paper 1 gas is equal to 0.00002 ethers.

2.2 Provenance Model

The *SmartProvenance* system represents the data provenance trails using Open Provenance Model (OPM) [26]. In the OPM methodology, each action of the current system is represented using three parameters: 1) artifact (e.g., documents, files) before and after change versions, 2) an agent which represents the initiator of the change and, 3) the process which is the process that changes the artifact from the previous version to the current version. In our project, we represent the OPM model as a triple describing what the agents, artifacts, and process are, and also number code relationship edges between them. For example, the action of modifying a file can be represented in OPM as a tuple *(user, file: old version, file: new version, the process used for modifications)*.

2.3 Threat Model

The *SmartProvenance* system can have two types of attackers: an external adversary and an internal adversary. An external adversary is a user who does not have access to the document/data in the system, but will actively try to corrupt the data provenance trails of a particular private document/data. An internal adversary has access to the document/data granted by the owner in the *SmartProvenance* system. The internal adversary is able to change the document and log the changes as provenance trails on the blockchain. The internal adversary tries to corrupt the provenance chain by logging incorrect details to the chain. For this work, we assume that the external adversary does not know the key to decrypt the document nor does he have access to the location in which the document is stored. The adversary only has knowledge of the document id and uses this information to mount an attack on the system. For the case of an internal adversary, we assume that he is not the owner of a document who can grant access to the document. The *SmartProvenance* guarantees truthful behavior if at least half of the users that can access the documents and associated provenance data are honest [13]. Finally, we assume that the cloud storage is not trustworthy and all the files version stored are encrypted through a shared key using a symmetric key encryption. We also assume that there exists a secure external key sharing platform through which the owner of the document can share the keys.

3 SYSTEM OVERVIEW

We consider a scientific setting where researchers keep their research records as a document stored in the cloud. The document (e.g., any data file) is encrypted by the owner of the document (e.g., the lead researcher). The owner of the research document provides access to the document to users by providing the key. For a user to log the provenance information in the *SmartProvenance* system, the owner of a document needs to grant access to the unique document log to the user. In the *SmartProvenance* system model, the changes to the documents are made through versioning. Each change related to a document is stored as a separate new version. The system assumes that only the latest version of the document/data file is used for modification. The system checks the condition that any document which contains changes not logged in the provenance data is ignored.

The system encourages truthful behavior by penalizing the users who submit wrong change provenance details. The voters are rewarded in the event they find a defective change submitted with a portion of the deposit amount for the change. The users log valid changes to the system using client applications running in each of the individual user's browser. Each of the client applications stores persistent data about the documents that the current user has access to using a database. For the current version of *SmartProvenance*, meteor JS [30] and MongoDB [25] are used to implement the client applications. The client applications communicate with the smart contract through a Geth node which is a program that Ethereum platform uses to communicate with the main blockchain network, running on the client side. The client applications monitor the relevant smart contracts for data change events and initiate verification process. The smart contract module implements functionalities such as access control policies and provenance trail storage.

4 SYSTEM DETAILS

The *SmartProvenance* system consists of two modules. The on-chain module which mainly consists of Ethereum Smart contracts for access control, generating and storing provenance trails and conducting voting process, and the off-chain module which consist of client application that interfaces with the smart contracts to log the changes, provide timers for voting processes and perform the verification of each file change using the cloud-based verification script.

4.1 On-chain module

The Ethereum blockchain provides executable programs, called Smart Contracts, that reside within the blockchain. The Smart Contracts execute only when called and are capable of maintaining state variables. *SmartProvenance* on-chain module mainly consists of two smart contracts which we discuss next.

4.1.1 Document Tracker contract. The Document Tracker smart contract is used to keep track of changes to a given document. Document Tracker contract implements access control policies and restricts user access to the document's provenance trails. The contract also provides methods for provenance trail generation for a particular document. The generated document trails are stored as events in the event log of the Document Tracker contract. Event log storage of data provenance trails is preferred due to cost per storage consideration in the Ethereum blockchain environment [4].

The format of the change event is described in our detailed paper [29]. Each change event also stores the digital signature of the initiator based on the message digest. The Document Tracker restricts access to all document functionalities such as *create* a document for tracking, *grant users rights* to add changes to a particular document provenance history, *revoke users access* rights to a particular document history and finally *generate and store provenance history* of a particular document to the log.

It is *important to note that, SmartProvenance does not store any sensitive information in plain text on the blockchain* because any information stored on the blockchain including the smart contract code is publicly accessible. In addition, due to storage costs and blockchain storage limits, actual data is stored off the blockchain, potentially in a cloud location.

The initial iteration of the provenance history is generated by the owner of a document when that document is added to the system. The contract enforces the constraint that granting access to adding provenance trails for a document is strictly controlled by the owner of the document. In the current implementation of *SmartProvenance*, access rights to a particular document are non-transferable. In addition to the main methods, Document Tracker also consists of helper methods for granting the user access to a document and methods to update the owner of the document. The Document Tracker rejects any unauthorized calls to the functions. Every provenance change event *has to be approved through a voting process by the vote contract*. The data trails are only logged if they are approved by the Vote contract.

We chose the *voting for verifying the submitted provenance information for two reasons*: 1) We want to efficiently prevent malicious changes that obviously violate data use constraints (e.g., not allow the deletion of a patient record from the drug trial data). 2) We do not want the verification process to leak any sensitive information. Unfortunately, verification process could vary in different settings. For example, for drug trials, main verification process could be to make sure that no patient is deleted (e.g., to boost the success rate of the drug) from the data set due to a fatal reaction. Also, if the verification is done in the contract, we need to do this in a way that discloses no information (e.g., using zero-knowledge proofs [20] since contract source code and execution are publicly observable). To our knowledge, the existing zero-knowledge techniques that are efficient are not general enough for all verification scenarios needed for our use case. At the same time, general zero-knowledge verification techniques are not efficient enough to implement for provenance capturing [3]. Due to these reasons, we allow each participant client program to run *the verification code automatically off-the-chain and use on-the-chain contract to vote for or against the change*. Below, we discuss the details of the voting process.

4.1.2 Vote contract. The vote contract implements the voting protocol. The contract implements two types of voting: simple majority voting and threshold voting which we discuss in Section 5. The initiator submits the change in an encrypted form along with his signature and document id to the vote contract. The vote contract receives the change and after verification generates a log event to initiate the voting phase for the change. The voting phase time interval is set as t_1 (t_1 is set to one hour in our experiments) during which the participant can vote on the change. For each vote that is submitted, the vote contract verifies whether the vote is valid for the current voting period. At the end of the voting period, based on the type of voting process, the vote contract rejects/accepts the change based on the voting results. The vote contract restarts the voting phase if the minimum threshold is not satisfied. At the end of the voting phase, if the decision is to accept the change, vote contract submits the change to the Document Tracker contract for generating the provenance event. The vote contract currently accepts only a single outstanding change for a particular document for ensuring the continuity of the data provenance chain and consistency. The current vote contract allows users to log provenance trails if the total count of users of a document is less than three.

4.2 Off-chain module

The off chain module, a JavaScript client, runs on the browser of each of the user machines. The client acts as an interface between the user and back-end smart contracts. The client is responsible for communicating with the smart contract for the storage of the changes, retrieval of the changes and verifying the validity of the changes. The client consists of different components such as the Client Interface module which mainly provides an interface for the user to interact with various functionalities of the on chain smart contracts. The Interface module implicitly generates the digital signature for all the operations that the user performs through the module. The client contains an event watcher component that monitors the vote contact for any change events. If a change is relevant to the current user, the event watch module calls a verification script and verifies the change. The watcher module uses a database to keep track of the documents that are relevant to the current user. In addition to the Javascript clients, *SmartProvenance* also has a verification script running at the cloud storage location, where versions of the documents are stored. The verification script verifies the validity of each change of a document submitted to the Document Tracker. Lastly, the client also has a timer module that is responsible for keeping track of the voting phases. The timer will trigger the termination of the voting process at the end of the voting interval.

4.2.1 Verification script: The verification script resides within the cloud storage of the system. The verification script validates the data file/document changes that are submitted to the *Smart-Provenance* system. The input to the verification script includes current and previous cryptographic hash of the document (from the changes submitted to *SmartProvenance*) and the link to the latest version of the file. The verification script first verifies whether the hashes submitted to the files are valid. It then compares the current unconfirmed data file with the last stable version of the file. If any other changes to the file other than the ones mentioned in the change request are identified, the verification script notifies the user of a mismatch. If there are no invalid changes in the file, the verification script confirms the change as valid to the user. Once the changes are verified as valid, to prevent further manipulation of the document version, the verification script restricts the write access to only the owner of the original document. The verification script *can be customized according to the usage scenario* of the *Smart-Provenance* system and is developed as a plug-in module. In the current implementation, we have developed the verification script based on Google appscript [14] to support Google Drive Storage. The verification script automates the verification of the changes without relying on a trusted third party. A well-written verification script allows for the secure generation, verification and logging of the provenance trails.

5 VOTING PROCESS

The overall view of the voting process is described in Figure 1. The voting process starts when the initiator submits a change to the vote contract. The initiator client triggers a timer to initiate the voting phase of the newly submitted change. The vote contract generates an event which indicates the commencement of the voting phase for the submitted change. The Event listener module in the

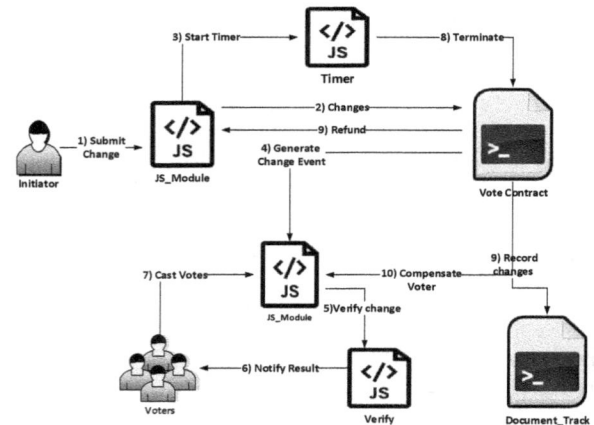

Figure 1: Voting procedure for a document change.

client applications reads the newly generated vote event. The client application verifies if it is a stakeholder in the current document change event. It then calls the verification script residing within the cloud along with the links to the current and previous versions of the file and the file hashes. The call to verification process occurs in every node based on the voting protocol policy. If the verification script returns as true then the client application notifies the user of the result and casts its *vote automatically* on the decision to accept or reject the changes. The vote contract on receiving the vote from a client application records the user decision. [1] The timer module will terminate the vote contract at the end of the voting period. The vote contract counts both for and against votes and rejects the change if the majority have voted against the change. If the change is accepted, the deposit by the initiator is refunded back. If the change is rejected then, the deposit is divided among the participants of the voting phase. This way we incentivize truthful behavior by the participants. If the majority is to accept the vote then the vote contract submit the changes to the Document Tracker contract for logging.

In our current implementation of *SmartProvenance*, we have implemented two types voting protocols: simple majority voting and randomized voting.

5.1 Randomized Threshold Voting

Every client voting for each and every change is not efficient for systems that contain a large number of changes and users. For such scenarios, we propose randomized threshold voting. In randomized threshold voting, the contract requires that a minimum percentage of votes accept or reject the change. Suppose the document has n users, to accept or reject a change, the vote contract threshold is s. To ensure that each voting phase for a change receives s votes, the contract tries to get expectedly t votes for $t \geq s$. The threshold t ensures that the minimum number of votes s is received for each change.

---

[1]We would like to stress that in our case, this entire voting process is automated using the verification script without any user manual input.

To determine whether to take part in change voting phase, each client generates a random number based on the formula:

$$Ks = Hash(Bno, ETxt, Diff, Glim, Addr) \bmod n$$

In the formula, Ks is the random number generated by the client by hashing Bno - the current block number, Etext - the encrypted text in the change event, Diff - the current gas limit and the Addr - the initiator's address. If the generated number is below the threshold number t set by the vote contract (i.e. $Ks < t$), the client votes based on the result of the verification script. Once a vote is submitted, the vote contract generates the random number for each vote in a similar manner and verifies that the submitted vote is legitimate.

In this technique, the voting for the change is based on secure pseudo-random numbers; and it is not feasible to know which clients vote on which changes since the inputs to the hash function differ for each vote almost in a random manner. At the end of a voting period, if the vote contract finds that the total number of votes is below the threshold s, the vote contract restart the voting process. The probability of a restart event can be bounded by choosing appropriate t and s values as described in our detailed paper [29]. If after a predefined maximum number of restarts, the required number of votes are not received, the change is rejected and the deposit is refunded to the initiator of the current change. We can set the system parameters t and s in such a way that this is very unlikely.

6 SYSTEM ANALYSIS

In this section, we analyze the security and privacy aspects of our *SmartProvenance* system. Specifically, we discuss how *SmartProvenance* system handles attacks from the two type of adversaries discussed in Section 2.3.

6.1 Security Analysis

An external adversary can try to attack the current system by submitting an invalid change request for a particular document ID. The *SmartProvenance* contract would stop any such attempts by enforcing access control policies on documents. The Document Tracker contract will only accept change requests from users who have been granted access by the owner of the document. All other change requests are simply rejected by the contract. The Document Tracker also penalizes the external adversary by withholding the deposit amount for the change for the attack attempt. Document Tracker prevents replay attack by keeping track of the latest change timestamp for a particular document. Any message carrying timestamp older than the latest timestamp for that document is ignored.

An internal user can be the owner of the document or one of the users who has been granted access to the document by the owner. An internal adversary who is not the owner of the document can try and corrupt the data provenance trails by submitting defective changes. Since *SmartProvenance* system requires each of the changes to be approved by a minimum number of users, this attack from the internal adversary succeeds only if he can control more than half of the total number of users allowed for the document. The randomized threshold voting further ensures that the adversary cannot know in advance who among all the voters can take part in the voting for a particular change, making it difficult to mount the

attack. The internal adversary who is an owner can corrupt the system if he colludes with other stakeholders and votes for the change. The owner is the only user who can grant access, the system can be at a disadvantage if the owner selects a group of users who are loyal to him and corrupts the provenance trail. Although this type of attack may be successful, it still leaves a traceable trail on the blockchain that could be used to detect the attack.

6.2 Privacy Analysis

The privacy protection for the provenance data trail is achieved by the use of hashing and encryption. An external user can infer only the document id and the number of changes that are made to a particular document id by looking at the event logs. Each change event encrypts the payload of the event so that all an external adversary could get is the document id, the ciphertext, and the signature. The link to the cloud location where the actual file is encrypted. The other information that an external user can deduce from watching the contract transaction trails are to see which users are associated with a particular document id. This information is deducible by observing iterations of the voting contract. The Ethereum platform provides anonymization of users through the use of random public addresses. The users of *SmartProvenance* do not reveal their identity in the environment but instead, use public addresses to perform operations on the system. In *SmartProvenance*, only the file owner will see the document user. An adversary observing multiple voting iterations could at most deduce the public addresses associated with each document.

In *SmartProvenance* system, each change in the document is represented as a separate record. In the current system, we take each change as a standalone change and do not allow multiple outstanding changes to the same document. This can be restrictive in certain use cases. The system could be modified to accept non-conflicting changes in different parts of the tracked document. The system could accept changes to the document as long as they are non-conflicting, thereby increasing the concurrency. The above modification may involve adding an extra step to the verification script to check for non-conflicting changes.

7 EXPERIMENTAL EVALUATION

To evaluate the *SmartProvenance* system, we test it on two real-life scenarios and calculate the average cost for each of the individual operations of the smart contract. In both scenarios, we find that *SmartProvenance* system performs at a constant cost for individual operations and within a reasonable overhead. We provide the details of one of the use cases below. The details of the other case can be found in our extended paper [29].

For all use cases, we use the following evaluation setup: the client applications implemented using Meteor JS ran in a laptop (Core i7 2.4GHZ) and a desktop computer (Core i7 3.40GHZ) running Ubuntu 16.04.2 LTS. The smart contracts developed using Solidity language ran on Ethereum Ropsten Testnet[2]. For all scenarios, we simulate the tests for a setting where we have 100 users for each of the document/data file. For the cloud-based storage, we used Google Drive and the verification scripts were developed using Google AppScript.

---

[2]https://ropsten.etherscan.io/

7.1 Clinical Drug trial

As the first use case, we consider the scenario of a clinical trial [10] of an experimental drug. In phase 3 of the drug trial process, the drug is tested with 300–1000 patients. The objective of the trial is to find the side effects of varying dosages on the patients. The drug trials are conducted by various doctors in various locations and each of the results is recorded in a common document. Each of the experiment group updates the same document every month for a twelve month period. In the research setting, some of the patients may show an adverse reaction to the drug. Researchers with a vested interest may try to remove those records that would show the side effects of the drug, and successive iterations of the same document will be missing records that would adversely affect the trustworthiness of the trails. To avoid the omission of records, the verification process for each change iteration should ensure that the original patient set is maintained. [3]

7.1.1 Add Document.
The *Add Document* function is used to add a document to the system for the purpose of maintaining its provenance. The owner of the document could be the head physician who initiates the whole process. The owner generates the initial form of the file that includes the entire initial set of patient details and initial drug dosage and adds it to the contract. The Add Document functions generate a unique document id for each file added. For the drug trials scenario, we need to add only a single file. The average gas cost per file added is 139552. Please note that in our setting, *SmartProvenance* keeps *fixed size provenance records irrespective of the original data file size.*

7.1.2 Add User.
The *Add User* function deals with granting access to users for a document. The user who creates a particular document is recorded as the owner of the contract. Access to a particular contract can only be granted by the owner of that contract. Figure 2 gives the gas used per user added for one document where each transaction is the addition of a new user. The average gas used per transactions is 90559. The user details are stored as the hash of the user address. The spikes in the figure 2 represent the difference in the hashing requirements for the inputs.

7.1.3 Initiate Change.
The *Initiate Change* function deals with triggering the voting process for logging a particular change. The Initiate Change requires the initiator of the change to deposit an amount with the contract while calling the contract. The Initiate Change function is called in the current scenario at the end of every month by the doctors to record the side effects (if any) of the current dosage. The average gas used for the changes is 731768. Figure 2 gives the gas distribution per initiation of voting phase for different transactions.

7.1.4 Voting phase.
Once the change has been initiated, the client programs running in the voting quorum will verify the changes and cast their votes. The vote of each of the participant is recorded by the smart contract and tallied up. The average gas used during this process is 89176. This is due to the initialization that occurs at the start of the voting intervals.

7.1.5 Termination.
The result of the voting process determines whether to accept or reject the changes. On rejection of a change, the voters who verified and voted are awarded the deposit amount of the initiator. On acceptance of the change, the change is recorded in the event log of the Document Track contract and the deposit is refunded to the initiator of the change. In Figure 2, we can see that there are two large spikes. These are the cases in which the changes are rejected after the voting process. The gas used for these are more because all the voters are awarded a part of the deposit in the case of a rejection. The average gas used for termination is 249812.

7.1.6 Verification Script:
In the drug trial scenario, the verification script verifies if the same set of patients given in the original trials are maintained across the various iterations of the data collection phase. The client initiates the verification script by providing it with the link to the current file version and hashes submitted with the change. The verification script generates its own hashes and compares with the submitted hashes. The script then compares patient identification columns with the previous files to ensure that none of the original patients have been omitted from the currently submitted version. The verification script then notifies the client of the result and votes accordingly. In the drug trials scenario, the verification script checks if all patient records are retained in subsequent iterations. The run times of the verification script which depends on the data file size and the verification complexity, for data files that contain 1000 to 5000 patients, the verification runtime vary from 7 to 31 secs.

7.2 Operation Cost

By observing the system contract executions in the above scenarios, we see that for an individual function such as add user or add document, the gas used per transaction remains almost constant. The cumulative gas used for any individual function is a nearly linear function (e.g., as shown in Figure 2 for vote function).

The gas usage is calculated at an average of 0.00000002 ethers per gas used. At the time of experimentation, a single ether cost is 90 US dollars. The Table 1 shows the average gas used for various operations of the *SmartProvenance* system. As the results indicate most operations can be executed with relatively little cost.

Table 1: Cost of operations in the *SmartProvenance* System.

Operation	Avg gas spent	cost (USD)
Vote	89176.33	0.1605173
Add User	90559	0.1630062
Add Document	139552	0.2511936
Record Change	249812	0.4496616
Initiate Change	731351.5	1.3164327

7.3 Contract Execution Duration

The time taken to perform each of the operations in the system is represented in the Table 2. We can see that all the operations take near constant time to perform. The time taken for each operation is reported as the average time taken per thousand operations.

---

[3]In our experiments, we choose only this constraint for the automatic verification process. Other constraints could be added for different scenarios.

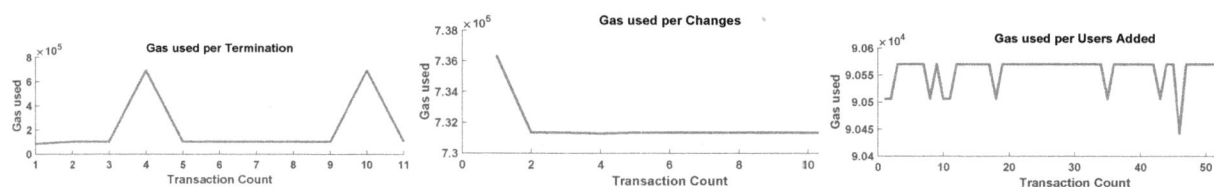

Figure 2: Gas used for various operations.

The execution time of each of the above operations depends on

Table 2: Time for operations in the *SmartProvenance* System.

Operation	Time Taken (ms)
Vote	829
Initiate Change	858
Add User	877
Add Document	926
Record Change	950

the network speed and the speed of mining of the blocks, but in long run, these times remain near constant and take less than a second in all of the usage scenarios. The experiments show that the *SmartProvenance* generates and stores provenance data in a secure trusted manner with moderate overhead.

8 RELATED WORK

Recently there have been several research studies that leverage Blockchain as a platform for building trusted systems. Below, we summarize this work and discuss its relationship to our work.

Access control: In [18], authors explain the use of Blockchain as a trans-organizational authentication system. The Medrec system [1] implements access control for medical records across medical institutions through the usage of the public blockchain. Fair access system [27] is a decentralized access control system for the Internet of things devices using blockchain technology. In our *SmartProvenance* system, we also implement access control policies, but our focus is in the capturing of provenance data.

Trusted Authority system: The legal aspect of using blockchain as a verifiable trusted source was further expanded upon by the Common Accords Group [2, 12]. These work describe leveraging data stored in a public blockchain as a verifiable evidence in a court of law. Namecoin [8] system uses the blockchain technology as a trusted source for the Domain Name System (DNS). Our *SmartProvenance* system eliminates the need for storing data on transactions by using the event logs of the smart contract to store the provenance trails. The smart contracts on top of the Ethereum platform act as a decentralized trusted authority regarding all provenance trails stored. The provenance trails generated by *SmartProvenance* is trustworthy as they are verified using the verification policy and stored. *SmartProvenance*, therefore, acts as a decentralized trust-based system for data provenance.

Privacy preserving blockchain systems: The DECENT system [22] uses the blockchain along with the smart contracts to implement key management services. It implements the idea of secret sharing to securely share keys in a public environment. The Hawk system [20] implements the concept of zero-knowledge proofs combined with encryption to implement privacy preserving blockchain systems. The Hawk system uses two components: an on-chain component which uses smart contracts and zero-knowledge proofs to facilitate betting protocols and the off-chain component which generates zero-knowledge proofs for the system. The Hawk system shows how secure computations can be implemented on top of a public system such as the blockchain.

The use of secret sharing techniques for protecting sensitive information is further discussed in [17]. Compared to these works, the *SmartProvenance* system utilizes encryption and hashing to preserve the privacy of the data stored in the public Ethereum blockchain and secure communication channels between the smart contract and client machines to preserve the privacy. For efficiency, verification of the captured provenance data is done off-the-chain.

The common security vulnerabilities in the smart contracts are discussed in [19]. This work illustrates a number of security issues in smart contracts such as call stack bug, block hash bug, and miners withholding the addition of blocks to gain an unfair advantage. This work further discusses how to avoid these pitfalls by including additional access verification and cryptographic primitives like encryption and hashing. Compared to these works, *SmartProvenance* implements digital signatures to avoid malicious logging of provenance data. It uses an encrypted form of the provenance trails to avoid revealing details such as the location of the files and the user access information. *SmartProvenance* further restricts the access to methods based on checks implemented on the user address.

Data provenance: Leveraging blockchain as a data provenance tracker was first discussed by the Project Provenance [23]. In this work, blockchain transactions are used to store provenance details of food products from production to the consumer. In addition, in [15], the use of blockchain as provenance platform is presented as one of the four breakout cases of the blockchain platform. The use of Bitcoin as a data provenance system for research scenario was further explored in [9]. The author suggested the idea of storing the research objectives as an encoded file in the data fields of Bitcoin transactions. Compared to these works, our the *SmartProvenance* system adopts the immutability of the blockchain environment and implements a full stack privacy-preserving, verified data provenance store with access control policies. The provenance chains that are generated by the *SmartProvenance* system are stored as event logs thereby saving costs on storage. The system facilitates the verification of these provenance events by any authorized users. *SmartProvenance* provides a platform to implement custom verification scripts suited for the application area. The system ensures privacy by using public key encryption and preserves integrity by the use of digital signatures.

The ProvChain [21] system provides a data provenance system based on Blockchain technology. The ProvChain system uses monitor programs called "hooks" to track the changes that occur in the cloud storage system and records each and generates events corresponding to the actions of the users. The user events thus recorded are then stored on the blockchain as transactions. The verification process is achieved by an external entity known as the auditor. The auditor generates transaction receipts using Tieron API [7]. The Provchain system verifies the changes after the information is logged on to the blockchain. The *SmartProvenance* differs from Provchain by implementing automated verification scripts and rejecting the invalid changes. The change hash-chain generated by the *SmartProvenance* records only the changes that are verified by the verification script. This guarantees that the changed document is always valid and prevents any chance of collusion between the auditor and the stakeholders. Another major difference compared to Provchain is that *SmartProvenance* implements incentivized voting using smart contracts to penalize the users who try to log invalid changes to the system. The use of randomized voting reduces the centralization of the verification process. Therefore, there is no need for a physical verifier as the verification script verifies the changes before voting on the changes. The advantage of developing verification script is that a verification script for a scenario could be reused by similar applications thereby reducing the cost of development.

9 CONCLUSION

The *SmartProvenance* is a Blockchain based system that provides access control based privacy-preserving data provenance trails. In the *SmartProvenance* system, an authorized user can verify the changes that are made to any data file. It also provides a proof of change with the use of digital signatures and timestamps. The system ensures that the change logs in the blockchain environment are only accessed by the authorized users with appropriate keys. The *SmartProvenance* system further enhances the trustworthiness of the data trails by implementing randomized voting for the captured change trails and any deviation is punished by a monetary penalty using smart contracts. The evaluation of the system based on two real-life scenarios shows that individual operations of the system run with acceptable cost in near constant time.

10 ACKNOWLEDGEMENT

The research reported herein was supported in part by NIH award 1R01HG006844, NSF awards CNS-1111529, CICI-1547324, and IIS-1633331 and ARO award W911NF-17-1-0356.

REFERENCES

[1] Thiago Vieira Andrew Lippman Ariel Ekblaw, Asaf Azaria. 2016. MedRec: Medical Data Management on the Blockchain. (2016). version: 57e013615dbf3f3300152554.

[2] David Bollier. 2015. Reinventing Law for the Commons. (2015). http://www.commonaccord.org/

[3] Zvika Brakerski, Jonathan Katz, Gil Segev, and Arkady Yerukhimovich. 2011. Limits on the Power of Zero-Knowledge Proofs in Cryptographic Constructions. In *Theory of Cryptography - 8th Theory of Cryptography Conference, TCC 2011, Providence, RI, USA, March 28-30, 2011. Proceedings*. 559–578. https://doi.org/10.1007/978-3-642-19571-6_34

[4] Jonathan Brown. 2015. Storing compressed text in Ethereum transaction logs. (2015). http://jonathanpatrick.me/blog/ethereum-compressed-text

[5] Vitalik Buterin. 2015. A Next-Generation Smart Contract and Decentralized Application Platform. (2015). September.

[6] Tim Clark, Paolo Ciccarese, and Carole A. Goble. 2013. Micropublications: a Semantic Model for Claims, Evidence, Arguments and Annotations in Biomedical Communications. *CoRR* abs/1305.3506 (2013). http://arxiv.org/abs/1305.3506

[7] Tierion coporation. 2017. Tierion API. (2017). https://tierion.com/

[8] Vincent Durham. 2010. *NAMECOIN.* https://namecoin.org/.

[9] The Economist. 2016. Better with bitcoin. (2016). http://www.economist.com/news/science-and-technology/21699099-blockchain-technology-could-improve-reliability-medical-trials-better.

[10] US Food and Drug Administration. 2017. *Clinical Research.* https://www.fda.gov/ForPatients/Approvals/Drugs/ucm405622.htm.

[11] Buyse M George SL. 2015. Data fraud in clinical trials. *PMC* 5, 2 (2015), 161–173. https://doi.org/10.4155/cli

[12] Bela Gipp, Jagrut Kosti, and Corinna Breitinger. 2016. Securing Video Integrity Using Decentralized Trusted Timestamping on the Blockchain. In *Proceedings of the 10th Mediterranean Conference on Information Systems (MCIS)*. Paphos, Cyprus.

[13] Oded Goldreich. 2004. *Foundations of Cryptography: Volume 2, Basic Applications.* Cambridge University Press, New York, NY, USA.

[14] Google. 2017. *Google Appscript.* https://developers.google.com/apps-script/.

[15] Gideon Greenspan. 2016. Four Genuine Blockchain Use Cases. (May 2016). http://www.coindesk.com/four-genuine-blockchain-use-cases/

[16] R. R. Downs R. Duerr J. C. Goldstein M. A. Parsons Hills, D. J. and H. K. Ramapriyan. 2015. The importance of data set provenance for science. (2015). version: doi:10.1029/2015EO040557.

[17] Roman JagomÄḡis, Peeter Laud, and Alisa Pankova. 2015. Preprocessing-Based Verification of Multiparty Protocols with Honest Majority. Cryptology ePrint Archive, Report 2015/674. (2015). http://eprint.iacr.org/2015/674.

[18] Cruz Jason, Paul and Kaji Yuichi. 2015. The Bitcoin Network as Platform for Trans-Organizational Attribute Authentication. *IPSJ SIG Notes* 2015, 12 (feb 2015), 1–6. http://ci.nii.ac.jp/naid/110009877764/en/

[19] Ahmed Kosba Andrew Miller Kevin Delmolino, Mitchell Arnett and Elaine Shi. 2015. Step by Step Towards Creating a Safe Smart Contract: Lessons and Insights from a Cryptocurrency Lab. Cryptology ePrint Archive, Report 2015/460. (2015). http://eprint.iacr.org/2015/460.

[20] Ahmed Kosba, Andrew Miller, Elaine Shi, Zikai Wen, and Charalampos Papamanthou. 2015. Hawk: The Blockchain Model of Cryptography and Privacy-Preserving Smart Contracts. Cryptology ePrint Archive, Report 2015/675. (2015). http://eprint.iacr.org/2015/675.

[21] Xueping Liang, Sachin Shetty, Deepak Tosh, Charles Kamhoua, Kevin Kwiat, and Laurent Njilla. 2017. ProvChain: A Blockchain-based Data Provenance Architecture in Cloud Environment with Enhanced Privacy and Availability. In *Proceedings of the 17th IEEE/ACM International Symposium on Cluster, Cloud and Grid Computing (CCGrid '17)*. IEEE Press, Piscataway, NJ, USA, 468–477. https://doi.org/10.1109/CCGRID.2017.8

[22] Peter Linder. 2016. DEcryption Contract ENforcement Tool (DECENT): A Practical Alternative to Government Decryption Backdoors. Cryptology ePrint Archive, Report 2016/245. (2016). http://eprint.iacr.org/2016/245.

[23] Project Provenance Ltd. 2015. Blockchain: the solution for transparency in product supply chains. (2015). https://www.provenance.org/whitepaper

[24] MeteorJs. 2016. (May 2016). https://www.meteor.com/

[25] MongoDB. 2017. MongoDB. (Jan. 2017). https://www.mongodb.com/

[26] Open Provenance model 2007. *Open Provenance Model.* Open Provenance model. http://openprovenance.org/.

[27] Aafaf Ouaddah, Anas Abou El Kalam, and Abdellah Ait Ouahman. 2016. FairAccess: a new Blockchain-based access control framework for the Internet of Things. *Security and Communication Networks* 9, 18 (2016), 5943–5964. https://doi.org/10.1002/sec.1748

[28] Eric F. Pettersen, Thomas D. Goddard, Conrad C. Huang, Gregory S. Couch, Daniel M. Greenblatt, Elaine C. Meng, and Thomas E. Ferrin. 2004. UCSF Chimera - A visualization system for exploratory research and analysis. *Journal of Computational Chemistry* 25, 13 (2004), 1605–1612. https://doi.org/10.1002/jcc.20084

[29] Aravind Ramachandran and Murat Kantarcioglu. 2017. Using Blockchain and smart contracts for secure data provenance management. (2017). https://arxiv.org/abs/1709.10000

[30] Gavin Wood. 2017. ETHEREUM: A secure decentralized generalized transaction ledger. (2017). http://gavwood.com/paper.pdf

Cross-App Tracking via Nearby Bluetooth Low Energy Devices

Aleksandra Korolova
University of Southern California
Los Angeles, California
korolova@usc.edu

Vinod Sharma
University of Southern California
Los Angeles, California
vinodsha@usc.edu

ABSTRACT

Today an increasing number of consumer devices such as head phones, wearables, light bulbs and even baseball bats, are Bluetooth-enabled thanks to the widespread support of the technology by phone manufacturers and mobile operating system vendors. The ability for any device to seamlessly connect and exchange information with smartphones via Bluetooth Low Energy (BLE) protocol promises unlimited room for innovation. However, it also brings about new privacy challenges. We show that the BLE protocol together with the Bluetooth permission model implemented in the Android and iOS operating systems can be used for cross-app tracking unbeknownst to the individuals.

Specifically, through experiments and analyses based on real-world smartphone data we show that by listening to advertising packets broadcasted by nearby BLE-enabled devices and recording information contained in them, app developers can derive fairly unique "fingerprints" for their users, which can be used for cross-app tracking, i.e., linking pseudonymous users of different apps to each other. We demonstrate that privacy protections put in place by the Bluetooth Special Interest Group, Google, and Apple are not sufficient to prevent such fingerprinting or to make cross-app tracking difficult to execute.

Our main contribution is to demonstrate the feasibility of cross-app tracking using nearby BLE and raise awareness that changes are needed in order to prevent it from becoming widespread. We also propose mitigation strategies to decrease the feasibility of tracking using nearby BLE devices while preserving the utility of the BLE technology.

ACM Reference Format:
Aleksandra Korolova and Vinod Sharma. 2018. Cross-App Tracking via Nearby Bluetooth Low Energy Devices. In *CODASPY '18: Eighth ACM Conference on Data and Application Security and Privacy, March 19–21, 2018, Tempe, AZ, USA.* ACM, New York, NY, USA, 10 pages. https://doi.org/10.1145/3176258.3176313

1 INTRODUCTION

Online tracking and profiling is one of the main privacy concerns of individuals today. The mechanisms of tracking when individuals access the Internet on their computers are well-understood

by privacy researchers, legal scholars, and individuals themselves, and there have been significant efforts in many communities to empower individuals to be able to limit or make choices about tracking. In the technological tools space that includes browser privacy settings to control and remove cookies, browser extensions that block cookie-based trackers and make other forms of fingerprinting difficult, and so on; in the research space – investigation of browser, canvas, and other types of fingerprinting and remediations against them; in the policy space – the Do Not Track initiative, the Network Advertising Initiative[I], and others.

However, with the recent shift to smartphones and the rise of mobile applications as the primary interface to the Internet and between individuals and businesses, the question of what is being done to track individuals and what can be done to restrict it or give individuals choices regarding it arises anew. In a sense, mobile tracking and its circumvention is a new arms-race between mobile app developers, ad tech companies and individuals. It is a high-stakes race for the former, because profile-based advertising is one of the main vehicles for online monetization and better tracking may result in better monetization; for the latter, because activity performed on smartphones has increasingly far-reaching privacy implications as the smartphone becomes the main device with which one interacts with the world.

From the app-developer and ad-tech perspectives, cookies, the most prevalent tracking mechanism for desktops, are less useful in the mobile context as typically each mobile application runs in a separate sandbox that cannot share information with others. Thus, different app developers interested in *cross-app tracking*, or linking their (anonymous or pseudonymous) users to each other, are constantly looking for new, smartphone-specific approaches, such as:

(1) Device-specific identifiers, such as Apple's Unique Device ID, Google's Android ID, MAC address, etc.
(2) Log-in credentials provided to the app, such as an email address, a phone number, or identity obtained through a set of authentication APIs (e.g., Facebook, OpenID, Google) provided by the user in order to sign up for the app.
(3) Fingerprints of the user device derived from its properties or activity using statistical or machine learning techniques.

Concurrently to the development of techniques for smartphone-specific user[1] tracking by app developers, mobile OS developers Apple and Google and individuals have been looking for techniques to curb or circumvent tracking. For example, to address (1), Apple has moved away from making the Unique Device ID accessible to apps through the developer API[II], replacing it with an Advertising Identifier that can be reset by the phone owner at any time[III]. To address

---

[1]In approaches (1) and (3) developers are tracking a device, not a user, i.e., they cannot easily differentiate between two different people using the same device.

(2), individuals often choose to provide different credentials to different apps. Numerous services have arisen to aid in the generation of one-time email addresses or phone numbers that can be used for this purpose (e.g., https://throttlehq.com, http://www.burnerapp.com). Finally, to address (3), privacy researchers investigate techniques that may be used for fingerprinting phones and develop countermeasures [5, 8, 10, 17, 26, 31].

Our work brings to light a novel tracking technique of the third type, and, by creating awareness of its feasibility, argues for modifications needed to protect privacy. Specifically, we observe that developer APIs on both Android and iOS do not require a user's permission for an app to run a scan that listens for presence announcements from nearby Bluetooth Low Energy (BLE) devices[2]. We hypothesize that, even though the Bluetooth Special Interest Group, Apple, and Google have taken some steps to decrease the potential privacy impact of such scans, those steps are not sufficient to prevent cross-app tracking. Specifically, we hypothesize that by running periodic scans for nearby BLE devices and recording the information contained in them, app developers could derive a fairly unique "fingerprint" for each of their users. Use of these fingerprints could power a new type of tracking, that would enable app developers to identify users across apps and across devices without reliance on shared log-in credentials or other device identifiers. We hypothesize that derivation of a fairly unique fingerprint from observations of packets from nearby BLE peripherals is feasible due to the rapidly increasing number and diversity of BLE devices, virtually unfettered access to BLE data in Android and iOS, and information-theoretic richness of that data.

To verify our hypothesis of the feasibility of cross-app tracking via nearby BLE devices, we build Android and iOS apps that run scans listening for presence announcements of BLE devices with fixed periodicity and record the results. We discover that due to Apple's design choices related to the Bluetooth API implementation, cross-app tracking is trivial for iPhone developers. We then incentivize 100 individuals from a university to install and keep our Android app running on their mobile devices for a week. We analyze the data obtained and find strong support for our hypothesis also on Android; namely, that the data of each scan is rich enough to make it feasible for multiple app developers to identify their shared users even in the absence of other identifiers.

Cross app-tracking using BLE data constitutes a serious privacy threat as under the current implementations of BLE protocol and mobile APIs and permission models it could happen without the individual's knowledge or consent, and with limited ability for them to detect or prevent it. Although one may argue that app developers can use advertising identifiers to track users, and thus there is hardly a need to worry about possible more sophisticated tracking, such as BLE tracking, that is not the case, at least conceptually, from the users' standpoint. The advertising identifier can be reset in Android and iOS, and its tracking implications are well-publicized and well-understood. Thus the privacy-conscious users have some recourse to limit advertising id-based tracking. Furthermore, removal of an advertising identifier altogether by Apple and Google, or automated frequent resets of it, is merely a matter of policy, not technology. Currently, there is no such recourse for BLE-based tracking, for two

reasons. First, the feasibility of such tracking prior to our work was unknown and, second, the mobile ecosystem does not provide tools to curb it (we consider the idea of keeping the phone's Bluetooth off at all times incompatible with functionality). We hope that as a result of this work, the privacy implications of BLE technology for tracking will become better understood and that the Bluetooth Special Interest Group, Bluetooth device manufacturers, and mobile OS developers Apple and Google will implement changes that will give individuals ability to limit such tracking if they so choose, without having to give up on using innovative technologies enabled by BLE.

The rest of the paper is organized as follows. Section 2 provides background on the BLE protocol and related privacy features put forth by the Bluetooth Consortium, Apple, and Google. Section 3 describes the Android app we built, the design of our data collection study, and relevant characteristics of the obtained dataset. Section 4 presents the data analyses and experiments we ran to support our hypothesis of feasibility of cross-app tracking using nearby BLE devices on Android. Section 5 explains why BLE-based tracking is trivial on iOS. We discuss the implications of our findings, including possible approaches to decreasing the feasibility of cross-app tracking using nearby BLE devices in Section 6. Finally, Section 7 describes related work.

2 BLE BACKGROUND & PRIVACY FEATURES

BLE (aka LE) is a Bluetooth protocol introduced in June 2010 by the Bluetooth Special Interest Group designed to enable a new set of devices with low power consumption [4][IV]. Under this protocol, each BLE *peripheral* device, such as a fitness tracker, announces its presence to all nearby *central* devices, such as phones or computers, through advertising. Advertising consists of 8-39 byte advertising packets broadcasted by BLE peripherals through three dedicated advertising channels in the 2.4GHz ISM band. The advertising packets are sent with a periodicity of 20ms to 10.24 seconds.[V] The distance range within which the advertising packets may be read varies depending on the transmit power of the peripheral device, and can be as large as 100 meters.[VI]

We refer to a central device that merely listens to the dedicated advertising channels and thus discovers nearby BLE devices as a *passive scanner*. In addition to learning information by listening for advertisements, a central device can also send *scan requests* and *connection requests* to peripherals. In this work, we focus on cross-app tracking that can be performed by passive scanning alone, and therefore, cannot be detected by peripherals as it does not communicate any information to peripherals. Subsequently, we refer to phones acting as central devices as scanners.

2.1 Data Available in Passive Scanning Phase

We now describe the information typically contained in advertising packets sent by peripherals. The contents of the advertising packet can vary, depending on the peripheral, but each advertisement always includes a 2-byte header and a 6-byte advertisement *address*, typically referred to as the Bluetooth MAC address or simply, the address of the peripheral, and, optionally, up to 31 bytes of other data[VII]. Besides the peripheral address, some of the data types frequently included that may be useful for cross-app tracking are:

---

[2]Starting with Android 6.0, a location permission is required, as discussed in Section 2.3.

- *Service UUID*: a unique identifier for each service provided by the peripheral. Each advertisement contains zero or multiple service UUIDs and the same service UUID can be advertised by different peripherals. For manufacturer-specific service UUIDs, only different peripherals which are of similar type (e.g., all fitness trackers of the same brand and type) will advertise the same service UUID.
- *Peripheral Name*: a name of the peripheral device. Different peripherals can have the same name if their manufacturer has assigned a fixed name to its devices.
- *Transmitting Power Level*: the current (numerical) transmitting power level of the peripheral device. Although this value can be changed by users, typically it remains unchanged from the value set by the manufacturer of the peripheral.
- *Manufacturer Data*: information provided by the specific manufacturer in binary format. This field contains two or more octets. The first two octets contain manufacturer IDs and the format of the other octets depends on the specific manufacturer and usually is not public knowledge. The manufacturer ID (aka company ID)[VIII] is a 16-bit number assigned to Bluetooth SIG members.
- *RSSI*: the current received signal strength indicator of the peripheral (in decibels). RSSI is a mandatory field and indicates the closeness of the peripheral to the scanner and changes continuously in every new advertisement.

2.2 Peripheral Address Privacy

The Bluetooth Special Interest Group recognized that much like MAC addresses transmitted in other contexts [18], Bluetooth peripheral addresses can pose a privacy risk[IX]. Specifically, they observed that a person who carries a BLE device with them throughout the day can be tracked using the MAC address that peripheral broadcasts in its advertisements. To remedy this, they introduced an "LE Privacy" feature that enables the peripheral MAC address broadcast within the advertising packets to be replaced with a random value that changes at timing intervals chosen by the manufacturer of the peripheral device. However, according to a recent survey by [19], many manufacturers do not properly implement this feature. A notable exception is Apple who ensures all their devices change their Bluetooth address every 15 minutes.

2.2.1 Treatment of Peripheral Addresses by Android and iOS.
Both Android and iOS implement APIs methods that enable app developers to obtain information contained in BLE advertising packets. The Android APIs provide app developers with the peripheral addresses as they are presented in advertising packets. In other words, all Android applications running on all phones receiving advertising packets from the same peripheral at the same time will obtain the same peripheral address.

Unlike on Android, applications installed on iOS are provided with a 128-bit number called `peripheral uuid` via the Core Bluetooth API[X] instead of the peripheral address. This is a privacy feature introduced by Apple as a countermeasure against tracking [16] – Apple replaces the BLE peripheral address with a randomized peripheral uuid. The randomization procedure for transforming peripheral addresses to reported uuids is not publicly known. However, through our experiments we observe the following pattern: if two apps are installed on the same phone, the peripheral uuids of a peripheral with address p that they receive through the API will be identical; if two apps are installed on different phones, the peripheral uuids of a peripheral with address p will be different. Table 1 schematically shows the values of the peripheral addresses reported through the APIs for a fixed peripheral with address p as observed by two different applications running on two iPhones and two Android Phones.

We will refer to the peripheral addresses that apps obtain through Android and iOS APIs as peripheral uuids in subsequent discussions in order to reflect the fact that the mobile OSes have the liberty to change the peripheral addresses that they present to app developers through their APIs.

As will become clear from subsequent discussion in Section 5, the fact that Apple's randomization ensures that a peripheral uuid of a particular peripheral is seen as the same for apps installed on the same phone, but as different for apps installed on different phones, makes cross-app tracking using nearby BLE devices on iOS trivial.

2.3 Application Permissions Needed for Scans

We now describe what is needed for an application installed on an iOS or Android-based phone to passively scan for nearby BLE devices, that is, obtain the contents of advertising packets broadcast by nearby BLE devices through the APIs.

2.3.1 iOS.
An iOS application does not require any permissions to run Bluetooth scans if the app is running in the foreground, allowing any application to conduct scans for nearby Bluetooth devices. Although an iOS application can also run scans in the background using bluetooth-central background mode provided by the iOS, scans in the background mode are limited, i.e., they can scan only for BLE devices supporting specific services[XI XII].

2.3.2 Android.
An Android application that wants to run scans requires the BLUETOOTH and BLUETOOTH_ADMIN permissions. However, these permissions are automatically granted to an app that declares them in their manifest, because they belong to the "normal" protection level. The Android divides system permissions into protection levels, the most common of which are *normal* and *dangerous*[XIII]. Normal permissions are those whose access, according to Android's documentation, poses "very little risk to the user's privacy", and thus are automatically granted.

Starting with Android 6.0 (API level 23), in addition to the BLUETOOTH and BLUETOOTH_ADMIN permissions, applications also need ACCESS_COARSE_LOCATION or ACCESS_FINE_LOCATION permissions to run BLE scans[XIV]. Both of these location-related

Apps	iOS		Android	
	phone1	phone2	phone3	phone4
app1	x	y	p	p
app2	x	y	p	p

Table 1: Addresses observed by two iOS and two Android applications running on four different phones for a peripheral advertising address p

permissions belong to the "dangerous" protection level and thus require an explicit approval from the user of the app.

However, a malicious application developer can overcome the need to obtain a user's explicit permission by exploiting forward compatibility[XV] features of Android. He can set the desired API level of 22 in the `targetSdkVersion` and thus bypass the need to ask a user's approval for accessing location when the app desires to run BLE scans. As of November 2016, 76.7% of Android devices are running with API 22 or lower[XVI], which suggests that many apps could be willing to give up on the new features of API level 23 to preserve ability to perform surreptitious cross-app tracking.

3 A REAL-WORLD DATASET OF BLE SCAN DATA

3.1 Data Collection

In order to perform a realistic evaluation of the feasibility of cross-app tracking using nearby BLE devices, we developed an Android app that uses Android's Bluetooth API[XVII] to conduct scans while running in the background. Our app conducted scans every 10 minutes as follows:

- Start a scan, scan for 1 minute, stop the scan
- Wait for 1 minute
- Start a scan, scan for 1 minute, stop the scan

In the period between April 25, 2016, and May 6, 2016 through our university's mailing lists we recruited 100 volunteers with phones running Android 5.1 lollypop or higher to install our app and leave it running on their phone for a week. 46 individuals installed the app between Apr 25-27, 20 – between Apr 28 - May 3, 34 – between May 4-6. Of those 100 individuals, 70 left our app running on their phone for a full week, and are the ones whose data we will be considering in subsequent analysis.

3.1.1 Ethics. Our institution did not require IRB approval since we took the following measures to protect privacy of volunteers:

- No registration of any kind was required, and thus we did not collect names, emails, phone numbers, or any other identifying information.
- The app was distributed through a public web page and required no interaction between study participants and researchers. The modest compensation for participation – an electronic gift card to a party unrelated to the researchers – was distributed by displaying its code in the user interface of the app a week after the app's installation.
- We disclosed the purpose of the app and collected only information needed for that purpose (i.e., only information contained in the Bluetooth advertisements). In particular, we did not collect location data, which limited the analyses we could run on the data obtained.

3.2 Dataset Characteristics

In the subsequent text, we refer to the phones on which the participants installed the app as scanners.

Our collected data provides evidence that most individuals (at least among those on a college campus) are near a variety of BLE-enabled devices much of the time.

Scanner #	# of non-empty scans observed by scanner	# of distinct peripheral uuids observed by scanner	# of scans in which the most frequently seen peripheral uuid of this scanner is observed	# of peripheral uuids not observed by any other scanner	fraction of non-empty scans that contain the same peripheral
1	2011	273	2011	273	1
2	1926	1148	1026	963	0.53
3	1848	1360	1388	1285	0.75
4	1842	965	1323	781	0.72
5	1834	1424	803	1290	0.44
6	1749	1350	1218	856	0.7
7	1721	1703	684	1204	0.4
8	1674	1228	1305	1200	0.78
9	1650	897	1407	612	0.85
10	1622	2429	795	2429	0.49
11	1612	2007	668	1443	0.41
12	1554	2216	935	1778	0.6
13	1491	424	1181	343	0.79
14	1450	1613	980	1127	0.68
15	1443	1003	608	932	0.42
16	1441	755	1021	409	0.71
17	1437	862	412	605	0.29
18	1433	333	1346	205	0.94
19	1407	1345	387	1120	0.28
20	1188	339	840	233	0.71
21	1168	1510	537	985	0.46
22	1152	282	521	163	0.45
23	1149	1269	89	946	0.08
24	1132	538	292	509	0.26
25	1130	963	561	875	0.5
26	1116	860	714	776	0.64
27	1112	1388	565	1190	0.51
28	1081	576	773	305	0.72
29	1076	922	397	680	0.37
30	1067	1333	83	885	0.08
31	1000	676	277	443	0.28
32	948	900	160	738	0.17
33	918	290	578	165	0.63
34	918	585	227	399	0.25
35	873	733	108	557	0.12
36	867	415	393	377	0.45
37	832	2040	313	1430	0.38
38	817	891	801	564	0.98
39	817	907	70	595	0.09
40	800	652	281	589	0.35
41	796	1254	73	1010	0.09
42	790	1116	333	805	0.42
43	735	404	129	240	0.18
44	732	702	394	596	0.54
45	694	446	559	369	0.81
46	674	1020	172	491	0.26
47	668	940	127	667	0.19
48	661	284	214	206	0.32
49	620	561	124	377	0.2
50	578	326	108	220	0.19
51	576	334	356	222	0.62
52	549	457	224	393	0.41
53	524	654	199	449	0.38
54	519	308	172	273	0.33
55	475	272	304	228	0.64
56	443	180	427	142	0.96
57	396	513	38	333	0.1
58	385	160	8	160	0.02
59	378	462	108	413	0.29
60	336	327	125	181	0.37
61	329	46	253	33	0.77
62	276	661	152	540	0.55
63	254	202	33	158	0.13
64	156	58	32	41	0.21
65	119	153	36	121	0.3
66	116	48	36	43	0.31
67	69	106	36	17	0.52
68	27	61	5	35	0.19
69	25	69	6	36	0.24
70	17	7	9	6	0.53

Table 2: Statistics, per scanner, on the number of non-empty scans, distinct peripheral uuids, frequency of the most frequent peripheral, number of peripherals unique to a scanner.

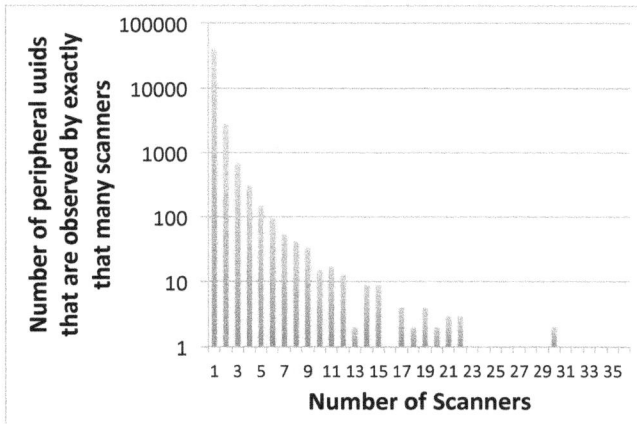

Figure 1: Characterizing how many scanners observe the same peripheral uuids

Given our app's scanning behavior, each scanner that used our app for a week conducted 2,016 scans (2 scans every 10 minutes for 7 days). We call a scan during which a scanner receives some BLE advertisements *non-empty*. Although each scanner had some non-empty scans, 57 out of the 70 scanners observed their first peripheral within 10 minutes of installing our app, 65 – within 1 hour of installing our app. The median number of non-empty scans for a scanner is 870, and 54 out of 70 scanners have carried out at least 504 non-empty scans, meaning that for 54 scanners, at least $\frac{1}{4}$-th of the scans conducted were non-empty.

The scanners together observed 45,283 distinct peripheral uuids.[3] Each scanner observed as few as 7 and as many as 2,429 distinct peripheral uuids, with the median number of distinct peripheral uuids observed by a scanner of 658. Most of the scanners observe a high number of peripheral uuids that are unique to them.

47 scanners observed the same peripheral uuid in 30% or more of their non-empty scans, suggesting that most scanners consistently and frequently see the same peripheral, and the peripheral uuid of the most commonly seen peripheral may provide a "fingerprint" or a unique identifier for the phone. Furthermore, most scanners see many peripheral uuids that are not seen by any other scanner in the dataset, suggesting that these peripherals can also meaningfully contribute to the fingerprint. Detailed information for each scanner is presented in Table 2.

Finally, for each of the peripheral uuids in our dataset, we compute the number of different scanners that see this peripheral uuid. There are a number of peripheral uuids that are seen by many scanners; for example, one of the peripheral uuids in our dataset is seen by 36 out of the 70 scanners, another – by 33 scanners, two others – by 30 scanners, and so on. Detailed information on the number of peripherals that are observed by a fixed number of distinct scanners is presented in Figure 1.

---

[3]Recall from our discussion in Section 2.2 that observing 45,283 distinct peripheral uuids does not imply that there were as many distinct bluetooth-enabled devices near our volunteers, as some peripherals (most notably, Apple's devices) implement the "LE privacy" feature of periodically changing the peripheral address advertised.

There are a number of reasons why a peripheral uuid may be observed by many scanners: it could be a stationary BLE device, such as a beacon, that many individuals pass by, or it could be a BLE device of some individual who meets many of the other individuals in our dataset (e.g., during a crowded campus-wide event). The fact that our dataset contains some peripheral uuids that are observed by more than one scanner is a good sanity check – it shows that our users are not completely disconnected from each other, and at least occasionally, are near each other or visit the same places. The peripheral uuids that are seen by many scanners make the task of fingerprinting harder, but as we will see next, not insurmountable. Furthermore, most peripheral uuids (41,064) are observed by at most one scanner.

4 TRACKING FEASIBILITY ON ANDROID

In this section, we present experiments based on the data collected aimed to illustrate that our hypothesis of the feasibility of cross-app tracking via nearby BLE devices holds. We do not utilize the full set of information available to app developers from BLE scans; rather, we demonstrate that the tracking is feasible even when the only information used are the peripheral uuids. Our goal is to present a proof-of-concept that uses only the most basic data and relies on the most basic algorithms. In practice, cross-app tracking can be more successful than shown in our experiments as app developers can build sophisticated algorithms that utilize the full set of data (Section 6.1).

4.1 Experimental Set-Up

We formulate the problem of cross-app tracking as a problem of finding matching users between two applications (App1 and App2) based on the BLE scan data applications possess for each user. We assume that the apps share the scan data with each other, and, for simplicity, that they are used by the same set of users. For ease of exposition, when we refer to a "user", we mean the BLE scan data an app has collected for that user. Specifically, for experiments in this section, each user U of an app A is represented by a (numpy) array, whose size is equal to the total number of distinct peripheral uuids observed in our data and whose array entry j corresponds to the number of scans in which app A running on user U's phone observed peripheral uuid j (we create a 1-1 mapping between peripheral uuids and array indexes for simplicity).

We assume the collaborating apps deploy the simple matching strategy described in Algorithm 1.

Algorithm 1: Match App1 Users with App2 Users

1 For each user U of App1 compute his similarity score with each user of App2.

2 Select the user of App2 with the highest similarity score to U as the matching user.

We next detail how we transform our data collected from a single app into simulated data from multiple apps and how we compute the similarity score between users.

4.1.1 Modeling Data From Multiple Apps. Our matching experiment requires data from multiple apps, but as explained in Section 3, the scan data collected by our volunteers came from one app. We could have chosen to ask our volunteers to install multiple apps, but the increased effort needed could have deterred some volunteers from participating in our study. Instead, we chose to use the data collected by our app that does very frequent scans, in order to model data collected by multiple apps doing less frequent scans.

Specifically, we model scan data that would be obtained from two applications running on the phone of the same user by splitting the data collected by our app on each scanner into two scanner instances. Suppose we want to model that each app is used by a user every $10x$ minutes, where x is an integer from 1 to 144. Then we assign data from scans numbered $i \cdot 2x$, where i is an integer starting at 0 to App 1, and data from scans numbered $x + i \cdot 2x$ to App2 (scans are numbered in the increasing order of the time at which they are run). Given the frequency with which our Android app runs scans (Section 3) this corresponds to Apps 1 and 2 being used by the user within 1 minute of each other when $x = 1$, and within $5x$ minutes of each other for larger values of x. By varying x between 1 and 144, we can model apps that are used as frequently as every 10 minutes, and as infrequently as once a day.

A distinct advantage of using the modeling approach, rather than asking our users to install multiple apps, is that we can model apps doing scans with different intervals between them. Via modeling, we also automatically obtain the "ground truth" of who are the matching users between apps. A disadvantage is that the simulated data results in scans at fixed intervals, which is more structured than what application developers might see in practice[4].

4.1.2 Similarity Score. Given two arrays representing the scan data of two users held by two different apps, we would like to estimate the likelihood that the scan data belongs to the same user. We do so by computing a similarity score between the arrays. We use the off-the-shelf *Cosine* similarity score.

Given two arrays x and y of size n, each containing the number of scans in which each peripheral uuid has occurred for that user, the *Cosine* similarity score are computed as follows:

If $(\forall i, x_i = 0) \vee (\forall j, y_j = 0)$ then $Cosine(x, y) = 0$; otherwise

$$Cosine(x, y) = \frac{\sum_{i=0}^{n-1} x_i y_i}{\left(\sum_{i=0}^{n-1} \sqrt{x_i^2}\right)\left(\sum_{i=0}^{n-1} \sqrt{y_i^2}\right)}.$$

The intuition behind using cosine similarity as a similarity measure is as follows. Two applications can see the same peripheral uuid during scans for BLE devices if: they are installed on the same phone OR they are installed on different phones, but the owners of those phones have passed by the same peripheral (not necessarily at the same time). If one application sees a particular peripheral uuid during scans, and another does not, it could be because the peripheral changes its address frequently or because these applications are running on different phones. The more common peripheral uuids the apps see and the more often it happens, the more likely these apps are to run on the same phone; the more distinct peripheral uuids the apps see and the more often that happens, the less likely these apps are to run on the same phone. The cosine similarity measure is just one option to encoding this, Jaccard similarity and many others would also be suitable. We deliberately do not optimize the

similarity measure in order to demonstrate that tracking is feasible even without any optimization.

4.2 Experiment Results

Our results unequivocally demonstrate that cross-app tracking using nearby BLE-devices is a realistic possibility.

Modeling frequency of app usage from every 10 mins to once a day, we split our data into two apps with 70 different users each. For each user of App 1, we compute his cosine similarity score with each user of App2 and select the user of App2 with the highest similarity score as the candidate matching user as per Algorithm 1. We present the number of correct matches (out of 70 possible) made by this algorithm depending on the app usage frequency in Figure 2. Even when the apps are used only once a day, more than half the users are matched correctly. This is a solid result, as the expected number of users matched correctly by a random matching is one.

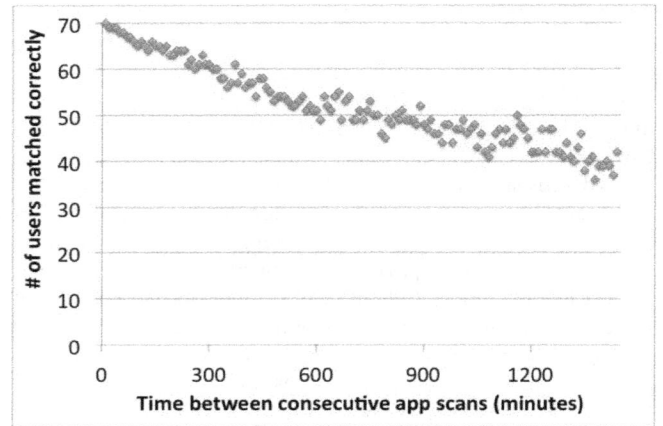

Figure 2: Number of correctly matched users (out of 70) using cosine similarity score as a function of app usage frequency.

5 TRACKING FEASIBILITY ON IOS

We also investigated the possibility of cross-app tracking using nearby BLE devices on iOS, and concluded that cross-app tracking is even easier on iOS than on Android, due to the differences in how Apple and Android transform the peripheral addresses received in advertisements before giving them to app developers through their APIs (Section 2.2.1 and Table 1) and lack of permissions needed to run scans (Section 2.3).

Since iOS limits the ability to run scans for all BLE devices when the application is in the background[XVIII], it makes frequent data collection by volunteers more difficult, as they have to actively engage with our app. Thus, rather than trying to collect large-scale iOS data from volunteers, we focused on identifying possible differences between BLE data presented to app developers in iOS vs in Android. To that end, we developed an app for iOS identical to the one described in Section 3 with the exception that an individual has to specify manually when the app should run a scan for BLE devices. In parallel, we modified our Android app to permit manual

---

[4]This disadvantage can be mitigated via modeling that sub-samples scans using a randomized, rather than a deterministic, process.

specification of when the scans should be run. For 4 days in May 2016, we manually ran two scans within one-minute interval of each other on an iPhone 5S running iOS 9.0 and on an Android device (Motorola Moto G3 running Android 6.0) at 18 distinct locations on our university's campus and recorded the data received. Our iOS application was compiled with *iOS Deployment Target* set to 9.0 and our Android application was compiled using *targetSDKVersion* set to 22. We observed no quantitative or qualitative differences in the data, except when scans were conducted at one particular location. In that location, our iOS app observed more distinct peripheral devices than our Android app, which can likely be attributed to a slight variation in the different vendor implementation of the BLE protocol for a particular BLE device located in that location.

We then ran two identical versions (differing only in the app's name) on two identical iPhones and two identical Android devices, performing scans both at various locations on campus, as well as in the authors' homes and offices, where the set of all BLE-enabled devices was known to us. It is through these experiments we discovered and verified the difference between Android's and iOS's Bluetooth APIs described in Section 2.2.1. Namely, a peripheral with address p will appear as having address p in (simultaneously run) scans of all apps installed on all Android phones, whereas the peripheral uuids seen by iPhone apps in advertisements coming from peripheral with address p will be different if these apps are installed on different iPhones but the same if they are installed on the same iPhone (see again Table 1). This feature, introduced by Apple for privacy [16], has the (presumably unintended) consequence of making cross-app tracking using nearby BLE devices trivial on iOS. Indeed, if there is even one peripheral uuid that appears in the scan data of both applications, these applications can with certainty conclude that the scan data belongs to the same user. If apps installed on the same phone are conducting scans within a short timeframe of each other or if the user is near the same BLE peripheral during large chunks of the day (which our data of Section 3.2 supports), the apps are virtually guaranteed to observe at least one common peripheral uuid.

6 DISCUSSION

6.1 Study Limitations

Our study has several limitations. We conducted the study with volunteers who visit a university campus, where one can presumably find more BLE devices than in a poor residential neighborhood. Our data collection was done using one app, and then we sub-divided this data to simulate data from multiple apps running on the same phone, resulting in scans that were done with more regularity than one would expect from typical mobile app usage. When computing matching accuracy scores, we assumed the apps trying to match users had the same set of users.

Some of these limitations can be addressed with additional research. However, it was not our goal to provide a definitive cross-app tracking technology for today's BLE device landscape. Rather, our goal was to demonstrate that the current treatment of BLE, if unchanged, will give rise to possibilities of fairly successful cross-app user tracking in the future, and thus, to argue for modifications needed from Bluetooth Special Interest Group, Apple, Google, and

BLE device manufacturers to safeguard user privacy before BLE-based tracking becomes widespread. The accuracy of tracking could likely be improved via more sophisticated approaches, such as:

- relying on a more complex similarity score, including one derived using machine learning on part of the data, as in practice, apps may know which of their users match through other means for a fraction of the users, and can use that data for training,
- distinguishing between advertisements received at nights vs during the day, to take advantage of the knowledge that users tend to be at home at night,
- building a more complex feature vector, that takes into account all information contained in advertisements (Section 2.1), including Service UUIDs, manufacturer data, the time when the advertisement is received, the RSSI, Transmitting Power Level, peripheral name and others, periodicity with which advertisements are received from a peripheral with a particular uuid, etc.,
- paying particular attention to paired BLE devices, rather than relying on passive scanning,[5]
- obtaining information about manufacturer specific settings for common BLE devices and incorporating it into our feature vector building and similarity scoring functions.

Furthermore, as the number and variety of BLE-enabled devices increases (13.9 billion such devices are estimated to be shipped by 2020[XIX]), so will the amount and variety of the data contained in scans, thus making cross-app tracking easier.

Our study was done using data of only 70 users who are all connected to our university. A natural question is what impact a larger number of users would have on cross-app tracking accuracy. We are interested in answering this question ourselves but a significantly more extensive study is not feasible in an academic setting[6]. However, even though our dataset is small, it has characteristics that make cross-app tracking in it more difficult than for an arbitrary set of users. Specifically, because our volunteers live or work or study in close proximity, observations of identical peripheral uuids from different phones are more likely than they would be for a population of users that never overlaps in space.

Finally, even if BLE data alone is not sufficient for tracking, we showed that it contains enough signal to amplify other surreptitious forms of tracking such as [28]. As many as 33% of iPhone users had Bluetooth turned on in 2014[XX], and the fraction is expected to increase. Thus, despite the limitations of our study, we believe that given the gravity of the privacy risk, the experiments presented are sufficient to confirm the viability of cross-app tracking and motivate a call for privacy-enhancing changes.

---

[5] Although omitted for brevity, we have experimentally established that *pairing*, a core primitive in LE communication, between a central and a peripheral device, although initiated at the application-level, is done at the device-level in iOS. This fact was already known for Android [24]. Thus, if one application on a phone has paired with a peripheral, then all other applications running on the same phone will see the same peripheral hardware address, effectively making cross-app tracking for users with at least one paired peripheral that can frequently be found near the user, trivial.

[6] Device Analyzer [29], the largest crowdsourced dataset of Android smartphone usage, does not initiate Bluetooth scans. Other available datasets we are aware of [11, 23] contain data collected by 100 and 12 devices, respectively.

6.2 Building Profiles using Nearby BLE Devices

Although it was not a focus of our study, we observe that information collected via nearby BLE devices can be used to refine a profile an app may have about the user. Specifically, our dataset contains more than 1,000 distinct peripheral names, some of which could be useful for profiling. For example,

- an app that observes a BLE device with name "Alice Smith's Fitbit" in most of its scans can conclude that the user's name is likely Alice Smith, a female,
- an app that often observes a BLE device with name "mama-Roo" in its evening and night scans can conclude that the user lives in a household with an infant,
- an app that observes a BLE device with name "[TV] Samsung 9 Series (65)" in its evening scans may make inferences about user's living room size and spending habits.

6.3 Mitigations of BLE Privacy Risks

We suggest modifications that would make tracking of the kind we describe more difficult without impacting the innovation capabilities of BLE-enabled devices.

Make device address and its derivates useless for tracking. Android and iOS should reveal a peripheral uuid rather than the device address to the applications using their Bluetooth APIs and these peripheral uuids should be randomized at the application and device levels. In other words, different apps should see different peripheral uuids for the peripheral with address P even if the apps are installed on the same phone, and the same app should see a different peripheral uuid for the peripheral P on each phone that it is installed on. Such a change would not significantly impact functionality of BLE devices, but would make peripheral uuids useless for tracking as apps would not see overlap in the uuids.

Increase the barrier for applications to perform scans via permissions and transparency. On Android, that would mean that instead of tying Bluetooth-related permissions to location ones (Section 2.3) and thus giving apps that only need access to Bluetooth data the additional highly sensitive location data, Bluetooth-related systems permissions should be classified as dangerous and require per-app user consent for the scans[7]. For Apple, that would mean introducing a user-controlled Bluetooth permission, analogous to the one iOS has for location. Introduce a user-visible indicator for when Bluetooth is being used and provide a list of apps that recently used it, similar to Apple's information on location usage by apps. Have the mobile OS keep track of which apps run BLE scans often, and surface these observations to the users with a nudge to reconfirm such scans by the app are desired. Such changes in the permission model would force apps to provide justification for their Bluetooth access, make the access transparent, and thus increase the barrier for abuse and likelihood of abuse detection.

Deploy data minimization [15] principles. Ensure that communication of other information contained in the BLE advertisements that may be useful for tracking (such as service uuid, peripheral name, manufacturer data) through the Android and iOS APIs to the apps is on a strictly as-needed bases. Further research is needed to find a practical way of doing this, but one approach could be to

require each BLE device to transmit its service uuid(s), for the apps to specify which service uuid(s) are relevant to their functionality, and for the mobile OS to provide each app with advertising data from only the BLE devices matching those services. In parallel, the mobile OSes could develop machine-learning and crowdsourcing-based approaches to verify whether the service uuid(s) specified by the app are needed for the app's functionality.

Enforce manufacturer utilization of the "LE privacy" feature provisioned by the Bluetooth Special Interest Group.

Policy and Legal Approaches. Make BLE-based cross-app tracking and profiling be a violation of the app store's terms of service, unless explicitly mentioned in the app's privacy policy.

The proposed modifications are simple, yet they could be very effective in preventing the use of nearby BLE device data for covert tracking by the majority of app developers. Furthermore, the changes would not negatively impact innovations that the BLE protocol aims to empower. Thus, this is a (relatively rare) case where significant privacy gains can be made without sacrificing much functionality.

7 RELATED WORK

The works most closely related to ours are the very recent works of [2, 9, 19], as they suggest that it may be possible to use fixed Bluetooth MAC addresses for tracking peripheral owners. Specifically, [2] presents a detailed analysis of MAC address persistence in advertising packets for a variety of fitness trackers. [9] also focuses on fitness trackers, shows that most do not change their MAC addresses, and further, demonstrates that the BLE traffic between the fitness tracker and the paired central device can serve as a fingerprint. Finally, [19] hypothesizes that other fields besides MAC addresses present in BLE advertisements can also be useful for tracking. We differ from these works in two ways: first, we collect real-world data and perform analyses to support the hypothesis that a particular kind of tracking, cross-app tracking, is indeed feasible in practice. Second, we do so without reliance on an individual owning a BLE device of a particular brand.

[13] and [30] aim to mitigate various privacy threats due to the BLE protocol but do not address the threat of cross-app tracking. In particular, both focus on preventing unauthorized scanner devices from accessing advertisement information transmitted by devices owned by the user (such as the phone itself), which is a different type of tracking risk than the one we consider. [27] demonstrates the feasibility of constructing botnets communicating via Bluetooth.

Recent work of [1, 14, 20, 28] considers the tracking risks due to Wi-Fi rather than BLE. [28] shows information contained in Wi-Fi probes can be used to fingerprint devices. Work of [1] explains Android's failure to assign the appropriate protection level to the ACCESS_WIFI_STATE permission and that decision's implications for user privacy, paralleling our observations regarding the BLUETOOTH and BLUETOOTH_ADMIN permissions on Android and no such permission on iOS. [14] quantifies the Wi-Fi probe requests' threat to privacy via an experimental study of popular smartphones.

[5, 8, 10, 17, 26, 31] present smartphone device fingerprinting techniques for user tracking which exploit hardware imperfections in the sensors introduced during manufacturing. [5] use hardware imperfections in the microphone and accelerometer to fingerprint

---

[7]This hurdle could be bypassed using forward compatibility, which is an argument for gradually stopping support of older API levels.

a device, [8] and [31] rely on microphone and speakers, [26] use diagnostic features such as hardware statistics and system settings extracted using the smartphone's operating system's API, [17] use the personalized device configuration created using the list of applications installed, songs frequently played, language settings, etc. The major difference between our works is in the choice of feature source used for fingerprinting. We rely on BLE sensor data, not previously discussed in this context.

Recent work by [32] and [7] study the conceptually related problem of cross-device tracking.

Significance of Findings. One may argue that the practical privacy implications of our findings are limited, since there exist other methods for cross-app tracking that are easier to implement, such as tracking via dedicated advertising identifiers provided by Apple and Google. We disagree. Firstly, using the advertising identifier for cross-app tracking is against Apple's policy[8], so apps that do not have advertising or want to covertly track may use the nearby BLE approach. Secondly, deterministic tracking methods such as device specific identifiers and log-in credentials are by now well-understood by privacy conscious users, and there is a clear recourse – the user can reset the advertising identifier as frequently as desired and use different credentials for different apps. Prior to this study, the possible tracking implications of nearby BLE devices were not well-understood. Furthermore, short of completely disabling Bluetooth functionality on one's phone (hardly a practical option in the world increasingly reliant on BLE devices), there is no recourse analogous to "clear cookies" or "reset an advertising identifier" or disable the "ask to join [wifi] networks" option in the BLE tracking context.

One may ask whether we have evidence that nearby BLE-based tracking is something apps already engage in. Doing such an analysis is beyond the scope of this work, and is research that could most easily be done by Apple and Google. However, very recent work by [6] demonstrates that much like the information from AC-CESS_WIFI_STATE that is very actively exchanged between apps, BLUETOOTH information exchange has also begun. Furthermore, it is irresponsible to wait until BLE-based tracking is widely deployed and only then implement mitigation techniques, as matches made before such protections are put in place can be exploited by the apps indefinitely. Finally, we've seen in the web context that tracking technologies used become increasingly more sophisticated as users, advocacy groups, and developers provide ways to circumvent known ones [12, 21]. There's every reason to expect a similar arms-race in mobile, and given the impending ubiquity of BLE-devices, it may become the next tracking and profiling frontier.

Although one might argue that our attack's feasibility is not surprising to the experts in the field, we believe that an actual demonstration of feasibility is a valuable contribution, as it is precisely such demonstrations that effect change in practice. For example, the work of [25] demonstrating the feasibility of tracking using battery status API led to Mozilla's withdrawal of support for it in Firefox[XXII]; the work of [22] demonstrating the feasibility of canvas fingerprinting led to introduction of a user-facing notice of such fingerprinting happening by the Tor browser[XXIII] and subsequent

de-legitimatization and drop of usage of this technique [3]; the work of [20, 28] led to changes in MAC address randomization for Wi-Fi scan traffic produced by Google Pixel and Nexus 5X devices[XXIV]. We hope that our findings can inform the new standards being developed, such as the Web Bluetooth protocol[XXV].

8 CONCLUSIONS

We presented a data-driven study demonstrating the feasibility of surreptitious cross-app user tracking using current BLE protocols and Android and iOS APIs. Through our analysis, we motivated the need for modest changes by Apple, Google, Bluetooth Special Interest Group, and BLE device manufacturers that would make such tracking difficult and give users meaningful control over it while preserving BLE functionality.

REFERENCES

[1] Jagdish Prasad Achara, Mathieu Cunche, Vincent Roca, and Aurélien Francillon. 2014. WifiLeaks: underestimated privacy implications of the access_wifi_state Android permission. In *Proceedings of the ACM conference on Security & Privacy in Wireless & Mobile Networks (WiSec)*. 231–236.

[2] Hilts Andrew, Parsons Christopher, and Knockel Jeffrey. 2016. *Every Step You Fake: A Comparative Analysis of Fitness Tracker Privacy and Security*. Open Effect Report. https://openeffect.ca/reports/Every_Step_You_Fake.pdf

[3] Julia Angwin. July 21, 2014. Meet the Online Tracking Device That is Virtually Impossible to Block. *ProPublica* (July 21, 2014). https://www.propublica.org/artic le/meet-the-online-tracking-device-that-is-virtually-impossible-to-block

[4] Bluetooth Special Interest Group. 2014. *Specification of the Bluetooth System Covered Core Package Version 4.2*.

[5] Hristo Bojinov, Yan Michalevsky, Gabi Nakibly, and Dan Boneh. 2014. Mobile device identification via sensor fingerprinting. *arXiv preprint arXiv:1408.1416* (2014).

[6] Amiangshu Bosu, Fang Liu, Danfeng Yao, and Gang Wang. 2017. Collusive Data Leak and More: Large-scale Threat Analysis of Inter-app Communications. In *Proceedings of the 12th ACM on Asia Conference on Computer and Communications Security (ASIA CCS)*.

[7] Justin Brookman, Phoebe Rouge, Aaron Alva, and Christina Yeung. 2017. Cross-Device Tracking: Measurement and Disclosures. *Proceedings on Privacy Enhancing Technologies* 2017, 2 (2017), 133–148.

[8] Anupam Das, Nikita Borisov, and Matthew Caesar. 2014. Do you hear what I hear?: fingerprinting smart devices through embedded acoustic components. In *Proceedings of the ACM SIGSAC Conference on Computer and Communications Security (CCS)*. 441–452.

[9] Aveek K Das, Parth H Pathak, Chen-Nee Chuah, and Prasant Mohapatra. 2016. Uncovering Privacy Leakage in BLE Network Traffic of Wearable Fitness Trackers. In *Proceedings of the 17th International Workshop on Mobile Computing Systems and Applications*. ACM, 99–104.

[10] Sanorita Dey, Nirupam Roy, Wenyuan Xu, Romit Roy Choudhury, and Srihari Nelakuditi. 2014. AccelPrint: Imperfections of Accelerometers Make Smartphones Trackable. In *NDSS*.

[11] Nathan Eagle and Alex Sandy Pentland. 2006. Reality mining: sensing complex social systems. *Personal and ubiquitous computing* 10, 4 (2006), 255–268.

[12] Steven Englehardt and Arvind Narayanan. 2016. Online tracking: A 1-million-site measurement and analysis. In *ACM Conference on Computer and Communications Security (CCS)*.

[13] Kassem Fawaz, Kyu-Han Kim, and Kang G. Shin. 2016. Protecting Privacy of BLE Device Users. In *25th USENIX Security Symposium*.

[14] Julien Freudiger. 2015. How talkative is your mobile device?: an experimental study of wi-fi probe requests. In *Proceedings of the ACM Conference on Security & Privacy in Wireless & Mobile Networks (WiSec)*.

[15] Seda Gürses. 2014. Can you engineer privacy? *Commun. ACM* 57, 8 (2014), 20–23.

[16] Frederic Jacobs. Jun 8, 2015. Apple iOS 9: Security and Privacy Features. *Medium* (Jun 8, 2015). https://medium.com/@FredericJacobs/apple-ios-9-security-priva cy-features-8d82d9da10eb#.5zspfi63t

[17] Andreas Kurtz, Hugo Gascon, Tobias Becker, Konrad Rieck, and Felix Freiling. 2016. Fingerprinting Mobile Devices Using Personalized Configurations. *Proceedings on Privacy Enhancing Technologies* 2016, 1 (2016), 4–19.

[18] John Leonard. Nov 9, 2015. MAC addresses: the privacy Achilles' Heel of the Internet of Things. *Computing* (Nov 9, 2015). http://www.computing.co.uk/ctg/news /2433827/mac-addresses-the-privacy-achilles-heel-of-the-internet-of-things

[19] Scott Lester and Paul Stone. 2016. Bluetooth LE - Increasingly popular, but still not very private. (2016). http://www.contextis.com/resources/blog/bluetooth-l

---

[8]Cross-app tracking is not listed among acceptable uses for the Advertising Identifier[XXI].

e-increasingly-popular-still-not-very-private/

[20] Célestin Matte. 2017. *Wi-Fi Tracking: Fingerprinting Attacks and Counter-Measures*. Theses. Université de Lyon. https://hal.archives-ouvertes.fr/tel-01659783

[21] Jonathan R Mayer and John C Mitchell. 2012. Third-party web tracking: Policy and technology. In *IEEE Symposium on Security and Privacy (S&P)*. 413–427.

[22] Keaton Mowery and Hovav Shacham. 2012. Pixel Perfect: Fingerprinting Canvas in HTML5. In *Proceedings of Web 2.0 Security & Privacy (W2SP)*. IEEE Computer Society.

[23] Anirudh Natarajan, Mehul Motani, and Vikram Srinivasan. 2007. CRAWDAD dataset nus/bluetooth (v. 2007-09-03). Downloaded from http://crawdad.org/nus/bluetooth/20070903. (Sept. 2007). https://doi.org/10.15783/C74K5N

[24] Muhammad Naveed, Xiao-yong Zhou, Soteris Demetriou, XiaoFeng Wang, and Carl A. Gunter. 2014. Inside Job: Understanding and Mitigating the Threat of External Device Mis-Binding on Android. In *21st Annual Network and Distributed System Security Symposium, NDSS*.

[25] Łukasz Olejnik, Gunes Acar, Claude Castelluccia, and Claudia Diaz. 2015. The leaking battery. In *International Workshop on Data Privacy Management*. Springer, 254–263.

[26] Anthony Quattrone, Tanusri Bhattacharya, Lars Kulik, Egemen Tanin, and James Bailey. 2014. Is this you?: identifying a mobile user using only diagnostic features. In *Proceedings of the 13th International Conference on Mobile and Ubiquitous Multimedia*. ACM, 240–243.

[27] Kapil Singh, Samrit Sangal, Nehil Jain, Patrick Traynor, and Wenke Lee. 2010. Evaluating bluetooth as a medium for botnet command and control. In *International Conference on Detection of Intrusions and Malware, and Vulnerability Assessment*. Springer, 61–80.

[28] Mathy Vanhoef, Célestin Matte, Mathieu Cunche, Leonardo S Cardoso, and Frank Piessens. 2016. Why MAC Address Randomization is not Enough: An Analysis of Wi-Fi Network Discovery Mechanisms. In *Proceedings of the 11th ACM on Asia Conference on Computer and Communications Security (ASIA CCS)*. 413–424.

[29] Daniel T Wagner, Andrew Rice, and Alastair R Beresford. 2013. Device analyzer: Understanding smartphone usage. In *International Conference on Mobile and Ubiquitous Systems: Computing, Networking, and Services*. Springer, 195–208.

[30] Ping Wang. 2014. *Bluetooth Low Energy-privacy enhancement for advertisement*. Ph.D. Dissertation. Norwegian University of Science and Technology, Department of Telematics. http://www.diva-portal.org/smash/get/diva2:750267/FULLTEXT01.pdf

[31] Zhe Zhou, Wenrui Diao, Xiangyu Liu, and Kehuan Zhang. 2014. Acoustic fingerprinting revisited: Generate stable device id stealthily with inaudible sound. In *Proceedings of the ACM SIGSAC Conference on Computer and Communications Security (CCS)*. 429–440.

[32] Sebastian Zimmeck, Jie S. Li, Hyungtae Kim, Steven M. Bellovin, and Tony Jebara. 2017. A Privacy Analysis of Cross-device Tracking. In *26th USENIX Security Symposium (USENIX Security 17)*. USENIX Association, Vancouver, BC, 1391–1408. https://www.usenix.org/conference/usenixsecurity17/technical-sessions/presentation/zimmeck

NOTES

I. https://www.networkadvertising.org/about-nai

II. http://now.avg.com/apple-ios-7-puts-unique-device-ids

III. https://support.apple.com/en-us/HT205223

IV. https://www.bluetooth.com/what-is-bluetooth-technology/bluetooth-technology-basics/low-energy

V. http://www.argenox.com/a-ble-advertising-primer

VI. https://www.sans.edu/research/security-laboratory/article/bluetooth

VII. https://www.bluetooth.org/en-us/specification/assigned-numbers/generic-access-profile

VIII. https://www.bluetooth.com/specifications/assigned-numbers/company-Identifiers

IX. http://blog.bluetooth.com/bluetooth-technology-protecting-your-privacy/, https://developer.bluetooth.org/TechnologyOverview/pages/le-security.aspx

X. https://developer.apple.com/library/mac/documentation/NetworkingInternetWeb/Conceptual/CoreBluetooth_concepts/AboutCoreBluetooth/Introduction.html

XI. https://developer.apple.com/library/ios/documentation/NetworkingInternetWeb/Conceptual/CoreBluetooth_concepts/CoreBluetoothBackgroundProcessingForIOSApps/PerformingTasksWhileYourAppIsInTheBackground.html

XII. https://developer.apple.com/library/ios/documentation/CoreBluetooth/Reference/CBCentralManager_Class/#//apple_ref/occ/instm/CBCentralManager/scanForPeripheralsWithServices:options:

XIII. https://developer.android.com/guide/topics/security/permissions.html#normal-dangerous

XIV. https://developer.android.com/about/versions/marshmallow/android-6.0-changes.html

XV. https://developer.android.com/guide/topics/manifest/uses-sdk-element.html#fc

XVI. https://developer.android.com/about/dashboards/index.html

XVII. https://developer.android.com/guide/topics/connectivity/bluetooth.html

XVIII. https://developer.apple.com/library/ios/documentation/CoreBluetooth/Reference/CBCentralManager_Class/#//apple_ref/occ/instm/CBCentralManager/scanForPeripheralsWithServices:options:

XIX. https://www.bluetooth.com/specifications/bluetooth-core-specification/bluetooth5

XX. http://beekn.net/2014/03/ibeacon-bluetooth-insights-empatika/

XXI. https://developer.apple.com/library/content/documentation/LanguagesUtilities/Conceptual/iTunesConnect_Guide/Chapters/SubmittingTheApp.html#//apple_ref/doc/uid/TP40011225-CH33-SW8

XXII. https://bugzilla.mozilla.org/show_bug.cgi?id=1313580

XXIII. https://trac.torproject.org/projects/tor/ticket/6253

XXIV. https://android-developers.googleblog.com/2017/04/changes-to-device-identifiers-in.html

XXV. https://webbluetoothcg.github.io/web-bluetooth/

Privacy-Preserving Certification of Sustainability Metrics

Cetin Sahin, Brandon Kuczenski, Omer Egecioglu, Amr El Abbadi
University of California, Santa Barbara
{cetin, omer, amr}@cs.ucsb.edu, bkuczenski@bren.ucsb.edu

ABSTRACT

Companies are often motivated to evaluate their environmental sustainability, and to make public pronouncements about their performance with respect to quantitative sustainability metrics. Public trust in these declarations is enhanced if the claims are certified by a recognized authority. Because accurate evaluations of environmental impacts require detailed information about industrial processes throughout a supply chain, protecting the privacy of input data in sustainability assessment is of paramount importance. We introduce a new paradigm, called *privacy-preserving certification*, that enables the computation of sustainability indicators in a privacy-preserving manner, allowing firms to be classified based on their individual performance without revealing sensitive information to the certifier, other parties, or the public. In this work, we describe different variants of the certification problem, highlight the necessary security requirements, and propose a provably-secure novel framework that performs the certification operations under the management of an authorized, yet untrusted, party without compromising confidential information.

ACM Reference format:
Cetin Sahin, Brandon Kuczenski, Omer Egecioglu, Amr El Abbadi University of California, Santa Barbara {cetin, omer, amr}@cs.ucsb.edu, bkuczenski@bren.ucsb.edu . 2018. Privacy-Preserving Certification of Sustainability Metrics. In *Proceedings of Eighth ACM Conference on Data and Application Security and Privacy, Tempe, AZ, USA, March 19–21, 2018 (CODASPY '18),* 11 pages.
https://doi.org/10.1145/3176258.3176308

1 INTRODUCTION

Organizations are often motivated to make public disclosures about their environmental performance. These motivations may be inspired by regulatory requirements, marketing initiatives, or as part of a broader project of corporate sustainability. The landscape of environmental and sustainability claims is largely standardized, as exemplified by the ISO 14000 series of standards. Often environmental disclosures take the form of certifications, which establish that some agency has reviewed the claim and confirmed its validity. A prominent example is the ISO 14001 certification, which simply establishes that a firm has an established policy to review and correct its environmental performance. To make a quantitative evaluation about the ecological sustainability of a product or service, approaches that consider the full life cycle of the product are often used [38]. This form of analysis, known as life cycle assessment (LCA), is codified in the ISO 14044 standard [23].

Sustainability certification has been shown to lead to potentially significant operational improvements in environmental performance [35]. Firms with more significant environmental impacts are more likely to have high-quality environmental management systems [16]. Life cycle approaches can improve the quality of environmental disclosures [24] and also provide a framework for firms to take broader responsibility for the impacts of the products they make or sell [22].

The ISO 14020 series of standards governs environmental product declarations (EPDs), which include public assertions about the sustainability of products, based on ISO 14044-style life cycle evaluation [15, 32]. EPDs can include both externally certified claims and self-reported results. Certified results can include both "pass-fail" binary assertions about a product or process with regard to a set of criteria, known as "eco-labels," as well as detailed quantitative results [17].

The data sets that provide input to these computations express essential information about the operation of a process or production step [10]. A typical data point could be the quantity of electricity required to output a reference unit of some product. These data are often regarded as confidential and are typically concealed through aggregation with other data sets [41, 44]. Engagement with stakeholders and supply chain partners [36] is often required for effective consideration of life cycle environmental sustainability, which accentuates confidentiality concerns and may limit the scope of information included in the assessment [24].

Despite the importance of data privacy, the LCA community lacks a formal framework for managing private data, and very limited number of techniques exist for computing sustainability metrics that preserve the privacy of input data. In [29], Kerschbaum et al. introduce a framework for sustainability benchmarking with the help of an untrusted third-party, however, the proposed solution has an assumption that the participants do not collude with the third-party or each other which not might be realistic in the LCA community. This can result in significant risk to the privacy of individual data since small organizations might collude with each other to gain private information against big competitors or vice versa. We seek to apply recent developments in security and privacy to the problem of certification of environmental claims even in the presence of colluding parties. Specifically, we aim to confront the following challenges: 1) mutually competitive firms want to gain private knowledge about their environmental performance by comparing their environmental impact against a statistical metric, which is a function of the competitors' performance, such as an average or maximum; 2) an association of firms wants to enable its members to make public, validated claims about their individual environmental performance in comparison to a cohort or to the full group, based on private data.

The first of these can be achieved using existing secure multiparty computation (SMC) protocols (see Section 2). However, to the best of our knowledge, SMC has never been applied to the case of sustainability assessment in a completely secure manner. The second use case is novel and has the distinct requirements that parties be provided with certificates validating qualitative assertions about their inputs without the inputs being known, unlike most SMC solutions, these parties *not* communicate directly with one another, instead by interacting through a certifying authority.

In this paper, we formally define the *privacy preserving LCA certification* paradigm along with its goals, security and computation requirements. A certification is a quantitative evaluation of the result of such a computation, or an evaluation of a given contribution with respect to the result. Unlike in the SMC context where the individual parties involved need to know some if not all of the other parties involved, in the LCA context, communication with other parties might not be possible or is even desirable. Hence, we propose a novel privacy-preserving certification framework that enables an authorized party, referred to as *certifier*, to certify participants based on industrially well agreed on set of criteria or a common function without compromising any sensitive/confidential information to any other parties even in the presence of colluding parties. Although the certifier is authorized in the LCA context, it is not assumed to be trusted, which explicitly requires hiding inputs from the certifier as well. Moreover, the certifier might collude with some of the parties. Unlike previous proposals like [29], our approach is secure even if parties collude with the certifier. Our framework **does not** require parties to communicate with each other and aims to minimize the rounds of communication between the parties and the certifier. We now highlight some of the distinctive features of the LCA problem domain and our contributions.

Certification with no trusted entities

Even though the computation is performed by a certifying authority, it cannot be assumed to act as a *trusted*, unbiased authority, since the parties may not want to reveal their individual inputs to any other entity, including the certifying authority. In general, the certifying authority might need to perform complex computations and comparisons. It might be possible to perform such computations with an untrusted authority using advanced cryptographic tools like fully homomorphic encryption [18], but such techniques are known to be quite inefficient [40]. An established, computationally efficient approach for performing the complex computations required for certification is to use secure co-processors [3]. A secure co-processor is a tamper-proof hardware, which provides a non-transparent and isolated computation environment. It creates a trusted computing environment in hostile environments and prevents any unauthorized access. Because of these advantages, secure co-processors have been adapted in different contexts such as encrypted database querying [6, 7] and secure multiparty computations [25]. However, such hardware is limited in terms of computational resources and their straightforward deployment does not solve all the problems. The design of a secure and efficient framework is still a challenge.

Certification Operations

The certifier will perform secure *mean* and *quantile* computations (will be discussed later in detail) to make public or private announcements about parties. These are quantitive computations that allow the certifier to benchmark the performance of parties. To perform such computations, the certifier needs to perform secure comparison which requires a set of private cryptographic and secure operations. Performing these computations without compromising security and privacy constraints is a challenge in the LCA context.

Veracity of LCA data

When multiple parties want to perform a joint computation, the accuracy and usefulness of the computation rely on the correctness of the inputs. Verifying the correctness of the inputs is an important challenge in many contexts. The standard approach in the LCA context is the assumption of the correctness of the provided inputs, since the correctness of the inputs are verified via an audit after the computation [8, 43]. Therefore, the verification of inputs and the audition of data are beyond the scope of this paper. The main motivation is to perform computations securely.

We propose efficient algorithms to perform certification operations for the certification problems-mean, quantile- using the proposed framework. We show that the proposed algorithms are correct and secure with the assumption of honest-but-curious parties. Furthermore, we discuss the efficiency of our algorithms both empirically and analytically.

2 RELATED WORK

Secure multiparty protocols (SMC) are known for computing functions jointly over a set of inputs without revealing any information about the inputs. In brief, a set of n parties with private inputs $x_1, x_2, \ldots, x_n$ wish to compute a function $f(x_1, x_2, \ldots, x_n)$ jointly without revealing any x_i to any other party. After an execution of this function, the parties learn the correct output but nothing else, even if some parties try to obtain more information by colluding. There are two-party computation protocols that execute generic functions [34, 46], but these constructions rely on heavy cryptographic computations and may not be practical [12]. Privacy-preserving statistics using SMC have been well-studied under the scope of privacy-preserving data mining[11, 19, 26, 27, 33]. For example, Rmind [11] is a tool that computes well-known statistics privately such as average, mean, median, while [19] proposes a secure dot product computation using SMC.

Although SMC has a wide spectrum of applications, most applications require interactive communication among the parties. Certification on the other hand focuses on a performance evaluation using some statistical analysis. Our protocols differ from existing SMC approaches in that they do not require communication and data exchange among the parties, and instead require the involvement of an authorized (but untrusted) party in the computations to regulate certification policies.

Involvement of an authorized party requires the establishment of trust between the participants and the authority. Establishing trust with an untrusted party is not a new problem in the literature and several works in different contexts [4–7, 39] rely on trusted hardware based solutions, e.g. Trusted Platform Modules (TPMs) [2] or secure co-processors [1, 3], to establish a trusted computing environment, which are shown to be quite efficient for specific applications [4, 6].

Unlike fully homomorphic encryption, which is computationally quite expensive, partial homomorphic encryption has been shown to be relatively efficient. Examples of partial homomorphic encryption are the additive homomorphic Paillier [37] and Quadratic Residues [20] public key cryptosystems and these will be explained in detail later in Section 4.2. The central component of our protocols is private comparison, which has been well studied previously [9, 13, 14, 28, 30, 42, 46]. Each technique is suitable to different settings. For example, while [42] performs comparison on encrypted data, [14] compares unencrypted values privately. It is important to note that providing a new private comparison technique is not in the scope of this paper, it is just one of the main building tools to develop our protocols for the certification problem. We adapted our private comparison protocol from Veugen's protocol [42] as discussed in Section 4.3. Several recent works [7, 12] also adopt Veugen's protocol to solve different problems. Bost et al. [12] construct machine learning classification protocols over encrypted data. On the other hand, Baldimtsi et al. [7] propose a framework, which also benefits from secure co-processors, that builds on top of searchable encryption techniques to return ranked results to queries. Our work follows in this tradition, and applies it to an important new domain, namely environmental certification.

To the best of our knowledge, the closest work to ours is [29]. In this work, Kerschbaum et al. propose a private benchmarking platform for environmental sustainability with the help of an untrusted third party. Although the overall setting seems similar to our setting, there are fundamental differences in the two approaches regarding the security of the systems. The assumption in [29] is that the parties do not collude with each other and the untrusted party. However, this is not a realistic assumption given the current competition in the market. The parties might collude with each other or with the untrusted party to gain private knowledge against the competitors. The proposed key management scheme in [29] either allows parties to share the same private key or distribute the private key among k parties which will later require at least t of them to be present to decrypt the output. In the case of key sharing, any party colluding with the untrusted party can reveal the private inputs of the other parties. Similarly, in the presence of t colluding parties, it is possible to infer the private inputs of others if the key distribution approach is applied. Our approach is secure against colluding parties. Additionally, the certification process heavily relies on private comparison of inputs. The proposed comparison protocol in [29] relies on [30] which ensures a weaker notion of security due to the usage of multiplicative hiding. Our protocols rely on semantically and cryptographically secure comparison protocols in the certification process.

3 PROBLEM DESCRIPTION

3.1 Privacy-Preserving Aggregation in LCA

Life Cycle Assessment (LCA) is critical for quantitative evaluations of the ecological sustainability of a product or service. The computation of results in LCA can be described as a series of matrix operations in which possible results are activity or output levels of industrial unit processes, quantities of emissions into the environment resulting from those processes, or measurements of environmental impact scores [21]. The calculation of any one of these values can be described as the inner product of a vector of input data with a weighting vector of environmental characteristics [31]. We formulate the private LCA aggregation problem as an inner product of two vectors

$$s = \mathbf{w} \cdot \mathbf{x} \qquad (1)$$

where s is an LCA metric, each element x_i of the input vector $\mathbf{x}$ is one party's private contribution, and the weighting vector $\mathbf{w}$ is determined separately and may be either public or private. In this paper, for simplicity, $\mathbf{w}$ will be taken to be 1, so that s is the sum of the parties' inputs.

Consider an international trade group in steel manufacturing that wants to issue a report that documents the industry's environmental performance, such as the World Steel Organization's LCA study [45]. In the World Steel Organization, the certifier is managed by a committee, with representatives of the different manufacturers. All the manufacturers want to have a certifier, but since it has reps for different manufacturers, any given manufacturer cannot trust the certifier with its info. Conventionally, a report can only be prepared if the member firms share their confidential information with the trade group, allowing it to perform the aggregation and report the results. If instead the report were determined using privacy-preserving aggregation, the inputs would remain private, and firms could use the results privately for benchmarking their own performance, or publish the results, individually or together. However, the veracity of the results would be difficult to establish to the public.

We define a new problem, called *private certification*, in which an authorized party, referred to as *certifier*, can certify the participants' inputs based on a set of criteria or a common function without compromising any sensitive or confidential information. The output of this private computation may be announced by the certifier publicly or held private; however, the certifier should not learn any sensitive information during its execution. The certifier would need to be "trusted" by the public to compute and report results accurately, but may not be trusted by the parties with respect to the private data. In the private certification framework, unlike in traditional SMC, parties *are not required to communicate with each other*, but only with the certifier. The parties is not realistic nor desirable in the certification model, since the parties might not know each other, and may not want to communicate with each other.

We introduce two new privacy preserving certification problems, namely *mean* and *quantile* based, which allow firms to make public or private announcements about their inputs to a secure aggregation. Here we describe the constraints and requirements of the two certification methods. The correctness of the certification relies on the correctness of the inputs. As we mentioned earlier, the parties are honest-but-curious, i.e. they are honest about executing the protocol correctly, but curious to learn other inputs. Hence, we can assume that the provided inputs are correct, which is a standard assumption in the LCA context, since the correctness of inputs are verified via an audit after the computation (e.g. [8, 43]). Please note that in describing the functionality, we use inputs in the clear and

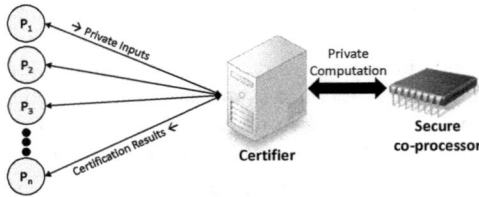

Figure 1: Overview of Framework Model

ignore cryptographic details. Later in Section 5, we will explain how to perform these certifications securely.

3.2 Mean Based Certification

In *mean based certification*, the certifier uses private aggregation to compute the average of a set of private inputs. Afterwards, the certifier compares each private input x_i with the average and performs the necessary certification operation, i.e. if a party generates less than the average, it can seek being labeled as more "eco-friendly" than its peers; otherwise it can forgo such labeling.

In mean based certification, the certifier computes the average of n inputs $x_1, x_2, x_3, ..., x_n$, and then certifies the parties either as *below* or *above* by comparing the individual values with the computed average value.

3.3 k-Quantile Based Certification

Grouping items into distinct groups based on predefined criteria is a well studied concept in statistics and can be utilized in different contexts. In the context of environmental impact assessment, this grouping technique provides performance information about a specific firm among the set of manufacturers. Being in the top quantile may be regarded as a prestigious certification that manufacturers can use to advertise their products with a greater confidence. By the nature of quantile based computation, the order information among the groups is revealed but it is hard to conclude which party is better inside the same group if the complete ranking information is hidden. It also allows parties increased flexibility to publish top performers' results while keeping others private.

In $k − quantile$ based certification, the certifier partitions the parties into k groups after ranking them based on the provided inputs. A party with the minimum input will be in the first group while a party with the maximum input will be in the kth group.

4 SYSTEM MODEL AND BUILDING BLOCKS

We now describe the system model and basic building blocks used in the paper.

4.1 System Model

The proposed framework contains three main entities: *parties*, a *certifier*, and a *computation helper* as illustrated in Figure 1.

Parties. Parties are end-users which are the main data (input) providers to the system. In reality, parties are the competitors in manufacturing the same product or providing the same service. To demonstrate the superiority of their product or service, they would like to be certified by an authorized party. Parties are not aware of the other participant parties and do not communicate directly with each other.

Certifier. In this context, the authorized party is called the *certifier*. It is the main computation unit of the framework and it communicates with all registered parties during the computation. Each party has to register through the certifier to be able to join the certification process. The certifier is trusted in performing operations but at the same time it might be curious to learn some information about the parties' data. Therefore, the framework aims to preserve the confidentiality of inputs throughout the computation against the certifier and all other external adversaries. To achieve this goal, the computation is split between two non-colluding computation units: *the certifier itself and a computation helper.*

Computation Helper. The framework needs an additional computation unit other than the certifier to satisfy privacy constraints. It is called *computation helper.*

The computation helper aids the certifier compute the certification function. The helper and the certifier must not collude, otherwise, they can reveal the secret data. The helper can be a server from a different service provider or a secure, tamper-proof hardware that can be deployed on the certifier site. As depicted in Figure 1, the framework deploys a specialized secure co-processor like IBM 4764 PCI-X Cryptographic co-processor [3]. These processors have relatively low resources in terms of memory and computation power, and are invoked to compute relatively small computations. Secure co-processors provide a non-transparent and isolated computation environment which fits directly into our model. We assume that the supplier of the co-processor is different than the certifier and their marketing interests do not intersect. Several privacy preserving solutions using a secure co-processor have already been proposed in different contexts such as encrypted database querying[6, 7] and secure multiparty computations [25]. Our framework requires only one round of communication between the parties and the certifier. Once a party submits a private input to the certifier, all the remaining communication happens between the certifier and the secure co-processor (the computation helper). The availability of fast network communication between the certifier and the secure co-processor is another advantage of our design. When the secure co-processor is deployed at the certifier's site, it is realistic to assume negligible network latency, since communication usually happens in the order of 1 millisecond.

4.2 Cryptosystems

The certifier needs two additively homomorphic cryptosystems: Paillier [37] and Quadratic Residues(QR) [20]. The cryptosystem is called *partially homomorphic* if it supports either addition (additive homomorphic) or multiplication (multiplicative homomorphic). Both Paillier and QR are additively homomorphic which means given two encrypted ciphertexts, $Enc(m_1)$ and $Enc(m_2)$, the application of the additive homomorphic operation will result in the decryption of $Enc(m_1 + m_2)$.

The Paillier cryptosystem is based on the Decisional Composite Residuosity assumption [37]. We use $[\![m]\!]$ to denote the encryption of message m with the Paillier cryptosystem using a public-secret key pair $K_P = (PK_P, SK_P)$. The plaintext space of Paillier is $\mathbb{Z}_N$ where N is the public modulus of Paillier and its homomorphic property is $[\![m_1]\!].[\![m_2]\!] = [\![m_1 + m_2]\!]$. In addition, the Paillier cryptosystem also supports multiplying ciphertext with a constant, which is actually the homomorphic summation of input with itself by n times. On the other hand, the plaintext space of Quadratic Residues (QR) is bits and $[m]$ denotes the encrypted bit m under QR. The key pair of QR is denoted by $K_{QR} = (PK_{QR}, SK_{QR})$. The homomorphic property of QR is $[m_1].[m_2] = [m_1 \oplus m_2]$.

Basically, Paillier implements the following three functions:

- $K_P(PK_P, SK_P) \leftarrow KEYGEN_{PL}(\lambda)$ generates a key pair. Note that λ is a security parameter.
- $[\![m]\!] \leftarrow \text{encPL}(m, PK_P)$ encrypts plaintext m using public key PK_P and outputs encrypted ciphertext $[\![m]\!]$.
- $m \leftarrow \text{decPL}([\![m]\!], SK_P)$ decrypts given ciphertext $[\![m]\!]$ using secret key SK_P and outputs m in the clear.

Similarly, QR implements the following functions:

- $K_{QR}(PK_{QR}, SK_{QR}) \leftarrow KEYGEN_{QR}(\lambda)$ generates a key pair.
- $[m] \leftarrow \text{encQR}(m, PK_{QR})$ encrypts clear bit m using public key PK_{QR} and outputs encrypted ciphertext $[m]$.
- $m \leftarrow \text{decQR}([m], SK_{QR})$ decrypts given ciphertext $[m]$ using secret key SK_{QR} and outputs m in the clear.

For the simplicity, we will omit including keys and security parameters in the function parameters in the rest of the paper. The reason for using two homomorphic cryptosystems is efficiency but only one cryptosystem can be used as long as it is homomorphic and semantically secure.

4.3 Comparison of Encrypted Data

A primitive module used by many of the problems addressed in this paper is "comparison". Take mean certification as an example. The certifier can compute the average using the homomorphic encryption scheme. However, the next step is challenging: the certifier has to compare secret values against the average without learning any information about neither the average nor the secret values. There is no efficient and secure way for a certifier to perform the comparison herself. Therefore, we need a *collaboration of two parties* such that both will not know the values, but *together* they will be able to do the comparison. The proposed framework fits this requirement and the certifier is able to perform the comparison protocol with the help of a computation helper.

The certifier has two encrypted numbers $[\![a]\!] \leftarrow \text{encPL}(a)$ and $[\![b]\!] \leftarrow \text{encPL}(b)$ of ℓ bits and the computation helper has private keys SK_P and SK_{QR}. Both $[\![a]\!]$ and $[\![b]\!]$ are sent by parties. The goal of the comparison protocol is to decide whether $a \leq b$ without revealing the actual values of a and b to neither the certifier or the computation helper. Our comparison protocol is adapted from Veugen's [42] protocol. The main idea is to compute $2^\ell + b - a$ and check the most significant bit ($\ell + 1$). If the most significant bit equals 1, then $a \leq b$, otherwise $a > b$. As a result of the protocol, the certifier gets the result of the comparison encrypted and the computation helper never learns the actual results of the inputs. Veugen's protocol has also been adapted and slightly modified by two recent works [7, 12].

To perform certification either with public or private outputs in our certification framework, we introduce two private comparison protocols, namely PRIVATECOMPARE and ENCRYPTEDPCOMPARE. They both takes encrypted inputs but PRIVATECOMPARE

Protocol 1 Two party private comparison with Public Output

Input A: $[\![a]\!]$, $[\![b]\!]$, PK_P, PK_{QR}, and SK_{QR}
Input B: SK_P
Output: bit t where $t = a \leq b$

1: **procedure** PRIVATECOMPARE($[\![a]\!]$, $[\![b]\!]$)
2:      A: $[\![x]\!] \leftarrow [\![b]\!].[\![2^\ell]\!].[\![a]\!]^{-1} \bmod N$ ▷ $x \leftarrow b + 2^\ell - a$
3:      A chooses a random number $r \leftarrow \{0,1\}^{\ell+\sigma}$
4:      A: $[\![z]\!] \leftarrow [\![x]\!].[\![r]\!] \bmod N$
5:      A sends $[\![z]\!]$ to B
6:      B: $z \leftarrow \text{decPL}([\![z]\!])$
7:      A: $c \leftarrow r \bmod 2^\ell$
8:      B: $d \leftarrow z \bmod 2^\ell$
9:      A and B privately compute the encrypted bit $[t']$ such that $t' = (d < c)$
10:      A: $[r_{\ell+1}] \leftarrow \text{encQR}(r_{\ell+1})$ and sends $[r_{\ell+1}]$ to B
11:      B: $[z_{\ell+1}] \leftarrow \text{encQR}(z_{\ell+1})$
12:      B: $[t] \leftarrow [z_{\ell+1}].[r_{\ell+1}].[t']$ ▷ $t \leftarrow z_{\ell+1} \oplus r_{\ell+1} \oplus t'$
13:      B sends $[t]$ to A
14:      A: $t \leftarrow \text{decryptQR}(t)$
15:      **return** t

---

announces the output of the comparison publicly, while ENCRYPTEDPCOMPARE keeps the result of the comparison secret. Both protocols require joint computations between the two parties, and both of them are secure under the honest-but-curious security model.

PRIVATECOMPARE compares two encrypted inputs and announces the result of the comparison publicly. The details of the protocol is summarized in Protocol 1. It is a joint computation of two parties, the certifier and the computation helper. The certifier has two encrypted numbers $[\![a]\!]$ and $[\![b]\!]$ and owns public keys PK_P, PK_{QR} and secret key SK_{QR}. On the other hand, the computation helper owns the secret key for Paillier, SK_P. The certifier initially computes $[\![x]\!] \leftarrow [\![b]\!].[\![2]\!]^\ell.[\![a]\!]^{-1} \bmod N$ and then hides it with a randomly chosen number, r. r should contain σ more bits than x. Next, the certifier sends $[\![z]\!]$ to the computation helper. Note that unless x was hidden by r, the computation helper could easily learn the comparison result. After receiving $[\![z]\!]$, the computation helper decrypts it and computes $d \leftarrow z \bmod 2^\ell$. In the meantime, the certifier computes $c \leftarrow r \bmod 2^\ell$. Then, the certifier and the computation helper cooperate to compare c and d ($t' \equiv d < c$) using a private input comparison protocol. Although Veugen also proposes a private integer comparison protocol in [42], Bost et al. [12] suggest using the DGK protocol[14] for better practicality. This private integer comparison procedure is a sub-procedure in the protocol and either of the proposed protocols can be used in this protocol. After the execution of the private input comparison, the computation helper receives the encrypted bit $[t']$ as a result. Later, the certifier encrypts and sends the $(\ell + 1)^{th}$ bit of r, $[r_{\ell+1}]$ to the computation helper. Finally, the computation helper computes the most significant bit of z by computing $[t] \leftarrow [z_{\ell+1}].[r_{\ell+1}].[t']$ and sends $[t]$ to the certifier. By using private key SK_{QR}, the certifier decrypts $[t]$ and announces t publicly.

Unlike PRIVATECOMPARE, ENCRYPTEDPCOMPARE aims to return both the comparison result and its negation privately. ENCRYPTEDPCOMPARE is summarized in Protocol 2. As in PRIVATECOMPARE, ENCRYPTEDPCOMPARE also requires the cooperation

---

Protocol 2 Two party private comparison with Private Output

Input A: $[\![a]\!]$, $[\![b]\!]$, PK_P, and PK_{QR}
Input B: SK_P and SK_{QR}
Output A: Encrypted Integer $[\![t]\!]$ where $(t = 1) \equiv a \le b$

9: **procedure** ENCRYPTEDPCOMPARE($[\![a]\!]$, $[\![b]\!]$)
    Run the steps 2-9 of Protocol 1
10: A: $[r_{\ell+1}] \leftarrow encQR(r_{\ell+1})$
11: B: $[z_{\ell+1}] \leftarrow encQR(z_{\ell+1})$ and sends $[z_{\ell+1}]$ to A
12: A: $[t] \leftarrow [z_{\ell+1}].[r_{\ell+1}].[t']$ ▷ $t \leftarrow z_{\ell+1} \oplus r_{\ell+1} \oplus t'$
    Run re-encryption procedure
13: $[\![t]\!]$, $[\![\overline{t}]\!] \leftarrow$ REENCFORPL($[t]$) from Protocol 3

---

of both the certification and the computation helper. Although the protocols appear quite similar, they feature crucial differences in terms of the initial setup and the computation. The certifier owns two encrypted numbers-$[\![a]\!]$, $[\![b]\!]$- and public keys for both Paillier and QR cryptosystem, PK_P and PK_{QR}. On the other hand, the computation helper owns private keys for both Paillier and QR, SK_P and SK_{QR}. Until the private integer comparison, both the certifier and the computation helper follow the same procedures as they execute in Protocol 1 (line 2 to 9). Once line 9 is executed, i.e. the certifier and the computation helper have privately computed the encrypted bit $[t']$ such that $(t' = 1) \equiv (d < c)$, the certifier receives the result of the comparison encrypted $[t']$, and computes $[r_{\ell+1}]$. In the meantime, the computation helper encrypts $[z_{\ell+1}]$ and sends it to the certifier. Finally, the certifier computes $[t] \leftarrow [z_{\ell+1}].[r_{\ell+1}].[t']$ and has the result encrypted. The result is encrypted with the QR cryptosystem. Thus, the certifier and the computation helper jointly run the re-encryption protocol that returns both the resulting bit and its negate to the certifier encrypted under Paillier, i.e. $(t = 1 \equiv a \le b) \Longleftrightarrow [\![t]\!] = [\![1]\!]$ and $[\![\overline{t}]\!] = [\![0]\!]$.

4.4 Re-encryption From QR to Paillier

PRIVATECOMPARE generates the result of the comparison encrypted under the QR cryptosystem (line 12 of Protocol 1). The plaintext space of QR is a bit, i.e. the result is either the encryption of 0 or 1. Although it is enough for learning the result of the comparison, to rank the inputs privately, our quantile based certification protocol needs to keep counters for comparison results without actually knowing the result. Therefore, we need to re-encrypt the resulting comparison bit to a corresponding integer value which is encrypted with Paillier. Re-encryption from the QR scheme to Paillier is performed such that the value of an encrypted bit is not revealed to any of the parties. Our implementation is adapted from [7] and slightly modified to meet the additional requirements. As presented in Protocol 3, to re-encrypt encrypted bit $[m]$, the certifier selects a random secret bit r, and then computes $[s_r] = [m].[0]$ and $[s_{1-r}] = [m].[1]$. The certifier sends $[s_r]$ and $[s_{1-r}]$ to the computation helper, thus, independently of the value of m, the computation helper receives the encryption of 0 and 1 every time. Then, the computation helper decrypts s_r and s_{1-r} under Paillier encryption, and sends $[\![s_r]\!]$ and $[\![s_{1-r}]\!]$ back together with their negates $[\![\overline{s_r}]\!]$, $[\![\overline{s_{1-r}}]\!]$ to the certifier in the same order as it received them. Since the certifier knows r, it uses $[\![s_r]\!]$ and $[\![\overline{s_r}]\!]$. $[\![s_{1-r}]\!]$ and $[\![\overline{s_{1-r}}]\!]$ are disregarded.

Note that our comparison and re-encryption protocols are correct and secure. Due to space constraints, we omit further details, but

---

Protocol 3 Re-encrypt from QR to Paillier

Input A: $[m]$, PK_P, and PK_{QR}
Input B: SK_P and SK_{QR}
Output: $[\![m]\!]$ where $[\![m]\!] = [\![1]\!]$ if $m \equiv 1$. Else, $[\![m]\!] = [\![0]\!]$.

1: **procedure** REENCFORPL($[m]$)
2: A chooses a random bit $r \leftarrow \{0, 1\}$
3: A: $[s_r] \leftarrow [m].[0]$ ▷ $s_r \leftarrow m \oplus 0$
4: A: $[s_{1-r}] \leftarrow [m].[1]$ ▷ $s_{1-r} \leftarrow m \oplus 1$
5: A sends $[s_0]$ and $[s_1]$ to B
6: B: $s_0 \leftarrow decrQR([s_0])$
7: B: $[\![s_0]\!] \leftarrow encPL(s_0)$, $[\![\overline{s_0}]\!] \leftarrow encPL(s_0 \oplus 1)$
8: B: $s_1 \leftarrow decrQR([s_1])$
9: B: $[\![s_1]\!] \leftarrow encPL(s_1)$, $[\![\overline{s_1}]\!] \leftarrow encPL(s_1 \oplus 1)$
10: B sends $[\![s_0]\!]$, $[\![s_1]\!]$, and their negates to A in the same order as received, i.e $([\![s_0]\!], [\![s_1]\!], [\![\overline{s_0}]\!], [\![\overline{s_1}]\!])$
11: A: $[\![m]\!] \leftarrow [\![s_r]\!]$ and $[\![\overline{m}]\!] \leftarrow [\![\overline{s_r}]\!]$

---

the intuitions for the correctness and the security can be found in [7, 42].

5 CERTIFICATION PROTOCOLS

This section outlines how to deploy and perform the certification operations described in Section 3 in a privacy-preserving manner on top of the proposed framework model. Basically, n parties want to be certified through a certifier. To satisfy security guarantees, the computation helper, an on-site secure co-processor, helps the certifier execute protocols securely. Note that each certification problem has its own computation and security requirements, and these are highlighted explicitly. For simplicity, we assume all n parties join the computation.

5.1 Private Mean Based Certification

To perform *mean based certification*, the certifier needs to overcome two main challenges: (1) computing the average of n encrypted ciphertexts, (2) comparing each private input with the computed average privately.

Initialization. The secure co-processor executes the $K_P \leftarrow KEYGEN_P$ function to generate a key pair for the Paillier cryptosystem and shares public key PK_P with the certifier. Then, the certifier executes the key generation algorithm for QR, $K_{QR} \leftarrow KEYGEN_{QR}$. After key generation, the certifier sends PK_P to all parties and sends PK_{QR} to the secure co-processor.

Security Requirements. The individual inputs x_i will be kept confidential throughout the certification. In addition to this, the average value of the provided inputs must also be hidden from both the certifier and the secure co-processor. The final result of the computation will be made public. The system should also be secure against the existence of colluding parties.

Protocol. The parties encrypt their inputs with the Paillier cryptosystem using public key PK_P, $[\![x_i]\!] \leftarrow encPL(x_i)$, and send the encrypted ciptertexts to the certifier. After receiving n inputs $[\![x_1]\!]$, $[\![x_2]\!]$, ..., $[\![x_n]\!]$, the certifier executes the MEAN-CERTIFY algorithm which is presented in Protocol 4. The protocol starts by computing the summation of the private inputs. Using the homomorphic property of Paillier, the certifier computes $[\![s]\!] \leftarrow [\![s]\!].X[i] \bmod N$. This operation yields $s \leftarrow s + x_i$ and after this is executed on all

Protocol 4 Mean Certification
___
Input Party$_i$: x_i and PK_P
Input Certifier: SK_{QR}, and PK_P
Input Secure Coprocessor: SK_P and PK_{QR}
Output: c_i (certification result for each party)
1: **procedure** SENDToCERTIFIER(x_i)
2:     $[\![x_i]\!] \leftarrow$ encPL(x_i)
3:     Send $[\![x_i]\!]$ to the certifier
4: Each party executes SENDToCERTIFIER(x_i)

   After receiving all inputs, $X[1..n] = \{[\![x_1]\!], [\![x_2]\!],...,[\![x_n]\!]\}$, the certifier executes the following procedure.
5: **procedure** MEAN-CERTIFY($X[1..n]$)
   Compute the sum of inputs
6:     $[\![s]\!] \leftarrow X[1]$
7:     **for** $i \leftarrow 2$ to n **do**
8:         $[\![s]\!] \leftarrow [\![s]\!].X[i] \bmod N$ ▷ $s \leftarrow s + x_i$
   Note that $s = \sum_{i=1}^{n} x_i$
9:     **for** $i \leftarrow 1$ to n **do**
10:        $[\![\tilde{x}_i]\!] \leftarrow X[i]^n \bmod N$ ▷ $\tilde{x}_i \leftarrow n \times x_i$
11:        $t_i \leftarrow$ PRIVATECOMPARE($[\![s]\!]$, $[\![\tilde{x}_i]\!]$)
12:        **if** $t_i == 1$ **then**
13:            $c_i \leftarrow$ Above
14:        **else**
15:            $c_i \leftarrow$ Below
16:        Sends c_i to P_i
___

inputs, the resulting computation will be the summation of all inputs encrypted with Paillier, $[\![s]\!]$. The Paillier cryptosystem does not support a division operation. Rather than computing the average, i.e. dividing the summation by n, the certifier normalizes the inputs by multiplying them by the number of participants, i.e. $[\![\tilde{x}_i]\!] \leftarrow [\![x_i]\!]^n \bmod N$. Recall that our main goal is to compare x_i with the average, ie, $x_i \leq sum/n$. The basic idea for this comparison is $x_i \leq \frac{sum}{n} \equiv x_i * n \leq sum$ where $\frac{sum}{n}$ is the average. Recall that the Paillier cryptosystem supports multiplying ciphertext with a constant. After normalizing the input, the certifier and the secure co-processor jointly execute the PRIVATECOMPARE function, introduced in Section 4.3, to compare $[\![s]\!]$ with the normalized input $[\![\tilde{x}_i]\!]$. The result of this comparison is known by the certifier in the clear and the certification is completed by labeling the party with input x_i as *above* or *below*.

Correctness. The certifier computes the summation of n private inputs using the additive homomorphic operation of Paillier which executes the summation operation over ciphertexts. Because of the homomorphic property of Paillier, lines 3 through 5 of Protocol 4 compute the encrypted summation of n inputs. Each encrypted input $[\![x_i]\!]$ is normalized by taking the power of n under modular arithmetic, which is equivalent to $[\![\tilde{x}_i]\!] \leftarrow [\![x_i \times n]\!]$ due to the Paillier properties. The comparison of each private input with the average of n private input is equal to the comparison of normalized input with the summation of n inputs, i.e. $\frac{sum}{n} \leq x_i \equiv sum \leq x_i \times n$ where $sum \leftarrow \sum_{i=1}^{n} x_i$. After executing the private comparison, a party is certified as *above* if $sum \leq x_i * n$. Otherwise, the label is *below*.

Intuition of Security Proof. The certifier receives the inputs encrypted with Paillier from the parties. Since, it does not own

the secret key SK_P, it cannot decrypt and learn the actual inputs. The homomorphic addition is semantically secure due to the Paillier cryptosystem, and the certifier computes the summation encrypted under Paillier. The comparison protocol is already proved secure [42] and does not reveal any information. Recall that the only restriction on collusion is between the certifier and the helper. Hence, we need to prove that collusion between the certifier and any number of parties will not reveal any private parties. Assume $n-1$ parties collude with the certifier except party P_1. In such a case, the certifier has $x_2, x_3, ..., x_n$ in the clear and x_1 encrypted, i.e. $[\![x_1]\!]$. Throughout the computation, the certifier computes *sum* encrypted which is denoted as $[\![s]\!]$ in Protocol 4. The certifier can compute $C_{sum} = \sum_{i=2}^{n} x_i$ in the clear. If *sum* was in clear, knowing C_{sum} would help computing $s - C_{sum} \equiv x_1$. However, since s is encrypted, the subtraction results in $[\![s]\!].[\![C_{sum}]\!]^{-1} \equiv [\![s - C_{sum}]\!] \equiv [\![x_1]\!]$. As it can be easily inferred from the result, the colluding parties do not provide any useful information to the certifier to reveal x_1. Hence, our private mean based certification protocol is secure even under the existence of colluding parties, since neither the certifier nor the secure co-processor learn any intermediary results throughout the computation.

5.2 Private k-Quantile Certification

To split parties into distinct groups privately, the quantile based certification is performed. Although the quantile computation is directly related to the ranking of a set of inputs, the certifier computes the k-quantiles privately without learning the ordering of the private inputs.

Initialization. The secure co-processor generates key pairs, K_P and K_{QR}, for both Paillier and QR. It owns *both* private keys SK_P and SK_{QR}, and sends the public keys, PK_P and PK_{QR}, to the certifier. Then, the certifier shares the public key for Paillier, PK_P, with the parties. We assume that the certifier knows the parameter k.

Security Requirements. Throughout the certification process, the individual inputs should be kept secret as in prior certifications. By the nature of quantile computations, the order information among different groups, i.e. the order of the parties in different groups, will be revealed. However, the ordering information of parties inside the same quantile group should not be revealed. We assume that the parties do not collude in this certification method[1].

Protocol. Parties encrypt their inputs with Paillier, $[\![x_i]\!]$, and send them to the certifier. After receiving n inputs, the certifier executes the QUANTILE-CERTIFY algorithm which is presented in Protocol 5. At a high-level, the protocol privately compares each possible pair securely. The aim is to construct a private comparison matrix, where the pairwise comparison is hidden from the certifier using Paillier. Later, by computing the sum of each column in the comparison matrix, the certifier figures out the rank of the corresponding parties, which will be used later to split parties into k groups.

The public pairwise comparisons of all pairs reveal the order of the inputs, which obviously violates the security constraint. Therefore, the protocol initially performs private pairwise comparison

___
[1]This is a natural problem of quantile based private grouping. If the parties from neighbor groups collude with each other, due to the ordering, it might be possible to reveal the input of non-colluding party in one of these groups.

Protocol 5 k-Quantile Certification

Input Party$_i$: x_i and PK_P
Input Certifier: k, PK_P, and PK_{QR}
Input Secure Coprocessor: SK_{QR}, SK_P and PK_{QR}
Output: c_i (certification result for each party)

1: Each party executes SENDTOCERTIFIER(x_i) from Protocol 4
   After receiving all inputs, $X[1..n] = \{[\![x_1]\!],...,[\![x_n]\!]\}$, the certifier
   executes the following.
2: **procedure** QUANTILE-CERTIFY($X[1..n]$, k)
   Private pairwise comparisons of inputs
3:     $C[1..n][1..n] \leftarrow$ empty
4:     **for** $i \leftarrow 1$ to n **do**
5:       **for** $j \leftarrow i+1$ to n **do**
6:         $[t_{ij}] \leftarrow$ ENCRYPTEDPCOMPARE($X[i]$, $X[j]$) $\triangleright t_{ij} \leftarrow$
   $x_i \leq x_j$
7:         $[\![t_{ij}]\!], \overline{[\![t_{ij}]\!]} \leftarrow$ REENCFORPL($[t_{ij}]$)
8:         $C[i][j] \leftarrow [\![t_{ij}]\!]$ and $C[j][i] \leftarrow \overline{[\![t_{ij}]\!]}$
9:     $c[1..n] \leftarrow$ empty
10:     **for** $j \leftarrow 1$ to n **do**
11:       $[\![sum]\!] \leftarrow [\![0]\!]$
12:       **for** $i \leftarrow 1$ to n **do**
13:         **if** $i \neq j$ **then**
14:           $[\![sum]\!] \leftarrow [\![sum]\!].C[i][j] \bmod N$
15:       $c[j] \leftarrow [\![sum]\!]$
16:     Choose a random permutation π over $\{1,..,n\}$
17:     **for** $i \leftarrow 1$ to n **do**
18:       $c_\pi[i] \leftarrow c[\pi(i)]$
19:     $R[1..n] \leftarrow$ COMPUTEBIN($c_\pi[]$, n, k)
20:     **for** $i \leftarrow 1$ to n **do**
21:       $j \leftarrow \pi^{-1}(i)$
22:       $c_j \leftarrow R[i]$
23:       Send c_j to party P_j
24: **procedure** COMPUTEBIN($V[1..n]$, n, k)
25:     $R[1..n] \leftarrow$ empty
26:     **for** $i \leftarrow 1$ to n **do**
27:       $v \leftarrow$ decPL($V[i]$)
28:       $R[i] \leftarrow \lceil \frac{n-v}{n/k} \rceil$
29:     **return** R

---

for all pairs using ENCRYPTEDPCOMPARE introduced earlier in Section 4.3 which returns the resulting bit $[t_{ij}]$ of comparison $x_i \leq x_j$ encrypted. Using the re-encryption function, the resulting bit is transformed to a Paillier scheme. Additionally, the negation of the result is also provided to the certifier. This will allow the certifier to construct a private comparison matrix C_{ij} where $i, j \in \{1,..,n\}$ as shown is Figure 2. Briefly, if $x_i \leq x_j$, then the comparison will return $[\![t_{ij}]\!] = 1$ and $\overline{[\![t_{ij}]\!]} = 0$. These results are stored in the indexes of C_{ij} and C_{ji}. Consider an example in Figure 2 where $x_1 = 3$ and $x_3 = 5$. The comparison of x_1 and x_3 is $x_1 \leq x_3 \equiv 3 \leq 5 \equiv 1$. Hence, $C_{13} = 1$ and $C_{31} = 0$. After comparing all pairs, the certifier computes the columnwise summation of all entries in the comparison matrix using homomorphic addition. The columnwise summation will give the number of ones, i.e. the input is greater than or equal to how many other inputs. Therefore, the summed values in the resulting vector show the ranking among n parties, i.e. if the entry

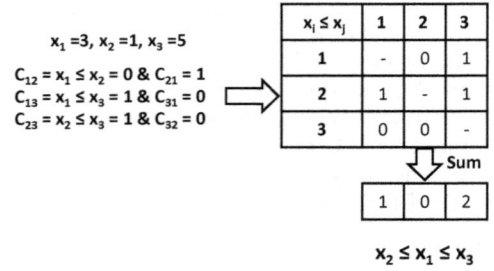

$x_1 = 3$, $x_2 = 1$, $x_3 = 5$

$C_{12} = x_1 \leq x_2 = 0$ & $C_{21} = 1$
$C_{13} = x_1 \leq x_3 = 1$ & $C_{31} = 0$
$C_{23} = x_2 \leq x_3 = 1$ & $C_{32} = 0$

$x_i \leq x_j$	1	2	3
1	-	0	1
2	1	-	1
3	0	0	-

Sum

1	0	2

$x_2 \leq x_1 \leq x_3$

Figure 2: Private Comparison for Ordering

in index i of the resulting vector is 0, that means the input x_i is the minimum input. If it is $n - 1$, that means x_i is greater than all other inputs and it is the maximum. Consider the example in Figure 2. After the columnwise summation, the resulting vector is $< 1, 0, 2 >$, which means x_i is greater than one input, x_2 is not greater than or equal to any of the other inputs, and x_3 is greater than equal to two parties. Hence, the resulting vector shows the ranking of the corresponding inputs. Recall the certifier does not own SK_P; thus, it cannot learn the ordering information. To prevent the secure co-processor from learning the order of the values in the resulting vector $c[1..n]$, the certifier applies a random permutation π. The ith element of c is stored at index $\pi(i)$, $c_\pi[i] \leftarrow c[\pi(i)]$. Then, the permuted result vector is sent to the secure co-processor. The secure co-processor decrypts the entries in the permuted resulting vector, and computes the group of the inputs. After computing groups for all inputs, the secure co-processor returns the group vector, R, to the certifier. The certifier can compute $j \leftarrow \pi^{-1}(i)$ which represents the jth index in the unpermuted order. After unpermuting the orders, the certifier returns the corresponding results to the parties, $c_j \leftarrow R[j]$, where c_j is the quantile rank of the jth party.

Correctness. Th certifier first compares all pairs and constructs a comparison matrix such that $\forall i, j x_i \leq x_j \Leftrightarrow C_{ij} \leftarrow 1$ and $C_{ji} \leftarrow 0$ where $i \neq j$. The comparison can be one of the followings: (1) $x_i < x_j$, (2) $x_i = x_j$, and (3) $x_i > x_j$. For cases 1 and 3, the numbers are distinct, and the output of comparisons are $C_{ij} \leftarrow 1$ and $C_{ij} \leftarrow 0$, respectively. In case 2, the numbers are equal and it returns $C_{ij} \leftarrow 1$. In this case, $C_{ji} \leftarrow 0$. This means x_i is not greater than x_j. Although $x_i = x_j$, the comparison selects x_j greater and ranks it higher. The columnwise summation of the comparison matrix will form a resulting vector which shows the ranking of the inputs among all n parties. The smallest input will have an entry of 0 and the maximum input will have an entry of $n - 1$ which says this input is greater than or equal to $n - 1$ other entries. Thus, the resulting vector will have entries from 0 to $n - 1$ which are the ranks of the inputs. The correctness of the rest of the protocol is straightforward. The resulting vector has entries $0, 1, ..., n - 1$ in some order. The secure co-processor decrypts the entries and split inputs into k groups (quantiles) based on their order among the n parties. For example, the inputs with entries $0, 1, ..., k - 1$ will be in the first group.

Intuition of Security Proof. The certifier receives the inputs encrypted with Paillier. The certifier initially compares all pairs using the function ENCRYPTEDPCOMPARE which is followed by the execution of the re-encryption function. The private comparison and re-encryption functions are already proved secure in [7] and they do not reveal any information. The results of the pairwise comparisons are encrypted with Paillier and the certifier cannot decrypt the results due to its lack of knowledge of the private key, SK_P. To rank the inputs, the certifier computes the columnwise summation of the comparison matrix using the additive homomorphic properties of Paillier. Therefore, it does not learn any information about the inputs and the pairwise comparisons. On the other hand, the secure co-processor receives the resulting vector permuted. Although it decrypts entries in the permuted vector, it cannot infer any information about the relationship between the results and the parties, since it does not know the permutation. At the end of the certification, groups(quantiles) of parties are public, but neither the certifier nor the secure co-processor learn any information about the ordering of parties inside the same group. Thus, the quantile based certification is secure.

5.3 Private Certification with Private Outputs

So far, the certification results are made public. As was discussed earlier, mutually competitive firms might want to gain private knowledge about their performances without revealing the result of the certification to the certifier, the computation helper and other parties. We now describe necessary modifications to perform such certifications with private outputs.

5.3.1 Mean Based Certifications with Private Outputs. The framework initializes the same setup as in the corresponding certification with public outputs except that a key pair K_{QR} is generated by the secure co-processor. SK_{QR} is only owned by the secure co-processor and PK_{QR} is shared with the certifier. To compare the private input with the encrypted threshold value, the certifier invokes the ENCRYPTEDPCOMPARE function from Protocol 2 until line 12 instead of the PRIVATECOMPARE function inside the MEAN-CERTIFY function. Line 12 from the ENCRYPTEDPCOMPARE function returns the result of the comparison encrypted with QR, $[t]$, to the certifier. Since, the certifier does not own SK_{QR}, it cannot decrypt and learn the result of the comparison. The certifier sends the resulting bits to the parties encrypted. The parties do not own the secret key SK_{QR}, thus, they need help from the secure co-processor to learn the actual results. To prevent the certifier and the secure co-processor from learning the actual results, the parties randomize their inputs by applying the same logic as in Protocol 3. In brief, each party chooses a random bit, r, and then computes $s_r \leftarrow [t].[0]$ and $s_{1-r} \leftarrow [t].[1]$. Both s_r and s_{1-r} are independent from the value of the resulting bit t. Each party sends their s_r and s_{1-r} to the certifier and the certifier sends them to the secure co-processor. The secure co-processor decrypts both of them and returns the unencrypted results to the certifier in the order received. The certifier also does the same and sends the unencrypted s_r and s_{1-r} to the corresponding party. Since the party knows r, it selects the correct result. If the result is 1, the party knows the label is *above*; otherwise, it is *below*.

5.3.2 Quantile based Certification with Private Outputs. The framework uses the same setup introduced in Section 5.2. The certifier executes the QUANTILE-CERTIFY functions as it is until line 21 in Protocol 5, where the secure co-processor computes the groups (quantiles) of inputs based on their order. After the secure

co-processor computes the groups, it encrypts the entries of R using the COMPUTEBIN function, which are the group numbers (quantiles) of the inputs, with Paillier. Then, the secure co-processor returns R to the certifier. Since the certifier does not own SK_P, it cannot decrypt and learn which party is placed in which group. The certifier executes the rest of the protocol as is and sends the results to the parties encrypted. The parties do not have the secret key SK_P. Therefore, they need help from the secure co-processor. To hide the real results (c in this case), each party selects a large enough random number r, and executes $[\![s]\!] \leftarrow [\![c]\!].[\![r]\!]$ which is equivalent to $[\![s]\!] \leftarrow [\![c+r]\!]$. Then, each party sends their inputs to the certifier and the certifier also sends these inputs to the secure co-processor. After decrypting $[\![s]\!]$, the secure co-processor sends s to the certifier in the clear. Note that since the random number r is hidden from both the certifier and the secure co-processor, they cannot learn the actual group number of the party. The certifier sends s back to the corresponding party. Upon receiving s, a party executes $c \leftarrow s - r$ and learns the group of the party.

6 PERFORMANCE

To show the performance analysis of our framework and algorithms, in this section, we present both empirical and complexity analysis for both the mean and k-quantile certifications.

6.1 Complexity Analysis

Mean and quantile based certifications rely on comparing encrypted data. This paper proposes two comparisons protocols, PRIVATE-COMPARE and ENCRYPTEDPCOMPARE, which are adapted from Veugen's [42] protocol. Veugen discusses the complexity analysis of the encrypted comparison protocol and shows that encrypted comparison has a very low computation complexity. The main computation complexity occurs while two private integers are being compared. In the same paper, Veugen proposes a Lightweight Secure Integer Comparison (LSIC) which requires l rounds of communications plus half a round at the beginning. Our prototype also implements the LSIC algorithm to compare two integers privately. Both PRIVATECOMPARE and ENCRYPTEDPCOMPARE have one more round for transferring z and $[t]$. Therefore, our comparison protocols require $l + 1.5$ rounds of communications between the certifier and the computation helper (e.g. assuming a 32-bit integer domain: 33.5). In addition, the re-encryption procedure requires one round of communications.

6.2 Empirical Analysis

We implemented a prototype of the proposed framework in Java. The certifier is run on a Windows machine with i5-2320 3 GHZ CPU and 8 GB memory. On the other hand, the computation helper is run on a machine running Linux with Intel Xeon(R) E31235 3.20 GHZ CPU and 32 GB memory. Both machines are on the same network and the average latency between them is 0.1 ms. The parties are run on the same machine with the certifier. The data domain is 32-bit integers. The conducted experiments measure the execution time to evaluate system performance by varying the number of participating parties. The size of the keys for both the Paillier and the QR cryptosystems are set to 2048 bits.

(a) Homomorphic sum   **(b) Time spent in comparisons**

(c) Total execution time

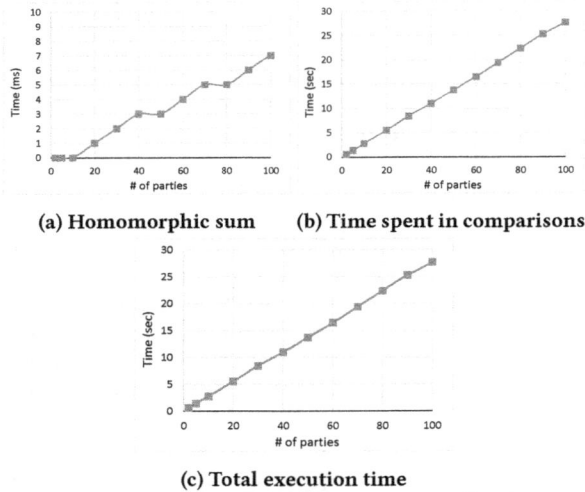

Figure 3: Results of Private Mean Certification

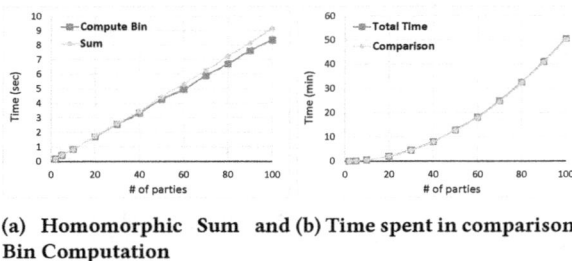

(a) Homomorphic Sum and (b) Time spent in comparisons
Bin Computation

Figure 4: Results of Private Quantile Certification

6.2.1 Mean Certification. The mean certification initially computes the average of inputs, and then compares each input with the average. Figure 3(a) and 3(c) present the execution times for homomorphic summation and total certification times, respectively.

Homomorphic summation is performed with modular multiplication. It is cheaper compared to encryption and decryption and this is also validated in our experiments. For very small number of parties, the average computation is performed in 0 or 1 ms. In the worst case, the homomorphic summation takes 7 ms (number of parties = 100). These results are very promising for other privacy-preserving database applications which need to perform aggregate operations as part of query executions.

The execution time of the mean based certification is dominated by the comparisons with the average (Figure 3(b)). The mean certification requires n comparisons against the computed average. In our implementation, the comparisons are sequential, therefore, both total execution time and time spent in comparisons have linear behavior. As the number of participating parties increases, the total execution time also increases. It is possible to perform comparisons in parallel which will decrease the total execution time, though this paper does not discuss and implement parallelism. Even without such an optimization, the total certification times take seconds, with a maximum of 27.6 seconds when 100 parties participate. This is still well below a minute, and hence for many applications, especially environmental certification, is very reasonable.

6.2.2 4-Quantile Certification. The quantile certification requires pair-wise comparison of each input data, which requires $(n^2 - n)/2$ comparisons. This quadratic behavior causes longer certification times as the number of participants increases as depicted in Figure 4(b). The other important sub-procedures inside the quantile certification protocol are the homomorphic summation of comparison values and the grouping computations. We set k to 4, that means the parties are split into 4 groups. The computation helper maps parties into groups in linear time. On the other hand, to get the final scores encrypted, the certifier performs $n^2 - n$ homomorphic summations before computing the bins. The certification of 20 participants is performed within 2 minutes though it takes slightly more than 50 minutes when there are 100 participants. Since this is an off-line operation, such execution times are reasonable. However, it is expected to have 20-30 participants most of the time and the quantile based certification can be done within a few minutes in such settings, which is pretty efficient.

Discussion. Our algorithms and framework enable achieving significant functionality with reasonable computation performance without sacrificing any performance. Our evaluations show the advantage of the usage of secure co-processors as a computation helper on site. Recall that the average network latency between the certifier and the computation helper is 0.1 ms in our experiments, which makes the cost of rounds of interactions among two parties negligible compared to the computation cost. An on site secure co-processor also makes the network transmission time negligible. Recall that the encrypted comparison operations require $l + 1.5$ rounds of communication and the mean certification requires n comparisons while the k-quantile comparison requires $(n^2 - n)/2$ comparisons, which makes $n(l + 1.5)$ and $(n^2 - n)(l + 1.5)/2$ rounds of communications, respectively. A setting where there is a non-negligible latency between the certifier and the computation helper will result in drastic performance degradation. Therefore, a secure co-processor perfectly fits the proposed model.

7 CONCLUSION

In this paper, we formally define the *privacy preserving certification* paradigm to evaluate the environmental impacts of industrial processes privately and propose solutions for two certification problems-mean, quantile. To perform privacy preserving certifications without compromising any sensitive information, we propose a framework, which enables a certifier to certify parties based on a well agreed upon set of criteria under realistic network setting. The paper also presents efficient and provably secure algorithms for the certification. Our prototype demonstrates that the proposed approach is not only secure but also efficient and practical.

Although the certification process is typically performed off-line, and hence might not require strict time constraints to complete the certification process, other applications might require instant feedback or certification based on the input, e.g., privacy preserving online auction system. Our framework is shown to be efficient for such application scenarios as well.

ACKNOWLEDGMENT

This work is partly funded by NSF grants CNS-1528178 and CCF-1442966.

REFERENCES

[1] Sean W. Smith and Steve Weingart (Eds.). 1999. Building a High-performance, Programmable Secure Coprocessor. *Comput. Netw.* 31, 9 (April 1999), 831–860. http://dl.acm.org/citation.cfm?id=324119.324128

[2] 2011. TPM Main Specification. (March 2011). http://www.trustedcomputinggroup.org/tpm-main-specification/.

[3] 2012. IBM 4764 product and PCIXCC feature overview. (March 2012). https://www-03.ibm.com/security/cryptocards/pcixcc/overview.shtml.

[4] Arvind Arasu, Spyros Blanas, Ken Eguro, Raghav Kaushik, Donald Kossmann, Ravi Ramamurthy, and Ramaratnam Venkatesan. 2013. Orthogonal security with cipherbase. In *Proc. of the 6th CIDR, Asilomar, CA.*

[5] Michael Backes, Aniket Kate, Matteo Maffei, and Kim Pecina. 2012. ObliviAd: Provably Secure and Practical Online Behavioral Advertising. In *Proceedings of the 2012 IEEE Symposium on Security and Privacy (SP '12)*. IEEE Computer Society, Washington, DC, USA, 257–271. DOI : https://doi.org/10.1109/SP.2012.25

[6] Sumeet Bajaj and Radu Sion. 2011. TrustedDB: a trusted hardware based database with privacy and data confidentiality. In *Proceedings of the ACM SIGMOD International Conference on Management of Data, SIGMOD 2011, Athens, Greece, June 12-16, 2011.* 205–216. DOI : https://doi.org/10.1145/1989323.1989346

[7] Foteini Baldimtsi and Olga Ohrimenko. 2015. Sorting and Searching Behind the Curtain. In *Financial Cryptography and Data Security - 19th International Conference, FC 2015, San Juan, Puerto Rico, January 26-30, 2015, Revised Selected Papers.* 127–146. DOI : https://doi.org/10.1007/978-3-662-47854-7_8

[8] Carsten Baum, Ivan DamgÃ¥rd, and Claudio Orlandi. 2014. Publicly Auditable Secure Multi-Party Computation. *Security and Cryptography for Networks* (2014), 175–196. DOI : https://doi.org/10.1007/978-3-319-10879-7_11

[9] Mihir Bellare, Viet Tung Hoang, Sriram Keelveedhi, and Phillip Rogaway. 2013. Efficient garbling from a fixed-key blockcipher. In *Security and Privacy (SP), 2013 IEEE Symposium on.* IEEE, 478–492.

[10] Beth R. Beloff, Jeanette M. Schwarz, and Earl Beaver. 2002. Use Sustainability Metrics to Guide Decision-Making. *Chemical Engineering Progress* 98, 7 (July 2002), 58–63.

[11] Dan Bogdanov, Liina Kamm, Sven Laur, and Ville Sokk. 2014. *Rmind: a tool for cryptographically secure statistical analysis.* Technical Report. Cryptology ePrint Archive, Report 2014/512.

[12] Raphael Bost, Raluca Ada Popa, Stephen Tu, and Shafi Goldwasser. 2015. Machine Learning Classification over Encrypted Data. In *22nd Annual Network and Distributed System Security Symposium, NDSS 2015, San Diego, California, USA, February 8-11, 2014.* http://www.internetsociety.org/doc/machine-learning-classification-over-encrypted-data

[13] Ivan Damgård, Martin Geisler, and Mikkel Krøigaard. 2007. Efficient and secure comparison for on-line auctions. In *Information security and privacy.* Springer, 416–430.

[14] Ivan Damgård, Martin Geisler, and Mikkel Krøigaard. 2009. A correction to 'efficient and secure comparison for on-line auctions'. *IJACT* 1, 4 (2009), 323–324. DOI : https://doi.org/10.1504/IJACT.2009.028031

[15] Adriana Del Borghi. 2012. LCA and communication: Environmental Product Declaration. *The International Journal of Life Cycle Assessment* 18, 2 (Oct 2012), 293–295. DOI : https://doi.org/10.1007/s11367-012-0513-9

[16] Magali Delmas and Vered Doctori Blass. 2010. Measuring corporate environmental performance: the trade-offs of sustainability ratings. *Bus. Strat. Env.* 19, 4 (Apr 2010), 245–260. DOI : https://doi.org/10.1002/bse.676

[17] Annik Magerholm Fet and Christofer Skaar. 2006. Eco-labeling, Product Category Rules and Certification Procedures Based on ISO 14025 Requirements (6 pp). *The International Journal of Life Cycle Assessment* 11, 1 (Jan 2006), 49–54. DOI : https://doi.org/10.1065/lca2006.01.237

[18] Craig Gentry. 2009. Fully homomorphic encryption using ideal lattices. In *STOC '09: Proceedings of the 41st annual ACM symposium on Theory of computing.* 169–178.

[19] Bart Goethals, Sven Laur, Helger Lipmaa, and Taneli Mielikäinen. 2005. On private scalar product computation for privacy-preserving data mining. In *Information Security and Cryptology—ICISC 2004.* Springer, 104–120.

[20] Shafi Goldwasser and Silvio Micali. 1984. Probabilistic encryption. *Journal of computer and system sciences* 28, 2 (1984), 270–299.

[21] Reinout Heijungs and Sangwon Suh. 2002. *The computational structure of life cycle assessment.* Vol. 11. Springer Science & Business Media.

[22] Eva Heiskanen. 2002. The institutional logic of life cycle thinking. *Journal of Cleaner Production* 10, 5 (Oct 2002), 427–437. DOI : https://doi.org/10.1016/s0959-6526(02)00014-8

[23] ISO 14044. 2006. *Environmental management — Life cycle assessment — Requirements and guidelines.* ISO, Geneva, Switzerland.

[24] Josef Kaenzig, Damien Friot, Myriam SaadÃI, Manuele Margni, and Olivier Jolliet. 2010. Using life cycle approaches to enhance the value of corporate environmental disclosures. *Bus. Strat. Env.* 20, 1 (Dec 2010), 38–54. DOI : https://doi.org/10.1002/bse.667

[25] Jonathan Katz. 2007. Universally composable multi-party computation using tamper-proof hardware. In *Advances in Cryptology-EUROCRYPT 2007.* Springer, 115–128.

[26] Florian Kerschbaum. 2008. Practical Privacy-Preserving Benchmarking. In *Proceedings of The IFIP TC-11 23rd International Information Security Conference, IFIP 20th World Computer Congress, IFIP SEC 2008, September 7-10, 2008, Milano, Italy.* 17–31. DOI : https://doi.org/10.1007/978-0-387-09699-5_2

[27] Florian Kerschbaum. 2011. Secure and Sustainable Benchmarking in Clouds - A Multi-Party Cloud Application with an Untrusted Service Provider. *Business & Information Systems Engineering* 3, 3 (2011), 135–143. DOI : https://doi.org/10.1007/s12599-011-0153-9

[28] Florian Kerschbaum, Debmalya Biswas, and Sebastiaan de Hoogh. 2009. Performance Comparison of Secure Comparison Protocols. In *Database and Expert Systems Applications, DEXA, International Workshops, Linz, Austria, August 31-September 4, 2009, Proceedings.* 133–136. DOI : https://doi.org/10.1109/DEXA.2009.37

[29] Florian Kerschbaum, Jens Strüker, and Thomas G. Koslowski. 2011. Confidential Information-Sharing for Automated Sustainability Benchmarks. In *Proceedings of the International Conference on Information Systems, ICIS 2011, Shanghai, China, December 4-7, 2011.* http://aisel.aisnet.org/icis2011/proceedings/breakthroughideas/4

[30] Florian Kerschbaum and Orestis Terzidis. 2006. Filtering for Private Collaborative Benchmarking. In *Emerging Trends in Information and Communication Security, International Conference, ETRICS 2006, Freiburg, Germany, June 6-9, 2006, Proceedings.* 409–422. DOI : https://doi.org/10.1007/11766155_29

[31] Brandon Kuczenski. 2015. Partial ordering of life cycle inventory databases. *The International Journal of Life Cycle Assessment* 20, 12 (Oct 2015), 1673–1683. DOI : https://doi.org/10.1007/s11367-015-0972-x

[32] K.M. Lee and H.D. Stensel. 1999. ISO standards on environmental labels and declarations and its implications on the market. *Proceedings First International Symposium on Environmentally Conscious Design and Inverse Manufacturing* (1999). DOI : https://doi.org/10.1109/ecodim.1999.747664

[33] Yehuda Lindell and Benny Pinkas. 2008. Secure Multiparty Computation for Privacy-Preserving Data Mining. *IACR Cryptology ePrint Archive* 2008 (2008), 197. http://eprint.iacr.org/2008/197

[34] Dahlia Malkhi, Noam Nisan, Benny Pinkas, Yaron Sella, and others. 2004. Fairplay-Secure Two-Party Computation System.. In *USENIX Security Symposium*, Vol. 4. San Diego, CA, USA.

[35] David Morrow and Dennis Rondinelli. 2002. Adopting Corporate Environmental Management Systems:. *European Management Journal* 20, 2 (Apr 2002), 159–171. DOI : https://doi.org/10.1016/s0263-2373(02)00026-9

[36] Katsuyuki Nakano and Masahiko Hirao. 2011. Collaborative activity with business partners for improvement of product environmental performance using LCA. *Journal of Cleaner Production* 19, 11 (Jul 2011), 1189–1197. DOI : https://doi.org/10.1016/j.jclepro.2011.03.007

[37] Pascal Paillier. 1999. Public-key Cryptosystems Based on Composite Degree Residuosity Classes. In *Proceedings of the 17th International Conference on Theory and Application of Cryptographic Techniques (EUROCRYPT'99)*. Springer-Verlag, Berlin, Heidelberg, 223–238. http://dl.acm.org/citation.cfm?id=1756123.1756146

[38] G. Rebitzer, T Ekvall, R. Frischknecht, D. Hunkeler, G. Norris, T. Rydberg, W. -P. Schmidt, S. Suh, B. P. Weidema, and D. W. Pennington. 2004. Life cycle assessment: Part 1: Framework, goal and scope definition, inventory analysis, and applications. *Environ. Int.* 30, 5 (July 2004), 701–720. DOI : https://doi.org/10.1016/j.envint.2003.11.005

[39] Nuno Santos, Rodrigo Rodrigues, Krishna P. Gummadi, and Stefan Saroiu. 2012. Policy-Sealed Data: A New Abstraction for Building Trusted Cloud Services. In *Presented as part of the 21st USENIX Security Symposium (USENIX Security 12)*. USENIX, Bellevue, WA, 175–188. https://www.usenix.org/conference/usenixsecurity12/technical-sessions/presentation/santos

[40] Bruce Schneier. 2009. Homomorphic Encryption Breakthrough. (2009). http://www.schneier.com/blog/archives/2009/07/homomorphic_enc.html, 2009.

[41] UNEP/SETAC. 2011. *Global Guidance Principles for Life Cycle Assessment Databases.* Technical Report. United Nations Environment Programme.

[42] Thijs Veugen. 2011. Comparing encrypted data. *Multimedia Signal Processing Group, Delft University of Technology, The Netherlands and TNO Information and Communication Technology, Delft, Tech. Rep* (2011).

[43] Cong Wang, Sherman S.M. Chow, Qian Wang, Kui Ren, and Wenjing Lou. 2013. Privacy-Preserving Public Auditing for Secure Cloud Storage. *IEEE Trans. Comput.* 62, 2 (Feb 2013), 362–375. DOI : https://doi.org/10.1109/tc.2011.245

[44] Gregor Wernet, Stavros Papadokonstantakis, Stefanie Hellweg, and Konrad HungerbÃ¼hler. 2009. Bridging data gaps in environmental assessments: Modeling impacts of fine and basic chemical production. *Green Chem.* 11, 11 (2009), 18–26. DOI : https://doi.org/10.1039/b905558d

[45] World Steel Association. 2011. *Life cycle inventory study for steel products.* Technical Report. World Steel Association.

[46] Andrew Chi-Chih Yao. 1982. Protocols for secure computations. In *FOCS*, Vol. 82. 160–164.

Capacity: an Abstract Model of Control over Personal Data

Daniel Le Métayer
Inria, Université de Lyon
daniel.le-metayer@inria.fr

Pablo Rauzy*
Université Paris 8 / LIASD
pablo.rauzy@univ-paris8.fr

ABSTRACT

While the control of individuals over their personal data is increasingly seen as an essential component of their privacy, the word "control" is usually used in a very vague way, both by lawyers and by computer scientists. This lack of precision may lead to misunderstandings and makes it difficult to check compliance. To address this issue, we propose a formal framework based on capacities to specify the notion of control over personal data and to reason about control properties. We illustrate our framework with social network systems and show that it makes it possible to characterize the types of control over personal data that they provide to their users and to compare them in a rigorous way.

KEYWORDS

privacy, control, formal model

ACM Reference Format:
Daniel Le Métayer and Pablo Rauzy. 2018. *Capacity*: an Abstract Model of Control over Personal Data. In *CODASPY '18: Eighth ACM Conference on Data and Application Security and Privacy, March 19–21, 2018, Tempe, AZ, USA.* ACM, New York, NY, USA, 12 pages. https://doi.org/10.1145/3176258.3176314

1 INTRODUCTION

Instead of the "right to be let alone", as originally coined by Samuel Warren and Louis Brandeis in their landmark article [16], privacy is increasingly seen as the ability for individuals to control their personal data[1]. The current trend is also to recommend the integration of privacy requirements in the earliest stages of the design of a product, following the privacy by design approach. However, even if the notions of *privacy as control* and *privacy by design* are predominant in the privacy literature, clear definitions of their meanings are still missing. The word "control" in particular is usually used in a very vague way in this context, both by lawyers and by computer scientists. This lack of precision may lead to misunderstandings and makes it difficult to check compliance. To address this issue, we propose a formal framework to specify the notion of control over personal data and to reason about control properties.

---

*Part of this work was done while Pablo Rauzy was a post-doc at Inria.

[1]This principle is often called "informational self-determination" after a ruling of the German Federal Constitutional Court related to the 1983 census.

The notion of control occurs in different contexts such as "access control" or "usage control" in computer science, but none of these variants really encapsulates the intuition underlying the notion of control over personal data. Previous work [8] has identified three dimensions of control over personal data corresponding to the capacities for an individual

(1) to perform actions on their personal data,
(2) to prevent others from performing actions on their personal data, and
(3) to be informed of actions performed by others on their personal data.

Actions can be of various kinds including, without limitation, consultation, modification, deletion and disclosure. In this paper, we build on this reflection to define a formal model of control and we show its relevance through the description of different options of implementation of a social network system. We show that each option provides a different type of control that can be characterized in a formal way.

Contributions and organization of the paper. In Section 2, we introduce an abstract model, called *Capacity*, which makes it possible to express, *inter alia*, the three capacities put forward in [8]. We proceed in Section 3 with the definition of requirements characterizing typical variants of control: action control, observability control, authorization control, and notification control. In Section 4, we introduce a concrete case study, a social network system, with its specification and describe it within the *Capacity* model. Section 5 presents three implementations of the specifications of the case study corresponding to different architectural choices (respectively centralized, peer to peer, and federated). We prove that they meet different control requirements in the *Capacity* model. In Section 6, we present previous works on control and compare them with our model before suggesting avenues for further research in Section 7. In Appendix B, we define an order relation which is useful to compare different systems based on the level of control that they provide (but not necessary to follow the body of the paper).

2 *CAPACITY*

The goal of the *Capacity* model is to make it possible to express, in a very general way, the three dimensions of controls (the *capacities*) introduced in Section 1 and to use them as a basis for reasoning about control. The guiding principles for the design of *Capacity* were therefore *abstraction* and *minimality*. Basically, the model is based on a set of *agents* that can perform *operations* on *resources*. These operations can be constrained by control *requirements* which form the core of the model. In this section, we first introduce the building blocks of the model in Sections 2.1 through 2.3 before defining the notion of requirement and its semantics in Section 2.4.

2.1 Objects

The *Capacity* model is based on four types of atomic objects drawn from finite distinct sets $\mathcal{A}, \mathcal{R}, O$ and C:

- *Agents*, noted $a_1, a_2, \ldots \in \mathcal{A}$, represent active entities (typically users or services).
- *Resources*, noted $r_1, r_2, \ldots \in \mathcal{R}$, typically include personal data.
- *Operations*, noted $o_1, o_2, \ldots \in O$, may typically include access, update, deletion, and communication operations.
- *Contexts*, noted $c_1, c_2, \ldots \in C$, denote the context in which an agent operates on a resource, i.e., any external factors relevant to the operation. Depending on the application, the context can include information such as location, time, or relationships between agents. Contexts can be used in particular to distinguish successive applications of an operation to the same arguments, or more high-level concepts such as the purpose for which personal data are processed.

2.2 Actions

We call an action the application of an operation to a list of parameters in a given context. By convention, we write[2] $o_c(x_1, \ldots, x_n)$ the action consisting of the application of operation o to arguments $x_1, \ldots, x_n$ in context c. The arguments x_i can be resources or agents. When the context is irrelevant, we omit the context and simply write $o(x_1, \ldots, x_n)$. Δ denotes the set of actions.

2.3 Relations

To be able to express privacy requirements, we need to introduce three relations on atomic objects:

- *Pers*(r, a) expresses that resource r is a personal data[3] of agent a,
- *In*(r, α) means that resource r is involved[4] in action α, and
- *Trust*(a, b) expresses that agent a trusts agent b.

The last relation can be useful to distinguish situations in which the control of an agent over their personal data depends only on trusted agents from situations in which it depends also on untrusted agents[5].

2.4 Requirements

We define a requirement R as a relation $Can^R(a, \alpha, E, W) \subseteq \mathcal{A} \times \Delta \times \mathcal{P}(\mathcal{A}) \times \mathcal{P}(\mathcal{A})$ such that $a \notin E$ and $a \notin W$. The intuition for $Can^R(a, \alpha, E, W)$ is that agent a can perform action α only if this action is enabled by all agents in E (the enablers), while all agents in W (the witnesses) have to be informed about the performance of this action by a. In other words, agents in E can prevent a from doing α.

By convention, we use $\perp$ to denote an undefined or phantom agent, which never performs nor enables any action. Therefore, $Can^R(a, \alpha, \{\perp\}, W)$ expresses the fact that requirement R prevents

a from performing action[6] α. Conversely, $Can^R(a, \alpha, \varnothing, W)$ expresses the fact that requirement R unconditionally allows a to perform action α.

Requirements make it possible to express the three capacities mentioned in the introduction, depending on the position of an agent x in the parameters of $Can^R(a, \alpha, E, W)$:

(1) a property with $x = a$ expresses the conditions under which x has the capacity to perform an action,
(2) a property with $x \in E$ expresses the capacity of x to prevent others from performing an action, and
(3) a property with $x \in W$ expresses the capacity of x to be informed of the performance of an action by another agent.

We further elaborate on these options in Section 3 in which we take a systematic approach and describe four types of control.

Definition 1 (Compact requirements). A requirement R is said to be *compact* if $\forall a \in \mathcal{A}, \forall \alpha \in \Delta, \exists E, W \subseteq \mathcal{A}, Can^R(a, \alpha, E, W)$, and $\forall a \in \mathcal{A}, \forall \alpha \in \Delta, \forall E, E', W, W' \subseteq \mathcal{A}, Can^R(a, \alpha, E, W) \wedge Can^R(a, \alpha, E', W') \implies E = E' \wedge W = W'$.

Without loss of generality, we only consider compact requirements in the rest of this paper, and to improve readability, we introduce the following functions:

- $\overline{Can}_e^R(a, \alpha) = E$ if $\exists W \subseteq \mathcal{A}$ s.t. $Can^R(a, \alpha, E, W)$,
- $\overline{Can}_w^R(a, \alpha) = W$ if $\exists E \subseteq \mathcal{A}$ s.t. $Can^R(a, \alpha, E, W)$,

which are well-defined because of the restriction to compact requirements.

In order to define the semantics of requirements, we characterize execution traces θ in a very abstract way (the type of θ remains opaque at this level of abstraction), in terms of the following properties:

(1) $\theta \vdash Requests(a, \alpha)$ means that, in trace θ, agent a attempts to perform action α.
(2) $\theta \vdash Enables(a, b, \alpha)$ means that, in trace θ, agent a enables the performance of action α by agent b.
(3) $\theta \vdash Does(a, b, \alpha)$ means that, in trace θ, agent a performs action α on behalf of agent b. *Does* makes it possible to distinguish the agent actually performing an action from the agent that has initiated this action, which is useful in many situations.
(4) $\theta \vdash Notifies(a, b, c, \alpha)$ means that, in trace θ, agent a notifies to agent b the performance of action α on behalf of agent c.

At this stage, we are content with an intuitive description of the above properties which are used below to define trace consistency and trace compliance. For each implementation, these properties will be defined precisely in terms of the corresponding execution traces (Section 5). It should be noted that this abstract level does not involve any notion of time or position in a trace: as suggested above, the context can be used to distinguish actions corresponding to different occurrences of application of an operation. At the implementation level, this information can be refined, for example, in terms of the position of an event in the trace.

---

[2]It should be noted that $o_c(x_1, \ldots, x_n)$ is not the result of the application of o_c to parameters $x_1, \ldots, x_n$. Formally speaking, it is just a convenient notation for the tuple $[o, c, x_1, \ldots, x_n]$.

[3]A resource can be the personal data of multiple agents. Therefore, we can have $Pers(r, a_1)$ and $Pers(r, a_2)$ with $a_1 \neq a_2$.

[4]More precisely, r is a parameter (or is included in one) of the operation of α.

[5]The notion of trust is intentionally left informal at our level of abstraction.

[6]Specifying that an action is not possible amounts to requiring that this action has to be enabled by an agent that does not exist or never enables any action.

Definition 2 (Trace consistency). Trace θ is said to be *consistent* if $\theta \vdash Does(c, a, \alpha) \implies \theta \vdash Requests(a, \alpha)$, and $\theta \vdash Notifies(a, b, c, \alpha) \implies \exists d, \theta \vdash Does(d, c, \alpha)$

Definition 2 expresses the fact that a trace is inconsistent if it includes an action performed on behalf of an agent that has not requested it or the notification of an action that has not been performed.

Definition 3 (Trace completeness). Trace θ is said to be *complete* with respect to requirement R if $\theta \vdash Requests(a, \alpha) \wedge \forall b \in \overline{Can}_e^R(a, \alpha), \theta \vdash Enables(b, a, \alpha) \implies \exists c, \theta \vdash Does(c, a, \alpha)$

Definition 3 characterizes a complete trace by the fact that a requested action is always performed if all the enabling agents have actually enabled it[7].

In the rest of this paper, we assume that traces are both complete and consistent.

We can now characterize the notion of compliance of a trace with a requirement.

Definition 4 (Trace compliance). Trace θ is *compliant* with requirement R, noted $\theta \models R$ if and only if $\forall a \in \mathcal{A}, \forall d \in \mathcal{A}, \forall \alpha \in \Delta$, $\theta \vdash Does(d, a, \alpha) \implies \forall b \in \overline{Can}_e^R(a, \alpha), \theta \vdash Enables(b, a, \alpha)$, and $\forall b \in \overline{Can}_w^R(a, \alpha), \exists c \in \mathcal{A}, \theta \vdash Notifies(c, b, a, \alpha)$.

In a nutshell, trace θ complies with requirement R if all Can^R constraints are met by θ: no action is performed unless it is enabled by all its enablers and all agents that have to be notified are notified.

3 TYPES OF CONTROL

Capacity requirements can be used to characterize different forms and levels of control which can typically be required or expected by data subjects. In the following, we introduce four types of control:

- **Action control**, characterizing an agent's control on the actions that it initiates.
- **Observability control**, characterizing an agent's capacity to perform actions that are not observable by others.
- **Authorization control**, characterizing an agent's control on the actions initiated by others.
- **Notification control**, characterizing an agent's capacity to be informed about actions performed by others.

For each type of control, we distinguish two levels: absolute control and relative control (in addition to level zero, or lack of control).

Definition 5 (Action control). Requirement R provides agent a *absolute action control* over action α, noted $AA_R(a, \alpha)$, if and only if $\overline{Can}_e^R(a, \alpha) = \varnothing$.

Requirement R provides agent a *relative action control* over action α, noted $RA_R(a, \alpha)$, if and only if $\forall b \in \mathcal{A}, b \in \overline{Can}_e^R(a, \alpha) \implies Trust(a, b)$.

$AA_R(a, \alpha)$ means that a can perform action α without needing any enabler. In other words, a does not depend on any other agent to perform α. In contrast, $RA_R(a, \alpha)$ means that a depends on other agents to perform α but all these agents are trusted by a.

Definition 6 (Observability control). Requirement R provides agent a *absolute observability control* over action α, which is noted $AO_R(a, \alpha)$, if and only if $\overline{Can}_w^R(a, \alpha) = \varnothing$.

Requirement R provides agent a *relative observability control* over action α, which is noted $RO_R(a, \alpha)$, if and only if $\forall b \in \mathcal{A}$, $b \in \overline{Can}_w^R(a, \alpha) \implies Trust(a, b)$.

$AO_R(a, \alpha)$ means that a can perform α discreetly, that is to say without being observable by other agents. In contrast, $RO_R(a, \alpha)$ means that other agents can know that a performs α but all these agents are trusted by a.

We should emphasize that we consider only observability of actions here and do not express other forms of observability or notions of implicit information flows for example.

Definition 7 (Authorization control). Requirement R provides agent a *absolute authorization control* over action α, which is noted $AH_R(a, \alpha)$, if and only if $\forall b \in \mathcal{A}$ such that $b \neq a$, $\overline{Can}_e^R(b, \alpha) = \{a\}$.

Requirement R provides agent a *relative authorization control* over action α, which is noted $RH_R(a, \alpha)$, if and only if $\forall b \in \mathcal{A}$ such that $b \neq a$, $a \in \overline{Can}_e^R(b, \alpha)$.

$AH_R(a, \alpha)$ means that a can enable the performance of action α by other agents and is the only agent having this power[8]. In other words, the possibility for another agent to perform α depends only on a. In contrast, $RH_R(a, \alpha)$ means that a is not the only agent having this power. In other words, the possibility for another agent to perform α depends not only on a but also on other agents.

Definition 8 (Notification control). Requirement R provides agent a *absolute notification control* over action α, noted $AN_R(a, \alpha)$, if and only if $\forall b \in \mathcal{A}$ such that $b \neq a$, $\overline{Can}_w^R(b, \alpha) = \{a\}$.

Requirement R provides agent a *relative notification control* over action α, noted $RN_R(a, \alpha)$, if and only if $\forall b \in \mathcal{A}$ such that $b \neq a$, $a \in \overline{Can}_w^R(b, \alpha)$.

$AN_R(a, \alpha)$ means that a is informed about the performance of action α by other agents and is the only agent having this power. In contrast, $RN_R(a, \alpha)$ means that a is not the only agent having this power.

Extensions. All the above definitions of control can be generalized to personal data and agents. For example:

- Requirement R provides a an *absolute action control* over r, noted $AA_R(a, r)$, iff $\forall \alpha \in \Delta$ s.t. $In(r, \alpha)$, then $AA_R(a, \alpha)$.
- Requirement R provides a an *absolute action control* over their personal data, noted $AA_R(a)$, iff $\forall r \in \mathcal{R}, Pers(r, a) \implies AA_R(a, r)$.

It is easy to check that, for each variant, absolute control implies relative control. Considering that action, observability, authorization, and notification are four independant variants of control, the above definitions give rise to a lattice (using the order defined by implication) made of 81 forms of control[9] (for each action, data, or agent).

---

[7]For the sake of simplicity, we consider that an agent requesting an action cannot change their mind and cancel the request before the actual performance of the action.

[8]We recall that $a \in \overline{Can}_e^R(b, \alpha)$ means that a has the capacity to *prevent* b from performing α.

[9]Which is equal to 3^4 considering that 3 levels are possible for each variant: absolute control, relative control, and lack of control.

4 SOCIAL NETWORK SYSTEM

The goal of the *Capacity* model presented in the previous sections is to capture the meaning of the notion of control in a very abstract and general way. In the rest of this paper, we describe the application of this model to a specific case study and show its relevance to assess different implementation choices. We choose a social network system ("SNS" in the sequel) to illustrate the model, not only because of the central role of social networks nowadays but also because they raise significant challenges in terms of control. We first introduce generic definitions allowing us to describe an SNS in the *Capacity* framework in Section 4.1 and define some requirements that have to be met by all SNS implementations in Section 4.2. Then, in Section 5, we respectively describe a centralized SNS implementation, a peer to peer SNS implementation, and a federated SNS implementation, and we show that they provide different types of control.

4.1 Generic Definitions

Due to space considerations, we focus on the following set of core SNS features in this paper: profile update, access to profiles, and connection with other users.

The first step to apply the *Capacity* framework is to define the sets $\mathcal{A}$ (agents), $\mathcal{R}$ (resources), O (operations) and C (contexts) introduced in Section 2, as well as the relations *Pers*, *Trust* and *In* introduced in the same section.

- $\mathcal{A}$ includes the users of the social network, noted u_i. Depending on the implementation, $\mathcal{A}$ may also include services such as the SNS agent itself (noted sn). In order to distinguish users from other agents, we introduce a unary relation *User* defined as $User(x) \iff \exists i \in \mathbb{N}, x = u_i$.
- $\mathcal{R}$ includes two resources per user u_i: their name, noted n_i, and their complete profile, noted p_i (which includes n_i).
- O consists of the operations update-profile, access-profile, and connect:
  - update-profile$_c(u_i)$ is the update of the profile p_i of user u_i in context c,
  - access-profile$_c(u_i)$ is the access to the profile p_i of user u_i in context c,
  - connect$_c(u_i)$ is the connection[10] to user u_i in context c.
  Note that an operation does not refer to the agent performing it. This information is provided by relations (such as *Can*, *Requests*, *Enables*, in which actions involving the operation appear.
- C is defined by $C \subseteq \mathbb{N}$. A context is simply a natural number corresponding to an index in an execution trace (allowing for disambiguation of otherwise similar events).
- *Pers* is defined by $Pers(r, a) \iff a = u_i \wedge (r = n_i \vee r = p_i)$, assuming for the sake of simplicity, that agents do not share personal data.
- *Trust* can take different values depending on the agents. For example, some users may trust the SNS agent while others do not, some users may trust some peers but not all other users, etc.
- *In* is derived from the definition of O:

$$In(r, \alpha) \iff (\alpha = \text{update-profile}_c(u_i) \wedge (r = p_i \vee r = n_i))$$
$$\vee \quad (\alpha = \text{access-profile}_c(u_i) \wedge (r = p_i \vee r = n_i))$$
$$\vee \quad (\alpha = \text{connect}_c(u_i) \wedge r = n_i).$$

4.2 Generic SNS Requirements

Some properties, which can be seen as the control oriented part of the SNS specification, have to be met by any SNS implementation. The most important generic requirements are the following:

(1) A user cannot prevent another user to update or access their own profile:
$$\forall u_i, u_j \in \mathcal{A}, User(u_i) \wedge User(u_j) \wedge u_i \neq u_j$$
$$\implies u_j \notin \overline{Can}_e^R(u_i, \text{update-profile}_c(u_i))$$
$$\wedge \quad u_j \notin \overline{Can}_e^R(u_i, \text{access-profile}_c(u_i)).$$

(2) A user cannot update the profile of another user:
$$\forall u_i, u_j \in \mathcal{A}, User(u_i) \wedge User(u_j) \wedge u_i \neq u_j$$
$$\implies \bot \in \overline{Can}_e^R(u_i, \text{update-profile}_c(u_j)).$$

(3) A user can always refuse a connection request from another user:
$$\forall u_i, u_j \in \mathcal{A}, User(u_i) \wedge User(u_j) \wedge u_i \neq u_j$$
$$\implies u_j \in \overline{Can}_e^R(u_i, \text{connect}_c(u_j)).$$

(4) A user cannot interfere in the action concerning two other users:
$$\forall u_i, u_j, u_k \in \mathcal{A}, u_i \neq u_j \neq u_k \neq u_i,$$
$$\wedge \ User(u_i) \wedge User(u_j) \wedge User(u_k)$$
$$\implies u_k \notin \overline{Can}_e^R(u_i, \text{access-profile}_c(u_j))$$
$$\wedge \quad u_k \notin \overline{Can}_e^R(u_i, \text{connect}_c(u_j))$$

Other properties which are not used in this paper[11] are not included in the above list for the sake of conciseness.

5 COMPARING THREE SNS IMPLEMENTATIONS

In this section we describe three SNS implementations: one centralized, one peer to peer, and one federated, and we show that they provide different types of control.

5.1 Centralized SNS Implementation

As a first example of architectural choice, we consider in this section the most common option, that is a centralized SNS implementation. This implementation involves, in addition to user agents u_i, the SNS agent sn.

In order to describe this implementation in the *Capacity* framework, we characterize its execution traces in Section 5.1.1 and define the *Requests*(a, α), *Enables*(a, b, α), and *Does*(a, b, α) trace properties[12] in Section 5.1.2. Then, we can establish the types and levels of control provided by this implementation in Section 5.1.3.

5.1.1 Execution Traces. Concrete traces in the centralized implementation are sequences of the following events. As a convention, events starting with "U" are those initiated by a user agent u_i and those starting with "S" are initiated by sn.

---

[10]What we mean by connection here is a link in the social network (e.g., following someone on Twitter or adding a friend on Facebook).

[11]For example, users cannot refuse access to their profiles to users that are connected to them.

[12]Due to lack of space, we chose to focus on certain aspects of control and thus voluntarily omit *Notifies*(a, b, c, α).

- U-req-upd-profile(u_i, p): u_i sends an update p of their profile p_i to sn.
- S-do-upd-profile(u_i, p): sn sets u_i's profile to p.
- U-req-acc-profile(u_i, u_j): u_i sends to sn a request to access u_j's profile.
- S-do-acc-profile(u_i, u_j): sn grants u_i's request to access u_j's profile.
- U-req-conn(u_i, u_j): u_i sends to sn a request to be connected to u_j.
- S-transfer-req-conn(u_i, u_j): sn forwards to u_j the connection request from u_i.
- U-accept-req-conn(u_i, u_j): u_i accepts u_j's connection request.
- U-reject-req-conn(u_i, u_j): u_i rejects u_j's connection request.
- S-do-conn(u_i, u_j): sn sets up the connection between u_i and u_j.

In the following, we note θ_n the nth event of an execution trace θ. The above events cannot occur in any order in a valid trace. Space considerations prevent us from presenting the full definition of valid C-traces[13] in the core of the paper. The interested reader can find it in Appendix A (Definition 12). To follow the paper, it is sufficient to understand that in a valid C-trace sn does not act spontaneously, in particular no action can be performed on behalf of an agent if this agent has not previously requested this action.

5.1.2 Trace Properties. In order to establish the control requirements provided by the centralized implementation as defined in Section 3, we first have to define the trace properties $Requests(a, \alpha)$, $Enables(a, b, \alpha)$, and $Does(a, b, \alpha)$ in terms of execution traces. In the following, the relation Ω_θ is used to relate an event to its trigerring request in trace θ:

$$\Omega_\theta(n, m, \alpha) \iff \theta_n = \alpha \wedge n < m \wedge$$
$$\forall k, n < k < m \implies \theta_k \neq \alpha.$$

- $\theta \vdash Requests(u_i, \text{update-profile}_n(u_i))$
  $\iff \exists p \in \mathcal{R}, \theta_n = \text{U-req-upd-profile}(u_i, p)$
- $\theta \vdash Requests(u_i, \text{access-profile}_n(u_j))$
  $\iff \theta_n = \text{U-req-acc-profile}(u_i, u_j)$
- $\theta \vdash Requests(u_i, \text{connect}_n(u_j))$
  $\iff \theta_n = \text{U-req-conn}(u_i, u_j)$

- $\theta \vdash Enables(sn, u_i, \text{update-profile}_n(u_i))$
  $\iff \exists p \in \mathcal{R}, \exists m \in \mathbb{N},$
  $\theta_m = \text{S-do-upd-profile}(u_i, p) \wedge$
  $\Omega_\theta(n, m, \text{U-req-upd-profile}(u_i, p))$
- $\theta \vdash Enables(sn, u_i, \text{access-profile}_n(u_j))$
  $\iff \exists m \in \mathbb{N}, \theta_m = \text{S-do-acc-profile}(u_i, u_j) \wedge$
  $\Omega_\theta(n, m, \text{U-req-acc-profile}(u_i, u_j))$
- $\theta \vdash Enables(sn, u_i, \text{connect}_n(u_j))$
  $\iff \exists m \in \mathbb{N},$
  $\theta_m = \text{S-transfer-req-conn}(u_i, u_j) \wedge$
  $\Omega_\theta(n, m, \text{U-req-conn}(u_i, u_j))$
- $\theta \vdash Enables(u_i, u_j, \text{connect}_n(u_i))$
  $\iff \exists m \in \mathbb{N}, \theta_m = \text{U-accept-req-conn}(u_i, u_j) \wedge$
  $\Omega_\theta(n, m, \text{U-req-conn}(u_j, u_i))$

---

[13]Valid traces for the centralized implementation.

- $\theta \vdash Does(sn, u_i, \text{update-profile}_n(u_i))$
  $\iff \exists p \in \mathcal{R}, \exists m \in \mathbb{N},$
  $\theta_m = \text{S-do-upd-profile}(u_i, p) \wedge$
  $\Omega_\theta(n, m, \text{U-req-upd-profile}(u_i, p))$
- $\theta \vdash Does(sn, u_i, \text{access-profile}_n(u_j))$
  $\iff \exists m \in \mathbb{N}, \theta_m = \text{S-do-acc-profile}(u_i, u_j) \wedge$
  $\Omega_\theta(n, m, \text{U-req-acc-profile}(u_i, u_j))$
- $\theta \vdash Does(sn, u_i, \text{connect}_n(u_j))$
  $\iff \exists m \in \mathbb{N}, \theta_m = \text{S-do-conn}(u_i, u_j) \wedge$
  $\Omega_\theta(n, m, \text{U-req-conn}(u_i, u_j))$

We assume that these conditions define entirely $Requests(a, \alpha)$, $Enables(a, b, \alpha)$, and $Does(a, b, \alpha)$, which means that these properties are false in all other cases. The context n associated with an action is defined as the index in the trace when this action was requested. Remark that the same event may implement several properties: e.g., event S-do-acc-profile(u_i, u_j) implements both $Enables(sn, u_i, \text{access-profile}_n(u_j))$ and $Does(sn, u_i, \text{access-profile}_n(u_j))$ at the same time because granting profile access and providing profile is implemented in a single step by sn in this architecture.

5.1.3 Control Properties. As discussed in Section 2 and 3, control can be considered from different perspectives (action, observability, authorization, and notification) and analyzed for each agent and with respect to each action. For the sake of conciseness, we focus on two types of control here:

- Action control of users u_i over the update of their profiles.
- Authorization control of users u_i over the connections to their profile (requested by other users).

Thus we introduce the following control requirement.

Definition 9 (*Rc* Requirement). Requirement *Rc* is defined by:
(1) $\overline{Can_e}^{Rc}(u_i, \text{update-profile}_n(u_i)) = \{sn\}$
(2) $\overline{Can_e}^{Rc}(u_i, \text{connect}_n(u_j)) = \{sn, u_j\}$

All other sets are considered empty, which means that we focus only on these two conditions in *Rc*, i.e., that $Can^{Rc}(a, \alpha, \varnothing, \varnothing)$ holds for all other cases.

It is easy to check that *Rc* satisfies the generic properties presented in Section 4.2. We can now prove that the centralized implementation meets the *Rc* requirements.

Theorem 1 (Consistency and compliance of C-traces). *Any valid C-trace is consistent and compliant with Rc.*

Consistency follows directly from Definition 2 (trace consistency) and Definition 12 (validity).

In order to prove compliance, we consider a valid C-trace θ and show that it complies with the two conditions of Definition 9. From Definition 4 (compliance):

- For the first condition, we have to show:
  $\forall u_i \in \mathcal{A}, \forall d \in \mathcal{A}, \theta \vdash Does(d, u_i, \text{update-profile}_n(u_i))$
  $\implies \theta \vdash Enables(sn, u_i, \text{update-profile}_n(u_i))$

  From the definitions of $Does(a, b, \alpha)$ and $Enables(a, b, \alpha)$, this property can be expanded into:

  $\exists p \in \mathcal{R}, \exists m \in \mathbb{N}, \theta_m = \text{S-do-upd-profile}(u_i, p) \wedge$
  $\Omega_\theta(n, m, \text{U-req-upd-profile}(u_i, p))$
  $\implies \exists p \in \mathcal{R}, \exists m' \in \mathbb{N},$

$\theta_{m'} = \mathsf{S\text{-}do\text{-}upd\text{-}profile}(u_i, p) \wedge$
$\Omega_\theta(n, m', \mathsf{U\text{-}req\text{-}upd\text{-}profile}(u_i, p))$

which is obviously true.

- For the second condition, we have to show:

$\forall u_i \in \mathcal{A}, \forall d \in \mathcal{A}, \theta \vdash Does(d, u_i, \mathsf{connect}_n(u_j))$
$\implies \theta \vdash Enables(sn, u_i, \mathsf{connect}_n(u_j)) \wedge$
$\theta \vdash Enables(u_j, u_i, \mathsf{connect}_n(u_j))$

From the definitions (Section 5.1.2) of $Does(a, b, \alpha)$ and $Enables(a, b, \alpha)$ the above property can be expanded into:

$\exists m \in \mathbb{N}, \theta_m = \mathsf{S\text{-}do\text{-}conn}(u_i, u_j) \wedge$
$\Omega_\theta(n, m, \mathsf{U\text{-}req\text{-}conn}(u_i, u_j))$
$\implies \exists m' \in \mathbb{N}, \theta_{m'} = \mathsf{S\text{-}transfer\text{-}req\text{-}conn}(u_i, u_j)$
$\wedge \, \Omega_\theta(n, m', \mathsf{U\text{-}req\text{-}conn}(u_i, u_j))$
$\wedge \, \exists m'' \in \mathbb{N}, \theta_{m''} = \mathsf{U\text{-}accept\text{-}req\text{-}conn}(u_j, u_i)$
$\wedge \, \Omega_\theta(n, m'', \mathsf{U\text{-}req\text{-}conn}(u_i, u_j))$

This property follows from the third item of Definition 12 (valid C-traces).

Theorem 2 (Control under centralized SNS). *The centralized implementation provides:*

- *Relative action control on* $\mathsf{update\text{-}profile}_n(u_i)$ *to agents* u_i *such that* $Trust(u_i, sn)$.
- *No action control on* $\mathsf{update\text{-}profile}_n(u_i)$ *to agents* u_i *such that* $\neg Trust(u_i, sn)$.
- *Relative authorization control to agents* u_i *on* $\mathsf{connect}_n(u_i)$.

Theorem 2 follows directly from the definitions of relative action control and relative authorization control in Section 3 (Definition 5 and Definition 7 respectively), the definition of Rc (Definition 9) and Theorem 1. It expresses the fact that:

- Agents u_i may consider that they control the updates of their profile only if they trust the social network sn.
- Agents u_i can forbid connections to their profiles but they are not the only actors with this ability.

5.2 Peer to Peer SNS Implementation

In this section, we consider a fully decentralized implementation of the social network described in Section 4, in which each agent manages their profile on their own node. In contrast with the previous one, this implementation does not involve any dedicated sn agent.

As was done in the previous section, we first characterize the execution traces of the peer to peer implementation in Section 5.2.1 before defining the trace properties $Requests(a, \alpha)$, $Enables(a, b, \alpha)$, and $Does(a, b, \alpha)$ in Section 5.2.2. Then, we can establish the types and levels of control provided by the peer to peer implementation in Section 5.2.3.

5.2.1 Execution Traces. Concrete traces in the peer to peer implementation are sequences of the following events.

- $\mathsf{U\text{-}do\text{-}upd\text{-}profile}(u_i, p)$: u_i sets their profile to p.
- $\mathsf{U\text{-}req\text{-}acc\text{-}profile}(u_i, u_j)$: u_i sends to u_j a request to access their profile.
- $\mathsf{U\text{-}do\text{-}acc\text{-}profile}(u_i, u_j)$: u_i grants u_j's request to access their profile.
- $\mathsf{U\text{-}req\text{-}conn}(u_i, u_j)$: u_i sends to u_j a request to be connected to u_j.

- $\mathsf{U\text{-}accept\text{-}req\text{-}conn}(u_i, u_j)$: u_i accepts u_j's connection request.
- $\mathsf{U\text{-}reject\text{-}req\text{-}conn}(u_i, u_j)$: u_i rejects u_j's connection request.

We remark that all event names start with "U" as users are assimilated to their node of the social network in this fully decentralized model.

A definition of valid P-traces is given in Appendix A (Definition 13). To follow the paper, it is sufficient to understand that in a valid P-trace a user does not address requests that have not been emitted by another agent.

5.2.2 Trace Properties. In order to establish the control requirements provided by the peer to peer implementation as defined in Section 3, we must first define the trace properties $Requests(a, \alpha)$, $Enables(a, b, \alpha)$, and $Does(a, b, \alpha)$ in terms of execution traces.

- $\theta \vdash Requests(u_i, \mathsf{update\text{-}profile}_n(u_i))$
  $\iff \exists p \in \mathcal{R}, \theta_n = \mathsf{U\text{-}do\text{-}upd\text{-}profile}(u_i, p)$
- $\theta \vdash Requests(u_i, \mathsf{access\text{-}profile}_n(u_j))$
  $\iff \theta_n = \mathsf{U\text{-}req\text{-}acc\text{-}profile}(u_i, u_j)$
- $\theta \vdash Requests(u_i, \mathsf{connect}_n(u_j))$
  $\iff \theta_n = \mathsf{U\text{-}req\text{-}conn}(u_i, u_j)$
- $\theta \vdash Enables(u_i, u_j, \mathsf{access\text{-}profile}_n(u_i))$
  $\iff \exists m \in \mathbb{N}, \theta_m = \mathsf{U\text{-}do\text{-}acc\text{-}profile}(u_i, u_j)$
  $\wedge \, \Omega_\theta(n, m, \mathsf{U\text{-}req\text{-}acc\text{-}profile}(u_j, u_i))$
- $\theta \vdash Enables(u_i, u_j, \mathsf{connect}_n(u_i))$
  $\iff \exists m \in \mathbb{N}, \theta_m = \mathsf{U\text{-}accept\text{-}req\text{-}conn}(u_i, u_j)$
  $\wedge \, \Omega_\theta(n, m, \mathsf{U\text{-}req\text{-}conn}(u_j, u_i))$
- $\theta \vdash Does(u_i, u_i, \mathsf{update\text{-}profile}_n(u_i))$
  $\iff \exists p \in \mathcal{R}, \theta_n = \mathsf{U\text{-}do\text{-}upd\text{-}profile}(u_i, p)$
- $\theta \vdash Does(u_i, u_j, \mathsf{access\text{-}profile}_n(u_i))$
  $\iff \exists m \in \mathbb{N}, \theta_m = \mathsf{U\text{-}do\text{-}acc\text{-}profile}(u_i, u_j)$
  $\wedge \, \Omega_\theta(n, m, \mathsf{U\text{-}req\text{-}acc\text{-}profile}(u_j, u_i))$
- $\theta \vdash Does(u_i, u_j, \mathsf{connect}_n(u_i))$
  $\iff \exists m \in \mathbb{N}, \theta_m = \mathsf{U\text{-}accept\text{-}req\text{-}conn}(u_i, u_j)$
  $\wedge \, \Omega_\theta(n, m, \mathsf{U\text{-}req\text{-}conn}(u_j, u_i))$

5.2.3 Control Properties. As was done in Section 5.1.3, we focus on two types of control here:

- Action control of users u_i over the update of their profiles.
- Authorization control of users u_i over the connections to their profile (requested by other users).

To express these types of control, we introduce the following requirement.

Definition 10 (Rp Requirement). Requirement Rp is defined by:

(1) $\overline{Can}_e^{Rp}(u_i, \mathsf{update\text{-}profile}_n(u_i)) = \varnothing$
(2) $\overline{Can}_e^{Rp}(u_i, \mathsf{connect}_n(u_j)) = \{u_j\}$

All other sets are considered empty, which means that we focus only on these two conditions in Rp, i.e., that $Can^{Rp}(a, \alpha, \varnothing, \varnothing)$ holds for all other cases.

It is easy to check that Rp satisfies the generic properties presented in Section 4.2. We can now prove that the peer to peer implementation meets the Rp requirements.

Theorem 3 (Consistency and compliance of P-traces). *Any valid P-trace is consistent and compliant with Rp.*

Consistency follows directly from Definition 2 (trace consistency) and Definition 13 (validity).

In order to prove compliance, we consider a valid P-trace θ and show that it complies with the two conditions of Definition 10.

- The first condition is straightforward (empty set).
- To prove the second condition, we need (Definition 4):

$$\forall u_i \in \mathcal{A}, \forall d \in \mathcal{A}, \theta \vdash Does(d, u_i, \text{connect}_n(u_j))$$
$$\implies \theta \vdash Enables(u_j, u_i, \text{connect}_n(u_j))$$

From the definitions (Section 5.1.2) of $Does(a, b, \alpha)$ and $Enables(a, b, \alpha)$, the above property can be expanded into:

$$\exists m \in \mathbb{N}, \theta_m = \text{U-accept-req-conn}(u_j, u_i) \land$$
$$\Omega_\theta(n, m, \text{U-req-conn}(u_i, u_j))$$
$$\implies \exists m' \in \mathbb{N}, \theta_{m'} = \text{U-accept-req-conn}(u_j, u_i)$$
$$\land \Omega_\theta(n, m', \text{U-req-conn}(u_i, u_j))$$

which is obviously true.

Theorem 4 (Control under peer to peer SNS). *The peer to peer implementation provides:*

- *Absolute action control on* update-profile$_n(u_i)$ *to agents* u_i.
- *Absolute authorization control to agents* u_i *on* connect$_n(u_i)$.

Theorem 4 follows directly from the definitions of absolute action control and absolute authorization control in Section 3 (Definition 5 and Definition 7 respectively), the definition of Rp (Definition 10) and Theorem 3. It expresses the fact that:

- Agents u_i do not depend on others to update their profile.
- Agents u_i can forbid connections to their profiles and they are the only actors with this ability.

5.3 Federated SNS Implementation

In this section, we consider a partially decentralized implementation of the social network system described in Section 4, where each agent potentially shares their node with others, and may or may not trust their node.

Again, we characterize the execution traces of the federated implementation in Section 5.3.1 before defining the trace properties $Requests(a, \alpha)$, $Enables(a, b, \alpha)$, and $Does(a, b, \alpha)$ in Section 5.3.2. Then, we can establish the types and levels of control provided by the federated implementation in Section 5.3.3.

In this implementation, there are a number of nodes running an instance of the SNS software, which we model by adding:

- a number of agents $s_0, s_1, \ldots$ to $\mathcal{A}$, and
- a $Node(u_i, s_j)$ relation meaning that $User(u_i)$ holds and u_i uses the social network via the node s_j.

For the sake of simplicity, each user uses only one node, i.e., we have that $\forall u_i, s_j, s_k \in \mathcal{A}, Node(u_i, s_j) \land Node(u_i, s_k) \implies s_j = s_k$. In addition, some users may trust their node (e.g., if they are among the node's administrator and the implementation they run is open source). In such cases we have $Node(u_i, s_j) \land Trust(u_i, s_j)$.

5.3.1 Execution Traces. Concrete traces in the federated implementation are sequences of the following events.

- U-req-upd-profile(u_i, p, s_j): u_i sends an update p of their profile p_i to s_j.
- S-do-upd-profile(s_j, u_i, p): s_j sets u_i's profile to p.

- U-req-acc-profile(u_i, u_j, s_k): u_i sends to s_k a request to access u_j's profile.
- S-req-profile(s_k, s_l, u_i, u_j): s_k requests u_j's profile to s_l on behalf of u_i.
- S-send-profile(s_l, s_k, u_j, u_i): s_l sends u_j's profile to s_k for u_i.
- S-do-acc-profile(s_k, u_i, u_j): s_k gives access to u_j's profile to u_i.
- U-req-conn(u_i, u_j, s_k): u_i sends to s_k a request to be connected to u_j.
- S-req-conn(s_k, s_l, u_i, u_j): s_k forwards to s_l the connection request from u_i to u_j.
- S-transfer-req-conn(s_l, u_j, u_i): s_l asks u_j about the connection request from u_i.
- U-accept-req-conn(u_i, u_j): u_i accepts u_j's connection request.
- U-reject-req-conn(u_i, u_j): u_i rejects u_j's connection request.
- S-do-conn(s_l, s_k, u_i, u_j): s_l sets up the connection between u_i and u_j via s_k.

A definition of valid F-traces is given in Appendix A (Definition 14). To follow the paper, it is sufficient to understand that in a valid F-trace the nodes do not act spontaneously, in particular no action can be performed on behalf of an agent if this agent has not previously requested this action.

5.3.2 Trace Properties. In order to establish the control requirements provided by the federated implementation as defined in Section 3, we must first define the trace properties $Requests(a, \alpha)$, $Enables(a, b, \alpha)$, and $Does(a, b, \alpha)$ in terms of execution traces.

- $\theta \vdash Requests(u_i, \text{update-profile}_n(u_i))$
  $\iff \exists s_j \in \mathcal{A}, Node(u_i, s_j), \exists p \in \mathcal{R},$
  $\quad \theta_n = \text{U-req-upd-profile}(u_i, p, s_j)$
- $\theta \vdash Requests(u_i, \text{access-profile}_n(u_j))$
  $\iff \exists s_k \in \mathcal{A}, Node(u_i, s_k),$
  $\quad \theta_n = \text{U-req-acc-profile}(u_i, u_j, s_k)$
- $\theta \vdash Requests(u_i, \text{connect}_n(u_j))$
  $\iff \exists s_k \in \mathcal{A}, Node(u_i, s_k),$
  $\quad \theta_n = \text{U-req-conn}(u_i, u_j, s_k)$

- $\theta \vdash Enables(s_j, u_i, \text{update-profile}_n(u_i))$
  $\iff Node(u_i, s_j) \land \exists p \in \mathcal{R}, \exists m \in \mathbb{N},$
  $\quad \theta_m = \text{S-do-upd-profile}(s_j, u_i, p) \land$
  $\quad \Omega_\theta(n, m, \text{U-req-upd-profile}(u_i, p, s_j))$
- $\theta \vdash Enables(s_k, u_i, \text{access-profile}_n(u_j)) \land Node(u_i, s_k)$
  $\iff \exists s_l \in \mathcal{A}, Node(u_j, s_l), \exists m \in \mathbb{N},$
  $\quad \theta_m = \text{S-req-profile}(s_k, s_l, u_i, u_j) \land$
  $\quad \Omega_\theta(n, m, \text{U-req-acc-profile}(u_i, u_j, s_k))$
- $\theta \vdash Enables(s_l, u_i, \text{access-profile}_n(u_j)) \land Node(u_j, s_j)$
  $\iff \exists s_k \in \mathcal{A}, Node(u_i, s_k), \exists m \in \mathbb{N},$
  $\quad \theta_m = \text{S-send-profile}(s_l, s_k, u_j, u_i) \land$
  $\quad \Omega_\theta(n, m, \text{U-req-acc-profile}(u_i, u_j, s_k))$
- $\theta \vdash Enables(s_k, u_i, \text{connect}_n(u_j)) \land Node(u_i, s_k)$
  $\iff \exists s_l \in \mathcal{A}, Node(u_j, s_l), \exists m \in \mathbb{N},$
  $\quad \theta_m = \text{S-req-conn}(s_k, s_l, u_i, u_j) \land$
  $\quad \Omega_\theta(n, m, \text{U-req-conn}(u_i, u_j, s_k))$
- $\theta \vdash Enables(s_l, u_i, \text{connect}_n(u_j)) \land Node(u_j, s_l)$

$\Longleftrightarrow \exists s_k \in \mathcal{A}, Node(u_i, s_k), \exists m \in \mathbb{N},$
$\qquad \theta_m = \text{S-transfer-req-conn}(s_l, u_j, u_i) \wedge$
$\qquad \Omega_\theta(n, m, \text{U-req-conn}(u_i, u_j, s_k))$

- $\theta \vdash Enables(u_i, u_j, \text{connect}_n(u_i))$
$\Longleftrightarrow \exists s_k \in \mathcal{A}, Node(u_i, s_k), \exists m \in \mathbb{N},$
$\qquad \theta_m = \text{U-accept-req-conn}(u_i, u_j) \wedge$
$\qquad \Omega_\theta(n, m, \text{U-req-conn}(u_j, u_i, s_k))$

- $\theta \vdash Does(s_j, u_i, \text{update-profile}_n(u_i))$
$\Longleftrightarrow Node(u_i, s_j), \exists p \in \mathcal{R}, \exists m \in \mathbb{N},$
$\qquad \theta_m = \text{S-do-upd-profile}(s_j, u_i, p) \wedge$
$\qquad \Omega_\theta(n, m, \text{U-req-upd-profile}(u_i, p, s_j))$

- $\theta \vdash Does(s_k, u_i, \text{access-profile}_n(u_j))$
$\Longleftrightarrow Node(u_i, s_k), \exists m \in \mathbb{N},$
$\qquad \theta_m = \text{S-do-acc-profile}(s_k, u_i, u_j) \wedge$
$\qquad \Omega_\theta(n, m, \text{U-req-acc-profile}(u_i, u_j, s_k))$

- $\theta \vdash Does(s_l, u_i, \text{connect}_n(u_j))$
$\Longleftrightarrow Node(u_j, s_l), \exists s_k \in \mathcal{A}, Node(u_i, s_k), \exists m \in \mathbb{N},$
$\qquad \theta_m = \text{S-do-conn}(s_l, s_k, u_i, u_j) \wedge$
$\qquad \Omega_\theta(n, m, \text{U-req-conn}(u_i, u_j, s_k))$

5.3.3 Control Properties. As for the centralized and peer to peer implementations, we focus on two types of control here:

- Action control of users u_i over the update of their own profiles.
- Authorization control of users u_i over the connections to their profile (requested by other users).

Thus we introduce the following control requirement.

Definition 11 (Rf Requirement). Requirement Rf is defined by:

(1) $\overline{Can}_e^{Rf}(u_i, \text{update-profile}_n(u_i)) = \{s_j\}$,
where $Node(u_i, s_j)$,

(2) $\overline{Can}_e^{Rf}(u_i, \text{connect}_n(u_j)) = \{s_k, s_l, u_j\}$,
where $Node(u_i, s_k)$ and $Node(u_j, s_l)$

All other sets are considered empty, which means that we focus only on these two conditions in Rf, i.e., that $Can^{Rf}(a, \alpha, \varnothing, \varnothing)$ holds for all other cases.

It is easy to check that Rf satisfies the generic properties presented in Section 4.2. We can now prove that the centralized implementation meets the Rf requirements.

Theorem 5 (Consistency and compliance of F-traces). *Any valid F-trace is consistent and compliant with Rf.*

Consistency follows directly from Definition 2 (trace consistency) and Definition 14 (validity).

In order to prove compliance, we consider a valid F-trace θ and show that it complies with the two conditions of Definition 11. From Definition 4 (compliance):

- For the first condition, we have to show:
$\forall u_i, s_j \in \mathcal{A}, Node(u_i, s_j), \forall d \in \mathcal{A},$
$\theta \vdash Does(d, u_i, \text{update-profile}_n(u_i))$
$\implies \theta \vdash Enables(s_j, u_i, \text{update-profile}_n(u_i))$

From the definitions (Section 5.3.2) of $Does(a, b, \alpha)$ and $Enables(a, b, \alpha)$, the above property can be expanded into:
$\exists d \in \mathcal{A}, Node(u_i, d), \exists p \in \mathcal{R}, \exists m \in \mathbb{N},$
$\theta_m = \text{S-do-upd-profile}(d, u_i, p) \wedge$

$\Omega_\theta(n, m, \text{U-req-upd-profile}(u_i, p, d))$
$\implies \exists p \in \mathcal{R}, \exists m' \in \mathbb{N},$
$\qquad \theta_{m'} = \text{S-do-upd-profile}(s_j, u_i, p) \wedge$
$\qquad \Omega_\theta(n, m', \text{U-req-upd-profile}(u_i, p, s_j))$

which is obviously true.

- For the second condition, we have to show:
$\forall u_i, u_j, s_k, s_l \in \mathcal{A}, \forall d \in \mathcal{A},$
$\theta \vdash Does(d, u_i, \text{connect}_n(u_j))$
$\implies \theta \vdash Enables(s_k, u_i, \text{connect}_n(u_j)) \wedge$
$\qquad \theta \vdash Enables(s_l, u_i, \text{connect}_n(u_j)) \wedge$
$\qquad \theta \vdash Enables(u_j, u_i, \text{connect}_n(u_j))$

From the definitions (Section 5.3.2) of $Does(a, b, \alpha)$ and $Enables(a, b, \alpha)$, the above property can be expanded into:
$\exists d \in \mathcal{A}, Node(u_j, d), \exists s_k \in \mathcal{A}, Node(u_i, s_k), \exists m \in \mathbb{N},$
$\theta_m = \text{S-do-conn}(d, s_k, u_i, u_j) \wedge$
$\Omega_\theta(n, m, \text{U-req-conn}(u_i, u_j, s_k))$
$\implies \exists s_l \in \mathcal{A}, Node(u_j, s_l), \exists m \in \mathbb{N},$
$\qquad \theta_m = \text{S-req-conn}(s_k, s_l, u_i, u_j) \wedge$
$\qquad \Omega_\theta(n, m, \text{U-req-conn}(u_i, u_j, s_k))$
$\wedge \; \exists m \in \mathbb{N},$
$\qquad \theta_m = \text{S-transfer-req-conn}(s_l, u_j, u_i) \wedge$
$\qquad \Omega_\theta(n, m, \text{U-req-conn}(u_i, u_j, s_k))$
$\wedge \; \exists m \in \mathbb{N}, \theta_m = \text{U-accept-req-conn}(u_i, u_j) \wedge$
$\qquad \Omega_\theta(n, m, \text{U-req-conn}(u_j, u_i, s_k))$

This property follows from the third item of Definition 14 (valid F-traces).

Theorem 6 (Control under federated SNS). *The federated implementation provides:*

- *Relative action control on* update-profile$_n(u_i)$ *to agents* u_i *such that* $Node(u_i, s_j) \wedge Trust(u_i, s_j)$.
- *No action control on* update-profile$_n(u_i)$ *to agents* u_i *such that* $Node(u_i, s_j) \wedge \neg Trust(u_i, s_j)$.
- *Relative authorization control to agents* u_i *on* connect$_n(u_i)$.

Theorem 6 follows directly from the definitions of relative action control and relative authorization control in Section 3 (Definition 5 and Definition 7 respectively), the definition of Rf (Definition 11) and Theorem 5. It expresses the fact that:

- Agents u_i may consider that they control the updates of their own profile only if they trust their node s_j.
- Agents u_i can forbid connections to their profiles but they are not the only actors with this ability.

5.4 Discussion

We have presented three architectural choices for implementing the social network system introduced in Section 4, namely a centralized implementation (Section 5.1), a peer to peer implementation (Section 5.2), and a federated implementation (Section 5.3). The *Capacity* model makes it possible to highlight the different types of control provided by these architectural choices.

The centralized implementation gives users relative control over the update over their profile and connections to them, provided that they trust the social network. This would argue in favor of free and open source software for example, as transparency and auditable code is likely to be more trustworthy for users.

The peer to peer implementation gives users the best control over their personal data: they have absolute control over the update of their profile and over who can connect to them.

The federated implementation is, in terms of control, very close to the centralized implementation. Note however that the assumption $Trust(u_i, s_j)$ when $Node(u_i, s_j)$ in the federated case is much more realistic than the assumption $Trust(u_i, sn)$ in the centralized case, as nodes may be operated by users themselves or by people they trust (friends, associations, etc.). In practice, the federated implementation is also more likely to be open source, as its developers do not intend to keep users locked-in their own centralized service.

Because the case study used here is very simple, none of these remarks is really surprising. Nevertheless, it confirms that the intuitive notion of control is well captured by *Capacity*. The added-value of the approach is the fact that these results have been obtained formally through a systematic study of the different implementations. The same approach can be applied to the analysis of more complex and realistic systems. For example, the CNIL[14] recently stated[15] that biometric access control on smartphones is acceptable because the biometric data processing is performed under the control of the user. It is not clear, however, in what sense users really control their biometric template, what actions they can perform, enable or observe and what actors they have to trust (in addition to the smartphone provider). The same questions hold for many devices in the internet of things.

The fact that the three implementations studied here implement the generic SNS requirement presented in Section 4.2 suggests the potential benefit of defining relation orders on requirements in *Capacity*. This is further studied in Section B.

Due to lack of space, many aspects of *Capacity* have not been illustrated in this paper. For example, the only type of context used in our case study is the index of an action in a trace. Contexts can actually be used to express different types of contextual information, in the spirit of contextual integrity [1].

Other possibilities which have not been illustrated here include personal data of multiple agents, such as pictures involving several friends, and more complex information flows. The first situation can be expressed in a natural way in *Capacity* as the *Pers* relation is not exclusive. As far as complex information flows are concerned, we can consider, for instance, a situation where agent A grants permission to agent B to access a data d but prohibits C to do so. If B is able to grant access to this data to C, a model of the system in *Capacity* would show that A can only have *relative* control on this data (if they trust B).

6 RELATED WORK

The two main bodies of work related to the *Capacity* model presented in this paper concern respectively formal privacy policy languages and usage control models. We sketch successively these two trends of work before discussing the main points of departure of the approach followed in this paper.

Policy languages. Several languages have been proposed for the definition of privacy policies. They differ mostly in terms of scope

(general purpose or specific), target (individual privacy policies, corporate rules, legal rules), and semantics. For this kind of tools to be considered as legitimate means to deliver user consent from a legal point of view, they must be able to express unambiguous choices. One of the criticisms raised against early privacy frameworks such as P3P[16] was precisely their lack of clarity and the divergent interpretations of privacy policies. An option to solve the ambiguity problem is to resort to a sound, mathematical definition of the semantics of the language. This approach has been followed in several proposals. For example, CI [1] is a dedicated linear temporal logic language inspired by the notion of contextual integrity, which makes it possible to express the conditions that have to be met for an agent, acting in a given role and context, to be allowed to transmit a piece of information. CI makes it possible to express both positive and negative norms, and focuses on the transfer of personal data which forms the core of contextual integrity. Another example of temporal logic based privacy policy language is the language proposed in [2] which relies on alternating-time temporal logic.

Other languages such as S4P [3] and SIMPL [10] rely on a trace semantics. For example, in SIMPL, users can express their policies using sentences such as "I consent to disclose my CV to a third party only if their privacy policy includes the following commitments: only use this data for the purpose of human resource management; delete this data within a maximum delay of three months; do not transfer this data to any third party".

Particular attention has been paid to privacy policy languages in the specific context of social networks. These proposals are welcome considering that social networks generally provide many privacy options or parameters whose combinations are difficult to grasp. For example, the models presented in [6] (which generalizes the access control paradigm) and [12] (based on epistemic and deontic properties) can be used not only to better understand the effect of a privacy policy but also to investigate alternative options that are not necessarily supported by existing social networks.

Because they are endowed with a formal semantics in a mathematical framework, the above privacy policy languages make it possible to prove certain properties about the policies (e.g., that a given third party may never receive a given piece of data) and to prove that a given implementation is consistent with the semantics — in other words, that the system behaves as expected by the user.

Access and usage control models. The other most relevant body of literature concerns access and usage control models [9, 13, 14]. Many models have been proposed in the computer security area to characterize the conditions under which subjects can access (or use) certain resources. These models include, *inter alia*, Mandatory Access Control, Discretionary Access Control, and Role-Based Access Control. Usage Control models have been proposed to make it possible to define not only the access rules but also conditions on the use of a resource (e.g., obligations, limitations, etc.). One of the most ambitious frameworks for usage control is the $UCON_{ABC}$ model, which makes it possible to express authorizations, obligations, and conditions (contextual constraints) at different points of time (before, during, and after usage). Other major features of $UCON_{ABC}$ are mutable attributes (e.g., actions changing the value

---

[14]French data protection authority.
[15]https://www.cnil.fr/fr/biometrie-dans-les-smartphones-loi-informatique-et-libertes-exemption-ou-autorisation

[16]https://www.w3.org/P3P/.

of an attribute) and the continuity of decisions (i.e., rights may be terminated during the usage when attributes have changed). $UCON_{ABC}$ is very general and can be used to define several families of models. Different approaches have been proposed to define its semantics (or the semantics of a subset of its features), including temporal logic frameworks such as TLA [17] or ITL [4], and process algebra [9].

Capacity. The main point of departure between all the above works and the approach followed in this paper is the fact that the objective of *Capacity* is not to specify privacy policies or usage control policies, but to define the notion of control itself and to characterize different types of control. For example, $UCON_{ABC}$ being a usage control framework it focuses on the users of a system rather than on the data subjects as it is necessary to properly express privacy requirements and properties. Moreover, *Capacity* can be seen as a metamodel with respect to privacy policy or usage control models in the sense that it makes it possible to talk about (express, manipulate) notions which are hardwired in these frameworks. Let us take some examples to illustrate this difference of points of view:

Firstly, neither in privacy policy languages nor in usage control models is it possible to express that an agent depends (or does not depend) on other agents to exercise their rights. Some dependencies could be expressed by temporal properties in privacy policy languages (such as, for example, action α performed by agent a cannot occur unless action β performed by agent b – which could be used to express consent for example – has occurred before). But this would have to be done on a case by case basis, for each relevant action and data (the types of control defined in Section 3, for example, cannot be expressed in these frameworks).

Secondly, both $UCON_{ABC}$ and privacy policy languages assume the existence of an underlying system to manage the rights. The fact that an agent depends on this system to exercise their rights cannot therefore be expressed within the framework itself. This point was raised as the "administrative issues" in $UCON$ and left for further work [13]. Similarly, the privacy languages mentioned above do not make it possible to refer explicitly to the social network itself (the administrator, in $UCON$ terminology). Therefore it is not possible to express the fact that a user can be more or less dependent on the social network. We believe that this possibility is essential in the context of privacy because data controllers (such as social network providers) can in many cases represent the main source of risk for the user[17]. It is therefore necessary to be able to include them in any model of control. In *Capacity*, the social network is an agent and it is possible to express the level of dependency of the users with respect to this agent just like their dependencies with respect to other users.

Finally, because *Capacity* is a metamodel rather than a model, it does not make sense to talk about an architecture to implement it (akin, for example, to reference monitors, as discussed in [9]). Requirements in *Capacity* define abstract control constraints on systems and these constraints have to be refined to establish a link

with an actual implementation. For example, the notion of an agent enabling an action is not limited to a matter of granting rights. Enabling can be implemented in many different ways (e.g., forwarding a message, modifying a data on behalf of the requestor, etc.). Access or usage rights are just particular cases for the implementation of *Capacity* requirements.

7 CONCLUSION

The main objective of this paper was to introduce the *Capacity* framework and to show its relevance to provide a formal account of the notion of control. The goal of the social network example developed in the previous sections was only to make the *Capacity* framework more concrete and to show its use to compare different implementations of a system according to control criteria. We have considered only simple social network functionalities and two aspects of control in this example (action control and authorization control). Other aspects of control corresponding to more complex privacy policies can be represented in the same spirit. Other dimensions of privacy can also be expressed in the *Capacity* framework. In particular, the purpose for which personal data are processed is very important with regard to privacy, and contexts of actions in *Capacity* can be used to specify such information. Contexts can also be more complex, including, for example, time, space, or environment (work, family, medical, etc.).

Going one step further, additional developments allowing refinements in the use of the *Capacity* framework to formally capture the notion of exposure [11] better than using contexts would be beneficial. Indeed, from a legal point of view, for an event to happen in the public space or in a private space depends on the existence of a *community of interest* (e.g., on a social network, direct contacts of a particular user that this user has manually approved one by one), which can be modeled using relations as defined in Section 2.3. However, from a privacy point of view, this legal definition is not sufficient as for example the size of a community may be as important as its public or private characterization.

The study of non compact requirements, such as what could be implemented with some types of secret sharing techniques [15] (typically with (t, n)-threshold scheme), would also be interesting.

A complementary aspect which has not been discussed in this paper is the verification that a given implementation actually meets the validity properties (Definition 12 and 13) and the completeness property (Definition 3), which ensures that a requested action is always performed if all the enabling agents have actually enabled it. This task pertains to traditional code verification techniques [5].

Another perspective would be the use of the classification of control properties presented in this paper to structure the privacy design space and select appropriate strategies according to the objectives in terms of control [7].

An interesting avenue for further research would be to exploit the systematic classification of control properties presented in Section 3 to help data subjects in the definition of their privacy policies. Indeed, provided that they are supported by user-friendly interfaces, the abstract definitions made possible by the *Capacity* framework could provide a more systematic and intelligible way to grasp user-defined privacy requirements.

---

[17]As an illustration, according to its privacy policy (as of 2017), Facebook retains the right to use the personal data of its users to deliver ads and measure their effectiveness, to provide location-based services, to make suggestions and to provide innovative features and services it develops in the future. In addition, Facebook may change its terms, and the continued use of the service following changes to the terms constitutes acceptance of the amended terms.

REFERENCES

[1] Adam Barth, Anupam Datta, John C. Mitchell, and Helen Nissenbaum. 2006. Privacy and Contextual Integrity: Framework and Applications. In *IEEE Symposium on Security and Privacy*. https://crypto.stanford.edu/~jcm/papers/barth-datta-mitchell-nissenbaum-2006.pdf

[2] Adam Barth, Anupam Datta, John C. Mitchell, and Sharada Sundaram. 2007. Privacy and Utility in Business Processes. In *20th IEEE Computer Security Foundations Symposium (CSF07)*.

[3] Moritz Y. Becker, Alexander Malkis, and Laurent Bussard. 2010. S4P: A Generic Language for Specifying Privacy Preferences and Policies. (2010). https://research.microsoft.com/pubs/122108/main.pdf

[4] Antonio Cau and Hussein Zedan. 1997. Refining Interval Temporal Logic specifications. In *Transformation-Based Reactive Systems Development*. http://antonio-cau.co.uk/ITL/publications/pubs/1997-2.pdf

[5] Vijay D'Silva, Daniel Kroening, and Georg Weissenbacher. 2008. A Survey of Automated Techniques for Formal Software Verification. In *IEEE Trans. on CAD of Integrated Circuits and Systems*. http://www.kroening.com/papers/tcad-sw-2008.pdf

[6] Philip W.L. Fong, Mohd Anwar, and Zhen Zhao. 2009. A Privacy Preservation Model for Facebook-Style Social Network Systems. In *ESORICS*.

[7] Jaap-Henk Hoepman. 2014. Privacy Design Strategies. In *ICT Systems Security and Privacy Protection*. https://www.cs.ru.nl/~jhh/publications/pdp.pdf

[8] Christophe Lazaro and Daniel Le Métayer. 2015. Control over Personal Data: True Remedy or Fairy Tale? *SCRIPTed* (2015). http://script-ed.org/?p=1927

[9] Aliaksandr Lazouski, Fabio Martinelli, and Paolo Mori. 2010. Usage control in computer security: A survey. *Computer Science Review 4 (2)* (2010).

[10] Daniel Le Métayer. 2008. A formal privacy management framework. In *Formal Aspects in Security and Trust (FAST 2008)*.

[11] Mainack Mondal, Peter Druschel, Krishna P. Gummadi, and Alan Mislove. 2014. Beyond Access Control: Managing Online Privacy via Exposure. In *Workshop on Useable Security*. https://www.mpi-sws.org/~mainack/papers/usec2014-final46.pdf

[12] Raul Pardo and Gerardo Schneider. 2014. A Formal Privacy Policy Framework for Social Networks. In *12th International Conference on Software Engineering and Formal Methods (SEFM)*.

[13] Jaehong Park and Ravi Sandhu. 2004. The $UCON_{ABC}$ Usage Control Model. *ACM Transactions on Information and System Security* (2004).

[14] Jaehong Park and Ravi Sandhu. 2010. A Position Paper: A Usage Control (UCON) Model for Social Networks Privacy. (2010). https://www.w3.org/2010/policy-ws/papers/17-Park-Sandhu-UTSA.pdf

[15] Adi Shamir. 2008. How to share a secret. *Communications of the ACM* (2008).

[16] Wikipedia. [n. d.]. The Right to Privacy. ([n. d.]). https://en.wikipedia.org/wiki/The_Right_to_Privacy_%28article%29 Accessed on 2015-11-24.

[17] Xinwen Zhang, Francesco Parisi-Presicce, Ravi Sandhu, and Jaehong Park. 2005. Formal Model and Policy Specification of Usage Control. *ACM Transactions on Information and System Security* (2005). https://profsandhu.com/journals/tissec/p351-zhang.pdf

A   FORMAL VALIDITY DEFINITIONS

In this appendix, we present the full definitions of valid C-traces, valid P-traces and valid F-traces referred to in Section 5.1.1, Section 5.2.1 and Section 5.3.1 respectively.

Definition 12 (Valid C-trace). A valid trace for the centralized implementation, or *valid C-trace*, is a sequence of events (as defined in Section 5.1.1) meeting the following properties:

(1) $\forall m \in \mathbb{N}, \theta_m = \mathsf{S\text{-}do\text{-}upd\text{-}profile}(u_i, p)$
$\implies \exists n \in \mathbb{N}, n < m \wedge$
$\quad \theta_n = \mathsf{U\text{-}req\text{-}upd\text{-}profile}(u_i, p)$

(2) $\forall m \in \mathbb{N}, \theta_m = \mathsf{S\text{-}do\text{-}acc\text{-}profile}(u_i, u_j)$
$\implies \exists n \in \mathbb{N}, n < m \wedge$
$\quad \theta_n = \mathsf{U\text{-}req\text{-}acc\text{-}profile}(u_i, u_j)$

(3) $\forall m \in \mathbb{N}, \theta_m = \mathsf{S\text{-}do\text{-}conn}(u_i, u_j)$
$\implies \exists n, m', m'' \in \mathbb{N}, \theta_n = \mathsf{U\text{-}req\text{-}conn}(u_i, u_j) \wedge$
$\quad \theta_{m'} = \mathsf{S\text{-}transfer\text{-}req\text{-}conn}(u_i, u_j) \wedge$
$\quad \theta_{m''} = \mathsf{U\text{-}accept\text{-}req\text{-}conn}(u_j, u_i) \wedge$
$\quad n < m' < m'' < m \wedge$
$\quad \forall k \in \mathbb{N}, n < k < m, \theta_k \neq \mathsf{U\text{-}req\text{-}conn}(u_i, u_j)$

Definition 13 (Valid P-trace). A valid trace for the peer to peer implementation, or *valid P-trace*, is a sequence of events (as defined in Section 5.2.1) meeting the following properties:

(1) $\forall m \in \mathbb{N}, \theta_m = \mathsf{U\text{-}do\text{-}acc\text{-}profile}(u_i, u_j)$
$\implies \exists n \in \mathbb{N}, n < m \wedge$
$\quad \theta_n = \mathsf{U\text{-}req\text{-}acc\text{-}profile}(u_j, u_i)$

(2) $\forall m \in \mathbb{N}, \theta_m = \mathsf{U\text{-}accept\text{-}req\text{-}conn}(u_i, u_j)$
$\implies \exists n \in \mathbb{N}, n < m \wedge \theta_n = \mathsf{U\text{-}req\text{-}conn}(u_j, u_i)$

(3) $\forall m \in \mathbb{N}, \theta_m = \mathsf{U\text{-}reject\text{-}req\text{-}conn}(u_i, u_j)$
$\implies \exists n \in \mathbb{N}, n < m \wedge \theta_n = \mathsf{U\text{-}req\text{-}conn}(u_j, u_i)$

Definition 14 (Valid F-trace). A valid trace for the federated implementation, or *valid F-trace*, is a sequence of events (as defined in Section 5.3.1) meeting the following properties:

(1) $\forall m \in \mathbb{N}, \theta_m = \mathsf{S\text{-}do\text{-}upd\text{-}profile}(s_j, u_i, p)$
$\implies Node(u_i, s_j) \wedge \exists n \in \mathbb{N}, n < m \wedge$
$\quad \theta_n = \mathsf{U\text{-}req\text{-}upd\text{-}profile}(u_i, p, s_j)$

(2) $\forall m \in \mathbb{N}, \theta_m = \mathsf{S\text{-}do\text{-}acc\text{-}profile}(s_k, u_i, u_j)$
$\implies Node(u_i, s_k) \wedge Node(u_j, s_l) \wedge$
$\quad \exists n', n'' \in \mathbb{N}, n' < n'' < m \wedge$
$\quad \theta_{n'} = \mathsf{S\text{-}req\text{-}profile}(s_k, s_l, u_i, u_j) \wedge$
$\quad \theta_{n''} = \mathsf{S\text{-}send\text{-}profile}(s_l, s_k, u_j, u_i) \wedge$
$\quad \Omega_\theta(n, m, \mathsf{U\text{-}req\text{-}acc\text{-}profile}(u_i, u_j, s_k))$

(3) $\forall m \in \mathbb{N}, \theta_m = \mathsf{S\text{-}do\text{-}conn}(s_l, s_k, u_i, u_j)$
$\implies Node(u_i, s_k) \wedge Node(u_j, s_l) \wedge$
$\quad \exists n', n'', m' \in \mathbb{N}, n' < n'' < m' < m \wedge$
$\quad \theta_{n'} = \mathsf{S\text{-}req\text{-}conn}(s_k, s_l, u_i, u_j) \wedge$
$\quad \theta_{n''} = \mathsf{S\text{-}transfer\text{-}req\text{-}conn}(s_l, u_j, u_i) \wedge$
$\quad \theta_{m'} = \mathsf{U\text{-}accept\text{-}req\text{-}conn}(u_j, u_i) \wedge$
$\quad \Omega_\theta(n, m, \mathsf{U\text{-}req\text{-}conn}(u_i, u_j, s_k))$

B   RELATION ORDERS ON REQUIREMENTS

In order to make it possible to reason about the level of control provided by a requirement, we introduce several order relations between requirements in Section B.1 and notions of trace compliance with respect to personal data in Section B.2.

B.1   Comparing Requirements

We first define a general order between requirements before introducing specific orders capturing the notion of level of control over personal data.

Definition 15 ($R_1 \succeq R_2$). The *general order* relation between requirements, noted $\succeq$, is defined as follows: $R_1 \succeq R_2$ if and only if $\forall a \in \mathcal{A}, \forall \alpha \in \Delta$,

$$\overline{Can}_e^{R_1}(a, \alpha) \subseteq \overline{Can}_e^{R_2}(a, \alpha) \wedge \overline{Can}_w^{R_1}(a, \alpha) \subseteq \overline{Can}_w^{R_2}(a, \alpha)$$

Intuitively, $R_1 \succeq R_2$ means that R_1 is more permissive than R_2: it requires less enablers and less witnesses to perform an action. This first order is very generic and it does not deal specifically with personal data. The next definitions allow us to distinguish requirements based on their contraints on personal data.

Definition 16 ($R_1 \succeq_\oplus^a R_2$). The *positive preorder* relation between requirements, noted $\succeq_\oplus^a$, is defined as follows: $R_1 \succeq_\oplus^a R_2$ if and only if $\forall \alpha \in \Delta, \forall r \in \mathcal{R}, Pers(r, a) \wedge In(r, \alpha) \implies$

$$\overline{Can}_e^{R_1}(a, \alpha) \subseteq \overline{Can}_e^{R_2}(a, \alpha) \wedge \overline{Can}_w^{R_1}(a, \alpha) \subseteq \overline{Can}_w^{R_2}(a, \alpha)$$

Intuitively, $R_1 \succeq_\oplus^a R_2$ means that R_1 is more permissive than R_2 for the manipulation of their personal data by agent a: it requires less enablers and less witnesses for a to perform an action on their own personal data.

Definition 17 ($R_1 \succeq_\ominus^a R_2$). The *negative preorder* relation between requirements, noted $\succeq_\ominus^a$, is defined as follows: $R_1 \succeq_\ominus^a R_2$ if and only if $\forall b \in \mathcal{A}, \forall \alpha \in \Delta, \forall r \in \mathcal{R}$,

- $Pers(r, a) \wedge In(r, \alpha) \wedge a \in \overline{Can_e}^{R_2}(b, \alpha) \implies a \in \overline{Can_e}^{R_1}(b, \alpha)$
- $Pers(r, a) \wedge In(r, \alpha) \wedge a \in \overline{Can_w}^{R_2}(b, \alpha) \implies a \in \overline{Can_w}^{R_1}(b, \alpha)$

Intuitively, $R_1 \succeq_\ominus^a R_2$ means that R_1 provides a greater scrutiny than R_2 to agent a on the manipulation of their personal data by others: a can enable or witness more actions performed by other agents on a's personal data.

Definition 18 ($R_1 \succeq_C^a R_2$). The *control preorder* relation between requirements, noted $\succeq_C^a$, is defined as follows: $R_1 \succeq_C^a R_2$ if and only if $R_1 \succeq_\oplus^a R_2 \wedge R_1 \succeq_\ominus^a R_2$.

Intuitively, $R_1 \succeq_C^a R_2$ means that R_1 provides a greater control than R_2 over their personal data to agent a: it is more permissive about what a can do with their personal data and provides a a greater scrutiny over what others can do with a's personal data.

The above preorders can be generalized to all agents in a natural way. For example, $\succeq_C$ is defined as follows: $R_1 \succeq_C R_2$ if and only if $\forall a \in \mathcal{A}, R_1 \succeq_C^a R_2$.

Theorem 7 (Preorders). $\succeq$ *is an order relation and* $\succeq_\oplus^a, \succeq_\ominus^a, \succeq_C^a, \succeq_\oplus, \succeq_\ominus, \succeq_C$ *are preorder relations.*

PROOF. The property of $\succeq$ results from the facts that $\subseteq$ is an order relation and the functions $\overline{Can_w}^R$ and $\overline{Can_e}^R$ together define completely R. The other relations are only preorders because their definitions involve only subsets of Δ (actions involving personal data). As usual, it is possible to derive order relations from these preorders using the quotient sets of the associated equivalence relation. □

B.2 Relative Trace Compliance

Let us now introduce notions of trace compliance relative to the personal data of a given agent a.

Definition 19 ($\theta \models_\oplus^a R$). The *positive compliance* of a trace θ with respect to a requirement R and agent a is defined as follows: $\theta \models_\oplus^a R$ if and only if $\forall \alpha \in \Delta, \forall d \in \mathcal{A}$,
$\theta \vdash Does(d, a, \alpha) \wedge Pers(r, a) \wedge In(r, \alpha) \implies$

- $\forall b \in \overline{Can_e}^R(a, \alpha), \theta \vdash Enables(b, a, \alpha)$, and
- $\forall b \in \overline{Can_w}^R(a, \alpha), \exists c \in \mathcal{A}, \theta \vdash Notifies(c, b, a, \alpha)$.

Intuitively, $\theta \models_\oplus^a R$ means that in the execution represented by θ, all actions performed by agent a on their personal data have been enabled by the required agents (members of $\overline{Can_e}^R(a, \alpha)$) and all the necessary witnesses have been notified (members of $\overline{Can_w}^R(a, \alpha)$).

Positive trace compliance can be generalized to all agents as follows: $\theta \models_\oplus R$ if and only if $\forall a \in \mathcal{A}, \theta \models_\oplus^a R$.

Definition 20 ($\theta \models_\ominus^a R$). The *negative compliance* of a trace θ with respect to a requirement R and agent a is defined as follows: $\theta \models_\ominus^a R$

if and only if $\forall b \in \mathcal{A}, b \neq a, \forall \alpha \in \Delta, \forall d \in \mathcal{A}$,
$\theta \vdash Does(d, b, \alpha) \wedge Pers(r, a) \wedge In(r, \alpha) \implies$

- $a \in \overline{Can_e}^R(b, \alpha) \implies \theta \vdash Enables(a, b, \alpha)$, and
- $a \in \overline{Can_w}^R(b, \alpha) \implies \exists c \in \mathcal{A}, \theta \vdash Notifies(c, a, b, \alpha)$.

Intuitively, $\theta \models_\ominus^a R$ means that in the execution represented by θ, any action performed by another agent b on the personal data of a has been enabled by a (if a is a member of $\overline{Can_e}^R(b, \alpha)$) and notified to a (if a is a member of $\overline{Can_w}^R(b, \alpha)$).

Negative trace compliance can be generalized to all agents as follows: $\theta \models_\ominus R$ if and only if $\forall a \in \mathcal{A}, \theta \models_\ominus^a R$.

Definition 21 ($\theta \models_C^a R$). The *control trace compliance* to a requirement with regard to an agent, is defined as follows: $\theta \models_C^a R$ if and only if $\theta \models_\oplus^a R \wedge \theta \models_\ominus^a R$.

The control trace compliance is defined as the conjunction of positive and negative trace compliances. The intuition is that the control of an agent over their personal data is greater when they have less constraints on their own actions on their data and more powers to prevent actions from other agents on their data. Control trace compliance can be generalized to all agents as follows: $\theta \models_C R$ if and only if $\forall a \in \mathcal{A}, \theta \models_C^a R$.

Theorem 8 (Orders and relative trace compliance). *For all requirements R_1, R_2, trace θ, and agent a, we have:*

(1) If $R_1 \succeq R_2$ then $\theta \models R_1 \implies \theta \models R_2$
(2) If $R_1 \succeq_\oplus^a R_2$ then $\theta \models_\oplus^a R_2 \implies \theta \models_\oplus^a R_1$
(3) If $R_1 \succeq_\oplus R_2$ then $\theta \models_\oplus R_2 \implies \theta \models_\oplus R_1$
(4) If $R_1 \succeq_\ominus^a R_2$ then $\theta \models_\ominus^a R_1 \implies \theta \models_\ominus^a R_2$
(5) If $R_1 \succeq_\ominus R_2$ then $\theta \models_\ominus R_1 \implies \theta \models_\ominus R_2$
(6) If $R_1 \succeq_C^a R_2$ then $\theta \models_\oplus^a R_2 \implies \theta \models_\oplus^a R_1$ and $\theta \models_\ominus^a R_1 \implies \theta \models_\ominus^a R_2$
(7) If $R_1 \succeq_C R_2$ then $\theta \models_\oplus R_2 \implies \theta \models_\oplus R_1$ and $\theta \models_\ominus R_1 \implies \theta \models_\ominus R_2$

PROOF. In order to prove the first property, we assume $R_1 \succeq R_2$ and $\theta \models R_1$. In order to show $\theta \models R_2$, let us consider $a \in \mathcal{A}, d \in \mathcal{A}, \alpha \in \Delta$ such that $\theta \vdash Does(d, a, \alpha)$. From $\theta \models R_1$, we have:

- $\forall b \in \overline{Can_e}^{R_1}(a, \alpha), \theta \vdash Enables(b, a, \alpha)$, and
- $\forall b \in \overline{Can_w}^{R_1}(a, \alpha), \exists c \in \mathcal{A}$ s.t. $\theta \vdash Notifies(c, b, a, \alpha)$

$R_1 \succeq R_2$ entails $\overline{Can_e}^{R_2}(a, \alpha) \subseteq \overline{Can_e}^{R_1}(a, \alpha)$, which allows us to derive:

- $\forall b \in \overline{Can_e}^{R_2}(a, \alpha), \theta \vdash Enables(b, a, \alpha)$, and
- $\forall b \in \overline{Can_w}^{R_2}(a, \alpha), \exists c \in \mathcal{A}$ s.t. $\theta \vdash Notifies(c, b, a, \alpha)$

and therefore $\theta \models R_2$. The proofs of the other properties are similar with the switch of order for properties 2 and 3 due to the definition of $R_1 \succeq_\oplus R_2$. As explained above, more privacy for agents means more possibilities to act on their own data and less possibilities for others. □

An Empirical Study on Online Price Differentiation

Thomas Hupperich
University of Twente, The Netherlands

Dennis Tatang
Ruhr-University Bochum, Germany

Nicolai Wilkop
Ruhr-University Bochum, Germany

Thorsten Holz
Ruhr-University Bochum, Germany

ABSTRACT

Price differentiation describes a marketing strategy to determine the price of goods on the basis of a potential customer's attributes like location, financial status, possessions, or behavior. Several cases of online price differentiation have been revealed in recent years. For example, different pricing based on a user's location was discovered for online office supply chain stores and there were indications that offers for hotel rooms are priced higher for Apple users compared to Windows users at certain online booking websites. One potential source for relevant distinctive features are *system fingerprints*, i. e., a technique to recognize users' systems by identifying unique attributes such as the source IP address or system configuration. In this paper, we shed light on the ecosystem of pricing at online platforms and aim to detect if and how such platform providers make use of price differentiation based on digital system fingerprints. We designed and implemented an automated price scanner capable of disguising itself as an arbitrary system, leveraging real-world system fingerprints, and searched for price differences related to different features (e. g., user location, language setting, or operating system). This system allows us to explore price differentiation cases and identify those characteristic features of a system that may influence a product's price.

ACM Reference format:
Thomas Hupperich, Dennis Tatang, Nicolai Wilkop, and Thorsten Holz. 2018. An Empirical Study on Online Price Differentiation. In *Proceedings of Eighth ACM Conference on Data and Application Security and Privacy, Tempe, AZ, USA, March 19–21, 2018 (CODASPY '18),* 8 pages.
https://doi.org/10.1145/3176258.3176338

1 INTRODUCTION

Pricing policies of (online) business providers are typically not transparent to customers and are based on parameters that a customer is not aware of. This opens up a number of opportunities for so-called *price differentiation* and *price discrimination*. Price differentiation is a pricing policy in which providers demand different prices for the same asset, including special offers or discounts. In contrast, adjusting a product's price based on a customer's *personal* information (e. g., gender, wealth, home address, or other feature)

is called price discrimination. In the past, suspected cases of online price discrimination captured headlines, including different pricing at Staples based on a user's location [14] and indications that offers for hotel rooms are priced higher for Apple users compared to Windows users at Orbitz [20].

From a technical point of view, an online platform can leverage many kinds of techniques to identify a user, which would be the starting point for price discrimination. Generally speaking, the term *fingerprinting* refers to the process of obtaining characteristic attributes of a system and determining attribute values that can be leveraged to recognize or identify a single system among others. In the context of online user tracking, this technique complements cookie-based recognition, which has been ubiquitously deployed for many years [4]. In practice, browser fingerprinting provides more information about a customer compared to cookie-based methods, including software attributes (i.e., the used user-agent, installed plugins, and supported mimetypes [1, 5, 15, 19]). Previous research demonstrated that browser-based system fingerprinting performs well for most types of commodity systems such as desktop computers and mobile devices [4, 11, 24].

Our assumption is that information about a user's system—obtained via browser fingerprinting—is leveraged by online providers for price discrimination as it leaks information about the system configuration and the user himself. While flight tickets have been found to be subject to too many influence factors to be able to identify methodical price discrimination [27], there has been no systematic investigation of the existence of systematic price discrimination in online commerce. In particular, hotel booking websites are often criticized for non-transparent pricing and have been suspected of price differentiation. Unfortunately, not all details about leveraged price differentiation mechanisms can be determined without detailed insight into the inner working of such platforms, and thus we need to adopt a black-box strategy to explore abnormalities.

In this paper, we apply real-world *browser fingerprints* to simulate different systems and analyze corresponding price changes. To achieve this goal, we implemented an automated price scanner capable of disguising itself as an arbitrary system leveraging real-world system fingerprints and searched for price differences related to (i) user location represented by the IP address, (ii) specific systems represented by their fingerprints, and (iii) single features of fingerprints. This enables us to expose the impact of these features on asset prices. Generally speaking, we aim to expose system configuration features that may influence prices and perform a repeatable empirical analysis to measure the effects of fingerprint changes.

In an empirical study, we examined several accommodation booking websites and a rental car provider platform to identify which parameters affect an asset's price. Our results show the existence of location-based price differentiation while price changes based on system fingerprints are found in single cases and do not reveal systematic discrimination. We also shed light on how changing single attributes in a system fingerprint affects an asset's price. Associating reproducible price changes with specific attribute values allows users to change their system fingerprint and start hunting for the best prices for hotel rooms.

In summary, we make the following contributions:

- We developed and implemented a method to find and analyze price differentiation by automatically testing different system configurations against online providers.
- We conducted an empirical study to explore price differentiation based on user location and system configuration.
- We provide insights into which specific system features influence pricing strategies and how a user can potentially affect them.

To foster additional research we present several examples of online price discrimination detected by our analysis framework at https://rawgit.com/ananonymousauthor/examples/master/index.html. A more detailed technical report about this research and results is available on arXiv [12].

2 BACKGROUND

First we introduce both *price discrimination* and *system fingerprinting* in more detail and explain why and how both concepts are related to each other.

As noted above, there is a small yet important difference between price discrimination and price differentiation: while price differentiation describes a strategy to determine a product's or service's price based on a potential customer's needs, it does not depend on a customer's characteristics. In price discrimination, however, the price is determined on the basis of a potential customer's *attributes*, such as location, financial status, possessions, gender, or behavior. According to Varian [26], price discrimination is defined as specific pricing for specific groups and has been a common technique since 1920. Traditionally, price discrimination and differentiation can be subdivided into three different degrees [26]:

First degree: Involves individualization of prices for all customers. Second degree: Prices differ based on additional services. It is possible to distinguish between service-related, quantitative, and price-pack forms. Third degree: Involves individual prices for groups of people. They can be individual, location, or time-related.

Online commerce has widely been resistant to price discrimination as customers typically decide to buy a product for the lowest price possible. Furthermore, few customer characteristics were customarily revealed during an online purchase (like residential area) and there are usually no negotiations (at least for standard products). Today, however, a client's computer system reveals more information about its user [1, 4, 11, 24]. This presents new opportunities for online shop operators to personalize their content for each individual customer [16, 18]. From their perspective, price discrimination is a way to maximize their profits and thus they have an incentive to utilize such techniques.

To implement such a strategy, they can use system fingerprinting methods to identify user groups that are likely willing to pay more than other user groups.

Fingerprinting is a technique to obtain characteristic attributes of a given system, enabling the recognition or identification of a single system among others. While this is a general method and can be applied to different kinds of systems, including servers, mobile devices, or websites, we focus in this work on client-side systems, especially browsers on commodity systems like desktop computers and smartphones. This approach enables Web platform providers to fingerprint—and consequently recognize or identify—a user's system and improves on classical cookie-based user tracking to enhance the reliability of tracking techniques [24].

In practice, the attributes of a system are examined and analyzed if they are unique compared to the attributes of other systems. Such characteristic attributes serve as so-called *features* that can be used to create a fingerprint that is as unique as possible. Consequently, every system is assigned a fingerprint which describes the system's characteristic attributes (e. g., configuration items like a browser's settings, display size, or the IP address). As our work is in the context of online shopping, we focus on attributes accessible from the Web and hence use browser attributes as our browser fingerprints. Common browsers reveal adequate information to generate this kind of fingerprint [24], and web-based fingerprinting of personal computers and mobile devices is a common technique that has been investigated by other researchers [4, 11, 17, 24, 28].

3 SEARCHING FOR PRICE DISCRIMINATION

Below, we outline goals, workflow, and functionality of our method for searching the Web for potential cases of price discrimination. For more details of our approach for searching for price discrimination, we kindly refer to our technical report [12].

3.1 Design Goals

We want to conduct a systematic study as well as an objective analysis to clarify the existence of online price discrimination based either on location information or on system configuration. Therefore, we define the following goals for our implementation of systematic, non-offensive scans: (i) fingerprint variety, (ii) simulation of user behavior, (iii) robustness, and (iv) deterministic behavior.

Besides these design goals, we also follow three additional principles. First, as we aim to include multiple platforms in our study, the implementation needs to be modular. For every scan, the platforms, search parameters, fingerprints, etc. can be chosen freely, which also enables us to extend the system with additional scrapers so more websites and product categories may be scanned for fingerprint-based price discrimination in future work. Second, we strive for minimal invasiveness and avoid to produce too many requests to a given website at once. As we certainly do not want to disturb legitimate services, we apply a time delay to our low-traffic implementation and hence ensure that our scans will be tolerable to platform providers and do not interfere with their daily business. Third, we want to be transparent about our work and thus plan to publish the code and data obtained by our scanning practice.

3.2 High-level Overview of Workflow

We begin by providing a high-level overview of the system's workflow. We have two data sources (system fingerprints and provider websites), three data processors (scanner, scraper, and price analysis), and result data (cases of price discrimination).

First, we build system profiles, each including four components: (i) a real-world fingerprint, (ii) a proxy server to be used, (iii) search parameters, such as the dates of arrival and departure for hotels, and (iv) the providers and websites to be examined. Bundles of such profiles are loaded by the scanner.

The scanner's duty is to automatically browse the website of a given provider to end up on certain product result pages. Our scraper implementations then extract the relevant price information from these pages. Finally, we analyze the extracted price information; this analysis of the collected data can point to cases of price discrimination.

In the following sections, we describe each of these steps in more detail and provide information about implementation aspects.

3.3 System Fingerprints

The real-world systems fingerprints that we use for our study are derived from two data sources: First, a previous study [11] providing 385 fingerprints, primarily from mobile devices, and second a project partner that has provided 15,000 fingerprints to a large browser gaming platform.

We re-grouped these fingerprints in order to identify the most and fewest common feature values (see Sec. 3.1). This set of most common and uncommon system fingerprints is suitable for our purpose: we need to include in our study those systems that are frequently found in the wild, but we also need to include special systems with unusual appearances in order to test how such rare fingerprints may influence a product's price. We also reduced the set, since many features' values were identical across several fingerprints. Following this re-grouping and reduction, our set includes a total of 332 real-world fingerprints for scanning Web platforms.

As noted above, a fingerprint may encompass manifold features of a system. However, we include only the following features, **AvailHeight**, **AvalWidth**, **ColorDepth**, **CookieEnabled**, **Height**, **Language**, **Languages**, **MimeTypes**, **PixelDepth**, **Platform**, **Plugins**, **ProductSub**, **UserAgent**, **Vendor**, and **Width**. All features were gathered either from the Browser Object Model (BOM) or the HTTP header, as these have been proven to be common features used for browser fingerprinting [4, 24].

In addition to all of these device-level features, we also need to consider the network location (i. e., IP address), as this represents an important feature for location analyses. We opted to use free proxy servers and rent VPN gateways to enable a flexible routing of requests. As a result, we can issues queries from different network locations and observe changes in responses.

3.4 Scanner and Scraper

Figure 1 depicts the components of our scanner implementation.

The real-world fingerprints, the proxies, the provider websites, and the search parameters serve as input data for the scanner, which uses Selenium to communicate with the custom PhantomJS browser via its extended GhostDriver implementation.

The scraper, in general, extracts product information from selected websites.

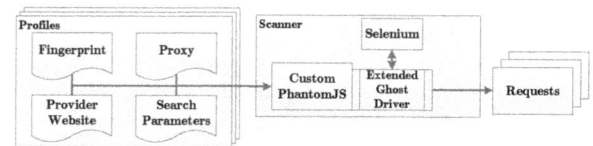

Figure 1: Scanner components operation chart

When extracting price information from a website, one has to handle different price presentation formats, currencies, and the meaning of the displayed prices. Therefore, this data must be converted to a common format for use in subsequent data analysis.

4 EVALUATION

Based on the implementation of the scanning infrastructure, we performed several empirical tests. We focus on two specific types of business: hotel booking platforms and rental car suppliers.

4.1 Price Analyses

We scanned different providers for hotels and rental cars, namely *Booking.com*, *Hotels.com*, *Hrs.com*, *Orbitz.com*, and *Avis.com* and conduct three kinds of analyses: (i) location-based, (ii) fingerprint-based, and (iii) fingerprint-feature-based price differentiation analyses.

First, we investigate location-based price differentiation. We consider several countries (including France, Germany, the United States, Russia, Pakistan, and the Netherlands) to determine how realistic it is that a higher or lower price for the same asset will be obtained when requesting it from a different country. For these countries, we obtained proxy servers or VPN gateways and re-routed our search requests through these servers. The target websites will treat these as search requests coming from the corresponding country. Furthermore, we randomly picked six fingerprints from our set to repeat these scans with different system configurations. Note that we focus in this analysis on hotel providers.

Second, we shed light on price differentiation based on system configurations. This analysis is normalized to France, the United Kingdom, Germany, and the United States because we aim to highlight the systems' fingerprints instead of different originating countries and because we obtained complete result sets for our scans for these countries. While we generally do not consider single fingerprints for location-based analyses, we do so in this step. We used our set of 332 representative system fingerprints for the following analyses and utilized them to disguise our scanner.

Third, these fingerprints are leveraged to create pairs in which one fingerprint yields a high price and the other yields a low price for the same asset with significant frequency. Intermediate fingerprints are then forged, simulating single feature changes. By re-scanning the providers' platforms, we harvest insights on which specific system attributes affect online pricing policies.

Note that we are always searching for one person and one single night in the case of hotel booking websites, hence, the search parameters described in Sec 3.4 are kept constant in the following analyses. After sending a search request, we scrape the top offer prices per hotel for every provider as our ground data for analysis. Finally, we repeat search requests and confirm that using the same configuration reproduces the same prices, so that we can exclude randomness and consider only reproducible price changes.

4.2 Location-based Price Differentiation

We sent search requests for different parameters, e. g., dates of arrival and departure, to all accommodation providers, querying assets in four major cities, namely Los Angeles (USA), London (United Kingdom), Berlin (Germany), and Tokyo (Japan). Each scan lasted about one hour in order to not overwhelm a given site with queries. As a result of these scans, we obtained over 455,500 data records, including an accommodation's name, its provider, and the normalized price in Euro.

Figure 2 shows boxplots for all providers, including the countries we re-routed the search requests through, on the X-axis and the prices in Euro on the Y-axis. Each box depicts the median, quartiles as well as minimum and maximum values of prices for the corresponding country. Note that the prices for each country refer to the same set of hotels in all cities, while there may be differences when comparing providers, as some of them may not cooperate with specific accommodations. This set is used for all location-based analyses and contains only hotels that were found in all single scans for all configurations. We omitted results with fewer than 1,000 responses per provider to avoid bias and keep the results representative; therefore the number of countries varies in Figure 2.

Summary. The result of our price differentiation analysis regarding location is mixed: Not all providers seem to leverage price adjustments based on a user's location. On Orbitz.com, all examined countries were treated the same in our study, giving no indication that this platform performs systematic price differentiation. In contrast, we see for the other accommodation search providers a medium variance of prices for the same assets. The USA received privileged prices at Booking.com and Hotels.com, while the Netherlands and Pakistan were given rather high prices at Booking.com, as was Germany at Hotels.com. At Hrs.com, prices tend to be higher for requests from the Georgian Republic, whereas requests from Germany and Russia likely achieve lower prices. Finally, we can confirm the existence of price adjustment based on a user's location, though prices seem to vary within a limited range only.

4.3 Fingerprint-based Price Differentiation

We scanned the providers mentioned above instrumenting our fingerprint set containing 332 system fingerprints. As a result, we obtained over 4,370,000 data records, including an asset's name, its provider, the used fingerprint, and the normalized price in Euro within about 19 hours total. In this iteration the request country has been set to a fixed parameter, as are the destination and dates of travel. In particular, we tested how much prices vary for every single hotel when the fingerprint of a request changes.

For every product (hotel or car) we obtained two lists: (i) fingerprint(s) which yield a maximum price for this asset, and (ii) fingerprint(s) which achieve a minimum price for it. This results in almost 50,000 cases showing price differences, which is only about 1.12 % of all scanning results.

For Booking.com, we recorded 20,868 cases, representing a share of 0.48 %. Hrs.com and Orbitz.com show almost the same amount of

cases with 9,786 and 9,600 both being a share of 0.22 % of all scanning results. Hotels.com produced 9,174 cases, meaning a share of 0.21 %. Finally, for Avis.com, we found 181 cases which are negligible as their share is below 0.01 %. Hence, we see that fingerprint-based pricing is applied to different extents. While we found the majority of suspected price variation based on fingerprints at Booking.com, the other three providers seem to deploy price differentiation at about the same intensity. However, the share of suspicious cases that exhibit a high price variance is rather small compared to the over 4 million scanned prices. We speculate that these are individual cases, as a systematic price differentiation—or even price discrimination—usually has a greater impact and is not limited to a small share of cases.

Building on these initial findings, we perform a statistical significance analysis to further investigate how changing a system's fingerprint affects prices. For this purpose, we conduct the Friedman test [6, 7]. We used the Friedman test because it is a parameter-free alternative to classical analysis of variance (ANOVA). The result of both analysis variants is equivalent. An ANOVA requires data in a normal distribution which we do not have. The Friedman test does not necessarily need it and is therefore suitable for our significance analysis. We assembled nearly 600 hotels and a selection of 130 fingerprints that yield price results for all of the assembled hotels, so that there is a scanned price for every combination of fingerprint, hotel, request country, and provider. The Friedman test calculates the significance of price changes resulting from these fingerprints. By reducing the number of fingerprints to only those which occur in all records of our data gathering, we guarantee the comparability between the various characteristics.

However, before the Friedman test can be performed, additional cleaning of the input data is necessary. Hotels with no free rooms must be removed. This keeps the sample size (number of hotels) identical for each fingerprint, which is important for statistical analysis. Altogether we use a data matrix including the numeric hotel prices of the fingerprints as our input data. Each record has 130 columns for 130 fingerprints and a certain number of lines for hotels. We made sure that the hotels used for comparison occur in all records. Due to proxy availability, we scanned Hotels.com from France, Germany, and Romania, adding the United States for HRS.com and Orbitz.com. Unfortunately, we could not include Booking.com, as we did in the previous tests, since the Web application changed during our research, making scraping hotel prices impossible. In total we conducted eleven Friedman tests—one for each combination of provider and country. In almost all cases, the p-value was lower than 0.05, representing a significant difference between at least two fingerprints in the corresponding subset. Only one test (Hotels.com from Romania) produced a p greater than 0.05, presumably because the median values are all equal. We calculated the median of medians directly for this single case instead of the post-hoc tests we conducted for all other cases. Using a post-hoc test in this case could possibly lead to false positives. Table 1 shows an excerpt of the Friedman test results, showing the median of each fingerprint for all combinations of provider and country. More results of the Friedman test can be found in the appendix of our technical report [12]. Note that only intra-column comparisons

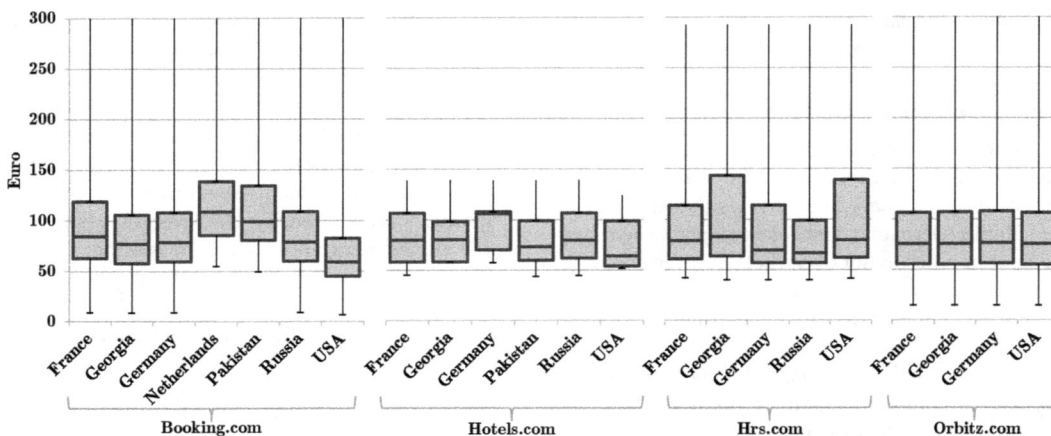

Figure 2: Location-based price discrimination by provider

are allowed as the sample sizes, i.e., the number of hotels, varies between 397 and 594.

In these results, we see isolated price changes for Hotels.com regardless of the requesting country. In fact, only a few fingerprints were found to be disadvantaged. With France as request country, only one fingerprint (FP 171) deviates by €6, while all other fingerprints yield a median price value of €74. For Germany, there are three fingerprints (FP 105, FP 169, and FP 183) which deviate by €5.50 and €8, and for Romania all fingerprints yield the same median price of €74. While these fingerprints resulted in reproducible and significant price changes, the majority of prices remained the same or showed only little variation for all other fingerprints. More significant price variations among fingerprints can be found at HRS.com. Generally, there are many different prices in the median for every request country, which means that the provider's website responded with different prices for different fingerprints. However, almost all of these significant price differences are less than one Euro, so currency conversions cannot be excluded as the cause. Only two fingerprints (FP 35 and FP 95) deviated by about €2.70 and €2.80. Again, these price differences are significant according to the Friedman test, but as such deviations occur only twice, it is questionable whether a price differentiation system exists.

These findings also apply for Orbitz, as there are also many price variances for this site. But again, the differences among the prices is about one Euro or less, and not a single fingerprint delivered a significant price difference of several Euro. In fact, the price differences were found to be significant, but the reasons for these differences may lie in rounding errors rather than being an indication of systematic price discrimination.

4.4 Price-influencing Features

To investigate the individual cases of price changes due to system fingerprints, we dissected those fingerprints that we suspected of price changes in the previous section. Although these are rare and individual cases, we aim to learn which of these features are involved in price changes. We therefore created pairs combining a fingerprint that resulted in a low price with a fingerprint that resulted in a high price. Then we built intermediate fingerprints for

all these pairs, so-called *morphprints*, fading from one fingerprint to another by successively changing their attribute values. The morphprints are naturally not real-world fingerprints, they are only intended to compare single feature changes. Combining these morphprints (M_x) with the two original fingerprints (O1, O2) results in a pack of feature changes. This matched-pairs design enables a precise analysis of which feature values influence an asset's price and in what way.

To find the correct order for feature replacement, we applied the *information gain* algorithm, instrumenting the Kullback-Leibler divergence [9], to our data set, revealing every feature's importance to distinguish all data records. It provides an order of how important and descriptive each feature is in relation to our data. We instrument this output to set the order for successive feature value replacement. In total, we created 111 morphprints and re-scanned accommodation websites, resulting in over 14,000 records. These additional scans took about six hours each. To test for reproducibility, every fingerprint and morphprint has been re-scanned twice.

First, we examine which features affect an asset's price most often. Second, we shed light on how these features' values influence online pricing.

Features. While previous research identified a system's user agent string to be the top feature for fingerprinting (see Sec. 6), we see that a system's language is the most frequently occurring price changing feature in our empirical data set. About one third of all discovered cases in our study include a language feature. However, we confirm `navigator.userAgent` to be of particular importance, occurring in about 8 % of all cases in our data set. The screen resolution as well as the property `navigator.vendor` were found to be involved in about 6 % of cases. This indicates that these attributes might only play a minor role in pricing policies. Surprisingly, plugins and mime types are not often involved in price changes, as they occurred in fewer than 4 % of all price changes. Usually these attributes are considered to be highly personalized and should therefore have a greater affect on price customization. This, however, cannot be confirmed on the basis of our data. Table 2 lists each feature's share in price changes.

Table 1: Excerpt of Median Hotel Prices as Result of the Friedman Test

	Hotels			HRS				Orbitz			
FP	Fr	De	Ro	Fr	De	Ro	USA	Fr	De	Ro	USA
1	74	74	74	70	69.9	70	70.2	62.93	62.93	62.93	62.93
3	74	74	74	70	69.9	70	70.2	63.24	63.24	64.19	64.19
5	74	74	74	70.83	70.73	70.83	70.2	63.25	63.25	64.2	64.2
. . .	. . .	. . .	. . .	. . .	. . .	. . .	. . .	. . .	. . .	. . .	. . .
165	74	74	74	70.4	70.24	70.4	70.65	63.24	63.24	64.19	64.19
167	74	74	74	70.34	70.19	70.4	70.41	63.25	63.25	64.2	64.2
169	74	79.5	74	70.53	70.3	70.4	70.41	62.93	62.93	63.87	63.87
171	80	74	74	70	69.9	70	70.2	63.24	63.24	64.19	64.19
173	74	74	74	70	69.9	70	70.2	63.25	63.25	64.2	64.2
175	74	74	74	70.53	70.3	70.4	70.41	62.93	62.93	63.87	63.87
. . .	. . .	. . .	. . .	. . .	. . .	. . .	. . .	. . .	. . .	. . .	. . .
295	74	74	74	70	69.9	70	70.2	62.93	62.93	63.87	63.87
297	74	74	74	70.4	70.24	70.4	70.65	63.24	63.24	64.19	64.19

Table 2: Features share (price change cases)

Feature	Share
httpHeader.acceptLanguage	14.57 %
navigator.languages	9.73 %
navigator.language	9.05 %
navigator.userAgent	7.95 %
screen.availHeight	6.90 %
navigator.vendor	6.77 %
screen.height	6.50 %
navigator.platform	6.31 %
screen.availWidth	6.17 %
screen.width	5.37 %
screen.colorDepth	4.63 %
navigator.productSub	4.26 %
screen.pixelDepth	4.04 %
navigator.plugins	3.97 %
navigator.mimeTypes	3.79 %

Feature Values. Given these findings, we now investigate which feature changes result in a price difference. For the following analysis, we only consider reproducible cases with just one single feature changing its value. Due to irregular website responses more than one feature may have changed before scraping these websites, but we eliminated these cases beforehand. Table 3 presents the feature changes, their occurrences, and average price changes.

Summary. Our results show that language settings and user agent strings are the most influential of all features. Changing these features to specific values may increase the chance of receiving a lower price for online hotel bookings. Adjusting other attributes, like vendor and screen resolution, may also affect online pricing policies, but only to a small degree and in specific cases.

Although we cannot make a general claim about how certain feature values should be set to optimize a search for the best price, our results indicate that features which are closer to the user (like language settings, operating system, and browser) have a greater impact when it comes to fingerprint-based pricing policies.

Nevertheless, our findings—especially regarding single features and their values—refer to individual cases in our data set. Although we have shown the statistical significance of these cases, we cannot claim a systematic third-degree price differentiation or price discrimination. Small price changes of a few Eurocent may be related to currency conversions, and price changes of more than one Euro are rare and cannot be proven to be based on system fingerprinting.

5 THREATS TO VALIDITY

Although we handled both the data collection and analysis phases thoroughly, there are limitations and threats to validity.

First, there are various sources that can influence prices, which is why we cannot be completely sure to produce deterministic results with our method. However, in the gathered data the same input parameters, e. g., fingerprint, destination and travel date, produced the same price in all corresponding scans. Hence, we may consider deterministic behaviour concerning our analysis.

Our findings are not omni-valid as we examined only a subset of all available accommodation booking platforms and one rental car provider. Our results and conclusions are in general only valid for our data set, and investigating other providers, product categories, countries, or fingerprints may verify or refute them. However, our data and results derive from realistic search requests and their valid responses, including real-world prices. To foster research on this topic, we plan to publish all data collected during this study.

Our analysis regarding location-based price differentiation sheds light on differences in pricing on a per-country basis determined by the geolocation of IP addresses. Such differences might also exist intra-nationally, i. e., between regions and cities. This type of fine-grained analysis is not within the scope of this work.

Probably the greatest threat to validity are special offers, hidden price boosters or discounts and other secret price-fixing agreements. In a worst case scenario, a discount is offered during only parts of our scan, so that fingerprints which are applied early in the scanning order, for example, would get a lower special offer price than all fingerprints later on receive. To remedy this threat, we applied a filter to catch these cases and to ensure that only nonlinear price changes are taken into account. For instance, if a hotel cost €100 per night for fingerprints 1 to i, but only €80 per night for fingerprints $i + 1$ to n, it is possible that this price change is due to a special offer. In contrast, if a hotel cost €100 per night for fingerprints 1 to i, but €140 per night for fingerprints $i + 1$ to n, we cannot exclude the possibility that the price has risen just because of our scanning, since the first fingerprints simulate a high demand for this asset: the price could have been increased as a reaction, meeting supply and demand. The exceeding of a room quota may be another cause for such artifacts. All these ambiguous cases are omitted in our analyses. However, we cannot guarantee that we caught all potential external influence factors.

Another possible source of distortion may be the hotel providers' booking conditions. During the scraping process, we obtain the price offered at first sight per accommodation regardless of room type and amenities, e. g., breakfast. It is reasonable to assume that this is the best price for an offer as a lower price attracts more customers than would a price for a premium suite including amenities. Hence, we assume that a provider's platform would always list this best price for all search requests. In practice, if a hotel offered

Table 3: Most influencing features value changes

Feature	Old Value	New Value	Occurrence	Change
language	en-US	de	11.87 %	8.88 %
language	ru	de-de	14.16 %	1.27 %
language	ru-RU	en-US	9.32 %	0.83 %
language	en-US	it-IT	8.48 %	0.77 %
language	ko-KR	en-US	9.10 %	0.30 %
language	de	es-ES	4.01 %	0.06 %
navigator.productSub	20030107	None	4.01 %	0.06 %
navigator.userAgent	Android 4.4.2 Android Browser	Windows 7 Firefox	0.10 %	17.33 %
navigator.userAgent	Mac OS X 10.9.4 Safari	iPad OS 7.0.4 Safari	0.18 %	14.69 %
navigator.userAgent	Android 5.0.1 Chrome	iPad OS 8.1 Safari	0.35 %	10.81 %
navigator.userAgent	Android 4.1.2 Android Browser	Linux Iceweasel	0.34 %	10.67 %
navigator.userAgent	Windows 10 Chrome	Android 4.1.2. Android Browser	0.95 %	8.89 %
navigator.userAgent	Android 4.4.2 Chrome	Windows Phone 8.1 IE Mobile	0.26 %	0.06 %
navigator.userAgent	Android 4.4.4 Android Browser	Windows Phone 8.1 IE Mobile	4.01 %	0.06 %
navigator.vendor	Google Inc.	null	13.10 %	0.06 %
screen.availHeight	588	942	4.43 %	0.06 %
screen.availWidth	384	338	2.17 %	0.06 %

For better readability we present only operating system and browser instead of the complete user agent string. The column *Change* represents the average price change in percent.

standard rooms and premium rooms at different prices, and the standard room price is advertised for the first search request, we presume that the prices shown in response to other requests by our scan are also the advertised standard room price. This does not apply to providers of rental cars, as there are fewer car types than there are possible room types. Although there are typically several room types available, it is possible that during a scan, standard rooms are fully booked and only premium suites are offered at a higher price. Such incidents are also detected by our filter described above and excluded from our data set.

Although we normalized the accommodation prices to compensate changes in currency exchange rates, there may be external factors we cannot consider without insider knowledge. For instance, additional transaction fees for providers may differ based on their bank or foreign exchange company.

With respect to our analyses of the ability of single features to increase or decrease a price depending on their specific values, we have analyzed the most striking fingerprints and created artificial morphprints. Due to the huge amount of data, a complete analysis of all possible feature changes considering all possible values in all possible combinations is not feasible. However, our findings are derived from real-world data, though additional feature values may be seen in the wild, meaning that additional value changes may occur, influencing online pricing policies.

In this study, we instrumented browser fingerprints as well as proxy connections/VPN gateways to create profiles. While unlikely, it might be possible for a cross-layer fingerprinting mechanism to discover a profile, e. g., if a user agent shows a Windows machine, but a TTL (Time To Live) value in the IP header analysis reveals a Linux system. Note that our results show clear price variations based on browser fingerprints, regardless of whether or not such a complex mechanism was in place.

Future enhancements could take into account additional providers, as well as more fingerprints, in order to enlarge the data set and gain additional insights. In addition, a longitudinal analysis of possible price differentiation behavior by several providers is another possible direction for future work. Including different product categories also seems promising.

6 RELATED WORK

Several studies have revealed that online price discrimination is a common technique for online shop operators [2, 10, 22, 23, 27].

Hannak et al. recently analyzed several e-business websites which personalize their content. They found that while personalization on e-business websites can provide their users with advantages, aspects such as price customization, for example, can also create disadvantages for those users [10]. Their results provide evidence of price steering and discrimination practices in 9 of 16 analyzed websites. Vissers et al. analyzed price discrimination in online airline tickets. Their results, however, demonstrate that it was not possible to find any evidence for systematic price discrimination on such platforms. This result may be due to the fact that airlines utilize highly volatile pricing algorithms for their tickets [27]. Another empirical study was performed by Mikians et al.; they were among the first to empirically demonstrate the existence of price discrimination [22]. With this knowledge, they started another large-scale crowd-source study and they were able to confirm that there are price differences in e-business based on location [23]. One more recent study by Chen et al. takes a closer look at the algorithmic pricing on Amazon Marketplace [2]. Our work concentrates on price discrimination on hotel booking and car rental websites. In addition, we make use of system fingerprints and analyze which fingerprinting features are the main attributes causing price changes.

Web personalization work continues to improve the quality of Web search requests and their personalized site content [16, 18]. Personalization is important for our work because we analyze the levels on which system fingerprinting methods are used for personalization. To the best of our knowledge, we are the first to extract specific fingerprinting attributes which cause price changes.

Finally, system fingerprinting of clients is a conventional method wielded for user tracking and identification, among other objectives [4, 8, 11, 17, 24, 28]. In this work, we discuss our assumption that client fingerprinting methods are also utilized for price discrimination. The economic fundamentals are extensively discussed by several economists [25, 26].

Iordanou et al. presented a system to detect e-commerce price discrimination [13]. Although the authors faced a similar challenge, they did not inspect fingerprint-based pricing policies explicitly. Additionally, our approach does not require user interaction as we automatically scan provider websites and scrape their contents.

Datta et al. found that user profile information is instrumented for gender discrimination in the context of advertising [3]. Although this indicates the existence of discrimination on the Internet, this study does not include price differentiation.

Melicher et al. have shown that users are uncomfortable especially with invisible methods of user-tracking, such as price discrimination [21]. In contrast, noticeable effects (e. g., advertising) are experienced as tolerable. This shows the importance of secret price differentiation based on user behavior or system fingerprints.

7 CONCLUSION

In this paper, we proposed a method to search for online price differentiation in a systematic way. To this end, we implemented a system capable of disguising itself as different systems based on real-world fingerprints. Utilizing this system, we sent search requests from several locations and systems to four accommodation booking websites and one rental car provider. The returned prices of all found assets (hotel rooms and cars) were examined regarding systematic price differentiation behavior. We ensured that only reproducible cases of online pricing were considered to exclude randomness and external factors.

Despite recent articles about possible price discrimination based on a user's system, we could not prove the existence of such a system for the examined providers. Getting a lower (or higher) price for an asset based on a digital system fingerprint is probably limited to individual cases. Our data show that such cases are rare or may be the result of currency conversions. Nevertheless, it is possible that price differentiation based on other attributes and factors is applied in the wild, such as regional price discrimination.

Furthermore, we investigated single attributes to find which values will provoke a reproducible price change. We found that a user's language settings and user agent (containing information about the operating system and browser) to be the most promising attributes to manipulate when searching for an asset's best price. In contrast to other attributes like screen resolution, these features represent a user's choice and may, therefore, be more frequently instrumented for fingerprint-based price discrimination. Though price discrimination does exist, we found price fluctuations based on changed feature values to be individualized, specific cases. Our study shows that systematic price differentiation is applied by booking providers for locations while system fingerprints do not affect pricing of online accomodation bookings in our setup.

REFERENCES

[1] Gunes Acar, Marc Juarez, Nick Nikiforakis, Claudia Diaz, Seda Gürses, Frank Piessens, and Bart Preneel. 2013. FPDetective: Dusting the Web for fingerprinters. In *ACM Conference on Computer and Communications Security (CCS)*.

[2] Le Chen, Alan Mislove, and Christo Wilson. 2016. An Empirical Analysis of Algorithmic Pricing on Amazon Marketplace. In *World Wide Web Conference (WWW)*. 11. https://doi.org/10.1145/2872427.2883089

[3] Amit Datta, Michael Carl Tschantz, and Anupam Datta. 2015. Automated experiments on ad privacy settings.

[4] Peter Eckersley. 2010. How Unique is Your Web Browser?. In *Proceedings on Privacy Enhancing Technologies (PETS)*. 18.

[5] Christian Eubank, Marcela Melara, Diego Perez-botero, and Arvind Narayanan. 2013. Shining the Floodlights on Mobile Web Tracking – A Privacy Survey. In *Web 2.0 Security & Privacy Conference (W2SP)*.

[6] Milton Friedman. 1937. The use of ranks to avoid the assumption of normality implicit in the analysis of variance. *J. Amer. Statist. Assoc.* 32, 200 (1937), 675–701.

[7] Milton Friedman. 1940. A comparison of alternative tests of significance for the problem of m rankings. *The Annals of Mathematical Statistics* 11, 1 (1940), 86–92.

[8] Gábor György Gulyás, Gergely Acs, and Claude Castelluccia. 2016. Near-Optimal Fingerprinting with Constraints. *Proceedings on Privacy Enhancing Technologies (PoPETs)* 4 (2016), 1–17.

[9] Mark Hall, Eibe Frank, Geoffrey Holmes, Bernhard Pfahringer, Peter Reutemann, and Ian H. Witten. 2009. The WEKA Data Mining Software: An Update. *SIGKDD Explor. Newsl.* 11, 1 (Nov. 2009), 10–18. https://doi.org/10.1145/1656274.1656278

[10] Aniko Hannak, Gary Soeller, David Lazer, Alan Mislove, and Christo Wilson. 2014. Measuring Price Discrimination and Steering on E-commerce Web Sites. In *Internet Measurement Conference (IMC)*. 14. https://doi.org/10.1145/2663716.2663744

[11] Thomas Hupperich, Davide Maiorca, Marc Kührer, Thorsten Holz, and Giorgio Giacinto. 2015. On the Robustness of Mobile Device Fingerprinting: Can Mobile Users Escape Modern Web-Tracking Mechanisms?. In *Anual Computer Security Applications Conference (ACSAC)*.

[12] Thomas Hupperich, Dennis Tatang, Nicolai Wilkop, and Thorsten Holz. 2017. An Empirical Study on Price Differentiation Based on System Fingerprints. *arXiv preprint arXiv:1712.03031* (2017).

[13] Costas Iordanou, Claudio Soriente, Michael Sirivianos, and Nikolaos Laoutaris. 2017. Who is Fiddling with Prices?: Building and Deploying a Watchdog Service for E-commerce. In *Proceedings of the Conference of the ACM Special Interest Group on Data Communication (SIGCOMM '17)*.

[14] Jeremy Singer-Vine Jennifer Valentino-Devries and Ashkan Soltani. 2017. Websites Vary Prices, Deals Based on Users Information. (2017). http://www.wsj.com/articles/SB10001424127887323777204578189391813881534.

[15] Samy Kamkar. 2010. Evercookie – never forget. (2010). http://samy.pl/evercookie/.

[16] Chloe Kliman-Silver, Aniko Hannak, David Lazer, Christo Wilson, and Alan Mislove. 2015 Location, Location, Location: The Impact of Geolocation on Web Search Personalization. In *Internet Measurement Conference (IMC)*.

[17] Andreas Kurtz, Hugo Gascon, Tobias Becker, Konrad Rieck, and Felix C. Freiling. 2016. Fingerprinting Mobile Devices Using Personalized Configurations. *Proceedings on Privacy Enhancing Technologies (PoPETs)* (2016).

[18] Mathias Lecuyer, Riley Spahn, Yannis Spiliopolous, Augustin Chaintreau, Roxana Geambasu, and Daniel Hsu. 2015. Sunlight: Fine-grained targeting detection at scale with statistical confidence. In *ACM CCS*.

[19] Bin Liang, Wei You, Liangkun Liu, Wenchang Shi, and M. Heiderich. 2014. Scriptless Timing Attacks on Web Browser Privacy. In *Annual IEEE/IFIP International Conference on Dependable Systems and Networks (DSN)*.

[20] Dana Mattioli. 2017. On Orbitz, Mac Users Steered to Pricier Hotels. (2017). http://www.wsj.com/articles/SB10001424052702304458604577488822667325882.

[21] William Melicher, Mahmood Sharif, Joshua Tan, Lujo Bauer, Mihai Christodorescu, and Pedro Giovanni Leon. 2016. (Do Not) Track Me Sometimes: Users' Contextual Preferences for Web Tracking.

[22] Jakub Mikians, László Gyarmati, Vijay Erramilli, and Nikolaos Laoutaris. 2012. Detecting Price and Search Discrimination on the Internet. In *ACM Workshop on Hot Topics in Networks*. 6. https://doi.org/10.1145/2390231.2390245

[23] Jakub Mikians, László Gyarmati, Vijay Erramilli, and Nikolaos Laoutaris. 2013. Crowd-assisted Search for Price Discrimination in E-Commerce: First results. *CoRR* abs/1307.4531 (2013). http://arxiv.org/abs/1307.4531

[24] Nick Nikiforakis, Alexandros Kapravelos, Wouter Joosen, Christopher Kruegel, Frank Piessers, and Giovanni Vigna. 2013. Cookieless monster: Exploring the ecosystem of web-based device fingerprinting. In *IEEE S&P*.

[25] Benjamin Reed Shiller et al. 2014. First degree price discrimination using big data. *Presented at The Federal Trade Commission* (2014).

[26] Hal R Varian. 1989. Price discrimination. *Handbook of industrial organization* 1 (1989).

[27] Thomas Vissers, Nick Nikiforakis, Nataliia Bielova, and Wouter Joosen. 2014. Crying wolf? On the price discrimination of online airline tickets. In *Workshop on Hot Topics in Privacy Enhancing Technologies (HotPETs)*.

[28] Ting-Fang Yen, Yinglian Xie, Fang Yu, Roger Peng Yu, and Martin Abadi. 2012. Host Fingerprinting and Tracking on the Web: Privacy and Security Implications.. In *Symposium on Network and Distributed System Security (NDSS)*.

Remote Attestation for Low-End Prover Devices with Post-Quantum Capabilities

Xiruo Liu
Intel Labs, Intel Corporation
Hillsboro, Oregon, United States
xiruo.liu@intel.com

Rafael Misoczki
Intel Labs, Intel Corporation
Hillsboro, Oregon, United States
rafael.misoczki@intel.com

Manoj R. Sastry
Intel Labs, Intel Corporation
Hillsboro, Oregon, United States
manoj.r.sastry@intel.com

ABSTRACT

Remote attestation is a well-established interactive technique to establish trust in the realm of connected devices. It allows a Prover device to attest its platform integrity to a Verifier device. Existing remote attestation protocols rely on classical asymmetric cryptography, which are too heavy for low-end Prover devices, and vulnerable to quantum attacks (a serious concern due to the long lifespan of IoT devices). Hash-Based Signatures (HBS) offer attractive performance and have capabilities to defeat quantum attacks. This paper presents several contributions in this context. First, we present an efficient remote attestation protocol that requires the Prover to perform only one-time HBS operations, which are very lightweight. Our protocol also proposes robust embedded techniques to refresh one-time keys that allow multiple attestations. Second, we present a simpler construction based on multi-time HBS scheme which does not depend on a trusted-third-party. Third, to demonstrate the feasibility of our protocols, we developed prototypes based on state-of-the-art HBS schemes (XMSS and WOTS+) for highly constrained platforms (Arduino 101) in both classical and post-quantum security settings. Finally, we present a comprehensive comparison between these strategies, including guidance on suitable use cases for each one of them. To summarize, our work demonstrates the feasibility of modern HBS constructions for remote attestation of highly-constrained devices.

CCS CONCEPTS

• Security and privacy → Security protocols; *Digital signatures*; Trusted computing;

KEYWORDS

Remote Attestation; Hash-Based Signatures; Post-Quantum Cryptography; Internet of Things; Security

ACM Reference Format:
Xiruo Liu, Rafael Misoczki, and Manoj R. Sastry. 2018. Remote Attestation for Low-End Prover Devices with Post-Quantum Capabilities. In *CODASPY '18: Eighth ACM Conference on Data and Application Security and Privacy, March 19–21, 2018, Tempe, AZ, USA.* ACM, New York, NY, USA, 11 pages. https://doi.org/https://doi.org/10.1145/3176258.3176324

1 INTRODUCTION

Internet of Things (IoT) is becoming the foundation of the "smart" world. It spans from everyday life to military usages, from public utilities to smart home, from factory automation to environment monitoring. IoT devices are being deployed at an increasing speed. These devices, collectively or individually, sense the environment, collect information, process data and provide feedback to the environment.

On one hand, trustworthy IoT devices can significantly improve the productivity and the quality of our lifes. On the other hand, malfunctioning or compromised devices may bring severe consequences. Take smart grid for example: privacy and security issues arise along with the modernization process of the power supply systems. Compromising a few devices can jeopardize an entire network. A group of compromised smart meters may form botnets and launch distributed Denial-of-Service (DoS) attacks. Power usage misinformation might be injected into control systems, resulting in serious damages to the electrical infrastructure [31]. As a result of the inter-connectivity of cyber-physical systems, the threats to only a few IoT devices may propagate and exacerbate, resulting in severe consequences at large scale.

Given these threats and consequences, platform security has become a major concern. As the cornerstone of platform security, the device integrity is a prerequisite to achieve trustworthiness. As a means to validate the integrity of a device, remote attestation allows a device to report the proof of its internal state (e.g., current firmware, hardware or software) to another remote party. It is an important building block for critical operations, such as secure boot, trusted firmware update, etc. For example, the smart meter installations in U.S. exceeded 50 million units by July 2014, which covered more than 43% households [48]. Due to the large scale deployment, frequent on-site inspections to validate the integrity of smart meters become a quite expensive or even unfeasible process. As an alternative, remote attestation is an effective and efficient approach to ensure the integrity of those meters.

Typically, remote attestation adopts a challenge-response paradigm involving two parties: a *Verifier*, the remote challenger who wants to verify the state of the Prover; and a *Prover*, an entity who provides a cryptographic measurement of its state as a proof of its integrity to the Verifier. In general, to initiate an attestation, the Verifier sends a challenge to the Prover. Then the Prover signs the proof of its integrity (e.g., the hash of its firmware or a segment of the memory, depending on the specific attestation request) with its private key, and sends the signature to the Verifier as the response. Digital signatures are used to ensure the integrity and the authenticity of the attestation response from the Prover.

Most of the widely used remote attestation schemes are based on classical digital signatures, such as RSA [40] and ECC [26, 34], which, unfortunately, are vulnerable to quantum attacks [46]. Note that years are usually required for the transition from a crypto algorithm to its actual practical implementation and deployment. Therefore, it is of utmost importance to develop and experiment with quantum-resistant solutions much before the upcoming rise of quantum technologies. Particularly, IoT devices will have much longer lifespan (e.g., the life span of smart meters are typically fifteen years [27]) with little or even no maintenance. For this reason, devising quantum-resistant solutions for IoT is an even more critic topic of investigation. There exist digital signatures that can defeat quantum computers [1, 8, 14, 19, 21, 33]. Particularly, Post-Quantum Cryptography (PQC) standardization efforts have already begun [35, 39] as the community realized the urgency of transition to quantum-resistant solutions.

Contributions: This paper introduces remote attestation protocols that imposes only a minimum overhead at the Prover side, and are thus suitable for IoT devices. Specifically, Hash-Based Signatures (HBS) are chosen as the underlying cryptography in order to ensure post-quantum capabilities. We examine the features of different HBS designs with special focus on one-time HBS. Additionally, we present a simple design based on multi-time HBS. We develop prototypes of our protocols instantiated with state-of-the-art HBS schemes (XMSS and WOTS+) targeting highly-constrained devices (Arduino 101) and present a comprehensive comparison regarding their practical performance. Finally, we present recommendations on use cases that are suitable to our protocols. In short, our work demonstrates the feasibility of modern HBS constructions for remote attestation of highly-constrained devices.

Organization: The paper is organized as follows: Section 2 discusses the related work. Section 3 introduces Hash-Based Signatures, which serves as the crypto basis for this work. We leverage the characteristics of different HBS schemes and propose two remote attestation protocols for Provers with different capabilities and requirements in Section 4. Section 5 presents the prototypes and the performance evaluation. Protocol comparison and usage recommendations are provided in Section 6. Section 7 concludes the paper.

2 RELATED WORK

There are two main categories of remote attestation schemes: software-based attestation and hardware-based attestation.

Software-based attestation schemes [28, 42–45] typically depend on the intrinsic physical constraints on the Prover's hardware and communication channels, such as time and memory constraints [7], and require very specific settings, such as the Verifier communicating to the Prover *directly*. Consequently, those strong assumptions limit the usage of software-based remote attestation schemes in practice.

Hardware-based remote attestation techniques tackle the issue from another angle to overcome the limitations of the software-based counterparts. They rely on dedicated hardware, such as Trusted Platform Modules (TPM) [22], which is a prevalent security hardware. TPM provides commands to support the local attestation service, which uses RSA in early versions and adds ECC in

the newest version. Many existing remote attestation protocols [11, 17, 25, 37, 47] are based on TPM. As an enhancement to TPM, several other security architectures (e.g., Flicker [30], TrustVisor [29], Trusted Execution Environment [38]) introduce extended mechanisms to enable dynamic attestation. Unfortunately, the digital signature schemes used in current hardware-based remote attestation schemes are restricted by the choices of the underlying hardware architectures, all of which adopt traditional asymmetric cryptography (typically RSA or ECC). Hence, the existing hardware-based remote attestation schemes naturally inherit the post-quantum vulnerability [46].

In face of the threats posed by quantum attacks, finding replacements for the currently widely-used asymmetric algorithms became a topic of great relevance. There are two techniques that overcome quantum attacks: quantum-cryptography and post-quantum cryptography. The former requires a quantum infrastructure (i.e., with very high cost) and is limited to key exchange [9]. For this reason, it has been restricted to government deployments, such as Defense Advanced Research Projects Agency (DARPA) [20] and European Union-funded initiatives [2]. The latter, known as Post-Quantum Cryptography (PQC)[10], consists of using cryptographic schemes based on different mathematical problems (other than integer factorization or discrete log) that are not disruptively affected by quantum computers. PQC can replace current cryptography with minimum investment and some schemes may even offer performance advantages (e.g., better latency or memory-wise cost).

There are various existing PQC digital signature schemes in the literature, e.g. Lattices-based schemes [1, 8, 19], Code-based schemes [21] and Hash-Based Signatures (HBS) [14, 33]. Differently to all other candidates, HBS relies its security solely on well-known security notions related to hash functions, which are only marginally affected by quantum computers [23], thus are quantum-resistant.

The literature exploring PQC-based attestation is not vast yet. One of the few existing works [4] proposes a quantum-secure TPM by replacing RSA with one-time HBS. It investigates the feasibility of applying one-time HBS on the TPM and provides suggestions for system parameters. However, it confines itself to the TPM platforms and local attestation operations.

Additionally, little of the current work focuses on the Prover's perspective: cost of operations at the Prover, and protections for the Prover against malicious Verifiers. [13] identifies several attacks against Provers and proposes mitigation methods, but it does not provide an end-to-end solution for remote attestation and the piecewise solution relies on conventional cryptographic algorithms that are vulnerable to quantum attacks.

3 HASH-BASED SIGNATURES

HBS schemes offer advantages from both security and efficiency perspectives. Regarding the former, HBS schemes rely solely on the security of hash functions (collision-resistance [33] and target-collision resistance [10]). This is an extremely important advantage as all other digital signature schemes (pre-quantum or post-quantum) need to rely not only on the security of hash functions (to map messages of arbitrary length into fixed length digests that are actually signed) but additionally on some other computational problem (commonly, the venue for attacks). Moreover, even in the unexpected event that a well-known hash function family is broken, the security of HBS is not affected at all because this would only show the non-suitability of such a hash function. In short, HBS schemes are secure as long as there exists at least one secure hash function, which is a minimal assumption when compared to all other assumptions that need to be met by other schemes.

Regarding efficiency, HBS operations consist of hash calls which are simpler and faster than operations required by conventional asymmetric cryptography (exponentiation, arbitrary precision arithmetic, among others). Besides, the flexibility of selecting the appropriate underlying hash function allows it to satisfy distinctive performance requirements.

The best-known HBS schemes belong to two main categories: *one-time signature (OTS)* schemes and *multi-time signature (MTS)* schemes. In the OTS schemes, each private key must be used to sign only a single message. If the same private key is used to sign a second message, the scheme loses its security guarantees. On the other hand, MTS schemes allows for signing multiple messages with the same key pair. In terms of computational cost, OTS schemes are much more efficient than MTS schemes. However, since we are usually interested in signing multiple messages with a same key, OTS-based solutions need to be enhanced by some robust mechanism to update the OTS key pairs after being used.

In this work, we are particularly interested in the WOTS+ one-time HBS scheme [24] and the XMSS multi-time HBS scheme [14] because they are the cryptographic foundations of our remote attestation protocols. Therefore, before diving into the remote attestation protocols, we will recap the WOTS+ and XMSS schemes.

3.1 WOTS+ One-Time Signature Scheme

The WOTS+ scheme [24] is a variant of the Winternitz scheme [33] that allows shorter hash lengths given the same security level. This leads to smaller signature sizes, which is often seen as the main drawback of HBS.

Winternitz-like signature schemes have a straightforward rationale. In a simplified description, the private key is a set of random bits. The public key is computed from applying a one-way function on the private key a fixed number $N \in \mathbb{N}$ of times (the output of one iteration works as the input of the next iteration). To sign a message, seen as an integer $m \in \mathbb{N}$, $0 < m < N$, the one-way function is applied m times on the private-key. To verify a signature σ, the one-way function is applied more $(N - m)$ times on σ. If the result matches the public key, the signature is authentic; otherwise, it will be rejected. From this simple rationale, it is possible to design OTS schemes that solely rely on well-known security properties of the one-way function (e.g. collision resistance).

More formally, the WOTS+ schemes uses the following parameters: $w, n, m \in \mathbb{N}$, which are respectively the Winternitz parameter, the hash digest size and the message size. Subsequently, the sub-parameters are defined as $\ell_1 = \lceil m/\log(w) \rceil$, $\ell_2 = \lfloor \log(\ell_1(w - 1))/\log(w) \rfloor$, $\ell = \ell_1 + \ell_2$. It also uses a family of functions $\mathcal{F}_n : \{f_k : \{0,1\}^n \to \{0,1\}^n | k \in \mathcal{K}_n\}$, with key space $\mathcal{K}_n$, which can be seen as a non-compressing hash function, and a function $c_k^i(x, \mathbf{r}) = f_k(c_k^{i-1}(x, \mathbf{r}) \oplus r_i)$, called chain function, where $x \in \{0,1\}^n$, $i \in \mathbb{N}$, $k \in \mathcal{K}$, $\mathbf{r} = (r_1, ..., r_j) \in \{0,1\}^{n \times j}$, with $j > i$, for $i > 0$, and

$c_k^0(x, \mathbf{r}) = x$, for $i = 0$. In short, the chain function encapsulates the calls to the hash function.

Key generation consists of generating the private key $\mathbf{sk} = (sk_1, ..., sk_\ell) \in \{0,1\}^{\ell \times n}$ and the randomization elements $\mathbf{r} = (r_1, ..., r_j) \in \{0,1\}^{n \times j}$, both uniformly at random. Then, a key $k \leftarrow \mathcal{K}$ is randomly chosen and the public verification key is computed as $\mathbf{pk} = (pk_1, ...pk_\ell) = ((\mathbf{r}, k), c_k^{w-1}(sk_1, \mathbf{r}), ..., c_k^{w-1}(sk_\ell, \mathbf{r}))$. Essentially, the private key is a uniformly random bit stream and the public key is the result of applying the chain function over the private key chunks $(w - 1)$ times.

To sign a message M of m bits, the signing algorithm computes the base-w representation of $M = (M_1, ..., M_\ell)$, $M_i \in \{0, ..., w-1\}$, a checksum $C = \Sigma_{i=1}^{\ell_1}(w - 1 - M_i)$, its base-$w$ representation $C = (C_1, ..., C_{\ell_2})$, and it sets $B = (b_1, ..., b_\ell) = (M||C)$. Finally, the signature is computed as $\sigma = (\sigma_1, ..., \sigma_\ell) = (c_k^{b_1}(sk_1, \mathbf{r}), ..., c_k^{b_\ell}(sk_\ell, \mathbf{r}))$. The verification procedure recomputes B as described above and accepts the signature if pk is equal to:

$$((\mathbf{r}, k), c_k^{w-1-b_1}(\sigma_1, \mathbf{r}_{b_1+1, w-1}), ..., c_k^{w-1-b_\ell}(\sigma_\ell, \mathbf{r}_{b_\ell+1, w-1})).$$

All three algorithms require at most ℓw calls to the chain function. Both the signature and the private key have the size of ℓn bits (although the private key can be just an n-bits seed, if a cryptographically secure pseudo-random number generator is used). The public key has $(\ell + w - 1)n + |k|$ bits, where $|k|$ denotes the number of bits to represent an element of $\mathcal{K}$.

3.2 XMSS Multi-Time Signature Scheme

The XMSS scheme [14] is a variant of the classical Merkle scheme [33] that allows shorter hash lengths given the same security level. As a result, it also leads to smaller signatures.

Merkle-like signature schemes focus on enabling multi-time signatures from the limited one-time schemes. They bind in a secure way a large number of one-time public keys into a single public key. Each one-time key pair is used to sign a single message, but all signatures are verified using the same overall public key. This is realized through a Merkle tree, which is a binary tree data structure. The root of this tree is the overall public key, while the leaf nodes are constructed from the one-time public keys. The rule to build this tree from the leaf nodes up to the root note depends on the security property of the one-way function. Figure 1 shows a toy-size Merkle tree for the classical Merkle scheme, which has the leaf nodes computed as the hash of the one-time public keys and the non-leaf nodes are constructed by hashing the concatenation of the two children nodes.

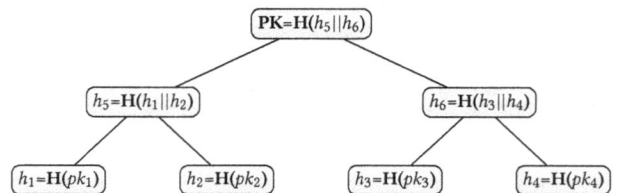

Figure 1: Merkle-Tree of height 2 and 4 leaf nodes.

To sign a message, it is necessary to sign it with a one-time key and then compute the so-called authentication path, which includes the $\mathcal{H}$ (tree nodes in a tree of height $\mathcal{H}$) needed to reconstruct the root node from the one-time public key using the tree construction rule described earlier. As an example, consider Figure 1 and assume that the first (the left most, of index 1) one-time key pair is used. The authentication path will include nodes h_2 and h_6. The tree height determines the number of maximum signature per Merkle key pair: $2^{\mathcal{H}}$. To verify a signature, one needs to at first verify the one-time signature in order to produce the one-time public key. Then, with the assistance of the authentication path and the hash of the one-time public key, it is possible to reconstruct the root of the tree. If the result matches the Merkle public key, then the signature is accepted; otherwise, it is rejected.

Note that a one-time key pair must never be re-used as the security of the scheme will be lost, as seen in the one-time schemes. This turns such scheme into a stateful scheme. In other words, a state needs to be securely maintained by the signer in order to prevent duplicate usages of one-time keys. This represents an additional requirement for the HBS when compared with traditional signature schemes, and there are works how to satisfy this requirement in practice [32].

Having presented the intuition behind Merkle-like schemes, we now proceed to formally define the XMSS scheme, which is a variant of the Merkle scheme. The XMSS scheme uses a different rule to build the tree and relies on the WOTS+ scheme, instead of the classical Winternitz. The parameters are the same as for WOTS+ ($w, n, m \in \mathbb{N}$), plus $\mathcal{H}$, the tree height. The XMSS tree is built using the following rule:

$$Node_{i,j} = h_k((Node_{2i,j-1} \oplus bm_{l,j})||(Node_{2i+1,j-1} \oplus bm_{r,j})),$$

$0 < j < \mathcal{H}$, $0 < i < 2^{\mathcal{H}-j}$. The bitmasks $(bm_{l,j}, bm_{r,j}) \in \{0,1\}^{2n}$ are sampled uniformly at random and h_k is chosen randomly from the set $\{h_k : \{0,1\}^{2n} \to \{0,1\}^n | k \in \{0,1\}^n\}$.

Key generation consists of generating $2^{\mathcal{H}}$ W-OTS+ key pairs. Each WOTS+ public-key is used to build an L-Tree, which is a binary tree of ℓ leaf nodes that follows the tree building rule described above, and is used to compress an Ln bits one-time public key into an n-bits. The root nodes of the L-Trees are used as leaf nodes of the (main) Merkle tree. The XMSS public key is the root of the Merkle tree plus the bitmasks. The private key is either the $2^{\mathcal{H}}$ WOTS+ private keys or, more conveniently, an n-bit seed used to generate all one-time private keys assuming that a secure pseudo random number generator is available.

To sign the i-th message, the i-th WOTS+ private key is used and the signature is $SIG = (i, \sigma, Auth)$, where i is an index between $0 < i < 2^{\mathcal{H}} - 1$, σ is the the WOTS+ signature, and $Auth \in \{0,1\}^{\mathcal{H} \times n}$ is the authentication path. Althoug there are several candidate techniques to compute the authentication path, [15] is suggested as it provides optimal balanced runtime with little memory requirement.

To verify a signature SIG, the WOTS+ signature σ is verified in order to produce the WOTS+ public key **pk**. Then using both WOTS+ public key and the authentication path, the verifier is able to reconstruct the root of the Merkle tree. If the result matches the XMSS public key, the signature is valid; otherwise, the signature is rejected.

Having explained how WOTS+ and XMSS schemes work, we will present our remote attestation protocols that use the aforementioned HBS schemes as the cryptographic foundations.

4 HBS-BASED REMOTE ATTESTATION PROTOCOLS

In this section, we present two remote attestation protocols that utilize HBS schemes as the cryptographic foundation. For the sake of generality, we refer to the WOTS+ scheme simply as OTS and to the XMSS scheme simply as MTS (although the parameters and peformance results presented in Section 5 are related to the protocols instantiated with WOTS+ and XMSS schemes). Firstly, we introduce a remote attestation protocol that requires from the Prover only OTS operations. This is an important advantage as OTS operations have very low cost and hence are suitable for IoT resource constrained devices which may not be able to afford expensive cryptography. Since our focus is in the Prover's perspective, we name this protocol as "OTS-based Remote Attestation", although other entities in this protocol still require MTS operations. Then, we introduce another (simpler) protocol based on MTS operations for all parties involved. This protocol is simpler than our OTS-based protocol given the fact that MTS do not have the limitation of signing a single messages per key.

Threat Model: For all protocols, we assume network adversaries that follow the classic Dolev-Yao Intruder model [18], which allows an active network adversary to take full control of all the communication channels. For example, the adversary can eavesdrop on messages, modify them at will, inject its own messages, delete messages, delay message delivery, duplicate any message and/or replay it later. Furthermore, the adversary may be able to initiate new protocol sessions and interleave messages from different sessions. In the local scope, a weak software adversary is assumed such that the attacker can only access and/or overwrite regular applications or the operating system, but not the non-volatile secure storage, which is required for storing HBS private keys. Secure hardware modules may be used to keep the HBS private keys from being compromised.

4.1 OTS-Based Remote Attestation Protocol

Common remote attestation protocols use a challenge-response mechanism that only involves a Verifier and a Prover. This paradigm is simple, yet it still carries a drawback particularly relevant for IoT: the Prover is subject to Denial-of-Service attacks, i.e. malicious Verifiers can trigger several attestation requests and exhaust the resource of the victim constrained resource Prover. Moreover, in a simplistic OTS-based remote attestation protocol, the Prover would need to maintain one key pair per Verifier, which would limit the number of Verifiers the Prover can accommodate. In this section, we introduce an OTS-based remote attestation that intends to address both aforementioned issues.

The usage of OTS-based schemes for remote attestation is challenging. The main issue refers to the fact that OTS can only sign a single message per key, while in remote attestation applications we are usually interested in generating large/unlimited number of attestations. To address this problem, we propose the introduction of a trusted third party that is responsible to validate the attestation request and authenticate Prover's freshly generated one-time keys for the Verifier. Therefore, our protocol involves the following three parties:

- *P*: the Prover who needs to prove its current device integrity status to another party Verifier.
- *V*: the Verifier who wants to check whether the Prover's platform has its integrity preserved.
- *TTP*: a third party that is trusted by both the Prover and the Verifier, playing facilitation role in the protocol.

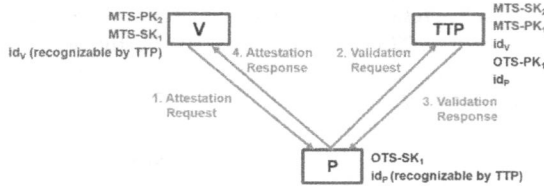

Figure 2: Model of the One-Time HBS Remote Attestation.

Figure 2 shows the main objectives of each message (in green) sent by V, P and TTP that enable the remote attestation between V and P with the help from TTP. With more details, V initiates an *Attestation Request* with P, who then contacts TTP with a *Validation Request* to verify the legitimacy of this request originated from V. If TTP verifies (in a possibly expensive process) the validity of this request and sends the result within the *Validation Response*. In case it is a valid request, then P computes the proof of its device integrity and sends it in the *Attestation Response* to V.

Prior to the attestation, V and TTP should share pairs of MTS keys to authenticate each other. This design allows more flexibility to serve various remote Verifier entities, without increasing the overhead for the resource-constrained Provers as this workload is shifted to the trusted third party. Some of the existing works, such as [3], also adopt similar approach. The benefits of introducing such a TTP include:

- *Access control*: access control mechanisms may be enforced at TTP, instead of P. From the Prover's perspective, introducing TTP may offload the complexity on P and therefore minimize the DoS risks for P.
- *Protect P's privacy from V*: removing the trust assumption between P and V so that they do not need to know the identity of each other.
- *Attestation service availability*: As P is considered as a resource-constrained device, it may be unable to maintain too many trust relationships with various Verifiers concurrently, which limits the number of Verifiers it can serve. With a TTP, P only needs to maintain one trust relationship with TTP, who is typically more powerful and hence capable of accommodating more Verifiers than P itself.

Our protocols assume a few things about the parties and what they share before the execution of the protocol, namely:

- P and TTP have established a trusted relationship in terms of an OTS key pair (P holds the private key $OTS\text{-}SK_1$ and TTP holds the corresponding public key $OTS\text{-}PK_1$); P and TTP have identifiers to uniquely identify each other.

Symbol	Notation
$A \rightarrow B : m$	Entity A sends entity B message m
$\|\|$	Concatenation
N	Nonce generated in the protocol session
id_X	Identifier of the protocol participant X
$MTS\text{-}PK_i$	Multi-time HBS public key
$MTS\text{-}SK_i$	Multi-time HBS private key
$OTS\text{-}PK_i$	One-time HBS public key
$OTS\text{-}SK_i$	One-time HBS private key
rng	Random number generation
$sig_X(M)$	Signature on material M using the private key of X
P_{attr}	Prover's attributes (e.g., address, model number)
$attr$	Attributes specifying what to be attested
α, γ	Multi-time HBS signature
β	One-time HBS signature
att_resp	Attestation response
FW_{attr}	Attestation content identified by parameter $attr$

Table 1: Notation for the OTS-Based Protocol

- V and TTP have established a trusted relationship in terms of two MTS key pairs (V holds one private key $MTS\text{-}SK_1$ and one public key $MTS\text{-}PK_2$, while TTP holds the corresponding public key $MTS\text{-}PK_1$ and the private key $MTS\text{-}SK_2$); V and TTP have identifiers to uniquely identify each other.
- P and V may not have any prior trusted relationship: the authentication for V and the authorization to the attestation service on P should be realized by the protocol.
- P may be resource-constrained and only be able to support OTS operations. V and TTP are relatively more powerful and capable of handling expensive cryptographic computations, such as MTS operations.
- Secure key store: the private keys are protected properly in the key store and are not accessible to adversaries.

Figure 3 presents the format and the exchange flows of four messages in the OTS-based remote attestation protocol. Table 1 lists the notations used in Figure 3. Next, we present the description of each message exchanged in our protocol and its security purpose.

(1) $V \rightarrow P$: $\{N, id_V, id_T, P_{attr}, attr, \alpha\}$

Message 1 is an attestation request from V to P. To initiate a new protocol session, V first generates a fresh nonce N to prevent replay attack and uniquely identify this new protocol session. Then V specifies what to be attested (e.g., the firmware image or memory region) by setting proper $attr$. Note that the format and the content of $attr$ depend on the attestation content P can support. It may follow the convention or a pre-defined agreement, and is out of the scope of this paper. To bind this attestation request to the intended P, V includes its knowledge of P, P_{attr}, in Message 1. P_{attr} can be replaced by P's identifier, if the privacy is not a concern. But in the case where P wants to protect its privacy (i.e., do not want to let V identify itself) or V does not have any knowledge of P's identifier, V may use P's feature P_{attr} (e.g., IP address, device type or model number) to locate P at TTP for the service authorization later. Lastly, to guarantee the integrity of Message 1, V computes the signature α on all

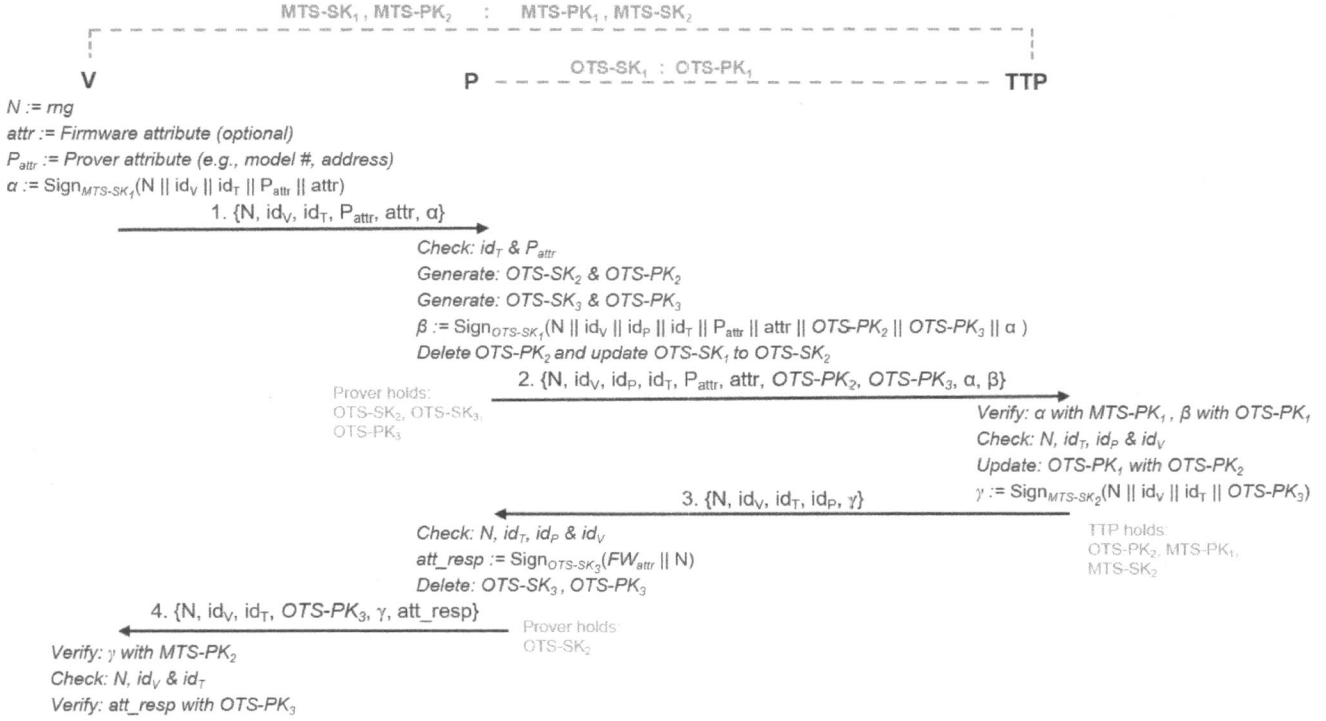

Figure 3: OTS-based remote attestation protocol details.

the previous components using a MTS private key $MTS\text{-}SK_1$ and attaches it at the end of Message 1.

(2) $P \rightarrow TTP$: $\{N, id_V, id_P, id_T, P_{attr}, attr, OTS\text{-}PK_2, OTS\text{-}PK_3, \alpha, \beta\}$

Message 2 is a validation request from P to TTP for verifying V's eligibility to the attestation service. After receiving Message 1, P first checks if he knows a TTP with id_T and verifies if it matches P_{attr}. If id_T and P_{attr} are correct, P forwards the attestation request to TTP for further verification with Message 2. P clearly indicates id_P to prevent misbinding attack and prepares two OTS key pairs: $OTS\text{-}PK_2/OTS\text{-}SK_2$ and $OTS\text{-}PK_3/OTS\text{-}SK_3$. $OTS\text{-}PK_2/OTS\text{-}SK_2$ are used to replace $OTS\text{-}PK_1/OTS\text{-}SK_1$ as they will be consumed when signing Message 2. $OTS\text{-}PK_3/OTS\text{-}SK_3$ will be used to protect the integrity of the attestation measurement taken by P in Message 4. Then P computes the OTS signature β with $OTS\text{-}SK_1$ as in Equation 1 to protect the integrity of Message 2 as well as authenticate itself to TTP. P constructs Message 2 as indicated above and sends it to TTP. Lastly, P deletes its local copy of $OTS\text{-}PK_2$ and update $OTS\text{-}SK_1$ to $OTS\text{-}SK_2$.

$$\beta = Sign_{OTS\text{-}SK_1}(N||id_V||id_P||id_T||P_{attr} \\ ||attr|| OTS\text{-}PK_2 || OTS\text{-}PK_3 ||\alpha) \tag{1}$$

(3) $TTP \rightarrow P$: $\{N, id_V, id_T, id_P, \gamma\}$

Message 3 is the validation response from TTP to P. TTP verifies the information carried in Message 2 regarding to

V's attestation request and replies its assessment to P. Specifically, TTP will conduct the following verifications: ① Verifies the signature β with $OTS\text{-}PK_1$ and the signature α with $MTS\text{-}PK_1$. ② If both signatures are correct, checks the nonce N with its local database. If N is fresh, TTP adds N to the local nonce database; otherwise, it informs P to reject the attestation request as it is a replay attack. ③ TTP verifies all the three identifiers. ④ TTP checks whether the P identified by id_P has matching attributes indicated in P_{attr}. ⑤ TTP determines if V, identified by id_V, has the attestation privilege regarding to the content specified by $attr$ on P. If all the verifications pass, TTP updates its local copy of $OTS\text{-}PK_1$ with $OTS\text{-}PK_2$. To prepare the validation response, TTP computes the signature γ on $(N||id_V||id_T|| OTS\text{-}PK_3)$ with $MTS\text{-}SK_2$. Note that $OTS\text{-}PK_3$, which will be used for V to verify the attestation response from P, is protected by the multi-time signature and hence has TTP's guarantee.

(4) $P \rightarrow V$: $\{N, id_V, id_T, OTS\text{-}PK_3, \beta, att\_resp\}$

Message 4 is the attestation response from P to V. If TTP approves V's attestation request in Message 3, P takes the attestation measurement and sends the result to V. P computes its attestation response, att_resp, as one-time HBS signature on $(FW_{attr}||N)$ with $OTS\text{-}SK_3$. Note that FW_{attr} is the attestation content specified by $attr$, which can be firmware, software version, etc. Message 4 includes two signatures: the one-time HBS signature att_resp, which carries attestation results, and the multi-time HBS signature γ from TTP, which

protects the important session information and carries the
OTS public key used to verify the attestation response.

(5) V parses Message 4

Upon receiving Message 4, V first verifies the signature γ
with $MTS\text{-}PK_2$. Then V checks if the session information
(id_V, id_T, N) is correct. V uses $OTS\text{-}PK_3$ to verify att_resp
and infer P's device integrity.

Besides the basic attestation goal, this protocol also provides
desired features and security protections, including lightweight,
integrity, authenticity and privacy. To meet the lightweight demand
from P, we customize the protocol so that P only needs to deal with
the lightweight OTS operations, while V and TTP support both
OTS and MTS operations.

To enhance the resilience against DoS attacks, this protocol shifts
the workload from P to TTP as much as possible. For example, the
access control is enforced at TTP so that P does not need to validate
the V's identity and the attestation privilege. TTP also takes the
responsibility of checking the nonce (to prevent replay attack) so
that P can save storage from maintaining a local database.

The integrity property is achieved through proper signatures that
protects the critical elements of the messages. And using correct
private keys to generate the signatures also provides authenticity
guarantees. To prevent misbinding and impersonating attacks, the
protocol should explicitly include the identity of the protocol participants when necessary. However, in certain application scenarios,
P's privacy is of most interest and needs to be protected from V.
One effort to provide "partial privacy" for P against V is eliminating
P's identity information from the message exchanges with V, which
might leave a room for man-in-the-middle attack. To resolve the
conflict between the privacy requirement and preventing man-in-
the-middle attack, P's attribute P_{attr} is used to help identify the
correct P at TTP. This mitigation method is not perfect and may not
provide the comprehensive privacy-preserving features. To achieve
full privacy protection, further investigation is needed.

4.2 Multi-time HBS-based Remote Attestation

In use cases where Prover devices are able to support more expensive operations, an MTS-based remote attestation protocol might
be more convenient (and simpler) than our OTS-based protocol.
For this reason, we decided to present alternative MTS-based protocols that will allow us a fair comparison and a complement to our
OTS-based proposal.

One of the benefits of using a MTS scheme at the Prover is that it
may be able to support multiple verifiers without sharing one pair of
public/private keys with each of them. This is because MTS schemes
are similar to the classic asymmetric cryptography and do not
suffer from the limitation in OTS schemes, which require updating
the OTS key pair per signature. Therefore, with MTS operations
supported by both the Prover and the Verifier, it is reasonable to
assume that the Prover holds the MTS private key for protecting
its attestation measurement, while the corresponding MTS public
key is known to all Verifiers. As a result, we simplify the remote
attestation scheme by removing the trusted third party and follow
the classical challenge-response model as shown in Figure 4. For
the intruder model, we assume again the Dolev-Yao Intruder model
[18].

**Figure 4: System model of multi-time HBS-based remote at-
testation.**

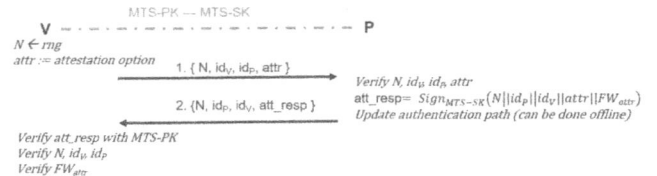

Figure 5: MTS-based remote attestation protocol details.

The MTS-based remote attestation protocol replaces the underlying conventional asymmetric crypto algorithm with the hash-
based MTS signatures scheme. The MTS-based approach has the
following assumptions:

- V and P have an established trusted relationship in terms of
a pair of MTS keys (P holds the private key $MTS-SK$ and V
holds the corresponding public key $MTS-PK$); $MTS-SK$
is not accessible by attackers and only P can read/update it.
- P and V have identifiers that can uniquely identify each
other; and they are different.

The protocol flow is straightforward and includes two message
exchanges between V and P as in Figure 5.

(1) $V \rightarrow P$: $\{N, id_V, id_P, attr\}$

Message 1 is an attestation request from V to P. V generates a fresh nonce N to initiate a fresh protocol session and
specifies $attr$.

(2) $P \rightarrow V$: $\{N, id_P, id_V, att\_resp\}$

Message 2 is the attestation response from P to V. P computes
its attestation response as in Equation 2.

$$att\_resp = Sign_{MTS\text{-}SK_1}(N||id_P||id_V||FW_{attr}) \qquad (2)$$

The signature att_resp guarantees the integrity and authenticity of the attestation response message. Also, all the session
information is confirmed and protected by P's signature so
that misbinding attack and spoofing attack are mitigated.
After sending Message 2 to V, P may update its local authentication path. Note that this path update can be performed
off-line, at a convenient time. The only restriction is that
it should be completed before the next time using the MTS
private key $MTS-SK$. Alternatively, we remark that a set
containing a certain number of future authentication paths
can be pre-computed, if this is convenient for the application.

(3) V parses Message 2

Upon receiving Message 2, V first verifies the signature
att_resp with $MTS-PK$. Then V verifies if id_V is its own
identifier and if N and id_P in Message 2 are from Message 1.
The output of the protocol is the attestation response FW_{attr}
protected by the signature.

Parameter	m	n	w	h
128-bit classical security	16	16	4	16
128-bit post-quantum security	32	32	16	16

Table 2: Suggested HBS parameters

Algorithm	ECDSA	OTS	MTS (Classical)	MTS (PQC)
Parameter n	–	16	16	32
Parameter w	–	4	4	16
KeyGen (ms)	1657	221	N/A	N/A
Sign (ms)	1777	2	90	600
Verify (ms)	3315	140	157	594
UpAuthPath (ms)	N/A	N/A	721	3800

Table 3: Latency of HBS and ECDSA on Arduino 101

5 PROTOTYPE AND PERFORMANCE EVALUATION

Prototypes of the proposed protocols have been developed in C language to validate the feasibility of the HBS-based remote attestation on resource-constrained devices. Specifically, in the prototype, the three parties have the following settings:

- P: Arduino 101 (32 MHz clock, 24 kB SRAM) [5] + WiFi 101 Shield [6]
- V and TTP: Laptop (Ubuntu) (2.4 GHz Intel Core i7)
- Communication technology: WiFi

The main challenge relates to P's limited hardware capabilities. Our focus is to validate whether even an Arduino 101 would be able to execute the protocols and then evaluate their overhead (both latency and memory-wise). The protocols presented in this paper can provide different security levels, i.e., classical security or post-quantum security, depending on the parameters chosen by the underlying HBS crypto algorithms shown in Table 2 [14]. Thus, different values of n and w with the same $\mathcal{H} = 16$ are explored. Here $\mathcal{H}$ is the height of the XMSS tree and indicates the ability to issue up to 2^{16} signatures, which is considered acceptable for most applications. The employed hash function is SHA2-256 [36], which has the output truncated to 128 bits for the classical security level setting and fully consumed (256 bits) in the post-quantum setting.

We investigated WiFi, Bluetooth and Bluetooth Low Energy (BLE) [12] as candidate communication methods. Bluetooth adopts a master-slave paradigm, which assigns to a communicating entity either a master role or a slave role. However, the OTS-based scheme requires P to act as both master (with respect to TTP) and slave (with respect to V). Few Arduino Bluetooth Shields on the market support two or more Bluetooth connections at the same time and switching roles between the master and the slave usually takes considerable time. Hence, Bluetooth did not meet the requirements for our prototype. BLE inherits the communication paradigm of Bluetooth (with energy-saving features) and limits the maximum packet payload to 20 bytes, which is too small comparing to the size of the messages our protocols exchange (see Table 4 and Table 6). Therefore, BLE is not suitable for the prototype either. Finally, we chose WiFi as the underlying communication method given its easy setup and high throughput. The network topology used in the prototype is straightforward: one LAN is setup to enable the communication between an Arduino 101 and a laptop. V is one hop away from P with minimum, maximum and average ping times of 5.7 ms, 268.3 ms, and 15.9 ms over 100 trials.

5.1 Performance Evaluation

In the performance evaluation of our protocols, we first benchmarked the high level OTS and MTS operations (i.e., key generation, signing, verifying, updating authentication path) on Arduino 101.

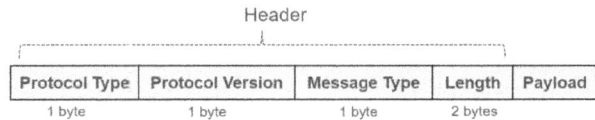

Figure 6: Message format of HBS-based attestation protocols.

Parameter	Msg 1	Msg 2	Msg 3	Msg 4
$w = 4$	1426	2612	1407	2541
$w = 16$	898	1556	879	1485

Table 4: Size of messages (bytes) for the OTS-based remote attestation protocol ($n = 16, h = 16$).

As a comparison, we also include the benchmark of EC-DSA operations to provide a comparison with classical schemes. Table 3 shows the results of the average of 100 tests. One of the bottlenecks is the MTS key generation (since it requires building the associated Merkle tree), which would take approximately 7.4 hours on Arduino 101. Therefore, in the prototype, MTS keys are expected to be generated in a large platform and then transferred (hard-coded) to the constrained device. Note that the latency of signature generation and verification tends to be stable across the tests, but the latency of updating authentication path varies significantly depending on which leaf node is being used to sign the message. In our work, we use the method described in [15] to update the authentication path. This method is efficient and has a well-defined worst-case cost (see Theorem 1 in [15]): it requires storing at most $(3.5\mathcal{H} - 4)$ nodes and the computation of at most $\mathcal{H}/2$ leaf nodes and $3/2(\mathcal{H} - 3) + 1$ inner nodes. Note that the worst case happens after signing with the $2^{\mathcal{H}} - 1$ leaf node, i.e. the center of the tree, as the authentication path is significantly different from the previous one. In the following assessment, we only present the average of updating authentication path for the first 100 leaf nodes. From our experiments, it is possible to conclude that the OTS operations are more efficient than ECDSA in terms of latency.

The network packets implemented in the prototype follows the format specified in Figure 6: *Header* includes protocol type, protocol version, message type and message length; and *Payload* is the contents defined in Section 4.1 and Section 4.2.

The OTS-based remote attestation protocol includes four messages. The protocol is implemented on Arduino 101 (with WiFi 101

Parameter	Msg 1	Msg 2	Msg 3	Msg 4	Overall
$w = 4$	7	586	31	118	742
$w = 16$	5	1059	51	232	1347

Table 5: Latency (ms) of OTS-based remote attestation protocol on Arduino 101 ($n = 16, h = 16$).

MTS Remote Attestation	Classical		Post-quantum	
	Latency (ms)	Size (bytes)	Latency (ms)	Size (bytes)
Msg 1	2	45	37	45
Msg 2 (include update_auth_path)	890	1405	4414	2733
Msg 2 (exclude update_auth_path)	169	1405	653	2733
Update authentication path	721	N/A	3761	N/A
Overall (exclude update_auth_path)	171	N/A	690	N/A

Table 6: Performance of the MTS-based remote attestation protocol on the Arduino 101 using classical security parameters ($n = 16, w = 4, h = 16$) and post-quantum security parameters ($n = 32, w = 16, h = 16$)

Shield) as P, and a Linux laptop (both V and TTP). Table 4 shows the size of each message (with HBS parameter $n = 16$) and Table 5 shows the average processing time of 100 tests on P. From both storage and latency viewpoint, Message 2 has the largest overhead and is the bottleneck.

For the MTS-based approach, the prototype is implemented using HBS parameters with classical security strength ($n = 16$ and $w = 4$) and post-quantum security strength ($n = 32$ and $w = 16$). As it is impractical to let the Arduino 101 (P) generate the MTS key pair(s), hard-coded MTS private/public keys are used to satisfy the trust assumptions. In practice, we can allow other powerful devices to generate the MTS key pairs for the embedded device.

Table 6 shows the performance of the MTS-based scheme on Arduino 101. The latency is the average of 100 consecutive tests. We use the first 100 nodes of the XMSS tree (with height $h = 16$). The authentication path update is a process that can happen off-line (at any time before the next signature is issued) as stressed in Section 4.2. However, for the purpose of the simulation, the authentication path was being executed immediately after constructing Message 2. Table 6 shows that the biggest concern comes from updating authentication path.

6 PROTOCOL COMPARISON AND ANALYSIS

In this section, we present a comprehensive comparison on the HBS-based remote attestation proposals with respect to latency and memory performance, and security. Finally, recommendations on the usage of the protocols are provided.

6.1 Latency

The performance evaluation focuses on the Prover side as we consider it a resource-constrained device. The execution time of the underlying signature operations are discussed and compared here as they intrinsically relate to the overall protocol performance.

In terms of latency, OTS operations are more efficient than MTS operations. As shown in Table 3, the OTS key generation is much faster than the MTS key generation, which becomes impractical on Arduino 101. OTS signing is also much more efficient than MTS signing, while OTS signature verification is slightly faster than the MTS counterpart. The execution time for most HBS operations is quite stable, except for the authentication path update, which varies significantly depending on which leaf node is being used. From the benchmark conducted on Arduino 101, the minimum time for the authentication path update (e.g., using the first leaf node) is more than twice of the MTS signing time.

However, if we consider the remote attestation protocol as a whole, the MTS-based remote attestation scheme (excluding updating authentication path operation) is faster than the OTS-based scheme. Note that, in certain scenarios (e.g., DoS attack), P might be forced to update the authentication path frequently. As the latency of the authentication path update varies significantly and can be very slow at certain points, it might become a deal killer for the adoption of the MTS-based scheme in the scope of certain applications. To mitigate the impact of updating the authentication path, one possible option is to use a smaller XMSS tree in the MTS scheme (thus ensuring an always-fast authentication path update) at the cost of refreshing MTS key pair(s) regularly. In this context, once the key is approaching its limit of signatures, a private key could be used to sign the public key of a new XMSS key pair instead of a message. Then, new attestations could be achieved by signing messages using this new key pair. This approach of course leads to an important stateful requirement (i.e. keep track of the current MTS key pair). In case the key generation time is critical, the protocol can be instantiated with $XMSS^{MT}$, which offers a virtually unlimited number of signatures per key pair (2^{60}). On the other hand, the protocol execution time of the OTS-based scheme is completely stable and simply avoids all complications related to the authentication path update in the MTS-based approach.

Comparing to traditional TPM-based attestation approaches with similar classical security level, our approaches show very competitive results. According to [41], many TPM commands, including the TPM quote, take approximately one second to complete. This conclusion is consistent with the benchmark collected in [30], where the latency measurement of the TPM quote is 972.7 ms on an HP dc5750 PC, which uses an AMD Athlon64 X2 Dual Core 4200+ processor running at 2.2 GHz, and a v1.2 Broadcom BCM0102 TPM. [16] investigates trusted computing on embedded systems and provides measurements of the TPM quote, which takes about 6000 ms on a Raspberry Pi with 700MHz ARMv6 core in a Broadcom BCM283 SoC with 256 MB. With a much less powerful embedded device Arduino 101 (32 MHz Curie core), our OTS-based remote attestation scheme costs approximately 742 ms with $w = 4$, and the MTS-based scheme is even faster as shown in Table 6 when assuming that the authentication path update is done offline.

6.2 Memory Consumption

Different HBS parameter settings lead to distinctive performance in terms of latency and memory. For $n = 32$, thus providing 128 bits of post-quantum security, the memory requirement is always larger than for $n = 16$. As for the OTS-based attestation scheme, Table 4 and Table 5 show that $w = 4$ has faster execution time at the cost of larger message sizes; while $w = 16$ makes the protocol more memory efficient yet less latency efficient. All these available trade-offs should also be considered an interesting advantage to our HBS-based remote attestation protocols as they allow users to chose parameter w so that it meets certain storage/latency requirements. Comparing to the MTS-based scheme (with same $w = 4, n = 16$), the OTS-based scheme has bigger messages and requires larger memory for the message processing. But on the other side, the MTS-based approach may require the maintenance of the XMSS tree locally (depending on its height) or some other quantities to facilitate the authentication path update process as needed for the method in [15].

6.3 Security Property

The two HBS-based remote attestation protocols may accommodate different security requirements. The proper use of hash-based signatures provides integrity and authenticity guarantees. Most importantly, these protocols are able to provide an affordable post-quantum protection with proper HBS parameters. The Arduino 101's limited SRAM (24kB) is the bottleneck for supporting HBS post-quantum parameters. Table 6 shows that enabling post-quantum protection leads to a significant increase in memory and latency requirements. Besides, the OTS-based scheme is resistant to DoS attacks and offers privacy protection in a lightweight and scalable fashion as discussed in Section 4.1.

Overall, our HBS-based attestation schemes outperform TPM-based attestation solutions as our constructions offer post-quantum security capabilities. Another benefit is that with the underlying HBS cryptographic algorithms, the proposed schemes can support both classical and post-quantum security requirements. With that being said, it is possible to deploy the HBS-based protocol on devices with classical security parameters as an initial configuration. When post-quantum protection becomes effectively required, it will be easy to upgrade the security protections by simply tuning the parameters accordingly.

6.4 Usage Recommendations

As discussed previously, due to the intrinsic features of OTS operations and MTS operations (e.g., signing, verification and updating authentication path), the OTS-based remote attestation protocol and the MTS-based remote attestation protocol are suitable for different application scenarios.

The OTS-based scheme is suitable for the usages that require a constant latency or, more importantly, when the frequency of the remote attestation requests is high. This is because in the OTS-based scheme the Prover does not need to update the authentication path, whose performance has significant variation. Besides, when privacy is concerned, the OTS-based protocol can provide privacy preserving through the TTP's assistance. One exemplar usage of the OTS-based scheme is Vehicle-to-Everything (V2X) networks. The On-Board-Unit (OBU) in the vehicle sends *periodic* beacon messages (e.g., Basic Safety Message, Cooperative Awareness Message), which puts a limit on the execution time of the remote attestation

operation, requires constant latency, and ideally should protect the privacy of the user associated to such vehicle.

On the other hand, the MTS-based scheme can accommodate use cases that require an infrequent but fast attestation service. For example, it is suitable for applications that require the Prover to react fast to an attestation request and allow the Prover to leave the authentication path update operation to be done later. These characteristics make the MTS-based remote attestation scheme suitable for mission-critical emergency tasks that are executed infrequently. In such an emergency task, both the correct execution of the task, which requires the platform integrity as a prerequisite, and the fast response are essential. With these requirements, the MTS-based remote attestation may provide a fast and accurate guarantee of the platform integrity.

7 CONCLUSION

Trustworthiness is a critical requirement in IoT applications and remote attestation is one effective way to achieve it. Existent remote attestation protocols do not satisfy all requirements for future IoT applications, such as quantum resistance and performance that meets the limited low-end devices capabilities.

In this work, two remote attestation protocols based on Hash-Based Signatures (HBS) schemes are presented to solve the aforementioned problems. One is based on one-time HBS and requires from the Prover solely one-time HBS operations (i.e. very efficient operations). This protocol also proposes robust embedded techniques to refresh one-time keys that allow multiple attestations. The other protocol is based on multi-time HBS and does not require a TTP. On the other hand, it requires the execution of the authentication path update process which can be seen a more expensive operation. We remark, however, that this process can be performed offline as it does not depend at all on the attestation content.

Both schemes are tailored for IoT devices. Our prototypes based on state-of-the-art HBS schemes (XMSS and WOTS+) running on highly constrained devices (Arduino 101) show that the proposed schemes are more efficient than traditional TPM-based attestation for the same (classical) security level. Additionally, our protocols based on HBS schemes can accommodate post-quantum capabilities depending on the selected parameters, something impossible to current TPM-based attestation mechanisms based on classical cryptography.

In short, the proposed protocols and the comprehensive assessment presented in this work represent a promising framework for future IoT remote attestation mechanisms.

REFERENCES

[1] Sedat Akleylek, Nina Bindel, Johannes Buchmann, Juliane Krämer, and Giorgia Azzurra Marson. 2016. An Efficient Lattice-based Signature Scheme with Provably Secure Instantiation. In *International Conference on Cryptology in Africa*. Springer, 44–60.
[2] R. Alleaume. 2007. SECOQC White Paper on Quantum Key Distribution and Cryptography. (2007).
[3] Moreno Ambrosin, Hossein Hosseini, Kalikinkar Mandal, Mauro Conti, and Radha Poovendran. 2016. Despicable me (ter): Anonymous and Fine-grained Metering Data Reporting with Dishonest Meters. In *IEEE Conference on Communications and Network Security (CNS)*. 163–171.
[4] Megumi Ando, Joshua D Guttman, Alberto R Papaleo, and John Scire. 2016. Hash-Based TPM Signatures for the Quantum World. In *International Conference on Applied Cryptography and Network Security*. Springer, 77–94.

[5] Arduino. [n. d.]. Arduino 101. ([n. d.]). https://www.arduino.cc accessed 2018-01-03.
[6] Arduino and ATMEL. [n. d.]. Arduino WiFi 101 Shield. ([n. d.]). https://www.arduino.cc/en/Main/ArduinoWiFiShield101 accessed 2017-09-12.
[7] Frederik Armknecht, Ahmad-Reza Sadeghi, Steffen Schulz, and Christian Wachsmann. 2013. A Security Framework for the Analysis and Design of Software Attestation. In Proceedings of ACM Conference on Computer & Communications Security. 1–12.
[8] Paulo S. L. M. Barreto, Patrick Longa, Michael Naehrig, Jefferson E. Ricardini, and Gustavo Zanon. 2016. Sharper Ring-LWE Signatures. IACR Cryptology ePrint Archive (2016), 1026.
[9] C. H. Bennett and G. Brassard. 1984. Quantum Cryptography: Public Key Distribution and Coin Tossing. In Proceedings of IEEE International Conference on Communication Systems and Signal Processing. New York, 175–179.
[10] Daniel J. Bernstein, Johannes Buchmann, and Erik Dahmen. 2009. Post-Quantum Cryptography. Springer-Verlag.
[11] Benoît Bertholon, Sébastien Varrette, and Pascal Bouvry. 2011. Certicloud: a Novel TPM-based Approach to Ensure Cloud IaaS Security. In IEEE International Conference on Cloud Computing (CLOUD). 121–130.
[12] SIG Bluetooth. 2010. Bluetooth Core Specification version 4.0. Specification of the Bluetooth System (2010).
[13] Ferdinand Brasser, Kasper B Rasmussen, Ahmad-Reza Sadeghi, and Gene Tsudik. 2016. Remote Attestation for Low-End Embedded Devices: the Prover's Perspective. In IEEE Design Automation Conference (DAC). 1–6.
[14] Johannes Buchmann, Erik Dahmen, and Andreas Hülsing. 2011. XMSS – a Practical Forward Secure Signature Scheme Based on Minimal Security Assumptions. In PQCrypto. Springer, 117–129.
[15] Johannes Buchmann, Erik Dahmen, and Michael Schneider. 2008. Merkle Tree Traversal Revisited. 63–78.
[16] Bernard Candaele, Dimitrios Soudris, and Iraklis Anagnostopoulos. 2015. Trusted Computing for Embedded Systems. Springer.
[17] Anupam Datta, Jason Franklin, Deepak Garg, and Dilsun Kaynar. 2009. A Logic of Secure Systems and its Application to Trusted Computing. In Security and Privacy, 2009 30th IEEE Symposium on. IEEE, 221–236.
[18] Danny Dolev and Andrew Yao. 1983. On the Security of Public Key Protocols. IEEE Transactions on Information Theory 29, 2 (1983), 198–208.
[19] Léo Ducas, Alain Durmus, Tancrède Lepoint, and Vadim Lyubashevsky. 2013. Lattice Signatures and Bimodal Gaussians. Springer, Berlin, Heidelberg, 40–56.
[20] C. Elliott, A. Colvin, D. Pearson, O. Pikalo, J. Schlafer, and H. Yeh. 2005. Current status of the DARPA Quantum Network. (2005). https://arxiv.org/ftp/quant-ph/papers/0503/0503058.pdf accessed 2018-01-03.
[21] Matthieu Finiasz. 2011. Parallel-CFS. Springer, Berlin, Heidelberg, 159–170.
[22] Trusted Computing Group. 2011. TPM Main Specification. (2011). https://trustedcomputinggroup.org/tpm-main-specification accessed 2018-01-03.
[23] Lov K. Grover. 1996. A Fast Quantum Mechanical Algorithm for Database Search. In Proceedings of the 28th ACM symposium on Theory of Computing. 212–219.
[24] Andreas Hülsing. 2013. W-OTS+ – Shorter Signatures for Hash-Based Signature Schemes. Springer, Berlin, Heidelberg, 173–188.
[25] Chongkyung Kil, Emre C Sezer, Ahmed M Azab, Peng Ning, and Xiaolan Zhang. 2009. Remote Attestation to Dynamic System Properties: Towards Providing Complete System Integrity Evidence. In IEEE International Conference on Dependable Systems & Networks. 115–124.
[26] N. Koblitz. 1987. Elliptic Curve Cryptosystems. Math. Comp. 48, 177 (1987), 203–209.
[27] Tom Lawton. 2014. Meter Operations in A Post AMI World. (2014).
[28] Yanlin Li, Jonathan M McCune, and Adrian Perrig. 2011. VIPER: Verifying the Integrity of PERipherals' Firmware. In Proceedings of the 18th ACM Conference on Computer and Communications Security. 3–16.
[29] Jonathan M McCune, Yanlin Li, Ning Qu, Zongwei Zhou, Anupam Datta, Virgil Gligor, and Adrian Perrig. 2010. TrustVisor: Efficient TCB Reduction and Attestation. In IEEE Symposium on Security and Privacy. 143–158.
[30] Jonathan M McCune, Bryan J Parno, Adrian Perrig, Michael K Reiter, and Hiroshi Isozaki. 2008. Flicker: An Execution Infrastructure for TCB Minimization. In ACM SIGOPS Operating Systems Review, Vol. 42. ACM, 315–328.
[31] Patrick McDaniel and Stephen McLaughlin. 2009. Security and Privacy Challenges in the Smart Grid. IEEE Security & Privacy 7, 3 (2009).
[32] David McGrew, Panos Kampanakis, Scott Fluhrer, Stefan-Lukas Gazdag, Denis Butin, and Johannes Buchmann. 2016. State Management for Hash-Based Signatures. Springer International Publishing, 244–260.
[33] Ralph C. Merkle. 1979. Secrecy, Authentication and Public Key Systems. Ph.D. Dissertation. Stanford.
[34] V. S. Miller. 1986. Use of Elliptic Curves in Cryptography. In Advances in Cryptology. Springer-Verlag, New York, USA, 417–426.
[35] National Institute of Standards and Technology. [n. d.]. Post-quantum Crypto Project. ([n. d.]). http://csrc.nist.gov/groups/ST/post-quantum-crypto/ accessed 2017-09-12.
[36] National Institute of Standards and Technology. 2012. FIPS 180-4 - Secure Hash Standard (SHS). (2012). http://csrc.nist.gov/publications/fips/fips180-4/fips-180-4.pdf accessed 2018-01-03.
[37] Siani Pearson, Marco Casassa Mont, and Stephen Crane. 2005. Persistent and Dynamic Trust: Analysis and the Related Impact of Trusted Platforms. In International Conference on Trust Management. Springer, 355–363.
[38] Global Platform. 2011. The Trusted Execution Environment: Delivering Enhanced Security at a Lower Cost to the Mobile Market. White Paper (February 2011).
[39] European Comission CORDIS Community Research and Development Information Service. [n. d.]. PQCrypto Project. ([n. d.]). http://cordis.europa.eu/project/rcn/194347_en.html accessed 2017-09-12.
[40] R. L. Rivest, A. Shamir, and L. M. Adleman. 1978. A Method for Obtaining Digital Signatures and Public-Key Cryptosystems. In Communications of the ACM, Vol. 21. 120–126.
[41] Nuno Santos, Rodrigo Rodrigues, Krishna P Gummadi, and Stefan Saroiu. 2012. Policy-Sealed Data: A New Abstraction for Building Trusted Cloud Services.. In USENIX Security Symposium. 175–188.
[42] Arvind Seshadri, Mark Luk, and Adrian Perrig. 2008. SAKE: Software Attestation for Key Establishment in Sensor Networks. In International Conference on Distributed Computing in Sensor Systems. Springer, 372–385.
[43] Arvind Seshadri, Mark Luk, Adrian Perrig, Leendert van Doorn, and Pradeep Khosla. 2006. SCUBA: Secure Code Update by Attestation in sensor networks. In Proceedings of the 5th ACM Workshop on Wireless Security. 85–94.
[44] Arvind Seshadri, Adrian Perrig, Leendert Van Doorn, and Pradeep Khosla. 2004. SWATT: SoftWare-based ATTestation for Embedded Devices. In IEEE Symposium on Security and Privacy. 272–282.
[45] Mark Shaneck, Karthikeyan Mahadevan, Vishal Kher, and Yongdae Kim. 2005. Remote Software-based Attestation for Wireless Sensors. In European Workshop on Security in Ad-hoc and Sensor Networks. Springer, 27–41.
[46] P. W. Shor. 1997. Polynomial-Time Algorithms for Prime Factorization and Discrete Logarithms on a Quantum Computer. Society for Industrial and Applied Mathematics Journal on Computing 26, 5 (1997), 1484–1509.
[47] Hailun Tan, Wen Hu, and Sanjay Jha. 2011. A TPM-enabled Remote Attestation Protocol (TRAP) in Wireless Sensor Networks. In Proceedings of the 6th ACM Workshop on Performance Monitoring and Measurement of Heterogeneous Wireless and Wired Networks. 9–16.
[48] Song Tan, Debraj De, Wen-Zhan Song, Junjie Yang, and Sajal K Das. 2016. Survey of Security Advances in Smart Grid: A Data Driven Approach. IEEE Communications Surveys & Tutorials (2016).

IoTVerif: An Automated Tool to Verify SSL/TLS Certificate Validation in Android MQTT Client Applications

Khalid Alghamdi, Ali Alqazzaz, Anyi Liu, Hua Ming
Oakland University
Rochester, MI, USA
{kaalgham,aalqazzaz,anyiliu,ming}@oakland.edu

ABSTRACT

Developing secure Internet of Things (IoT) applications that are free of vulnerabilities and resilient against exploit is desirable for software developers and testers. In this paper, we present IoTVerif, an automated tool that can verify SSL/TLS (Secure Socket Layer/Transport Layer Security) X.509 certificate validation of IoT messaging protocols utilized by real-world IoT client applications. IoTVerif does not require any prior knowledge about the messaging protocol, but simply correlates the observed network trace of an application with its execution context. IoTVerif helps IoT client application developers identify the SSL/TLS vulnerabilities based on certificate validation. We specifically target MQTT, a broker-based protocol that has attracted increasing popularity in the IoT application market.

We used IoTVerif to analyze the server X.509 certificate validation in 15 well-known MQTT client applications. Our result revealed that 5 (33.3%) of the applications examined are vulnerable to man-in-the-middle (MITM) and/or TLS renegotiation attacks. Our result also shows that IoTVerif can generate a Finite State Machine (FSM) that depicts the interaction between the application and the IoT broker and automatically identifies various attacks. It has the potential to reverse-engineer the emerging IoT messaging protocols and identify the vulnerabilities in the IoT applications.

CCS CONCEPTS

• Security and privacy → Mobile and wireless security; • Networks → *Protocol testing and verification*;

KEYWORDS

MQTT protocol; Model checking; SSL/TLS; Certificate validation

ACM Reference format:
Khalid Alghamdi, Ali Alqazzaz, Anyi Liu, Hua Ming. 2018. IoTVerif: An Automated Tool to Verify SSL/TLS Certificate Validation in Android MQTT Client Applications. In *Proceedings of Eighth ACM Conference on Data and Application Security and Privacy, Tempe, AZ, USA, March 19–21, 2018 (CODASPY '18)*, 8 pages.
https://doi.org/10.1145/3176258.3176334

1 INTRODUCTION

The importance of IoT security is widely understood and agreed upon [16]. SSL/TLS protocols are the most commonly used mechanisms for ensuring the security and privacy of the network communication and the user data integrity from MITM [23] attack. They have gone through a lot of upgrading since they were first introduced, for instance, SSLv1.0, SSLv2.0, SSLv30, and TLSv1.0. SSL/TLS security depends on the validation of the server X.509 certificate in the MQTT client application. The server sends the X.509 certificate to the client during the TLS handshake phase, which is responsible for authentication and exchanging certificates between the MQTT client and the broker for necessary secure sessions. Certificate validation depends on verifying the certificate chain, subjectCN (Common Name), signature, and certificate validity.

In this paper, we present IoTVerif, an automated tool that aims at verifying SSL/TLS X.509 certificate validation of IoT messaging protocols utilized by real-world IoT MQTT client applications and thus identifying the vulnerabilities in the applications. IoTVerif is based on the key observation that the network traffic of an application is *highly correlatable* with the execution context of an IoT applications (e.g., the API calls). By monitoring the execution of applications and their network trace, a finite state machine (FSM), which depicts the interaction between the application and the message broker via the protocol, is generated and then streamlined to a formal tool to be verified. Because IoTVerif learns the inbound and outbound messages and infers the states of the protocol, it does not require any prior knowledge about the protocol. We have tested IoTVerif with real-world applications that use the popular protocol, namely MQTT. We show that our tool can generate the FSM accurately. Furthermore, it leverages the general model checking tool to automatically identify various attacks, such as MITM and TLS Renegotiation.

The reminder of this paper is organized as follows. Section 2 briefly describes the MQTT protocol and other techniques used in this paper. Section 3 describes the scope of the problem and defines the terminologies. Section 4 presents the system architecture of IoTVerif and details its working mechanism. Section 5 evaluates the effectiveness of IoTVerif. Section 6 covers the related work. Section 7 concludes the paper.

2 BACKGROUND

Our security verification focuses on verifying the validation of SSL/TLS certification of Android IoT applications utlizing MQTT protocol. These applications used Eclipse Paho project. To perform the task of verifying these MQTT clients applications, we need to have a deep understanding of the MQTT protocol, SSL/TLS protocol, and the tools used in this work.

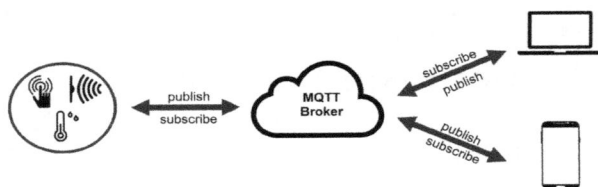

Figure 1: MQTT architecture for publishing and subscribing

2.1 MQTT

MQTT is a asynchronous, lightweight, and based on publish-subscribe architecture protocol. According to the way messages are delivered, MQTT messaging protocols can be categorized as *broker-based* protocol [2] and designed for machine-to-machine (M2M) communication. The broker controls the distribution of the information as illustrated in Fig. 1. It stores, forwards, filters, and prioritizes publish requests from the *publisher* (the message producer) to the *subscriber* (the message consumer). Clients switch the role between publisher and subscriber depending on their objectives. MQTT provides Three levels of quality of service (QoS), QoS 0, 1, and 2. The QoS is an agreement between the message sender and receiver regarding the guarantees of delivering the message [18].

According to a recent survey [16], MQTT protocol has been ranked the most popular broker-based protocol among IoT messaging protocols, which demonstrates its advantages for interacting with resource-constrained IoT devices over low bandwidth and unreliable environments.

2.2 SSL/TLS & Android

The SSL and its successor TLS are cryptographic protocols. The fundamental goal of SSL/TLS is to protect network communication and data integrity from tampering. To start a secure connection, the client must securely obtain the server X.509 certificate and extract the server public key, which must be signed by a Certificate Authority (CA). When the client receives the X.509 certificate from the server, the client must check and validate the certificate components [9]. The certificate basic validation includes a) validating that the subject (CN) of X.509 certificate and the URL matches; b) validating that the certificate is signed by the trusted CA; c) validating that the signature is correct; and d) validating that the certificate is not expired. Furthermore, most of the messaging providers of MQTT, such as HiveMQ [14] and Microsoft Azure [5], recommend MQTT client developers use the highest TLS version and not use SSLv3 or any prior versions. The reason is that all SSL versions are considered broken and vulnerable to well-known attacks, while TLSv1.0 is exposed to TLS Renegotiation attack.

Android SDK 4.0 and later provides several packages to establish the connection and access the network, such as java.net, javax.net, android.net or org.apache.http. Android allows developers to customize the SSL/TLS environment. However, if the SSL/TLS is not correctly implemented, the user sensitive data may leak via vulnerable SSL. Fahl *et al.* [12] describe SS/TLS (mis-)use cases, such as trusting all certificates and allowing all host names, of such customization that could cause a broken SSL channel.

3 PROBLEM SCOPE & TERMINOLOGIES

The primary goal of IoTVerif is to generate a finite state machine that depicts the interaction between an IoT application and the message broker, verifies the security properties with respect to the usage of SSL/TLS and identifies the vulnerabilities in IoT applications. In particular, we analyzed the applications' vulnerabilities against *TLS Renegotiation* [21] and MITM attacks. The *key* observation is that the Android application level API invocations essentially lead to communication traffic that can be monitored at the network layer, and vice versa.

3.1 Motivating Example

To understand our problem better, we illustrate these concepts with an actual attacking scenario that leverages the vulnerability of MQTT applications and launches an *MITM* attack through the Android application, MQTT Viewer (IoT Client). It is a simple client-side application that controls various IoT sensors, such as reading from humidity sensors and sound sensors, and turns on/off LED lights through Wi-Fi. Fig. 2 shows the code snippet of MyMQTT and the network traffic between the application and MQTT broker, the major responsibility of which is to exchange data between the application and IoT sensors through the broker through publishing and subscribing. The publishing- and subscribing-related *Paho* API calls are highlighted. For simplicity, we omit the functionalities of the application, such as data processing, and their corresponding network traffic. In addition, we abstract away some details such as the class definition, and consolidate relevant application-side API calls.

As illustrated in Fig. 2(a), a normal session between the application and MQTT broker always starts with a client-side API invocation connect that triggers the TCP handshake (packets 1 - 3) followed by MQTT connection (packets 4 - 7). Then, the invocations of publish cause the traffic that publishes the data with the broker (packets 8 and 9). After that, the network traffic (packets 10 and 11) cause the API invocation of messageArrived. Finally, the invocations of disconnect terminates the session with the broker (packets 12-18). Fig. 2(b) shows a *TLS Renegotiation* attack [21] on the same application, which use an TLS port. The invocation of connect triggers the TCP handshake (packets 1 - 3) followed by TLS handshake (packets 4 - 13). TLS handshake allows the application and broker to authenticate each other and negotiate the encryption algorithm and cryptographic keys. Then the application and broker exchange data (packet 14 - 18). The circled network packets (packets 19 and 20) show the beginning of the TLS renegotiation handshake. The cause of the second TLS handshake is that we inject plain text in packet 18 payload to force the client to renegotiate the TLS handshake with the broker. Then MITM attacker blocks *Hello Client* packet and form a new *Hello Client* using the client IP address. When the attacker finishes communicating with the broker, the blocked *Hello Client* will be released and sent to the broker. We performed the attack by creating our own Ruby module atop of BetterCap [6] tool.

We notice some security issues of MQTT client applications caused by either the developers' carelessness or malicious intention. For example, some applications are still using old versions of SSL/TLS, such as SSLv3 and TLSv1.0 which are known to be broken nowadays and vulnerable to various attacks [22]. TLSv1.1

Figure 2: MQTT-related Paha API calls and Network Trace

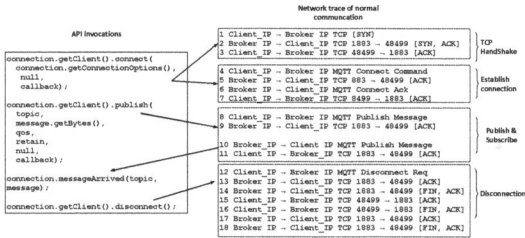

(a) MQTT-related Paha API calls and Network Trace of Normal Communication Over the Default Port (1883)

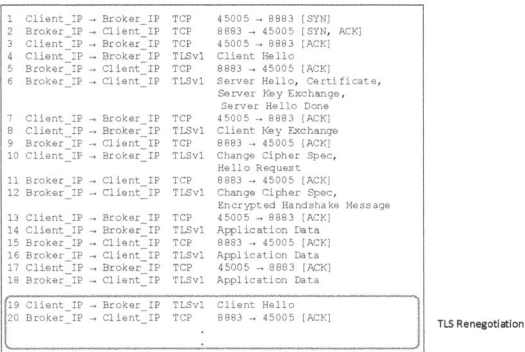

(b) Network Trace of Anomalous Communication Over Secure Port (8883)

and TLSv1.2 solve the security issue of renegotiation by adding a *renegotiation_info* extension to the *Client Hello* and *Server Hello* packets. If the extension is not present, the server does not support secure renegotiation [21]. Although most applications provide secure communication over TLSv1.1 or TLSv1.2, some do not validate the server certificate components as described in Section 2.2. Such checking prevents MITM attacks by ensuring the certificate was not changed during the transmission. If the application does not provide certificate checking, the attacker can replace the certificate during the transmission with his own and pretend to be the broker.

As mentioned, the primary goal of IoTVerif is to verify the security properties with respect to use of SSL/TLS by correlating the observed network traffic of an application with its execution context. From the network's perspective, we can easily identify the SSL/TLS version as illustrated in Fig. 2(b), which is too difficult to obtain from the application layer by using code instrumentation. However, the network traffic does not provide any information about whether the application validates the X.509 certificate components. Thus, to check the application certificate validation, we need to analyze and instrument the application layer. Therefore, we consider both network traffic and execution context layers to generate the finite state machine and verify the SSL/TLS validation of the application.

3.2 Terminologies

Let us consider the interaction between an application and the message broker. In particular, we focus on those APIs that directly

engage broker-based IoT protocol activities such as establishing connection, publishing, subscribing, and disconnecting the connection. We use $A = \{\alpha_1, \alpha_2, ..., \alpha_i\}$ to represent those APIs. The execution state of an application is closely related to the particular order of API invocations and their context. We extract the execution states using the technique of code instrumentation as described in Section 4.2. As a result, we propose the execution state of Android applications with regard to their respective API invocations, and define it as a four-tuple $S = \langle \Phi, M, I, R \rangle$, where Φ denotes the method that encompasses an API call, M denotes the certificate subjectCN validation, I denotes the certificate signature validation, and R denotes the certificate expiration.

From the network's perspective, we use $P = \{p_1, p_2, ..., p_j\}$ to represent the set of MQTT-based network packets. Correspondingly, an IoT connection session is denoted as $CS = \langle p_1, p_2, ..., p_l \rangle$, which is comprised of all the network packets in that session. A network packets fragment with the length of k is denoted as $NPF_{i,k} = \langle p_i, ..., p_{i+k} \rangle$, where $1 \leq i \leq l$. Based on these definitions, we formulate the finite state machine that depicts the interaction between the application and the message broker as MQTT-FSM, which is a five-tuple $\mathcal{F} = \langle Q, \Sigma, \delta, I, F \rangle$, where:

- Q is a finite set of states S;
- Σ is the set of session fragments $S_{i,k}$;
- $\delta \subseteq Q \times \Sigma \times Q$ is a set of transitions;
- $I \in Q$ is the initial state; and
- $F \in Q$ is the final state.

4 SYSTEM DESIGN

4.1 System Architecture

The system architecture of IoTVerif is illustrated in Fig. 3 and is comprised of four main components shown in shaded boxes. There are in total seven major steps to verify the security properties of MQTT application. The *Instrumentation Engine* takes the application (.apk) file as an input and statically analyzes the application and identifies and instruments the APIs that are directly involved in IoT-related functionalities, such as establishing connecting, publishing, subscribing, and ending connection (**step ❶**). It also identifies whether the application validates the broker X.509 certificate or not. Then IoTVerif launches the emulator, installs, and starts the instrumented application (**step ❷**). After that, a special Android application installed in the emulator, namely, Android tcpdump, sniffs the network traffic between the application and the broker (**step ❸**) and forwards it to the *Network Traffic Parser*. The *Network Traffic Parser* parses the traffic and identifies the SSL/TLS version and other network traffic related to communication between the client and broker. Using the result of the *Network Traffic Parser* (**step ❹**) and the *Instrumentation Engine* (**step ❺**), the *FSM Generator* generates MQTT-FSM and forwards it to the *Symbolic Model Checker* (**step ❻**), which takes security specifications and determines whether the IoT application is vulnerable to certain security exploits such as MITM and/or TLS Renegotiation attack (**step ❼**). The following subsections present the technical details of IoTVerif.

4.2 Instrumenting IoT App

To generate and verify the correct model, we need to properly answer at least three key questions: 1) how to *identify* all the relevant

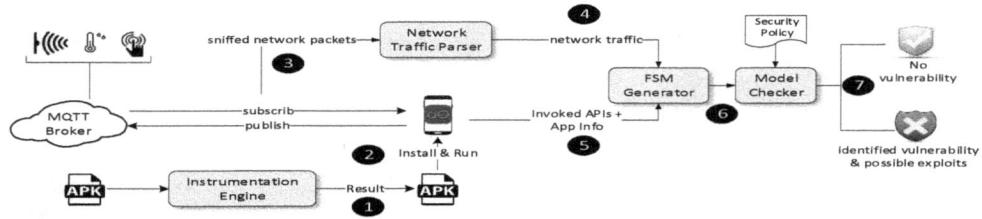

Figure 3: The system architecture of IoTVerif.

APIs with invocations that directly trigger the IoT-related network traces?; 2) how to *infer* the states of an application during its execution?; and 3) how to *correlate* these APIs with the particular network packets in a trace?

To answer the first two questions, we leverage the technique of code instrumentation, which has been widely used in Android application testing and security [3], and has demonstrated its advantages of enhancing testing with no knowledge of the code. In particular, because the Android SDK provides a set of IoT-related packages (e.g., Paho APIs), our instrumentation engine covers the well-defined IoT API calls. Based on their specification as well as our manual analysis with a number of IoT applications, we have obtained 4 commonly used IoT-related Paho APIs, *paho.android.service.MqttService.connect*, *paho.android.service.MqttService.publish*, *paho.client.mqttv3.internal.CommsCallback.messageArrived*, and *paho.android.service.MqttService.disconnect*. We found that most applications directly use them to facilitate IoT-related functionalities. In addition, the *instrumentation engine* instruments the server certificate validation methods in the application, for instance, `verify`, and `checkValidity` methods from *javax.security* library. These methods validate the certificate subject distinguish name (DN), and the certificate expiration, respectively.

To answer the third question, it is important to collect a substantial amount of network trace packets that achieve high code coverage for the IoT functionalities. To do that, we developed a simple and fully automated tool based on Monkey [25] to generate the network traces automatically. The manual effort is to provide the configuration settings for connecting the application with the broker. Specifically, we invoke the am command provided by Monkey to run the application and stop executing it after 60 seconds. To correlate the APIs α_i and the packet p_j, we define two heuristic relationships, namely, *prepare-for* and *lead-to*. The relationship *prepare-for* states that α_i triggers p_j. It can be observed in Fig. 2(a), when the invocation of *publish* triggers a segment of the network traffic (packet 8). The relationship *lead-to* states that α_i is triggered by p_j and can be observed in Fig. 2(a) when the invocation of *messageArrived* is triggered by a segment of the network traffic (packet 10).

We define the relationships of *prepare-for* and *lead-to* as follows:

- $\alpha_i \xmapsto{prepare-for} p_j$: $p_j.time - \alpha_i.time < \gamma$ and $\alpha_i.time \leq p_j.time \leq \alpha_{i+1}.time$
- $\alpha_i \xmapsto{lead-to} p_j$: $\alpha_i.time - p_j.time < \gamma$ and $\alpha_{i-1}.time \leq p_j.time \leq \alpha_i.time$

where $\alpha_i.time$ and $p_j.time$ refer to the time stamps of the API calls and the packet, respectively; while γ is a user-defined parameter for the timing window size. Because the mapping between α_i and p_j is one-to-many, a total number of k packets that satisfies the criteria *prepare-for* α_i or *lead-to* α_i forms the session segment $S_{j,k}$.

Algorithm 1 Constructing MQTT-FSM

1: **Inputs:**
    A network trace P and the set of states $\mathbb{S}$.
2: **Output:**
    The *MQTT-FSM* as a five-tuple, $\mathcal{F} = \langle Q, \Sigma, \delta, I, F \rangle$.
3: **Initialize:**
    $Q = \phi; \Sigma = \{\varepsilon\}; \delta = \phi; I = \phi; F = \phi;$
    $pre = NUL; post = NUL; e = \phi; i = 0;$
4: **loop:**
5: **for** *next* $p_i \in P$
6: **if** observe a $S_i \in \mathbb{S}$ && $S_i \notin Q$ **then**
7:     $Q = Q \cup \{S_i\};$
8:     /*Identifying different transitions*/
9:     **if** $S_i.I ==$ disconnect **then**
10:         $pre=S_i; F = post = S_F;$
11:     **else**
12:         $pre=S_i; post = look\_ahead(pre);$
13:     **end if**
14:     /*Combining session fragments*/
15:     Let NPF_1 and NPF_2 be two empty lists;
16:     $len1 = 0; len2 = 0;$
17:     **if** $\forall p_i \in P : \alpha_i \xmapsto{prepare-for} p_i$ **then**
18:         $NPF_1 = append(NPF_i, p_i); len1$++;
19:     **end if**
20:     **if** $\forall p_j \in P : \alpha_{i+1} \xmapsto{lead-to} p_j$ **then**
21:         $NPF_2 = append(NPF_i, p_i); len2$++;
22:     **end if**
23:     /*Updating alphabet set*/
24:     $e = concat(NPF_{i,len1}, NPF_{j,len2});$
25:     $\Sigma = \Sigma \cup \{e\};$
26:     /*Updating transition set*/
27:     $\delta = \delta \cup \{((pre, e), post)\};$
28:     i++;
29: **end if**
30: **end loop:**
31: Return $\langle Q, \Sigma, \delta, I, F \rangle;$

4.3 Generating MQTT-FSM

In essence, the key to constructing an FSM that depicts interaction between an IoT application and message broker is determining the states of the interaction. As we mentioned, we use a four-tuple S to approximate the states of the interaction, which is generated by the component of model generator.

Algorithm 1 describes the process of constructing the MQTT-FSM with the information of network trace and application state. Before running the algorithm, we first define a function, namely, *look_ahead*, which is looks ahead of the string and returns the next states. This function is similar to the *lookahead* function that is widely adopted in compiler-related techniques [13]. Two string functions, namely, *append* and *concat*, are also used. We further define a hypersthenic final state S_F. The algorithm treats the strings of the network traffic P and the API calls $\mathbb{S}$ as the input and the five-tuple $\langle Q, \Sigma, \delta, I, F \rangle$, i.e., the MQTT-FSM, as the output. First, it scans the packets and API calls and determines different transitions (lines 9 - 13). Then it identifies the network packets fragments NPF_1 and NPF_2 for two adjacent API calls, namely, α_i and α_{i+1}, respectively (lines 17 - 19 and lines 20 - 22). After that, it concatenates NPF_1 and NPF_2 as a new symbol e and includes it in the alphabet (lines 24 and 25). It also includes the transition $\{((pre, e), post)\}$ into the transition set Σ (line 27). Finally, it returns the constructed MQTT-FSM as a five-tuple.

Table 1: General CTL formulas

1	$\mathcal{M}, S \vDash AG(R = connect \rightarrow AX(R = publish$ $\vee \quad R = messagArrived$ $\vee \quad R = disconnect))$
2	$\mathcal{M}, S \vDash AG(R = connect \rightarrow AX(NT = e1e2$ $\vee \quad NT = e1e2e4))$
3	$\mathcal{M}, S \vDash AG(R = publish \rightarrow AX(R = publish$ $\vee \quad R = messageArrived$ $\vee \quad R = disconnect))$
4	$\mathcal{M}, S \vDash AG((NT = e1e2e4$ $\vee \quad NT = e3e4$ $\vee \quad NT = e3) \rightarrow AX(R = messageArrived))$
5	$\mathcal{M}, S \vDash AG(R = publish \rightarrow AX(NT = e3 \vee NT = e3e4))$

Table 2: Security CTL formulas

1	$\mathcal{M}, S \vDash AG(TLS = TRUE)$
2	$\mathcal{M}, S \vDash AG(TLSv >= 1)$
3	$\mathcal{M}, S \vDash AG(certCheckCN = TRUE)$
4	$\mathcal{M}, S \vDash AG(SignedCA = TRUE)$
5	$\mathcal{M}, S \vDash AG(checkSigCorr = TRUE)$
6	$\mathcal{M}, S \vDash AG(checkCAEXP = TRUE)$
7	$\mathcal{M}, S \vDash AG(\neg NT = RST \quad AU \quad R = disconnect)$
8	$\mathcal{M}, S \vDash AG(R = connect \rightarrow AF(R = connect \quad AU$ $R = disconnect))$
9	$\mathcal{M}, S \vDash AG(NT = e2 \rightarrow (TLS \wedge TLSv >= 1 \wedge SignedCA$ $\wedge \quad certCheckCN$ $\wedge \quad checkCAEXP))$

4.4 MQTT Security Properties

After MQTT-FSM is generated, the component of symbolic model checker converts it to a symbolic model and verifies the security properties for the model.

The properties are expressed in CTL [11]. Such properties can be used to check whether the MQTT application is vulnerable to security attacks, such as MITM and TLS Renegotiation attacks. We developed 14 CTL formulas based on the existence of the SSL/TLS certificate validation in the client applications and the interaction between the application and the network. The CTL formulas are divided into 2 categories. The first category verifies general properties such as the application API execution order and the network behavior, while the second category verifies security properties such as the existence of the TLS, the TLS version, the certificate validation, and the connection integrity.

Table 1 shows the general CTL formulas. In all formulas, $\mathcal{M}$ and S represent MQTT-FSM and the current state of MQTT-FSM, respectively. R is the variable that represents the API call and NT is used to denote the network traffic fragment. In the following, we explain the CTL formulas in Table 1. The first formula holds for all paths and future states, the connect API call will be followed by either publish or messageArrived or disconnect API call. Similarly with the third formula, the publish API call will be followed by either publish, messageArrived, or disconnect API call. The second formula holds for all paths and future states, the connect API call will be followed by network traffic e1e2 or e1e2e4. Similarly with the fifth formula, the publish API call will be followed by network traffic e3 or e3e4. The fourth formula holds for all paths and states, the network traffic e1e2e4 or e3e4 or e4 will trigger messageArrived API in the application.

Table 2 shows the security CTL formulas. These formulas use notations similar to the general CTL formulas. The first and second formulas hold for all paths and all states if the application provides TLS connection and the application use the latest TLS version respectively. The next four formulas hold for all paths and all states if the application validates the certificate subjectCN, certificate signature, signature correctness, and the validity of the certificate. The seventh formula, which verifies the connection integrity, holds for all paths and all states, the reset (RST) network packet will not appear *until* disconnect API call appears. The TCP RST flag is used to terminate the connection immediately, mostly because of a fatal error in the communication. The eighth formula holds for all paths and all future states, there is no second connect API call until disconnect API call appears. The last formula checks the TLS renegotiation handshake. It holds for all paths and future states, the TLS renegotiation network packet *e2* occurs over TLSv1.1 or TLSv1.2, and the application validates the server X.509 certificate.

5 EVALUATION

5.1 Experimental Setup

To evaluate the effectiveness of IoTVerif, we use real-world Android IoT applications as illustrated in Table 3. To obtain the appropriate apps for our evaluation, we first use Google Play Crawler [1] to crawl mobile applications from Google Play, and then only keep those with installation counts greater than 1000 and that were developed with MQTT Paho API. As a result, we eventually had 15 apps to test. The API calls are triggered by Monkey and executed inside Genymotion Emulator. The instrumentation engine of IoTVerif is developed based on FlowDroid [4]. The model generator is implemented by Java. The symbolic model check leverages *NuSMV* [8].

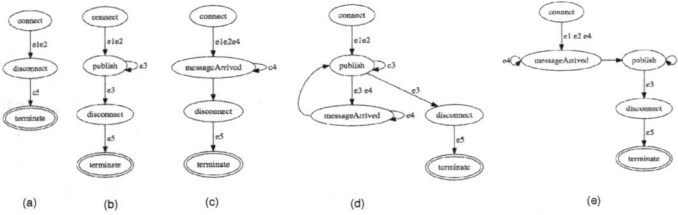

Figure 4: MQTT-FSM, which models both sides of application and network of Android application, namely, `MQTT Dashboard`.

Table 4: The Notations of MQTT-FSM Transitions

Notation	Structure of Traffic
e1	SYN(A, B)→SYN,ACK(B, A)→ACK(A, B)
e2	ClientHello(A, B)→
	ServerHello, Certificate, ServerKeyExchange, ServerHelloDone(B, A)→
	ACK(A, B)→ ClientKeyExchange(A,B)→ACK(B,A) →
	ChangeCipherSpec, HelloRequest(A,B) → ACK(B,A) →
	ChangeCipherSpec, EncryptedHandshakeMessage(B,A) → ACK(A,B)
e3	ApplicationData (A, B)→ACK (B, A)
e4	ApplicationData (B, A)→ACK (A, B)
e5	ApplicationData (A, B) →ACK (B, A) →FIN,ACK (B, A)→
	FIN,ACK (A, B) → ACK (B, A)→ACK (A, B)
NOTE : A = app , B = broker	

Table 3: The category, installs, app Name, version, size, and total number of activities for the 15 tested apps

Category	#install	App Package Name	Version	App size	Total # of Activities
Comm	50,000	net.routix.mqttdash	4.4	5.1 M	12
Tools	50,000	com.deepeshc.mqttrec	2.4	480 K	5
Tools	50,000	at.tripwire.mqtt.client	1.0	1.1 M	2
Tools	50,000	ru.esp8266.iotmanager	1.5.5	8.3 M	3
Tools	50,000	com.thn.iotmqttdashboard	1.9.3	3.3 M	20
Tools	10,000	net.nosybore.mqttpublishplugin	1.4.0	1.2 M	1
L&D	5,000	com.codifythings.universalmqttclient	1.1	5 M	7
Tools	5,000	com.vinmacro.vinmacromqtt	1.0	3.6 M	5
Tools	5,000	info.laptrinhpic.easycontrol.mqttplugin	1.0.2	1.2 M	2
Tools	5,000	net.sabamiso.android.simplemqttviewer	1.3	100.9 K	2
Tools	1,000	br.com.bintechnology.mqttclient	0.4.1	3.5 M	2
Comm	1,000	com.patterns.io.mqttpatterns	1.0	4.3 M	7
Tools	1,000	com.cmmakerclub.iot.cmmciotswitch	1.0	1.7 M	4
Tools	1,000	in.dc297.mqttclpro	2.3.1	2.7 M	9
Tools	1,000	com.hanzycanada.mqttspeed	0.05	7.5 M	8

The IoT platform is constructed on both Arduino Yun and Raspberry Pi, which comprises the sensors for temperature, humidity, LED, metal touch, and sound.

5.2 The Construction of MQTT-FSM

The design of Android applications is based on event-driven, depends on asynchronous programming [26], and is executed by a single event-loop thread [17]. Event-driven programming relies on the user activities and events, such as button presses, touch screens, and receiving network packets. During the running of Android applications, these events are delivered to the applications in non-deterministic order [7]. As a result, IoTVerif generates non-deterministic state machines based on the execution order of the events and the network traffic.

Fig.4 illustrates the generated MQTT-FSM, which models the benign activities on both sides of application and network of MQTT Dashboard Android application. For simplicity, we only keep the API names of each state. The network traffic fragments as the elements of the alphabet are shown in Table 4.

As Fig.4(b) shows, it is obvious that the API connect triggers the network fragment e1 e2, which includes the packets relevant to the task of establishing TCP handshake and SSL/TLS handshake. Then, Monkey tool publishes multiple messages to the broker. The invocation of publish triggers the network traffic e3. Then the disconnect method is invoked, which triggers the network traffic e5 and ends the connection.

Fig.4(c) illustrates different behavior of the application events caused by the network traffic. To invoke messageArrived, we published multiple messages from Amazon Web Services (AWS) broker to the application. To ensure message delivery, we use QoS 1. After that, we connected the application to the broker. That invokes connect method and triggers e1 e2, followed by network traffic fragment e4, which is triggered by publishing the message from the broker. Then, messageArrived method is invoked. Because the invocation of messageArrived does not trigger any network traffic, the transition between messageArrived to publish or disconnect has no input.

5.3 NuSMV model and MQTT Security Verification

The conversion of the state machine to symbolic model generates that NuSMV file that contains 4 modules: main, Security, States, and Transitions. The following listings show the code snippet of main, Security, States, Transitions modules that model the state machine in Fig.4(d) for MQTT Dashboard application. The main module creates an instance of the other modules using the VAR declaration.

```
MODULE main
VAR
   security : Security;
   s        : States(n.NT);
   n        : Transitions(s.R);
```

The Security module defines the security properties of the application. These properties check whether the MQTT application validates the server X.509 certificate.

```
MODULE Security
DEFINE
   TLS          := TRUE;
   TLSv         := TRUE;
   certCheckCN  := TRUE;
   SignedCA     := TRUE;
   checkSigCorr := TRUE;
   checkCAEXP   := TRUE;
```

The States module models the states of the MQTT-FSM of the application. Because of the messageArrived API invocation triggered by network traffic, we passed the network traffic NT as a parameter to this module.

```
MODULE States(NT)
VAR
R : {connect,publish,mesageArrived,disconnect,terminate};
ASSIGN
init(R) := connect;
next(R) := case
R = connect                     : {publish};
R = publish & NT = e3           : {publish, disconnect};
```

```
R = publish & NT = e3e4      : {mesageArrived};
R = mesageArrived & NT = e4  : {ma};
R = mesageArrived & NT = nop : {publish};
R = disconnect               : terminate;
TRUE                         : R;
esac;
```

The Transitions module models the transition of the MQTT-FSM of the application and takes API call as parameter.

```
MODULE Network(R)
VAR
NT : {e1e2,e3,e3e4,e4,e5,nop};
ASSIGN
init(NT) := e1e2;
next(NT) := case
R = connect      : e1e2;
R = publish      : {e3e4, e3};
R = ma           : {e4, nop};
R = disconnect   : e5;
TRUE             : NT;
esac;
```

After converting the MQTT-FSM to the symbolic model, the model checker of IoTVerif verifies both the general and security properties of the application. If MQTT client application provides secure connection over the latest version of SSL/TLS protocol and validates the certificate subjectCN, signature, and the certificate validity, the evaluation of all security specifications must all be *true*. Fig.5 illustrates the snippet of the specifications evaluation using the symbolic model above and the described specifications in Section 4.4 for IoT MQTT Dashboard application. It is clear that the application provides TLS and validates all the certificate components. Thus, all specifications are evaluated as *true*. However, Fig.6 illustrates the snippet of the specifications evaluation of MQTT Viewer (IoT Client) application. Although that application provides TLS, it does not validate the certificate , which exposes the application to MITM attack. Consequently, some security specifications, such as checking the certificate subjectCN and the signature, are evaluated as *false* and counter examples are given.

We have tested IoTVerif using 15 real-world Android MQTT applications. The detailed result of the tested 15 applications is presented in Table 4. We also include the statistics of network packets obtained from Monkey and the Paho API coverage. It is clear that the automation of network traces generation has high rates of API coverage for all apps: all are higher than 69%. We can notice from Table 4 that 5 (33.3%) of the applications are vulnerable to MITM. Only 1 application does not provide secure connection over SSL/TLS; hence, the application is vulnerable to various attacks. In addition, 3 applications provide secure connection over SSL/TLS, but they do not check the server certificate. Therefore, these 3 applications are vulnerable to MITM and TLS renegotiation attacks. Interestingly, 1 application provides secure connection and certificate validation, but the application uses TLSv1.0, which is vulnerable to various attacks as described in Section 2.2.

6 RELATED WORK

Verifying security properties of network protocols, including IoT protocols, is still undergoing research. Some works are closely related to our approach in terms of inferring a state machine of a protocol. De Ruiter and Poll [10] used automata algorithms to infer the TLS protocol model and inspected the state machine to find bugs and vulnerability. This work focused on the generated

```
-- specification AG TLS = TRUE IN security is true
-- specification AG TLSv >= 1 IN security is true
-- specification AG certCheckCN = TRUE IN security is true
-- specification AG SignedCA = TRUE IN security is true
-- specification AG checkSigCorr = TRUE IN security is true
-- specification AG certCheck = TRUE IN security is true
-- specification AG(! NT = RST AU R = disconnect) IN s is true
-- specification AG(R = connect -> AF (R = connect AU R = disconnect))
IN s is true
-- specification AG(NT = e2 -> (TLS ∧TLSv >= 1 & SignedCA &
certCheckCN & checkCAEXP)) IN security is true
          ·
          ·
```

Figure 5: The result of IoTVerif model checker of Android application, namely, MQTT Dashboard

```
-- specification AG TLS = TRUE IN security is true
-- specification AG TLSv >= 1 IN security is true
-- specification AG (certCheckCN = TRUE) IN secure is false
-- as demonstrated by the following execution sequence
Trace Description: CTL Counterexample
Trace Type: Counterexample
  -> State: 1.1 <-
     s.R = connect
     n.NT = e1
     security.TLS = TRUE
     security.TLSv = 1
     security.certCheckCN = FALSE
     secure.SignedCA = FALSE
     secure.checkSigCorr = FALSE
     secure.checkCAEXP = FALSE
```

Figure 6: The result of IoTVerif model checker of Android application, namely, MQTT Viewer (IoT Client)

TLS state machine during the handshake. Leita *et al.* [19] attempted to infer protocol state machine from the network traffic based on rebuilding TCP flows. Wang *et al.* [27] described the model probabilistically as the state machine based on the network trace of a specific application. In contrast, our system is based on both network traffic and application-level events, which can produce more accurate results.

There have been several efforts to investigate SSL/TLS security problems. Fahl *et al.* [12] statically analyzed Android applications from Google Play to find applications, which allow all host names and trust all certificates, vulnerability to MITM attack. Similarly, Sounthiraraj *et al.* [24] and FireEye [15] searched for TrustManager and HostnameVerifier issues to find applications vulnerability to MITM attack. Montelibano and Dormann [20] used CERT Tapioca tool to dynamically analyzed Android applications to find SSL/TLS vulnerabilities. The scope of these works does not include the study of the used SSL/TLS versions in the applications and their impact on SSL/TLS security. In contrast, our approach identifies SSL/TLS vulnerabilities based on the existence of the server certificate validation and the used SSL/TLS version in the client application.

7 CONCLUSION

In this paper, we presented IoTVerif, an automated tool that learns and identifies secure vulnerabilities, with respect to the usage of SSL/TLS, of IoT applications that utilize MQTT messaging protocol. IoTVerif simply correlates the observed network trace of an IoT applications with its execution context. IoTVerif does not require prior knowledge of protocols and is still able to identify various security vulnerabilities in software and enumerate the possible exploits. IoTVerif can help MQTT Android client developers to identify security vulnerability related to SSL/TLS certificate validation before they distribute their application through any marketplace. Our analysis of the 15 most popular free applications from the Google

Table 4: The detailed result for the 15 tested Android applications

App Package Name	Step ❶	Step ❸				Step ❹		Step ❺				Step ❼	
	# instrumented Paho Methods	# Network Packets by Monkey				Provide TLS?	TLS Version	Certificate Validation				vulnerable?	
		Min	Max	Average	Paho API Coverage Rate			Subject CN	Trusted Signature	Correct Signature	Certificate Validity	MITM	Renego
net.routix.mqttdash	1411	42	180	103	100%	✓	1.2	✓	✓	✓	✓	✗	✗
com.deepeshc.mqttrec	1245	25	117	71	82%	✓	1.2	✓	✓	✓	✓	✗	✗
com.patterns.io.mqttpatterns	1754	19	95	57	71%	✓	1.1	✓	✓	✓	✓	✗	✗
com.codifythings.universalmqttclient	621	25	125	75	88%	✓	1.0	✗	✗	✗	✗	✓	✓
br.com.bintechnology.mqttclient	785	27	135	81	78%	✗	N/A	✗	✗	✗	✗	✓	N/A
at.tripwire.mqtt.client	838	48	130	84	98%	✓	1.2	✓	✓	✓	✓	✗	✗
ru.esp8266.iotmanager	1656	27	119	73	75%	✓	1.2	✓	✓	✓	✓	✗	✗
com.thn.iotmqttdashboard	1083	58	200	119	71%	✓	1.2	✓	✓	✓	✓	✗	✗
com.vinmacro.vinmacromqt	941	51	119	68	69%	✓	1.1	✗	✗	✗	✗	✓	✓
com.cmmakerclub.iot.cmmciotswitch	1768	23	115	69	84%	✓	1.1	✓	✓	✓	✓	✗	✗
info.laptrinhpic.easycontrol.mqttplugin	702	40	160	108	88%	✓	1.1	✓	✓	✓	✓	✗	✗
net.nosybore.mqttpublishplugin	1318	21	105	63	75%	✓	1.2	✓	✓	✓	✓	✗	✗
net.sabamiso.android.simplemqttviewer	758	44	110	75	88%	✓	1.0	✓	✓	✓	✓	✗	✗
in.dc297.mqttclpro	1226	27	135	81	72%	✓	1.1	✓	✓	✓	✓	✗	✗
com.hanzycanada.mqttspeed	1661	44	110	74.8	84%	✓	1.1	✗	✗	✗	✗	✓	✓

Play Market has shown that 5 applications are vulnerable to MITM and/or TLS Renegotiation attacks.

ACKNOWLEDGMENTS

This work is supported by the funding from National Science Foundation under award Grant No. DGE-1723707, DGE-1623713, and Michigan Space Grant Consortium.

REFERENCES

[1] Akdeniz. 2017. GitHub - Akdeniz/Google Play Crawler). https://github.com/Akdeniz/google-play-crawler. (2017).

[2] Ala Al-Fuqaha, Mohsen Guizani, Mehdi Mohammadi, Mohammed Aledhari, and Moussa Ayyash. 2015. Internet of Things: A Survey on Enabling Technologies, Protocols, and Applications. *IEEE Communications Surveys Tutorials* 17, 4 (Fourthquarter 2015), 2347–2376. https://doi.org/10.1109/COMST.2015.2444095

[3] Aisha Ali-Gombe, Irfan Ahmed, Golden G. Richard, III, and Vassil Roussev. 2016. AspectDroid: Android App Analysis System. In *Proceedings of the Sixth ACM Conference on Data and Application Security and Privacy (CODASPY '16)*. ACM, New York, NY, USA, 145–147. https://doi.org/10.1145/2857705.2857739

[4] Steven Arzt, Siegfried Rasthofer, Christian Fritz, Eric Bodden, Alexandre Bartel, Jacques Klein, Yves Le Traon, Damien Octeau, and Patrick McDaniel. 2014. Flow-Droid: Precise Context, Flow, Field, Object-sensitive and Lifecycle-aware Taint Analysis for Android Apps. In *Proceedings of the 35th ACM SIGPLAN Conference on Programming Language Design and Implementation (PLDI '14)*. ACM, New York, NY, USA, 259–269. https://doi.org/10.1145/2594291.2594299

[5] Microsoft Azure. 2017. Microsoft Azure IoT Hub. (2017). https://azure.microsoft.com/en-us/free/

[6] BetterCAP. 2017. MITM Tool and Framework. (2017). https://www.bettercap.org/

[7] Pavol Bielik, Veselin Raychev, and Martin Vechev. 2015. Scalable Race Detection for Android Applications. In *Proceedings of the 2015 ACM SIGPLAN International Conference on Object-Oriented Programming, Systems, Languages, and Applications (OOPSLA 2015)*. ACM, New York, NY, USA, 332–348. https://doi.org/10.1145/2814270.2814303

[8] Alessandro Cimatti, Edmund M. Clarke, Enrico Giunchiglia, Fausto Giunchiglia, Marco Pistore, Marco Roveri, Roberto Sebastiani, and Armando Tacchella. 2002. NuSMV 2: An OpenSource Tool for Symbolic Model Checking. In *Proceedings of the 14th International Conference on Computer Aided Verification (CAV '02)*. Springer-Verlag, London, UK, 359–364. http://dl.acm.org/citation.cfm?id=647771.734431

[9] David Cooper, Stefan Santesson, Stephen Farrell, Sharon Boeyen, Russell Housley, and Tim Polk. 2008. *Internet X.509 Public Key Infrastructure Certificate and Certificate Revocation List (CRL) Profile.* RFC 5280. RFC Editor. http://www.rfc-editor.org/rfc/rfc5280.txt

[10] Joeri de Ruiter and Erik Poll. 2015. Protocol State Fuzzing of TLS Implementations. In *Proceedings of the 24th USENIX Security Symposium, USENIX Security 15, Washington, D.C., USA, August 12-14, 2015.* 193–206. https://www.usenix.org/conference/usenixsecurity15/technical-sessions/presentation/de-ruiter

[11] Ernest Allen Emerson. 1990. Temporal and Modal Logic. MIT Press, Cambridge, MA, USA, Chapter Handbook of Theoretical Computer Science (Vol. B), 995–1072. http://dl.acm.org/citation.cfm?id=114891.114907

[12] Sascha Fahl, Marian Harbach, Thomas Muders, Lars Baumgärtner, Bernd Freisleben, and Matthew Smith. 2012. Why Eve and Mallory Love Android: An Analysis of Android SSL (in)Security. In *Proceedings of the 2012 ACM Conference on Computer and Communications Security (CCS '12)*. ACM, New York, NY, USA, 50–61. https://doi.org/10.1145/2382196.2382205

[13] Simos Gerasimou, Radu Calinescu, and Alec Banks. 2014. Efficient Runtime Quantitative Verification Using Caching, Lookahead, and Nearly-optimal Reconfiguration. In *Proceedings of the 9th International Symposium on Software Engineering for Adaptive and Self-Managing Systems (SEAMS 2014)*. ACM, New York, NY, USA, 115–124. https://doi.org/10.1145/2593929.2593932

[14] HiveMq. 2017. MQTT Security Fundamentals: TLS/SSL. (2017). http://www.hivemq.com/blog/mqtt-security-fundamentals-tls-ssl

[15] FireEye Inc. 2014. SSL Vulnerabilities: Who listens when Android applications talk? (August 2014). https://www.fireeye.com/blog/threat-research/2014/08/ssl-vulnerabilities-who-listens-when-android-applications-talk.html

[16] IEEE IoT. 2016. IoT Developer Survey 2016 Final Report. (2016). https://iot.ieee.org/images/files/pdf/iot-developer-survey-2016-report-final.pdf

[17] Casper S. Jensen, Anders Møller, Veselin Raychev, Dimitar Dimitrov, and Martin Vechev. 2015. Stateless Model Checking of Event-driven Applications. In *Proceedings of the 2015 ACM SIGPLAN International Conference on Object-Oriented Programming, Systems, Languages, and Applications (OOPSLA 2015)*. ACM, New York, NY, USA, 57–73. https://doi.org/10.1145/2814270.2814282

[18] Ravi Kishore Kodali. 2016. An implementation of MQTT using CC3200. In *2016 International Conference on Control, Instrumentation, Communication and Computational Technologies (ICCICCT)*. 582–587. https://doi.org/10.1109/ICCICCT.2016.7988017

[19] Corrado Leita, Ken Mermoud, and Marc Dacier. 2005. ScriptGen: an automated script generation tool for Honeyd. In *21st Annual Computer Security Applications Conference (ACSAC'05)*. 12 pp.–214. https://doi.org/10.1109/CSAC.2005.49

[20] Joji Montelibano and Will Dormann. 2015. How We Discovered Thousands of Vulnerable Android Apps in One Day. https://www.rsaconference.com/events/us15/agenda/sessions/1638/how-we-discovered-thousands-of-vulnerable-android RSA Conference.

[21] Eric Rescorla, Marsh Ray, Steve Dispensa, and Nasko Oskov. 2010. *Transport Layer Security (TLS) Renegotiation Indication Extension.* RFC 5746. RFC Editor. http://www.rfc-editor.org/rfc/rfc5746.txt

[22] Yaron Sheffer, Ralph Holz, and Peter Saint-Andre. 2015. *Summarizing Known Attacks on Transport Layer Security (TLS) and Datagram TLS (DTLS).* RFC 7457. RFC Editor. http://www.rfc-editor.org/rfc/rfc7457.txt

[23] Preeti Sirohi, Amit Agarwal, and Sapna Tyagi. 2016. A comprehensive study on security attacks on SSL/TLS protocol. In *Proceedings of the 2016 2nd International Conference on Next Generation Computing Technologies (NGCT)*. 893–898. https://doi.org/10.1109/NGCT.2016.7877537

[24] David Sounthiraraj, Justin Sahs, Garret Greenwood, Zhiqiang Lin, and Latifur Khan. 2014. Smv-hunter: Large scale, automated detection of ssl/tls man-in-the-middle vulnerabilities in android apps. In *Proceedings of the 21st Annual Network and Distributed System Security Symposium (NDSS 14)*. Citeseer.

[25] Android Studio. 2017. UI/Application Exerciser Monkey | Android Studio. (2017). https://developer.android.com/studio/test/monkey.html

[26] Heila van der Merwe, Brink van der Merwe, and Willem Visser. 2014. Execution and Property Specifications for JPF-android. *SIGSOFT Softw. Eng. Notes* 39, 1 (Feb. 2014), 1–5. https://doi.org/10.1145/2557833.2560576

[27] Yipeng Wang, Zhibin Zhang, Danfeng Daphne Yao, Buyun Qu, and Li Guo. 2011. Inferring Protocol State Machine from Network Traces: A Probabilistic Approach. In *Proceedings of the 9th International Conference on Applied Cryptography and Network Security (ACNS'11)*. Springer-Verlag, Berlin, Heidelberg, 1–18.

Keyboard Emanations in Remote Voice Calls: Password Leakage and Noise(less) Masking Defenses

S Abhishek Anand
University of Alabama at Birmingham
anandab@uab.edu

Nitesh Saxena
University of Alabama at Birmingham
saxena@uab.edu

ABSTRACT

Keyboard acoustic side channel attacks to date have been mostly studied in the context of an adversary eavesdropping on keystrokes by placing a listening device near the intended victim creating a *local* eavesdropping scenario. However, being in close physical proximity of the victim significantly limits the applicability of the attack.

In this paper, we study the keyboard acoustic side channel attacks in *remote* attack settings and propose countermeasures in such attack settings. Specifically, we introduce an *offense-defense* system that: (1) highlights the threat of a *remote* adversary eavesdropping on keystrokes while the victim is on a VoIP call, and (2) builds a way to *mask* the leakage through the use of system-generated sounds. On the offensive side, we show the feasibility of existing acoustic side channel attacks adapted to a remote eavesdropper setting against sensitive input such as random passwords, PINs etc. On the defensive side, we demonstrate a software-based approach towards masking the keystroke emanations as a defense mechanism against such attacks and evaluate its effectiveness. In particular, we study the use of white noise and *fake keystrokes* as masking sounds and show the latter to be an effective means to cloak such side channel attacks. Finally, we discuss a novel way of masking by virtually inserting the masking signal in remote voice calls without distracting the user.

ACM Reference Format:
S Abhishek Anand and Nitesh Saxena. 2018. Keyboard Emanations in Remote Voice Calls: Password Leakage and Noise(less) Masking Defenses. In *CODASPY '18: Eighth ACM Conference on Data and Application Security and Privacy, March 19–21, 2018, Tempe, AZ, USA.* ACM, New York, NY, USA, 8 pages. https://doi.org/10.1145/3176258.3176341

1 INTRODUCTION

Acoustic side channel attacks have been shown to be successful at decoding keystrokes by exploiting keystroke emanations from the victim's typing, by placing a covert listening device in vicinity of the victim.[1] The fundamental insight of these attacks is that, due to the mechanical characteristics of the keyboard, each key on the keyboard produces a unique sound on press and release. Studies

---

[1]We use the terms "victim" and "user" interchangeably throughout this work.

have indicated that such attacks are reasonably accurate at decoding typed words by using methods described in [5–7, 11, 16]. As such, they pose a viable threat to highly sensitive information such as (random or non-random) passwords and other natural language text input by the user.

Given the huge concern about privacy issues in the digital world, these threats pose a serious risk to a user's interactions in an insecure environment. However, the existing acoustic emanation attacks have all been studied only in a *local setting* where the victim is being eavesdropped by a covert listening device placed in its vicinity. Such a setting may limit the applicability of the attack since the attacker is forced to be in close physical proximity of the victim user. The proximity-based attacks may also be detected/prevented via physical means, for example, with closer inspection of the space around the user such as through bug sweeping [3]. It is also important to note that, in such proximity settings, there may be other, simpler and more effective mechanisms to learn sensitive information from the user, such as simple shoulder-surfing attacks that monitor the user as she types her confidential information.

In this paper, our goal is to expand the research on keyboard acoustic emanations by exploring other attack avenues for the adversary and investigating defensive scenarios, especially when the victim is typing sensitive information such as passwords and PINs. First, since acoustic emanation attacks have already been studied extensively in a local setting where the victim is being eavesdropped by a covert listening device placed in its vicinity, we investigate the behavior of such attacks in a more broader *remote eavesdropper* setting. In this setting, the victim is unknowingly being eavesdropped by an attacker from a remote location while the victim is on a call with a malicious or compromised entity, or by a wiretapper who is sniffing the VoIP traffic containing the keystrokes between two honest parties. We also concentrate on attacks against random passwords and PINs as they demand more security and are supposed to be harder to decode due to their randomness. When compared to the localized attack setting, the remote attacks give immense flexibility to the attacker and are harder to detect, and therefore can be more devastating in practice.

Second, while the study of acoustic side channel attacks have been extensively highlighted, there is a scarcity of adequate defense techniques that can thwart such attacks. Most of the proposed defense revolves around improved hardware and a sanitized environment to suppress the acoustic emanations. However, these methods come with an expensive implementation making them impractical in assisting a common user, especially in a remote eavesdropping setting. In the face of such challenges, we examined the efficiency of system generated sounds in suppressing or masking the acoustic emanations to make the proposed remote acoustic side channel attacks ineffective. We investigate two types of defense mechanisms: noisy defense mechanism that generates masking signal at the victim's end using speakers and noiseless defense that virtually mixes the masking signal with the victim's microphone output and directs it seamlessly to the remote calling application. While noiseless defense is user transparent, noisy defense can be utilized to counteract the threat of a local eavesdropping adversary (in addition to a remote attacker).

Our Contributions: In this paper, we show that keyboard acoustic eavesdropping is possible in remote voice calling applications like VoIP scenarios, where the attacker is eavesdropping while the victim is typing during the call. Moreover, we show that such attacks can be thwarted with acoustic masking mechanisms. We also introduce the idea of noiseless masking where the masking mechanism is used without distracting the victim from the important task of password entry. Our contributions are summarized below:

- **Leakage of Password Keystrokes:** We utilize similar attack methodology as in [8] and show in Section 5 that traditional attack vectors (like *time-frequency distance* and machine learning tools) provide a reasonable accuracy at decoding single keystrokes (74.33% for lowercase alphabet keys and 77.33% for numeric keys), 6-character length random passwords (46.67%), and 4-digit PIN (70.00%) using the keystroke sounds transmitted over VoIP calls.
- **Noisy Masking Defense:** We propose a noisy defense mechanism based on sound masking in Section 6 to hide the keystroke acoustic emanations during password (and PIN) entry. We study the effectiveness of white noise and *fake keystrokes* in hiding the keystrokes typed by the victim.
- **Noiseless Masking Defense:** We introduce the idea of a novel defense mechanism in Section 7 that silently injects masking signal into the audio stream of a voice call during password (or PIN) entry. This setup allows a noise free environment at victim's end while preventing an eavesdropping attacker at the other end from exploiting leaked password keystroke emanations.

2 BACKGROUND AND RELATED WORK

Acoustic eavesdropping over keystrokes has been a well researched area in computer security. The acoustic emanations resulting from the keystrokes were identified as leaking significant amount of information about the keys being pressed. Asonov et al.[5] used neural networks with labeled keystroke samples to identify a keystroke using Fast Fourier Transformation (*FFT*) as a feature from the key press regions. They were able to identify the keystrokes with an accuracy of 80%. Zhuang et al.[16] improved upon this work by using non labeled training samples and *Cepstrum* features to achieve accuracy up to 96%.

Berger et al.[7] exploited the correlation between keystrokes based on their physical location on the keyboard to decode single words of length 7-13 using dictionary attack. Halevi et al.[11] studied keyboard acoustic emanations attacks by using *time-frequency decoding* that provided improved accuracy over previous methods. They also explored the effect of a user's typing style on keystroke identification in the context of decoding random passwords. They inferred that different typing styles affect the accuracy of keyboard acoustic attacks and random passwords are less vulnerable to such attacks as language modeling techniques and dictionary based attacks are not applicable. Context free attack was proposed by Zhu

et al. [14] that utilized multiple microphones placed strategically around a keyboard to identify keystrokes based on time difference of arrival (TDoA) of the keystroke emanation at each microphone.

Compagno et al. [8] explored the issue of a remote adversary eavesdropping on keystrokes through VoIP calls. They used *MFCC* features for keystroke detection and investigated the impact of bandwidth as well as presence of speech on the accuracy of their classifier. Our work re-investigates this issue with a focus on random passwords and PINs while proposing a defense mechanism against a remote eavesdropping adversary. Similar to [8], our work does not consider geometry based attacks such as [14] because remote eavesdropping removes the distance factor between the eavesdropping device and the keyboard. This renders these class of attacks infeasible in our threat model as distance i.e. TDoA can not be used as a unique identifying factor.

3 ATTACK MODEL AND OVERVIEW

In this section, we give an overview of the acoustic eavesdropping attack system, which is a reincarnation of existing localized keyboard acoustic attacks [5, 7, 11, 16] for remote voice call setting. We describe in detail our threat model for the voice call scenario elaborating the capabilities of the attacker.

In our threat model, we consider the victim to be in a voice call while typing sensitive information such as random passwords, PINs, or credit card information. We assume the user at the other end of the call is using speakers to listen to the victim. This allows the attacker to remotely eavesdrop on the voice call. In this scenario, the attacker could be a malicious application exploiting the microphone on the other end of the victim's call or it could be a dishonest user itself communicating with the victim. The attacker could also install a hidden listening device near the benign user (using speakers) who is on call with the victim. The voice call in our model could be a VoIP call, a video call or a normal phone call. In this work, we will limit ourselves to the VoIP scenario that can easily be extended to any types of calls with the victim.

Our threat model assumes that the victim is typing sensitive information during the call. One way to ensure this scenario could be using social engineering trickeries to influence the victim into logging to a website or authentication system while on the voice call. For example, in a customer service call, the customer service agent may ask the user to login to test if his account is accessible. The victim may also log into an authentication service even without the attacker's prompt while on the call.

To obtain training samples for the victim's keyboard, we assume the attacker has access to prior calls from the victim that allows building a keystroke feature set to be used for keystroke identification. Other ways for the attacker to build a training model for the victim's keyboard involve an exchange of chat messages between the attacker and the victim, online editing of a shared document (e.g. Google Docs) or coercing the victim to send an email while on call. In all of these scenarios, the attacker can record victim's keystrokes through VoIP call and match them against the written text. This is in contrast to prior keyboard emanations attacks [5, 7, 11, 16] where the attacker had physical access to victim's keyboard. As an analogy, this constitutes a type of known-plaintext attack against

(a) Malicious end point attacker   (b) Network sniffing attacker

Figure 1: Eavesdropping attack scenarios

encryption systems where the attacker has the general knowledge of the keys on the victim's device but not the actual typed keys.

We also consider a scenario where the attacker builds the training model by eavesdropping locally on the victim's keystrokes and then using the obtained training model to recognize the remotely eavesdropped keystrokes of the same victim. This scenario assumes that attacker may have one-time access to victim's keyboard (similar to lunch-time attack) that allows him to build a training model using the exact keyboard of the victim. This training model is later used to decode victim's keystroke over VoIP call.

In our model, we limit ourselves to eavesdropping on random passwords and numerical data (like PINs, credit card number, and date of birth). Hence, we eliminate the effect of individual typing style from the recorded keystrokes as such data is generally not entered using touch typing[2]. Also, HMM (Hidden Markov Model) language-based models and dictionary attack can not be useful in this case as random passwords and numbers are devoid of language features that make such attacks possible. To give the attacker a realistic chance for decoding the keystrokes, we allow multiple samples of the sensitive data to be collected by the attacker (e.g., the same password typed multiple times).

In line with prior acoustic side channel attacks, we design our environment to be free of noise to evaluate the maximum likelihood of a successful attack. While it is realistic for the victim to converse during the call while entering the sensitive information, we do not consider this scenario in our threat model. Note that the attacker side noise/speech does not affect our attacks, only the victim's side is important. Another important scenario in our threat model involves the attacker sniffing on the network traffic of the VoIP call between two honest parties. When a VoIP call is made to or from the victim, the attacker monitors the network traffic for VoIP packets. One amendable setting for this attack involves unencrypted VoIP communication, or third-party encryption (who themselves can be the attacker). However, even if VoIP services employ end-to-end encryption, VoIP packets have been shown to be vulnerable and can still be decoded as shown by Wright et al.[13]. Thus, our work may apply to both encrypted and cleartext VoIP communications.

4 ATTACK SETTINGS & TECHNIQUES

In this section, we lay out the design of the experiment that was conducted to study the feasibility of the attacker eavesdropping

remotely on an unaware victim during a voice call while she enters some sensitive information (password or PIN).

4.1 Experiment Design

In our experiments, we study the following scenarios based on the threat model: a) An attacker (a malicious user) communicating with the victim, or a compromised machine on call with the victim, b) an attacker sniffing and capturing the audio packets directly from the network, and c) the attacker obtains a training model of the keystrokes locally and later eavesdrops remotely intending to use the training model for decoding. The first scenario is depicted in Figure 1a and the second scenario is depicted in Figure 1b.

4.2 Keystroke Processing

The keystroke processing done by the attacker for audio signals eavesdropped over voice calls is in line with keystroke extraction and processing done in previous works [5, 7, 11, 16]. The process is divided in two phases: keystroke extraction, and keystroke classification and recognition. We restrict our signal processing (that uses Fast Fourier transform) to the frequency band 400Hz-12kHz as we obtained best results in this band. For classification and recognition, we compared single character detection accuracy for existing methods in literature such as MFCC with neural networks [16], cross-correlation [7], frequency distance measure [7], frequency-time distance measure [11] and machine learning methods described in [8], and chose the method that gave us the best accuracy.

Our threat model differs from previous works in the sense that the eavesdropping is done remotely and not in the proximity of the victim, the eavesdropped signal is *not* the same signal that emanated from the keystrokes at the victim's end. The eavesdropped keystroke signal is a result of an encoding-decoding (defined by the underlying VoIP protocol) of the original keystroke emanation from the keyboard that is transmitted over the network. Therefore we implement and test all the previously described methods and choose the method that provides us with the best accuracy.

5 ATTACK EXPERIMENT AND RESULTS

This section describes the setup details of our experiments and the results that show the threat of an acoustic eavesdropping attack.

Table 1: Single key classification using time-domain and frequency-domain distance estimates

Classification Method	Accuracy (in %)
Alphabet keys (a-z)	
Cross-correlation	56.00
Frequency Distance	64.70
Frequency Time	**67.30**
Numpad keys (0-9)	
Cross-correlation	73.30
Frequency Distance	70.00
Frequency Time	**83.30**

Table 2: Single key classification using FFT coefficients

Classification Algorithm	Accuracy (in %)
Alphabet keys (a-z)	
J48	15.79
Random Forest	32.35
Linear Nearest Neighbor Search	20.92
SMO	21.95
Simple Logistic Regression	**39.54**
Multinomial Logistic Regression	**38.89**
Numpad keys (0-9)	
J48	39.67
Random Forest	49.67
Linear Nearest Neighbor Search	42.33
SMO	38.67
Simple Logistic Regression	**53.00**
Multinomial Logistic Regression	**53.67**

Table 3: Single key classification using MFCC

Classification Algroithm	Accuracy (in %)
Alphabet keys (a-z)	
J48	34.40
Random Forest	66.88
Linear Nearest Neighbor Search	53.91
SMO	**74.33**
Simple Logistic Regression	**73.17**
Multinomial Logistic Regression	62.52
Numpad keys (0-9)	
J48	44.67
Random Forest	**73.67**
Linear Nearest Neighbor Search	62.00
SMO	**77.33**
Simple Logistic Regression	**70.67**
Multinomial Logistic Regression	56.33

5.1 Single Character Detection

Single character detection involves determining the accuracy of correctly recognizing a keystroke. For this purpose, two sets of keystroke samples are used: a labeled training set and a testing set. The testing set is evaluated against the training set using the methods described in Section 4.2 for determining the single character detection accuracy.

5.1.1 Experimental Setup. For our experiment, we collected 20 keystroke samples for each of the lowercase alphabetical keys *(a-z)* and each of the numpad keys *(0-9)*. The keyboard used was Dell SK-8125 and the recording was performed by a PC microphone (DX-USBMIC13). The scenario involved victim typing each key *(a-z; 0-9)* twenty times while communicating with the attacker on Skype. The typing was done in hunt and peck style where the victim used right hand index finger to press each key individually. The victim and the attacker are not present on the same network connection.

As per our attack model, no other sounds were present except the keystroke sounds. The keystroke sounds generated at the victim's end were transmitted through the microphone of the victim to the attacker by Skype. The microphone was placed at a distance of 15cm from the victim's keyboard to allow the attacker to have the best quality recording. The attacker recorded the victim's keystroke using a microphone from the other end of the Skype call. This captured our first attack setting involving a malicious end point.

5.1.2 Processing and Results. We divided the collected samples for each keystroke into training set (14 samples) and testing set (6 samples). We extracted the key press and the key release regions from each keystroke sample as detailed in Section 4.2. To get the best possible accuracy, we built models for each of the methods described in Section 4.2 and trained them on the obtained training set for each of the keys *(a-z; 0-9)*. The testing set for each key was then used to determine the accuracy of the models. The results are enumerated in Table 1.

For applying supervised machine learning, we used FFT coefficients and MFCC as classifying features for each keystroke. We calculated FFT features with a window of 441 samples with overlap of half the window size. We also used *"melfcc"* code provided at [4] with frequency wrap of type htkmel and used the first 32 channels in our calculations. We performed 10 fold cross validation on the collected samples of keystrokes with following algorithms: Simple Logistic Regression, Multinomial Logistic Regression, J48, Random Forest, SMO and Linear Nearest Neighbor Search.

The results are compiled in Table 2 and 3. From the results, we observe that MFCC provide a better classification accuracy than FFT coefficients. The best accuracy achieved by FFT coefficients was 39.54% using Simple Logistic Regression while using MFCC as features, the classification accuracy was 74.33% (SMO) and 73.17% (Simple Logistic Regression).

We compared the results obtained using multiple machine learning algorithms that use MFCC features against time domain methods like cross-correlation or derived features in frequency domain such as frequency-distance or frequency-time distance estimate. We clearly observe from Table 1 and Table 3 that machine learning method using MFCC delivers better results for a single keystroke accuracy for both alphabets and numpad keys. Hence, we utilize machine learning using MFCC features in our subsequent analysis of decoding random passwords and PINs over VoIP calls.

5.2 Random Passwords and PIN Detection

We now focus on the feasibility of decoding random passwords and PINs using same technique as in single character detection. Random passwords are difficult to decode as the accuracy of the attack method depends only on the single character detection rate as we can not use language models and dictionaries to deduce the correct word from a partially decoded word.

5.2.1 Experimental Setup. In order to test for random passwords, we allowed the victim to type 5 randomly generated 6-character passwords consisting of only lowercase alphabets *(a-z)*. The length of 6 characters is the minimum requirement for a password on most of the authentication systems. The victim typed each of the 5 passwords for a total of 10 times with a time interval of 5 seconds between successive password inputs for the same password. For testing PINs, we allowed the victim to type 5 randomly generated PINs of length 4, which is the standard length in most PIN authentication systems. Each PIN was typed 10 times allowing for an interval of 5 seconds between successive PIN entries for the same PIN similar to random passwords.

5.2.2 Processing and Results. For decoding random passwords, we used MFCC features extracted from password keystrokes, eavesdropped over the remote call. We used previously collected samples of single keystrokes (30 instances per key) to build the training model and keystrokes from each password attempt were used as the testing set. We used all ten attempts of each of the five random passwords against our training model and recorded the best obtained accuracy for each password over ten samples.

The results for password decoding is shown in Appendix Table 4 that indicate that SMO and Simple Logistic Regression algorithms were able to decode, on an average, more than 40% of the password over ten samples for each of the five random passwords. Single keystroke accuracies observed in Table 3 collaborate the effectiveness of these two algorithms when used with MFCC features. In terms of search space, SMO algorithm is able to decode almost half of the password, averaging about 3 characters for a 6-character length password. Since the experiments were performed over ten samples for each password, the required search space is $C_1^{10} \times C_3^6 \times 26^3$ guesses. A brute force attack would require 26^6 guesses which means our attack reduces the search space by a factor of 88, for a 6-character length password.

If we consider a 10-character password, a brute force attack would require 26^{10} guesses. Using our best accuracy for password decoding (approximately 46.67%), the required number of guesses would be $C_1^{10} \times C_5^{10} \times 26^5$ reducing the search space by a factor of 4716. While the accuracies are not very high, they still show an underlying threat that has the potential to compromise user's security if the password is not truly random.

The decoding accuracy for 4-digit PINs is also shown in Appendix Table 4 demonstrating average accuracies using SMO, Simple Logistic Regression and Linear Nearest Neighbor Search. For a 4-digit PIN, the attacker can reveal as many as 3 digits contained in the PIN. The search space for this attack would be $C_1^{10} \times C_3^4 \times 10^1$. When compared to a brute force attack (a search space of 10^4), the attacker's search space has been reduced by an order 10^3.

5.3 Network Sniffing

For this scenario, we assumed that the attacker had direct access to the network and can sniff audio packets from it. To emulate this scenario, we installed the recorder plugin for Skype named Supertintin [1] that can directly record the audio from Skype instead of relying upon the user's speaker to get access to the keystroke sounds. This also removes the need for the use of a microphone for the attacker as the recording was now done through the software.

We performed the experiment with no explicit limit imposed on the network bandwidth. Compagno et al. [8] showed that classification of remote keystrokes using MFCC suffers noticeable loss at and under 40 Kbits/s. Thus, we perform the experiment where the Skype conversation was working at almost best possible quality thereby creating the most favorable scenario for the attacker.

Top 5 Matching Character List: In this technique, we find the 5 most frequently matching characters for each of the characters *(a-z)*. We match each of the samples for each keystroke against the samples of remaining 25 keystrokes using our classification algorithms and arrange the matching candidates in decreasing order of frequency during the matching process. The matching character list describes the similarity of a given alphabetical key with other alphabetical keys. Thus, for each decoded character in our attack, we get a possible search space of 5 characters that could replace the decoded characters. If the replaced character resulted in a successful

match, i.e. it was the same character typed by the victim, we count it as a correctly decoded character in the 6-character password.

For random passwords decoding, the attack was able to decode 2 out 6 characters for random passwords with a single character accuracy of 8.0% for the raw samples and after the application of top 5 matching list, it rose to 24.0%. For the 4 digit PIN, it was able to decode 3 out of 4 characters with the single character detection rate of 20.0% for the raw samples that rose to 50% after applying the top 5 matching character list. These results are in line with those of the end point attack setting and again demonstrate the feasibility for a network sniffing attacker, which will give rise to a significant factor reduction in the search space for passwords and PINs.

5.4 Local and Remote Eavesdropping Attacker

We used the same setup as used in the experimental setup described in Section 5.1.1. However, on this occasion, we also recorded the keystrokes locally at the victim's end by placing a microphone near the victim's keyboard. This setup mimics the threat scenario for eavesdropping on keystrokes locally as studied in previous literature ([5], [7], [9], [11], [15],[16]).

We build the training model as per Section 4.2 by using the keystrokes signals recorded locally at the victim's end. We then tested the remotely recorded keystrokes against this local eavesdropping based training model. We found out that using the top 5 matching character list as described in Section 5.2.2, we could only achieve a single character detection accuracy of 18.6% as compared to 32.7% as achieved in Section 5.2.2. This indicates that the steps involved in the transmission of the audio signal from victim's to attacker's end affect the features of signal to an extent that is lowers the accuracy of the classifier. This is to be expected when VoIP applications need to compress and encode the signals that may result in loss of some information about the signals.

6 NOISY AUDIO MASKING DEFENSE

Audio masking is used to hide susceptible sounds by introducing a different sound in the environment that should be able to cloak the susceptible sounds. In acoustic side channel attacks, the attacker exploits the sounds emanated from the victim's device (keyboard) to recover sensitive information. In our setup, the attacker records keystroke emanations that are transmitted over the VoIP call and decode them to extract random passwords, PINs, etc.

The main principle behind audio masking is to decrease signal to noise ratio (SNR) making it hard to separate the signal from noise. The audio emanations from the keystrokes constitute the signal and the masking sound is the background noise. If the loudness of the background noise is comparable to the signal, it becomes hard for an adversary to filter out the noise. To implement audio masking, an audio signal could be introduced in the victim's environment coexisting with the keystroke audio emanations. The masking signal could be generated from the victim's device or it could come from an external source.

6.1 Types of Masking Sound

For our defense based on masking keystroke emanations, we explore the masking ability of two types of masking sounds: white noise and *fake keystrokes*. We evaluate the masking signals on their ability to cloak keystroke emanations by measuring the accuracy of the adversary in decoding the keystrokes typed by the victim.

6.1.1 White Noise. Theoretically, white noise is defined as a random signal of constant spectral density and infinite bandwidth. However, in practice the bandwidth of white noise is regulated for the noise generator and is dependent on the context of generation. In our work, we are interested in masking keystroke sounds so we limit white noise to the frequency range of keystroke sounds. White noise is often used in office environments to drown out distracting sounds. While white noise is a simple masking signal, it lacks sophistication due to uniform frequency distribution leading to poor frequency spectrum overlap with keystroke sounds. It is also susceptible to filtering by most of the VoIP applications for enhancing speech and hence merely serves a baseline in our work from which we build upon more sophisticated masking signals.

6.1.2 Fake Keystrokes. Fake keystrokes refer to a pre-recorded sound of keystroke emanations where random keystrokes are typed without any pause between successive keystrokes. *Fake keystrokes* have similar frequency spectrum as the keystrokes typed by the victim during the VoIP call hence they lie in the same frequency spectrum. Due to this property, it may become difficult to filter *fake keystrokes* from real keystrokes for an attacker. In order to have maximum efficiency at masking the real keystrokes, the *fake keystrokes* should aim to overlap with the real keystrokes as much as possible. The overlap of the real and *fake keystrokes* may change the frequency features of the real keystrokes causing the resultant keystroke sound to be different than the real keystroke sound. Most VoIP applications, in our knowledge, do not filter out keystrokes during a call making the *fake keystrokes* a viable defense mechanism.

6.2 Experimental Setup

Our experimental setup for implementing the noisy defense mechanism was similar to the attack's experimental setup. The victim was in a VoIP call (Skype) with a malicious end user while entering sensitive information (passwords or PINs) at the same time on a computer terminal. The call from the victim was recorded at the malicious user's end using a PC microphone. In addition, we generated the masking sound using the victim's computer speaker. We divided the experiment in two stages: the first stage involved the use of white noise as the masking signal, and the second stage involved the usage of fake keystrokes as the masking signal.

The victim was instructed to type five unique 6-character random passwords, with each password being typed 30 times. Similarly, five unique 4-digit PINs were entered by the victim using the computer's keyboard, with each PIN being entered 30 times. We increased the number of samples for each password/PIN compared to the attack setup in order to test the defense against a more determined adversary. For the first stage of the experiment involving white noise, we generated white noise using the "wgn" function of Matlab in the frequency range 400Hz-12kHz at a sampling frequency of 44.1kHz. The resulting audio was played back using Windows Media Player by the inbuilt speaker at a sound level of 60dB. This is considered to be the sound level for a normal speech conversation and therefore any noise at the same level should probably be not distracting to the conversation. The keystroke sound was also measured and found to be around similar audio level.

For the second stage of the experiment, *fake keystrokes* were recorded offline by the victim locally, prior to the VoIP conversation with the malicious end point attacker. Since each keystroke lasts around 100ms and an average time duration between two successive keystrokes while entering a random password (we assume touch typing is not used for random passwords) is significantly more than 100ms, the victim presses random keys on the keyboard as fast as she can while recording the resulting keystroke sounds at the same time. Once the recording is complete, any part or whole of it can be played during the sensitive information entry event making sure that the masking sound is present during the entirety of this event.

6.3 Experimental Results

In order to test the viability of masking signals in cloaking acoustic emanations of keystrokes, we used our attack described in Section 5.2.2 to recover information from the eavesdropped signal.

6.3.1 In Presence of White Noise. Our results from the testing of white noise as a masking signal point out to the fact that white noise is recorded at a very low volume as compared to the keystrokes at the attacker's end. Hence in the presence of white noise, for the 6-character random passwords, we were able to recover on an average 5 out of 6 characters. Out of the 180 decoded characters (30 samples × length of a single password), we were able to correctly decode 9.2%, i.e, 16 characters correctly. After using the top 5 matching list, the percentage of correctly decoded characters went up to 35.9%.

For 4-digit PINs, we were able to recover almost all of the 4 digits of the PIN. Out of the 120 decoded numbers (30 samples × length of a single PIN), 12.5%, of digits were correctly decoded. Applying the top 5 matching list made the percentage of correctly decoded digits rise up to 67.2%. Thus, we can see that white noise has no effect upon the accuracy of the attack.[2] This is not surprising as most of the microphones and voice calling software implement some type of background noise suppression for improving the quality of the call. In other words, our experiments confirm that white noise as masking signal is not effective to defeat eavesdropping attack.

6.3.2 In Presence of Fake Keystrokes. Our recordings of the victim's keystrokes in the presence of *fake keystrokes* show that Skype does not filter out the fake keystrokes. This means that the real keystrokes typed by the victim may get obfuscated by the fake keystrokes that were played at the victim's end.

From the spectrum analysis, we observe that it may be difficult to identify *fake keystrokes* from real keystrokes as they lie in the same frequency spectrum. There may be cases of complete overlap of fake and real keystrokes, partial overlap between the fake and real keystrokes or no overlap between the fake and real keystrokes. In the first two cases, where there is a complete or a partial overlap between the fake and real keystrokes, the resultant keystroke signal will have different characteristics than the original real keystroke that was typed by the victim. In the case of no overlap between the fake and the real keystrokes, the *fake keystrokes* will still be mapped to some alphabetical key *(a-z)* and hence result in a false positive detection/insertion of a character.

---

[2] These accuracies are a bit higher compared to the ones reported in our attack section, which could be attributed to the independent setting in which this new data set was collected.

We tested the resultant keystroke audio signal captured by the attacker consisting of both real and *fake keystrokes*. The first challenge was to determine the correct number of samples. According to the experimental setup, 30 samples were recorded for a 6-character random password. However, the number of detected characters was fairly higher (261) than the number of characters actually typed by the victim (180). This results indicated that the recorded signal contains a high number of false positives in addition to the false negatives that may occur due to the overlapping of real and *fake keystrokes* as explained above.

Since there seems to be no viable way to identify the real keystrokes from the attack perspective, we can assume that the search space would increase drastically for an attacker trying to separate *fake keystrokes* from real keystrokes and the attack would fail. Also the randomness of *fake keystrokes* prevents the attacker from building up a profile of *fake keystrokes* over repeated trials. Thus we may say that *fake keystrokes* possess the capability of thwarting an acoustic side channel attack.

6.4 Keystroke Eavesdropping with Speech

While our threat model did not consider speech to be present during the eavesdropping of keystrokes, we examined the effect of speech on the accuracy of the remote eavesdropping attack. If speech has a detrimental effect on the attack's accuracy, it may have the potential to be used as a defensive measure against such attacks.

We tested the passwords and the PINs (2 instances randomly generated each) with 20 samples per instance. For each password/PIN entry on the victim's side, the victim also read aloud an English language text from a newspaper clip. The attack could deduce only 2 out of 6 characters for the password using the top 5 matching character list and 3 out of 4 for the PIN. This result indicates that the attack accuracy drops in presence of speech as compared to the scenario when no speech or masking signal is present. When compared to masking signals (white noise and fake keystrokes), speech may be more effective at masking keystrokes than white noise but less effective than the fake keystrokes over the VoIP channel.

7 NOISELESS AUDIO MASKING DEFENSE

While the approach of generating a masking sound at the victim's end may be able to hide keystroke sounds from a potential eavesdropper, it may also distract the victim from typing password. Since the malicious eavesdropper is not in proximity to the victim and the only feedback he can get is the from VoIP application itself, it may be beneficial for the victim if the masking signal is injected directly into the audio stream of VoIP application while being inaudible to the victim. In this manner, the masking sound will only be heard by the attacker and the victim will face no distraction while typing.

A virtual audio driver that provides the capability of rerouting the audio from a media software (the masking signal) to the audio input of the VoIP software while mixing it with audio from the user's microphone would be ideal for setting up a noiseless masking defense mechanism. Such a system would allay the usability concerns that arise when the masking signal is played through speakers on the user's end and affects the microphone output. This may be distracting to the user especially while trying to enter sensitive information that requires user's full attention.

Masking Signal: Same type of masking signal could be used in this setup as in noisy defense. White noise was not found to be very efficient at masking keystrokes in our noisy defense setup as Skype filters the noise in order to provide speech clarity. In our noiseless setup, we aim to inject white noise directly into Skype without it being relayed to Skype via microphone. We also use fake keystrokes in a similar manner since fake keystrokes seemed to have provided efficient masking to actual keystrokes from the victim's device. The experiments and evaluation of this approach are deferred to the full version of this paper.

8 DISCUSSION AND FUTURE WORK

We studied the feasibility of a remote eavesdropping acoustic side channel attack and demonstrated that such attack was able to reduce the search space for guessing the correct password/PIN when compared to a random guess. We also demonstrated that it is possible for an attacker to directly sniff the audio packets from the network with similar accuracy as a malicious end point attacker. We proposed two defense mechanisms based on sound masking to mitigate the investigated attacks. In our noisy defense setup, we generated the masking signal at the victim's end while the victim was typing the sensitive information. In the noiseless defense setup, a virtual audio driver can be used to mix the masking signal with the output from the victim's microphone and transmit it over the communication channel.

We evaluated two types of masking signal: white noise and fake keystrokes. We found out that white noise was not a suitable candidate to defend against our attack system due to noise suppression mechanisms deployed by the microphone and the voice calling applications. *Fake keystrokes* proved to be a better candidate against our attack system by effectively masking the keystroke emanations from the victim due to similarity of the *fake keystroke* signal and the real keystroke signal in the frequency domain which increased the search space for an attacker (more false negatives) during the attack. However, they should be randomly generated with random time intervals (none lasting more than 100ms) between successive *fake keystrokes* for effective overlap with real keystrokes. Longer passwords also increase the effectiveness of *fake keystrokes* due to increase in typing duration and are also harder to guess.

Continuous speech may also have potential as a defensive measure as it performs better than white noise since VoIP applications are configured to allow speech to be transmitted and suppress background noise. Compagno et al. [8] showed that the accuracy of their classifier decreased when speech became louder than keystroke sounds. When speech was 20dB higher than the keystroke sounds, their classifier reached a random guess baseline. We measured the loudness of keystrokes for three different keyboards (Dell SK-8125, Dell L100 and) using a sound meter and the average sound pressure level was 62dB. If the speech needs to be around 20db higher than the keystroke sound, it needs to be at 80dB which is beyond normal conversation loudness level (around 65-70db). Compared with the fake keystroke sounds that only need to be as loud as the keystroke themselves, we believe that speech as a masking signal may suffer from usability issue as the victim would only be conversing at a normal loudness level most of the time.

Real-world Defense Implementation: The design of our noise-less defense requires the masking signal generation capability to be in-built within the system (the source of the audio leakage) and the ability to inject the masking signal directly into the communication channel of VoIP call while being inaudible to the user. One such tool for virtual mixing and injection of audio into VoIP channel has already been introduced and utilized in our experiments. However, there needs to be a mechanism that allows the user to activate and deactivate the defense by the click of a button without explicitly going through audio settings of each involved application.

An alternative and zero-effort design for a real life implementation of the noiseless defense would be to detect the first key press for the password or sensitive input entry that will act as a trigger for the defense mechanism to activate and start injecting masking signal into the audio stream. In scenarios such as web login through passwords and PINs, the trigger can also be bound to the URL of the website, in particular to the login webpage. In our experiments, a Java swing based UI was constructed to test the defense mechanism. However, the defense mechanism can also be deployed as a browser plugin that can generate the masking sounds based on the visited URL. It is also possible to allow the user to enable or disable the defense mechanism at his discretion (e.g., by typing in a special character sequence such as "@@" as in an existing password manager application [12]).

Beyond Random Passwords and PINs: The focus of this paper was centered on short and sensitive input (e.g., random passwords and PINs). However, any arbitrary input containing sensitive data can be protected by our proposed defense. This may include, for example, email messages or documents prepared by the user while on a call that may be sensitive to the user. However, given these tasks are longer in time duration, further usability studies need to performed to analyze the effect of background noise generation on arbitrary text input in case of noisy defense. Our proposed noiseless defense remedies this issue and therefore is capable of working with even longer inputs and gets better at thwarting attacks with longer time duration as discussed before.

Other Acoustic Side Channels Attacks and Defenses over VoIP: The idea of applying acoustic side channel attacks to remote voice call setting is not limited to keyboard inputs alone. CPU acoustic emanations [10] and printer acoustic emanations [6] would also be potentially significant threats in a general remote setting explored in the paper. Further work, however, would be needed to study the impact of VoIP transmission over voice channel to these audio emanations. In the similar vein, our defense idea involving masking sounds would be applicable to defense against these attacks too that need to be studied in future work as well.

9 CONCLUSION

In this paper, we highlighted and quantified the threat of keyboard acoustic side channel attacks in the context of remote eavesdropping over voice calls. We showed the feasibility of the attack against short-length sensitive input, random passwords and numeric PINs based on off-the-shelf signal processing techniques. In contrast to localized attacks considered in prior work, our remote attack presents a threat to users' private information inadvertently leaked over a simple phone call unbeknownst to the user. We also proposed

defense mechanisms against such attacks that attempt to obfuscate the acoustic leakage by inserting system-generated sounds while the user provides any sensitive input. Our noisy defense generates user-audible masking signal while noiseless defense silently combines the masking signal with microphone output while being inaudible to the user. The results for noiseless defense are deferred to the full version of the paper. The significance of our work lies in systematically investigating a known threat in a broader application setting and coming up with a near practical and user-transparent defense against this threat.

REFERENCES

[1] 2016. Supertintin. The Most Advanced Skype Video Recorder. http://http://www.supertintin.com/. (2016). Accessed: 2016-06-07.
[2] 2016. Touch typing. Wikipedia, available at. https://en.wikipedia.org/wiki/Touch_typing. (2016). Accessed: 2016-05-08.
[3] 2016. USA Bug Sweeps: We Will Find Hidden Audio Microphones & Recorders! http://usabugsweeps.com/tscm-debugging-audio/. (2016). Accessed: 2016-06-07.
[4] 2017. PLP and RASTA (and MFCC, and inversion) in Matlab using melfcc.m and invmelfcc.m. http://www.ee.columbia.edu/ln/rosa/matlab/rastamat/. (2017). Accessed: 2017-08-07.
[5] Dmitri Asonov and Rakesh Agrawal. 2004. Keyboard Acoustic Emanations. In IEEE Symposium on Security and Privacy.
[6] Michael Backes, Markus DÃ¼rmuth, Sebastian Gerling, Manfred Pinkal, and Caroline Sporleder. 2005. Acoustic Side-Channel Attacks on Printers. In USENIX Security Symposium.
[7] Y. Berger, A. Wool, and A. Yeredor. 2006. Dictionary Attacks Using Keyboard Acoustic Emanations. In ACM Conference on Computer and Communications Security.
[8] Alberto Compagno, Mauro Conti, Daniele Lain, and Gene Tsudik. 2016. Don't Skype & Type! Acoustic Eavesdropping in Voice-Over-IP. https://arxiv.org/abs/1609.09359. (2016).
[9] A.H.Y. Fiona. 2006. Keyboard Acoustic Triangulation Attack. http://citeseerx.ist.psu.edu/viewdoc/download?doi=10.1.1.100.3156&rep=rep1&type=pdf. (2006). Final Year Project.
[10] Daniel Genkin, Adi Shamir, and Eran Tromer. 2014. RSA Key Extraction via Low-Bandwidth Acoustic Cryptanalysis. In Advances in Cryptology - CRYPTO.
[11] Tzipora Halevi and Nitesh Saxena. 2012. A Closer Look at Keyboard Acoustic Emanations: Random Passwords, Typing Styles and Decoding Techniques. In ACM Symposium on Information, Computer and Communications Security.
[12] Blake Ross, Collin Jackson, Nick Miyake, Dan Boneh, and John C Mitchell. 2005. Stronger password authentication using browser extensions. In USENIX Security Symposium.
[13] Charles Wright, Lucas Ballard, Scot Coulls, Fabian Monrose, and Gerald Masson. 2008. Spot me if you can: recovering spoken phrases in encrypted VoIP conversations. In IEEE Symposium on Security and Privacy.
[14] T. Zhu, Q. Ma, S. Zhang, and Y. Liu. 2014. Context-free attacks using keyboard acoustic emanations. In ACM SIGSAC Conference on Computer and Communications Security. 453–464.
[15] Tong Zhu, Qiang Ma, Shanfeng Zhang, and Yunhao Liu. 2014. Context-free Attacks Using Keyboard Acoustic Emanations. In ACM Conference on Computer and Communications Security.
[16] Li Zhuang, Feng Zhou, and J. D. Tygar. 2009. Keyboard Acoustic Emanations Revisited. ACM Transactions on Information and System Security 13, 1 (2009).

A APPENDIX

Table 4: Decoding accuracy using MFCC features

Password	Accuracy in %					
	J48	Random Forest	Linear Nearest Neighbor Search	SMO (SMV)	Simple Logistic Regression	Multinomial Logistic Regression
hfkgml	33.33	50.00	50.00	33.33	33.33	33.33
jotfnk	16.67	33.33	16.67	50.00	33.33	33.33
loughl	16.67	33.33	66.67	50.00	50.00	50.00
mlcabd	33.33	33.33	33.33	33.33	50.00	33.33
vaorkg	33.33	33.33	33.33	66.67	50.00	33.33
Average accuracy	26.67	36.66	40.00	46.67	43.33	36.66
PIN						
0075	75.00	75.00	75.00	75.00	75.00	50.00
1282	50.00	100.00	75.00	75.00	50.00	50.00
1446	50.00	50.00	75.00	50.00	75.00	75.00
3684	50.00	50.00	75.00	75.00	75.00	75.00
4793	50.00	50.00	50.00	50.00	75.00	50.00
Average accuracy	55.00	65.00	70.00	65.00	70.00	60.00

SPEED: Secure Provable Erasure for Class-1 IoT Devices

Mahmoud Ammar
imec-DistriNet, KU Leuven
mahmoud.ammar@cs.kuleuven.be

Wilfried Daniels
imec-DistriNet, KU Leuven
wilfried.daniels@cs.kuleuven.be

Bruno Crispo
imec-DistriNet, KU Leuven
University of Trento, Trento, Italy
bruno.crispo@cs.kuleuven.be

Danny Hughes
imec-DistriNet, KU Leuven
danny.hughes@cs.kuleuven.be

ABSTRACT

The Internet of Things (IoT) consists of embedded devices that sense and manage our environment in a growing range of applications. Large-scale IoT systems such as smart cities require significant investment in both equipment and personnel. To maximize return on investment, IoT platforms should support multiple third-party applications and adaptation of infrastructure over time. Realizing the vision of shared IoT platforms demands strong security guarantees. That is particularly challenging considering the limited capability and resource constraints of many IoT devices.

In this paper, we present SPEED, an approach to secure erasure with verifiability in IoT. *Secure erasure* is a fundamental property when it comes to share an IoT platform with other users which guarantees the cleanness of a device's memory at the beginning of the application deployment as well as at the time of releasing the underlying IoT device. SPEED relies on two security primitives: memory isolation and distance bounding protocol. We evaluate the performance of SPEED by implementing it on a simple baremetal IoT device belongs to Class-1. Our evaluation results show a limited overhead in terms of memory footprint, time, and energy consumption.

ACM Reference Format:
Mahmoud Ammar, Wilfried Daniels, Bruno Crispo, and Danny Hughes. 2018. SPEED: Secure Provable Erasure for Class-1 IoT Devices. In *CODASPY'18: Eighth ACM Conference on Data and Application Security and Privacy, March 19–21, 2018, Tempe, AZ, USA*. ACM, New York, NY, USA, 8 pages. https://doi.org/10.1145/3176258.3176337

1 INTRODUCTION

The IoT envisions a future where billions of Internet-connected devices are deployed in our environment to support novel Cyberphysical applications. Contemporary IoT networks are large and growing in scale from smart buildings to smart cities. Research deployments such as City of Things [20] already incorporate tens of thousands of IoT devices. The majority of such devices are very tiny and belong to Class-1 [7]. The Internet Engineering Task Force

(IETF) identifies Class-1 IoT devices with 10KB RAM and 100KB ROM as having the minimal resources necessary to communicate securely with the Internet [7]. The ideal multi-app IoT platform would execute efficiently on typical Class-1 embedded devices and enable the secure execution of coexisting third-party applications.

However, commercial deployments of similar scale have been slow to appear. One reason for this slow adoption is the unclear Return-on-Investment (RoI) for large-scale IoT networks that demand significant upfront investment in the infrastructure as well as technical staff to deploy, manage and maintain the system. Supporting multiple applications enables IoT infrastructure providers to increase their RoI. Multi-app nodes allow an IoT deployment to satisfy multiple stakeholders and therefore to cover hardware and associated staff costs arising from the deployment, management and maintenance of the infrastructure. IoT infrastructure providers could, for example, lease out resources on underutilized devices to third parties to increase revenue or specialize in deploying IoT infrastructure as a service. Realizing the idea of shared IoT platforms requires security mechanisms that ensure among other things that: (i) the memory of a public shared IoT device does not store any unwanted software or malware, (ii) the user can delete the entire memory footprint when he releases the IoT device, and (iii) any user can use the public IoT platform, so no complex key distribution and management is required.

This paper addresses the problem of *secure remote erasure of IoT with verifiability* without depending on pre-shared secret keys. A proof of secure erasure (PoSE) is the ability of the end user to verify the outcome of the erasure operation of a black-box system such as a remote IoT device. In spite of its importance, the topic of the provable secure erasure in IoT has been neglected and started to attract attention recently by some proposals [15]. This is an important omission that we aim to address in this research work. Our approach, SPEED, targets Class-1 IoT devices [7]. We build on two security primitives: (i) *memory isolation* and (ii) *distance bounding protocol* (DB). An isolated and secure portion of memory is needed to store the security-relevant functions for deletion and communication with the outside world. DB is implemented in this trusted part of the memory, and needed for proximity-based authentication and preventing man-in-the-middle (MITM) attack, as explained in Section 5. Henceforth, the term *verifier* refers to the user who wants to erase the memory of a target IoT device and verify the outcome of this remote erasure operation; and the term *prover* refers to the target IoT device that has to give a proof of erasure. In particular, the verifier should be able to securely erase the prover's memory and get a proof of erasure if he is in vicinity. The prover has to verify the distance of the verifier and give a proof of secure erasure if the verifier's distance is less than the predefined maximum threshold, where the threshold is an application-dependent value. Please, notice that there is an interesting swap of roles between the verifier and the prover, where the verifier has to verify the secure erasure and the prover has to verify the distance bounding.

To sum up, the chief contributions of this paper are:

- Overcoming the security limitation of the majority of Class-1 IoT devices, identified by the lack of the memory protection unit (MPU), by designing and developing an efficient memory isolation technique for low-end embedded devices that acts as a software-based MPU.
- Designing a flexible and secure memory erasure primitive, that can guarantee the deletion of any memory contents without any predefined information about the device (e.g. type, size of memory, shared keys, etc.). The only requirement is that the device should run our software-based memory isolation mechanism or some related functions only if it has a hardware-based MPU.
- Advancing the secure erasure in the IoT by brining it closer to reality through a proper implementation of SPEED on one of the Class-1 IoT devices and showing the efficiency and practicality of using DB to prevent MITM attack instead of selective jamming, as assumed by other research papers.

Paper outline. The remainder of this paper is organized as follows. Section 2 reviews the related work. Design principles of memory isolation are presented in Section 3. Section 4 describes the chosen distance bounding protocol. Section 5 proposes SPEED, our approach to secure erasure. Implementation details and evaluations are reported in Section 6 and 7 respectively. Section 8 concludes and gives directions for future work.

2 RELATED WORK

In 2010, Perito and Tsudik proposed an approach called Proofs of Secure Erasure (PoSE) [15]. PoSE is a protocol to perform secure erasure and secure code update. Both mechanisms are interleaved since the secure erasure can be considered as a prelude to secure code update. Remote attestation can be applied by erasing the memory each time and updating the code again. PoSE takes advantage of the flash memory which is common in all embedded devices by designating a small portion of it to be read-only. This small ROM on the prover side hosts the main functions needed for interacting with the verifier and erasing the contents of memory. The verifier starts the protocol by sending true randomness in order to fill and overwrite the prover's memory. The last k bits of these randomness are used as a session key by the prover to compute the message authentication code (MAC) of the memory and send it back to the verifier. On the other side, the verifier computes his own MAC and compares it with the received one. If they match, then proof of secure erasure holds. The security parameter k is known in advance to both parties. Also, the size of prover's memory has to be known in advance to the verifier. To prevent man-in-the-middle attack, PoSE relies on the assumption of jamming all other nearby devices during the run of the protocol. Moreover, the protocol incurs high overhead in terms of communication as the verifier has to send

random bytes equal to the size of the entire writable memory of the target IoT device.

Dziembowski et al. [10] proposed a cryptographic scheme that minimizes the communication complexity of PoSE [15]. The verifier sends a few number of bits (seed) to the prover. Using this seed, the prover performs a set of deterministic computations and expansion functions (e.g. calculation of a hash function recursively) that require the usage of the whole memory and thus overwriting its content. The secure erasure is proved if the computed hash value is correct as it can only be generated once. The idea behind this is that the prover stores a secret key in its memory. The size of this key should be at least half of the size of the available memory. Assuming bounded-retrieval model and restricted write/read operations, the adversary can not leak the key or make a copy of it internally due to its size. This key will be (at least partially) destroyed after recursively executing a set of hash functions. Therefore, the adversary can not preform the computations again. The main drawback of this solution is the computational complexity. It is quadratic on the size of the prover's memory.

Karame et al. [12] introduced a lightweight version of the previously mentioned PoSE [15] approach which reduces the overhead of computations. This scheme does not rely on the computation of MAC but on the correct structure of data in the prover's memory. The verifier selects a random secret K and a seed s of size m bits each. Then, he generates n random data blocks of length m bits each, where the result of multiplying m and n equals the size of the writable memory at the prover side. The verifier computes K' after performing a procedural set of cyclic shifts and XOR functions. The prover has to compute and send K back after receiving the n random data blocks in addition to the s and K' from the verifier. If both values of K match, the proof of secure erasure holds due to the idea of designing the ShiftXOR function, where K can not be computed correctly on the fly without storing the random data blocks in their exact locations. Similarly to PoSE, this approach still depends on the assumption of selective active jamming of nearby devices and does not solve the high overhead of the number of the transmitted packets.

In nutshell, we show that SPEED enhances over all of the proposed approaches in the following:

- Excluding the assumption of selective jamming to prevent MITM attack. Selective jamming of all other nodes around the prover is difficult to implement and suffers from some limitations (e.g. illegal at the standard wireless bands, not fully secure and can be bypassed [16], cost ineffective which requires an extra hardware, etc.).
- The communication overhead required is very minimal which limited to the exchange of few bytes regardless the size of the remote IoT device's memory. The computational overhead also is limited to the computation of a simple MAC function. Moreover, no prior keys have to be stored and known in advance.
- Suitable for a wide range of legacy IoT devices, where the implementation of SPEED requires a minimal memory footprint and takes into account the lack of hardware security features.

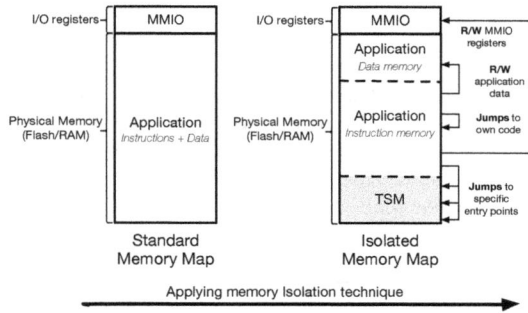

Figure 1: Overview of the unrestricted standard memory map and the restricted memory map after applying isolation technique.

3 MEMORY ISOLATION

Memory isolation is a security feature that provides a way to control memory access rights and prevent damage or leakage of private data through the unauthorized access that could happen by a software bug or a malware infection. The class of IoT devices (e.g. IETF Class-1), we are targeting, depends on the commercial off-the-shelf (COTS) microcontrollers that are optimized for low cost and low power consumption. So, they are deployed without any security properties. Furthermore, the existing hardware protection mechanisms can not be applied on such devices due to the restrictions of their own hardware architectures.

The basic property required to implement any form of secure erasure is memory isolation. It allows to control the memory addresses and reserve a part of it to store the private data and the security-related functions. Therefore, as a first step to build the secure erasure approach, we had to overcome the problem of lacking MPUs in Class-1 IoT devices by designing and implementing a pure software-based memory isolation technique. This security feature is required to isolate and guarantee the integrity of the Trusted Software Module (TSM) that running within a single address space from other untrusted software modules. The TSM refers to the cryptographic primitives, secrets keys, private data, and all other helping functions that we trust to execute. Our technique can be easily applied to any MCU with the following characteristics: (i) has no memory protection unit, (ii) supports disabling of global interrupts to ensure atomic execution of SPEED, (iii) does not support multi-threading, and (iv) still has sufficient flash memory to store the TSM code as a requirement of SPEED.

Design of Software-based Memory Isolation. Our design of the memory isolation shares similarities with the Software-based Fault Isolation (SFI) approach proposed by Whabe et al. [19]. As SFI approach has been designed for computer systems, we are taking advantages of it by designing and implementing a pure software-based memory isolation approach for embedded systems in an optimized way.

We use selective software virtualization and assembly-level code verification to provide sandboxing between software modules. At initialization time, the TSM should be installed using a physical programming device (e.g. JTAG) through an edited toolchain. Upon

successful installation, the occupied portion of the memory by TSM acts like an isolated and *virtual* ROM. The TSM memory can not be written or even read after the deployment of the microcontroller without a physical access. Furthermore, the execution of this area is only allowed from specific entry points as we see later. Therefore, the access to this part of the memory is protected by the employed virtualization mechanism. The TSM has no restrictions at all and has full access over other parts of the memory. As shown in Figure 1, the remaining part of the memory, denoted as *Application Memory*, should host other (untrusted) software modules. It consists of two subareas: the *Instruction Memory*, that holds the application code, and the *Data Memory* for data. In contrast to the TSM memory, the *Application Memory* is subject to the following restrictions:

- *Control Transfer:* branch and jump operations can only target either the instruction memory or specific entry points in the TSM memory.
- *Read and Write:* read and write operations address only the data memory and Memory Mapped IO (MMIO) registers.
- *Deployment:* updating the application memory can only occur by the TSM. Restrictions on the application code are enforced at the instructions level by *verifying* the adherence of the instructions to the listed rules and replacing unsafe and essential instructions by *safe virtualized* ones. Applications that violate the rules are rejected instantly by the TSM.

During the deployment process of an application, the TSM takes care of checking each instruction at the assembly level. Two types of illegal instructions can be identified:

- *static jump operations:* instructions that have a target address encoded in it statically, and this target address refers to a restricted point of memory.
- *dynamic jump operations:* instructions that access any memory dynamically as the target address is encoded in a pointer register.

Any application with at least one unsafe instruction will be rejected by the TSM. The vast majority of the control transfer instructions (e.g. program counter relative branches) have a direct target address and thus they can be checked statically at deployment time. Dynamic jump operations that use indirect addressing mode will be replaced by virtual safe instructions. The actual verification of their safety takes place at runtime rather than the deployment time. If at least one of these operations is unsafe (e.g. access restricted memory), the MCU will perform a soft reset preventing illegal operation. From a practical point of view, replacing the unsafe indirect call with a safe virtual indirect call takes place between the assembly and linking stages, as we add a post-processor to do this substitution during the compilation of the application code.

4 DISTANCE BOUNDING PROTOCOL

Distance Bounding (DB) protocols allow to establish an upper-bound on the physical distance between two parties which are typically denoted as *verifier* and *prover*. The first DB protocol was introduced by Brands and Chaum [8] in order to prevent mafia fraud (relay) attacks on bank ATMs [9], a special version of MITM attack. Brands and Chaum's DB is a challenge-response protocol which estimates the distance between two entities by measuring the round-trip time (RTT) of challenges and responses that travel at

Prover

$m_i \in_R \{0,1\}$

Verifier

$a_i \in_R \{0,1\}$

$commit(m_1 \mid .... \mid m_k)$

Start of rapid bit exchange

a_i

$B_i \leftarrow a_i \oplus m_i$

B_i

End of rapid bit exchange

$X \leftarrow a_1 \mid B_1 \mid ... \mid a_k \mid B_k$ $X \leftarrow a_1 \mid B_1 \mid ... \mid a_k \mid B_k$

(open commit), sign(X)

Verify commit
Verify sign(X)

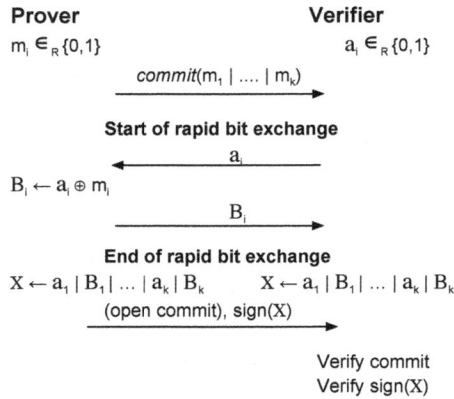

Figure 2: Distance bounding protocol of Brands and Chaum

the speed of light. Relying on this fact, we guarantee to obtain the upper bound of the distance between two parties, as the dishonest party can not claim to be closer than he really is because nothing propagates faster than the light. Thus preventing distance fraud attack too. The relay attack is prevented by forcing the adversary to come closer to the victim, which increases the possibility of being detected even by offline methods (i.e. visual detection).

An important feature of implementing distance bounding protocol is to rule out the assumption of selective jamming. To the best of our knowledge, all related approaches depend on this assumption. Jamming techniques work in theory as they depend on the noise level or channel properties, and such methods are not easy to implement [11]. Also, jamming techniques have a negative impact on the network performance and can be bypassed as demonstrated in [16]. On the other hand, Time Of Flight (ToF) based distance bounding protocols (e.g. the one we use) are more reliable, and often used to authenticate and evaluate the distance of the node in many applications such as keyless entry systems in vehicles, RFID door access systems, payment systems, and real time location systems (e.g. RADAR) [6].

Figure 2 shows the basic principles of the distance bounding protocol proposed by Brands and Chaum. The protocol encompasses three general phases. In the first phase, both the verifier and the prover generate a series of random bits. The number of bits depends on a chosen security parameter, k, that expresses the degree of confidence desired. The prover has to commit to the chosen values using a secure commitment scheme in order to avoid cheating. The backbone of the protocol is the second phase, which is the rapid exchange of bits to measure the distance, where both parties exchange challenges and responses represented as single bits. The basic idea is to precisely measure the round-trip time between two unpredictable messages (a challenge and a response). The process is repeated k times and each time the verifier computes the elapsed time. The verifier's challenges are unpredictable and each response has to be computed as a function of the corresponding challenge to ensure sending it after receiving the correct challenge. This helps in estimating the upper bound of the real distance of the prover node. Since we are interested in the propagation time, the processing

delay should be very small and negligible compared to the time of flight, taking into account that 1 nanosecond processing time yields 30 cm accuracy of RTT (15 cm of propagation time). This prevents a computationally powerful malicious node claiming false position. The proposed operation in the protocol is a simple XOR between two bits. In the last phase, the prover opens the commit. The verifier verifies it and computes the upper bound of the distance according to the following equation:

$$\left(\frac{max(RTT_i) - \alpha}{2}\right) \times C$$

where α is the processing time and C is the speed of the light.

If node authentication is required, public key cryptography can be used in the last phase to sign and verify the exchanged nonces. Public key identification schemes such as Fiat-Shamir can also be used for authentication, as described in the original paper [8].

5 SPEED

SPEED is a challenge-response protocol dedicated for secure erasure by allowing a node (e.g. a user of mobile phone) to securely and remotely delete the memory of another node (e.g. IoT device) and to get a proof of secure erasure without any pre-knowledge in advance. PoSE is given by the construction of SPEED itself without the requirement to run other protocols. Node authentication occurs by verifying the proximity of the two corresponding nodes through the implementation of a secure version of the DB protocol.

We start by outlining the attacker model. We then introduce and analyze SPEED, and explain the working mechanism behind the integration of the aforementioned building blocks in Section 3 and Section 4.

5.1 Adversarial Model

As a consequence of the advances in the IoT domain, attention started to shift from designing architectures relying on dedicated infrastructure to new trends of design using shared and distributed infrastructure [3, 14]. Hence, our case reference is that a single infrastructure provider deploy a set of smart devices for the public use as a shared hardware where any user can deploy his software and data over a custom IoT device for a period of time. Upon accomplishing the work, the user releases the underlying IoT device after verifying the cleanness of its memory and that nothing is left in it. Also, the user can perform the secure erasure of the memory before the software deployment in order to ensure that it doesn't store any unwanted software or malware.

We consider two types of adversaries based on the recently proposed taxonomy [1]:

- Remote adversary: exploits software bugs remotely at the prover side to infect it with malware.
- Local adversary: a standalone device, located in vicinity of the prover to eavesdrop on and interfere with the prover's communication.

As most other related work, we rule out all types of physical attacks. Also, denial-of-service (DoS) attacks are beyond the scope of this paper. Furthermore, we assume that TSM code is bug and exploit free and is deployed on the IoT device by a trusted party.

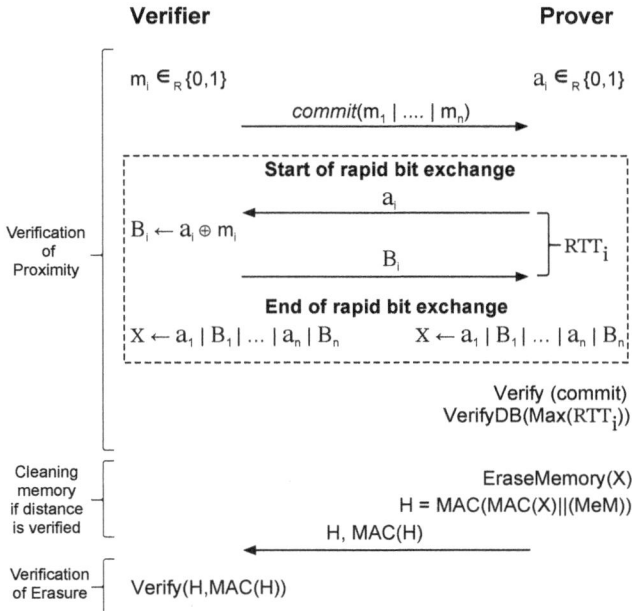

Figure 3: Overview of SPEED

5.2 Design Rationale

SPEED relies on the integration of two security primitives; memory isolation and distance bounding protocol. The latter is needed for the prover to verify the distance of the verifier, where the verifier is the node that wants to clean the memory of another node (prover) and get a proof of erasure. If the verifier is within range, the target device (prover) executes the request of secure erasure, otherwise, no change occurs. All necessary functions needed to run SPEED are located in the TSM. Memory isolation is guaranteed by the sandboxing technique we designed and implemented in Section 3.

Measuring the round-trip-time (RTT) of a given message provides a bound on the distance and this helps in preventing MITM attack and all of its related forms (e.g. mafia-fraud attack) since the simplest technique of relaying messages consumes an extra time and consequently results in a longer distance. The security of the DB protocol, we implement, is verified in [17] and thus it prevents against MITM attack as measuring RTT according to the speed of light can't be spoofed even if the adversary has a powerful hardware. This advantage of the DB replaces the assumption of using selective jamming, where DB is simpler to implement on the resource-constraint devices and easier to prove its security.

Figure 3 illustrates SPEED. Denoting the verifier as v and the prover (target device) as ρ, the protocol starts by generating random nonces of length n bits at both sides. v sends to ρ the hash value (the commit) of the chosen nonce to avoid cheating of sending responses in the future. Upon receiving the commit, ρ starts the rapid bit exchange phase by sending a challenge composed of one bit and wait for a response from v. The rapid bit exchange process is repeated n times. Assuming that we are in the ith iteration, the response is the result of XORing the two corresponding bits (the ith challenge bit and the ith bit in v's nonce). By the end of this

phase, ρ knows the maximum round-trip time (RTT) and is able to compute the hash value of the nonce generated by v. Hence, ρ can verify the received commit (e.g. *Verify(commit)*) and establish an upper bound of v's distance (e.g. *VerifyDB(Max(RTT$_i$))*). If both verification steps are passed successfully, the secure erasure of the memory takes place by resetting the value of each byte in the memory to be equal to either a default value or to a value of one of the random bytes in the nonces (e.g. *EraseMemory(X)*). In the last step, ρ generates a session key by computing the MAC value of the alternating bits-concatenated nonces and then computes the message authentication code (MAC) of the entire memory using this key (e.g. $H = MAC(MAC(X)||(MeM))$). ρ sends the result back to v along with its MAC value to ensure integrity. Finally, v verifies the outcome by following the same deterministic steps of computing the MAC. If both values are equal, secure erasure has occurred. We notice that our protocol has minor modifications with regards to the original DB v does not have to open the commit after the rapid bit exchange phase, as we use the same public hash function used for computing the MAC of the memory to compute the hash value of the chosen randomness by v in the initial phase. ρ can verify it easily after the second phase. Moreover, we do not consider the authentication using public key cryptography since our scenario simulates the case where there is no prior knowledge between v and ρ. Any v close to any ρ can execute the secure erasure of the memory. The execution of SPEED occurs only from a valid entry point and is not interruptible as all global interrupts are disabled prior to the start and activated again after clearing the RAM from all temporary variables used during the run of the protocol.

5.3 Security Analysis

To analyse the security of SPEED, we first present the existing and related attacks on both Distance bounding [6] and similar challenge-response (e.g. Remote Attestation) protocols [18] and then defend against them considering the aforementioned adversarial model (Section 5.1) and under the following assumptions:

- *AS1*: We assume a source of true and unpredictable randomness on both sides, and all responses depends on the corresponding challenges (e.g. $r = f(c)$).
- *AS2*: The cryptographic hash function used for commitment and computing MAC is secure.
- *AS3*: The TSM guarantees that the prover device can only communicate with the verifier during the run of SPEED (e.g. single uninterruptible thread of execution).

5.3.1 Security of TSM. The software-based memory protection unit (TSM), that we implement, is the core of providing the security of SPEED. SPEED, similarly to all other challenge-response protocols, can be vulnerable to one or more of the following attacks [18]:

- Precomputation attack: The ability of the adversary to predict the challenges sent by the IoT device (e.g. the node (ρ) that wants to verify the distance of another node (v)) and precompute valid responses in advance.
- Replay attack: The ability of the adversary to eavesdrop to the correct outcome of the erasure routine from a non-compromised node (ρ), store it, and then reply it when needed.

- Forgery attack: The adversary may alter the erasure routine to forge a real but not valid outcome from (ρ) in order to give a fake proof of erasure.
- Impersonation attack: The adversary might impersonate a genuine node (ρ) and send valid but fake proofs of erasure to v.
- Proxy attack: A dishonest node (v) might relay the challenges to a more powerful node that is able to compute a valid response in its behalf.
- Collusion attack: The ability of a compromised node (ρ) to collude with other nodes to provide a valid proof of erasure without erasing the actual content of memory.
- Memory copy attack: If there is an enough free space in the prover's memory, the adversary can keep a copy of the original memory contents. Then, he can modify the erasure routine so it computes a response over the memory locations where his copy is not maintained.
- Compression attack: The adversary might save a compressed version of the prover's memory in a random location and decompress it after the execution of the erasure routine. It is a special case of the memory copy attack.
- Return-oriented programming (ROP) attack: the adversary may modify the control-flow of the prover's code to execute arbitrary operations by linking together small sequences of instructions, called gadgets, without making any changes to the program memory.

Precomputation and replay attacks are no longer feasible as *AS1* guarantees that the challenges are unpredictable and the hash value of the memory is variable since it depends on the nonce generated by these challenges.

The forgery attack aims to overcome the secure erasure routine itself and tamper with the TSM code. This is prevented by the access rules enforced by the TSM at deployment time, where read and write operations to this part of the memory are not allowed, whereas execution can only occur from specific entry points after disabling all global interrupts to ensure atomicity. Moreover, *AS1* and *AS2* guarantee that MAC values can't be forged.

Impersonation attack is prevented and can easily be detected using either offline methods (e.g. visual detection) as we are considering small distances or by the responses which would reflect an invalid value of MAC.

Proxy and collusion attacks are not valid under the adapted threat model and *AS3*. Moreover, Proxy attack is already prevented by the countermeasure of the terrorist fraud attack as we see later.

Memory-copy, compression, and ROP attacks have the same goal as the forgery attack, aiming to modify the TSM code and alter with the secure erasure routine. This is totally prevented by the employed sandboxing mechanism under the aforementioned threat model (e.g. No physical access). Nevertheless, any bug of the deployed user application (e.g. stack overflow) increases the possibility of ROP attack to occur. However, this attack is implementation-specific and requires high efforts to cause damage. The security of the TSM still can not be broken by this attack. However, if succeeded, it executes arbitrary lines of the TSM code without modifying or altering it. This means that TSM still guarantees to provide a valid proof of erasure by the end of a correct execution of the secure erasure routine.

5.3.2 Security of Distance Bounding.
There are four major attacks that threaten the security of the DB protocol:

- Impersonation: An impersonation fraud is an attack where an adversary acting alone purports to be a legitimate prover.
- Distance fraud: The claim of a dishonest party (v) to be closer than (s)he really is.
- Mafia fraud: A special type of man-in-the-middle attack, in which, the third party is passive and simply relays messages regardless of their content.
- Terrorist fraud: A variant of mafia fraud attack, in which, the prover (e.g. in our case: v) colludes with the adversary to deceive the verifier (e.g. in our case: ρ) that (s)he in vicinity without disclosing the secret key to the adversary, where the adversary performs the first two phases of the protocol (e.g. see Figure 2) and the dishonest prover (v) performs only the signing phase.

Countermeasures to such attacks are already proposed and discussed in literature [6, 17] and hence we just implement them.

In our case, the impersonation attack is useless as all devices can act as legitimate provers (v) since authentication using secret/private key is not required.

The RTT distance-estimation technique, that we use, depends on precise timing, as a deviation of a few nanoseconds affects negatively on the estimated distance (e.g. 6 ns add an extra 1 meter). Depending on this strict timing property and taking into account *AS1*, we prevent mafia fraud attack as even a simple relay of messages unavoidably adds an extra time and thus results in longer distance. Accordingly, distance fraud attack is prevented too.

In SPEED, we do not depend on secret or private keys to authenticate the prover as we demonstrate our scenario in the public space and anyone in vicinity of the IoT device can delete it's memory. Therefore, in this case, terrorist fraud attack is the same as mafia fraud attack and thus it is implicitly prevented.

6 IMPLEMENTATION

We implemented a prototype of SPEED on an 8-bit AVR ATmega 1284p microcontroller (MCU) [4] mounted on the MicroPnP IoT platform [22]. This MCU belongs to Class-1 devices which runs at 10 MHz, with 16 KB of SRAM, 4 KB of EEPROM, and 128 KB of flash memory. In addition to the MCU, MicroPnP offers an IEEE 802.15.4e [21] radio for wireless communication. In contrast to *von Neumann* architecture, the AVR family of microcontrollers uses the modified Harvard architecture, where MMIO, instructions and data memory are physically separated and not mapped on to a single address space. The sandboxing techniques we implement, in SPEED, can be applied to both architectures without any limitations.

The secure erasure of a device's memory may be considered as a prelude or a consequence of software deployment. We consider the secure deployment of software out of scope in this paper. However, in the implementation of the memory isolation, we take care that the current untrusted application in the *Instruction memory* should not violate the restricted rules explained in Section 3. This means that the software installation should pass through some functions in the TSM in order to ensure the adherence to the rules and the success of secure erasure later on.

From a programming point of view, we have two entry points in the TSM (e.g. two public functions), from which we can execute the code. The first entry point is called the *Loader*. The *Loader* function is responsible to load the produced binary image of the application in a temporary area in the application memory and verify its instructions to see if they adhere to the rules or not. Verification is done line by line at the assembly level. If even only one statement violates the rules (e.g. jump to a restricted point in the TSM), the whole application is rejected. As argued before, in a standard toolchain, producing the binary image of the user application goes through the compiler, the assembler, and then the linker. We edited the toolchain by adding a post-processor between the assembler and the linker in order to replace all unsafe dynamic instructions with safe virtual ones. These instructions cannot be checked statically by the *Loader* function at the deployment time and therefore they are checked at runtime. Any violation caused by one of these instructions makes the device restarting itself in order to avoid the unauthorized execution of the malicious code.

The second entry point is the *SecureErasure* function, using which, we execute the erasure routine described in Figure 3. All related functions are located in the TSM memory and can be executed through this entry point. The protocol starts by disabling all global interrupts. Therefore, the correct and atomic execution of this function is guaranteed. The verification of secure erasure requires the computation of the message authentication code (MAC) of the entire memory. We developed two versions of our system. In the first one, we use an optimized implementation of the sponge Keccak-256 (SHA-3 standard) function in the assembly level to compute the MAC. In the second, HMAC-SHA1 is used. The same hash function is used for computing the commit in DB and verifying it. The output of Keccak is 256 bits long, whereas HMAC-SHA1 output is 160 bits long. We considered a length of 128 bytes for generating nonces which can be adjusted according to the specific domain of application. At the end of the rapid exchange bytes process, both parties have a nonce of length *2n* (256 bytes).

7 EVALUATION

We evaluate SPEED according to many factors: (i) performance, (ii) memory footprint, (iii) power consumption, and (iv) the accuracy of estimating the distance between two parties.

7.1 Performance

The main parameters that affect the time overhead of SPEED are:

- **Number of exchanged bits**. Launching SPEED requires exchanging a limited number of bits (seed) between the verifier and the prover. The length of this seed does not depend at all on the size of the memory and can be adjusted by the user, where the longer the sequence of bits exchanged, the more accurate the measurement is. In our experiment, we considered a length of 128 bytes as a seed. The objectives of this seed are manifold: (i) establishing the upper-bound of the distance between the verifier and the prover, (ii) using it as a nonce to satisfy the freshness property, and (iii) generating a session key to compute the corresponding MAC.

Table 1: Evaluation of MAC constructions

MAC	Memory footprint		Performance
	ROM (bytes)	RAM (bytes)	Time (sec)
HMAC-SHA1	1296	86	6.8
Keccak-256	1512	174	12.9

In contrast to other existing approaches [12, 15], SPEED has the advantage that it does not require exchanging a number of bits equals to the size of prover's memory to overwrite it. Thus, it incurs very small communication overhead.

- **Memory access time**. SPEED requires accessing each byte address in the memory twice. First, to erase it's content. Second, to compute the MAC. The speed of accessing the memory mainly relies on the clock rate of the MCU. In our experiment, the microcontroller operates at 10 MHz. This means that the total time of accessing the memory accounts just for a small fraction of the total run time of SPEED.

- **Computation of MAC**. Table 1 shows the time required to compute the MAC of the application memory using either HMAC-SHA1 or Keccak-256. It is clear that total time consumed by running SPEED mainly depends on the time of computing the MAC. This metric is approach-independent which relies on the device capabilities (e.g. the speed of the clock), the type of MAC selected, and the performance of the MAC implementation used.

7.2 Memory overhead

- **Flash Memory** The TSM code has to be placed in the bootloader section which is part of the flash memory. SPEED requires no more than 4 KB of the flash memory. The exact code size of SPEED using HMAC-SHA1 is 2866 bytes, whereas it is 3102 bytes when using Keccak-256.

- **RAM** The overhead of using RAM is limited only to the use of the stack for holding temporary buffers and variables. In AVR, execution of instructions is only allowed from the Flash memory. Our evaluation shows that SPEED requires either 494 bytes or 582 bytes of RAM when using HMAC-SHA1 or Keccak-256 respectively. Table 1 presents the memory overhead of the MAC constructs without other helping functions in the TSM.

7.3 Power Consumption

The MicroPnP IoT platform, where we perform our experiment, consumes 3.54 mA when operating on 10 MHz in the active mode, and 54.5 μA in the idle mode. Every MicroPnP platform is powered by a standard 3000 mAh battery pack. The baseline battery lifetime, if the MCU is in the sleeping mode constantly, is 6.5 years. Considering these values, Figure 4 shows the estimated lifetime of the battery when running SPEED using either HMAC-SHA1 or Keccak-256 under different rates of time.

7.4 Accuracy of measuring the distance

The DB primitive in SPEED aims to establish the upper bound on the distance of the other party and does not target the exact location

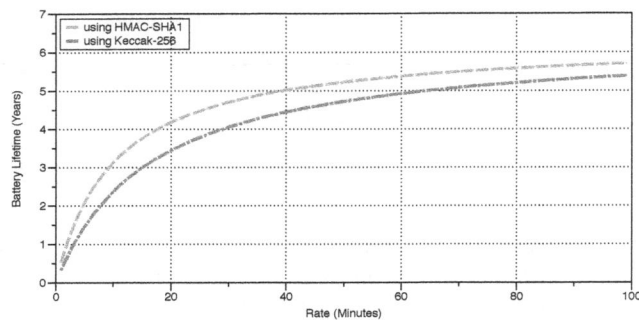

Figure 4: The impact on battery lifetime when using either HMAC-SHA1 or Keccak-256 primitives in SPEED.

of this party. We measure according to the speed of the light. So, a delay of 1 *ns* affects the distance of 15 cm. The microcontroller between hands (e.g. ATmega 1284p) operates on 10 MHz frequency and this means having a resolution of 100 *ns* in the ideal condition (e.g. The processing time is identified accurately on both sides, etc.), where a device with a distance of 1 *m* is detected as 15 *m* farther. Longer the range the more accurate is the measurement. For example, with this resolution, all devices within a range of 1 *m* to 14 *m* will be labeled with a distance of around 15 *m*. Since we are conducting our experiment within close range, this resolution does not help us. Therefore, we depend on the distance measurement functionality in the transceiver module itself. The IEEE 802.15.4 transceiver [5] between hands has a *time-of-flight* facility built into the hardware that improves the accuracy of measuring distance. Experimentally, we got an accuracy of 3 meters, which means a resolution of 20 *ns*. However, there are some distance measurement technologies [13] that integrate the aforementioned transceiver with a custom firmware to acquire special features like a RADAR system, thus giving a high accuracy where the resolution is near 1 *ns*.

Nevertheless, not all microcontrollers are integrated with such type of transceivers. In this case, the microcontroller should rely on the internal capabilities to calculate RTT accurately. Though recent work has yielded some proposals for establishing the upper bound on the distance between wireless sensor nodes with standard hardware [2], we still believe that this research problem is hardware-dependent and remains an open issue.

8 CONCLUSION & FUTURE WORK

Secure remote decommissioning (e.g. erasure) is as important as secure remote provisioning (e.g. deployment), and should be a key requirement for IoT devices. This paper proposed SPEED, an approach to secure provable erasure for embedded devices. It can be applied to all Class-1 IoT devices without any limitations. Our approach depends on isolating part of the flash memory using selective software virtualization and assembly level verification to store the trusted software module. We then build the secure erasure mechanism using DB protocol to prevent man-in-the-middle attack. The evaluation results show that SPEED incurs an acceptable overhead in terms of memory footprint, power consumption and

performance. A fundamental limitation of SPEED is that it is limited to small (visual) distances.

In future work, we plan to investigate SPEED with a stronger attacker model where physical attack (e.g. the invasive one) should be taken into account by implementing some techniques in the TSM to detect it (e.g. detecting loss of power). Finally, a formal verification of the TSM code and a demonstration of a real and complete scenario including secure software deployment as well is another future goal.

REFERENCES

[1] Tigist Abera, N Asokan, Lucas Davi, Farinaz Koushanfar, Andrew Paverd, Ahmad-Reza Sadeghi, and Gene Tsudik. 2016. Things, trouble, trust: on building trust in IoT systems. In *Proceedings of the 53rd Annual Design Automation Conference*. ACM, 121.
[2] Stephan Adler, Stefan Pfeiffer, Heiko Will, Thomas Hillebrandt, and Jochen Schiller. 2012. Measuring the distance between wireless sensor nodes with standard hardware. In *Positioning Navigation and Communication (WPNC), 2012 9th Workshop on*. IEEE, 114–119.
[3] Muneeb Ahmad, Jalal S Alowibdi, and Muhammad U Ilyas. 2017. vIoT: A first step towards a shared, multi-tenant IoT Infrastructure architecture. In *Communications Workshops (ICC Workshops), 2017 IEEE International Conference on*. IEEE, 308–313.
[4] Atmel. 2009. AVR Atmega 1284p 8-bit microcontroller. http://www.atmel.com/images/doc8059.pdf. (2009). [Online; accessed 13-April-2017].
[5] Atmel. 2014. AT86RF233 . http://ww1.microchip.com/downloads/en/DeviceDoc/Atmel-8351-MCU_Wireless-AT86RF233_Datasheet.pdf. (2014). [Online; accessed 13-July-2017].
[6] G Avoine, MA Bingol, Ioana Boureanu, S Capkun, G Hancke, S Kardas, CH Kim, C Lauradoux, B Martin, J Munilla, et al. 2017. Security of Distance-Bounding: A Survey. *Comput. Surveys* (2017).
[7] Carsten Bormann, Mehmet Ersue, and A Keranen. 2014. *Terminology for constrained-node networks*. Technical Report.
[8] Stefan Brands and David Chaum. 1993. Distance-bounding protocols. In *Workshop on the Theory and Application of of Cryptographic Techniques*. Springer, 344–359.
[9] Yvo Desmedt. 1988. Major security problems with the âĂŸunforgeableâĂŹ(Feige)-Fiat-Shamir proofs of identity and how to overcome them. In *Proceedings of SECURICOM*, Vol. 88. 15–17.
[10] Stefan Dziembowski, Tomasz Kazana, and Daniel Wichs. 2011. One-time computable self-erasing functions. In *Theory of Cryptography Conference*. Springer, 125–143.
[11] Kanika Grover, Alvin Lim, and Qing Yang. 2014. Jamming and anti–jamming techniques in wireless networks: a survey. *International Journal of Ad Hoc and Ubiquitous Computing* 17, 4 (2014), 197–215.
[12] Ghassan O Karame and Wenting Li. 2015. Secure erasure and code update in legacy sensors. In *International Conference on Trust and Trustworthy Computing*. Springer, 283–299.
[13] metirionic. 2015. ATSAMR21-XPRO. http://www.metirionic.com/en/technology.html. (2015). [Online; accessed 13-July-2017].
[14] Job Noorman. 2017. Sancus: A Low-Cost Security Architecture for Distributed IoT Applications on a Shared Infrastructure. (2017).
[15] Daniele Perito and Gene Tsudik. 2010. Secure code update for embedded devices via proofs of secure erasure. In *European Symposium on Research in Computer Security*. Springer, 643–662.
[16] Alejandro Proano and Loukas Lazos. 2012. Packet-hiding methods for preventing selective jamming attacks. *IEEE Transactions on dependable and secure computing* 9, 1 (2012), 101–114.
[17] Dave Singelee and Bart Preneel. 2005. Location verification using secure distance bounding protocols. In *Mobile Adhoc and Sensor Systems Conference, 2005. IEEE International Conference on*. IEEE, 7–pp.
[18] Rodrigo Vieira Steiner and Emil Lupu. 2016. Attestation in Wireless Sensor Networks: A Survey. *ACM Computing Surveys (CSUR)* 49, 3 (2016), 51.
[19] Robert Wahbe, Steven Lucco, Thomas E Anderson, and Susan L Graham. 1993. Efficient software-based fault isolation. *ACM SIGOPS Operating Systems Review* 27, 5 (dec 1993), 203–216. https://doi.org/10.1145/173668.168635
[20] Nils Walravens. 2016. Operationalising the Concept of the Smart City as a Local Innovation Platform: The City of Things Lab in Antwerp, Belgium. In *International Conference on Smart Cities*. Springer, 128–136.
[21] Thomas Watteyne, M Palattella, and L Grieco. 2015. *Using ieee 802.15. 4e time-slotted channel hopping (TSCH) in the Internet of Things (IoT): Problem statement*. Technical Report.
[22] Fan Yang, Nelson Matthys, Rafael Bachiller, Sam Michiels, Wouter Joosen, and Danny Hughes. 2015. μ PnP: plug and play peripherals for the internet of things. In *Proceedings of the Tenth European Conference on Computer Systems*. ACM, 25.

Identifying Relevant Information Cues for Vulnerability Assessment Using CVSS

Luca Allodi
Eindhoven University of Technology
l.allodi@tue.nl

Sebastian Banescu
Henning Femmer
Munich Technical University
name.surname@tum.de

Kristian Beckers
Social Engineering Academy (SEA)
GmbH
kristian.beckers@social-engineering.
academy

ABSTRACT

The assessment of new vulnerabilities is an activity that accounts for information from several data sources and produces a 'severity' score for the vulnerability. The Common Vulnerability Scoring System (CVSS) is the reference standard for this assessment. Yet, no guidance currently exists on *which information* aids a correct assessment and should therefore be considered. In this paper we address this problem by evaluating which information cues increase (or decrease) assessment accuracy. We devise a block design experiment with 67 software engineering students with varying vulnerability information and measure scoring accuracy under different information sets. We find that baseline vulnerability descriptions provided by standard vulnerability sources provide only part of the information needed to achieve an accurate vulnerability assessment. Further, we find that additional information on assets, attacks, and vulnerability type contributes in increasing the accuracy of the assessment; conversely, information on known threats misleads the assessor and decreases assessment accuracy and should be avoided when assessing vulnerabilities. These results go in the direction of formalizing the vulnerability communication to, for example, fully automate security assessments.

CCS CONCEPTS

• **Security and privacy** → **Vulnerability management**; • **Software and its engineering** → **Risk management**; • **General and reference** → *Empirical studies*;

KEYWORDS

software vulnerability assessment; vulnerability information; CVSS

ACM Reference Format:
Luca Allodi, Sebastian Banescu Henning Femmer, and Kristian Beckers. 2018. Identifying Relevant Information Cues for Vulnerability Assessment Using CVSS. In *CODASPY '18: Eighth ACM Conference on Data and Application Security and Privacy, March 19–21, 2018, Tempe, AZ, USA*. ACM, New York, NY, USA, 8 pages. https://doi.org/10.1145/3176258.3176340

1 INTRODUCTION

Addressing software vulnerabilities is an important process in any software development project [17] to maintain software quality and mitigate risk of attack for the users. Several standards, such as PCI-DSS for the management of credit card information and NIST's SCAP protocol (adopted for example by the U.S. DoD directive 8500.01), require the use of the Common Vulnerability Scoring System [12], CVSS, as the metric of choice for vulnerability measurement and prioritisation [1, 25]. The CVSS specification [12] describes a framework that the assessor follows to transform information about the vulnerability into a CVSS score, and provides a number of 'dimensions' or 'metrics' over which the assessor performs his or her evaluation. For example, the assessor may evaluate that the vulnerability can be remotely accessed, and assign a Network value to the CVSS metric Attack Vector; similarly, he or she may conclude that a successful attack requires the victim user to perform specific actions for the attack to be successful, and assign a Required value to the CVSS metric User Interaction.

The result of these assessments depends strongly on what information on the vulnerability is available to the assessor. Notably, this information may vary substantially, ranging from general descriptions such as *"Unspecified vulnerability in [..] allows local users to affect availability via vectors related to Kernel"*,[1] to more technically detailed information [6]. Whereas the type of information one can gather generally covers type of vulnerability, attack procedure, and existence of threats [14], no guidance currently exists on the mapping of which information should be considered when performing an assessment over the CVSS metrics. For example, analysing the attack procedure may provide details on the position of the attacker w.r.t. the vulnerable software component (captured by the Attack Vector CVSS metric), but may not reveal useful information to evaluate which privileges are required to exploit the vulnerability (captured by the Privileges Required metric). This prevents the development and use of automatic tools that can provide useful summaries of available information that the assessor can use when performing his or her CVSS evaluation of the vulnerability.

In this study we evaluate which information cues can aid the vulnerability assessment process as guided by the CVSS standard, and should therefore be readily provided to the assessor. This paper's contributions can be summarized as follows:

(1) Following guidelines from current standards [20] and recent literature [14, 26], we identify four information categories over which vulnerabilities are described: Assets [29], Attack [26], Vulnerability type [20], and Known threats [14].

---

[1] https://web.nvd.nist.gov/view/vuln/detail?vulnId=CVE-2016-5469

(2) Building on recent research on the automatic identification of 'requirement smells' [10], we evaluate the number of *information cues* (i.e. phrases consisting of one or more words) associated with each of the identified information categories, and their affect on assessment error.

(3) We ask 67 students to score a set of 16 vulnerabilities using CVSS. To evaluate the effect of different information cues, we devise a block experiment design in which each student is assigned randomly to a treatment[2] group, and compare assessment errors to identify which information cues are effective in aiding the final assessment and which are not.

This paper unfolds as follows: Section 2 discusses related work. Section 3 outlines our research goal and questions, experiment setup, metrics, and hypotheses. We then presents our results (Section 4) and discuss their implications (Section 5). Section 6 and 7 discusses threats to validity and conclude.

2 BACKGROUND AND RELATED WORK

In security engineering controlled experiments have been performed to measure the effectiveness and efficiency of vulnerability analysis techniques and applications [3, 4, 27], security patterns in helping software designers [32], and the application of different security methods for risk assessment [21].

Similarly, several authors studied the relation between vulnerability measures and risk scenarios. The operative aspects integrating security measures in production environments have been studied, among others, by Dashevskyi et al. [7] (who investigate settings where vulnerabilities are included in third party components), Zhang et al. [33] (who predict bug fixing times by employing a Markov model based on field data), Zimmermann et al. [35] (who investigate the discrepancies between user-supplied bug information and information needed by the developers), and Zhao et al. [34] (who evaluate the effect of early discussion on bug fixing). We integrate these findings by focusing on vulnerability information and evaluating which information aids the vulnerability fixing process.

Proposed measures for the identification of vulnerabilities in code rely on features of code such as code complexity and code churn [28], whereas other authors propose keyword-based text-mining procedures to forecast vulnerabilities [31]. Thompson et al. [30] investigated the cognitive effort spent when breaking down software engineering tasks such as bug fixing.

To aid a correct understanding of software requirements, natural language processing techniques such as keyword extraction have been used to detect quality defects in natural language specification [10]. Experimentation often relates to factors such as the correctness and the positive or negative tone of requirements [22], and grammatical features such as passive or active voice requirements. While our approach is similar, we detect information cues in vulnerability description text to associate it with assessment errors, as opposed to measuring 'bad wording' in software requirements.

2.1 The Common Vulnerability Scoring System

The CVSS framework specification is the worldwide standard for vulnerability assessment and has been drafted by the dedicated *First.org*

Table 1: Summary description of CVSS v3 Base metrics

	Exploitability metrics		
ID	Metric	Description	Values
AV	Attack Vector	Reflects how remote the attacker can be, to deliver the attack against the vulnerable component. The more remote, the higher the score.	Physical, Local, Adj. Net., Network.
AC	Attack Complexity	Reflects the existence of conditions that are beyond the attacker's control for the attack to be successful.	High, Low.
PR	Privileges Required	Reflects the privileges the attacker need have on the vulnerable system to exploit the vulnerable component.	High, Low, None.
UI	User Interaction	Reflects the need for user interaction to deliver a successful attack.	Required, None.
	Impact metrics		
ID	Metric	Description	Values
C	Confidentiality	Measures the impact to the confidentiality of information.	None, Low, High.
I	Integrity	Measures the impact to the integrity of information.	None, Low, High.
A	Availability	Measures the impact to the availability of the impacted component.	None, Low, High.

Special Interest Group (SIG). The CVSS framework provides a number of dimensions over which a vulnerability is assessed based on available information on the vulnerability. These dimensions are classified into three groups, or metrics: Base Metric (captures technical characteristics of the vulnerability), Temporal Metric (captures vulnerable conditions that change in time), and Environmental Metric (captures conditions that change by deployment environments). The Base Metric Group is by far the most commonly used in practice [16, 23] and is the one officially used to describe vulnerabilities in the NIST's *National Vulnerability Database* (NVD) [2].

The Base Score assessment is organized in two conceptually different groups of sub-metrics [3]; *Exploitability* metrics reflect the means by which an attacker can deliver a successful attack, whereas *Impact* metrics provide an assessment of the consequences of a successful attack on the impacted system.

Exploitability metrics under CVSS v3 are measured over four dimensions: Attack Vector (AV), Attack Complexity (AC), Privileges Required (PR) and User Interaction (UI). Impact metrics in CVSS v3 are measured over the triad Confidentiality, Integrity and Availability. Table 1 provides a summary description of the CVSS v3 Base metrics. Full reference can be found at the official *First.org* specification documentation [12].

2.2 Information categories for vulnerability measurement

We evaluate the effect of the following information categories on the accuracy of CVSS assessments:

---

[2]Treatments integrate baseline vulnerability descriptions with information provided by the standard body for CVSS.

[3]A third metric group, Scope, is not reported here for brevity as it is not used in this study.

`Assets`. Security assessment and management standards such as NIST 800-30 and Common Criteria [19, 29] define the concept of 'asset' as key to correctly evaluate the severity of the vulnerability impact. Information in this category includes details on type of affected system (e.g. a server or a client) or the component affected by the vulnerability (e.g. an operating system or a virtual machine).

`Attack`. Expert interviews conducted by Holm et al. [14], alongside other studies [13], identify information regarding attack procedures as important to conduct an accurate vulnerability assessment. Attack procedures describe the actions that an attacker must perform to exploit the vulnerability: for example, the attacker may need to launch a *man-in-the-middle* attack, or inject code in a webpage.

`Vulnerability type`. ISO 29147 [20] conceptualizes vulnerability information as related to a description of the vulnerability and its impact. This includes information on the type of vulnerability and its causes in the program's code. For example, an erroneous bound checking of a memory array may lead to *memory corruption* vulnerabilities; similarly, erroneous input validation on a web form may lead to *cross-site-scripting* (XSS) vulnerabilities.

`Known threat`. Several studies [5, 14, 26] suggest that information on existing threats should also be provided to aid a better vulnerability assessment. This information includes details on the existence of *proof-of-concept* exploit (*PoC*), active exploitation in the wild, or incidents linked to the specific vulnerability.

3 METHODOLOGY

In this paper, following the discussion in Sec. 2.2, we investigate the following research question: *How does information on {*`Asset`*,* `Attack`*,* `Vuln. type`*,* `Known threat`*} impact assessment errors?*

3.1 Experimental settings

To address these four research questions, we perform an experiment where subjects are asked to score sixteen vulnerabilities using CVSS. Each vulnerability is associated with its description from the National Vulnerability Database (NVD)[2] and a treatment consisting of *additional information* on the vulnerability (on top of its baseline NVD description) provided by the CVSS SIG [11]. Table 2 reports example vulnerability descriptions and treatments used for the experiment. The column 'Treatment effect' reports the effect of the treatment on the accuracy of the assessment, which is discussed in detail in Section 4.

Subjects were given 90 minutes to complete the assessment irrespective of the treatment selection. Hence, each subject had on average about 6 minutes per vulnerability. In accordance with literature on the subject [24], the time was selected on the basis of previous trial experiments previously conducted in similar settings.

3.2 Vulnerabilities and Subject Selection

The sixteen vulnerabilities employed in the experiment are obtained from the official CVSS v3 Example document drafted by the First.org SIG for CVSS [11]. The vulnerabilities included by the SIG have been chosen to represent the full set of CVSS metrics, and are actively used for training purposes by members of the SIG consortium within the respective organizations. Each vulnerability in the document is associated with its official public description from

the National Vulnerability Database [2] and additional information added by the CVSS SIG. The subjects of this study are 67 students enrolled in the software engineering study program, who registered for a software security course.

3.3 Measures

Information cues. To quantify the amount of information in a vulnerability description (for each information category identified in Sec. 2.2: `Asset`, `Attack`, `Vulnerability type`, `Known threat`) we employ a methodology originally developed to automatically identify 'smells' in software requirement specifications [10]. The original methodology employs keyword-matching to identify standard-defined criteria for quality of requirements in the analysed text. As no such standard exists for software vulnerability descriptions, in our study we identify keywords relevant to each of the identified information categories by manually analysing over 100 randomly sampled vulnerabilities from NVD. Keywords are selected as indicators of what information is present in the description. For example, the keyword '*remote attacker*' indicates that the vulnerability description explicitly reports information relative to the information category `Attacker`. Information cues are measured as the number of keyword matches in a baseline vulnerability description and in the corresponding treatment. Table 3 reports a sample of the keywords identified for each information category. The full keyword list is available in the online appendix.[4]

Assessment errors. To evaluate assessment errors, we compare the subjects' CVSS assessments on the vulnerabilities with those performed by the CVSS SIG. In this study we do not consider magnitude or directionality of error, but only the presence of a correct (*error* = 0) or wrong (*error* = 1) assessment for each CVSS metric (`AV`, `AC`, `UI`, `PR`, `C`, `I`, `A`), for all vulnerabilities.

Subject characteristics. Each subject was asked to complete a background questionnaire. We collected data relative to: security expertise of the student; software engineering expertise; years of prior work experience; years of enrollment in a Computer Science major; university courses completed. Students where asked to perform both a self-assessment on their expertise and to answer a set of multiple-choice technical questions on relevant areas of software security and engineering. Each technical question has only one correct answer. The questionnaire is available in the online appendix. Results are discussed in Section 4.1.

3.4 Hypotheses

`Asset`. Because `Asset` provides information regarding the target of the attack (e.g. a browser, or a server) we expect this information category to reduce error assessments on the impact metrics `C`, `I` and `A`. For example, an attack on a browser may violate the Confidentiality of information stored in cookies or browsing history, whereas an attack on a server may affect the service Availability. We formulate the following *null* hypothesis:

HYPOTHESIS 1. H_0: *The* `Asset` *information category does not reduce error rates for the* `C`, `I`, `A` *metrics.*

---

[4]https://github.com/tum-i22/information-cues

Table 2: Example of vulnerability descriptions and treatments given to the students.

Example of four CVE descriptions and treatments assigned to students. We obtained this descriptions from the NVD. Treatment are obtained from the official CVSSv3 example guide [11]. The column 'Treatment effect' outlines the effect on error rate of the treatment. Indicated p-values are Holm-corrected for multiple comparisons over CVSS metrics. We highlighted in bold relevant excerpts that explain the treatment effect. Significance of the treatment effect is evaluated with a Wilcoxon rank-sum test.

CVE	NVD Description	Treatment	Treatment effect
CVE-2014-3566	The SSL protocol 3.0, as used in OpenSSL through 1.0.1i and other products, uses nondeterministic CBC padding, which makes it easier for man in the middle attackers to obtain plaintext data via a padding-oracle attack, aka the "POODLE" issue.	A typical treatment is that a **victim has visited a web server and her web browser now contains a cookie** that an attacke wishes to steal. For a successful attack, the **attacker must be able to modify network traffic between the victim and this web server**, and both victim and system must be willing to use SSL 3.0 for encryption.	Decrease error on AC ($p < 0.10$) Decrease error on UI ($p < 0.01$)
CVE-2012-0384	Cisco IOS 12.2 through 12.4 and [..] before 3.2.2SG, when AAA authorization is enabled, allow remote authenticated users to bypass intended access restrictions and execute commands via a (1) HTTP or (2) HTTPS session, aka Bug ID CSCtr91106.	**This vulnerability is post authentication on the administrative interface of the Cisco device.** Therefore to attack a typical installation, the attacker would need access to the trusted / internal side of the IOS.	Increase error on PR ($p < 0.01$)

Table 3: Definitions of information categories and selection of respective keywords.

Information categories	Definition	Reference	Keywords
Asset	Assets are entities that users or vendors value and contain vulnerabilities.	[12, 18, 29]	hardware, guest virtual machine, host, vm, device, client, server, operating system, version, product, affected version, affected product, vulnerable, vulnerable software, vulnerable hardware, affected software, affected hardware, software
Attack	Actions and entities that can adversely act on assets by exploiting vulnerabilities.	[5, 14, 26]	attacker, malicious user, remote authenticated user, remote user, man in the middle, unauthenticated remote attacker, spoofing, inject code, manipulate pointers, cache poisoning, open malicious file, birthday attack
Vulnerability type	Describes the technical flaws that can be exploited and the impact of the exploitation.	[20]	improper bounds checking, insufficient randomness, memory corruption, buffer overflow, cross-site scripting, broken authentication, insecure cryptographic storage, failure to restrict URL access, cross-site request forgery (CSRF)
Known threat	Describe known threats that can exploit the vulnerability	[5, 14]	known threats, threat, known attacks, information about known threats, exploit, proof-of-concept, incident activity, incident, known incident

Attack. Information on Attack adds details on the actions that the attacker has to perform to exploit the vulnerability. Therefore, we expect this information category to reduce assessment error for the AV metric (position of the attacker with respect to the vulnerable component), and the AC metric (reflecting conditions outside of the attacker control). Additionally, indications on the attacker actions may give significant indications for the impact of the vulnerability. For example, performing a *cache poisoning attack*[5] has clear repercussions on C and I. Denial of service attacks may indicate losses on A. We formulate the following *null* hypothesis:

HYPOTHESIS 2. H_0: *The* Attack *information category does not* reduce *error rates for the* AV, AC, C, I, A *metrics.*

Vulnerability type. Information on Vulnerability type provides information on the complexity of an attack, e.g. by specifying that the vulnerability is due to insufficient randomness in a

specific variable. Information regarding specific vulnerability types (e.g. cross-site-scripting vulnerabilities) and required authentication levels give information on PR and UI. We formulate the following *null* hypothesis:

HYPOTHESIS 3. H_0: *The* Vulnerability type *information category does not* reduce *error rates for the* AC, PR, UI *metrics.*

Known threat. From the CVSS specification, the Base Metric should only consider information relative to the technical characteristics of the vulnerability. Specifically, Known threat information may be relevant in subsequent assessments to evaluate risk of attack (e.g. involving the CVSS temporal metrics [12]), but may confuse the baseline assessment of the vulnerability. For example, Known threat information may increase error on AC as the existence of known threats may suggest that the vulnerability can be easily exploited, e.g. building up on the existing PoC. Similarly, information on known attacks may influence impact assessments to reflect those of the known incidents. Therefore, we expect Known threat to be generally detrimental to the assessment of AC and C,I,A. We formulate the following *null* hypothesis:

---

[5]A cache poisoning attack requires the attacker to modify some cached record (e.g. a DNS response) such that at the next request the victim will receive the counterfeit information added by the attacker. This may lead to spoofing attacks with possible losses on at least Confidentiality and Integrity.

HYPOTHESIS 4. H_0: *The* `Known threat` *information category does not increase error rates for the* `AC, C, I, A` *metrics.*

3.5 Experimental procedure

Before the experiment subjects were given a lecture on vulnerability assessment with CVSS. The lecture covered all aspects of the standard required for the experiment. With the objective of increasing subject's confidence in the procedure, a demo session scoring five vulnerabilities from the CVSS documentation (not included in the experiment) was performed during the lecture.

Subjects were given a handout with the official CVSS specification, and a printout spreadsheet containing the sixteen vulnerability descriptions. Subjects were randomly assigned to a treatment group and received additional information on each vulnerability together with the NVD description. Subjects had to 1) complete the questionnaire described in Sec. 3.3; 2) read each vulnerability description; 3) indicate which value for each of the CVSS metrics in Tab. 1 better reflect the vulnerability description.

3.6 Analysis procedure

To test our hypotheses we employ a set of multilevel mixed effect regression models of the form: $y_{s,c}^m = \mathbf{Z}_s\boldsymbol{\beta}_1 + \mathbf{X}_c\boldsymbol{\beta}_2 + u_s + v_c + \epsilon_{s,c}^m$, where $y_{s,c}^m$ reflects the presence or absence ($y_{s,c}^m \in \{1,0\}$) of an assessment error on the metric $m \in \{$AV, AC, UI, PR, C, I, A$\}$ by student s, over vulnerability c; $\mathbf{Z}_s$ is the control vector of subject characteristics, and $\mathbf{X}_c$ is the vector of information cues for each category measured on vulnerability c. The remaining terms account for random effects for the first level in the hierarchy, students (u_s); and the second, vulnerability (v_c). Each hypothesis is evaluated in accordance with the respective coefficient sign and its significance.

4 RESULTS

4.1 Overview of subjects

Before executing the experiment, we asked students to fill out a questionnaire that provides an overview of their background (twenty multiple-choice questions) and relevant security and software engineering expertise (six self-assessment questions and six technical questions). All questions where divided in *security* and *software engineering* questions. From the 67 participants, 14 were Bachelor students, the rest were Master students. 36% of the participants have part-time work occupations. Looking at the technical security questions, the mean score was 0.57, with 1 indicating all correct answers and 0 no correct answer. The standard deviation is relatively small at 0.27 points. Similar scores are identified for the software engineering technical questions.

4.2 Illustrative analysis example

Table 2 reports two example vulnerability descriptions for which treatments have a significant effect on assessment errors for at least one CVSS metric. We report one vulnerabilities where we observe negative effects on the error (CVE-2014-3566), and one where we observe positive effects (CVE-2012-0384). Information that explains the difference is highlighted in bold in the Table. In the following, the correct metric assessment is reported next to the CVE vulnerability identifier:

CVE-2014-3566 (AC:High, UI:Required). Students that received the treatment were less likely to err at identifying: (a) conditions outside of the attacker control ($p < 0.10$), as the treatment specifies that "*[the] attacker must be able to modify network traffic between the victim and this web server*", suggesting a man-in-the-middle condition; (b) the requirement on UI, specifying that the attack is possible only after "*[the victim] has visited a web server*" ($p < 0.01$).

CVE-2012-0384 (PR:Low). The treatment significantly increases chances of error over PR ($p < 0.01$). The treatment states that to trigger the vulnerability "*the attacker would need access to the trusted / internal side of the IOS.*". Any user authenticated in the network would be able to access the interface (i.e. only non-privileged authentication to the network is required). However, the additional information that "*the vulnerability is post authentication on the administrative interface of the Cisco device*", can be misleading in that the attacker does not need to be logged in the administrative panel, but only capable of reaching it from the network (in which he/she must be authenticated).

In our examples, additional information could either aid or hinder a correct assessment by, for example, misleading wording of relevant information (e.g.CVE-2012-0384): in accordance with previous findings in sw engineering [9, 24], both *quantity* and *quality* of information may affect task execution. Unfortunately, neither can be a realistic requirement for an informative vulnerability description as they do not provide a clear guidance on *which* information cues should be provided.

4.3 Tratment effect on assessment error

To identify the effect of the measured information cues we employ a set of mixed-effect regression analyses. For the model selection we relied on the Akaike Information Criterion[6]. The only significant student characteristic is *security expertise* (E^{sec}). Correlation between the independent variables is always below 0.2.

We first check for the possible correlation between length of vulnerability description (expressed as word counts) and error rates, and find that neither the length of the original NVD description nor the length of the treatment text have significant effects on the observed error. We therefore proceed with the analysis of the effect of the information cues.

For our final regression, the regressors are count of information cues measured in the original NVD description and those added by the assigned treatments T. All variables are standardized. The final regression equation over the binomial response variable representing assessment error $\hat{y} = y_{s,c}^m$ is:

$$\hat{y}_i = \beta_0 + \beta_1 E_i^{sec} + \boldsymbol{\beta}_2\mathbf{Cues}_i^{NVD} + \boldsymbol{\beta}_3\mathbf{Cues}_i^{T} + u_s + v_c + \epsilon_i$$

Results are reported in Table 4. A negative, significant coefficient indicates a decrease in the chances of error. Positive, significant coefficients indicate an increase in chances of error. Security expertise tends to reduce error although it is not a significant factor for all metrics. Overall, we find consistent estimations for each information category. In general, information cues on `Attack` and `Vulnerability` type aid the scoring for all metrics. `Asset` creates

---

[6]Considered control variables: $Z1$: security expertise of the student; $Z2$: software engineering expertise; $Z3$: work experience; $Z4$: years of enrollment in a Computer Science major $Z5$: university courses completed.

Table 4: Regression results

Regression results for our equations. p-values for the fixed effects are computed by using Satterthwate's estimation for degrees of freedom as provided by the R package lmerTest. Standard errors are indicated in parenthesis. Regression coefficients are reported for the information cues all students received (as provided in the original NVD description of the vulnerability) and for the additional information cues included in the treatment. All variables are standardized. The original NVD descriptions do not have any information regarding Known threats, which is therefore only relevant for the provided treatments. An anova test of variance indicates that the intercepts for students and CVEs significantly vary between subjects and vulnerabilities.

Fixed effects	model AV	model AC	model UI	model PR	model C	model I	model A
(Intercept)	-0.804***	-0.667***	-2.035***	-1.008***	0.504**	0.088	-0.511
	(0.203)	(0.200)	(0.376)	(0.331)	(0.224)	(0.246)	(0.312)
E^{sec}	-0.088	-0.007	-0.233**	-0.137	-0.190*	-0.246***	-0.080
	(0.081)	(0.098)	(0.110)	(0.128)	(0.100)	(0.093)	(0.095)
Information cues from original description							
Assets	0.384*	0.097	-0.550	0.246	-0.035	0.314	-0.696**
	(0.198)	(0.192)	(0.383)	(0.328)	(0.221)	(0.232)	(0.320)
Attack	-0.555***	0.062	0.111	-0.209	-0.013	-0.034	0.388
	(0.211)	(0.196)	(0.386)	(0.333)	(0.228)	(0.238)	(0.327)
Vulnerability type	0.085	-0.330**	-0.362	-0.530***	0.169	0.032	-0.150
	(0.149)	(0.135)	(0.228)	(0.166)	(0.143)	(0.139)	(0.163)
Additional information cues from treatment							
Assets	-0.191	0.169	-0.282	-0.054	0.121	-0.069	-0.100
	(0.129)	(0.123)	(0.175)	(0.131)	(0.113)	(0.125)	(0.108)
Attack	-0.036	-0.280**	-0.238	-0.031	-0.313***	-0.202*	-0.183
	(0.116)	(0.127)	(0.183)	(0.139)	(0.112)	(0.114)	(0.120)
Vulnerability type	-0.108	-0.067	-0.563***	-0.103	-0.015	-0.072	-0.052
	(0.098)	(0.116)	(0.171)	(0.125)	(0.100)	(0.100)	(0.112)
Known threats	0.176	0.528***	0.494***	-0.206	0.325***	0.017	0.278**
	(0.128)	(0.138)	(0.177)	(0.138)	(0.121)	(0.127)	(0.131)
Variance of random intercepts							
Student	0.045	0.263	0.101	0.637	0.314	0.210	0.200
CVE	0.464	0.436	1.821	1.473	0.636	0.706	1.400
Pseudo-R^2 (Fixed effect)	0.09	0.09	0.14	0.09	0.03	0.05	0.09
Pseudo-R^2 (Fixed and random eff.)	0.22	0.25	0.46	0.44	0.25	0.26	0.39

Signif. codes: '***' 0.001; '**' 0.01; '*' 0.05; '.' 0.1.

mixed results, whereas Known threat is always counter-productive. The fixed effects account for about 10% of the overall variance in the model across all metrics, with only a few exceptions in either direction (14% for UI, 3% for C). The inclusion of the random effects accounts for in between 22% and 46% of the variance, indicating a good overall fit.

RQ1: How does information category Asset *impact assessment errors?* Error rates on A are negatively impacted by this information category; for example, if the vulnerable asset is a server, service availability can be likely compromised by an attack. Additionally, we find that information on Assets *increase* the error on the AV metric, albeit the effect is only weakly significant. Some assets (e.g. a router or a server) may be correlated with AV:Network assessments, whereas in specific cases the attacker may need be locally authenticated on the asset. We provide two examples of this from our experiment in the next Section. We reject the null hypothesis of Hyp. 1 for A and accept the alternative that there is a decrease in error. We do not reject the null for C,I.

RQ2: How does information category Attack *impact assessment errors?* This information category improves accuracy on AV, as it

can clearly indicate the position of the attacker. Similarly, we find a negative effect on error for AC. For example, a *man-in-the-middle* attack suggests a high condition for this metric [12]. For the CVSS impact triad CIA, information regarding the attack decreases error for Confidentiality and Integrity. For example, a cache poisoning attack implies an impact on the integrity of the cached information. We reject the null hypothesis of Hyp. 2 for AV,AC,C,I and accept the alternative that there is a decrease in error. We do not reject the null for A.

RQ3: How does information category Vulnerability type *impact assessment errors?* For AC, information on the type of vulnerability favours assessment accuracy. For example, specifying that the vulnerability is caused by insufficient randomness (e.g. of a hash function) may indicate that the attacker will typically have to find a collision before actively exploiting the vulnerability. Vulnerability type also reduces chances of error on UI. For example, a cross-site-scripting vulnerability typically requires the user to click on a malicious link. The effect on PR is similar: this information cue may clarify whether some level of privilege is required to launch the attack. For example, privilege escalation vulnerabilities typically require some level of authentication. We reject the null hypothesis of Hyp. 3 for AC,PR,UI, and accept the alternative that there is a decrease in error.

RQ4: How does information category Threat *impact assessment errors?* In general, we find that this information cue increases the chances of error. From the CVSS specification, the Base Metric should only consider information relative to the technical characteristics of the vulnerability. Hence, the existence of an exploit or of a demonstrated attack is unnecessary information that need be processed by the assessor. For example, information on the existence of a demonstrated attack may increase the error on AC, as previously discussed (cf. 3.4). Similar considerations can be made for the other metrics. We reject the null hypothesis of Hyp. 4 for AC,C,A, and accept the alternative that there is an increase in error. We do not reject the null for I.

Hyp.	Inf. Cue	H_0		H_1
		Reject	No reject	
Hyp. 1	Assets	A	C,I	Err. Decrease
Hyp. 2	Attack	AV,AC,C,I	A	Err. Decrease
Hyp. 3	Vuln. Type	AC,PR,UI	-	Err. Decrease
Hyp. 4	Known threats	AC,C,A	I	Err. Increase

5 DISCUSSION

Our results indicate that 'baseline' vulnerability descriptions can be significantly improved by including additional information. Information of type Attack and Vulnerability type are particularly effective in increasing the accuracy of vulnerability assessment by reducing error on the whole set of Exploitability metrics (cf. Table 1) AV, AC, UI, PR.

In our sample, additional information on attacker actions significantly decrease error on AC, indicating that additional information on Attack was missing from the original text. Similarly, the Attack information added by our treatments also significantly decrease the error for C and I. Our results suggest that security expertise helps interpreting this information (e.g. a 'cache poisoning' attack).

The information on Vulnerability type conveyed by standard vulnerability descriptions seem not to be significantly improved by our treatment for AC and PR, whereas there is a highly significant improvement in assessment accuracy for UI. Information regarding the type of vulnerability such as a file-based buffer overflow or a cross-site-scripting vulnerability should be included in vulnerability descriptions. This is again in accordance with the negative significant coefficient for E^{sec}, indicating that security expertise is significant in correctly understanding the type of vulnerability.

An interesting finding is that Asset contribute in *increasing* error on AV. Certain information on Asset may correlate with certain AV values; for example, if the vulnerable asset is a server, AV:Network assessments may be more likely. For example, 42% of the students erroneously classified CVE-2014-6271 as AV:Local, likely as the vulnerability is specified, in the original NVD description, to affect *"GNU Bash through 4.3 [..] [in] situations in which setting the environment occurs across a privilege boundary from Bash execution"*. Here the vulnerable asset is clearly the GNU Bash, which may suggest that the user need be authenticated locally to reach the vulnerability. However, in the worst case this is possible without any local

access to the environment, as specified in the description: *"the vulnerability can be exploited by [..] mod_cgid modules in the Apache HTTP Server, scripts executed by unspecified DHCP clients [..]"*, which indicates a Network vector for the attack. Similarly, in our sample, 89% of the students erroneously categorized CVE-2012-1516 as AV:Local. The description reports that *"it is possible to manipulate data pointers within the Virtual Machine Executable (VMX) process"*, which suggests that the user need be locally authenticated on the machine to access the process. This is not a condition for AV:Local as the vulnerability can be reached by the *"handler function for RPC commands"* [11], a procedure to send remote commands to a process. Both examples suggest that a more precise definition of Attacker actions may contribute in decreasing the effect.

Finally, information on Known threats is regarded by security experts as of primary importance to assess vulnerability risk [14]. However, we find first evidence that it consistently increases chances of error, as the CVSS Base metric should only consider technical details on the vulnerability.

Following Devanbu et al.'s recommendations on the impact of empirical findings on software practices [8], we further discuss practical implications of this work.

Implications for vulnerability communication. Our results suggest that baseline vulnerability descriptions contain only a limited set of the information that leads to an accurate CVSS assessment. Additional information on Attack, Vulnerability type, and Assets may result in more informative vulnerability descriptions. Following our results, standards and best practices for vulnerability communication, including CVSS itself, may provide guidelines for the communication of informative vulnerability descriptions [20]. Our results suggest that inclusion of information of the Threat category should be discouraged. Further, our results identify dimensions over which vulnerability information can be automatically categorized and provided to vulnerability assessors.

Implications for software security practices. Our findings can help practitioners in identifying information that is significant for a vulnerability assessment over each specific metric [24]. For example, the assessor performing an evaluation of the AV metric may look specifically for Attack information. Similar considerations can be made for the other metrics (cf. Table 4). Additionally, the assessor should deliberately ignore any information on Known threats, if present. By replicating this work, it could be possible to build 'confidence intervals' around vulnerability assessment that account for errors in the estimate. These intervals could then be accounted for when prioritizing vulnerability fixing.

6 THREATS TO VALIDITY

Conclusion validity. To avoid introducing noise in the vulnerability descriptions and treatments used in the experiment, all descriptions and treatments have been chosen from the official documentation released by the the First.org standardisation team, used for official training for the standard.

Internal validity. Results may be confounded by order of treatment or learning effects. As we can not cover all treatment combinations, our experiment design is not full-factorial. However, we accounted for all combinations of treatments for similar vulnerabilities that might confound results. The identification of our keywords for the measurements of information cues in the vulnerability descriptions was performed independently by three authors of the paper. To minimize chances of bias, the experiment was performed before the final example documentation was publicly released.

External validity. Following [15] we consider students suitable subjects for relative performance measures. Students were informed that the exercise is not graded. All received the same training on the CVSS scoring system at the beginning of our experiment. We controlled for potentially relevant characteristics of our subjects, including security expertise and work experience.

7 CONCLUSIONS

In this paper we investigate which information cues aid vulnerability assessment by humans. We based our definition of relevant information on current standards and best practices [20, 29], and recent research findings by other authors [14, 26]. Our results provide first indication that, in general, additional information cues on Asset, Attack, and Vulnerability type on top of the baseline vulnerability descriptions may aid the assessment process, whereas information cues on Threat hinders it.

An interesting venue for future research is to explicitly consider the effect of information security knowledge by devising experiments with security professionals. Additionally, this work opens toward research considering measures of complexity to evaluate whether there exist boundaries over which the cognitive performance of the assessor decays.

8 ACKNOWLEDGMENTS

This project has been partly supported by the University of Trento, Italy, through the EIT Digital Master School 2016 - Security and Privacy programme, and by the NWO through the SpySpot project no. 628.001.004.

REFERENCES

[1] 2010. PCI Council PCI DSS Requirements and Security Assessment Procedures, Version 2.0. (2010). https://www.pcisecuritystandards.org/documents/pci_dss_v2.pdf

[2] 2015. NIST National Vulnerability Database (NVD). (2015). http://nvd.nist.gov [online] http://nvd.nist.gov.

[3] Luca Allodi and Fabio Massacci. 2014. Comparing vulnerability severity and exploits using case-control studies. *ACM Transaction on Information and System Security (TISSEC)* 17, 1 (August 2014).

[4] Luca Allodi, Shim Woohyun, and Fabio Massacci. 2013. Quantitative assessment of risk reduction with cybercrime black market monitoring.. In *In Proc. of IWCC'13*.

[5] Sean Barnum and Gary McGraw. 2005. Knowledge for software security. *IEEE Security & Privacy* 3, 2 (2005), 74–78.

[6] Steve Christey and Brian Martin. 2013. Buying into the bias: why vulnerability statistics suck. https://www.blackhat.com/us-13/archives.html#Martin. (July 2013).

[7] Stanislav Dashevskyi, Achim D Brucker, and Fabio Massacci. 2016. On the Security Cost of Using a Free and Open Source Component in a Proprietary Product. In *International Symposium on Engineering Secure Software and Systems*. Springer, 190–206.

[8] Prem Devanbu, Thomas Zimmermann, and Christian Bird. 2016. Belief & Evidence in Empirical Software Engineering. In *Proceedings of the 38th International Conference on Software Engineering (ICSE '16)*. ACM, New York, NY, USA, 108–119. https://doi.org/10.1145/2884781.2884812

[9] Martin J Eppler and Jeanne Mengis. 2004. The concept of information overload: A review of literature from organization science, accounting, marketing, MIS, and related disciplines. *The information society* 20, 5 (2004), 325–344.

[10] Henning Femmer, Daniel Méndez Fernández, Stefan Wagner, and Sebastian Eder. 2016. Rapid quality assurance with Requirements Smells. *Journal of Systems and Software* (2016). https://doi.org/10.1016/j.jss.2016.02.047

[11] First.org. 2015. *Common Vulnerability Scoring System v3.0: Example Document.* Technical Report. FIRST, Available at https://www.first.org/cvss/examples.

[12] First.org. 2015. *Common Vulnerability Scoring System v3.0: Specification Document.* Technical Report. FIRST, Available at http://www.first.org/cvss.

[13] Christian Fruhwirth and Tomi Mannisto. 2009. Improving CVSS-based vulnerability prioritization and response with context information. In *Proceedings of the 2009 3rd international Symposium on Empirical Software Engineering and Measurement*. IEEE Computer Society, 535–544.

[14] Hannes Holm and Khalid Khan Afridi. 2015. An expert-based investigation of the Common Vulnerability Scoring System. *Computers & Security* 53 (2015), 18–30.

[15] Martin Höst, Björn Regnell, and Claes Wohlin. 2000. Using students as subjects—a comparative study of students and professionals in lead-time impact assessment. *Empirical Software Engineering* 5, 3 (2000), 201–214.

[16] Siv Hilde Houmb, Virginia NL Franqueira, and Erlend A Engum. 2010. Quantifying security risk level from CVSS estimates of frequency and impact. 83, 9 (2010), 1622–1634.

[17] Michael Howard and Steve Lipner. 2006. The Security Development Lifecycle. Microsoft Press.

[18] ISO/IEC. 2005. *Information technology - Security techniques - Information security management systems - Requirements.* ISO/IEC 27001. International Organization for Standardization (ISO) and International Electrotechnical Commission (IEC).

[19] ISO/IEC. 2012. *Common Criteria for Information Technology Security Evaluation.* ISO/IEC 15408. International Organization for Standardization (ISO) and International Electrotechnical Commission (IEC).

[20] ISO/IEC. 2014. *Information technology - Security techniques - Vulnerability disclosure.* ISO/IEC 29147. International Organization for Standardization (ISO) and International Electrotechnical Commission (IEC).

[21] Katsiaryna Labunets, Fabio Massacci, Federica Paci, et al. 2013. An experimental comparison of two risk-based security methods. In *2013 ACM/IEEE International Symposium on Empirical Software Engineering and Measurement*. IEEE, 163–172.

[22] Jakob Mund, Henning Femmer, M Daniel, and Jonas Eckhardt. 2015. Does Quality of Requirements Specifications matter ? Combined Results of Two Empirical Studies. In *Proc. of the 9th International Symposium on Empirical Software Engineering and Measurement (ESEM '15)*.

[23] Mendes Naaliel, Duraes Joao, and Madeira Henrique. 2014. Security Benchmarks for Web Serving Systems. In *Proc. of ISSRE'14*.

[24] Robin Pennington and Brad Tuttle. 2007. The effects of information overload on software project risk assessment. *Decision Sciences* 38, 3 (2007), 489–526.

[25] Stephen D. Quinn, Karen A. Scarfone, Matthew Barrett, and Christopher S. Johnson. 2010. *SP 800-117. Guide to Adopting and Using the Security Content Automation Protocol (SCAP) Version 1.0.* Technical Report. NIST.

[26] Sebastian Roschke, Feng Cheng, Robert Schuppenies, and Christoph Meinel. 2009. *Towards Unifying Vulnerability Information for Attack Graph Construction.* Springer Berlin Heidelberg, Berlin, Heidelberg, 218–233. https://doi.org/10.1007/978-3-642-04474-8_18

[27] R. Scandariato, J. Walden, and W. Joosen. 2013. Static analysis versus penetration testing: A controlled experiment. In *Software Reliability Engineering (ISSRE), 2013 IEEE 24th International Symposium on*. 451–460.

[28] Yonghee Shin, Andrew Meneely, Laurie Williams, and Jason A. Osborne. 2011. Evaluating Complexity, Code Churn, and Developer Activity Metrics as Indicators of Software Vulnerabilities. 37, 6 (2011), 772–787. https://doi.org/10.1109/TSE.2010.81

[29] Gary Stoneburner, Alice Y. Goguen, and Alexis Feringa. 2002. *SP 800-30. Risk Management Guide for Information Technology Systems.* Technical Report. Gaithersburg, MD, United States.

[30] C. Albert Thompson, Gail C. Murphy, Marc Palyart, and Marko Gašparič. 2016. How Software Developers Use Work Breakdown Relationships in Issue Repositories. In *Proceedings of the 13th International Conference on Mining Software Repositories (MSR '16)*. ACM, New York, NY, USA, 281–285. https://doi.org/10.1145/2901739.2901779

[31] James Walden, Jeff Stuckman, and Riccardo Scandariato. 2014. Predicting vulnerable components: Software metrics vs text mining. In *2014 IEEE 25th International Symposium on Software Reliability Engineering*. IEEE, 23–33.

[32] Koen Yskout, Riccardo Scandariato, and Wouter Joosen. 2015. Do Security Patterns Really Help Designers?. In *Proceedings of the 37th International Conference on Software Engineering - Volume 1 (ICSE '15)*. IEEE Press, 292–302.

[33] Hongyu Zhang, Liang Gong, and Steve Versteeg. 2013. Predicting bug-fixing time: an empirical study of commercial software projects. In *Proceedings of the 2013 International Conference on Software Engineering*. IEEE Press, 1042–1051.

[34] Yu Zhao, Feng Zhang, Emad Shihab, Ying Zou, and Ahmed E Hassan. 2016. How Are Discussions Associated with Bug Reworking?: An Empirical Study on Open Source Projects. In *Proceedings of the 10th ACM/IEEE International Symposium on Empirical Software Engineering and Measurement*. ACM, 21.

[35] Thomas Zimmermann, Rahul Premraj, Nicolas Bettenburg, Sascha Just, Adrian Schroter, and Cathrin Weiss. 2010. What makes a good bug report? *IEEE Transactions on Software Engineering* 36, 5 (2010), 618–643.

Malware Analysis of Imaged Binary Samples by Convolutional Neural Network with Attention Mechanism

Hiromu Yakura*, Shinnosuke Shinozaki, Reon Nishimura, Yoshihiro Oyama, Jun Sakuma*†

University of Tsukuba

Tsukuba, Japan

{hiromu,s1511382,s1511392}@coins.tsukuba.ac.jp,oyama@cc.tsukuba.ac.jp,jun@cs.tsukuba.ac.jp

ABSTRACT

This paper presents a proposal of a method to extract important byte sequences in malware samples to reduce the workload of human analysts who investigate the functionalities of the samples. This method, by applying convolutional neural network (CNN) with a technique called attention mechanism to an image converted from binary data, enables calculation of an "attention map," which shows regions having higher importance for classification in the image. This distinction of regions enables extraction of characteristic byte sequences peculiar to the malware family from the binary data and can provide useful information for the human analysts without a priori knowledge. Furthermore, the proposed method calculates the attention map for all binary data including the data section. Thus, it can process packed malware that might contain obfuscated code in the data section. Results of our evaluation experiment using malware datasets show that the proposed method provides higher classification accuracy than conventional methods. Furthermore, analysis of malware samples based on the calculated attention maps confirmed that the extracted sequences provide useful information for manual analysis, even when samples are packed.

KEYWORDS

Malware analysis; Convolutional neural network; Attention mechanism.

ACM Reference Format:

Hiromu Yakura, Shinnosuke Shinozaki, Reon Nishimura, Yoshihiro Oyama, Jun Sakuma. 2018. Malware Analysis of Imaged Binary Samples by Convolutional Neural Network with Attention Mechanism. In *CODASPY '18: Eighth ACM Conference on Data and Application Security and Privacy, March 19–21, 2018, Tempe, AZ, USA.* ACM, New York, NY, USA, 8 pages. https://doi.org/10.1145/3176258.3176335

---

*Also with RIKEN Center for Advanced Intelligent Project.

†Also with JST CREST.

Figure 1: Examples of correspondences between the region in images and the underlined word in captions obtained from the feature map (cite from [33]).

1 INTRODUCTION

Malware, a major threat to the security of computer users, causes huge financial losses [2]. To address diverse types of malware that evolve from moment to moment, it is important to acquire deep knowledge related to the behavior of malware samples instantly. For static analysis, the target malware sample is reverse-engineered. The function is analyzed by interpreting disassembled instructions line-by-line.

When a new variant of malware is acquired, experts commonly analyze the sample manually because the knowledge about the functions of malware is necessary for its removal [21]. Such manual analysis requires several hours to several weeks, depending on the malware complexity [4]. One reason that malware analysis is so time-consuming is that it is not easy to identify the region in the binary data that characterizes the functionality of the malware. We expect that human analysts could analyze the functions of malware more efficiently if they were able to find such important regions in the malware samples automatically.

Recently, image classification technology has improved with the development of deep learning. Reportedly, a method using a convolutional neural network (CNN) demonstrated better classification performance than humans [14]. Its achievement is attributable to its ability to earn feature representations that show regions having important information for classification in the middle layer of the network. In addition, the information can be visualized using the *attention mechanism* [33]. An *attention map* obtained from CNN with the attention mechanism presents specific regions that are expected to characterize the target. Figure 1 represents highlighted regions corresponding to each word in the caption. These highlights are made based on attention maps obtained from the network [33], which aims at generating captions from images.

Our major motivation of this paper is to exploit CNN with the attention mechanism for making manual analysis efficient. In our framework, we convert binary data of malware samples into images and then apply the CNN with the attention mechanism for

Table 1: Correspondence between the malware sample file size and the converted image width (cite from [23]).

File size	Width	File size	Width
< 10KB	32	100 KB – 200 KB	384
10 KB – 30 KB	64	200 KB – 500 KB	512
30 KB – 60 KB	128	500 KB – 1000 KB	768
60 KB – 100 KB	256	100 KB ≤	1024

the images. In doing so, the important part for malware classification in the binary data is obtained automatically without a priori information about the functionalities of the samples. Using such information as a hint, the workload for analysis would be reduced.

1.1 Related Works

In this section, as related works, we describe malware classification methods by converting binary data into an image. We also present malware classification methods using deep learning, with similar sequence detection methods for malware comparison.

1.1.1 Malware classification by converting binary data into an image. Malware classification by converting binary data into an image has been proposed by Nataraj et al. [22, 23]. This method classifies malware samples into malware families as follows.

(1) Read each byte of the binary data of the target malware sample and store it in a numeric array (range 0 ~ 255).
(2) Determine the image width based on the malware sample file size (Table 1) and transform the array into a grayscale image.
(3) Stretch the obtained image to a resolution of 64 × 64.
(4) From the stretched image, extract 320-dimensional GIST features [24], which are used as feature vectors.

After converting labeled malware samples following the procedures above, classification of unlabeled malware samples is performed using the *k*-nearest neighbor method. More specifically, given an unlabeled malware sample, we convert it into an image following the procedures. Then predict the malware family using the *k*-nearest neighbor method with feature vectors and labels.

As a result of experimental evaluation using various malware datasets, Nataraj et al. [22] concluded that the method achieves higher accuracy than existing methods against samples including obfuscated binary data, which are produced by an obfuscation program called *packer*. Kirat et al. [17] proposed another image-based classification method and demonstrated that the method shows higher accuracy than methods using *n*-gram of the binary data and methods based on control flow graphs against datasets including packed samples. Ahmadi et al. [1] proposed a classification method that aggregates multiple features including image-based features and concluded that the image-based features are effective to improve the accuracy against a dataset including packed samples.

In general, binary data obfuscated by packers is expected to become a nearly random binary sequence. Consequently, it might appear to be meaningless to train a classifier directly with binaries or images obtained from packed samples. However, when malware samples in the same family are compressed by packers using

dictionary-based compression method (e.g., UPX[1]), the resulting files often include common sequences [16]. This occurs because the dictionary-based packer obfuscates files using similar dictionaries, yielding features that help to identify the malware family of obfuscated malware samples.

Unfortunately, these methods that classify samples based on hand-crafted features extracted from images do not clarify which binary data region affected the classification. Consequently, it cannot be used to improve the efficiency of manual analysis.

1.1.2 Malware classification using deep learning. Several methods have been proposed for applying deep learning to malware detection and malware classification [15, 26, 30]. For example, Saxe et al. [30] presented a malware detection method using Deep Neural Network (DNN) on a histogram of byte sequences and metadata extracted from headers. Pascanu et al. [26] trained Recurrent Neural Network (RNN) using API call history and performed a detection using multilayered neural network based on feature vectors obtained from the RNN. Huang et al. [15] used bag-of-words feature consisting of API call *n*-gram as an input of multi-task DNN, which simultaneously predicts whether a given sample is malware or not and to which family it belongs.

Other methods targeting Android apps are also proposed [20, 32, 34, 35]. Su et al. [32] proposed a method using Deep Belief Network (DBN) on metadata of apps. Yuan et al. [34, 35] also used the occurence of specific API calls as an input of DBN. MacLaughlin et al. [20] presented a detection method that applies one-dimensional CNN to instruction sequences of Java Virtual Machine.

These methods are divisible into two types: static analysis and dynamic analysis. Here, static analysis refers to a method using only information obtained without executing malware. It is applicable only to [20, 30, 32]. Dynamic analysis refers to a method using information obtained by executing malware such as [15, 26, 34, 35]. These methods use API call information.

Although dynamic analysis can use deeper knowledge related to the target compared to static analysis, it can be pointed out that many malware samples change their behavior by detecting the presence of virtual machine monitor and other systems used to record the API call information, to disturb the analysis [7, 25]. Consequently, the possibility exists that they are undetectable and classified incorrectly because of their anti-analysis mechanisms. In addition, the methods using static analysis [20, 30, 32] are aimed at discrimination as to whether the sample is malware or not. Therefore, they cannot be used for making manual analysis efficient by finding information peculiar to the malware family.

1.1.3 Similar sequences detection method for malware comparison. Methods of detecting similar sequences between malware samples have been proposed [3, 8–10] for making manual analysis efficient when a human-annotated analysis result for another malware sample of the same family is available. Farhadi et al. [9] presented a detection method by normalizing disassembled instructions to generate feature vectors and comparing them. The others [3, 8, 10] calculate control flow graphs from disassembled instructions and compares the graphs to find the corresponding nodes.

---
[1]https://upx.github.io/

However, all of them use the information only from the code section of the malware samples. They cannot use the information in the data section. Therefore, if the sample is packed and important information related to its behavior is placed in the data section, then these methods cannot be used.

For comparison including the data section, we can use a tool to compare all binary data such as [27]. However, it outputs all differences including small modifications produced by the difference of compilers. Therefore, they are unsuitable for malware comparison.

1.2 Contributions

The contributions of this paper are three-fold.

First, we propose a method to extract byte sequences peculiar to the malware family from the binary data automatically. It makes the manual analysis more efficient. We remark that such automatic extraction is not achievable using the conventional methods described in Section 1.1.1 and Section 1.1.2. We realize it by applying CNN with the attention mechanism to malware classification.

Second, this method can deal with packed malware, which places obfuscated code in the data section. It is enabled by using all binary data including the data section to extract sequences, whereas the conventional methods described in Section 1.1.3 use only the code section. Moreover, this method does not require any a priori knowledge of the malware behavior in contrast to the conventional methods, which use existing analysis results to specify the important sequences before searching similar sequences.

Finally, we show that the attention maps obtained by this method characterize malware families by evaluating the classification accuracy and that the information obtained from the attention maps is useful for manual analysis. For example, in the case of *Backdoor. Win32.Agobot.lt* as described in Section 4.5.1, the region with the highest importance in the attention map points at a function to receive commands from a remote server via IRC. This result characterizes the behavior of its family, *Worm:Win32/Gaobot*, which executes commands sent via IRC to construct a botnet.

2 BACKGROUND

In this section, we describe details of CNN and the attention mechanism, techniques used in the proposed method.

2.1 Convolutional Neural Network

CNN is a deep learning model and has shown successful results particularly in the field of image classification. CNN consists of multilayered neural networks as well as other deep learning methods and has a specific structure called a convolution layer.

As shown in Figure 2, *convolution layer* performs convolutional filtering on the input map using a small filter. The convolution layer limits the number of the input elements used in the calculation of one output element, whereas all the input elements are used in the fully connected layer. In addition to the technique called *sparse connectivity*, the convolution layer attains *parameter sharing*, a technique to apply same small filters to all elements of the input, in order to enable CNN to extract the local features in the image efficiently [13].

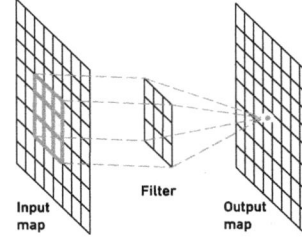

Figure 2: Outline of the convolutional layer.

2.2 Attention Mechanism in CNN

The attention mechanism is a well-known technique aiming at improving the translation performance by introducing it to select important features dynamically. The mechanism was proposed originally in an application of deep learning to natural language processing [5, 19]. By combining the mechanism with CNN, it is useful as a method to visualize important regions [33], as shown in Figure 1.

Figure 3 presents the outline of the attention mechanism. First, let $z_{i,j} \in \mathbb{R}^N$ ($0 \leq i < W, 0 \leq j < H$) be the output map of the middle convolution layer of CNN. The map is propagated to the next layer as the input map in the regular CNN. The attention mechanism calculates $\hat{z} \in \mathbb{R}^N$ and the weighted average of $z_{i,j}$, and then propagates $\hat{z}$ to the next layer. To calculate $\hat{z}$, the attention mechanism estimates $a_{i,j} \in \mathbb{R}$, the importance of each $z_{i,j}$, using the neural network as follows.

$$A = \text{softmax} \circ \text{Fc}_{W_m, b_m} \circ \text{ReLU} \circ \text{Fc}_{W_z, b_z}(Z)$$

Here $A = (a_{i,j})$ and $Z = (z_{i,j})$. Because $a_{i,j}$ is calculated using the softmax function to satisfy $\sum_i \sum_j a_{i,j} = 1$, the weighted average is calculated as shown below.

$$\hat{z} = \sum_{i=1}^{W} \sum_{j=1}^{H} a_{i,j} z_{i,j} \tag{1}$$

In terms of training, the attention mechanism optimizes the weights W_m, W_z and the biases b_m, b_z so that $a_{i,j}$ represents the importance of $z_{i,j}$. Here, all operations in the mechanism, including calculations of the weighted averages, are (sub)differentiable. Consequently, these parameters in the attention layer are updated using optimization algorithms like stochastic gradient descent in the same manner as other layers in the regular CNN.

From above, we see that $z_{i,j}$ is obtained from the convolution layer and represents a feature extracted from a specific region of the input image. Thus, $a_{i,j}$ can be interpreted as a value representing the importance of the region. The size of the region each $a_{i,j}$ referring to becomes small, and only the local features of the input are used for the calculation if $z_{i,j}$ is obtained from a shallow layer. The size of the region each $a_{i,j}$ refers to becomes large, and the global features are also used for the calculation if $z_{i,j}$ is obtained from a deeper layer.

3 PROPOSED METHOD

In this section, we describe the overview and the requirements of the proposed method, and details of its workflow.

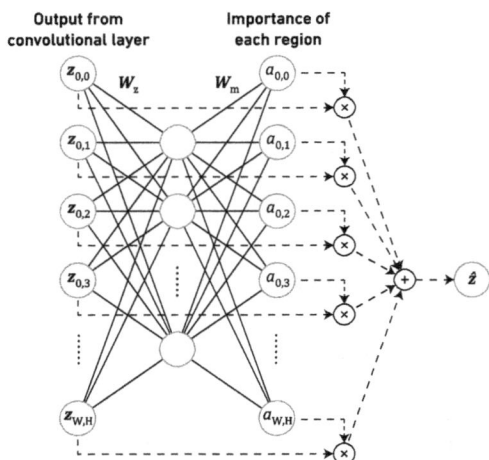

Figure 3: Outline of the attention mechanism. Straight lines represent the calculation of the fully connected layers. Dashed lines represent the calculation of the weighted average in Equation 1.

3.1 Overview

We propose a method to extract important byte sequences from malware samples for making manual analysis efficient. An overview of the proposed method is shown in Figure 4. The method takes a sample as input and outputs byte sequences peculiar to the malware family of the sample (Figure 4, (1)–(3)). By analyzing how functions contained in the sequences perform (Figure 4, (4) and (6)), or how asset files contained in the sequences are used (Figure 4, (5)), human analysts can understand the sample behavior.

3.2 Requirements

The followings are the requirements of the proposed system:

(1) **Detection against the data section**
To deal with packed malware, which places obfuscated code in the data section, we want our method to detect the important sequences not only from the code section but also the data section.

(2) **Location invariance**
To confront attackers who try to deceive anti-virus software by creating new variants with small modifications, we want our method to preserve location invariance.

(3) **Specified detection**
To reduce the cost of post-analysis by human analysts, we want the length of the extracted sequence to remain small.

To satisfy (1), we used a method that converts the binary data of malware samples into images because it can deal with both the code section and the data section in a unified way. It is supported by the fact that its effectiveness to packed malware is already confirmed in [1, 17, 22]. It seems nonintuitive to convert one-dimensional binary data into two-dimensional images and use them for training a classifier, but that point is discussed in Section 4.4.

To satisfy (2), we used CNN since it is known for earning location invariant features by the characteristics described in Section 2.1.

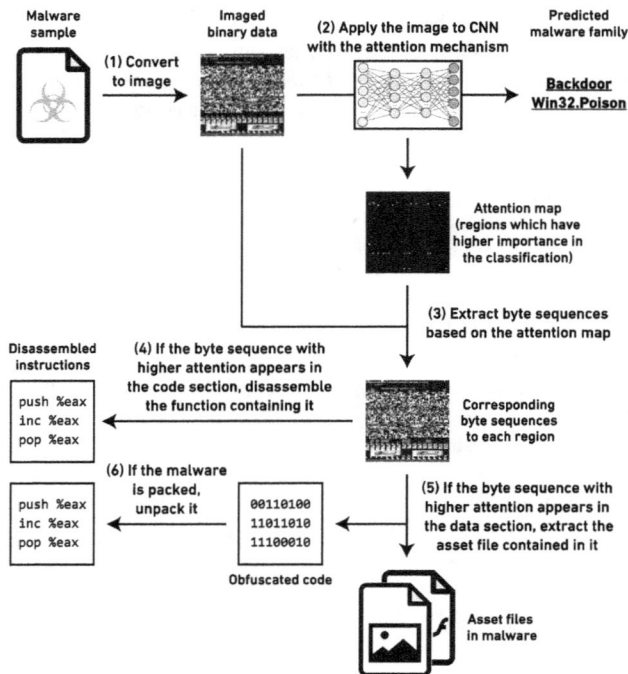

Figure 4: Overview of the proposed method.

Moreover, performance improvement on the conventional methods can be expected to CNN because it can acquire suitable features automatically instead of using hand-crafted features such as GIST in [22, 23]. For example, experimental results in [29] demonstrated that a method using CNN achieved much better performance than that with GIST features in general image classification tasks.

To satisfy (3), we used a shallow architecture compared to recent networks such as [14]. That is, images converted from the binary data of malware samples are expected not to have salient global features, whereas the size of the region indicated by the attention maps is expected to remain compact. Consequently, as described in Section 2.2, connecting the shallow convolution layer to the attention layer is preferred for our purpose.

3.3 Workflow

3.3.1 Conversion of malware sample into an image. First, the input malware sample is converted to an image. We used the same conversion methodology as that by Nataraj et al. [22, 23], which is described in Section 1.1.1. As shown in Table 1, the data are converted to a two-dimensional image.

3.3.2 Applying image to CNN with attention mechanism. Next, the converted image is applied to CNN with the attention mechanism. The network is trained with the pair of the images of known malware samples and their labels representing the family to which each malware sample belongs. Then, the network predicts the malware family of the input and outputs the attention map.

The structure of the CNN is shown in Table 2. Here, attention of Table 2 refers to the attention mechanism described in Section 2.2. Then, $a_{i,j}$ in Equation 1, the importance of each region in the input

Table 2: Structure of CNN in the proposed method.

Layers	Filter (size/stride)	Output map size	Activation function
input	-	$64 \times 64 \times 1$	-
conv1	$3 \times 3/1$	$62 \times 62 \times 128$	ReLU
conv2	$3 \times 3/1$	$60 \times 60 \times 256$	ReLU
attention	-	256	ReLU
fc1	-	512	ReLU
fc2	-	Number of classes	softmax

image, is used as the attention map. The attention map is expected to show regions having patterns peculiar to its malware family.

3.3.3 Extract important byte sequences based on the attention map. Byte sequences peculiar to the malware family of the input sample are shown on the attention map. Because the conversion method from binary data to images has a correspondence relation of the positions, the byte sequence corresponding to each region in the attention map is specified and extracted.

The function containing the sequence is determined and disassembled if the extracted sequence is located in the code section of the input malware sample. The asset file containing the sequence is determined and extracted if the extracted sequence is located in the data section of the sample.

When the input sample is packed, the byte sequence in the data section would be obfuscated code. It is therefore necessary to unpack it for additional analysis. In such a case, the corresponding position in the unpacked data to the extracted sequence can usually be determined because most packers use typical compression algorithms, as described in Section 1.1.1.

3.3.4 Analyze malware manually using extracted information. From the procedure described in earlier subsections, the proposed method enables us to specify the functions or the asset files that are likely to distinguish the corresponding malware family. Then, human analysts would reveal how the functions perform or how the asset files are used in the input malware sample.

In addition, when a human-annotated analysis for the same family malware is available, it is possible to identify the positions of the specific functions and data directly by matching the annotation on the binary data with the attention maps, which further improves the efficiency of the manual analysis.

4 EVALUATION

To confirm the effectiveness of the proposed method, we conducted an evaluation experiment. First, we compared the accuracy of malware classification with conventional methods to ascertain whether the attention maps obtained using the proposed method has a certain level of reliability. Then, we ascertained whether the attention maps provide useful information, or not, for the manual analysis by assessing codes and assets specified by the attention maps.

In this section, we describe detailed procedures and the results.

Table 3: Comparison of classification accuracies. The proposed method shows higher accuracy than the conventional methods.

	Top-1 error	Top-5 error
GIST + k-NN [22]	53.53%	41.78%
2D-CNN	**50.97%**	**31.34%**

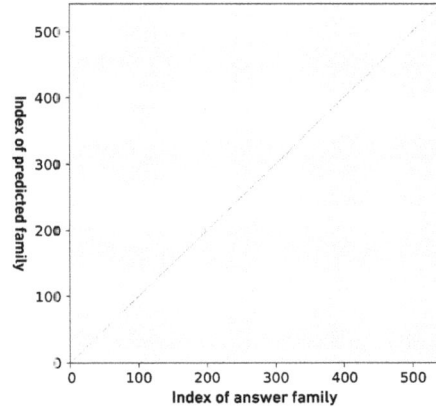

Figure 5: Confusion matrix of 2D-CNN.

4.1 Dataset

In the experiment, VX Heaven[2] malware dataset was used because it has numerous samples and because it is used in many research efforts including [22]. As the ground-truth information of which malware family to which each sample belongs, detection results by Microsoft Security Essentials[3] was used in the manner described in [22]. By excluding families with a small population (the threshold was set to 60), we obtained 147,803 samples from 542 families.

4.2 Implementation

We prepared two implementations as below. In both cases, the classification accuracy was measured by five-fold cross-validation.

GIST + k-NN We implemented the conventional method (k-nearest neighbor with GIST features) proposed by [22], as a baseline for comparison. The value of k of the k-nearest neighbor was set to 3, as suggested in [22].

2D-CNN We implemented the proposed method applying two-dimensional CNN with the attention mechanism to the images converted from the binary data, as described in Section 3.

4.3 Classification Accuracy

Table 3 shows classification accuracies obtained using the experiment and Figure 5 shows the confusion matrix of **2D-CNN**. From the above, it was confirmed that the automatically acquired features in the CNN are useful for classification, as described in Section 3.2. Overall, the classification performance of the proposed method is verified. These observations justify that the attention maps obtained using the proposed method well characterizes the target malware family.

[2]http://vxheaven.org/
[3]https://www.microsoft.com/security/portal/mmpc/

4.4 Limitations

It is not intuitive that **2D-CNN** works effectively with the binary data of malware samples, because it originally forms one-dimensional binaries. In particular, a small insertion or deletion in the binary data appears to change the positional relations of binary data in the vertical direction of the converted image completely. In fact, the vertical relationships collapse only around the position of the modification. The vertical relations located after the modified position will not be significantly collapsed because bytes in each row just shift toward the same distance. In addition, since the proposed method does not use global features, we observed no serious impact had been caused by a small modification.

In contrast, it is vulnerable to adversaries who intentionally obfuscate their malware specifically for defeating this method. For example, by inserting nop instructions between each two consecutive instruction, the texture of the image converted from the binary data can be completely changed. On the other hand, other static analysis methods such as the *n*-gram based classification method are also affected. In other words, this problem is generic to methods that classify based on the similarity of the binary data.

If packers use strong cryptographic methods such as AES or RSA, it will be hard to find important byte sequences from encrypted data. However, such malware are rare because it require to re-implement a decryption algorithm to avoid the use of easily-detected cryptographic APIs and subsequently become slower [16].

4.5 Analysis

This section presents results obtained from analyzing several malware samples to ascertain whether the byte sequences extracted by the proposed method provide useful information for manual analysis. If we can specify a byte sequence that contains important information for analysts for every sample, we can numerically evaluate the performance of the attention map. However, it is almost impossible to specify such byte sequences for all samples. We remark that we prepared about 1.5×10^6 malware samples and we need to disassemble them and interpret their instructions line-by-line to specify such sequences.

Thus, we manually chose several samples considering the following two criteria. First, we picked up samples having significantly large value on the corresponding attention map. This means that the region pointed out in the attention map is likely to indicate byte sequences having important information. Second, in order to justify the analysis result, we picked up samples in which the behavior of the malware family has been extensively described in scientific literature.

We used IDA Pro[4] to analyze how extracted functions perform or how extracted asset files are used, as described in Section 3.3.4.

4.5.1 Case of Worm:Win32/Gaobot. Worm:Win32/Gaobot (also called *Agobot*) is the name of a malware family that spread explosively around 2004 to construct a large botnet [18]. In addition to executing commands sent from a remote server over IRC, it also intercepts HTTP communication to steal login information [12].

In Figure 6, left and right respectively show images of *Backdoor.Win32.Agobot.lt*, a sample belonging to Worm:Win32/Gaobot,

---

[4]https://www.hex-rays.com/products/ida/

Figure 6: Image converted from binary data of Backdoor.Win32.Agobot.lt (left half) and the corresponding attention map obtained using the proposed method (right half).

Figure 7: Image converted from the binary data of Backdoor.Win32.Agobot.on (left half) and the corresponding attention map obtained using the proposed method (right half).

and the attention map of the sample obtained using the proposed method. As a result of analyzing the sample manually, it is confirmed that the region with the highest importance in the attention map (red) points at sub_401356, a function to connect to an IRC server and enter a chat room to receive commands from the remote server. The region with the second highest importance (yellow) points at sub_410F80, a function to receive the contents of the intercepted HTTP communication and checks whether the contents include strings "PAYPAL," "paypal.com," and others.

Figure 7 is an image of *Backdoor.Win32.Agobot.on*, another sample belonging to Worm:Win32/Gaobot, and its attention map. In this attention map, the region with the highest importance (red) points at sub_401356, a function to connect to an IRC server and enter a chat room, and the region which has the third highest importance (yellow) points at sub_4108AC, a function to ascertain whether the contents of the intercepted HTTP communication include strings "PAYPAL," "paypal.com," and others. In addition, the region with the second highest importance (green) points at sub_4258B7, a function to redirect TCP and GRE packets to designated destinations to perform DDoS attacks.

The analysis results confirmed that the regions with high importance according to the proposed method point to byte sequences that provide useful information for analyzing the malware sample behavior. Furthermore, even if their positions are changed for each sample, the proposed method can extract them. Moreover, results suggest correspondence of the extracted sequences between malware samples of the same family.

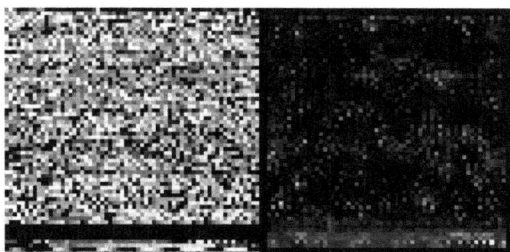

Figure 8: Image converted from the binary data of Trojan-Banker.Win32.Banbra.r (left half) and the corresponding attention map obtained using the proposed method (right half).

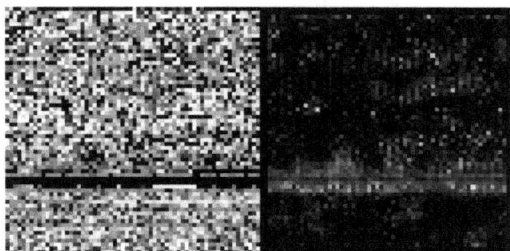

Figure 9: Image converted from the binary data of Trojan-Banker.Win32.Banbra.as (left half) and the corresponding attention map obtained using the proposed method (right half).

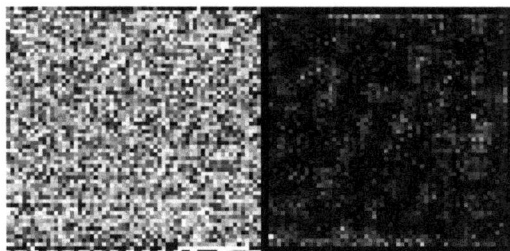

Figure 10: Image converted from the binary data of Trojan-Banker.Win32.Banbra.ghf (left half) and the corresponding attention map obtained using the proposed method (right half).

4.5.2　Case of TrojanSpy:Win32/Banker. *TrojanSpy:Win32/Banker* is the name of the malware family designed to steal bank account information by recording the keyboard and mouse input [11]. Its variants were prevalent around 2006–2007, especially in Brazil [31].

In Figure 8, left and right respectively show images of *Trojan-Banker.Win32.Banbra.r*, a sample belonging to TrojanSpy:Win32/Banker, and the attention map of the sample obtained using the proposed method. Results obtained from analyzing the sample manually confirmed that the region with the highest importance in the attention map (red) points at sub_480A84, a function to send information of OS version, the history of the entered key, the captured screen shot, etc. via e-mail. In addition, the region with the second highest importance (yellow) points at bitmap data of "✓" and "✗", which are contained in executable files produced by Delphi for

button icons. The bitmap data are regarded as having high importance because Delphi is frequently used especially for TrojanSpy: Win32/Banker. It was verified from a report [28] issued by ESET, a vendor of anti-virus software, which concludes that Delphi is the programming language used in almost all the samples to steal bank account information collected in Brazil.

Figure 9 is an image of *Trojan-Banker.Win32.Banbra.as*, another sample belonging to TrojanSpy:Win32/Banker, and its attention map. In this attention map, the region with the highest importance (red) points at sub_46596C, a function to send collected information via e-mail. The region with the second highest importance (yellow) points at the same bitmap data of the button icons. In addition, the region with the third highest importance (green) points at sub_42F778, a function to check whether specific keys are pressed using GetKeyState to acquire the input information.

Figure 10 is an image of *Trojan-Banker.Win32.Banbra.ghf*, another sample belonging to TrojanSpy:Win32/Banker, and its attention map. This sample is packed using UPX, but by unpacking it manually, it is possible to obtain the original binary data implemented by Delphi. A byte sequence in the unpacked binary corresponding to the region has the highest importance in the packed binary (yellow) points at the same bitmap data of the button icons. In addition, a byte sequence corresponding to the region with the second highest importance (green) points at sub_4755F8, a function to check the status of the keys using GetKeyState.

The analysis results confirmed in the same way as Section 4.5.1 that the regions with high importance point to byte sequences that provide useful information for analyzing the malware behavior. Furthermore, even for a sample packed with UPX, the proposed method was able to extract the sequences, and correspondence of the extracted sequences exists between malware samples of the same family.

4.5.3　Case of Trojan:Win32/Sisron!gmb. *Trojan:Win32/Sisron!gmb* is the family name generically assigned to Trojan, which downloads executable files from the Internet and installs them to be executed at startup [6].

In Figure 11, left and right respectively show images of *Trojan-Downloader.Win32.Banload.aafw*, a sample belonging to Trojan:Win32/Sisron!gmb, and the attention map of the sample obtained using the proposed method. As a result of analyzing the sample manually, the region with the highest importance in the attention map (red) points at an icon image (Figure 13) included in the binary data to spoof users.

Figure 12 is an image of *Trojan-Downloader.Win32.Banload.aapn*, another sample belonging to Trojan:Win32/Sisron!gmb, and its attention map. In this attention map, the region with the highest importance (red) points at the same icon image (Figure 13).

From the analysis results, and those from Section 4.5.1 and Section 4.5.2, correspondence is confirmed to exist with extracted sequences between malware samples of the same family. By contrast, the extracted sequences have importance in terms of the classification of families. In the case of generically used families such as Trojan:Win32/Sisron!Gmb, the sequences are not useful for behavior analysis.

Figure 11: Image converted from binary data of Trojan-Downloader.Win32.Banload.aafw (left half) and the corresponding attention map obtained using the proposed system (right half).

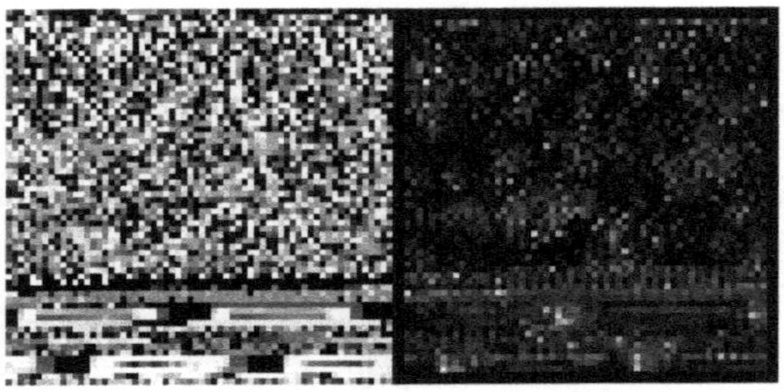

Figure 12: Image converted from the binary data of Trojan-Downloader.Win32.Banload.aapn (left half) and the corresponding attention map obtained using the proposed system (right half).

Figure 13: Icon image included in both Trojan-Downloader. Win32.Banload.aafw and Trojan-Downloader.Win32. Banload.aapn.

5　CONCLUSION

As described herein, we proposed a method to extract important byte sequences in malware samples for making manual analysis efficient by application of the CNN with the attention mechanism for images converted from binary data. Results of the evaluation experiment reveal that the proposed method demonstrates higher classification accuracy than that of the conventional methods. Furthermore, the results show that the extracted sequences provide useful information for the behavior analysis by human analysts. Because correspondence relations are found in the attention maps of different malware samples in the same family, analysts can identify the positions of functions or data that characterizes the target malware family by matching the binary data with the attention maps when a human-annotated analysis is available for the same family malware.

As an avenue for future work, we expect to conduct a user study with experts to verify the usefulness of the proposed method.

ACKNOWLEDGMENTS

The work is supported by JSPS KAKENHI 16H02864.

REFERENCES

[1] Mansour Ahmadi et al. 2016. Novel Feature Extraction, Selection and Fusion for Effective Malware Family Classification. In *ACM CODASPY*. 183–194.
[2] Mamoun Alazab et al. 2011. Cybercrime: The Case of Obfuscated Malware. In *ICGS3*. 204–211.
[3] Saed Alrabaee et al. 2015. SIGMA: A Semantic Integrated Graph Matching Approach for identifying reused functions in binary code. *Digital Investigation* 12, Supplement-1 (2015), S61–S71.
[4] Blake Anderson et al. 2014. Automating Reverse Engineering with Machine Learning Techniques. In *ACM AISec*. 103–112.
[5] Dzmitry Bahdanau et al. 2015. Neural Machine Translation by Jointly Learning to Align and Translate. In *ICLR*.
[6] Raymond Canzanese et al. 2015. Run-time classification of malicious processes using system call analysis. In *MALWARE*. 21–28.
[7] Xu Chen et al. 2008. Towards an understanding of anti-virtualization and anti-debugging behavior in modern malware. In *IEEE/IFIP DSN*. 177–186.
[8] Thomas Dullein and Rolf Rolles. 2005. Graph-based comparison of Executable Objects. In *SSTIC*.
[9] Mohammad Reza Farhadi et al. 2014. BinClone: Detecting Code Clones in Malware. In *SSIRI*. 78–87.
[10] Debin Gao et al. 2008. BinHunt: Automatically Finding Semantic Differences in Binary Programs. In *ICICS*. 238–255.
[11] Manuel García-Cervigón and Manel Medina Llinàs. 2012. Browser function calls modeling for banking malware detection. In *CRiSIS*. 1–7.
[12] Sanjay Goel et al. 2006. Botnets: the anatomy of a case. *J. of Information Systems Security* 1, 3 (2006), 1–12.
[13] Ian Goodfellow et al. 2016. *Deep Learning*. MIT Press.
[14] Kaiming He et al. 2015. Delving Deep into Rectifiers: Surpassing Human-Level Performance on ImageNet Classification. In *IEEE ICCV*. 1026–1034.
[15] Wenyi Huang and Jack W. Stokes. 2016. MtNet: A Multi-Task Neural Network for Dynamic Malware Classification. In *DIMVA*. 399–418.
[16] Grégoire Jacob et al. 2012. A Static, Packer-Agnostic Filter to Detect Similar Malware Samples. In *DIMVA*. 102–122.
[17] Dhilung Kirat et al. 2013. SigMal: a static signal processing based malware triage. In *ACSAC*. 89–98.
[18] Zhiyin Liang et al. 2007. Component similarity based methods for automatic analysis of malicious executables. In *VB*. 283–299.
[19] Zhouhan Lin et al. 2017. A structured self-attentive sentence embedding. In *ICLR*.
[20] Niall McLaughlin et al. 2017. Deep Android Malware Detection. In *ACM CODASPY*. 301–308.
[21] Andreas Moser et al. 2007. Exploring Multiple Execution Paths for Malware Analysis. In *IEEE SP*. 231–245.
[22] Lakshmanan Nataraj et al. 2011. A comparative assessment of malware classification using binary texture analysis and dynamic analysis. In *ACM AISec*. 21–30.
[23] Lakshmanan Nataraj et al. 2011. Malware images: visualization and automatic classification. In *IEEE VizSec*. 4.
[24] Aude Oliva and Antonio Torralba. 2001. Modeling the Shape of the Scene: A Holistic Representation of the Spatial Envelope. *Int. J. of Comput. Vision* 42, 3 (2001), 145–175.
[25] Yoshihiro Oyama. 2017. Trends of anti-analysis operations of malwares observed in API call logs. *J. of Comput. Virology and Hacking Techniques* 14 (2017), 1–17.
[26] Razvan Pascanu et al. 2015. Malware classification with recurrent networks. In *IEEE ICASSP*. 1916–1920.
[27] Colin Percival. 2006. *Matching with mismatches and assorted applications*. Ph.D. Dissertation. University of Oxford, UK.
[28] Matías Porolli and Pablo Ramos. 2015. CPL Malware in Brazil: Somewhere Between Banking Trojans and Malicious Emails. https://www.welivesecurity.com/wp-content/uploads/2015/05/CPL-Malware-in-Brasil-zx02m.pdf. (May 2015).
[29] Ali Sharif Razavian et al. 2014. CNN Features Off-the-Shelf: An Astounding Baseline for Recognition. In *IEEE CVPR*. 512–519.
[30] Joshua Saxe and Konstantin Berlin. 2015. Deep neural network based malware detection using two dimensional binary program features. In *MALWARE*. 11–20.
[31] Mika Ståhlberg. 2007. The Trojan Money Spinner. In *VB*. 234–241.
[32] Xin Su et al. 2016. A Deep Learning Approach to Android Malware Feature Learning and Detection. In *IEEE TrustCom*. 244–251.
[33] Kelvin Xu et al. 2015. Show, Attend and Tell: Neural Image Caption Generation with Visual Attention. In *ICML*. 2048–2057.
[34] Zhenlong Yuan et al. 2014. Droid-Sec: deep learning in android malware detection. In *ACM SIGCOMM*. 371–372.
[35] Zhenlong Yuan et al. 2016. Droiddetector: android malware characterization and detection using deep learning. *Tsinghua Sci. and Tech.* 21, 1 (Feb 2016), 114–123.

Automated Generation of Attack Graphs Using NVD

M. Ugur Aksu[1, 2], Kemal Bicakci[2], M. Hadi Dilek[1], A. Murat Ozbayoglu[2], E. İslam Tatlı[1]

[1]STM Defense Technologies Engineering and Trade Inc. Ankara, Turkey

[1]{mugur.aksu, mhdilek, emin.tatli}@stm.com.tr

[2]TOBB University of Economics and Technology Ankara, Turkey

[2]{m.aksu, bicakci, mozbayoglu}@etu.edu.tr

ABSTRACT

Today's computer networks are prone to sophisticated multi-step, multi-host attacks. Common approaches of identifying vulnerabilities and analyzing the security of such networks with naive methods such as counting the number of vulnerabilities, or examining the vulnerabilities independently produces incomprehensive and limited security assessment results. On the other hand, attack graphs generated from the identified vulnerabilities at a network illustrate security risks via attack paths that are not apparent with the results of the primitive approaches. One common technique of generating attack graphs requires well established definitions and data of prerequisites and postconditions for the known vulnerabilities. A number of works suggest prerequisite and postcondition categorization schemes for software vulnerabilities. However, generating them in an automated way is an open issue. In this paper, we first define a model that evolves over the previous works to depict the requirements of exploiting vulnerabilities for generating attack graphs. Then we describe and compare the results of two different novel approaches (rule-based and machine learning-employed) that we propose for generating attacker privilege fields as prerequisites and postconditions from the National Vulnerability Database (NVD) in an automated way. We observe that prerequisite and postcondition privileges can be generated with overall accuracy rates of 88,8 % and 95,7 % with rule-based and machine learning-employed (Multilayer Perceptron) models respectively.

CCS CONCEPTS

• **Security and privacy** → **Systems security**; *Vulnerability management*;

KEYWORDS

attack graph generation, CVE, CVSS, NVD, vulnerability

1 INTRODUCTION

Today's computer networks are facing complicated and increased numbers of attacks. In order to evaluate such threats, using vulnerability scanners to identify the number, type, and location of

the vulnerabilities that exist at our networks is a common practice. However, such tools consider the vulnerabilities independently and do not show how one relate to another to reveal combinations of them that may pose significant threats to our networks. Defending such networks requires identification of each path into the networks and blocking any malicious access through those paths. To assess overall vulnerability of a network, vulnerabilities need to be grouped showing the multi-step and multi-host nature of them [1].

Generating attack graphs is very useful in combining low-level vulnerabilities to show the attack paths leading to the targets in the enterprise networks. Security professionals might focus on patches or configuration errors that pose greater risks, by analyzing the attack paths that might be exploited. Risk assessments generated from probabilistic attack graphs assist further such decisions [2][3].

A number of attack graph generation techniques have been proposed, though not all of them are feasible or accurate enough to be adopted in practice. We classify these attack graph generation approaches in three general categories:

- Prerequisite/Postcondition (Requires/Results-In) Models,
- Artificial Intelligence Based Models,
- Ontology-Based Models.

Attack graph generation techniques are reviewed in further detail in Section 2. In this paper, we firstly aim to define a prerequisite and postcondition classification scheme regarding attacker privileges for generating attack graphs in the context of the requires/results-in model. We define attacker privileges in a way to distinguish between privileges relating to physical and virtual machines. We also describe attacker prerequisite and postcondition privileges with the same set so that prerequisites and postconditions can be easily related one to another in attack graph generation. Then, we describe two different approaches, one with a rule-based method, and another with employing machine learning (ML), for generating these labels from the National Vulnerability Database (NVD) [4] in an automated way. The need for the automation arises from the fact that manually determining the attacker privileges corresponding to all vulnerabilities and continuing this effort as new vulnerabilities emerge seem impractical and require significant effort and time. Currently NVD hosts more than 92.000 vulnerability entries (In 2016 alone, 6.517 new vulnerabilities were identified) and the amount of identified vulnerabilities each year almost doubles.

The paper is organized as follows: Section 2 reviews the related work with a focus on attack graph generation approaches. Section 3 explains an enhanced prerequisite and postcondition model. Section 4 describe our rule-based and ML-employed automation approaches for generating prerequisite and postcondition labels and evaluates the results of these two approaches. Section 5 concludes the paper and discusses the future work.

2 RELATED WORK

A number of attack graph generation approaches have been proposed, each with different maturity and applicability levels. Among them, prerequisite/postcondition models are intuitive and simplistic in nature. Necessary conditions of exploiting the vulnerabilities are defined as *prerequisites*. Effects and the capabilities obtained by the attackers as a result of the exploitations are named as *postconditions*. TVA (Topological Analysis of Network Attack Vulnerability) [1] and NETSPA (Network Security Planning Architecture) [5][6][7] are two of the well-known examples of this approach [3].

In order to generate attack graphs, TVA utilizes a knowledge database of exploit conditions in terms of preconditions and postconditions that relate to exploitation steps. Preconditions and postconditions specify in detail the network connectivity requirements and attacker privileges using natural language descriptions. Its shortcoming is that the preconditions and postconditions are manually generated from the vulnerability information available in natural language descriptions [7]. This approach demands intensive manual effort and requires the conditions database be enriched manually as new vulnerabilities emerge. Thus scalability and practicality are of significant concerns for this methodology.

NETSPA takes an approach of *attacker state*, which is a combination of the locality and effect information. Locality is processed as a precondition and categorized as *remote* and *local*. Effect information represents the postconditions of exploits and categorized into four levels: *user, administrator, DoS* and *other*. Combining vulnerability information from multiple sources, they generate preconditions and postconditions via a logistic regression model trained with a sample manual data. Their work is outdated since the vulnerability database (VDB) of ICAT is not maintained anymore and its replacement, the CVSS database provides fields of information significantly different than that of the ICAT. Secondly, their precondition and postcondition classification schemes seem to be limited, such that only locality knowledge of the attacker is used as a prerequisite, disregarding the privilege status. Lastly, their privilege classification scheme does not cover application level privileges.

In their work of analyzing NVD for the composition of vulnerabilities to generate attack scenarios, Franqueria and van Keulen [8] describe an approach of *access-to-effect* with little enhancements to the *attacker state* definition of the NETSPA. They describe access in the same way defined in the NETSPA. They name the effects in five categories, adding *runCode* and *obtainCred* to the previously defined *user, admin* and *DoS* categories of the NETSPA. Their model has similar shortcomings pointed out for the NETSPA.

For the category of artificial intelligence based models, MULVAL is a notable work. Relevant information to generate attack graphs, such as vulnerability descriptions and system configuration information are fed to the MULVAL as Datalog facts. Attack graphs are generated via a reasoning engine that correlates the facts given to the MULVAL [3][9][10]. Our experiment with the MULVAL produces significant rates of false positive and negatives.

Ontology-based attack graphs, which have been worked on recently, provide some valuable information, such as interrelations among concepts, not available in the taxonomy based information classification approaches. For the downside, although some initial ontologies for attack graph generation have been proposed [11][12],

they require a lot more effort to be comprehensive enough for generating attack graphs deployed for real-life computer networks.

Rather than focusing on prerequisite and postcondition information for attack graph generation, a number of works elucidate specifically on extracting relevant information from the VDBs, which could aid the process of attack graph generation. Among these, Weerawardhana et al. [13] present two different solutions (machine learning based and linguistic patterns based) for information extraction from online VDBs. Though they identify a number of useful vulnerability information categories and show ways of extracting them automatically, their work lacks the privilege prerequisite and postcondition information categories that are essential to our approach. Secondly, Roschke et al.[14] investigate extraction of vulnerability information from textual descriptions for attack graph construction, in addition to analyzing and comparing the features of multiple VDBs. However, their work gives a few examples of keywords that can be extracted from textual descriptions rather than describing a complete and categorized list of them.

3 DESCRIPTION OF THE PROPOSED REQUIRES/RESULTS-IN MODEL

3.1 Overview of the Model

In this section, we define a generic requires/results-in model, that improves upon the previous works of [5][6] and [8] to depict a way of generating attack graphs. A comparison of our approach and the early works is given at Table 1. Requires/results-in models typically define exploits in terms of a set of prerequisite and postcondition rules. The resulting set of all the rules for the exploits are used as a knowledge base for attack graph generation [7].

Our model takes a set of information in four categories as its input and relates them to the privileges gained knowledge as its output via a reasoning engine that makes use of the knowledge base. The set of input information are:

- Vulnerability scan results that can be produced by tools such as NESSUS or OPENVAS,
- Topology and reachability information of the network,
- Attack Vector (AV) for each vulnerability and the locality of the attacker,
- Privilege of the attacker at their initial/current state and privilege prerequisites for the vulnerabilities.

Among this set of input information, vulnerabilities at a computer network can be identified by vulnerability scanning tools, and their results as CVE ids can be fed into the model. Regarding the network information, topology discovery tools can be used to identify the number and type of the assets and map their connectivity.

Reachability information, which indicates whether there exist logical connections among the network hosts given the physical connections, can be derived from the active network components, such as, routers, switches, firewalls and IDS/IPSs.

The third input, AV for a vulnerability defines how a vulnerability can be exploited in terms of the attacker's current location at the network and takes the values of *Physical, Local, Adjacent Network* and *Network* as described in [15].

The data of privileges required for the input set and the privileges gained as the model's output are not readily available to

Table 1: Comparison Of Prerequisite/Postcondition Models

Model	Access Vector Prereq.	Privilege Prereq.	Privilege Postcondition	Database	Automation
TVA [1]	Exploitation steps are defined in natural language. No formal prerequisite or postcondition definitions. No linkage between prerequisites and postconditions.			N/A	N/A
NETSPA [3][4]	Remote Local	N/A	User Admin DoS Other	ICAT (Obsolete)	Uses logistic regression trained with a sample data for automation.
Franqueria & Van Keulen [7]	Remote Local	N/A	User Admin RunCode ObtainCred DoS	NVD	N/A
Our Model	Network Adjacent Local Physical [15]	OS(Admin)/VOS(Admin) OS(User)/VOS(User) APP(Admin) APP(User) None		NVD	1. Rule-based automation. 2. Machine Learning-based automation.

extract from the open VDBs. Nor there exists a formal definition or categorization accepted generally to characterize privileges of the attackers as prerequisites and postconditions. In the next subsection, we describe a novel privilege classification scheme and show two different approaches to classify vulnerabilities defined by the NVD with our privilege labels in Section 4.

The model that we propose is a multi-prerequisite approach since it considers not only the locality, but also the privilege level of the attacker, which is used only as a postcondition of an exploitation by the earlier works, as shown in Table 1. The reasoning for using attacker privileges as exploitation prerequisites can be captured from the textual descriptions (i.e. "a local authenticated user ..." or "a remote authenticated administrator ...") of vulnerabilities that imply attacker privileges as exploitability requirements.

3.2 Privilege Classification

We define a set of five general privilege categories. The types and ordering of privilege classes are depicted in Figure 1. According to the capability levels, privileges are depicted in descending order from *OS* level to the *None*. Additionally, privileges at *Admin* levels are more capable than *User* level privileges.

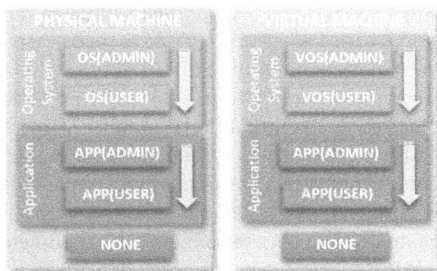

Figure 1: Categorization of Attacker Privilege Levels

In addition to the operating system level privilege classification of the earlier works, we use application level privileges and differentiate privileges inside and outside the virtual machines. Application level privileges indicate privilege requirements/gains for specific applications for which the names can be derived from the

CPE (Common Product Enumeration) fields of the vulnerabilities. They are useful in modeling the authentication requirements/gains for applications with or without regard to operating system level privileges.

The benefit of using application level privileges can be explained with an example. For *CVE-2016-1990* the *AV* property is *Local* and its textual description is given as *"HPE ArcSight ESM ... allows local users to gain privileges for command execution via unspecified vectors."* If only the locality property of this CVE were used, being local at an asset would be enough to exploit it. However, our model requires the adversary to be both local and to have APP(USER) privilege by possessing authentication knowledge for the *ArcSight ESM* in order to exploit the vulnerability successfully.

To differentiate attacker privileges at the virtual machines from the physical ones, another set of labels starting with the letter "V" are defined. Since the privileges gained at either the physical or virtual machines do not have the same capabilities, we find it useful to differentiate between where exploitations start and where their impacts (privilege gains) occur, in terms of their physical or virtual locations. The need for and usefulness of such distinction can be explained with two chosen CVE examples as illustrated in Figure 2.

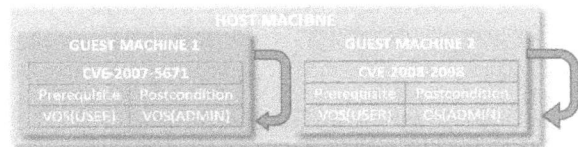

Figure 2: Host/Guest Machine Exploitation Example

In the examples, exploiting CVE-2007-5671 gives the attacker operating system level ADMIN privilege only on the same guest machine whereas CVE-2008-2098 is more dangerous since it provides ADMIN privilege on the physical machine hosting the guest machine.

3.3 Attack Graph Generation

Using attacker privileges both as exploitation prerequisites and postconditions in our model, vulnerabilities can be easily related to each other for attack graph generation. In order to exploit a given vulnerability that requires any attacker privilege, an attacker must have one or more of the required privileges at the operating system or application level, either as an administrator or a user. NONE, as a privilege prerequisite, implies the attacker does not need any of the four privileges listed at the operating system or application level. After exploiting a vulnerability, one or more of the categories of privileges can be acquired. The semantics of the NONE as a postcondition is that none of the privileges at the operating system or application level is gained after exploiting a vulnerability, disregarding any impact that might be caused by the exploitation. An exploitation with NONE as its privilege postcondition might cause any of the confidentiality, integrity and availability impacts, as described at [15] and such impact information for each known vulnerabilities can be derived from the NVD.

In our model, attack graphs can be generated by the *Reasoning Engine* that interacts with the *Knowledge Base* of enriched vulnerability information, using the Algorithm 1 that is based on the earlier work [5]. Nodes in this algorithm represents the states of the attackers as a pair of locality and privilege information. Starting from the initial node, for each node that is physically and logically reachable, vulnerabilities existing at the target nodes are examined to determine if they are exploitable. If both the attack vector and privilege level parameters at a given node suffice to exploit a given vulnerability, then a directed edge that represents an attack path is added between the current and target nodes.

Algorithm 1: Attack Graph Generation Algorithm

1   $priv \leftarrow \{OS/VOS(Adm.), OS/VOS(User), APP(Adm.), APP(User), None/VNone\}$;
2   $AV \leftarrow \{Physical, Local, Adjacent, Network\}$;
3   $curNod.priv \leftarrow initial\ privilege\ of\ the\ attacker \in priv$;
4   $curNod, destNod, currentNod.av, v \leftarrow null$;
5   $attackerNodes \leftarrow \{SET - attacker's\ initial\ node\}$;
6   $destNodes, V1, V2 \leftarrow \{null\}$;

7   **while** $attackerNodes$ *is not empty* **do**
8     $curNod \leftarrow attackerNodes.pop()$;
9     $V1 \leftarrow \{SET - vulnerabilities\ at\ the\ curNod\}$;
10   **foreach** $v \in V1$ **do**
11   **if** $curNod.priv >= curNod.v.privPre$ **then**
12   **if** $curNod.v.privPost > curNod.priv$ **then**
13           $curNod.priv \leftarrow curNod.v.privPost$;
14   **end**
15   **end**
16   **end**
17     $destNodes \leftarrow \{SET - nodes\ reachable\ from\ the\ curNod\}$;
18   **foreach** $destNod \in destNodes$ **do**
19       $V2 \leftarrow \{SET - vulnerabilities\ at\ the\ destNod\}$;
20   **foreach** $v \in V2$ **do**
21   **if** $curNod.av >= destNod.v.av$ **then**
22   **if** $(destNod.v.privPre == NONE)\ OR\ (destNod.priv >= destNod.v.privPre)$ **then**
23   **if** $destNod.v.privPost > destNod.priv$ **then**
24               $destNod.priv \leftarrow destNod.v.privPost$;
25               $addEdgeBtw(curNod, destNod)$;
26               $attackerNodes.add(destNod)$;
27   **end**
28   **end**
29   **end**
30   **end**
31   **end**
32 **end**

Using the Algorithm 1, example attack graphs generated on a simple network are shown in Figure 3. On the sample network, firewall rules allow the outsiders only to communicate with the Apache HTTP Server. Inside the network, there exist a trust relationship between the Apache HTTP Server and the Red Hat Server. Other than than, host are denied any communication among them by the router rules. Linux Server hosts a Guest Machine which is highly untrusted, thus the Guest Machine is not allowed to communicate with any other host on the network, including the host machine on which it resides. For this simple scenario, there exist two malicious adversaries, one outside the local network, and another inside the local network, at the untrusted Guest Machine.

From the attack graphs depicted in Figure 3, it can be observed that the *Attacker 1* can exploit Device 1, 2 and 5 with OS(ADMIN) privileges and causes a Denial of Service impact on the Device 3. On the other hand, the *Attacker 2*, who is a malicious insider with access only to a virtual machine with no connection to the other devices in the network, can exploit the Device 3 with OS(ADMIN) privilege in addition to the devices exploitable by the *Attacker 1*.

4   AUTOMATED GENERATION OF THE PRIVILEGES

Given the many on-line and public VDBs, extracting or generating the prerequisites and postconditions for attacker privileges for known vulnerabilities might seem to be a trivial task. However, firstly, analysis of VDBs and listings reveals considerable amount of missing, inconsistent or incorrect data [7]. Secondly, such data are not readily available to extract from the data fields supported by the public VDBs, such as NVD. The available VDBs have no defined formal languages and they generally define the vulnerability information in terms of taxonomies and rely on natural language text for a considerable part of the definitions [7]. These findings lead us to investigate for an automated way of capturing the semantics of exploit prerequisites and postconditions in terms of attacker privileges, which is then fed into a knowledge base to generate attack graphs practically with the proposed requires/results-in model.

In the following subsections, we describe in detail the two different approaches of rule-based and ML-employed for generating attacker privilege labels and compare their results on the confusion matrices using metrics of accuracy rates as well as precision and recall values. Accuracy rates are defined as the ratio of correctly identified classes compared with the total number of vulnerabilities. Precision values show the ratio of total number of correct identifications given the total number of predictions for each class, while the recall values demonstrate the ratio of total number of correctly identified classes given the actual total numbers of the classes. The results of the models are checked against an experimental dataset given at Table 2 in order to determine their accuracy rates. This evaluation dataset of NVD vulnerabilities has been generated manually by carefully analyzing more than 550 vulnerabilities out of the 92000 currently available at the NVD and has been chosen in a way to cover most of the different types of vulnerabilities, such as with varying impacts, weaknesses or attack types.

We note that we have not included incorrect data, such as the data for *CVE-2008-0840* described by [14], in this dataset. Specifically, 20 vulnerability entries for postcondition and 1 entry for

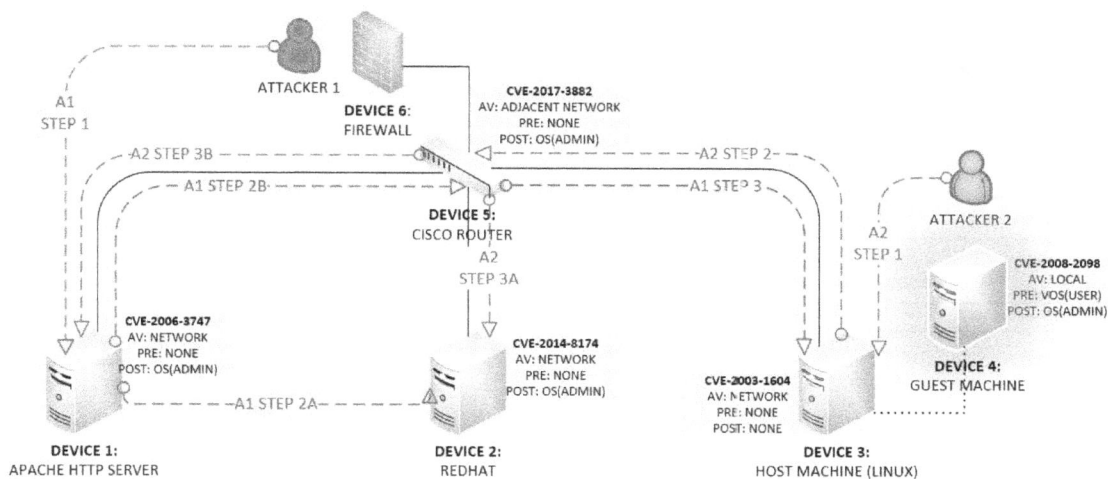

Figure 3: Examples of Attack Graphs on a Sample Network

prerequisite determination have been excluded. However, we handle the inconsistencies where the same information is expressed with varying vocabulary or when the relevant information is expressed sporadically. For instance CVE-2005-1207 has the textual description *"Buffer overflow in the Web Client service in MS Windows XP and Windows Server 2003 allows remote authenticated users to execute arbitrary code via a crafted WebDAV request containing special parameters."* with no usage of *"root"* and we still correctly identify the privilege postcondition through checking another expression (buffer overflow) together with the CVSS Impact score.

4.1 Rule-Based Generation of the Privileges

As our first method, we generate privilege information relating to the vulnerabilities with a rule based reasoning engine. Rules at the reasoning engine have been defined manually by analyzing the experimental data given at Table 2. The manually generated rules are static in that they do not dynamically change or increase in size as the vulnerability data imported from the NVD enlarges in quantity. The defined rules process both taxonomy-based and textual data to capture the semantics of the vulnerabilities. Below, we give an overview of the fields of data employed in our rules. The detailed definitions of the fields can be found at CVSS 2.0 [16] and CVSS 3.0 [15] specifications.

As described in the previous sections, *Attack Vector (AV)* (CVSS 2.0 and 3.0) denotes the locality of the attacker with regard to the network asset on which a vulnerability exists. It takes the values of *Physical, Local, Adjacent Network* and *Network*.

Authentication (only CVSS 2.0) field shows the number of times an attacker must authenticate to a vulnerable target and it takes the values of *None, Single* and *Multiple*. In the context of their usage in our rules, we are interested in only if a vulnerability requires any authentication or not. A *Not None* value implies that the related vulnerability requires an attacker privilege at either the operating system or application level.

Privilege (only CVSS 3.0) field expresses the level of privilege an attacker must possess and it takes the values of *None, Low* and *High*.

A value of *Low* denotes basic user capabilities while a value of *High* indicates significant control over the vulnerable asset. From this parameter, attacker privilege level as a prerequisite can be inferred as either *Administrator* or *User*. But it is not possible to determine its privilege level as operating system or application level only by analyzing this field.

Common Platform Enumeration (CPE) [17] data shows a set of vulnerable products with regard to each known vulnerabilities. The vulnerable platforms are represented in three categories, such as *operating systems, firmwares* and *applications*. Correlating the CPE data with the *Authentication* and *Privilege* data enables us to derive further knowledge on these fields that are not explicit when they are analyzed on their own.

The *Impacts* (CVSS 2.0 and 3.0) data with regard to the three pillars (Confidentiality, Integrity, Availability) of the information security show the damage induced at the victim and takes the values of *None, Partial,* and *Complete*. This field is especially useful in determining the privilege gained after exploiting a vulnerability.

Another field of information, *Security Protection*, which is not defined formally as a data field by the NVD in the CVSS 2.0 and 3.0 specifications, have been discovered by our manual analysis of the NVD data feed of XML 2.0. This field denotes the attacker privilege postconditions as *Admin, User,* or *Other*. However, labeling vulnerabilities with this field is not continued by the NVD and only a minority of them have been labeled with this field.

In addition to the above explained taxonomy of data, natural language descriptions are also used by the NVD to explain the vulnerabilities. A number of single words or sequences of words that we have identified through our manual analysis of the description are also employed in our rules and proves to be very useful in determining attacker privileges.

Table 3 and 4 depict the rules to produce attacker privilege prerequisites and postconditions, respectively. Rules in both categories process both taxonomy and natural language-based data for determining the privileges. The ellipsis in the keywords represent any number of words residing in the same sentence.

Table 2: Distribution of Privilege Classes on the Experimental Dataset

	OS (Admin)	VOS (Admin)	OS (User)	VOS (User)	App (Admin)	App (User)	None	Total
Prerequisite	31	72	160	49	31	77	150	570
Postcondition	168	1	100	0	60	23	199	551

Table 3: Rules For Producing Attacker Privilege Prerequisites

#	Vocabulary	Impacts	CPE	Post-Condition
1	'gain root' | 'gain unrestricted, root shell access' | 'obtain root'	All Complete	-	OS(ADMIN)
2	'gain privilege' | 'gain host OS privilege' | 'gain admin' | 'obtain local admin' | 'obtain admin' | 'gain unauthorized access' | 'to root' | 'to the root' | 'elevate the privilege' | 'elevate privilege' | 'root privileges via buffer overfow'	All Complete	-	OS(ADMIN)
3	'unspecified vulnerability' | 'unspecified other impact' | 'unspecified impact' | 'other impacts'	All Complete	-	OS(ADMIN)
4		Partial	Only OS	OS(USER)
5	'gain privilege' | 'gain unauthorized access'	Partial	Only OS	OS(USER)
6	'gain admin' | 'obtain admin'	Partial	-	APP(ADMIN)
7	'hijack the authentication of admin' | 'hijack the authentication of super admin' | 'hijack the authentication of moderator'	-	-	APP(ADMIN)
8	'hijack the authentication of users' | 'hijack the authentication of arbitrary users' | 'hijack the authentication of unspecified victims'	-	-	APP(USER)
9	'obtain password' | 'obtain credential' | 'sniff ... credentials' | 'sniff ... passwords' |'steal ... credentials' | 'steal ... passwords'	All Complete	Only OS	OS(ADMIN)
10		Partial	Only OS	OS(USER)
11		Partial	APP/ HW	APP(ADMIN)
12	'cleartext credential' | 'cleartext password' | 'obtain plaintext' | 'obtain cleartext' | 'discover cleartext' | 'read network traffic' | 'un-encrypted' | 'unencrypted' | 'intercept transmission' | 'intercept communication' | 'obtain and decrypt passwords' | 'conduct offline password guessing' | 'bypass authentication'	All Complete	Only OS	OS(ADMIN)
13		Partial	Only OS	OS(USER)
14		Partial	APP/ HW	APP(ADMIN)
15	'buffer overflow' | 'command injection' | 'write arbitrary,file' | 'command execution' | 'execute command' | 'execute root command' | 'execute commands as root' | 'execute arbitrary' | 'execute dangerous' | 'execute php' | 'execute script' | 'execute local' | 'execution of arbitrary' | 'execution of command' | 'remote execution' | 'execute code' & ! 'execute arbitrary SQL'	All Complete	-	OS(ADMIN)
16		Partial	-	OS(USER)
17	'SQL injection'	-	APP/HW	APP(ADMIN)
18	-	Any None	-	NONE

Table 4: Rules For Producing Attacker Privilege Postconditions

#	AV	Authentication	Privilege	CPE	Pre-Condition
1	-	-	None	-	NONE
2	Local	-	Low	Only OS	OS(USER)/VOS(USER)
3	Local	-	High	Only OS	OS(ADMIN)/VOS(ADMIN)
4	Local	! None	Low	APP/HW	APP(USER)
5	Local	! None	High	APP/HW	APP(ADMIN)
6	Local	None	Low	APP/HW	OS(USER)/VOS(USER)
7	Local	None	High	APP/HW	OS(ADMIN)/VOS(ADMIN)
8	! Local	! None	Low	Only OS	OS(USER)/VOS(User)
9	! Local	! None	High	Only OS	OS(ADMIN)/VOS(ADMIN)
10	! Local	! None	Low	APP/HW	APP(USER)
11	! Local	! None	High	APP/HW	APP(ADMIN)
#			Vocabulary		
12			'allow ... guest OS user' | 'allow ... PV guest user' | 'user on a guest operating system'	-	VOS(USER)
13			'allow ... guest OS admin' | 'allow ... PV guest admin' | 'allow ... guest OS kernel admin'	-	VOS(ADMIN)
14			'allows local users' | 'allowing local users' | 'allow local users' | 'allows the local user'	-	OS(USER)/VOS(USER)
15			'allows local administrators' | 'allow local administrators' | 'allows the local administrator'	-	OS(ADMIN)/VOS(ADMIN)
16			'remote authenticated user' & ! 'remote authenticated users with administrative privileges'	APP/HW	APP(USER)
17			'remote authenticated admin' | 'remote authenticated users with administrative privileges'	APP/HW	APP(ADMIN)
18			'remote authenticated users'	Only OS	OS(USER)/VOS(USER)
19			'remote authenticated admin'	Only OS	OS(ADMIN)/VOS(ADMIN)

Regarding the application of the rules, *Logical And* is used for reasoning, such that, only if all the fields of a given rule satisfy for a given vulnerability, then the privilege level of the rule is assigned to that vulnerability as a prerequisite or postcondition. If more than one rule apply to a given vulnerability, the rule with the highest privilege level overrides. In case none of the rules applies for a given vulnerability, a default value (*None* for prerequisites, *OS(Admin)* for postconditions) is assigned as its privilege level. Our rule-based model generates privilege prerequisite and postcondition labels with accuracy rates of 87,7 % and 89,8 % respectively. These accuracy rates are defined as the ratio of correctly identified classes compared with the total number of vulnerabilities. Confusion matrices given at Tables 6 and 7 can be used to further investigate the precision and recall values for each privilege level.

4.2　ML-Employed Generation of the Privileges

To further investigate the possibility of increasing the accuracy rate of the rule-based model for determining attacker privileges, we have experimented on four different ML-employed approaches listed below:

- Radial Basis Function (RBF) Networks,
- Support Vector Machines (SVM),
- Neuro Evolution of Augmenting Topologies (NEAT),
- Multi Layer Perceptron (MLP).

Among these approaches, RBF networks is known for its ability to respond well to fast local changing borders between classes, but it might not be as good generalizer as an MLP [18]. SVM, on the other hand, is one of the best classifiers for binary classification problems, since it finds the optimum discriminative function that maximizes the margin between the classes, but might be difficult to implement in multiclass problems, as is in our case [18]. NEAT is a neural network which uses evolutionary algorithms to dynamically alter its topology and connections to achieve better results than static networks [19]. The last of these approaches, MLP, is a widely used model due to its success in various different application areas and its well-defined implementation methodology [18].

MLP has one input layer, one or more hidden layers, and one output layer. Basically, MLP takes the inputs and assigns them to the desired outputs by mapping through the hidden layer neurons. The mapping process is implemented through an iterative optimization process called gradient descent based error backpropagation [18]. The iterative process continues until the sum of error squares between the desired and the model outputs drops below an acceptable threshold level (or the cross validation error starts increasing, as used in our model).

Among these ML models, we focus on the MLP as our ML-employed model due to its significantly better results than the other three approaches. Thus we compare in detail only the results of the MLP model with the rule-based model and give an accuracy comparison chart of these four ML-employed models at Table 5.

Table 5: Accuracy Rates of the ML-Employed Models

	RBF	SVM	NEAT	MLP
Privilege Prerequisite	58.6	90,7	91,8	96,1
Privilege Postcondition	54,3	91,6	92,1	95,7

As input to our MLP model, we use the same set of taxonomy-based and vocabulary-based categories of information applied in our rule-based model. Additionally, we utilize CVSS 2.0 scores ranging from 0 to 10 as an extra information. As the output, the privilege categories are determined.

Given the dataset at Table 2, 5-fold Cross Validation (CV) and Testing of the data is implemented. 60 % of the data was used for training, 20 % is used for CV and 20 % is used for testing in all 5 cases. As a result, all available data is tested. The corresponding Confusion Matrix for privilege prerequisites is provided in Table 6 and for privilege postconditions in Table 7.

The Confusion Matrix rows represent the actual appearance of any class, i.e., in the privilege prerequisite model (Table 6), out of 570 data points, *OS(User)* is seen 160 times (sum of the terms in row 3 of the confusion matrix). In a similar fashion, the columns of the confusion matrix represent how many times the model predicts a certain class. For example, the model predicts *OS(User)* 158 times (sum of the terms in column 3 of the confusion matrix).

Precision is defined as the ratio of the correct predictions of a certain class. In the privilege prerequisite model (Table 6), out of the 158 *OS(User)* predictions, 152 of them are correct (and 6 of them are wrong). As a result, the precision value for *OS(User)* class is 0.96. Of the 6 wrong predictions 5 are actually *VOS(User)*, and 1 is *None*.

Recall represents the ratio of the actual class instances within the predictions that the model made for a certain class. In the privilege prerequisite model (Table 6), out of the 160 OS(User) data points that exist in the dataset, the model is able to determine 152 of them correctly. Thus the recall value for OS(User) is 152/160 = 0.95.

Overall accuracy is defined as the ratio of correctly identified classes (sum of the diagonal values in the confusion matrix) compared with the total number of points. In our study, we are able to achieve 96,1 % overall accuracy for privilege prerequisite model and 95,4 % for the privilege postcondition.

4.3　Comparison of the Models

The rules we defined can produce privilege prerequisite and postconditions labels with accuracy rates of 87,7 % and 89,8 %, respectively. The rule-based privilege generation method proposed in our work is not completed. We show that such a rule based approach can be used to enhance the data derived from the NVD, so that attack graphs that are consistent and with minimized false positive/negative rates can be automatically generated. By adding more rules, the accuracy of the this approach can be increased further.

For the ML model, we get the accuracy rates of 96,1 % and 95,7 % for privilege prerequisites and postconditions, respectively. Comparing the results of these two models, ML-employed model achieves significantly better results for both the privilege prerequisites and postconditions. This promising result of our MLP model indicates that ML techniques can be also used successfully for privilege determination in order to generate attack graphs.

In addition to the higher overall accuracy rate, the feature of generating the privileges with confidence levels, compared to the *1 (found)* or *0 (not found)* nature of the rule based-model is a significant advantage of the MLP model. This feature is especially useful in manually evaluating the generated privileges that are below a defined confidence threshold level.

Table 6: Confusion Matrix For Privilege Prerequisites

	Predicted															
	OS (ADMIN)		VOS (ADMIN)		OS (USER)		VOS (USER)		APP (ADMIN)		APP (USER)		NONE		Recall Values		TOTAL
	RB	ML	RB	ML	RB	ML	RB	ML	RB	ML	RB	ML	RB	ML	RB	ML	
OS(ADMIN)	31	30	0	1	0	0	0	0	0	0	0	0	0	0	100	0,97	31
VOS(ADMIN)	25	0	45	72	0	0	0	0	1	0	0	0	1	0	0,63	100	72
OS(USER)	5	1	0	0	141	152	0	0	0	0	2	2	12	5	0,88	0,95	160
VOS(USER)	0	0	0	0	7	5	38	43	0	0	1	0	3	1	0,78	0,88	49
APP(ADMIN)	0	1	0	0	0	0	0	0	30	29	1	1	0	0	0,97	0,94	31
APP(USER)	0	0	0	0	7	0	0	0	1	1	66	73	3	3	0,86	0,95	77
NONE	0	0	0	0	0	1	0	0	0	0	0	0	150	149	100	0,99	150
Precision Values	0,51	0,94	100	0,99	0,91	0,96	100	100	0,94	0,97	0,94	0,96	0,88	0,94			
TOTAL	61	32	45	73	155	158	38	43	32	30	70	76	169	158			570
Overall Accuracy															0,88	0,96	

Table 7: Confusion Matrix For Privilege Postconditions

	Predicted															
	OS (ADMIN)		VOS (ADMIN)		OS (USER)		VOS (USER)		APP (ADMIN)		APP (USER)		NONE		Recall Values		TOTAL
	RB	ML	RB	ML	RB	ML	RB	ML	RB	ML	RB	ML	RB	ML	RB	ML	
OS(ADMIN)	161	163	0	0	3	2	0	0	1	2	0	1	3	0	0,96	0,97	168
VOS(ADMIN)	1	0	0	0	0	0	0	1	0	0	0	0	0	0	0	0	1
OS(USER)	6	5	0	0	92	93	0	0	0	0	0	0	2	2	0,92	0,93	100
VOS(USER)	0	0	0	0	0	0	0	0	0	0	0	0	0	0	-	-	0
APP(ADMIN)	8	3	0	0	10	1	0	0	39	55	0	0	3	1	0,65	0,92	60
APP(USER)	11	0	0	0	0	3	0	0	2	0	9	20	1	0	0,40	0,87	23
NONE	5	0	0	0	0	2	0	0	0	1	0	1	194	195	0,97	0,98	199
Precision Values	0,84	0,95	-	-	0,88	0,92	-	0	0,93	0,95	100	0,91	0,96	0,98			
TOTAL	192	171	0	0	105	101	0	1	42	58	9	22	203	198			551
Overall Accuracy															0,90	0,95	

5 CONCLUSION AND FUTURE WORK

In this work, we first defined a generic requires/results-in model and an algorithm based on the early work for attack graph generation. Then, we defined an enhanced categorization of attacker privileges and showed two different methods, rule-based and ML-employed, for generating attacker privileges as prerequisites and postconditions from the vulnerability in the NVD. ML-employed MLP model achieved an accuracy of 96,1 % and 95,4 % for privilege prerequisite and postconditions, respectively, compared to the accuracy rates of 87,7 % and 89,8 % we get from the rule-based model.

The promising results of the models we have demonstrated urge us to further explore using a hybrid model as a future work. Possible usage scenarios for such a model are as listed below:

- Using the ML-employed model only for the vulnerabilities for which rule-based model does not cover,
- Using the results of the rule-based model as an additional feed to the ML-employed model,
- Comparing the results of the two models and alerting for manual analysis when the outputs of the models disagree.

REFERENCES

[1] S Jajodia, Steven Noel, and B O'Berry. Topological analysis of network attack vulnerability. *Managing Cyber Threats*, pages 247–266, 2005.
[2] M.U Aksu, M.H Dilek, E.İ Tatlı, K Bicakci, H. İ Dirik, M.U Demirezen, and T Aykır. A Quantitative CVSS-Based Cyber Security Risk Assessment Methodology For IT Systems. In *The 51st Int. Carnahan Conference on Security Technology*, 2017.
[3] Anoop Singhal and Ximming Ou. Security Risk Analysis of Enterprise Networks Using Probabilistic Attack Graphs. *Computer*, page 24, 2011.
[4] National Institute of Standards and Technology (NIST). National Vulnerability Database (NVD): Summary, 2016.
[5] Kyle Ingols, Richard Lippmann, and Keith Piwowarski. Practical attack graph generation for network defense. *Proceedings, ACSAC*, pages 121–130, 2006.
[6] Richard Lippmann, Kyle Ingols, Chris Scott, Keith Piwowarski, Kendra Kratkiewicz, Mike Artz, and Robert Cunningham. Validating and restoring defense in depth using attack graphs. *Proceedings - IEEE Military Communications Conference MILCOM*, 2007.
[7] K Ingols, C Scott, K Piwowarski, and K Kratkiewicz. Evaluating and Strengthening Enterprise Network Security Using Attack Graphs. *Technical report, MIT Lincoln Laboratory, Lexington, MA, ESC-TR-2005-064*, 2005.
[8] V.N.L. Franqueira and M van Keulen. Analysis of the nist database towards the composition of vulnerabilities in attack scenarios. *Technical report, TR-CTIT-08-08,University of Twente, Enschede*, 2008.
[9] Xinming Ou, Sudhakar Govindavajhala, and Andrew W. Appel. MulVAL: a logic-based network security analyzer. *Proceedings of the 14th conference on USENIX Security Symposium - Volume 14*, 2005.
[10] Xinming Ou, Wayne F. Boyer, and Miles a. McQueen. A scalable approach to attack graph generation. *Proceedings of the 13th ACM conference on Computer and communications security - CCS '06*, (March 2016):336, 2006.
[11] Andrew Simmonds, Peter Sandilands, and L. van Ekert. An ontology for network security attacks. *Lecture notes in computer science*, pages 317–323, 2004.
[12] Ahmad Salahi and Morteza Ansarinia. Predicting Network Attacks Using Ontology-Driven Inference. *arXiv preprint arXiv:1304.0913*, 2013.
[13] Sachini Weerawardhana, Subhojeet Mukherjee, Indrajit Ray, and Adele Howe. Automated Extraction of Vulnerability Information for Home Computer Security. In *Foundations and Practice of Security*, volume 8930, pages 356–366, 2015.
[14] Sebastian Roschke, Feng Cheng, Robert Schuppenies, and Christoph Meinel. Towards Unifying Vulnerability Information for Attack Graph Construction. In *12th International Conference on Information Security*, pages 218–233, 2009.
[15] FIRST. Common Vulnerability Scoring System v3.0: Specification Document. *Forum of Incident Response and Security Teams (FIRST)*, pages 1–21, 2015.
[16] Peter Mell, Karen Scarfone, and Sasha Romanosky. A Complete Guide to the Common Vulnerability Scoring System Version 2.0. *FIRST Forum of Incident Response and Security Teams*, pages 1–23, 2007.
[17] Andrew Buttner. Common Platform Enumeration (CPE): Specifications. *MITRE*, page 21, 2007.
[18] S. Haykin. *Neural Networks and Learning Machines*. Prentice Hall, New Jersey, USA, 3rd edition, 2008.
[19] Kenneth O. Stanley and Risto Miikkulainen. Evolving Neural Networks through Augmenting Topologies. *Evolutionary Computation*, 10(2):99–127, 2002.

Effectiveness of Android Obfuscation on Evading Anti-malware

Melissa Chua
Defence Science and Technology Agency
Singapore
cwanjunm@dsta.gov.sg

Vivek Balachandran
Singapore Institute of Technology
Singapore
vivek.b@singaporetech.edu.sg

ABSTRACT

Obfuscation techniques have been conventionally used for legitimate applications, including preventing application reverse engineering, tampering and protecting intellectual property. A malware author could also leverage these benign techniques to hide their malicious intents and evade anti-malware detection. As variants of known malware have been regularly found on the Google Play Store, transformed malware attacks are a real problem that security solutions today need to address. It has been proven that mainstream security tools installed on smartphones are mainly signature-based; our work focuses on evaluating the efficiency of a composite of obfuscation techniques in evading anti-malware detection. We further verified the trend of transformed malware in evading detection, with a larger and more updated database of known malware. This is also the first work to-date that presents the instability of some anti-malware tools (AMTs) against obfuscated malware. This work also proved that current mainstream AMTs do not build up resilience against obfuscation methods, but instead try to update the signature database on created variants.

ACM Reference format:
Melissa Chua & Vivek Balachandran. 2018. Effectiveness of Android Obfuscation on Evading Anti-malware. In *CODASPY '18: Eighth ACM Conference on Data and Application Security and Privacy, March 19–21, 2018, Tempe, AZ, USA.* ACM, NY, NY, USA, 3 pages. DOI: https://doi.org/10.1145/3176258.3176942

1 INTRODUCTION

The Android platform continues to dominate the mobile platform market with an approximate market share of 84.3% [1]. As mobile devices capabilities improve with better hardware, devices today are able to perform more sensitive operations like mobile banking. These functionalities come in the form of applications (APKs), which can be created by third-party developers and distributed on Google Play. Malware authors have begun tapping the openness of application markets to proliferate malicious APKs. Due to the rising threat of malicious APKs, mainstream commercial solutions have proposed similar methodologies to defend against malware. G. Hatchimonji proved that approximately 5% of all smartphones have some form of security tool installed [2]. Y. Xue added that as mainstream security tools are signature-based, they can only effectively detect malware when a comprehensive list of malware signature is provided [3]. Malware authors are then able to develop more complex obfuscation techniques to better evade signature-based detection. This phenomenon

was observed in [4], where over 3000 mutated versions of a known ransomware called SLocker were cited.

As security tools on most smartphones today perform signature-based analysis, this work focuses on proposing detailed obfuscation tactics that malware authors might leverage to obstruct or evade analysis. Additionally, recent malware found are not yet updated with evasion techniques yet. This work obfuscates recent malware with potential evasion methods that are proposed in this paper. The results also confirms that recent malware are able to evade signature-based analysis with the obfuscation techniques proposed in this paper. To our knowledge, this is the only paper to-date that has proven the instability of some anti-malware tools (AMTs) detection results. We were able to conclude that current mainstream AMTs are not resilient against the obfuscation method, but merely build up their signature database to detect mutated malware.

2 PREVIOUS WORKS

Works like [5] designed frameworks with various obfuscation techniques to transform the original malware into a different form. However, the obfuscation techniques implemented were trivial transformations including renaming of identifiers, methods and files, introducing junk codes, code reordering and string encoding. Although [5] mentioned more complicated obfuscation techniques like reflection or bytecode encryption, the effectiveness of such techniques is not evaluated in the paper. The framework that is proposed in this work explains more detailed techniques to perform code reordering, for example method overloading, opaque predicate, a try-catch or switch function. Additionally, the previous works were evaluating malware created before 2013. The malware dataset in this work is larger and more updated (e.g. malware from 2013 to 2015). Malware found in 2016 were not used due to the instability of AMTs in detecting them; for a better comparison of their ability to evade detection, malware should be consistently detected by AMTs used. Cani et. al. [6] performed generic programming to mutate malware samples into new possible variants. One critical flaw in these mutated malware is that its malicious behaviour might not be retained after transformation. Due to this, we will avoid using generic programming to perform obfuscation.

3 OBFUSCATION TECHNIQUES

To evaluate the effectiveness of techniques used on malware samples in avoiding detection by AMTs, we developed an automated framework consisting of several obfuscation techniques that could potentially be used by malware authors to obfuscate their malware. Based on the framework, we were able to send large numbers of known malware through these obfuscation techniques to generate a new variants, which were verified to possess the original malicious operations. In the following paragraphs, we discuss in detail the obfuscation techniques that our automated system contains.

3.1 Method Overloading

Method overloading uses polymorphism to divert the malware's flow by defining new functions to invoke functions that are originally in the malware. Dummy methods would be cloned with similar method names as the original method calls. For the malware to be executed correctly, the obfuscation method needs to ensure that function invocation is unique. The dummy method distinguishes itself from the original method by modifying the parameters and return type. This obfuscation provides a trivial means to manipulate the call graph of the application to defeat cryptographic hash matching detection.

3.2 Opaque Predicate

Opaque predicate uses conditional expressions to ensure one branch always gets executed. In this obfuscation method, we combined it with junk codes to further conceal the control flow of the malware. This technique inserts an opaque predicate statement between the original source code and sets it to always execute a particular branch. The malware's original codes are added to the branch that gets executed, while junk codes are added to the remaining branches.

3.3 Try-catch

Try-catch is scripted to always execute the "catch" block, by deliberately introducing an exception error such as arithmetic exception in the "try" block. This technique first identifies the smali codes within the method call and then adds an exception statement to the try-catch structure. Lastly, the return statement of the method call is included at the end of the catch block. This technique creates an illusion that the "catch" block would occasionally get executed when the error is invoked. However, the error would always get invoked as the try-catch structure contains an additional statement to deliberately cause the error.

3.4 Switch Statement Obfuscation

Switch statement obfuscation uses the concept of switches to break up the smali codes from a method call and insert them into the different branches of the switch accordingly. The switch structure is modified such that a "goto" instruction is added at the end of each branch, enabling all branches to be executed instead of one. This allows the dynamic program flow to be similar to the original malware, but makes it harder for static analysis.

4 DATASET

This section describes the malware samples that were selected and AMTs that were used for the study. An important criterion of this investigation is that the AMT detection should also be stable enough such that the AMTs detect the malware samples consistently.

4.1 Malware Dataset

Figure 1 provides an overview of the malware families in our malware dataset contributed from the Drebin dataset [7], Contagio Mobile [8] and open source downloads. It is evident that the majority of pre-2013 malware attempted to make money from the victims through sending premium SMS without user control. After 2013, malware samples have shifted from sending premium SMS to spywares, ransomwares and banking trojan. To ensure that the work is applicable with future malwares, we focus our evaluation on popular malware. Table 1 lists the top three malware types that this paper would be evaluating.

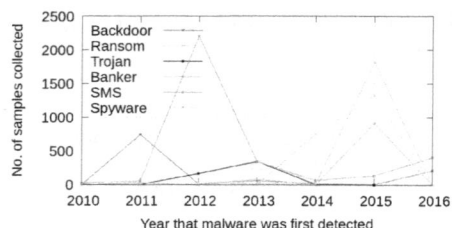

Figure 1: Evolution of malware types

Table 1: Malware dataset used to evaluate efficiency of obfuscation techniques on AMT

Malware Type	Families of Malwares	Samples	Detection Date
Spyware	SmsZombie, Vmvol, Finspy, Mecor	1851	2012–2015
Ransomware	Koler, SimpleLocker, Aples, Fusob, Roop	1560	2014–2015
Banking Trojan	Zitmo, Svpeng, Bankun, BankBot, Slembunk	1021	2011–2015

4.2 Anti-malware Tools used for Analysis

Akin to [9] and [10], our automation tool leverages VirusTotal API [11] to classify the malware samples. Using the 57 AMTs listed on VirusTotal, we evaluate the effectiveness of our proposed transformation techniques. To make the evaluation scalable for a large number of malware samples, we used the command line version of VirusTotal, which might be performing static analysis with a certain degree of signature database.

5 EVALUATION

The evaluation in this research work has two aims. First, we aim to evaluate the ability of a new variant of a known malware, transformed with a composite of obfuscation techniques, to evade detection from AMTs. The second part of the work investigates how detection results for mutated malware change over time. We wish to remark that the AMTs version would be updated across time as well. To the best of our understanding, there have been no citations that provide detection rate changes across time. This section illustrates the instability in detection results for AMTs and proved that these AMTs do not have resilience against our proposed obfuscation methods.

5.1 Effectiveness of Obfuscation

In order to quantitatively measure the ability of AMTs to detect the new malware variants, we create a measure called escape detection rate (EDR) defined by $EDR(AMT_i) = \frac{N}{T}$, where N is the number of mutated malware that manage to evade detection by AMT_i and T represents the number of original malware samples detected by AMT_i. The results of the resilience of the 57 AMTs listed in VirusTotal is tabulated in Table 2. The high proportion of AMTs with EDR greater than 0.8 proved that the obfuscation techniques highlighted

Table 2: Distribution of 57 AMTs' EDR.

EDR	0.0-0.2	0.2-0.4	0.4-0.6	0.6-0.8	0.8-1.0
No. of AMTs	7	9	2	6	33

in this work allowed the new variants of the malware to conclusively evade signature-based detection.

5.2 Detection Results Over Time

The next investigation analyses the change of AMT detection results over time. We took 4432 malware samples tabulated in Table 1. The detection of 30 out of 57 AMTs remained unchanged across a time period of nine days. There were 21 AMTs that managed to detect all obfuscated malwares after one version update, when they were initially unable to do so. The remaining six AMTs had unstable detection rate for obfuscated malware. The instability is illustrated in the top four graphs in Figure 2, whereas the bottom four graphs illustrate the results of AMTs that produced stable results. This instability in the detection results of AMTs against mutated malware is beneficial for malware authors.

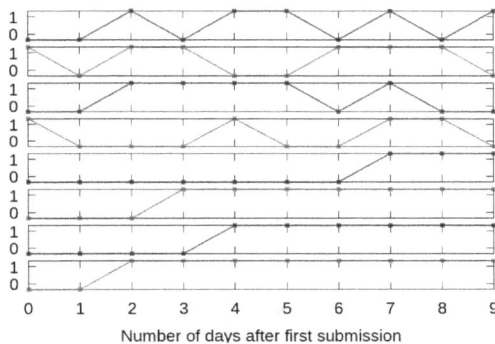

Figure 2: Detection pattern of AMTs across 9 days.

5.3 Resilience of AMTs against Obfuscation Methods

The last part of the investigation evaluates the resilience of AMTs against the proposed obfuscation techniques. We tested all malware from Table 1 and ensured that the samples are detected as malware by VirusTotal. After obfuscation, the number of malware that are detected has reduced from 4432 to 2274, a 48.69% detection rate decrease. The obfuscated malware were continuously submitted to VirusTotal for nine days. After this period, we can see from Table 3 that the number of malware detected has reduced from 4432 to 3878. This is a 12.5% reduction in detection rate as compared to the original malware samples. It is evident that obfuscated malware were able to initially evade detection. As the malware samples are continuously resubmitted for analysis, the number of obfuscated malware samples that are able to evade AMT detection is reduced.

When the original malware samples were re-obfuscated with the same techniques to produce a different hash value, it resulted in a decrease in detection rate of 48.44% from the original samples. This implies that the AMTs on VirusTotal do not build resilience against the obfuscation technique, but

Table 3: Malware dataset used to evaluate efficiency of obfuscation techniques on AMT

Description	SHA(input)	AM detected	Decrease
Submitted after obfuscation	x_1	2274	48.69%
Submitted same variant 9 days later	x_1	3878	12.50%
Submitted after re-obfuscation	x_2	2285	48.44%

instead use signature-based analysis to detect obfuscated malware. Such a detection scheme would imply that AMTs are constantly playing catch up with the malware authors, who could easily evade signature-based detection by using trivial obfuscation techniques to quickly change the cryptographic hash of a malware and mutate it.

6 CONCLUSIONS

This study proved that malware authors can increase a malware's evasion rate by performing obfuscation techniques that were highlighted in this study. In our analysis, we managed to confirm the trend of mutated malware evading detection with a larger and more updated pool of known malware. The novelty in this work identified the instability in detection results for some AMTs. We also highlighted that the AMTs do not build resilience against the technique used to obfuscate the malware, but only update their signature database to be resilient to the specific variant of the malware. The trends highlighted here emphasised the ease of eventually evading current mainstream security tools for a malware author.

REFERENCES
[1] Inc. IDC Research. Smartphone os market share, August 2016.
[2] G. Hatchimonji. Is mobile anti-virus even necessary?, September 2013.
[3] Y. Xue et al. Auditing anti-malware tools by evolving android malware and dynamic loading technique. *IEEE Transactions on Information Forensics and Security*, 12(7):1529–1544, July 2017.
[4] TrendMicro. Ransomware recap: Slocker copycats wannacry, July 2017.
[5] V. Rastogi et al. Droidchameleon: Evaluating android anti-malware against transformation attacks. *Proceedings of the 8th ACM SIGSAC symposium on Information, computer and communications security*, pages 329–334, 2013.
[6] A. Cani et al. Towards automated malware creation: Code generation and code integration. *Proceedings of the 29th Annual ACM Symposium on Applied Computing*, pages 329–334, 2014.
[7] A. Daniel et al. Drebin: Effective and explainable detection of android malware in your pocket. *Symposium on Network and Distributed System Security*, Feb 2014.
[8] M. Parkour. Contagio mobile: Mobile malware minidump, July 2017.
[9] M. Spreitzenbarth. The evil inside a droid - android malware: Past, present and future. In *Proceedings of the BALTIC CONFERENCE Network Security and Forensics*, 2012.
[10] M. Spreitzenbarth et al. Mobile-sandbox: having a deeper look into andrcid applications. In *Proceedings of the 28th Annual ACM Symposium on Applied Computing*, pages 1808–1815, Mar 2013.
[11] VirusTotal. Virustotal public api v2.0, September 2012.
[12] V. Balachandran et al. Function level control flow obfuscation for software security. *Proceedings of the IEEE 8th International Conference on Intelligent and Software Intensive Systems*, pages 133–140, Oct 2014.
[13] V. Balachandran et al. Control flow obfuscation for android applications. *IEEE International Conference on Systems, Man and Cybernetics*, pages 463–469, Dec 2014.
[14] V. Balachandran et al. Control flow obfuscation for android applications. *Computer and Security*, 61 Issue C:72–93, Aug 2016.

AEON: Android Encryption based Obfuscation

D Geethanjali
Singapore Institute of
Technology
Singapore
d.geethanjali_2015@sit.singapor
etech.edu.sg

Tan Li Ying
Singapore Institute of
Technology
Singapore
liying.tan_2015@sit.singaporete
ch.edu.sg

Chua Wan Jun Melissa
Defence Science and
Technology Agency
Singapore
cwanjunm@dsta.gov.sg

Vivek Balachandran
Singapore Institute of
Technology
Singapore
vivek.b@singaporetech.edu.sg

ABSTRACT

Android applications are vulnerable to reverse engineering which could result in tampering and repackaging of applications. Even though there are many off the shelf obfuscation tools that hardens Android applications, they are limited to basic obfuscation techniques. Obfuscation techniques that transform the code segments drastically are difficult to implement on Android because of the Android runtime verifier which validates the loaded code. In this paper, we introduce a novel obfuscation technique, Android Encryption based Obfuscation (AEON), which can encrypt code segments and perform runtime decryption during execution. The encrypted code is running outside of the normal Android virtual machine, in an embeddable Java source interpreter and thereby circumventing the scrutiny of Android runtime verifier. Our obfuscation technique works well with Android source code and Dalvik bytecode.

ACM Reference Format:

D Geethanjali, Tan Li Ying, Chua Wan Jun Melissa, Vivek Balachandran. 2018. AEON: Android Encryption based Obfuscation. In CODASPY '18: Eighth ACM Conference on Data and Application Security and Privacy, March 19–21, 2018, Tempe, AZ, USA. ACM, NY, NY, USA, 3 pages. https://doi.org/10.1145/3176258.3176943

1 INTRODUCTION

A mass migration from desktop computing devices to mobile computing devices has been seen in the recent years. The number of smartphones sold in 2015 is over 1.5 billion, with Android dominating the market with an 86. 1% share in the first quarter of 2017 [1].

The alarming rate at which computing tasks, both personal and professional, performed on the mobile platform calls for better security measures to the applications run on these platforms. A major threat to the Android application is reverse engineering.

There are various off the shelf tools that can enable easy reverse engineering of Android apps that will result in application tampering and repackaging of applications with malicious content.

A classic technique to make reverse engineering harder is obfuscation [2, 3]. Obfuscation is the process of attaining security through obscurity, where the original code is transformed into a more complex and harder to understand form while maintaining its semantics. Existing Android obfuscation tools such as DexGuard [4], DashO [5], etc., provides various obfuscation techniques like identifier renaming, control flow obfuscation, excessive overloading etc. Dexguard provides encryption of dynamic data. However, Android architecture does not support obfuscation techniques that manipulate the program code or static data. Both Android Runtime (ART) and Dalvik Virtual Machine (DVM) uses a runtime verifier to verify that the code is valid before executing it. Thus, obfuscation involving code manipulations at runtime are harder to implement.

Thus, a large part of the source code can still be recovered, with reverse engineering tools, incomprehensible form despite the obfuscation techniques performed on it. In this paper, we discuss a new method of performing obfuscation that decrypts and executes encrypted Android code at runtime. This obfuscation technique can be performed on both source code and Dalvik bytecode or smali code. Hence, the obfuscation technique can be performed on applications that are developed by third-party developers.

2 Proposed Technique - AEON

In this section, we discuss our proposed method AEON (Android Encryption based Obfuscation), which obfuscates Android applications by encrypting and decrypting the code at runtime. The basic idea is to move the code outside of Android Virtual Machine into an embeddable Java source interpreter. Since the code is running on an external interpreter the Android verifier will not flag any issues and run the program comfortably. The encrypted code is decrypted during runtime before it is moved to the external interpreter. Figure 1 shows an overview of our proposed technique.

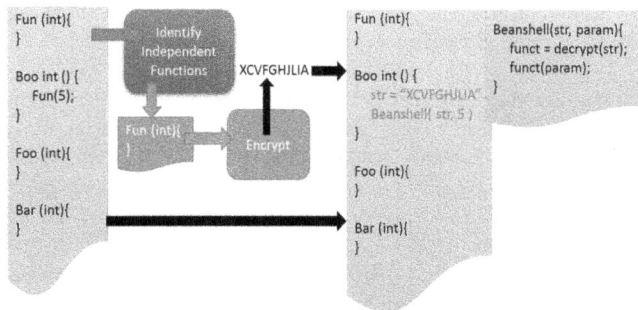

Figure 1. Overview of AEON Technique

2.1 Beanshell

We have used Beanshell [6] as our embeddable Java source interpreter. It provides many features such as dynamic execution of Java syntax and java code fragments. It also provides access to Java Objects and API. Beanshell works well in security constrained environments without classloader or bytecode generation for most features. The level of flexibility provided by Beanshell makes it a perfect choice for an embeddable source interpreter.

2.2 Identifying Independent Java Functions

A lot of Android programs are written in Java and hence if we can move independent Java functions into Beanshell instead of running it on Dalvik Virtual Machine or Android runtime then the code does not have to go through the scrutiny of the Android verifier. However, many functions in an Android program will be using Android libraries which cannot be ran independently in the Beanshell. Hence, the first step in AEON is identifying functions independent of Android library calls in the Android program. When source code is not available, and the obfuscator is working on Dalvik bytecode, then the bytecode is the first reverse engineered into Java source code using a reverse engineering tool.

Identifying independent code segments is not a trivial task. We define an independent code segment as a function/class which can be ran independently without depending on objects defined outside of the function/class and not making changes to objects defined outside its scope.

This intricate problem of identifying independent code segments has been sorted with a simple method identification program that we have used. Given the source code of an Android application, the program will first identify each package, classes and methods in them. A basic set of dependent methods are identified based on the following 3 criteria:

1. Void Method
2. Method modifies Global Variable.
3. Method calls on a Method which matches criteria 1 or 2

After initial classification of dependent and independent classes, we check if an independent method is dependent on another independent method or an object class from the project. This

check is done iteratively until all the methods are classified into independent and dependent.

Finally, we check if the independent methods can be executed properly on Beanshell. Based on the input parameters, an invoke method statement would be crafted. For example, if the input parameter for an invoking method is a primitive Java type the input value would be 0 or false (if boolean) and for any other variable type the input value would be null. The method is then run on the Beanshell with the crafted inputs. Based on the returned error, we would be able to determine whether that particular method can be ran on Beanshell or not.

2.3 Using Beanshell to run Encrypted Methods

Following the independent method filtering process, the program would then encrypt the independent methods. These methods would be removed from the smali code or the Java source code. A new string will be declared with the encrypted function as the value, where the independent function initially was invoked. A method call statement to invoke the Beanshell function will also be declared.

The Beanshell function will take in the encrypted method as a string and the input parameter of the original method. For Beanshell to be able to decrypt the encrypted string and execute it, a decrypt function must be pushed into the embeddable source interpreter. The key used for decryption can be embedded in the function that is pushed into the Beanshell instance. The Beanshell instance would then be invoked with the encrypted string as a parameter. The decrypted string would then be passed again to an instance of Beanshell and to be executed. The output will then be returned.

3 Implementation

We have developed a tool implementing the aforementioned technique written mainly using python and bash scripts. The tool is publically available [8] on GitHub. It takes in either an APK file or the path to an android applications source code as input. If the input is an APK file our tool decompiles it using jadx[7] to get the Java source of the application.

Upon gathering the Java source codes of the Android application, it is analyzed with a script that identifies and creates a mapping of each method to the respective classes and packages. This mapped collection of the Java source code would then go through the process of identifying independent Java functions as mentioned in section 2.2.

Each of these independent methods or independent methods dependent on other independent methods are passed as input parameter to 'beanshellTesting.class' file as a string, where it is executed as an independent method. The parameters to invoke independent methods in Beanshell would be crafted based on the input type of the independent method. The default values for the input parameters datatypes will be used to craft a statement to execute the method. Based on the error message returned by Beanshell, the program will decide if this function can be ran on Beanshell.

```
String SampleFunc(String param1, int param2, User param3){
    //Code
    return null;
}
```

Figure 2. Sample Function

For example, the method 'SampleFunc', shown in Figure 2, takes three arguments of type *String, int* and *User* (user-defined object type) and return an object of type *String*. The execute statement crafted and run on the Beanshell will be the following:

String output = SampleFunc(null, 0, null)

The decision to encrypt this function is based on the output error generated when the function is executed. If the output error is a Beanshell runtime error, the program will determine that the code cannot be executed at runtime and remove it from the encryptable independent method list. On the contrary, if the output error is a Java-based error the program will determine that the code can be encrypted and run at runtime. Once the independent methods are identified they are encrypted using an encryption algorithm. We are using AES-256 bit encryption for encrypting the independent methods. The encrypted method is stored as a string. The method invocation encountered in the original program is then replaced by the string declaration with the encrypted method as a string value. This is followed by a new function invocation, whose parameters are, the encrypted string and the parameters to the encrypted method. A Beanshell instance is invoked within this function and the decrypt function is called. The encrypted string is then decrypted and invoked with the input parameters and interpreted by the Beanshell. The returned value from the method is then returned to the Android program.

One method in a Java program can have only one return type. Therefore, if a class has multiple independent methods returning values of various return types, multiple methods of Beanshell need to be invoked. The last step performed by the obfuscation tool would be to add the Beanshell library. Following which the application would be repackaged to create the obfuscated APK.

4 Future Work

AEON is the first step in attempting to encrypt and run Android code without the verifier blocking the execution of the program. There are various additional changes to be made to the tool to make it more potent and stealthy. The following are some of the areas that we are currently working on to improve AEON.

4.1 Develop a Java interpreter. Beanshell is a Java interpreter that was sought out as a quick solution. As effective as Beanshell is there are still certain things that Beanshell can't do. An example would be the fact that in Beanshell, arrays are to be declared as strings before they can be split to form an array. A self-developed Java interpreter could also mean that the decryption process and

invocation of methods can be built in the new interpreter making reverse engineering of encrypted methods harder.

4.2 Dynamic Key. Currently, in AEON, the key used for encryption of independent function is a static key that has been hardcoded into the decrypt function. However, we are currently working on implementing the use of a dynamic key for encryption/decryption in AEON. The basic idea is to change the encryption key during runtime using the phone specifications such as IMEI number or Phone number. The independent methods get decrypted and re-encrypted each run making it harder for the reverse engineers to narrow down the encryption key or the decrypted methods.

4.3 Better technique to identify independent methods. We are also working on a better technique for identifying independent methods using dependency graphs. In this dependency graph technique, a set of code can be converted to a graph of instructions based on the dependency of the instruction. The vertex of the graph would be the instructions and the edges would represent the dependency on other instructions. We can easily identify independent methods by finding disconnected graphs.

4.3 AEON on obfuscated APK. In terms of efficiency, AEON works best on applications which follows good coding practice such as simple functions and classes. This means if the function is already obfuscated AEON will be having difficulty in finding if it is independent or not. This has an undesirable outcome of keeping AEON as the first obfuscation technique to be used in obfuscation order. We are also working on mitigating this shortcoming by making AEON work better with obfuscated APKs.

5 CONCLUSION

In this paper, we proposed an alternative obfuscation technique using encryption, AEON. This technique hopes to make static and dynamic analysis of Android applications harder by encrypting portions of the code and running it without getting flagged by the Android runtime verifier. AEON is the first step on achieving bytecode level obfuscation with encryption that is capable of bypassing the inbuilt code verifier in Android systems.

REFERENCES

[1] GartnerGartner Says Worldwide Sales of Smartphones Grew 9 Percent in First Quarter of 2017, https://www.gartner.com/newsroom/id/3725117
[2] V. Balachandran, Sufatrio, DJJ Tan, and V. L. L. Thing. "Control flow obfuscation for Android applications." Computers & Security 61 (2016): 72-93.
[3] V. Balachandran, S. Emmanuel, and Ng Wee Keong. "Obfuscation by code fragmentation to evade reverse engineering." In IEEE International Conference Systems, Man and Cybernetics (SMC), 2014.
[4] Dexguard, https://www.guardsquare.com/en/dexguard (accessed on 12 Nov 2017)
[5] DashO, https://www.preemptive.com/ (accessed on 12 Nov 2017)
[6] Beanshell, http://www.beanshell.org/ (accessed on 12 Nov 2017)
[7] JADX, https://github.com/skylot/jadx (accessed on 12 Nov 2017)
[8] AEON Source code, https://github.com/SITSecureSoftwareDevelopmentTeam/AEON_Obfuscation (accessed on 12 Nov 2017)
[9] V. Balachandran, S. Emmanuel, and Ng Wee Keong. "Obfuscation by code fragmentation to evade reverse engineering." In IEEE International Conference Systems, Man and Cybernetics (SMC), 2014.

An Empirical Study of Differentially-Private Analytics for High-Speed Network Data

Oana-Georgiana Niculaescu
UMass Boston
onic@cs.umb.edu

Gabriel Ghinita
UMass Boston
gabriel.ghinita@umb.edu

ACM Reference Format:
Oana-Georgiana Niculaescu and Gabriel Ghinita. 2018. An Empirical Study of Differentially-Private Analytics for High-Speed Network Data. In *Proceedings of Eighth ACM Conference on Data and Application Security and Privacy (CODASPY'18).* ACM, New York, NY, USA, 4 pages. https://doi.org/10.1145/3176258.3176944

1 INTRODUCTION

High-speed research networks are essential to support scientific projects and applications that have high bandwidth demands. These networks differ from conventional ones as they provide much higher line rates (up to 100Gbps), which are often required by scientific research. To efficiently run and maintain such networks, it is necessary to develop monitoring tools that provide usage statistics and information about network health status. Such data are important to researchers who develop new transport protocols, or to network engineers who must maintain the network infrastructure within optimal working parameters. However, collecting and sharing such high-speed network data also poses serious privacy risks. Through careful analysis of network data, an adversary may be able to determine the identity of a user associated to a specific network flow, and can subsequently infer potentially sensitive information about that individual from her usage pattern, e.g., health status, political affiliation, personal lifestyle, etc.

To counter such threats, it is important to sanitize network data before making them available for analysis. The current de-facto standard in privacy protection is the *differential privacy (DP)* model [3]. DP provides formal protection guarantees, and ensures that an adversary cannot learn with significant probability if a certain individual's data is included or not in a dataset (in our case, an individual's data consist of the network flows generated by a user). DP achieves protection by adding noise to the data, so one must be careful when deploying this model in practice, such that the distortion is minimized. In the case of high-speed network data, accurate and efficient sanitization is even more challenging, due to the high volumes of generated data.

In our work, we aim to achieve fast and accurate sanitization of high-speed network data, by focusing on network analytics in the form of statistical queries. For instance, one important use of such data is to determine the amount of total traffic flowing between distinct autonomous systems (AS), which are segments of the network under the management of a single organization. This is an important problem to solve for two reasons: (i) organizations are interested how much traffic goes to/from their peers, which is useful for equipment provisioning or billing, and (ii) there is typically no established relationship of trust among peer organizations, to the extent that allows them to directly share internal information about their users, hence the need for privacy. In this context, we present an empirical study of a differentially-private analytics system for high-speed research networks that we developed. We consider two different aspects the accuracy of answers returned by our system compared to non-sanitized data and the response time to return the query results. Our proposed system uses Apache HDFS and HBase for data storage and indexing, and builds contingency (i.e., summary) tables to support fast and accurate private analytics.

2 BACKGROUND

2.1 HDFS and HBase. High-speed research networks generate large amounts of data that need to be collected and processed efficiently. We use Apache Hadoop and HBase for processing and storing network data at flow granularity. Hadoop and HBase run atop the *Hadoop Distributed File System (HDFS)* environment [1]. HDFS is a Java-based file system that provides scalable and reliable data storage across large clusters of commodity servers. The *MapReduce* computation model [2] is a popular model for distributed big data processing. The core idea behind MapReduce is *mapping* data into a collection of <key, value> pairs, and then *reducing* over all pairs with the same key. Both operations can be done in parallel. The overall concept is simple, but it is very powerful when we consider that: (i) most datasets can be meaningfully mapped into <key, value> pairs, and (ii) the keys and values can be of any type (e.g., strings, integers, etc.). Both map and reduce phases use HDFS files as input and output. However, HDFS is designed for sequential access, and does not work well for random access. Since flexible network analytics may need to access multiple data regions, we use HBase for effective data indexing. HBase is a column-oriented, highly-distributed NoSQL solution that runs on top of Hadoop and HDFS. HBase supports efficient random access to data.

2.2 Autonomous System (AS) is a collection of networks managed and supervised by a single entity or organization. An AS comprises heterogeneous networks governed by a large enterprise, and has different subnetworks with combined routing logic and common policies. Each AS is assigned a globally unique 16 digit identification number (ASN).

2.3 Contingency Tables summarize data into a set of counts corresponding to all value combinations across certain attributes. A two-dimensional contingency table is based on two variables, one determining the row categories and the other defining the column categories. The combinations of row and column categories are

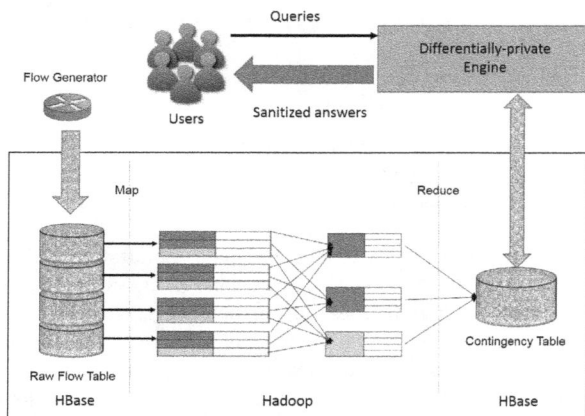
Figure 1: System Architecture

Row Key	CF1	CF2	CF3
ts|1|srcAS|md5	destAS, port	destAS, protocol	BC,PC
ts|2|destAS|md5	srcAS, port	srcAS, protocol	BC,PC
ts|3|port|md5	srcAS	destAS, protocol	BC,PC

Table 1: HBase schema for AS raw flow tables

terminated. The flows contain information about AS numbers that we save using the HBase schema presented in Table 1. In our schema, *ts* is the flow time stamp, and BC and PC are bytes and packet counts for that flow, respectively. The other attributes are source and destination AS numbers, and service ports.

TimeStamp	Src AS	Protocol	Port	Dst AS
4 bytes (int)	4 bytes (int)	1 byte	2 bytes (short)	4 bytes (int)

Table 2: HBase schema for AS contingency table

After storing network flows into HBase raw tables, a query engine computes differentially-private results. However, using the raw flow table directly requires intensive disk scans, slowing performance. Since each flow is stored as an individual row in the table, the size of the table is too large, and the required processing may take a long time to complete. Furthermore, if multiple queries are executed against the dataset such that their result sets contain a common record, it would be difficult to keep track of the sensitivity associated with that query set. Therefore, creating contingency tables that summarize the dataset on different attribute value combinations allows us to keep track of sensitivity and allocate appropriately the privacy budget. These summaries may include aggregating the flows based on source/destination AS number, service, or time resolution.

To illustrate how these network flows can be aggregated, consider the following example queries for a given time range:

(1) What is the total amount of traffic between all pairs of ASs?
   - This query is best answered by a table with schema ordered by timestamp at the front of the row key.
(2) How many packets originate from AS number 10437?
   - A table whose row keys are ordered by source AS number would best serve this query.
(3) What is the total amount of DNS traffic served by AS 10437?
   - A table whose row keys are ordered by protocol and port (protocol UDP, port 53), followed by the destination network for the DNS server, would answer this query most efficiently.

Given the above examples, it is clear that no single schema can serve well all queries. Each of these queries is best answered by scanning tables with different schemas. Query 1 does not specify any non-time predicates, and could be answered by tables whose row keys begin with timestamp, whereas queries 2 and 3 specify non-time predicates, and could be answered by tables whose row keys begin with such information, followed by timestamp.

Next, we focus on efficiently supporting type 1 queries. To that extent, we create a HBase table with the schema from Table 2 for

called cells. In order to use the statistical methods usually applied to such tables, subjects must fall into one and only one row and column category. Such categories are said to be exclusive and exhaustive. Exclusive means the categories don't overlap, so a subject falls into only one category. Exhaustive means that the categories include all possibilities, so every subject falls within a category.

2.4 Differential privacy (DP) [3] guarantees that for any two *sibling* datasets $\mathcal{D}_1, \mathcal{D}_2$ that differ in a single net flow π, the probability of an adversary learning which of the two datasets was used to obtain a certain output $\mathcal{A}$ is bounded by $\left| \ln \frac{Pr[\mathcal{A}(\mathcal{D}_1)]}{Pr[\mathcal{A}(\mathcal{D}_2)]} \right| \leq \epsilon$, where parameter $\epsilon > 0$ represents the *privacy budget*. To achieve privacy for numerical queries, the Laplace mechanism [3] adds to each query result noise randomly distributed according to a Laplace distribution with parameter $\lambda = S/\epsilon$ where S is the *sensitivity* of the query, i.e., the maximum change in the result of the query for any two sibling databases. *Sequential composability* guarantees that executing algorithm $\mathcal{A}_1$ with privacy budget ϵ_1 followed by algorithm $\mathcal{A}_2$ with budget ϵ_2 produces a differentially private algorithm with parameter $\epsilon_1 + \epsilon_2$. This allows composing algorithms which use the results of simpler queries to produce a more accurate result for a highly sensitive query/algorithm.

3 SYSTEM OVERVIEW

The proposed system architecture is presented in Figure 1 (the high-level system architecture was introduced in [4], but this submission brings design and implementation details, as well as evaluation results that represent new contributions compared to [4]). The input flows are collected from network devices such as switches or routers compliant with the NetFlow v9 standard. The flow attributes are saved in a HBase column store that provides efficient random access data. Contingency tables are created and maintained using MapReduce jobs on top of the raw flow data. At query time, instead of querying directly the raw data, we answer queries using contingency tables, which are more compact due to their summarizing role. The challenge is to find an appropriate set of contingency tables to materialize, such that the disk I/O is reduces at query time, while at the same time the sensitivity, and implicitly the amount of noise required by differential privacy, are kept low.

Flow data are collected from a series of devices located at several Internet2 academic participants. Each flow is being stored in the raw flow table repository after the generation of the flow has been

Column Family	size	
Qualifier	bytes	packets
Type	8 bytes (long)	8 bytes (long)

Table 3: HBase schema for AS raw flow tables

the row key, and a single column family as illustrated in Table 3, with two columns: bytes and packets. This schema affords for the creation of different versions of tables with varying time granularities and network addresses. These summaries have three types of fixed alignment for timestamps: minute (granule=60), hour (granule=3600), and day (granule=86400). Each timestamp is represented according to Unix time value. For example, aligned timestamps for 1492287912 are 1492287900 (minute), 1492286400 (hour), and 1492214400 (day). So, for hourly aligned timestamps, the contingency table for hours aggregates all flows with timestamps within the range [1492286400, 1492290000) into the row with aligned timestamp 1492286400. Considering those three granules (day, hour, minute) we create three contingency tables that allow to flexibly answer query type 1, while reducing the amount of rows scanned.

In terms of differential privacy protection, each contingency table increases sensitivity by one (as time granularities overlap). So for three granularities, the respective sensitivities for bytes/packets are multiplied by 3. We believe that summarizing all these three levels can increase accuracy for broader queries (in such cases, the error would be too large if considering only minute counts when answering a multi-day query). However, for specific scenarios, one can alter the design by only materializing a subset of these contingency tables. The decision would depend on the length of expected time ranges to analyze, and also the skewness of data over time. According to the Laplace mechanism outlined in Section 2 [3], the noise added to a query result is proportional to the sensitivity of the entire query set. In turn, sensitivity is proportional to the maximum number of queries that overlap a specific region of the attribute space. Thus, to maintain data accuracy, it is important to limit the amount of overlap. For our experiment the overlapping data is equal to the number of granules that we are interested in, in this case 3. The noise added to each of the answers to query type 1 are proportional to the value of the maximum difference that adding or removing one flow from the database will produce. Since we are interested in the number of bytes and the number of packets, the noise is proportional to the maximum value of bytes or packets that a flow can contain.

4 EXPERIMENTAL EVALUATION

We evaluated our proposed system using real flow data collected over a period of 24 hours from an Internet2 site, resulting in a raw dataset of 25GB. We measure the total amount of traffic (in terms of both packets and bytes) across all pairs of AS in a specified time period, ranging from one to ten hours. Our testbed consists of a dual Xeon E5-2430 v2 2.5GHz CPU system with 128GB of RAM running Ubuntu 16, HBase 1.2.4 and Hadoop 2.7.3. We compare our approach against a baseline which uses MapReduce to compute analytics directly from the raw data. The baseline is similar in accuracy to our method, so the direct comparison is done only with respect to performance.

Fig. 2(a)-(b) shows the accuracy of the proposed approach for top-10 talker AS systems, i.e., the AS pairs with the highest amount of traffic across them, for a privacy budget $\epsilon = 0.4$. We note that the error incurred by our approach is small, and that the precision and recall are at 100% for both bytes and packets (i.e., even after adding noise, the relative order of AS pairs when ordered according to traffic does not change). Fig. 2(c) presents the relative error for

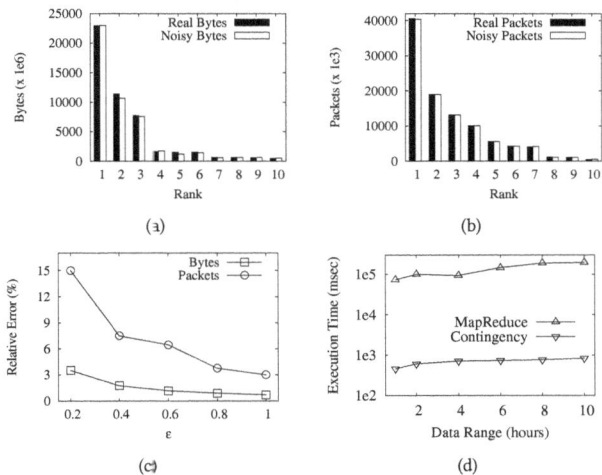

Figure 2: Evaluation Results

a wide range of privacy budgets, ranging from 0.2 to 1.0 (lower values correspond to stricter privacy constraints). We observe that the relative error is below 10% for most of the range, with slightly larger values at the lowest $\epsilon = 0.2$ setting. The relative error is lower for bytes, since the absolute data values are considerably larger than those of packets.

Fig. 2(d) show the performance of our approach (measured in *msec*) in comparison with the MapReduce-only baseline (without contingency tables). Even for queries with small time range (1 hour), the baseline performs quite poorly, requiring close to 30 seconds of processing. This increases to several minutes for the longer time ranges. In contrast, our approach is able to keep the response time below 1 second in all cases, or two orders of magnitude lower than the baseline.

5 CONCLUSION

We proposed a system for computing private flow-level granularity analytics on top of high-speed network data. Using the de-facto standard of differential privacy, our system builds on open-source tools like Apache Hadoop/HBase, and maintains contingency tables that summarize data on relevant attributes. It significantly outperforms benchmarks in terms of performance, while keeping data accuracy high. In future work, we will investigate approaches to efficiently support more complex query types by building more advanced contingency tables, while at the same time keeping sensitivity (and hence added noise) at low levels.

Acknowledgment: work supported by NSF grant 1450975.

REFERENCES

[1] R. Chansler, H. Kuang, S. Radia, K. Shvachko, and S. Srinivas. *The Architecture of Open Source Applications*. 2011.
[2] J. Dean and S. Ghemawat. Mapreduce: Simplified data processing on large clusters. In *Proceedings of the 6th Symposium on Operating Systems Design & Implementation*, pages 10–10, 2004.
[3] C. Dwork, F. McSherry, K. Nissim, and A. Smith. Calibrating noise to sensitivity in private data analysis. In *TCC*, pages 265–284, 2006.
[4] O.-G. Niculaescu, M. Maruseac, and G. Ghinita. Differentially-private big data analytics for high-speed research network traffic measurement. In *Proceedings of the Seventh ACM on Conference on Data and Application Security and Privacy*, CODASPY '17, pages 151–153, New York, NY, USA, 2017. ACM.

A Low Energy Profile: Analysing Characteristic Security on BLE Peripherals

Pallavi Sivakumaran*
Centre for Doctoral Training in Cyber Security,
Royal Holloway University of London
pallavi.sivakumaran.2012@live.rhul.ac.uk

Jorge Blasco Alis
Information Security Group,
Royal Holloway University of London
jorge.blascoalis@rhul.ac.uk

ABSTRACT

Bluetooth Low Energy is a ubiquitous technology, with applications in the fitness, healthcare and smart home sectors, to name but a few. In this paper, we present an open-source Profiler for classifying the protection level of data residing on a BLE device. Preliminary results obtained by executing the tool against several devices show that some BLE devices allow unauthenticated reads and writes from third party devices. This could expose them to a number of attacks and compromise the privacy, or even the physical safety, of the device owner.

KEYWORDS

Bluetooth Low Energy, attribute security, pairing, Just Works, Passkey

ACM Reference Format:
Pallavi Sivakumaran and Jorge Blasco Alis. 2018. A Low Energy Profile: Analysing Characteristic Security on BLE Peripherals. In *CODASPY '18: Eighth ACM Conference on Data and Application Security and Privacy, March 19–21, 2018, Tempe, AZ, USA.* ACM, New York, NY, USA, 3 pages. https://doi.org/10.1145/3176258.3176945

1 INTRODUCTION

Bluetooth Low Energy (BLE) is a wireless data communication technology which is rapidly increasing in popularity. Its focus on low-power and low-cost devices has resulted in the technology being implemented in a variety of use cases, ranging from personal health and fitness devices, such as glucose monitors and fitness trackers, to home automation and security systems, such as smart locks and energy monitors.

Data on these devices may reveal personal information about their users, and may directly or indirectly enable critical functionality. As such, a range of attacks may be possible against data that is not suitably protected. Passive eavesdropping on the wireless interface, or unauthorised data access requests made directly to the device, violate a user's expectation of confidentiality. In addition,

*The author was supported by the EPSRC and the UK government as part of the Centre for Doctoral Training in Cyber Security at Royal Holloway, University of London (EP/P009301/1)

active MitM eavesdropping and data modification, as well as inducing unexpected behaviour via fuzzing, may all be viable attacks against unprotected data.

With the increased proliferation of BLE into everyday devices, there is a greater likelihood that attacks on devices will not only affect the devices' functionality, but also cause harm in the "physical world". For example, recent research into BLE-enabled hover-boards has shown that unprotected data on the device can be overwritten, enabling an attacker to gain control of the board and potentially cause injury to the user [3].

Mechanisms have been described in the Bluetooth specification [1] for protecting data on BLE devices by allowing communicating devices to authenticate themselves to each other. However, oftentimes these security measures are not implemented. This may be due to device constraints or increasing competition and the pressure to reduce time-to-market. Difficulty in navigating the somewhat complicated Bluetooth specification may also be a factor.

In this paper, we present a novel Profiler (Section 3) for identifying the minimum level of security applied to data on a low energy device, to assess the safety and reliability of device-resident data. This can then be translated to possible attacks that the device may be vulnerable to. The tool does not identify the default security level supported by the target device, but instead aims to determine the *lowest* possible level at which the data can be accessed. This is important because an attacker would not be confined to normal operating conditions or default security behaviour.

The Profiler may also be able to identify whether a static PIN code is used by the BLE device during its authentication process, by testing against a dictionary of commonly-used PIN codes. Static PINs are typically used when a device does not have the input/output capabilities required for dynamic PINs. However, they reduce the security of the authentication process, as a known value can simply be reused at a later time.

Our tool may be useful for developers to validate their security implementations, for security analysts as a starting point into their testing, or even for end users to determine how secure their data is.

We also present preliminary results obtained from executing our code against a number of test devices (Section 4). Finally, we briefly discuss limitations of our method, potential avenues for future work, and recommendations for improving BLE data security.

2 BLE BACKGROUND

BLE is a technology that enables the wireless transfer of small amounts of data between two devices. The devices operate in an asymmetric Central-Peripheral configuration, where typically the more resource-constrained will assume the role of Peripheral and the more powerful device will act as the Central. As an example, in the case of a smart lock communicating with a mobile phone, the lock would function as the Peripheral and the phone as the Central.

Attributes: BLE devices store data as attributes, where attributes may be read or written if appropriate permissions are set. *Characteristics* are a type of attribute that contain the actual user or application data. Characteristics have associated *properties* that describe how the characteristic value can be accessed. Examples include "read", "write", "notify" and "indicate". Only "read" and "write" properties are considered for the purpose of this paper. Some characteristics on a device may need to be protected, and to access a protected characteristic, the two devices will typically need to communicate over an encrypted link. The keys required for link encryption are established during a process known as *pairing*.

Pairing: There are two methods or "generations" of pairing: LE Legacy and LE Secure Connections (LESC), where LE Legacy was the original pairing method for BLE and is still the most widely used. The pairing process also uses one of four *association models*: Just Works, Passkey Entry, Out-Of-Band (OOB) and Numeric Comparison. With the exception of Numeric Comparison, which can only be used with LESC, all association models can be used with both generations of pairing.

The level of protection applied to a connection depends on the method as well as the association model used for pairing. LESC uses FIPS-compliant Elliptic-Curve Diffie-Hellman for key generation and is generally considered to be the more secure of the two pairing methods, as the key establishment protocol in LE Legacy has been shown to be vulnerable to passive eavesdropping attacks [5].

Of the four association models, Numeric Comparison provides the most protection against eavesdropping and MitM attacks, but is rarely used. OOB requires a non-Bluetooth channel for transmitting keys and is also not widely seen in practice. The most commonly used association models are Passkey Entry and Just Works. Passkey Entry requires manual user intervention in terms of PIN code entry and is therefore considered to result in an "authenticated" key. Just Works uses an all-zero PIN code with no user input, and the resultant key is considered to be "unauthenticated". When used with LE Legacy, neither Just Works nor Passkey Entry provide protection against passive eavesdropping. However, Passkey Entry offers better protection against MitM attacks.

Attacks: A BLE device that has rudimentary or no authentication requirements may expose its readable characteristics' values to unauthorised third parties, which could be a violation of the device owner's privacy. Writeable characteristics are more critical, as they could be overwritten to cause unexpected behaviour and possibly harm to the owner. For example, overwriting a glucose measurement on a monitoring device may cause the user to think they needed an insulin shot when they did not, which could have serious consequences.

3 THE SECURITY PROFILER

We have developed a Profiler[1] for identifying the lowest level of security required to access the value of a characteristic attribute. The tool is written on top of a modified version of *noble*[2], an open-source Node.js implementation of a BLE Central device.

The Profiler scans for and connects to a user-specified BLE Peripheral device. It then attempts to access (i.e., read or write) every applicable characteristic, where a characteristic is applicable if the access type is present in its properties set.

If access is denied because the characteristic is protected, then the tool will attempt to pair with the test device using the lowest level of security. If pairing is successful, then it will re-attempt characteristic access. If pairing fails, then the tool will increment the security level and re-attempt pairing. The Profiler will continue to increase security and attempt characteristic access until either all characteristics have been accessed or the highest level of security (as implemented in code) has been reached.

The Profiler has four such security levels: None - No security; Low - Unauthenticated pairing with 64-bit key; Medium - Unauthenticated pairing with 128-bit key; High - Authenticated pairing with 128-bit key. In our code, unauthenticated pairing corresponds to Just Works and authenticated pairing indicates Passkey Entry. The code attempts to reach these levels of security by using custom pairing requests with different security requirements and purported capabilities in each request. It should be noted that these are levels that are requested by the Profiler code, but, depending on the capabilities of the target device, some levels may not be achievable.

The output of the code is a JSON file containing details of all characteristics on the test device and the results from access attempts against applicable characteristics. Each such characteristic will have a security key which specifies the level of security at which the characteristic value was accessed (or an indication of why it could not be accessed), as well as the final pairing method and association model that were used.

Dictionary "attack" with static PINs: Some BLE devices utilise fixed PIN codes with the Passkey Entry model. This somewhat defeats the purpose of passkeys since a known fixed PIN can be entered programmatically, with no need for the user intervention that is required with dynamically generated PINs. The Profiler provides the option for trying to identify whether a BLE device uses a static PIN. It does this by making repeated pairing attempts using a dictionary of commonly used passkeys, derived in part from an analysis of six-character passwords [4]. If a match is found, then this will be indicated in the output file, but the PIN itself will only be available from the code execution terminal.

4 DEVICE TESTING

Preliminary tests were conducted against four fitness trackers of different prices and capabilities, a posture monitoring device, and a smart lock. All devices were under our ownership and control.

The number of characteristics on each device accessible at each security level has been graphed in Figure 1. The level "Unknown" on the graph refers to when a characteristic was not accessible due to a non-security related reason, while "Custom" indicates potential application-layer security.

The graphs show that 83% of the tested devices allowed at least one unauthenticated write. Further, three out of the six devices allowed all their characteristics to be read, and one also allowed all of its characteristics to be written, without any authentication required. These devices will therefore likely be vulnerable to unauthorised data read/writes and perhaps also MitM attacks.

---

[1]https://github.com/projectbtle/att-profiler
[2]https://github.com/sandeepmistry/noble

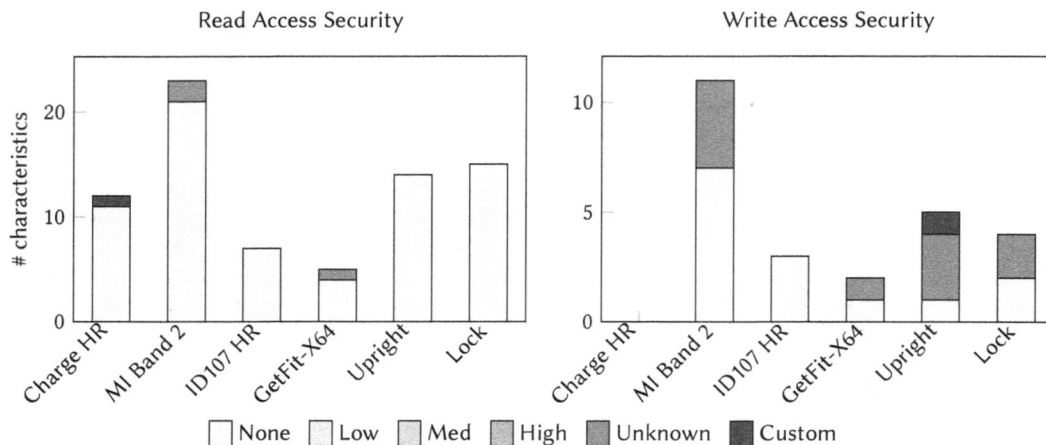

Figure 1: Security Levels for Read/Write Access

The devices that supported standard BLE pairing primarily used Just Works, which is the least secure association model, offering no MitM protection. Those that used Passkey Entry employed static, commonly-used PINs (000000 and 123456 were observed). This again would allow MitM attacks against these devices, if the attacker had previous knowledge of the static PIN.

The results appear to indicate that the Fitbit Charge HR has implemented application-layer security, which is consistent with previous findings [2]. Another fitness tracker, the Mi Band 2, responded to some write requests with an Application Error, which also may be indicative of protection applied at the application layer.

We also found that not all devices implemented the BLE specification exactly. While non-standard behaviour and services may reduce the amount of information that is immediately available to an attacker, they run the risk of being not as well defined or tested as standardised methods, which in turn could potentially result in security vulnerabilities.

5 DISCUSSION

5.1 Recommendations

We propose the following recommendations for BLE developers.

If the data stored in a characteristic is sensitive or enables critical functionality, developers should enforce security, particularly in the case of a writeable characteristic. Passkey Entry should be used at a minimum, preferably with dynamic passkeys. In the case of new developments, LESC with Numeric Comparison is preferred over LE Legacy pairing. This may require the use of new libraries and additional hardware. Further, the amount of data that can be accessed from the device should be reduced to the absolute minimum that is necessary for functionality, and standard, well-tested code or libraries should be used where possible.

5.2 Limitations and Future Work

While the Profiler can aid in understanding the security applied to some characteristics on a device, it has certain limitations which prevent it from testing the security of *all* characteristics. This is due

to the characteristic properties mentioned in Section 2. The Profiler is currently able to test characteristics that have properties "read" and "write". However, a characteristic value can also be obtained via "notifications" and "indications" and can be written using a "write without response" method. These are not handled in the code at present, but will be included in a future version.

Another potential avenue for future work is to fuzz test unprotected writeable characteristics identified by the Profiler, to determine if unexpected behaviour can be elicited.

Further, in its present form, the Profiler analyses how much data can be read from or written to a resource-constrained BLE Peripheral by a Central device or Central emulator. We aim to also explore whether a Peripheral can access data that it is not authorised to, from a connected Central device.

6 CONCLUSION

This paper describes a custom profiling tool for determining the minimum level of security applied to characteristics on a Bluetooth Low Energy device. Preliminary tests against some consumer devices show that several of the devices allow data to be read, and in some cases written, by a connected device without the device first authenticating itself. This translates to potential attacks that could be detrimental to user privacy and, in some cases, safety. The paper also presents some recommendations for reducing the attack surface of a device. The code for our tool is freely available, and we welcome suggestions and execution results.

REFERENCES

[1] Bluetooth Special Interest Group. 2016. Bluetooth Core Specification v5.0. (2016).
[2] Britt Cyr, Webb Horn, Daniela Miao, and Michael Specter. 2014. Security Analysis of Wearable Fitness Devices (Fitbit). *Massachusetts Institute of Technology* (2014).
[3] Thomas Kilbride, James Thomas, and Stefan Boesen. 2017. Ninebot by Segway miniPRO Vulnerabilities. (2017). Retrieved September 21, 2017 from https://www.ioactive.com/pdfs/IOActive-Security-Advisory-Ninebot-Segway-miniPRO_Final.pdf.
[4] David Malone and Kevin Mahern. 2011. Investigating the Distribution of Password Choices. (2011). Retrieved from https://arxiv.org/pdf/1104.3722.pdf.
[5] Mike Ryan. 2013. Bluetooth: With Low Energy Comes Low Security. In *WOOT '13: 7th USENIX Workshop on Offensive Technologies, Washington, D.C., USA, August 13, 2013.*

Secure Display for FIDO Transaction Confirmation

Yongxian Zhang[†], Xinluo Wang[†], Ziming Zhao[‡], Hui Li[†]
† Beijing University of Posts and Telecommunications
‡ Arizona State University
{yongxian.zhang, wangxinluo, lihuill}@bupt.edu.cn, ziming.zhao@asu.edu

ABSTRACT

FIDO protocols enable online services to leverage native authenticators of end-user computing devices including fingerprint readers for authentication to replace or complement passwords. FIDO protocols also offer support for prompting a user to confirm a specific transaction. However, due to the lack of a trusted display module in most Authenticators, operating systems of user devices display transaction contents directly on the main screen. In the paper, we demonstrate an attack on FIDO transaction confirmation in which malicious applications leverage the disparity between the displayed and actual transaction contents to trick users into confirming falsified transactions. In addition, we propose a lightweight secure display mechanism for FIDO transaction confirmations on mobile devices by leveraging the ARM TrustZone technology.

CCS CONCEPTS

• Security and privacy → Authentication;

KEYWORDS

FIDO, Transaction Confirmation, Secure Display

ACM Reference format:
Yongxian Zhang[†], Xinluo Wang[†], Ziming Zhao[‡], Hui Li[†]. 2018. Secure Display for FIDO Transaction Confirmation. In *Proceedings of Eighth ACM Conference on Data and Application Security and Privacy, Tempe, AZ, USA, March 19–21, 2018 (CODASPY '18)*, 3 pages.
https://doi.org/10.1145/3176258.3176946

1 INTRODUCTION

Fast IDentity Online (FIDO) is a public key cryptography based authentication framework developed in the quest of replacing passwords [4]. FIDO protocols enable online services and websites to leverage native security features including biometric authenticator of end-user computing devices for strong user authentication. By November 2017, there are already 383 certified FIDO products in the market [2].

FIDO has two specifications: universal authentication framework (UAF) and universal second factor (U2F). In UAF, users register their devices to online services by selecting a local authentication scheme such as swiping a finger, entering a PIN, etc [3]. Once registered, users can leverage the local authentication whenever they need to login to online services. U2F allows services to add another layer of authentication to their existing password infrastructure [5].

In addition to authentication, FIDO protocols provide a feature named transaction confirmation, which offers support for prompting a user to confirm a specific transaction. Using this feature online services can ensure the user is given additional information, such as the total of an order, regarding a transaction to confirm.

In the ideal case, a local authenticator with trusted display module shows the transaction content and triggers the user verification. However, most authenticators in the market do not have a trusted display module. Instead, operating systems of user devices display transaction contents directly on the main screen. Because there is no trusted path between an authenticator and the main screen, malicious applications can leverage the disparity between the displayed and actual transaction contents to trick users into confirming falsified transactions.

Even though local authenticators do not have trusted display modules, modern mobile devices are all equipped with the ARM Security Extensions, marketed as TrustZone [1]. TrustZone splits the system-on-chip systems into two security worlds, namely normal world and secure world, which can be leveraged to build trusted display.

In this paper, we propose a lightweight secure display mechanism for FIDO transaction confirmations. Our scheme only needs a slight modification of the current FIDO protocol by adding an digital signature of the transaction content. The signature is verified in the secure world of end-user devices. The secure world is also responsible for displaying the trusted transaction content on the main screen even when the normal world applications and OS are compromised.

2 TRANSACTION CONTENT DISPLAY TAMPERING ATTACK

Transaction confirmation is a feature, which offers support for prompting a user to confirm a specific transaction. It is a part of the authentication operation in the FIDO UAF protocol. Using this feature relying parties can ensure the user is given additional information, such as the total of an order, regarding a transaction to confirm. As shown in Figure 1, we use a simplified online shopping example to explain how transaction confirmation works and how this feature could be exploited. For simplicity, we intentionally omit several steps that are not related to transaction confirmation in the authentication operation, such as authenticator selection.

In this example, we assume the user has already registered her FIDO authenticator to the relying party, which means the relying party has a record of the user' account and public key and the authenticator has the user's corresponding private key. We use the

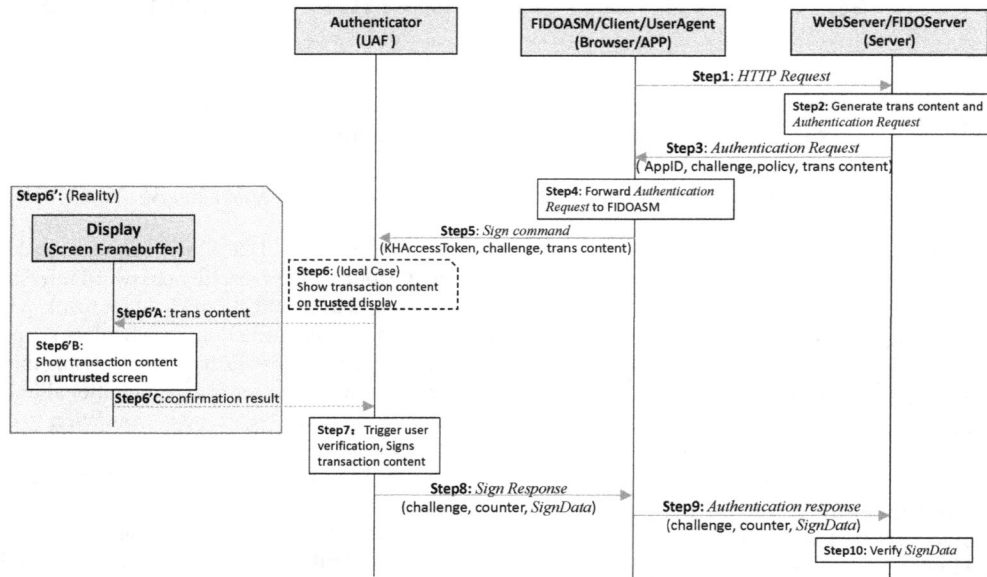

Figure 1: Original FIDO Transaction Confirmation Workflow

verb font to denote entities and the *italic* type to denote message types in the FIDO protocol.

Step 1: The user browses the online shopping website either using a browser or an application, which we call an UserAgent. Once the user decides to purchase anything, he/she clicks the corresponding button on the UserAgent before it sends an HTTP Request to the WebServer. Note that the communications between the WebServer and the UserAgent is secured through TLS/SSL.

Step 2: The WebServer of the online shopping site receives the HTTP GET message and generates a transaction content, which includes the total of the order, and sends it to the FIDOServer. We assume the communications between the WebServer and the FIDOServer is secure given that they belong to the same trust domain. Then The FIDOServer generates an *Authentication Request* message, which includes a challenge nonce and the transaction content, back to the WebServer.

Step 3: The WebServer forwards the message received from the FIDOServer to the UserAgent.

Step 4: The UserAgent forwards the *Authentication Request* to the FIDOClient, which forwards it to a FIDOASM based on which Authenticator is selected.

Step 5: The FIDOASM sends a *Sign Command* to the Authenticator in hopes that the Authenticator can digitally sign the challenge nonce upon user's approval.

Step 6: (Ideal Case) In the ideal case, a physical Authenticator with trusted display shows the transaction content and trigger the user verification.

Step 6: (Reality) In reality, physical authenticators in the market do not have a trusted display module. Therefore, the untrusted display module displays the transaction content directly on the main screen of the system using the APIs provided by the operating system. If the user confirms the displayed transaction content

is correct, she interacts with the Authenticator by swiping her finger or enter her PIN to authenticate herself and approve the transaction.

If an application or operating system is compromised, the transaction content display can be easily tampered.

Step 7: The Authenticator unlocks the user's private key and signs the challenge nonce and transaction content after a successful authentication of the user. The signed content is called the *SignData* in the FIDO protocol. Step 8: The Authenticator sends the *SignData* to the FIDOASM as part of the *Sign Response*.

Step 9: The *SignData* is eventually sent to the FIDOServer through FIDOClient, UserAgent and WebServer as a part of the *Authentication Response*.

Step 10: The FIDOServer verifies the *SignData* with the user's corresponding public key and sends the results back to the WebServer.

3 A SECURE DISPLAY MECHANISM FOR FIDO TRANSACTION CONFIRMATION

We propose a secure display mechanism for FIDO transaction confirmations. Our scheme only needs a slight modification of the current FIDO protocol by adding a digital signature of the transaction content. The signature is verified in the trusted execution environment of end-user devices enabled by the ARM TrustZone technology. The trusted execution environment is also responsible for displaying the verified transaction content on the main screen even when the rich execution environment is compromised.

In our proposed system, a rich OS like Android runs in the normal world. And, a trusted OS runs in secure world that is isolated from the normal one. The normal world runs most of FIDO modules. The secure world is used to protect the transaction content from

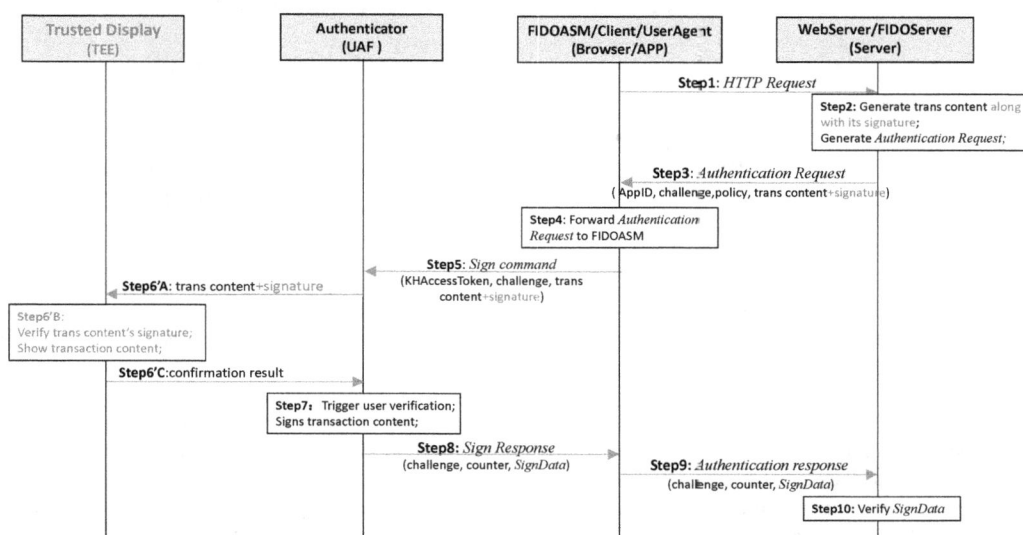

Figure 2: Modified FIDO Transaction Confirmation Workflow

being tampered when it displays in screen and to wait for user verification.

3.1 Signed Transaction Content

As shown in Figure 2 Step 2, in our proposed protocol WebServer not only generates the transaction content but also digitally sign the content using its private key when generating the *Authentication Request*. For convenience, the private key could be the same key used for the TLS connections. The transaction content along with the signature is sent to the user device as part of the *Authentication Request* message.

Different from the original system, in the proposed system the transaction content is not handled and displayed by the normal world OS. Instead, the normal world OS will send the unverified transaction content to the secure world OS through cross-world communication channels.

Then, the secure world verifies the integrity and authenticity of transaction content using the corresponding public key in Step 6'B. After display and user verification, the Authenticator generates *Sign Response* using the private key. And, the message is sent back to the WebServer and verified as the *SignData* in *Authentication Response* as in the original protocol.

3.2 TEE Assisted Trusted Display

For secure display, the secure world manipulates the physical memory access attributes to make sure part of the framebuffer cannot be modified by the normal world OS. It is achieved by configuring TrustZone controllers. The secure word also maps this area of the framebuffer into its own address space.

After receiving the message and successfully verifying the signature of transaction content, the secure world converts the transaction content to a displayable format, such as a BMP image. Then

the secure world directly writes the image to the start address of framebuffer of the normal world OS. As a result, the verified transaction content can be displayed on the screen of the device and waiting for user's verification. The secure world returns the display result to Authenticator as Figure 2, Step 6'C.

4 CONCLUSION

FIDO protocols offer support for prompting a user to confirm a specific transaction. In the paper, we demonstrated an attack on FIDO transaction confirmation in which malicious apps leverage the disparity between the displayed and actual transaction contents to trick users into confirming falsified transactions. We also proposed a lightweight secure display mechanism for FIDO transaction confirmations on mobile devices by leveraging the ARM TrustZone technology.

ACKNOWLEDGMENT

This research is supported in part by the National Natural Science Foundation of China grant (61628202) and the Center for Cybersecurity and Digital Forensics at Arizona State University.

REFERENCES

[1] ARM. 2016. ARM Architecture Reference Manual ARMv8, for ARMv8-A architecture profile. http://infocenter.arm.com/help/topic/com.arm.doc.ddi0487a.k/index.html. (2016).
[2] Justin Lee. 2017. FIDO Alliance announces new round of FIDO certified products. (2017). http://www.biometricupdate.com/201710/fido-alliance-announces-new-round-of-fido-certified-products
[3] Rolf Lindemann, Davit Baghdasaryan, Eric Tiffany, D Balfanz, B Hill, and J Hodges. 2014. FIDO UAF Protocol Specification v1. 0. *FIDO Alliance* (2014).
[4] Salah Machani, Rob Philpott, Sampath Srinivas, John Kemp, and Jeff Hodges. 2014. FIDO UAF Architectural Overview. *FIDO Alliance* (2014).
[5] Sampath Srinivas, Dirk Balfanz, and Eric Tiffany. 2014. FIDO Universal 2nd Factor (U2F) Overview. *Version v1. 0-rd-20140209, FIDO Alliance, February* (2014).

Misusing Sensory Channel to Attack Industrial Control Systems

Farhad Rasapour
Department of Computer Science
College of Engineering
Boise state university
Boise, Idaho
farhadrasapour@u.boisestate.edu

Hoda Mehrpouyan
Department of Computer Science
College of Engineering
Boise state university
Boise, Idaho
hodamehrpouyan@boisestate.edu

ABSTRACT

Industrial control systems (ICS) are used to control and manage critical infrastructures and protecting these complex system and their interfaces, which can be exploited by internal and external attackers, are a vital security task. Sensors, as an interface device, are used by ICS to collect information about the physical environment and should be guarded against cyber attacks. This paper investigates how sensors can be used as a communication channel by hackers to send a malicious command and control into the ICS. Further, we examine how abusing sensory channel would lead to a data pattern, which can be detected by a proper signature-based intrusion detection system (IDS).

KEYWORDS

Industrial Control System, Cyber-Security, Sensory Channel Misuse

ACM Reference Format:
Farhad Rasapour and Hoda Mehrpouyan. 2018. Misusing Sensory Channel to Attack Industrial Control Systems . In *CODASPY '18: Eighth ACM Conference on Data and Application Security and Privacy, March 19–21, 2018, Tempe, AZ, USA.* ACM, New York, NY, USA, 3 pages. https://doi.org/10.1145/3176258.3176947

1 INTRODUCTION

Industrial control systems (ICS) are used to control and manage critical infrastructures like transportation systems, nuclear facilities, power plants, and water refineries. ICSs are complicated systems composed of sensors, actuators, Programmable Logic Controllers (PLC) , Human Machine Interfaces(HMI), supervisory systems, and communication media, which makes them hard to defend. Being high-value targets and challenging to be secured accurately make the ICSs attractive targets for the cyber hackers. Hence, industrial control System cyber emergency response team (ICS-Cert) reported 295 attack incident against ICSs in the U.S. for 2015, and 290 for 2016[14]. Two attack incidents from 2016 are Kemuri Water Company network breach attack, which the attacker was able to take control of the flow of toxic chemicals that are used to treat water [13]. Second, the San Francisco transit system ransom-ware attack, which the hackers had the potential of compromising the service or cause collisions [13]. Considering how dangerous and life-threatening attacks against ICS can be, it is crucial to guard every hardware and software that provide access to the ICS. Normally,

the ICS access points are data interfaces like network interface cards (NIC) and HMIs. But there are devices that can be used or misused as an communication interfaces into ICS like sensors.

Sensors provide the ICS with information about the physical process, which can be consider as data interfaces and like any other data interface can be targeted or misused by hackers. There is a great deal of studies about detecting attacks which targeting the sensor itself or targeting components that rely on the sensor data [1, 3, 6, 7, 10, 11]. However, there is not enough work on *how to detect the sensory channel attack when the sensor is misused as an auxiliary device as a communication channel to inject data into the system.* In [15], the author shows the feasibility of sensory channel misuse in cyber-physical systems (CPS). Uluagac et al. injected data through an IR sensor to activate an already implanted malware inside a robot. The author finalized the study by recommending an Intrusion Detection System (IDS) architecture that is consist of sensory receptors, contextual analyzer, pattern analyzer, anomaly analyzer, and activity analyzer can detect the sensory channel misuse [15]. This paper studies the sensory channel misuse and possible injection data patterns in the ICS context by adding industrial control components like PLC and HMI to [15] study. Many of sensor in high-risk ICS like pressure and temperature sensors providing contiguous information of the physical phenomena. To match them and have a proper understanding of sensory channel data pattern caused by the attack, we used an IR sensor with continuous data output. Further, the contribution of this paper is to show the feasibility of misusing the sensory channel in the ICS and examine how an attacker can encode a control command for a malware utilizing the sensory channel to plan an accurate attack of PLC and tamper with the control process. In addition, the data patterns produced by the attack is studied to build a proper IDS in the future work.

One example scenario of misusing sensory channel is establishing a command and control path to send an instruction to an implanted malicious code inside the ICS. The attacker can encode a small chunk of data by leveraging the time between two changes in the sensory data. For example, if the time between tow transition is greater than S second, that bit is translated to one and if it is less than S seconds, it represents a bit 0. This type of attacks creates a data patterns that can be predicted before the attack happens and can be detected via pattern recognition systems. It is fair to anticipate that the instruction for a malware contains critical values like emergency shutdown port address, the maximum speed of a train or a command to compromise the safety management system. Hence, there is a great possibility of detecting the sensory channel misuse by constructing a bank of critical values in the ICS as a possible

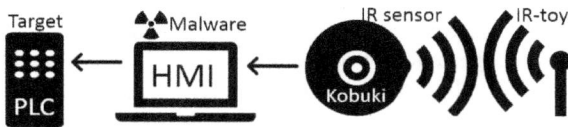

Figure 1: Injecting data through an IR sensor

Number of Reads	In 400 - 600 Range	In 0 - 200 Range
4-9	0	1
10-15	00	11
16-22	000	111
23-29	0000	1111
30-35	00000	11111
36-41	000000	111111
42-49	0000000	1111111
50-60	00000000	11111111

Table 1: Mapping injected data to bits.

attack signature. Then using a signature-based intrusion detection algorithm to verify these signatures in the sensory channel.

The rest of the paper is organized as below: the second section reviews the related work in the field of sensor security and sensory channel data injection attacks. The third section describes a case study of misusing the sensory channel to inject instruction for a malware and discusses data patterns caused by encoding malicious data into the sensory channel. In section fourth, a signature-based detection framework is proposed to detect the sensory channel misuse for future study, the last section provides the conclusion.

2 RELATED WORK

Previous works on sensor security can be categorized into three different groups: The first group of studies focus on the robustness of the system against the attacks and to examine the system can continue with the normal operation while the sensors are under attack [7]. The second group uses different types of algorithms to detect if the data on the sensory channel is false [1, 3, 5, 6, 10, 11, 17]. The second group proposed solution can be categorized into two classes: the first class uses the relations between different sensors which measures the same physical variable to detect the anomaly in the sensors reading [3, 6]. The second class takes advantage of different data coding techniques to validate the integrity of the data and detect the false data injection [1, 10]. The third group focus is on detecting the misuse of the sensory channel for purposes different than what the sensors are designed for or are built to do. [8, 15]. The authors of [8] show how Electromagnetic Interference (EMI) can be used to inject data into analog sensors and give some level of control over the system to the attacker. In [15], the authors showed a malware could be activated by sending an activation code through a sensory channel. Uluagac et al. also showed sensory channels could have enough bandwidth to transmit malware. The [15] calculated that a 1K malware could be transmitted in less than 82s over a light sensor channel, and even it could be done in less time by using combinations of different sensor channels.

3 CASE STUDY
3.1 Emulating an Injection Attack

To study the sensory channel misuse in ICS, we conduct an attack experiment by emulating a communication between a sensor, physical process, HMI, and a PLC as it shown in Figure 1. We monitored a Sharp GP2Y0A21 IR deep sensors on an iClebo Kobuki robot[12]. Kobuki is a mobile research base robot with several sensors and actuators which emulates an ICS physical process in the experiment. Kobuki can be controlled through a USB or serial ports. A device needs Kobuki driver to communicate and send a command to Kobuki. Kobuki driver is an open source application written in C++. Kobuki uses GP2Y0A21 IR deep sensor for detecting cliffs or ramps. This experiment shows misusing the GP2Y0A21 IR deep sensor to inject instruction for a malware into the ICS. GP2Y0A21 IR sensor emits IR light and base on the angle of reflected IR light

estimate the distance to the facing surface. GP2Y0A21 IR sensor is a analog sensor with output voltage in -0.3 ~ 0.3 V range. Kobuki uses an analog digital converter (ADC) to convert the sensor output voltage to a value in $0 \sim 2^{12} - 1$ range. The Kobuki sends a sample reading of all its sensors to the driver every 20ms (50Hz).

In addition, a Velocio Ace-11[16] programmable logic controller (PLC) is used as a target system. A PLC is a specialized digital computer that can be programmed to control a physical process. An Ace-11 has six output pins to send commands to communicate with physical devices. These output pins can be set to 1 or 0. An Ace-11 supports Modbus network protocol for input/output addressing and communicate with other devices. The 6th output is assigned 0x0F as a Modbus address. An Ace-11 also can be connected to supervisory or user interface devices via a USB port. A user interface devices like a human-machine interface (HMI) can send commands to Ace-11 and force it to set an output pin to 0 or 1. We programmed the Ace-11 to control a simple chemical mixing process. The chemical mixing has an emergency procedure, which would shut down the whole system in emergency cases by setting its 6th output pin to 1.

The Kobuki and the Ace-11 are both connected to a laptop through USB ports. The laptop is used as an HMI and engineering workstation in the ICS. Now the laptop has access to the IR sensors data, and also it can send commands to the Ace-11 [Figure 1].

Malware has been installed on the laptop, which can read the IR sensor data and send control commands to ACE-11. The goal of the experiment is to send the emergency pin address(0x0F) and the emergency activation value (0x01) through the sensory channel to the malware. Then the malware reads the IR sensor output and interprets the values based on the range of data and the number of sample data received in the corresponding range. Further, it converts the sensory channel output into the binary value based on the mapping depicted in Table 1. To the malware, the attacker sends a start signal by creating an immediate change from 400-600 range to 0-200 range and keeps the sensor sample reading in 0-200 range for about 1 to 3 sample reads.

Then we used an IR-toy[4] to manipulate the IR sensor and create the desired pattern on the sensory channel. IR-toy is a USB dongle which can be used to send a sequence of IR light. In this experiment, IR-toy was placed in a specific distance from the Kobuki IR deep sensor without emitting any IR light, so that Kobuki can provide sample data in the range of 400-600. On the other hand, in order for the Kobuki to provide a sample data in the range of 0-200, IR-toy is required to emit the IR light directly into the Kobuki sensor. The IR-toy emitted and blank sequence and created Kobuki IR sensor output is shown in Table 2.

Time (us)	Emit IR	Blank	Output range	Number of sample
5119.2		X	400-600	28
5119.2	X		0-200	24
8958.6		X	400-600	47
1279.8	X		0-200	5

Table 2: IR-toy emitting light and blank sequence.

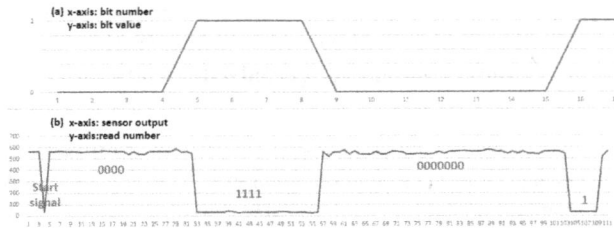

Figure 2: (a) Emergency address and emergency activation value bits pattern (b) Injected data pattern

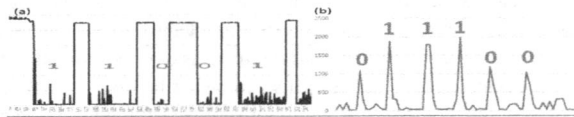

Figure 3: Encoding data in the sensory channel data range and sample read time

If there were an intrusion detection system (IDS) which monitored the sensory channel for the attack pattern, it would be possible to catch the attack. The figure 2 (b) shows Kobuki the IR sensor output data pattern and the figure 2 (a) shows the bits pattern for emergency address (0x0f) and its emergency activation value(0x01). As is depicted in figure 2, the two patterns are quite similar. A signature-based IDS could use the bits pattern as an attack signature to detect the sensory channel misuse.

3.2 Sensory Channel Misuse Patterns

As it is shown in the case study, the sensor value and the number of sensor sample reads between a rise and fall are used to encode data into the sensory channel [Table 1]. The sensor output value and the number of sensor read can be used independently to encode data into the sensory channel [Figure 3]. Figure 3 (a) shows an example of using the sample read values to encode 11001 in a sensory channel. If the sampling value between a rise and fall is less than 100 reads means 0 otherwise it means 1. Figure 3 (b) shows an example of using the sensor output value to encode 011100 in a sensory channel. If the sensor output value is less than 1450, it represents value 0. And if it is higher than 1550, it represents 1.

4 FUTURE WORKS

Signature-based intrusion detection (SID) systems monitor communication channels looking for attack signatures. The signature is a data pattern or string which an attacker uses or creates during the attack process. A SID uses a bank of signatures belong to known attacks. Misusing the sensory channel to inject instruction also creates a pattern in the sensory channel data which can be predicted and used as an attack signature. The only difference is that the signature does not represent a pattern caused by a known attack. Instead, the signature refers to a pattern caused by a possible

attack. Critical commands and values like the emergency controller address or the shutdown command are good signature candidates to look for in the sensory channel.

General IT signature-based detection system using fast string searching algorithm like Boyer-Moore [2] and Aho-Corasick [9] algorithms for detecting an attack in the communication channels. The next step is to experiment if sensory channel misuse detection can use the fast string matching algorithms by mapping sensory channel data to a string or sequence of 0s and 1s. And build a SID framework for the sensory channel by creating a bank of ICS critical values as signatures and designing a matching algorithm to detect the signatures in the sensory channel.

5 CONCLUSION

Attackers can misuse sensors and sensory channel as a command and control path for conducting a more accurate attack. Misusing the sensors for a purpose that they are not designed for would create a data pattern on the sensory channel that can be detected by a SID. By creating a bank of critical values as attack signatures and adapting a SID matching algorithm to the sensory channel behavior, it is possible to adopt a SID to the sensory channel.

REFERENCES

[1] Sulabh Bhattarai, Linqiang Ge, and Wei Yu. 2012. A novel architecture against false data injection attacks in smart grid. In *Communications (ICC), 2012 IEEE International Conference on*. IEEE, 907–911.
[2] Robert S Boyer and J Strother Moore. 1977. A fast string searching algorithm. *Commun. ACM* 20, 10 (1977), 762–772.
[3] Hang Cai and Krishna K Venkatasubramanian. 2016. Detecting Signal Injection Attack-Based Morphological Alterations of ECG Measurements. In *Distributed Computing in Sensor Systems (DCOSS), 2016 International Conference on*. IEEE, 127–135.
[4] dangerous prototype. [n. d.]. USB Infrared Toy. ([n. d.]).
[5] Hamza Fawzi, Paulo Tabuada, and Suhas Diggavi. 2012. Security for control systems under sensor and actuator attacks. In *Decision and Control (CDC), 2012 IEEE 51st Annual Conference on*. IEEE, 3412–3417.
[6] Minsu Jo, Junkil Park, Youngmi Baek, Radoslav Ivanov, James Weimer, Sang Hyuk Son, and Insup Lee. 2016. Adaptive Transient Fault Model for Sensor Attack Detection. In *Cyber-Physical Systems, Networks, and Applications (CPSNA), 2016 IEEE 4th International Conference on*. IEEE, 59–65.
[7] Marina Krotofil, Alvaro A Cárdenas, Bradley Manning, and Jason Larsen. 2014. CPS: driving cyber-physical systems to unsafe operating conditions by timing DoS attacks on sensor signals. In *Proceedings of the 30th Annual Computer Security Applications Conference*. ACM, 146–155.
[8] Denis Foo Kune, John Backes, Shane S Clark, Daniel Kramer, Matthew Reynolds, Kevin Fu, Yongdae Kim, and Wenyuan Xu. 2013. Ghost talk: Mitigating EMI signal injection attacks against analog sensors. In *Security and Privacy (SP), 2013 IEEE Symposium on*. IEEE, 145–159.
[9] Tsern-Huei Lee. 2007. Generalized aho-corasick algorithm for signature based anti-virus applications. In *Computer Communications and Networks, 2007. ICCCN 2007. Proceedings of 16th International Conference on*. IEEE, 792–797.
[10] Fei Miao, Quanyan Zhu, Miroslav Pajic, and George J Pappas. 2014. Coding sensor outputs for injection attacks detection. In *Decision and Control (CDC), 2014 IEEE 53rd Annual Conference on*. IEEE, 5776–5781.
[11] Junkil Park, Radoslav Ivanov, James Weimer, Miroslav Pajic, and Insup Lee. 2015. Sensor attack detection in the presence of transient faults. In *Proceedings of the ACM/IEEE Sixth International Conference on Cyber-Physical Systems*. ACM, 1–10.
[12] YUJIN ROBOT. [n. d.]. about. ([n. d.]).
[13] Michael Shalyt. 2017. How Vulnerable are Our Industrial Control Systems? What We Learned From ICS Attacks of 2016. (2017). http://www.icscybersecurityconference.com/ust-vulnerable-industrial-control-systems-learned-ics-attacks-2016/
[14] Industrial Control System Cyber Emergency Response Team. 2017. ICS-CERT Monitor. (2017). https://ics-cert.us-cert.gov/sites/default/files/Monitors/ICS-CERT_Monitor_Nov-Dec2016_S508C.pdf
[15] A Selcuk Uluagac, Venkatachalam Subramanian, and Raheem Beyah. 2014. Sensory channel threats to cyber physical systems: A wake-up call. In *Communications and Network Security (CNS), 2014 IEEE Conference on*. IEEE, 301–309.
[16] velocio.net. [n. d.]. Ace. ([n. d.]).
[17] Wenyuan Xu, Ke Ma, Wade Trappe, and Yanyong Zhang. 2006. Jamming sensor networks: attack and defense strategies. *IEEE network* 20, 3 (2006), 41–47.

SeCore: Continuous Extrospection with High Visibility on Multi-core ARM Platforms

Penghui Zhang, Bernard Ngabonziza, Haehyun Cho, Ziming Zhao, Adam Doupé, Gail-Joon Ahn
Arizona State University
{pzhang57,bngabonz,hcho67,zmzhao,doupe,gahn}@asu.edu

ABSTRACT

We present SeCore, which is a novel continuous extrospection system on multi-core ARM platform. SeCore leverages ARM Trust-Zone technology to keep one core in the secure world and assure the integrity of the static kernel data and code in the normal world. By breaking the original time-sharing paradigm of such systems, SeCore enables continuous coprocessor-like monitoring with high visibility into the rich execution environment on mobile and IoT platforms. By ensuring that secure tools execute on certain physical CPU cores, the system's attack surface is also significantly reduced.

ACM Reference Format:
Penghui Zhang, Bernard Ngabonziza, Haehyun Cho, Ziming Zhao, Adam Doupé, Gail-Joon Ahn. 2018. SeCore: Continuous Extrospection with High Visibility on Multi-core ARM Platforms. In *Proceedings of Eighth ACM Conference on Data and Application Security and Privacy, Tempe, AZ, USA, March 19–21, 2018 (CODASPY '18)*, 3 pages.
https://doi.org/10.1145/3176258.3176948

1 INTRODUCTION

Existing mobile and IoT systems and applications are fraught with vulnerabilities and prone to many attacks. In particular, attacks that can compromise OS kernels are a growing threat. When attackers take the control of an OS kernel, they can hide their traces, steal sensitive information, and install backdoors. Therefore, monitoring and protecting OS kernel has received significant attention. Existing techniques of monitoring and protecting the security of OS can be categorized into two classes:

1) Host based intrusion detection, where the intrusion detection system (IDS) runs as a monitor on its host from a higher privileged mode, such as a hypervisor and collects information used to identify possible intrusions on that host [2, 5]. The approach, which is named virtual machine introspection (VMI), significantly increases the size of the trusted computing base (TCB).

Hardware-isolated execution environment (HIEE), such as ARM TrustZone, enables another way of host based kernel protection on mobile and IoT platforms by running kernel protection tools in an isolated execution environment called the trusted execution environment (TEE), whose memory and peripherals can be physically isolated from a rich execution environment (REE) [1, 4, 7].

However, existing HIEE based solutions suffer from many if not all following limitations: i) a compromised REE kernel can

perform many types of denial-of-service attacks (DoS) on the TEE by refusing to relinquish the control of CPU [6]; ii) it is required that the security world returns as soon as possible. Otherwise, running inside the TEE for a long time could jeopardize the stability and usability of the normal world commodity OS; iii) the context switches from the TEE to the REE, and vice versa are very expensive, which significantly increase the performance overhead and power consumption.

2) Secure coprocessor based intrusion detection, where the state and data of the host is collected and processed by monitoring software running on an external hardware coprocessor [3]. Secure coprocessors have many advantages including isolated and continuous monitoring and low interaction with the target OS. However, compared with VMI they retain relatively low visibility into the host, since they only play the role of an outside peer.

In this paper, we present a hardware-based security framework, namely SeCore, in which one or more general purpose computing cores will stay in a hardware-isolated or safe execution environment to monitor the system running in the rich execution environment. Different from the existing paradigm of hardware-isolated environments, where CPU cores switch between a privileged mode (secure world in TrustZone) and a normal mode (normal world in TrustZone), the proposed idea breaks the time-sharing paradigm of cores, which enables both coprocessor-like continuous monitoring and host-based-solution-like high visibility into the rich execution environment within a CPU. Different from virtual machine introspection where the guest OSes run inside the hypervisor, in SeCore the monitored OS or hypervisor do not run directly inside the monitoring system and tools. Indeed, the inspection tools run outside the rich execution environment but retain high visibility of the rich execution environment. We call this kind of inspection *extrospection*.

2 DESIGN AND IMPLEMENTATION OF SECORE

SeCore has three major steps in achieving extrospection: In Step 1, SeCore changes the boot process of the dedicated cores and make sure world switching instructions will never be executed on this cores. In Step 2: SeCore accesses the monitored system from the monitoring Cores. The challenges in enabling monitoring cores to access the monitored system include configuring the undocumented on-chip registers, since most vendors do not implement the standard memory space controller. We reverse engineer available firmware to understand how different SoCs support the memory configurations. In Step 3: SeCore monitors the normal world continuously.

SeCore has three features. First, tamper-resistance. Since SeCore and the nomral world are isolated via the ARM TrustZone security extension, the normal world does not have the authority

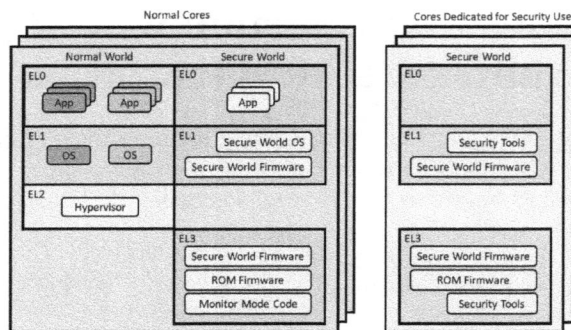

Figure 1: SeCore Architecture.

to access any resouces in SeCore, which makes SeCore tamper-resistant. Second, Continuous. We do not need to stop the normal world's execution for SeCore to perform extrospection. Both SeCore and the normal world operating system run concurrently. Third, stealty. It is difficult for the normal world to detect SeCore's extrospection is executing, which makes SeCore stealthy.

We implement SeCore on a Hikey board which has 8 ARM Cortex-A53 1.2GHz cores and 2GB of memory. Regarding the software stack, the secure world side runs OP-TEE, combined with ARM Trusted Firmware (ATF), while the normal world runs Linux.

2.1 SeCore Boot Process

In the normal boot process of a TrustZone-enabled platform, all cores boot in the secure world monitor mode <mon|s>. The cores are divided into one primary core and secondary cores. The system initializes the primary core first and let the primary core to wake the secondary cores up to get initialized. A bootloader that runs in <mon|s> sets up the environment, such as the stack for each mode, before it transfers control to the secure world operating system. The secure world operating system finishes its own initialization in <svc|s> and gives control back to a monitor by executing the SMC instruction. The code that runs in <mon|s> then switches the core's state from secure to non-secure. Then, the operating system running in the normal world, such as Linux and Windows, takes over and starts executing in <svc|ns> mode. When the normal world operating system needs services from the secure world, it executes SMC that forces the core to enter <mon|s> mode. Then, the monitor code will dispatch the request accordingly.

SeCore's initialization is different from the normal cores since the secure world operating system does not gives control to the normal world after finishing the initialization of SeCore.

Listing 1 shows how we implement SeCore during the booting procedure inside function vector_cpu_on_entry. Register x0 stores the number of CPU after the execution of function get_core_pos. Function vector_cpu_on_entry allows us to select one or more secondary cores as SeCore according to our needs. In this example, we just select one core as SeCore and SeCore is implemented to initialize the 7th core which should stay in the secure world from Line 9. After selecting 7th core as SeCore, it jumps to secore_func which goes to execute SeCore functions.

2.2 Accessing Normal World Memory

SeCore first needs to allow the secure world to access all the memory space, which includes RAM, peripherals, etc., at boot time. Note that SeCore will also make sure some memory address space, such as the secure world's physical memory, cannot be accessed from the normal world at this step. This can be done by configuring Trust-Zone Address Space Controller (TSC). However, on some platforms the TSC is replaced by a vendor-specific address space controller, which normally does not come with documentations.

We identified such as a memory controller on HiKey board at memory address 0xF7121000 that is very similar with TSC. Even though it is undocumented, the PIs were able to reverse engineer the associated code and perform several experiments to understand how it works. It turns out that, when secur_boot_lock signal is high, its register SEC_LOCKDOWN_SELECT will be set as read-only. Also, other registers specified in SEC_LOCKDOWN_SELECT will be set as read-only. And, they can only be unset by a poweron reset. So, SeCore software module can first configures the controller at address 0xF7121000 including SEC_RGN_MAP, SEC_RGN_ATTRIB, and others to specify secure world can see the whole physical memory space and normal world can only see some of it. Then, SeCore lock the registers, which cannot be reverted until next power-on reset.

2.3 Continuous Extrospection

SeCore monitors the normal world kernel static memory by staying outside the environment. SeCore functions execute in the secure world exception level 3 (EL3), which has the highest privilege to monitor all the memory in the normal world. Therefore, SeCore has the ability to extrospect the static memory regions of the normal world kernel, which stays in the normal world exception level (EL1).

Even though TrustZone architecture allows the secure world to access all the memory of the normal world, the memory area still needs to be mapped before the secure world can actually access it. After the initialization of cores, SeCore needs to access the static code and data in the normal world kernel memory. However, the addresses SeCore has are the virtual addresses. To solve the problem, SeCore needs to translate these virtual addresses to the physical addresses first, and then it can access the static memory region of the normal world kernel using the physical addresses. We implemented a function called va2pa_in_sec() to translate the starting and ending virtual addresses of the static kernel memory regions

```
1   LOCAL_FUNC vector_cpu_on_entry , :
2       adr    x16, thread_cpu_on_handler_ptr
3       ldr    x16, [x16]
4       blr    x16
5       mov    x19, x0
6       bl get_core_pos
7
8       /* select SeCore*/
9       cmp    x0, #7
10      beq    secore_func
11
12      mov    x1, x19
13      ldr    x0, =TEESMC_OPTEED_RETURN_ON_DONE
14      smc    #0
15      b  .   /* SMC should not return */
16  END_FUNC vector_cpu_on_entry
17
18  ...
19
20  LOCAL_FUNC secore_func , :
21  /* execute functionalities of SeCore */
22      b  secore_func_in_c
23      b  .
24  END_FUNC secore_func
```

Listing 1: Code of Core Initialization in SᴇCᴏʀᴇ

in the normal world to physical addresses so that SᴇCᴏʀᴇ can read the static code and data in the normal world kernel memory.

After SᴇCᴏʀᴇ gets the virtual address corresponding to the static memory region of the normal world kernel, it has the ability to monitor the normal world kernel and to check its integrity. In SᴇCᴏʀᴇ, integrity checking and monitoring take place continuously. As the static data in the normal world kernel memory is consecutively mapped, binaries in the static memory regions of the normal world kernel are read by accessing through the starting to the ending physical addresses which are converted from the virtual addresses by SᴇCᴏʀᴇ at first. To measure the integrity of static data and code, we compute the original hash values of the binaries using a cryptographic hash function before all processes begin to execute.

We store these hash values in order to check the integrity of static code and data later. After this, processes start being executed, and we implement a function integrity_check() running in SᴇCᴏʀᴇ to check the integrity continuously, by hashing the memory regions of the normal world kernel again, and comparing the hash values with the original one. If the hash values match with each other, the integrity of static code and data is guaranteed. If the hash values do not match with each other, it means that the static kernel memory region in the normal world has been tampered.

3 FUTURE WORK

The current version of SᴇCᴏʀᴇ checks the static code and data in the normal world kernel memory, which is linearly mapped in the memory. This feature offers us a convenient way to read all the data in binary as long as we know the starting and ending addresses of one specific memory region. However, the attackers would attempt to tamper the dynamic code to make the attacks successful. Unlike the static code and data, it is much more difficult to check the

integrity of dynamic data memory region, as the data is changing all the time when the system is running. It is a challenge for an integrity check to distinguish between a normal operation and a potential tampering behaviour. In the future, we plan to enhance SᴇCᴏʀᴇ to monitor dynamic areas as well.

Given the number of vulnerabilities discovered in hypervisors, it is imperative to design a framework that is not only able to perform virtual machine introspection but also hypervisor inspection. However, no existing solution that can provide an unified framework to monitor and protect kernel and hypervisor simultaneously. We plan to extend SᴇCᴏʀᴇ for hypervisor inspection in the future.

A major limitation of secure coprocessors based intrusion detection systems is their visibility into the host is limited due to the fact that they play the role of outside peers. This characteristic makes it impossible to perform event-triggered monitoring without modifying the host system. We plan to extend SᴇCᴏʀᴇ with the functionality of event-triggered extrospection in the future.

4 CONCLUSION

We presented SᴇCᴏʀᴇ, an innovative continuous high visibility extrospection technique on multi-core ARM platform in this paper. SᴇCᴏʀᴇ exploits ARM TrustZone technology to keep one core in the secure world forever, assuring the computing integrity of data. By breaking the original time-sharing paradigm of such systems, SᴇCᴏʀᴇ enables continuous coprocessor-like monitoring with high visibility into the rich execution environment on such mobile and IoT platforms. And by ensuring that secure tools execute on certain physical CPU cores, the system's attack surface is significantly reduced. Also, with the increasing number of mobile CPU cores and based on the results of evaluation, SᴇCᴏʀᴇ only introduces a negligible overhead.

5 ACKNOWLEDGEMENT

This work is partially supported by a grant from the Center for Cybersecurity and Digital Forensics at Arizona State University.

REFERENCES

[1] Ahmed M Azab, Peng Ning, Jitesh Shah, Quan Chen, Rohan Bhutkar, Guruprasad Ganesh, Jia Ma, and Wenbo Shen. 2014. Hypervision Across Worlds: Real-time Kernel Protection from the ARM TrustZone Secure World. In *Proceedings of the 2014 ACM SIGSAC Conference on Computer and Communications Security*. ACM, 90–102.
[2] Tal Garfinkel, Mendel Rosenblum, et al. 2003. A Virtual Machine Introspection Based Architecture for Intrusion Detection.. In *Ndss*, Vol. 3. 191–206.
[3] Hojoon Lee, Hyungon Moon, Ingoo Heo, Daehee Jang, Jinsoo Jang, Kihwan Kim, Yunheung Paek, and Brent Kang. 2017. KI-Mon ARM: A Hardware-assisted Event-triggered Monitoring Platform for Mutable Kernel Object. *IEEE Transactions on Dependable and Secure Computing* (2017).
[4] Hyungon Moon, Hojoon Lee, Jihoon Lee, Kihwan Kim, Yunheung Paek, and Brent Byunghoon Kang. 2012. Vigilare: toward snoop-based kernel integrity monitor. In *Proceedings of the 2012 ACM conference on Computer and communications security*. ACM, 28–37.
[5] Nick L Petroni Jr and Michael Hicks. 2007. Automated detection of persistent kernel control-flow attacks. In *Proceedings of the 14th ACM conference on Computer and communications security*. ACM, 103–115.
[6] Himanshu Raj, Stefan Saroiu, Alec Wolman, Ronald Aigner, Jeremiah Cox, Paul England, Chris Fenner, Kinshuman Kinshumann, Jork Loeser, Dennis Mattoon, et al. 2016. fTPM: A Software-Only Implementation of a TPM Chip. In *USENIX Security Symposium*. 841–856.
[7] He Sun, Kun Sun, Yuewu Wang, Jiwu Jing, and Sushil Jajodia. 2014. Trustdump: Reliable memory acquisition on smartphones. In *European Symposium on Research in Computer Security*. Springer, 202–218.

Model Checking of Security Properties in Industrial Control Systems (ICS)

Roshan Shrestha
Department of Computer Science
Boise State University
Boise, Idaho 83725
roshanshrestha@u.boisestate.edu

Hoda Mehrpouyan
Department of Computer Science
Boise State University
Boise, Idaho 83725
hodamehrpouyan@boisestate.edu

Dianxiang Xu
Department of Computer Science
Boise State University
Boise, Idaho 83725
dianxiangxu@boisestate.edu

ABSTRACT

With the increasing inter-connection of operation technology to the IT network, the security threat to the Industrial Control System (ICS) is increasing daily. Therefore, it is critical to utilize formal verification technique such as model checking to mathematically prove the correctness of security and safety requirements in the controller logic before it is deployed on the field. However, model checking requires considerable effort for regular ICS users and control technician to verify properties . This paper, provides a simpler approach to the model checking of temperature process control system by first starting with the control module design without formal verification. Second, identifying possible vulnerabilities in such design. Third, verifying the safety and security properties with a formal method.

ACM Reference format:
Roshan Shrestha, Hoda Mehrpouyan, and Dianxiang Xu. 2018. Model Checking of Security Properties in Industrial Control Systems (ICS). In *Proceedings of Eighth ACM Conference on Data and Application Security and Privacy, Tempe, AZ, USA, March 19–21, 2018 (CODASPY '18)*, 3 pages.
https://doi.org/10.1145/3176258.3176949

1 INTRODUCTION

Supervisory Control and Data Acquisition (SCADA) are widely used for managing Industrial Control System(ICS). SCADA focuses on the supervisory level and is not a full control system in itself. It is a software package that is positioned on top of the hardware to which it is interfaced usually using Programmable Logic Controllers (PLCs), or other commercial hardware modules[7]. A PLC is a microprocessor-based controller used to control machines and processes. According to IEC 61131[8], Instruction Lists (IL), Ladder Diagrams (LD), Structured Text (ST), Function Block Diagrams (FBD) and Sequential Function Charts (SFC) are commonly used specifications for programming PLC.

While constructing the LD (alternately FBD, SFC, ST or IL) for the control module, most of the end users put emphasis on making the control strategy/logic work for the functional requirements of the control process [3]. In such, no verification is used to validate the behavior of the code written in the PLC from the safety and

security perspective before it is deployed on the field. However, in many cases, there are implicit requirements pertaining to safety and security measures, which are not included as part of the control module design and implementation. As a result, the designed control module may have loopholes making it vulnerable to unprecedented execution sequences and/or from cyber attacks. Hence, some form of model checking[4] is required to tackle such hidden safety and security-related issues. Model checking means verifying whether the model of the system at hand satisfies certain properties or not.

Model checking typically needs deep expertise in formal methods to construct the model of the system and formally specify security properties. Many research studies ([9], [10], [11]) have been done to verify control module design; however, it requires considerable effort and exploration for a field technician to start model verification of the control module. The objective of this paper is to present a simplified case study of control module design for the temperature control process and its model checking for safety and security properties so that the model checking in ICS becomes more accessible to a field technician and readers.

This paper examines a control module that is designed in Honeywell Experion PKS [1], uses Linear Temporal Logic(LTL)[12] to formally specify properties and uses NuSMV[6] as a tool for model checking. The rest of the paper is organized as follows: Section II of the paper discusses related work. Section III presents the case study of control module design for the temperature control system. Section IV examines the possible vulnerabilities(attack vector) in the designed model. Section V presents how LTL and NuSMV can be used for model verification, and Section VI draws the conclusion.

2 CASE STUDY

2.1 Control System

This study examines a temperature control system which is responsible for maintaining the temperature of a designated space at the temperature set by a user. In addition to a heater and a cooler for the regulation of temperature, the system also includes a window that can be controlled to be opened or closed to maintain the temperature. The objective of the control system is to open the window and let external air flow inside for controlling the temperature whenever feasible. However, opening the window to regulate the temperature is not always feasible, and the control process should also operate the heater or the cooler to regulate temperature whenever opening a window is not feasible. The window can be opened whenever the set temperature as well as external temperature is higher (or lesser) than the inside temperature; otherwise the window should be closed and either the heater or the cooler should be turned on

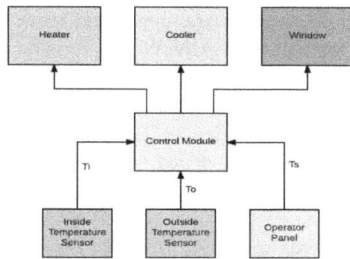

Figure 1: State transition diagram for planned control module to be designed

to regulate the temperature. The control system also consists of an alarm signal which is activated when there is a storm, heavy rainfall or faulty air outside, indicating that the window should be closed and the heater or the cooler should be used.

As shown in figure 1, the control system consists of i) two sensors - one inside the designated space and one outside of the space, ii) three actuators - heater, cooler, and window, iii) an operator panel - which consists of three LEDs showing the status of each actuator, three buttons that allows operator to overwrite the status of actuators, and a field to set the desired temperature iv) three analog inputs - two corresponding to the sensor readings and one from the set temperature in the operator panel and v) three outputs - each corresponding to one of the actuators to control its operation.

2.2 Testbed

The case study is performed in a Honeywell C300 simulator testbed which is simulator for Honeywell's C300 controller. C300 provides powerful and robust control capabilities for the Experion PKS (Process Knowledge System) platform[2]. It should be noted that we have used a C300 to design a control module just like the regular PLC, however, it is more capable and robust controller than the regular PLC. Experion PKS is the first enterprise-wide Distributed Control System (DCS) targeting to unify people with the process, business requirements, and asset management[1]. The C300 can address demanding process control requirements from integration with complicated batch systems to controlling devices on a variety of networks such as Fieldbus, Profibus, or Modbus[2].

2.3 Control Module Design

The paper now presents the control module design procedure that we followed to develop the control module. If end users do not verify safety and security properties, most of them would follow nearly similar procedure which involves the following:

2.3.1 Develop Control Strategy and Control Logic. The objective of temperature process control is to determine the difference between the actual temperature and the set temperature (referred as an error) and then guide actuators to minimize it. Hence, the closed-loop control scheme is to be designed for the control module. Let T_o, T_i represent the temperature reading from the outside temperature sensor and inside temperature sensor respectively. T_s corresponds to the temperature set by the user in the operator's panel.

If the difference between T_s and T_i is positive, then the temperature needs to be increased. In this case, if the outside air is also warmer than the inside air (T_o - T_i is positive), then opening the window to regulate the temperature is feasible and hence the heater and cooler should be disabled. Similarly, if the difference between T_s and T_i is negative, the temperature needs to be decreased and if outside air is cooler than the inside air ($T_o - T_i$ is negative), then the window should be opened and the cooler should be disabled. In any other cases, the window should be closed and the heater needs to be turned on if $T_s - T_i$ is positive; otherwise cooler needs to be turned on as shown in Table 1.

T_s-T_i	T_o - T_i	Heater	Cooler	Open window
+ve	+ve	disable	disable	open
+ve	-ve	enable	disable	close
-ve	+ve	disable	enable	close
-ve	-ve	disable	disable	open

Table 1: control logic - when alarm is off

This is the control logic for process control when the alarm is off. When the alarm is on, the window should be closed and the temperature should be regulated using the heater or cooler.

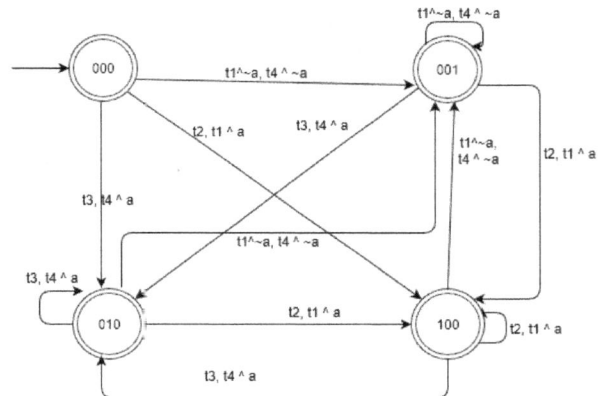

Figure 2: State transition diagram for planned control module to be designed

2.3.2 Behavior of the control module planned to be designed. Let 'hcw' represent the state of the system where h is 1 if the heater is on, c is 1 if the cooler is on and w is 1 if the window is open. h, w and c are 0 when corresponding actuators are off. Let us define predicates P1 as ts − ti > 0 and P2 as to − ti > 0 and combined propositions 'P1 ∧ P2' as t1, 'P1 ∧ ~P1' as t2, '~P1 ∧ P2' as t3 and finally '~P1 ∧ ~P2' as t4. Similarly, let proposition 'a' represent that the alarm is on. Hence, initially when the system is not started and nothing is turned on, the state of the system is **000** as show in Figure 2. If t1 is true (ts − ti > 0 and to − ti > 0), it is feasible to open the window if there is no alarm signal (~a holds). Hence, if t1 and ~a holds, then the window should be opened which will change the state of system changes from **000** to **001**. However, if there is an alarm signal (a is true), then the system will close the window and turn on the heater instead. This will change the state from **000** to **100**. Similarly, the behavior of the system in other situations is shown in Figure 2.

2.3.3 Design of the control module. With the aforementioned behavior of the control module in mind, the control module is designed in the Honeywell Experion PKS control module builder. Further, to enable the operator to overwrite the status of the actuator, the overwrite switches for each of the actuators are added into the design. This requirement is incorporated by simply adding the XOR gate in front of the control signal to the actuator such that the inputs to the XOR gate are - i) the control signal for the actuator from the control logic and, ii) the signal from the overwrite switch. The output of XOR gate is now the control signal for the actuator.

3 POSSIBLE VULNERABILITIES (ATTACK VECTORS) IN THE DESIGNED CONTROL MODULE

When we simulated the run in the testbed, the objective of the control module seems fulfilled since it behaved as shown in Figure 2. In addition, the overwrite switch is able to toggle the status of corresponding actuator. When the overwrite switch toggles the status of each actuator, it is actually changing the state of the control system but the state transition system diagram that we developed to analyze the behavior of the control module never considered such possible state transitions. So, various undesired states are possible because of potential state transitions from overwrite switches and could lead to harmful states in the system. For example, opening the window while the alarm is on using the overwrite switch for the window would lead to an undesired state. As a result, the operator could directly toggle the overwrite switch without the control process being informed of the potential undesired state. The operator with malicious intent (attacker) can use this direct (uncontrolled) capability provided by the overwrite switch as an attack vector.

4 MODEL VERIFICATION

For model checking, the model corresponding to the designed control module needs to be constructed and then presented to the model checking tool along with the formal specifications of the safety and security properties that we want to verify. As specified in Section 2.3.2, the state of the model is represented by ' **hcw**'.

The model specification for NuSMV begins with the MODULE keyword followed by the name. It consists of two parts - i) VAR and ii) ASSIGN. In VAR section, the possible states of the model and events that could trigger the state transitions are defined. Besides the four possible states planned in section 2.3.2, all eight possible combinations of ' **hcw**' are possible in the real design due to the overwrite switches. As a result, there are eight states defined in the bottom of VAR section in the NuSMV file. In addition, VAR section consists of event definitions of t1, t2, t3, t4, **alarm**, o1, o2, and o3 where o1, o2, and o3 correspond to the action of turning on the overwrite switch for the heater, cooler, and window respectively.

The first line in the ASSIGN section specifies the initial state of the system which is **000**. The second line *next(state):= case* begins the state transition function of the model which consists of multiple statements of the form *current-state and events : next-state* , each corresponding to the possible state transitions in the model. Finally, the ESAC keyword is used to end the transition function. For background on NuSMV model, refer to the Chapter 2 of the NuSMV manual [5].

The next step is to specify the safety and security properties of the system that we want to verify. We are considering two properties - i) the cooler and heater could not be on at the same time and ii) the window must be closed when the alarm is on. In the LTL specification, property ' **i** ' is specified as "G!(**state = 110 | state = 111**)", and property *'ii'* as "F!(**state = 001 & a**)". For background on the LTL specification, refer to the article "The temporal logic of programs" [12].

Finally, model checking is performed for the specified model and properties. For technical details to run model checking on NuSMV with LTL specification, refer to Chapter 6 of the NuSMV manual [5]. While model checking, we found the counter examples for both properties. The counter example for property '**i**' implies that the cooler and heater are on at the same time. Hence, the designed model does not satisfy property '**i**'. Similarly, the counter example for property '**ii**' implies that it is also not satisfied by the designed control module.

5 CONCLUSION AND FUTURE WORK

This paper presents a case study of formal verification of security properties in control module design for the temperature control system, specifying required background in model design, LTL, and NuSMV in a more succinct and precise way so that the model checking in ICS will be more accessible to a field technician and readers. In this work, we manually translated the design of the control module into model specifications for the NuSMV, however, in the future, we aim to construct such a model automatically from the control module's FBD program specification.

REFERENCES

[1] *Experion   PKS   Orion - Process   Control   Beyond   Distributed   Control   Systems.*   https://www.honeywellprocess.com/en-US/explore/products/control-monitoring-and-safety-systems/integrated-control-and-safety-systems/experion-pks/Pages/experionpks.aspx.
[2] *Honeywell C300 controller.*   https://www.honeywellprocess.com/en-US/explore/products/control-monitoring-and-safety-systems/integrated-control-and-safety-systems/experion-pks/controllers/Pages/c300.aspx.
[3] Zachry Basnight, Jonathan Butts, Juan Lopez, and Thomas Dube. 2013. Firmware modification attacks on programmable logic controllers. *International Journal of Critical Infrastructure Protection* 6, 2 (2013), 76–84.
[4] Béatrice Bérard, Michel Bidoit, Alain Finkel, François Laroussinie, Antoine Petit, Laure Petrucci, and Philippe Schnoebelen. 2013. *Systems and software verification: model-checking techniques and tools.* Springer Science & Business Media.
[5] Roberto Cavada, Alessandro Cimatti, Gavin Keighren, Emanuele Olivetti, Marco Pistore, and Marco Roveri. 2004. NuSMV 2.2 Tutorial. *ITC-irst-Via Sommarive* 18 (2004), 38055.
[6] Alessandro Cimatti, Edmund Clarke, Fausto Giunchiglia, and Marco Roveri. 1999. NuSMV: A new symbolic model verifier. In *International conference on computer aided verification.* Springer, 495–499.
[7] Axel Daneels and Wayne Salter. 1999. What is SCADA? (1999).
[8] Karl Heinz John and Michael Tiegelkamp. 2010. *IEC 61131-3: programming industrial automation systems: concepts and programming languages, requirements for programming systems, decision-making aids.* Springer Science & Business Media.
[9] Egor Vladimirovich Kuz'min and Valery Anatolievich Sokolov. 2012. On verification of PLC-programs written in the LD-language. *Modelirovanie i Analiz Informatsionnykh Sistem* 19, 2 (2012), 138–144.
[10] Kingliana Loeis, Mohammed Bani Younis, and Georg Frey. 2005. Application of symbolic and bounded model checking to the verification of logic control systems.. In *ETFA*
[11] Olivera Pavlovic and Hans-Dieter Ehrich. 2010. Model checking PLC software written in function block diagram. In *Software Testing, Verification and Validation (ICST), 2010 Third International Conference on.* IEEE, 439–448.
[12] Amir Pnueli. 1977. The temporal logic of programs. In *Foundations of Computer Science, 1977., 18th Annual Symposium on.* IEEE, 46–57.

Privacy-aware Data Assessment of Online Social Network Registration Processes

Christine Schuppler*
AIT Austrian Institute of Technology
Center for Digital Safety & Security
Vienna, Austria

Maria Leitner[†]
AIT Austrian Institute of Technology
Center for Digital Safety & Security
Vienna, Austria
maria.leitner@ait.ac.at

Stefanie Rinderle-Ma
University of Vienna
Faculty of Computer Science
Vienna, Austria
stefanie.rinderle-ma@univie.ac.at

ABSTRACT

Privacy and security research has been very active concerning online social networks (OSN) as a vast amount of personal information is used and published (by users) within OSNs. However, most people do not pay attention on what personal information they provide during registration. Depending on what information is provided in (public) OSN profiles, that data might be misused by attackers e.g., for cross-site profile cloning. This paper assesses data provided by the user during the registration of OSNs. Therefore, it is investigated how OSN registration processes are typically modeled, which information is needed to create a profile in OSNs and which attack scenarios can occur based on the provided data. The results contribute to the understanding of OSN registration process design as well as requested data and to replicate and reuse processes for further privacy and security investigations.

CCS CONCEPTS

• **Security and privacy** → **Social network security and privacy**; *Social aspects of security and privacy*; • **Applied computing** → Business process modeling;

KEYWORDS

privacy, online social networks, data assessment, business process

ACM Reference Format:
Christine Schuppler, Maria Leitner, and Stefanie Rinderle-Ma. 2018. Privacy-aware Data Assessment of Online Social Network Registration Processes. In *CODASPY '18: Eighth ACM Conference on Data and Application Security and Privacy, March 19–21, 2018, Tempe, AZ, USA.* ACM, New York, NY, USA, 3 pages. https://doi.org/10.1145/3176258.3176950

1 INTRODUCTION

Online social networks (OSN) are widely used by millions of people in everyday lives. OSNs are defined by Boyd and Ellison [4] as *"a web-based services that allow individuals to (1) construct a public or semi-public profile within a bounded system, (2) articulate a list*

---

*Contribution during work at AIT Austrian Institute of Technology.
[†]Corresponding Author.

of other users with whom they share a connection, and (3) view and traverse their list of connections and those made by others within the system". Privacy and security are major concerns when it comes to OSNs as a vast amount of personal information is used and published within OSNs. However, most people do not pay attention on what personal information they provide during the registration process [8]. Personal information is extremely valuable and can be sold on black markets (e.g., Dark web). For this reason the personal data is not only interesting for OSNs and third-party domains but also for malicious actors (e.g., hackers or thieves for selling data or identity theft). Already several security attacks were specified for OSNs ins [2, 7, 10]. For example, cloning an existing profile and sending friend requests to friends of the impersonated profile to steal personal data is called same-site and cross-site profile cloning attacks. While same-site profile cloning copies and inserts the profile within the same network, cross-site profile cloning is about copying the profile from OSN A into another network (OSN B). Copying a profile to a new OSN raises less suspicion and therefore is harder to detect. Further examples of attacks are phishing attacks where personal information from OSNs is reused for phishing. For example in [9], it is shown that phishing attacks with information from OSN profiles are four times more effective. Further security attacks include spamming, creation of an digital dossier of personal data, sybil attacks, malware attacks, information leak or de-anonymizing (see [2, 7, 10]). These attacks can have a significant impact on the use of personal information. In this paper, we start our investigation at the beginning - the **OSN user registration**. It is the first process where users "share" personal information with registering in the OSN and further with other OSN users (e.g., friends).

In particular, we want to investigate the following research questions:

(1) How are registration processes of OSNs typically modeled?
(2) Which information is generally needed to create a profile in an OSN?
(3) Which attack scenarios can occur based on the data attributes in OSN registration processes?

The first question (1) will investigate how registration processes are structured in OSNs and if there are differences between OSNs of different domains (e.g., business, leisure, research). This will further support the understanding of processes in OSNs and how online registration is typically designed. With the second question (2), we investigate which minimum data requirements exist to create OSN profiles. This information can be valuable for prospective users having privacy and security concerns for deciding whether or not to register in OSNs. The last question (3) analyzes which threats or attacks may occur due to the sharing of personal data.

The methodology is outlined as follows. First, we investigate the processes and data use in OSN registration processes. Therefore, we select eleven popular OSNs. In order to identify the structure of registration processes of OSNs, we create and register an avatar and further investigate the process and the information that is required during the registration process. In addition, we examine how existing OSN profiles can be used during the registration process in another OSN. Further we investigate which data attributes are interesting for malicious actors and which attack can occur in which OSN due to declaration of data in the examined registration processes. Based on the results from the analysis, we derive two aggregated registration processes. Due to page limitations we only focus on the reference process model based on all data fields that must be specified or are an optional field of at least fifty percent of all registrations. Business process modeling can be used to analyze security measures (cmp. [14]).

The analysis of the eleven OSN registration processes was conducted between November 17th and 21st, 2015. OSN and their registration processes might have changed since then the analysis results provide a still relevant picture for the current state and future development of OSNs.

The results of this paper can contribute to foster and deepen the understanding of the design of registration processes in OSNs, provide an overview on which mandatory or optional data can be entered by users who want to register a profile in an OSN, simulate OSN registration processes using the two derived processes, and replicate or reuse processes for further privacy and security investigations.

2 METHODOLOGY

As outlined in Figure 1, the methodology consisted of three steps. The first step *Selection of OSNs* focused on identification and selection of OSNs according the defined characteristics in the study. The second step, *Avatar Creation*, established an avatar and all data attributes required (e.g., name, username, email). Furthermore, the step *Investigation of OSN Registration Processes* focused on the privacy-aware data assessment of selected OSNs using the avatar. In the last step *Investigating Potential Threats and Attacks* potential attack scenarios (derived by literature) are investigated based on the attributes found in the previous step. The attacker model in this paper is based on information that is provided (sometimes carelessly) by the users in OSNs and later retrieved by attackers.

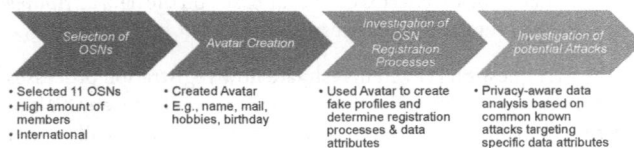

Figure 1: Methodology

3 BACKGROUND

In recent years, OSNs have gained importance and the number of users having an OSN account has increased dramatically as shown in [4, 5, 15].

During the registration process of an OSN, user have to declare personal information (further known as data attributes on e.g., name, birthday, city, profession). This can establish a social identity that requires management. For example in [16], the management of the identities itself is discussed focusing also on e.g., the control of data of an identity or ways to get in contact or restriction of profile views. In this paper, we focus only on the process when an identity is created and first data attributes specified for the social identity.

The use and sharing of personal information in OSNs has been investigated in literature. For example [17] discovered that there are design conflicts between the security and privacy goals and the traditional goals of OSNs such as usability and sociability. Gross and Acquisti [8] show that most users of online social networks do not worry about their privacy and provide their personal information carelessly. For instance, exceedingly few users change their default privacy settings, therefore the standard-visibility of the profile is selected which purpose is to maximize the visibility. This creates physical and cyber risks such as stalking social security numbers, stealing identities (identity theft) or creating digital dossiers of the behavior of the user [12].

Moreover [11] and [13] have found that users are not aware of third-party advertisers, data aggregators, external applications and users on the OSN which are not friends having access to private information. External actions while logged into an OSN are tracked and can be used for marketing purposes and more. For example, [11] discovers the role of third party domains in aggregating user related data. Privacy protection for future OSNs has been identified e.g. the minimum and maximum of information which have to be specified for a particular set of interactions must be declared.

4 RESULTS

This paper focused on the investigation of registration processes of OSNs. We examined which information is required (or optional) to create a profile, how profiles can be reused and how data attributes can be misused for attacks. Based on the research questions in Section 1 we came to the following principle findings.

How are registration processes of OSNs typically modeled? We constructed two registration processes illustrating a *reference process model* and aggregated process model for OSN registration. The *reference process model* represents the common behavior of the 11 individual registration processes (Facebook, Twitter, Google+, Instagram, Habbo, Hi5, Twoo, Xing, LinkedIn, Academia.edu and ResearchGate). If we consider the smallest common denominator of the individual OSN registration processes with respect to the data attributes (which would contain the data which has to be specified or is an optional field in all processes), this would comprise only the *password* and *e-mail* attributes. The resulting reference process model would consist of only one step, i.e., a process activity *input personal information*. Thus the definition of considered data attributes is extended to all data attributes that are mandatory or optional in the registration processes of at least **fifty percent** of all analyzed OSNs. As a result, the *first name, last name, e-mail*

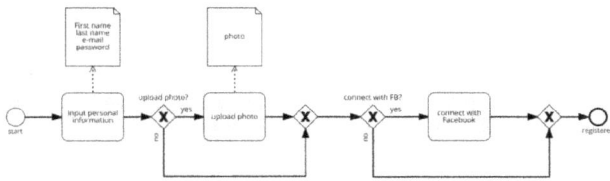

Figure 2: Reference OSN Registration Process Model for Mandatory and Optional Data Attributes in at least 50 percent of the Individual Registration Processes (in BPMN using Signavio)

Table 1: Assessing Data Attributes that can be misused for Attacks (Excerpt)

	Phishing [2, 6, 7, 10]	Profile Cloning [2, 6, 7]	Fake Profiles [6, 8]	Face Recognition [2, 6, 8]
Public profile	✓	✓	✓	
Account Username	✓			
E-Mail	✓			
Birthday	✓			
Photographs				✓
Passwords	✓			
Friendslist		✓	✓	
Credit Card Data	✓			
PIN	✓			
TAN	✓			

✓... utilized data for threat

Public profile: name, location and contact information, educational and employment history, personal preferences, interests and profile photo

and *password* are mandatory fields and are shown in Figure 2. In addition, *connect the profile with Facebook* and *upload a photo* were also optional in most selected OSNs.

Which information is generally necessary to create a profile in an OSN?. We investigated which personal data has to be declared during the registration processes OSNs. The only data which has to be specified in every registration process is the password and e-mail. The first name and last name have to be declared in more than fifty percent of the OSNs, the birthday and gender in exactly half of the selected networks. Uploading a photo or connect the profile with an e-mail account is mostly optional.

Which attack scenarios can occur based on the data attributes in OSN registration processes? Based on a literature review, we analyzed several attacks, i.e. phishing, profile cloning, fake profiles, face recognition (see Table 1) as potential attack scenarios (based on e.g., [2, 6–8, 10]). Luckily, we found that most personal information is optional to specify within the OSN registration processes. However, this does not signify that most users will or will not specify this information during registration. Further analysis would be required. It can be seen for example that many data attributes in OSNs are mandatory or optional. Hence, more publicly specified information can be misused by others and can lead to potential attacks (e.g., fake profiles).

Interpretation of Findings. The most investigated OSNs demand rights of personal information and data of the user during the registration process. The current state of registrations shows that there are possible improvements for the security of the personal information of users. Future OSNs should focus on user privacy and security. For instance, [3] show an approach of an OSN where the user defines the policy over access to private data instead of the OSN by using attribute-based encryption. We are currently not aware of any commercial OSNs using such approaches. One reason could be that personal information is extremely valuable for marketing purposes. For this reason it could be crucial to minimize sharing personal information in the internet to protect the data against third party applications (or use adequate OSN settings).

Finally, it will always depend on the user and which information he/she will share with others in an OSN. The behavior of this changes over time such as shown in [1]. As this paper is mostly about sharing and handling personal information, we feel it is our duty to refer to recommendations on how to handle personal information carefully. We found that recommendations given in [6] help to minimize the usage of personal information and to prevent misuse in general.

REFERENCES

[1] Alessandro Acquisti, Laura Brandimarte, and George Loewenstein. 2015. Privacy and human behavior in the age of information. *Science* 347, 6221 (Jan. 2015), 509–514. https://doi.org/10.1126/science.aaa1465

[2] Abdullah Al Hasib. 2009. Threats of online social networks. *IJCSNS International Journal of Computer Science and Network Security* 9, 11 (2009), 288–93.

[3] Randy Baden, Adam Bender, Neil Spring, Bobby Bhattacharjee, and Daniel Starin. 2009. Persona: an online social network with user-defined privacy. In *ACM SIGCOMM Computer Communication Review*, Vol. 39. ACM, 135–146.

[4] Danah M. Boyd and Nicole B. Ellison. 2007. Social Network Sites: Definition, History, and Scholarship. *Journal of computer-mediated communication* 13, 1 (2007), 210–230. https://doi.org/10.1111/j.1083-6101.2007.00393.x

[5] Maeve Duggan, Nicole B Ellison, Cliff Lampe, Amanda Lenhart, and Mary Madden. 2015. Social media update 2014. *Pew Research Center* 9 (2015).

[6] Michael Fire, Roy Goldschmidt, and Yuval Elovici. 2014. Online social networks: threats and solutions. *IEEE Comm. Surveys Tutorials* 16, 4 (2014), 2019–2036.

[7] Hongyu Gao, Jun Hu, Tuo Huang, Jingnan Wang, and Yan Chen. 2011. Security issues in online social networks. *IEEE Internet Computing* 15, 4 (2011), 56–63.

[8] Ralph Gross and Alessandro Acquisti. 2005. Information Revelation and Privacy in Online Social Networks. In *Proceedings of the 2005 ACM Workshop on Privacy in the Electronic Society (WPES '05)*. ACM, New York, NY, USA, 71–80.

[9] Tom N Jagatic, Nathaniel A Johnson, Markus Jakobsson, and Filippo Menczer. 2007. Social phishing. *Commun. ACM* 50, 10 (2007), 94–100.

[10] Prateek Joshi and C-C Jay Kuo. 2011. Security and privacy in online social networks: A survey. In *2011 IEEE Int. Conf. on Multimedia and Expo.* IEEE, 1–6.

[11] Balachander Krishnamurthy and Craig E. Wills. 2008. Characterizing Privacy in Online Social Networks. In *Proceedings of the First Workshop on Online Social Networks (WOSN '08)*. ACM, New York, NY, USA, 37–42.

[12] Katharina Krombholz, Heidelinde Hobel, Markus Huber, and Edgar Weippl. 2015. Advanced social engineering attacks. *Journal of Information Security and Applications* 22 (2015), 113 – 122.

[13] Katharina Krombholz, Dieter Merkl, and Edgar Weippl. 2012. Fake identities in social media: A case study on the sustainability of the facebook business model. *Journal of Service Science Research* 4, 2 (2012), 175–212.

[14] Maria Leitner and Stefanie Rinderle-Ma. 2014. A systematic review on security in Process-Aware Information Systems – Constitution, challenges, and future directions. *Information and Software Technology* 56, 3 (March 2014), 273–293.

[15] Alan Mislove, Hema Swetha Koppula, Krishna P Gummadi, Peter Druschel, and Bobby Bhattacharjee. 2008. Growth of the flickr social network. In *Proceedings of the first workshop on Online social networks*. ACM, 25–30.

[16] Moritz Riesner, Michael Netter, and Günther Pernul. 2013. Analyzing settings for social identity management on Social Networking Sites: Classification, current state, and proposed developments. *Inf. Sec. Technical Report* 17, 4 (May 2013), 185–198.

[17] Chi Zhang, Jinyuan Sun, Xiaoyan Zhu, and Yuguang Fang. 2010. Privacy and security for online social networks: challenges and opportunities. *IEEE Network* 24, 4 (2010), 13–18.

CSP & Co. Can Save Us from a Rogue Cross-Origin Storage Browser Network! But for How Long?

Juan D. Parra Rodriguez
University of Passau
dp@sec.uni-passau.de

Joachim Posegga
University of Passau
jp@sec.uni-passau.de

ABSTRACT

We introduce a new browser abuse scenario where an attacker uses local storage capabilities without the website's visitor knowledge to create a network of browsers for persistent storage and distribution of arbitrary data. We describe how security-aware users can use mechanisms such as the Content Security Policy (CSP), sandboxing, and third-party tracking protection, i.e., CSP & Company, to limit the network's effectiveness. From another point of view, we also show that the upcoming Suborigin standard can inadvertently thwart existing countermeasures, if it is adopted.

CCS CONCEPTS

• **Security and privacy** → **Browser security**; • **Networks** → **Web protocol security**;

KEYWORDS

Web Security; WebRTC; PostMessage; Browser Security; Content Security Policy; Suborigins; Parasitic Computing

ACM Reference Format:
Juan D. Parra Rodriguez and Joachim Posegga. 2018. CSP & Co. Can Save Us from a Rogue Cross-Origin Storage Browser Network! But for How Long?. In *CODASPY '18: Eighth ACM Conference on Data and Application Security and Privacy, March 19–21, 2018, Tempe, AZ, USA.* ACM, New York, NY, USA, 3 pages. https://doi.org/10.1145/3176258.3176951

1 INTRODUCTION

Browsers provide access to computational resources such as local storage, network and processing power. This can be helpful for several applications; however, rogue developers can also abuse browser's resources, e.g., for mining crypto-currencies in the browser (crypto-jacking). Meanwhile, the Web security community is engaged in an arms race against attackers exploiting data or session related vulnerabilities such as cross-site scripting (XSS), therefore leaving the browser resource abuse problem unattended.

We discuss how malicious third-party code can make its way into honest Web applications and force their visitor's browsers to join a browser network to store and distribute arbitrary data without letting the browser's user know. Also, we show that some CSP directives, and other mechanisms, can be effective to thwart the browser network attack, even though their rationale protects

against other attacks. Further, countermeasures presented are analyzed from the perspective of the two potential victims of a browser resource attack, namely the browser's user visiting the website, and the website (developer or administrator). From another point of view, we show that existing countermeasures are threatened by upcoming standards and can be reversed as their attacker model does not include browser resource abuse scenarios.

2 EXTERNAL SCRIPTS ON THE WEB

Websites commonly instruct the browser to fetch resources from different servers across the Internet. Thus, to cope with various security threats, the browser has an **Origin-based security model** which isolates resources. In most cases, an important factor is whether the code is served by a different Origin[1] than the site visited by the user. For brevity, we call this an *external resource*.

Nonetheless, in the Origin-based security model *external resources* **can inherit the Origin from the page including them** depending on how the resources are included. As shown by rows 1 and 2 of Table 1, sites including external resources with a script tag share their Origin with the resource. Conversely, Iframes obtain their Origin from their source location, i.e., rows 3 and 4 of Table 1, regardless of the Origin of the website including them.

Also, Table 1 shows the Origin assigned to the resource, which determines the Local Storage instance available for it. For example, the Iframe of row number 4 of Table 1 obtains a different storage object than the site including it. On the contrary, scripts included as shown by rows 1, 2 and 3 share the Local Storage instance with the site including them.

Leaving aside how external scripts are executed, **external code can go rogue and abuse a website visitor**. In our case, it is important to mention that abusive external code can be included in a website by a developer either intentionally or unintentionally. Some sites may intentionally sacrifice their reputation by using "unconventional" means to earn money, e.g., crypto-jacking. However, popular sites are not keen to destroy their reputation by intentionally abusing browsers. All in all, there are a number of ways leading to abusive code execution because developers include external code without being aware of the consequences; for example, through CMS widgets[2], advertisements, or JavaScript libraries.

---

[1] An Origin can be seen as a tuple containing the protocol, host and port for a particular website; for example, the origin for https://a.com/home/ the tuple (https, a.com, 80)
[2] Wordpress removed a plugin from their marketplace, as it abused thousands of browsers to do crypto-jacking without the website's owners and browser's users knowledge. For more information see https://www.wordfence.com/blog/2017/11/wordpress-plugin-banned-crypto-mining/

Row No.	Inclusion code from visited site: code from Origin https://a.com	Same Origin as the visited site	Local Storage Instance
1	`<script src="https://a.com/script.js" ... >`	yes	https://a.com (shared)
2	`<script src="https://b.com/script.js" ... >`	yes	https://a.com (shared)
3	`<iframe src="https://a.com/script.js" >`	yes	https://a.com (shared)
4	`<iframe src="https://b.com/script.js" >`	no	https://b.com (not shared)

Table 1: External resource inclusion (from a site hosted by https://a.com), its Origin and Local Storage

3 THE ATTACK

In addition to inadvertently including malicious external code, developers can introduce XSS vulnerabilities allowing the execution of malicious scripts abusing local storage, i.e., *Abusive Scripts*.

As shown by row 4 in Table 1, the **Origin-based security model** introduced in Section 2 provides Iframes loaded from a different Origin with a Local Storage instance in a different Origin as the site including them. Although this Local Storage separation is beneficial for data isolation, it can be abused when a website includes n Iframes from different Origins consuming up to n times the Local Storage quota (see Figure 1). This approach has already been used to fill the user's disk[3].

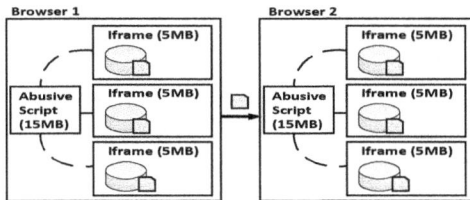

Figure 1: Rogue Storage Network (using 30 MB)

This way of bypassing the storage quota can be extended by using a cross-Origin **inter-window messaging** mechanism, i.e., postMessage represented by dotted lines. This lets each Iframe communicate with the parent window (Abusive Script) allowing it to access their Local Storage to create a database with n frames, and therefore using n times the Iframe quota.

Furthermore, an attacker can coerce browsers to share information from Local Storage with other browsers executing the Abusive Script without the user's knowledge through **inter-browser messaging communication**, i.e., WebRTC Data Channels. In the case of WebRTC, the Same Origin Policy is not applicable when browsers interact with each other, so an attacker can connect browsers he controls through different sites in a single cross-Origin browser network.

We have previously evaluated the feasibility of the browser network through several experiments with real-life browsers and automation tools in a technical report [1]. We analyzed how visitor return rates and time between visits affect availability of the information distributed across browsers. Further, we also analyzed the amount of traffic exchanged between browsers and servers to conclude that network overhead for servers is significantly less than for browsers.

---
[3]http://www.bbc.com/news/technology-21628622

4 ATTACKER MODEL

Before defining countermeasures, we analyze possible attack scenarios. Figure 2 depicts how an attacker can use a site (marked with X) to deliver malicious code while making the Origin-based isolation implemented by browsers explicit.

The **first scenario** shows an attacker compromising the website visited by the user. This scenario takes place when the attacker embeds the Abusive Script directly within the Origin of the visited site. This can, for example, happen when an attacker controls a third-party library included using the script tag or when an attacker exploits an XSS bug. The **second and third scenario** show when the Abusive Script included in a "safe" manner, i.e., different Origin than the website being visited. These cases happen when the external content is included in an Iframe, e.g., advertisements. The main difference between attack scenario 2 and 3 is that an attacker could make a site host the Abusive Script or the Iframes performing storage. In practice the attacker can do both in one Origin, but we separate them for the sake of clarity in relation to the possible countermeasures.

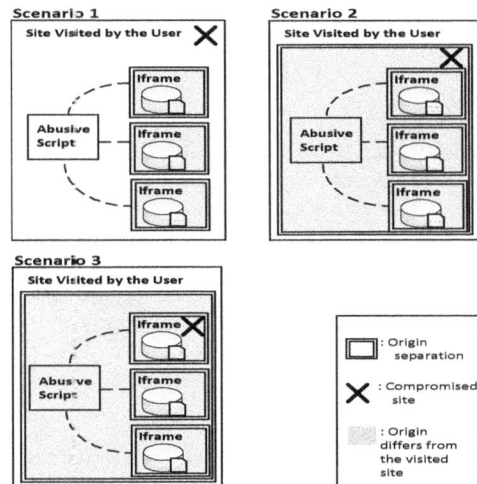

Figure 2: Scenarios based on compromised sites and Origin separations

5 COUNTERMEASURES

The victim most affected by browser resource attacks is the browser's user. However, sites used to host Abusive Scripts without their knowledge can be considered victims of the attack also as their reputation could suffer. Thus, we split countermeasures based on who can take action (browser's user or website developers); further, for each actor deploying a countermeasure, we reference for which attack scenarios from Figure 2 they are protected.

Users can protect themselves against all attack scenarios if they enable their browser's third-party tracking protection. This protects the user's privacy from advertisements by blocking persistence APIs for JavaScript running in Origins different from the site loaded. This removes any persistent storage mechanism available for resources outside of the visited website's Origin, i.e. row number 4 on Table 1. Practically speaking, this measure denies local storage access to any resource with gray background in Figure 2.

Website's developers can use HTTP response headers or HTML keywords for security directives when they include external resources. For instance, the `sandobx` HTML keyword ensures that an Iframe is not allowed to execute JavaScript, unless the `allow-scripts` keyword is used. Moreover, even if developers use the `allow-scripts` keyword, sand-boxed Iframes cannot use their Local Storage instance because each Iframe gets assigned to a random, invalid, origin. As a result, all Origin checks fail and prevent the Iframe from using Local Storage or cookies. By including the `sandbox` directive when including the site containing the Abusive Script, developers can prevent the second and third attack scenarios.

Developers can use the `script-src` and `frame-src` CSP directives in the HTTP response headers to specify which scripts or frames are loaded by a particular site. Thus, a restrictive policy allowing only secure scripts makes it impossible for the attacker to execute his Abusive Script or the storage Frame functionality. If this countermeasure is properly implemented, it would protect the site against the first and second attack scenarios. Although it is less likely, an attacker compromising a website to host the Iframe source (Local Storage part) would not be prevented by the `script-src` directive from including this compromised script in another Origin, i.e., third scenario.

When an attacker has compromised a site and is using it as an Iframe within an Abusive Script, i.e., third scenario, a developer could set the `frame-ancestors` CSP directive in the HTTP response headers to ensure that the site can only be embedded in resources loaded from a list of origins. Therefore, if a security-aware developer specifies a restrictive list of frame ancestors for his site, this would prevent an attacker who has compromised the site from including this particular site as the storage Iframe in the Abusive Script.

6 CONCLUSION

Currently, security-aware users and developers can configure browsers and their websites to avoid being used by a rogue cross-Origin storage network such as the one described in this paper. However, there are three issues that could revert existing advantages. *First*, CSP directives are designed for different purposes than preventing an attack such as the one presented in this paper. For instance, `script-src` and `frame-ancestors` protect against XSS and click-jacking; therefore, there is no guarantee that future countermeasures, e.g., future specifications of CSP, will still protect users against resource abuse attacks. *Second*, the most successful mechanism from CSP, i.e., `script-src`, has faced challenges when

retrofitting existing applications [3]; moreover, most of the CSP policies using script-src are easily circumvented today [2]. *Third*, the browser's third-party tracking protection currently prevents all attack scenarios; however, if the Suborigins[4] specification is adopted, attackers can abuse browsers with less effort than today and overcome the third-party tracking protection. The main problem with the Suborigins specification is that it allows a single Origin to define separate Suborigins. Each Suborigin is provided with a Local Storage instance and inter-window communication capabilities. Therefore, an attacker can increase the number of Iframes used to store information on the browser side without constraints. More to the point, separate Suborigins created from the same Origin are not considered third-party content[5], so the third-party tracking protection would not prevent the attack when Suborigins are used. However, this kind of attack requires a more powerful attacker who can set HTTP response headers.

ACKNOWLEDGMENTS

This research has been supported by the EU under the H2020 AGILE (Adaptive Gateways for dIverse muLtiple Environments), grant agreement number H2020-688088.

REFERENCES

[1] Juan David Parra Rodriguez and Joachim Posegga. 2016. *Abusing Web Browsers for Hidden Content Storage and Distribution*. Technical Report MIP-1603. University of Passau. http://www.fim.uni-passau.de/fileadmin/files/forschung/mip-berichte/MIP_1603.pdf
[2] Lukas Weichselbaum, Michele Spagnuolo, Sebastian Lekies, and Artur Janc. 2016. CSP Is Dead, Long Live CSP! On the Insecurity of Whitelists and the Future of Content Security Policy. In *Proceedings of the 2016 ACM SIGSAC Conference on Computer and Communications Security (CCS '16)*. ACM, New York, NY, USA, 1376–1387. https://doi.org/10.1145/2976749.2978363
[3] Michael Weissbacher, Tobias Lauinger, and William Robertson. 2014. Why is CSP failing? Trends and challenges in CSP adoption. *Lecture Notes in Computer Science (including subseries Lecture Notes in Artificial Intelligence and Lecture Notes in Bioinformatics)* 8688 LNCS (2014), 212–233. https://doi.org/10.1007/978-3-319-11379-1_11

---

[4]https://w3c.github.io/webappsec-suborigins/
[5]https://github.com/w3c/webappsec-suborigins/issues/43

Ɔobɘ Odʇuɔƨɒifou

Why is This Still a Thing?

Christian Collberg
Department of Computer Science
University of Arizona
collberg@gmail.com
http://collberg.cs.arizona.edu

ABSTRACT

Early developments in code obfuscation were chiefly motivated by the needs of Digital Rights Management (DRM) [7]. Other suggested applications included intellectual property protection of software [4] and code diversification to combat the monoculture problem of operating systems [2].

Code obfuscation is typically employed in security scenarios where an adversary is in complete control over a device and the software it contains and can tamper with it at will. We call such situations the *Man-At-The-End* (MATE) [3] scenario. MATE scenarios are the best of all worlds for attackers and, consequently, the worst of all worlds for defenders: Not only do attackers have physical access to a device and can reverse engineer and tamper with it at their leisure, they often have unbounded resources (time, computational power, etc.) to do so. Defenders, on the other hand, are often severely constrained in the types of protective techniques available to them and the amount of overhead they can tolerate.

In other words, there is an asymmetry between the constraints of attackers and defenders. Moreover,

- DRM is becoming less prevalent (songs for sale on the Apple iTunes Store are no longer protected by DRM, for example);
- there are new cryptographically-based obfuscation techniques [1] that promise provably secure obfuscation;
- secure enclaves [5] are making it into commodity hardware, providing a safe haven for security sensitive code; and
- recent advances in program analysis [12] and generic deobfuscation [13] provide algorithms that render current code obfuscation techniques impotent.

Thus, one may reasonably ask the question: "Is Code Obfuscation Still a Thing?"

Somewhat surprisingly, it appears that the answer is yes. In a recent report, Gartner [14] lists 19 companies active in this space (8 of which were founded since 2010) and there are still (in 2017) many papers published on code obfuscation, code de-obfuscation, anti-tamper protection, reverse engineering, and related technologies.

One of the reasons for this resurgence of code obfuscation as a protective technology is that, more and more, we are faced with applications where security-sensitive code needs to run on unsecured

endpoints. In this talk we will show MATE attacks that appear in many novel and unlikely scenarios, including smart cars [6], smart meters [9], mobile applications such as *Snapchat* and smartphone games, Internet of Things applications [8], and ad blockers in web browsers [11]. We will furthermore show novel code obfuscation techniques that increase the workload of attackers [10] and which, at least for a time, purport to restore the symmetry between attackers and defenders.

CCS CONCEPTS

• **Security and privacy** → **Digital rights management**; **Software reverse engineering**; *Malware and its mitigation*; *Hardware attacks and countermeasures*;

KEYWORDS

Software protection, code obfuscation, reverse engineering, Man-At-The-End, diversification, digital rights management, software watermarking, anti-tamper

BIOGRAPHY

Christian Collberg is a Professor in the Department of Computer Science at the University of Arizona. Prior to arriving in Tucson he worked at the University of Auckland, New Zealand, and before that got his Ph.D. from Lund University, Sweden. He has also held a visiting position at the Chinese Academy of Sciences in Beijing, China, and taught at universities in Russia and Belarus.

Dr. Collberg's main research interest is Software Protection, the use of code obfuscation, software watermarking, anti-tamper, and related techniques to protect software that runs on endpoints under the control of an adversary. He is the co-author of the first book on software protection, *Surreptitious Software: Obfuscation, Watermarking, and Tamperproofing for Software Protection*, published in Addison-Wesley's computer security series. It has also been translated into Portuguese and Chinese.

In addition to his security research, Dr. Collberg is an advocate for Reproducibility, Repeatability, and Sharing in Computer Science. He maintains the site FindResearch.org which aims to be the most authoritative and complete catalog of research artifacts (i.e., code and data) related to Computer Science publications.

ACKNOWLEDGMENTS

This work was funded in part by the NSF under grants CNF-1145913 and CNF-1145913.

REFERENCES

[1] Boaz Barak. 2016. Hopes, Fears, and Software Obfuscation. *Commun. ACM* 59, 3 (Feb. 2016), 88–96. https://doi.org/10.1145/2757276

[2] Frederick B. Cohen. 1993. Operating system protection through program evolution. *Computers & Security* 12, 6 (1993), 565–584.

[3] Christian Collberg and Jasvir Nagra. 2009. *Surreptitious Software: Obfuscation, Watermarking, and Tamperproofing for Software Protection.* Addison-Wesley. 816 pages.

[4] Christian S. Collberg and Clark D. Thomborson. 2002. Watermarking, Tamper-Proofing, and Obfuscation-Tools for Software Protection. *IEEE Trans. Software Eng.* 28, 8 (2002), 735–746.

[5] Victor Costan and Srinivas Devadas. 2016. Intel SGX Explained. *IACR Cryptology ePrint Archive* (2016), 86.

[6] European Union Agency for Network and Information Security. 2016. Cyber Security and Resilience of Smart Cars — Good practices and recommendations. (Dec. 2016).

[7] Karl L. Ginter, Victor H. Shear, W. Olin Sibert, Francis J. Spahn, and David M. Van Wie. 1996. US Patent 5,892,900: Systems and methods for secure transaction management and electronic rights protection. (1996).

[8] Shohreh Hosseinzadeh, Sami Hyrynsalmi, and Ville Leppänen. 2016. *Obfuscation and Diversification for Securing the Internet of Things (IoT).* Elsevier, 259–274.

[9] Parks R.C. 2007. Sandia Report: Advanced Metering Infrastructure Security Considerations. (Nov. 2007).

[10] Jon Stephens, Babak Yadegari, Christian Collberg, Saumya Debray, and Carlos Scheidegger. 2018. Probabilistic Obfuscation through Covert Channels. In *3rd IEEE European Symposium on Security and Privacy.*

[11] Grant Storey, Dillon Reisman, Jonathan Mayer, and Arvind Narayanan. 2017. The Future of Ad Blocking: An Analytical Framework and New Techniques. *CoRR* abs/1705.08568 (2017).

[12] Fish Wang and Yan Shoshitaishvili. 2017. Angr - The Next Generation of Binary Analysis. In *SecDev.* IEEE, 8–9.

[13] Babak Yadegari, Brian Johannesmeyer, Ben Whitely, and Saumya Debray. 2015. A Generic Approach to Automatic Deobfuscation of Executable Code. In *IEEE Symposium on Security and Privacy.* IEEE Computer Society, 674–691.

[14] Dionisio Zumerle and Manjunath Bhat. 2017. Market Guide for Application Shielding. (2017).

Access Control Model for Virtual Objects (Shadows) Communication for AWS Internet of Things

Asma Alshehri, James Benson, Farhan Patwa and Ravi Sandhu
Institute for Cyber Security (ICS),
Center for Security and Privacy Enhanced Cloud Computing (C-SPECC), and
Department of Computer Science, University of Texas at San Antonio, San Antonio, Texas, US
{nmt366,james.benson,farhan.patwa,ravi.sandhu}@utsa.edu

ABSTRACT

The concept of Internet of Things (IoT) has received considerable attention and development in recent years. There have been significant studies on access control models for IoT in academia, while companies have already deployed several cloud-enabled IoT platforms. However, there is no consensus on a formal access control model for cloud-enabled IoT. The access-control oriented (ACO) architecture was recently proposed for cloud-enabled IoT, with virtual objects (VOs) and cloud services in the middle layers. Building upon ACO, operational and administrative access control models have been published for virtual object communication in cloud-enabled IoT illustrated by a use case of sensing speeding cars as a running example.

In this paper, we study AWS IoT as a major commercial cloud-IoT platform and investigate its suitability for implementing the afore-mentioned academic models of ACO and VO communication control. While AWS IoT has a notion of digital shadows closely analogous to VOs, it lacks explicit capability for VO communication and thereby for VO communication control. Thus there is a significant mismatch between AWS IoT and these academic models. The principal contribution of this paper is to reconcile this mismatch by showing how to use the mechanisms of AWS IoT to effectively implement VO communication models. To this end, we develop an access control model for virtual objects (shadows) communication in AWS IoT called AWS-IoT-ACMVO. We develop a proof-of-concept implementation of the speeding cars use case in AWS IoT under guidance of this model, and provide selected performance measurements. We conclude with a discussion of possible alternate implementations of this use case in AWS IoT.

KEYWORDS

Security; Access Control; Internet of Things (IoT); AWS IoT; IoT Architecture; Devices; Virtual Objects; ACL; RBAC; ABAC;

ACM Reference Format:
Asma Alshehri, James Benson, Farhan Patwa and Ravi Sandhu. 2018. Access Control Model for Virtual Objects (Shadows) Communication for AWS Internet of Things. In *CODASPY '18: Eighth ACM Conference on Data and* Application Security and Privacy, March 19–21, 2018, Tempe, AZ, USA. ACM, New York, NY, USA, 11 pages. https://doi.org/10.1145/3176258.3176328

1 INTRODUCTION

The Internet of Things (IoT) raises new security challenges, which require significant revisions and enhancements of existing security solutions, including access control systems. Recently an access-control oriented architecture (ACO) [2] for cloud-enabled IoT has been developed, which includes four layers: an object layer, a virtual object (VO) layer, a cloud services layer, and an application layer (see Section 2.1). The ACO recognizes the need for communication control within each layer and across adjacent layers, as well as the need for data access control at the cloud services and application layers. Multiple and diverse access control models are required at various points in this architecture, which must collectively enforce over-arching access control policies reflecting the complexity of cloud-enabled IoT. Towards this end, a set of access control models for VO communications has been published [3], referred to as ACO-IoT-ACMsVO. These models are developed in two layers: operational models and administrative models. Also, the style of communication among VO is based upon publish/subscribe topic-based communication interaction scheme. The ACO-IoT-ACMsVO models are illustrated by a use case of sensing speeding cars as a running example [3] which we will utilize in this paper (see Section 2.2).

The principal goal of this paper is to reconcile the afore-mentioned academic models with a major commercial cloud-IoT platform, viz., AWS IoT. While AWS IoT has a notion of digital shadows closely analogous to VOs, it lacks explicit capability for VO communication and thereby for VO communication control. Thus, there is a significant mismatch between AWS IoT and these academic models. Nevertheless, as we will show, it is possible to use AWS IoT mechanisms to effectively realize and control VO communications. This demonstrates on one hand that academic models developed independent of AWS IoT can be enforced using this commercially significant platform. It also suggests enhancements to AWS IoT that would be beneficial to facilitate such enforcement. We believe that in the rapidly developing ecosystems of cloud, IoT and their intersection, it is crucial to place academic work within major industry developments. This is the primary motivation for this research.

The rest of the paper is organized as follows. First, we review the ACO architecture for cloud-enabled IoT, the published ACO-IoT-ACMsVO [3] access control models for VO communication within ACO, and the general access control model for AWS IoT called AWS-IoTAC [5] in Section 2. Then, within AWS IoT, we develop an access control model for virtual object communication (AWS-IoT-ACMVO)

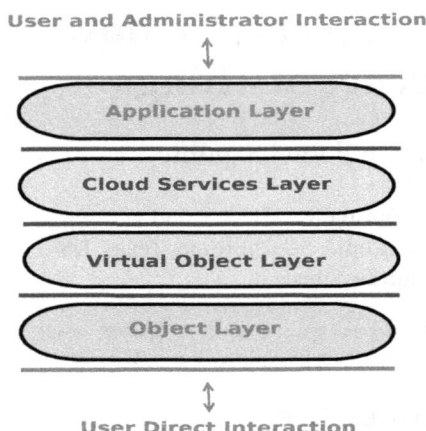

Figure 1: ACO Architecture for Cloud-Enabled IoT

in Section 3. Section 4 discusses the use case of ACO-IoT-ACMsVO within the AWS-IoT-ACMVO model. Section 5 discusses proof-of-concept implementations of the use case in two scenarios in AWS IoT platform. Selected performance aspects of our implementation are described in Section 6. A discussion of some issues of AWS IoT and possible enhancements are explained in Section 7. Finally, Section 8 concludes the paper.

2 BACKGROUND

2.1 ACO Architecture

The Access Control Oriented (ACO) Architecture for IoT was proposed in [2], consistent with various published IoT architectures [1, 6, 7, 9–14]. ACO architecture comprises four layers: an object layer, a virtual object layer, a cloud services layer, and an application layer, as shown in Figure 1. We briefly discuss each layer below.

The object layer comprises heterogeneous physical objects such as sensors, actuators, cameras, cellphones, etc. Users can directly communicate with objects by pressing a button, changing a device, powering on an object, etc. Also, objects can communicate directly to each other through communication technologies, or indirectly through virtual objects.

A virtual object represents the persistent current status of a physical object, when the two are connected. Otherwise, a virtual object could represent the last received state, desired future state, or both. A virtual object can have a subset of a physical object's services, all of a physical object's services, or a subset of a physical object's services. Virtual objects can uniformly communicate with each other regardless of heterogeneity and locality in the object layer. Virtual to physical object association can be one-to-one, many-to-one, one-to-many, or many-to-one [2].

The cloud services layer assists in storing and processing the collected data. This data can be used intelligently for smart monitoring and actuation, and it can be visualized in ways that are more meaningful for users. Thus, policymakers (or administrators) can utilize the visualized data to help them to modify or add policies that are kept in the cloud, so the communication and access between applications and objects are managed through the cloud. In

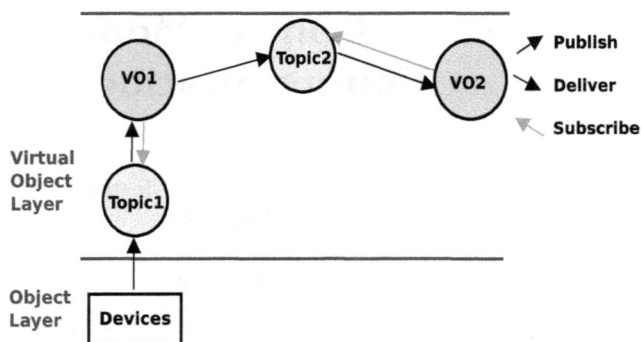

Figure 2: The Publish/Subscribe Topic-Based Scheme in the ACO-IoT-ACMsVO

addition, multiple IoT clouds can also communicate with each other, ranging from only providing services and information at a local level to collaborating with other connected IoTs in order to share information at a broad level and pursue common goals.

The application layer is the topmost layer of the proposed ACO IoT architecture and offers an interface through which users can easily communicate with objects and visualize the analyzed information. Administrators can also interact with applications to generate policies or to update/add policies based on the obtained information. Moreover, configuring and managing the communication of objects and virtual objects is organized by administrators through applications. General users and administrators can remotely communicate with IoT objects and virtual objects only through applications.

2.2 Access Control Models for VO Communication in Cloud-Enabled IoT

The ACO architecture emphasizes the need for communication control and data access control within and across ACO layers [2]. One of the communication points that needs to be controlled is virtual object communication. Alshehri and Sandhu used the ACO architecture for IoT to propose access control models for virtual object communication (ACO-IoT-ACMsVO) [3]. The developed access control models are in two layers: operational models and administrative models. The current dominant access control models, viz., access control lists (ACLs), capability lists, and role-based access control (RBAC), are formally defined in both operational and administrative models for VO communication. Also, attribute-based access control (ABAC) models are proposed, because ABAC encompasses the benefits of previous traditional models, as well as brings new features appropriate for dynamic and open environments such as IoT.

The ACO-IoT-ACMsVO models are developed utilizing publish/subscribe communication interaction scheme. This scheme is appropriate for large-scale distributed interactions such as the IoT. The basic implementation style of publish/subscribe paradigm is topic-based scheme. The topic-based scheme is comparable to the idea of groups, where producers (publishers) publish data to a topic and consumers (subscribers) become members of a topic (a group) [4, 8]. Figure 2 shows the general idea of publish/subscribe topic-based scheme that is used in ACO-IoT-ACMsVO.

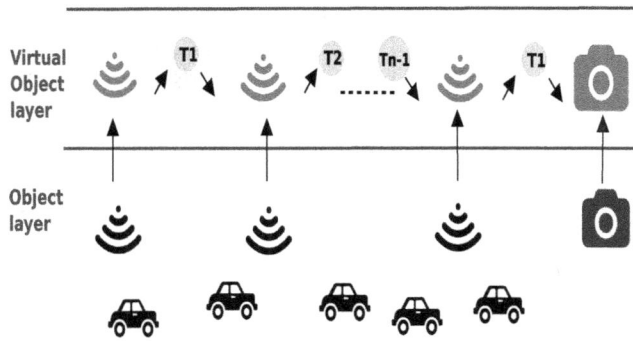

Figure 3: The Sensing Speeding Cars Use Case within ACO Architecture [3]

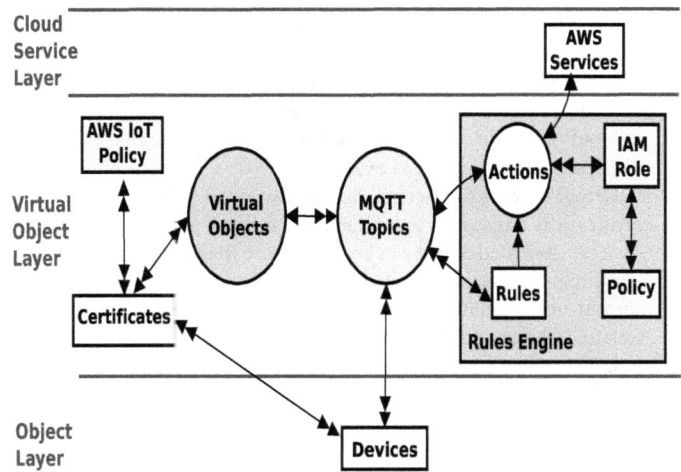

Figure 4: The Components of AWS-IoT-ACMVO

The operational AC models specified in [3] focus in placing the control on both VO side and topic (T) side to authorize VO to VO communications via topics. In other words, the operational AC models address the following questions. Which VOs are allowed to publish or send a subscription request to a topic? Which VOs should a topic forward data to? Which topic should VOs publish to or send a subscription request to? Which topics should VOs receive data from? This dual scheme permits unauthorized actions to be denied at the earliest possible moment, rather than postponing the decisions until later. Therefore, the decision of the VO communication in Figure 2 will be upon both of VO and T access control list and capability list (ACL-Cap Operational Model) or upon both of VO and T attributes (ABAC Operational Model).

A use case of sensing speeding cars is employed in [3] as a running example. Figure 3 shows a simplified picture of the employed use case. One car is recognized to be speeding if two sensors within a specified distance sense the speed to be over limit, and a camera will report pictures of the over-limit cars. Physical sensors and the camera identify cars by attached RFIDs and push collected data (e.g. RFID and Speed) to their virtual objects where more powerful computations and communication could happen. The use case assumes that sensors can only communicate within the virtual object layer, and they cannot communication directly with each other.

2.3 The General Access Control Model for AWS-IoT (AWS-IoTAC)

Bhatt et al [5] study AWS IoT as a major commercial cloud-IoT platform, and develop a formal access control model for AWS-IoT called AWS-IoTAC. This access control model is an extension of AWS access control (AWSAC) model previously developed by Zhang et al [15] for AWS access control in general.

AWS-IoTAC comprises all the components and relations of AWSAC with modified or extra set of components and relations related to the AWS IoT service. The main component of AWSAC are Accounts (A), Users (U), Groups (G), Roles (R), Services (S), Object Types (OT), and Operations (OP). The additional components in AWS-IoTAC, which are related to AWS IoT service, are Certs (C), IoT Objects (IO), IoT Operations (IOP), Rules (Ru), Virtual Permission Assignment (VPA), and Devices (D). The functionality of these entities and their relationship to each other is formally described in [5].

3 THE AWS-IOT-ACMVO MODEL FOR AWS IOT SHADOWS COMMUNICATION

In this section, based on our extensive exploration of AWS IoT platform, its documentation, and our implemented use cases, we propose an access control model for virtual objects (shadows) communication called AWS-IoT-ACMVO as an abstracted view of AWS IoT capabilities. Figure 4 shows the major components of this model, viz., certificates, AWS IoT policies, virtual objects (device shadows), Message Queuing Telemetry Transport (MQTT) topics, and rules engine and its action. The details of their functionalities are discussed below.

AWS IoT uses X.509 certificates as an identity credential for devices authentication [5]. Certificates can be either an AWS IoT generated certificate or a certificate signed by a AWS IoT registered external certification authority. Generally, one certificate can be given to many **devices**, but it is recommended that each device has a unique certificate to enable fine-grained device management. Figure 4 shows that each certificate can be given to more than one device, and each device can have multiple certificates (the arrow with double end means a multiplicity). However, every time a device connects it can only activate one certificate.

Once a certificate is generated, there are two AWS IoT entities that need to be attached to the certificate in order to authenticate and authorize AWS IoT devices, which desire to communicate with virtual objects (device shadows), viz., **AWS IoT policy** and **virtual objects**. An AWS IoT policy is a JSON document that is attached to a certificate for authorization purpose. It comprises one or more policy statements, each of which specifies effect, action, resources, and optional condition. An action is an operation that can be granted or denied to a resource as determined by the effect value. Actions can be MQTT policy actions or thing shadow policy actions. The MQTT policy actions are the operations that deal with connecting, sending, or receiving data, which are iot:Connect, iot:Publish, iot:Subscribe, and iot:Receive. On the other hand, thing shadow policy actions deal with permissions to handle virtual objects (device shadows), which are iot:DeleteThingShadow, iot:GetThingShadow, and iot:UpdateThingShadow. Figure 4 shows that each AWS IoT policy can be attached to more than one certificate, and each certificate can attach multiple AWS IoT policies. Generally, the AWS IoT policy is attached to a certificate to authorize any kind of actions (e.g. iot:Publish and iot:GetThingShadow) to devices that hold that certificate (and its private key).

Virtual objects (device shadows) also need to be attached to a certificate as a resource that a device is fully or partially authorized to access. A virtual object can be given more than one certificate, and a certificate can attach to more than one device. Figure 4 shows the many-to-many relationship between certificates and virtual objects. A virtual object is also a JSON document that stores information about the current state of a connected device and the desired future state of the connected device (there is no recent or historical state). One of the benefits of the device shadow is that its information can be used to set or get the state of its device, even if the device is not connected. In general, a device that holds a certificate with attached policies and virtual objects has the rights to communicate and access to the attached virtual objects (one virtual object at each connection) based on the attached policies.

In AWS IoT, applications cannot directly update or retrieve data of devices. Virtual objects in AWS work as an intermediate point of communication among applications and physical devices. The only way for applications or devices to interact with a virtual object is to communicate with its **MQTT topics**. In other words, MQTT topics of a virtual object allow applications and devices to get, update, or delete the state information of the virtual object (device shadow) by publishing or subscribing to its MQTT topics. The name of each MQTT topic begin with $aws/things/thingName/shadow/\#$, where the thingName is the name of a virtual object, and the symbol \# could be one of the thingName MQTT topics that can be used to interact with the thingName. There are reserved thingName MQTT topics for each virtual object that can be used to publish or subscribe to the virtual object. In order to send a request to a thingName (a virtual object), we only can use /update, /get, or /delete as thingName MQTT topics of that thingName. While /update/accepted, /update/reject, /update/delta, /update/documents, /get/accepted, /get/rejected, /delete/accepted, and /delete/rejected MQTT topics are used by the thingName itself to publish an acknowledgement about accepting or rejecting the received request. Generally, AWS IoT service generates reserved MQTT topics for each created virtual object. The reserved MQTT topics is the only way to communicate with the created virtual object. Figure 4 shows that each virtual object has specific reserved MQTT topics, and each reserved MQTT topic is only related to one virtual object. Moreover, each device can communicate with more than one MQTT topic as long as it has an authorized certificate, and each MQTT topic can be used by more than one device if devices are authorized.

A powerful mechanism in AWS IoT is that a message sent to an MQTT topic can be recognized and analyzed by a rule. **Rules** provide processing for the arrived messages to MQTT topics and enable interactions with various AWS services. A rule consists of a rule name, optional description, SQL statement, SQL version, and one or more actions. The SQL statement is used to filter received messages to MQTT topics, and then the rule engine forwards it to AWS services or republishes it to other MQTT topics by using the action field specified in the rule. There are fixed AWS actions that

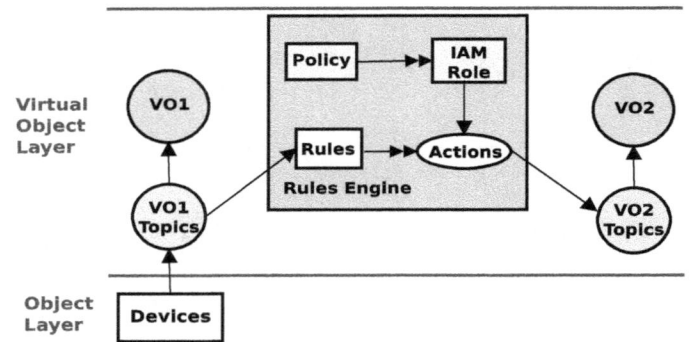

Figure 5: The Rules Engine as a Communication Channel in AWS-IoT-ACMVO

can be selected, such as inserting a message into a DynamoDB table, invoking a Lambda function, and republishing messages to AWS IoT topics. Thus, rules that are attached to MQTT topics provide ways for virtual objects to interact with AWS services or republish the received messages to other MQTT topics (reserved or unreserved). Figure 4 shows that each rule can be triggered by more than one topic, and each topic can trigger more than one rule. Also, when a rule is triggered, one or multiple actions can be executed.

When rules forward the published messages to another AWS service, such as AWS Lambda, the authorization to access the other service and the actions of other service can be controlled via AWS identity and access management **(IAM) role**. Each IAM role is attached with at least one **policy** that grants permissions to access resources specified in the action of the rule or to control actions toward the received data. For example, when an Amazon SNS rule is created, an IAM role will be attached to that SNS rule to authorize access to SNS resources. The attached role will have policies that allow actions (e.g. sns:Publish) toward specific resources in Amazon SNS. Similarly, when a lambda rule is created, an IAM role will be attached to the lambda function. This attached IAM role will have policies that authorize actions (e.g. iot:Publish, iot:GetThingShadow) toward specific resources in AWS Lambda. Thus, we can see that IAM role and its attached policies are a part of the AWS IoT rule definition to control actions. Figure 4 shows that each action of a rule can only attach one IAM role, but each IAM role can be used by many rule actions. Also, one IAM role can attach many policies, and one policy can be attached to many IAM roles.

4 ISSUES IN ENFORCING ACO-IOT-ACMSVO WITHIN AWS-IOT-ACMVO

AWS IoT does not support direct communication among VOs, because a VO is only allowed to communicate directly with its reserved topics. The AWS-IoT-ACMVO model is one way to effect VOs communication via rules within AWS IoT. AWS-IoT-ACMVO keeps the transient data within the virtual object layer without persistent storage, while only data about actual speeding cars is propagated to the higher layers. Thus, the privacy of data can be preserved. All components of VOs communication that contribute in this communication are shown in Figure 4. Figure 5 show how

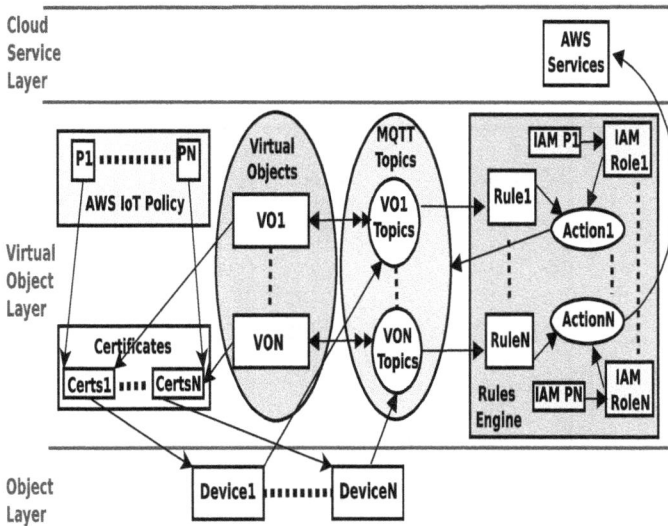

Figure 6: The Sensing Speeding Cars Use Case within AWS-IoT-ACMVO

the rules engine of AWS IoT serves as a communication channel between VOs in the AWS-IoT-ACMVO model. The ACO-IoT-ACMsVO academic model assumes the communication regime shown in Figure 2 where the communication channel between two VOs is a shared topic to which VO1 publishes and VO2 subscribes. The rules engine enables a similar effect to be achieved in AWS IoT as shown in Figure 5.

The control points to authorize VOs communication via topics in ACO-IoT-ACMsVO is placed on both VO side and topic (T) side [3]. For example, in case of ACL-Cap operational model, a VO can have a right to publish to a topic only if the topic in the capability list of the VO and the VO is in the access control list of T. In case of the ABAC operational model, a publish permission will be authorized if the topic is within VO-Publish attribute values and the VO is within T-Publish attribute values. The subscription right is similarly authorized on both sides.

In case of AWS-IoT-ACMVO, the control point to authorize reserved topics of a VO to communicate with other reserved topics of another VO is placed in rules engine. For example, when a data arrived to a reserved topic of a VO, a lambda rule will trigger a lambda function as an action if the Select Clause and Where Clause in the SQL statement of the lambda rule evaluate to true. When the lambda function is triggered, an attached IAM role with lambda function will comply with a coupled policy or policies to authorize AWS-IoT to access to the lambda function and authorize the lambda function to execute actions with the received data. IAM role policy could authorize lambda function to forward data to other reserved/unreserved topics. Thus, other topics will receive data as long as it is in an appropriate format without checking where the data came from or rejecting the received data, and as a result, the received data will be forwarded to subscribers. So, a question like "which resources should a topic receives data from?" is only controlled via IAM role that is attached within an action of a rule, and topics has no control over what they receive.

We investigated applying the use case of sensing speeding cars, which is employed in ACO-IoT-ACMsVO, within AWS-IoT-ACMVO. But as we discussed above, the communication style, access control points, access control models are not precisely alike. Although, AWSnIoT does not support direct VOs communication, we were able to develop AWS-IoT-ACMVO that allows effect VOs communication. So, the use case of sensing speeding cars within ACO architecture in Figure 3 can be applied and enforced within AWS IoT as shown in Figure 6. The details of configuration, scenario, and authorization policy are discussed in the following section.

5 A USE CASE: THE SENSING SPEEDING CARS WITHIN AWS-IOT-ACMVO

In this section, we present two scenarios of the use case of sensing cars speed. The two scenarios will have number of sensors and a camera in the physical layer. All devices on the physical layer will push collected data to their virtual objects (shadows). In our scenarios, we focus on the communication among virtual objects and how this communication can be controlled.

5.1 Sensing the Speed of One Car

We will discuss the configuration and the scenario of our simple use case as follow.

5.1.1 Setup and Configuration. In this simple scenario, we will have two physical sensors and one physical camera each with one virtual object connected to it. Figure 7 shows the connected devices, virtual objects (shadows), certificates, AWS IoT policy, rules, actions and their IAM roles, and AWS services.

First, we create one virtual object for each physical object using AWS IoT management console and attach one X.509 certificate for each virtual object. For each one certificate, we attached an AWS IoT policy. Certificates are copied into their corresponding physical objects to allow authentication and authorization of physical objects when they communicate with the corresponding virtual objects. In other words, the attached AWS IoT policy authorizes specific actions (connect and publish) for physical objects. When certificates are given to the corresponding physical objects, they are accompanied by the private key of the certificate and an AWS root CA certificate.

We simulated sensors and camera physical objects using AWS SDK for JavaScript (Node.js). There is an attached rule for each MQTT update topic $aws/things/Sensor_i/shadow/update$ that triggers a Lambda function. Lambda functions are responsible about republishing the coming reported data that arrived to a virtual object ($Virtual\ Sensor_i$ or $Virtual\ Camera$) from its corresponding physical object ($Sensor_i$ or $Camera$) to the next virtual object ($Virtual\ Sensor_{(i+1)}$ or $Virtual\ Camera$) as shown in Figure 7. Also, each Lambda function is attached with IAM role that authorizes AWS IoT to access AWS and AWS IoT resources and services. The IAM role also controls Lambda function operations, such as republishing data to another topic or getting the current state of a shadow.

5.1.2 Senario. $Sensor_1$ sends RFID and Speed of the over speeding car as a *reported* message to $Virtual\ Sensor_1$ ($VS1$) by publishing to $Sensor_1$ MQTT update topic $aws/things/Sensor_1/shadow/update$. $Rule_1$ that is attached with the $Sensor_1$ MQTT update topic will

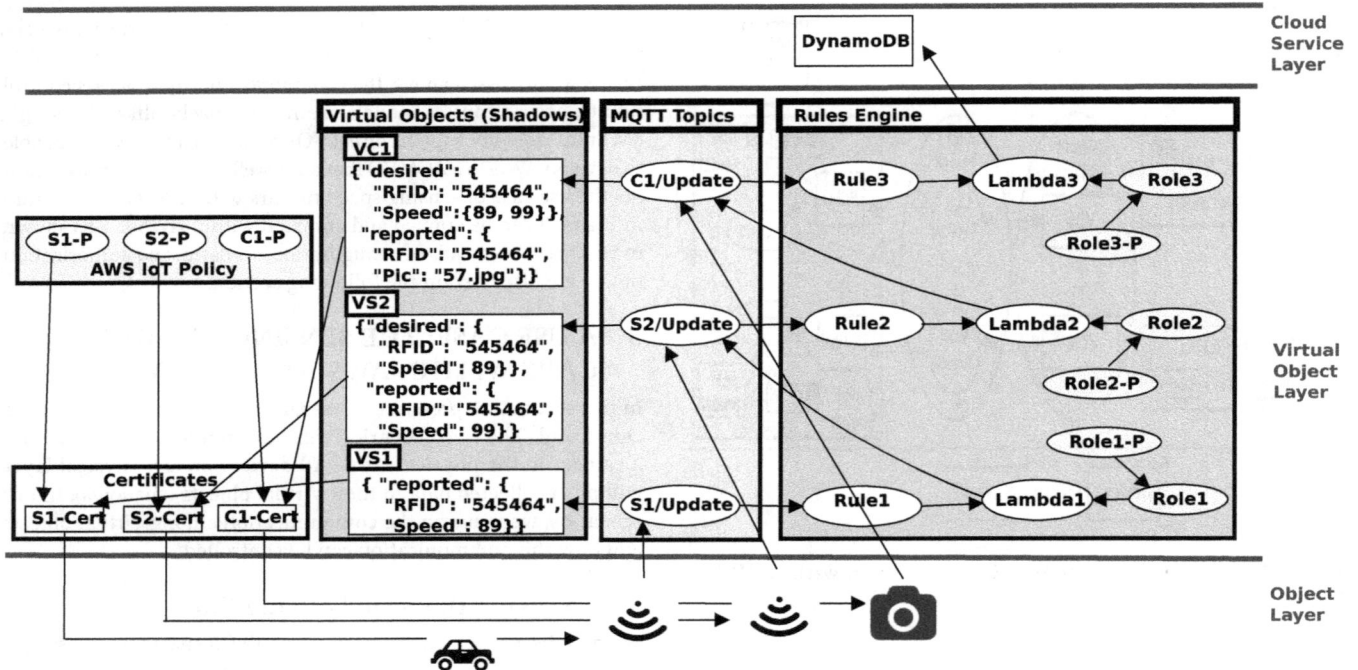

Figure 7: A Simple Use Case of Sensing the Speed of One Car

trigger $Lambda_1$ $function$ every time data arrived to MQTT update topic of $VS1$. $Lambda_1$ $function$ republishes the arrived data to $Virtual$ $Sensor_2$ ($VS2$) with a $desired$ tag. Figure 7 shows that the $reported$ RFID and Speed to $VS1$ is republished to $VS2$ as $desired$ state by $Lambda_1$ $function$.

$Sensor_2$ also sends RFID and Speed of the over speeding car as a $reported$ message to $VS2$ by publishing to the following MQTT update topic: $\$aws/things/Sensor_2/shadow/update$. $Rule_2$ is going to trigger $Lambda_2$ $function$ every time data arrived to MQTT update topic of $VS2$. $Lambda_2$ $function$ check if the coming data is with $reported$ tag, it compares the saved $desired$ RFID with the coming $reported$ RFID from $Sensor_2$. If the two RFIDs are matched, $Lambda_2$ $function$ combines the two speeds and one RFID and publish it with a $desired$ tag to the $Virtual$ $Camera$ ($VC1$). Figure 7 shows that the $reported$ RFID matches the $desired$ RFID in $Virtual$ $Sensor_2$. Thus, $VC1$ will receive from $Lambda_2$ $function$ two speeds that are reported from $Sensor_1$ and $Sensor_2$ for the same RFID.

$Camera$ also sends RFIDs and pictures (Pic) of the passed cars as a $reported$ message to $Virtual$ $Camera$ by publishing to MQTT update topic $\$aws/things/Camera/shadow/update$. $Rule_3$ is going to trigger $Lambda_3$ $function$ every time data arrived to MQTT update topic of $VC1$. $Lambda_3$ $function$ check if the coming data is with a $reported$ tag, it compares the saved coming $desired$ RFID from $Sensor_2$ with the coming $reported$ RFID from $Camera$. If the two RFIDs are matched, $Lambda_3$ $function$ combines the RFID, Speeds, and Pic and store them to the Amazon DynamoDB. Figure 7 shows that the $reported$ RFID matches the $desired$ RFID in $VC1$. Thus, the combined RFID, Speeds, and Pic will be stored in in the Amazon DynamoDB.

```
{ "Version": "2012-10-17",
 "Statement":
 [
   { "Effect": "Allow",
     "Action": [ "iot:Connect" ],
     "Resource": ["arn:aws:iot:us-west-2:760000000000:
     client/Sensor2"]
   },
   { "Effect": "Allow",
     "Action": [ "iot:Publish"],
     "Resource": [ "arn:aws:iot:us-west-2:76000000000:
     topic/$aws/things/Sensor2/shadow/update"]
   }
 ]
}
```

Figure 8: $S2$-P that is Attached to $S2$-$Cert$

5.1.3 Authorization policy. There is an AWS IoT policy attached with each certificate to authorize specific actions for physical objects. For example, $Sensor_1$ are only allowed to connect and publish to $VS1$ in order to send the collected RFID and Speed of the over speed cars. Thus, the AWS IoT $S1$-P and $VS1$ are attached with $S1$-$Cert$ which is copied to $Sensor_1$. The policy states that connect and publish actions are allowed to the specified resources, which is $VS1$ (the shadow of $Sensor_1$). Similarly, the AWS IoT $S2$-P in Figure 8 and $VS2$ will be attached to $S2$-$Cert$, which is copied to $Sensor_2$, and the AWS IoT $C1$-P and $VC1$ will be attached to $C1$-$Cert$, which is copied to $Camera_1$. AWS IoT defines policy variables, which can be used in AWS IoT policies within the resource or condition block. The basic variable $IoT : ClientID$ can be used to generate a policy

```
{
    "Version": "2012-10-17",
    "Statement": [
        { "Effect": "Allow",
            "Action": "iot:GetThingShadow",
            "Resource": "arn:aws:iot:us-west-2:760000000000:
            thing/Sensor2"
        },
        { "Effect": "Allow",
            "Action": "iot:Publish",
            "Resource": "arn:aws:iot:us-west-2:760000000000:
            topic/$aws/things/Camera/shadow/update"
        }
    ]
}
```

Figure 9: $Role_2$ *Policy* **that is Attached to** $Role_2$

that can be attached to all certificates. However, certificates is not coupled with an ID of physical sensor that should connect and publish to the attached shadows, so malicious sensor could change their ID to connect and publish to any other MQTT update topic. Therefore, we preferred to specify and hard-coded one different policy for each certificate as shown in Figure 7, and each AWS IoT policy is similar to $S2$-P shown in Figure 8 but with different sensor names.

Also, There is an IAM role attached to each Lambda function to authorize it accessing to AWS services and AWS IoT resources. For example, $Role_1$ is attached to $Lambda_1$ to authorize it publishing to the update topic of $VS2$. Also, $Role_2$ is attached to $Lambda_2$ to authorize it getting the *desired* state of $VS2$ and publishing to the MQTT update topic of $VC1$. Figure 9 shows the IAM $Role_2$ *Policy* that is attached to $Role_2$. Also, $Role_3$ is attached to $Lambda_3$ to authorize it getting the *desired* state of $VC1$ and publishing to Amazon DynamoDB.

5.2 Sensing the Speed of Multiple Cars

The previous simple use case introduces the basic idea of implementing and controlling the virtual object communication within AWS IoT. However, in realty there is a need to track multiple cars, where different cars pass a sensor at a time. A VO (shadow) in AWS IoT has different reserved topics that are used by the VO to subscribe to them. So, any time a sensor publish a new list of RFIDs/Speeds, the old list is deleted and a new one is saved. However, our use case with multiple cars needs to keep track of the historical data (old and new RFIDs).

In this use case, for every VO corresponding to a physical object, we propose to have another relative VO that works as storage of historical data. The only way to push or get data from the VO storage is by using a lambda function that is triggered by publishing data from a sensor to the MQTT update topic of the corresponding VO. Figure 10 shows sensors ($S1, S2, ..., Sn, C1$) and their corresponding virtual objects ($VS1, VS2, ..., VSn, VC1$) and the storage for each of them ($VS1S, VS2S, ..., VSnS, VC1S$).

5.2.1 Setup and Configuration.
As pervious simple use case, we create one virtual object and one virtual object storage for our physical objects and attached one X.509 certificate for each

virtual object. Certificates that are attached with AWS IoT policies are copied into their corresponding physical objects. The AWS IoT policy states that sensors and the Camera are only allowed to connect and publish to the corresponding VO (similar to the mentioned policy in Figure 8).

We simulated Sensors and the Camera using AWS SDK for JavaScript (Node.js). Lambda functions are triggered by rules that are attached with MQTT update topics of VOs. For example, $Lambda_1$ is triggered by $rule1$ that is attached to MQTT update topic of VS1. In general, Lambda functions are responsible about the complex computations, such as getting the stored data, comparing and consolidating the coming and the stored data, and republishing data to the current storage or next VO. Figure 10 describes the functionality of each lambda function.

5.2.2 Senario.
$Sensor_1$ sends a list of RFIDs/Speeds of over speeding cars as a *reported* message to $VS1$ by publishing to $VS1$ MQTT update topic. $Rule_1$ triggers $Lambda_1$ *function* when a published request arrived to MQTT update topic. $Lambda_1$ *function* will consider the reported RFIDs/Speeds as a suspicious list, that will be handled as described in Figure 10.

$Sensor_2$, ..., $Sensor_i$, .., $Sensor_n$ also send a list of RFIDs/Speeds of over speeding cars as a *reported* message to their corresponding VO by publishing to VO_i MQTT update topic, where $2 \leq i \leq n$. The reported RFIDs/Speeds from physical objects is considered as a suspicious list (stored in $VSiS$ under reported tag) beside the suspicious list that is coming from a previous VO (stored in $VSiS$ under desired tag with RFID1). The matched RFIDs in both of the suspicious lists will be stored as SavePic list (stored in $VSiS$ under desired tag with RFID2). $Rule_i$ triggers $Lambda_i$ *function* when a published request arrived to MQTT update topic of VS_i. $Lambda_i$ *function* will deal with the arrived data as suspicious lists and handle it to generate the SavePic list as descried in Figure 10. Note that $Lambda_3$ to $Lambda_{(n-1)}$ will do the same computations.

$Camera$ sends RFIDs and pictures (Pic) of the passed cars as a *reported* message to $Virtual Camera$ ($VC1$) by publishing to MQTT update topic of $VC1$. $Rule_{(n+1)}$ triggers $Lambda_{(n+1)}$ *function* when a published request arrived to $VC1$ MQTT update topic. $Lambda_{(n+1)}$ *function* will deal with the coming data as descried in Figure 10.

5.2.3 Authorization policy.
As pervious simple use case, we will have an AWS IoT *Policy* that is attached with $S1$-$Cert$, .., Sn-$Cert$, $C1$-$Cert$. The policy state that physical objects can only connect to their corresponding VO and publish to MQTT update topic of the VO. Figure 8 is an example of an attached AWS IoT policy that authorizes physical objects to connect and publish.

Also, The IAM roles are attached to Lambda functions. For example, $Role_1$ is attached to $Lambda_1$ to authorize it publishing to the update topic of $VS2$. $Role_2$ is attached to $Lambda_2$ to authorize it getting the data of the storage of $VS2$ and publishing only to the update topic of the $VS2S$ and $VS3$. $Role_{(n+1)}$ is attached to $Lambda_{(n+1)}$ to authorize it getting the data of the storage of $VC1$ and publishing only to its storage and then to the Amazon DynamoDB. Figure 11 shows the $Role_5$ *Policy* of the IAM $Role_2$ that is attached to $Lambda_5$ to authorize it getting the data that is saved in the storage of $VS5$ ($n = 5$ in our implementation) and publishing only to the update topic of the $VS5S$ and to the update topic of $VC1$.

DynamoDB

Cloud
Service layer

λ1

If Reported:
1- Publish suspicious list to the next sensor with a desired tag and RFID1/Speed1.

λ2

If Desired with RFID1:
1- Combine current (in the VS2S) and comming suspicious lists.
2- Publish the combined suspicious list to current storage (VS2S) and the next sensor with a desired tag and RFID1/Speed1.

If Reported:
1- Compare current and comming suspicious lists, and if there are similar RFIDs:
   A- Generate a SavePic list with the similar RFIDs, and puplish it to the next sensor with a desired tag and RFID2/Speed2.
   B- Restore current suspicious list without the similar RFIDs
2- Publish the reported suspicious list without the similar RFIDs to the next sensor with a desired tag and RFID1/Speed1.

λi (where 2 < i < n)

If Desired with RFID1:
1- Combine current (in the VSiS) and comming suspicious lists.
2- Publish the combined suspicious list to current storage (VSiS) and the next sensor with a desired tag and RFID1/Speed1.

If Desired with RFID2:
1- Publish the SavePic list to next sensor
2- Delete current suspicious RFIDs/Speeds that are in the SavePic list.

If Reported:
1- Compare current and comming suspicious lists, and if there are similar RFIDs:
   A- Generate a SavePic list with the similar RFIDs, and puplish it to the next sensor with a desired tag and RFID2/Speed2.
   B- Restore current suspicious list without the similar RFIDs
2- Publish the reported suspicious list without the similar RFIDs to the next sensor with a desired tag and RFID1/Speed1.

λn

If Desired with RFID1:
1- Combine current (in the VSnS) and comming suspicious lists
2- Publish the combined suspicious list to current storage (VSnS).

If Desired with RFID2:
1- Publish the SavePic list to next sensor
2- Delete current suspicious RFIDs/Speeds that are in the SavePic list.

If Reported:
1- Compare current and comming suspicious lists, and if there are similar RFIDs:
   A- Generate a SavePic list with the similar RFIDs, and puplish it to the next sensor with a desired tag and RFID2/Speed2.
   B- Restore current suspicious list without the similar RFIDs
2- Publish the reported suspicious list without the similar RFIDs to the next sensor with a desired tag and RFID1/Speed1.

λn+1

If Desired with RFID2:
1- Combine the curent SavePic list and the comming SavePic list
2- Publish the Combined SavePic list to current sotrage (VC1S)

If Reported:
1- Compare the current SavePic list and the comming suspicious list, and if there are similar RFIDs:
   A- Consolidate the two lists, and publish it to the Amazon DynamoDB
   B- Remove the similar RFIDs/Speeds that are saved in the current SavePic list.

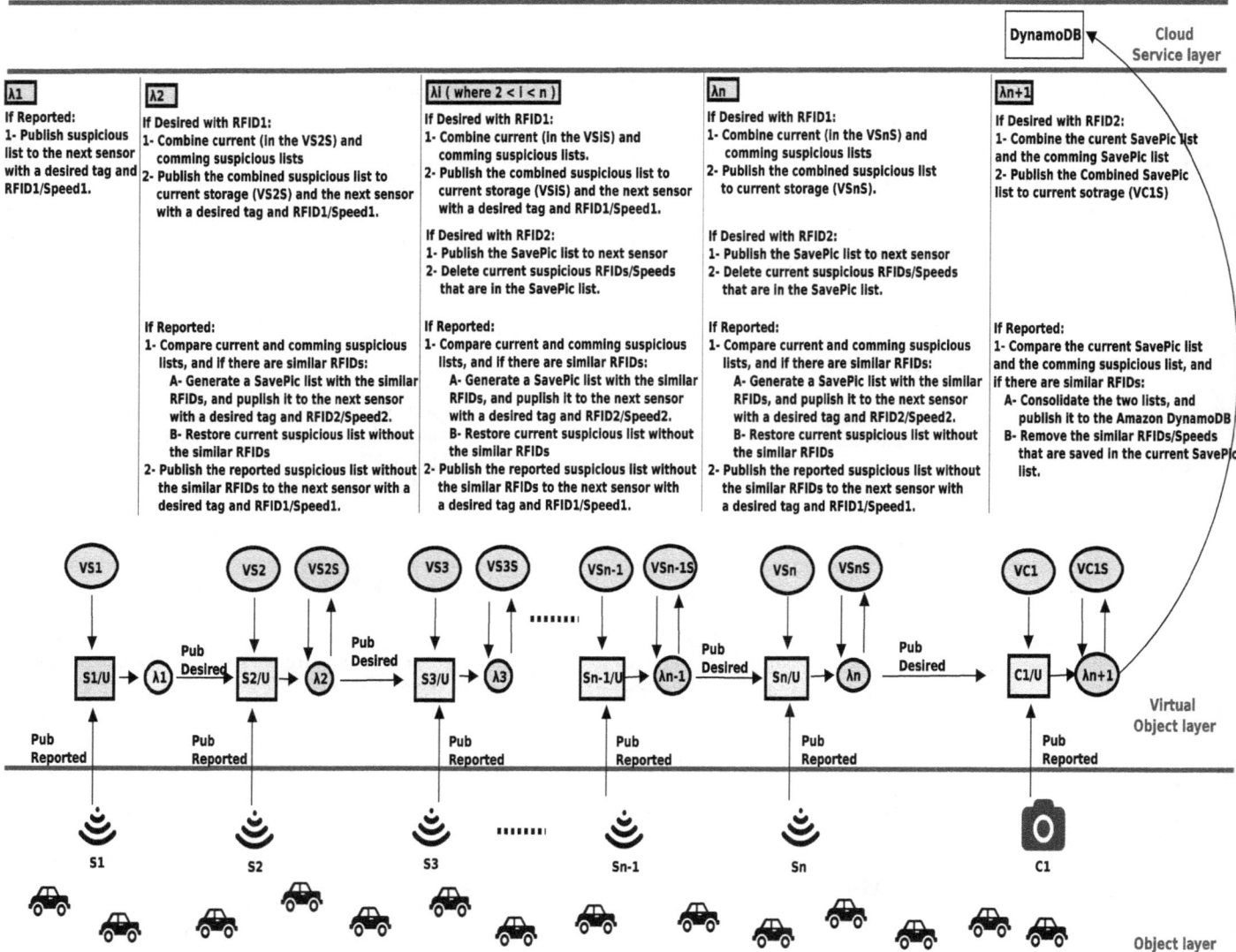

Figure 10: A Use Case of Sensing the Speed of Multiple Cars

```
{"Version": "2012-10-17",
  "Statement": [
    { "Effect": "Allow",
      "Action": "iot:Publish",
      "Resource": "arn:aws:iot:us-west-2:760000000000:
        topic/$aws/things/Sensor5_Storage/shadow/update"
    },
    { "Effect": "Allow",
      "Action": "iot:GetThingShadow",
      "Resource": "arn:aws:iot:us-west-2:769000000000:
        thing/Sensor5_Storage"
    },
    { "Effect": "Allow",
      "Action": "iot:Publish",
      "Resource": "arn:aws:iot:us-west-2:769000000000:
        topic/$aws/things/Camera/shadow/update"}
  ]
}
```

Figure 11: $Role_5$ that is attached to $Lambda_5$

6 PERFORMANCE

Our scenario propagates the Suspicious list published by any sensor until the last virtual sensor, and it propagates the SavePic list from the moment of generation until the camera. The first possible generated Suspicious list starts from $Sensor_1$, and the first possible SavePic list starts when $Sensor_2$ publishes similar Suspicious list to the published Suspicious list by $Sensor_1$, so the SavePic list will be generated by $lambda_2$ $function$ that is triggered when $Sensor_2$ publishes to its virtual object. In this section, we calculate the time of propagating the Suspicious and the SavePic list to their final destination.

The use case with multiple sensors and cars is employed in computing the propagation time. we set the number of sensors to five. We used two AWS SDKs for JavaScript (Node.js) to subscribe to $Virtual$ $Sensor_5$ $Storage$ (VS5S) and $Virtual$ $Camera_1$ $Storage$

($VC1S$), so we can get an acknowledgement whenever the Suspicious and the SavePic list are reached. A bash script is written to run $Sensor_1$, start the timer, run $VS5S$, and end the timer whenever we get an acknowledgement from $VS5S$. Similarly, the bash script will run $Sensor_2$ (with simillar RFIDs of $Sensor_1$), start the timer, run $VC1S$, and end the timer whenever we get an acknowledgement from $VC1S$. Thus, we were able to calculate the propagation time of the Suspicious and the SavePic list to their final destination.

We run $Sensor_1$ that publish the Suspicious list with $\{1, 10, 20, 30, 40\}$ RFIDS. For the Suspicious list with one RFID, we calculate the propagation average time of 10 times run. Thus, the propagation time of the Suspicious list with one RFID from S_1 until $VS5S$ in Figure 12, which is 5915 millisecond, is the average of 10 times run. Similarly, the propagation time of the Suspicious list with 10, 20, 30, 40 RFIDs from S_1 until $VS5S$, which is 6335, 7131, 7519, and 8109 millisecond, is also the average of 10 times run. However, we get rid off outliers, which is the time values that exceed 10000 or less than 3000 millisecond.

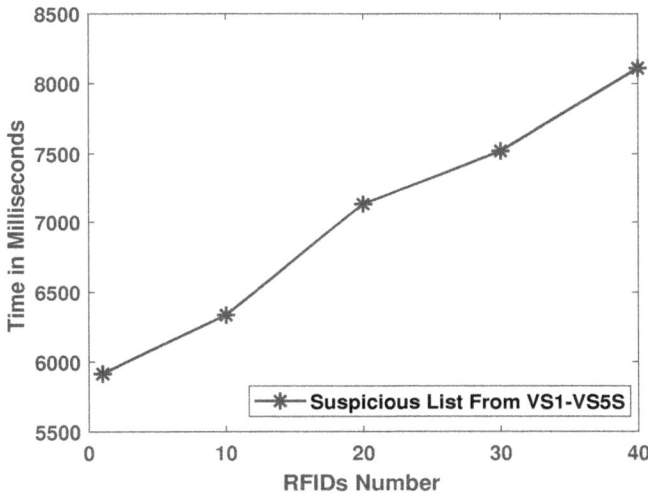

Figure 12: Propagation Time of Suspicious List from S_1 until $VS5S$

After a Suspicious list is published by S_1 and an acknowledgement is received from $VS5S$, $Sensor_2$ is also run to publish a Suspicious list, similar to the Suspicious list that is published by S_1, with $\{1, 10, 20, 30, 40\}$ RFIDS. The propagation time of the SavePic list with $\{1, 10, 20, 30, 40\}$ RFID from S_2 until $VC1S$ in Figure 13, which is 7774, 8100 , 8405, 8694 , 8851 millisecond, is the average of 10 times run. However, we get rid off outliers, which is the time values that exceed 14000 or less than 4000 millisecond.

The algorithms of our Lambda functions that we used within our use case in Figure 10 shows more computation and steps when a Lambda function gets the Suspicious list than when a Lambda function gets the SavePic list. However, our results in Figure 12 and 13 show that the propagation time of the Suspicious lists are less than the propagation time of the SavePic lists. This different is because of the larger payload of the SavePic list, which has two

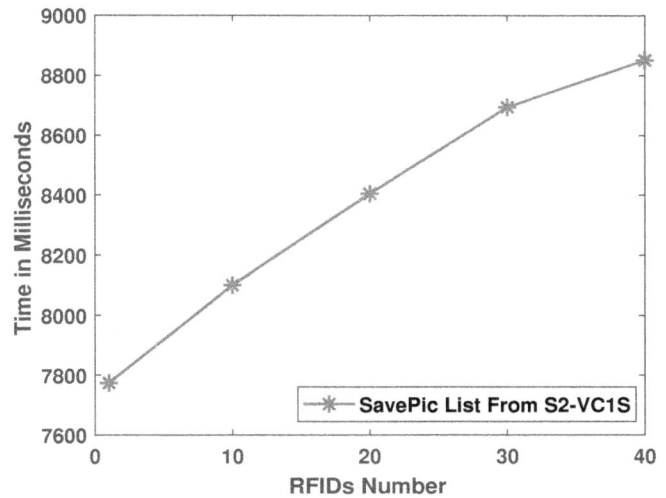

Figure 13: Propagation Time of SavePic List from S_2 until $VC1S$

speeds for each one RFID, than the Suspicious list, which has only one speed for each RFID.

7 DISCUSSION

AWS IoT does not have full capability to implement our use case that we employed in [3]. First, virtual objects (shadows) in AWS IoT can not communicate directly to each other. Since virtual objects can only subscribe to their reserved topics update, get, and delete. So, they receive data through their reserved topics. Also, virtual objects can publish to their reserved topics only whenever they receive data. As a result, publishing and subscribing of virtual objects is only to their reserved topics and direct publishing to unreserved topics or irrelevant topics is not applicable.

There are several indirect ways to allow virtual objects communication in AWS IoT. One way to allow two virtual objects to communication is to attach a rule with the update topic of first virtual object that triggers a republish action to the second virtual object update topic. The Republish ction can be also used to forward data to AWS services as shown in Figure 14. Another way is to attach a rule with a topic of first virtual object that trigger a lambda function, which can do complex computation, such as publishing data, getting data, and comparing data. Thus, lambda function can republish the received data to another topic, which could be the update topic of the second virtual object. We employed the second way in our use cases.

In addition to indirect communication among virtual objects, virtual objects in AWS IoT cannot keep track of old data. For example, if a new suspicious list is published to a virtual object, the current suspicious list will be deleted and the new one will be saved. However, our use case needs to combine the coming suspicious list from previous sensor and the current saved one. Since the process of deleting and saving list is very fast, triggering a lambda function that get the current suspicious list from virtual object and then combine it with the coming one did not work. Thus, virtual objects in AWS IoT can not save old data.

There are several ways to keep track historical data in AWS IoT. One way to keep track historical data of a virtual object is to have another relative virtual object that works as storage. The only way to get or publish data to the relative virtual object is by allowing one lambda function to publish and get data from it. This lambda function is triggered whenever data is published to update topic of the virtual object. Thus, the *coming* suspicious list arrived to the update topic of a virtual and the *current* suspicious list that is saved in the virtual object can be combined and republished by the lambda function. We used this way in our use case to keep transit data within the virtual object layer, so the privacy of data can be reserved. Another way to reach the historical data of a virtual object is to trigger a republish action to AWS DynamoDB whenever data is published to update topic of the virtual object. Thus, authorized virtual objects can get the historical data from AWS DynamoDB as needed. However, our use case tends to keep the suspicious lists within the virtual object until at least two sensors report the speed of a car to be over limit. Figure 14 shows the way of republishing suspicious lists, which come from S_1 and S_2, to AWS DynamoDB in the cloud service layer. Then, $lambda_1$ is authorized to get all suspicious lists and check if there are duplicated RFIDs within the saved suspicious lists and also within the suspicious list coming from the camera. If so, this RFID is declared to be an over-limit car, and it is reported along with consolidate information from all suspicious lists (speed, picture).

Another issue with the AWS IoT is that virtual objects cannot do complex computation on the data they receive. They only save the recent published desired or reported data. Such a computation in our use case can not be implemented within only AWS IoT. Thus, since we need the transit data to be only within AWS IoT, we used AWS Lambda service to support doing the needed computation. Another way to do that is to send data to DynamoDB and allow an application or a third party to do the needed computation.

Moreover, in our use case, we could have up to n sensors. $Lambda_3$ to $Lambda_{(n-1)}$ functions are repetitive functions that can be triggered by the update topic of $VS3$ to $VS_{(n-1)}$. We can get rid of this repetition If we have only one Lambda that accept passing the name of the published sensor. However, triggering same lambda is not working within our use case, because to our knowledge there is no way to pass the name of the published sensor to a lambda function. Thus, repeated copies of $Lambda_{(n-1)}$ will be increased by increasing the number of sensors, which is n.

8   CONCLUSION

In this paper, we studied AWS IoT and developed the access control model for virtual objects (shadows) communication in AWS IoT (AWS-IoT-ACMVO). We used the AWS-IoT-ACMVO to implement two scenarios of the use case that is employed in ACO-IoT-ACMsVO: the simple use case of sensing the speed of one car with two sensors and the use case of sensing the speed of multiple cars with multiple sensors. By implementing these two scenarios using ACO-IoT-ACMsVO, we determined how to configure the policies and control virtual object communication of our proposed model. The time to propagate information about suspicious cars and over-limit

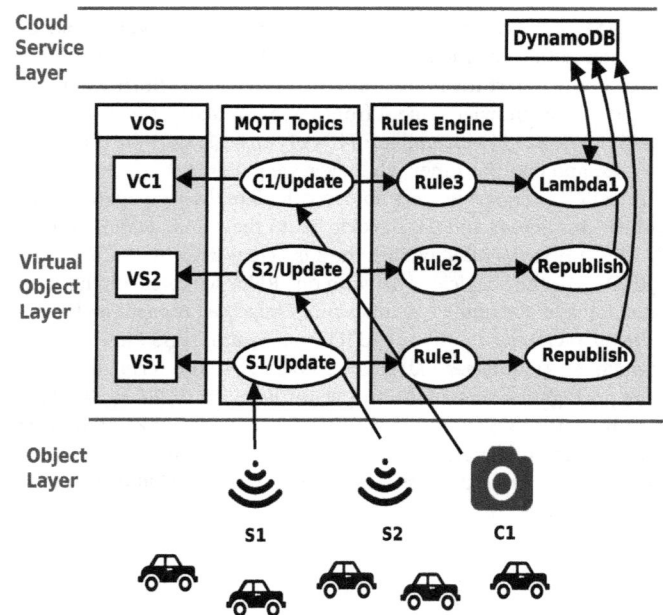

Figure 14: A Different Way of VOs Communication and Data Computation

cars through all virtual objects is measured and discussed. Finally, upon our study and implementation, we offered a discussion of AWS IoT issues and suggestions of enhancing VOs communication and their access control.

ACKNOWLEDGMENT

This research is partially supported by NSF CREST Grant HRD-1736209, NSF Grants CNS-1111925, CNS-1423481, CNS-1538418, and DoD ARL Grant W911NF-15-1-0518.

REFERENCES

[1] Ala Al-Fuqaha, Mohsen Guizani, Mehdi Mohammadi, Mohammed Aledhari, and Moussa Ayyash. 2015. Internet of things: A survey on enabling technologies, protocols, and applications. *IEEE Comm. Surveys & Tutorials* 17, 4 (2015), 2347–2376.
[2] Asma Alshehri and Ravi Sandhu. 2016. Access Control Models for Cloud-Enabled Internet of Things: A Proposed Architecture and Research Agenda. In *the 2nd IEEE International Conference on Collaboration and Internet Computing (CIC)*. IEEE, 530–538.
[3] Asma Alshehri and Ravi Sandhu. 2017. Access Control Models for Virtual Object Communication in Cloud-Enabled IoT. In *The 18th International Conference on Information Reuse and Integration (IRI)*. IEEE.
[4] Jean Bacon, David M Eyers, Jatinder Singh, and Peter R Pietzuch. 2008. Access control in publish/subscribe systems. In *the Second International Conference on Distributed Event-Based Systems*. ACM, 23–34.
[5] Smriti Bhatt, Farhan Patwa, and Ravi Sandhu. 2017. Access Control Model for AWS Internet of Things. In *International Conference on Network and System Security*. Springer, 721–736.
[6] Alessio Botta, Walter De Donato, Valerio Persico, and Antonio Pescapé. 2014. On the integration of cloud computing and internet of things. In *IEEE Int. Conf. on Future Internet of Things and Cloud (FiCloud)*. 23–30.
[7] Li Da Xu, Wu He, and Shancang Li. 2014. Internet of things in industries: A survey. *IEEE Trans. on Indust. Informatics* 10, 4 (2014), 2233–2243.
[8] Patrick Th Eugster and et all. 2003. The many faces of publish/subscribe. *ACM computing surveys (CSUR)* 35, 2 (2003), 114–131.
[9] Jayavardhana Gubbi, Rajkumar Buyya, Slaven Marusic, and Marimuthu Palaniswami. 2013. Internet of Things (IoT): A vision, architectural elements, and

future directions. *Future Generation Computer Systems* 29, 7 (2013), 1645–1660.

[10] Rafiullah Khan, Sarmad Ullah Khan, Rifaqat Zaheer, and Shahid Khan. 2012. Future internet: the internet of things architecture, possible applications and key challenges. In *10th IEEE Int. Conf. on Frontiers of IT.* 257–260.

[11] Michele Nitti, Virginia Pilloni, Giuseppe Colistra, and Luigi Atzori. 2015. The Virtual Object as a Major Element of the Internet of Things: a Survey. *IEEE Communications Surveys & Tutorials* 18, 2 (2015), 1228–1240.

[12] Pritee Parwekar. 2011. From internet of things towards cloud of things. In *2nd IEEE Int. Conf. on Comp. and Comm. Tech.* 329–333.

[13] BB Prahlada Rao, Paval Saluia, Neetu Sharma, Ankit Mittal, and Shivay Veer Sharma. 2012. Cloud computing for Internet of Things and sensing based applications. In *Sixth IEEE Int. Conference on Sensing Technology (ICST).* 374–380.

[14] Rodrigo Roman, Jianying Zhou, and Javier Lopez. 2013. On the features and challenges of security and privacy in distributed internet of things. *Computer Networks* 57, 10 (2013), 2266–2279.

[15] Yun Zhang, Farhan Patwa, and Ravi Sandhu. 2015. Community-based secure information and resource sharing in AWS public cloud. In *2015 IEEE International Conference on Collaboration and Internet Computing (CIC).* IEEE, 46–53.

Security Analysis of Relationship-Based Access Control Policies

Amirreza Masoumzadeh
University at Albany – SUNY
Albany, NY
amasoumzadeh@albany.edu

ABSTRACT

Relationship-based access control (ReBAC) policies can express intricate protection requirements in terms of relationships among users and resources (which can be modeled as a graph). Such policies are useful in domains beyond online social networks. However, given the updating graph of user and resources in a system and expressive conditions in access control policy rules, it can be very challenging for security administrators to envision what can (or cannot) happen as the protection system evolves.

In this paper, we introduce the *security analysis* problem for this class of policies, where we seek to answer security queries about future states of the system graph and authorizations that are decided accordingly. Towards achieving this goal, we propose a state-transition model of a ReBAC protection system, called RePM. We discuss about formulation of security analysis queries in RePM and present our initial results for a limited version of this model.

CCS CONCEPTS

• **Security and privacy** → **Access control**; **Authorization**;

KEYWORDS

relationship-based access control; security analysis; safety

ACM Reference Format:
Amirreza Masoumzadeh. 2018. Security Analysis of Relationship-Based Access Control Policies. In *CODASPY '18: Eighth ACM Conference on Data and Application Security and Privacy, March 19–21, 2018, Tempe, AZ, USA.* ACM, New York, NY, USA, 10 pages. https://doi.org/10.1145/3176258.3176323

1 INTRODUCTION

Several relationship-based access control (ReBAC[1]) models have been developed in recent years [5, 12, 13, 9, 7]. While they were initially inspired by online social networks (OSNs) and Web 2.0 applications, it has been also shown that their expressive power is useful in other domains such as healthcare [25]. In ReBAC models, authorizations are specified based on relationship patterns between users and resources that are involved in an access control scenario. Such patterns are typically captured as paths or topological constraints in a graph structure of entities and relationships among them. For example, access control policy options in an OSN, which allows a user to share with "friends" or "friends of friends," are expressed as paths of different lengths in the OSN graph based on friendship relationships between users.

ReBAC policies are very expressive (e.g., see various intricate examples expressible in Fong's ReBAC [13]). However, such expressiveness also complicates understanding a ReBAC policy. For example, consider this question: given a set of actions that users can perform and policies that they can configure in an OSN, can a certain leak of information happen? (e.g., can a stalker obtain access to a victim's information after performing a series of actions?) There are several factors that makes answering such a question challenging in ReBAC environments, such as interaction of rules, updates to graph and policies, and distributed administration. A ReBAC policy is composed of individual rules, each authorizing some action(s) according to relationship-based conditions in a system. In any sizable ReBAC policy, it will be hard to comprehend and ensure that protection requirements are met as interactions between rules may lead to unknown situations and some security gaps might be even left undetected. Even if protection requirements are confirmed at one moment, future updates to the policy may result in unexpected situations. The problem is even more complicated since as the underlying graph of relationships is updated it will also affect the authorization decisions in a ReBAC environment. We need to also consider that often times in modern systems, updates happen in a distributed fashion (not by a central security administrator). For example, each user is in charge of specifying her own access control options (privacy settings) in an OSN, and the policy of an OSN as a whole is a combination of such policies (along with other rules set by the OSN provider).

In this paper, we investigate the *security analysis* problem [19] in the context of ReBAC models. The goal of security analysis is to verify properties of a protection system as it

---

[1] We use the term *ReBAC* to refer to the class of access control models based on relationships. In order to avoid confusion, we refer to the seminal work proposed in [12, 13] as Fong's ReBAC.

may evolve: i.e., starting from a given secure state, and based on a given set of state transitions (or constraints that control them), whether an (undesirable) state is reachable (i.e., existential query) or a (desirable) property is always held (i.e., universal query). The existential flavor of this problem, known as *safety* problem, has been studied whether leakage of a specific right can happen in a discretionary access control model [14, 28, 26]. It was then extended to include universal questions as well, and thus, called *security analysis* [19] in the context of trust management systems. The security analysis problem has also been investigated in the context of administrative role-based access control [18, 29]. It is worthwhile to note that security analysis is essentially a more complex problem than verifying properties of a protection system at a given state, e.g., whether certain undesirable authorization exists. The latter problem can be referred to as policy analysis [23, 21] or proof of compliance [19].

While there have been formal approaches to the specification/enforcement (e.g, [13, 9]), and more recently administration [30, 8] of ReBAC policies, to the best of our knowledge, this is the first work to study the security analysis problem in this context. In particular we make the following contributions in this paper:

- We propose a formal relationship-based protection model, called RePM, that captures the essence of ReBAC policies as a state-transition system. The model captures an underlying graph of entities, ReBAC policy that controls authorizations on the graph, and administrative ReBAC policy that governs changes to the ReBAC policy itself. In addition to providing a generalizable model, RePM addresses a major gap in previous formal ReBAC models [13, 9] by supporting authorization policies for "viewing" edges in the system graph.
- We present, for the first time, the security analysis problem for ReBAC policies, formulated in the context of the proposed protection model. We propose two versions of the problem which have different security analysis query targets (graph and authorization).
- We study the safety problem in a limited version of our model and prove its decidability.

The rest of the paper is organized as follows. In Section 2, we briefly review the related work on ReBAC policies and security analysis. We begin Section 3 with presentation of a running example and the design considerations for our protection model. We then propose a formal model of ReBAC protection system, called RePM. We formulate the security analysis in the context of RePM in Section 4, and finally illustrate decidability result for a simplified model in Section 5.

2 RELATED WORK

Our work is closely related to two bodies of work, namely, relationship-based access control and safety/security analysis. Among them, we review the most relevant work to this paper in the followings.

2.1 Relationship-Based Access Control

The early work on ReBAC models focused on specifying simple path conditions based on relationships among users in OSNs and other web applications [17] which may be also composed with trust evaluation along such paths [4]. Other models involved including more rich relational semantics available in Semantic Web [3, 22], conflict resolution on shared resources by multiple parties [16, 15], and including objects in addition to users in the network [6, 22]. Fong et al. [13, 12, 2] proposed a series of access control policy models (named "ReBAC") which are capable of expressing sophisticated topological relationships among users based on modal/hybrid logics. While the models consider only positive authorization rules, exceptions can be handled using negative conditions. Inspired by the notion of principals in Unix and ReBAC, the RPPM model [9, 10] proposed a two-step authorization process for an access request. Access subjects are first matched to the known principals in the policy based on path-based conditions. Then, further path-based conditional rules determine authorizations (after resolving conflicts if needed). Finally, a recent work shows how conversion of Fong's ReBAC to Datalog programs [24] can help extending it to include negative authorizations and temporal policies, and additionally support simple policy analysis (in the same protection state). Unlike the above mentioned models, the focus of our work is to provide a clear formal model of a ReBAC protection system as a state transition machine which can be used for security analysis. In other words, we are not seeking to provide a better expressiveness power for ReBAC policies. In fact, our goal is to keep the model compatible (to the extent possible) with existing condition specification approaches. In describing our model, we use path expressions similar to RPPM [9].

Almost all of the work mentioned so far, consider only using topology-based conditions in policies without addressing how such topology itself might evolve. The recent ReBAC administrative models [30, 8] based on RPPM [9] have focused on this missing aspect. While we also adopt ideas from these recent models in formalizing our protection system, a clarification is needed with regards to the use of terminology in our model versus the previous work. While both RPPM2 [30] and ARPPM [8] consider changes to graph of entities by users as "administration," we consider those as user-level changes. We believe that only updates to ReBAC policy rules should be considered as administrative actions, and provide a full justification as we present our model in Section 3.

2.2 Safety and Security Analysis

The safety problem was first introduced in the context of the access matrix protection system [14]. It was shown that for a given access matrix (protection state) and set of commands that make changes to the matrix (transition to new protection states), it is generally undecidable whether a certain right will be entered in the matrix in future (i.e., leaking). Here, leakage of the right represents an undesirable situation that should be avoided in a safe and secure system. Also, it was shown while there are decidability results for restricted versions of the problem, they are still hard problems (to solve in polynomial time). Subsequently, other protection models were developed with improved decidability results [28] and it was shown that considering entity types in an access matrix model will lead to decidable cases for safety [26]. The problem was revisited later in the context of trust management (a distributed approach to access control based on roles) by Li and Winsborough [19]. They showed that universal queries can be verified beyond existential queries such as "simple safety" (e.g., is there a reachable state in which a user has certain access?). For example one can query about "simple availability" (e.g., can a certain access happen in all reachable states?), or "containment" (e.g., will every principal having certain access will have certain property in all reachable states?) Therefore, the problem was renamed to "security analysis" to include all such queries. They also showed that, in the context of a simplified version of RT language [20], simple safety, availability, and containment (only when language contains simple delegations) are answerable in polynomial time. In the context of RT, protection state is described by a set of policy statements (membership to a role, delegation of a role, etc.), and state transitions involve addition and removal of such statements while the analysis prevents addition or removal of statements about certain roles. Security analysis has been also studied in the context of role-based access control (RBAC) [18, 29]. Here, the protection state includes the RBAC policy configuration (i.e., current assignments) while transitions can be performed based on *can_assign* and *can_remove* policies in administrative model, ARBAC [27].

3 RePM: RELATIONSHIP-BASED PROTECTION MODEL

We propose a formal model of a ReBAC protection system, which we call *RePM*. Following the construction of safety/security analysis problems in the literature [14, 19], our model will be a state-transition system. Before discussing the model, we present a running example and our design considerations in order to facilitate discussions in the rest of the paper. Then, we define the notion of protection state in RePM which captures the changing components of the system. And finally, we show how the protection system model is formed together with the non-changing parts.

3.1 Running Example

ReBAC policies are useful in many application domains. In order to facilitate a focused discussion as we present the model and discuss its analysis, we choose a simple running example in a healthcare information environment. Suppose Alice is being treated for cancer. She is receiving treatment by her oncologist, Jane, at M-Hospital. Jane happens to be Alice's primary physician as well. Alice has specified Bob and Carol as her contacts and has specifically designated Bob as her emergency contact. Figure 1 portrays the entities and relationships as a graph in such a scenario. We consider

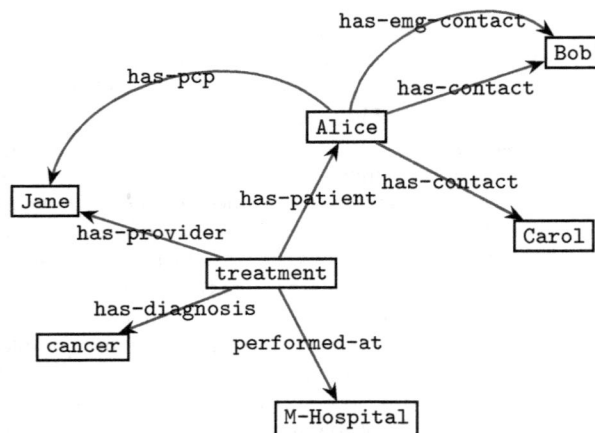

Figure 1: Running Example – A Healthcare Scenario

the following access control policy statements applied in this scenario:

(a) a doctor and a patient should know everything about a treatment in which they're involved
(b) a patient's provider in a treatment case should know about the patient's primary care doctor
(c) a patient can add contacts
(d) a patient can designate contacts as emergency contact
(e) a facility at which a patient is being treated can inform a patient's emergency contact about the patient's diagnosis when needed

The above rules may not capture all security requirements. However, we note that the number of rules even for such a simple scenario increases fast, which demonstrates the need for policy and security analysis.

In the rest of the paper we refer to the above scenario as *the running example* and omit an explicit reference to this section.

3.2 Design Considerations

Our main goal in the design of the RePM model is to formalize the necessary elements and structure in a ReBAC environment that are important in reasoning about its security properties. Therefore, RePM is not supposed to be yet another model to capture more expressive authorization or administrative policies. It is rather designed to be a comprehensive model that can incorporate or be easily extended based on various proposals in the literature. As a fundamental design principle, we intend to keep the proposed model as simple as possible, mainly to avoid overcomplicated presentation and to facilitate compatibility with the existing ReBAC models in the literature. For example, as we define policies, we avoid using keywords such as "*" that may match with any values. While such notions are useful for convenience purpose, they are not necessary for analysis purpose as long as policies can be equivalently expressed without them.

We also intend to maintain some separation between functional and security aspects of a system. Since ReBAC policies can benefit from a rich amount of information about entities and their relationships in the system, typically, there will be a significant overlap between information model from a functional perspective (for providing application functions) and information model from a security perspective (for deciding about authorizations). However, we intentionally avoid inclusion of any non-security requirement in our protection model in order to keep the model simple. For example, some data integrity requirements such as functional validity of a specific type of relationship between two types of entities may be accommodated by mechanisms other than access control (e.g., in a database environment) and so they will be excluded from our model. However, we acknowledge that any restrictions enforced on evolution of a system may affect its security analysis and we plan to address such considerations as future work.

3.3 System Graph

A protection state in RePM needs to capture the current state of user authorizations. Authorizations in ReBAC are derived based on the authorization rules which test some specified conditions about entity relationships in the system. Entities include users as well other logical resources in the application that need to be represented in the protection state. Therefore, a protection state needs to capture entities, relationships among them, and authorization policy.

A natural way to capture entities and their relationships is a graph structure. For this purpose, we follow a similar formulation as in RPPM [9, 10].

Definition 3.1 (System Graph). Given a set of relationship labels L_R, a system graph is a pair of vertices and edges $\langle V, E \rangle$, where V is the set of entities, and $E \subseteq L_R \times V \times V$ is the set of labeled relationships between entities.

We previously illustrated the system graph for our running example in Figure 1. We should note that in the rest of the paper we use dot notation to refer to elements within a concept. For instance, $G.V$ refers to the set of vertices in system graph G.

The system graph, as defined above, is limited to directed and typed edges. We note that it can be extended by notions such as symmetric relationships and typed vertices [10] among other possibilities (e.g., see the variations explored in [1]). However, for simplicity we limit our model as above. Also, it is noteworthy that unlike RPPM [9] we do not consider a *system model* alongside an instantiated system graph. From a logics point of view, a model and its instantiated version can be seen as TBox and ABox, respectively. The integrity constraints that need to be enforced according to a TBox (e.g., a *has-pcp* relationship is only meaningful between two users and not between a user and a resource) will be trivial to enforce and will be outside of the scope of our model.

One of the features of applications that benefit from ReBAC policies is the overlap between application and protection state. For instance, while the system graph for the running example (Figure 1) is part of the protection state it also captures data that will be utilized in the application (e.g., in order to look up contacts of a patient). In RePM, we assume the overlap is complete in the way that the application resources that need to be protected have been already represented in the system graph. This assumption has been validated in application areas beyond online social networks such as in an open-source medical record system [25].

Moreover, we consider edges (or relationships) as the main protected resources. This allows RePM to be able to specify authorizations for "viewing" edges; for instance, that Jane is Alice's PCP in the running example (i.e., seeing relationship **has-pcp** between Alice and Jane). Existing formal ReBAC models such as Fong's ReBAC [12] and RPPM [9] consider only vertices as access objects while specifying policies according to relationship-based conditions. Such models are not be able to model authorization policies for edges as mentioned in the above example. It should be noted that while recent ReBAC administrative models such as RPPM2 [30] and ARPPM [8] include update to edges as part of administration, the administrative actions naturally include "insertion"/ "removal" of edges and exclude "viewing" edges.

3.4 Authorization Policy

Since the system graph captures the protected resources, we consider any access attempt to the graph (including modification to it) as an access request. Modification to system graph has been termed as "administrative action" by recent works such as RPPM2 [30] and ARPPM [8]. However, we see it as modification of the application resources which also happens to be part of the information used to decide about authorization (known as ADI or access decision information in standard access control frameworks [11]). We consider six *primitive operations* that capture the basic modes of access to the graph. They include viewing, inserting, or deleting a vertex or an edge. In order to simplify presentation, following the approach in ARPPM [8], we focus on the operations on edges only (although ARPPM only considers them in the context of "administrative actions"). We assume that a vertex is inserted upon creation of its first edge and removed when all of its edges have been removed. Furthermore, we assume that viewing a vertex without its edges would not reveal any sensitive information.

Definition 3.2 (Access Request). An access request is a triple $\langle s, \langle rl, v_s, v_d \rangle, op \rangle$, where subject $s \in V$ is requesting to perform operation op (view/insert/remove) on an edge expressed as a tuple of type $rl \in L_R$ between $v_s, v_d \in V$.

A sample access request in the running example is as follows.

$$\langle \texttt{M-Hospital}, \langle \texttt{has-emg-contact}, \texttt{Alice}, \texttt{Bob} \rangle, \texttt{view} \rangle$$

We clarify that an access request is not directly formulated by a subject in the system, but rather by the reference monitor that authorizes the request. The mention of Bob in the above request does not mean that M-Hospital already knows about Alice's emergency contact; the reference monitor has formulated the request to authorize revealing the relationship to M-Hospital.

An access request needs to be evaluated against an authorization policy comprising of authorization rules. Authorization rules in ReBAC test relationship-based conditions based on an incoming access request.

Definition 3.3 (Authorization Rule). An authorization rule is a tuple $\langle \phi, rl, op, d \rangle$, where ϕ is a matching condition based on an access request, rl is the relationship label, op is a primitive operation on system graph (`view`/`insert`/`remove`), and d is an authorization decision (`grant`/`deny`).

Relationship label rl and primitive operation op in an authorization rule are matched against their counterparts in an incoming access request in order to determine the applicability of the rule. Various proposals exist in the literature for expressing the matching condition ϕ stated above, including modal/hybrid logic approach of Fong's ReBAC [12, 2] and path expressions in ARPPM [8]. While we envision RePM to be neutral in the choice of matching conditions, the choice of language is important in determining the complexity of its security analysis. In this paper, we will adopt a slightly simplified version of path expressions of ARPPM [8] in order to formulate our examples and discuss results further below.

Definition 3.4 (Path Condition). A path is constructed using the following syntax:

$$\pi ::= \top \mid \diamond \mid rl \mid rl; \pi \mid \overline{\pi}$$

where $rl \in L_R$ is a relationship label. A path condition is a a logical conjunction of one or more expressions of format $u.\pi.v$ where given a system graph G, an access request q, $u, v \in G.V$ we have:

- $G, q \models \top$;
- $G, q \models u.\diamond.v$ iff $u = v$;
- $G, q \models u.rl.v$ iff $\langle rl, u, v \rangle \in G.E$;
- $G, q \models u.rl; \pi.v$ iff there exists $w \in G.V$ such that $G, q \models u.rl.w$ and $G, q \models w.\pi.v$;
- $G, q \models u.\overline{\pi}.v$ iff $G, q \models v.\pi.u$.

Informally, the expressions above, respectively model the always-true condition, test for same vertices, a relationship, concatenation of a relationship and a path, and the inverse of a path.

In the above definition, u and v can either represent specific vertices (e.g., `Alice`) or vertex elements of access request tuple q (i.e., s, v_s, and v_d). For instance, the following captures the authorization rule corresponding to the policy statement (c) in the running example. Here, $s.\diamond.v_s$ means that subject s is the same as the source vertex for the edge:

$$\langle s.\diamond.v_s, \texttt{has-contact}, \texttt{insert}, \texttt{grant} \rangle$$

Given a set of authorization rules, an authorization policy is defined as follows.

Definition 3.5 (Authorization Policy). An authorization policy is a pair $\langle R, \sigma \rangle$, where R is a set of authorization rules and σ is a conflict resolution strategy.

When multiple rules within set R with conflicting decisions become applicable to an access request, we use strategy σ to resolve the conflict. For example, *deny-takes-precedence* is a well-known access control conflict resolution approach that adheres to the principle of fail-safe defaults in security.

3.5 Protection State

We formally define a protection state based on system graph and authorization policy as follows.

Definition 3.6 (Protection State). A protection state is a pair $\langle G, P \rangle$, where G is the system graph capturing entities and relationships among them, and P is an authorization policy which controls operations on G.

Note that the protection state as defined above encompasses both authorization decision information (system graph) and authorization policy. The authorization policy needs to be enforced when changes to the system graph are requested. Furthermore, the authorization policy may be updated over time by performing administrative operations.

3.6 Administrative Policy

The RePM protection system comprises of the protection state and an administrative policy that allows modifications to the authorization policy (a component in the protection state). In terms of modifications to authorization policy, we define two *primitive administrative operations*: namely, insertion and removal of an authorization rule. We assume the administration is distributed and performed by entities represented in the system graph.

Definition 3.7 (Admin Request). An admin (access) request is a triple $\langle s, pr, op \rangle$, where subject $s \in V$ is requesting to perform primitive administrative operation op (`insert`/`remove`) on authorization rule pr, which is specified as a tuple as in Definition 3.3.

We define the administrative authorization rules and policy analogous to their non-administrative counterparts.

Definition 3.8 (Administrative Rule). An administrative rule is a tuple $\langle \phi, \phi_{pr}, rl_{pr}, op_{pr}, d_{pr}, op, d \rangle$, where ϕ is a matching condition based on an admin request, op is a primitive administrative operation (`insert`/`remove`), and d is an administrative decision (`grant`/`deny`). The elements with pr subscript indicate matching component in the authorization rule pr provided in the administrative request.

Based on an incoming administrative request $\langle s, pr, op \rangle$, four sets of checks need to be completed in order to determine applicability of an administrative rule to the request. First, the primitive operation of an administrative rule should be the same as in the request. Second, condition ϕ is tested which may include tests on relationships about subject s in the admin request. Third, components rl_{pr}, op_{pr}, and d_{pr} are checked for equivalence against their counterparts within the requested pr rule in the request. Finally, ϕ_{pr} is tested to establish if it is less than or equally specific to its counterpart in the request's pr. Here, the idea is that an administrative request is allowed as long as it is more specific than what an administrative rule authorizes. In other words, ϕ_{pr} specifies the most generic authorization rule (based on relationship-based conditions) that can be inserted/removed from the policy by the specified administrators. This captures the *strictness order* proposed in RPPM2 [30].

The policy statement (e) in the running example is an administrative policy which updates the authorization policy by allowing emergency contact of a patient to see the diagnosis. For instance, when needed, M-Hospital needs to add the following authorization rule to the policy so that Alice's emergency contact, Bob, can view her diagnosis:

$$\langle \texttt{Alice.has-emg-contact}.s \wedge v_s.\texttt{has-patient.Alice},$$
$$\texttt{has-diagnosis}, \texttt{view}, \texttt{grant} \rangle$$

Note that the above rule is an authorization rule according to Definition 3.3 which ensures that subject s is Alice's emergency contact, and the starting vertex v_s of the protected resource (**has-diagnosis** edge) is Alice's treatment. Now, an administration rule that authorizes addition of the above rule to the authorization policy is as follows.

$$\langle s.\overline{\texttt{performed-at}}; \texttt{has-patient}.\$x,$$
$$\$x.\texttt{has-emg-contact}.s \wedge v_s.\texttt{has-patient}.\$x,$$
$$\texttt{has-diagnosis}, \texttt{view}, \texttt{grant}, \texttt{insert}, \texttt{grant} \rangle$$

Note that we consider free variables such as $\$x$ in the syntax for administrative rules in order to support flexible administrative policies. It should be clear that when $\$x$ in the above administrative rule is bound to **Alice**, M-Hospital will be able to insert the previous authorization rule.

Finally, given a set of administrative rules, an administrative policy is defined as follows.

Definition 3.9 (Administrative Policy). An administrative authorization policy is a pair $\langle AR, \sigma \rangle$, where AR is a set of administrative rules and σ is a conflict resolution strategy.

3.7 Protection System

We now formally define a RePM protection system as follows.

Definition 3.10 (Protection System). A RePM protection system is defined by a pair $\langle PS, AP \rangle$, where PS represents the possible protection states and AP is an administrative policy. AP authorizes administrative operations applicable to the authorization policy at a state ps, i.e., $ps.P$.

In each state of the system ps, exercise of an operation on system graph $ps.G$ is authorized by $ps.P$, and if allowed, will result in transition to a new protection state (with an updated $ps.G$). At the same time, each exercise of an administrative action authorized by AP will also result in transition to a new protection state (with an updated $ps.P$).

4 SECURITY ANALYSIS IN RePM

In this section, we formulate security analysis problem in the context of RePM. In order to facilitate discussions about security analysis, we first provide an illustration of a the RePM protection model. Figure 2 depicts a fairly complex state-transition system of RePM using a small synthetic example. In the figure, each node (ellipse shape) represents a protection state, which includes both system graph G and authorization policy P. Each solid arrow indicates possibility of transition from one state to another. The dashed circles show logical groupings of states based on same authorization policy p_i. The transitions in the protection system are controlled by the enforced policies. While transitions within a logical group are restricted by authorization policy p_i, transitions across logical groups are restricted by administrative policy AP. Note that administrative policy AP is considered constant (or only updated by trusted users). However, authorization policy can be updated according to AP, and for that reason, it is considered constant only within each logical circle in the figure.

4.1 Factors Affecting Analysis

In this section, we informally discuss about the security analysis problem in the context of RePM and contributing factors to its expressiveness and complexity.

Query target A security analysis query should be about properties of protection states. In RePM, given the structure of a protection state $\gamma = \langle G, P \rangle$ the query can be about system graph G, or valid authorizations based on authorization policy P. We call them *graph queries* and *authorization queries*, respectively. In the context of the running example, "whether a person can be a patient's PCP and her emergency contact at the same time" is a graph query. An example of authorization query is that whether a regular contact will be able to learn about a patient's illness.

Query formulation One of the strengths of ReBAC is its ability to specify powerful conditions based on system graph. This feature can be utilized in security analysis queries to precisely characterize an entity (group of entities) of interest based on its (their) relationships at the desired level of specificity. For example, one can ask if at any point any doctor will have more access to treatment information than the involved patients. While this enables much more flexible queries compared to the existing security analysis approaches (for example in case of ARBAC [18]), it adds to the complexity of answering such queries.

Existential vs. universal query We expect both existential and universal queries to be useful. Such quantifiers are applicable both to system states and queries.

Policy syntax The richness of both authorization and administrative policies in RePM will affect the complexity of security analysis. That includes support for expressions based on system graph in the conditions, and whether rules will be positive-only or a mixture of positive and negative rules accompanied by a conflict resolution strategy.

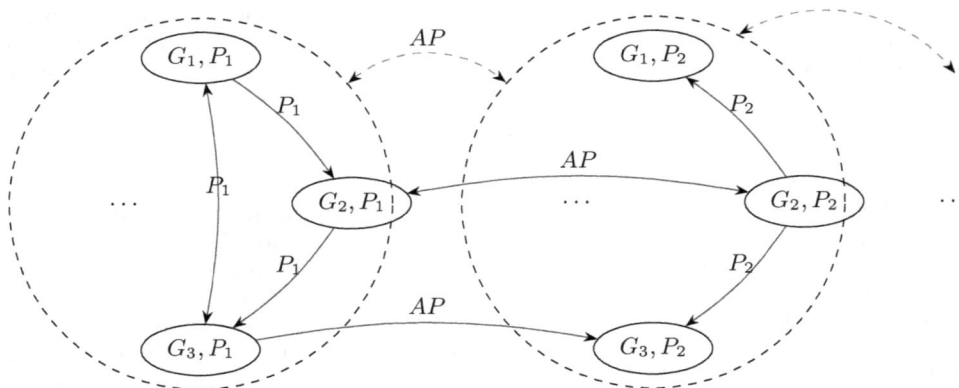

Figure 2: RePM State Transition System

Authorization policy update RePM supports modification of the authorization policy using the administrative policy, which is assumed to be constant itself (or modified only by trusted users). This is natural in ReBAC environments. For example, OSN users may specify their own authorization policies for their data (privacy settings). At the same time, they only have a fixed amount of administrative power on specifying such policies. We also envision ReBAC systems which may not need such administrative capability. We therefore, consider and analyze a class of systems with no administrative policy as well.

4.2 Security Analysis Problem

In order to formulate the security analysis problem in the context of RePM, we adopt the following two definitions of access control scheme and security analysis, originally presented in the context of RBAC [19].

Definition 4.1 (Access Control Scheme [19]). An access control scheme is a state-transition $\langle \Gamma, Q, \vdash, \Psi \rangle$, where Γ is set of states, Q is set of queries, $\vdash$ is an entailment relation $\vdash: \Gamma \times Q \to \{\texttt{true}, \texttt{false}\}$ that determines whether a query is true or not in a given state, and Ψ is the set of the possible schemes for state transitions.

In the above definition, $\psi \in \Psi$ is a state-change rule, i.e., a policy. We write $\gamma \overset{*}{\mapsto}_\psi \gamma_1$ if starting from state γ we reach state γ_1 after zero or more transitions allowed by ψ.

Definition 4.2 (Security Analysis [19]). Given an access control scheme $\langle \Gamma, Q, \vdash, \Psi \rangle$ a security analysis instance takes the form $\langle \gamma, q, \psi, \Pi \rangle$, where $\gamma \in \Gamma$ is a starting state, $q \in Q$ is a query, $\psi \in \Psi$ is a state-change rule, and $\Pi \in \{\exists, \forall\}$ is a quantifier. An instance $\langle \gamma, q, \psi, \exists \rangle$ asks whether there exists γ_1 where $\gamma \overset{*}{\mapsto}_\psi \gamma_1$ and $\gamma_1 \vdash q$. An instance $\langle \gamma, q, \psi, \forall \rangle$ asks whether for every γ_1 such that $\gamma \overset{*}{\mapsto}_\psi \gamma_1$ and $\gamma_1 \vdash q$.

As discussed in Section 4.1, there are many contributing factors to security analysis problem for ReBAC policies which can lead different formulations of the problem. In the followings, we introduce RePM-specific security analysis problems by specifying elements of an access control scheme (Definition 4.1). In particular, we define two classes of security analysis problems in the context of RePM based on different query targets. The first class uses graph queries as targets.

Definition 4.3 (RePM Security Analysis with Graph Query Target). A RePM security analysis based on a graph query is defined according to the following access control scheme:

states A state γ is a pair $\langle G, P \rangle$ of a system graph and an authorization policy.

state-transition rules A state transition ψ includes both authorization policy P and administrative policy AP.

queries A graph query is a tuple $q_g = \langle \phi, rl, \Pi' \rangle$, where ϕ is a matching condition based on Definition 3.4, rl is a relationship label, and $\Pi' \in \{\exists, \forall\}$ is a quantifier. Variables v_s and v_d can be used in ϕ to express beginning and ending vertices of an edge with label rl.

entailment An *existential graph query* (where $\Pi' = \exists$) entails true if and only if there exists an edge $\langle rl, v_s, v_d \rangle$ in the system graph that satisfies matching condition ϕ. A *universal graph query* (where $\Pi' = \forall$) entails true if and only if all edges $\langle rl, v_s, v_d \rangle$ in the system graph satisfy matching condition ϕ.

Note the distinction between quantifiers Π and Π' in Definitions 4.2 and 4.3, respectively. While the former quantifies future states, the latter quantifies edges in the system graph at a given state. The combination of the two quantifiers leads to four different types of analysis.

As an example of an existential security analysis ($\Pi = \exists$), based on an existential graph query ($\Pi' = \exists$), we may ask: "Would it be possible that some patient's PCP be her emergency contact as well?" Such an analysis can be formulated as follows.

$$\langle \gamma, \langle v_s.\texttt{has-emg-contact}.v_d, \texttt{has-pcp}, \exists \rangle, \psi, \exists \rangle$$

The other variations of the above analysis that can be formulated are as follows. For brevity, we avoid repeating the analysis expressions.

- $(\Pi = \forall; \Pi' = \exists)$ Is it always the case that some patient's PCP is her emergency contact as well?
- $(\Pi = \exists; \Pi' = \forall)$ Would it be possible that every patient's PCP be their emergency contacts as well?
- $(\Pi = \forall; \Pi' = \forall)$ Is it always the case that every patient's PCP are their emergency contacts as well?

We present our second RePM-specific security analysis problem based on authorization queries.

Definition 4.4 (RePM Security Analysis with Authorization Query Target). A RePM security analysis based on an authorization query is defined according to the following access control scheme:

states A state γ is a pair $\langle G, P \rangle$ of a system graph and an authorization policy.

state-transition rules A state transition ψ includes both authorization policy P and administrative policy AP.

queries An authorization query is a tuple $q_a = \langle \phi, rl, op, d, \Pi' \rangle$, where ϕ, rl, op, and d are same as in an authorization rule (Definition 3.3), and $\Pi' \in \{\exists, \forall\}$ is a quantifier.

entailment An *existential authorization query* q_a entails true if and only if $\gamma_1.P$ (authorization policy in state γ_1) and corresponding authorization elements in q_a result in consistent authorization decision for an applicable access request. A *universal authorization query* q_a entails true if and only if $\gamma_1.P$ and q_a result in consistent authorization decisions for every applicable access request.

Consistent decisions for a policy and q_a means that either both grant or both deny the applicable access(es).

As an example of a universal analysis, based on a universal authorization query, we may ask: "Will patients always be able to see their diagnosis?" The analysis will be formulated as follows.

$$\langle \gamma, \langle v_s.\texttt{has-patient}.s, \texttt{has-diagnosis}, \texttt{view}, \texttt{grant}, \forall \rangle, \psi, \forall \rangle$$

5 SAFETY ANALYSIS IN RePM$_G$

As a sample security analysis problem for ReBAC policies, we study a safety problem in a limited version of RePM, which we call RePM$_G$. In RePM$_G$, there is no administrative policy, i.e., $AP = \emptyset$. This means that authorization policy is never updated or only updated by trusted administrators. Actions taken by trusted administrators are excluded from security analysis as they are assumed to avoid any breach of security.

The safety problem in RePM$_G$ that we consider in this section is a graph query that asks whether at any future state a certain edge will exist in the system graph. We define the problem as follows, as a subclass of the problem in Definition 4.3.

Definition 5.1 (Edge Safety Problem in RePM$_G$). Edge safety problem in RePM$_G$ is a simplified version of RePM security analysis problem with graph query target according to the following access control scheme:

states A state γ is modeled as system graph G.

state-transition rules A state transition ψ is modeled using authorization policy P.

queries The edge safety query q_g can be formulated as the following graph query: $\langle \top, rl, \exists \rangle$

THEOREM 5.2. *The edge safety problem in RePM$_G$ is decidable.*

We can prove the above theorem by reducing the safety problem in RePM$_G$ to the safety in the mono-operational case of the HRU model [14]. A sketch of the proof is as follows.

PROOF SKETCH. Given an instance of safety problem in RePM$_G$, we build an HRU protection system by converting system graph G to an access control matrix and each authorization rule with `insert/remove` primitive operations to a command in the context of HRU model. We note that an authorization rule with a `view` primitive operation does not result in changing the protection state. It is sufficient to represent system graph G as its adjacency matrix in order to convert it to its access matrix equivalent. The result will be a square matrix M, where $l \in M[x, y]$ if and only if $\langle l, x, y \rangle \in G.E$. Note that in terms of access matrix this means subject x will have right l on object y. Given the structure of an access request $\langle s, \langle rl, v_s, v_d \rangle, op \rangle$, an authorization rule $pr = \langle \phi, rl, op, \texttt{grant} \rangle \in P$ is converted to the following command:

```
command auth_cmd_pr(s, rl, vs, vd, w1,...,wt)
{
    if Φ then
        OP(rl, vs, vd)
}
```

In the above, primitive operation OP will correspond to op in the authorization rule. The condition Φ will translate path condition ϕ in the authorization rule into a series of tests for presence of rights in the access matrix as follows. Let $\phi_i = u_i.\pi_i.v_i$ be the ith operand of the conjunction in ϕ. According to Definition 3.4, ϕ_i has format $u.l_1; l_2; \ldots; l_k.v$, which can be unfolded into a conjunction

$$u.l_1.w_1 \wedge w_1.l_2.w_2 \ldots \wedge w_{k-1}.l_k.v$$

We create a conjunctive expression consisting of tests on access matrix corresponding to each operand $x.l_i.y$ as follows:

- $x = y$ if $l_i = \diamond$;
- $l_i \in M[x, y]$ if $l_i \in L_R$;
- $l_i \in M[y, x]$ if $l_i = \overline{l'_i}$ and $l'_i \in L_R$.

This will capture ϕ_i in terms of access matrix. Finally, we consider Φ to be the conjunctive statement containing all such corresponding ϕ_is. Arguments $w_1 \ldots w_t$ in the command correspond to placeholder vertices that are used in the construction of individual tests described above. The count of them will depend on the length of the paths tested in the path condition. Now, test Φ on access matrix is equivalent to matching condition ϕ in RePM$_G$.

In this setting, leaking a right in the context of the constructed HRU model is equivalent to insertion of the equivalent edge in system graph G. The constructed HRU model is a mono-operational HRU protection system, therefore the same process that can decide about it [14] can decide about safety in RePM$_G$. □

Note that, in the above proof sketch, we have slightly deviated from the syntax of commands in the HRU model. The HRU commands do not consider tests for equivalency of arguments. However, including such tests will not compromise the original proof of decidability presented in [14]. We recall that the main argument of the original proof is that by considering the creation of only one new subject instead of many possible creations, the leak can be still achieved (if possible at all). If we substitute the newly created subject s_1 in place of any other subject that might have been potentially created, say s_2: as long as tests for an equivalency test $x = s_2$ is replaced with $x = s_1$, if $x = s_2$ was able to a leak a right, $x = s_1$ will lead to a leak too.

6 CONCLUSION

It is critical to formally analyze safety and security of an access control policy system in order to ensure that it provides the expected security. Reasoning about security of complex ReBAC policy systems as they evolve can mitigate many challenges with which such systems are already facing. For example, it can potentially resolve uncertainties that both users and provider of an online social network may have about future security and privacy behaviors in the system. In this work, we presented a first formulation of security analysis problem in the context of ReBAC systems by formalizing a ReBAC protection system, RePM. We also showed the decidability of edge safety problem in a limited version of RePM.

There are many exciting challenges to be addressed as future work including improving generalizability of the RePM model, investigating various subclasses of the security analysis problem in this context, and studying application of such analysis on real-world systems.

ACKNOWLEDGMENTS

We would like to thank the anonymous reviewers for their valuable comments and helpful suggestions that guided us in improving the final manuscript.

REFERENCES

[1] T. Ahmed, R. Sandhu, and J. Park. Classifying and Comparing Attribute-Based and Relationship-Based Access Control. In *Proceedings of the Seventh ACM on Conference on Data and Application Security and Privacy*, CODASPY '17, pages 59–70, New York, NY, USA. ACM, 2017.

[2] G. Bruns, P. Fong, I. Siahaan, and M. Huth. Relationship-based Access Control: Its Expression and Enforcement Through Hybrid Logic. In *Proceedings of the Second ACM Conference on Data and Application Security and Privacy*, CODASPY '12, pages 117–124, New York, NY, USA. ACM, 2012.

[3] B. Carminati, E. Ferrari, R. Heatherly, M. Kantarcioglu, and B. Thuraisingham. A semantic web based framework for social network access control. In *Proc. 14th ACM Symposium on Access Control Models and Technologies*, pages 177–186. ACM, 2009.

[4] B. Carminati, E. Ferrari, and A. Perego. Enforcing access control in Web-based social networks. *ACM Trans. Inf. Syst. Secur.*, 13(1):1–38, Nov. 2009. ISSN: 1094-9224.

[5] B. Carminati, E. Ferrari, and A. Perego. Rule-Based Access Control for Social Networks. In R. Meersman, Z. Tari, and P. Herrero, editors, *Proc. OTM 2006 Workshops (On the Move to Meaningful Internet Systems)*, volume 4278 of *LNCS*, pages 1734–1744. Springer, Oct. 2006.

[6] Y. Cheng, J. Park, and R. Sandhu. Relationship-Based Access Control for Online Social Networks: Beyond User-to-User Relationships. In *Proc. 2012 International Conference on Privacy, Security, Risk and Trust and 2012 International Confernece on Social Computing*, pages 646–655, Sept. 2012.

[7] M. Cramer, J. Pang, and Y. Zhang. A Logical Approach to Restricting Access in Online Social Networks. In *Proceedings of the 20th ACM Symposium on Access Control Models and Technologies*, SACMAT '15, pages 75–86, New York, NY, USA. ACM, 2015.

[8] J. Crampton and J. Sellwood. ARPPM: Administration in the RPPM Model. In *Proceedings of the Sixth ACM Conference on Data and Application Security and Privacy*, CODASPY '16, pages 219–230, New York, NY, USA. ACM, 2016.

[9] J. Crampton and J. Sellwood. Path Conditions and Principal Matching: A New Approach to Access Control. In *Proceedings of the 19th ACM Symposium on Access Control Models and Technologies*, SACMAT '14, pages 187–198, New York, NY, USA. ACM, 2014.

[10] J. Crampton and J. Sellwood. Relationships, Paths and Principal Matching: A New Approach to Access Control. arXiv:1505.07945 [cs], May 29, 2015. arXiv: 1505.07945;.

[11] eXtensible Access Control Markup Language (XACML) Version 3.0, OASIS, 2013.

[12] P. W. Fong. Relationship-based access control: protection model and policy language. In *Proc. CODASPY '11*, pages 191–202, San Antonio, TX, USA. ACM, 2011.

[13] P. W. Fong and I. Siahaan. Relationship-based access control policies and their policy languages. In *Proc. 16th ACM Symposium on Access Control Models and Technologies*, SACMAT '11, pages 51–60, Innsbruck, Austria. ACM, 2011.

[14] M. A. Harrison, W. L. Ruzzo, and J. D. Ullman. Protection in operating systems. *Commun. ACM*, 19(8):461–471, Aug. 1976. ISSN: 0001-0782.

[15] H. Hu, G. J. Ahn, and K. Kulkarni. Discovery and Resolution of Anomalies in Web Access Control Policies. *IEEE Transactions on Dependable and Secure Computing*, 10(6):341–354, Nov. 2013. ISSN: 1545-5971.

[16] H. Hu and G.-j. Ahn. Multiparty Authorization Framework for Data Sharing in Online Social Networks. In Y. Li, editor, *Proceedings of the 25th Annual IFIP WG 11.3 Conference on Data and Applications Security and Privacy*, volume 6818 of *Lecture Notes in Computer Science*, pages 29–43. Springer Berlin / Heidelberg, 2011.

[17] S. R. Kruk. FOAF-Realm: control your friends access to the resource. In Workshop on Friend of a Friend, Social Networking and the Semantic Web, 2004.

[18] N. Li and M. V. Tripunitara. Security Analysis in Role-based Access Control. In *Proceedings of the Ninth ACM Symposium on Access Control Models and Technologies*, SACMAT '04, pages 126–135, New York, NY, USA. ACM, 2004.

[19] N. Li and W. H. Winsborough. Beyond proof-of-compliance: safety and availability analysis in trust management. In *Proceedings of the 2003 Symposium on Security and Privacy*, pages 123–139, May 2003.

[20] N. Li, W. H. Winsborough, and J. C. Mitchell. Distributed credential chain discovery in trust management. *Journal of Computer Security*, 11(1):35–86, Jan. 1, 2003. ISSN: 0926-227X.

[21] D. Lin, P. Rao, E. Bertino, N. Li, and J. Lobo. EXAM: a comprehensive environment for the analysis of access control policies. *International Journal of Information Security*, 9(4):253–273, Aug. 2010. ISSN: 1615-5262.

[22] A. Masoumzadeh and J. Joshi. OSNAC: An Ontology-based Access Control Model for Social Networking Systems. In *Proc. 2nd IEEE Int'l Conference on Information Privacy, Security, Risk and Trust (PASSAT 2010)*, pages 751–759, Minneapolis, MN, USA, Aug. 2010.

[23] T. Nelson, D. J. Dougherty, C. Barratt, and K. Fisler. The Margrave Tool for Firewall Analysis. In *Proceedings of the 24th USENIX Large Installation System Administration Conference (LISA 2010)*, 2010.

[24] E. Pasarella and J. Lobo. A Datalog Framework for Modeling Relationship-based Access Control Policies. In *Proceedings of the 22Nd ACM on Symposium on Access Control Models and Technologies*, pages 91–102, New York, NY, USA. ACM, 2017.

[25] S. Z. R. Rizvi, P. W. Fong, J. Crampton, and J. Sellwood. Relationship-Based Access Control for an Open-Source Medical Records System. In *Proceedings of the 20th ACM Symposium on Access Control Models and Technologies*, SACMAT '15, pages 113–124, New York, NY, USA. ACM, 2015.

[26] R. S. Sandhu. The typed access matrix model. In *Proceedings 1992 IEEE Computer Society Symposium on Research in Security and Privacy*, pages 122–136, May 1992.

[27] R. S. Sandhu, V. Bhamidipati, and Q. Munawer. The ARBAC97 Model for Role-Based Administration of Roles. *ACM Transactions on Information and Systems Security*, 2(1):105–135, 1999.

[28] R. S. Sandhu. The Schematic Protection Model: Its Definition and Analysis for Acyclic Attenuating Schemes. *J. ACM*, 35(2):404–432, Apr. 1988. ISSN: 0004-5411.

[29] A. Sasturkar, P. Yang, S. D. Stoller, and C. R. Ramakrishnan. Policy analysis for administrative role based access control. In *Proceedings of the 19th IEEE Computer Security Foundations Workshop (CSFW'06)*, 13 pp.–138, 2006.

[30] S. D. Stoller. An Administrative Model for Relationship-Based Access Control. In *SpringerLink*. IFIP Annual Conference on Data and Applications Security and Privacy, pages 53–68. Springer, Cham, July 13, 2015.

The Next Domino to Fall: Empirical Analysis of User Passwords across Online Services

Chun Wang, Steve T.K. Jan, Hang Hu, Douglas Bossart, Gang Wang
Department of Computer Science, Virginia Tech, Blacksburg, VA, 24060
{wchun, tekang, hanghu, bossartd, gangwang}@vt.edu

ABSTRACT

Leaked passwords from data breaches can pose a serious threat if users reuse or slightly modify the passwords for other services. With more services getting breached today, there is still a lack of a quantitative understanding of this risk. In this paper, we perform the first large-scale empirical analysis of password reuse and modification patterns using a ground-truth dataset of 28.8 million users and their 61.5 million passwords in 107 services over 8 years. We find that password reuse and modification is very common (observed on 52% of the users). Sensitive online services such as shopping websites and email services received the most reused and modified passwords. We also observe that users would still reuse the already-leaked passwords for other online services for years after the initial data breach. Finally, to quantify the security risks, we develop a new training-based guessing algorithm. We show that more than 16 million password pairs (including 30% of the modified passwords) can be cracked within just 10 guesses.

ACM Reference Format:
Chun Wang, Steve T.K. Jan, Hang Hu, Douglas Bossart, Gang Wang. 2018. The Next Domino to Fall: Empirical Analysis of User Passwords across Online Services. In *CODASPY '18: Eighth ACM Conference on Data and Application Security and Privacy, March 19–21, 2018, Tempe, AZ, USA*. ACM, New York, NY, USA, 8 pages. https://doi.org/10.1145/3176258.3176332

1 INTRODUCTION

Today's data breaches (*e.g.*, Equifax, Yahoo, Myspace, Office of Personnel Management, Ashley Madison) are reaching unprecedented scale and coverage. In 2016 alone, there were more than 2000 confirmed breaches causing a leakage of billions of user records [37]. Many of the leaked datasets contain sensitive information such as *user passwords*, which are often made publicly available on the Internet by the attackers [25, 26, 29, 31, 42].

Leaked passwords can pose serious threats to users, particularly if the passwords are reused somewhere else by the users. Reusing the *same* or even slightly *modified* passwords allows attackers to further compromise the user's accounts in other unbreached services [23, 28]. Even worse, if the target user happened to be the administrator of another service, password reuse may lead to new massive data breaches (*e.g.*, Dropbox [4]).

With more and more passwords being leaked [8, 38], there is an urgent need to systematically assess users' password reuse and modification patterns and quantify the security risks. This is not only instrumental to protecting user accounts after data breaches, but can also help to develop more effective tools to manage users' passwords. Due to a lack of large-scale empirical data, most existing works rely on surveys or interviews to study password reuse [7, 14, 30, 32, 34, 40]. The problem is that user studies are often limited in scale (*e.g.*, a few hundred users), and users' self-reported results may contradict their actual behavior in practice [40].

Recently, researchers start to analyze empirical data to understand users' password reuse and modification patterns [5, 6, 24, 40, 43]. However, the scale of existing empirical studies is still very limited. The largest study so far that focuses on both password reuse and modification only covers 6,077 users [5]. The limited scope of the dataset (sample size, service type, user demographics) makes it challenging to examine the generalizability of the observations and quantify the actual security risks.

In this paper, we seek to fill in the gaps by gathering and analyzing a large collection of leaked password datasets across multiple years and various online services[1]. By linking the userID (*i.e.*, email address) in different password datasets, we construct a ground-truth mapping for the same users' passwords and study their reuse and modification patterns. The resulting ground-truth dataset contains 28,836,775 users and their 61,552,446 passwords from 107 online services across 8 years.

Our study has two goals. 1) We seek to empirically understand how users reuse and modify their passwords across online services at a *large-scale*. 2) We want to quantify the security risks introduced by password reuse and modifications after data breaches. To achieve these goals, we have addressed a number of technical challenges. First, while password reuse is easy to determine, password modification is not obvious. To this end, we develop a measurement framework to automatically determine whether two passwords are modified from each other, and extract the transformation rules. This framework enables a deeper analysis of users' password habits and cross-examining our results with the existing small-scale user studies. Second, we develop a new *training-based* password guessing algorithm to guess a target user's password based on her leaked ones. We empirically examine the possibility of password guessing in an *online* fashion. We have a number of key findings:

1. Password reuse and modification are still very common. Among the 28.8 million users, 38% have once reused the same password in two different services and 21% once modified an existing password to sign up a new service (52% collectively). In addition, we find that users with more total passwords are more likely to

---

[1]Our study has received IRB approval (Protocol #17-393).

reuse/modify passwords. The reused/modified passwords are statistically shorter but more complex. These results echo and help to confirm early findings of small-scale user studies [24, 40].

2. Sensitive online services have a high ratio of reused and modified passwords. A surprising new finding is that "shopping" services have the highest ratio (>85%) of reused and modified passwords, while "email" services are at the second place (>62%). Shopping services often store users' credit card information and home address, and thus reusing their passwords have key security implications. The problem with email services can be even more serious, given that attackers can use the email address to reset the user's passwords in other accounts (*e.g.*, online banking).

3. Users still reuse the already-leaked passwords for years after the data breach. We find a long delay before users change their already leaked passwords *in other services*. More than 70% of the users are still reusing the already-leaked passwords in other services 1 year after the leakage. 40% of the users are reusing the same passwords leaked more than 3 years ago. This indicates a persistent threat of the leaked passwords from data breaches.

4. Modified passwords are highly predictable. Among a large user population, there is only a small set of rules that users often apply to modify their passwords. Such "low variance" makes the modified passwords highly predictable. Our training-based algorithm can guess 30% of the modified passwords within 10 attempts (46.5% within 100 attempts). If we consider both the reused and modified passwords, we estimate that more than 16 million password pairs in our dataset can be cracked within 10 guesses. Our algorithm achieves a similar performance even if it is trained with only 0.1% of the data.

In summary, our work makes 3 key contributions.

- We perform the first large-scale empirical analysis on password reuse and modification behavior across online services (28.8 million users, 107 online services). Our analysis provides new insights into how user reuse and modify passwords in practice.

- We develop a new training-based password guessing algorithm to quantify the risk of password modification. Our algorithm can guess a large portion of modified passwords within 10 guesses.

- To facilitate future research, we share the dataset with the research community with carefully designed data sharing policies.

2 RELATED WORK

Password Reuse and Modification. Text-based password is still the primary authentication method for today's online services. Due to the difficulties of memorizing a large number of passwords, users often *reuse* the same passwords or slightly *modify* existing passwords when creating new ones [5, 7, 40]. Attackers may leverage the reused passwords to compromise new user accounts, or link user identities by mining the leaked password datasets [22].

Table 1 lists the key related works on password reuse and modification. On one hand, due to a lack of empirical datasets, most existing works rely on user surveys or interviews to understand password usage [5, 7, 14, 21, 30, 32, 34, 40]. For example, Das et al. [5] have reported that 51% of the users re-use passwords across online services. Stobert and Biddle's interview [32] suggests that password reuse often happens on "less important" services.

	PW Reuse	PW Modify	Methods	# Users
[21]	✓	✗	Survey	26
[32]	✓	✗	Survey	27
[40]	✓	✗	Empirical+Survey	134
[6]	✓	✗	Empirical	544,960
[7]	✗	✓	Survey	80
[30]	✗	✓	Survey	470
[43]	✗	✓	Empirical	7,700
[34]	✓	✓	Survey	49
[24]	✓	✓	Empirical+Survey	154
[14]	✓	✓	Survey	5,000
[5]	✓	✓	Empirical+Survey	6,077
Our	✓	✓	Empirical	28,836,775

Table 1: Related works on password reuse and modification.

Inevitably, user studies suffer from key limitations due to the small user population. A recent work also shows that user self-reported results may contradict their real behavior in practice [40]. To these ends, empirical analysis is needed to understand users' real-world behavior [5, 6, 24, 40, 43]. To date, existing empirical studies are still limited in scale, most of which only cover a few hundred (or a few thousand) users. The only exception is a measurement study [6] conducted 10 years ago by Microsoft (500K users), which, however, only analyzed password reuse not password modification across services. In our work, we seek to fill in the gap by collecting and analyzing a large-scale empirical password dataset (61.5 million passwords across 107 services). We focus on both *password reuse* and *modification*, and cross-examine our results with early findings from small-scale studies.

Online & Offline Password Guessing. Another related body of work is password guessing, which can be roughly divided into online guessing and offline guessing. Online guessing has a strict limit on the number of guessing attempts. For example, Trawling based approach simply guesses the most popular passwords chosen by users [18]. More targeted guessing exploits the fact that users may reuse the same or similar passwords [5, 43]. More recently, target guessing also incorporates users' personal information such as name and birthday [15, 39].

Offline guessing can easily reach trillions of guessing attempts [9, 10, 12, 19, 20, 36, 41]. A common scenario is to use offline guessing algorithms to recover plaintext passwords from a hashed password dataset. Over the last decades, a number of guessing methods have been proposed, including Markov Model [16, 20], Mangled Wordlist method [35], Probabilistic Context-Free Grammars Method (PCFGs) [12, 20, 36, 41], and Deep Neural Networks [19]. Offline guessing has also been used to measure password strength [13].

3 DATASET

To study password usage across online services, we gathered a large number of password datasets and linked the same user's passwords.

Data Collection In January 2017, we searched through various online forums and data archives for *public* password datasets. We looked for candidate datasets that meet two criteria. First, the dataset should contain email addresses so that we can link a user's passwords across different services. Second, we exclude datasets that only contain *salted hashes* since it is difficult to recover their

Category	#Plain PWs (#Datasets)	Top 3 Largest Datasets
Social	286M (7)	Myspace, VK.com, LinkedIn
Adult	75.2M (9)	Zoosk, Mate1, YouPorn
Game	40.8M (13)	Neopets, 7k7k, Lbsg
Entertain	30.7M (4)	Lastfm, Swingbrasileiro, LATimes
Internet	16.4M (18)	000webhost, Comcast, Yahoo
Email	9.6M (3)	Gmail, Mail.ru, Yandex
Forum	1.1M (25)	CrackingForum, Abusewith.us, Gawker
Shopping	340K (12)	RedBox, 1394store, Myaribags
Others	210K (7)	Data1, Data2, Data3
Business	10K (9)	Movatiathletic, Hrsupporten, 99Fame
Total	460M (107)	Myspace, VK, LinkedIn

Table 2: Categories and statistics of the collected datasets.

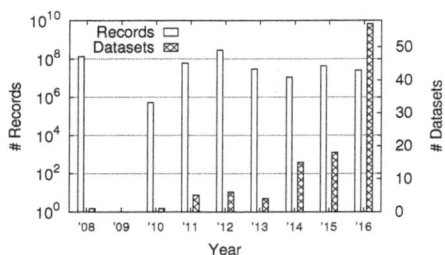

Figure 1: # of datasets and total # records per year.

passwords. In total, we collected 107 datasets leaked between 2008–2016, which contain 497,789,976 passwords and 428,199,842 unique users (email addresses). 14 datasets contain hashed passwords, and we spent a week to recover the plaintext using offline guessing tools [10, 11, 35]. This effort returned 460,874,306 plaintext passwords (93% of all passwords). We have carefully checked each dataset to make sure there are no duplicate records.

Data Statistics. In Table 2, we manually classify the 107 online services into 10 categories based on their category information in Alexa[2]. The "unknown" category contains 7 password datasets with no information about their leakage source. We double checked to make sure the 7 "unknown" datasets did not overlap with any existing ones. The password datasets vary in size. Large datasets from *LinkedIn* and *Myspace* contain hundreds of millions of records, while small datasets such as *InternetFamous* only have a few hundred records. Note that the password dataset may not cover the entire leaked data — attacker might only publish part of the dataset publicly.

We manually label the year *when each dataset was leaked* (excluding "unknown" datasets). We confirm the year of the data breach based on various sources such as reputable news reports and data breach reports [1, 2, 8, 38]. Figure 1 shows the number of datasets and the number of user records in different years. Note that year 2016 covers most of our datasets since it is easier to find datasets that were leaked more recently. For older datasets, they are primarily related to large data breaches.

Ethic Guidelines. Our work involves analyzing leaked datasets that contain sensitive information. We have worked closely with our local IRB and obtained the approval for our research. Our study

[2]https://www.alexa.com/topsites

is motivated by the following considerations. First, we only analyze datasets that are already publicly available. Analyzing such data does not add additional risks other than what already exists. Second, these datasets are also publicly available to potential attackers. Failure to include the data for research may give attackers an advantage over researchers that work on defensive techniques. In the past decades, leaked password datasets have been extensively used in academic research [5, 15, 35, 36, 39] to develop security mechanisms to protect users in the long run.

Primary Dataset (28.8 Million Users) To study cross-site password usage, we focus on users who appear in at least two different services. We construct a *primary* dataset of 28,836,775 users who have at least two plaintext passwords (61,552,446 passwords in total). Note that users outside of the primary dataset are not necessarily risk-free: they might still have accounts in services that we didn't cover. In this study, a *user* is defined by an email address, which helps us to link the same user's passwords together. In practice, it is possible for a person to have multiple email addresses. Our study will only estimate a lower-bound.

4 PASSWORD REUSE & MODIFICATION

Our dataset provides a unique opportunity to study password reuse and modifications across *a large user population* and *a variety of online services*. At the same time, we also seek to cross-compare our results with those from smaller-scale studies [5, 7, 24, 32, 34, 40] to provide a more complete view of this problem.

In the following, we first develop a framework to measure password reuse and modification behavior across online services (current section). Then we use this framework to perform an in-depth analysis to understand how users manage their passwords and generate the statistical patterns of password reuse and modification (Section 5). Finally, we empirically quantify the security risks of password reuse/modifications by performing password guessing experiments (Section 6 and Section 6.2), and discuss the implications of our results to the increasingly frequent data breaches (Section 7).

4.1 Reusing the Same Password

Human brains can only memorize a limited number of passwords, and thus users often reuse their passwords for different online services [6]. To understand the password reuse in practice, we perform a quick measurement on the *primary* dataset. For each user, we cross-examine all the possible password pairs (*e.g.*, if a user has 4 passwords, then we get 6 pairs). In total, we extract 37,301,406 password pairs for the 28.8 million users. We find that 34.3% of the pairs are identical pairs, meaning that the password is reused by the user. At the user level, 38% of the users (10.9 million) have at least one identical pair. This ratio is slightly lower than the self-reported results (51%) from a prior user study [5].

4.2 Classifying Password Modification

In addition to reusing the same password, users may also modify an existing password to sign up for a new service. We refer this type of behavior as *password modification*. Unlike password reuse, password modification is more difficult to measure because users may apply different rules to make the transformation. To this end,

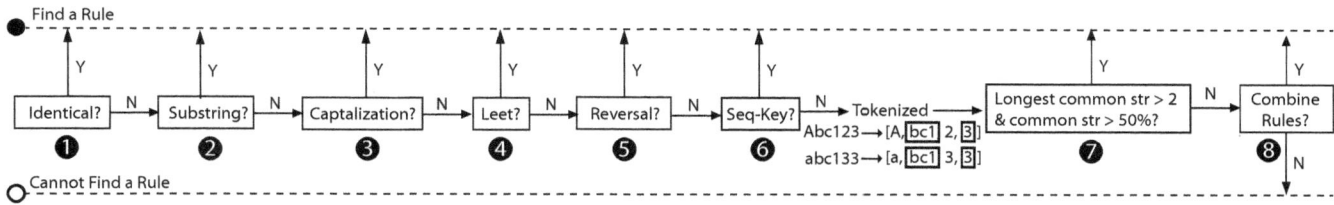

Figure 2: The workflow to measure a user's password transformation patterns.

Rule	# Pairs of Passwords	Ratio (%)
❶. Identical	12,780,722	34.3%
❷. Substring	3,748,258	10.0%
❸. Capitalization	478,233	1.3%
❹. Leet	93,418	0.3%
❺. Reversal	5,938	< 0.1%
❻. Sequential keys	12,118	< 0.1%
❼. Common Substring	2,103,888	5.7%
❽. Combination of Rules	754,393	2.0%
Can Not Find A Rule	17,324,438	46.4%
Total	37,301,406	100%

Table 3: Distribution of password transformation rules.

we first develop a method to automatically identify and classify modified passwords.

Given a pair of passwords, our goal is to detect if one password is modified from the other password and infer the rule of the transformation. Figure 2 shows the high-level workflow. In total, we construct 8 rules for password transformation based on our manual examinations of 1000 random password pairs and the results from prior studies [5, 43, 44]. We test these rules against the password pairs in the *primary dataset*, and the results are shown in Table 3.

We find that the majority of the password pairs (55.6%) can be explained by one of the transformation rules. To translate the numbers to the user level, 38% of the users have reused the same password at least once, and 21% of the users have once modified an existing password to create a new one. Collectively, these users count for 52%. Below, we discuss each of the rules in detail.

Identical. For completeness, we consider reusing the same password as one of the rules (12 million password pairs, 34.3%).

Substring. This rule indicates that one password is a substring of the other one (*e.g.*, "abc" and "abc12"). This rule matches 3.7 million password pairs (10%), indicating that users have inserted/deleted a string to/from an existing password to make a new one. As shown in Table 4, most insertions/deletions happened at the tail (87.2%). Most inserted/deleted strings are pure digits (74%) and short (1–2 characters), *e.g.*, "1", "2", and "12".

Capitalization. Users may simply capitalize certain letters in a password. Even though the ratio of matched pairs is not high (1.3%), the absolute number is still significant (478,233 pairs). We observe that users commonly capitalize letters at the beginning of the password (73%), particularly the first letter (68.6%).

Leet. 93,418 password pairs match the leet rule (0.3%) [27]. Leet transformation refers to replacing certain characters with other similar-looking ones. Our analysis shows the top 10 most common transformations are: 0↔o, 1↔i, 3↔e, 4↔a, 1↔!, 1↔l, 5↔s,

Insert/Delete Position	Ratio	Inserted/Deleted Length	Ratio
Tail	87.2%	1	48.3%
Head	11.0%	2	28.0%
Both Ends	1.8%	3+	23.7%
Insert/Delete Type	Ratio	Top Inserted/Deleted Str.	Ratio
Digit	74.0%	"1"	24.2%
Letter	17.8%	"2"	4.0%
Combined	4.5 %	"12"	2.1%
Special Char	3.7%	"123"	1.9%

Table 4: Substring rule: insertion/deletion patterns.

Longest Comm. Substring	Ratio	Transformation Rules	Ratio
Letter	63.8%	Substitution	84.7%
Digit	22.0%	Insertion/Deletion	32.4%
Combined	13.7%	Capitalization	3.2%
Special Char	0.5%	Switching Order	2.2%

Table 5: Common substring rule: longest common substring and transformation patterns.

@↔a, 9↔6, and $↔s. These 10 transformations already cover 96.6% of the leet pairs.

Reversal. Reversal rule is rarely used (5938 pairs, <0.1%), which means reversing the order of the characters in a password, *e.g.*, abcd↔dcba. Intuitively, reversed passwords are hard to memorize.

Sequential Keys. Sequential keys include alphabetically-ordered letters (abcd), sequential numbers (1234) and adjacent keys on the keyboard (qwert, asdfg, !@#$%). The matched pairs (*i.e.*, both passwords are sequential keys) are also below 0.1%.

Common Substrings. When a user modifies an existing password to create a new one, we assume the majority of the password remains the same. As shown in Figure 2, we extract the longest common substrings from the two passwords to learn how they transform the rest parts. To avoid accidental character overlaps, we require the longest common string to be >2 characters, and all the common substrings should cover >50% characters of a password (*i.e.*, the majority). This rule matches 2.1 million password pairs (5.7%). To make sure the thresholds make sense, we manually examine a random sample of 1000 matched pairs. For ethical considerations, we use a script to remove the email addresses before manually looking at the passwords. We find only 44 out of 1000 pairs appear to be accidental overlaps. For example, "fighter51" and "nightfall" share a common substring "ight", but do not look like a password modification case. At this point, we can allow false negatives since we have one more rule to check. Based on the false positive rate (4.4%), we estimate that the common substring rule should match at least 5.4% of all password pairs (lower bound).

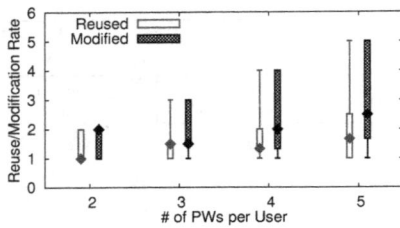

Figure 3: Password reuse/modification rate for users of different # of total passwords. The box plot quantiles are 5%, 25%, 50%, 75%, 95%.

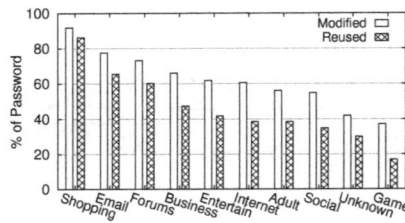

Figure 4: Ratio of reused and modified password under different services. Shopping and email services received the most reused and modified passwords.

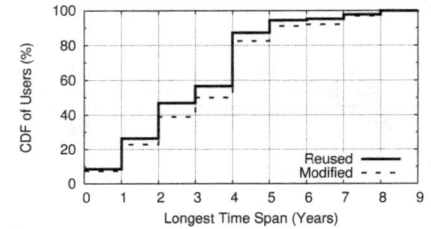

Figure 5: Longest time span between any pair of reused/modified passwords for each user.

Rule Combination	Ratio	Rule Combination	Ratio
Capitalization+Substring	26.2%	Reversal+CSS	6.1%
Leet+CSS	21.8%	Leet+SubString	5.6%
Seqkey+CSS	13.2%	Seqkey+SubString	4.2%
Reversal+Leet+CSS	7.1%	Seqkey+Leet+CSS	2.9%
Capitalization+CSS	6.2%	Others	6.8%

Table 6: Rule combinations (CSS: Common SubString).

Table 5 shows characteristics of the longest common substrings for the matched password pairs. The longest common substring represents the "unmodified" part of the password, most of which are pure letters (63.8%) or pure digits (22%). The majority (56.7%) of the pure-letter substrings are actually English words or English names (based on NLTK corpus [3]). Table 5 shows that the most common transformation is substitution, followed by insertion and deletion. Note that one password pair may have multiple transformations (the accumulated ratio exceeds 100%).

Combination of Rules. As a final step, we combine possible rules to find a match. Note that rule3 – rule6 modify the characters (or the sequence of characters) in a password, while rule2 and rule7 operate on substrings. Our approach is to use a combination of rule3 – rule6 to modify the password first, and then test if rule2 or rule7 can declare a match. In this way, we further matched another 754,000+ pairs (2.0%). As shown in Table 6, "Capitalization" and "Substring" are the most common combination (26.2%), followed by the combination of "Leet" and "Common substring" rules.

Unmatched Password Pairs. After testing all the above rules, there are still 46.4% password pairs remain unmatched. To make sure we did not miss any major rules, we randomly sample 1000 unmatched pairs for manual examination. Through our manual analysis, we did not find any of the 1000 password pairs exhibiting a meaningful transformation. Some example password pairs are: (samsungi5700, nokiae61), (phone80720, computer7), (iloveyou12, 12081999), and (sleepwalker, 123456). We regard the remaining 46.4% of password pairs as the result of users "making new passwords from scratch".

5 MEASURING PASSWORD HABITS

Next, we leverage the labeled data to answer key questions about users' password habits. We focus on the *individual users* to explore a series of key questions. *Firs*, how often do users reuse (modify) the same password for different services? *Second*, what types of online services receive the most reused (modified) passwords? *Finally*, how long do users wait before changing their reused passwords in other services after a data breach?

User-level Reuse and Modification Rate. To measure password reuse and modification at the *per-user* level, we calculate a *reuse rate* and a *modification rate* for each user. Given a user u_i, we define her online services as $S_i = [s_{i,1}, s_{i,2}, s_{i,3}, ..., s_{i,K_i}]$, where K_i is user u_i's total number of services. The corresponding passwords are $P_i = [p_{i,1}, p_{i,2}, p_{i,3}, ..., p_{i,K_i}]$. First, *reuse rate* describes how many times a user's password is reused in different services on average. $RR(i) = \frac{|S_i|}{|Set(P_i)|}$. $RR=1$, if the user sets a unique password for each service. A higher value of RR indicates a more severe password reuse. Second, *modification rate* describes how many times a user's password is reused or modified for different services. $MR(i) = \frac{|S_i|}{|Cluster(P_i)|}$, where $Cluster()$ groups the user's passwords based on whether one password is modified from the other. Based on the transformation rules in Section 4, we group passwords into the same cluster if they match with one of the transformation rules. The resulting clusters don't overlap, representing independent password groups. A higher value of MR indicates more frequent password reuse and modifications.

Figure 3 shows the distribution of RR and MR for users with different numbers of total passwords. We examine whether users with more passwords (*i.e.* online accounts) are more likely to reuse their passwords. The intuition is that a user can only memorize a limited number of passwords. The more online services she has, the more likely her passwords are reused. Our result supports this intuition. As shown in Figure 3, both the reuse rate and modification rate are increasing as users have more total passwords. Our results agree with prior user studies (100+ users) that examine this intuition on *password reuse* [21, 40]. Figure 3 also shows that the black bars (modification) are consistently higher than the blue bars (reuse). This indicates that password modification is broadly applied by users. Analysis that does not consider password modification will under-estimate the security risks.

Impact of Online Services. In Figure 4, we examine what types of online services have received the most reused or modified passwords. We find that "shopping" services have the most reused/-modified passwords with a ratio over 85%. Shopping services usually store users' credit information and home address information.

Reusing passwords of shopping services have key security implications. A possible explanation is that users may have too many accounts for various online stores, making it difficult to memorize a unique password for each one.

More surprisingly, we find that "email services" contain the second-most reused and modified passwords. This result has more serious security implications. First and foremost, an email account can be used to reset the password for other online services (*e.g.*, banking accounts). Many of the online accounts will be in danger if the user's email account is compromised. The ratio of reused email passwords is over 62% and the ratio of modified email passwords is an even higher 78%. Noticeably, our observation contradicts with the results from a prior user study (154 users) [24], which shows that "email" is among categories with the least password reuse.

Delay of Changing Passwords. Finally, we examine the password reuse and modification *across time*. More specifically, we examine how long it takes before users change their reused passwords in other services after data breaches. For example, suppose service A was breached in year t_A and service B was breached later in year t_B. If a user has the same password for both A and B in our dataset, it means this user did not bother to change the reused password for $t_\delta = t_B - t_A$ years. Another interpretation is that the user still signs-up new services using the same password leaked t_δ years ago. For users who have reused/modified passwords, we calculate the largest time-span between her reused/modified password pairs. The result is shown in Figure 5.

Surprisingly, our results indicate that after a service was breached, a large number of users did not reset their reused passwords in *other services* for a long time. More than 70% of the users with reused passwords are still reusing the leaked passwords 1 year after the initial leakage. 40% of users are still reusing the same passwords leaked 3 years ago. Not too surprisingly, slightly modified passwords are continuously used for a longer time than the reused passwords. Our result indicates a persistent threat from reused/modified passwords after data breaches. Attackers may still use the leaked passwords to compromise user accounts in other services after a long time.

6 PASSWORD GUESSING EXPERIMENT

So far, the measurement results suggest that password reuse and modification have potential security risks. Next, we seek to *quantify* the security risks by performing password guessing experiments. In this section, we develop a new *training-based* password guessing algorithm and answer the following key questions. First, how quickly can attackers guess a modified password based on a known one? Second, can attackers use a small training data (*e.g.*, 0.1%) to achieve an effective guessing?

6.1 Guessing Algorithm

We build a new password guessing algorithm to quantify the security risks of password reuse and modification. The algorithm seeks to guess a target user's password by transforming a known password of the same user. The high-level idea is to test different password transformation rules (*e.g.*, rules in Table 3) on the known password. This idea is similar to DBCBW [5], a popular algorithm for targeted password guessing. DBCBW's focuses on *simplicity* which, however, has to make a few compromises. First, due to the

18 Features Extracted from a Password
PW (password) length, # Lowercase letters, # Uppercase letters, # Digits, # Special chars, Letter-only pw?, Digit-only pw?, # Repeated chars, Max # consec. letters, Max # consec. digits, Max # sequential keys, Englishword-only pw?, # Consec. digits (head), # Consec. digits (tail), # Consec. letters (head), # Consec. letters (tail), # Consec. special-chars (head), # Consec. special-chars (tail)

Table 7: Feature list of the Bayesian model.

lack of training data, the DBCBW uses hand-crafted transformation rules. Second, it tests these rules in a *fixed order*, which may not be optimal for individual passwords. For example, given "l0ve", the most probable rule should be leet ($0 \rightarrow o$);

Our algorithm overcomes these drawbacks by introducing a *training phase*. Using ground-truth password pairs, we learn two things: (1) the transformation procedure for each rule, and (2) a model to customize the ordering of the rules for each password.

Training 1: Transformation Procedures. A transformation procedure describes how to transform a password to a new one. For each rule in Table 3, we seek to learn a list of possible transformations during the training phase. For each rule R_i, the learned transformation is $T_i = [t_{i1}, t_{i2}, ...t_{iN_i}]$, which is sorted by the frequency of each transformation in the training dataset. For the "substring rule", t is characterized by *<insert/delete><position><string>*. For the "capitalization rule", t is characterized by *<position><#chars>*. In a similar way, we learn the lists of transformations for "leet", "sequential keys" and "reversal". For the "identical" rule, no transformation is needed, and we simply test if the password is reused.

There are special designs for the "common substring" rule and the "combination" rule. For the common substring rule, we can learn and sort the transformations (*e.g.*, insert, delete, replace, substitute, switch orders) based on the training data. However, when applying the transformation to a given password, we need to split the password to detect potential common substrings. In our design, we test 3 types of candidates: (1) substrings of pure digits/letters/special characters, (2) English words/names, and (3) popular common substrings in the *training data*. For the "combined rule", T is a sorted list of rule-combinations where each rule-combination has a sorted list of transformations to be tested.

Training 2: Rule Ordering. For a given password, we also learn which rule should be applied first. We treat this as a multiple-class classification problem. Given a password, we train a model to estimate the likelihood that the password can be transformed by each rule. To achieve a quick training, we choose the Naive Bayes classifier (multinomial model) [17], which produces the *probability* that a data point (password) belong to a class (rule). Based on the probability, we customize the ordering of the rules for this password. Table 7 shows the 18 features used in the Bayesian model.

Password Guessing Method. For a password pair (pw_1, pw_2), we seek to test how many attempts are needed to guess pw_2 by transforming a known pw_1. We first use the Bayesian model to generate a customized order of rules for pw_1. Following the ordered rule list, we have two options for guessing:

- **Sequential**: testing one rule at a time. After testing all the transformations under a rule, we move to the next rule. Since certain rules have a significantly longer list than others, we set a

(a) 5000 Guesses

(b) 10 Guesses

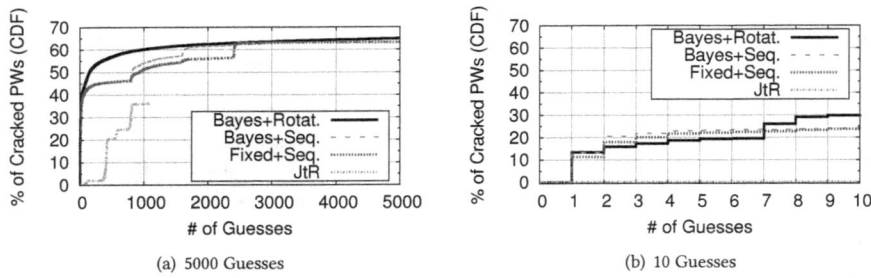

Figure 6: Password guessing with 50% of the data for training.

Figure 7: Password guessing with different training data sizes.

threshold M as the maximum number of guesses under each rule ($M = 800$ for our experiment).

- **Rotational:** testing one rule and one transformation at a time. After testing one transformation under a rule, we move to the next rule to test another transformation. We rotate to test each rule for just one guess.

Note that sequential guessing requires a higher accuracy of the predicted order. If the predicted order is wrong, it will waste many guesses on the wrong rule before moving on.

Baselines. When choosing baselines, we ruled out algorithms that don't fit our threat model. First, we rule out non-targeted guessing algorithms [19, 35], since non-targeted algorithms are primarily for offline guessing (*e.g.*, 10^{12} guesses needed). Second, we also rule out targeted guessing algorithms that require the user's PII information (*e.g.*, real name, date of birth) [15, 39]. Such PII information is not available in our datasets.

For our experiment, we run two baseline algorithms for comparison purposes. First, instead of customizing the order of rules for each password, we apply these rules with *a fixed order* for "sequential guessing". The fixed order is based on the overall rule popularity in the training data. Our second baseline is a widely used password cracking tool John the Ripper (JtR) [11]. We use the "single" mode and follow the default setting. Given a password, JtR applies a list of mangling rules to transform the password. It stops when all the mangling rules have been exhaustively tested.

6.2 Password Guessing Results

We use the proposed algorithm to evaluate the risks of *modified passwords*. For this experiment, we exclude identical password pairs (34.3%) since they only take one guess, and 46.4% of the pairs that don't match a rule. This leaves us 7,196,242 password pairs that represent password modifications (*exp dataset*). Our experiment contains two parts. First, we split the *exp dataset* randomly to use 50% for training and the other 50% for testing. Second, we use a much smaller training dataset to train the guessing algorithm. During the password guessing phase of our experiment, we test both directions for each password pair ($pw_1 \rightarrow pw_2$ and $pw_2 \rightarrow pw_1$), which doubles the size of the testing data.

Training on 50% of the Data. As shown in Figure 6, our best algorithm guessed 46.5% of the passwords within just 100 attempts. Figure 6(b) shows that 10 guesses already cracked 30% of the passwords. In comparison, the JtR baseline almost got nothing in the first 10 attempts and exhausted all the mangling rules after 1081

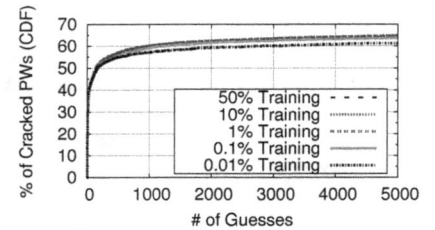

guesses. Since we evaluate an online-guessing scenario, we stopped our algorithm after 5000 guesses for each password.[3]

Comparing different algorithms, we show that the Bayesian model outperforms the fixed ordering method. This confirms the benefits of prioritizing the more likely rules for each password. In addition, we show that rotational guessing is better than sequential guessing. Sequential guessing has a clear stair-step increase of the hit rate after switching to a new rule. This indicates that the first few transformations under each rule are the most effective ones. Rotational guessing has an overall better performance due to switching the rules more frequently.

We argue that Bayesian-based sequential guessing still has its value, especially for *online guessing* attacks. As shown in Figure 6(b), sequential guessing's advantage is in the first 7 guesses — if the Bayesian prediction is correct, sticking to the right rule helped to guess the password more quickly. Within the first 7 guesses, Bayesian-based sequential guessing can guess 3% more passwords than rotational guessing. Given the large number of passwords being tested (3.6 million pairs, 7.2 million passwords), 3% still involve a large number of passwords (216K).

Using Smaller Training Data. Next, we try to use smaller datasets to train our algorithm (Bayesian+rotational). We vary the size of the training data from 0.01% to 10% of the *exp dataset*. To be consistent, we use the same 50% as the testing data (training and testing data has no overlap). As shown in Figure 7, the 0.1%-training curve is still overlapped with the 50%-curve, suggesting that extremely small training data can achieve a comparable performance. The result suggests that users are following a small number of consistent rules to modify their passwords. This is likely to make the modified passwords more predictable.

To measure the number of vulnerable password pairs, we use the 0.1%-trained model to guess the rest 99.9% of the password pairs. Since we guess both directions, the testing data essentially has 14 million passwords. Within 10 attempts, we guessed 30% (4.2 million passwords) — 3.8 million *password pairs* are cracked for at least one direction. Together with the identical password pairs (12.8 million), over 16.6 million pairs can be cracked within 10 attempts.

7 DISCUSSION & CONCLUSION

In this paper, we perform a large-scale empirical analysis on leaked password datasets over 8 years. We find that a majority of users have reused the same password or slightly modified an existing password for multiple services. Particularly, "shopping" and "email"

---

[3] Our experiment shows that 50,000 guesses can crack 70%.

services received the most reused and modified passwords (contradicting with existing results [24, 32]). In addition, users are still reusing their leaked passwords in other online services for years after the initial data breach, which introduces a persistent threat. More importantly, we find that the password modification patterns are highly consistent across various user populations, allowing attackers to quickly guess a large number of passwords with minimal training. Moving forward, we believe more proactive steps should be taken to protect user accounts after data breaches. Major online services such as Google have made an initial progress along this direction to proactively detect and stop malicious login attempts using the leaked passwords [33].

Limitations. Our study has a few limitations. First, our dataset is by no means complete, even for the 107 online services. For a given user, there are likely more reused or modified passwords in other services outside of our dataset. Our results can only be interpreted as a lower bound. Second, we treat each email address as a "user", but in practice, a user may have multiple email addresses. Again, the estimated password reuse and modification rates may be only a lower bound. Finally, our password guessing algorithms requires training data. We argue that such training data is relatively easy to obtain, and only a small training dataset is needed.

Data Sharing. To facilitate future research, we share our password dataset with the research community[4]. Although these datasets are already public on the Internet, it will still take a significant effort to search, collect, and clean the datasets. Sharing the dataset will benefit the research community as a whole. At the same time, we believe careful steps are needed to make sure the dataset is not misused by malicious parties. To this end, we follow a conservative data sharing policy that is commonly used by password researchers [10, 35]. First, we remove the email address from all the datasets, and use a hashed string as the identifier. Second, we remove the service name of each dataset. Finally, we will carefully verify the data requester's identity (*e.g.*, based on his/her institutional email address) before sharing the dataset.

ACKNOWLEDGMENTS

This project was supported by NSF grant CNS-1717028. Any opinions, conclusions or recommendations expressed in this material do not necessarily reflect the views of the funding agency.

REFERENCES

[1] Abusewith. 2017. Abusewith. http://abusewith.us/. (2017).
[2] Breach Alarm. 2017. Breach Alarm. https://breachalarm.com/all-sources/. (2017).
[3] Steven Bird, Ewan Klein, and Edward Loper. 2009. *Natural Language Processing with Python* (1st ed.). O'Reilly Media, Inc.
[4] Kate Conger. 2016. Dropbox employee's password reuse led to theft of 60M+ user credentials. TechCrunch. (2016).
[5] Anupam Das, Joseph Bonneau, Matthew Caesar, Nikita Borisov, and XiaoFeng Wang. 2014. The Tangled Web of Password Reuse. In *Proc. of NDSS'14*.
[6] Dinei Florencio and Cormac Herley. 2006. A Large Scale Study of Web Password Habits. In *Proc. of WWW'06*.
[7] S.M. Taiabul Haque, Matthew Wright, and Shannon Scielzo. 2013. A Study of User Password Strategy for Multiple Accounts. In *Procs. of CODASPY'13*.
[8] HIBP. 2017. Have I Been Pwned. https://haveibeenpwned.com/. (2017).
[9] Shouling Ji, Shukun Yang, Xin Hu, Weili Han, Zhigong Li, and Beyah. 2015. Zero-Sum Password Cracking Game: A Large-Scale Empirical Study on the Crackability, Correlation, and Security of Passwords. *IEEE TDSC* PP, 99 (2015), 1–1.
[10] Shouling Ji, Shukun Yang, Ting Wang, Changchang Liu, Wei-Han Lee, and Raheem Beyah. 2015. PARS: A Uniform and Open-source Password Analysis and Research System. In *Proc. of ACSAC'15*.
[11] JtR. 2017. John the Ripper. http://www.openwall.com/john/. (2017).
[12] Patrick Gage Kelley et al. 2012. Guess Again (and Again and Again): Measuring Password Strength by Simulating Password-Cracking Algorithms. In *Proc. of IEEE S&P'12*.
[13] Johannes Kiesel, Benno Stein, and Stefan Lucks. 2017. A Large-scale Analysis of the Mnemonic Password Advice. In *Proc. of NDSS'17*.
[14] Saranga Komarduri et al. 2011. Of Passwords and People: Measuring the Effect of Password-composition Policies. In *Proc. of CHI'11*.
[15] Yue Li, Haining Wang, and Kun Sun. 2016. A Study of Personal Information in Human-chosen Passwords and Its Security Implications. In *Proc. of INFOCOM'16*.
[16] Jerry Ma, Weining Yang, Min Luo, and Ninghui Li. 2014. A Study of Probabilistic Password Models. In *Proc. of IEEE S&P'14*.
[17] Christopher D. Manning, Prabhakar Raghavan, and Hinrich Schütze. 2008. *Introduction to Information Retrieval*. Cambridge University Press.
[18] Michelle L. Mazurek et al. 2013. Measuring Password Guessability for an Entire University. In *Proc. of CCS'13*.
[19] William Melicher, Blase Ur, Sean M. Segreti, Saranga Komanduri, Lujo Bauer, Nicolas Christin, and Lorrie Faith Cranor. 2016. Fast, Lean, and Accurate: Modeling Password Guessability Using Neural Networks. In *Proc. of USENIX Security'16*.
[20] Arvind Narayanan and Vitaly Shmatikov. 2005. Fast Dictionary Attacks on Passwords Using Time-space Tradeoff. In *Proc. of CCS'05*.
[21] Gilbert Notoatmodjo and Clark Thomborson. 2009. Passwords and Perceptions. In *Proc. of AISC'09*.
[22] Heen Olivier and Neumann Christoph. 2017. On the Privacy Impacts of Publicly Leaked Password Databases. In *Proc. of DIMVA'17*.
[23] Pierluigi Paganini. 2016. Reuse of login credentials put more than 20M Alibaba accounts at risk. Security Affairs. (2016).
[24] Sarah Pearman, Jeremy Thomas, Pardis Emami Naeini, Hana Habib, Lujo Bauer, Nicolas Christin, Lorrie Faith Cranor, Serge Egelman, , and Alain Forget. 2017. Let's go in for a closer look: Observing passwords in their natural habitat. In *Proc. of CCS'17*.
[25] Roi Perez. 2017. Hacker publicly releases 900GB of data stolen from Cellebrite. SC Magazine. (2017).
[26] Sarah Perez. 2016. 117 million LinkedIn emails and passwords from a 2012 hack just got posted online. TechCrunch. (2016).
[27] QNTM. 2017. Leet Transformation. https://qntm.org/l33t. (2017).
[28] Steve Ragan. 2015. Mozilla's bug tracking portal compromised, reused passwords to blame. CSO. (2015).
[29] TOBIAS SALINGER. 2015. Hackers post personal data stolen from adultery website Ashley Madison to dark web: reports. NY DailyNews. (2015).
[30] Richard Shay et al. 2010. Encountering Stronger Password Requirements: User Attitudes and Behaviors. In *Proc. of SOUPS'10*.
[31] OLIVIA SOLON. 2014. NHS patient data made publicly available online. Wired. (2014). http://www.wired.co.uk/article/care-data-leaks.
[32] Elizabeth Stobert and Robert Biddle. 2014. The Password Life Cycle: User Behaviour in Managing Passwords. In *Procs. of SOUPS'14*.
[33] Kurt Thomas, Frank Li, Ali Zand, Jake Barrett, Juri Ranieri, Eric Severance, Luca Invernizzi, Yarik Markov, Oxana Comanescu, Vijay Eranti, Angelika Moscicki, Dan Margolis, Vern Paxson, and Elie Bursztein. 2017. Data Breaches, Phishing, or Malware? Understanding the Risks of Stolen Credentials. In *Proc. of CCS'17*.
[34] Blase Ur et al. 2015. "I Added '!' at the End to Make It Secure": Observing Password Creation in the Lab. In *Proc. of SOUPS'15*.
[35] Blase Ur et al. 2015. Measuring Real-world Accuracies and Biases in Modeling Password Guessability. In *Proc. of USENIX Security'15*.
[36] Rafael Veras, Christopher Collins, and Julie Thorpe. 2014. On Semantic Patterns of Passwords and their Security Impact. In *Proc. of NDSS'14*.
[37] Verizon. 2017. Verizon's Data Breach Investigations Report. http://www.verizonenterprise.com/verizon-insights-lab/dbir/2017/. (2017).
[38] Vigilante. 2017. Vigilante. https://www.vigilante.pw/. (2017).
[39] Ding Wang, Zijian Zhang, Ping Wang, Jeff Yan, and Xinyi Huang. 2016. Targeted Online Password Guessing: An Underestimated Threat. In *Proc. of CCS'16*.
[40] Rick Wash, Emilee Rader, Ruthie Berman, and Zac Wellmer. 2016. Understanding Password Choices: How Frequently Entered Passwords Are Re-used across Websites. In *Proc. of SOUPS'16*.
[41] Matt Weir, Sudhir Aggarwal, Breno de Medeiros, and Bill Glodek. 2009. Password Cracking Using Probabilistic Context-Free Grammars. In *Proc. of IEEE S&P'09*.
[42] Joon Ian Wong. 2016. Stolen Dropbox passwords are circulating online. Here's how to check if your account's compromised. Quartz. (2016).
[43] Yinqian Zhang, Fabian Monrose, and Michael K. Reiter. 2010. The Security of Modern Password Expiration: An Algorithmic Framework and Empirical Analysis. In *Proc. of CCS'10*.
[44] Leah Zhang-Kennedy, Sonia Chiasson, and Paul van Oorschot. 2016. Revisiting password rules: facilitating human management of passwords. In *Proc. of eCrime'16*.

---

[4]Project website: https://people.cs.vt.edu/gangwang/pass

Efficient Authorization of Graph Database Queries in an Attribute-Supporting ReBAC Model

Syed Zain R. Rizvi
University of Calgary
szrrizvi@ucalgary.ca

Philip W. L. Fong
University of Calgary
pwlfong@ucalgary.ca

ABSTRACT

Neo4j is a popular graph database that offers two versions; a paid *enterprise edition* and a free *community edition*. The enterprise edition offers customizable Role-Based Access Control (RBAC) features through custom developed *procedures*, while the community edition does not offer any access control support. Being a graph database, Neo4j is a natural application for Relationship-Based Access Control (ReBAC), an access control paradigm where authorization decisions are based on relationships between subjects and resources in the system. In this paper we present AReBAC, an attribute-supporting ReBAC model for Neo4j (applicable to both editions) that provides finer grained access control. AReBAC employs Nano-Cypher, a declarative policy language based on Neo4j's Cypher query language, the result of which allows us to weave database queries with access control policies and evaluate both simultaneously. Evaluating the combined query and policy produces a result that i) matches the search criteria, and ii) the requesting subject has access to. Our experiments show that our evaluation algorithm performs faster than Neo4j's query evaluation engine when evaluating queries that are expressible using Nano-Cypher.

CCS CONCEPTS

• **Security and privacy** → **Access control**; **Authorization**;

KEYWORDS

Relatioship-Based Access Control, Attributes, Graph Database, Neo4j

ACM Reference Format:
Syed Zain R. Rizvi and Philip W. L. Fong. 2018. Efficient Authorization of Graph Database Queries in an Attribute-Supporting ReBAC Model. In *CODASPY '18: Eighth ACM Conference on Data and Application Security and Privacy, March 19–21, 2018, Tempe, AZ, USA.* ACM, New York, NY, USA, 8 pages. https://doi.org/10.1145/3176258.3176331

1 INTRODUCTION

Access control is a corner stone of application security. Databases such as MySQL offer built-in access control features so that applications do not have to develop their own mechanisms for controlling what user has access to which resources [13]. Following this example, Neo4j, a popular graph database, recently introduced

Role-Based Access Control (RBAC) features for its paid *enterprise edition* while the free-to-use *community edition* still suffers from a lack of access control. The enterprise edition ships with five roles, *reader, editor, publisher, architect,* and *admin*. A limitation of this approach is that the capabilities provided by each role span the whole database. For example, a *reader* can read all of the data stored in the database. To remedy this limitation, Neo4j allows the implementers to define their own roles and *procedures*, and assign role requirements to procedures. A procedure is a mechanism that allows Neo4j to be extended by writing custom code that can operate on the database and can be invoked directly from the query language. Thus, instead of being able to query the whole database, a user may only be able to invoke a limited number of procedures.

We argue that Neo4j is capable of even finer grained access control by restricting access to resources rather than procedures. For example, if a procedure allows a requestor to access a certain type of resource, then she can access all resources of that type, regardless of her connection, or lack thereof, with the resources. A similar limitation was encountered by Rizvi *et al.* [23] for their work with OpenMRS, an open source medical records system. OpenMRS restricts access to its *Application Programming Interface* (API) by requiring specific permissions. Therefore, if a user has the capability to invoke the method that returns patient records, then she has access to all patient records in the system. They implemented Relationship-Based Access Control (ReBAC) into OpenMRS, thereby providing finer grained access control so that the user only had access to records of the patients she was treating. However, for methods that returned a collection of resources (e.g., searching for patients by name), authorization checking was performed one resource at a time. Rizvi *et al.* reported that on average each authorization check took between 0.016 - 0.037 seconds under a specific authorization profile [23, §10]. If a method invocation returns a large collection, we immediately see a drawback to their approach. Given the performance reported by Rizvi *et al.* with only 100 members in the query result set, it would take between 1.6 - 3.7 seconds for the requestor to get the result of her method invocation. Such a performance is unacceptable where users expect results within a second [18].

The above challenge serves as the primary motivation for this work. One way to remedy the limitation is to have a declarative access control policy language, which can then be translated into database queries. We can then merge the original search query with the applicable policy and obtain a single query for which the result set is already filtered to the resources the requestor has access.

In this paper we present AReBAC, an attribute-supporting ReBAC model for controlling access in Neo4j [2], a graph database. Along with the model we present **Nano-Cypher** and **graph patterns** as two languages for specifying database queries and access control policies. The former is a subset of the original Cypher query language supported by Neo4j, and the latter is the internal data structure used by our query evaluation algorithm. Being able to specify policies in more than one way demonstrates that ReBAC models are not necessarily restricted to their specific policy language. An important feature of these languages is that they do not require writing logic formulas [7] and variations of regular expressions [8, 11], but leverage the user's knowledge of the underlying database query language. This paper is accompanied by tools that translate queries and policies between both languages. Easing policy specification serves as the secondary motivation for our work. The contributions of this paper are as follows:

- We present **Nano-Cypher**, a subset of the Cypher query language supported by Neo4j. We limit our focus to Nano-Cypher instead of the original Cypher language so that we can provide compatibility with graph patterns for specifying queries and policies (§2).
- We present AReBAC, an attribute-supporting ReBAC model for controlling access in Neo4j [2], a graph database (§3). What distinguishes AReBAC from existing ReBAC models (with attribute support) is that 1) it is rooted in existing technology used in industry, and 2) instead of using the traditional definition of an authorization request (s, o, a), where subject s requests of execute action a on object o, authorization requests in AReBAC are a pair (m, s), where subject s requests to execute method m (a database query). This new definition allows us to combine database queries with access control policies so that we can simultaneously perform query execution and authorization checking.
- We define **graph patterns** (§3.1), access control policies (§3.2), and the process of weaving queries with policies (§3.3). Weaving queries with policies allows us to overcome the two-step process (query execution followed by authorization checking) by evaluating a single graph pattern. The combined graph pattern specifies the requirements of the query as well as the policy.
- We define i) how multiple graph patterns can be combined into a single graph pattern that maintains requirements of each of the original graph patterns (§4.1), and ii) *GP-Eval*, an intelligent backtracking algorithm algorithm for evaluating a graph pattern against a database (§4.2). *GP-Eval* employs a novel approach to forward checking [20] that focuses on minimizing the number of database accesses.
- We evaluate the performance of *GP-Eval* and demonstrate that it performs faster than Neo4j's query evaluation engine when evaluating queries that are expressible using Nano-Cypher. (§5).
- We provide the implementation of the proposed model, the experiment test cases, and the raw results of the experiments [21].

Notation. Given a function f, we use the notations $Dom(f)$ and $Ran(f)$ to refer to the domain and range of f, respectively. $f \mid_X$, with $X \subseteq Dom(f)$, specifies the restriction of f to a smaller domain X. These notations are used throughout this paper.

2 GRAPH DATABASE

Graph databases present a database model in which the data is structured as a possibly edge-labelled and directed graph [6]. Data retrieval and manipulation are expressed as graph oriented operations: i.e., operations that operate on graph features such as paths, neighbourhoods, subgraphs, and graph patterns. The graph model

allows for a topology-based approach of data representation that can be exploited by the system for assessing connectivity of entities rather than depending on costly join operations, such as in relational databases. One popular example of graph databases is Neo4j [2]. Neo4j structures data as a directed and edge-labelled graph that supports properties for nodes and relationships. We use the term *property* in the context of Neo4j, otherwise we use the term *attribute*. The database exposes two interfaces, an embedded *Java API* and a SQL-inspired query language *Cypher*.

"Cypher is a declarative, SQL-inspired language for describing graph patterns using ascii-art syntax" [1]. A Cypher query describes a graph pattern which is then matched against the data store for data retrieval and manipulation. The language uses Match statements for specifying nodes and relationships to match against the data store. Where statements with one or more clauses (conjuncted together) are used to specify further restrictions for matching the already specified nodes and relationships, such as property requirements. Return statements describe the result set of executing a query, which can contain nodes, relationships, properties for both nodes and relationships, paths in the subgraph, and aggregation functions. Cypher also supports statements for manipulating the data store; Create statements for creating nodes and relationships, Set statements for setting properties for nodes and relationships, and Delete statements for deleting nodes and relationships.

2.1 Nano-Cypher

In this work we focus our attention on a susbet of the Cypher query language that we dubbed **Nano-Cypher**. The limited scope allows us to work with a language that is compatible, in terms of expressiveness, with Graph Patterns (§3.1), so that database queries can be merged with access control policies (§3.2) in order to simultaneously perform query execution and authorization checking. In this section we describe the syntax and semantics for Nano-Cypher.

Nano-Cypher is a subset of the Cypher query language supported by Neo4j [2]. Much like Cypher queries, Nano-Cypher queries are executed against edge-labelled and directed graphs that support attributes for node and relationships. We define a graph as $G = (V, E, ID)$ where V, E, and ID represent the nodes, relationships, and edge labels respectively. An edge $id(u, v) \in E$, with $u, v \in V$ and $id \in ID$ specifies an edge from u to v with label id. An attribute-supporting edge-labelled directed graph is a triple (G, A_V, A_E). A_V represents the set of attributes associated with nodes. An attribute $a_v \in A_V$, with valid values X_{a_v} is a function $a_v : V \rightarrow X_{a_v} \cup \{\bot\}$ which assigns a value from X_{a_v} to a node $v \in V$, if v has the attribute a_v; otherwise $a_v(v)$ returns $\bot$. A_E is similar to A_V, except it represents attributes associated with relationships instead of nodes. To avoid confusion we use the terms nodes and relationships when referring to the elements of a graph, and the terms vertices and edges when referring the to elements of a query. A query execution is satisfied by a set of models where each model maps the vertices and edges from the query to nodes and relationships in the graph respectively, such that each instance of mapping preserves the constraints specified in the query.

Abstract Syntax. A Nano-Cypher query, Q, consists of a set of vertex variables $V'(Q)$, a set of edge variables $E'(Q)$ (which are mapped to nodes and relationships in the graph), and a set of edge labels $ID'(Q)$. A query is composed of three components; multiple Match statements, each followed by an optional Where statement, and a single Return statement. We first describe the internal structures of each of these components and then describe the how they fit together.

A Nano-Cypher query starts off with a Match statement with a body ϕ.

$$\phi ::= (v) \mid (v)\text{-}[e : id]\text{->}\phi \mid (v)\text{<-}[e : id]\text{-}\phi$$

Where $v \in V'(Q)$ is a vertex variable, $e \in E'(Q)$ is an edge variable, and $id \in ID'(Q)$ is an edge label. $(v)\text{-}[e : id]\text{->}(u)$ specifies an outgoing relationship from v to u with label id[1], and $(v)\text{<-}[e : id]\text{-}(u)$ specifies an incoming relationship for v from u labelled id.

We can specify *mutual exclusion constraints* and *attribute requirements* using the Where statements with a condition ψ.

$$\psi ::= v\text{<>}u \mid v.attr_v\ OP_v\ val_v \mid e.attr_e\ OP_e\ val_e \mid \psi\ AND\ \psi$$

Where $v, u \in V'(Q)$ are vertex variables that have appeared before in a ϕ statement, $attr_n$ is a vertex attribute, OP_v is an operation defined over $attr_v$ (e.g., $OP_v \in \{<, \leq, =, \neq, \geq, >\}$), and val_v is a valid value for $attr_v$. Similarly, $e \in E'(Q)$ is an edge variable that has appeared before in a ϕ statement, $attr_e$ is an edge attribute, OP_e is an operation defined over $attr_e$, and val_e is a valid value for $attr_e$. $v <> u$ specifies a **mutual exclusion constraint**, i.e., the same node cannot be assigned to both v and u, $v.attr_v\ OP_v\ val_v$ specifies an attribute requirement for v, and $e.attr_e\ OP_e\ val_e$ specifies an attribute requirement for e.

Once we have specified all requirement, we can specify the Return statement of the query using the following syntax:

$$\mu ::= v \mid v, \mu$$

Where $v \in V'(Q)$ is a vertex that has appeared before in a ϕ statement. Intuitively the Return statement specifies the set $\mathcal{V}'(Q) \subseteq V'(Q)$ that composes the result set of the query execution.

Combining all three of these components together to form a complete Nano-Cypher query, we get the following syntax.

$$Q ::= \alpha\ \text{Return}\ \mu \quad \alpha ::= \beta \mid \beta\ \alpha$$
$$\beta ::= \text{Match}\ \phi\ \delta \quad \delta ::= \epsilon \mid \text{Where}\ \psi$$

Given a Match statement with body ϕ, the function $hd : \phi \rightarrow V$ returns the left most vertex (i.e., the head) in ϕ, which allows us to extract specific vertices from the query in order to evaluate it.

Example 2.1. $hd((v)\text{-}[a : friend]\text{->}(u)\text{<-}[b : friend]\text{-}(w)) = v$.

Semantics. A Nano-Cypher query Q is executed against an attribute-supporting edge-labelled directed graph (G, A_V, A_E), and is satisfied by a set of models where each model maps the vertices and edges from Q to nodes and relationships in G respectively, such that each instance of mapping preserves the constraints specified in Q. We define the product of query evaluation as $result\text{-}set((G, A_V, A_E), Q)$ where each model $M \in result\text{-}set((G, A_V, A_E), Q)$ is a function with $M : V'(Q) \cup E'(Q) \rightarrow V \cup E$ that maps vertex and edge variables from Q to nodes and relationships in G.

Example 2.2. $M = \{v_1 \mapsto 123, v_2 \mapsto 124, \ldots e_1 \mapsto gp(125, 126), e_2 \mapsto parent(127, 128), \ldots\}$

---

[1] e is used to refer to the edge $(v)\text{-}[e : id]\text{->}(u)$.

Where $v_1, v_2 \in V'(Q)$, $e_1, e_2 \in E'(Q)$, $123, \ldots, 128 \in V$, and $gp(125, 126)$, $parent(127, 128) \in E$. $M \in result\text{-}set((G, A_V, A_E), Q)$ iff M can satisfy the sequence of Match and Where statements. A Match statement is satisfied iff its body ϕ is satisfied, and a Where statement is satisfied iff its condition ψ is satisfied. The satisfaction relationship between M and ϕ and ψ is defined as follows:

$M \models v$ iff $M(v)$ is defined.

$M \models e$ iff $M(e)$ is defined.

$M \models v\text{-}[e : id]\text{->}\phi$ iff $M \models v$, $M(e) = id(M(v), M(hd(\phi)))$ and $M \models \phi$.

$M \models v\text{<-}[e : id]\text{-}\phi$ iff $M \models v$, $M(e) = id(M(hd(\phi)), M(v))$ and $M \models \phi$.

$M \models v_1\text{<>}v_2$ iff $M \models v_1$, $M \models v_2$ and $M(v_1) \neq M(v_2)$.

$M \models v.attr_v\ OP_v\ val_v$ iff $M \models v$ and $attr_v(M(v))OP_v\ val_v$ is true.

$M \models e.attr_e\ OP_e\ val_e$ iff $M \models e$ and $attr_e(M(e))\ OP_e\ val_e$ is true.

$M \models \psi_1\ AND\ \psi_2$ iff $M \models \psi_1$ and $M \models \psi_2$.

The intuition behind the satisfaction relationship is that each vertex is mapped to a node and each edge is mapped to a relationship such that the connectivity structure, mutual exclusion constraints and attribute requirements are satisfied. Once we have all the models that satisfy the query, we restrict the domain of each model to only consist of vertices specified in the Return statement. The set of restricted models is the result set of the query execution.

3 AReBAC

Traditional authorization requests are a triple (s, o, a), where subject s requests to perform action a on resource o. A limitation of this paradigm is that if one wishes to perform authorization checking on a collection of resources, then the authorization checking would need to be performed one resource at a time. For example, a query is first invoked which returns the result set, and then authorization checking is performed on each entry in the result set. An approach to address this limitation is to weave the query evaluation with the authorization checking, thereby performing both tasks simultaneously and obtaining the result that 1) match the search parameters, and 2) the requester has access to. In this section we present AReBAC, an attribute-supporting ReBAC model that is able to perform query evaluation and authorization checking simultaneously due to its declarative policy language. We will first describe the ontology of the model, followed by descriptions and examples for the components to demonstrate their purpose.

DEFINITION 1. *The protection state of AReBAC has the following components.*

- *O: The set of objects (resources).*
- *$S \subseteq O$: The set of subjects (users).*
- *ID: The set of relation identifiers (i.e., relationship types).*
- *$AG \subseteq ID \times O \times O$: The directed and edge-labelled graph, in which $(id, u, v) \in AG$ refers to a relationship from object u to object v that is labelled with the relation identifier id.*
- *MD: The set of methods (actions) that a subject can invoke. Each method represents a database query specified using Nano-Cypher.*
- *C: The set of categories. Categories are used to describe the types of methods (discussed below).*
- *$CH \subseteq C \times C$: A partial ordering on C called the category hierarchy. We use the shorthand $c \geq c'$ if $(c, c') \in CH$.*

- $MC : MD \rightarrow C$: A mapping from a method to a category.
- ACT: The finite set of actors. The actors represent special verticies specified in queries (§3.1).
- $CA : C \rightarrow 2^{ACT}$: A mapping from a category to a set of actors.
- $Attr_O$: The set of attributes that are associated with objects. An attribute $\varphi_O \in Attr_O$, with valid values X_{φ_O}, is a function $\varphi_O : O \rightarrow X_{\varphi_O} \cup \{\perp\}$ which assigns an attribute value from X_{φ_O} to an object $o \in O$, if o has the attribute φ_O, otherwise $\varphi_O(o)$ returns $\perp$.
- $Attr_R$: Similar to $Attr_O$, except $\varphi_R \in Attr_R$ assigns attributes to relationships.
- P: The set of all graph patterns recognized by the system (§3.1).
- $CP : C \nrightarrow P$: A partial function that assigns some categories to system recognized graph patterns.

DEFINITION 2. An **authorization request** (or simply a **request**) is a pair, $(m, s) \in MD \times S$, whereby subject s requests to invoke method m.

Example 3.1. Alice, a doctor, wishes to read the health record of Bob, her patient. To do this, she invokes the method read_hr(bob_hr), where bob_hr is the identifier for Bob's health record, and provided to the method read_hr as a parameter. This method invocation gets translated to the authorization request (read_hr(bob_hr), Alice).

Each method has an associated **category** that describes the type of the method. Additionally, the category also specifies the **actors** involved in the method. Actors represent the important objects involved in the method, however not all involved objects are associated with actors. During the request evaluation objects are assigned to appropriate actors.

Example 3.2. Once the authorization request of Example 3.1 is issued, the category $c_{\text{read\_hr}} = MC(\text{read\_hr})$ is looked up. Based on the category, the system finds the important actors involved in the method, $CA(c_{\text{read\_hr}}) = \{\text{requestor, health\_record, patient}\}$. In this case, the important actors for $c_{\text{read\_hr}}$ are the requestor, health_record, and the patient.

The underlying database query for the method is designed in such a way that it is intuitive to observe how the actors are involved in the query[2]. At this stage the query contains variables that are replaced by parameters to complete the query. Additionally, when the developer creates the method she also specifies the category for the method by updating MC.

Example 3.3. The Nano-Cypher query for the read_hr method has the form:

```
Match (requestor)
Match (patient) – [: patient_record]– > (health_record)
Where requestor.id = REQ_ID AND health_record.id = HR_ID
Return health_record
```

Where REQ_ID and HR_ID are variables to be replaced by Alice's unique identifier and the parameter *bob_hr* respectively. The query also specifies the actor to vertex mapping through the variable names. Notice that the vertex requestor is not associated with any edges. However, the developer still specifies that requestor vertex

---

[2]For the remainder of this paper we assume that the "important actor" variables in Nano-Cypher queries are named the same as their actor name.

because it is a specified actor for the category, and its requirements will be specified in the corresponding access control policy.

The category is not only used for specifying the types of the methods, but also the types of the access control policies. The system uses the categories and the category hierarchy in order to find the appropriate access control policy for the authorization request. The category hierarchy, CH, is a partially ordered set that represents a refinement relationship between the categories. For $c_1, c_2 \in C$, if $c_1 \geq c_2$, then c_1 is more refined than c_2 and thus all of the actors associated with c_2 are also associated with c_1. The relation also asserts the requirement that it must be the case that c_1 is at least as restrictive as c_2. The process for finding the access control policy for an authorization request is defined in §3.2.

Finally, the system weaves the policy with the method and invokes the combined database query. The result of the query is the set of resources that 1) match the initial search query, and 2) the requestor has access to. The process of weaving access control policies with methods is described in §3.3.

3.1 Graph Patterns

Since AReBAC uses graph databases as its back end data store, we use **graph patterns** to specify database queries internally. Intuitively, graph patterns represent Nano-Cypher queries, with additional information regarding the type of the query (categories) and specific vertices (actors). Recall that a Nano-Cypher query Q consists of a set of vertices $V'(Q)$, directed and labelled edges $E'(Q)$, edge labels $ID'(Q)$, mutual exclusion constraints, attribute requirements for vertices and edges, and a return statement $\mathcal{V}'(Q) \subseteq V'(Q)$. A graph pattern models these requirements through a graph $G = (V, E, ID)$, mutual exclusion constraints Σ, vertex attribute requirements Γ_V, edge attribute requirements Γ_E, and the return statement $Ret \subseteq V$. A graph pattern also contains a category c for describing the type of the graph pattern, and a mapping G_{ACT} from actors in $CA(c)$ to V.

DEFINITION 3. A graph pattern is a seven tuple, $GP = (G, \Sigma, \Gamma_V, \Gamma_E, c, G_{ACT}, Ret)$, which consists of an edge-labelled directed graph $G = (V, E, ID)$, a set of mutual exclusion constraints $\Sigma \subseteq V \times V$, a set of vertex attribute requirements Γ_V, a set of edge attribute requirements Γ_E, a category c, an function $G_{ACT} : CA(c) \rightarrow V$ that maps the actors in $CA(c)$ to the vertices in V, and a set of vertices $Ret \subseteq V$ specifying the return statement. In order to simplify notation, we use $V(GP)$, $E(GP)$, $ID(GP)$, $\Sigma(GP)$, $\Gamma_V(GP)$, $\Gamma_E(GP)$, $C(GP)$, $G_{ACT}(GP)$, and $Ret(GP)$ to refer to the components of the graph pattern GP.

A graph, $G = (V, E, ID)$, consists of a set of vertices, V, a set of directed and labelled edges, E, and a set of relation identifiers ID (i.e., edge labels), as defined in §2.1.

Mutual exclusion constraints $\Sigma \subseteq V \times V$ are used to specify further restrictions for query evaluations. The intuition behind a mutual exclusive constraint $(u, v) \in \Sigma$, with $u \neq v$, is that during a query evaluation, if n_1 is mapped to u and n_2 is mapped to v, where $n_1, n_2 \in O$, then it must be the case that $n_1 \neq n_2$.

Γ_V specifies the vertex attribute requirements for the graph pattern. A vertex attribute requirement, $\gamma_v \in \Gamma_V$, is a function $\gamma_v : O \rightarrow \{0, 1\}$, which specifies all of the attributes required for the vertex v. $\gamma_v(o)$ returns 1 if o satisfies all of the required attributes specified for v, else it returns 0. The intuition behind vertex attribute requirements is that, during a query execution, if an object o is mapped to the vertex v, then it must satisfy the attribute requirements for v[3]. Similarly, Γ_E specifies edge attribute requirements for the graph pattern.

A graph pattern query is executed against a AReBAC protection state and is satisfied by sets of objects and relationships that together satisfy the graph pattern. We refer to each set as a map, $M : V \cup E \to O \cup AG$, which is a complete function that maps a vertices and edges from the graph pattern to objects and relationships in the protection state (see Example 2.2). The set $Ret \subseteq V$ is used to form a restriction on each map, $M \mid_{Ret}: V \to O$, which forms the return value of the query.

For a fixed protection state, a map M satisfies a graph pattern $GP = (G, \Sigma, \Gamma_V, \Gamma_E, c, G_{ACT}, Ret)$, denoted $M \vDash GP$ if and only if the following statements are true

(1) $\forall v \in V, M(v)$ is defined. Each vertex is mapped to a node in O.
(2) $\forall i(u, v) \in E, M(i(u, v)) = i(M(u), M(v))$. Each edge is mapped to a relationship in AG, with u and v mapped to $M(u)$ and $M(v)$.
(3) $\forall (u, v) \in \Sigma, M(u) \neq M(v)$. Any two mutually exclusive vertices are not mapped to the same object.
(4) $\forall \gamma_v \in \Gamma_V, \gamma_v(M(v)) = 1$. The mapping preserves attribute requirements between vertices and objects.
(5) $\forall \gamma_e \in \Gamma_E, \gamma_e(M(e)) = 1$. The mapping preserves attribute requirements between edges and relationships.

3.2 Policies

In this section we discuss access control policies and related concepts. We first define access control policies, followed by the process of computing the **enforced policy** for an authorization request.

An access control policy is a graph pattern used for specifying authorization requirements for accessing resources. The requirements are specified in the form of a graph along with mutual exclusion constraints and attribute requirements. Essentially, a policy is a graph pattern.

Definition 3.4. A policy is a graph pattern used for specifying authorization requirements for access resources. $CP : C \twoheadrightarrow P$ provides the policy specified for a given category.

The above definition ensures that each category has at most one policy specified. A result of this requirement is that methods of the same category are restricted in the same way. Recall that the category hierarchy is a refinement relationship (partial ordering) between the categories in C. Thus, for two categories $c_i, c_j \in C$, if $c_i \geq c_j$ then c_i is more refined than c_j and $CA(c_i) \supseteq CA(c_j)$. This relation implies that methods with higher level categories provide access to more specific resources and therefore require stricter restrictions.

To address this situation one could demand that policy designers ensure this restriction manually when designing policies, however, it is much simpler to leverage the category hierarchy to achieve the same result. This is obtained by the superior category policies inheriting all of the requirements from their inferior counterparts.

The function $\sqcup_C : 2^P \to P$ combines a set of graph pattern into a single graph pattern that specifies all of the requirements from input set. $\sqcup_C$ is formally defined in §4.1. For a category c_i, we use $\sqcup_C$ to combine $CP(c_i)$ with all $CP(c_j)$ such that $c_i \geq c_j$. For an authorization request (m, s) with $MC(m) = c$, the function $Pol : C \to P$ returns the **enforced policy**[4].

DEFINITION 4. $Pol(c) = \sqcup_c \{GP_i \mid c_i \in C, c \geq c_i \wedge CP(c_i) = GP_i\}$

Being able to combine graph patterns allows us to have implicitly defined policies. A combined policy will enforce the requirements of all of its components thereby ensuring the most relevant requirements are enforced based on what is explicitly defined in the protection state. There exists one and only one enforced policy for each category, however $CP(c)$ does not need to be defined for every $c \in C$. If a category c does not require any new restrictions that have not already been specified by the policies of its inferior categories, then $CP(c)$ is undefined.

If the access control policies are explicitly defined for all $\geq$-minimal categories then we say that CP is sufficient for C. We denote this relationship by sufficient$_C(CP)$. The sufficiency condition allows us to ensure that the enforced policy for each category is composed of explicitly defined requirements. For a protection state to be usable, it must be the case that CP is sufficient for the category set (i.e., sufficient$_C(CP)$). The sufficiency condition can be checked in time linear to the size of the category hierarchy.

3.3 Weaving Policies and Methods

Now that we have defined access control policies and the process of computing enforced policies, we can define how to weave methods with their corresponding enforced policies.

We first translate the authorization request, $(m, s) \in MD \times S$, which is specified using Nano-Cypher, to a pair, $(GP_r, Info)$, where GP_r is the Nano-Cypher query translated to a graph pattern and $Info : CA(C(GP_r)) \twoheadrightarrow O$ is a partial function used to assign some of the vertices to objects for the query evaluation. Intuitively, $Info$ represents the contextual information gleaned from the request (e.g., the identity of the requestor) to reduce the search space for the query evaluation. In the next step, we combine GP_r with the enforced policy $Pol(MC(m)) = GP_p$ and obtain the resulting graph pattern, GP_{rp}. More formally:

$$GP_{rp} = \sqcup_{MC(m)} \{GP_r, GP_p\}$$

We evaluate the pair, $(GP_{rp}, Info)$, using the *GP-Eval* algorithm (§4.2) to find mappings from the protection state that satisfy the graph pattern. During this step, we also generate the result sets by collecting the vertices stated in the return statement.

This model can be simplified if we express both the methods and policies using either Nano-Cypher or graph patterns. In fact, if we also express the policies using Nano-Cypher, then we will need to translate the policies to the internal graph pattern data structure that we use for evaluating queries. Alternatively, we can express the methods using graph patterns, in which case we no longer require the translating step as we are working with graph patterns directly. We chose to present the model in this manner so

---

[3]We abstracted away the details for the attribute requirement functions since they do not add to the complexity of the model.

[4]This process can be optimized by the system computing $Pol(c)$ for each category once and storing them alongside the protection state.

that we can cover both cases and provide a very brief description on how to switch to one of the variations.

Although using Nano-Cypher adds an additional step in the whole process, it has been reported that the Cypher query language is easy to use for specifying graph traversals [25]. Since Nano-Cypher is a based on the Cypher query language, it should not be any more complicated than Cypher for specifying simple graphs.

4 WORKING WITH GRAPH PATTERNS

In this section we present how to combine a set of graph patterns into a single graph pattern, and the algorithm for evaluating a graph pattern, that is, finding all of the mappings for a given graph pattern.

4.1 $\sqcup_C : 2^P \to P$

$\sqcup_C : 2^P \to P$ combines a set of graph patterns into a single graph pattern. The general idea here is that the combined graph pattern has a match if and only if every component pattern has a match. This is achieved by having a corresponding vertex in the combined graph pattern for each of the original vertices, where the vertices that represent the same actor are mapped together, and then generating the rest of the elements based on the vertex mapping.

Intuitively, we start by generating the set V_1, where each element ($\{v\}$) is a singleton set containing a vertex. This set collects a subset of vertices from each input graph pattern where these vertices are not mapped to by an actor. We then define the set V_2 and the function G'_{ACT} that ensures that the vertices that represent the same actor are mapped together. Note that since c is superior to all of the input graph pattern categories, then for $1 \leq i \leq k$ $CA(C(GP_i)) \subseteq CA(c)$. We then generate the set V_2, using G'_{ACT}, where each element ($\{v_1, \ldots, v_m\}$) is a set of vertices (from the input graph patterns) that are mapped to by the same actor. Once we have the sets V_1 and V_2, which are pairwise disjoint, we can generate V' as the union of the two sets. This ensures that the set V' consists of all of the vertices from the input graph patterns, and the vertices that are mapped to the same actor are mapped together to the same vertex in V'. Once we have generated V', we can define the function $f : V(GP) \to V'$ that maps a vertex from an input graph pattern to a vertex in V'. Specifically, it maps a vertex v to a vertex Π such that $v \in \Pi$. We can now generate the rest of the components, using the function f when needed. A declarative definition of this function is provided in [21].

4.2 Graph Pattern Evaluation

The graph pattern evaluation problem is essentially a *Constraint Satisfaction Program (CSP)* [20] which asks, given a set of variables and constraints, assign values to those variables such that the assignments satisfy the constraints. Here vertices of the graph pattern $V(G)$ are the variables, the edges $E(G)$, mutual exclusion constraints Σ, and attribute requirements Γ_V, Γ_E are the constraints, and the vertices of the graph $V(G')$ are the possible assignment values.

GP-Eval (Algorithm 1) is a forward-checking algorithm [20], and employs the *smallest domain size* variable ordering. It describes how to find the mappings that satisfy the graph pattern and are restricted based on *Ret*. For our problem, *GP-Eval* improves upon regular forward-checking in two main ways. 1) *GP-Eval* focuses on

---

Algorithm 1 *GP*-Eval

Global: Attribute-supporting edge-labelled and directed graph: (G', A'_V, A'_E).
Global: The result set: $RS : 2^{(Ret \to V(G'))}$.
Input: The graph pattern: $GP = (G, \Sigma, \Gamma_V, \Gamma_E, c, G_{ACT}, Ret)$.
Input: Context information: $Info : CA(c) \to V(G')$.

1: **function** INIT(GP, $Info$)
2:     $(Assn : V(G) \to V(G')) \leftarrow \emptyset$
3:     $(Cand : V(G) \to 2^{V(G')}) \leftarrow \emptyset$
4:     **for all** $v \in Dom(Info)$ **do**
5:         $Assn(v) \mapsto Info(v)$
6:     PRECHECK(GP, $Assn$, $Cand$)
7:     **for all** $v \in Dom(Assn)$ **do**
8:         $(Cand, valid) \leftarrow$ FC(GP, $Assn$, $Cand$, v)
9:         **if** $valid = \bot$ **then return** FAIL
10:     GRAPHEVAL(GP, $Assn$, $Cand$)
11:     **return** result set.

12: **procedure** GRAPHEVAL(GP, $Assn$, $Cand$)
13:     **if** $| V(GP) | = | Dom(Assn) |$ **then**
14:         $RS = RS \cup Assn |_{Ret}$
15:         **return**
16:     $v \leftarrow$ PICKNEXTVERTEX(GP, $Assn$, $Cand$)
17:     $Cand(v) \leftarrow$ MEXFILTER($Assn$, $Cand(v)$)
18:     **for all** $n \in Cand(v)$ **do**
19:         $Cand' \leftarrow Cand \setminus \{v\}$
20:         $Assn' \leftarrow Assn \cup \{v \mapsto n\}$
21:         $(Cand'', valid) \leftarrow$ FC(GP, $Assn'$, $Cand'$, v)
22:         **if** $valid = \top$ **then**
23:             GRAPHEVAL(GP, $Assn'$, $Cand''$)
24:     **return**

---

reducing/minimizing the number of database accesses. This idea was motivated by the performance evaluation conducted by Rizvi *et al.* for their implementation of ReBAC in OpenMRS [23]. In their experiments it was revealed that the majority of the performance overhead came not from the backtracking within the hybrid logic model checker, but rather database accesses. 2) Given a graph pattern $GP = (G, \Sigma, \Gamma_V, \Gamma_E, c, G_{ACT}, Ret)$, we are not interested in all of the mappings that satisfy the graph pattern, but rather only the mappings that are unique in mapping the members of *Ret*.

5 PERFORMANCE EVALUATION

We conducted an empirical study to compare the proposed query evaluation and authorization checking algorithm (§4.2) to the traditional authorization scheme. We compared the performances under various configurations. The study was conducted in a simulated environment using synthetic data. Below we describe our experimental set-up followed by the results of the experiments comparing the authorization schemes.

The Protection State. For the protection state we used the *"soc-Slashdot0922"* social network dataset, obtained from the Stanford Large Network Dataset Collection [4], to construct the authorization graph. The graph consisted of 82,168 nodes and 948,464 directed edges. We generated seven relationship identifiers and randomly

	$\lvert GP_r \rvert$	$\lvert GP_p \rvert$	Combined	Two-Step	Cypher
			Finished	Finished	Finished
			Avg. Time	Avg. Time	Avg. Time
Profile 1	1	5	999	368	998
			0.010 sec	0.737 sec	0.308 sec
Profile 2	1	7	946	377	919
			0.087 sec	0.893 sec	0.833 sec
Profile 3	1	10	656	281	409
			0.487 sec	1.068 sec	2.092 sec
Profile 4	5	5	925	215	797
			0.198 sec	1.542 sec	1.537 sec
Profile 5	5	7	795	227	362
			0.409 sec	1.705 sec	2.272 sec
Profile 6	7	5	769	167	304
			0.353 sec	1.700 sec	2.285 sec
Profile 7	7	7	616	174	71
			0.630 sec	1.606 sec	3.063 sec

Table 1: The size of the test cases as well as the performance for each evaluation scheme.

assigned a relation identifier to each edge[5]. In addition to an identifier, each edge was also randomly assigned a *weight* attribute with an integer value (between 1 to 10). The attributes for each node were provided by *"Census-Income (KDD) Dataset"*, obtained from the UCI Machine Learning Repository [17]. This dataset consisted of 199,523 (non-test) nodes and 40 attribute types, however not every node had all 40 attributes. For a single node, each attribute had at most one value which was treated as either a String or an integer. Since this dataset consisted more nodes than the number of vertices in the authorization graph, we randomly chose 82,168 nodes from the dataset and assigned attributes to vertices using a randomly generated bijective mapping.

Generating Test Cases. We extracted a subset of the authorization graph to generate the authorization requests and access control policies. Each test case consists of three graph patterns; the database query graph pattern (GP_r), the policy graph pattern (GP_p), and the combined database query and policy graph pattern (GP_{rp}). Table 1 summarizes the various profiles for generating the tests, where the profiles are ordered based on the number of nodes in GP_r and GP_p. We vary the graph pattern sizes for the query as well as the policy to observe the impact of the graph pattern size on the algorithm. In addition to the graph size, we require a minimum of 50% connectivity between the vertices for graphs with specified size 7 or less, and a minimum 25% connectivity between the vertices for graphs with specified size 10 [6]. For each graph, we also randomly pick 1, 2, or 4 vertex attribute requirements, 1, 2, or 4 edge attribute requirements, and 0, 1, or 2 mutual exclusion constraints. Graph patterns of size 1 are an exception and do not contain any mutual exclusion constraints. GP_r and GP_p always share one source node that functions as the common actor between the graph patterns, as well as the vertex for *Ret*.

Running Test Cases. We first ran 250 randomly generate tests of various sizes to warm up the cache. After the warmup tests, we ran each test three ways. First, we evaluated the test through the two-step process. We evaluated GP_r using our algorithm, followed

---

[5]We followed the experimental design of Rizvi *et al.* [22, 23] and chose seven relation identifiers, which were based on the case study presented by Fong [14].

[6]Two vertices are considered connected if there is at least one edge between them, regardless of the identifier and direction.

by evaluating GP_p by fixing the seed node for each entry provided by the query result set. Second, we evaluated the combined graph pattern using *GP-Eval*. Third, we translated the combined graph pattern to a Nano-Cypher query and executed it against the Neo4j Cypher evaluation engine.

Results and Discussions. The experiments were conducted on a desktop machine with Intel Xeon CPU E5-1650 v3 @3.5GHz (6 cores) processor with 64 GB RAM and 1 TB SSD, running Fedora release 24 OS. The project was implemented in Java 8 using Neo4j version 3.2.1. 1000 test cases were generated for each profile and a six second time limit was set for each of the three testing schemes. Table 1 also shows the number of instances that were evaluated within the six second time limit, for each evaluation scheme, as well as the average time over the completed instances. For Profiles 1 - 6 the two-step process failed most often, while in Profile 7 the Cypher engine failed most often. We refer the reader to [21] for the raw data and test cases.

There is a significant performance difference between the traditional two-step process and the proposed combined scheme. In several cases, the GP_r result set consists of hundreds of entries, however the final result set, after authorization checking, contains only a single entry. This suggests that the two-step process did a lot of work that was thrown away. Avoiding such work is indeed the motivation behind the proposed combined scheme.

A surprising result is that *GP-Eval performed faster than Neo4j's Cypher evaluation engine for the combined graph patterns.* We do realize that since Nano-Cypher is a sub-language of Cypher, *GP-Eval* does not support several of the features supported by Neo4j's Cypher query engine. However *GP-Eval* seems to be the better choice for simpler queries. The performance of the Cypher engine is also affected by the syntactical structure of the query. For a given Nano-Cypher query q, if we permute the ordering of the Match and Where statements, while maintaining the syntax requirements, we obtain a new query q' which has the same semantic meaning as q. However, the evaluation processes of q and q' might be different (depending on the level of permutation), thereby having one query being evaluated faster than the other. This allows users to manually refine queries to obtain the desired performance. *GP-Eval*, on the other hand, mostly bases its evaluation process on the semantic structure of the query and uses syntactical structure for only breaking ties. This approach shifts the responsibility of optimizing queries from the user to the algorithm.

6 RELATED WORKS

A number of ReBAC models have been proposed in the literature. Fong [14] proposed a ReBAC model social network as its protection state. This model supports modal logic as its policy language, and with an extension to hybrid logic [7]. [15] added a temporal dimension to the model, and [24] extended the hybrid logic policy language to impose relationship constraints over people located in certain geographical neighbourhoods.

Crampton and Sellwood [11] proposed *RPPM*, a ReBAC model which tracks relationships between users and resources. This allowed for a wider class of relationships than [7, 14]. RPPM uses *path conditions*, which are similar to regular expressions, as its policy language. [11] also proposed *authorization principals* which are a relationship-based analog of roles. Administrative RPPM [12] extended RPPM by being able to handle operational and administrative requests.

Rizvi *et al.* [23] combined *RPPM* [11] with hyrbid logic [7] and demonstrated for the first time that ReBAC can be implemented in a production scale medical records system. They chose OpenMRS [3] as their subject and maintained backwards compatibility with the system's original RBAC mechanism. [23] also included an empirical evaluation of computing authorization decisions under various profiles, and reported that the fastest profiles took between 0.016 to 0.037 seconds per authorization check on average. Rizvi *et al.* then extended their model to interoperate with RBAC, and formalized their model as *ReBAC2015* [22].

Pasarella and Lobo [19] also combined [11] with [7] by extending hybrid logic to express the path conditions, and dubbed the language Extended Hybrid Logic (EHL). Along with the extension, they presented a subset of Datalog with equality constraints for specifying ReBAC policies, which was then extended to allow negative authorization and handle temporal policies. While discussing the performance of their proposed system, they mention how fixing one or two of the variables to specific nodes in the dataset significantly impacts the search space and thus the performance of executing a query. This phenomenon is also exploited in *GP-Eval*.

Attribute-Based Access Control (ABAC) is an access control paradigm that bases its authorization decisions on attributes [16]. Ahmed *et al.* [5] presented a comparative analysis of ABAC and ReBAC. They presented a family of ReBAC models and a family of ABAC models, and demonstrated how the ABAC models were either equally or more expressive than ReBAC models. Other extensions to ReBAC have also been proposed to support attributes. Cheng *et al.* proposed an attribute-aware ReBAC model [10], as an extension to user-to-user relationship-based access control (UURAC) [9].

7 CONCLUSION AND FUTURE WORKS

AReBAC is an attribute-supporting ReBAC model for controlling access in Neo4j, a graph database, and is motivated by three factors; i) combine database queries with authorization checking in order to obtain acceptable performance for query executions coupled with authorization checking, ii) connect the model with technologies that are used in industry, and iii) promote usability by providing the required tools. Our performance evaluation demonstrated that *GP-Eval* performs faster than Neo4's query evaluation engine when evaluating queries that are expressible using Nano-Cypher.

There are still a few explorable areas in this work. First, *GP-Eval* can be optimized by exploiting techniques used in constraint satisfaction problems such variable ordering and back jumping. The insights learned from AReBAC can be used to create similar models for other database systems. Nano-Cypher can also be extended to incorporate more features offered by Cypher, such as attribute comparison between vertices instead of comparison to strict values. In order for AReBAC to be usable, we also need to introduce capabilities for manipulating the database.

ACKNOWLEDGMENTS

This work is supported in part by an NSERC Discovery Grant (RGPIN-2014-06611) and a Canada Research Chair (950-229712).

REFERENCES

[1] Intro to Cypher. https://neo4j.com/developer/cypher-query-language/.
[2] Neo4J. http://neo4j.com/.
[3] OpenMRS. http://openmrs.org/.
[4] Stanford Large Network Dataset Collection. http://snap.stanford.edu/data.
[5] AHMED, T., SANDHU, R., AND PARK, J. Classifying and comparing attribute-based and relationship-based access control. In *Proceedings of the Seventh ACM on Conference on Data and Application Security and Privacy* (New York, NY, USA, 2017), CODASPY '17, ACM, pp. 59–70.
[6] ANGLES, R., AND GUTIERREZ, C. Survey of graph database models. *ACM Comput. Surv. 40*, 1 (Feb. 2008), 1:1–1:39.
[7] BRUNS, G., FONG, P. W. L., SIAHAAN, I., AND HUTH, M. Relationship-based access control: Its expression and enforcement through hybrid logic. In *Proceedings of the 2nd ACM Conference on Data and Application Security and Privacy (CODASPY'12)* (San Antonio, TX, USA, Feb. 2012).
[8] CHENG, Y., PARK, J., AND SANDHU, R. Relationship-based access control for online social networks: Beyond user-to-user relationships. In *Proceedings of the 4th IEEE International Conference on Information Privacy, Security, Risk and Trust (PASSAT'12)* (Amsterdam, Netherlands, Sept. 2012).
[9] CHENG, Y., PARK, J., AND SANDHU, R. A user-to-user relationship-based access control model for online social networks. In *Proceedings of the 26th Annual IFIP WG 11.3 Working Conference on Data and Applications Security and Privacy (DBSec'12)* (Paris, France, July 2012), vol. 7371 of *LNCS*.
[10] CHENG, Y., PARK, J., AND SANDHU, R. Attribute-aware relationship-based access control for online social networks. In *Proceedings of the 28th Annual IFIP WG 11.3 Working Conference on Data and Applications Security and Privacy XXVIII - Volume 8566* (New York, NY, USA, 2014), DBSec 2014, Springer-Verlag New York, Inc., pp. 292–306.
[11] CRAMPTON, J., AND SELLWOOD, J. Path conditions and principal matching: A new approach to access control. In *Proceedings of the 19th ACM Symposium on Access Control Models and Technologies (SACMAT'14)* (New York, NY, USA, 2014), ACM, pp. 187–198.
[12] CRAMPTON, J. AND SELLWOOD, J. Arppm: Administration in the rppm model. In *Proceedings of the Sixth ACM Conference on Data and Application Security and Privacy* (New York, NY, USA, 2016), CODASPY '16, ACM, pp. 219–230.
[13] FERRARI, E. *Access Control in Data Management Systems*. Morgan and Claypool Publishers, 2010.
[14] FONG, P. W. Relationship-based access control: Protection model and policy language. In *Proceedings of the First ACM Conference on Data and Application Security and Privacy (CODASPY'11)* (New York, NY, USA, 2011), ACM, pp. 191–202.
[15] FONG, P. W. L., MEHREGAN, P., AND KRISHNAN, R. Relational abstraction in community-based secure collaboration. In *Proceedings of the 20th ACM Conference on Computer and Communications Security (CCS'13)* (Berlin, Germany, Nov. 2013), pp. 585–598.
[16] HU, V. C., FERRAIOLO, D., KUHN, R., SCHNITZER, A., SANDLIN, K., MILLER, R., AND SCARFONE, K. Guide to Attribute Based Access Control (ABAC) Definition and Considerations. *NIST Special Publication* (Jan. 2014).
[17] LICHMAN, M. UCI machine learning repository, 2013.
[18] NIELSEN, J. Powers of 10: Time scales in user experience. https://www.nngroup.com/articles/powers-of-10-time-scales-in-ux/.
[19] PASARELLA, E., AND LOBO, J. A datalog framework for modeling relationship-based access control policies. In *Proceedings of the 22Nd ACM on Symposium on Access Control Models and Technologies* (New York, NY, USA, 2017), SACMAT '17 Abstracts, ACM, pp. 91–102.
[20] PROSSER, P. Hybrid algorithms for the constraint satisfaction problem. *Computational Intelligence 9*, 3 (1993), 268–299.
[21] RIZVI, S. Z. R. Attribute-supporting ReBAC model. http://pages.cpsc.ucalgary.ca/~szrrizvi/projectAReBAC/, 2018.
[22] RIZVI, S. Z. R., AND FONG, P. W. Interoperability of relationship- and role-based access control. In *Proceedings of the Sixth ACM on Conference on Data and Application Security and Privacy* (New York, NY, USA, 2016), CODASPY '16, ACM, pp. 231–242.
[23] RIZVI, S. Z. R., FONG, P. W., CRAMPTON, J., AND SELLWOOD, J. Relationship-based access control for an open-source medical records system. In *Proceedings of the 20th ACM Symposium on Access Control Models and Technologies* (New York, NY, USA, 2015), SACMAT '15, ACM, pp. 113–124.
[24] TARAMESHLOO, E., AND FONG, P. W. Access control models for geo-social computing systems. In *Proceedings of the 19th ACM Symposium on Access Control Models and Technologies* (New York, NY, USA, 2014), SACMAT '14, ACM, pp. 115–126.
[25] VICKNAIR, C., MACIAS, M., ZHAO, Z., NAN, X., CHEN, Y., AND WILKINS, D. A comparison of a graph database and a relational database: A data provenance perspective. In *Proceedings of the 48th Annual Southeast Regional Conference* (New York, NY, USA, 2010), ACM SE '10, ACM, pp. 42:1–42:6.

Hyperagents: Migrating Host Agents to the Hypervisor

Micah Bushouse
Department of Computer Science
North Carolina State University
Raleigh, NC, USA
mbushou@ncsu.edu

Douglas Reeves
Department of Computer Science
North Carolina State University
Raleigh, NC, USA
reeves@ncsu.edu

ABSTRACT

Third-party software daemons called host agents are increasingly responsible for a modern host's security, automation, and monitoring tasks. Because of their location within the host, these agents are at risk of manipulation by malware and users. Additionally, in virtualized environments where multiple adjacent guests each run their own set of agents, the cumulative resources that agents consume adds up rapidly. Consolidating agents onto the hypervisor can address these problems, but places a technical burden on agent developers.

This work presents a development methodology to re-engineer a host agent in to a *hyperagent*, an out-of-guest agent that gains unique hypervisor-based advantages while retaining its original in-guest capabilities. This three-phase methodology makes integrating Virtual Machine Introspection (VMI) functionality in to existing code easier and more accessible, minimizing an agent developer's re-engineering effort. The benefits of hyperagents are illustrated by porting the GRR live forensics agent, which retains 89% of its codebase, uses 40% less memory than its in-guest counterparts, and enables a 4.9x speedup for a representative data-intensive workload. This work shows that a conventional off-the-shelf host agent can be feasibly transformed into a hyperagent and provide a powerful, efficient tool for defending virtualized systems.

CCS CONCEPTS

• **Security and privacy** → Virtualization and security;

KEYWORDS

Cloud security, virtual machine introspection, computer forensics

ACM Reference Format:
Micah Bushouse and Douglas Reeves. 2018. Hyperagents: Migrating Host Agents to the Hypervisor. In *Proceedings of Eighth ACM Conference on Data and Application Security and Privacy (CODASPY '18)*. ACM, New York, NY, USA, 12 pages. https://doi.org/10.1145/3176258.3176317

1 INTRODUCTION

Third-party host agents are pervasive in modern computing, where it is common practice to install multiple adjacent agents on production systems to monitor performance [2], conform to regulations and industry standards [18], and scale system administration [9].

These agents perform their duties locally on a host on the behalf of a centralized management server. Agents specializing in security-related areas such as intrusion detection, policy enforcement, forensics, and incident response are employed at a system's highest privilege level, where they have unrestricted access to the host, can intercept and mediate undesirable activities, and resist subversion.

However, even when agents are running as kernel modules or privileged processes, they can still be subverted through vulnerabilities found elsewhere in the kernel [21]. Although more privileged hardware-enforced modes are available (e.g., virtualization and processor management modes), their use is uncommon in production due to framework immaturity, performance, perceptions of complexity, and uneven hypervisor support [21]. Integrating an existing agent with one of the few security frameworks that does take advantage of these hardware-enforced modes is complicated by the requirement to re-write agent code against unique APIs [23, 27, 43]. Therefore, despite the potential benefits of running in the hypervisor, host agents have continued to be implemented on the "guest side" of the virtualization layer.

This paper presents a methodology to assist agent developers in making a simple, well-defined set of changes to port an existing security agent to the hypervisor. Once ported, the agent is completely removed from the guest, and instead performs the same functionality as it did "in guest" from a layer below. This methodology relies on the observation that the core functionality of a host agent does not rely upon which side of the virtualization layer it executes in. As a result, porting only requires that the agent code that interacts with host APIs (this work terms these *actuators*) be replaced with hypervisor-based Virtual Machine Introspection (VMI) equivalents.

The porting methodology has three software development phases:

Phase 1: An agent's source code is examined to identify code sections that interact with the host. These sections are refactored to make use of libhyperagent, a library we specifically designed to simplify the integration of VMI functionality into an agent.

Phase 2: Agent code is further modified to allow multiple agents, for different guests, to execute under the control of a single process (the hyperagent) in the hypervisor.

Phase 3: New features are built into the hyperagent to take advantage of its environment. These features take advantage of the broad cross-VM view of a hyperagent and new opportunities to move server-side work forward to the hyperagent.

The proposed methodology is illustrated by porting the GRR Rapid Response (GRR) [1] live forensics C++ agent into a hyperagent. This GRR hyperagent is compared with its in-guest counterpart in terms of the developer effort required to port the agent's code, resource usage, execution time, and performance. The evaluation is conducted on two platforms: the Xen hypervisor and Qubes.

This work also ported the ClamAV virus scanner and discusses how three other agents could be re-engineered.

This work makes the following contributions:

(1) A development methodology to convert host agents into hyperagents that execute in the hypervisor's administrative domain.
(2) A VMI library of useful hyperagent functions, including a new VMI technique to sync a guest's cached disk writes.
(3) The implementation and evaluation of the GRR hyperagent.

2 MOTIVATION

This work presents a methodology that assists agent developers with the technical hurdles associated with the re-engineering, or *porting*, of a third-party host agent, ensuring the agent can do the same job executing under control of the hypervisor as it could under control of a guest OS (see Figure 1). There are several compelling benefits to re-engineering a host agent in this manner [17], as described below.

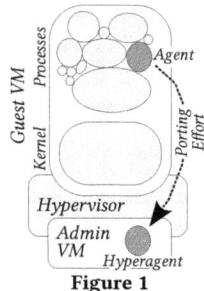

Figure 1

Better Isolation. It is more difficult for malicious code in a guest to both identify and resist a hypervisor-based security agent. The hardware-enforced isolation and smaller exposed interface between a hypervisor and its guests is also more difficult to subvert than the interface between a user process and its kernel [16, 21]. An agent running beneath the guest is both isolated (and to a degree [10], concealed) from the guest and operates at a higher privilege level than the guest kernel, so the agent is less likely to be tampered with or disabled by users or malware.

Enhanced Agent Capability. An agent running on the hypervisor combines the best architectural strengths of both host agents and network security devices. A hypervisor-based agent has the host-level advantages of fine-grained visibility into a host and the ability to interpose on guest execution (e.g., hook and mediate host actions), but also the network-level advantages of broad visibility across hosts, independence from host influence, and centralized administration.

From its position beneath guests, a hyperagent takes advantage of two concepts unavailable to in-guest agents. The first is *locality*, where a more trusted hyperagent performs analysis that is normally kept server-side. This delegation to the hyperagent cuts out network round trips and speeds up analysis by co-locating the analysis with VMI-acquired guest data. The second is *cross-VM visibility*, where work is consolidated and executed centrally at the hyperagent instead of once-per-guest as is the case with in-guest agents.

Resource Efficiency. Collapsing multiple per-guest copies of a normal host agent into a single hyperagent reduces the system's overall memory footprint.

Centralized Administration. In a guest-dense environment with tens-to-hundreds of guests per hypervisor, administrative effort is reduced if a single hyperagent replaces many guest agents.

Additionally, a hyperagent can be managed independently of the virtual machines it inspects [17]. The agent can be activated, reconfigured, or deactivated without regard to the guest's state [14].

3 BACKGROUND

This section introduces the concepts upon which this work is based, including agents, VMI, and live forensics, then concludes with assumptions and threat model.

3.1 Host Agents

A *host agent* is a third-party software daemon or kernel module that acts on behalf of an external agent *controller* (e.g., server) to access or control local host resources. Using agents, the agent controller can gather or change local system state, update or back up files, start or stop processes, and control policy enforcement. An *agent-based system* includes the agents, the controller (i.e., agent server), and the protocols by which they communicate.

Security-focused host agents in particular are designed to extend or supplant the host operating system's security functionality. These agents often consist of components which proactively hook into the operating system in order to intercept and mediate actions, such as preventing the execution of malicious code.

System administrators are often compelled to run multiple agents on the same host. For example, compliance requirements often mandate that a security agent (such as an anti-virus product) protect each host, a host configuration management agent may be needed to allow remote, centralized administration, and a monitoring agent may be needed to ensure service level agreements are met. The following are major categories of agents that may be required, with examples of each.

Category	Examples
Security	OSSEC, ClamAV, and centrally-managed anti-virus systems
Forensics	GRR, Mozilla MIG, Access Data agent, Encase Enterprise servlet
Monitoring	Nagios NRPE, Zabbix, Ganglia
Cloud Mon.	AWS CloudWatch, GCE Stackdriver, DataDog
Cfg. Mgmt.	SaltStack, Puppet, Chef
Hypervisor	QEMU guest agent, VMware tools, Hyper-V LIS, Xen/Qubes util.

The impacts of these agents on resource utilization can quickly add up. In a virtualized environment, that cost is multiplied by the number of virtual machines that are executing in parallel.

3.2 Hypervisor-based Security Agents

Hypervisor-based security agents often use *Virtual Machine Introspection* (VMI) to inspect and influence guests. VMI is generally defined as the direct external observation of a guest's internal state [16]. This *out-of-guest* (sometimes called *agentless*) approach enables security functionality at a privilege level higher than the guest kernel. VMI and clever re-use of processor virtualization extensions has been recently leveraged for such purposes as malware analysis [27], forensics [34], debugging [23], and browser security [8].

In the context of Xen, the hypervisor used in this work, running "on the hypervisor" means executing from Xen's privileged management domain, dom0.

An agent developer seeking to leverage VMI for hypervisor-based security would survey the available frameworks and likely conclude that the porting effort either must require extensive knowledge of low-level guest OS details or require significant refactoring to conform their agent into a VMI framework's API such as those provided by *DRAKVUF* [27], *XMHF* [43], and others [23, 41].

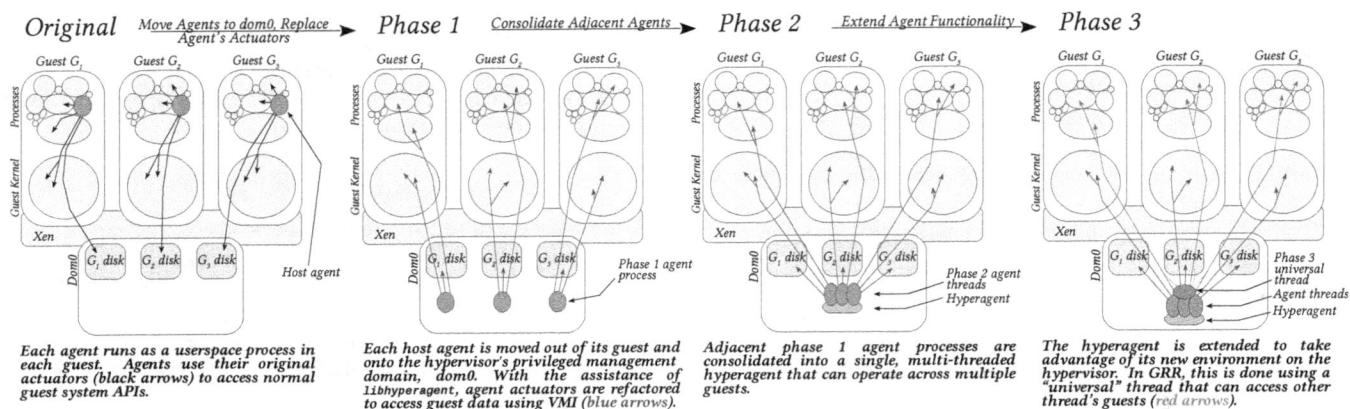

Figure 2: The three-phase methodology to re-engineer host agents into hyperagents.

3.3 Live Forensics

The methodology introduced in this paper is validated by applying it to the GRR live forensics agent [1]. Live forensics is the ability to access volatile forensic artifacts in a potentially compromised machine while it is still running. These artifacts include its network connections, opened files, and userspace processes [7, 30]. Live forensics can be contrasted with dead box forensics, which is focuses on analyzing data on persistent storage.

Software-based live forensics is accomplished using one of two general approaches. Either privileged forensics software is pre-emptively installed on the host (e.g., GRR), or the host is *hyper-jacked* [38], transplanting its OS in-place into a virtual machine on top of a specially-built forensics hypervisor (an on-the-fly approach introduced by *HyperSleuth* [34]).

VMI is often used by forensics tools [30]. Examples include combinations of LibVMI and Volatility by *Dolan-Gavitt et al.* [13] and *MiniSecHV* [32].

3.4 Assumptions and Threat Model

This work considers an adversary who seeks to gain control of a host by exploiting a weakness in userspace software and escalating to root via a kernel vulnerability. The adversary establishes persistence on the host using a rootkit with anti-forensic and anti-debugging capabilities and has awareness of how security agents are designed.

Our approach assumes the integrity of the hardware, the hypervisor, and the agent system.

It is advisable for security reasons that the ported agent code remain outside of the hypervisor's trusted computing base (TCB). Our work is based upon the Xen hypervisor, where isolating a hyperagent would be accomplished using XSM [40] and others [42] to encase the hyperagent in a privileged VM. This has been shown to exert acceptable overheads (≤3.0% [42]). Hyperagent code could also be sandboxed (e.g., chroot, seccomp-bpf, and Linux namespaces) or otherwise constrained by the dom0 OS.

Some of the hypervisor-based techniques used to replace an agent's actuators depend on guest OS invariants [44] that implicitly assume that the guest kernel remains in a state where the invariants hold [3, 26]. Guaranteeing this assumption is equivalent to solving the strong semantic gap problem [21], an open problem out of the scope of this work. We assume, as do others, that only a small fraction of malware samples are capable of identifying and deliberately manipulating the specific OS invariants relied on in this work.

4 DESIGN AND METHODOLOGY

This section introduces a three-phase methodology for porting host agents across the virtualization barrier:

Phase 1. The agent is moved out of the guest and into the hypervisor's administrative domain (dom0). A LibVMI-based [37] VMI library, called libhyperagent, is used to selectively replace agent components with their hypervisor-based equivalents. This grants an agent with the **higher privilege, isolation, and concealment** security benefits associated with an out-of-guest approach.

Phase 2. The multiple adjacent phase 1 agent processes (one per guest) now running in dom0 are collapsed into threads inside a single multithreaded hyperagent process. This consolidation makes **more efficient use of memory**, and facilitates the next phase.

Phase 3. New features are added to the hyperagent to take advantage of functionality offered by its new hypervisor environment. By exploiting locality and cross-VM visibility, the hyperagent is able to **outperform in-guest agents**.

Figure 2 depicts these phases. The term *hyperagent* is distinguished from an agent at the conclusion of phase 2, and is taken to mean a single process running and controlling multiple agent threads within the hypervisor.

4.1 Methodology Goals

The proposed methodology has three goals. The first goal is to faithfully preserve the original agent's functionality. Any action the agent was able to take inside the guest as a standalone process should also be possible by the hyperagent. The second goal is to minimize the amount of source code changes required during re-engineering, especially changes that require specialized VMI expertise. The final goal is to measurably improve the agent's effectiveness and efficiency.

4.2 Phase 1: Porting Agent Actuators

In phase 1, portions of an agent's source code are refactored to use VMI so that the agent can be moved to the hypervisor and inspect and influence a guest virtual machine. With Xen, dom0 is typically

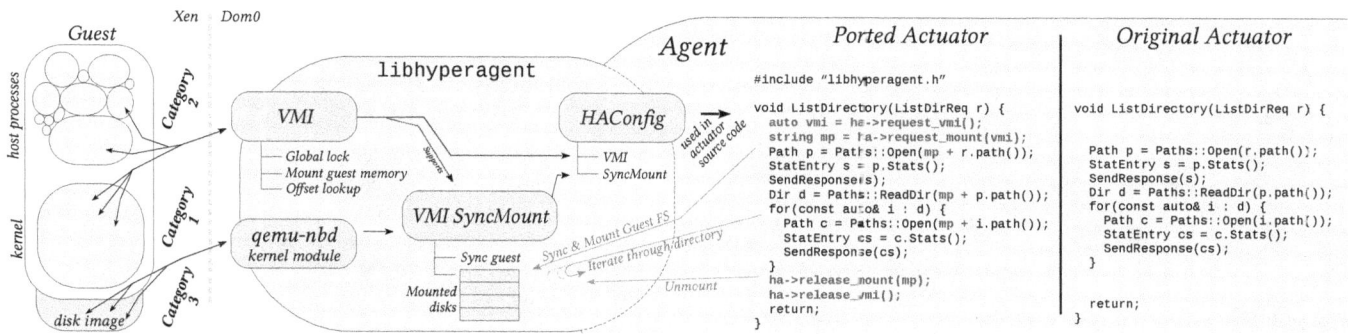

Figure 3: Adding libhyperagent **enables agent actuators to access a guest's kernel data structures (category 1), process memory (category 2), and file system (category 3). This example GRR actuator iterates through a guest directory's contents. The guest file system is temporarily mounted in dom0 using** libhyperagent's **VMI SyncMount component.**

Linux. Once a few necessities are resolved (e.g., library dependencies and network connectivity) a host agent will run equally as well in the hypervisor as it would in any Linux-based guest.

Once on dom0, the agent's actuators must be refactored to use VMI techniques. An agent's actuators are where its purpose is realized. For example, if an agent exists to read a local file and send its contents to the agent controller, the block of agent code that reads the file would be considered an actuator. Examples of actuators include accessing file systems, making system calls, and using ptrace to access data in other processes.

A developer must identify these actuator sites in the agent's source code. Our experience has shown that code modularity and common software design patterns makes actuators straightforward to identify. For example, actuators may occur in all derived classes of a certain class, or actuators might only occur in source code files containing unique imported libraries (e.g., an actuator that uses ptrace imports the ptrace header file).

This work introduces libhyperagent, a LibVMI-based [37] memory and guest file system introspection library that presents an API for hypervisor-based agents to use. Through libhyperagent, actuators can interact with guest kernel data structures, access a guest process's memory, and read from the guest file system. Internally, libhyperagent enables each of these categories of capabilities using a combination of VMI techniques as described below.

Category 1: Kernel Data Structures. Normal host agents typically access kernel data structures by interacting with /proc or /sys, two pseudo file systems that essentially represent useful kernel data structures as files and directories that are easily accessible by userspace programs.

In the case of VMI, kernel information is instead accessed directly in guest memory, based on location information gleaned from the guest's kernel debugging symbols. For objects stored common kernel data structures such as linked lists and binary trees, the typical VMI approach is to find the exported kernel symbol address for the "anchoring" statically-addressed kernel object, then to traverse object pointers on the kernel's heap (much like the kernel does) until reaching the desired kernel object instance [27, 37].

Category 2: Process Memory. Kernel memory objects can be predictably accessed via debugging symbols made available by the OS distribution, but the analogous symbols for userspace processes

may not be available [5]. The approach normally taken by forensics software is to carve up process memory into its memory areas (as defined in kernel data structures). These areas are then accessed by the agent without further VMI-specific semantic interpretation.

Category 3: File System Operations. Host agents routinely interact with a host's file systems. This may be necessary both to fulfill the agent's specific purpose or for tasks such as loading the agent's configuration file and writing log files. When porting the agent on to dom0, it is challenging to provide equivalent access to the guest's file system while minimizing the work required to refactor the agent's actuators. In the worse case, agent actuators might have to be completely re-written against a disk introspection API (e.g., libguestfs[1]).

The approach taken by libhyperagent is to shadow mount the guest file system locally on dom0, essentially causing the guest file system to be mounted a second time (the file system has already been mounted once by the guest OS).[2] As a result, actuator code that performs file system operations needs only to be directed to the guest file system's local mount point in dom0. Figure 3 shows the minor changes required to refactor an actuator that lists the contents of a directory.

Since the guest has already mounted (and is actively using) the same file system, this mounting process must be transparent to the guest and should be read-only.

Solving the Problem of Delayed Writes. Ensuring an up-to-date and consistent view of the guest file system is complicated by the layers of caching performed by modern operating systems. Guest writes are often delayed before being committed to disk, creating a temporary inconsistency between in-guest and out-of-guest views. To flush writes to disk and avoid this problem, a hyperagent needs the ability to perform the equivalent of sys_sync, the Linux kernel's sync system call, immediately prior to an actuator's work in the guest file system. Since synchronizing to disk must be blockable, any VMI technique seeking to induce sys_sync must avoid interacting with the guest kernel at an undesirable time, such as when interrupts are disabled.

---

[1] http://libguestfs.org/

[2] For raw and QCOW2 file-based image formats, libhyperagent uses qemu-nbd, a Linux kernel module, to mount guest file systems in dom0.

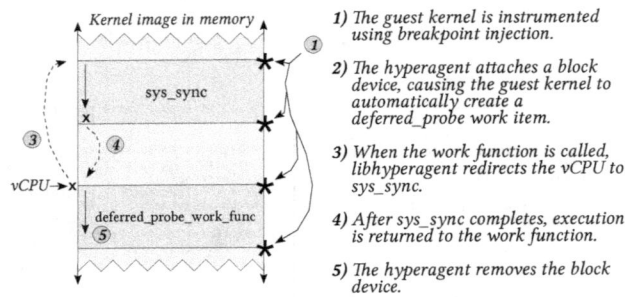

1) *The guest kernel is instrumented using breakpoint injection.*

2) *The hyperagent attaches a block device, causing the guest kernel to automatically create a deferred_probe work item.*

3) *When the work function is called, libhyperagent redirects the vCPU to sys_sync.*

4) *After sys_sync completes, execution is returned to the work function.*

5) *The hyperagent removes the block device.*

Figure 4: The predictability of work queue behavior enables the hyperagent to divert a guest vCPU to sys_sync.

To flush outstanding writes to disk, we propose a new VMI technique for Linux,[3] called *Work Queue Interception (WQI)*. Inspired by *SYRINGE* [6], WQI is useful because it does not introduce new code into the guest, is simpler than stack-based code-injection [27] or syscall redirection [15], and can be reliably triggered by the hyperagent. While WQI is specifically used here to call sys_sync, it is general enough to be used to call other functions elsewhere in existing kernel code.

Work queues are usually used by kernel interrupts to perform low-priority work outside of interrupt context [31]. They are interesting with regard to guest file system introspection because they allow arbitrary work to be performed in kernel process context, in which sys_sync can be safely executed. During normal use, when work is to be added to a work queue, a *work struct* is allocated and populated with the kernel function pointer to be called. Later, a kernel *work process* will run down its work queue and dutifully call each work struct function pointer.

An examination of the Linux kernel identified a work item that can be reliably triggered by the hypervisor. It happens that the deferred_probe work item is generated by kernel device hotplug code when a new block device is attached to a guest (this same code runs when a USB device is inserted into a physical machine). libhyperagent uses VMI to interrupt the guest when this work item is processed in order to redirect the guest vCPU to sys_sync. The procedure is described below in detail and illustrated in Figure 4:

(1) libhyperagent configures the guest vCPU to trap to the hypervisor when an injected breakpoint is encountered at the beginning and end of each sys_sync and deferred_probe function call.

(2) libhyperagent attaches a dummy block device to the guest, inducing the guest kernel into enqueuing a deferred_probe work item.

(3) A guest kernel work process calls deferred_probe. At the first instruction of this function, the guest vCPU encounters the injected breakpoint and traps to the hypervisor. libhyperagent saves the vCPU's register state, then directly alters the guest vCPU registers to jump to sys_sync.

(4) As sys_sync's breakpoints are encountered, libhyperagent receives confirmation the guest disks are synchronized. libhyperagent returns control to the calling agent actuator so that it can perform work on the guest file system. Afterwards,

libhyperagent restores the original vCPU state and allows deferred_probe to execute normally.

(5) Finally, libhyperagent detaches the block device, returning the guest to its original state.

Phase 1 Summary. At the conclusion of the first phase, the agent's actuators have been replaced with their out-of-guest equivalents made available by the libhyperagent library. The agent can then run inside the hypervisor, and connect to the (unchanged) agent controller as before. With the exception of the VMI-enabled actuators, the body of the agent behaves precisely as it did inside the guest.

The primary benefit of this phase is security. The agent is now isolated and concealed from the guest. As an additional benefit, because each guest's phase 1 agent now runs inside dom0, agent management is centralized within the hypervisor.

4.3 Phase 2: Consolidating Adjacent Agents

Modern hypervisors often host many guests, which after phase 1 would mean that multiple agent processes run inside the hypervisor. It is intuitively appealing to eliminate redundancy between multiple agent processes by consolidating them into a single process.

A simple solution is to encapsulate the original agent's functionality in a thread, running as part of a new multi-threaded process, termed the hyperagent. Each time an agent is to be ran for a guest, this process creates a new agent thread. The translation from process to thread requires a management mechanism to spawn and supervise agent threads. This approach eliminates process-level overheads and allows agent threads to share the expensive VMI-related library objects.

Depending on how the agent is ported, synchronization mechanisms may be needed to mediate each agent thread's access to shared objects. The scope and effort required to add these synchronization mechanisms is dependent on how the agent was originally designed. libhyperagent itself is thread safe and handles synchronization internally.

Phase 2 Summary. The immediate benefit of phase 2 is memory savings, achieved by replacing independent agent processes by threads.

4.4 Phase 3: New Agent Functionality

In addition to the described security and efficiency benefits, the hyperagent can support powerful new features that take advantage of its new position beneath its guests.

Compared to an in-guest agent, a hyperagent is dramatically less visible to in-guest malware, and is difficult to affect even if detected. This allows the hyperagent to safely assume functionality that is normally executed by the agent controller. Additionally (from phase 2), the hyperagent has the ability to monitor and control the agent threads for all guests, further motivating a migration of functions from the server to the hyperagent.

While the specific features introduced in phase 3 largely depend on the agent's purpose, in general, these features take advantage of a combination of two related ideas:

---

[3]Although this implementation is Linux-specific, Windows has equivalent *work items*.

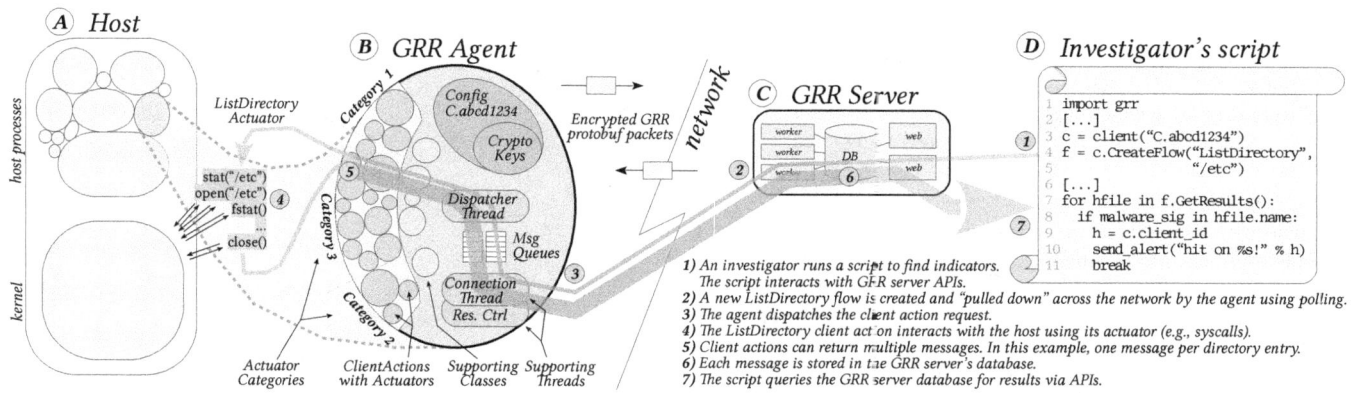

Figure 5: The GRR architecture. From left to right: (A) **a host contains a kernel and userspace processes. One of these processes is** (B) **the GRR C++ agent. The agent registers with** (C) **the GRR server across the network.** (D) **An investigator's script interacts with GRR server APIs to create a** *flow* **that directs the agent to perform one or more of its client actions.**

Locality refers to the benefits of migrating work from the server to the hyperagent. This delegation of work can help eliminate processing bottlenecks at the server. In addition, communication with the server is reduced, saving network bandwidth and eliminating some round-trip latencies. The combination of these makes hyperagents more attractive for applications requiring quick response times.

Cross-VM visibility refers to benefits achieved when a single hyperagent can interact with multiple guest VMs. This direct, cross-VM access can benefit any application that aggregates agent information. The hyperagent can compute and communicate to the server only aggregated results, rather than raw data collected from the individual VMs.

Due to its position on dom0, a hyperagent also has the potential to support VMI applications described in prior VMI work [4] and link into the hypervisor APIs responsible for controlling guests (e.g., to roll back a guest when a security problem is detected).

New functionality introduced in phase 3 should be a well-behaved extension of the original agent system. Migrating server functionality to the hyperagent requires understanding the server's purpose and organization, and requires changes to the server as well. The challenge becomes introducing these new features in a way that preserves the norms and internal rules of the agent system's design.

Phase 3 Summary. Phase 3 introduces new agent features which leverage the greater access and scope provided by the hyperagent environment, including synchronous local access to each guest and a suitable platform for moving analysis to the hyperagent.

5 RE-ENGINEERING GRR

The previous section described a methodology for porting agent system functionality into the hypervisor. In this section, the methodology is illustrated by re-engineering the GRR live forensics C++ agent in to a hyperagent.

Figure 5 shows GRR's client-server model where GRR agents are installed across an enterprise on workstations, servers, and virtual machines. These agents run as daemons on each host and poll the GRR server for work. Forensics investigators use the GRR server to query the agent "fleet" during an investigation.

Table 1: A matrix of GRR agent actuators (columns) matched against the libhyperagent **components (rows) used to function on a guest.**

Actuator	EnumerateFilesystems	EnumerateInterfaces	ListProcesses	GetPlatformInfo	DumpProcessMemory	SysDiff*	ListDirectory	StatFile	GetInstallDate	EnumerateUsers	Find	FingerprintFile	GetConfiguration	GetClientInformation	GetLibraryVersions	DeleteGRRTempFiles	Grep	TransferBuffer
#	1	2	3	4	5	-	6	7	8	9	10	11	12	13	14	15	16	17
Kernel	■	■	■	■														
Process				■		■												
Disk	■					■	■	■	■	■		■						
Minor													■	■	■	■		■

SysDiff is a new GRR flow enabled by phase 3.
Minor: Actuator required few changes.

Each agent can perform a set of primitive tasks (called *client actions* [7]) to collect evidence, triage, and respond to an incident. These client actions are triggered remotely by *flows*, pre-built GRR server procedures that are invoked by an investigator's analysis scripts. An example GRR flow, ListDirectory, is shown in Figure 5.

GRR supports two types of host agents. The first, written in Python, is the default agent used in nearly all cases, and is compatible with Windows, Linux, and OS X. The second, an experimental C++ variant built for a minimal footprint, is limited to Linux. To demonstrate the methodology, the C++ agent was ported into a hyperagent.

5.1 Phase 1

In this phase, each of the GRR agent's actuators were identified and modified to perform the same in-guest function using VMI. The rest of the agent remained as before, and the GRR agent configuration file was unchanged.

The GRR C++ agent's actuators all inherit from a single class that defines the agent's client actions. In the source files for these child classes, libhyperagent was included. The actuator was either replaced with equivalent VMI code (such as when accessing guest userspace or kernel memory) or wrapped in libhyperagent function calls that SyncMount a guest file system. Figure 3 shows how an actuator (the ListDirectory client action) was wrapped in a call to libhyperagent to mount a guest's file system. Table 1 shows the results of phase 1 porting of the GRR C++ agent's 17 client actions.

5.2 Phase 2

The objective of the second phase is to replace agent processes with threads running inside a single consolidated hyperagent process.

The GRR C++ agent's main class, called directly by the agent's main function (int main()) in the original agent, was reimplemented to instead be started as a thread. Each agent's main class was self-contained (i.e., did not use global variables or shared objects) so did not require additional locking mechanisms. A new management process (the hyperagent) was implemented to spawn these agent threads according to a configuration file. This configuration file identifies the guests to be monitored, their disk path, and their kernel symbols (all required for VMI).

5.3 Phase 3

This phase integrates a new GRR workflow that takes advantage of the hyperagent's new position on the hypervisor to dramatically increase the efficiency of a common incident response task.

New Feature Integration. Before adding any new features, the GRR hyperagent requires a workable framework for adding new code into the established GRR system. This was accomplished by defining an additional agent thread called the universal thread (UT). This thread accommodates new phase 3 features as its client actions.

The UT is an entity designed to work within the GRR system to house new hyperagent functionality, and appears to the GRR server as an agent running alongside other normal agent threads. When an investigator wishes to use a new feature introduced in this phase, the investigator includes a call to the UT and its desired client action in their GRR server script.

Any server-side analysis code migrated to the hyperagent gains *locality*, and can now access guest data directly. To further enable the concept of *cross-VM visibility*, the UT is granted access to the data structures of every other agent thread in the hyperagent, allowing it to "borrow" the VMI and guest file system introspection handles of adjacent (normal) agent threads in order to work with their assigned guests.

The functions of the GRR server that will gain the most from migration to the hypervisor are those that involve substantial data transfer from multiple guests. With slight modifications the analysis portions of these scripts can be executed on the hyperagent instead.[4] GRR investigator scripts were examined for such cases.

Figure 6 shows evidence of this migration of work. ① In the original agent system in the top pane, an investigator's script performs high-level analysis by directing the GRR server to issue a series of flows to each agent. In the bottom pane, this high-level analysis will instead be performed directly by the hyperagent using a single GRR flow. ② The GRR server signals agents to initiate each flow's corresponding client actions. In the bottom pane, because there are fewer hyperagents (1 per hypervisor) responding to a single flow,

---

[4]To avoid re-writing the script in C++, the UT can invoke it through an embedded Python interpreter linked into the hyperagent for this purpose.

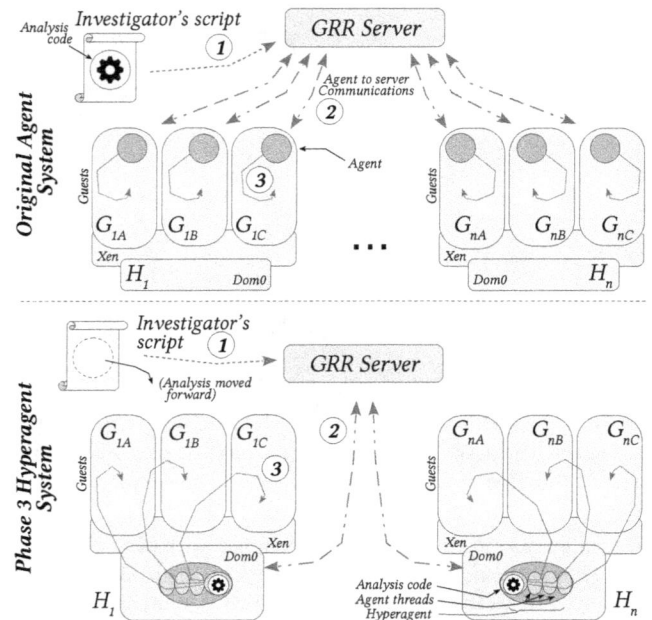

Figure 6: New phase 3 features take advantage of *locality* (moving work forward to the hyperagent) and *cross-VM visibility* (centralized work against all guests).

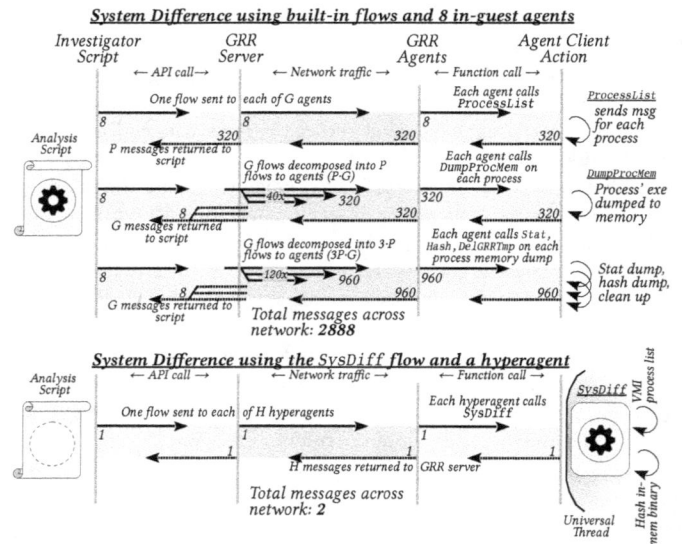

Figure 7: Comparing network activity between a script using the built-in GRR flows (top) and the UT performing computation forward on the hyperagent (bottom). By moving server-side analysis code forward to the hyperagent, multiple network round trips are avoided. Message counts in this figure are based on a single hypervisor ($H = 1$) running 8 guests ($G = 8$), each with 40 processes ($P = 40G = 320$).

network traffic is greatly reduced. ③ The agent's actuators interact with the guest and perform the desired task.

The SysDiff Flow. To illustrate phase 3, we introduce the SysDiff flow, a hyperagent-unique GRR flow that detects anomalous processes across a set of guests. The SysDiff flow implements the common forensics task of identifying hosts running unique (i.e., potentially anomalous) processes. For this purpose, the in-memory executable sections of each guest's running processes are collected, and a hash for each page is computed. These hashes can then be compared to detect differences between guest processes; two processes are considered identical if their intersecting set of resident page hashes match.

For example, if three guests were running the same process binary, but a fourth guest ran an altered version, SysDiff might produce the following output:

```
Exe SHA256:    Exe Path:                            Exe running in:
a9b8c7d6e5...  C:/Windows/System32/notepad.exe      vm-1, vm-2, vm-3
e5d4c3b2a1...  C:/Windows/System32/notepad.exe      vm-4
```

The UT SysDiff client action uses VMI to retrieve the in-memory executable sections of each guest's running processes, computes the hash of each resident page, and compares the hashes. The hyperagent then returns just the final result (resembling the SysDiff output above) to the GRR server.

Figure 7 contrasts the hyperagent's approach with an analogous number of standard GRR agents performing the equivalent of SysDiff using a scripted combination of built-in client actions. This script requires three flows: the first collects the list of active processes; the second dumps the in-memory executables of these processes to the local file system; and, the last flow computes the hashes. This sequence illustrates normal GRR execution, and clearly results in additional round trips to the GRR server.

When compared to server-side analysis, the hyperagent's SysDiff performance should be superior because repeated communication with the server is avoided, and because SysDiff can directly access each guest's memory.

6 EVALUATION AND RESULTS

Several experiments quantify the usability, resource usage, and performance of a GRR hyperagent. The effort required to port the agent into the hypervisor was also evaluated. The security benefits of an out-of-guest approach are adequately addressed by numerous prior VMI works [4], and are not evaluated further here.

6.1 Evaluation Environment

The environment for the *Xen* portion of the performance evaluation consisted of a single Dell R920 hypervisor. The hypervisor ran Xen version 4.7.1 with a Fedora 25 dom0 and was furnished with four 2.3GHz Intel Xeon E7-4870 processors and 256GB RAM. The *Qubes* portion of the performance evaluation consisted of a single Dell Latitude 3340 hypervisor with two 1.6GHz Intel i5-4200U processors and 8GB RAM running Qubes 3.2. In both hypervisor environments, hyperagents ran in dom0 and communicated with the GRR server using a dom0 network interface. Each guest in the evaluation was a fully virtualized Fedora 25 guest with 1 vCPU, 1GB RAM, and 5GB of storage.

6.2 Development Work Factor

The effort required to port the GRR agent into a hyperagent was assessed first. For this purpose, the ported hyperagent's codebase was compared to that of the original GRR C++ agent. Source code differences were then manually classified as belonging to the body

Table 2: Source Code Changes

Component	Body	Source Code Lines Actuators	libhyperagent	SysDiff
GRR Server	109.3k	-	-	+148
				(+0.1%)
C++ IG	4.3k	2.1k	-	-
Hyperagent	+182	+510	+857	+517
	(+2.8%)	(+7.9%)	(+13.5%)	(+8.0%)

Hyperagent code additions were made to the C++ In-Guest (IG) agent.
For reference, Python agent: 7.2k lines body, 5.1k lines actuators.

Table 3: SysDiff Performance

	t	Δ%	Msgs	Δ%	Per Agent Net. payload	Δ%
IG	22.2	-	s→1185.6	-	s→255.2 kB	-
			s←2320.0	-	s←322.0 kB	-
HA	4.5	20.3%	s→ 1.0	0.08%	s→ 0.1 kB	0.06%
			s← 1.0	0.04%	s← 1.3 kB	0.41%

In Guest (IG) agent, Hyperagent (HA), GRR server "s."
Network payloads exclude GRR keep-alives. Averaged across 10 trials.
Time in seconds. On 8 idle Linux guests with ≈35 processes each.

of the agent, its actuators, the libhyperagent library, or features added in phase 3.

Table 2 shows the changes by category. In total, phases 1 and 2 modified 11% of the agent codebase (692 lines). The libhyperagent library itself accounted for another 857 lines. Note that the library can be shared by many other porting efforts. Finally, a combined 665 lines were added to the agent and server to support the SysDiff flow added in phase 3. A large majority of the GRR agent code was unchanged by the re-engineering process.

The re-engineering effort requires a developer who is able to identify actuators in the agent, and who should have a conceptual understanding of how VMI primitives work (e.g., read, write, and using kernel symbols). The availability of the libhyperagent library significantly reduces the effort required to use VMI.

6.3 Execution Time and Network Bandwidth

This experiment compared the performance of the hyperagent's SysDiff flow with an equivalent GRR script that relies on in-guest agents. Figure 7 shows these two scenarios in detail. The same set of 8 Linux guests was used for both parts of this evaluation.

During this evaluation, GRR message types and sizes were recorded as they were sent and received by agents. The GRR messages and their size are used to quantify the difference in network traffic between the two approaches. The end-to-end duration (wall clock time) of the flow was also recorded.

Table 3 shows that locality and cross-VM visibility clearly benefit the hyperagent's SysDiff flow, which returned results to the server 4.9x faster than the built-in flows. In addition, for the same end result, the hyperagent generated roughly three orders of magnitude less traffic than the in-guest approach.

6.4 Performance and Overhead

In another set of experiments, the memory and processing impact of a hyperagent was assessed. For this purpose, the GRR *interrogate*

Table 4: Agent Memory Usage

		Mean Cumulative Memory Usage (RSS)				
		In-Guest Agents		Hyperagent		
		Python	C++	C++	MB/Guest	Δ% IG C++
Guests	1	70.1	52.9	60.3	60.3	114.0%
	2	140.2	105.8	105.8	52.9	100.0%
	4	280.4	211.6	160.9	40.2	76.0%
	8	560.8	423.2	233.4	29.2	55.2%
	16	1,121.6	846.4	505.6	31.6	59.7%
	32	2,243.2	1,692.8	1,031.7	32.2	60.9%

Memory units in MB. Statistics across 100 samples.
Shaded values are extrapolated.

Table 5: In-guest Overheads

Scenario	Sysbench Score	Δ%
No agent	7246.0 ± 19.2	100.0%
"Hot" hyperagent	7223.0 ± 11.1	100.3%
In-guest agent	7200.9 ± 10.5	100.6%
"Cold" hyperagent	6071.2 ± 262.0	119.3%

Units in events/sec at 0.95 Confidence Interval.
Higher is better. Statistics across 10 samples.

flow was used. This flow collects basic host information when new agents register with the server. Due to its complexity, this flow is useful for comparing approaches. The interrogate flow exercises many of the code paths in the GRR agent, including most of the actuators. An interrogate flow consists of nine subordinate flows, which themselves trigger a total of 16 unique client actions on an agent, each retrieving information about a host's network interfaces, disks, and users.

The first experiment in the set measured the duration of the interrogate flow for the Python GRR agent, the C++ GRR agent, and the hyperagent. The second experiment ran the interrogate flow across increasingly large sets of guests in order to quantify hyperagent memory consumption. Since agents running on separate guests are independent, memory is not shared and may be extrapolated for increasing numbers of in-guest agents. The hyperagent's memory usage, however, was directly measured. The third experiment measured overheads by comparing the results of Sysbench's[5] CPU benchmark across three scenarios: the benchmark running on a guest without agents, on a guest with an in-guest agent, and on a guest with the hyperagent running underneath.

The latency results are shown in Table 6. For Xen, the hyperagent requires slightly more time to complete, which is expected due to the use of VMI. This is unlike Qubes, where the hyperagent performs much better than the in-guest agents due to the delays induced by the additional networking components in Qubes' design (these only impact the in-guest agent's traffic stream). Both results fall into ranges that would not likely be noticed by investigators.

The results of evaluating memory usage are shown in Table 4. For these conditions, there was a 40% improvement in hyperagent memory efficiency compared with 8 or more in-guest agents, illustrating the benefits of consolidating agents into a single hyperagent.

Lastly, Table 5 shows each agent's in-guest performance overhead. The hyperagent measurements are broken into two cases,

---

[5]https://github.com/akopytov/sysbench

Table 6: Interrogation Latency

	Xen			Qubes		
	Py IG	C++ IG	Hyperagent	Py IG	C++ IG	Hyperagent
(box max)	15.48	11.35	14.22	16.52	19.26	13.16
	11.86	10.3	12.16	13.39	16.2	11.13
(median)	10.3	9.3	11.17	11.34	14.19	9.12
	8.82	9.28	10.17	9.3	13.16	8.12
(box min)	6.21	8.25	8.11	7.24	9.13	7.09
μ	10.41	9.84	10.14	11.56	14.83	9.58
σ	2.27	1.99	1.16	2.26	5.31	1.12

In Guest (IG) agent. HA (Hyperagent).
Units in seconds. Statistics across 100 samples.

"hot" and "cold," which indicate whether the guest's disk had already been mounted by the hyperagent prior to the interrogate flow. The "hot" hyperagent impacts the guest less than the in-guest agent because the hyperagent's flow processing is performed by the hypervisor, freeing up the guest vCPU to work on the benchmark. This experiment shows that once mounted, a hyperagent has little effect on in-guest overheads.

7 DISCUSSION

7.1 Other Agents

The GRR agent was one of several agents studied as at part of this work. The methodology was also informed by incorporating libhyperagent into the ClamAV anti-virus scanner. A source code review of three other host agents (OSSEC, Nagios NRPE, and the Datadog agent) was also performed. Although these agents differ in terms of purpose, design, and programming language, the methodology's core re-engineering ideas applies equally to them. Each agent has discrete, identifiable actuators, and each is also amenable to a consolidated, single-process hyperagent approach. See the appendix for additional details.

7.2 Tradeoffs

A hyperagent gains its security and efficiency benefits as a tradeoff for increasing the complexity of the hypervisor. This tradeoff should be considered carefully. Good agent candidates include monitoring or security-related agents that gain the most from the increased privilege and concealment offered by a hyperagent.

7.3 Beyond the Datacenter

In addition to evaluating the GRR hyperagent on Xen, the evaluation included Qubes, a standalone desktop OS that encourages users to separate their computing tasks into workflows. These workflows are encapsulated inside disposable virtual machines. This concept of security by compartmentalization means that if one of the Qubes VMs becomes compromised, the damage is contained and unlikely to also compromise the underlying hypervisor and adjacent guests.

In-guest agents can be particularly cumbersome in Qubes. At the hypervisor level, Qubes VMs are designed such that the majority of their file system is backed by a shared copy-on-write root partition. Because this root partition typically houses the agent binaries and configuration file, multiple guests will run an identical agent configuration (a *software identity* [17] problem). While there are multiple ways to fix this problem, using a hyperagent may be the simplest.

7.4 Memory Deduplication

Modern hypervisors offer optional memory sharing features, where identical physical pages owned by adjacent guests are deduplicated and shared between guests. Memory sharing has been shown to offer significant savings [19], so if this sharing is enabled, the potential for memory savings from agent consolidation may be lessened. However, while deduplication works well for certain classes of pages (e.g., read-only code pages), it induces computational overheads and has also been associated with security vulnerabilities [20], leading some hypervisor vendors to disable it by default.

7.5 Adding VMI Functionality

libhyperagent contains the set of VMI-enabled functions that were required to port the GRR agent's actuators. Other agents would likely require different VMI functionality that does not yet exist in the library, and adding this functionality would require VMI experience. Several works [11, 12] have demonstrated methods to automate VMI development, but manual development remains one of the most straightforward methods available [4]. There are several disadvantages to manual development, including building VMI functions that only work against certain generations of guest kernels. As a part of this work, a repository of manually-derived VMI procedures has been made available to assist developers in extending libhyperagent.

7.6 Related Work

Hypervisor-based Frameworks. Existing hypervisor-based tools such as *DRAKVUF* [27], *Stackdb* [23], and *NFM* [41] allow plugins or customizations that could support agent functionality, but each would require an agent to be more thoroughly refactored against the framework's unique APIs. These frameworks were also not designed to host an entire agent, much less the agent consolidation that occurs during phase 2, and lack capabilities such as disk introspection. Forensics-specific hypervisors, such as *MiniSecHV* [32] and *HyperSleuth* [34], have similar issues.

The *XMHF* [43] hypervisor introduced the concept of hypapps through a extensible interface that was used to port several other hypervisor-oriented security systems [35, 39] to run in its framework. While conceptually similar, this work and *XMHF* have divergent objectives and different intended use cases. First, *XMHF*'s execution model supports exactly one guest (such as a nested guest hypervisor). Furthermore, hypapps are integrated into *XMHF* at compile time and activated during system boot, meaning that making changes to a hypapp requires a system-wide disruption. From a development perspective, hypapps cannot take advantage of the standard libraries inherent in Xen's dom0, its ability to mount guest file systems, or its network stack for communication, each of which would require a far-reaching overhaul of an agent's codebase. Unlike the various sandboxing and containment options available in Xen, hypapps are an integral part of XMHF and operate at its highest privilege level. Finally, *XMHF*'s single-guest execution model

precludes both agent consolidation and any analysis seeking to take advantage of cross-VM visibility.

Guest File System Introspection. *Atomizer* [22] and *VMI-Honeymon* [28] both use libguestfs to access a guest's disk. Other out-of-guest disk access methods include intercepting and interpreting file systems and raw disk operations as was done by *vMON* [29], *DIONE* [33], open source tools such as *TSK*,[6] and LibVMI's predecessor, *XenAccess* [37]. Work which handles file systems directly must have a built-in understanding of each file system format likely to be encountered. Alternatively, libhyperagent, *KVMonitor* [24], and *V-Met* [36] use the qemu-nbd kernel module or dm-thin provisioning to mount the guest file system locally, transferring this burden to the dom0 OS and its file system drivers. The qemu-nbd approach also avoids the overheads of libguestfs's supermin appliance.

Regardless of the disk access approach, these other methods are also affected by the implications of delayed writes to disk. *DIONE* [33] specifically acknowledges delayed writes as a factor in their evaluation. Similarly, the work of *Krishnan et al.* [25] introduced a heuristic, time-sensitive method to correlate system calls with disk activity, which might have been made more reliable if extraneous delayed writes were reduced.

8 CONCLUSION

This work introduced a methodology to port host agents to the hypervisor. These newly re-engineered hypervisor-based agents, called hyperagents, offer better isolation and concealment against in-guest threats. In return for a minimal impact on in-guest overhead, hyperagents are easier to administer across lots of guests, save memory and network bandwidth, and can meet and improve upon an in-guest agent's effectiveness. The effort to port an agent is acceptable, and is significantly aided by our structured methodology and accompanying libhyperagent library. This work shows that hyperagents represent a powerful and practical approach to defending virtualized systems.

9 ACKNOWLEDGMENTS

We thank the anonymous reviewers, the Wolfpack Security and Privacy Research Laboratory, Nathan Hicks, Luke Deshotels, and Isaac Polinsky for their reviews.

REFERENCES

[1] GRR Rapid Response. https://github.com/google/grr.
[2] G. Aceto, A. Botta, W. De Donato, and A. Pescapè. Cloud Monitoring: A Survey. *Computer Networks*, 57(9):2093–2115, 2013.
[3] S. Bahram, X. Jiang, Z. Wang, M. Grace, J. Li, D. Srinivasan, J. Rhee, and D. Xu. DKSM: Subverting Virtual Machine Introspection for Fun and Profit. In *29th IEEE Symposium on Reliable Distributed Systems*, Oct 2010.
[4] E. Bauman, G. Ayoade, and Z. Lin. A Survey on Hypervisor-Based Monitoring: Approaches, Applications, and Evolutions. *ACM Computing Surveys*, 2015.
[5] M. Bushouse, S. Ahn, and D. Reeves. Arav: Monitoring a Cloud's Virtual Routers. In *Proceedings of the 12th Annual Conference on Cyber and Information Security Research*.
[6] M. Carbone, M. Conover, B. Montague, and W. Lee. Secure and Robust Monitoring of Virtual Machines Through Guest-assisted Introspection. In *International Workshop on Recent Advances in Intrusion Detection (RAID)*. Springer, 2012.
[7] M. I. Cohen, D. Bilby, and G. Caronni. Distributed Forensics and Incident Response in the Enterprise. *Digital Investigation*, 8:S101–S110, 2011.
[8] S. Cristalli, M. Pagnozzi, M. Graziano, A. Lanzi, and D. Balzarotti. Micro-Virtualization Memory Tracing to Detect and Prevent Spraying Attacks. In

---

[6]http://www.sleuthkit.org/

25th USENIX Security Symposium (USENIX Security 16), pages 431–446, Austin, TX, 2016. USENIX Association.

[9] T. Delaet, W. Joosen, and B. Van Brabant. A Survey of System Configuration Tools. In *Proceedings of the 23rd Conference on Large Installation System Administration*, volume 10 of *LISA'10*, pages 1–8, 2010.

[10] A. Dinaburg, P. Royal, M. Sharif, and W. Lee. Ether: Malware Analysis via Hardware Virtualization Extensions. In *Proceedings of the 15th ACM Conference on Computer and Communications Security, CCS '08*, 2008.

[11] B. Dolan-Gavitt, T. Leek, J. Hodosh, and W. Lee. Tappan Zee (North) Bridge: Mining Memory Accesses for Introspection. In *Proceedings of the 2013 ACM SIGSAC Conference on Computer and Communications Security, CCS '13*. ACM, 2013.

[12] B. Dolan-Gavitt, T. Leek, M. Zhivich, J. Giffin, and W. Lee. Virtuoso: Narrowing the Semantic Gap in Virtual Machine Introspection. In *IEEE Symposium on Security and Privacy (SP)*, pages 297–312. IEEE, 2011.

[13] B. Dolan-Gavitt, B. Payne, and W. Lee. Leveraging Forensic Tools for Virtual Machine Introspection. Technical report, Georgia Institute of Technology, 2011.

[14] Y. Fu. *Bridging the Semantic Gap in Virtual Machine Introspection via Binary Code Reuse*. PhD thesis, The University of Texas at Dallas, May 2016.

[15] Y. Fu and Z. Lin. Bridging the Semantic Gap in Virtual Machine Introspection via Online Kernel Data Redirection. *ACM Transactions on Information System Security*, 16(2):7:1–7:29, Sept. 2013.

[16] T. Garfinkel and M. Rosenblum. A Virtual Machine Introspection Based Architecture for Intrusion Detection. In *Proceedings of the Network and Distributed Systems Security Symposium*, 2003.

[17] T. Garfinkel and M. Rosenblum. When Virtual Is Harder than Real: Security Challenges in Virtual Machine Based Computing Environments. In *HotOS*, 2005.

[18] C. Gikas. A General Comparison of FISMA, HIPAA, ISO 27000 and PCI-DSS Standards. *Information Security Journal: A Global Perspective*, 19(3):132 – 141, 2010.

[19] D. Gupta, S. Lee, M. Vrable, S. Savage, A. C. Snoeren, G. Varghese, G. M. Voelker, and A. Vahdat. Difference Engine: Harnessing Memory Redundancy in Virtual Machines. In *Proceedings of the 8th USENIX Conference on Operating Systems Design and Implementation*, OSDI'08, pages 309–322, Berkeley, CA, USA, 2008. USENIX Association.

[20] G. Irazoqui, M. S. Inci, T. Eisenbarth, and B. Sunar. Wait a minute! A fast, Cross-VM attack on AES. In *International Workshop on Recent Advances in Intrusion Detection (RAID)*, pages 299–319. Springer, 2014.

[21] B. Jain, M. B. Baig, D. Zhang, D. E. Porter, and R. Sion. SoK: Introspections on Trust and the Semantic Gap. In *2014 IEEE Symposium on Security and Privacy*, May 2014.

[22] S. Javaid, A. Zoranic, I. Ahmed, and G. G. Richard III. Atomizer: Fast, Scalable and Lightweight Heap Analyzer for Virtual Machines in a Cloud Environment. In *6th Layered Assurance Workshop, 2012*.

[23] D. Johnson, M. Hibler, and E. Eide. Composable multi-level debugging with Stackdb. In *Proceedings of the 10th ACM SIGPLAN/SIGOPS International Conference on Virtual Execution Environments*, VEE '14, pages 213–225, Salt Lake City, UT, Mar. 2014.

[24] K. Kourai and K. Nakamura. Efficient VM introspection in KVM and Performance comparison with Xen. In *20th Pacific Rim International Symposium on Dependable Computing (PRDC)*, pages 192–202. IEEE, 2014.

[25] S. Krishnan, K. Z. Snow, and F. Monrose. Trail of Bytes: Efficient Support for Forensic Analysis. In *Proceedings of the 17th ACM Conference on Computer and Communications Security*, pages 50–60. ACM, 2010.

[26] T. K. Lengyel, T. Kittel, G. Webster, J. Torrey, and C. Eckert. Pitfalls of Virtual Machine Introspection on Modern Hardware. In *1st Workshop on Malware Memory Forensics (MMF)*, 2014.

[27] T. K. Lengyel, S. Maresca, B. D. Payne, G. D. Webster, S. Vogl, and A. Kiayias. Scalability, Fidelity and Stealth in the DRAKVUF Dynamic Malware Analysis System. In *Proceedings of the 30th Annual Computer Security Applications Conference*, ACSAC '14. ACM, 2014.

[28] T. K. Lengyel, J. Neumann, S. Maresca, B. D. Payne, and A. Kiayias. Virtual Machine Introspection in a Hybrid Honeypot Architecture. In *5th Workshop on Cyber Security Experimentation and Test (CSET)*, 2012.

[29] N. Li, B. Li, J. Li, T. Wo, and J. Huai. vMON: An Efficient out-of-VM Process Monitor for Virtual Machines. In *10th International Conference on High Performance Computing and Communications*, pages 1366–1373. IEEE, 2013.

[30] M. Ligh, A. Case, J. Levy, and A. Walters. *The Art of Memory Forensics: Detecting Malware and Threats in Windows, Linux, and Mac Memory*. Wiley, 2014.

[31] R. Love. *Linux Kernel Development*. Pearson Education, 2010.

[32] D. Lutas, A. Colesa, S. Lukács, and A. Lutas. Secure Virtual Machine for Real Time Forensic Tools on Commodity Workstations. In *Innovative Security Solutions for Information Technology and Communications*, pages 193–208, Cham, 2016. Springer International Publishing.

[33] J. Mankin and D. Kaeli. Dione: A Flexible Disk Monitoring and Analysis Framework. In *International Workshop on Recent Advances in Intrusion Detection (RAID)*, pages 127–146. Springer, 2012.

[34] L. Martignoni, A. Fattori, R. Paleari, and L. Cavallaro. Live and Trustworthy Forensic Analysis of Commodity Production Systems. In *International Workshop on Recent Advances in Intrusion Detection (RAID)*, pages 297–316. Springer, 2010.

[35] J. M. McCune, Y. Li, N. Qu, Z. Zhou, A. Datta, V. Gligor, and A. Perrig. TrustVisor: Efficient TCB Reduction and Attestation. In *Security and Privacy (SP), 2010 IEEE Symposium on*, pages 143–158. IEEE, 2010.

[36] S. Miyama and K. Kourai. Secure IDS Offloading with Nested Virtualization and Deep VM Introspection. In *22nd European Symposium on Research in Computer Security*. ESORICS, 2017.

[37] B. D. Payne, M. de Carbone, and W. Lee. Secure and Flexible Monitoring of Virtual Machines. *Proceedings of the 23rd Annual Computer Security Applications Conference (ACSAC)*, 2007.

[38] J. Rutkowska. Introducing Blue Pill. *Invisible Things Laboratory*, 2006.

[39] A. Seshadri, M. Luk, N. Qu, and A. Perrig. SecVisor: A Tiny Hypervisor to Provide Lifetime Kernel Code Integrity for Commodity OSes. In *ACM SIGOPS Operating Systems Review*, volume 41, pages 335–350. ACM, 2007.

[40] R. Spencer, S. Smalley, P. Loscocco, M. Hibler, D. Andersen, and J. Lepreau. The Flask Security Architecture: System Support for Diverse Security Policies. In *Proceedings of the 8th Conference on USENIX Security Symposium - Volume 8*, SSYM'99, pages 11–11, Berkeley, CA, USA, 1999. USENIX Association.

[41] S. Suneja, C. Isci, V. Bala, E. de Lara, and T. Mummert. Non-intrusive, Out-of-band and Out-of-the-box Systems Monitoring in the Cloud. In *The 2014 ACM International Conference on Measurement and Modeling of Computer Systems*, SIGMETRICS '14, pages 249–261, New York, NY, USA, 2014. ACM.

[42] B. Taubmann, N. Rakotondravony, and H. P. Reiser. CloudPhylactor: Harnessing Mandatory Access Control for Virtual Machine Introspection in Cloud Data Centers. In *2016 IEEE Trustcom/BigDataSE/ISPA*, pages 957–964, Aug 2016.

[43] A. Vasudevan, S. Chaki, L. Jia, J. McCune, J. Newsome, and A. Datta. Design, Implementation and Verification of an eXtensible and Modular Hypervisor Framework. In *Proceedings of the 2013 IEEE Symposium on Security and Privacy*, SP '13, pages 430–444, Washington, DC, USA, 2013. IEEE Computer Society.

[44] C. Wang, X. Yun, Z. Hao, L. Cui, Y. Han, and Q. Zou. Exploring Efficient and Robust Virtual Machine Introspection Techniques. In *Algorithms and Architectures for Parallel Processing*. Springer, 2015.

A APPENDIX: OTHER AGENTS

This appendix describes how four other agents could be re-engineered into hyperagents. For brevity, a discussion on phase 3 is omitted and the diagrams accompanying each agent focus on the "top" and "bottom" portions of the figure on the right.

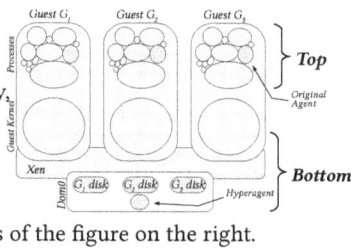

A.1 Security: ClamAV Scanner

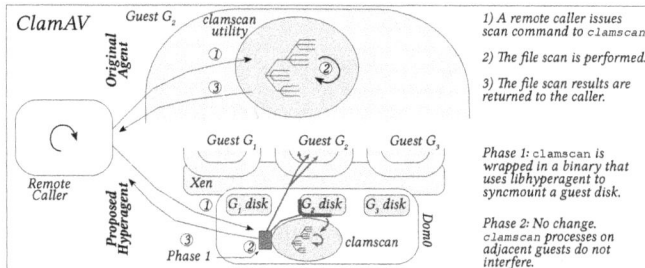

ClamAV[7] is a file-based anti-virus scanner that iteratively scans files in a guest file system hierarchy. ClamAV scanning activity can be controlled by a GUI, a standalone command line utility, or a networked agent daemon called clamd. **Phase 1:** A small libhyperagent-enabled binary is used to "wrap" the ClamAV command line utility, clamscan, such that a guest filesystem is temporarily SyncMounted immediately prior to initiating a scan. **Phase 2:** Since multiple clamscan instances can already run concurrently without interference, phase 2 did not require changes.

A.2 Security: OSSEC Intrusion Detection

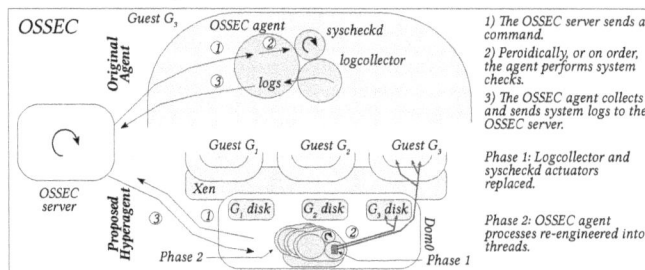

OSSEC[8] is an open source log analysis project that consists of several interrelated programs which collect, parse, analyze, and respond to the contents of a host's log messages. OSSEC can also initiate file integrity scans that look for configuration problems and indicators of rootkits. **Phase 1:** OSSEC's core log collection and analysis functionality relies on file-system-based actuators which are already supported by libhyperagent. Other OSSEC features would require additions to libhyperagent, including inotify-like VMI functionality to detect changes in files, VMI functions that walk a guest's device tree, and the ability to spawn in-guest binaries (or temporarily hijack existing processes in a manner similar to

work queue interception). Examples of these techniques can be found in prior work [23, 27]. **Phase 2:** Much like the GRR agent, a hyperagent management layer could be introduced to instantiate OSSEC agent threads that monitor each guest.

A.3 Traditional Monitoring: Nagios NRPE

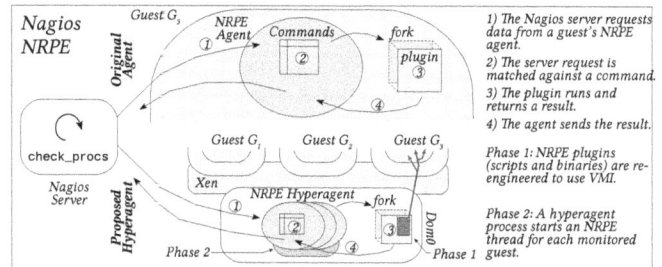

The Nagios Remote Plugin Executor[9] (NRPE) host agent allows a remote Nagios server to query local host state. The NRPE agent responds to a server's requests by looking up and invoking the the request's corresponding NRPE plugin (a binary) as a child process. **Phase 1:** Because each plugin communicates with the main NRPE process via standard output, the plugins are the only agent components that need to be re-engineered in phase 1. The majority of the official plugins are written in C and contain a single actuator site that could be re-engineered to leverage libhyperagent to inspect a guest. **Phase 2:** A hyperagent management layer would be introduced to instantiate a NRPE thread for each monitored guest. Unlike the GRR agent, the NRPE agent makes use of global variables, which would need to be isolated on a per thread basis.

A.4 Cloud Monitoring: Datadog

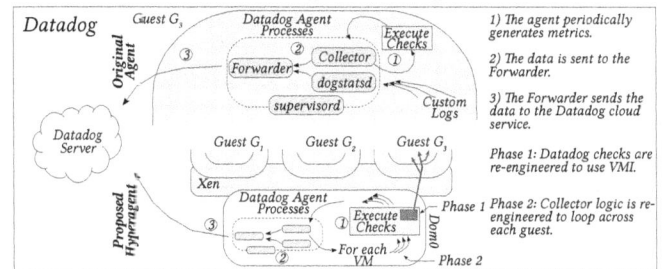

The Datadog agent[10] sends host metrics and events to the Datadog cloud-based monitoring service. At runtime, the Datadog agent collector periodically loops through a configurable series of AgentCheck objects, each of which gathers metrics by reading /proc (or equivalent), invoking a program, or interacting with a local service. **Phase 1:** Each AgentCheck object contains an actuator site, and most sites simply wrap a shell command. libhyperagent could be leveraged in building a second set of VMI-enabled binaries that mimic the syntax of the original commands. **Phase 2:** Unlike GRR, the DataDog agent's design does not require a new management layer. Instead, modifications could be made to the agent loop that calls each AgentCheck object. A second outer loop could be added that calls the set of AgentCheck objects for each monitored VM.

---

[7] https://github.com/vrtadmin/clamav-devel

[8] https://github.com/ossec/ossec-hids

[9] https://github.com/NagiosEnterprises/nrpe

[10] https://github.com/DataDog/dd-agent

CacheShield: Detecting Cache Attacks through Self-Observation

Samira Briongos
Universidad Politécnica de Madrid
samirabriongos@die.upm.es

Gorka Irazoqui
Worcester Polytechnic Institute
Nagravision Iberica
girazoki@wpi.edu

Pedro Malagón
Universidad Politécnica de Madrid
malagon@die.upm.es

Thomas Eisenbarth
Worcester Polytechnic Institute
University of Lübeck
thomas.eisenbarth@uni-luebeck.de

ABSTRACT

Microarchitectural attacks pose a great threat to any code running in parallel to other untrusted processes. Especially in public clouds, where system resources such as caches are shared across several tenants, microarchitectural attacks remain an unsolved problem. Cache attacks rely on evictions by the spy process, which alter the execution behavior of the victim process. Similarly, all attacks exploiting shared resource access will influence these resources, thereby influencing the process they are targeting. We show that hardware performance events reveal the presence of such attacks. Based on this observation, we propose *CacheShield*, a tool to protect legacy code by self-monitoring its execution and detecting the presence of microarchitectural attacks. *CacheShield* can be run by users and does not require alteration of the OS or hypervisor, while previously proposed software-based countermeasures require cooperation from the hypervisor. Unlike methods that try to detect malicious processes, our approach is lean, as only a fraction of the system needs to be monitored. It also integrates well into today's cloud infrastructure, as concerned users can opt to use *CacheShield* without support from the cloud service provider. Our results show that *CacheShield* detects attacks fast, with high reliability, and with few false positives, even in the presence of strong noise.

KEYWORDS

Cache attacks; Hardware performance counters; Change point detection

ACM Reference format:
Samira Briongos, Gorka Irazoqui, Pedro Malagón, and Thomas Eisenbarth. 2018. CacheShield: Detecting Cache Attacks through Self-Observation. In *Proceedings of Eighth ACM Conference on Data and Application Security and Privacy, Tempe, AZ, USA, March 19–21, 2018 (CODASPY '18),* 12 pages.
https://doi.org/10.1145/3176258.3176320

1 INTRODUCTION

Modern computing technologies like cloud computing build on shared hardware resources opaquely accessible by independent tenants, ensuring protection through sandboxing techniques. However, microarchitectural attacks are able to extract information across VM boundaries even if hypervisors are correctly implemented and otherwise secure. These attacks exploit shared hardware resources such as caches to observe effects of co-located processes, allowing them to extract sensitive data or to decrease quality of service.

Various variants of practical cache attacks have been applied in cloud environments: Prime+Probe [13, 22, 36, 51, 52], Prime+Abort [12], Flush+Reload [4, 17, 18, 46], and Flush+Flush [15]. All of them can recover cryptographic keys, break security protocols or compromise the end users privacy. Similarly, Degradation of Service attacks create contention in shared hardware resources such as caches or the memory bus to degrade services of co-located VMs [20, 49]. All these attacks have been demonstrated in contemporary public cloud systems, with severe consequences to sensitive data or service quality of cloud customers.

Several techniques for detection and/or mitigation of cache attacks and other microarchitectural attacks have been proposed. Most of the proposed *mitigation techniques* succeed in stopping cache based attacks, but are not being adopted by cloud service providers. Proposed hardware countermeasures require making modifications to the hardware that may induce severe performance penalties and take years to integrate and deploy into the infrastructure. Cloud hypervisors, on the contrary, can implement any of the proposed hypervisor based countermeasures [24, 26, 42] by making small modifications to the kernel configuration. While effective, the countermeasures are not being adopted by cloud service providers, presumably due to the performance overhead that they add to their systems, irrespective of the actual presence of attacks.

Another approach is to first *detect* ongoing attacks and then react with a countermeasure. The advantage is that system changes are less severe and countermeasure overhead is only invoked when an attack occurs. One way to detect cache attacks is by monitoring hardware performance counters (HPCs) for attack features such as increased cache miss rates. HPCs are available on all modern CPUs and have been successfully used for security applications such as detecting malware and security breaches [5, 11, 39, 43]. Libraries such as PAPI (Performance Application Programming Interface) [30], facilitate the task of configuring and reading those hardware counters. Several methods to detect cache attacks using HPCs have been proposed [10, 34, 48], but these approaches have drawbacks. Some works require the hypervisor to periodically monitor all existing VMs, which introduces a great overhead in CPU usage and detection capabilities depend on how efficiently an attacker can hide from the monitoring tool [34, 48]. Other works which offer solutions applicable to multi-process environments [10, 15], require information for each neighboring process which is not feasible in cloud environments, or are simply too costly [50]. Furthermore, if tools operate at the hypervisor level, they need support from the Cloud service provider. Hence, tenants have to rely on goodwill from hardware and hypervisor designers or cloud service providers to protect themselves against cache attacks.

Thus, we observe the necessity of giving those tenants that need protection against cache attacks, tools to defend themselves independently from other parties. So far, all known cache attacks have in common that they cause cache misses *in the victim VM process*. Intuitively, detecting anomalies in the number of cache misses in the victim can indicate an ongoing cache attack and allow the victim to react with appropriate precautionary measures.

All major hypervisors, including VMware, Xen and KVM, now provide virtualized access to performance counters [37] from inside the VMs. This access can be enabled only in the VMs that request the service. The virtualized counter values provided to the VM by the hypervisor, refer uniquely to this VM. That is, one VM cannot read counters referring to another co-resident VM. Until recently, access to HPCs was out of reach for cloud tenants. However, at this time, all major cloud providers have added functionality to provide secure and transparent access to HPCs to their VMs [1, 2]. Tenants can monitor performance events for *their* own processes and resources. We propose to use this monitoring capability inside the VM to detect anomalies in performance rates such as the cache miss rate *only on the victim side*: A tenant can detect the presence of an attack by monitoring itself.

Our work demonstrates for the first time, that performance counter access for tenant VMs can indeed be utilized to *improve security* of the tenants. We offer tenant VMs a new monitoring service, *CacheShield*, to detect cache attacks. *CacheShield* can be activated before running sensitive processes. *CacheShield* detects attacks quickly, with high reliability and low CPU overhead, due to the use of Page's cumulative sum method [33]. The CUSUM method is an unsupervised anomaly detection method, ensuring that even new attack techniques can be detected with high confidence. *CacheShield* automatically turns off if the monitored process is idle by detecting the lack of activity, resulting in a significant reduction in CPU processing overheads. In summary, our work

- presents a performance counter based monitoring service that users can voluntarily activate to detect cache attacks.
- only monitors the victim process upon when active, i.e., the cloud service provider does not waste cycles continuously monitoring all VMs running in the same host.
- only requires the hypervisor to enable VM access to the performance counters, a feature commonly supported by all major hypervisor systems, including KVM, VMware and Xen. No other additional help from the underlying system is needed.
- implements an efficient algorithm that maximizes fast and reliable attack detection, while minimizing false positives and

keeping the performance overhead minimal and restricted to the protected VM.
- succeeds detecting all existing cache attacks, including stealthy attacks that are miss-detected by other solutions, e.g. Flush+Flush, since our detection technique uses attack characteristics.
- shows that it can be adapted and extended to detect other attacks based on abuses of shared resources such as DoS attacks.

2 BACKGROUND AND RELATED WORK

2.1 Cache Attacks

In the last years cache attacks have shown to pose a big threat in those systems in which the underlying hardware architecture is shared with a potential attacker. Cache attacks monitor the utilization of the cache to retrieve information about a co-resident victim. Indeed, if the utilization of such a hardware piece is directly correlated with a security-critical piece of information (e.g., a cryptographic key) the consequences of the attack can be as devastating as an impersonation of the victim.

Two main cache attack designs out-stand over the rest: the Flush+Reload and the Prime+Probe attacks. The first was first introduced in [17], and was later extended to target the LLC to retrieve cryptographic keys, TLS protocol session messages or keyboard keystrokes across VMs [16, 23, 46]. Further, Zhang et al. [52] showed that Flush+Reload is applicable in several commercial PaaS clouds. Despite its popularity and resistance to micro-architectural noise, the Flush+Reload presents a main drawback, as it can only be applied in systems in which memory deduplication mechanisms are in place, and further, can only recover information coming from statically allocated data.

The Prime+Probe attack design, contrary to the Flush+Reload attack, is agnostic to special OS features in the system, and therefore it can not only be applied in virtually every system, but further, it can additionally recover information from dynamically allocated data. This attack was first proposed for the L1 data cache in [32], while later was expanded to the L1 instruction cache [3]. Recently, it has been shown to also bypass several difficulties to target the LLC and recover cryptographic keys or keyboard typed keystrokes [13, 22, 27]. Even further, the Prime+Probe attack was used to retrieve a RSA key in the Amazon EC2 cloud [21].

Variations of both attacks have also been proposed to bypass specific difficulties found in some systems (e.g., lack of a flush instruction in the Instruction Set Architecture). Perhaps the one that most directly influences this work is the design of the Flush+Flush attack, as it was proposed to be stealthy and bypass attack monitoring systems [15]. This attack retrieves information by measuring the execution time of the flush instruction, thus avoiding direct cache accesses. As we will see, although this design might be effective against some of the proposed detection systems, ours correctly identifies when such an attack is being executed. The recent Prime+Abort attack removes the need for a timer, but requires set priming (like Prime+Probe) [12]. Priming results in detectable cache evictions for the victim process, as shown in this work, thus rendering Prime+Abort detectable by *CacheShield*.

2.2 Performance Counters

The performance counters are special purpose hardware registers that count a broad spectrum of low-level hardware events related to code execution. The selection of observable events is usually larger than the number of actual counters, hence, counters must be configured in advance. All events associated with a counter are recorded in parallel. As the PMU allows detailed insight into the state of the processor in real-time, it is a valuable tool for debugging applications and their performance.

All main micro-processor architectures, i.e., Intel, AMD and ARM, include a bigger or a smaller number of these configurable registers. However, while monitoring of these hardware events in Intel and AMD processors is usually possible from user mode (when referring to an application also being run in user mode), ARM devices require root rights to enable them. Emulating the behavior in ARM devices, cloud providers might disable the utilization of performance counters from guest VMs. Indeed we find two main reasons why they would do this

- Performance counters might be utilized with malicious purposes and retrieve information from collisions in shared resources co-resident user hardware utilization [8].
- As performance counters are hardware dependent, giving a guest VM access to benign utilization of performance counters might be problematic if guest VMs are migrated over different architectures, as customers would have to design code for different hardware architectures.

We do not believe that these facts should make cloud providers disable the usage of performance counters from guest VMs, specially when one can use them as a protection mechanism as we will see later in this work. First, VMs can only retrieve information about their own hardware usage, and thus, *users can not directly gather information from their neighbors utilization*. The only possibility for such a malicious approach is to create collisions and infer this utilization through the information given by their counters. However, even if performance counters are not enabled, attackers have already found alternative ways to retrieve the same information performance counters give. For instance, attackers can read the cycle counter or an incremental thread to know when TLB or cache misses occur. Thus, disabling the counters does not prevent the leakage of hardware events information. As for the second claim, a possible solution could be to create clusters with the same hardware configuration, and migrate VMs within this cluster. Thus, we do not believe the above concerns are strong enough arguments against the guest VM performance counter usage. In this paper, we will further show that such a usage can indeed offer more protection to cloud infrastructure customers.

2.3 Detection, Mitigation and Other Countermeasures

HPCs have been used to detect generic malware [5, 38, 39] as well as microarchitectural attacks [10, 15, 34, 48]. Their success mostly depends on the ability to correctly identify cache (and other resource) attack patterns by *continuously* monitoring the associated event in the HPC. This approach is usually implemented at the OS or hypervisor level that has enough permissions to monitor what is running in the system. However, we observe two main problems with these detection-based approaches:

- Most of these detection approaches incur severe performance overheads that hypervisors or OSs do not seem willing to pay,

as to the best of our knowledge no OS is implementing such a mechanism. This leaves the user of the system with few resources to know whether his code will be executed in a safe environment.

- As these detection countermeasures base their success on the monitoring of both the victim and the attacker processes, the attacker can vary patterns in a smart way to try to bypass the detection mechanisms.

These facts are observed, for instance in [10, 34, 48]. All three works incur significant overheads on all applications. CloudRadar, for example, requires three dedicated cores for its detection [48]. In addition, they usually assume the ability to monitor the attacking process [10, 15], which is not possible across VM boundaries (except for the hypervisor), and not possible for user-level processes.

Detection-based countermeasures are not the only possibility shown to prevent cache timing attacks. Preemptive approaches can be taken at the hardware, software and application level. The first usually requires changes in the hardware pieces such that collisions in the cache can not happen, or if they do, they do not carry information [44]. The second involves the utilization of specific software features (e.g., page allocation) to prevent two processes from colliding in the cache [24]. Finally, the latter is achieved by utilizing specific tools to ensure a security sensitive binary does not leak information, even if it is under attack [47].

3 VICTIM-BASED ATTACK DETECTION

Our objective is to build an attack detection tool that detects any abuse of the LLC without any modifications to the hypervisor, OS, or the CPU hardware. Unlike previous approaches, we show that monitoring the behavior of a victim application is sufficient for the detection of cache attacks. To that end, we first analyze the behavior of these *victim applications* by monitoring several critical hardware performance counters.

For the sake of simplicity, we base our analysis on cryptographic algorithms, which are the most popular target for cache attacks. Our approach can also detect attacks on other security-critical pieces of code like SSL/TLS protocol stacks. There are different types of cryptographic algorithms in use, which traditionally have been classified as symmetric cryptography and public-key cryptography. AES is the most widely used symmetric encryption algorithm. Software implementations of AES usually rely on table look-ups, unless hardware support such as AES-NI is available. The popularity of AES together with the secret-dependent use of table look-ups make AES a popular target for cache attacks [4, 7, 17, 22, 32]. For public key cryptography, RSA, ECC and ElGamal are currently the prevailing schemes. While mathematically quite different, their implementations follow similar strategies, resulting in similar leakage behavior. We chose RSA, which has also been a popular target for cache attacks [3, 8, 46], for the preliminary analysis.

We only collect information about the victim processes, i.e. the processes operating on sensitive data. This approach avoids the need of monitoring other processes or VMs running in the same host. This approach also avoids relying on the information gathered from an attacker who might try to hide changes on its behavior to avoid triggering an alarm and bypass current detection systems.

3.1 Analyzing Hardware Performance Events

In this preliminary step, we followed a similar approach as they did in [9]. We used PAPI to collect data from 30 accessible hardware event counters on our test platform, for sample public and private key algorithms, in the presence and the absence of cache attacks. The counters referring to our process were read before and after each cryptographic operation, that is, we got detailed information for a single encryption or decryption execution. Since the number of counters that can be read in parallel is limited, we collected the data for different groups of counters at different times, then joined the data altogether and carried further study to determine which counters provide meaningful information for our purpose.

For this initial analysis, we have chosen the software AES T-Table implementation and the RSA sliding window implementation of OpenSSL , which give representative results for public key and symmetric key cryptography. As sample attack we have used the Flush+Reload against both implementations. One difference between these two implementation is that the attack targets data in the case of AES and instructions in the case of RSA. These experiments were performed on an Intel Core i7-4790 CPU 3.60 GHz machine with 8 MB of L3 cache with Centos 7 OS, collecting 1 million samples for each counter for encryption or decryption operations.

In order to perform the analysis of the information gained from the counters, we have used the WEKA tool [19], designed with the purpose of allowing researchers to easily access state-of-the-art techniques in machine learning. To this end, we have randomly selected 50000 instances of each of the groups, that is for AES attack and non-attack and for RSA attack and non-attack, obtaining 200000 samples (balanced between attack and non-attack "classes") with information about 30 counters, each labeled with '1' for attacks and '0' for non-attacks. We have used the infoGain function, which evaluates the worth of an attribute by measuring the information gain with respect to the class according with "InfoGain(Class,Attribute) = H(Class) - H(Class | Attribute)", where H is the entropy. We have also evaluated the relief algorithm [25] for feature selection. Unlike the InfoGain, which only evaluates information gained from each attribute individually, the relief algorithm outputs a score of the predictive value of an attribute relative to other attributes.

Table 1 presents a summary of the counters which give most relevant information for detection according to the mentioned algorithms. The table states their mean values for the considered scenarios, and the differences between attacks and the *expected* behavior. Note that in our case H(Class)= 1, thus an ideal attribute would gain 1 bit. Values of infoGain around 0.5 may indicate the attribute carries meaningful information, but only for one of the algorithms or one of the attacks. Thus, L3 cache misses are not only the most meaningful predictions, as highlighted by both tests, but also work across the considered scenarios. In fact, the relief algorithm scores all other attributes with very low scores, implying only little additional gain from using them.

3.2 Concurrent Signal Assessment

Tracking hardware performance events for each cryptographic operation showed that victim-based attack detection is feasible and helped identifying relevant counters. However, with this approach,

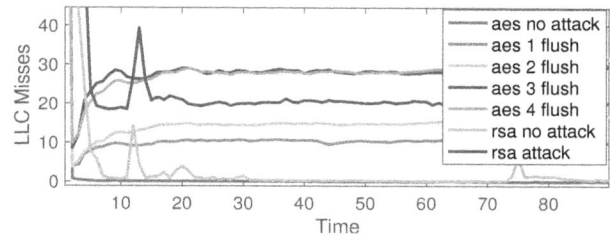

Figure 1: Mean LLC miss traces over time for AES and RSA executions in the presence and absence of cache attacks. The numbers next to *flush* indicate the number of lines flushed at a time. After the start up peaks, the misses go to zero in the absence of a cache attack,and remain high under attack.

achieving detection fast enough to detect attacks that succeed during the execution of a single call to the sensitive function, e.g. the attacks presented in [45, 46], would require adding instructions in the middle of the code we want to protect. Hence, it requires alteration of the target code, which adds unnecessary burden on the user and diminishes practicality. For more effective attack detection, it is preferable to read performance counters concurrently to the execution of the sensitive process.

During our initial experiments we have observed that all implementations feature a *start up* behavior, where data is loaded into the cache for the first time and the frequency of the CPU might be adjusted. The subsequent executions feature a more constant behavior. When we switch to continuous monitoring, the start-up behavior is restricted to a short time at the beginning of the executions. Figure 1 represents the mean value of the L3 miss counter in our initial scenario setup, for Flush+Reload attacks as well as *normal* executions of the mentioned processes. The average is computed over 1000 encryptions and counters are read every 100 μs. It can be clearly observed that after the initial transient state, the number of misses goes to zero in the absence of attacks (aes no attack and rsa no attack) for both crypto primitives. Thus, both algorithms behave similarly for *normal* execution. It can also be observed that the mean number of misses in the case of an attack varies with the number of lines flushed each time aes 1 flush, aes 2 flush....

To ensure the information of the other counters mentioned in Table 1 is still optimal for attack detection when using concurrent monitoring, we performed a new analysis considering each sample collected at a period of 100μs as an independent input to the selection attribute algorithms. We have observed that the infoGain increases up to 0.92 for the L3 cache misses counter, while values for the other counters decrease. Additionally, the relief algorithm still gives the highest score for the L3 cache misses (0.18), a value 5 times higher than the weight of the next counter, indicating the L3_TCM is still the one counter of choice for cache attack detection.

We performed additional experiments to determine how well a cluster algorithm would distinguish between attacks and non-attacks with the periodically sampled data from several counters at once. We tested *EM* and *Self Organizing Maps* using WEKA, setting the number of clusters to two. The most interesting result of these experiments is that while these algorithms were able to classify in the same cluster respectively 84% and 91% of the *attack* samples when using only the LLC misses counter, this number decreases to

Table 1: Overview of most relevant hardware performance counters in the presence and absence of attacks, over 1 million calls to RSA and AES, as well as their rankings according to the InfoGain and relief metrics. Level 3 cache misses, PAPI_L3_TCM, clearly have the strongest information for cache attacks.

Performance Counter	AES Normal	AES w/ Attack				RSA Normal	RSA Attack		Joint Evaluation Algorithms	
		1 line		4 lines					infoGain	Relief
	μ_n	μ_{a1}	$\mu_{a1} - \mu_n$	μ_{a2}	$\mu_{a2} - \mu_n$	μ_n	μ_a	$\mu_a - \mu_n$		
PAPI_L3_TCM	0.0002	0.92	0.9189	3.56	3.5598	1.12	2601.4	2600.28	0.885	0.245
Cycles (rdtsc)	612.33	828.60	216.27	1151.71	539.38	8.840e+07	8.956e+07	1.151e+06	0.714	0.014
PAPI_REF_CYC	61.93	71.01	9.08	79.93	18	2.453e+06	2.484e+06	3.1e+04	0.683	0.005
PAPI_CA_SNP	21.95	28.77	6.82	30.35	8.4	727.87	3417.5	2689.63	0.531	0.034
PAPI_CA_INV	21.99	28.83	6.86	30.45	8.46	727.88	3417.6	2689.72	0.530	0.033
PAPI_L3_TCR	24.65	24.73	0.08	25.90	1.25	490.47	3253.6	2763.13	0.528	0.029
PAPI_L2_ICM	15.51	9.16	-6.35	11.86	-3.65	381.12	3149.2	2768.08	0.510	0.056

around 50-60% when adding other counters. These results indicate that cache attacks can be detected, regardless of the algorithm the victim process runs, by only using information gathered from the L3 cache miss counter. The algorithms feature zero misses after the initial warm-up, unless an attacker is forcing misses. Given that all known cache attacks, including Flush+Flush, cause cache misses on the victim process to obtain information, the results obtained here for the Flush+Reload attack are applicable for other attacks.

4 CACHE SHIELD

So far, techniques proposed to detect cache attacks imply monitoring the victim VM, the attacker VM, and any other VM running in the same host [10, 48]. Monitoring all VMs at rates which vary from 1 μs to 5 ms results in huge overheads which increases with each new virtual machine allocated in the same host. As a difference with previous approaches, *CacheShield* avoids monitoring all other processes or VMs running in the same host, i.e., we only focus on the one process needing protection. By leaving the choice of deciding which processes should be monitored and protected and when in the hands of the user, we avoid the need to detect when a sensitive process is executed. Also, from the cloud provider's point of view, this way of facing detection also means no waste, as it does not have to dedicate extra resources and only affects the implied VM and only when it is necessary reducing the impact in performance of such monitoring to a minimum.

Figure 2 presents a diagram of our proposed solution. Whenever a user wants to protect a process, he informs the *CacheShield* module, which utilizes the information gathered from the counters to decide whether the user is being attacked. If *CacheShield* detects an attack, an appropriate response mechanism to prevent the information leakage is put in place. Although we mainly focus on the detection phase, we discuss potential countermeasures in Section 6.

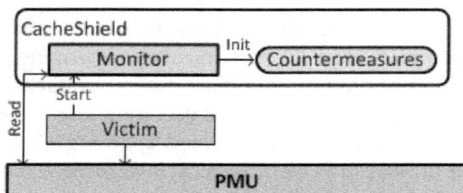

Figure 2: Overview of *CacheShield*.

4.1 Detection Algorithm

CacheShield should detect attacks independently of the protected algorithm and can detect all known types of cache attacks, and, potentially, currently unknown attacks.

Supervised learning algorithms such as neural networks, have already been used to detect certain cache attacks. As any supervised algorithm, they require a labeled data set including data from different attacks we want to detect, to build meaningful models and to identify their characteristic features. As a drawback of this approach, new attacks, or attacks with different patterns would be non-detectable without training.

The alternative is using unsupervised techniques. They do not receive labeled data, by themselves try to cluster the received data into different groups. We briefly explored clustering in section 3.2 to select the counters which can identify an attack. Other kind of unsupervised techniques are anomaly-based detection algorithms, which in theory could detect "zero-day" attacks. To the best of our knowledge, no successful cache detection fully based on anomaly-detection techniques has been yet demonstrated.

Change-point detection methods are designed to deal with the problem of detecting abrupt changes in distributions. Under the assumption that cache attacks have an effect in the performance of the protected algorithms, change-point detection algorithms stand as great candidates to detect LLC attacks. We propose an algorithm based on change point-detection techniques which is self-learning so it adapts itself to detect different attack patterns, allows us to fix the attack detection delay, is computationally simple, and respects the constraint of minimum impact in performance.

4.2 Cache Shield Design

CacheShield monitors the counters for LLC misses and for total cycles. The former gives information about the use of the LLC of the protected process while the latter gives information about when it is running or when it has finished. Based on Figure 2, the *CacheShield* module needs the PID of the process we desire to protect so it can attach the counters to gather the data referring to this single process. Similarly, this process needs the PID of the *CacheShield* process so they can communicate with each other.

On Unix systems, the easiest way to use *CacheShield* is to use the fork operation, and then to use the *exec* system call to run the module and to give it the PID of the parent process. The parent process then executes the desired operation while being monitored. If the parent process stops or gets paused, *CacheShield* automatically stops after noticing the parent has not been running for a while.

Change Point Detection: Change point detection theory (CPD) [6] can be used to construct the commonly known as quick detection algorithms. CPD has successfully been applied for quality control, signal-processing, anomaly or intrusion detection tasks, among other problems [29, 31, 40, 41]. The assumption in these scenarios is that the parameters describing the monitored system do not change or change very slowly under normal conditions. The parameters can, however, change at unknown time instants (including at startup) into anomalous conditions. Thus, CPD algorithms are used to detect significant changes in the characteristic parameters of the monitored system, quickly and with high confidence.

CPD algorithms feature optimality properties, in the sense that for a given false-alarm rate (FAR) they minimize the average time it takes to detect the change in the descriptive system's features [31]. CPD algorithms are easy to implement, do not require much memory and, as a consequence do not have significant computational overhead. In the following, we describe the parameters of the algorithm and how we assess key issues, such as the choice of models or the use of prior information.

The sequence of observations of N variables monitored in parallel is denoted as $X(t) = (X_1(t), ..., X_N(t)), t \geq 1$. Before a change occurs, the joint probability distribution (pdf) of the random variables $X_1, ..., X_N$ also known as *prechange distribution*, can be denoted as $p_0(X_1, ..., X_N)$. If a change occurs at an unknown time instant λ, the observations will follow a different distribution $p_1(X_1, ..., X_N)$, also called *postchange distribution*. That is, when $t < \lambda$ the observations $X(t)$ will have conditional pdf $p_0(X(t)|X(1), ..., X(t-1))$, and pdf $p_1(X(t)|X(1), ..., X(t-1))$ for $t \geq \lambda$. Under the hypothesis that a change has occurred, the stopping time τ at which the alarm is triggered gives a measurement of the detection time. It is typically defined as the first time the change sensitive statistic watching the system, exceeds a threshold. Naming E_0 and E_λ the expectations for the sequence of observations prior and after the change at time λ, and assuming that no alarm occurred, the mean time between false alarms will be given by the expression $E_0\tau$. As a consequence of this definition, the average frequency of false alarms or false alarm rate (FAR) is defined as:

$$FAR(\tau) = \frac{1}{E_0\tau}$$

For a good detection procedure it is expected low FAR. Page's cumulative sum (CUSUM) detection algorithm [33] is one of the most popular CPD algorithms: with a full-knowledge of the pre-change and post-change distributions it provides an optimal scheme minimizing the worst-case detection delay. Page's CUSUM algorithm utilizes the log-likelihood ratio (LLR) to check the hypothesis that a change occurred, LLR is defined as:

$$s(t) = ln\frac{p_1(X(t)|X(1), ..., X(t-1))}{p_0(X(t)|X(1), ..., X(t-1))}$$

A change in the parameter under study will also cause a change in the sign of the log-likelihood ratio. In other words, $s(t)$ shows a negative drift before change and a positive drift after change. Based on a recursive comparison with a threshold h, the decision rule is

$$g_k = \max\left\{0, g_{k-1} + \ln\frac{p_1(X(k))}{p_0(X(k))}\right\} \geq h$$

Then the detection time for the given threshold is

$$\tau(h) = \min\{k \geq 1 : g_k \geq h\}$$

Although this first approach considers that both distributions are known, this assumption is usually not true, and as a consequence this proposal has to be adapted for each situation. We may know one distribution in advance or none, so it may be necessary to estimate the parameters of the algorithm during the runtime. As long as the estimators for the distributions and the real observation meet certain convergence conditions, we will be able to fix the parameters such as the desired detection delay or the FAR.

Change Point Detection in *CacheShield*: Attacks either start after the detection algorithm has been started or they are already running when the detection starts. Both situations are efficiently managed by the proposed CUSUM algorithm. Each new sample is classified into one of two different groups or clusters, namely "attack" and "non-attack". The "non-attack" cluster represents how we expect the protected process to behave under normal conditions. Based on the information gained from previous experiments, this assumption is that after a few samples corresponding to the initialization of the protected process, the number of L3 cache misses will be around 0, then $\mu_{na} = 0$. On the other hand, when there is an attack, we have observed that the mean number of misses is μ_a. Then each new sample belonging to the "attack" cluster will be around μ_a. The value of μ_a is unknown and depends on the attack so it needs to be computed and recalculated with each new sample.

We denote each new sample that the *CacheShield* module gets as $miss_i$, referring to the protected process. We need to decide if it belongs to one cluster or to the other. To do so, we compute the value of the "probability" that $miss_i$ belongs to each one, making use of the distance metric. We define the distance from $miss_i$ to μ_{na} as: $d_{na}(i) = miss_i - \mu_{na} = miss_i$ Then, the distance with the "attack" cluster is $d_a(i) = |miss_i - \mu_a|$. As stated before, the value of μ_a is unknown when we start to monitor the process. We select an arbitrary initial value, and whenever a new sample $miss_i$ is obtained, if $miss_i \geq 0$ we update the value of μ_a as follows:

$$\mu_a = (1 - \beta) * \mu_a + \beta * miss_i$$

This method is known as exponentially weighted moving average, where the weight of the older datum decreases exponentially. This way of estimating the mean of the "attack cluster" makes the election of the initial arbitrary value irrelevant after collecting a few misses samples. However, If the initial value is chosen too low, we may trigger false positives. In our experiments we set $\beta = 0.05$ and the initial value to 12.5. While $\beta = 0.05$ is a commonly used value, 12.5 was selected to not to trigger false positives during the initialization step and still allow convergence of the "attack" cluster mean in the desired time.

We can now define the probability of belonging to each cluster:

$$p_{na}(miss_i) = \frac{d_a(i) + 1}{|d_{na}(i)| + |d_a(i)|}, \quad p_a(miss_i) = \frac{d_{na}(i) + 1}{|d_{na}(i)| + |d_a(i)|}$$

The value 1 has been added to avoid divisions by 0 in the LLR calculation that has to be performed as part of the detection algorithm.

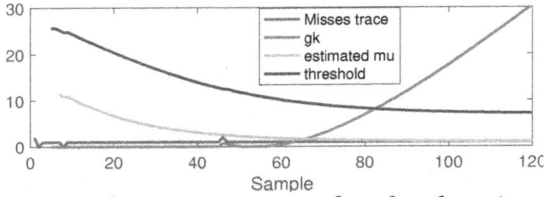

Figure 3: Relevant parameters for the detection task, prime+probe attack on AES

Thus, for every sample $k \geq 1$ we can express the detection rule as:

$$g_k = \max \left\{ 0, g_{k-1} + \log \frac{d_{na}(k) + 1}{d_a(k) + 1} \right\} \geq h$$

When the number of misses is 0 or close to 0, the distance between the sample and the "non-attack" cluster $d_{na}(k)$ will be lower than the distance to the attack cluster $d_a(k)$, so the value of the metric g_k decreases or stays at zero. On the other hand, readings from the LLC miss counter approaching to the attack cluster will increase the value g_k. Note that when the error in the estimation of the mean ϵ approaches zero, $d_a(i) = \epsilon$ also tends to zero. Then, the increase in the value of g_k is also limited

$$\log \frac{d_{na}(k) + 1}{d_a(k) + 1} \leq \log(\mu_a + 1)$$

Given a threshold h, the minimum expected detection time is:

$$\tau_e(h) \geq \frac{h}{\log(\mu_a + 1)}$$

or, as a consequence of reformulating this equation, the threshold h, for a minimum expected delay τ_e

$$h_\tau \leq \tau_e * \log(\mu_a + 1)$$

The unit of the $\tau_e(h)$ is *number of samples*. Since the most effective cache attacks can potentially extract most of the key with just one execution of the victim, the sampling rate must be chosen lower than the execution time of the victim. As the execution time of these algorithms is in the order of few milliseconds, a sampling rate of $100\,\mu s$ is sufficient to provide evidence of the attack, it allows to collect enough samples to accurately distinguish attacks and non-attacks. This frequency can be increased at additional load for the system. For an expected detection delay of 1 ms with a sampling rate of $100\,\mu s$ we define the threshold as $h = 10 * \log(\mu_a + 1)$. The choice of the threshold h also determines the tolerance to noisy frames, and as a consequence the false positive rate. Higher threshold values imply greater detection times and also lower false positive rates.

Algorithm 1 summarizes our *CacheShield* implementation. An example of the values of the parameters considered in the detection process is given in Figure 3 for a real attack trace.

5 EVALUATION OF *CACHESHIELD*

Once we have defined and described the relevant parameters of the detection algorithm, we evaluate its performance. To this end we ran several experiments in different environments and machines. We have selected two of the major hypervisors (KVM and VMware) and only changed the settings of the selected VM to be able to read the performance counters.

KVM-based Hypervisor These experiments were performed in an Intel Core i7-4790 CPU with 8 MB of L3 cache and 8 GB of

---

Algorithm 1 CacheShield detection algorithm

Input: Process PID
Output: *Attack detected*
  read_counters(misses,cpu_cycles);
  wait;
  while *victim_is_running* **do**
    read_counters(misses,cpu_cycles);
    if misses> 0 **then**
      update μ_a;
      update h;
    end if
    calculate g_k
    if $g_k > h$ **then**
      trigger_alarm;
      trigger_countermeasure;
    end if
    wait;

RAM, within a VM with Centos 7 hosted in KVM as hypervisor. Each victim VM instance had 2 VCPUs and 2 GB of RAM.

VMware-based Cloud Server We have also executed experiments in a host managed with VMware, this machine is equipped with a Intel XeonE5-2670 v2 processor, 25Mb of L3 cache and 32GB of RAM. The OS in these VMs was Ubuntu 12.04. Similarly, the target VM was configured with 2 VCPUs and 2 GB of RAM.

In a controlled environment, e.g., when a user is executing the crypto algorithm in his own machine, *CacheShield* does not trigger any false positives. Users can also get information about the utilization of their machine or about other tasks running concurrently. However, when executing the crypto algorithms in cloud environments they cannot get any information about what their neighbors are doing. In such scenarios, it becomes mandatory to study how the execution of different applications running in parallel with the protected process affects the behavior of *CacheShield*. Note that as we use the LLC misses counter to decide if there is an attack going on, applications consuming high amount of memory resources are likely to cause the LLC misses indicator to rise, and thus are the most likely to trigger false positives. For this reason, we have selected several worst case scenario applications, which can be found in cloud environments, and with high memory activity, to run in parallel with the *victim* and *CacheShield*:

Yahoo Cloud Serving Benchmark This benchmark provides a common evaluation framework and a set of common workloads to test the performance of different serving stores as elastic search, Cassandra, MongoDB and others [35] in cloud environments. That is, it imitates the behavior of a database running in a VM. In our experiments, we use this benchmark with the Apache Cassandra database and example workload *workloada*.

Video Streaming Another application that generates cache misses is video streaming. The video streaming VM continuously streams and plays back Youtube videos on the Firefox browser.

Randmem Benchmark randmem is intended to test the impact of burst reading and writings [28]. In our experiments, we launch each randmem instance configured to use 2 Gb of RAM memory.

Table 2: Mean detection time (ms) per attack and scenario for the evaluated crypto algorithms. Note that in all cases *Cache-Shield* has the same configuration and that detection times are much lower than the ones required for the attack to succeed

Scenario	AES				RSA			ElGamal		
	F+R (1)	F+R (4)	F+F (1)	P+P	F+R	F+F	P+P	F+R	F+F	P+P
KVM	7.38	7.05	6.64	9.53	4.08	3.92	4.93	3.76	3.45	3.98
Vmware	8.75	5.98	10.74	13.42	4.43	3.87	4.51	4.83	5.06	7.08

Table 3: False positive rate across scenarios and algorithms. (Y: Yahoo Cloud Serving, V: Video Streaming; R: Randmem)

Scenario	Noise Instances			False Positives		
	Y	V	R	AES	RSA	ElGamal
KVM	1	0	0	1.2%	4.5%	2.8%
KVM	0	1	0	1.1%	3.4%	0.6%
KVM	0	0	1	12.2%	21.4%	15.4%
VMware	1	2	10	0.1%	5.9%	4.1%

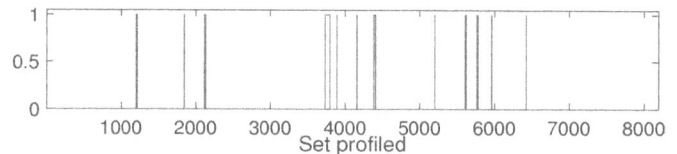

Figure 4: Output of *CacheShield* when the cache is profiled accessing each set. "1" indicates a positive attack detection.

To show the applicability of *CacheShield* to a broad range of implementations that require protection against cache attacks, we chose from a range of crypto primitives and implementations, though focusing on vulnerable ones, since such legacy implementations actually require protection. The three crypto algorithms considered as *victims* are AES (Openssl 1.0.1f T-Table implementation), 2048 bit RSA (Openssl 1.0.1f with RSA_FLAG_NO_CONSTTIME flag) and El Gamal (Libgcrypt 1.5.0). ElGamal was not considered during the design of *CacheShield*, and hence shows how *CacheShield* performs for other types of algorithms. These algorithms differ quite significantly in their particular implementation and usage of cache. Many other potentially leaky codes might require protection, and we are confident that *CacheShield* will perform well.

To evaluate the effectiveness of *CacheShield* across different types of cache attacks, we implemented and performed three popular attacks, namely Flush+Reload, Flush+Flush and Prime+Probe. We collected data for the above-mentioned algorithms under attack as well as from normal executions, as baseline behavior. Under each configuration, we collected data for more than 1000 executions of the crypto primitives, and in the case of the AES attack we also considered different attack rates (number of lines flushed at a time), as the attacker may try to gain different amount of information from the T-tables per execution [14]. As stated in previous sections, the main characteristics defining the detection algorithm are the mean detection time, and the false positive rate. Table 2 presents the results for mean detection time under different configurations, for the different attacks and algorithms and table 3 shows the results related with false positives in noisy environments.

Requirements for Flush+Flush/Flush+Reload and Prime+Probe attacks differ significantly. While Flush+X attacks are faster and more precise, they require shared data, i.e. deduplication between attacker and victim. All the attacks performed in virtualized scenarios were across VMs so we enabled deduplication features (KSM and TPS for KVM and Vmware respectively) to perform Flush+X attacks. Prime+Probe attacks work across VMs even without deduplication, so we disabled deduplication and enabled huge pages. Prime+Probe attacks require, prior to the information extraction, a *profiling* of the cache [13, 21, 22]. The profiling stage reveals the

sets the victim process is accessing and that carry the necessary information to succeed in the attack. In this situation, the detection tool will trigger an alarm whenever the set being tested by the attacker was actually used by the victim. Figure 4 visualizes the output of the detection algorithm, for the cache profiling stage of an 8 MB L3 cache when the target is the T-table implementation of AES. The x-axis represents each set of the cache being evicted during the Prime+Probe profiling step; a 1 on the the y-axis indicates that an alarm has been triggered. Thus, alarms are only triggered when the cache attack affects the target.

For all evaluated attacks, the detection rates are 100%. Note that the sampling rate is 100 μs and that we want to detect the attack before the end of each decryption (for public key cryptography). If we wished to detect attacks against algorithms whose duration is below 5 or 6 ms, we will need to increase the sampling rate, since mean number of samples required to detect the attack cannot be lowered arbitrarily without increasing the FAR too much. The duration of the decryption/encryption depends on frequency of the processor, and as a consequence on the machine. For example, ElGamal encryption takes around 11 ms when being attacked on the i7 machine, and 24 ms on the Xeon machine. Thus, we are able to detect attacks against ElGamal when less than the 37% of the encryption has been performed for the i7 machine, and 30% for the second machine in the worst case. Regarding to RSA its mean execution times are around 18 ms for the i7 machine and around 37 ms for the other. In the worst case, on average, we detect the attacks with less than 50% of the decryption performed in the first case and with about 37% of decryption in the second one.

Regarding to the existing differences between false positive rates for AES and public crypto algorithms, these are easy to explain. While between AES encryptions exists some time in which the processor does nothing, the others execute uninterruptedly. This fact increases the probability of other processes accessing the cache during the same interval. While the AES encryption in the period of 100 μs is only active during around 7000 cycles, the RSA process is active during about 30000 cycles for the VMware machine when there is no attack. Figure 5 depicts the LLC misses for one noisy RSA encryption, besides the initialization steps, it can be observed a high amount of cache misses during the whole decryption. Similarly,

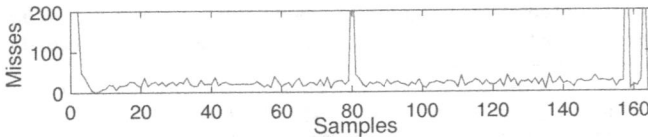

Figure 5: LLC misses for a noisy RSA execution under rand-mem benckmark.

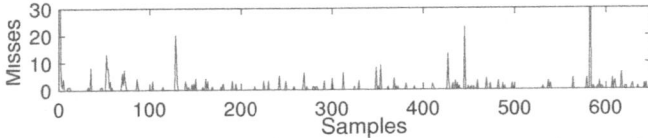

Figure 6: Sample of a noisy execution of AES under rand-mem benchmark.

Figure 6 corresponds to one process performing AES encryptions concurrently with noisy VMs.

The results also show that the tolerance to noise of the detection algorithm is more dependent on the hardware than on the virtualizing technology: It can be observed that the results are significantly better on the Xeon machine. The Xeon machine did not trigger any false positives when there were one or two VMs generating "noise" concurrently, until we launched several more instances. As this machine is more similar to the kind of machine cloud providers utilize, these results show that the tool is practical in these environments.

Randmem generates more misses on the i7 machine. Because of its smaller cache, it is more likely that both applications access to the same cache sets. It is not possible to distinguish whether these misses were generated with malicious purposes or not. However, noisy samples present more variance than attack samples and only appear when the memory sets accessed are also used by the "victim", that is, for shorter time than attacks. Thus, considering the variance in the CUSUM algorithms proposed and increasing detection times will reduce the false positive rate. Particularly, randmem traces show that it accesses the same sets as the crypto algorithm for a short time and then accesses a different cache region. Since our detection times are quite restrictive, and shorter than the period of time both applications share the cache, we observe some false positives that could be avoided increasing the detection time.

To ensure our tool also meets the requirement of low CPU utilization, we have measured the amount of CPU our tool utilizes, when running, to monitor the victim and compute the detection algorithm. Figure 7 show the mean CPU utilization of *CacheShield* for different sampling rates. To obtain the CPU utilization we have measured the time it takes to read the counters and perform the calculations and the total time elapsed, then the utilization is given by its division. In both cases, the total utilization of our tool is below 5% of CPU. Note that sampling rates of 10 μs are not always achievable as sometimes (around 10% of the time) it takes more time to read the counters.

6 CACHE ATTACK COUNTERMEASURES

Once an attack has been detected, *CacheShield* needs to react in some way. One way is to simply interrupt the monitored process and to purge used keys. While this approach ensures high security, it decreases the usability, as any false positives will result a total cryptosystem shutdown. More viable alternatives are:

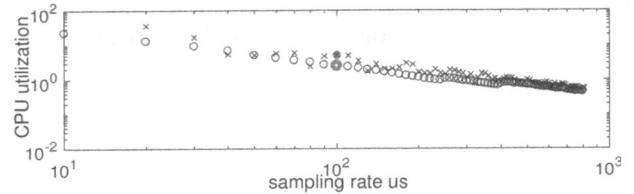

Figure 7: CPU utilization of the i7-4790 (o) in native environment and of the Xeon machine in virtualized environment (x) for different sampling rates in microseconds. Highlighted the 100 us rate, the one we use in our experiments

Adding Noise A simple method to hinder cache attacks is making the channel noisier, e.g. through frequently flushing cache lines used by the protected process, or by performing additional reads on data. This approach works particularly well if critical data is known, e.g. the tables of an AES implementation.

Dummy Operations An alternative approach is to perform dummy operations on meaningless secrets. In practice this can mean to run the protected process with a newly generated secret. The original process can be paused, or continue in parallel to the dummy process. Parallel processing obfuscates the true leakage. Certain attacks might still succeed when increasing the number of observations. While the performance degradation is not negligible, but ît only is incurred in the presence of an attack.

Protected Implementations The reason why leakage is still observed in security solutions is the performance overhead that pure constant time implementations present. A way of avoiding such a scenario is to use protected implementations *only* when *CacheShield* detects an attack behavior. When no attack is detected, faster (less secure) implementations can be used.

7 EXTENDING OUR APPROACH TO OTHER MICRO-ARCHITECTURAL ATTACKS

While cache side-channel attacks are an immediate threat due to their ability to extract sensitive information from co-located VMs, they do not represent the only threat in shared environments. Another class of attacks are performance degradation attacks, by inducing intense resource contention, attackers are able to degrade neighboring applications performance. We show that *CacheShield* can also be configured to detect these degradation attacks.

7.1 Memory DoS Attacks

Memory DoS attacks refer to the Degradation of Service caused by contention of hardware memory resources as the ring bus that connects elements in some processor sockets (e.g Intel architectures). This bus is hard to saturate and difficult to lock with normal operations. However, there are certain operations known as exotic atomic operations which can lock the internal memory buses. Since the processor has to ensure atomicity while processing these operations, it has to lock the memory. Thus, an attacker continuously performing these operations effectively degrades performance of real cloud applications in commercial clouds [49] and Android devices [20].

Assuming that an attacker has the ability of placing a VM with its victim, he can intentionally abuse hardware resources to degrade the performance of all the VMs running on the same host.

Previous works have also considered the cache as a possible mean of degrading the performance of the victim by accessing the same sets it is using. However, as we have previously demonstrated the feasibility of our approach to detect cache attacks or abuses, we focus on exotic atomic locking attacks. We demonstrate that when performance counters access is enabled inside the VM we can measure the performance of the process we want to protect, and as a consequence, we are able to detect deviations in the expected behavior caused by attacks, just adapting the *CacheShield* approach.

7.2 Detection Algorithm

As we did for cache attacks, we have first determined which counters are useful in this scenario, and which are the requirements for our detection system. Further details about these experiments are provided in Appendix A. We have considered two applications commonly found in cloud environments: web servers and databases, Apache web server and Apache Cassandra (NoSQL database).

Unlike for cryptographic processes, we cannot assume the normal or expected behavior of these applications. Instead, it is necessary to profile the applications we want to protect. Additionally, the values of the counters depend on the number of requests the applications are processing. However, we have found out that some ratios such as cycles stalled per L3 access, are almost invariant with the number of requests while changing significantly under attacks. Then, they are useful to detect memory DoS attacks. The desired detection time that determines the threshold h, depends on the users of the application and for how long they are willing to wait (1 second in our system).

As we did for cache attacks, for each collected sample we calculate its distance to μ_a and μ_{na} and consequently, the probability of this sample to belong to each cluster. μ_{na} has to be obtained in the profiling step, this value gives an idea about the performance that can be expected. We also calculate the variance of these samples, since we define the "limit" of degradation we are able to tolerate as the mean μ_{na} plus certain times this variance. Note that if we are too restrictive with this limit, the number of false positives will increase. In our experiments, we had set this limit as three times the variance. Each new sample below this limit will be used to update the "non-attack" distribution mean, while samples over it, will be used to compute the "attack" distribution. With all these values we are in condition to obtain g_k.

7.3 Evaluation

Results regarding detection time and false positives are shown in tables 4 and 5. All the experiments were performed in VMs allocated in the i7 and Xeon machines. We have considered different request rates, monitored the whole VM, run each experiment for at least 10 seconds and executed more than 1000 simulations per scenario (application-hardware-attack/non-attack). In all cases, we have achieved a detection rate of 100%.

The false positive rate for DoS attacks is lower than for cache attacks. This is mainly due to two factors, one is that we are more permissive with the degradation and the other is that the fact that performance is much more degraded by the attack than it is by neighbor applications. As before, randmem is the most degrading application, however considering both the information referred

Table 4: Mean detection time (s) per attack and scenario for the evaluated cloud applications.

Scenario	Web server	no-SQL database
KVM	1.78	1.85
Vmware	1.97	2.04

Table 5: False positive rate for different scenarios and applications. (Instances: Y - Yahoo Cloud Serving, V - Video Streaming; R - Randmem)

Scenario	Noise Instances			False Positives	
	Y	V	R	Web server 1/2 counters	Cassandra 1/2 counters
KVM	1	0	0	0 %	0%
KVM	0	1	0	0%	0%
KVM	0	0	1	4.3%/0%	3.1%/0%
VMware	1	2	10	1.6%/0%	2.3%/0%

to cycles stalled per LLC access and to cycles per instruction, we achieve a false positive rate of 0%. When such attack is detected, the victim should inform the provider about the degradation it is suffering and request a migration of its VM as soon as possible.

8 CONCLUSION

In this work we have introduced *CacheShield*, a tool that is able to detect all known types of cache attacks targeting cryptographic applications as well as DoS attacks. The analysis of various hardware performance counters revealed which counters carry enough information to detect each attack. We take advantage of change point detection algorithms and adapt them to detect attacks based on the information retrieved from the counters. *CacheShield* was designed to detect attacks based on the characteristics of two particular algorithms, AES and RSA. However, *CacheShield* can also be used to protect other algorithms (as demonstrated for ElGamal) without further modification. It is also effective against "unknown" attacks, as all cache attacks force cache misses on the victim. In addition, we have shown that CacheShield tolerates considerably high amount of noise while only triggering a few false positives in machines similar to the ones cloud providers use.

Previously proposed cache attack detection tools involve continuously monitoring all running processes or VMs, resulting in huge performance overheads. *CacheShield* only needs access to the protected victim process or VM, greatly reducing the waste. As Cloud Service Providers are now providing transparent access to performance counters to their tenants, *CacheShield* opens a lean and effective way to enable tenants to protect themselves against cache attacks and, as also demonstrated, against degradation attacks.

9 ACKNOWLEDGMENTS

Visit of Samira Briongos to Vernam group at Worcester Polytechnic Institute has been supported by a collaboration grant from HiPEAC. This work was in part supported by the National Science Foundation under Grant No. CNS-1618837 and by the Spanish Ministry of Economy and Competitiveness under contracts TIN-2015-65277-R, AYA2015-65973-C3-3-R and RTC-2016-5434-8.

A   APPENDIX

As stated before, we consider two different applications commonly found in cloud environments: web servers and databases. As representative applications of each group we have selected Apache web server and Apache Cassandra (NoSQL database). These applications once installed and started launch multiple threads to answer the requests they get. This means there can be multiple PIDs associated with the application, so we changed our initial approach. Since we still want to monitor the applications concurrently with its execution without modifying them, we decided to monitor the whole VM. Additionally, in this scenario detection time is not as critical as for cache attacks, so we have selected a new sampling rate of 100ms. PAPI allows to detect the number of cores and to attach a group of counters to each core similarly as it does for each PID. However, monitoring the whole VM it requires root privileges, privileges that any user monitoring its own VM has.

We gathered the information for the analysis in the VMs virtualized with KVM running in the i7 processor and the VMs virtualized with VMware running in the Xeon machine. For both applications we have considered different request rates and in the case of Cassandra, different kinds of operations (adding, removing, retrieving and modifying entries of a database). For each application we had a dedicated VM, the attack was performed from a neighboring VM and requests were sent from a different machine not affected by the attack. Figure 8 shows the distributions of the values of relevant counters gathered every 100 ms referred to the Apache web server in the i7 machine, including more than 50000 samples each. Both applications and machines behave similarly, in the sense that the values of the counters are different but the trend is the same. Based on these experiments, we can derive the following conclusions:

- The values of the counters depend on the number of requests the application is processing. If the request rate is unknown, the values read from the counters by themselves are not indicative of an attack, while if it is known the counters evidence an increase of cache misses, cycles stalled and total cycles employed by the monitored process and a drop in the number of instructions executed and L3 cache accesses (col. 1 of fig. 8).

- If we consider ratios as cycles stalled per L3 cache access, or cycles per instruction we can distinguish between attack and non-attack regardless of the request rate. This means that getting once the model for our application is enough, avoiding the need to acquire a different model per request rate (col. 2 of fig. 8).

Note that the ratios considered are also a measure of the efficiency of a processor (its architecture) executing the profiled application. The number of cycles per instruction or the number of cycles per memory access are parameters that depend on the architecture, and on the application. Although for these two particular applications it is still possible to distinguish between attack and non attack regardless of the application, we need two different models for the two architectures (i7 and Xeon). For other applications, we should get one model per architecture and application.

REFERENCES

[1] 2017. Amazon CloudWatch. Web Site. (2017). https://aws.amazon.com/cloudwatch/.
[2] 2017. The PMCs of EC2: Measuring IPC. (2017). http://www.brendangregg.com/blog/2017-05-04/the-pmcs-of-ec2.html.

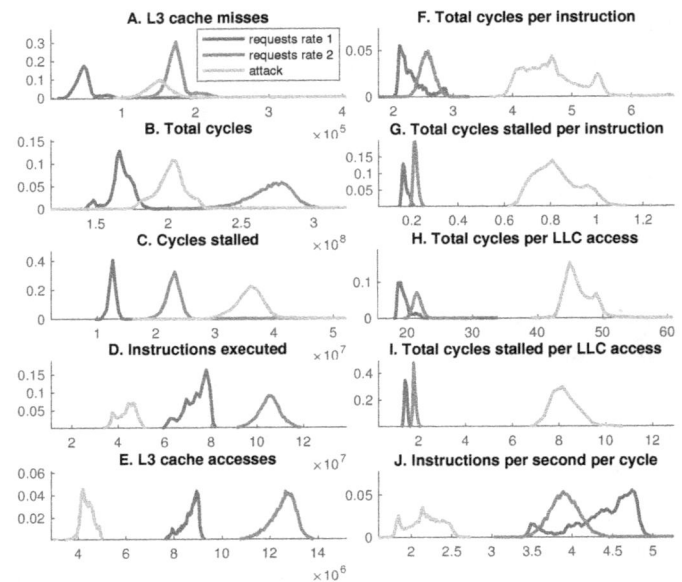

Figure 8: Distributions of the values of different counters gathered each 100 ms for different request rates related to the Apache web server application with and without DoS attack executed in the i7 machine virtualized with KVM

[3] Onur Acıiçmez and Werner Schindler. 2008. A Vulnerability in RSA Implementations Due to Instruction Cache Analysis and its Demonstration on OpenSSL. In *Topics in Cryptology–CT-RSA 2008*. Springer, 256–273.
[4] Gorka Irazoqui Apecechea, Mehmet Sinan Inci, Thomas Eisenbarth, and Berk Sunar. 2014. Wait a Minute! A fast, Cross-VM Attack on AES. In *Research in Attacks, Intrusions and Defenses - 17th International Symposium, RAID 2014, Gothenburg, Sweden, September 17-19, 2014. Proceedings*. 299–319.
[5] M. B. Bahador, M. Abadi, and A. Tajoddin. 2014. HPCMalHunter: Behavioral malware detection using hardware performance counters and singular value decomposition. In *2014 4th International Conference on Computer and Knowledge Engineering (ICCKE)*. 703–708.
[6] Michèle Basseville and Igor V. Nikiforov. 1993. *Detection of Abrupt Changes: Theory and Application*. Prentice-Hall, Inc., Upper Saddle River, NJ, USA.
[7] Daniel J. Bernstein. 2005. *Cache-timing attacks on AES*. Technical Report.
[8] Sarani Bhattacharya and Debdeep Mukhopadhyay. 2015. *Who Watches the Watchmen?: Utilizing Performance Monitors for Compromising Keys of RSA on Intel Platforms*. Springer Berlin Heidelberg, Berlin, Heidelberg, 248–266. https://doi.org/10.1007/978-3-662-48324-4_13
[9] Samira Briongos, Pedro Malagón, José L. Risco-Martín, and José M. Moya. 2016. Modeling Side-channel Cache Attacks on AES. In *Proceedings of the Summer Computer Simulation Conference (SCSC '16)*. Society for Computer Simulation International, San Diego, CA, USA, Article 37, 8 pages. http://dl.acm.org/citation.cfm?id=3015574.3015611
[10] Marco Chiappetta, Erkay Savas, and Cemal Yilmaz. 2016. Real time detection of cache-based side-channel attacks using hardware performance counters. *Applied Soft Computing* 49 (2016), 1162 – 1174.
[11] John Demme, Matthew Maycock, Jared Schmitz, Adrian Tang, Adam Waksman, Simha Sethumadhavan, and Salvatore Stolfo. 2013. On the Feasibility of Online Malware Detection with Performance Counters. In *Proceedings of the 40th Annual International Symposium on Computer Architecture (ISCA '13)*. ACM, New York, NY, USA, 559–570.
[12] Craig Disselkoen, David Kohlbrenner, Leo Porter, and Dean Tullsen. 2017. Prime+Abort: A Timer-Free High-Precision L3 Cache Attack using Intel TSX. In *26th USENIX Security Symposium (USENIX Security 17)*. USENIX Association, Vancouver, BC, 51–67. https://www.usenix.org/conference/usenixsecurity17/technical-sessions/presentation/disselkoen
[13] Fangfei Liu and Yuval Yarom and Qian Ge and Gernot Heiser and Ruby B. Lee. 2015. Last level Cache Side Channel Attacks are Practical. In *Proceedings of the 2015 IEEE Symposium on Security and Privacy (SP '15)*. IEEE Computer Society, Washington, DC, USA, 605–622. https://doi.org/10.1109/SP.2015.43

[14] Marc Green, Leandro Rodrigues Lima, Andreas Zankl, Gorka Irazoqui, Johann Heyszl, and Thomas Eisenbarth. 2017. AutoLock: Why Cache Attacks on ARM Are Harder Than You Think. *CoRR* abs/1703.09763 (2017). http://arxiv.org/abs/1703.09763

[15] Daniel Gruss, Clémentine Maurice, Klaus Wagner, and Stefan Mangard. 2016. Flush+Flush: A Fast and Stealthy Cache Attack. In *13th Conference on Detection of Intrusions and Malware & Vulnerability Assessment (DIMVA)*.

[16] Daniel Gruss, Raphael Spreitzer, and Stefan Mangard. 2015. Cache Template Attacks: Automating Attacks on Inclusive Last-Level Caches. In *24th USENIX Security Symposium (USENIX Security 15)*. USENIX Association, Washington, D.C., 897–912. https://www.usenix.org/conference/usenixsecurity15/technical-sessions/presentation/gruss

[17] David Gullasch, Endre Bangerter, and Stephan Krenn. 2011. Cache Games – Bringing Access-Based Cache Attacks on AES to Practice. In *Proceedings of the 2011 IEEE Symposium on Security and Privacy (SP '11)*. IEEE Computer Society, Washington, DC, USA, 490–505. https://doi.org/10.1109/SP.2011.22

[18] Berk Gülmezoglu, Mehmet Sinan Inci, Gorka Irazoqui Apecechea, Thomas Eisenbarth, and Berk Sunar. 2015. A Faster and More Realistic Flush+Reload Attack on AES. In *Constructive Side-Channel Analysis and Secure Design - 6th International Workshop, COSADE 2015, Berlin, Germany, April 13-14, 2015. Revised Selected Papers*. 111–126. https://doi.org/10.1007/978-3-319-21476-4_8

[19] Mark Hall, Eibe Frank, Geoffrey Holmes, Bernhard Pfahringer, Peter Reutemann, and Ian H. Witten. 2009. The WEKA Data Mining Software: An Update. *SIGKDD Explor. Newsl.* 11, 1 (Nov. 2009), 10–18. https://doi.org/10.1145/1656274.1656278

[20] Mehmet Sinan Inci, Thomas Eisenbarth, and Berk Sunar. 2017. Hit by the Bus: QoS Degradation Attack on Android. In *Proceedings of the 2017 ACM on Asia Conference on Computer and Communications Security (ASIA CCS '17)*. ACM, New York, NY, USA, 716–727. https://doi.org/10.1145/3052973.3053028

[21] Mehmet Sinan İnci, Berk Gulmezoglu, Gorka Irazoqui, Thomas Eisenbarth, and Berk Sunar. 2016. Cache Attacks Enable Bulk Key Recovery on the Cloud. In *Cryptographic Hardware and Embedded Systems – CHES 2016: 18th International Conference, Santa Barbara, CA, USA, August 17-19, 2016, Proceedings*, Benedikt Gierlichs and Axel Y. Poschmann (Eds.).

[22] Gorka Irazoqui, Thomas Eisenbarth, and Berk Sunar. 2015. S$A: A Shared Cache Attack that Works Across Cores and Defies VM Sandboxing and its Application to AES. In *36th IEEE Symposium on Security and Privacy (S&P 2015)*. 591–604.

[23] Gorka Irazoqui, Mehmet Sinan Inci, Thomas Eisenbarth, and Berk Sunar. 2015. Lucky 13 Strikes Back. In *Proceedings of the 10th ACM Symposium on Information, Computer and Communications Security (ASIA CCS '15)*. ACM, New York, NY, USA, 85–96. https://doi.org/10.1145/2714576.2714625

[24] Taesoo Kim, Marcus Peinado, and Gloria Mainar-Ruiz. 2012. STEALTHMEM: System-Level Protection Against Cache-Based Side Channel Attacks in the Cloud. In *Presented as part of the 21st USENIX Security Symposium (USENIX Security 12)*. USENIX, Bellevue, WA, 189–204. https://www.usenix.org/conference/usenixsecurity12/technical-sessions/presentation/kim

[25] Kenji Kira and Larry A Rendell. 1992. The feature selection problem: Traditional methods and a new algorithm. In *AAAI*, Vol. 2. 129–134.

[26] Peng Li, Debin Gao, and Michael K Reiter. 2014. Stopwatch: a cloud architecture for timing channel mitigation. *ACM Transactions on Information and System Security (TISSEC)* 17, 2 (2014), 8.

[27] Moritz Lipp, Daniel Gruss, Raphael Spreitzer, Clémentine Maurice, and Stefan Mangard. 2016. ARMageddon: Cache Attacks on Mobile Devices. In *25th USENIX Security Symposium, USENIX Security 16, Austin, TX, USA, August 10-12, 2016*. 549–564. https://www.usenix.org/conference/usenixsecurity16/technical-sessions/presentation/lipp

[28] Roy Longbottom. 2016. RandMem Benchmark. http://www.roylongbottom.org.uk/. (2016). [Online; accessed 19-May-2017].

[29] David McDonald. 1990. A cusum procedure based on sequential ranks. *Naval Research Logistics (NRL)* 37, 5 (1990), 627–646. https://doi.org/10.1002/1520-6750(199010)37:5<627::AID-NAV3220370504>3.0.CO;2-F

[30] Philip J. Mucci, Shirley Browne, Christine Deane, and George Ho. 1999. PAPI: A Portable Interface to Hardware Performance Counters. In *In Proceedings of the Department of Defense HPCMP Users Group Conference*. 7–10.

[31] Veronica Montes De Oca, Daniel R. Jeske, Qi Zhang, Carlos Rendon, and Mazda Marvasti. 2010. A cusum change-point detection algorithm for non-stationary sequences with application to data network surveillance. *Journal of Systems and Software* 83, 7 (2010), 1288 – 1297. https://doi.org/10.1016/j.jss.2010.02.006 {SPLC} 2008.

[32] Dag Arne Osvik, Adi Shamir, and Eran Tromer. 2006. Cache Attacks and Countermeasures: The Case of AES. In *Topics in Cryptology – CT-RSA 2006: The Cryptographers' Track at the RSA Conference 2006, San Jose, CA, USA, February 13-17, 2005. Proceedings*. Springer Berlin Heidelberg, Berlin, Heidelberg, 1–20. https://doi.org/10.1007/11605805_1

[33] ES Page. 1954. Continuous inspection schemes. *Biometrika* 41, 1/2 (1954), 100–115.

[34] Mathias Payer. 2016. HexPADS: A Platform to Detect "Stealth" Attacks. In *Engineering Secure Software and Systems: 8th International Symposium, ESSoS 2016, London, UK, April 6–8, 2016. Proceedings*, Juan Caballero, Eric Bodden, and Elias Athanasopoulos (Eds.). Springer International Publishing, Cham, 138–154.

[35] Yahoo research. 2010. Yahoo! Cloud System Benchmark (YCSB). https://github.com/brianfrankcooper/YCSB. (2010). [Online; accessed 19-May-2017].

[36] Thomas Ristenpart, Eran Tromer, Hovav Shacham, and Stefan Savage. 2009. Hey, you, get off of my cloud: exploring information leakage in third-party compute clouds. In *ACM Conference on Computer and Communications Security, CCS 2009, Chicago, Illinois, USA, November 9-13, 2009*. 199–212. https://doi.org/10.1145/1653662.1653687

[37] Benjamin Serebrin and Daniel Hecht. 2012. Virtualizing Performance Counters. In *Proceedings of the 2011 International Conference on Parallel Processing (Euro-Par'11)*. Springer-Verlag, Berlin, Heidelberg, 223–233. https://doi.org/10.1007/978-3-642-29737-3_26

[38] Baljit Singh, Dmitry Evtyushkin, Jesse Elwell, Ryan Riley, and Iliano Cervesato. 2017. On the Detection of Kernel-Level Rootkits Using Hardware Performance Counters. In *Proceedings of the 2017 ACM on Asia Conference on Computer and Communications Security*. ACM, 483–493.

[39] Adrian Tang, Simha Sethumadhavan, and Salvatore J. Stolfo. 2014. Unsupervised Anomaly-Based Malware Detection Using Hardware Features. In *Research in Attacks, Intrusions and Defenses*, Angelos Stavrou, Herbert Bos, and Georgios Portokalidis (Eds.). Lecture Notes in Computer Science, Vol. 8688. Springer International Publishing, 109–129.

[40] A. G. Tartakovsky, B. L. Rozovskii, R. B. Blazek, and Hongjoong Kim. 2006. A novel approach to detection of intrusions in computer networks via adaptive sequential and batch-sequential change-point detection methods. *IEEE Transactions on Signal Processing* 54, 9 (Sept 2006), 3372–3382. https://doi.org/10.1109/TSP.2006.879308

[41] Alexander G. Tartakovsky, Boris L. Rozovskii, Rudolf B. Blaž̌ek, and Hongjoong Kim. 2006. Detection of intrusions in information systems by sequential change-point methods. *Statistical Methodology* 3, 3 (2006), 252 – 293. https://doi.org/10.1016/j.stamet.2005.05.003

[42] Venkatanathan Varadarajan, Thomas Ristenpart, and Michael Swift. 2014. Scheduler-based Defenses against Cross-VM Side-channels. In *23rd USENIX Security Symposium (USENIX Security 14)*. USENIX Association, San Diego, CA, 687–702. https://www.usenix.org/conference/usenixsecurity14/technical-sessions/presentation/varadarajan

[43] X. Wang and R. Karri. 2013. NumChecker: Detecting kernel control-flow modifying rootkits by using Hardware Performance Counters. In *2013 50th ACM/EDAC/IEEE Design Automation Conference (DAC)*. 1–7.

[44] Zhenghong Wang and Ruby B. Lee. 2007. New cache designs for thwarting software cache-based side channel attacks. In *34th International Symposium on Computer Architecture (ISCA 2007), June 9-13, 2007, San Diego, California, USA*. 494–505. https://doi.org/10.1145/1250662.1250723

[45] Yuval Yarom and Naomi Benger. 2014. Recovering OpenSSL ECDSA Nonces Using the FLUSH+RELOAD Cache Side-channel Attack. *IACR Cryptology ePrint Archive* 2014 (2014), 140.

[46] Yuval Yarom and Katrina Falkner. 2014. FLUSH+RELOAD: A High Resolution, Low Noise, L3 Cache Side-Channel Attack. In *23rd USENIX Security Symposium (USENIX Security 14)*. 719–732. https://www.usenix.org/conference/usenixsecurity14/technical-sessions/presentation/yarom

[47] Andreas Zankl, Johann Heyszl, and Georg Sigl. 2017. Automated Detection of Instruction Cache Leaks in Modular Exponentiation Software. In *Smart Card Research and Advanced Applications: 15th International Conference, CARDIS 2016, Cannes, France, November 7–9, 2016, Revised Selected Papers*, Kerstin Lemke-Rust and Michael Tunstall (Eds.). Springer International Publishing, Cham, 228–244. https://doi.org/10.1007/978-3-319-54669-8_14

[48] Tianwei Zhang, Yinqian Zhang, and Ruby B. Lee. 2016. *CloudRadar: A Real-Time Side-Channel Attack Detection System in Clouds*. Springer International Publishing, Cham, 118–140. https://doi.org/10.1007/978-3-319-45719-2_6

[49] Tianwei Zhang, Yinqian Zhang, and Ruby B. Lee. 2017. DoS Attacks on Your Memory in Cloud. In *Proceedings of the 2017 ACM on Asia Conference on Computer and Communications Security (ASIA CCS '17)*. ACM, New York, NY, USA, 253–265. https://doi.org/10.1145/3052973.3052978

[50] Y. Zhang, A. Juels, A. Oprea, and M. K. Reiter. 2011. HomeAlone: Co-residency Detection in the Cloud via Side-Channel Analysis. In *2011 IEEE Symposium on Security and Privacy*. 313–328. https://doi.org/10.1109/SP.2011.31

[51] Yinqian Zhang, Ari Juels, Michael K. Reiter, and Thomas Ristenpart. 2012. Cross-VM side channels and their use to extract private keys. In *ACM Conference on Computer and Communications Security, CCS'12, Raleigh, NC, USA, October 16-18, 2012*. 305–316. https://doi.org/10.1145/2382196.2382230

[52] Yinqian Zhang, Ari Juels, Michael K. Reiter, and Thomas Ristenpart. 2014. Cross-Tenant Side-Channel Attacks in PaaS Clouds. In *Proceedings of the 2014 ACM SIGSAC Conference on Computer and Communications Security (CCS '14)*. ACM, New York, NY, USA, 990–1003. https://doi.org/10.1145/2660267.2660356

Secure, Consistent, and High-Performance Memory Snapshotting

Guilherme Cox
Rutgers University

Zi Yan
Rutgers University

Abhishek Bhattacharjee
Rutgers University

Vinod Ganapathy
Indian Institute of Science

ABSTRACT

Many security and forensic analyses rely on the ability to fetch memory snapshots from a target machine. To date, the security community has relied on virtualization, external hardware or trusted hardware to obtain such snapshots. These techniques either sacrifice snapshot consistency or degrade the performance of applications executing atop the target. We present SnipSnap, a new snapshot acquisition system based on on-package DRAM technologies that offers snapshot consistency without excessively hurting the performance of the target's applications. We realize SnipSnap and evaluate its benefits using careful hardware emulation and software simulation, and report our results.

CCS CONCEPTS

• **Security and privacy** → **Tamper-proof and tamper-resistant designs**; *Trusted computing*; *Virtualization and security*;

KEYWORDS

Cloud security; forensics; hardware security; malware and unwanted software

ACM Reference Format:
Guilherme Cox, Zi Yan, Abhishek Bhattacharjee, and Vinod Ganapathy. 2018. Secure, Consistent, and High-Performance Memory Snapshotting. In *CODASPY '18: Eighth ACM Conference on Data and Application Security and Privacy, March 19–21, 2018, Tempe, AZ, USA.* ACM, New York, NY, USA, 12 pages. https://doi.org/10.1145/3176258.3176325

1 INTRODUCTION

The notion of acquiring memory snapshots is one of ubiquitous importance to computer systems. Memory snapshots have been used for tasks such as virtual machine migration and backups [4, 19, 21, 23, 31, 34, 39, 45, 63, 71, 94] as well as forensics [18, 81], which is the subject of this paper. In particular, memory snapshot analysis is *the* method of choice used by forensic analyses that determine whether a target machine's operating system (OS) code and data are infected by malicious rootkits [10, 17, 24, 25, 43, 72–74, 80]. Such forensic methods have seen wide deployment. For example, Komoku [72, 74] (now owned by Microsoft) uses analysis of memory snapshots in its forensic analysis, and runs on over 500 million hosts [8]. Similarly, Google's open source framework, Rekall Forensics [2], is used to monitor its datacenters [68]. Fundamentally, all these techniques depend on secure and fast memory snapshot acquisition. Ideally, a memory snapshot acquisition mechanism should satisfy three properties:

① **Tamper resistance.** The target's OS may be compromised with malware that actively evades detection. The snapshot acquisition

mechanism must resist malicious attempts by an infected target OS to tamper with its operation.

② **Snapshot consistency.** A consistent snapshot is one that faithfully mirrors the memory state of the target machine at a given instant in time. Consistency is important for forensic tools that analyze the snapshot. Without consistency, different portions of the snapshot may represent different points in time during the execution of the target, making it difficult to assign semantics to the snapshot.

③ **Performance isolation.** Snapshot acquisition must only minimally impact the performance of other applications that may be executing on the target machine.

The security community has converged on three broad classes of techniques for memory snapshot acquisition, namely *virtualization-based*, *trusted hardware-based* and *external hardware-based* techniques. Unfortunately, none of these solutions achieve all three properties (see Figure 1).

With virtualization-based techniques (pioneered by Garfinkel and Rosenblum [35]), the target is a virtual machine (VM) running atop a trusted hypervisor. The hypervisor has the privileges to inspect the memory and CPU state of VMs, and can therefore obtain a snapshot of the target. This approach has the benefit of isolating the target VM from the snapshot acquisition mechanism, which is implemented within the hypervisor. However, virtualization-based techniques:

• *impose a tradeoff between consistency and performance-isolation.* To obtain a consistent snapshot, the hypervisor can pause the target VM, thereby preventing the target from modifying the VM's CPU and memory state during snapshot acquisition. But this consistency comes at the cost of preventing applications within the target from executing during snapshot acquisition, which is disruptive if snapshots are frequently required, *e.g.*, when a cloud provider wants to monitor the health of the cloud platform in a continuous manner. The hypervisor could instead allow the target VM to execute concurrently with memory acquisition, but this compromises snapshot consistency.

• *require a substantial software trusted computing base (TCB).* The entire hypervisor is part of the TCB. Production-quality hypervisors have more than 100K lines of code and a history of bugs [26–30, 55, 79] that can jeopardize isolation.

• *are not applicable to container-based cloud platforms.* Virtualization-based techniques are applicable only in settings where the target is a VM. This restricts the scope of memory acquisition only to environments where the target satisfies this assumption, *i.e.*, server-class systems and cloud platforms that use virtualization. An increasing number of cloud providers are beginning to deploy lightweight client isolation mechanisms, such as those based on containers (*e.g.*, Docker [1]). Containers provide isolation by enhancing the OS. On container-based systems, obtaining a full-system snapshot would require trusting the OS, and therefore placing it in the TCB. However, doing so defeats the purpose of snapshot acquisition if the goal is to monitor the OS itself for rootkit infection.

Hardware-based techniques reduce the software TCB and are applicable to any target system that has the necessary hardware support.

Property→ Method↓	① Tamper resistance	② Snapshot consistency	③ Performance isolation
Virtualization	✓	Tradeoff: ② ✓ ⇔ ③ ✗	
Trusted hardware	✓	Tradeoff: ② ✓ ⇔ ③ ✗	
External hardware	✗	✗	✓
SnipSnap	✓	✓	✓

Figure 1: Design tradeoffs in snapshot acquisition.

Methods that use trusted hardware rely on the hardware architecture's ability to isolate the snapshot acquisition system from the rest of the target. For example, ARM TrustZone [5, 9, 36, 85] partitions the processor's execution mode so that the target runs in a deprivileged world ("Normal world"), without access to the snapshot acquisition system, which runs in a privileged world ("Secure world") with full access to the target. However, because the processor can only be in one world at any given time, this system offers the same snapshot consistency versus performance isolation tradeoff as virtualized solutions. The situation is more complicated on a multi-processor TrustZone-based system, because the ARM specification allows individual processor cores to independently transition between the privileged and deprivileged worlds [5, §3.3.5]. Thus, from the perspective of snapshot consistency, care has to be taken to ensure that when snapshot acquisition is in progress on one processor core, all the other cores are paused and do not make concurrent updates to memory. This task is impossible to accomplish without some support from the OS to pause other cores. Trusting the OS to accomplish this task defeats the purpose of snapshot acquisition if the goal is to monitor the OS itself.

External hardware-based techniques use a physically isolated hardware module, such as a PCI-based co-processor (*e.g.*, as used by Komoku [8]), on the target system and perform snapshot acquisition using remote DMA (*e.g.*, [10, 16, 50, 58, 59, 65, 67, 72, 74]). These techniques offer performance-isolation by design—the co-processor executes in parallel with the CPU of the target system and therefore fetches snapshots without pausing the target. However, this very feature also compromises consistency because memory pages in a single snapshot may represent the state of the system at different points in time. Further, a malicious target OS can easily subvert snapshot acquisition despite physical isolation of the co-processor [78]. Co-processors rely on the target OS to set up DMA. On modern chipsets with IOMMUs, a malicious target OS can simply program the IOMMU to reroute DMA requests away from physical memory regions that it wants to hide from the co-processor (*e.g.*, pages that store malicious code and data). Researchers have also discussed address-translation attacks that leverage the inability of co-processors to view the CPU's page-table base register (PTBR) [51, 56]. These attacks enable malicious virtual-to-physical address translations, which effectively hide memory contents in the snapshot from forensic analysis tools.

Contributions. We propose and realize **S**ecure and **N**imble **In-Package Snapshotting** or SnipSnap, a hardware-based memory snapshot acquisition mechanism that achieves all three properties. SnipSnap frees snapshotting from the shackles of the consistency-performance tradeoff by leveraging two related hardware trends—the emergence of high-bandwidth DRAM placed on the same package as the CPU [15, 41, 60, 61], and the resurgence of near-memory processing [6, 7, 44]. Specifically, processor vendors have embraced technologies like embedded on-package DRAM in products including IBM's Power 7 processor, Intel's Haswell, Broadwell, and Skylake processors, and even in mobile platforms like Apple's iPhone [32]. More recently, higher bandwidth on-package DRAM has been implemented on Intel's Knight's Landing chip, while emerging 3D and 2.5D die-stacked DRAM is expected to be widely adopted [60]. On-package DRAM has in turn prompted flurry of research on near-memory

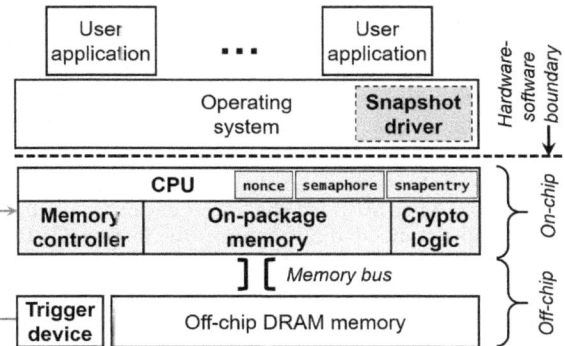

Figure 2: Architecture of SnipSnap. Only the on-chip hardware components are in the TCB.

processing techniques that place logic close to these DRAM technologies. Consequently, near-memory processing logic for machine learning, graph processing, and general-purpose processing has been proposed [6, 7, 44] for better system performance and energy.

SnipSnap leverages these hardware trends to realize fast and effective memory snapshotting. SnipSnap leverages on-package DRAM by realizing a fully hardware-based TCB. With modest hardware modifications that increase chip area by under 1%, SnipSnap captures and digitally signs pages in the on-package DRAM. The resulting snapshot captures the memory and CPU state of the machine faithfully, and any attempts by a malicious target OS to corrupt the state of the snapshot can be detected during snapshot analysis. Because SnipSnap's TCB consists only of the hardware, it can be used on target machines running a variety of software stacks, *e.g.*, traditional systems (OS atop bare-metal), virtualized systems, and container-based systems. We identify *consistency* as an important property of memory snapshots and present SnipSnap's memory controller that offers both consistency and performance isolation. We implement SnipSnap using real-system hardware emulation and detailed software simulation atop state-of-the-art implementations of on-package die-stacked DRAM (*e.g.*, UNISON cache [52]). We vary on-package die-stacked DRAM from 512MB to 8GB capacities. We find that Snip-Snap offers 4-25× performance improvements while also ensuring consistency. Finally, we verify SnipSnap's consistency guarantees using TLA+ [57].

In summary, SnipSnap securely obtains consistent snapshots while offering performance-isolation using non-exotic hardware that is already being implemented by chip vendors. This makes SnipSnap a powerful and general approach for snapshot acquisition, with applications to memory forensics and beyond.

2 OVERVIEW AND THREAT MODEL

SnipSnap allows a forensic analyst to acquire a complete snapshot of a target machine's off-chip DRAM memory. SnipSnap's mechanisms are implemented in a hardware TCB and an untrusted snapshot driver in the target's OS. The hardware TCB consists of on-package DRAM, simple near-memory processing logic, and requires modest modification of the on-chip memory controller and CPU register file. In concert, these components operate as described below.

A forensic analyst initiates snapshot acquisition by triggering the hardware to enter *snapshot mode*. Subsequently, the memory controller iteratively brings each physical page frame from off-chip DRAM to the on-package DRAM. SnipSnap's on-chip near-memory processing logic creates a copy of the page and computes a cryptographic digest of the page. The untrusted snapshot driver in the target OS then commits the snapshot entry to an external medium, such as persistent storage, the network, or a diagnostic serial port.

The hardware exits snapshot mode after the near-memory processing logic has iterated over all page frames of the target's off-chip DRAM. A well-formed memory snapshot from SnipSnap contains one snapshot entry per page frame and one entry with CPU register state and a cryptographic digest. Figure 2 shows the components of SnipSnap:

① The *trigger device* is an external mechanism that initiates snapshot acquisition. When activated, the trigger device toggles the hardware into snapshot mode. It also informs the target's OS that the hardware has entered snapshot mode.

② The *memory controller* brings pages from off-chip DRAM into on-package DRAM to be copied into the snapshot when the hardware is in snapshot mode (as discussed above). The memory controller maintains internal hardware state to sequentially iterate over all off-chip DRAM page frames. The main novelty in SnipSnap's memory controller is a copy-on-write feature that allows snapshot acquisition to proceed without pausing the target.

③ The *near-memory processing logic* implements cryptographic functionality for hash and digital-signature computation in on-package DRAM [20]. As we show, such near-memory processing is readily implemented atop, for example, die-stacked memory [60]. As such, we assume that the hardware is endowed with a public/private key pair (as are TPMs—trusted platform modules). Digital signatures protect the integrity of the snapshot even from an adversary with complete control of the target's software stack.

④ The *snapshot driver*, SnipSnap's only software component, is implemented within the target's OS. Its sole responsibility is to copy snapshot entries created by the hardware to a suitable external medium.

⑤ The *hardware/software interface* facilitates communication between the snapshot driver and the hardware components. This interface consists of three special-purpose registers and adds minimal overhead to the existing register file of modern processors, which typically consists of several tens of architecturally-visible and hundreds of physical registers.

Threat Model. Our threat model is that of an attacker who controls the target's software stack and tries to subvert snapshot acquisition. The attacker may try to corrupt the snapshot, return stale snapshot entries, or suppress parts of the snapshot. A snapshot produced by SnipSnap must therefore contain sufficient information to allow a forensic analyst to verify integrity, freshness, and completeness of the snapshot. We assume that the on-chip hardware components described above are trusted and are part of the TCB. We exclude physical attacks on off-chip hardware components, *e.g.*, those that modify contents of pages either in off-chip DRAM via electromagnetic methods, or as they transit the memory bus.

SnipSnap's snapshot driver executes within the target OS, which may be controlled by the attacker. We will show that despite this, a corrupt snapshot driver cannot compromise snapshot integrity, freshness, or completeness. At worst, the attacker can misuse his control of the snapshot driver to prevent snapshot entries (or the entire snapshot) from being written out to the external medium. However, the forensic analyst can readily detect such denial of service attacks because the resulting snapshot will be incomplete. Once the forensic analyst obtains a snapshot, he can analyze it using methods described in prior work (*e.g.*, [10, 17, 24, 25, 33, 43, 72, 73]) to determine if the target is infected with malware.

SnipSnap's main goal is secure, consistent, and fast memory snapshot acquisition. Forensic analysts can perform offline analyses on these snapshots, *e.g.*, to check the integrity of the OS kernel or to detect traces of malware activity. While analysts can use SnipSnap to

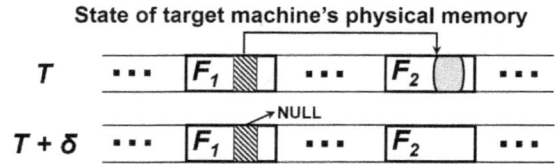

Figure 3: Example showing need for snapshot consistency. *Depicted above is the memory state of a target machine at two points in time, T and T+δ. At T, a pointer in F_1 points to an object in F_2. At T+δ, the object has been freed and the pointer set to NULL. Without consistency, the snapshot could contain a copy of F_1 at time T and F_2 at time T+δ (or vice-versa), causing problems for forensic analysis.*

request snapshots for offline analysis as often as they desire, it is not a tool to perform continuous, event-based monitoring of the target machine. To our knowledge, state of the art forensic tools to detect advanced persistent threats (*e.g.*, [8, 10, 17, 24, 25, 43, 72–74, 80]) rely on offline analysis of memory snapshots.

3 DESIGN OF SNIPSNAP

We now present SnipSnap's design, beginning with a discussion of snapshot consistency.

3.1 Snapshot Consistency

A snapshot of a target machine is *consistent* if it reflects the state of the target machine's off-chip DRAM memory pages and CPU registers at a given instant in time. Consistency is an important property for forensic applications that analyze snapshots. Without consistency, different memory pages in the snapshot represent the state of the target at different points in time, causing the forensic analysis to be imprecise. For example, consider a forensic analysis that detects rootkits by checking whether kernel data structures satisfy certain invariants, *e.g.*, that function pointers only point to valid function targets [73]. Such forensic analysis operates on the snapshot by identifying pointers in kernel data structures, recursively traversing these pointers to identify more data structures in the snapshot, and checking invariants when it finds function pointers in the data structures. If a page F_1 of memory contains a pointer to an object allocated on a page F_2, and the snapshot acquisition system captures F_1 and F_2 in different states of the target, then the forensic analysis can encounter a number of illogical situations (Figure 3). Such inconsistencies can also be used to hide malicious code and data modifications in memory [51]. Prior work [10, 73] encountered such situations in the analysis of inconsistent snapshots, and had to resort to unsound heuristics to remedy the problem. A consistent snapshot will capture the state of the target's memory pages at either T or at T+δ, thereby allowing the forensic analysis to traverse data structures in memory without the above problems.

As discussed in Section 1, prior systems have achieved snapshot consistency at the cost of performance isolation, or vice versa. SnipSnap acquires consistent memory snapshots without pausing the target machine in the common case. Snapshot acquisition proceeds in parallel with user applications and kernel execution that can actively modify memory. SnipSnap's hardware design ensures that the acquired memory snapshot reflects the state of the target machine at the instant when the hardware entered snapshot mode.

Consistency versus Quiescence. While SnipSnap ensures that an acquired snapshot faithfully mirrors the state of the machine at a given time instant, we do not specify what that time instant should be. Specifically, while snapshot consistency is a *necessary* property for client forensic analysis tools, it is not *sufficient*, *i.e.*, not every consistent snapshot is ideal from the perspective of client forensic analyses. For example, consider a consistent snapshot acquired when the kernel is in the midst of creating a new process. The kernel may have created a structure to represent the new process but may not have finished adding it to the process list, resulting in a snapshot where the process list is not well-formed.

In response, prior work suggests collecting snapshots when the target machine is in *quiescence* [43], *i.e.,* a state of the machine when kernel data structures are likely to be well-formed. Quiescence is a domain-specific property that depends on which data structures are relevant for the forensic analysis and what it means for them to be well-formed. SnipSnap only guarantees consistency, and relies on the forensic analyst to trigger snapshot acquisition at an instant when the system is quiescent. Because SnipSnap guarantees consistency, even if the target enters a non-quiescent state after snapshot acquisition has been triggered, *e.g.,* due to concurrent kernel activity initiated by user applications, the snapshot will reflect state of the target at the beginning of the snapshot acquisition. Triggering snapshot acquisition when the system is in *non-quiescent* state may require a forensic analyst to retake the snapshot.

3.2 Triggering Snapshot Acquisition

An analyst requests a snapshot using SnipSnap's trigger device. This device accomplishes three tasks: ① it toggles the hardware TCB into snapshot mode; ② it informs the target's OS that the hardware is in snapshot mode; and ③ it allows the analyst to pass a random nonce that is incorporated into the cryptographic digest of the snapshot.

Task ① requires direct hardware-to-hardware communication between the trigger device and the hardware TCB that is transparent to, and therefore cannot be compromised by, the target OS. Commodity systems offer many options to implement such communication, and SnipSnap can adapt any of them. For example, we could connect a physical device to the programmable interrupt controller, and have it deliver a non-maskable interrupt to the processor when it is activated. Upon receipt of this interrupt, the hardware TCB examines the IRQ to determine its origin, and switches to snapshot mode. Since this triggering mechanism piggybacks on the standard pin-to-bus interface, we find that implementing it requires less than 1% additional area on the hardware TCB.

Task ② is to inform the OS, so that it can start executing the snapshot driver. This task can be accomplished by raising an interrupt. The target OS invokes the snapshot driver from the interrupt handler.

To accomplish task ③, we assume that the trigger device is equipped with device memory that is readable from the target OS. The analyst writes the nonce to device memory, and the OS reads it from there, *e.g.,* after mounting the device as /dev/trigger_device.

3.3 DRAM and Memory Controller Design

SnipSnap relies on on-package DRAM for secure and consistent snapshots. Today, research groups are actively studying how best to organize on-package DRAM. Research questions focus on whether on-package DRAM should be organized as a hardware cache of the off-chip DRAM *i.e.,* the physical address space is equal to the off-chip DRAM capacity [52, 62, 77], or should extend the physical address space instead, *i.e.,* the physical address space is the sum of the off-chip DRAM and on-chip memory capacities [22, 93]. While SnipSnap can be implemented on any of these designs, we focus on die-stacked DRAM caches as they have been widely studied and are expected to represent initial commercial implementations [52, 53, 62, 77].

DRAM caches can be designed in several ways. They can be used to cache data in units of cache lines like conventional L1-LLCs [52, 62, 77]. Unfortunately, the fine granularity of cache lines results in large volumes of tag metadata stored in either SRAM or DRAM caches themselves [52, 53, 62, 77]. Thus, architects generally prefer to organize DRAM caches at page-level granularity. While SnipSnap

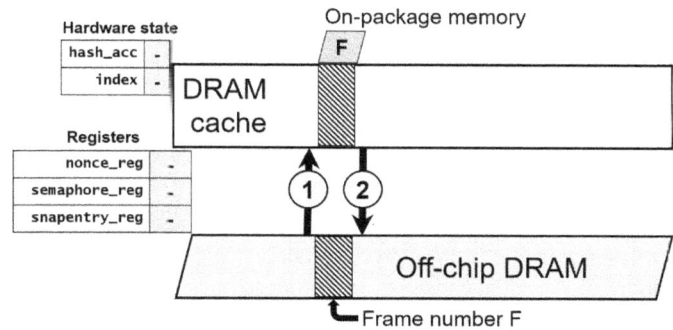

4(a) During regular operation, on-chip memory is a cache of off-chip DRAM pages. (1) Accesses by the CPU to a DRAM page brings the page to the on-chip memory, where it is tagged using its frame number (F). (2) Pages are evicted from on-chip memory region when it reaches its capacity.

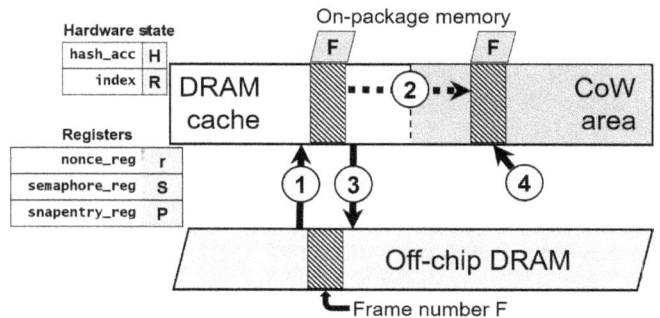

4(b) In snapshot mode, on-chip memory is split in two. (1) The DRAM cache works as in Figure 4(a) (2) If there is a write to a page that has not yet been snapshot (*i.e.,* F ≥ R), it is copied into the CoW area. (3) The page may be evicted if the DRAM cache reaches capacity (4) The CoW area copy of the page remains until it has been included in the snapshot (*i.e.,* F < R), after which it is overwritten with other pages that enter the CoW area. In snapshot mode H and R are initialized to 0.

Figure 4: Layout of on-chip memory.

can be built using any DRAM cache data granularity, we focus on such page-level data caching approaches.

Overall, as a hardware-managed cache, the DRAM cache is not directly addressable from user- or kernel-mode. Further, all DRAM references are mediated by an on-chip memory controller, which is responsible for relaying the access to on-package or off-chip DRAM. That is, CPU memory references are first directed to per-core MMUs before being routed to the memory controller, while device memory references (*e.g.,* using DMA) are directed to the IOMMU before being routed to the memory controller.

Regular Operation. When snapshot acquisition is not in progress, SnipSnap's on-package memory acts as a hardware DRAM cache, before off-chip DRAM (see Figure 4(a)). The DRAM cache stores data in the unit of pages, and maintains tags, as is standard, to identify the frame number of the page cached and additional bits to denote usage information, like valid and replacement policy bits. When a new page must be brought into an already-full cache, the memory controller evicts a victim using standard replacement policies.

Snapshot Mode. When the trigger device signals the hardware to enter snapshot mode, several hardware operations occur. First, the hardware captures the CPU register state of the machine (across all cores). Second, all CPUs are paused, their pipelines are drained, their cache contents flushed (if CPUs use write-back caches), and their load-store queues and write-back buffers drained. These steps ensure that all dirty cache line contents are updated in main memory before snapshot acquisition begins. Third, SnipSnap's memory controller reconfigures the organization of on-package DRAM to ensure that a consistent snapshot of memory is captured. It must track any modifications to memory pages that are not yet included in the snapshot and keep a copy of the original page till it has been copied to the snapshot.

To achieve this goal, the memory controller splits the on-package DRAM into two portions (Figure 4(b)). The first portion continues to serve as a cache of off-chip DRAM memory. Since only this portion of on-package DRAM is available for caching in snapshot mode, the memory controller tries to fit in it all the pages that were previously cached during regular operation into the available space. If all pages cannot be cached, the memory controller selects and evicts victims to off-chip DRAM. The second portion of die-stacked memory serves as a copy-on-write (CoW) area. The CoW area allows user applications and the kernel to modify memory concurrently with snapshot acquisition, while saving pages that have not yet been included in the snapshot. We study several ways to partition on-package DRAM into the CoW and DRAM cache areas in Section 6.

Recall that a snapshot contains a copy of all pages in off-chip DRAM memory. However, the hardware creates a snapshot entry one page of memory at a time. It works in tandem with the snapshot driver to write this snapshot entry to an external medium and then iterates to the next page of memory until all pages are written out to the snapshot. As this iteration proceeds, other applications and the kernel may concurrently modify memory pages that have not yet been included in the snapshot. If SnipSnap's memory controller sees a write to a memory page that the hardware has not yet copied, the memory controller creates a copy of the original page in the CoW area, and lets the write operation proceed in the DRAM cache area. A page frame is copied *at most once* into the CoW area, and this happens only if the page has to be modified by other applications before it has been copied into the snapshot.

The memory controller maintains internal hardware state in the form of an *index* that stores the frame number (R in Figure 4(b)) of the page that is currently being processed for inclusion in the snapshot. The hardware initializes the index to 0 when it enters snapshot mode. The memory controller uses the index as follows. It copies a frame F from the DRAM cache to the CoW area when it has to write to that frame and $F \geq R$, indicating that the hardware has not yet iterated to frame F to create a snapshot entry for it. If $F < R$, then it means that the frame has already been included in the snapshot, and can be modified without copying it to the CoW area. SnipSnap requires that page frames be copied into the snapshot sequentially in ascending order by frame number.

To create a new snapshot entry for a page frame, the memory controller first checks whether this page frame is in the CoW area. If it exists, the hardware proceeds to create a snapshot entry using that copy of the page. The memory controller can then reuse the space occupied by this page in the CoW area. If the page frame is not in the CoW area, the memory controller checks to see if it already exists in the DRAM cache. If not, it brings the page from off-chip DRAM into the DRAM cache, from where the hardware creates a snapshot entry for that page. It places the newly-created entry in a physical page frame referenced by the *snapshot entry register* (snapentry_reg in Figure 4), and informs the snapshot driver using the *semaphore register* (semaphore_reg in Figure 4). The driver then writes out the entry to a suitable external medium and informs the hardware, which increments the index and iterates to the next page frame.

The hardware exits snapshot mode when the index has iterated over all the frames of off-chip DRAM. At this point, the hardware creates a snapshot entry containing the CPU register state (captured on entry into snapshot mode), and appends it as the last entry of the snapshot. We leverage die-stacked logic to capture and record register

state. SnipSnap's approach is inspired by prior work on introspective die-stacked logic [69], where hardware analysis logic built on die-stacked layers uses probes or "stubs" on the CPUs to introspect on dynamic type analysis, data flight recorders, *etc.* Similarly, we design hardware support to capture register state, using: ① stubs that allow the contents of the register file to be latched into the logic on the die-stack; and ② logic on the die-stack that copies the contents of register files into the last snapshot entry.

The memory controller's use of CoW ensures that concurrent applications can make progress, while still maintaining the original copies of memory pages for a consistent snapshot. The hardware pauses a user application during snapshot acquisition only when the CoW area fills to capacity and when that application attempts to write to a page that the hardware has not yet included in the snapshot. In this case, the hardware can resume these applications when space is available in the CoW area, *i.e.*, when a page from there is copied to the snapshot.

Our implementation of SnipSnap has important design implications on recently-proposed DRAM caches. Research has shown that DRAM caches generally perform most efficiently when they use page-sized allocation units to reduce tag array size requirements [52, 53]. However, they also employ memory usage predictors (e.g., footprint predictors [52, 53]) to fetch only the relevant 64B blocks from a page, thereby efficiently using scarce off-chip bandwidth by not fetching blocks that will not be used. This means the following for SnipSnap. During regular operation, SnipSnap continues to employ page-based DRAM caches with standard footprint prediction. However, to simplify our design, SnipSnap does not use footprint prediction during snapshot mode and moves entire pages of data with their constituent cache lines in both the CoW and DRAM cache partitions. Naturally, this does degrade performance of applications running simultaneously with snapshotting; however, our results (see Section 6) show that performance improvements versus current snapshotting techniques remain high.

3.4 Near-Memory Processing Logic

Near-memory processing logic implements cryptographic functionality to create the snapshot. On a target machine with N frames of off-chip DRAM memory, the snapshot itself contains N+1 entries. The first N entries store, in order, the contents of page frames 0 to N-1 of memory (thus, an individual snapshot entry is 4KB). The last entry of the snapshot stores the CPU register state and a cryptographic digest that allows a forensic analyst to determine the integrity, freshness and completeness of the snapshot.

The near-memory processing logic maintains an internal *hash accumulator* that is initialized to zero when the hardware enters snapshot mode. It updates the hash accumulator as the memory controller iterates over memory pages, recording them in the snapshot. Suppose that we denote the value of the hash accumulator using H_{idx}, where idx denotes the current value of the memory controller's index (thus, $H_0 = 0$). When the memory controller creates a snapshot entry for page frame numbered idx, the near-memory processing logic updates the value of the hash accumulator to $H_{idx+1} = Hash(idx \| r \| H_{idx} \| C_{idx})$. Here:

① The value idx is the hardware's index. It records the frame number of the page that included in the snapshot;

② The value r denotes a random nonce supplied by the forensic analyst using the trigger device and stored in the on-chip *nonce register* (nonce_reg in Figure 4(b)). The use of the nonce ensures freshness of the snapshot;

③ H_{idx} denotes the current value of the hash accumulator;

④ C_{idx} denotes the actual contents of page frame idx.

Snapshot Driver	Hardware/Software Interaction
A.　/* Initialization, done at kernel startup */	
B.　`char *plocal = kmalloc (SNAPSHOT_ENTRY_SIZE);`	
C.　`%snapentry_reg = virt_to_phys (plocal);` ←	OS sets **%snapentry_reg** to point to the physical page frame reserved for snapshot entries.
1.　/* Runs when hardware enters snapshot mode */ ←	Hardware's **index** and **hash_acc** are initialized to 0 when hardware enters snapshot mode.
2.　`void snapshot_driver (void) {`	
3.　　`%semaphore_reg = 0xFF...FF;`	
4.　　`%nonce_reg = read (/dev/trigger_device);` ←	Hardware starts processing first page frame when **%nonce_reg** is set to a non-zero value.
5.　　/* Iterate in sync with hardware */	
6.　　`for (int ctr=0; ctr < NUM_FRAMES; ctr++) {`	Software waits for new snapshot entry to become ready. Hardware creates the entry either from a copy of the
7.　　　`while (%semaphore_reg != 0x0);` ←	page in CoW area or after bringing the page frame to die-stacked memory from off-chip DRAM. Hardware
8.　　　`write_out (plocal, SNAPSHOT_ENTRY_SIZE);`	updates **hash_acc** using page contents and sets **%semaphore_reg** to 0 after creating the snapshot entry.
9.　　　`%semaphore_reg = 0xFF...FF;` ←	Software signals the hardware to proceed to next page frame by setting **%semaphore_reg** to a non-zero
10.　　`}`	value. Hardware increments its **index** and proceeds to process the page frame referenced by it.
11.　　`while (%semaphore_reg != 0x0);`	Hardware exits snapshot mode when **index** reaches the value NUM_FRAMES. It then places the CPU
12.　　`write_out (plocal, SNAPSHOT_ENTRY_SIZE);`	register state, which was recorded at the instant when the hardware entered snapshot mode, together with a
13.　`}`	digitally-signed copy of the value of **hash_acc** in the frame referenced by **%snapentry_reg**.

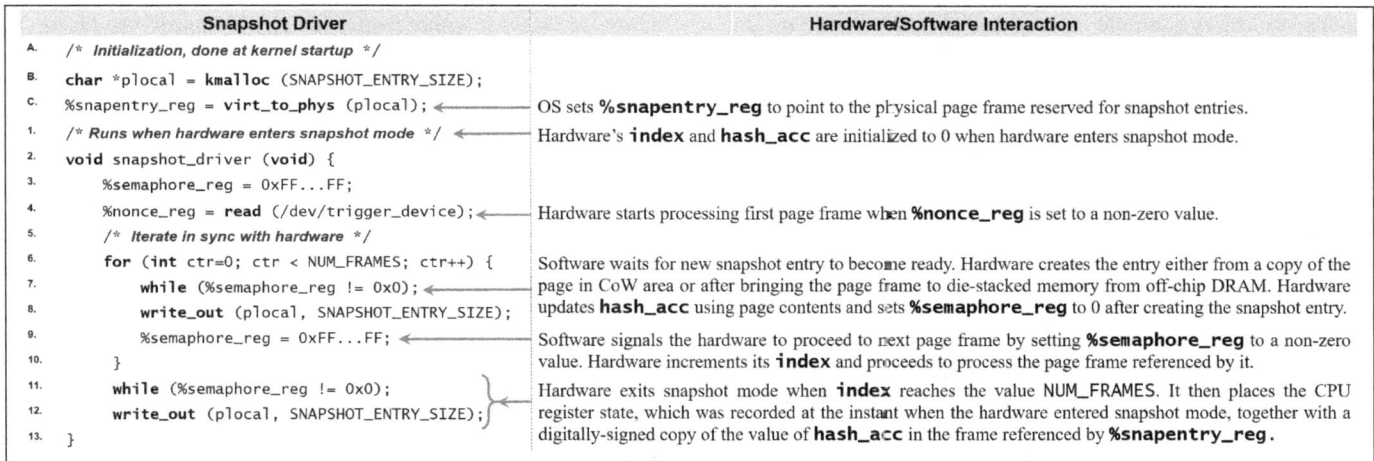

Figure 5: Pseudocode of the snapshot driver and the corresponding hardware/software interaction.

All these values are readily available on-chip.

When the memory controller finishes iterating over all N memory page frames, the value H_N in the hash accumulator in effect denotes the value of a *hash chain* computed cumulatively over all off-chip DRAM memory pages. The final snapshot entry enlists the values of CPU registers as recorded by the hardware when it entered snapshot mode—let us denote the CPU register state using C_{reg}. The near-memory logic updates the hash accumulator one final time to create $H_{N+1} = Hash(N \parallel r \parallel H_N \parallel C_{reg})$. It digitally signs H_{N+1} using the hardware's private key, and records the digital signature in the last entry of the snapshot. This digital signature assists with the verification of snapshot integrity (Section 4). We use SHA-256 as our hash function, which outputs a 32-byte hash value. The size of the digital signature depends on the key length used by the hardware. For instance, a 1024-bit RSA key would produce a 86-byte signature for a 32-byte hash value with OAEP padding.

3.5　Snapshot Driver and HW/SW Interface

The hardware relies on the target's OS to externalize the snapshot entries that it creates. We rely on software support for this task because it simplifies hardware design, and also provides the forensic analyst with considerable flexibility in choosing the external medium to which the snapshot must be committed. Although we rely on the target OS for this critical task, we do not need to trust the OS and even a malicious OS cannot corrupt the snapshot created by the hardware.

The hardware and the software interact via an interface consisting of three registers (nonce, snapshot entry and semaphore registers), which were referenced earlier. Figure 5 shows the software component of SnipSnap and the hardware/software interaction. SnipSnap's software component consists of initialization code that executes at kernel startup (lines A–C) and a snapshot driver that is invoked when the hardware enters snapshot mode (lines 1–13). The implementation of the snapshot driver in the target OS depends on the trigger device and executes as a kernel thread. For example, if the trigger device raises an interrupt to notify the target OS that the hardware has switched to snapshot mode, the snapshot driver can be implemented within the corresponding interrupt handler. If the trigger device instead uses ACPI events for notification, the snapshot driver can be implemented as an ACPI event handler.

In the initialization code, SnipSnap allocates a buffer (the plocal buffer) that is the size of one snapshot entry. This buffer serves as the temporary storage area in which the hardware stores entries of the snapshot before they are committed to an external medium. It

then obtains and stores the physical address translation of plocal in snapentry_reg, The hardware uses this physical address to store computed snapshot entries into the plocal buffer and the snapshot driver writes it out. Pages allocated using kmalloc cannot be moved, ensuring that the buffer is in the same location for the duration of the snapshot driver's execution. If the page moves, *e.g.*, because of a malicious implementation of kmalloc, or if virt_to_phys returns an incorrect virtual to physical translation, the snapshot will appear corrupted to the forensic analyst.

When hardware enters snapshot mode, it initializes its internal index and hash accumulator, captures CPU register state, and invokes SnipSnap's snapshot driver. The goal of the snapshot driver is to work in tandem with the hardware to create and externalize one snapshot entry at a time. The snapshot driver and the hardware coordinate using the semaphore register, which the driver first initializes to a non-zero value on line 3. It then reads the nonce value that the forensic analyst supplies via the trigger device. Writing this non-zero value into nonce_reg on line 4 activates the near-memory processing logic, which creates a snapshot entry for the page frame referenced by the hardware's internal index.

In the loop on lines 6–10, the snapshot driver iterates over all page frames in tandem with the hardware. Each iteration of the loop body processes one page frame. The hardware begins processing the first page of DRAM as soon as line 4 sets nonce_reg, and stores the snapshot entry for this page in the plocal buffer. On line 7, the driver waits for the hardware to complete this operation. The hardware informs the driver that the plocal buffer is ready with data by setting semaphore_reg to 0. The driver then commits the contents of this buffer to an external medium, denoted using write_out on line 8. The driver then sets semaphore_reg to a non-zero value on line 9, indicating to the hardware that it can increment its index and iterate to the next page for snapshot entry creation. Note that the time taken to execute this loop depends on the number of page frames in off-chip DRAM and the speed of the external storage medium.

When the loop completes execution, the hardware would have iterated through all DRAM page frames and exited snapshot mode. When it exits, it writes out the CPU register state captured during snapshot mode-entry and the digitally-signed value of the hash accumulator to the plocal buffer, which the snapshot driver can then output on line 12.

3.6　Formal Verification

We used TLA+ [57] to formally verify that SnipSnap produces consistent snapshots. To do so, we created a system model that mimics

241

SnipSnap's memory controller in snapshot mode and during regular operation. Our TLA+ system model can be instantiated for various configurations, such as memory sizes, cache sizes, and cache associativities. We encoded consistency as a safety property by checking that the state of the on-package and off-chip DRAM at the instant when the system switches to snapshot mode will be recorded in the snapshot at the end of acquisition. We verified that our system model satisfies this property using the TLA+ model checker. Our TLA+ model of SnipSnap is open source [3].

4 SECURITY ANALYSIS

When a forensic analyst receives a snapshot acquired by SnipSnap, he establishes its integrity, freshness, and completeness. In this section, we describe how these properties can be established, and show how SnipSnap is robust to attempts by a malicious target OS to subvert them.

① INTEGRITY. An infected target OS may attempt to corrupt snapshot entries to hide traces of malicious activity from the forensic analyst. To ensure that the integrity of the snapshot has not been corrupted, an analyst can check the digital signature of the hash accumulator stored in the last snapshot entry. The analyst performs this check by essentially mimicking the operation of SnipSnap's memory controller and near-memory processing logic, i.e., iterating over the snapshot entries in order to recreate the value of the hash accumulator, and verify its digital signature using the hardware's public key. Since the hash accumulator is stored and updated by the hardware TCB, which also computes its digital signature, a malicious target cannot change snapshot entries after they have been computed by the hardware.

② FRESHNESS. The forensic analyst supplies a random nonce via the trigger device when he requests a snapshot. SnipSnap's hardware TCB incorporates this nonce into the hash accumulator computation for each memory page frame, thereby ensuring freshness. Note that SnipSnap uses the untrusted snapshot driver to transfer the nonce from trigger device memory into the hardware's nonce register (line 4 of Figure 5). A malicious target OS cannot cheat in this step, because the nonce is incorporated into the hardware TCB's computation of the hash accumulator.

③ COMPLETENESS. The snapshot should contain one entry for each page frame in off-chip DRAM and one additional entry storing CPU register state. This criterion ensures that a malicious target OS cannot suppress memory pages from being included in the snapshot. Each snapshot entry is created by the hardware, by directly reading the frame number and page contents from die-stacked memory, thereby ensuring that these entities are correctly recorded in the entry.

Our attack analysis focuses on how a malicious target OS can subvert snapshot acquisition. A forensic analyst uses the trigger device to initiate snapshot acquisition by toggling the hardware TCB into snapshot mode. The trigger device communicates directly with SnipSnap's hardware TCB using hardware-to-hardware communication, transparent to the target's OS, and therefore cannot be subverted by a malicious OS. The hardware then notifies the OS that it is in snapshot mode, expecting the snapshot driver to be invoked.

A malicious target OS may attempt to "clean up" traces of infection before it jumps to the snapshot driver's code so that the resulting snapshot appears clean during forensic analysis. However, once the hardware is in snapshot mode, SnipSnap's memory controller, which mediates all writes to DRAM, uses the CoW area to track modifications to memory pages. Even if the target's OS attempts to overwrite the contents of a malicious page, the original contents of the page are saved in the CoW area to be included in the snapshot. Thus, any attempts by the target OS to hide its malicious activities after the

hardware enters snapshot mode are futile. Of course, the target OS could refuse to execute the snapshot driver, which will prevent the snapshot from being written out to an external medium. Such a denial of service attack is therefore readily detectable.

A malicious OS may try to interfere with the execution of the initialization code in lines A–C of Figure 5. The initialization code relies on the correct operation of kmalloc and virt_to_phys. However, we do not have to trust these functions. If kmalloc fails to allocate a page, snapshots cannot be obtained from the target, resulting in a detectable denial of service attack. If the pages allocated by kmalloc are remapped during execution or virt_to_phys does not provide the correct virtual to physical mapping for the allocated space, the write_out operation on line 8 will write out incorrect entries that fail the INTEGRITY check.

Once the snapshot driver starts execution, a malicious target OS can attempt to interfere with its execution. If it copies a stale or incorrect value of the nonce into nonce_reg from trigger device memory on line 4, the snapshot will violate the FRESHNESS criterion. It could attempt to bypass or short-circuit the execution of the loop on lines 5–10. The purpose of the loop is to synchronize the operation of the snapshot driver with the internal index maintained by SnipSnap's memory controller. If the OS short-circuits the loop or elides the write_out on line 8 for certain pages, the resulting snapshot will be missing entries, thereby violating COMPLETENESS. Attempts by the target OS to modify the virtual address of plocal or the value of snapshot_reg during the execution of the snapshot driver will trigger a violation of INTEGRITY for the same reasons that attacks on the initialization code triggers an INTEGRITY violation.

Finally, a malicious target could try to hide traces of infection by creating a synthetic snapshot that glues together individual entries (with benign content in their memory pages) from snapshots collected at different times. However, such a synthetic snapshot will fail the INTEGRITY check since the hash chain computed over such entries will not match the digitally-signed value in the last snapshot entry.

The last entry records the values of all CPU registers at the instant when the hardware entered snapshot mode. For forensic analysis, the most useful value in this record is that of the page-table base register (PTBR). As previously discussed, forensic analysis of the snapshot often involves recursive traversal of pointer values that appear in memory pages [10, 17, 25, 72–74, 80]. These pointers are virtual addresses but the snapshot contains physical page frames. Thus, the forensic analysis translates pointers into physical addresses by consulting the page table, which it locates in the snapshot using the PTBR. External hardware-based systems [10, 16, 58, 59, 67, 72, 74] cannot view the processor's CPU registers. Therefore, they depend on the untrusted target OS to report the value of the PTBR. Unfortunately, this results in address-translation redirection attacks [51, 56]. The target OS can create a synthetic page table that contains fraudulent virtual-to-physical mappings and return a PTBR referencing this page table. The synthetic page table exists for the sole purpose of defeating forensic analysis by making malicious content unreachable via page-table translations—it is not used by the target OS during execution. SnipSnap can observe and record CPU register state accurately when the hardware enters snapshot mode and is not vulnerable to such attacks. It captures the PTBR pointing to the page table that is in use when the hardware enters snapshot mode.

5 EXPERIMENTAL METHODOLOGY

5.1 Evaluation Infrastructure

We use a two-step approach to quantify SnipSnap's benefits. In the first step, we perform evaluations on long-running applications with full-system and OS effects. Since this is infeasible with software simulation, we develop hardware emulation infrastructure similar to

① **Canneal**	Simulated annealing from PARSEC [11]
② **Dedup**	Storage deduplication from PARSEC [11]
③ **Memcached**	In-memory key-value store [66]
④ **Graph500**	Graph-processing benchmark [38]
⑤ **Mcf**	Memory-intensive benchmark/SPEC 2006 [83]
⑥ **Cifar10**	Image recognition from TensorFlow [87]
⑦ **Mnist**	Computer vision from TensorFlow [87]

Figure 6: Description of benchmark user applications.

recent work [70] to achieve this. This infrastructure takes an existing hardware platform, and through memory contention, creates two different speeds of DRAM. Specifically, we use a two-socket Xeon E5-2450 processor, with a total of 32GB of memory, running Debian-sid with Linux kernel 4.4.0. There are 8 cores per socket, each two-way hyperthreaded, for a total of 16 logical cores per socket. Each socket has two DDR3 DRAM memory channels. To emulate our DRAM cache, we dedicate the first socket for execution of our user applications, our kernel-level snapshot driver, and our user-level snapshot process. This first socket hosts our "fast" or on-package memory. The second socket hosts our "slow" or off-chip DRAM. The cores on the second socket are used to create memory contention (using the memory contention benchmark memhog, like prior work [75, 76]) such that the emulated die-stacked memory or DRAM cache is 4.5× faster compared to the emulated off-chip DRAM. This provides a similar memory bandwidth performance ratio of a 51.2GBps off-chip memory system compared to a 256GBps of die-stacked memory, consistent with the expected performance ratios of real-world die-stacking [62, 70]. We modify Linux kernel to page between the emulated fast and slow memory, using the libnuma patches. We model the timing aspects of paging to faithfully reproduce the performance that SnipSnap's memory controller would sustain. Since our setup models CPUs with write-back caches, we include the latencies necessary for cache, load-store queue, and write buffer flushes on snapshot acquisition. Finally, we emulate the overhead of marshaling to external media by introducing artificial delays. We vary delay based on several emulated external media, from fast network connections to slower SSDs.

While our emulator includes full-system effects and full benchmark runs, it precludes us from modeling SnipSnap's effectiveness atop recently-proposed (and hence not available commercially) DRAM cache designs. Therefore, we also perform careful software simulation of the state-of-art UNISON DRAM cache [52], building SnipSnap atop it. Like the original UNISON cache paper, we assume a 4-way set-associative DRAM cache with 4KB pages, a 144KB footprint history table, and an accurate way predictor. Like recent work [93], we use an in-house simulator and drive it with 50 billion memory reference traces collected on a real system. We model a 16-core CMP and with ARM A15-style out-of-order CPUs, 32KB private L1 caches, and 16MB shared L2 cache. We study die-stacked DRAM with 4 channels, and 8 banks/rank with 16KB row buffers, and 128-bit bus width, like prior work [53]. Further, we model 16-64GB off-chip DRAM, with 8 banks/rank and 16KB row buffers. Finally, we use the same DRAM timing parameters as as the original UNISON cache paper [52].

5.2 Workloads

We study the performance implications of SnipSnap by quantifying snapshot overheads on several memory-intensive applications. We evaluate such workloads since these are the likeliest to face performance degradation due to snapshot acquisition. Even in this "worst-case," we show SnipSnap does not excessively hurt performance.

Figure 6 shows our single- and multi-threaded workloads. All benchmarks are configured to have memory footprints in the range of 12-14GB, which exceeds the maximum size of die-stacked memory we emulate (8GB). To achieve large memory footprints, we upgrade the inputs for some workloads with smaller defaults (*e.g.*, Canneal,

Dedup, and Mcf), so that their memory usage increases. We set up memcached with a snapshot of articles from the entire Wikipedia database, with over 10 million entries. Articles are roughly 2.8KB on average, but also exhibit high object size variance.

6 EVALUATION

We now evaluate the benefits of SnipSnap. We first quantify performance, and then discuss its hardware overheads.

6.1 Performance Impact on Target Applications

A drawback of current snapshotting mechanisms is that they *must* pause the execution of applications executing on the target to ensure consistency. SnipSnap does not suffer from this drawback. Figures 7 and 8 quantify these benefits. We plot the slowdown in runtime (lower is better) with benchmark averages, minima, and maxima, as we vary on-package DRAM capacity. We separate performance based on how we externalize snapshots: NICs with 100Gbps, 40Gbps, and 10Gbps throughput, and a solid-state storage disk (SSD) with sequential write throughput of 900MBps. Larger on-package DRAM (and hence, larger CoW areas) offer more room to store pages that have not yet been included in the snapshot. Faster methods to externalize snapshot entries allow the CoW area to drain quicker. Some of the configuration points that we discuss are not yet in wide commercial use. For example, the AMD Radeon R9, a high-end chipset series supports only up to 4GB of on-package DRAM. Similarly, 40Gbps and 100Gbps NICs are expensive and not yet in wide use.

Figure 7 shows results collected on our hardware emulator, assuming that 50% of on-package DRAM is devoted to the CoW area during snapshot mode. We vary the size on-package DRAM from 512MB to 8GB, and assume 16GB off-chip DRAM. Further, our hardware emulator assumes that on-package DRAM is implemented as a page-level fully-associative cache. We show the performance slowdown due to idealized current snapshotting mechanisms, as we take 1 and 10 snapshots. By idealized, we mean approaches like virtualization-based or TrustZone-style snapshotting which require pausing applications on the target to achieve consistency, but which assume unrealizable zero-overhead transition times to TrustZone mode or zero-overhead virtualization. Despite idealization, current approaches perform poorly. Even with only one snapshot, runtime increaseas by 1.2-2.4× using SSDs. SnipSnap fares much better, outperforming the idealized baseline by 1.2-2.2×, depending on the externalization medium and on-package DRAM size. Snapshotting more frequently (*i.e.*, 10 snapshots) further improves performance by 10.5-22×. Naturally, the more frequent the snapshotting, the more SnipSnap's benefits, though our benefits are significant even with a single snapshot.

Similarly, Figure 8 quantifies SnipSnap's performance improvements versus current snapshotting, assuming a baseline with state-of-the-art UNISON cache implementations of on-package DRAM [52], as UNISON cache sizes are varied from 512MB to 8GB. Some key differences between UNISON cache and our fully-associative hardware emulated DRAM cache is that UNISON cache also predicts 64B blocks within pages that should be moved on a DRAM cache miss, and also is implemented as 4-way set associative (as per the original paper). Nevertheless, Figure 8 (collected assuming SSDs as the externalizing medium) shows that SnipSnap outperforms idealized versions of current snapshotting mechanisms by as much as 22×, and by as much as 3× when just a single snapshot is taken.

SnipSnap's performance also scales far better than idealized versions of current snapshotting with increasing off-chip DRAM capacities. Figure 9 compares the performance slowdown due to one snapshot, as off-chip DRAM varies from 16GB to 64GB. These results are collected using UNISON cache (8GB in normal operation, 4GB in snapshot mode, with 4GB CoW), and assuming SSDs. Consider

Normalized Slowdown for 1 and 10 Snapshot Acquisitions on Hardware Emulator

CoW-nonCoW split 50-50

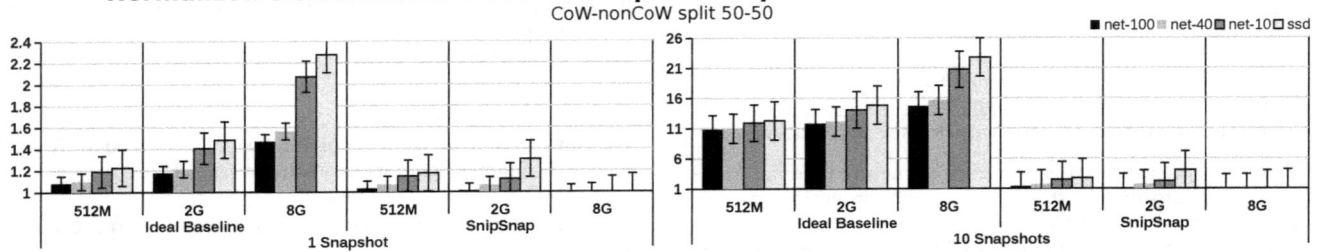

Figure 7: Performance impact of snapshot acquisition from hardware emulator studies. *Slowdown caused by modern snapshot mechanisms that also assure consistency, and compare against SnipSnap. We plot results for 1 and 10 snapshots separately (note the different y axes), showing averages, minima, and maxima amongst benchmark runtimes. X-axis shows the amount of on-package memory available on the emulated system. SnipSnap provides 1.2-22× performance improvements against current approaches.*

Normalized Slowdown for 1 & 10 Snapshot Acquisitions on UNISON Cache

CoW-nonCoW split 50-50 - SSD

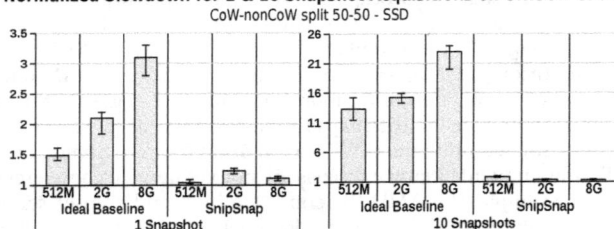

Figure 8: Performance impact of snapshot acquisition from simulator studies with UNISON cache [52]. *SnipSnap outperforms idealized versions of current snapshotting approaches by as much as 22× (graphs show benchmark averages, maxima, and minima).*

Normalized Slowdown for One Snapshot Acquisition on UNISON Cache for Different Off-Chip Memory Sizes

CoW-nonCoW split 50-50 - SSD

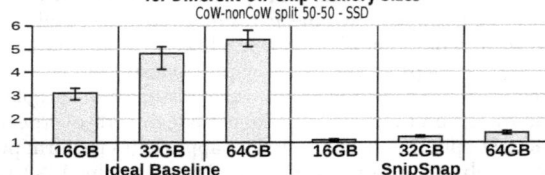

Figure 9: Average performance with varying off-chip DRAM size. *Bigger off-chip DRAM takes longer to snapshot, so SnipSnap becomes even more advantageous over current idealized approaches. These results assume UNISON cache with 8GB, split 50:50 in CoW:non-CoW mode during snapshot acquisition and SSDs, taking just one snapshot.*

idealized versions of current snapshotting approaches – runtime increases from 3× with 16GB off-chip DRAM to as high as 5.3× with 64GB of memory, when taking just a single snapshot. More snapshots further exacerbate this slowdown. While SnipSnap also suffers slowdown with larger off-chip DRAM, it still vastly outperforms current approaches by as much as 5× at 64GB of off-chip DRAM.

So far, we have shown application slowdown comparisons of Snip-Snap versus current approaches. Figure 10 focuses, instead, on per-benchmark runtime slowdown using SnipSnap, when varying the size of on-package DRAM and the externalizing medium. Results show that most benchmarks, despite being data-intensive, remain unaffected by SnipSnap's snapshot acquisition. The primary exceptions to this are memcached, cfar, and mnist, though their slowdowns vastly outperform current approaches (see Figures 7 and 8).

6.2 CoW Analysis

As discussed in Section 3, benchmark runtime suffers during snapshot acquisition only if the CoW area fills to capacity. When this happens,

the benchmark stalls until some pages from the CoW area are copied to the snapshot. Figure 11 illustrates this fact, and explains the performance of memcached. Figure 11 shows the fraction of the CoW area utilized over time during the execution of memcached. The fraction of time for which the CoW area is at 100% directly corresponds to the observed performance of memcached. When CoW utilization is below 100%, as is the case in Figure 11(b) the performance of memcached is unaffected.

Next, Figure 12 quantifies the performance impact of varying the percentage of die-stacked memory devoted to the CoW area. We vary the split from 50-50% to 25-75% and 75-25% for CoW-nonCoW portions, for various externalization techniques. We present the average results across all workloads for various total die-stacked memory sizes (individual benchmarks follow these average trends). Figure 12 shows that performance remains strong across all configurations, even when the percentage of DRAM cache devoted to CoW is low, which potentially leads to more stalls in the system. Furthermore, low CoW only degrades performance at smaller DRAM cache sizes of 512MB, which are smaller than DRAM cache sizes expected in upcoming systems.

Finally, note that the set-associativity of the DRAM cache devoted to the CoW region influences SnipSnap's performance. Specifically, consider designs like UNISON cache [52] (and prior work like Footprint cache [53]), which use 4-way set-associative (and 32-way set-associative) page-based DRAM caches. In these situations, if an entire set of the DRAM cache becomes full (even if other sets are not), applications executing on the target must pause until pages from that set are written to the external medium (i.e., SSD, network, etc.). Even in the worst case (all the application's data maps to a single set so the CoW region always stalls application execution and writing pages to the external medium takes as long as the entire snapshot time) this is *no worse* that idealized versions of current approaches. However, we find that this scenario does not occur in practice. Figure 13 quantifies SnipSnap's performance versus an ideal baseline for one snapshot, as off-chip DRAM capacity is varied from 16GB to 64GB, on-chip DRAM capacity is varied from 512MB to 8GB, and associativity is varied between 2-way and 4-way. Larger DRAM caches and higher associativity improve SnipSnap's performance, but even when we hamper UNISON cache to be 512MB and 2-way set-associative, it outperforms idealized current approaches by ~2×. More frequent snapshots further increase this number.

Beyond these studies, we also considered quantifying SnipSnap's performance on a direct-mapped UNISON cache. However, as pointed out by prior work, the conflict misses induced by direct-mapping in baseline designs without snapshotting are so high, that no practical page-based DRAM cache design is direct-mapped [52, 53]. Therefore,

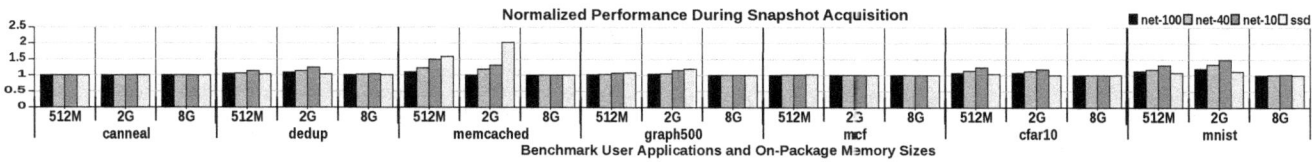

Figure 10: Performance impact of snapshot acquisition. *This chart reports the observed performance of user applications executing on the target during snapshot acquisition, normalized against their observed performance during regular execution, i.e., no snapshot acquisition. For each of the seven benchmarks, we report the performance for various sizes of die-stacked memory (50% of which is the CoW area), and for different methods via which the* write_out *in Figure 5 writes out the snapshot.*

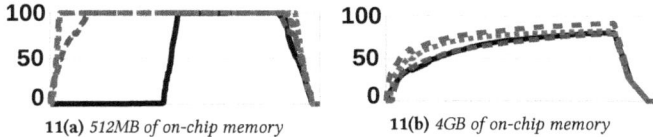

Figure 11: CoW area utilization over time for memcached. *Y-axis shows CoW area percentage used to store page frames that have not yet been included in the snapshot. X-axis denotes execution progress. We measured CoW utilization for every 1024 snapshot entries recorded. The two charts show CoW utilization trends for various sizes of die-stacked memory and for different methods to write out the snapshot:* ▬net-100 • • net-40 ▬net-10 ▬ ▬ssd. *Snapshot acquisition does not impact memcached performance when CoW utilization is below 100%.*

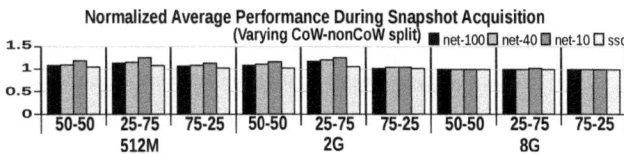

Figure 12: Performance impact of snapshot acquisition for different CoW-Cache partitions. *Y-axis shows average performance impact of all benchmarks to take a snapshot, varying CoW-nonCoW partition for different cache sizes. X-axis shows different total sizes of die-stacked memory and various ways in which to partition die-stacked memory for CoW (50%, 25% and 75% for CoW).*

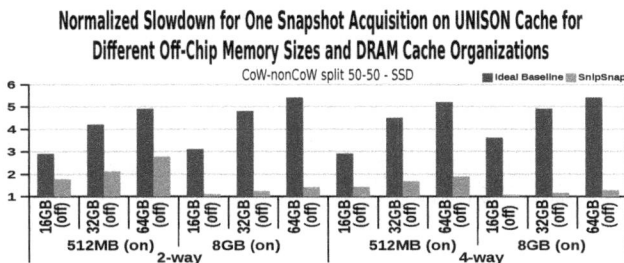

Figure 13: Performance as size and set-associativty of UNISON cache changes. *Lower UNISON cache size and set-associativity increases the chances that a set in the CoW region fills up and pauses execution of applications on the target. Results are shown using SSDs, varying off-chip DRAM capacity from 16GB to 64GB, UNISON cache size from 512MB to 8GB, and set-associativity from 2 to 4 way.*

we begin our analysis with 2-way set-associative DRAM caches, showing that SnipSnap consistently outperforms alternatives.

7 RELATED WORK

As Section 1 discusses, there is much prior work on remote memory acquisition based on virtualization, trusted hardware and external hardware. Figure 1 characterizes the difference between SnipSnap and this prior work. Aside from these, there are other mechanisms to

fetch memory snapshots for the purpose of debugging (*e.g.*, [37, 42, 54, 84, 86]). Because their focus isn't forensic analysis, these systems do not assume an adversarial target OS.

Prior work has leveraged die-stacking to implement myriad security features such as monitoring program execution, access control and cryptography [46–48, 64, 69, 89–91]. This work observes that die-stacking allows processor vendors to decouple core CPU logic from "add-ons," such as security, thereby improving their chances of deployment. Our work also leverages additional circuitry on the die-stack to implement the logic needed for memory acquisition. Unlike prior work, which focused solely on additional processing logic integrated using die-stacking, our focus is also on die-stacked memory, which is beginning to see deployment in commercial processors. While SnipSnap also uses the die-stack to integrate additional cryptographic logic and modify the memory controller, it does so to enable near-data processing on the contents of die-stacked memory.

Prior work has also used die-stacked manufacturing technology to detect malicious logic inserted into the processor. The threat model is that of an outsourced chip manufacturer who can insert Trojan-horse logic into the hardware. This work suggests various methods to combat this threat using die-stacked manufacturing. For example, one method is to divide the implementation of a circuit across multiple layers in the stack, each manufactured by a separate agent, thereby obfuscating the functionality of individual layers [49, 88]. Another method is to add logic into die-stacked layers to monitor the execution of the processor for maliciously-inserted logic [12–14].

There is prior work on near-data processing to enable security applications [40] and modifying memory controllers to implement a variety of security features [82, 92]. There is also work on using programmable DRAM [59] to monitor systems for OS and hypervisor integrity violations. Unlike SnipSnap, which focuses on fetching a complete snapshot of DRAM, and must hence consider snapshot consistency, this work only focuses on analysis of specific memory pages, *e.g.*, those that contain specific kernel data structures. It also cannot access CPU register state, making it vulnerable to address-translation attacks [51, 56].

8 CONCLUSION

Vendors are beginning to integrate memory and processing logic on-chip using on-package DRAM manufacturing technology. We have presented SnipSnap, an application of this technology to secure memory acquisition. SnipSnap has a hardware TCB, and allows forensic analysts to collect consistent memory snapshots from a target machine while offering performance isolation for applications executing on the target. Our experimental evaluation on a number of data intensive workloads shows the benefit of our approach.

Dedication and Acknowledgments. We would like to dedicate this paper to the memory of our friend, colleague and mentor, Professor Liviu Iftode (1959-2017). This work was funded in part by NSF grants 1319755, 1337147, 1420815, and 1441724.

REFERENCES

[1] [n. d.]. Docker – Build, Ship and Run Any App, Anywhere. ([n. d.]). https://www.docker.com/.

[2] [n. d.]. Rekall Forensics – We can remember it for you wholesale! ([n. d.]). http://www.rekall-forensic.com/.

[3] [n. d.]. TLA+ model of SnipSnap. ([n. d.]). http://bit.ly/2mOCY23.

[4] [n. d.]. Volatility – An advanced memory forensics framework. ([n. d.]). https://github.com/volatilityfoundation/volatility.

[5] 2009. ARM Security Technology – Building a Secure System using TrustZone Technology. (2009). ARM Technical Whitepaper. http://infocenter.arm.com/help/topic/com.arm.doc.prd29-genc-009492c/PRD29-GENC-009492C_trustzone_security_whitepaper.pdf.

[6] J. Ahn, S. Hong, S. Yoo, O. Mutlu, and K. Choi. 2015. A Scalable Processing-in-Memory Accelerator for Parallel Graph Processing. In *International Symposium on Computer Architecture (ISCA)*.

[7] J. Ahn, S. Yoo, O. Mutlu, and K. Choi. 2015. PIM-Enabled Instructions: A Low-Overhead, Locality-Aware Processing-in-Memory Architecture. In *International Symposium on Computer Architecture (ISCA)*.

[8] William Arbaugh. [n. d.]. Komoku. In https://www.cs.umd.edu/~waa/UMD/Home.html.

[9] A. Azab, P. Ning, J. Shah, Q. Chen, R. Bhutkar, G. Ganesh, J. Ma, and W. Shen. 2014. Hypervision Across Worlds: Real-time Kernel Protection from the ARM TrustZone Secure World. In *ACM Conference on Computer and Communications Security (CCS)*.

[10] A. Baliga, V. Ganapathy, and L. Iftode. 2011. Detecting Kernel-level Rootkits using Data Structure Invariants. *IEEE Transactions on Dependable and Secure Computing* 8, 5 (2011).

[11] C. Bienia, S. Kumar, J. P. Singh, and K. Li. 2008. The PARSEC benchmark suite: characterization and architectural implications. In *Parallel Architectures and Compilation Techniques (PACT)*.

[12] M. Bilzor. 2011. 3D execution monitor (3D-EM): Using 3D circuits to detect hardware malicious inclusions in general purpose processors. In *6th International Conference on Information Warfare and Security*.

[13] M. Bilzor, T. Huffmire, C. Irvine, and T. Levin. 2011. Security Checkers: Detecting Processor Malicious Inclusions at Runtime. In *IEEE International Symposium on Hardware-oriented Security and Trust*.

[14] M. Bilzor, T. Huffmire, C. Irvine, and T. Levin. 2012. Evaluating Security Requirements in a General-purpose Processor by Combining Assertion Checkers with Code Coverage. In *IEEE International Symposium on Hardware-oriented Security and Trust*.

[15] B. Black, M. Annavaram, E. Brekelbaum, J. DeVale, L. Jiang, G. Loh, D. McCauley, P. Morrow, D. Nelson, D. Pantuso, P. Reed, J. Rupley, S. Shankar, J. P. Shen, and C. Webb. 2006. Die Stacking 3D Microarchitecture. In *International Symposium on Microarchitecture (MICRO)*.

[16] A. Bohra, I. Neamtiu, P. Gallard, F. Sultan, and L. Iftode. 2004. Remote Repair of Operating System State Using Backdoors. In *International Conference on Autonomic Computing (ICAC)*.

[17] M. Carbone, W. Cui, L. Lu, W. Lee, M. Peinado, and X. Jiang. 2009. Mapping Kernel Objects to Enable Systematic Integrity Checking. In *ACM Conference on Computer and Communications Security (CCS)*.

[18] Andrew Case and Golden G. Richard. 2017. Memory forensics: The path forward. *Digital Investigation* 20 (2017), 23 – 33. https://doi.org/10.1016/j.diin.2016.12.004 Special Issue on Volatile Memory Analysis.

[19] Michael Chan, Heiner Litz, and David R. Cheriton. 2013. Rethinking Network Stack Design with Memory Snapshots. In *Proceedings of the 14th USENIX Conference on Hot Topics in Operating Systems (HotOS'13)*. USENIX Association, Berkeley, CA, USA, 27–27. http://dl.acm.org/citation.cfm?id=2490483.2490510

[20] R. Chaves, G. Kuzmanov, L. Sousa, and S. Vassiliadis. 2006. Improving SHA-2 Hardware Implementations. In *IACR International Cryptology Conference (CRYPTO)*.

[21] David Cheriton, Amin Firoozshahian, Alex Solomatnikov, John P. Stevenson, and Omid Azizi. 2012. HICAMP: Architectural Support for Efficient Concurrency-safe Shared Structured Data Access. In *Proceedings of the Seventeenth International Conference on Architectural Support for Programming Languages and Operating Systems (ASPLOS XVII)*. ACM, New York, NY, USA, 287–300. https://doi.org/10.1145/2150976.2151007

[22] C.-C. Chou, A. Jaleel, and M. K. Qureshi. 2012. CAMEO: A Two-Level Memory Organization with Capacity of Main Memory and Flexibility of Hardware-Managed Cache. In *International Symposium on Microarchitecture (MICRO)*.

[23] Lei Cui, Tianyu Wo, Bo Li, Jianxin Li, Bin Shi, and Jinpeng Huai. 2015. PARS: A Page-Aware Replication System for Efficiently Storing Virtual Machine Snapshots. In *Proceedings of the 11th ACM SIGPLAN/SIGOPS International Conference on Virtual Execution Environments (VEE '15)*. ACM, New York, NY, USA, 215–228. https://doi.org/10.1145/2731186.2731190

[24] W. Cui, M. Peinado, S. K. Cha, Y. Fratantonio, and V. P. Kemerlis. 2016. RETracer: Triaging Crashes by Reverse Execution from Partial Memory Dumps. In *International Conference on Software Engineering (ICSE)*.

[25] W. Cui, M. Peinado, Z. Xu, and E. Chan. 2012. Tracking Rootkit Footprints with a Practical Memory Analysis System. In *USENIX Security Symposium*.

[26] CVE-2007-4993. [n. d.]. Xen guest root escapes to dom0 via pygrub. ([n. d.]).

[27] CVE-2007-5497. [n. d.]. Integer overflows in libext2fs in e2fsprogs. ([n. d.]).

[28] CVE-2008-0923. [n. d.]. Directory traversal vulnerability in the Shared Folders feature for VMWare. ([n. d.]).

[29] CVE-2008-1943. [n. d.]. Buffer overflow in the backend of XenSource Xen ParaVirtualized Frame Buffer. ([n. d.]).

[30] CVE-2008-2100. [n. d.]. VMWare buffer overflows in VIX API let local users execute arbitrary code in host OS. ([n. d.]).

[31] Bernhard Egger, Erik Gustafsson, Changyeon Jo, and Jeongseok Son. 2015. Efficiently Restoring Virtual Machines. *International Journal of Parallel Programming* 43, 3 (2015), 421–439. https://doi.org/10.1007/s10766-013-0295-0

[32] Wikipedia entry. [n. d.]. eDRAM. In https://en.wikipedia.wiki/EDRAM.

[33] Q. Feng, A. Prakash, H. Yin, and Z. Lin. 2014. MACE: High-Coverage and Robust Memory Analysis for Commodity Operating Systems. In *Annual Computer Security Applications Conference (ACSAC)*.

[34] H. Fujita, N. Dun, Z. A. Rubenstein, and A. A. Chien. 2015. Log-Structured Global Array for Efficient Multi-Version Snapshots. In *2015 15th IEEE/ACM International Symposium on Cluster, Cloud and Grid Computing*. 281–291. https://doi.org/10.1109/CCGrid.2015.80

[35] T. Garfinkel and M. Rosenblum. 2003. A Virtual Machine Introspection Based Architecture for Intrusion Detection. In *Network and Distributed System Security Symposium (NDSS)*.

[36] X. Ge, H. Vijayakumar, and T. Jaeger. 2014. SPROBES: Enforcing Kernel Code Integrity on the TrustZone Architecture. In *IEEE Mobile Security Technologies Workshop (MoST)*.

[37] Google. [n. d.]. Using DDMS for debugging. ([n. d.]). http://developer.android.com/tools/debugging/ddms.html.

[38] Graph500. [n. d.]. http://www.graph500.org.

[39] Mariano Graziano, Andrea Lanzi, and Davide Balzarotti. 2013. *Hypervisor Memory Forensics*. Springer Berlin Heidelberg, Berlin, Heidelberg, 21–40. https://doi.org/10.1007/978-3-642-41284-4_2

[40] A. Gundu, A. S. Ardestani, M. Shevgoor, and R. Balasubramonian. 2014. A Case for Near Data Security. In *3rd Workshop on Near Data Processing*.

[41] M. Healy, K. Athikulwongse, R. Goel, M. Hossain, D. H. Kim, Y. Lee, D. Lewis, T. Lin, C. Liu, M. Jung, B. Ouellette, M. Pathak, H. Sane, G. Shen, D. H. Woo, X. Zhao, G. Loh, H. Lee, and S. Lim. 2010. Design and Analysis of 3D-MAPS: A Many-Core 3D Processor with Stacked Memory. In *IEEE Custom Integrated Circuits Conference (CICC)*.

[42] A. P. Heriyanto. 2013. Procedures and tools for acquisition and analysis of volatile memory on Android smartphones. In *11th Australian Digital Forensics Conference*.

[43] O. S. Hofmann, A. M. Dunn, S. Kim, I. Roy, and E. Witchel. 2011. Ensuring Operating System Kernel Integrity with OSck. In *International Conference on Architectural Support for Programming Languages and Operating Systems (ASPLOS)*.

[44] K. Hsieh, E. Ebrahimi, G. Kim, N. Chatterjee, M. O'Connor, N. Vijaykumar, O. Mutlu, and S. Keckler. 2015. Transparent Offloading and Mapping (TOM): Enabling Programmer-Transparent Near-Data Processing in GPU Systems. In *International Symposium on Computer Architecture (ISCA)*.

[45] Y. Huang, R. Yang, L. Cui, T. Wo, C. Hu, and B. Li. 2014. VMCSnap: Taking Snapshots of Virtual Machine Cluster with Memory Deduplication. In *2014 IEEE 8th International Symposium on Service Oriented System Engineering*. 314–319. https://doi.org/10.1109/SOSE.2014.45

[46] T. Huffmire, T. Levin, M. Bilzor, C. Irvine, J. Valamehr, M. Tiwari, and T. Sherwood. 2010. Hardware Trust Implications of 3-D Integration. In *Workshop on Embedded Systems Security*.

[47] T. Huffmire, T. Levin, C. Irvine, R. Kastner, and T. Sherwood. 2011. 3-D Extensions for Trustworthy Systems. In *International Conference on Engineering of Reconfigurable Systems and Algorithms (ERSA)*.

[48] T. Huffmire, J. Valamehr, T. Sherwood, R. Kastner, T. Levin, T. Nguyen, and C. Irvine. 2008. Trustworthy System Security through 3-D Integrated Hardware. In *International Workshop on Hardware-oriented Security and Trust*.

[49] F. Imeson, A. Emtenan, S. Garg, and M. Tripunitara. 2013. Securing Computer Hardware using 3D Integrated Circuit Technology and Split Manufacturing for Obfuscation. In *USENIX Security Symposium*.

[50] InfiniBand. [n. d.]. The InfiniBand Trade Association—The InfiniBand™ Architecture Specification. ([n. d.]). http://www.infinibandta.org.

[51] D. Jang, H. Lee, M. Kim, D. Kim, D. Kim, and B. Kang. 2014. ATRA: Address Translation Redirection attack against Hardware-based External Monitors. In *ACM Conference on Computer and Communications Security (CCS)*.

[52] D. Jevdjic, G. Loh, C. Kaynak, and B. Falsafi. 2014. Unison Cache: A Scalable and Effective Die-Stacked DRAM Cache. In *International Symposium on Microarchitecture (MICRO)*.

[53] D. Jevdjic, S. Volos, and B. Falsafi. 2013. Die-stacked dram caches for servers: Hit ratio, latency, or bandwidth? have it all with footprint cache. In *International Symposium on Computer Architecture (ISCA)*.

[54] Joint Test Action Group (JTAG). 2013. 1149.1-2013 - IEEE Standard for Test Access Port and Boundary-scan Architecture. (2013). http://standards.ieee.org/findstds/standard/1149.1-2013.html.

[55] K. Kortchinsky. 2009. Hacking 3D (and Breaking out of VMWare). In *BlackHat USA*.

[56] Y. Kinebuchi, S. Butt, V. Ganapathy, L. Iftode, and T. Nakajima. 2013. Monitoring System Integrity using Limited Local Memory. *IEEE Transactions on Information Forensics and Security* 8, 7 (2013).

[57] L. Lamport. 2002. *Specifying Systems: The TLA+ Language and Tools for Hardware and Software Engineers*. Pearson Education.

[58] H. Lee, H. Moon, D. Jang, K. Kim, J. Lee, Y. Paek, and B. Kang. 2013. KI-Mon: A hardware-assisted event-triggered monitoring platform for mutable kernel objects. In *USENIX Security Symposium*.

[59] Z. Liu, J. Lee, J. Zeng, Y. Wen, Z. Lin, and W. Shi. 2013. CPU-transparent protection of OS kernel and hypervisor integrity with programmable DRAM. In *International Symposium on Computer Architecture (ISCA)*.

[60] G. Loh. 2008. 3D-Stacked Memory Architectures for Multi-Core Processors. In *International Symposium on Computer Architecture (ISCA)*.

[61] G. Loh. 2009. Extending the Effectiveness of 3D-Stacked DRAM Caches with an Adaptive Multi-Queue Policy. In *International Symposium on Microarchitecture (MICRO)*.

[62] G. Loh and M. D. Hill. 2011. Efficiently Enabling Conventional Block Sizes for Very Large Die-Stacked DRAM Caches. In *International Symposium on Microarchitecture (MICRO)*.

[63] Ali José Mashtizadeh, Min Cai, Gabriel Tarasuk-Levin, Ricardo Koller, Tal Garfinkel, and Sreekanth Setty. 2014. XvMotion: Unified Virtual Machine Migration over Long Distance. In *Proceedings of the 2014 USENIX Conference on USENIX Annual Technical Conference (USENIX ATC'14)*. USENIX Association, Berkeley, CA, USA, 97–108. http://dl.acm.org/citation.cfm?id=2643634.2643645

[64] D. Megas, K. Pizolato, T. Levin, and T. Huffmire. 2012. A 3D Data Transformation Processor. In *Workshop on Embedded Systems Security*.

[65] Mellanox Technologies. 2014. Introduction to InfiniBand. (September 2014). http://www.mellanox.com/blog/2014/09/introduction-to-infiniband.

[66] Memcached. [n. d.]. https://memcached.org.

[67] H. Moon, H. Lee, J. Lee, K. Kim, Y. Paek, and B. Kang. 2012. Vigilare: Toward a Snoop-based Kernel Integrity Monitor. In *ACM Conference on Computer and Communications Security (CCS)*.

[68] Andreas Moser and Michael I. Cohen. 2013. Hunting in the enterprise: Forensic triage and incident response. *Digital Investigation* 10, 2 (2013), 89 – 98. https://doi.org/10.1016/j.diin.2013.03.003 Triage in Digital Forensics.

[69] S. Mysore, B. Agrawal, N. Srivastava, S-C. Lin, K. Banerjee, and T. Sherwood. 2016. Introspective 3D Chips. In *International Conference on Architectural Support for Programming Languages and Operating Systems (ASPLOS)*.

[70] M. Oskin and G. Loh. 2015. A Software-managed Approach to Die-Stacked DRAM. In *International Conference on Parallel Architectures and Compilation Techniques (PACT)*.

[71] Eunbyung Park, Bernhard Egger, and Jaejin Lee. 2011. Fast and Space-efficient Virtual Machine Checkpointing. In *Proceedings of the 7th ACM SIGPLAN/SIGOPS International Conference on Virtual Execution Environments (VEE '11)*. ACM, New York, NY, USA, 75–86. https://doi.org/10.1145/1952682.1952694

[72] N. Petroni, T. Fraser, A. Walters, and W. A. Arbaugh. 2006. An architecture for specification-based detection of semantic integrity violations in kernel dynamic data. In *USENIX Security Symposium*.

[73] N. Petroni and M. Hicks. 2007. Automated Detection of Persistent Kernel Control-flow Attacks. In *ACM Conference on Computer and Communications Security (CCS)*.

[74] N. L. Petroni, T. Fraser, J. Molina, and W. A. Arbaugh. 2004. Copilot: A Coprocessor-based Kernel Runtime Integrity Monitor. In *USENIX Security Symposium*.

[75] B. Pham, V. Vaidyanathan, A. Jaleel, and A. Bhattacharjee. 2012. CoLT: Coalesced Large-Reach TLBs. In *International Symposium on Microarchitecture (MICRO)*.

[76] B. Pham, J. Vesely, G. Loh, and A. Bhattacharjee. 2015. Large Pages and Lightweight Memory Management in Virtualized Environments: Can You Have it Both Ways?. In *International Symposium on Microarchitecture (MICRO)*.

[77] M. K. Qureshi and G. H. Loh. 2012. Fundamental latency trade-off in architecting DRAM caches: Outperforming impractical SRAM-tags with a simple and practical design. In *International Symposium on Microarchitecture (MICRO)*.

[78] J. Rutkowska. 2007. Beyond the CPU: Defeating Hardware based RAM Acquisition, part I: AMD case. In *Blackhat Conf*.

[79] J. Rutkowska and R. Wojtczuk. 2008. Preventing and detecting Xen hypervisor subversions. In *Blackhat Briefings USA*.

[80] K. Saur, M. Hicks, and J. S. Foster. 2015. C-Strider: Type-aware Heap Traversal for C. *Software, Practice, and Experience* (May 2015).

[81] Bradley Schatz and Michael Cohen. 2017. Advances in volatile memory forensics. *Digital Investigation* 20 (2017), 1. https://doi.org/10.1016/j.diin.2017.02.008 Special Issue on Volatile Memory Analysis.

[82] A. Shafiee, A. Gundu, M. Shevgoor, R. Balasubramonian, and M. Tiwari. 2015. Avoiding Information Leakage in the Memory Controller with Fixed Service Policies. In *International Symposium on Microarchitecture (MICRO)*.

[83] Spec. [n. d.]. Https://www.spec.org/cpu2006/.

[84] A. Stevenson. [n. d.]. Boot into Recovery Mode for Rooted and Un-rooted Android devices. ([n. d.]). http://androidflagship.com/605-enter-recovery-mode-rooted-un-rooted-android.

[85] H. Sun, K. Sur., Y. Wang, J. Jing, and S. Jajodia. 2014. TrustDump: Reliable Memory Acquisition on Smartphones. In *European Symposium on Research in Computer Security (ESORICS)*.

[86] J. Sylve, A. Case, L. Marziale, and G. G. Richard. 2012. Acquisition and analysis of Volatile Memory from Android Smartphones. *Digital Investigation* 8, 3-4 (2012).

[87] TensorFlow. [n. d.]. https://www.tensorflow.org.

[88] Tezzaron Semiconductors. 2008. 3D-ICs and Integrated Circuit Security. (2008). http://www.tezzaron.com/media/3D-ICs_and_Integrated_Circuit_Security.pdf.

[89] J. Valamehr, T. Huffmire, C. Irvine, R. Kastner, C. Koc, T. Levin, and T. Sherwood. 2012. A Qualitative Security Analysis of a New Class of 3-D Integrated Crypto Co-Processors. In *Cryptography and Security: From Theory to Applications, LNCS volume 6805*.

[90] J. Valamehr, M. Tiwari, T. Sherwood, R. Kastner, T. Huffmire, C. Irvine, and T. Levin. 2010. Hardware Assistance for Trustworthy Systems through 3-D Integration. In *Annual Computer Security Applications Conference (ACSAC)*.

[91] J. Valamehr, M. Tiwari, T. Sherwood, R. Kastner, T. Huffmire, C. Irvine, and T. Levin. 2013. A 3-D Split Manufacturing Approach to Trustworthy System Development. *IEEE Transactions on Computer-aided Design of Integrated Circuits and Systems* 32, 4 (April 2013).

[92] Y. Wang, A. Ferraiuolo, and G. E. Suh. 2014. Timing Channel Protection for a Shared Memory Controller. In *IEEE International Conference on High-performance Computer Architecture (HPCA)*.

[93] Zi Yan, Jan Vesely, Guilherme Cox, and Abhishek Bhattacharjee. 2017. Hardware Translation Coherence for Virtualized Systems. In *International Symposium on Computer Architecture (ISCA)*.

[94] Ruijin Zhou and Tao Li. 2013. Leveraging Phase Change Memory to Achieve Efficient Virtual Machine Execution. In *Proceedings of the 9th ACM SIGPLAN/SIGOPS International Conference on Virtual Execution Environments (VEE '13)*. ACM, New York, NY, USA, 179–190. https://doi.org/10.1145/2451512.2451547

URLs in references were last accessed January 10, 2018

Fidelius Charm: Isolating Unsafe Rust Code

Hussain M. J. Almohri
Department of Computer Science
Kuwait University and University of Virginia
almohri@ieee.org

David Evans
Department of Computer Science
University of Virginia
evans@virginia.edu

ABSTRACT

The Rust programming language has a safe memory model that promises to eliminate critical memory bugs. While the language is strong in doing so, its memory guarantees are lost when any unsafe blocks are used. Unsafe code is often needed to call library functions written in an unsafe language inside a Rust program. We present Fidelius Charm (FC), a system that protects a programmer-specified subset of data in memory from unauthorized access through vulnerable unsafe libraries. FC does this by limiting access to the program's memory while executing unsafe libraries. FC uses standard features of Rust and utilizes the Linux kernel as a trusted base for splitting the address space into a trusted privileged region under the control of functions written in Rust and a region available to unsafe external libraries. This paper presents our design and implementation of FC, presents two case studies for using FC in Rust TLS libraries, and reports on experiments showing its performance overhead is low for typical uses.

CCS CONCEPTS

• **Security and privacy** → **Systems security**;

KEYWORDS

Isolation, Rust, Compartmentalization, Sandboxing

ACM Reference Format:
Hussain M. J. Almohri and David Evans. 2018. Fidelius Charm: Isolating Unsafe Rust Code. In *CODASPY '18: Eighth ACM Conference on Data and Application Security and Privacy, March 19–21, 2018, Tempe, AZ, USA.* ACM, New York, NY, USA, 8 pages. https://doi.org/10.1145/3176258.3176330

1 INTRODUCTION

Rust is designed to provide strong memory safety, but provides a way to escape its strict checking rules using an explicit unsafe keyword. This enables systems-level Rust programming, and supports easy integration with libraries written in unsafe languages such as C. Code within an unsafe region can use all memory in the Rust program's process in arbitrary ways, jeopardizing all the safety guarantees made by the Rust compiler. Unsafe regions enable calling unsafe and untrustworthy external libraries through Rust's foreign function interface (FFI). When using FFI, the Rust compiler cannot reason about memory vulnerabilities, repudiating all the safety guarantees Rust programmers work so hard to obtain.

ACM acknowledges that this contribution was authored or co-authored by an employee, contractor or affiliate of a national government. As such, the Government retains a nonexclusive, royalty-free right to publish or reproduce this article, or to allow others to do so, for Government purposes only.
CODASPY '18, March 19–21, 2018, Tempe, AZ, USA
© 2018 Association for Computing Machinery.
ACM ISBN 978-1-4503-5632-9/18/03...$15.00
https://doi.org/10.1145/3176258.3176330

The goal of this work is to enable FFI calls while isolating some of the already allocated memory, limiting the potentially-vulnerable external code (running within the same address space) from reading sensitive data. Rust has no mechanism to isolate an unsafe external function or limit its impact. A practical isolation mechanism must be able to limit the data available to an unsafe external function while allowing it to execute normally without the need to modify or even inspect the unsafe code (which may only be available as a binary). Traditional ways to address this problem use computationally-intensive runtime systems for compartmentalization of untrustworthy code, or complex (and seldom usable) modifications of the language's compiler for monitoring and sandboxing vulnerable or unsafe regions of the code. These solutions would require major changes to either the Rust compiler or the unsafe code itself, both of which we want to avoid. Instead, we focus on a solution that leverages existing language and operating system mechanisms.

While no prior work addressed memory isolation for unsafe Rust regions in particular, several previous works have sought to confine code executing within a single address space. Recent work such as Shreds [7], lwC [14], and SpaceJMP [12] provide thread-like abstractions for isolating memory. Codejail [29], a memory sandbox system, has fewer dependencies and provides a sandbox of the memory for unsafe libraries. Our approach reverses the sandbox model by isolating a subset of the trusted region of the program and providing the rest of the memory to the unsafe libraries.

All the previous works, except Codejail, require some static analysis or special abstractions. We aim to have a practical and lightweight solution that allows programmers to make choices about which parts of the memory to protect, that requires only memory page permissions that are supported by modern hardware, and that avoids hard modifications to the operating system, only involving simple kernel extensions. Our approach is to (i) move sensitive program data to protected pages before entering unsafe code, (ii) allow unsafe code to run normally without modifications, (iii) restore visibility of the protected state when unsafe code execution completes, and (iv) incorporate a precise and efficient kernel-level monitor to ensure unsafe code cannot circumvent protections.

Threat Model Our solution assumes a trusted starting state in which the operating system, and underlying hardware, are not malicious and are implemented correctly. FC is designed to protect the memory of processes executing *FC-ified* Rust programs, in which sensitive memory regions are protected by isolated secure compartments when interacting with foreign function interfaces. Thus, we assume the code written in Rust is trusted except when using an unsafe block to call an external library function.

We assume attackers are remote and do not have root privileges on the target machine (that is, the machine on which FC operates and is subject to attacks) or any way to interfere with program execution other than through the foreign function called by the Rust program. We assume the attacker can use memory vulnerabilities in the unsafe code to access data allocated by the trusted program region, for example, using poorly checked memory boundaries. Thus, the attacker has access to all memory pages available to the process in which the untrusted code executes, except memory pages that are under FC's protection. The attacker aims to exploit vulnerabilities in untrusted code to gain control over the program state in a Rust program.

Contributions We present Fidelius Charm[1], a Rust language library and kernel extension support for creating in-memory *secure compartments* by protecting sensitive data in memory from an unsafe function execution. We discuss the design decisions made for developing FC, which intends to hide a subset of the trusted memory regions allocated while executing Rust code. In particular, our work has four primary contributions:

- **Extending Rust's memory ownership** by allowing functions to own their allocated data in *secure compartments* and limit access from unauthorized functions (Section 2).
- **Designing strong kernel-level protection** to maintain the integrity of FC's secure compartments by monitoring and protecting the underlying APIs, such as mprotect, as well as performing stack inspection to ensure that access can be re-enabled only by the intended safe Rust code (Section 2.4).
- **Controlling data sharing** between a Rust function and a unsafe library function while providing strong isolation of the safe and unsafe code using a narrow and controlled data interface (Section 2).
- **Testing FC in case studies** to explore its effectiveness and implementation efforts (Section 3).

FC's on-demand secure compartments ensure memory protection and isolation within a single process using architectural support for memory page permissions. FC's design is cross-platform and thread-safe, and requires no modification to the Rust compiler. Our implementation uses a Rust library and kernel extension, both of which are available under an open source license. Using FC involves mostly simple modifications to the program's source code, and low run-time overhead (Section 4).

2 DESIGN

To control access to memory allocated in Rust while calling an unsafe code, we designed a compartmentalization technique which splits the address space into three regions: (i) a *private region* that is inaccessible from unsafe functions and is fully accessible from safe functions, (ii) an *immutable region* that could be read from any part of the program, and (iii) an *exposed region*, which is accessible from any part of the program. The private and the immutable regions comprise *secure compartments*, which are collections of continuous memory pages with specific permission bits. These compartments isolate sensitive data from unsafe code by arranging memory appropriately on pages and changing their permission bits to read-only or no access. When an unsafe function executes, depending on the program's policies (specified by the programmer), it has limited access to the secure compartments.

---

[1]The name Fidelius Charm is inspired by Harry Potter's Fidelius Charm, which is a complex spell to conceal a secret in a person.

2.1 Motivating Example

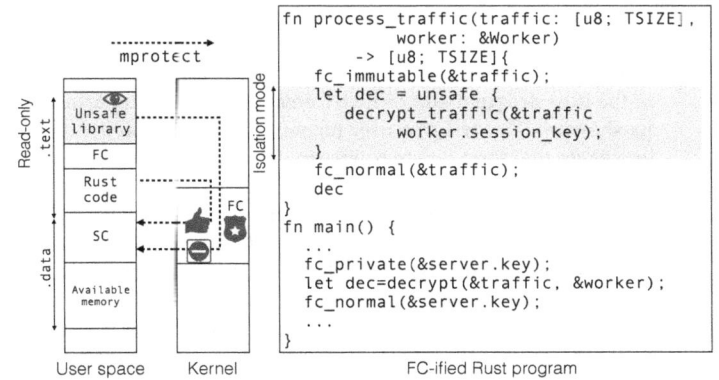

```
fn process_traffic(traffic: [u8; TSIZE],
        worker: &Worker)
    -> [u8; TSIZE]{
  fc_immutable(&traffic);
  let dec = unsafe {
    decrypt_traffic(&traffic
        worker.session_key);
  }
  fc_normal(&traffic);
  dec
}
fn main() {
  ...
  fc_private(&server.key);
  let dec=decrypt(&traffic, &worker);
  fc_normal(&server.key);
  ...
}
```

Figure 1: FC's user space and kernel components create and maintain secure compartments in the Rust program's process. Access to mprotect calls is restricted to a specific region in the code, which controls the secure compartments. The FC-ified program shows a simplified usage of FC's interfaces to create a private (no permission) secure compartment and an immutable (read-only) secure compartment.

Consider developing a TCP server using worker threads, excerpted in Figure 1. It uses a Worker structure to hold data for a client session, and a Server structure to hold data for the main server program. To store client's message for processing, define an array, let traffic = [0; TSIZE]. Also, consider a Rust function process_traffic that invokes the unsafe external function decrypt_traffic, which decrypts traffic using Worker.session_key.

This simple example includes several aspects that motivate the need for FC. First, when decrypting the traffic using an unsafe library function, the Rust function only needs to share the client's session key in Worker.session_key, hiding the server's private key (Server.key). Second, the Rust function must protect the original copy of the client's traffic and send it as a read-only input to decrypt_traffic. Third, when processing a Worker's client, the Rust function must isolate the sensitive data, for example the session keys of another Worker's client. Also, the list of Workers, and other server-related data stored in an instance of Server should be secured before executing unsafe code.

Since the external library implemented in an unsafe language may have serious security flaws that could allow arbitrary access to memory [25], any call to decrypt_traffic using unsafe in Rust potentially exposes all of program's memory. FC isolates data objects (i.e., individual variables, referred to as bindings in Rust) to minimize the exposure when calling unsafe code. For example, when calling decrypt_traffic to decrypt a client's message using its session key, only the worker.session_key is exposed to the unsafe code; Server.key and all other sensitive data objects stay in an isolated secure compartment and are temporarily inaccessible throughout the entire program.

2.2 Architecture of FC

FC consists of a user space library, a modified Rust program that links to the library, and a kernel module that maintains access control for the program's safe (written in Rust) and unsafe code (arbitrary libraries) regions. Prior to an unsafe call, the programmer adds calls to FC's user space component, which are interfaces linked to the Rust program and facilitate creating secure compartments. As shown in Figure 1, the user memory's data section is divided into pages that form secure compartments and exposed pages with read and write access.

The second component of FC is the modified Rust program that wraps unsafe calls with invocations of FC's functions. For example, in the FC-ified program of Figure 1, process_traffic creates a read-only secure compartment. The code following a call to fc_immutable changes the program's state to the *isolated mode*, in which some of the original memory page permission bits are modified. A subsequent call to fc_normal reverses the program's state to *exposed mode* with all data section page permissions are reversed to read and write. The main function creates a private secure compartment that hides the server's sensitive data.

FC's user space library serves as a client for its third component, a kernel module that implements a mandatory access control by separating the code section of the user space into two groups: (i) the code written in Rust that has the right to issue mprotect calls and modify page permissions, and (ii) the code written in arbitrary languages, which cannot make mprotect calls on pages that are tagged as secure compartments. As detailed in Section 2.4, the kernel module maintains the secure compartments and mediates access to memory page permissions.

2.3 Secure Compartments

FC enables two memory permission modes for its secure compartments: *immutable* (read-only) and *private* (inaccessible). The default memory permissions are set by the process at the time of allocating memory pages, which FC does not change. The design of FC faces a key challenge to maintain the integrity of the secure compartments within a single virtual address space by preventing the unsafe foreign functions from accessing the enclosed memory pages. The problem is that both the trusted Rust code and the untrustworthy foreign function are sharing a process, giving them equal operating system-level privileges for modifying memory page permissions. A seemingly simple solution would be to isolate the unsafe code in a separate process. However, this solution requires nontrivial changes to existing code, and can potentially interfere with concurrency in existing Rust programs, which benefit from Rust's clear and memory-safe concurrency model. Our solution preserves the current concurrency structure of the code while providing an inexpensive mechanism to maintain the integrity of secure compartments, specifically by disabling the unsafe code from subverting the policies set by the Rust code.

Creating and Reversing Secure Compartments As shown in the FC-ified code of Figure 1, one private secure compartment holds server.key and an immutable secure compartment holds traffic and worker.session_key (since both are on the same memory page, one call to FC will create a shared secure compartment for traffic and worker.session_key).

Creating the secure compartments starts with a trusted Rust function call to fc_immutable(var) (or fc_private(var)) to provide protection for all data objects in the memory page where var exists. In the example code of Figure 1, this is repeated twice since the secure compartments must be separated by the level of access provided to the unsafe code (a secure compartment cannot be both immutable and private). First, FC examines the number of allocated pages, determines the page addresses, and applies the appropriate permissions to the pages (i.e., PROT_READ for immutable and PROT_NONE for private), creating two secure compartments. Next, FC issues a system call, sending the kernel a list of page addresses that will be in the program's secure compartments (regardless of being in immutable or private compartments) to deny using mprotect on the specified pages. FC also makes a system call to specify a *designated trusted region* (an address in the code section pointing to a function in FC) in the code, which will be allowed (by the kernel) to make mprotect calls for reversing page permissions in the secure compartments. The kernel records the trusted region's address and page addresses in a protected address table (Section 2.4) and monitors requests to modify permissions of the protected pages.

2.4 Kernel Module

To designate a trusted region for kernel protection, we implemented a Linux kernel module that traps all mprotect calls (from those processes carrying a special signal from FC) and monitors the protected memory pages.

The kernel extension determines when a call to change page access permissions is legitimate based on code regions. The idea is to designate a specific address range within the Rust code at the time FC creates a secure compartment. The designated address range is communicated to the kernel extension, which will subsequently only allow modifications of the secure compartments to originate and return to the specified address range. The address range is computed at run time according to the fully linked executable.

For security, FC's kernel extension requires that (i) the loaded code to be immutable across the process, except by the operating system or the program loader, (ii) an address A in the code section (address of a function in FC's code, linked to the Rust program), which the kernel can trust to allow mprotect calls to return to, and (iii) the *first* system call from the user space FC, which explicitly asks the kernel to restrict access to mprotect except those returning to A, is trustworthy (done before any unsafe code is executing).

Code Section Permissions The page permissions for the code section (.text in the linked ELF) must be set to PROT_READ, which is ensured by the Rust compiler.[2] FC's kernel extension monitors the page permissions for the code section and deny all mprotect calls to them. This monitoring is only for the parts of the Rust code, which must be given the rights to call mprotect, which is a small subset of the READONLY .text section that fits in a memory page.

Designating the Trusted Region As described in Section 2.3, FC's user space component invokes the kernel component with a system call (FC reuses existing system calls to avoid modifying the kernel) before executing an unsafe function. After creating secure compartments, a call to fc_protect(var) will send the page address on which var exists along with the address of the trusted

---

[2]As tested with the Rust's compiler rustc 1.14.0 (e8a012324 2016-12-16).

region to the kernel (through a system call). fc_protect(var) computes the address of the trusted region as a fixed offset relative to the linked address of fc_protect(var) itself. That is, depending on the number of instructions in fc_protect(var), the offset is manually computed and hard coded in FC's code and is relative to the address given to fc_protect(var) by the linker. The off-

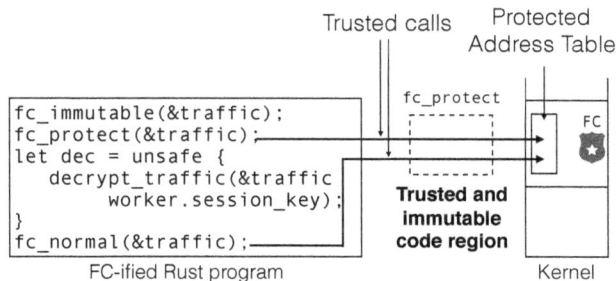

Figure 2: The trusted region is an address (in the code of FC's user space library) to which calls from mprotect must return to, which is ensured by FC's kernel module.

Designating the trusted region must come from a trusted part of the code, which is code written in Rust and is assumed to have compile-time memory guarantees. As the programs must always start execution in Rust's main function, assuming the programmer has FC-ified the program around all calls to unsafe foreign functions, the first use of fc_protect(var) is trusted to be from the Rust program. In the example shown in Figure 2, a new line of code is added to the body of process_traffic (from Figure 1), which performs the trusted call. Upon receiving the call, FC's kernel module disables mprotect and records the address of the protected page and the trusted region's address in the protected address table. The trusted code region's address is the address to which subsequent mprotect calls on the protected memory pages must return. The call to fc_normal perfroms a system call asking FC's kernel module to first allow calls to mprotect and then reverse page permissions. Before re-enabling mprotect, the kernel checks the instruction pointer of the requesting task to verify the return address from the call against the recorded address in the protected address table. When a malicious call to fc_normal is made, the instruction pointer has an invalid address, and FC's kernel module's policy policy is to kill the process (although other actions could be used for applications where fail safety is important). We will further analyze the security of FC's kernel module and possible attacks in Section 2.5.

2.5 Security Analysis

We examine the security guarantees achieved by FC from an attacker's perspective. According to our threat model, the attacker is only capable of a remote attack, for example by crafting requests to a server. FC's effectiveness depends on both the attackers goals and capabilities, and how much data the program exposes to vulnerable unsafe components.

Protection Against Data Attacks The main goal of FC's design is to thwart attacks that depend on reading or modifying sensitive data in the program's memory. The attacker's gateway to the program's memory is through unchecked memory boundaries in the unsafe external library. Once exploited, the attacker can potentially search through all accessible memory to find the target data. The attacker's task is easier when the calling frame from the trusted region can be identified (for accessing stack data), and when a reference to memory allocated on heap is passed to the unsafe function.

First, identifying the calling frame enables the attacker to access data allocated in the trusted region. This data is completely protected by FC, except for any data that is on the calling frame's page. Provided that the programmer does not violate FC's intended usage (by not declaring sensitive data objects in the calling frame), the attacker cannot manipulate or read data on the stack. Second, when the unsafe function has a pointer to a memory allocated in the heap, the attacker can identify the region of the memory that is likely to contain sensitive data. As heap is allocated on consecutive memory addresses, the attacker can attempt to access pages that may belong to the heap. FC protects memory in the heap as requested by the programmer. Thus, all memory pages that were designated to move to secure compartments are not accessible by the attacker, when executing in isolation mode. One limitation of FC is that there may be heap memory allocated for libraries that are not visible to the programmer. It is also important to note that any data in memory that is used as indirect jump location or memory reference is potentially sensitive; if such references are exposed to the adversary, they may be corrupted to allow jumps that bypass FC protections or to copy sensitive data into locations that are not protected in a future unsafe call.

Bypassing FC's protection Bypassing FC involves issuing calls to mprotect with a list of addresses to be set to PROT_READ OR PROT_WRITE. First, the attacker is required to identify which memory pages are of interest. Second, a separate call to mprotect is needed for each memory page. An alternative is that the attacker brute-forces the range of all virtual memory addresses and sets the protection for all pages to PROT_READ OR PROT_WRITE.

FC's primary line of defense is the kernel-level discretionary access control based on code regions. As explained in Section 2.4, FC's kernel module only allows mprotect to succeed on memory pages that are not in the list of the task's secure compartments. Also, FC will not allow such calls to succeed if the current task's instruction pointer does not indicate the address of FC's library function in the trusted region, which renders the attack unfeasible. There is, however, a possibility of launching a return-oriented programming attack by chaining a set of gadgets within the trusted region to call mprotect and trick the kernel to releasing secure compartments. The limitation of this attack is that the only possibility of an execution path is to re-execute the calling trusted function to first release the secure compartments and then make a call to the unsafe library function allowing the attacker to continue execution within the unsafe function. Such an attack is not possible as calls to FC should always create the secure compartments first and then release them, calling the unsafe function in between. Repeating this execution only trigger's FC's kernel module to be cautious of the process and terminate it as this will involve multiple consequent calls to create secure compartments.

3 CASE STUDIES

FC assumes a knowledgeable programmer who uses its core functions to perform the necessary protections. In general, FC's protections could be highly automated, but our current implemention only automates stack protection. As automating heap protection involves many low-level details including implementing a custom memory allocator, we leave it for future work. We present here our experience in FC-ifying a server based on Rust's openssl crate (https://github.com/sfackler/rust-openssl); we also FC-ified a similar Rust TLS server based on the hyper crate (https://github.com/ctz/hyper-rustls/) but since the experience and results were similar we only describe openssl in detail here. We show performance results for both in Section 4.

FC-ifying openssl The openssl crate relies heavily on the foreign function interface to fully implement a TLS server based on the functionality provided in the original openssl library implemented in C. Similar to hyper, the server using openssl can be FC-ified for protecting the acceptor object when handling a client.

An acceptor object contains the server's credentials. The acceptor is stored in a Mutex, which is in turn managed by a heap memory under an instance of Arc. The objective of the FC-ified openssl implementation is to secure the heap page that contains the server's private key. For each incoming connection, at the time the client is served in a dedicated thread, the program no longer needs access to the acceptor. Thus, after the thread receives a pointer to the acceptor (acceptor.clone), locks the Mutex (acceptor.lock), and finally accepts the connection (acceptor.accept(stream)), a call to fc_protect(acceptor_addr) will result in a secure compartment for the heap page on which the acceptor resides. This secures the private key which will be inaccessible to the unsafe code. The call to fc_auto_stack and the corresponding call to fc_auto_stack_reverse will automatically protect the stack pages, and the call to kernel_disable! and kernel_enable! (kernel_disable! and kernel_enable! are macros to facilitate using FC's interface with the kernel fc_protect as described in Section 2.4) that restrict access to sys_mprotect. The call to a helper macro, stack_padding! allocates auxiliary memory on stack, ensuring that the data allocated prior to the call remains on a separate virtual memory page.

Attacks Thwarted FC can be used in various ways depending on the needs. The main goal is to prevent exposing the server's credentials and the program's state (mainly on stack) when interacting with untrustworthy clients and executing unsafe code. For complex servers, the handling function may include references to commodity unsafe libraries that can jeopardize the security guarantees of the program, causing arbitrary data leak. FC guarantees that the explicitly protected data remains unreachable when such an attack occurs. FC releases the secure compartments, when called through fc_normal, after completing a client processing. This ensures that the server's credentials are only accessible when the server can make sure a malicious client is no longer connected. A slight limitation of this implementation is when serving clients for long periods, which can cause long delays for concurrently connecting clients

```
1   fn openssl_listener() {
2       let acceptor = load_ssl_acceptor();
3       stack_padding!();
4       let acceptor = Arc::new(Mutex::new(acceptor));
5       let acceptor_ptr = acceptor.clone();
6       let acceptor_addr = memory_page_addr!(*acceptor_ptr);
7       let listener = TcpListener::bind(SERVER_IP).unwrap();
8       for stream in listener.incoming() {
9           match stream {
10              Ok(stream) => {
11                  let acceptor = acceptor.clone();
12                  let child = thread::spawn(move || {
13                      let acceptor = acceptor.lock().unwrap();
14                      let mut stream = acceptor.accept(stream).unwrap();
15                      fc_private_u(acceptor_addr);
16                      fc_auto_stack();
17                      kernel_disable!(acceptor_addr as usize);
18                      handle_client(&mut stream);
19                      kernel_enable!();
20                      fc_auto_stack_reverse();
21                      fc_normal_u(acceptor_addr);
22                  });
23                  child.join().unwrap();
24              }
25              Err(_) => { /* connection failed */ }
26          }
27          break;
28      }
29  }
```

Figure 3: Starts a FC-ified server, while protecting the server's private key after a new client connection is established. This function is thread-safe and does not cause segmentation fault for accessing the protected acceptor.

(as the acceptor object is locked while serving the client). One can prevent this limitation by generating multiple copies of the acceptor with a pool of worker threads model. Each thread would use FC to protect its own copy.

4 PERFORMANCE

This section reports on our experiments to evaluate the run-time cost of FC, first showing results on a set of microbenchmarks, and then reporting application-level performance measurements on the openssl and hyper case study applications from Section 3.

4.1 Microbenchmarks

For the microbenchmarks, our goal is to understand the cost of each of the operations involved in using FC. We use Rust's benchmarking interface to measure the cost for creating secure compartments, launching and processing a plain openssl request, and launching and processing a FC-ified openssl request, as implemented in Figure 3.

Table 1 reports the cost of using FC's main interfaces. The *Base* benchmark is an empty closure for measuring the benchmarking interface's cost. The *Padding* benchmark is a closure which isolates two memory pages using 512×64 byte arrays. *Creating Secure Compartment* is a closure that introduces padding, modifies the isolated page's permissions, communicates the page address to the kernel module, and reverses page permissions and requests the kernel to re-enable access to the specified page address.

The last two rows in Table 1 compare the time require to launch an openssl-based HTTP server and processing a single client using a plain Rust implementation and a FC-enabled implementation. The results shown are the average over multiples of multi-iteration tests, in which some of the tests did not distinguish the difference at all. FC's cost is negligible relative to the overall cost of openssl. The cost of FC is slightly more noticeable in the system benchmarks presented next. We performed the tests on a vmware Workstation virtual machine on a local disk with Ubuntu 15 as the host system, configured to use two of the available four cores and two GBs of memory.

Experiment	Time (ms)
Base	0.000024
Padding	0.0054
Creating Secure Compartment	0.0105
openssl server	14.342
FC-ified openssl server	14.385 (0.29% increase)

Table 1: Microbenchmark results.

4.2 System Benchmarks

In the second and third settings, we test the performance of unsafe operations in TLS-based HTTP servers, which either use unsafe operations for invoking openssl operations or make calls to Rust's ring library, which in turn makes unsafe calls to cryptographic functions. We perform a time comparison between a plain HTTP server that doesn't use FC and an FC-ified HTTP server. FC's latency includes the small overhead of the kernel module, which is disabled in experiments without FC.

HTTP server Measuring the throughput of a openssl-based and a hyper-based HTTP server required implementing benchmarking tools for a precise measuring of the contribution of each thread in processing the requests. In the openssl-based server, for each request three secure compartments are created prior to handling the process and one secure compartment is created for handling the process. We measure the throughput by running the test for 60 seconds while automatically sending HTTP requests in intervals of 10 milliseconds, collecting the number of successfully processed requests at the end of the experiment. In each iteration, all four secure compartments are created and destroyed. FC maintains modest overhead even when handling 128 simultaneous request threads, reaching a pick decrease of 5% in the number of requests processed in 60 seconds. FC's overhead was noticeable when every request involved 50 calls to ring for computing a file's digest, with an average decrease of 13.69% processed requests occurred. Finally, when using a duration of 30–100 seconds with a fixed number of 16 simultaneous requests processed in intervals of 10 milliseconds, the average decrease in the number of requests processed was 8.30% (Figure 4.

In the hyper-based server, the throughput was measured similar to the benchmark of Figure 4 in which a growing number of threads

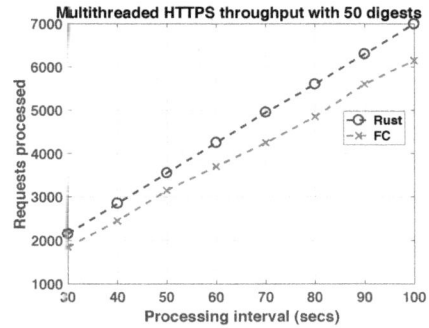

Figure 4: Throughput of an openssl HTTP in 30–100 seconds. Each request has 50 calls to ring's digest. In the FC-enabled server, each digest iteration creates and releases a secure compartment.

send simultaneous requests. All requests were implemented as echo requests. In the FC-enabled version, during the time the client is served, the server's private key is totally isolated and is unusable. To serve multiple clients, for each request, the private key is cloned and once the shared key is established, the cloned private key will be kept in a separate secure compartment. The result of the experiment is in Figure 5, showing an average decrease of 1.38% in the number of requests processed.

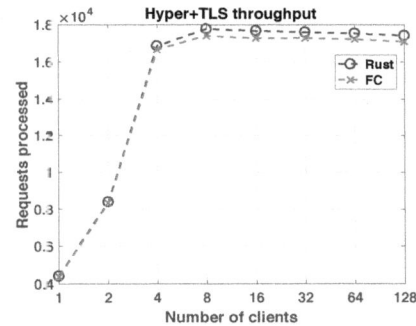

Figure 5: Throughput of a Hyper server using Rust TLS in 60 seconds. Requests are sent locally using 2^k threads for $k \in [0,7]$.

5 RELATED WORK

The goal of isolating code components (also referred to as application compartmentalization) is a long-standing goal of our community and has been the focus of extensive research in operating systems, programming languages, and architecture. This is the first work to focus on isolating unsafe code within a single address space for Rust programs.

In terms of our memory model and isolation techniques, previous works most similar to FC include Native Client [30], Codejail [29], HideM [9], SeCage [15], Shred [7], lwC [14], and SpaceJMP [12]. We discuss these next, followed by a brief account of classical work on software fault isolation and the principle of least privilege.

Sandboxing Libraries Native Client [30] provided memory sandboxing for libraries, allowing limited interaction with the trusted program using remote procedure calls. Fidelis Charm and Native Client (NaCI) share the main objective of limiting external libraries, however, differ in approach and applicability. In contrast with NaCI's approach for loading libraries in limited containers, FC contains the trusted memory when interacting with unsafe libraries. Codejail [29] proposed an enhancement of the idea by sandboxing a library by disallowing write access to the program's data, making the sensitive memory read-only. The program would selectively allow write access to its data, when a tight interaction with the library is needed. Codejail shares FC's goals in (i) proposing a secure memory sharing model that does not require modifications to the library and (ii) supporting tight and limited interactions with an untrustworthy library. Aside from focusing on Rust, FC is distinguished in that the memory of the trusted program is the sandbox, instead of the library, and unless a data object must be shared with the library, the entire memory allocated either on stack or heap of the trusted Rust code is inaccessible to the library. This key difference in memory sandboxing model overcomes Codejail's limitation of libraries within a specific memory regions.

Various techniques have been developed for confining and limiting processes or groups of processes (e.g., [1, 8, 10, 13, 18, 19, 23]), aiming for isolating vulnerable software from critical system resources. In the design of FC, a sandbox would avoid incuring unnecessary latency as our goal is to isolate code at the fine level of (often frequent) unsafe calls. That said, sandboxing using Intel enclaves [13] can provide improved security for FC's kernel module.

Memory partitioning Shared memory among distrustful threads within a single process is addressed by Arbiter [27], which proposes to use memory permission bits to protect a thread's data from another. Arbiter uses to a policy manager that understands programmer-annotated privileges and enforces them. FC uses memory page padding to separate and isolate data objects based on a simple binary permission system (immutable or private). The kernel component in FC only enforces FC's integrity and does not need to enforce application-level policies. HideM [9] takes a radical approach by using split-TCB to show different contents of a page for different CPU operations, hiding data when a specified code region should not have access to it. In contrast, FC temporarily hides the actual memory page and isolates the data when an explicit interaction with an untrustworthy library function occurs. SeCage [15] is similar to HideM in providing different views of the memory according to separated privileges. Using hardware virtualization, SeCage targets a strong adversary model in which the operating system does not need to be trusted.

Shred [7], light-weight context (lwC) [14], and SpaceJMP [12] are new methods for splitting the virtual address space into multiple distinct sections aiming for isolating untrustworthy code. Shreds and lwC introduce abstractions similar to threads. To protect data across a program, Shred provides a set of programming interfaces to request creating and moving data into separate Shreds. At runtime, Shreds are implemented using Intel's memory protection keys. A lwC, in contrast, does not work with memory permissions directly but creates separate address spaces, when the programmer requests that using the programming interfaces. SpaceJMP is similar to lwCs in using multiple virtual address space, differing from lwCs in that

SpaceJMP enables memory sharing across multiple processes. While FC is similar to these in that it provides an interface for isolating memory regions, it does not propose a new operating system model and does not require switches between address spaces.

Other related work but farther away have provided interesting contributions for application compartmentalization, mainly with narrow and specific applicability. For example, Mimosa specifically targets cryptographic keys and uses hardware transactional memory to ensure that no process, other than Mimosa, can access the keys. Mimosa uses encryption to hide the keys, when the system is idle. Although FC and Mimosa agree on a high level goal of hiding data objects in memory, FC differs in that it uses memory isolation without the need for hardware transactional memory and works with arbitrary data. DataShield [5] protects data in C++ programs by disallowing pointer dereferencing based on programmer annotations. Song et al. propose a data-flow integrity approach to infer and enforce correct flow of sensitive data in kernel space [24]. Lastly, SOAAP [11] is a reasoning tool for assisting programmers in using application compartmentalization to avoid security and correctness errors. We envision a similar tool for our future work to support programmers with FC and automate the task of locating unsafe regions and the data objects that must be isolated.

Software fault isolation has consistently received attention during the past decades. Simple solutions such as placing the faulty code, or the unsafe code, in a separate address space seem viable, although for merely a call to an unsafe function, the unnecessary context switches are too much of a burden. Wahbe et al. pioneered the design of logically separated fault domains within a single address space [26], which was followed by an effort to isolate addressability from accessibility in Opal, a single-address-space 64-bit architecture [6]. The work in [26] described a model in which fault domains are separated based on the code region through restricting the execution of one to jump to another. This model inspired our kernel-centric code region discrimination design, with a fundamental difference; FC would not require an RPC interface to enable cross-domain interactions. In fact, FC imposes no particular paradigm on the program and automates code region separation through a kernel extension.

The principle of least privilege [22] is the theme of a number of previous work that promised least privilege isolation. With resource containers [2] separating access control from execution, isolation progressed further towards decoupling scheduling from security requirements, which were a fundamental design issue with process management in modern monolithic kernels. The work by Provos et. al set a clear goal: privilege separation within an application forbids programming errors in the lower privileged code from abusing higher privileged code [20]. However, privilege separation was a return back to the use of processes as basic blocks for isolation, reusing UNIX per-process protection domains. Privtrans [4] automated privilege separation using programmer annotations, partitioning a program into a monitor and a slave program, continuing the efforts of isolation at the process level. Sthreads in Wedge [3] introduced default-deny compartments within a single monolithic program, spawning new threads, not entire processes, for isolating parts of the program. Sthreads enjoy programmer tagged memory access rights, which are enforced at runtime. Programmer annotated privileges were also introduced for isolating kernel modules [17] from core kernel services to prevent privilege escalation. Similarly, Trellis [16] allows code-annotated privileges (mainly for memory allocations), which are enforced by the kernel at runtime. CHERI [28], a hardware extension relying on a capability co-processor, supports compartmentalization for in-address-space memory isolation targeting the C language.

Finally, RustBelt [21] develops a subet of Rust, namely λ_{Rust}, and uses to prove the safety of Rust programs. An important result provided by RustBelt is verification of safety while using unsafe interactions with linked libraries. Rustbelt verifies a λ_{Rust} program with unsafe code has safely encapsulated the externally linked library using within Rust wrappers.

6 CONCLUSION

Rust provides strong memory guarantees using zero-cost abstractions, but any non-trivial Rust program today includes unsafe code and most fall back on using libraries in unsafe languages. A long-range goal should be to eliminate the need for any unsafe code— developing native Rust libraries when possible, and when arbitrary memory operations are needed using more powerful formal methods to prove the safety of code that cannot be proven safe by Rust's compiler. A practical path to dramatic improvements in program safety and reliability, however, requires combining safe and unsafe code. Incorporating any unsafe code into a Rust program, however, abandons all of the safety guarantees. Fidelius Charm provides a step towards safe incorporation of unsafe code by isolating sensitive data in memory from the unsafe code. We achieved a high level of isolation, without requiring any compiler changes or complex abstractions, and in a way that can be applied to any Rust program when interacting with any unsafe library function.

Acknowledgements

This work was partially supported by a grant from the National Science Foundation (SaTC, #1422332).

REFERENCES

[1] Hussain M. J. Almohri, Danfeng Yao, and Dennis G. Kafura. 2014. Process Authentication for High System Assurance. *IEEE Trans. Dependable Secur. Comput.* 11, 2 (March 2014), 168–180. https://doi.org/10.1109/TDSC.2013.29

[2] Gaurav Banga, Peter Druschel, and Jeffrey C. Mogul. 1999. Resource Containers: A New Facility for Resource Management in Server Systems. In *Proceedings of the Third Symposium on Operating Systems Design and Implementation.* 45–58.

[3] Andrea Bittau, Petr Marchenko, Mark Handley, and Brad Karp. 2008. Wedge: Splitting Applications into Reduced-Privilege Compartments. In *Proceedings of the 5th USENIX Symposium on Networked Systems Design and Implementation (NSDI'08).* 309–322.

[4] David Brumley and Dawn Xiaodong Song. 2004. Privtrans: Automatically Partitioning Programs for Privilege Separation. In *USENIX Security Symposium.*

[5] Scott A. Carr and Mathias Payer. 2017. DataShield: Configurable Data Confidentiality and Integrity. In *Proceedings of the 2017 ACM Asia Conference on Computer and Communications Security (ASIA CCS '17).* ACM, New York, NY, USA, 193–204. https://doi.org/10.1145/3052973.3052983

[6] Jeffrey S. Chase, Henry M. Levy, Michael J. Feeley, and Edward D. Lazowska. 1994. Sharing and Protection in a Single-Address-Space Operating System. *ACM Trans. Comput. Syst.* 12 (1994), 271–307.

[7] Y. Chen, S. Reymondjohnson, Z. Sun, and L. Lu. 2016. Shreds: Fine-Grained Execution Units with Private Memory. In *Proceedings of the 2016 IEEE Symposium on Security and Privacy (SP).* 56–71. https://doi.org/10.1109/SP.2016.12

[8] Bryan Ford and Russ Cox. 2008. Vx32: Lightweight User-level Sandboxing on the x86. In *USENIX 2008 Annual Technical Conference (ATC'08).* USENIX Association, Berkeley, CA, USA, 293–306. http://dl.acm.org/citation.cfm?id=1404014.1404039

[9] Jason Gionta, William Enck, and Peng Ning. 2015. HideM: Protecting the Contents of Userspace Memory in the Face of Disclosure Vulnerabilities. In *Proceedings of the 5th ACM Conference on Data and Application Security and Privacy (CODASPY '15).* ACM, New York, NY, USA, 325–336. https://doi.org/10.1145/2699026.2699107

[10] Anitha Gollamudi and Stephen Chong. 2016. Automatic enforcement of expressive security policies using enclaves. In *Proceedings of the 2016 ACM SIGPLAN International Conference on Object-Oriented Programming, Systems, Languages, and Applications (OOPSLA 2016).* ACM, New York, NY, USA, 494–513. https://doi.org/10.1145/2983990.2984002

[11] Khilan Gudka, Robert N. M. Watson, Jonathan Anderson, David Chisnall, Brooks Davis, Ben Laurie, Ilias Marinos, Peter G. Neumann, and Alex Richardson. 2015. Clean Application Compartmentalization with SOAAP. In *ACM Conference on Computer and Communications Security.*

[12] Izzat El Hajj, Alex Merritt, Gerd Zellweger, Dejan S. Milojicic, Reto Achermann, Paolo Faraboschi, Wen mei W. Hwu, Timothy Roscoe, and Karsten Schwan. 2016. SpaceJMP: Programming with Multiple Virtual Address Spaces. In *ASPLOS.*

[13] Dmitrii Kuvaiskii, Oleksii Oleksenko, Sergei Arnautov, Bohdan Trach, Pramod Bhatotia, Pascal Felber, and Christof Fetzer. 2017. SGXBOUNDS: Memory Safety for Shielded Execution. In *EuroSys.*

[14] James Litton, Anjo Vahldiek-Oberwagner, Eslam Elnikety, Deepak Garg, Bobby Bhattacharjee, and Peter Druschel. 2016. Light-weight Contexts: An OS Abstraction for Safety and Performance. In *Proceedings of the 12th USENIX Conference on Operating Systems Design and Implementation (OSDI'16).* USENIX Association, Berkeley, CA, USA, 49–64. http://dl.acm.org/citation.cfm?id=3026877.3026882

[15] Yutao Liu, Tianyu Zhou, Kexin Chen, Haibo Chen, and Yubin Xia. 2015. Thwarting Memory Disclosure with Efficient Hypervisor-enforced Intra-domain Isolation. In *ACM Conference on Computer and Communications Security.*

[16] Andrea Mambretti, Kaan Onarlioglu, Collin Mulliner, William Robertson, Engin Kirda, Federico Maggi, and Stefano Zanero. 2016. Trellis: Privilege Separation for Multi-user Applications Made Easy. In *International Symposium on Research in Attacks, Intrusions, and Defenses.* Springer, 437–456.

[17] Yandong Mao, Haogang Chen, Dong Zhou, Xi Wang, Nickolai Zeldovich, and M. Frans Kaashoek. 2011. Software fault isolation with API integrity and multi-principal modules. In *SOSP.*

[18] Erman Pattuk, Murat Kantarcioglu, Zhiqiang Lin, and Huseyin Ulusoy. 2014. Preventing Cryptographic Key Leakage in Cloud Virtual Machines. In *USENIX Security Symposium.*

[19] David S. Peterson, Matt Bishop, and Raju Pandey. 2002. A Flexible Containment Mechanism For Executing Untrusted Code. In *USENIX Security Symposium.*

[20] Niels Provos, Markus Friedl, and Peter Honeyman. 2003. Preventing Privilege Escalation. In *USENIX Security Symposium.*

[21] Robbert Krebbers Derek Dreyer Ralf Jung, Jacques-Henri Jourdan. 2018. RustBelt: Securing the Foundations of the Rust Programming Language. In *Proceedings of the 45th ACM SIGPLAN Symposium on Principles of Programming Languages (POPL 2018)* ACM, New York, NY, USA. https://doi.org/10.1145/3158154

[22] J. H. Saltier and M. P. Schroeder. 1975. The Protection of information in computer systems. *IEEE CSIT Newsletter* 3, 12 (Dec 1975), 19–19. https://doi.org/10.1109/CSIT.1975.6498831

[23] Rohit Sinha, Manuel Costa, Akash Lal, Nuno P. Lopes, Sriram K. Rajamani, Sanjit A. Seshia, and Kapil Vaswani. 2016. A design and verification methodology for secure isolated regions. In *PLDI.*

[24] Chengyu Song, Byoungyoung Lee, Kangjie Lu, William Harris, Taesoo Kim, and Wenke Lee. 2016. Enforcing Kernel Security Invariants with Data Flow Integrity. In *NDSS.*

[25] Laszlo Szekeres, Mathias Payer, Tao Wei, and Dawn Xiaodong Song. 2013. SoK: Eternal War in Memory. In *Proceedings of the 2013 IEEE Symposium on Security and Privacy (SP '13).* IEEE Computer Society, Washington, DC, USA, 48–62. https://doi.org/10.1109/SP.2013.13

[26] Robert Wahbe, Steven Lucco, Thomas E. Anderson, and Susan L. Graham. 1993. Efficient Software-Based Fault Isolation. In *SOSP.*

[27] Jun Wang, Xi Xiong, and Peng Liu. 2015. Between Mutual Trust and Mutual Distrust: Practical Fine-grained Privilege Separation in Multithreaded Applications. In *USENIX Annual Technical Conference.*

[28] Robert N. M. Watson, Jonathan Woodruff, Peter G. Neumann, Simon W. Moore, Jonathan Anderson, David Chisnall, Nirav H. Dave, Brooks Davis, Khilan Gudka, Ben Laurie, Steven J. Murdoch, Robert Norton, Michael Roe, Stacey D. Son, and Munraj Vadera. 2015. CHERI: A Hybrid Capability-System Architecture for Scalable Software Compartmentalization. *2015 IEEE Symposium on Security and Privacy* (2015), 20–37.

[29] Yongzheng Wu, Sai Sathyanarayan, Roland H. C. Yap, and Zhenkai Liang. 2012. Codejail: Application-Transparent Isolation of Libraries with Tight Program Interactions. In *ESORICS.*

[30] Bennet Yee, David Sehr, Gregory Dardyk, J. Bradley Chen, Robert Muth, Tavis Ormandy Shiki Okasaka, Neha Narula, and Nicholas Fullagar. 2009. Native Client: A Sandbox for Portable, Untrusted x86 Native Code. *2009 30th IEEE Symposium on Security and Privacy* (2009), 79–93.

A Multi-Enterprise Containerization Approach with an Interoperable Position-Based System

Oyindamola Oluwatimi
Purdue University
West Lafayette, Indiana
ooluwati@gmail.com

Elisa Bertino
Purdue University
West Lafayette, Indiana
bertino@purdue.edu

ABSTRACT

In this paper, we present our position-based, **M**ulti-**E**nte**R**rise **C**ontainerization (MERC) architecture for BYOD security. The MERC architecture leverages positional data to grant context-aware capabilities to container-based systems. We grant enterprises the ability of defining location- and proximity-based conditions that must be met in order for users to securely access enterprise container content. First, we provide a scalable location-based scheme that allows multiple enterprise context-aware systems to securely coexist and activate policies and personas on an end-user's device. Second, the MERC incorporates proximity-based constraints to modify a persona's behavior. We evaluate our prototype using preexisting infrastructures, and our experimental results show that MERC is an effective and practical solution for BYOD security.

KEYWORDS

Access Control; Android; BYOD; Containerization;Micro-location

ACM Reference Format:
Oyindamola Oluwatimi and Elisa Bertino. 2018. A Multi-Enterprise Containerization Approach with an Interoperable Position-Based System. In *CODASPY '18: Eighth ACM Conference on Data and Application Security and Privacy, March 19–21, 2018, Tempe, AZ, USA.* ACM, New York, NY, USA, 11 pages. https://doi.org/10.1145/3176258.3176311

1 INTRODUCTION

Bring-your-own-device (BYOD) scenarios enable employees to utilize their personal mobile device for enterprise purposes, thereby allowing sensitive enterprise content to be stored and accessed on end-users' devices *anywhere* and *anytime*. However, security is an important, and the most significant, barrier to wide adoption of such dual-use scenarios. In 2016, conducted research found that the top two security concerns of cybersecurity practitioners, such as enterprise IT admins, were data leakage (72%) and unauthorized access to enterprise resources (56%)[34]. In fact, nearly one out of five organizations (21%) experienced a security breach via BYOD vectors. IT admins attempt to mitigate such threats by employing Enterprise Mobility Management (EMM) systems which administer secure containers (e.g., work personas) to end-users' devices[28],

but enterprises continue to suffer due to EMM systems lack of or ineffective access control and monitoring solutions. In this paper, we present MERC to address practical contextual access control requirements that many enterprises encounter.

We identify a few shortcomings of contemporary EMM systems in which this paper is motivated by. First, EMM systems do not consider the context in which personas are employed. EMM systems, such as KNOX[28], do not provide enterprises a means to specify or enforce contextual constraints to control access to or influence the behavior of personas. Second, modern EMM systems assume that each end-user uses her device for only one enterprise. We argue that EMM systems need to support *multi-enterprise* environments, as end-users may interface with a variety of first/third-parties with potentially conflicting contextual access control policies. To limit risks of unauthorized access, it is imperative that organizations employ secure means of *contextual authentication and authorization* to protect enterprise content after it is downloaded to end-users' devices. As contextual information can be quite encompassing, in the rest of the discussion, we limit context to its most common representation, that is, positional information. Section 2 provides motivating scenarios that require position-based services (PBS) to be secure and flexible in multi-enterprise BYOD scenarios.

In this paper, we present the design of our MERC context-aware system (CAS) that utilizes our PBS to influence the behavior of containers. The MERC architecture limits employees' accesses to work personas and enterprise content within them dynamically and passively through the enforcement of context-based constraints. The novelty of our system is twofold. First, our system is the first to apply both location- *and* proximity-based (hereinafter, context/ual) constraints to containers. Second, we utilize sound to determine a device's logical location. We observe that many proposed PBSs are radio-based, and objects of various size, shape, and material in the environment can obstruct the propagation path of radio signals, thus diminishing the accuracy. For example, the work by Bocca et al.[8] demonstrates the effect of human interference on the propagation path of radio signals. Instead, we leverage the unique characteristics of sound that make it suitable for supporting PBSs. First, unlike radio signals, sound is inherently localized as it cannot penetrate walls or propagate over long distances. Second, it does not require a line-of-sight, as with GNSS systems whose signal degrades if a device is within a building. Third, the audio frequency of sound can be shifted so that it is inaudible to the human ear (i.e., ultrasound). To detect the proximity of other users, we also leverage Bluetooth low energy (BLE) capabilities of mobile devices as standardized BLE protocols provide proximity ranging measurements. We implemented our custom Android operating system (OS), MERCOS, on Pixel C and Nexus 6P, which OEMs can readily incorporate into their proprietary EMMs (e.g., Samsung KNOX[28]). Enterprises can also readily deploy our custom PBS using devices with microphones, speakers, and Bluetooth pervaded in existing mobile IT and building infrastructures[18]. Last, we extend Android Device Administration policies with proximity-based constraints to influence persona behavior.

The contributions of this work can be summarized as followed:

(1) *Position-Based Containerization:* We propose a context-based containerization policy enforcement scheme to control BYOD devices based upon positional constraints. Different from existing containerization architectures, our approach is the first to introduce proximity-based constraints to Android containers.

(2) *Position-Based Service:* We investigate the feasibility of a novel application of ultrasound to determine a user's location. We also evaluate proximity-based detection via BLE. Our results produced high accuracy, with 100% location detection accuracy and a maximum false negative rate of 4% in proximity detection accuracy while introducing a minor impact on battery life, thus demonstrating the feasibility and effectiveness of our solution.

(3) *Secure Beacon Protocol:* We propose an acoustic-based protocol that addresses several significant challenges in supporting a multi-enterprise position-based architecture, including interoperability, privacy, and security.

The paper is organized as follows. Section 2 introduces position-based scenarios that motivate this work. We provide background information on PBSs, proximity-based access control, and Android in Section 3. Sections 4 and 5 introduce the architecture of our approach followed by the implementation and technical details in Section 6. We next report our experimental results in Section 7. We analyze the security of our approach in Section 8. Next, we further discuss relevant work in Section 9. Section 10 concludes the paper.

2 MOTIVATING SCENARIOS

Pervasive computing has enabled CASs to be leveraged in a variety of settings, including enterprise organizations[35]. Our paper specifically targets enterprises that are currently using EMM systems to manage employees' devices, but require that such systems be context-aware. In terms of access control, such systems aim to secure access to sensitive content on employees' devices by adapting access authorizations to the current context *without* explicit user intervention. Below, we describe two scenarios motivating the need to incorporate context-aware capabilities within EMM systems.

Consider an enterprise setting in which two, but independent enterprise organizations exist. Each enterprise allows enterprise containers, containing sensitive content, to exist on employees' devices. Each employee, regardless of the enterprise, is assigned a role that reflects the privileges granted to that employee within the respective organization. *NekSec*, the first enterprise, is a network security consulting agency whose objective is to identify security vulnerabilities within a client's computer network infrastructure. *Banker*, the second enterprise, is a financial institution that provides online banking facilities to its customers. Two relevant roles within *NekSec* and *Banker* are (network) *Supervisor* and *Consultant.*

With respect to accessing enterprise content, the role Supervisor grants an employee many privileges. The privileges assigned to the Consultant role vary depending on whether the consultant is an external or internal entity to the organization. However, we focus on the former in our paper, which is further discussed below.

Location-based Containerization Scenario. *An enterprise container belonging to NekSec is deployed to Alice's, a NekSec Consultant, smartphone. The container's content is highly sensitive as it contains confidential information regarding NekSec's clients. The enterprise requires that the container must only be accessible on NekSec's campus.* The scenario reflects a real world circumstance in which an employee only has access to resources while the employee is on premise. For example, an employee would normally only be able to access his/her enterprise user account via *stationary* terminals; the terminals do not leave the work premise. However, implications of BYOD must be considered. The dual use of mobile devices allows employees to remotely access resources that otherwise would not be accessible outside of the enterprise setting. Therefore, such circumstances require that containers (e.g., user accounts or personas) must only be accessible at specific locations.

Proximity-based Containerization Scenario. *Banker's network Supervisor has hired Alice to investigate the possible existence of insider threats and the leakage of confidential financial information through the institution's network-enabled computing devices. Similarly, to conduct her investigation, a Banker container with confidential network security data has been deployed to Alice's smartphone, but can only be accessed within a designated office on Banker's campus. In addition, only employees with the role of Supervisor or higher are authorized to be within Alice's immediate proximity while in the office.*

This scenario also reflects real world circumstances; in fact, 23% of enterprises make BYOD available to contractors[34]. Consultants are often hired to temporarily provide their expertise on an on-going project, but are only granted a limited set of privileges required to execute their duties. In addition, investigating the existence of nefarious activities executed by employees is of a sensitive nature; Banker should be extremely cautious not to alert low level employees that are concluded to have malicious intent. Consequently, such circumstances require that containers must only be accessible depending on proximity-based information.

3 BACKGROUND

3.1 Position-based Services

PBSs[39] have the ability to detect the current position of user devices, and such services are important in variety of settings including BYOD access control enforcement. PBSs vary with respect to many parameters, such as the position technologies on which they are based, security, privacy, affordability, resource requirements (e.g., memory or power consumption), and precision level of positional data, and therefore have their inherent advantages and disadvantages. For example, geofencing PBSs are able to place a user within a predefined area such as with the use of GPS. Microlocation PBSs can locate a user with high accuracy such as with the use of Ultra Wide-Band radios to provide an accuracy as high as 10 cm. Other positioning techniques based on different technologies include Infrared (IR), Radio Frequency (RF), Radio Frequency Identification (RFID)[22], magnetic field[25], acoustic mediums[23, 31], Bluetooth[9], and WiFi [6, 8, 33, 35].

Acoustic communication is a possible technology for both geofencing and microlocation PBSs[10, 23]. By applying coding schemes, data can be transmitted and received through the air using acoustic hardware in mobile devices. Various coding schemes (e.g., on-off keying) have been proposed that encode data into sound by modulating sound wave properties, such as frequency, amplitude, or phase which affect the bit rate, bit error rate, and range of transmission [10, 23]. As our work targets BYOD, we are particularly interested in encoding mechanisms that allow reliable acoustic communication using audio signals not perceivable to humans. That is, we embed location-based information in ultrasonic signals that operate at frequencies above 18 kHz, which is understood to be frequencies at which adult humans are unable to detect. Developing or determining the optimal encoding scheme that allows efficient transmission of ultrasonic signals is outside the scope of the paper. We utilize a third-party sound-based, data communication SDK [30] to embed and extract location information within ultrasonic signals. With such a SDK, we are able to transmit data at the speed of sound, which is approximately 340 m/s[31] at standard temperature and pressure.

Leveraging widely-used microlocation BLE-based beacon protocols, a beacon region or the proximity of other BLE-enabled devices can be detected in an energy efficient manner[39]. Detection is achieved by periodically broadcasting BLE beacons. Each beacon protocol has a different beacon construction, but we utilize Google's Eddystone implementation as it incorporates features that our MERCOS leverages (c.f. Section 5). The Eddystone UID is 16 bytes long and consists of two values: Namespace (10 bytes) and Instance (6 bytes). The Namespace value is a UUID (Universally Unique Identifier) that identifies a top-level beacon region. The Instance value identifies sub-beacon regions and can be constructed using any scheme. For example, semantically, a beacon construction could represent the *auditorium within building 10* (i.e., Instance) at NekSec's campus (i.e., Namespace). The beacon also provides two measurements. The distance measurement is an indicator of the proximity of one device to another which is provided by the received signal strength indicator (RSSI). The ranging measurement is an intuitive, user-friendly indicator of the distance between two devices which falls into one of the following ranges: *Immediate* (very close), *Near* (at a distance of 1-3m), *Far* (greater than 3m), or *Unknown* (the distance cannot be accurately determined).

3.2 Proximity-Based Access Control

Role-based access control (RBAC) systems are used in enterprise environments in order to streamline access control policies. In such environments, each user is assigned different roles whereby each role is granted predefined access privileges to enterprise resources. Various access control models and systems have been proposed that augment the RBAC model so that privileges associated with a role can only be exercised if contextual parameters are adhered to. The most common extensions to RBAC are the inclusion of spatial and temporal constraints. GEO-RBAC is an extension of the RBAC model that introduces the concept of spatial roles which

allow an authorized user to assume a role (i.e., role enabling) and exercise its associated privileges (i.e., role activation) only if the user is at a designated location specified by physical coordinates[7]. LoT-RBAC and STARBAC are other augmented RBAC models that incorporate spatio-temporal constraints for role enabling and role activation[2, 11]. Each of these access control models, however, do not have an implemented system able to enforce their policies on EMM containerization solutions.

Proximity-based Access Control (PBAC) [17] is an access control model developed specifically for Smart-Emergency Environments that takes into account the user's proximity to a resource (e.g., a computer). Prox-RBAC [20] builds upon GEO-RBAC with proximity constraints. That is, access control decisions are not solely based on the requesting user's location, but also on the location of other users in the physical space. CASSEC [27] is a system that leverages techniques from previous proximity-based systems to restrict access to enterprise resources by uniquely using WiFi signal interference and Bluetooth as its underlying technique/technology. However, each of these systems do not provide EMM support and relies on PBSs that are costly or ineffective (c.f. Section 9).

3.3 Android Overview

Android for Work (AFW), which has been integrated into Android since version 5.0, is a platform-level EMM system. It introduces the ability for a device to have multiple user profiles (i.e., personas) to isolate content for different device users. A device owner is provided with a default persona, but can create up to a preset limit of personas for her device. A newly created persona, which can be provisioned by Device Administration APIs, is provided with its own clean userspace that includes all the applications from the device owner's persona. These applications do not retain any application data from the original profile, and therefore, once activated, execute as if they were just installed. Each persona is assigned an ID, and from this point forward, we will refer to this as *persona ID*.

4 DESIGN GOALS, CHALLENGES, AND ASSUMPTIONS

The design of a multi-enterprise CAS that utilizes a PBS to influence the behavior of containers introduces several challenges:

Interoperability: We consider the dynamic nature of users in BYOD scenarios involving individuals using their devices for multiple enterprises. The CAS must therefore address the *occupancy detection problem*[15], that is, *who* is and/or *how many* people are in a given space. As such, we aim to make our position-based architecture and secure beacon protocol interoperable so to allow a device's secure container to be influenced even when the device owner moves from one enterprise environment to another.

Privacy: Another design goal is to ensure the confidentiality of enterprise building infrastructures. Some PBSs (e.g., iBeacons) transmit cleartext positional data divulging information particular to a given enterprise. Our system protects such information as enterprises may desire confidentiality.

Security: One design goal is to minimize the trust placed in users of the system. Specifically, we do not rely on users, possibly malicious, to manually report their location or proximity to others. Instead, the system takes a proactive approach by automatically monitoring entities within the environment. In that way, we make access to personas secure and as fluid as possible.

Ease of Integration: Another design goal is to maximize ease of integration into enterprises' IT infrastructures. First, we must consider the method in which we incorporate context-based constraints into existing OEMs' containerization solutions. Second, we intentionally employ sensor technology already integrated into IT infrastructures, thereby removing deployment costs.

Flexibility: As each enterprise environment is unique, we also aim to make the specification of locations as flexible as possible.

Performance: Given that users are assumed to be mobile, continuity of access must be considered; CASs should be readily updated when context changes. For instance, a persona should be quickly activated/deactivated once an employee enters/leaves the workplace. As such, we aim to minimize and simplify the steps in the communication process between the architectural components while not impacting system performance.

4.1 Assumptions

We make the following assumptions about the proposed system and the adversary attempting to view content (i.e., information regarding the current investigation) on Alice's device. Each employee/contractor, including the adversary, has full access to his/her device. Each device has been preauthorized by the IT admin for BYOD use. Preauthorization consists of (1) deploying a work persona to the device in which the IT admin controls and (2) verifying that the device's acoustic and Bluetooth sensors are functioning correctly. Consequently, we assume IT admins can be trusted. We trust the Android access control system, which includes the Android middleware and Linux Kernel, to correctly enforce all security policies. Our ultrasonic beacon protocol requires the exchange of cryptographic keying material between MERC's architectural components to protect communication. We assume that such material is secured. Physical security or video monitoring is employed to prevent the adversary from compromising positioning modules and entering the environment with foreign objects such as a non-secured phone/camera so as to configure a remote monitoring device within Alice's designated office room.

5 MERC SYSTEM ARCHITECTURE

In this section, we describe the MERC architecture. We first describe the architectural components for the sake of defining terms. Next, we provide an overview of the system.

5.1 Client-Server Architecture

Client: A Client is a device that is operated by a user to access enterprise content, and in our work, content includes persona, applications, and data. We focus on smartphones, but the same techniques are also applicable to desktops.

Enterprise Policy Server (EPS): The EPS component hosts policies and disseminates them to employees' devices when required. By designing this component as a server, a heterogeneous network of end-users' devices can be serviced. Therefore, access to resources can be requested from desktop terminals or mobile devices.

Positioning Module (PM): The role of the PM is to detect the positions (i.e., location and proximity) of Clients by periodically collecting and analyzing contextual information.

We note that the various components of MERC's architecture may not be integrated into the same physical component. In our proof-of-concept implementation, for example, the PM only provides location verification support by transmitting periodic ultrasonic beacons, which Clients consume. In addition, a Client consumes/emits BLE beacons to determine the proximity of other Clients. We depict the prototype's architecture in Figure 1.

5.2 Overview

The operations of the MERC are centered around enterprises' mobile IT management. Each enterprise has enterprise members that deploy personas. We define an *enterprise member* as the entity which deploys, controls, and manages a persona. An enterprise member could be either the IT admin (of a business/corporation) or simply an end-user; we, however, focus only on the duties of the former because enterprises desire to have full control over employees' personas.

Client Registration. Each enterprise has an Enterprise ID (EID)[1] that is communicated to Clients. This EID serves two purposes: (1) as an unique identifier for an enterprise; (2) as information regarding the top-level locations that belong to the particular enterprise.

Persona Deployment. We leverage Android facilities to deploy personas on our platform. The persona deployment is achieved through the development of a custom device admin application built using Android's Device Administration APIs. Use of such APIs increases the MERCOS's ease of adoption as current IT admins would have already built a device admin to control their employees' devices running AFW, which MERCOS is built upon. Once the device admin is downloaded to an employee's device, the device admin creates a new persona dedicated to work-related activities. At this point, a clean userspace containing the same list of applications as the default persona, including the device admin, will be instantiated. However, unlike the rest, the device admin is the only application that is removed completely from the default persona as its duties only lie in the created persona. Once the persona-creation process is completed, the device admin must register a legitimate EID, acting as a persona ID, via our custom interface.

Activating Personas & Deploying Policies. End-users authenticate their logical location by passively consuming, via Clients, an ultrasonic beacon that is partially encrypted with two different keys. The Ultrasonic Beacon (Figure 1) contains several pieces of information, including an EID, a Location ID (LID), timestamps, and a policy number. The ultrasonic beacons are periodically sent every 10 seconds by a PM. The EID and LID describe a Client's general (e.g., NekSec's campus) and specific (building 10, room 100) location, respectively.

We apply defense-in-depth by employing three layers of defense to access content on the Client. First, the Client extracts the EID from the beacon, and compares the identifier with previously registered EIDs. If there is a matching EID, the Client activates the associated persona, otherwise, the default persona is activated. We use the term "activate" to simply indicate that a persona is brought

---

[1] The creation and management of unique EIDs are neither delegated to MERCOS or enterprises. AFW, through Google Enterprise solutions, handles such operations[5].

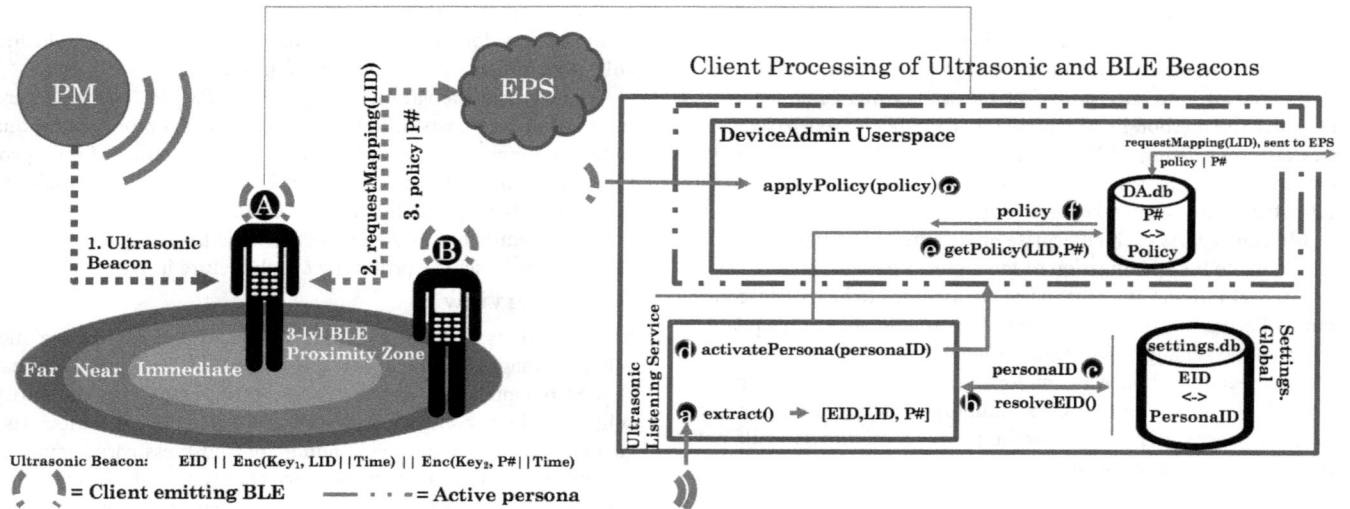

Figure 1: The access control process between the major components of the MERC architecture, in which ultrasonic and bluetooth low energy beacons are processed. Such beacons influence which persona is active and the level of accessibility Client A has to that persona and its contents.

to the foreground, and thus, all other personas are not visible since they execute in the background. Unlike the first defense layer, the second and third layers are handled by the device admin. Android delegates the responsibility of screen-locking a persona to the device admin[4]. However, the device admin allows the screen lock to receive user input *only* if the policy number is decipherable. Such defense-in-depth ensures legitimate access authorizations, regardless of an attacker attempting a replay or denial-of-service attack (see Section 8).

At this point, the Client forwards the beacon's LID to the device admin, which is within the Client's active persona. As the device admin is built by the enterprise, it is aware of the EPS' remote address, and thus forwards the LID to the EPS for processing (NetMsg in Figure 1). The content of the LID dictates the content of the EPS' response message. Each LID is tied to a unique policy, and this association is configured by the enterprise member. The EPS responds with the policy number and the policy itself.

To minimize communication between the Client and the EPS, the device admin stores the policy number sent by the EPS. Whenever the device admin extracts a policy number from the ultrasonic beacon, the device admin compares it with previously stored values. If a value previously exists, the matching policy is adhered to, otherwise, the device admin forwards the LID to the EPS to retrieve the appropriate policy.

Encryption Keys. As previously stated, ultrasonic beacons are partially encrypted using two keys (Figure 1): Key_1 is a periodically updated symmetric key generated by and stored on the EPS. It is used to encrypt a LID and a timestamp. Such encryption ensures the confidentiality of an enterprise's building infrastructure as per our design goal. Key_2 is the private key component of an asymmetric pair generated by the EPS. The private key is used to encrypt a policy number and a timestamp. The public component, which is stored within an X.509 certificate downloaded to a Client device, is

used for decryption. Such encryption minimizes the communication between the Client and EPS while maintaining high security since the policy number is used to apply an associated policy previously downloaded to the Client, and therefore obviating the need to contact the EPS as frequently as ultrasonic beacons are broadcasted.

Detecting Proximity. The policies a system can enforce are dependent on the underlying technology. Similarly to ultrasonic beacons, each Client scans for BLE beacons every 10 seconds. Particularly, we utilize BLE to detect if other users are within *Near* reach (c.f. to Section 3). That is, the proximity zone (Figure 1) encompasses the area within 3 meters around a Client. We selected *Near* for the maximum range as we believe that if, for example, any employee with an inferior role to that of the Supervisor is within 3 meters of Alice, then it is a clear indication that the employee is able to visually observe content on Alice's device he/she is unauthorized to view. We emphasize that this hard-coded metric of proximity is implementation specific as we rely on BLE's four-step ranging measurements. We assume that the device admin maintains a database that maps Bluetooth MAC addresses to user IDs, which can be easily retrieved from an enterprise's preexisting RBAC system that is incorporated into the EPS. We chose the Client (rather than the EPS) to track user movements so that Clients can immediately react to proximity violations and minimize communication with the EPS.

5.3 Proximity-Based Device Admin Policies

Much work has been done in the design of policy languages[3, 7, 20, 27]. However, we extend CASSEC's PrBAC policy specification [27] and integrate it into Android's existing Device Administration policy specification (MercBAC), thereby enabling MERC to enforce restrictions based on Separation of Duty and Absence of Other Users. The device admin is solely responsible for enforcing policies on the persona such as password configuration or device force lock, and similar to Android's permission model, the device admin must request the privilege to exercise such capabilities through a security metadata file stored within the application's binary. We do not modify this file. Instead, the device admin reads a MercBAC policy, written by the IT admin, which is stored within the application's data directory. The device admin must ensure the current context violates the policy's contextual constraints prior to exercising force lock (*DevicePolicyManager.lockNow()*), for example, thereby applying proximity-based access control to personas. In this way, we increase the ease-of-adoption and resiliency to change in MERCOS as a subset of these policy features are pre-built into the stock Android OS. Figure 2 provides an example MercBAC device admin policy that reflects the scenario presented in Section 2.

```
<device-admin
xmlns:android="http://schemas.android.com/apk/res/android">
    <uses-policies>
        <force-lock >
        <context>
            <obligation>ongoing</obligation>
            <proximity-constraints>
                <proximity-constraint>
                    <cardinality>at_least</cardinality>
                    <digit>1</digit>
                    <role>inferior(Supervisor)</role>
                </proximity-constraint>
            ...
</device-admin>
```

Figure 2: A MercBAC policy that specifies a persona should forcefully lock if there is at least one individual with an inferior role to Supervisor in proximity of the requesting user.

5.4 The EID and LID

We take advantage of preexisting data structures for EIDs. An IT admin is required to perform a registration process with Google which entails claiming and verifying an enterprise domain name (e.g., www.example.com) to use Android For Work (AFW). In addition, an Eddystone UID Namespace is generated by selecting the first 10 bytes of a SHA-1 hash of the domain name. The MERC uses the Eddystone UID as the EID to describe top-level locations.

The intentional naming system proposed by Adjie-Winoto et al. [1] is an attribute-value naming system with nested attribute-value pairs. Such a naming architecture provides significant flexibility in defining location-based information of broad resolutions. As such, we adopt this attribute-value system to construct a LID. The advantage is that the particular construction of a LID is defined by each enterprise IT admin instead of uniformly. In this paper, we use a simple construction of the following form: [building = B [floor = F [room = R]]].

6 PROTOTYPE IMPLEMENTATION

6.1 Client

We made minor modifications to the Android OS to support MERCOS. We first created and exposed a new system API called *switchPersona(string eid)*. This API switches the persona, and is called whenever a new EID is detected from an ultrasonic beacon. For simplicity, we allow device admins to register an EID within Android's "settings.db", which is a database managed by the Settings

application, via the *Settings.Global* interface. In this way, the database can be globally accessed no matter which persona is currently active. Normally, third-party applications can only read from Settings.Global, and not write. To ensure that the device admins are the only entities with the write privilege, we call Android's *DevicePolicyManager.getActiveAdmins()* function. It returns a package name list of all device admin applications, but only *one* should exist as the enterprise controls the list of applications that exist within the work persona. Prior to updating the EID database, we verify that the package name of the entity attempting to update the EIDs is authorized to do so. Read access to EIDs is not a privacy concern since they are constructed based on enterprises' public web domain[4].

To send/receive ultrasonic beacons, we integrate a third-party sound-based, data communication SDK [30] into our custom device admin which operates at frequencies above 18 KHz (i.e., frequency range inaudible to the human ear). The reader may wonder why we integrate such a feature at the application level rather than the system level. We believe that this is sufficient as modern smartphones already silently process audio in the background via application-level programs. For example, the Google Now application allows the Android OS to respond to voice-commands[29]. So in reality, the ability to read ultrasonic beacons would be integrated into the Google Now application so that it can be a system-wide functionality. The device admin also periodically scans for BLE beacons every 10 seconds using the *android.bluetooth.le* APIs[4]. Nearby users are identified by maintaining a SQL database which contains a mapping from BLE MAC addresses to user IDs.

6.2 EPS

The EPS was implemented in PHP and hosted on a remote commercial server. It disseminates policy files to Clients. The EPS provides a function that can be remotely invoked via URL: *getPolicy(NetMsg)* (Figure 1). The function is invoked by Clients whenever a new policy number is detected in ultrasonic beacons.

7 EXPERIMENTAL RESULTS

7.1 Deployment

In this section, we report experimental results. First, we deployed our MERC prototype in one of our campus buildings. Figure 3 displays the schematics of our tested area. The green (benign) and red (malicious) circles and arrows indicate the placements and facing directions of PMs, respectively. A large, grid-patterned rectangle points out a sub-area of an enterprise environment that contains only one PM. The gray-filled circles indicate the current positions of Clients. The gray, circular outlines indicate the possible positions of Clients during testing. Second, our modifications to the Android source code were tested on the Android Pixel C tablet device running Android Nougat (API 22 v7.0). Last, each PM was a Dell A215 Multimedia Speaker, and each speaker was connected to a device capable of playing MP3s. All experiments were conducted in areas in which the ambient noise were minimal.

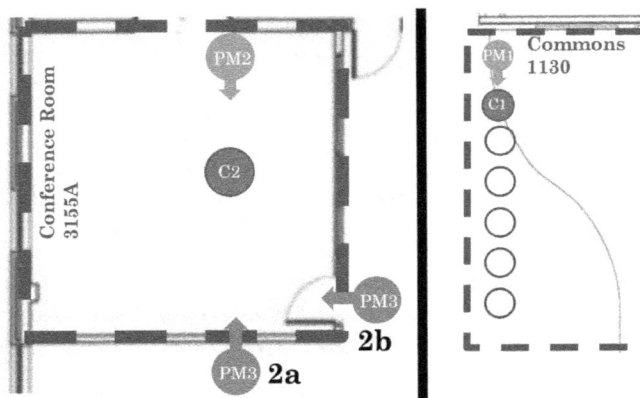

Figure 3: The map of a campus building which contains our positioning module (PM#) and Clients (C#). Arrows indicate the directions PMs are facing.

7.2 Experiments

Experiment 1: Enterprise Setting Suitability. An enterprise may place PMs in arbitrary locations such as an office or a large sitting area (e.g., auditorium). Therefore, it is necessary to understand how messages embedded in ultrasounds will propagate. Specifically, the goal of the experiment is to determine if the Client is able to capture location information at varying distances away from a PM. The Client ($C1$) was placed at six different positions away from the PM ($PM1$), and at each position, $PM1$ transmitted 10 ultrasonic beacons at its maximum possible amplitude.

Figure 4 shows results of this experiment. $C1$ was able to detect beacons with strong accuracy, at least 90%, up to 30m away from $PM1$. However, at a distance of 36m, $C1$ was only able to detect beacons with 60% accuracy. The lower detection rate at 36m was expected as it is a natural phenomena that everyone observes on a daily basis. That is, there is a direct correlation between the distance between a source of sound and a listener and the likelihood of the sound being heard. Therefore, a speaker that can emit sounds at larger volumes would be able to transmit beacons to Clients at farther distances. Nevertheless, this experiment has demonstrated that ultrasonic beacons can be detected with 100% accuracy in most enterprise settings since such settings (i.e., offices and meetings rooms) are significantly smaller than 24m on the longest sides[18].

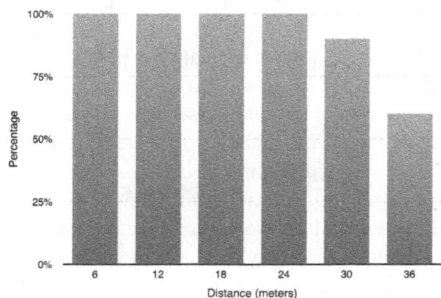

Figure 4: Using commodity devices to capture location information at varying distances.

Experiment	PM2	PM3
2a	100%	0%
2b	100%	6%
2b′	77%	57%

Table 1: Location detection rates when two positioning modules, one benign and one malicious, are in proximity.

Experiment 2a and 2b: Collisions. Sound waves can transmit arbitrarily far, and sounds from varying sources can mesh together. If multiple PMs are placed in relatively close proximity, the ultrasounds may also blend together. We must determine if placing PMs in isolated areas that are in proximity, but demarcated by walls or closed doors will cause any interference with Clients. We explain in the security analysis below that an adversary is unable to transmit *valid* ultrasonic beacons. However, we temporarily relax our video monitoring assumption (Section 2), thereby enabling an attacker to transmit beacons on the same ultrasonic frequency to cause collisions via malicious PMs (red PMs in Figure 3) from adjacent rooms/areas. We perform two experiments to determine the extent in which an adversary can perform a Denial-of-Service attack with the constraint that the adversary is using the same hardware deployment acquired by hijacking legitimate PMs. In Experiment 2a, $C2$ and $PM2$ are placed within a closed-door room situated roughly 3 and 6 meters away from $PM3$, respectively. $PM3$ is pressed against and facing a 1 ft (~0.3 m) thick wall. In Experiment 2b, $C2$ and $PM2$ remain in the same positions, but $PM3$ is now pressed against and facing the room's door. A notable difference between the two experiments is that, although still demarcated by some obstruction, $PM3$ may have a likelier chance to permeate through the room as cracks exist around the door that sound can travel through.

In each experiment (Table 1), each PM begins transmission, at maximum volume, of 30 ultrasonic beacons at a specified time using a time-based activation program. In Experiment 2a, $C2$ did not detect beacon collisions as it identified 100% of $PM2$'s beacons and 0% of $PM3$'s beacons. Such results demonstrate that sound is indeed inherently localized as the attacker could not successfully penetrate the obstructing wall(s). In Experiment 2b, $C2$ detected beacon collisions as it identified 100% and 6% of $PM2$'s and $PM3$'s beacons, respectively. We performed Experiment 2b once more (i.e., 2b′), but we instead increase the adversary's attack power by leaving $PM3$ at full volume while reducing $PM2$'s volume by half. As a result, $C2$ identified 77% and 57% of $PM2$'s and $PM3$'s beacons, respectively. Such results demonstrate that under a certain adversarial model, an attacker can cause collisions. Given the unprecedentedly fine-grained nature of BYOD scenarios that we envision for MERC (e.g., different LID per room), processing beacons from adjacent rooms/areas would cause the Client to continuously switch containers or apply the wrong policies. Such erratic behavior is a major issue w.r.t. security, and it would also potentially ruin the user experience. To address this issue, we implemented a temporal localization analysis mechanism to determine the correct candidate to enforce in a set of beacons recently heard by a Client. We first determine which beacon is consumed more frequently, but using only this criteria is insufficient as an attacker could simply increase the rate of transmission of malicious beacons. Therefore, beacons must also be consumed at a valid transmission rate, otherwise the attack is detectable. We discuss this further in Section 8.

Distance	Rm1	Rm2	Rm3
2m	FNR: 0%	FNR: 0%	FNR: 4%
4m	FPR: 2%	FPR: 0%	FPR: 0%

Table 2: Proximity detection rates when two stationary BLE devices are situated at varying distances.

Experiment 3: Proximity Detection. We test the proximity detection method which relies on BLE beacons. The device admin is configured to enforce the MercBAC policy in Figure 2. In particular, we test if Alice's Client can accurately determine the distance to the unauthorized user. Two BLE-enabled devices were used to conduct the experiment: a Nexus 6P smartphone (*C1*) and a Pixel C tablet (*C2*) acting as Alice's and the unauthorized user's Clients, respectively. We repeated this experiment twice; differentiating the two by placement of the stationary Clients: a distance of 2m (< *Near*) and 4m (>= *Near*) between each other which indicates attack and non-attack instances, respectively. We use the following metric to evaluate the effectiveness of the proximity detection. False negative rate (FNR) is defined as the percentage of attack instances in which *C1* mistakenly evaluates as non-attack instances. False positive rate (FPR) is defined as the percentage of non-attack instances in which *C1* mistakenly evaluates *C2* as attack instances. We performed the experiment three times, each on the 1st, 2nd, and third (Figure 3) floor of an isolated room. *C2* emitted 100 BLE beacons with each five seconds apart.

Table 2 presents the false positive rates and false negative rates of proximity detection under varying distances. *C1* precisely evaluated *C2* as *Near* when *C2* was placed 2m away, with a 4% FNR in the worst case. When Clients were situated 4m apart, a FPR of 2% was observed in the worst case. Such occurrences can be attributed to possible interferences caused by the environment since BLE is a radio-based technology, and such technology is susceptible to signal attenuation. The experiment has demonstrated that if unauthorized employees enter Alice's vicinity, with high accuracy, the device admin would be able to force lock the persona. However, an enterprise may consider a 4% FNR non-negligible as personas would be inaccessible in such instances. We leave the investigation of alternative proximity technologies for future work.

Experiment 4: Battery Consumption. Mobile devices are resource constrained, and continually probing sensors can tax the device. The Clients are continually listening for ultrasonic and BLE beacons. The goal of this experiment is to observe the consumption of the device's battery. We monitored the device's battery percentage when running both the unmodified OS and our customized system, separately. We performed this experiment three times on each system. Towards this goal, we set *WindowManager* class's FLAG_KEEP_SCREEN_ON which is an Android mechanism to force the screen to never turn off. It is vital that this flag is set as it ensures that the listening service is not temporarily halted or shutdown by the stock Android resource management system. We logged the battery consumption every hour.

Figure 5 shows results of this experiment. As observed from the graph, the average performance impact of MERCOS is minimal as compared to the non-modified OS. The maximum difference observed each hour was 2%. An explanation for this result is that Android already silently processes audio in the background when the unmodified OS is used (e.g., Google Now application's

voice-activation services). The processing of ultrasonic beacon in MERCOS takes precedent over the voice-activation services. Thus, the only additional processing that is performed in our custom OS is the scanning of BLE beacons. Therefore, integrating features of our CAS into resource-constrained devices is practical.

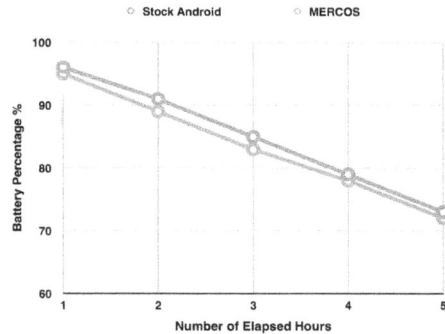

Figure 5: Average battery consumption of a Client when continuously listening for ultrasonic and Bluetooth beacons.

8 SECURITY ANALYSIS

We discuss possible attacks to our system, and means to to prevent or mitigate them.

8.1 Attacking Ultrasonic Beacons

Replay Attack. An attacker may attempt a simple replay attack. The goal of the attack is to confuse the MERC system to activate an incorrect persona and policy on a Client. The attack is executed by recording a previously transmitted ultrasonic message and re-transmitting it at a different time or location. We protect the system from replay attacks by embedding temporal information within the beacon. The components in the system must have loosely synchronized clocks. We extract the timestamps and compare them to the current time, and then determine if the time difference exceeds a specified threshold. In the midst of Experiment 1, at a distance of 24m, prior to signal degradation at 30m, we averaged the elapsed time in milliseconds to transmit, receive, and process 30 ultrasonic beacons. The longest sides of most offices or meeting rooms are significantly smaller than 24m, which we believe reflects the maximum distance an ultrasonic beacon must travel. On average, the complete process took approximately 1.33 seconds. Although the longest elapsed time recorded was 2.5 seconds, all other recorded times fell well below two seconds. As a result, we set our threshold to two seconds. Therefore, the system would be able to detect malicious activity under the threat of a simple attacker.

In this paper, we do not consider a sophisticated attacker that is able to execute a wormhole attack[19]. A wormhole attack is similar to a replay attack except that the adversary tunnels the beacon through a "wormhole". Defending against such an attack is quite challenging as the wormhole allows the re-transmission at a different location with minimal delay, possibly within milliseconds. A sophisticated method to address both attacks would be to employ ultrasonic distance-bounding techniques [24, 31]. Such techniques were not investigated for several reasons. First, recently proposed techniques require special hardware, and modern smartphones are not currently capable of handling such a task. Second, given the scenarios that we envision for MERC, such a feature would incur significant overhead for each architectural component. For these reasons, MERC would not satisfy the main goals of the paper as ease of integration and interoperability would be significantly reduced.

Denial-of-Service. In Experiment 2, we addressed the issue of collisions as result of *benign* position modules in adjacent rooms. However, an attacker can execute a denial-of-service (DOS) attack by physically tampering with or altering the beacons that are transmitted from PMs. For example, an attacker may tamper with a benign PM to transmit audio shifted to a frequency that will negate legitimate ultrasonic beacons. If this occurs, the Clients may consume data that is corrupted and indecipherable; persona activation and policy deployment will not function properly. It is difficult to defend against such a DOS attack, but it can be detected. The results in Experiment 1 and 2 demonstrate high accuracy with respect to detecting beacons. Consequently, repetitive consumption of indecipherable beacons can be inferred as malicious activity, especially if enterprises appropriately place benign PMs as to minimize collisions between those devices. Another practical method that can be immediately employed is Android's Geofences APIs[4]. A geofence is a circular area defined by a latitude, longitude, and radius, which can be specified by the device admin. The device admin thus becomes more context aware as it is alerted whenever a user enters/exits the geofence. Experiencing GPS signal attenuation is not a cause for concern since the device admin would instead place a geofence to entirely encompass, for example, NekSec's campus. An expected EID is thus established once a Alice enters the campus, otherwise, a DOS attack can be inferred. Last, physical security could also be utilized by delegating the responsibility of monitoring for malicious location devices to sentries placed throughout the campus. Nevertheless, the security of personas would still be ensured if enterprises apply defense-in-depth as described in Section 5.2.

8.2   Attacking BLE Beacons

Rooting. A possible attack to our system involves a user rooting his/her Client, and maliciously modifying the Bluetooth MAC address. In this way, the Client can impersonate another user of the system. To mitigate such an attack, an enterprise must employ hardware and software mechanisms (e.g., Android's dm-verity) that enhance device security. For example, Samsung KNOX 2.0 is a custom Android OS which has a low-level security feature that leaves the device inoperable once it detects a root attack[28], which is a sufficient mechanism to defend against malicious modification of the MAC address (or any root-based attack targeting MERC).

Masking BLE. The simplest attack malicious users could execute is to mask their MAC address by either disabling the Bluetooth peripheral on the Client or simply leaving it in another room. By doing so Clients will be unable to correctly enforce proximity constraints. There are several measures that can be taken against such attack. First, an enterprise simply has to enforce mandatory enabling of Bluetooth through the device admin application, which completely controls the settings and configurations of the Clients.

Second, accidental or malicious misplacing of the Client can be addressed by supplementing the system with a facility to detect the number of individuals in a room. For example, the system by Oluwatimi et al. [27] takes an infrastructure-based approach (i.e., independent of the Clients) utilizing signal attenuation of WiFi radios caused by human interference to achieve occupant localization. Therefore, if the number of individuals in a room and the number of MAC addresses do not match, the system will infer malicious behavior, and subsequently revoke access to resources.

Unauthorized Device User. Another attack vector involves an unauthorized individual obtaining an authorized user's phone, whether by theft or voluntary provision. Such an attack would allow an individual to gain unauthorized access to persona content. To mitigate such a threat, biometric techniques can be employed. For example, Draffin et al. [12] demonstrate that it is possible to passively detect that a mobile device is being used by a non-authorized user by modeling user keyboard interactions. Wang et al. [38] explore biometric signatures using WiFi-based techniques to determine the identity of an individual. Using such techniques, it is therefore possible to associate an individual with a device.

9   RELATED WORK

Most EMM-based systems cannot address the scenarios in Section 2 for two reasons: (1) they do not support position-based containerization and/or (2) they utilize a PBS that does not provide an effective and efficient method to acquire contextual information.

9.1   Containerization

There are several existing EMM-like systems that utilize multi-partition techniques to isolate private and corporate content. Contrary to our work, most fail to consider the context in which they are employed. Gupta et al[16] created a custom Android OS that supports dual-mode personas. In enterprise mode, the system could enforce policies that disable a subset of device communication peripherals, force the device to only communicate via an enterprise VPN, and ensure an encrypted external storage is utilized. TrustDroid proposed the use of domains and their isolation by monitoring and limiting data exchanged via IPC (Inter-Process Communication), files, databases, and socket connections.

IdentiDroid [36] is an application level privacy-enhancing tool based on Android that addresses the shortcomings of network anonymizers (e.g., Tor and Hotspot Shield). IdentiDroid uses configuration profiles which are analogous to personas that relocate application data when a profile is de/activated. Unlike other platform-level systems, IdentiDroid also contain application-level containerization through the utilization of several device content protection techniques. DroidARM [26] builds upon the work in IdentiDroid by developing upon Android Lollipop. In this way, DroidARM is able to use native multi-user containerization to isolate applications and data as well as support EMM-based management features. Samsung KNOX 2.0[28], the system AFW actually adopted its persona-based approach from, incorporates significantly more hardware and platform security than any other platform-level EMM system, thus providing stronger guarantees of preventing root attacks.

Cellrox[28] uses a lightweight virtualization technology called ThinVisor. ThinVisor resides in the OS and allows multiple instances of the Android OS, which Cellrox calls Virtual Mobile Instances (VMIs), using the same kernel. Cellrox's VMIs can be made portable allowing a VMI to be decoupled from the device and placed in another device without needing to reconfigure the VMI. None of the aforementioned solutions support the activation of a container via location-based constraints or the restriction of the container's content via proximity-based constraints.

Several other solutions have been proposed that rely on the data tagging and information-flow tracking capabilities of TaintDroid[13]. In the work by Kodeswaran et al. [21], applications are classified as enterprise-related via parameters such as market source or developer signature. In addition, the data that is generated or processed by these applications are consequently tainted as enterprise. However, the proposed system does not incorporate contextual constraints. The work by Feth et al.[14] proposes a data-driven usage control architecture in which data is tainted by an enterprise-provided tag. The system supports context-aware policies by monitoring various device sensors such as location, WiFi, accelerometer, battery, Bluetooth, etc. Moses[32] isolates sensitive content from different personas by tainting data at the OS level with the name of the persona the data is associated with. Moses supports passive persona activation via GPS tracking, and therefore it is the closest, to the best of our knowledge, to our work. However, Moses, as well as the work proposed by Feth et al. [14], is not suitable for indoor environments as a result of GPS signal attenuation caused by construction materials. Furthermore, all of these solutions require significant modifications to the Android OS.

We emphasize that our work is orthogonal to application-level containerization solutions. Such solutions, such as role-based single-sign-on access control mechanisms, deploy enterprise content in password-protected app-level containers. In fact, enterprises currently apply defense-in-depth by employing both application- and platform-level containerization simultaneously[28]. With respect to MERC, the app-level container would exist within an Android persona, thereby having two password-based authorization methods to access enterprise content. Thus, our solution can be integrated into enterprises existing mobile IT solutions.

9.2 Position-Based Services

Over the years, researchers have proposed the use of various PBSs[39], which can be applied to containerization. However, many of these services have significant drawbacks that leave them unsuitable for such BYOD scenarios. Some PBSs require installing dedicated infrastructures[20], use specialized hardware[31], have significant energy consumption footprints on resource-constrained devices, are computationally intensive, and/or are highly susceptible to signal attenuation in indoor environments[6, 8, 33, 35]. In addition, most often than not, each proposed PBS is so unique that a PBS can be only deployed in specific and sporadic enterprise environments. As a result, containers that rely on these PBSs cannot move from one environment to the next since the underlying technologies are often different across different environments. For example, CASSEC[27], the first PBS to uniquely incorporate occupant WiFi signal interference and Bluetooth as part of a PrBAC system, has

several drawbacks. First, it does not take into account that radio signals permeate through walls. Multiple proximity modules residing in adjacent proximity zones would simultaneously detect the same user's Bluetooth-enabled smartphone, when in fact, the user and his/her smartphone were completely encapsulated within one of said proximity zones. Consequently, the number of falsely detected attacks may increase in standard enterprise settings. Second, to detect the number of occupants within a room using the WiFi component, occupants were required to stand in the line of sight (between a wireless transmitter and receiver) for at least one second. Even more, when the system was moved from one room to another identical room, a 46% decrease in occupancy detection accuracy was observed, possibly as a result of solely relying on radio wave-based occupancy detection techniques, which are highly susceptible to environmental signal attenuation[8]. Such drawbacks hinder the practicality and ease-of-adoption of CASSEC and other radio wave-based techniques. In direct contrast, the solutions presented in this paper are driven by design challenges presented in Section 4 such as security, privacy, and interoperability. Our intent was to demonstrate to enterprises the means to immediately implement a reliable positioning technology using devices integrated into existing infrastructures. In fact, 60% of conference attendees join a conference (audio, video and/or web) in conference rooms integrated with acoustic mediums such as speakers[18]. Consequently, Alice, who is employing our MERC system, would be able to securely migrate between Banker's and NekSec's campuses since such mediums are common to most enterprises.

10 CONCLUSION

In this paper, we investigate the feasibility of introducing context-based constraints to containers under a multi-enterprise context. Contextual information is supplied by our prototype PBS that relies on ultrasonic[2] and Bluetooth low energy beacons to address occupancy detection. With such information, proximity-based constraints can be effectively and efficiently enforced on Android's personas, which, to the best of our knowledge, has never been investigated. We also demonstrate how to allow multiple context-aware systems from different enterprises to serve a fleet of devices while maintaining privacy, security, scalability, and interoperability. Serving devices in such a manner is accomplished via our secure ultrasonic beacon protocol. In the future, we will investigate how to enhance system security by incorporating more contextual information – such as biometric signatures[12, 38] and redundant, Client-independent localization[27] – to ensure that users are not colluding and attempting to circumvent the system. Experiment 2 in Section 7 demonstrates that adjusting the amplitude affects the transmission distance. We can exploit this phenomena to support micro-position policies. For example, in a large sitting area containing tens of employees, a single high-level employee may instead use his smartphone device as a positioning module to support micro-position transmission of ultrasonic beacons. In this way, the high-level employee may adjust the device's volume to minimal levels to impose temporary restrictions on only low-level employees' devices that are within a few feet.

---

[2]Careful construction and transmission of ultrasonic signals must be taken to prevent adverse effects on the human body[37].

REFERENCES

[1] William Adjie-Winoto, Elliot Schwartz, Hari Balakrishnan, and Jeremy Lilley. 1999. The Design and Implementation of an Intentional Naming System. *SIGOPS Oper. Syst. Rev.* 33, 5 (Dec. 1999), 186–201. https://doi.org/10.1145/319344.319164

[2] Subhendu Aich, Shamik Sural, and Arun K Majumdar. 2007. STARBAC: Spatiotemporal role based access control. In *On the Move to Meaningful Internet Systems 2007: CoopIS, DOA, ODBASE, GADA, and IS.* Springer, 1567–1582.

[3] Anne Anderson. 2004. XACML profile for role based access control (RBAC). *OASIS Access Control TC committee draft* 1 (2004), 13.

[4] Android. [n. d.]. Android Developer's Guide. http://developer.android.com. ([n. d.]).

[5] Android. [n. d.]. Android Enterprise. https://enterprise.google.com/android. ([n. d.]).

[6] Bharathan Balaji, Jian Xu, Anthony Nwokafor, Rajesh Gupta, and Yuvraj Agarwal. 2013. Sentinel: occupancy based HVAC actuation using existing WiFi infrastructure within commercial buildings. In *Proceedings of the 11th ACM Conference on Embedded Networked Sensor Systems.* ACM, 17.

[7] Elisa Bertino, Barbara Catania, Maria Luisa Damiani, and Paolo Perlasca. 2005. GEO-RBAC: a spatially aware RBAC. In *Proceedings of the tenth ACM symposium on Access control models and technologies.* ACM, 29–37.

[8] Maurizio Bocca, Ossi Kaltiokallio, and Neal Patwari. 2012. Radio tomographic imaging for ambient assisted living. In *Evaluating AAL Systems Through Competitive Benchmarking.* Springer, 108–130.

[9] Raffaele Bruno and Franca Delmastro. 2003. Design and analysis of a bluetooth-based indoor localization system. In *IFIP International Conference on Personal Wireless Communications.* Springer, 711–725.

[10] Brent Carrara and Carlisle Adams. 2014. On acoustic covert channels between air-gapped systems. In *International Symposium on Foundations and Practice of Security.* Springer, 3–16.

[11] Suroop Mohan Chandran and James BD Joshi. 2005. LoT-RBAC: a location and time-based RBAC model. In *Web Information Systems Engineering–WISE 2005.* Springer, 361–375.

[12] Benjamin Draffin, Jiang Zhu, and Joy Zhang. 2013. Keysens: Passive user authentication through micro-behavior modeling of soft keyboard interaction. In *Mobile Computing, Applications, and Services.* Springer, 184–201.

[13] William Enck, Peter Gilbert, Seungyeop Han, Vasant Tendulkar, Byung-Gon Chun, Landon P Cox, Jaeyeon Jung, Patrick McDaniel, and Anmol N Sheth. 2014. TaintDroid: an information-flow tracking system for realtime privacy monitoring on smartphones. *ACM Transactions on Computer Systems (TOCS)* 32, 2 (2014), 5.

[14] Denis Feth and Christian Jung. 2012. Context-aware, data-driven policy enforcement for smart mobile devices in business environments. In *International Conference on Security and Privacy in Mobile Information and Communication Systems.* Springer, 69–80.

[15] Sunil Kumar Ghai, Lakshmi V Thanayankizil, Deva P Seetharam, and Dipanjan Chakraborty. 2012. Occupancy detection in commercial buildings using opportunistic context sources. In *Pervasive Computing and Communications Workshops (PERCOM Workshops), 2012 IEEE International Conference on.* IEEE, 463–466.

[16] Akhilesh Gupta, Anupam Joshi, and Gopal Pingali. 2010. Enforcing security policies in mobile devices using multiple personas. In *International Conference on Mobile and Ubiquitous Systems: Computing, Networking, and Services.* Springer, 297–302.

[17] Sandeep KS Gupta, T Mukheriee, K Venkatasubramanian, and TB Taylor. 2006. Proximity based access control in smart-emergency departments. In *Pervasive Computing and Communications Workshops, 2006. PerCom Workshops 2006. Fourth Annual IEEE International Conference on.* IEEE, 5-pp.

[18] Bill Haskins, Andy Nilssen, and Andrew Davis. [n. d.]. The Evolution of the Conference Room and the Technology Behind it. http://cp.wainhouse.com/content/evolution-conference-room. ([n. d.]).

[19] Yih-Chun Hu, Adrian Perrig, and David B Johnson. 2006. Wormhole attacks in wireless networks. *IEEE journal on selected areas in communications* 24, 2 (2006), 370–380.

[20] Michael S Kirkpatrick, Maria Luisa Damiani, and Elisa Bertino. 2011. Prox-RBAC: a proximity-based spatially aware RBAC. In *Proceedings of the 19th ACM SIGSPATIAL International Conference on Advances in Geographic Information Systems.* ACM, 339–348.

[21] Palanivel Kodeswaran, Vikrant Nandakumar, Shalini Kapoor, Pavan Kamaraju, Anupam Joshi, and Sougata Mukherjea. 2012. Securing enterprise data on smartphones using run time information flow control. In *2012 IEEE 13th International Conference on Mobile Data Management.* IEEE, 300–305.

[22] Andrey Larchikov, Sergey Panasenko, Alexander V Pimenov, and Petr Timofeev. 2014. Combining RFID-based physical access control systems with digital signature systems to increase their security. In *Software, Telecommunications and Computer Networks (SoftCOM), 2014 22nd International Conference on.* IEEE, 100–103.

[23] Anil Madhavapeddy, David Scott, and Richard Sharp. 2003. Context-aware computing with sound. In *International Conference on Ubiquitous Computing.* Springer, 315–332.

[24] Carlos Medina, José C Segura, and Sverre Holm. 2012. Feasibility of ultrasound positioning based on signal strength. In *Indoor Positioning and Indoor Navigation (IPIN), 2012 International Conference on.* IEEE, 1–9.

[25] M Moreno, Jose L Hernandez, and Antonio F Skarmeta. 2014. A New Location-Aware Authorization Mechanism for Indoor Environments. In *Advanced Information Networking and Applications Workshops (WAINA), 2014 28th International Conference on.* IEEE, 791–796.

[26] Oyindamola Oluwatimi and Elisa Bertino. 2016. An Application Restriction System for Bring-Your-Own-Device Scenarios. In *Proceedings of the 21st ACM on Symposium on Access Control Models and Technologies.* ACM, 25–36.

[27] Oyindamola Oluwatimi, Daniele Midi, and Elisa Bertino. 2016. A Context-Aware System to Secure Enterprise Content. In *Proceedings of the 21st ACM on Symposium on Access Control Models and Technologies.* ACM, 63–72.

[28] Oyindamola Oluwatimi, Daniele Midi, and Elisa Bertino. 2016. Overview of Mobile Containerization Approaches and Open Research Directions. *Under submission* (2016).

[29] Giuseppe Petracca, Yuqiong Sun, Trent Jaeger, and Ahmad Atamli. 2015. AuDroid: Preventing Attacks on Audio Channels in Mobile Devices. In *Proceedings of the 31st Annual Computer Security Applications Conference.* ACM, 181–190.

[30] prontoly [n. d.]. ultrasonic handsfree authentication technology. http://www.prontoly.com/. ([n. d.]).

[31] Kasper Bonne Rasmussen, Claude Castelluccia, Thomas S Heydt-Benjamin, and Srdjan Capkun. 2009. Proximity-based access control for implantable medical devices. In *Proceedings of the 16th ACM conference on Computer and communications security.* ACM, 410–419.

[32] Giovanni Russello, Mauro Conti, Bruno Crispo, and Earlence Fernandes. 2012. MOSES: supporting operation modes on smartphones. In *Proceedings of the 17th ACM symposium on Access Control Models and Technologies.* ACM, 3–12.

[33] Thanathat Saelim, Prawit Chumchu, and Thawatchai Mayteevarunyoo. 2015. Design and Performance Evaluation of Novel Location-Based Access Control Algorithm Using IEEE 802.11 r. *Journal of Convergence Information Technology* 10, 4 (2015), 33.

[34] Holger Schulze. 2016. BYOD & Mobile Security 2016 Spotlight Report. http://crowdresearchpartners.com/wp-content/uploads/2016/03/BYOD-and-Mobile-Security-Report-2016.pdf. (March 2016).

[35] Bilal Shebaro, Oyindamola Oluwatimi, and Elisa Bertino. 2015. Context-based Access Control Systems for Mobile Devices. *Dependable and Secure Computing, IEEE Transactions on* 12, 2 (2015), 150–163.

[36] Bilal Shebaro, Oyindamola Oluwatimi, Daniele Midi, and Elisa Bertino. 2014. Identidroid: Android can finally wear its anonymous suit. *TRANSACTIONS ON DATA PRIVACY* 7 (2014).

[37] Bożena Smagowska and Małgorzata Pawlaczyk-Łuszczyńska. 2013. Effects of ultrasonic noise on the human bodyâĂŤa bibliographic review. *International Journal of Occupational Safety and Ergonomics* 19, 2 (2013), 195–202.

[38] Wei Wang, Alex X Liu, Muhammad Shahzad, Kang Ling, and Sanglu Lu. 2015. Understanding and modeling of wifi signal based human activity recognition. In *Proceedings of the 21st Annual International Conference on Mobile Computing and Networking.* ACM, 65–76.

[39] Faheem Zafari, Ioannis Papapanagiotou, and Konstantinos Christidis. 2016. Microlocation for Internet-of-Things-Equipped Smart Buildings. *IEEE Internet of Things Journal* 3, 1 (2016), 96–112.

DialerAuth: A Motion-assisted Touch-based Smartphone User Authentication Scheme

Attaullah Buriro
University of Trento
Trento, Italy
attaullah.buriro@unitn.it

Bruno Crispo
University of Trento
Trento, Italy
bruno.crispo@unitn.it

Sandeep Gupta
University of Trento
Trento, Italy
sandeep.gupta@unitn.it

Filippo Del Frari
University of Trento
Trento, Italy
filippo.delfrari@unitn.it

ABSTRACT

This paper introduces DialerAuth - a mechanism which leverages the way a smartphone user taps/enters any "*text-independent*" 10-digit number (replicating the dialing process) and the hand's micro-movements she makes while doing so. DialerAuth authenticates the user on the basis of timing differences in the entered 10-digit strokes. DialerAuth provides enhanced security by leveraging the transparent and unobservable layer based on another modality - user's hand micro-movements. Furthermore, DialerAuth increases the usability and acceptability by utilizing the users' familiarity with the dialing process and the flexibility of choosing any combination of 10-digit number. We implemented DialerAuth for both data collection and proof-of-concept real-time analysis. We collected, in total ≈10500 legitimate samples involving 97 users, through an extensive unsupervised field experiment, to evaluate the effectiveness of DialerAuth. Analysis using one-class Multilayer Perceptron (MLP) shows a TAR of 85.77% in identifying the genuine users. Security analysis involving ≈240 adversarial attempts proved DialerAuth as significantly resilient against random and mimic attacks. A usability study based on System Usability Scale (SUS) reflects a positive feedback on user acceptance (SUS score = 73.29).

CCS CONCEPTS

• **Security and privacy** → **Authentication**; **Biometrics**; • **Human-centered computing** → **Mobile devices**;

KEYWORDS

Smartphone Authentication, Behavioral biometrics, Sensors

ACM Reference format:
Attaullah Buriro, Bruno Crispo, Sandeep Gupta, and Filippo Del Frari. 2018. DialerAuth: A Motion-assisted Touch-based Smartphone User Authentication Scheme. In *Proceedings of Eighth ACM Conference on Data and*

Application Security and Privacy, Tempe, AZ, USA, March 19–21, 2018 (CODASPY'18), 10 pages.
https://doi.org/10.1145/3176258.3176318

1 INTRODUCTION

Smartphone user authentication is the process of verifying the identity of the claimant and to ensure that only the authenticated and authorized user is granted access to the smartphone. Popular smartphone user authentication schemes, based on "something the user knows" (e.g., PINs/passwords, graphical patterns), have shown to have usability issue (because they cause inconvenience) [15] and also security issues (due to their vulnerability to different attacks) [24]. A recent study reported that users considered login with PINs and passwords more annoying than any other technology related problems, such as lack of coverage, small screen size or low voice quality [18].

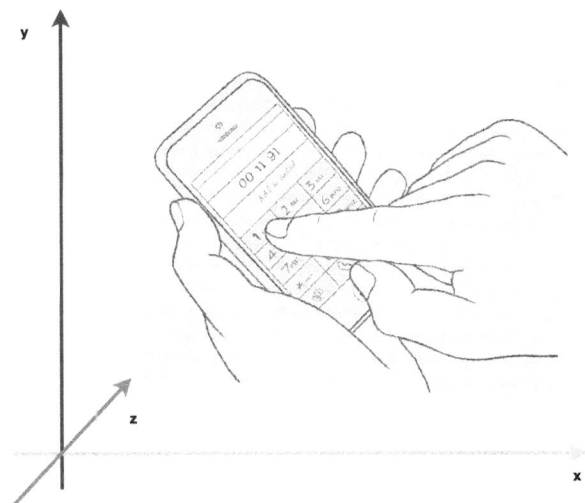

Figure 1: Dialing process in 3d space.

The recent introduction of physiological biometrics based on "something the user is", i.e., facial, fingerprint and iris recognition, have somehow mitigated the problems with the user input, however, some usability [10] and security [1] issues still remain unsolved.

This led researchers to investigate the feasibility of methods based on something the user does - often termed as behavioral biometrics. Behavioral biometrics offer various advantages over physiological counterparts. One of the main advantages is that the behavioral patterns can be used transparently. More importantly, data collection does not require any special dedicated hardware. Consequently, researchers have analyzed and tested several human behaviors for smartphone user authentication. For example, the way a user walks [11], the way a user types (touch-stroke) her secret [2], and how she interacts with the touchscreen [7, 12, 20].

This paper presents a bimodal smartphone user authentication scheme based on two human behaviors - the way a user taps a combination of 10-digits *"text-independent"* number, not necessarily secret (replicating dialing behavior) and the phone's micro-movements during the dialing process (see Figure 1). We chose 10-digits length because we empirically found this length more accurate and resilient compared to 4, 6, 8, 12, and 14 digits. The system profiles the users based on (i) the differences in the tap-timings, and (ii) the phone micro-movements during the entire process of dialing, to authenticate the users. DIALERAUTH does not require users to remember anything, and hence users can tap any combination of 10-digit number. An attacker has to successfully mimic the two invisible and inherently secure human behaviors, i.e., the invisible timings and the phone micro-movements of the legitimate user, to access the phone.

We registered users' generated phone micro-movements using accelerometer and gyroscope sensors, commonly available on most of the commercially available smartphones. DIALERAUTH starts these sensors when the user taps the first digit and stops when the user taps the last. We evaluated DIALERAUTH on our collected dataset of 93 (97, in total) qualified users, by applying anomaly detection (one-class classification) approach. Results show that MLP verifier outperformed other chosen verifiers and performed well in all the postures, i.e., *sitting, standing, walking and walking downstairs*.

The main contributions of this work are:

- The proposal of a bimodal smartphone user authentication scheme - DIALERAUTH, which authenticates the user based on the differences in the tap-timings while she taps/enters 10-digit *"text-independent"* number, and the phones micro-movements while doing so.
- Prototype implementation of the proposed solution on a smartphone.
- Collection and sharing of collected data set of 93 qualified participants, for further research.
- The security evaluation of DIALERAUTH to assess its robustness against the most common (random and mimic) attacks.
- The usability evaluation of DIALERAUTH to assess how users reacted to the solution and estimation of user acceptance.

Paper Organization. The rest of the paper is organized as follows: Section 2 surveys the related work which motivates why there is a need for an improvement. Section 3 explains the threat model and the main technologies used by our solution. Section 4, reports the detailed methodology, i.e., protocols for data collection, feature

extraction and selection, analysis, etc., of our conducted experiments. Section 5, explains the proof-of-concept application that we developed based on our findings. Sections 6 and 7 presents the results of security and usability evaluation of DIALERAUTH. Finally, Section 8 concludes the paper with the summary of our findings and future work.

2 RELATED WORK

Behavioral biometrics have increasingly been used for transparent and frictionless user authentication schemes on smartphones. Research on user authentication has been reshaped due to the inclusion of sufficiently sensitive mobile sensors, i.e., accelerometer, gyroscope, touchscreen, etc. As a result, multiple schemes leveraging these sensors have been introduced. Among all, the two behavioral biometric schemes, i.e., the way a user walks (gait) [11, 23], and the way the user interacts with the touchscreen [6, 7, 22, 32]) have dominated the research in the smartphone user authentication domain.

Most of the available smartphones nowadays are equipped with inertial sensors, e.g., accelerometer, gyroscope, etc., which can be used to fingerprint the device movement. This unique movement has explicitly been exploited for smartphone user authentication in recent studies [4]. The proposed solutions are either unimodal [8], bi-modal [6, 9, 14, 16], one-shot [6, 7] and continuous [13, 26].

Since, DIALERAUTH is a bimodal one-shot (i.e., at login stage) authentication scheme which leverages *"text-independent"* tapping behavior and hand micro-movements, we consider sensor-assisted one-shot schemes [6, 7, 14, 16] closer to our work and we compare our work with them.

Ho [16] besides collecting the touch-based data, i.e., hold and dwell time, key-tap size, etc., also investigated the effectiveness of accelerometer readings generated during the process of entering the pre-defined 4-digit PIN. The study involving 55 users showed that motion-based features performed the best as compared to other feature types, while with the fusion of all the feature types, the accuracy was drastically improved (FAR =4.4% and FRR = 5.3%) using SVM as the classifier.

UNAGI, introduced by Giuffrida et al., [14], presents a sensor-enhanced fixed-text scheme for user authentication on Android smartphones. They reported an EER of 4.97% on fixed-text passwords and 0.08% on sensory data. Later, Buriro et al., [6] modified this scheme by introducing the concept of a 4-digit *"text-independent"* secret in addition to the sensory readings. They achieved 1% EER on a dataset of 12 users on fused bimodal data. Similarly, the scheme introduced in [7] leverages the sensory readings while a user writes her name on the smartphone touchscreen. This bimodal system achieved ≈ 95% TAR at 3.1% FAR.

Our proposed scheme DIALERAUTH is different from the existing state of the art in several ways. First, in terms of the input method, all the schemes [6, 14, 16] require text entry using the soft-keyboard, whereas DIALERAUTH uses the dialer for text entry, which is quite important in terms of user experience. Second, our experiments are based on a comparatively large-scale dataset involving 97 users (93 qualified in *sitting*, 90 qualified in *standing* and *walking*, and 72 in *walking downstairs*) activity, while [14], [6], [7], and [16] involved only 20, 12, 30, and 55 users, respectively and testing only partially the different postures. As the users in these studies were less, it is difficult to assess how their achieved error-rates would have varied, given that the number of users is a very important factor in assessing the confidence on the analysis. Third, all the schemes in [6, 7, 14, 16] performed experimentation in a controlled way, i.e., in a lab and in one session. Whereas, DIALERAUTH leverages the collection of data in multiple sessions and data was collected in totally un-controlled and un-supervised manner.

3 PROPOSED METHOD

3.1 Threat Model

We consider the situation where an attacker is already in possession of the smartphone. This scenario is common because the user might forget her smartphone somewhere, i.e., in her office, canteen, etc., or an attacker manages to steal the smartphone (e.g., through pickpocketing, etc). More specifically, we target three scenarios: (i) an attacker accidentally finds the smartphone, (ii) the attacker is victim's friend or colleague (who knows about the implemented mechanism), and (iii) an attacker who tries to mimic the user behaviors (e.g., using recorded video, etc) to unlock the victim's smartphone.

3.2 Our Approach

DIALERAUTH requires its users to enter or tap any combination of 10-digits long number to replicate their dialing process and the way the user holds the device in her hand while tapping. We expect that most of the users are familiar with the dialing process. The first authentication factor in DIALERAUTH is how the user enters her *"text-independent"* number. The second authenticating factor is the hold behavior (profiled using the extracted features from the accelerometer and gyroscope sensors). Hence, imitating the two inherently invisible behavioral characteristics, is quite difficult. DIALERAUTH exploits hand micro-movements and the classical keystroke features, i.e., hold and dwell time to authenticate the user. DIALERAUTH captures the key-hold and inter-stroke timings from the 10-digit long number. Similarly it extracts statistical features from the phone's micro-movements to profile the genuine user (as shown in Figure 2). The extracted feature vectors are concatenated together to form a final fused vector to model a bimodal system. Since, the target device is the smartphone, we apply feature selection scheme to (i) improve the system's accuracy, and to (ii) improve the performance (as processing of smaller feature vector may incur less computational cost and processing, making decision time comparatively shorter).

DIALERAUTH also includes the parameter optimization block in which we choose the best parameter, i.e., *number of hidden layers* in MLP. Since, we need to implement the proof-of-concept app, we need to finalize the best features and best parameters. DIALERAUTH creates user templates on the selected features set and trains the verifiers on those templates and saves those templates in the database. Later, the testing template is formed similarly to the training templates and matched with the pre-enrolled templates to authenticate the user.

4 METHODOLOGY

In this section, we discuss the steps taken to design DIALERAUTH.

4.1 Data Collection

We developed a customized Android application, namely *StrokeCollector*, to collect stroke timings and the sensory readings while doing so. Our application can be installed on any Android smartphone having Android 4.4 or higher version. Our app collects sensory readings at 50Hz because this rate was empirically found suitable, for user behavior profiling, in recent studies [6, 7].

We involved "UBERTESTERS[1]" - a crowd-sourcing platform to collect unsupervised field data. "UBERTESTERS" recruited 97 testers and made sure that each tester uses one and always the same smartphone for the whole experiment.

StrokeCollector collected users' interactions in 3 sessions in 3 consecutive days. It required an interaction of 30 minutes on the first day and 15 minutes on the two subsequent days. In this way, each participant had to test the app for 1 hour but including also cool down periods.

4.1.1 Participants. All the recruited testers were application testers and had IT background but not security experts. We set up a webpage, explaining the purpose, the methodology of the experiment, the user consent, and the procedure to install/uninstall the application. Out of 97 recruited users by "UBERTESTERS", some of them were disqualified because of (i) the non-availability of gyroscope sensors, (ii) their samples have Not A Number (NaNs) values, and (iii) the users had less than 30 observations in an activity. Most of the users (72), finished the whole experiment in $40 - 45$ minutes and some of them (25, users) could not finish in their allocated time of 1 hour. To test the impact of different postures in the chosen behavioral traits, the data were collected in 4 different postures (*sitting, standing, walking,* and *walking downstairs*). The posture was explicitly indicated by the tester during the experiment.

We obtained the usable data of 93 participants in *sitting*, 90 in *standing* and *walking* and 72 users in *walking downstairs* activities. The volunteers were required to install the application, answer to the demographic questions, and perform dialing actions 30 times in four activities. In total, we collected 120 samples from each user in all four activities in first two days. On the third day, the previously collected samples were used to train the dummy classifier and users had to test the app by 30 testing samples in any activity as per their preference. After each testing attempt, the result of the dummy classifier (either accept or reject) was shown as the toast message to give the tester an idea of the scheme. Since, we are not sure about the activity of testing, we do not use this data, in this paper.

Our demographics questionnaire included 4 questions. Volunteers were free to answer those or choose if they did not want to disclose. The demographics questions, and options to answer these questions, are listed in the appendix A and the summary of collected dataset and corresponding demographics is tabulated in Table 1.

Lastly, the users' had to record their experience with our scheme using System Usability Scale (SUS)[2] questionnaire. All the users who completed the whole experiment filled in the SUS questionnaire embedded in our app. Additionally, we sent a link to all the remaining participants to know their opinion about our scheme.

---

[1] https://ubertesters.com/
[2] https://www.usability.gov/how-to-and-tools/methods/system-usability-scale.html

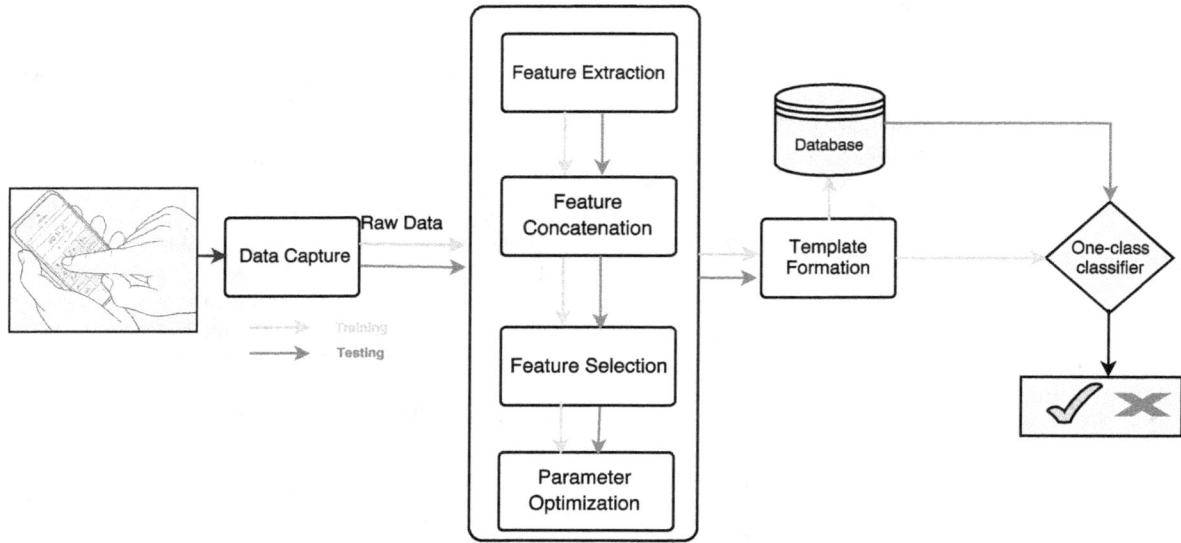

Figure 2: Model diagram of DIALERAUTH.

All the participants provided their feedback and so our usability analysis is based on the feedback of all 97 users.

Table 1: User demographics (M = Male, F = Female, U = Undisclosed, R = Right, L = Left, B = Both)

Information	Description
No. of Users	93 qualified (100, in total)
Sample Size	**Sitting** 2790 (93 **X** 30)
	Standing 2700 (90 **X** 30)
	Walking 2700 (90 **X** 30)
	Downstairs 2, 160 (72 **X** 30)
Devices	Android Smartphones with 4.4.x version
No. of Sessions	3
Gender	77(M), 20(F), 0 (U)
Handedness	91(R), 6(L) 0 (U)
Age Groups	92 (20 − 40), 5 (41 − 60)

4.2 Feature Extraction

Accelerometer and gyroscope are both 3-dimensional sensors commonly available on all the smartphones available today. We also calculated the magnitude (like the previous studies [6, 7]) using the following equation:

$$S_M = \sqrt{(a_x^2 + a_y^2 + a_z^2)} \qquad (1)$$

where S_M is the magnitude and a_x, a_y and a_z are the accelerations along the X, Y and Z directions.

All the four dimensions are processed to extract the following statistical features: Mean, Standard Deviation (STD), Skewness, Kurtosis, from each of the dimension. In this way, 16 statistical features

were extracted from each sensor (see Table 2). The final feature vector of hold behavior is 32 features long, formed by concatenating the features from two chosen sensors: accelerometer and gyroscope. Similarly, dialing behavior is profiled using the 38 timing-based features (dwell and flight time), as shown in Figure 3.

Table 2: List of selected features from sensory readings.

No.	Lift Features			
1-4	MeanX	MeanY	MeanZ	MeanM
5-8	STDX	STDY	STDZ	STDM
9-12	SkewX	SkewY	SkewZ	SkewM
13-16	KurtX	KurtY	KurtZ	KurtM

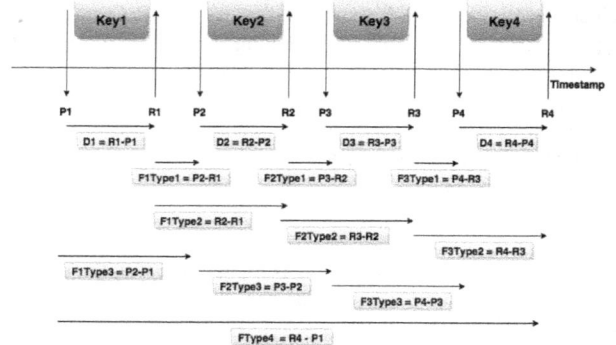

Figure 3: Features of dialing adapted from [6](for 4 digits).

4.3 Feature Fusion

The acquired biometric-data can be fused at 5 different stages, namely, sensor, feature, score, rank, and decision. The literature recommends the fusion of data as early as possible to obtain higher accuracy [17]. We preferred feature fusion over sensor level because at sensor level presence of noise could have affected, significantly, the recognition accuracy. Since, both the modalities are independent of each other, we concatenated the features of hold and dialing behavior, as suggested in [25], to form a final feature vector of 70 features to profile the user.

4.4 Feature Subset Selection

Feature subset selection is the process of selecting the most productive feature subset (based on higher accuracy) out of the full feature set. We considered feature selection because processing smaller feature vector incurs less computational time and cost. Additionally, smaller vector makes easier for the verifier to learn quickly as compared to learning on the redundant and irrelevant features.

We evaluated our combined feature set (70 features long) with a Weka-based feature selection scheme - the Information Gain Attribute Evaluator (IGAE) - a mutual-information based feature selection scheme, which ranks the features based on their contained information gain with respect to the class. The outcome of this scheme provides the feature ranking based on their feature weights (higher the better). We computed the threshold by taking the ratio of the number of features (i.e., 70) to the number of users per activity. For example, for sitting activity, the computed threshold was $70/93 = 0.75$. The features above this threshold are taken for further analysis. The list of selected features for all the activities is shown in Table 3. Motion-based features have dominated the touch-based features (see Table 3) because the touch-based features are computed on typing of arbitrary keys (independent of the content of the key) and this makes them a bit weak.

Table 3: List of selected features from fused (bi-modal) data.

Sitting	Standing	Walking	Downstairs
Acc_MeanX	Acc_MeanX	Acc_MeanX	Acc_MeanMag
Acc_MeanY	Acc_MeanY	Acc_MeanY	Acc_MeanX
Acc_MeanZ	Acc_MeanZ	Acc_MeanZ	Acc_MeanY
Acc_MeanMag	Acc_MeanMag	Acc_MeanMag	Acc_MeanZ
Acc_SkewX	Acc_SkewX	Acc_SkewX	Acc_STDMag
Acc_SkewZ	Acc_SkewZ	Acc_SkewZ	Acc_STDY
Acc_SkewMag	Acc_SkewMag	Acc_SkewMag	Acc_STDZ
Gyro_MeanX	Gyro_MeanX	Gyro_MeanX	Gyro_MeanMag
Gyro_MeanMag	Gyro_MeanMag	Gyro_MeanMag	Gyro_STDZ
Gyro_SkewX	Gyro_SkewX	Gyro_SkewX	FType4
Gyro_SkewY	Gyro_SkewY	Gyro_SkewY	-
Gyro_MeanZ	Gyro_MeanZ	Gyro_MeanZ	-
Gyro_SkewMag	Gyro_SkewMag	Gyro_SkewMag	-
-	-	F4Type2	-
-	-	F4Type3	-

4.5 Verifier Selection

We consider user authentication as one-class classification (anomaly detection) problem [7, 26], where the data from the "+ve" class

(owner), is used to train the system and is tested against the data from all other "-ve" (non-owners) classes. Trained verifier checks for the deviation between the testing sample to the training samples and decides, accordingly. Less different samples (with smaller deviation) are accepted as the patterns belonging to the "owner" and vice versa.

We used Weka - a gui-based workbench to perform one-class classification. We used multiple verifiers, namely, Bayesian Networks, K-Nearest Neighbors, Multilayer Perceptron (MLP) and Random Forest (RF), wrapped into the Weka meta-classifier -the OneClass-Classifier[3].

Bayesian classifiers such as Belief Networks (BN) use probabilistic techniques for classification. These classifiers/verifiers are widely used because of their super simplicity and faster learning capability. K-Nearest Neighbor (KNN) classifier is a density based simple and fast learner classifier [28] which can perform pretty well on any kind of a dataset and thus was considered among the top 10 classification algorithms [30]. Random Forest (RF) classifier grows multiple classification trees and classifies by providing the input vectors to each of the tree and infers the label of the class based on the majority voting. RF classifier learns quickly and never overfits [3], however it requires more memory compared to other classifiers. Multilayer Perceptron (MLP) classifier, belongs to the neural network family, and is composed of different layers, i.e., input layer, hidden layer, and output layer. It trains a non-linear approximator by learning on the feature vectors and their corresponding labels. It is found extremely useful classifier in recent studies [7, 8].

4.6 Parameter Optimization

For designing an MLP neural network, the question *"how many hidden layers?"* is very important and the solution depends mainly on the characteristics of the dataset, e.g., is the data linearly separable, etc. For linearly separable dataset, the default settings, i.e., one hidden layer, could provide the optimum results. However, because of the non-linearity of the data, we tried a number of hidden layers between $1 tc 10$ to find out the best parameter. We achieved highest TAR with 9 hidden layers. It should be noted that we performed this evaluation on selected IGAE features and used the same protocol (i.e., owner vs all would-be attackers) for evaluating different parameters for the MLP verifier.

4.7 Analysis

Our analysis starts by profiling one of the testers as the "owner" and the remaining users as "non-owners". We applied 5-fold cross-validation on the data from "owner" class to obtain the True Acceptance Rate (TAR) and False Rejection Rate (FRR). TAR shows the rate of correctly accepted patterns, and FRR shows the rate of incorrectly rejected patterns, of the genuine users, i.e., "owner". Then, we train the verifiers on the data of the genuine user, i.e., "owner" and test it against the data of all the remaining "non-owner" classes. The result of this setting also provides the binary output, i.e., False Accept Rate (FAR) and True Reject Rate (TRR). FAR shows the rate of incorrectly accepted impostor patterns as the genuine

---

[3]http://weka.sourceforge.net/doc.packages/oneClassClassifier
/weka/classifiers/meta/OneClassClassifier.html

users patterns and TRR shows the correctly rejected impostors patterns. We repeated the testing for all the users and report the average results.

4.8 Results

We show the results of our chosen verifiers in terms of $TAR = 1 - FRR$, and $FAR = 1 - TRR$. We do not report FRR and TRR to avoid the redundancy. Table 4 summarizes the obtained results (with the default settings of the verifiers) with full feature sets prior to the feature selection. Since MLP performed well yielding comparatively better results (and defeating KNN in 3 activities), we take this verifier for further analysis.

Table 4: : Results of different classifiers on full (70) and features (averaged over 93 (*sitting*), 90 (*standing & walking*) and 72 (*downstairs*) participants) in different activities.

	Sitting		Standing		Walking		Downstairs	
Classifiers	TAR	FAR	TAR	FAR	TAR	FAR	TAR	FAR
BN	69.37	12.63	67.83	11.69	67.21	8.76	67.96	13.97
RF	70.05	12.22	68.79	11.34	68.21	8.48	68.40	13.58
MLP	71.84	12.63	71.05	11.66	69.87	8.71	70.59	13.89
KNN	72.11	12.61	70.38	11.76	68.45	8.81	69.74	14.23

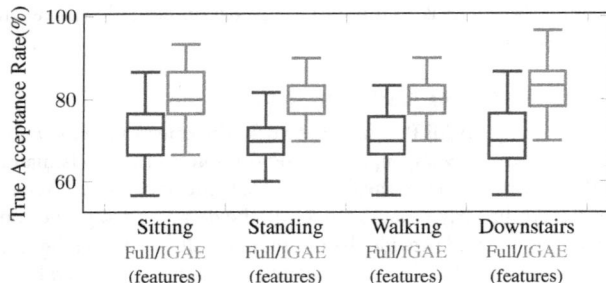

Figure 4: Comparison of TAR for full and extracted features.

With the most accurate verifier, i.e., MLP with full features, we obtained 69.87% to 71.84% TAR (see Table 4) in 4 different activities. The performance of the MLP verifier was increased on the selected IGAE features (see Figure 4). It is evident from the figure that the patterns of each of the participant are discriminated with higher accuracy. With the default parameters of MLP, i.e., with just one hidden layer, and using IGAE selected features, the achieved TAR is 81.63% compared to 71.84% (sitting), 81.13% compared to 71.05% (standing), 79.34% compared to 69.87% (walking), and 81.63% compared to 70.59% (walking downstairs). Furthermore, by applying the parameter optimization and using IGAE selected features, the TAR was improved to a significant level, i.e., from 71.84% to 85.77% in *sitting*, from 71.05% to 85.02% in *standing*, from 69.87% to 84.69% in *walking*, and from 70.59% to 84.36% in *walking downstairs*, activity.

Since we achieved the highest TAR for three activities with 9 hidden layers (see Figure 5) and lowest FAR with 8 hidden layers (see Figure 6), however, due to very less difference between the observed

FAR with 8 and 9 layers, we prototype final implementation with 9 hidden layers.

We accept that the overall performance of the system is less at this stage, compared to the sensor-enhanced fixed-text keystroke dynamics [14] however, it can be improved with the passage of time. This feature of dialing any arbitrary keys makes DIALERAUTH more usable because a user does not need to memorize the code.

5 PROOF-OF-THE-CONCEPT IMPLEMENTATION

Evaluating the accuracy of DIALERAUTH for intra-activity (training and testing in the same activity) is not enough. In real world situations, the user uses the smartphone in multiple situations, i.e., walking, biking, cycling, etc. So if the DIALERAUTH is trained in one activity, it will be useful only in that particular activity [7]. There are two solutions to this problem: firstly, the training needs to be done in multiple possible activities and their corresponding patterns needs to be saved separately in the database. During testing first the activity needs to be estimated using activity estimator (i.e., JigSaw [19]) and after determining the activity, the patterns needs to be compared with the pre-enrolled patterns of the corresponding activity. In this way, users have to train the system very well and it requires more training and end up in asking more training time and effort from the user. Additionally, this approach delays the decision time when the user logs in. Alternatively, as proposed in [7], multiple activities can be fused as well. For example, training the system with just 50 patterns in all possible activities could lead both to the user acceptance and the performance improvement. Similarly, the activities can be fused by creating a common feature vector based on the selected features, i.e., most of the features are common across activities (see Table 3).

The final proof-of-concept implementation of DIALERAUTH is based upon our findings discussed in the previous sections. It is worth repeating that MLP verifier performed well both on the full features, and selected features and provided highest TAR with 9 hidden layers. Thus, DIALERAUTH uses MLP with 9 hidden layers and the selected features (listed in Table 3) to authenticate the user. DIALERAUTH can be installed on any smartphone having in-built accelerometer and gyroscope sensors and running any Android version 4.4 or higher. DIALERAUTH requires minimal configuration at the time of installation. DIALERAUTH helps its user by displaying the suggested recommended value. At the end, the user is required to either only tap, or move (in the case of training over one modality) or do both to get authenticated.

6 SECURITY ANALYSIS

6.1 Considerations

DIALERAUTH cannot be easily attacked by a random attacker. The attacker can mount a side-channel attack using motion sensors [21], i.e., the attack can recover the entered text but not the stroke-timings. Therefore, despite having the knowledge of the entered text, the attacker would not be able to mimic the manner in which the text was entered.

As other keystroke-based schemes, DIALERAUTH too relies upon hidden features (i.e., timing-differences), it becomes than extremely hard to mount shoulder surfing, mimic attacks (through recorded

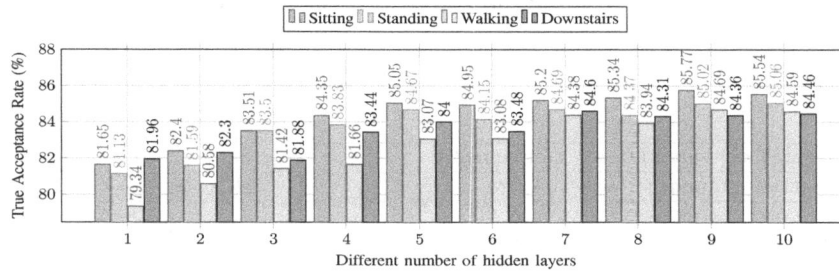

Figure 5: Parameter Optimization: highest TAR achieved is 85.77% with 9 hidden layers in sitting, 85.02% in standing, 84.69% in walking , and with 7 hidden layers 84.6% in walking downstairs. Obtained results are averaged over 93 (*sitting*), 90 (*standing*), 90 (*walking*), and 72 (*downstairs*) users.

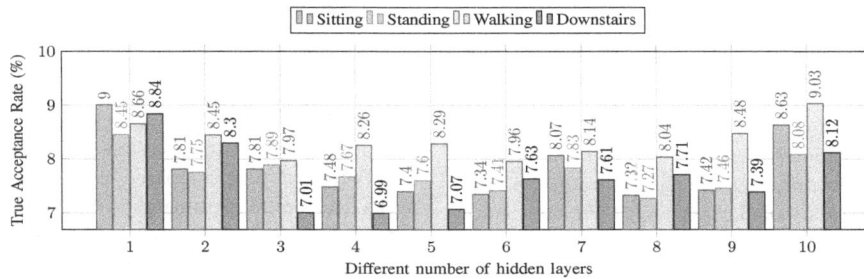

Figure 6: Parameter Optimization: Lowest FAR achieved is 7.32% with 8 hidden layers in sitting, 7.27% in standing, 8.04% in walking , and with 4 hidden layers 6.99% in walking downstairs. Obtained results are averaged over 93 (*sitting*), 90 (*standing*), 90 (*walking*), and 72 (*downstairs*) users.

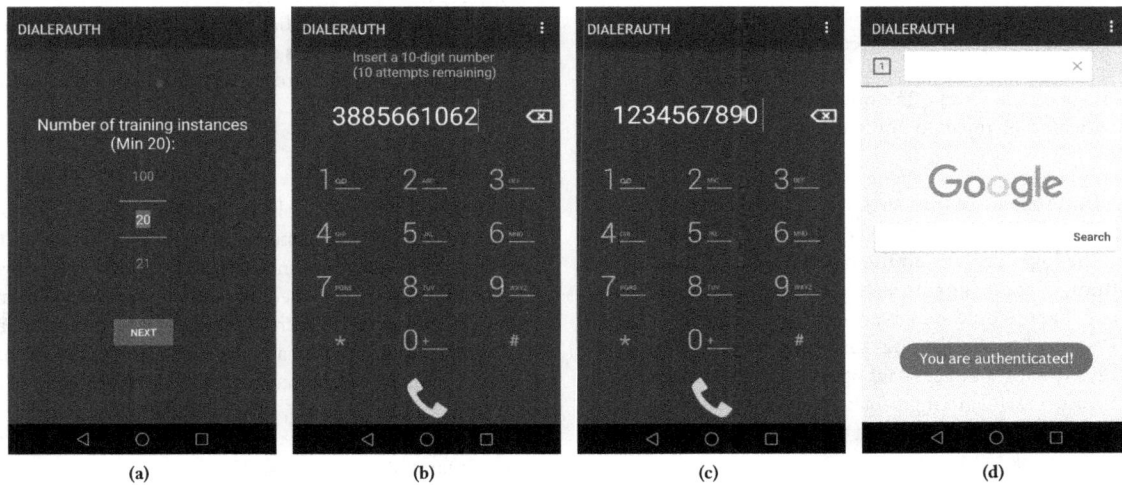

Figure 7: (a) & (b) Training the system, (c) & (d) testing the system.

videos, etc.), and other synthetic approaches [27]. Further DIALER-AUTH also depend upon the invisible phone's micro-movements the user makes while dialing. These movements are difficult to capture (at least using just naked eyes) and depend on various person-specific attributes such as height, weight, and length of the arm.

Hence mimicking these micro-movements could require to mount a quite expensive attack (i.e., using computer vision techniques). If that is considered a plausible attack, using a secret number rather than any number can be a way to mitigate such attack.

Table 5: Results of SUS-based usability study.

SUS Questions	Responses				
	Strongly Disagree	Disagree	Neutral	Agree	Strongly Agree
I think that I would like to use DIALERAUTH frequently	3	7	39	30	19
I found DIALERAUTH unnecessarily complex	34	21	28	10	4
I thought DIALERAUTH was easy to use	1	4	14	34	44
I think that I would need the support of a technical person to be able to use DIALERAUTH	59	18	11	7	2
I found the various functions in DIALERAUTH were well integrated	2	5	24	44	22
I thought there was too much inconsistency in DIALERAUTH	28	24	27	15	3
I would imagine that most people would learn to use DIALERAUTH very quickly	2	5	11	39	40
I found DIALERAUTH very cumbersome to use	28	21	31	12	5
I felt very confident using DIALERAUTH	1	5	14	36	41
I needed to learn a lot of things before I could get going with DIALERAUTH	56	21	11	8	1

6.2 Evaluation

In order to empirically determine the robustness of DIALERAUTH against possible attacks, we recruited 8 more testers (would-be adversaries) and performed the additional experiments. We installed the prototype application on three smartphones, i.e., HUAWEI GRA-L09, Samsung OnePlus One, and LG-Flex 2, trained their classifiers with the data of 3 randomly chosen participants of the main experiment. After the random attacks, the classifiers of these devices were re-trained in front of the testers with the intention that the testers would learn well the legit user's dialing behavior and attempt mimicking the trained behavior, effectively. We explained the complete experiment to the participants and requested them to dial any 10-digit number to impersonate the legit user. For each adversarial attempt, the trained classifier checks for the similarity between the testing and training samples and shows the decision as a Toast message on the screen. The outcome of the classifier was binary: authenticated or rejected and we save these outcomes as FAR and TRR.

6.2.1 Random Attacks. In this scenario, we requested the test-adversaries to dial any combination of 10-digit number and press enter to break the login process on the pre-trained classifier (over 30-dialing patterns of the legitimate user). The process was repeated for 3 legit users. Each would-be adversary tried 5 times on each smartphone (15 on all 3 smartphones and 120, in total, from all 8 testers). We tested with 5 adversarial attempts because Android devices after 5 unsuccessful attempts lock themselves for some time. All of the 120 adversarial attempts went unsuccessful, i.e., none of the attempt could break the login process.

6.2.2 Mimic Attacks. In this scenario, a valid user was asked to mimic the behaviors of the 3 legitimate users. The legit users trained their smartphones by dialing 10 times in three activities, i.e., *sitting*, *standing*, and *walking*, respectively, in front of the would-be attackers and later they were required to mimic the behaviors of the valid user. Some of the would-be adversaries also needed more demonstrations and practice and were allocated their required time slot. All 8 test adversaries were asked to mimic real user's behaviors in 5 attempts (15 total, on 3 smartphones) in any of their preferred

activity. 7 out of the 120 adversarial attempts went successful. It is worth-mentioning that 6 out of 7 successful attempts succeeded to spoof one legit user compared to 1 and 0 for other two legitimate users. The victim legitimate user might belonged to the "lambs[4]" family [31], however, majority of the users tend to be "sheeps[5]".

7 USABILITY ANALYSIS

We admit that the use of dialing process - user's action of entering telephone numbers, might be difficult for the enrollment to some, however, because of the (i) users' familiarity with the dialing process, and (ii) the flexibility to dial 10-digit *"text-independent"*, DIALERAUTH can get wide user acceptance. To assess our intuition related to usability, we relied on SUS to gather the testers reviews about DIALERAUTH. SUS is a 10-questions based questionnaire and considered as an standard tool to evaluate the usability of any system.

7.1 Methodology

The SUS[6] is a standard tool widely used to record user impressions about the usability of a system and has been also used in the context of smartphone user authentication [7, 22, 29]. The users' response to each question is recorded on a given 5-point scale ranging from "Strongly Disagree" to "Strongly Agree" as shown in Table 5. The outcome is computed as a score between 0 and 100 and termed as SUS score. The obtained score, x, is categorized as follows: (i) Best Imaginable ($x \geq 92$), (ii) Excellent ($92 < x \geq 85$), (iii) Good ($85 < x \geq 72$), (iv) OK ($72 < x \geq 52$), (v) Poor ($52 < x \geq 38$), and (vi) Worst Imaginable ($38 < x \geq 25$). We replaced the word "System" with 'DIALERAUTH'. In addition to the standard SUS questions, we also added some questions to know about testers' background and their feedback (see Appendix B).

---

[4]"Lambs are vulnerable to impersonation. When being matched against, they result in relatively high match scores, leading to potential false accepts."
[5]"Sheep make up the majority of the population of a biometric system. On average, they tend to match well against themselves and poorly against others".
[6]https://www.usability.gov/how-to-and-tools/methods/system-usability-scale.html

7.2 Responses

We report the usability analysis of DIALERAUTH on the basis of the feedback we received from all 97 study participants. The summary of the obtained responses is presented in Table 5. It is evident from the table (Question 1) that 49 users ($\approx$ 51%) were agreed or strongly agreed to use DIALERAUTH compared to just 10 (10%) who disagreed or strongly disagreed. On the simplicity and user-friendly point (Question 3), 78 (80%) of the users considered DIALERAUTH easy to use. Figure 8 illustrates the break up of obtained SUS score. Significant fraction of users (19.58%) rated DIALERAUTH as the best imaginable authentication solution, and 10.30% and 28.86% of users considered it as Excellent and Good, respectively. Overall, DIALER-AUTH was well accepted by the testers and it obtained a mean score of 73.29 (mean SUS score of 72 or higher is considered better with the higher probability of wide user acceptance).

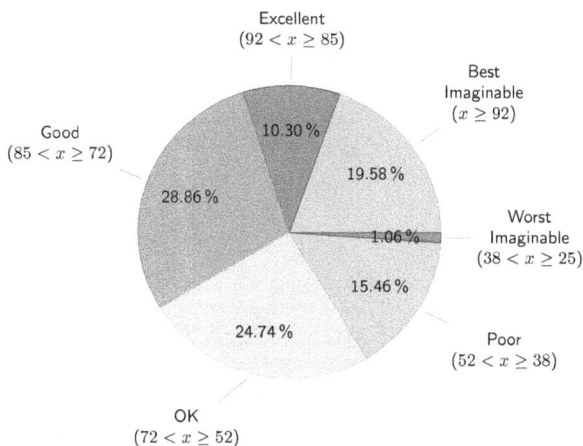

Figure 8: Break-up of the obtained SUS score.

In response to the question: "*How long have you been using the smartphone?*", 95 of 97 ($\approx$ 98%) users said they have been using it for more than 6 months. We assumed that most of the smartphone users could become the expert users after 6 months of regular usage.

Further, in response to the question "*Would you consider to use DIALERAUTH to replace the authentication mechanism you are using?*", $\approx$ 48% users replied with "Yes". More specifically, 75% of the users who did not have any authentication mechanism enabled, 38.46% slide-to-unlock users, 54.54% PIN/password users, 42.85% biometrics users, and 80% of the smartlock users, answered with "YES". This is positive indication of the user acceptance of DIALERAUTH.

As per the recorded feedback, most of the users looked satisfied mentioning DIALERAUTH as a simple, extremely convenient, user-friendly and intuitive authentication mechanism. The flexibility of tapping/dialing any number made users more comfortable.

We also got some negative responses related to the length of the digits and training the scheme. The scheme requires a fair amount of training patterns, i.e., 30 (as the users have to dial or tap multiple times for training compare to setting up a PIN or registering the face) and hence becomes unacceptable to some.

We will incorporate these suggestions into future version of DIALERAUTH before its deployment to the real world.

8 CONCLUSION AND FUTURE WORK

We have proposed a simple, secure and user-friendly, smartphone user authentication scheme leveraging the user's familiarity with the dialing process. The proposed scheme authenticates the users based on the timing differences in successive strokes while user taps 10-digit "*text-independent*" number. DIALERAUTH further adds an invisible and unobservable layer, based on the hand's micro-movement, to strengthen the security of the scheme. Hence, an attacker has to successfully mimic the two invisible and inherently secure human behaviors, i.e., the invisible timings and the phone micro-movements of the legitimate user, to access the phone.

DIALERAUTH counters the most common problems associated with different authentication schemes, e.g., user does not need to remember any secret (thus eliminating the problem of sharing and stolen passwords), it does not require any additional hardware (as the biometric technology, e.g., iris, fingerprint requires expensive dedicated hardware) and makes spoofing very difficult (as mimicking two invisible behaviors requires a lot of effort and time).

As a future work, we plan to check the effectiveness of DIALER-AUTH towards continuous authentication. We are also going to address the problem of seamless and fast detection of a user's current activity [5, 7], i.e., using Jigsaw [19], since this would allow authenticating users based on the best feature subset selected from that particular activity. We are also going to solve the DIALER-AUTH training problem (as its training in one go could be extremely cumbersome for some users) by collecting the dialing behavioral patterns in daily usage and after reaching a best number (e.g., 30), DIALERAUTH would notify the user about the availability of this modality for authentication.

9 ACKNOWLEDGEMENT

The authors would like to thank all the participants of the experiment for their time and effort, colleagues for valuable and insightful input and anonymous reviewers for their reviews and comments.

The work was partially supported by the European Training Network for CyberSecurity (NeCS) grant number 675320.

REFERENCES

[1] Zahid Akhtar. 2012. *Security of multimodal biometric systems against spoof attacks*. Ph.D. Dissertation. Department of Electrical and Electronic Engineering, University of Cagliari, Cagliari, Italy. Advisor(s) Fabio Roli.
[2] Francesco Bergadano, Daniele Gunetti, and Claudia Picardi. 2002. User authentication through keystroke dynamics. *ACM Transactions on Information and System Security (TISSEC)* 5, 4 (2002), 367–397.
[3] Leo Breiman and Adele Cutler. 2018. Random Forests. (2018). Retrieved January 8, 2018 from https://www.stat.berkeley.edu/~breiman/RandomForests/cc_home. htm#features/
[4] Attaullah Buriro. 2017. *Behavioral Biometrics for Smartphone User Authentication*. Ph.D. Dissertation. University of Trento, Italy. Advisor(s) Bruno Crispo.
[5] Attaullah Buriro, Bruno Crispo, Filippo Del Frari, Jeffrey Klardie, and Konrad Wrona. 2015. Itsme: Multi-modal and unobtrusive behavioural user authentication for smartphones. In *International Conference on Passwords*. Springer, 45–61.
[6] Attaullah Buriro, Bruno Crispo, Filippo Del Frari, and Konrad Wrona. 2015. Touchstroke: smartphone user authentication based on touch-typing biometrics. In *International Conference on Image Analysis and Processing*. Springer, 27–34.
[7] Attaullah Buriro, Bruno Crispo, Filippo Delfrari, and Konrad Wrona. 2016. Hold and Sign: A Novel Behavioral Biometrics for Smartphone User Authentication. In *IEEE Security and Privacy Workshops (SPW)*. 276–285.

[8] Attaullah Buriro, Bruno Crispo, and Yury Zhauniarovich. 2017. Please Hold On: Unobtrusive User Authentication using Smartphone's built-in Sensors. In *IEEE International Conference on Identity, Security and Behavior Analysis (ISBA-2017)*.

[9] Attaullah Buriro, Sandeep Gupta, and Bruno Crispo. 2017. Evaluation of Motion-based Touch-typing Biometrics for online Banking. (2017).

[10] Alexander De Luca, Alina Hang, Emanuel Von Zezschwitz, and Heinrich Hussmann. 2015. I Feel Like I'm Taking Selfies All Day!: Towards Understanding Biometric Authentication on Smartphones. In *Proceedings of the 33rd Annual ACM Conference on Human Factors in Computing Systems*. 1411–1414.

[11] Mohammad Omar Derawi, Claudia Nickel, Patrick Bours, and Christoph Busch. 2010. Unobtrusive user-authentication on mobile phones using biometric gait recognition. In *Proceedings of the 6th IEEE International Conference on Intelligent Information Hiding and Multimedia Signal Processing (IIH-MSP)*. 306–311.

[12] Mario Frank, Ralf Biedert, Eugene Ma, Ivan Martinovic, and Dawn Song. 2013. Touchalytics: On the applicability of touchscreen input as a behavioral biometric for continuous authentication. *IEEE transactions on information forensics and security* 8, 1 (2013), 136–148.

[13] Hugo Gascon, Sebastian Uellenbeck, Christopher Wolf, and Konrad Rieck. 2014. Continuous Authentication on Mobile Devices by Analysis of Typing Motion Behavior.. In *Sicherheit*. 1–12.

[14] Cristiano Giuffrida, Kamil Majdanik, Mauro Conti, and Herbert Bos. 2014. I sensed it was you: authenticating mobile users with sensor-enhanced keystroke dynamics. In *International Conference on Detection of Intrusions and Malware, and Vulnerability Assessment*. Springer, 92–111.

[15] Marian Harbach, Emanuel Von Zezschwitz, Andreas Fichtner, Alexander De Luca, and Matthew Smith. 2014. It's a hard lock life: A field study of smartphone (un) locking behavior and risk perception. In *Symposium on usable privacy and security (SOUPS)*. 213–230.

[16] Grant Ho. 2014. *Tapdynamics: strengthening user authentication on mobile phones with keystroke dynamics*. Technical Report. Stanford University.

[17] Anil Jain, Arun A Ross, and Karthik Nandakumar. 2011. *Introduction to biometrics*. Springer Science & Business Media.

[18] Markus Jakobsson, Elaine Shi, Philippe Golle, and Richard Chow. 2009. Implicit authentication for mobile devices. In *Proceedings of the 4th USENIX conference on Hot topics in security*. 9–9.

[19] Hong Lu, Jun Yang, Zhigang Liu, Nicholas D Lane, Tanzeem Choudhury, and Andrew T Campbell. 2010. The Jigsaw continuous sensing engine for mobile phone applications. In *Proceedings of the 8th ACM conference on embedded networked sensor systems*. 71–84.

[20] Yuxin Meng, Duncan S Wong, Roman Schlegel, et al. 2012. Touch gestures based biometric authentication scheme for touchscreen mobile phones. In *International Conference on Information Security and Cryptology*. Springer, 331–350.

[21] Emiliano Miluzzo, Alexander Varshavsky, Suhrid Balakrishnan, and Romit Roy Choudhury. 2012. Tapprints: your finger taps have fingerprints. In *Proceedings of the 10th ACM international conference on Mobile systems, applications, and services*. 323–336.

[22] Toan Van Nguyen, Napa Sae-Bae, and Nasir Memon. 2017. DRAW-A-PIN. *Computers and Security* 66, C (2017), 115–128.

[23] Claudia Nickel, Tobias Wirtl, and Christoph Busch. 2012. Authentication of smartphone users based on the way they walk using k-nn algorithm. In *Proceedings of the 8th IEEE International Conference on Intelligent Information Hiding and Multimedia Signal Processing (IIH-MSP)*. 16–20.

[24] Mudassar Raza, Muhammad Iqbal, Muhammad Sharif, and Waqas Haider. 2012. A survey of password attacks and comparative analysis on methods for secure authentication. *World Applied Sciences Journal* 19, 4 (2012), 439–444.

[25] Arun Ross and Anil Jain. 2003. Information fusion in biometrics. *Pattern recognition letters* 24, 13 (2003), 2115–2125.

[26] Zdenka Sitova, Jaroslav Sedenka, Qing Yang, Ge Peng, Gang Zhou, Paolo Gasti, and Kiran Balagani. 2015. Hmog: A new biometric modality for continuous authentication of smartphone users. *arXiv preprint arXiv* 1501 (2015).

[27] Deian Stefan, Xiaokui Shu, and Danfeng Daphne Yao. 2012. Robustness of keystroke-dynamics based biometrics against synthetic forgeries. *computers & security* 31, 1 (2012), 109–121.

[28] Saravanan Thirumuruganathan. 2010. A Detailed Introduction to K-Nearest Neighbor (KNN) Algorithm. (May 2010). Retrieved Nov 20, 2017 from https://goo.gl/qvgpwc

[29] Shari Trewin, Cal Swart, Larry Koved, Jacquelyn Martino, Kapil Singh, and Shay Ben-David. 2012. Biometric authentication on a mobile device: a study of user effort, error and task disruption. In *Proceedings of the 28th ACM Annual Computer Security Applications Conference (ACSAC 2012)*. 159–168.

[30] Xindong Wu, Vipin Kumar, J Ross Quinlan, Joydeep Ghosh, Qiang Yang, Hiroshi Motoda, Geoffrey J McLachlan, Angus Ng, Bing Liu, S Yu Philip, et al. 2008. Top 10 algorithms in data mining. *Knowledge and information systems* 14, 1 (2008), 1–37.

[31] Neil Yager and Ted Dunstone. 2010. The biometric menagerie. *IEEE transactions on pattern analysis and machine intelligence* 32, 2 (2010), 220–230.

[32] Heng Zhang, Vishal M Patel, Mohammed Fathy, and Rama Chellappa. 2015. Touch gesture-based active user authentication using dictionaries. In *Proceedings of the IEEE Winter Conference on Applications of Computer Vision (WACV)*. 207–214.

Appendices

A DEMOGRAPHIC QUESTIONNAIRE

(1) What is your gender?
- Male
- Female
- I don't want to disclose

(2) How old you are?
- ≤ than 20 years.
- > 20 years and ≤ 40 years.
- > 40 years and ≤ 60 years.
- > than 60 years.
- I don't want to disclose

(3) Tell us about your nationality.
- _____
- I don't want to disclose

(4) Which hand(s) do you use for interacting with your smartphone?
- Right
- Left
- Both
- I don't want to disclose

B ADDED QUESTIONS TO SUS QUESTIONNAIRE

(1) How long have you been using the smartphone?
- ≤ than 6 months.
- > than 6 months.

(2) Which authentication mechanism are you using on your smartphone?
- PIN/Password/Graphical Password
- Android Smartlock
- Biometrics (Face, Fingerprint, IRIS, Voice, etc)
- Slide-to-Unlock
- None

(3) Would you consider to use DialerAuth to replace the authentication mechanism you are using?
- Yes
- No

(4) Do you have any feedback you like to share with us?
- _____

Authorship Attribution of Android Apps

Hugo Gonzalez
Polytechnic University of San Luis
Potosi
San Luis Potosi, SLP, MX
hugo.gonzalez@upslp.edu.mx

Natalia Stakhanova
Faculty of Computer Science,
University of New Brunswick
Fredericton, New Brunswick, CA
natalia@unb.ca

Ali A. Ghorbani
Faculty of Computer Science,
University of New Brunswick
Fredericton, New Brunswick, CA
ghorbani@unb.ca

ABSTRACT

Since the first computer virus hit the Advanced Research Projects Agency Network (ARPANET) in the early 1970s, the security community interest revolved around ways to expose the identities of malware writers. Knowledge of the adversarial identities promised additional leverage to security experts in their ongoing battle against those perpetrators. At the dawn of computing era, when malware writers and malicious software were characterized by the lack of experience and relative simplicity, the task of uncovering the identities of virus writers was more or less straightforward. Manual analysis of source code often revealed personal, identifiable information embedded by authors themselves. But these times have long gone. Modern days malware writers extensively use numerous malware code generators to mass produce new variants and employ advanced obfuscation techniques to hide their identities. As a result the work of security experts trying to uncover the identities of malware writers became significantly more challenging and time consuming.

To gain insight into the identity of an adversary, we turn our attention to authorship attribution research, which offers a broad spectrum of techniques for identifying an author of a document, based on the analysis of an author's writing style. Equipped with these methods, we explore attribution of Android binaries and the role of features related to the development process on the determination of Android binary authorship.

Within this context, we propose an incremental approach to perform authorship attribution of Android apps. First to a set of known authors and then the generation of new profiles for unknown apps. We assess the effectiveness of our approach on several sets of malicious and legitimate Android binaries produced by actual developers, as opposed to using artificially created authors' data. We achieve 97.5% accuracy on these authors' data. We further evaluate our approach on more than 131,000 apps collected from various sources including 10 different markets around the globe.

CCS CONCEPTS

• **Security and privacy → Malware and its mitigation**; **Mobile and wireless security**;

KEYWORDS

Android, authorship attribution, suspicious authors

ACM Reference Format:
Hugo Gonzalez, Natalia Stakhanova, and Ali A. Ghorbani. 2018. Authorship Attribution of Android Apps. In *CODASPY '18: Eighth ACM Conference on Data and Application Security and Privacy, March 19–21, 2018, Tempe, AZ, USA.* ACM, New York, NY, USA, 10 pages. https://doi.org/10.1145/3176258.3176322

1 INTRODUCTION

Since the appearance of the first computer virus, the security community interest revolved around ways to expose an identity of an adversary. In the early days this was often possible due to relative simplicity of malicious software and inexperience of malware writers. Manual analysis of a code often revealed personal, identifiable information embedded by authors themselves [20]. However, with the extensive use of advanced obfuscation techniques and wide availability of malware code generators that allow malware authors to rapidly produce mass numbers of new variants, this process became significantly more challenging requiring advanced methodologies. These methods found in authorship attribution research, are referred to as stylometry. Well-established in social science, it offers a broad spectrum of techniques aiming to characterize an author of a document given a set of textual features that quantify an author's writing style [22]. The underlying assumption of attribution is an existence of an inherent distinctive writing style, unique to an author and easily distinguishable among others. Quantified representation of this style can be viewed as a fingerprint.

One of the main difficulties in the field lies in compiling such a fingerprint that provides efficient and accurate characterization of an author style. In the traditional setting, authorship attribution relies heavily on information that allows deeper linguistic analysis of author's works (e.g., richness of vocabulary, tense of verbs, semantic analysis of sentences). In software field, emphasis is mostly put on surface characteristics such as variable naming, program layout, and spacing, that reflect textual nature of source code [5]. Such approach is merely dictated by the nature of the field that in many cases fails to provide original source code of software (e.g., malware analysis, commercial software theft) leaving researchers with its binary representation. Unfortunately, such binary code retains very few of the surface characteristics. As a result in the recent years a few studies shifted its focus towards analysis of program binaries [7, 18, 19],

This shift was also driven by practical objectives. Such digital fingerprint of an author retrieved from a malicious program binary can potentially serve as a single signature for attributing suspicious executable to that author. From a practical perspective, the immediate benefit of malware author attribution is clear: instead of detecting every malware strain using narrow specialized signatures, we could effectively characterize all malware variants generated by its author. This approach allows us to significantly reduce the computational resources required for malware detection.

In this work, we explore this angle focusing specifically on mobile domain. Just in the first quarter of 2017 G-data labs reported registering around 8,400 new malware samples daily [16]. They estimated that 3.5 million of new malware samples will be discovered this year. In their analysis from 2016, Kaspersky Labs [15] reported a big grown in Banking malware and trojan-ransomware that are able to bypass security mechanisms in GooglePlay bouncer and new versions of Android.

In this study, we propose an approach for authorship attribution of Android apps using a set of features related to author's decision over an application development process, specifically, metrics about the structure of the app extracted from .dex files, such as number of employed methods, classes, fields, strings, etc. We specially focus on the usage of data structures and opcodes associated with data structures manipulations. Data structure features were among the basic set of programmer's attribution measures proposed in fundamental work of Spafford et al [21] for attribution of binary code.

We validate our approach on a set of manually collected Android applications published from 37 authors in different markets. We further evaluate it with over 30,000 apps from known different malicious sources, official market and eight third-party markets.

Finally, we perform a large-scale study of over 160,000 Android applications from official Google market and Virus Total stream service.

The remainder of the paper discusses the related work in Section 2. It introduces features employed in Section 3, presents the details of proposed approach in Section 4. Data employed is described in Section 5. Validation and evaluation results are in Section 6. Section 7 concludes the paper.

2 RELATED WORK

The problem of program authorship attribution is not new. Its feasibility has been shown in a small pilot study by [14] and has since revolved around the idea of attributing source code through various characteristics of a programmer style [11]. The consistency of programming style formed a foundation of software author attribution [11]. Recently, Burrows et al [4] systematized techniques for attributing source code. One of the largest focuses in this context is plagiarism detection [5,

header	Structural information
string_ids	Offset list for strings
type_ids	Index list into the string_ids for types
proto_ids	Identifiers list for prototypes
field_ids	Identifiers list for fields
method_ids	Identifiers list for methods
class_defs	Structure list for classes
data	Bytecode and data
link_data	Data for statically linked files.

Figure 1: The structure of a .dex file

23]. Since source code is available, such detection mostly entails analysis of syntactical features (e.g., format alterations, renaming, control replacement). However, due to the lack of malware source code, these features have limited applicability beyond the plagiarism domain.

In malware analysis, the majority of research focused on analysis of binaries, e.g., behaviour of the software [24], API calls [6], and control flow [12]. Although the primary focus of these approaches was extraction of 'software birthmark', i.e., a combination of unique software characteristics, the results of these studies can be complementary to author attribution and should be further explored in this context.

The problem of binary attribution has been explored by Rosenblum et al. in a series of studies [18, 19] that investigated tool-chain provenance. The studies confirmed feasibility of automating a discovery of details that characterize the production process of a given binary (e.g., the compiler family, versions, optimization options and source languages). This approach was later extended by Alrabaee et al. [1]. The authors employed a multilayer approach integrating syntax-based and semantics-based features. Binary analysis was also explored in attribution of metamorphic malware to malware generation engines by Chouchane et al. [7].

Although all these results showed high accuracy of attribution among well defined engines/tool-chain components, the question of applicability of these results to extracting unknown developers' fingerprints remains. We propose a framework to attribute Android apps to a known group of authors and to unknown groups.

3 BINARY ATTRIBUTION

One of the first cases of authorship attribution over malware binary code for forensics purposes was offered by Spafford and Weeber in 1992 [21]. Spafford and Weeber believed that every programmer has its own unique style. Investigating a security breach, this authors connected the manual writing recognition used by law-enforcement to identify people, with the task of analysis of residual code in a security incident to identify an adversary. As a result of this study, several groups of features for binary code attribution were proposed, among them are features related to programmer's style and expertise (e.g., presence of error handling) and features related to the development process (e.g., employed data structures, systems calls, tools).

The tell-tale signs of tools indicating the origin of executable have been successfully explored in previous studies [7, 9]. In this work we also focus on the features related to the development process and explore the impact of the number of employed methods, classes and data structures, and opcodes associated with data structures on attributing Android apps to an author.

Android background. An Android application, an apk file, is a compressed folder that contains a variety of files including an executable .dex file; AndroidManifest.xml file that describes the content of the package, resource files (e.g., image, sound files), and optional native code that is usually called from the classes.dex file.

A classes.dex file is a binary that results from compiling the app's Java source code. As illustrated by Figure 1, this file is partitioned into different sections that describe the structure of the file.

Among them are several identifier lists that contain offsets pointing to the corresponding entries in the data section. As such string identifiers list (string_ids section) provides offsets to all strings used by .dex file, while class identifier list contains offsets to the information related with classes. This class information list contains offsets pointing to method's information, this method's information contains offsets to the actual code that belongs to it. The code section include binary information (bytecode) about opcode and employed in-line data structures.

In this work, we focus on the use of types, methods, classes, fields, data structures employed and the opcodes related to data structure usage contained in method's code section. To reduce the amount of opcodes to analyze, we employ a filter to discard previously known or analyzed common code [10]. The statistics from this percentages of methods are also included in our feature vector.

Employed features. While programming in Java, an author could choose between several data structures to fulfill her purposes. After compiling the code data structures look different from basic arrays. Let us review as an example the Java code in Figure 2 that includes data structures and arrays. Line 28 that uses a hashtable is transformed in the following smali representation:

```
const/4 v8, 0x1
iget-object v1, p0,
        Lcom/gsg/test1/MainActivity;->
        numbers:Ljava/util/Hashtable;
const-string v2, "one"
invoke-static {v8}, Ljava/lang/Integer;->
        valueOf(I)Ljava/lang/Integer;
move-result-object v3
invoke-virtual {v1, v2, v3},
        Ljava/util/Hashtable;->
        put(Ljava/lang/Object;Ljava/lang/Object;)
        Ljava/lang/Object;
```

```
13  public class MainActivity extends ActionBarActivity {
14      Hashtable<String, Integer> numbers
15              = new Hashtable<String, Integer>();
16      ArrayList<String> MyArrayList
17              = new ArrayList<String>();
18
19      double aPowersOfTwo[] = new double[5];
20
21      int aNums[] = new int[5];
22      @Override
23      protected void onCreate(Bundle savedInstanceState) {
24          super.onCreate(savedInstanceState);
25          setContentView(R.layout.activity_main);
26
27
28          numbers.put("one", 1);
29          numbers.put("two", 2);
30          numbers.put("three", 3);
31
32          MyArrayList.clear();
33          MyArrayList.add("one");
34          MyArrayList.add("two");
35          MyArrayList.add("three");
36          MyArrayList.remove(2);
37
38
39          aNums = new int[]{2, 4, 6};
40          aPowersOfTwo[2] = 4;
41          aPowersOfTwo[3] = 9;
42          aPowersOfTwo[4] = 16;
43          String aStooges[] = {"Larry", "Moe", "Curly"};
44      }
45
```

Figure 2: Basic Android java code that include data structures and arrays.

The creation of array of integers in line 39 is represented in smali as:

```
const/4 v7, 0x3
new-array v1, v7, [I
fill-array-data v1, :array_0
:array_0
.array-data 4
    0x2
    0x4
    0x6
.end array-data
```

For the final example, string array from line 43 is represented in smali as:

```
new-array v0, v7, [Ljava/lang/String;
const/4 v1, 0x0
const-string v2, "Larry"
aput-object v2, v0, v1
const-string v1, "Moe"
aput-object v1, v0, v8
const-string v1, "Curly"
aput-object v1, v0, v6
.local v0, "aStooges":[Ljava/lang/String;
```

The decisions and experience of a developer will impact in the way data structures are used in the Android app. This usage could be related to the functionality of the app. However, it is our believe that developers decisions influence more on the usage of data structures than the functionality of the app. Basic arrays are meant to store data of similar type, these are very common in Android development and are used in almost all Android apps. A quick analysis of app extracted from GooglePlay market confirms this intuition. Figure 3 gives us an overview on how Android programmers

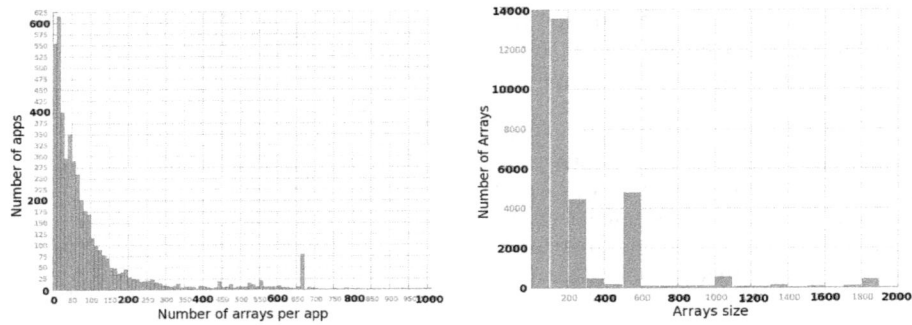

Figure 3: Array usage and array's size distribution from GooglePlay market.

Table 1: Array- unrelated features

total number of classes
total number of classes containing interfaces
total number of classes containing information about source file
total number of classes containing annotations
total number of classes containing data
total number of direct methods
total number of virtual methods
total number of abstract methods
total number of methods containing try and catch
total number of methods containing debug information
total number of static fields
total number of instanced fields
total size of instructions expressed in bytes

Table 2: Array related bytecode mnemonics

Opcode bytecode	Description
ARRAY LENGTH	Store the length of the indicated array in the given destination register .
NEW ARRAY	Construct a new array of the indicated type and size.
FILLED NEW ARRAY	Construct an array of the given type and size, filling it with the supplied contents.
FILLED NEW ARRAY RANGE	Similar as previous.
FILL ARRAY DATA	Fill the given array with the indicated data
AGET, AGET BOOLEAN, AGET BYTE, AGET CHAR, AGET SHORT, AGET WIDE, AGET OBJECT	Perform array operation at the identified index of the given array, loading into the value register.
APUT, APUT BOOLEAN, APUT BYTE, APUT CHAR, APUT SHORT, APUT WIDE, APUT OBJECT	Perform array operation at the identified index of the given array, storing into the value register.

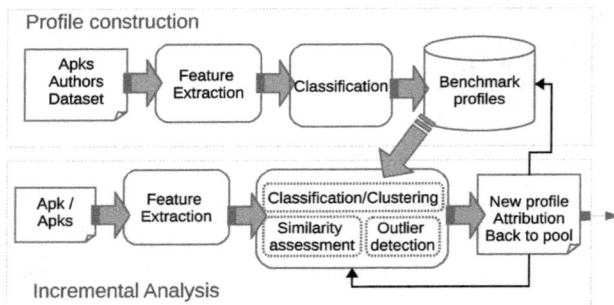

Figure 4: Automatic incremental learning for attribution framework

use array data structures in legitimate apps (see GooglePlay-2015 dataset in Table 3 for details). Out of 4517 apps only 106 (2%) did not employ arrays. Among the rest, the majority of apps use at least 300 array structures.

Figure 3 shows distribution of array's size. The largest size includes more than 14,000 elements while the smallest array has only 5 elements. The average size of an array is 37.54 elements with an standard deviation of 239.29 elements. This large deviation shows that the usage of arrays can be a potential indicator of an author's distinctive development style. Along with the rest of the data structures employed in the app.

4 AUTHORSHIP ATTRIBUTION FRAMEWORK

The goal of the proposed approach is to systematically attribute Android apps to corresponding author's profiles. Typically, attribution studies in literary domain focus on identifying an author of a sample out of a set of candidates based on sample's similarity to stylistic discriminators found in benchmark profiles. In malware domain, this has a limited value as benchmark profiles only represent a small set of known authors. As such, it is necessary to step beyond the known set and group stylistically similar binaries not attributed to the existing profiles as they might potentially be linked to a new author.

The proposed framework incorporates two components: a *profile construction* focusing on creating benchmark profiles for known authors, and an *incremental analysis*, responsible for a ongoing analysis of Android binaries, their attribution to the existing benchmark profiles and the generation of new profiles for stylistically similar binaries refereed to as emerging profiles. The overview of the framework is given in Figure 4.

The framework takes as an input an Android app. As the first step, the list of data structures used in the incoming app is extracted, then this app is parsed to retrieve bytecode from .dex file which is then analyzed to extract the rest of the features. To reduce the overhead in classification and speed up the process, common code is discarded. To determine and extract common code we follow a procedure explained in [10]. From the remaining bytecode, values related to array size, array operations (see Table 2), and values related to classes, methods and fields (Table 1) are extracted. These raw values are abstracted into a feature vector composed of four parts: (1) a fixed number of features from the numerical values of classes, methods, and fields; (2) the statistic values from size of array definitions, average, mean, median, standard deviation and variance; (3) variable length features extracted from the values of n-grams created from array operations opcodes and (4) the n-grams created from data structures detected. Since the resulting vector of features has variable lenght, we employ a mapping technique presented by Rieck et al [17] to convert it into a fixed length array. In this process each n-gram is hashed, then a number of bytes is chosen to represent the index on a sparse vector. This feature vector serves as a basis for grouping stylistically similar binaries.

Profile construction. The first framework component is responsible for generating the baseline model for further detection and clustering analysis. It can be viewed as a supervised authorship attribution problem; that is given a set of Android authors $A = a_1; a_2; a_3; \ldots; a_i; \ldots; a_n$ and their respective apps $a_i = app_1; app_2; app_3; \ldots; app_m$ to generate a model that can be used to attribute Android binaries to a given set of fixed authors. The aim is, given an apk file app_x, to determine who among these authors wrote it. We use machine learning techniques with prediction probability capabilities to build this model. We use Random Forest prediction as a classifier to build this model.

Random Forest classification algorithm was proposed as a bagging technique with an additional layer of randomness. When building standard trees, each node is split using the best split among all variables. In a Random Forest each node is split using the best split among a subset of variables randomly chosen at this node. Although this strategy might seem counter intuitive, it is quite robust and turns out to perform very well even in the presence of overfitting [3].

Incremental analysis. Once the model outlining benchmark profiles is generated, an incremental component is responsible for attributing new apps to the existing profiles (classification) and discovering new possible profiles (novelty detection and clustering) for Android apps that were not attributed yet to existing authors. Novelty detection of multiple classes is not studied as well as detection for one class at a time [8]. Here we propose an approach that let us create multiple classes from apps not seen before, and cluster them using same results from class prediction. This process is outlined in Algorithm 1. The algorithm takes as input apps to be processed (*apps*), thresholds (*NoveltyThreshold*,

GroupThreshold) and *buckets* to group similar apps. It offers as output apps attributed (*appsAttributed*) and apps to create new profiles (*appsForNewProfiles*). The assignment of new apps to a *bucket* is based on the probability score of an *app* belonging to an existing profile, or similarity between incoming apps, if a new profile needs to be formed.

Similar to profile construction step, we employ Random Forest classification to calculate a probability score of a given app being a part of each of the benchmark profiles. However, any machine learning method that gives a probability could be employed.

If a probability exceeds a defined *NoveltyThreshold* (we experimented with several values), we attribute this instance to a predicted author profile (line 9), otherwise this probability is used to analyze app similarity with other apps(line 12). In other words, if app is scored to be a part of profile A with 98%, it is automatically assigned to that author's profile. However, if the probability score is 20%, then it is clustered with other apps that are also given 20% probability of being a part of profile A. The intuition behind this is simple: even though these apps are not close enough to profile A, they share common attributes and can potentially form a new candidate profile. How the apps are clustered is guided by bucket size, e.g., with a bucket size of 10, for any given profile apps with a score 0-10%, 10-20%, 20-30%, etc. will be grouped together.

Algorithm 1 Minibatch Cluster and Classify algorithm

1: **function** INCREMENTAL PROFILE DISCOVERY
2:   input : *apps*
3:   input : *incrementalThreshold*
4:   input : *benchmarkThreshold*
5:   input : *buckets*
6:   output : *appsAttributed, appsNewProfiles*
7:   **for** each *app* in *apps* **do**
8:     Calculate *ProbabilityScore*
9:     **if** *ProbabilityScore > benchmarkThreshold* **then**
10:       Add *app* to *appsAttributed*
11:     **else**
12:       Grouping *app* into *buckets*
13:     **end if**
14:   **end for**
15:   **for** each *bucket* in *buckets* **do**
16:     **if** number of apps in *bucket > incrementalThreshold* **then**
17:       Remove outliers from *bucket*
18:       Create *NewProfile* from *bucket*
19:       add *NewProfile* to *appsNewProfile*
20:     **end if**
21:   **end for**
      return *appsAttributed, appsNewProfiles*
22: **end function**

The next step is to assess how similar these unassigned apps are within their respective groups and filter out potential outliers (line 17). The similarity between grouped apps is calculated based on Cosine Similarity ($K(X, Y)$) which computes the normalized dot product of X and Y as follows:

$$K(X,Y) = \frac{\langle X,Y \rangle}{(\|X\| * \|Y\|)} \quad (1)$$

To define outliers, first we found maximum distance among instances, calculate average, standard deviation, and quartiles $(q1, q2, q3)$. Then we decide on an outlier threshold between a naive approach inspired by standard deviation detection and the standard box plot rule (Equation 3). Instead of deciding 2 standard deviations as a threshold for upper outlier, we defined the average of maximun distance and average distances(Equation 2).

$$outlier = \frac{maximun\_distance + average}{2} \quad (2)$$

$$outlierboxplot = q3 + iqd * 3 \quad (3)$$

In Equation 3 $q1, q3$ represent lower and upper quartile, and $iqd = q3 - q1$ is interquartile distance.

Finally, an outlier is flagged if more than half of similarity distances are over this outlier threshold (we experiment with different outlier thresholds as such as maximum or minimum of the previous values, and with no outlier detection at all.)

If the resulting clusters of apps is over the $GroupThreshold$ (several values were explored), it forms a new candidate profile(line 18). It is important to note that this probability-based clustering is employed to avoid expensive pair-wise comparison among all unassigned apps. Apps not attributed in this round, will be assessed in next round, this time including new candidate profiles discovered in the last round.

Our model is retrained to incorporate new candidate profiles discovered in previous step. Note that as opposed to benchmark profiles that include validated information about their authors, these new profiles are limited to a label that is created automatically from originating profiles, probability, and number of apps in a newly created group.

5 DATA

To evaluate our proposed approach and study for the automatic creation of author label profiles, we gathered a large collection of 196,385 unique Android applications from different sources that we employed for various stages of analysis (Table 3).

To validate our approach we carefully selected some apps from "markets dataset" that contain the same serial certificate number used to sign these apps. We omitted public, leaked and debug certificates which anyone can have access to. Then we manually verified apps from the remaining 43 authors. To ensure that only unique apps were used in our analysis, all apps with duplicate .dex files were removed, authors with less than 20 apps were also removed. We finally obtained a set with 33 authors and 1428 apps.

Since these authors were deemed to be legitimate (verified through VirusTotal website), we also searched for those who produce malicious apps. For this purpose we employed Kooduos collaborative system [13], collecting groups of apps with the same certificates and flagged as malicious. This process produced a set of 222 apps from 10 different authors.

In addition to this, we retrieved 131 malware apps produced by Hacking Team, identified in Kooduos system by a community yara rule. These apps presumably from Hacking Team contain different certificates. If they are written by the same set of people, our system should be able to recognize this.

To explore the benefits of our approach in practice, we also collected apps from a number of other sources. Specifically, several malware families from Drebin dataset [2]; 1,395 apps from open source market Fdroid; 10 adware and ransomware families; 4,574 apps collected from Google Play; 23,656 apps from eight third-party markets; and 116,264 apps retrived from VirusTotal stream.

Details of datasets are shown in Table 3.

6 EXPERIMENTAL RESULTS

On our experiments, we aimed to evaluate several aspects of our approach:

(1) Validate the effectiveness of the proposed approach in attributing apps to the corresponding authors.

(2) Investigate the effect of $NoveltyThreshold$ and $GroupThresh$ on accuracy of attribution.

(3) Assess the ability of the incremental analysis component to attribute unknown apps and generate emergent profiles.

(4) Evaluate our approach capability to attribute a stream of wild data to the existing profiles.

6.1 Validating effectiveness

To validate the proposed approach, we employed our manually labeled $Authors\ dataset$ and performed 5-fold cross-validation in all experiments. The classification was based on authors' feature vectors composed of classes, fields and methods information, data structures employed and array related mnemonics. Since the amount of features containing application structure related values is stable, a major concern is a potentially significant amount of generated n-grams from data structures and array related opcodes. We evaluated the approach accuracy for values of n ranging from 1 to 8, then embedding the results into a fixed length array of 541, 1053, 2077, 4125, 8221, 16413, 32797, 65565 and 131101 features. The results are presented in Table 4.

The best result in terms of accuracy is 98.12%, with 8-gram and 65565 features, and 158 seconds in average to perform the classification. With a large number of features the time to perform training and testing increases. With a large number of n-grams the time to extract and represent the features increases. We decide to choose not the best accuracy, but the best trade-off between accuracy and time based on the n-grams and number of features. The selected parameters for future experiments are 3-grams with 2077 features, which lead to an accuracy of 97.7% and 68 seconds on average to perform classification.

6.2 Tunning thresholds

The proposed incremental analysis approach relies on three different thresholds for attributing binaries and forming

Table 3: Datasets

Name	Apps	Description
Authors dataset	1,444	Collected from eight different markets, this dataset contains information about 37 known authors with more than 20 apps in the markets, based on the assumption that same serial numbers certificates leads to same author (without considering public or leaked certificates)
Malicious authors	222	Collected from koodous system, this dataset contains at least 10 unique and malicious apps from 10 different authors. We use the same assumption that similar certificates lead to same author.
Hacking Team apps	131	Mobile apps offered by surveillance malware vendor Hacking Team. They were collected from koodous system from community ruleset 675.
Drebin partial dataset	3,181	From the original dataset, we only retained 47 malware families with more then 20 apps.
Adware dataset	211	Three related families (kemoge 90, shedun 97, shuanet 24) known to trojanize legitimate apps.
Ransomware dataset	408	Ransomware including the following seven families, fakeDefender 44, koler 74, Pletor 16, RansomBO 100, scarePakage 2, sLocker 72 and svpeng 100
Fdroid dataset	1,395	Open source apps without advertisement libraries.
GooglePlay-2015 dataset	4,574	Apps collected from Google Play in middle 2015 from all categories, top popular and top new.
Markets dataset	23,656	Apps collected from the following third-party markets: 360, 3gyu, anzhi, aptoide, mobomarket, nduoa, tencent, xiaomi.
GooglePlay-2016 dataset	898	Apps collected in January 2016.
VirusTotal stream	116,264	Suspicious apps provided by VirusTotal service.
Total	196,385	

Table 4: Accuracy results over 5-fold cross validation for different n-gram values

N-grams	# features	Performance (sec)	Accuracy
8	65565	158.61	98.12 %
5	32797	102.67	97.85 %
4	131101	92.49	97.84 %
7	65565	140.46	97.83 %
8	131101	171.01	97.77 %
6	65565	122.47	97.77 %
4	16413	84.83	97.76 %
5	16413	102.14	97.76 %
3	**2077**	**68.69**	**97.71** %
6	131101	128.21	97.71 %
5	131101	111.39	97.70 %
4	65565	86.27	97.70 %
5	4125	102.64	97.69 %
7	131101	149.31	97.69 %
5	8221	102.75	97.63 %

new profiles: *NoveltyThreshold* , *outliersThreshold* and *GroupThreshold*. We conducted a series of experiments to determine the impact of these thresholds on attributing apps using *Authors' dataset*. Our classifier was trained on 75% of the authors (i.e., 25 authors and their corresponding apps)

and tested on the remaining 8 authors. Since traditional metrics for evaluation of classification accuracy did not reveal enough information about how the apps were attributed, we used several other metrics to help us assess the behavior of thresholds. Specifically, we evaluated thresholds in terms of percentage of attributed apps AA, percentage of correctly attributed apps among all considered apps TCA, and a percentage of correctly attributed apps among those that were attributed to some profiles (CA).

$$AA = \frac{Apps\_attributed}{Total\_apps\_reviewed} \quad (4)$$

$$TCA = \frac{Apps\_correctly\_attributed}{Total\_apps\_reviewed} \quad (5)$$

$$CA = \frac{TCA}{AA} = \frac{Apps\_correctly\_attributed}{Apps\_attributed} \quad (6)$$

For this analysis, we also experimented with several bucket sizes: 10, 15, 20, 30 and three scenarios for filtering outliers: no outliers filtering (No), maximum (MAX) or minimum (MIN) between values defined to detect outliers. To avoid situations when 2-3 apps form a new profile, the minimum number of apps required to establish a profile was enforced as *GroupThreshold*, we experimented with 20, 15, 10, 7, 5 apps as minimum (20 is the least amount of apps in the dataset). The best results are showed in Table 5.

While we can achieve over 96% in correctly attribute apps (CA), AA and TCA values are below 80%. The highest

Table 5: Thresholds tuning using Authors' dataset

Bucket size	Min num of apps allowed	Outliers	Total apps	AA	TCA	CA
10	7	MIN	361	78.77 %	76.39 %	**96.97** %
10	10	MIN	396	74.82 %	71.61 %	95.71 %
10	5	MIN	387	83.87 %	80.64 %	96.15 %
10	5	NO	325	85.99 %	80.30 %	93.38 %
15	10	MIN	377	78.41 %	75.52 %	96.31 %
15	5	MAX	415	88.09 %	80.47 %	91.35 %
15	5	NO	374	87.10 %	**82.26** %	94.45 %
20	5	MIN	402	87.62 %	81.67 %	93.21 %
30	5	MIN	361	**88.43** %	79.48 %	89.89 %
30	10	NO	420	86.48 %	75.02 %	86.74 %

amount of attributed apps (AA=88.43%) was achieved with a bucket size of 30 and 5 apps as a minimum. Similar results were received with a bucket size of 15 and 5 minimum apps, that is 87% with no outlier detection, and 88.09% with maximum outlier detection. Since the difference between these results is insignificant, other factors have to be taken into consideration. One of these is the presence of outliers detection. Generally, additional processing of candidate profiles incurs an overhead on the system, so with equal performance, it is desirable to avoid this overhead. It is interesting to note though that these threshold settings (bucket size of 15, 5 minimum apps, and no outlier detection) also provide the highest amount of correctly attributed apps among these options (94.45%). These are the parameters we will employ throughout the rest of the experiments.

We repeat the same experiment, with Malicious authors data. The best 10 results based on TCA value are shown in Table 6. The performance under different settings is similar. The highest amount of apps is attributed with bucket size of 20, 5 minimum apps and no outlier detection (AA=80.47% with CA=70.70%). However, the threshold parameters selected in the previous experiments reached very similar result (AA=78% and CA=71%).

6.3 Incremental analysis

Given the optimal thresholds obtained in the previous round of experiments, we turned our attention to incremental analysis component.

Starting with benchmark profiles, we sequentially feed our system with the following datasets in this order: Hacking team, Drebin, Adware, Ransomware, Fdroid, GooglePlay-2015 and Markets datasets. This experiment was conducted in two phases: malicious data first, followed by the last 3 datasets. The results from the first phase are given in Table 7. The overall attribution rate for each of the datasets is fairly high, reaching 100% in case of apps coming from the Hacking Team. Out of attributed apps, the majority were assigned to labels (emergent profiles) generated for a given set (90% of attributed Hacking Team apps were part of 3 new profiles). For the malicious data, it is safe to assume that apps attributed to benchmark profiles are labeled incorrectly. Intuitively, this makes sense as original benchmark profiles were built on

benign data and thus attribution of malware to legitimate profile is likely to be an error. The overall percentage of these miss attributed apps across datasets in this phase ranged between 9-0%.

The second phase focused on the datasets thought to be primarily benign. As a result of this experiment, Fdroid dataset produced 124 emergent profiles, Googleplay2015 dataset produced 733 profiles and Markets data produced 94 new profiles. Even though we did not expect any apps to be attributed to profiles generated in the first phase, less than 10 apps overall were labeled as part of these malicious emergent profiles. Manual check of these apps revealed some suspicious behaviour and presence of adware. The percentage of apps attributed to emergent profiles also dropped compared to what we saw in case of malicious data. This is likely to be the result of authors' diversity, i.e., the number of different authors contributing to GooglePlay market is significantly larger than that in Hacking team, as an example.

6.4 Attributing a stream of apps

In practical setting, an analyst might be interested to identify apps in the wild that are potentially written by a given set of authors. Using multiple certificates and claiming different identities is not uncommon on the markets. However, figuring out whether or not apps belong to the same author is challenging. Having an easy way to attribute unknown apps to already established and well-known profiles is beneficial in practice. As such in this experiment we focus on a given scenario.

We evaluated a stream of over 160 000 wild apps obtained from GooglePlay and VirusTotal using defined thresholds, benchmark and emergent profiles generated by all other datasets. In this experiment we were not concerned with generation of new emergent profiles, but were rather interested to see if any apps captured in the wild can be attributed to already established profiles. The results are given in Table 8.

With the size of our datasets and the variety of potential authors, it is not surprising that much smaller percentage of apps were attributed. 6% of apps in GooglePlay data were attributed to overall 59 existing profiles and 9% of VirusTotal set to 104 profiles. Among them, 20% of GooglePlay apps and 25% of VirusTotal apps were attributed to original known

Table 6: Thresholds tuning for emerging profiles, attributing Malicious authors data

Bucket size	Min num of apps allowed	Outliers	AA	TCA	CA
10	5	MIN	75.34 %	**58.36** %	**77.46** %
10	5	MAX	76.96 %	56.76 %	73.75 %
10	5	NO	77.05 %	57.50 %	74.63 %
10	7	MIN	72.32 %	54.91 %	75.93 %
15	5	MIN	78.20 %	56.42 %	72.15 %
15	5	MAX	78.18 %	57.64 %	73.73 %
15	5	NO	78.29 %	55.81 %	71.29 %
15	7	MIN	75.56 %	54.86 %	72.61 %
20	5	MIN	78.99 %	56.73 %	71.83 %
20	5	MAX	80.29 %	54.53 %	67.91 %
20	5	NO	80.47 %	56.89 %	70.70 %
20	7	MIN	77.77 %	54.37 %	69.91 %
30	5	MIN	80.18 %	55.54 %	69.27 %
30	5	MAX	80.36 %	54.44 %	67.74 %
30	5	NO	**80.61** %	53.94 %	66.92 %

Table 7: Evaluation of incremental analysis

Dataset	Num of apps	Num of emerg. profiles	AA	Apps attrib. to emerg. profiles
Hacking team	131	3	100%	90% (118)
Drebin	3181	117	50% (1588)	91%(1442)
Adware	211	3	54% (113)	94%(106)
Ransomware	408	12	86% (349)	97%(338)
Fdroid	1395	124	18% (254)	100%(254)
Googleplay2015	4574	733	31% (1442)	20%(289)
Markets datasets	23 656	94	10% (2478)	68%(1681)

Table 8: Attributing stream of wild apps

Dataset	Num of apps	Num of attrib apps	Num of profiles	Num of apps attrib to bench profiles
Googleplay2016	44,915	6%(2921)	59	20%(598)
VirusTotal	116,264	9%(10 717)	104	25%(2721)

and verified benchmark profiles. The remaining attributed apps were labeled as parts of emergent profiles. As such 9 GooglePlay apps were attributed to a profile dominated by Hamob malware family. This profile was manually checked and all apps were verified through VirusTotal service. Our approach was not designed for malware detection, however this finding indicates that the same author was involved in development of samples of this malware family, or at least in part. This is common in practice and only confirms our results.

Similarly, among apps from VirusTotal repository 544 apps were attributed to 31 emergent profiles that were deemed suspicious. Checking these apps through VirusTotal service also confirmed their correct labeling. Among 544 apps, 96.51% (525) where correctly attributed to various malicious families, and only 16 apps were detected as benign. Their further manual analysis showed that all 16 apps had the same structure

and used the same set of advertisement libraries in exactly same way, as a result we assume that they probably belong to the same source/author and if we were generating emergent profiles, they would likely form one profile.

6.5 New labels for a known dataset

Using defined thresholds, benchmark and emergent profiles generated by all previous datasets, we attribute the whole Drebin dataset, not just the part that we use before to assign new labels based on possible author profiles.

From 5,555 apps 3,643 remain without known author. The rest of apps where attributed to 28 probable authors, with a close match between families and low mixture between families and profiles. The whole list of apps and labels could be downloaded from **github.com/hugo-glez/author-labels**.

7 CONCLUSION

In this work we presented an approach to attribute unlabeled apps to an established set of author profiles and generate Android developers' profiles for known apps. Our analysis is based on author's development style extracted from various features related to authors decisions about development process, number of employed methods, classes and data structures, and associated opcodes extracted from Android binary code. We design and present an incremental Mini batch classify and cluster algorithm, that employs Random Forest predictor to determine the probability of an app belonging to an existing profile. We analyzed almost 35,000 apps and created 259 profiles. From these profiles, 93 where related to malicious apps and authors.

We also evaluated over 160,000 apps to further assess the effectiveness of our approach in attributing apps. Since ground truth is not available for some employed data, we can not objectively evaluate accuracy, and thus measure the number of attributed apps and verify whether these apps are attributed to suspicious or legitimate profiles.

To the best of our knowledge there are no similar approaches to compare our work with. Previous works only work on close-source world where they identify author previously known. However, our evaluation over a set of known authors showed similar or better performance.

Our model is completely data driven and is able to create new author profiles from real Android apps and attribute unknown binaries to these newly established profiles. Our results are encouraging and offer an incentive to extend and continue the development in this area. To facilitate following research in this area, we release our created datasets to a broader research community.

REFERENCES

[1] Saed Alrabaee, Noman Saleem, Stere Preda, Lingyu Wang, and Mourad Debbabi. 2014. OBA2: an Onion approach to binary code authorship attribution. *Digital Investigation* 11 (2014), S94–S103.

[2] Daniel Arp, Michael Spreitzenbarth, Malte Hübner, Hugo Gascon, and Konrad Rieck. 2014. DREBIN: Effective and Explainable Detection of Android Malware in Your Pocket. In *Proceedings of the 21th Annual NDSS*.

[3] Leo Breiman. 2001. Random forests. *Machine learning* 45, 1 (2001), 5–32.

[4] Steven Burrows, Alexandra L Uitdenbogerd, and Andrew Turpin. 2014. Comparing techniques for authorship attribution of source code. *Software: Practice and Experience* 44, August 2012 (2014), 1–32. https://doi.org/10.1002/spe

[5] Aylin Caliskan-Islam, Richard Harang, Andrew Liu, Arvind Narayanan, Clare Voss, Fabian Yamaguchi, and Rachel Greenstadt. 2015. De-anonymizing Programmers via Code Stylometry. In *24th USENIX Security Symposium (USENIX Security 15)*. USENIX Association, Washington, D.C., 255–270.

[6] Dong-Kyu Chae, Sang-Wook Kim, Jiwoon Ha, Sang-Chul Lee, and Gyun Woo. 2013. Software plagiarism detection via the static API call frequency birthmark. *Proceedings of the 28th Annual ACM Symposium on Applied Computing - SAC '13* (2013), 1639. https://doi.org/10.1145/2480362.2480668

[7] Radhouane Chouchane, Natalia Stakhanova, Andrew Walenstein, and Arun Lakhotia. 2013. Detecting machine-morphed malware variants via engine attribution. *Journal of Computer Virology and Hacking Techniques* (2013). https://doi.org/10.1007/s11416-013-0183-6

[8] E. R. de Faria, I. R. Gonalves, J. Gama, and A. C. P. d. L. F. Carvalho. 2015. Evaluation of Multiclass Novelty Detection Algorithms for Data Streams. *IEEE Transactions on Knowledge and Data Engineering* 27, 11 (Nov 2015), 2961–2973. https://doi.org/10.1109/TKDE.2015.2441713

[9] Hugo Gonzalez, Andi A. Kadir, Natalia Stakhanova, Abdullah J. Alzahrani, and Ali A. Ghorbani. 2015. Exploring Reverse Engineering Symptoms in Android Apps. In *Proceedings of the Eighth European Workshop on System Security (EuroSec '15)*. ACM, New York, NY, USA, Article 7, 7 pages.

[10] H. Gonzalez, N. Stakhanova, and A. A. Ghorbani. 2016. Measuring code reuse in Android apps. In *2016 14th Annual Conference on Privacy, Security and Trust (PST)*. 187–195. https://doi.org/10.1109/PST.2016.7906925

[11] Jane Huffman Hayes and Jeff Offutt. 2010. Recognizing authors: an examination of the consistent programmer hypothesis. *Softw. Test. Verif. Reliab.* 20, 4 (Dec. 2010), 329–356. https://doi.org/10.1002/stvr.412

[12] Yoon-Chan Jhi, Xinran Wang, Xiaoqi Jia, Sencun Zhu, Peng Liu, and Dinghao Wu. 2011. Value-based program characterization and its application to software plagiarism detection. In *Proceedings of the 33rd International Conference on Software Engineering*. ACM, 756–765.

[13] Koodous. [n. d.]. Collaborative platform for APK analysis. https://koodous.com. ([n. d.]).

[14] Ivan Krsul and Eugene H. Spafford. 1996. Authorship Analysis: Identifying The Author of a Program. *Computers and Security* (1996).

[15] Kaspersky labs. 2017. MOBILE MALWARE EVOLUTION 2016. https://press.kaspersky.com/files/2017/02/Mobile_report_with-Interpol_2016_27-Feb-20172.pdf. (February 2017). Accessed May 27, 2017.

[16] Christian Lueg. 2017. 8,400 new Android malware samples every day. https://www.gdatasoftware.com/blog/2017/04/29712-8-400-new-android-malware-samples-every-day. (2017). Accessed May 27, 2017.

[17] Konrad Rieck, Christian Wressnegger, and Alexander Bikadorov. 2012. Sally: A tool for embedding strings in vector spaces. *Journal of Machine Learning Research* 13, Nov (2012), 3247–3251.

[18] N Rosenblum, X Zhu, and B Miller. 2011. Who wrote this code? Identifying the authors of program binaries. *Computer SecurityESORICS 2011* (2011). http://www.springerlink.com/index/C422JT41687VU470.pdf

[19] Nathan E. Rosenblum, Barton P. Miller, and Xiaojin Zhu. 2010. Extracting compiler provenance from program binaries. *Proceedings of the 9th ACM SIGPLAN-SIGSOFT workshop on Program analysis for software tools and engineering - PASTE '10* (2010), 21. https://doi.org/10.1145/1806672.1806678

[20] Eugene H Spafford. 1994. Computer viruses as artificial life. *Artificial life* 1, 3 (1994), 249–265.

[21] Eugene H. Spafford and Stephen A. Weeber. 1992. Software Forensics: Can We Track Code to its Authors? (1992).

[22] Efstathios Stamatatos. 2009. A Survey of Modern Authorship Attribution Methods. *JOURNAL OF THE AMERICAN SOCIETY FOR INFORMATION SCIENCE AND TECHNOLOGY* (2009), 538556.

[23] Benno Stein, Nedim Lipka, and Peter Prettenhofer. 2011. Intrinsic plagiarism analysis. *Lang. Resour. Eval.* 45, 1 (March 2011), 63–82.

[24] Zhi Wang, Xuxian Jiang, Weidong Cui, and Peng Ning. 2009. Countering kernel rootkits with lightweight hook protection. In *Proceedings of the 16th ACM conference on Computer and communications security*. ACM, 545–554.

Securing Wireless Neurostimulators

Eduard Marin[1], Dave Singelée[1], Bohan Yang[1], Vladimir Volski[2], Guy A. E. Vandenbosch[2]
Bart Nuttin[3] and Bart Preneel[1]
[1] imec-COSIC, KU Leuven, Belgium
{firstname.lastname}@esat.kuleuven.be
[2] ESAT-TELEMIC, KU Leuven, Belgium
{vladimir.volski,guy.vandenbosch}@kuleuven.be
[3] Neurosurgery, UZ Leuven, Belgium
{bart.nuttin}@kuleuven.be

ABSTRACT

Implantable medical devices (IMDs) typically rely on proprietary protocols to wirelessly communicate with external device programmers. In this paper, we fully reverse engineer the proprietary protocol between a device programmer and a widely used commercial neurostimulator from one of the leading IMD manufacturers. For the reverse engineering, we follow a black-box approach and use inexpensive hardware equipment. We document the message format and the protocol state-machine, and show that the transmissions sent over the air are neither encrypted nor authenticated. Furthermore, we conduct several software radio-based attacks that could compromise the safety and privacy of patients, and investigate the feasibility of performing these attacks in real scenarios.

Motivated by our findings, we propose a security architecture that allows for secure data exchange between the device programmer and the neurostimulator. It relies on using a patient's physiological signal for generating a symmetric key in the neurostimulator, and transporting this key from the neurostimulator to the device programmer through a secret out-of-band (OOB) channel. Our solution allows the device programmer and the neurostimulator to agree on a symmetric session key without these devices needing to share any prior secrets; offers an effective and practical balance between security and permissive access in emergencies; requires only minor hardware changes in the devices; adds minimal computation and communication overhead; and provides forward and backward security. Finally, we implement a proof-of-concept of our solution.

CCS CONCEPTS

• **Security and privacy** → **Embedded systems security**; *Key management*;

KEYWORDS

Proprietary wireless communication protocol, black-box reverse engineering, low-cost randomness source, security architecture.

ACM Reference format:
Eduard Marin[1], Dave Singelée[1], Bohan Yang[1], Vladimir Volski[2], Guy A. E. Vandenbosch[2] Bart Nuttin[3] and Bart Preneel[1] [1] imec-COSIC, KU Leuven, Belgium {firstname.lastname}@esat.kuleuven.be [2] ESAT-TELEMIC, KU Leuven, Belgium {vladimir.volski,guy.vandenbosch}@kuleuven.be [3] Neurosurgery, UZ Leuven, Belgium {bart.nuttin}@kuleuven.be . 2018. Securing Wireless Neurostimulators. In *Proceedings of Eighth ACM Conference on Data and Application Security and Privacy, Tempe, AZ, USA, March 19–21, 2018 (CODASPY '18)*, 12 pages.
https://doi.org/10.1145/3176258.3176310

1 INTRODUCTION

In the US, chronic pain already affects more people than those suffering from diabetes, heart disease and cancer altogether [1]. In recent years, the number of people with movement disorders such as Parkinson s disease or essential tremor has also increased. It is estimated that seven to ten million people worldwide are living with Parkinson's disease [6]. Many of these problems can be relieved with neurostimulators that deliver controlled electrical signals to specific targeted areas in the patient's brain.

The newest generations of neurostimulators often include wireless capabilities that enable remote monitoring and reprogramming through an external device programmer. While the wireless interface enables more flexible and personalized treatments for patients, it also opens the door for adversaries to conduct software radio-based attacks. If strong security mechanisms are not in place, adversaries could send malicious commands to the neurostimulator in order to deliver undesired electrical signals to the patient's brain. For example, adversaries could change the settings of the neurostimulator to increase the voltage of the signals that are continuously delivered to the patient's brain. This could prevent the patient from speaking or moving, cause irreversible damage to his brain, or even worse, be life-threatening.

Beyond attacks that can endanger the patient's safety, there are other attacks that can, for example, compromise the patient's privacy. On the one hand, adversaries could leverage the wireless nature of the communication to intercept the data transmitted over the air. The transmitted data is personal data, and some of it is sensitive medical data. On the other hand, a more sophisticated form of privacy attack would be to use signals extracted from the brain to make inferences about patients. While this is currently not possible, future generations of neurostimulators will use information extracted from patients brain signals for the development of more precise and effective therapies. In that case, adversaries could capture and analyze brain signals such as the P-300 wave, a brain response that begins 300 ms after a stimulus is presented to a subject. The P-300 wave shows the brain's ability to recognize familiar information. Martinovic et al. performed a side-channel attack on a Brain Computer Interface (BCI) while connected to several subjects, and showed that the P-300 wave can leak sensitive personal information such as passwords, PINs, whether a person is known to the subject, or even reveal emotions and thoughts [29]. All the attacks described above clearly show the need for analyzing the security and privacy of neurostimulators.

1.1 Problem statement and challenges

Several papers have demonstrated that implantable medical devices (IMDs) with wireless capabilities often lack strong security mechanisms. Halperin et al. were the first to identify some of the potential security and privacy threats on IMDs [19]. Hei et al. proposed simple yet effective denial-of-service (DoS) attacks against IMDs that cannot be prevented with traditional cryptographic approaches. The goal of these attacks is to deplete the IMD's resources such that the battery lifetime is reduced from several years to a few weeks [21]. These attacks are similar to the sleep deprivation torture attack proposed by Stajano and Anderson [38]. In 2008, Halperin et al. analyzed the proprietary protocol between a device programmer and an implantable cardioverter defibrillator (ICD) over a short-range communication channel (less than 10 cm) [20]. Because of the lack of security mechanisms, they were able to realize various attacks by replaying past transmissions sent by legitimate device programmers. Marin et al. fully reverse engineered the proprietary protocol between a device programmer and a latest generation ICD over a long-range communication channel (from 2 to 5 m) [27]. They also showed that it is possible to conduct attacks using only inexpensive hardware equipment without needing to be close to the patient. Similarly, Li et al. were able to emulate legitimate remote controls to perform attacks against insulin pumps [14]. Marin et al. extended the previous work by reverse engineering the proprietary protocol between an insulin pump and all its potential peripherals [28]. In previous work, Denning et al. and Rushanan et al. highlighted the need for evaluating the security and privacy of neurostimulators [15, 35]. In this paper, we tackle this problem and investigate the security of the proprietary protocol between a device programmer and a widely used commercial neurostimulator.

Securing the communication between IMDs and device programmers is a non-trivial task. Firstly, IMDs are resource-constrained devices with tight power and computational constraints, and a limited battery capacity. Furthermore, IMDs lack input and output interfaces, such as a keyboard or a screen, and cannot be physically accessed once they are implanted. Secondly, IMDs need to satisfy several important requirements for proper functioning, such as reliability, availability and safety. Adding security mechanisms into IMDs is challenging due to inherent tensions between some of these requirements and the desirable security and privacy goals. For example, IMDs should provide permissive access control such that

doctors can access the IMD in emergencies. A small delay when contacting care providers for device-specific cryptographic keys could prevent the patient from receiving care on time. However, if access control policies are not sufficiently strong, IMDs could be exposed to attacks. This shows the need for designing security solutions that achieve an effective balance between security and permissive access control in emergencies.

To bootstrap a secure communication channel between the IMD and the device programmer, cryptographic keys first need to be securely initialized and shared. This can be achieved using traditional approaches based on symmetric or public-key cryptography. For example, one could pre-install a device-specific symmetric key in each IMD during manufacturing, or use a key diversification protocol [20, 27]. However, as explained above, it may not be possible for medical personnel to contact care providers on the fly for requesting device-specific cryptographic keys. If a key diversification protocol is used, storing the master key in tamper-proof hardware in all device programmers would bring substantial security risks; if the master key is ever compromised, the security of millions of IMDs would be at risk. Instead, one could opt for storing the master key in the cloud but this is not a viable option since device programmers are required to operate at all times, including during Internet or cloud provider outages. Another solution would be to pre-install a public-private key pair in each IMD, and use any secure key transport or key agreement protocol. This approach would require a robust, worldwide infrastructure that keeps an updated list of trustworthy device programmers as well as a revocation mechanism that ensures that IMDs cannot communicate with untrustworthy device programmers [9]. Unfortunately, having such a robust worldwide infrastructure is difficult, and IMDs do not have an Internet connection to periodically get a certificate revocation list (CRL) or sufficient memory to store all the necessary certificates. This shows that traditional solutions may not be applicable for IMDs due to their unique functional requirements and limited resources.

1.2 Contributions

To the best of our knowledge, this is the first paper that evaluates the security of the wireless communication protocol between a device programmer and a widely used neurostimulator from one of the leading IMD manufacturers. In addition, we propose a practical and efficient security architecture that enables the device programmer and the neurostimulator to create a secure communication channel. In detail, our main contributions can be summarized as follows:

- **Security analysis.** We describe the process of how to reverse engineer the proprietary protocol between the device programmer and the neurostimulator. We follow a *black-box reverse engineering* approach and use inexpensive commercial hardware equipment.
- **Software radio-based attacks.** We assess the feasibility and demonstrate software radio-based attacks on neurostimulators. We also elaborate on how adversaries can overcome some of the limitations and challenges of these attacks.
- **Low-cost source of randomness for neurostimulators.** We explore the possibility of using a patient's brain physiological signal as a randomness source for generating keys,

and detail the process of extracting entropy from it. We evaluate our technique using real data extracted from the brain of 22 mice.

- **Security architecture for neurostimulators.** We present a complete security architecture that includes the generation of random session keys, the secure transportation of these keys from the neurostimulator to the device programmer and the cryptographic protocols to secure the communication flow.

Disclosure of results. We followed the principle of responsible disclosure and contacted the manufacturer six months before publishing our results. After discussing our findings with the manufacturer, we chose not to disclose the full details of the obtained results since this could help someone to mount these attacks on neurostimulators used by patients.

Paper outline. The remainder of this paper is organized as follows. Section 2 gives an overview of related work. Section 3 describes the devices that comprise the neurostimulation system, whereas our laboratory setup is shown in Sect. 4. Section 5 details the process of reverse engineering the proprietary protocol between the device programmer and the neurostimulator to discover the message format and the protocol state-machine. Section 6 shows several software radio-based attacks that we are able to conduct on the neurostimulator, while a security architecture to preclude these attacks is proposed in Sect. 7. Section 8 discusses possible limitations of our solution and provides some directions for future work. Section 9 gives concluding remarks.

2 RELATED WORK

There are two main categories of countermeasures to secure the communication between the IMD and the device programmer: (i) those based on using an external device as a proxy, and (ii) those relying on an out-of-band channel to allow the devices securely agree on a cryptographic key.

2.1 External devices

Gollakota et al. proposed an external device known as "shield", that jams the messages to/from the IMD to prevent others from decoding them, while still being able to successfully decode the messages itself [17]. While the shield can mitigate some of the existing security problems, it offers only very limited protection since adversaries could bypass it by transmitting messages with more power than those sent by the shield. Furthermore, a multiple-input multiple-output (MIMO) eavesdropper could suppress the jamming signal and recover the data sent by the devices, as shown by Tippenhauer et al. [39]. Xu et al. presented the "IMDGuard", a wearable proxy device that performs an authentication process on the ICD's behalf [41]. The IMDGuard relies on patient's electrocardiography (ECG) signals to generate a symmetric key that is valid for one session and is known only to the IMD and itself. However, Rostami et al. found that the IMDGuard is vulnerable to a man-in-the-middle (MiTM) attack which reduces its effective key length from 129 bits to 86 bits [33]. Overall, although external devices that use friendly jamming could help protecting legacy devices, they could also jam transmissions sent by legitimate devices. In some countries, jammers are illegal and their use can result in large fines.

Thus, it is unlikely that these solutions will be accepted by the US federal drug administration (FDA) and adopted by manufacturers.

2.2 Out-of-band channels

Another prominent family of countermeasures relies on establishing a cryptographic key between the device programmer and the IMD via an auxiliary or out-of-band (OOB) channel. OOB channels typically have low-bandwidth and are easy to set up. There exist two types of OOB channels: (i) *authentic* or (ii) *secret*. The former represents a channel where Bob is guaranteed that the message he receives was actually sent by Alice. The data can however be eavesdropped by others. The latter represents a channel where Alice is guaranteed that the message she sends is only received by Bob. However, Bob does not know that the data comes from Alice.

Halperin et al. proposed to use a radio-frequency identification (RFID) tag in combination with a piezo-element to achieve audio-based key distribution [20]. They were the first to introduce a countermeasure that does not consume energy from the IMD's battery. Nevertheless, the audio transmissions generated by the piezo-element can be eavesdropped, as shown by Halevi et al. [18]. As this technique uses a carrier frequency within the audible range so that it can be perceived by patients, it is unclear whether this technique could be applied in noisy environments. Kim et al. [24] and Abhishek Anand et al. [10] presented two similar vibration-based key transport protocols through which the device programmer and the IMD can agree on a cryptographic key [24]. Since vibration results in unintentional acoustic emanations, both solutions proposed that the device programmer generates a masking sound to hide the acoustic emanations. However, these solutions require the IMD to have extra hardware, and it is unclear whether the masking sound produced by the device programmer can have an effect in the data sent over the vibration channel. Furthermore, Trippel et al. showed that the integrity of audio and vibration sensor outputs can be compromised by injecting malicious analog acoustic signals [40]. This could allow adversaries to modify the key being sent over the audio/vibration channel in their favor so that the IMD establishes a key with a malicious device. Rasmussen et al. proposed an access control scheme based on ultrasonic distance bounding which enables the IMD to accept any device programmer that is in its close proximity [32]. The main limitation of this solution is that it requires dedicated analog hardware, which makes it not suitable for IMDs. Unfortunately, all the previous solutions have important limitations and drawbacks or have been proven to be vulnerable to security attacks.

The closest solution to ours is the heart-to-heart (H2H) protocol proposed by Rostami et al. [34]. H2H uses a novel access control policy called "touch-to-access" which ensures access to the IMD by any device programmer that can touch the patient's skin to measure his interpulse interval (IPI) (i.e. the time between heart beats). In H2H, both the device programmer and the IMD need to simultaneously measure the patient's heart rate. The heart rate is then used as a "fuzzy password" that is known only to the device programmer and the IMD. The authors state that one of the main advantages of using the patient's heart rate is that it can be measured anywhere in the patient's body just by touching his skin. However, this solution has several weaknesses and limitations. Firstly, Marin et al. showed that

H2H is vulnerable to a reflection and a MiTM attack [26]. Secondly, it is unclear how the authors transformed the IPI signal from analog to its digital form. Thirdly, the H2H protocol has a large communication and computation cost. It requires the IMD to transmit a substantial amount of messages and uses public-key cryptography, which can be too energy consuming for resource-constrained devices such as IMDs. Lastly, several articles have shown that the IPI can be measured remotely using a wide range of techniques. For example, Calleja et al. showed that it is possible to remotely gather information of cardiac signals using widely available inexpensive hardware [13]. Seepers et al. evaluated the feasibility of remote attacks using the existing remote photoplethysmography (rPPG) methods [36]. Their evaluation demonstrates that rPPG achieves similar accuracy as when measuring the heart rate by touching the patient's skin. Poh et al. proposed a simple, low-cost technique through which it is possible to measure the heart rate using a standard webcam [31]. Recently, Katabi et al. demonstrated that WiFi signals can be used to detect the breathing and heart rate of individuals [8]. All these papers render H2H (and other systems relying on the secrecy of the patient's heart rate such as the IMDGuard) insecure. This paper proposes a practical and effective solution that follows the "touch-to-access" principle, but overcomes all the previous limitations.

3 NEUROSTIMULATION SYSTEM

This section describes the devices that comprise the neurostimulation system. This includes device programmers used by doctors and patients as well as neurostimulators.

Device programmers: they are external portable devices used to read out patient's medical data stored on the neurostimulator or to reprogram its settings. There are two types of device programmer: those used by doctors and those used by patients. The former has full privileges to read data and modify the neurostimulator's settings, whereas the latter has restricted permissions, allowing only controlled therapy modifications, as established by the doctor.

Neurostimulators: they are devices implanted subcutaneously near the clavicle that are connected to the brain through several leads. They have limited memory storage, processing power and a battery with limited capacity that cannot be recharged or replaced. When the battery is depleted, the patient needs to undergo surgery in order to get a new implant. Such a surgery always introduces a small, but not negligible risk of infections, sometimes even with lethal consequences. We deliberately chose not to disclose how long the battery lasts because this could implicitly reveal the manufacturer and neurostimulator models that we investigated.

The device programmer contains a magnetic programming head that is used to communicate with the neurostimulator over a wireless bi-directional short-range communication channel (less than 10 cm). The programming head needs to be placed on the patient's chest in close proximity to the neurostimulator for the entire duration of the communication. In most cases, patients have their neurostimulators being interrogated and/or reprogrammed in isolated controlled locations, e.g. the doctor's office. However, patients also need to frequently use their own device programmer in order to adjust the stimulation configuration, for example, when lying, sitting or walking.

4 LABORATORY SETUP

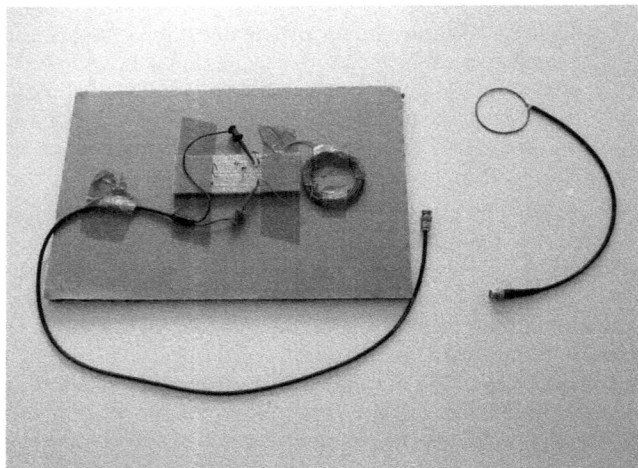

Figure 1: Antennas used for receiving and transmitting signals. The transmit antenna is shown on the left, the receive antenna on the right.

Our laboratory setup comprises inexpensive commercial hardware devices including a standard laptop and a USB-6351 data acquisition system (DAQ) from National Instruments [3]. Moreover, we built two antennas for receiving and transmitting messages respectively, as shown in Fig. 1. For receiving messages, we created a simple antenna by cutting a coaxial cable and connecting a circular piece of copper to it. Even though this antenna allowed us to capture messages exchanged between the devices, its impedance was too low to transmit signals with enough power. To overcome this problem, we designed our own antenna for transmitting signals (for more details, we refer the reader to Appendix A).

5 INTERCEPTING RF TRANSMISSIONS

This paper analyzes the security of the proprietary protocol between the device programmer and the neurostimulator to communicate wirelessly over a short-range communication channel. This is a challenging task because there is no information available about the protocol specifications. IMD manufacturers typically rely on keeping the protocol specifications secret as a means to provide security (i.e. security-through-obscurity). Protocol reverse engineering implies finding both the message format and the protocol state-machine without knowing the protocol specifications. Several articles [20, 27] have already shown that proprietary protocols can be reverse-engineered. While several techniques can be applied to reverse engineer proprietary protocols, physical access to the devices is often necessary, e.g. to extract the firmware.

In this paper, we follow a *black-box reverse engineering* approach which allows us to find the inner-workings of the protocol by only providing inputs to the devices and looking at their outputs. In other words, we change any of the neurostimulator's settings using the device programmer, and then inspect the format of the transmitted messages. Our black-box methodology is a labor-intensive and challenging process yet it is more realistic than other approaches. By following this approach, we assess the feasibility of reverse engineering the proprietary protocol by a weak adversary with limited resources and capabilities who cannot have physical access to the devices but can only intercept the messages sent wirelessly. We acknowledge that having access to the device programmer during our experiments in order to perform certain actions can speed up the process of reverse engineering the protocol. However, although this process may take longer when the actions being performed on the device programmer are not known, adversaries can still learn the inner-working of the protocol by intercepting and analyzing transmissions sent over the air by legitimate devices.

Next, we describe how to reverse engineer the proprietary protocol used by a specific neurostimulator model. However, we also conducted various experiments using other neurostimulator models, and came to similar findings as the ones described in this paper. Figure 3 shows the format of the messages sent by the device programmer.

5.1 Wireless communication parameters

Before capturing the messages exchanged between the device programmer and the neurostimulator, we first needed to discover several wireless communication parameters such as the transmission frequency, modulation and encoding scheme, and the symbol rate being used. This step is crucial as the use of slightly different parameters compared to those used by the devices would result in an incorrect demodulation of the captured messages, i.e. messages with erroneous bits.

The first step of our analysis was to find the frequency at which the devices transmit their messages. By entering the unique device programmer's federal communications commission identifier (FCC ID) in the FCC database [5], we determined that these devices transmit their messages at 175 KHz. We then captured several messages sent by the devices, and visualized the signals in the time domain. The waveform of these signals indicates that an on-off keying (OOK) modulation scheme is being used, as illustrated in Fig. 2. In an OOK modulation, the presence of a carrier wave is used to indicate a binary '1' and its absence indicates a binary '0'. Similarly to passive RFID devices, all messages are encoded to ensure that the neurostimulator receives enough power from the device programmer even when a long string of "0s" is sent. Encoding of '1' or '0' is based on a variable width high-pulse and a fixed width space. For security reasons, we decided not to reveal the symbol rate being used.

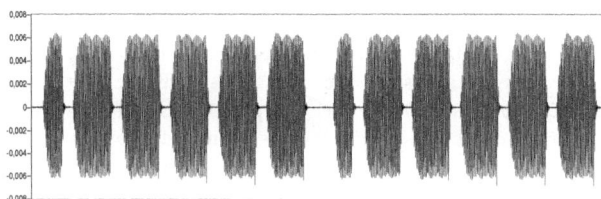

Figure 2: Waveform of a signal transmitted by the device programmer.

5.2 Reverse engineering the proprietary protocol

We intercepted messages exchanged between the two types of device programmer and several models of neurostimulator. However, we focused on analyzing the messages sent by the device programmer since understanding these transmissions would allow us to emulate a legitimate device programmer. (In Sect. 5.3 we show that most messages sent by neurostimulators are simply acknowledgements). After demodulating the captured messages, we observed that they all include a common synchronization sequence (not shown in Fig. 3) that consists of a series of alternating '1s' and '0s'. Subsequently, we found several message fields including headers, information data and checksums.

As a first experiment, we grouped the messages sent by the doctor's device programmers and patient's device programmers, respectively, in two different clusters. This experiment allowed us to determine that there is a 16-bit sequence at the beginning of each message which can take two values depending on the type of device programmer being used. Similarly, we compared the messages sent by each different device programmer, and discovered that there is a unique 16-bit sequence that varies depending on the device. This led us to conclude that this field represents the unique serial number (SN) of each device programmer. Following this approach, we also found two 16-bit sequences that denote the model and SN of the neurostimulator, respectively.

These headers are followed by a static x-bit sequence that is used to distinguish between three states of the communication including (i) unknown neurostimulator's SN, (ii) known neurostimulator's SN and (iii) confirmed neurostimulator's SN. More specifically, a sequence is used in the first message sent by the device programmer to indicate that the neurostimulator's SN is not yet known. A different sequence is used in the second message sent by the device programmer to indicate that both devices already know each other. From that point onwards, the device programmer uses a third sequence until the communication session finishes or expires. Subsequently, we intercepted the messages sent from the device programmer to the neurostimulator while performing different actions. By analyzing these messages, we observed that each message has a y-bit field that corresponds to the action being conducted by the device programmer, e.g. changing the patient's information or the therapy settings. Next, there is a payload field that contains different information depending on the settings being reprogrammed. Within the payload field, the data is encoded in ASCII and transmitted in reversed order, i.e. the least significant bit becomes the most significant bit and vice versa.

At the end of some messages, there are two 16-bit sequences that seem to be uniformly distributed. This made us think that they could be checksums to detect or correct bit errors. Our first hypothesis was that these sequences correspond to a cyclic redundancy check (CRC). This is because CRCs are widely used, easy to implement and very effective at detecting bit errors. Since CRCs are linear functions, we first checked whether the linearity property holds for the second 16-bit checksum. For this purpose, we computed the XOR of two messages and verified whether the result produces a valid message. As the linearity property was satisfied, the second step was to find

Programmer model	Programmer SN	Neurostimulator model	Neurostimulator SN	State	Action	Payload	Checksums
16 *bits*	16 *bits*	16 *bits*	16 *bits*	*x bits*	*y bits*	*z bits*	32 *bits*

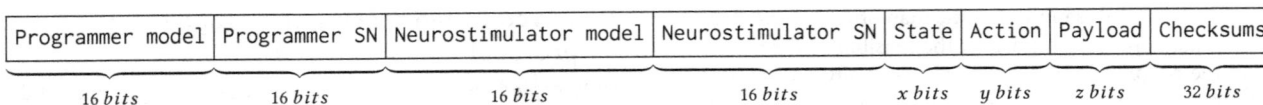

Figure 3: Device programmer's message format.

all the CRC parameters such as the polynomial, initial XOR value, final XOR value as well as whether the input and/or the output is reflected. To discover these parameters, we created a program that brute-forces all possible combinations of CRC parameters. This task required less than 5 minutes on a standard laptop. Following the steps described above, we discovered that the second 16-bit checksum corresponds to a CRC checksum that is computed over the entire message using the standard CRC-16-CCITT [25].

We then repeated this approach for the first 16-bit checksum but we did not succeed on finding the CRC parameters. A key observation was that this checksum remains identical when performing a specific action regardless of the device programmer and/or neurostimulators being used. In other words, this checksum depends only on the state, action and payload fields. To create messages with a valid checksum, we intercepted several messages sent by the device programmer, and XORed them to create new messages where only one bit is set to '1' and the rest of bits are set to '0'. We repeated this approach for each of the bits within these message fields, and created a code-book with all possible messages and their corresponding checksums. Let us give an example to describe how to compute the first 16-bit checksum of a message using our approach. Assuming that our message contains a '1' in the third, fifth and eleventh position, then we can compute this checksum by XORing the checksums of the third, fifth and eleventh messages, respectively, within our code-book.

5.3 Protocol state-machine

This section describes the three phases of the communication between the device programmer and the neurostimulator. This includes the initialization phase, the reprogramming phase and the termination phase.

Initialization phase: Initially, both devices exchange several messages so that the device programmer requests all the information stored on the neurostimulator.

We found that the device programmer always starts the communication by sending a message that is identical across sessions which contains the model and serial number of the device programmer. Within this message, the fields that denote the SN and model of the neurostimulator are kept empty. This is because the device programmer is not linked to any neurostimulator and does not yet know with which neurostimulator it is communicating. The neurostimulator then replies with a message containing its SN and model. From that point until the end of this phase, the device programmer always sends one message to request data whereas the neurostimulator replies back with two distinct messages. The former is an acknowledgment that indicates whether the message was received correctly, while the latter contains the data.

Reprogramming phase: After the initialization phase, the device programmer can be used to modify the neurostimulator's settings as many times as needed within the same protocol session. We discovered that the device programmer sends only one message to adjust the settings, to which the neurostimulator replies with two different messages that remain identical regardless of the action being performed.

Termination phase: Before an ongoing communication is terminated, the device programmer sends a message to the neurostimulator which enables the latter to switch to power saving mode. The neurostimulator replies back with the same two messages that it sends after it has been reprogrammed.

In the next section, we show that it is not necessary to follow the normal protocol flow in order to perform attacks on the neurostimulators.

6 SOFTWARE RADIO-BASED ATTACKS

This section details several software radio-based attacks that we are able to perform on the neurostimulator which could endanger the safety and compromise the privacy of patients. We conducted all these attacks with the device programmer turned off. We focus on an experiment where we changed the patient's name (programmed on the neurostimulator) since this allows us to easily verify whether the experiment succeeded. However, we want to emphasize that we can mimic the behavior of a legitimate device programmer to send valid messages to a neurostimulator to change any of its settings.

Replay attacks: We were able to modify any of the neurostimulator settings just by intercepting and replaying past transmissions sent from legitimate device programmers. However, this attack has two important practical limitations. The adversary needs to wait until there is an ongoing communication between a device programmer and a neurostimulator in order to intercept the messages. Furthermore, the adversary can only replay messages that were already transmitted by legitimate device programmers, which clearly limits the impact of the attack.

Spoofing attacks: Unlike the previous attack, spoofing attacks require to have partial or full knowledge of the protocol. After reverse engineering the protocol, we were able to create any arbitrary message and send it to the neurostimulator. One possible limitation that makes this attack less practical is that the adversary needs to know the neurostimulator's SN in order to create a valid message. Intuitively, adversaries could obtain the neurostimulator's SN by intercepting the exchanged messages while there is an ongoing communication. As the first message sent by the device programmer is always identical regardless of the neurostimulator, adversaries could also replay this message to a neurostimulator and intercept the response since this contains its SN.

We found a way to overcome even this limitation, which allows adversaries to send messages to a neurostimulator without knowing its SN. More specifically, we discovered that neurostimulators accept messages with an empty neurostimulator SN field. In our experiments, we were able to change the patient's name, programmed in the neurostimulator, by sending a single message with no neurostimulator's SN. The impact of this attack is quite large as an adversary could create a valid message, without a SN, and reuse it for all neurostimulators. The only challenge for adversaries is to be close enough to the victim in order to communicate to the neurostimulator. However, there are definitely several scenarios, such as a crowded subway, where this would be possible.

Privacy attacks: Since our reverse engineering on the proprietary protocol shows that the data sent over the air is unencrypted, passive adversaries can eavesdrop the wireless channel to infer private information about patients. Active adversaries can additionally send messages to the neurostimulator to request specific data. The data sent over the air between the device programmer and the neurostimulator includes diagnosis, symptoms, disease or therapy information. Moreover, all messages exchanged between the devices include a unique neurostimulator SN which could be used for adversaries to identify, locate and track patients. For this purpose, adversaries could install beacons in strategic locations (e.g. in hospitals or train stations) to learn the patients' movement pattern based on the signals transmitted by their neurostimulators.

DoS attacks: One would expect that neurostimulators switch to "sleep mode" once an ongoing communication is terminated. However, we found that neurostimulators always remain active and accept a message as long as its format and checksums are correct. We also observed that adversaries can send valid messages to the neurostimulator without needing to first execute the initialization phase. While we did not try to quantify the effect of performing a DoS attack against these devices, adversaries could repeatedly send malicious messages to the neurostimulator in order to deplete its resources faster, similarly to the attacks proposed by Hei et al. [21].

7 SECURITY ARCHITECTURE

In this paper, we propose a practical security architecture that allows the device programmer and the neurostimulator to securely exchange messages. Our solution consists of three main items: (i) session key initialization, (ii) key transport and (iii) secure data communication. The first two items are particularly challenging for medical implants.

To bootstrap a secure communication channel, a symmetric (session) key need to be shared between the devices. This key could be generated by the device programmer and transported from the device programmer to the neurostimulator using an OOB channel. However, this approach presents two limitations. Most OOB channels that allow to transport a key from the device programmer to the IMD, are shown to be vulnerable to security attacks or require to add extra hardware components in the neurostimulator. An alternative solution would be to generate the key in the neurostimulator and transport it to the device programmer. Halperin et al. presented a audio-based key transport solution where the IMD generates a random symmetric key and transports it to the device programmer through an acoustic channel [20]. Even though the authors stated

that the key can be received only by a device programmer that can make physical contact with the patient, Halevi et al. showed that it is possible to recover the key from far away by eavesdropping the acoustic channel [18].

We propose a solution where a symmetric (session) key is also generated in the IMD and transported to the device programmer using a secret OOB. Our solution overcomes the previous limitations and ensures that the key can only be picked up by a device programmer that touches the patient's skin for a few seconds. Below, we define our adversarial model and give an overview of all the building blocks of our solution.

7.1 Adversarial model

We consider the presence of strong adversaries who can eavesdrop or jam the wireless channel, as well as modify, replay or forge messages. Adversaries can be in close proximity with the patient and can possess any legitimate device programmer, even those that already interacted with the neurostimulator. However, adversaries cannot compromise the neurostimulator or the device programmer while being used, since this would make it impossible to protect the neurostimulator. Doctors are trusted and do not collude with adversaries. Adversaries can neither touch the patient's skin long enough (i.e. few seconds) without the patient noticing it, nor compromise any device that can make physical contact to the patient (e.g. a smart watch). Within the community, it is accepted to assume that physical contact to a patient means the ability to cure or harm [34]. When designing security solutions and defining the adversarial model for IMDs, it is important to note that their primary goal is to treat patients. Safety is of utmost importance and security should never interfere with this task.

7.2 Overview of the solution

Our solution involves three main steps: (i) key generation, (ii) key transport and (iii) secure data exchange. More concretely, our solution works as follows. Firstly, the neurostimulator uses a physiological signal from the patient's brain as a source of randomness for generating a 128-bit symmetric key. This key is valid only for a single session and is independent from old and future keys. Thus, if an adversary ever compromises a session key, he will not be able to compute past and future keys, i.e. backward and forward security are guaranteed. Secondly, this session key is transported securely and reliably from the neurostimulator to the device programmer through a secret OOB channel. Similarly to H2H [34], our solution follows a "touch-to-access" access control policy where access to the neurostimulator is granted only to device programmers that can touch the patient's skin for a few seconds. This provides a practical yet effective balance between security and permissive access in emergencies since it allows medical personnel to have immediate access to the neurostimulator without needing to contact care providers for device-specific cryptographic keys. In contrast to the existing solutions, key transportation can be achieved without adding extra hardware components on the neurostimulator. Once the key has been transported, the devices can optionally run a standard authentication protocol so that they can prove to each other that they posses the session key. Finally, this session key is used to bootstrap a secure communication channel between the devices.

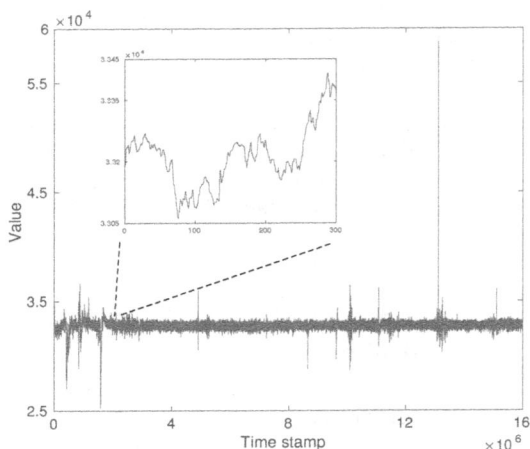

Figure 4: LFP data of one of our mice collected from one channel and sampled with 16-bit precision.

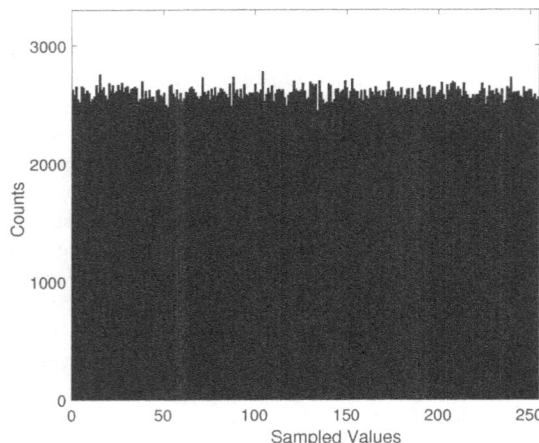

Figure 5: Histogram of bits (in groups of 8 consecutive bits) after applying the parity filter.

7.3 Key generation

True random number generators (TRNGs) are an essential building block of cryptographic systems for generating cryptographic keys, nonces and masks. Unfortunately, IMDs typically use microcontroller-based platforms and lack dedicated TRNGs, making it non-trivial to generate random numbers on these devices. Several articles have proposed to use the initial content of the static random-access memory (SRAM), on-chip RC oscillators and on-board external clocks as an alternative to TRNGs [22, 23]. However, these approaches need to be evaluated for each specific device since their performance depends on the platform and hardware components being used.

Recently, the use of physiological signals extracted from the patient's body has been proposed for generating cryptographic keys. This approach has several advantages with respect to traditional approaches based on PRNGs or TRNGs. Specifically, they allow to reuse signals that are already being gathered by the devices as a low-cost source of randomness. A possible limitation is that some physiological signals, such as those extracted from the patient's heart, can be predicted or measured remotely, which makes them vulnerable to attacks. In this paper, we explore the potential of using a signal from the patient's brain, that cannot be measured remotely by adversaries, as a randomness source for generating cryptographic keys. Our approach can be applied to any IMD that can measure the LFP signal from the patient's brain.

7.3.1 *LFP signal as a randomness source.* We propose to use a physiological signal from the patient's brain called *local field potential* (LFP), which refers to the electric potential in the extracellular space around neurons. The choice of the LFP for randomness extraction is based on the following reasons. Firstly, neurostimulators can easily measure signals in the patient's brain. There are already neurostimulators on the market that use the LFP to create feedback for the delivered stimulation. As the LFP can be collected with the existing lead configurations (i.e. without changing the

leads' position or requiring extra leads), future generations of neurostimulators will require only minor software changes to be able to measure this signal. Secondly, unlike other physiological signals such as the ECG, the LFP can be measured only through direct contact with the patient's brain, thus cannot be obtained remotely.

To analyze the feasibility of extracting randomness from the LFP to generate a 128-bit key in the neurostimulator, we used real LFP data collected from 22 mice[1]. Figure 4 shows LFP data collected from one of the 22 mice. While we recorded LFP data simultaneously from 16 electrode contacts connected to the mice brain using the W16 wireless recording device [7], we only looked at one of these channels. Our technique to extract randomness can be applied to LFP data collected from any of the 16 different channels. During each LFP recording, the mice were walking on a horizontal ladder. This is a well-known test that is used for many different purposes (for more details about this test, see Metz and Wishaw [30]).

The first step in our assessment was to extract the least significant bit of the sampled LFP data and used it as the raw random number. This is because the lower bits of LFP data seem to be quite noisy. Another possibility would be to extract multiple bits from the sampled LFP data but this would require to evaluate their joint probability distribution. We then computed the XOR of three consecutive bits using a simple two-stage parity filter to increase the entropy density. Figure 5 shows the histogram of 8 consecutive bits after applying the two-stage parity filter. Based on our results, these bits are to some extend uniformly distributed, which demonstrate the potential of the LFP as a randomness source for deriving a symmetric key. Following the test suites from NIST 800-90B [12], we estimated that the Shannon-entropy is around $0.91/bit$. The Shannon-entropy could be further improved by increasing the number of stages of the parity filter.

---

[1]Using data from mice to extract preliminary results to better understand the human brain is common practice in many scientific disciplines.

7.4 Key transport

Once a fresh cryptographic session key is generated in the neurostimulator, it has to be securely transported to the device programmer. Our technique for key transportation leverages the fact that both the patient's skin and the neurostimulator's case are conductive. We propose to apply an electrical signal (with the key bits embedded in it) to the neurostimulator's case such that the device programmer can measure this signal by touching the patient's skin, as shown in Fig. 6. To realize this technique, two extra short wires are needed from the microcontroller to the case of the neurostimulator. We discussed this technique with doctors and they claim that applying a signal of a few microvolts or millivolts to the neurostimulator's case would not cause any problem or be unpleasant to patients.

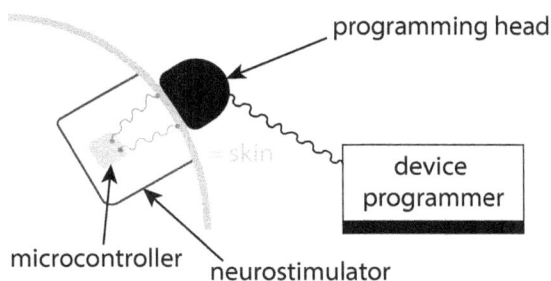

Figure 6: Technique to transport a session key from the neurostimulator to the device programmer.

To evaluate the suitability of this technique, we implemented a proof-of-concept using a NI USB-6351 DAQ and a neurostimulator. To emulate the human body, we used a 1 cm layer of bacon on a 4 cm layer of beef, as suggested by Kim et al. [24]. While this model does not account for changes in the skin conductance, for example, due to patient's emotions or sweat, all these factors can only make the patient's skin to be slightly more conductive than usual. In other words, none of these factors will affect the reliability of our technique. However, this could make it easier for adversaries to capture the EM radiations generated when transporting the key.

To preclude potential EM eavesdropping attacks, our system should be designed to minimize undesired EM radiation produced by the hardware components. This can be done by lowering the transmission power. While this comes at the cost of having a lower data rate, this would not be a problem in our solution. Another way of decreasing the EM emanations would be to use wires (from the microcontroller to the neurostimulator's case) that are sufficiently short and twisted. To further decrease the EM emanations, one could follow widely used electromagnetic compatibility (EMC) guidelines [4]. In addition, the undesired EM emanations generated from other devices that are in close proximity with the patient (e.g. his smart-phone) could be used to masquerade the EM radiations.

To simulate the process of transporting the key, we created a transmitter and a receiver LabVIEW program. We modulated the data using a standard OOK and set the symbol rate and the sampling rate to 100 symbols/s and 500 ksamples/s, respectively. Given that the duration of each symbol is 10 ms, the 128-bit key can be transported in less than 1.5 s. A few additional delays could be deliberately introduced in the key transport process such that access to the neurostimulator is guaranteed only to device programmers that can touch the patient's skin for a few seconds.

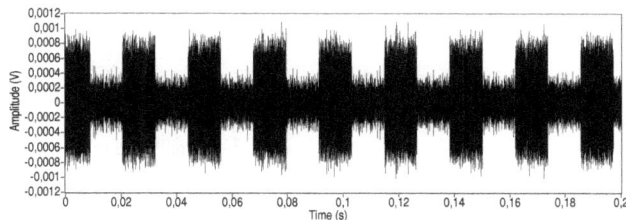

Figure 7: Waveform of the signal received by our DAQ at the other side of the meat.

For our experiments, we connected two wires from the transmission port of the DAQ to the neurostimulator's case. We then placed the meat on top of the neurostimulator, and attempted to measure the transmitted signal at the other side of the meat. Then we mimicked the behavior of a legitimate device programmer by using two wires to touch the meat while connected to the receiver port of the DAQ. The first step was to modulate the "1s" and "0s" corresponding to the 128-bit session key using the OOK modulator. Subsequently, we applied the modulated electrical signal to the neurostimulator's case using our transmitter. A short preamble sequence could be sent before the key is transmitted to help to synchronize the devices. Existing techniques to detect and correct bit errors could also be used to increase the robustness of our technique. Using our receiver, we measured and demodulated the signal to retrieve the key bits previously transmitted by the neurostimulator.

We conducted a series of experiments to determine the minimum signal power from which the device programmer can recover the key bits transmitted by the neurostimulator. It is important to note that the transmission power could be even further reduced by using an enhanced multi-feature OOK demodulation scheme, as the one proposed by Kim et al. [24]. Figure 7 illustrates the waveform of the signal (with the key bits embedded in it) that is received by our DAQ at the other side of the meat. This figure shows that it is possible to recover the key bits, which consists of a series of alternating '1s' and '0s', by demodulating a signal whose amplitude is less than 1 mV. Our results show that, when using the parameters mentioned above, the key can successfully be transported from the neurostimulator to the device programmer.

Furthermore, we tested whether it is possible to recover the key without needing to touch the patient's body when using the minimum signal power that we used in the experiment discussed above. For this, we connected two wires to the receiver port of the DAQ and used them as an antenna to try to measure the EM emanations. We repeated this experiment from several distances ranging from 3 meters to a few centimeters. In none of these cases, we were able to capture the transmitted key. This led us to conclude that the key can only be successfully received when touching the patient's skin.

Programmer model	Programmer SN	Neurostimulator model	Neurostimulator SN	Counter	State	Action	Payload	MAC
16 *bits*	16 *bits*	16 *bits*	16 *bits*	12 *bits*	*x bits*	*y bits*	*z bits*	64 *bits*

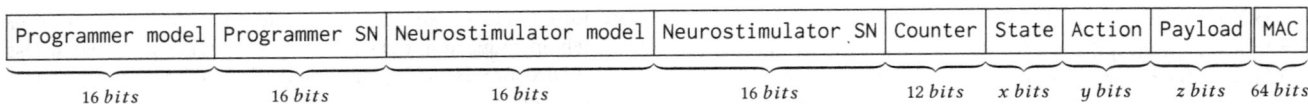

Figure 8: Optimized message format.

7.5 Secure data exchange

For the sake of completeness, we describe how to establish a secure communication channel once the session key has been transported from the neurostimulator to the device programmer. Firstly, both devices could optionally execute any authentication protocol to prove to each other knowledge of the shared session key. For efficiency reasons, we chose not to use an authentication protocol. Instead, both devices can implicitly demonstrate knowledge of the key during the first communication session.

The use of cryptography allows for secure data exchange between devices. However, it also increases the energy consumption in both the neurostimulator and the device programmer. This energy consumption can be divided into two components: (i) computation and (ii) communication cost. The former indicates the cost of performing cryptographic operations while the latter refers to the cost of transmitting/receiving bits to/from a device. However, several papers have shown that the computation cost is often negligible compared to the communication cost [28, 37]. Thus, we propose to use a new optimized message format that is slightly different from the original message format (see Fig. 3). This allows to build security mechanisms into the devices while keeping the additional energy consumption as low as possible in the neurostimulator.

Figure 8 shows the new optimized message format. It includes the same fields as those in the original message except for the two 16-bit checksums, and additionally has a 12-bit counter and a 64-bit MAC that is computed over the entire message. The reasoning behind the proposed message format optimization is the following. A 64-bit MAC offers a good trade-off between cost and security against both off-line and on-line attacks. To prevent replay attacks, the 12-bit counter is increased by one in each message and reset every time a new session key is generated. A message is accepted only if its counter is greater than the one in the previous received message. All these message optimizations lead to an increase of the message size of only 44 bits, which corresponds to an extra communication overhead of less than 10% compared to the original message format.

Since we need to encrypt all message fields except for the SN and model fields of both the device programmer and the neurostimulator, we recommend to use any secure authenticated encryption scheme [2].

8 LIMITATIONS AND FUTURE WORK

Lack of stochastic model for LFP. Our results indicate that the use of the LFP signal is a promising way for extracting randomness in neurostimulators. However, we conducted all our experiments without having a stochastic model on the entropy source or a physical model on the mechanism of the signal origin. In future work, we will develop a stochastic model for the LFP, and conduct a thorough analysis to gather more evidence that LFP can be used as a source of randomness in neurostimulators.

Consider a more powerful adversarial model. Our current solution assumes that adversaries cannot compromise any device that can make physical contact to the patient (e.g. a smart watch). In future work, we want to relax this requirement and also allow the adversary to compromise any wearable device of the patient.

9 CONCLUSIONS

In this work we have evaluated the security and privacy properties of a widely used commercial neurostimulator. For this, we fully reverse engineered the proprietary protocol between the device programmer and the neurostimulator over a short-range communication channel. We demonstrated that reverse engineering was possible without needing to have physical access to the devices by using a black-box approach. This allowed us not only to document the message format and the protocol state-machine, but also to discover that the messages exchanged between the devices are neither encrypted nor authenticated. We conducted several software radio-based attacks that could endanger the patients' safety or compromise their privacy, and showed that these attacks can be performed using inexpensive hardware devices. The main lesson to be learned is that security-through-obscurity is always a dangerous design approach that often conceals insecure designs. IMD manufacturers should migrate from weak closed proprietary solutions to open and thoroughly evaluated security solutions and use them according to the guidelines.

To preclude the above attacks, we presented a practical and complete security architecture through which the device programmer and the neurostimulator can agree on a session key that allows to bootstrap a secure communication channel. Our solution grants access to the neurostimulator to any device programmer that can touch the patient's skin for a few seconds. This allows to create a secure data exchange between devices while ensuring that medical personnel can have immediate access to the neurostimulator in emergencies. Our solution accounts for the unique constraints and functional requirements of IMDs, requires only minor hardware changes in the devices and provides backward and forward security.

10 ACKNOWLEDGEMENTS

The authors would like to thank the anonymous reviewers for their helpful comments and Stefanos Georgoutsos for his support. This work was supported in part by the Research Council KU Leuven: C16/15/058 and by FWO through SBO SPITE S002417N.

REFERENCES

[1] American Academy of Pain Medicine. http://www.painmed.org/patientcenter/facts_on_pain.aspx. [Online; accessed 5-June-2017].

[2] CAESAR competition. https://competitions.cr.yp.to/caesar.html. [Online; accessed 5-June-2017].

[3] DAQ NI USB-6351. http://www.ni.com/en-us/support/model.usb-6351.html. [Online; accessed 5-June-2017].

[4] EMC Improvement Guidelines. http://www.atmel.com/images/doc4279.pdf. [Online; accessed 5-June-2017].

[5] Federal Communications Commission (FCC) ID. http://www.fcc.gov/encyclopedia/fcc-search-tools. [Online; accessed 5-June-2017].

[6] Parkinson association. http://www.parkinsonassociation.org/facts-about-parkinsons-disease/. [Online; accessed 5-June-2017].

[7] W16 wireless recording device. http://www.multichannelsystems.com/products/wireless-systems. [Online; accessed 5-June-2017].

[8] WiFi system detects peoples breathing heart rate even through walls. https://www.medgadget.com/2014/06/mits-wifi-system-detects-peoples-breathing-heart-rate-even-through-walls.html. [Online; accessed 5-June-2017].

[9] C. Adams and S. Lloyd. *Understanding PKI: Concepts, Standards, and Deployment Considerations*. Addison-Wesley Longman Publishing Co., Inc., Boston, MA, USA, 2nd edition, 2002.

[10] S. A. Anand and N. Saxena. Vibreaker: Securing Vibrational Pairing with Deliberate Acoustic Noise. In *Proceedings of the 9th ACM Conference on Security and Privacy in Wireless and Mobile Networks*, WiSec, pages 103–108, NY, USA, 2016. ACM.

[11] C. A. Balanis. *Antenna Theory: Analysis and Design*. Wiley-Interscience, 2005.

[12] E. Barker and J. Kelsey. Recommendation for the entropy sources used for random bitgeneration. NIST DRAFT Special Publication 800-90B, 2016.

[13] A. Calleja, P. Peris-Lopez, and J. E. Tapiador. *Electrical Heart Signals can be Monitored from the Moon: Security Implications for IPI-Based Protocols*, pages 36–51. Springer International Publishing, Cham, 2015.

[14] L. Chunxiao, A. Raghunathan, and N. Jha. Hijacking an insulin pump: Security attacks and defenses for a diabetes therapy system. In *13th Int. Conf. on e-Health Networking Applications and Services*, pages 150–156, Jun 2011.

[15] T. Denning, Y. Matsuoka, and T. Kohno. Neurosecurity: security and privacy for neural devices. *Neurosurgical Focus*, 27(1):E7, 2009.

[16] C. F. *Capacitor tuning circuits for inductive loads*. PPG-1401, 1992.

[17] S. Gollakota, H. Hassanieh, B. Ransford, D. Katabi, and K. Fu. They Can Hear Your Heartbeats: Non-invasive Security for Implantable Medical Devices. *SIGCOMM Comput. Commun. Rev.*, 41(4):2–13, Aug. 2011.

[18] T. Halevi and N. Saxena. On pairing constrained wireless devices based on secrecy of auxiliary channels: the case of acoustic eavesdropping. In *Proc. 17th Conf. on Computer and Communications Security, October 4-8*, pages 97–108, 2010.

[19] D. Halperin, T. S. Heydt-Benjamin, K. Fu, T. Kohno, and W. H. Maisel. Security and Privacy for Implantable Medical Devices. *IEEE Pervasive Computing, Special Issue on Implantable Electronics*, 7(1):30–39, Jan. 2008.

[20] D. Halperin, T. S. Heydt-Benjamin, B. Ransford, S. S. Clark, B. Defend, W. Morgan, K. Fu, T. Kohno, and W. H. Maisel. Pacemakers and implantable cardiac defibrillators: Software radio attacks and zero-power defenses. In *Proc. 29th IEEE Symposium on Security and Privacy*, pages 129–142, May 2008.

[21] X. Hei, X. Du, J. Wu, and F. Hu. Defending resource depletion attacks on implantable medical devices. In *Global Telecommunications Conference*, pages 1–5, Dec 2010.

[22] J. Hlaváč and R. Ló. True random number generation on an Atmel AVR microcontroller. In *2nd Int. Conf. on Computer Engineering and Technology*, volume 2, pages V2–493–V2–495, April 2010.

[23] D. E. Holcomb, W. P. Burleson, and K. Fu. Power-up sram state as an identifying fingerprint and source of true random numbers. *IEEE Trans. Comput.*, 58(9):1198–1210, Sept. 2009.

[24] Y. Kim, W. S. Lee, V. Raghunathan, N. K. Jha, and A. Raghunathan. Vibration-based secure side channel for medical devices. In *Proceedings of the 52Nd Annual Design Automation Conference*, DAC '15, pages 32:1–32:6, New York, NY, USA, 2015. ACM.

[25] P. Koopman and T. Chakravarty. Cyclic redundancy code (CRC) polynomial selection for embedded networks. In *Int. Conf. Dependable Systems and Networks*, pages 145–154, June 2004.

[26] E. Marin, E. Argones Rúa, D. Singelée, and B. Preneel. A survey on physiological-signal-based security for medical devices. Cryptology ePrint Archive, Report 2016/188, 2016. http://eprint.iacr.org/.

[27] E. Marin, D. Singelée, F. D. Garcia, T. Chothia, R. Willems, and B. Preneel. On the (in)security of the latest generation implantable cardiac defibrillators and how to secure them. In *Proc. 32th Annual Conference on Computer Security Applications*, pages 226–236, 2016.

[28] E. Marin, D. Singelée, B. Yang, I. Verbauwhede, and B. Preneel. On the feasibility of cryptography for a wireless insulin pump system. In *Proc. 6th Conf. on Data and Application Security and Privacy*, pages 113–120, 2016.

[29] I. Martinovic, D. Davies, M. Frank, D. Perito, T. Ros, and D. Song. On the feasibility of side-channel attacks with brain-computer interfaces. In *Proc. 21st USENIX Conference on Security Symposium*, pages 34–34, 2012.

[30] G. A. Metz and I. Q. Whishaw. The ladder rung walking task: a scoring system and its practical application. *Journal of Visualized Experiments*, (28):e1204–e1204, 2009.

[31] M. Z. Poh, D. J. McDuff, and R. W. Picard. Advancements in Noncontact, Multi-parameter Physiological Measurements Using a Webcam. *IEEE Transactions on Biomedical Engineering*, 58(1):7–11, Jan 2011.

[32] K. B. Rasmussen, C. Castelluccia, T. S. Heydt-Benjamin, and S. Capkun. Proximity-based access control for implantable medical devices. In *Proc. 16th Conf. on Computer and Communications Security*, pages 410–419, 2009.

[33] M. Rostami, W. Burleson, F. Koushanfar, and A. Juels. Balancing security and utility in medical devices? In *50th Design Automation Conference, May 29 - June 07*, pages 13:1–13:6, 2013.

[34] M. Rostami, A. Juels, and F. Koushanfar. Heart-to-heart (H2H): authentication for implanted medical devices. In *Conf. on Computer and Communications Security, November 4-8 [34]*, pages 1099–1112.

[35] M. Rushanan, A. D. Rubin, D. F. Kune, and C. M. Swanson. Sok: Security and privacy in implantable medical devices and body area networks. In *Proc. IEEE Symposium on Security and Privacy*, pages 524–539, May 2014.

[36] R. M. Seepers, W. Wang, G. de Haan, I. Sourdis, and C. Strydis. Attacks on heartbeat-based security using remote photoplethysmography. *IEEE Journal of Biomedical and Health Informatics*, PP(99):1–1, 2017.

[37] D. Singelee, S. Seys, L. Batina, and I. Verbauwhede. The communication and computation cost of wireless security: Extended abstract. In *Proceedings of the Fourth ACM Conference on Wireless Network Security*, WiSec '11, pages 1–4, New York, NY, USA, 2011. ACM.

[38] F. Stajano and R. J. Anderson. The Resurrecting Duckling: Security Issues for Ad-hoc Wireless Networks. In *Proc. 7th Int. Workshop on Security Protocols*, pages 172–194. Springer-Verlag, 2000.

[39] N. O. Tippenhauer, L. Malisa, A. Ranganathan, and S. Capkun. On Limitations of Friendly Jamming for Confidentiality. In *Proc. IEEE Symposium on Security and Privacy*, pages 160–173, May 2013.

[40] T. Trippel, O. Weisse, W. Xu, P. Honeyman, and K. Fu. WALNUT: Waging Doubt on the Integrity of MEMS Accelerometers with Acoustic Injection Attacks. In *Proc. 2nd European Symposium on Security and Privacy*, Apr. 2017.

[41] F. Xu, Z. Qin, C. C. Tan, B. Wang, and Q. Li. IMDGuard: Securing implantable medical devices with the external wearable guardian. In *2011. 30th Int. Conf. on Computer Communications, 10-15 April*, pages 1862–1870, 2011.

A   DESIGN OF AN ANTENNA OPERATING AT 175 KHZ

Since there are no off-the-shelf antennas suitable for transmitting at 175 kHz, this component had to be designed and manufactured in house. The low working frequency points at a loop antenna as the optimal solution. A small loop antenna with N turns and a surface area S carrying an electric current I_o behaves similarly to a magnetic dipole with magnetic moment $I_m l$ given in Eqn. 1:

$$I_m l \approx NSI_o . \tag{1}$$

Thus, to maximize the magnetic field component, the equivalent dipole moment should be maximized. The conventional topology for near field communication systems assumes that the antenna size is comparable with the size of the neurostimulator antenna. Thus, the surface area S is determined by the size of the neurostimulator. The number of turns N can easily be adjusted. The electric current I_o depends on the output power and on the antenna matching. A small loop antenna behaves like an inductor with very small losses [11]. So it is not matched with a conventional 50 Ohm output and special antenna tuning is required. Due to the low frequency this tuning circuit can be constructed using lumped elements. The simplest type of matching network is a so called L matching network based on two reactive elements to match almost any load impedance to a 50 Ohm output at a single frequency [16].

Unfortunately, due to the large detuning of the antenna, the antenna impedance and the exact circuit model of the lumped elements, thus including parasitic components, should be known at the working frequency with a very high accuracy. Because the capacitor equivalent series resistance (ESR) can be comparable with the very small antenna resistance, the design of such a small loop antenna is typically based on a trial and error approach. We manufactured the loop antenna from a 4 m long blue 7 x 0.25 mm cable with PVC insulation from LappKabel. The antenna input impedance was measured using a low cost vector analyzer called miniVNA. The measured value was about 1.8 + j 79.4 Ω at 175 kHz. The input antenna resistance is determined mainly by the Ohmic wire resistance. A perfect matching can be obtained with two ideal capacitors of 2.4 nF and 9.4 nF. Since there were no such capacitors available, the actual tuning was performed by the consecutive testing of different capacitors. The final matching circuit contains two capacitors of 1 nF in parallel and 1 capacitor of 10 nF. All capacitors were fixed on a breadboard to ensure the possibility to easily re-tune if necessary. The magnetic field level was tested using a 6 cm H-field probe, Model 901 from the EMCO 7405 Near Field probe kit, and an Anritsu MS2721A spectrum analyzer. At first the field level of an original RF transmission was measured and recorded. Then the recorded message was re-transmitted using the set-up based on our antenna, and the magnetic field level was again measured. The new transmitter with the designed antenna provides a magnetic field level and a bandwidth comparable with those generated by the original neurostimulator.

SCLib: A Practical and Lightweight Defense against Component Hijacking in Android Applications

Daoyuan Wu
School of Information Systems,
Singapore Management University
dywu.2015@smu.edu.sg

Yao Cheng
Institute for Infocomm Research,
A*STAR, Singapore
cheng_yao@i2r.a-star.edu.sg

Debin Gao, Yingjiu Li, and
Robert H. Deng
Singapore Management University
{dbgao,yjli,robertdeng}@smu.edu.sg

ABSTRACT

Cross-app collaboration via inter-component communication is a fundamental mechanism on Android. Although it brings the benefits such as functionality reuse and data sharing, a threat called *component hijacking* is also introduced. By hijacking a vulnerable component in victim apps, an attack app can escalate its privilege for operations originally prohibited. Many prior studies have been performed to understand and mitigate this issue, but *no* defense is being deployed in the wild, largely due to the deployment difficulties and performance concerns. In this paper we present SCLib, a *secure component library* that performs in-app mandatory access control on behalf of app components. It does not require firmware modification or app repackaging as in previous works. The library-based nature also makes SCLib more accessible to app developers, and enables them produce secure components in the first place over fragmented Android devices. As a proof of concept, we design six mandatory policies and overcome unique implementation challenges to mitigate attacks originated from both system weaknesses and common developer mistakes. Our evaluation using ten high-profile open source apps shows that SCLib can protect their 35 risky components with negligible code footprint (less than 0.3% stub code) and nearly no slowdown to normal intra-app communication. The worst-case performance overhead is only about 5%.

ACM Reference Format:
Daoyuan Wu, Yao Cheng, and Debin Gao, Yingjiu Li, and Robert H. Deng. 2018. SCLib: A Practical and Lightweight Defense against Component Hijacking in Android Applications. In *Proceedings of Eighth ACM Conference on Data and Application Security and Privacy (CODASPY'18)*. ACM, New York, NY, USA, 8 pages. https://doi.org/10.1145/3176258.3176336

1 INTRODUCTION

Android has been the dominant player in smartphone markets in the last few years. On Android, different apps collaborate with each other via inter-component communication. Although such flexible cross-app collaboration brings the benefits of functionality reuse and data sharing, *component hijacking* [26] is also introduced in which an attack app hijacks a vulnerable component in victim apps to bypass Android sandbox and escalate its privilege [15], causing

confused deputy problems [22] such as permission misuse [21], data manipulation [26], and content leaks [43].

Many approaches have been proposed to mitigate component hijacking. One major line of the research [10, 12, 19, 30] is to modify and extend the Android operating system to supervise inter-component communication. The other direction [41] is to patch app binaries with repackaging [38]. Both are useful if they could be deployed in the wild, but nearly no proposal has been integrated into Android or adopted by Google Play to date, largely due to the compatibility and performance concerns. For example, repackaging violates Android's app verification mechanism and thus is not favorable by app markets and developers who own the source code. Consequently, component hijacking remains a serious open problem in the Android ecosystem. As one of our contributions, we make a comprehensive comparison on existing defenses in §3.2.

Key idea. In this paper, we provide a new perspective to practically defending against component hijacking. Our solution is a *secure component library*, shorted as SCLib, which performs in-app mandatory access control on behalf of app components. Due to its library-based nature, SCLib requires neither firmware modification nor app repackaging, significantly reducing the deployment difficulties. Specifically, we propose two deployment models as shown in Figure 1, the developer-driven and the end user-driven deployment.

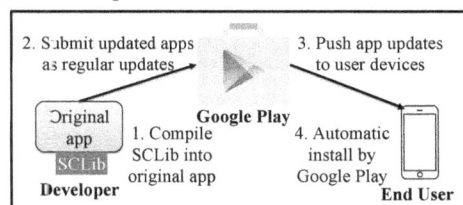

(a) Developer-driven deployment via regular app updates.

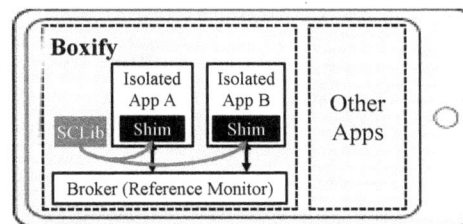

(b) End user-driven deployment via Boxify [11].

Figure 1: Two deployment models of SCLib.

Deployment models. SCLib can be compiled by app developers into their original apps via the regular app updates (e.g., for functionality improvement), which are then pushed to user devices and automatically installed by Google Play. This deployment model introduces minimal burden to developers because they have accumulated experiences to integrate third-party libraries, such as OkHttp [8] and advertisement libraries. Further, SCLib can help developers secure their apps in the first place (rather than applying patches after apps have been released) over fragmented Android devices [2] (a major limitation of firmware modification approaches).

To further enable end users to secure their apps directly, we envision the second deployment model through state-of-the-art app sandboxing technology, e.g., Boxify, which sandboxes any other app into its own process space and delegates their inter-component communication via a reference monitor called Broker. Note that Boxify does not require root privilege, firmware modification, or app repackaging. We refer interested readers to [11] for more details. As shown in Figure 1(b), SCLib can be plugged into Boxify as part of its policy module or its shim code in each isolated app. Since SCLib's design is generally the same for both deployment models, we present it under the first deployment in the rest of this paper.

SCLib design. As a major component of SCLib, we devise a set of practical in-app policies to defend against component hijacking. Our policy checking is based on enforcement primitives that previous efforts have not fully leveraged, including various component attributes and input data of incoming requests. SCLib automatically collects these primitives at entry points of the protected components, and enforces "just-enough" policies from the pre-defined policy set. As a proof of concept, we design six mandatory policies that either directly deny illegal requests or alert users via a pop-up dialog for suspicious requests. These policies can mitigate component hijacking originated from both system weaknesses and common developer mistakes, half of which have not been tackled by previous efforts. Moreover, we design SCLib to cover all four types of components for the first time (see §3.2).

In the course of implementing SCLib, we identify and overcome three major challenges that are unique in our context. First, Android currently fails to provide the caller identity information to most callee components, as explained in [10]. This caller identity, however, is essential in implementing our mandatory access control policies. Unlike the previous solution [10] that modifies Android source code, SCLib leverages the Binder side channel to recover caller app identities at the application layer (see §4.3). Second, it is nearly infeasible to pop up alert dialog in the intercepted components due to the lack of appropriate user interface context and limited function return timing thresholds. We solve this problem by a novel dialog-like Activity transition technique, which overcomes both context and timing restrictions while maintaining user experience and policy enforcement logic (see §4.4). Third, there is lack of API support to collect certain component attributes (e.g., whether an exported component is explicitly or implicitly exported). SCLib performs runtime Android manifest analysis by itself (see §4.5).

SCLib is a lightweight solution by design. It enforces policy checking only at the entry points, and thus has no additional overhead of information flow tracking that is required in some existing approaches, e.g., AppSealer [41]. In addition, SCLib only affects the performance of *certain* exported components that require protection. In contrast, hooking-based checking, e.g., Aurasium [38], adds overhead to both exported and non-exported components. Firmware modification approaches introduce overhead to all inter- and intra-app communications in all apps within the system.

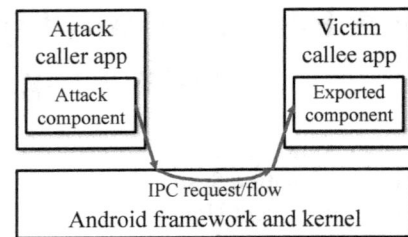

Figure 2: The threat model of component hijacking.

Evaluation. We evaluate SCLib using ten high-profile open source apps. We show that these well-tested apps contain 35 risky components that SCLib can contribute more protection. Our measurement further finds that SCLib introduces negligible code footprint — less than 0.3% stub code in all cases. Furthermore, by performing eight detailed security case studies, we demonstrate SCLib's unique values as compared to developers' own patches and Android platform updates. Finally, our performance evaluation shows that SCLib incurs modest overhead to those protected components (no overhead at all to other components).

The remainder of this paper is organized as follows. We first introduce the threat model in §2, outline the objectives and analyze existing solutions in §3. The design and implementation of SCLib are presented in §4. In §5, we evaluate SCLib's efficacy and efficiency. Finally, we conclude the paper in §6.

2 THREAT MODEL

Figure 2 presents our threat model of component hijacking on Android. The adversary is a *caller app*, and the victim is a *callee app* that contains a component that is *exported*. The attack component in the caller app sends a crafted *IPC* (inter-process communication)[1] request to the exported component to maliciously trigger its code execution for a privileged operation, e.g., permission misuse [21] and data manipulation [26]. In this sense, component hijacking belongs to the classic confused deputy problem [22]. Note that although Figure 2 shows only two parties, our defense can handle hijacking via one or multiple middle app(s).

More specifically, we underline two in-scope threats that are not considered in some related works.

- Unlike some existing work [21, 43], we do *not* assume that exported components protected with above-normal permissions [9] are always safe. We do not consider it safe because for an exported component protected with a dangerous-level permission, an attack app can still register the corresponding permission for sending IPC requests. Additionally, a recent report [5] showed that even components with a signature-level permission could be compromised, because the attack app can pre-claim that permission as normal if it is installed earlier than the victim app.

- Similarly, for the attack app, we do *not* assume that it always has zero or few permissions since it can claim the same permission as the misused permission in a victim app. The benefit for doing so is that it may deceive the IPC call chain-based permission checking [16, 19]. We *do* assume that the attack app has no root privilege though.

---

[1] A.k.a. ICC (inter-component communication) [29] on Android.

Note that unauthorized Intent receipt [14] and malicious app colluding [27] is out of the scope of this paper.

3 OBJECTIVES AND RELATED WORKS

3.1 Design Objectives

To defend against component hijacking in the wild, we identify the following four objectives:

O1 **No firmware modification.** The approach does not rely on firmware customization. It should also work without the root privilege.

O2 **No app repackaging.** The approach does not repackage target apps in bytecode or binary rewriting [25, 42].

O3 **Handling all four types of components.** The proposed solution shall protect all four types of Android components, including Intent-based components (i.e., Activity, Service, and Receiver) and non-Intent based components (i.e., Provider). Note that in this paper, we simplify BroadcastReceiver and ContentProvider as Receiver and Provider, respectively.

O4 **Minimal impact on normal operations.** The solution has minimal performance impact on normal app functionality and intra-app communication.

3.2 Analysis of Existing Solutions

We now analyze how existing solutions defend against component hijacking and the extent to which they achieve the aforementioned four objectives. Table 1 summarizes our analysis on major defenses against component hijacking.

First, most existing defenses require firmware modification (O1: ✗). This includes Saint [30] for adding install- and run-time policies that require developers to specify, IPC Inspection [19], Quire [16], TrustDroid [13], Scippa [10], Bugiel et al. [12] for using system-wide reference monitors to check inter-component call chains to prevent privilege (mainly permissions [21]) escalation, and Kantola et al. [24] for inferring and restricting unintentional component exposure. More recently, IEM [40] extends the Android framework to enable user-layer Intent firewall apps. All these prior works take advantage of the open-sourced nature of Android to make code changes and provide more secure OS design principles, but in the real world, they were not adopted by smartphone vendors. Additionally, end users have no capability to flash the modified firmware in general.

A particularly interesting example is IntentFirewall [1]. Although it was introduced into the Android Open Source Project (AOSP) repository over four years ago, it is still experimental and not an officially supported feature of the Android framework [39], probably due to its limitations [39]. The SEAndroid community is exploring the idea of using IntentFirewall as a potential replacement of their experimental Intent MAC mechanism [7], because in the original form of SEAndroid [32], it does not audit app-layer IPC. SEAndroid tries to reconstruct Android's sandbox from the previous Linux UID-based discretionary access control to the present SELinux-confined mandatory access control. It can restrict certain app flaws such as direct file leak [32] but not component hijacking or indirect file leak [33, 34], because it is challenging to efficiently audit every IPC at the system level without affecting normal app functionality. Even if one day a solid Intent MAC might be activated, it still faces the deployment challenges to protect fragmented and outdated devices.

Table 1: A comparison of major defenses against component hijacking.

Core Idea		Objectives (see §3.1)			
		O1	O2	O3	O4
Saint [30]	Adding install- and run-time policies	✗	✔	◗	✗
IPC Inspection [19]	Checking IPC call chains	✗	✔	✗	✗
Quire [16]	Checking IPC and RPC call chains	✗	✔	✗	✗
TrustDroid [13]	Mediating IPC in middleware layer	✗	✔	◗	✗
Bugiel et al. [12]	Mediating IPC in different layers	✗	✔	◗	✗
Aurasium [38]	Intercepting sensitive API calls	✔	✗	◗	◗
Kantola et al. [24]	Restricting component exposure	✗	✔	✗	✔
IntentFirewall [1]	A system-layer firewall to check Intents	◗	✔	✗	✗
AppSealer [41]	Flow checking of incoming Intents	✔	✗	✗	✗
Scippa [10]	Building system-centric IPC call chains	✗	✔	✗	✗
IEM [40]	Enabling user-layer Intent firewall apps	✗	✔	✗	✗

✔= applies; ◗= partially applies; ✗= does not apply.

Second, other defenses typically need to perform app repackaging (O2: ✗). Aurasium [38] and AppSealer [41] are the two notable examples. Specifically, Aurasium repackages apps to insert API hooking code to intercept sensitive API calls. It mainly aims to prevent malware but can also be used to mitigate component hijacking in which sensitive APIs (in a victim app) are triggered by an attack app. On the other hand, AppSealer is specialized to generate patched apps that introduce flow tracking to avoid critical APIs being triggered by malicious Intents. Both approaches are attractive from the security's perspective, but they also face the deployment difficulties: (i) repackaging is unlikely adopted by app developers because they own the source code and do not want repackaging to affect the original code quality; (ii) app stores are unlikely to deploy repackaging-based approaches because they (including Google Play) have no access to the developers' private signing keys.

Third, none of the prior efforts has fully handled all four types of components (O3: ✗; O3: ◗). Most of them only protect the Intent-based components, whereas the non-Intent based Provider component is largely under-treated. Although all underlying Android IPC communications go through the Binder driver [23, 31], Intent and Provider are two different higher-level abstractions of Binder [20]. Existing approaches either just modify the Android framework to supervise Intent IPC (e.g., [16, 19]), or only recover Intents' semantic from the kernel-layer Binder (e.g., [10, 12]). Approaches such as AppSealer [41] and IEM [40] also explicitly target at Intent-based components. Note that although some approaches (e.g., [13, 30]) mentioned the protection for Provider to some extent, the generic and broader app Provider vulnerabilities [43] were not touched because the problem itself was discovered only afterwards.

Fourth, nearly no defenses satisfy the requirement of minimal checking on normal operations (O4: ✗). Except the work from Kantola et al. [24], firmware modification approaches have to monitor all IPC communications in all apps within the system. Although they achieve the whole-system coverage, the performance was sacrificed by not focusing on apps or components that need protection. Moreover, they often need to retrieve the corresponding permission for each call chain, which also increases the overhead. On the other hand, Intent flow based repackaging approaches such as AppSealer [41] can concentrate on protecting risky app components, but its data flow tracking is expensive. Hooking-based API checking in Aurasium [38] is lightweight; however, it does not differentiate sensitive API calls resulting from user operations or malicious IPC.

4 SCLIB: SECURE COMPONENT LIBRARY

This section covers the design and implementation details of SCLib. We begin with an overview of SCLib in §4.1, and then present some important MAC policies that SCLib is capable of enforcing (§4.2). After that, we discuss the detailed implementation of SCLib with the focus on our novel ways of handling the challenges.

4.1 Design Overview

Figure 3 presents the overall design of SCLib. At the high-level view, SCLib is a regular user-space library that could be easily integrated into apps on different Android platforms. SCLib aims to be a secure component library that performs in-app mandatory access control (MAC) on behalf of app components to defend against component hijacking. With a set of pre-defined MAC policies in SCLib, developers can overcome the by-default system weaknesses and common mistakes. Moreover, as a library, SCLib inherently requires *no* firmware modification or app repackaging (O1: ✔; O2: ✔).

Using SCLib consists of two phases, i.e., the compile- and run-time phase as shown in Figure 3. Firstly in the compile-time phase, developers include SCLib into their app projects and run our tool suite to help SCLib identify risky components that need protection. Then limited amounts of stub codes are added into entry functions of risky components (usually two LOC per entry) so that SCLib can intercept incoming IPC flows. Note that the whole procedure could be automatic with just a run of our tool suite. Due to the page limit, we skip the details of compile-time designs in this paper, and leave them to the technical report version [35].

In the run-time phase, SCLib automatically collects enforcement primitives and enforces policy checking without developers' involvement. To make practical in-app policies to facilitate the access control, SCLib collects a number of enforcement primitives that previous efforts have not fully leveraged and takes all four types of Android components into consideration (O3: ✔). Considering that SCLib's checking is conducted only at entry points and only for risky components, it makes SCLib lightweight (O4: ✔). With SCLib, the incoming IPC flow no longer directly executes the component codes. Instead, it has to first go through SCLib's checking that could generate three possible outputs: deny, alert, and allow. Only in the allow case will the execution flow go back to the component code immediately. In the case of alert, SCLib pops up an alert dialog for users to make a decision — flow resumes if the users choose to allow the call. If SCLib determines to deny to call, control will return to the calling environment immediately.

4.2 In-app MAC Policy Design

It is important to understand the policies SCLib is designed to enforce before we present other details. Remember that our objective is to have mandatory access control (MAC) policies to stop common component hijacking issues that result from system flaws or developer mistakes. Table 2 lists six representative MAC policies (P1 to P6) we have designed. From a high-level view, policies P1 and P2 patch the system weaknesses, P3 to P5 mitigate common developer mistakes, and P6 filters a common attack. Note that we do not claim that they cover all hijacking issues; instead, our purpose is to show *how to design* in-app SCLib policies for major categories of attacks and for different components. Our policies thus serve as templates or baselines for more enhanced or customized policies.

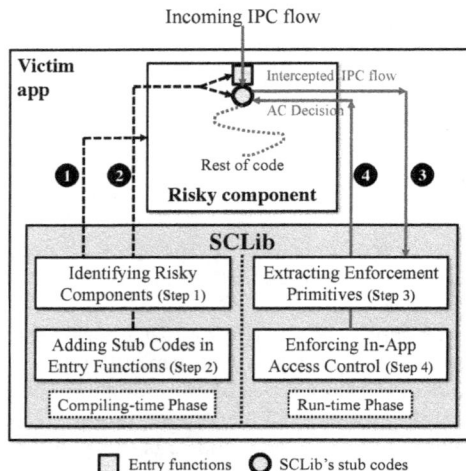

Figure 3: A high-level overview of SCLib.

Trusting intra-app IPC by default. A common point among all six policies is that we consider the IPC calls initiated from the same app/developer trusted. That is, only an external IPC call from a third-party app will be checked, i.e., $ID_a \neq ID_v$. This by-default rule is important in two aspects. First, it effectively minimizes the usability issues for normal user operations, because only the *external* IPC for certain exported components (i.e., risky components) will trigger the alerts. Second, it strengthens SCLib's access control capabilities because another app from the same developer now can be trusted through the app identity and its developer certificate checking. In contrast, solutions such as IntraComDroid [24] and Android Lint simply stop all incoming IPC calls, including those from the same developer, by un-exporting components.

Fixing system weaknesses with P1 and P2. We now show how to design SCLib policies to mitigate system flaws. To this end, we design policies P1 and P2 to fix two major weaknesses in Android. The first is that Android prior to 4.2 by default exports all Provider components even if they do not claim the exported attribute. This over-ambitious exposure rule led to thousands of vulnerable Provider components [43]. Although Google later disabled it, there are still many by-default exported Provider components in apps compiled with old SDK according to recent studies [28, 36]. To make the new rule available to all apps and all phones (including those under 4.2), we design policy P1 to mimic the current system rule at the app layer. Specifically, SCLib directly denies an external IPC request to the callee Provider that does not claim the exported attribute ($\neg ExportedAttr$).

P2, on the other hand, fixes a more complicated and less-known system flaw [5] where an attack app installed earlier can pre-claim a custom permission in the victim app with the purpose of downgrading its protection level, e.g., from signature to normal. Consequently, the attack app can hijack a "private" component that was originally protected with signature-level permissions. Based on this root cause, policy P2 first determines whether there is a custom permission defined in the callee component, i.e., $\exists (PermAttr_v \notin SysPerms)$. If it exists, we further check whether or not it has been pre-claimed by the caller app, i.e., $PermAttr_v = PermAttr_a$. In practice, we can simplify policy P2 for the signature-level custom permissions by leveraging the fact that an external IPC can come only when the signature permission has been downgraded.

Table 2: MAC policies in SCLib. Here are the six representative policies (P1 to P6) we have designed.

ID	Policy Name	†	Policy Representation	‡
P1	No By-default Exported Provider	P	**if** $ID_a \neq ID_v \wedge \neg ExportedAttr$: **deny**	◗
P2	No Pre-claimed Custom Permission	All	**if** $ID_a \neq ID_v \wedge \exists(PermAttr_v \notin SysPerms) \wedge PermAttr_v = PermAttr_a$: **deny**	◗
P3	Alerting Implicitly Exported Components with Custom Action	A, S, R	**if** $ID_a \neq ID_v \wedge \neg ExportedAttr \wedge ActionAttr \notin SysActions$: **alert**	✔
P4	Alerting Explicitly Exported Provider	P	**if** $ID_a \neq ID_v \wedge ExportedAttr = true$: **alert**	✗
P5	Checking System-only Broadcasts	R	**if** $ID_a \neq ID_v \wedge \exists(ActionAttr \in SysActions) \wedge InputAction \neq ActionAttr$: **deny**	✔
P6	Filtering Sql Injection for Provider	P	**if** $ID_a \neq ID_v \wedge \exists(AttackStr \in InputPara)$: **deny**	✗

† lists which components this policy is applicable to. All: all four components; A: Activity; S: Service; R: Receiver; and P: Provider.

‡ indicates whether a policy has been covered by previous efforts. ✔= covers by [24]; ✗= does not cover; ◗= partially covers by system updates. Note that [24] simply un-exports components in policy P3, which would cause incompatibility issues while ours will not.

Preventing developer mistakes with P3 to P5. In this part, we show that how SCLib prevents three common developer mistakes using policy P3 to P5. We first discuss policy P3 and P4 to take care of developers who mistakenly export their components or simply did not realize the threats from exported components. Specifically, for policy P3, our insight is that if developers register custom Intent actions for their implicitly exported components, very likely they do not intend to export those components. While policy P4 is based on the measurement results in [28, 43] that many explicitly exported Provider components can also leak sensitive data. To prevent these two types of mistakes, policy P4 checks *ExportedAttr* and policy P3 further checks the custom actions (*ActionAttr* ∉ *SysActions*). To reduce false positives, we choose the `alert` for policy P3 and P4. Moreover, since custom actions and Provider components are much less-called by inter-app IPC, we expect that our `alert` policies would not disrupt user experience.

Then we have policy P5 to mitigate a developer mistake that appears at the code level (instead of manifest). That is, a Receiver component that registers system-only broadcasts is still hijack-able if it does not check the incoming Intent action explicitly in the code [37]. Our measurement of ten high-profile open source apps in §5 shows that a couple of them made this mistake. To defend, policy P5 automatically checks the input action (on behalf of callee component) against the system-only action claimed in manifest, i.e., $\exists(ActionAttr \in SysAction) \wedge InputAction \neq ActionAttr$.

Stopping a common attack with P6. Finally, we propose policy P6 as a prominent example to show SCLib's capability of stopping common attacks. Specifically, policy P6 aims to filter SQL injection for Provider. As demonstrated in [43], an attack app can hijack a Provider component to inject malicious SQL statements. For example, the adversary sets the `projection` parameter of the query function as a special phase "`* from private_table;`". As these special inputs are different from normal queries, we use keyword-based filtering (such as the expression like "`xxx from yyy;`") to stop them. Similarly, we can stop the directory traversal attack [43] in `openFile` entry of Provider by leveraging some file path patterns. Furthermore, we can devise `alert` policies to protect permission-protected components to stop an adversary that claims corresponding `dangerous` permissions, as we will conduct case studies in §5.2.

4.3 Recovering Caller Identity via the Binder Side Channel

Having discussed the policies that SCLib is designed to enforce, we now turn to some implementation details to show how SCLib managed to overcome the design challenges. In this specific subsection, we show how SCLib recovers the caller identify (C2) via the Binder

ID	Action	PID (process id):TID (thread id)	Node (not important)

```
......           (attack app)    (/system/bin/surfaceflinger)
177341: call  from 7569:7590 to 173:0   node 176320 handle 17 size 156:4
177342: reply from 173:1462 to 597:624  node 0 handle -1 size 0:0
177343: async from 173:475 to 597:0     node 857 handle 2 size 68:0
177344: reply from 173:310 to 7569:7590 node 0 handle -1 size 20:0
177345: call  from 6767:6767 to 597:0   node 4298 handle 1 size 84:4
177346: reply from 597:1277 to 6767:6767 node 0 handle -1 size 24:4
......          (victim app)     (system_server)
```

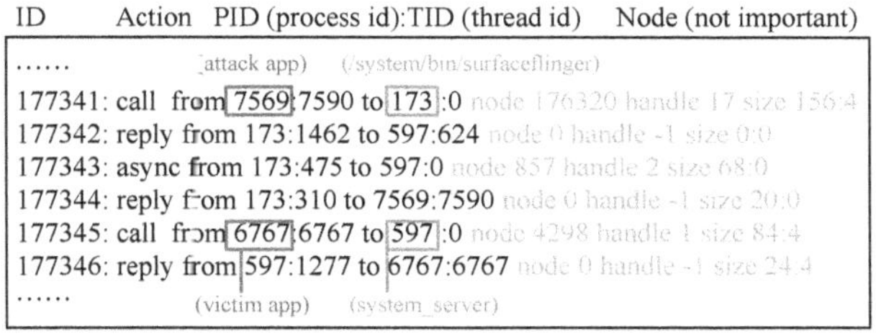

Figure 4: An example of the Binder transaction_log.

side channel at the path of `/sys/kernel/debug/binder/transaction_log`. More specifically, for each risky IPC call intercepted, we retrieve the recent Binder logs from this side channel and analyze them to recover the corresponding caller app identity. Figure 4 shows a `transaction_log` example when an attack app exploits an Activity component in the victim app. Each Binder log starts with a unique transaction ID followed by the Binder action and the process/thread IDs of the caller and callee processes. The last part, node information, is not important — so we skip here. Note that in the kernel-layer Binder driver, app processes do not directly interact with each other. Instead, the high-level IPC always involves a number of interactions between apps and system processes (see [10] for more details). For example, the attack app (PID: 7569) and the victim app (PID: 6767) here leverage the `surfaceflinger` and `system_server` processes to delegate their communication.

Our extensive tests of Binder logs in different components show that they all follow the same pattern, based on which we propose a simple yet effective algorithm to recover caller identities. We still use Figure 4 to illustrate this algorithm. The first step is to locate the Binder log that "calls from" the callee PID for the first time, i.e., the transaction 177345. Then we trace back to identify the first app process, i.e., PID 7569, which is the caller app we are looking for. Since there is no fixed PID pattern for non-system processes, we further extract the corresponding UID and package name for analysis. More specifically, if the UID is smaller than 10000 or if the package name is a system binary, it must be a system process.

Since there is a timing window to retrieve the recent Binder logs, SCLib performs the Binder analysis before other modules. To further decrease the delay, we focus on extracting and saving the logs first, and postpone the actual analysis. Our tests show that in this way, we can reliably retrieve the required Binder logs. Moreover, we found that accessing the Binder transaction log is allowed even in some smartphones with SEAndroid. We tested more than ten Android device models and found that the majority of them allow the access in the SEAndroid enforcing mode, including Samsung Galaxy S6 Edge+, Nexus 4/5/5X/6P, and several Huawei/Samsung/XiaoMi phones.

4.4 Popping Up Alerts via the Dialog-like Activity Transition

To enforce the `alert` policies, SCLib needs to pop up an alert dialog for users to choose "allow" or "deny". However, this is a challenging task due to the following reasons:

- Background components such as Provider and Service do not have an appropriate UI `Context` to display alert dialogs. Even for Activity, it cannot pop up dialogs when `onCreate()` is still being intercepted, (i.e., not return yet).
- Some components' entry functions (e.g., Activity's `onCreate()` and Receiver's `onReceive()`) need to return in a short time. Therefore, we cannot hold on the execution of these functions and wait for users' decisions.

To address these issues, we opt for a different strategy instead of directly displaying an alert dialog. The basic idea is to launch a dialog-like Activity from the intercepted component via the `startActivity()` API. For entry functions that are sensitive to execution time, SCLib immediately returns the execution flow to them by assuming users choosing "deny". If users select "allow" later, SCLib re-sends the same Intent[2] content on behalf of the original caller app. Since the callee app has no way to distinguish the caller identity, the original execution flow can resume. While for other time-insensitive entry functions, SCLib can pause their component execution and wait for users to make a decision on the alert dialog.

Due to the page limit, we refer interested readers to our technical report [35] for the implementation details of this dialog-like Activity transition approach.

4.5 Extracting Component Attributes by Run-time Manifest Analysis

To overcome the challenge that we do not have API support to collect certain component attributes, SCLib performs Android manifest analysis by itself. In particular, we choose the run-time analysis instead of compile-time analysis because it does not bother developers and neither needs the additional file storage. Also, it is immune to app updates and can handle new components well.

The basic procedure is to *dynamically* retrieve and parse Android `Manifest.xml` of the callee app. Specifically, for the callee component, we extract its raw `exported` status, the registered Intent actions, and the associated permissions. We then correlate the app permission entries to obtain their protection levels and determine whether an associated permission is defined by the system or the callee. We also build a list of system-defined and system-only Intent actions based on the Stowaway result [17] and Android source code so that we can determine whether a given component listens to system Intent actions or not.

5 EVALUATION

In this section, we evaluate SCLib in three aspects. Firstly in §5.1, we measure the component statistics of ten high-profile open source apps to find out how many risky components could benefit from SCLib and how much code footprint SCLib introduces. Then in

Table 3: Size of stub code to protect risky components.

Application	Lines of Java codes	Lines of stub codes	Extra code percentage
Telegram	222,074	32	0.014%
Zxing Barcode	43,221	24	0.056%
Terminal Emulator	11,507	30	0.261%
K-9 Mail	51,416	62	0.121%
WordPress	81,076	22	0.027%
Signal Messenger	63,137	34	0.054%
Wire	52,808	2	0.004%
Bitcoin Wallet	18,695	40	0.214%
ChatSecure	36,911	18	0.049%
Zirco Browser	9,638	26	0.270%

§5.2, we assess the security effectiveness of SCLib against attacks in different components. Finally in §5.3, we measure the performance overhead of SCLib under different scenarios.

5.1 Applying SCLib

We first get an idea about the extent to which typical Android apps export their components to others, and the corresponding code footprint when we apply SCLib to protect these components. To this end, we collect the latest source code of ten high-profile open source apps from their GitHub sites at the time of our research (November 2016). The detailed statistics of these apps are available in our technical report [35]. We find that every tested app exports some of its components, and 67.3% are *implicitly* exported. Moreover, a total of 35 component are risky and thus require SCLib's protection.

We further measure the additional stub code introduced by SCLib. Specifically, we calculate the number of additional lines of code based on the type of risky component and the number of entry functions of that type. The results in Table 3 show that the code footprint introduced by SCLib is negligible at less than 0.3% in all cases. Note that since SCLib is implemented in Java and will be instrumented in Java environments, we only compare our code footprint based on the number of lines of Java code in each apps, though some tested apps also contain many C/C++ codes. Additionally, the jar file of SCLib itself is also very small — only around 30KB before compression.

5.2 Security Evaluation

To perform security evaluation, we identify eight vulnerable or risky components from the aforementioned ten apps. As shown in Table 4, these cases cover all four types of Android components and all six policies we designed. In this subsection, we present our detailed analysis of the eight case studies to demonstrate SCLib's unique values in mitigating developer mistakes and system weaknesses when compared to developers' own patches and Android platform updates.

Case 1: Fixing vulnerable components without losing compatibility. The first case, Terminal Emulator (`jackpal.androidterm`), is a good example to illustrate that the developers' own patches sometimes could cause incompatibility issues that SCLib can avoid. Terminal Emulator contained a vulnerable component called `Remote Interface` in its version 1.0.63. The component is implicitly exported and can be triggered by a crafted Intent to execute arbitrary commands without any user interaction. To fix this vulnerability, the developers removed the programmatic command execution functionality in `RemoteInterface` [3, 4]. However, there were

---

[2]Provider's entry functions are not sensitive to execution time, so we focus on Intent-based communications here.

Table 4: Security case studies: Using SCLib to protect vulnerable/risky components.

ID	Target Component (†)	App	Policy
1	RemoteInterface (A; I)	Term Emulator	P3 (alert)
2	MessageProvider (P; E)	K-9 Mail	P4 (alert)
3	RemoteControlReceiver (R; I)	K-9 Mail	P3 (alert)
4	TermService (S; I)	Term Emulator	P3 (alert)
5	ZircoBookmarksProvider (P; I)	Zirco Browser	P1 (deny)
6	New/Clear KeyReceiver (R; I)	Signal	P2 (deny)
7	AppStartReceiver (R; I)	Telegram	P5 (deny)
8	WeaveContentProvider (P; I)	Zirco Browser	P6 (deny)

† means Type; Export, i.e., the component type (four types of components) and the export status (implicitly or explicitly exported).

other apps[3] that continue to utilize this programmatic interface and the patch thus caused an incompatibility issue[4] on those apps. Additionally, simply un-exporting the component as proposed by IntraComDroid [24] would cause the same incompatibility issue.

In contrast, SCLib fixes this vulnerability in a more elegant way that results in no incompatibility issue and no additional developer effort. Specifically, since RemoteInterface registers an Intent filter to take a custom Intent action, it satisfies our policy P3 (see Table 2). As a result, SCLib pops up an alert dialog when an external app tries to trigger the programmatic command execution in RemoteInterface. In this way, SCLib notifies users on potential attacks while keeping the app compatible with other legacy apps (that call RemoteInterface). SCLib also saves the developers' effort in making the patches — Terminal's developers performed around 200 lines of code changes to construct the patch [3].

Case 2 & 3 & 4: Enforcing security beyond Android's existing security mechanisms. In this part, we first present how SCLib enhances protection of two risky components in K-9 Mail (com.fsck.k9) — MessageProvider as in case 2 and RemoteControl Receiver as in case 3. Both components are exported and have self-defined dangerous-level permissions. The rationale behind this design is that K-9 Mail has a number of extension apps [6] which need to access these two components. To share components to other apps with different signatures, the most secure way Android currently provides is to define a dangerous-level permission, as what K-9 Mail did. However, this is too coarse-grained and cannot prevent a malicious app from claiming the corresponding permissions to steal users' emails via MessageProvider. Indeed, according to a comprehensive survey [18], users generally skip the permission inspection during app installation or simply cannot understand the permission meanings, which makes the attacks here realistic.

With SCLib, K-9 Mail now can achieve a more fine-grained access control by enabling users allow/deny a *particular* external app on the alert dialog. K-9 Mail would not have been capable of achieving such fine-grained security because: (i) Intent-based components such as RemoteControlReceiver have no existing method of obtaining caller identity, an important primitive Android currently fails to provide; and (ii) even though MessageProvider has an API to extract the caller identity, it cannot pop up alert dialogs.

---

[3]To name a few, see code snippets in https://goo.gl/HK3HgJ, https://goo.gl/0t78J8, https://goo.gl/xPjlv3, and https://goo.gl/xOs5zN.
[4]A bug report was actually issued after the patch, but the developers of Terminal closed all links after the project was finished.

Further, TermService in case 4 demonstrates a clearer example where developers actually demand the capability of differentiating different caller app identities. According to its code at http://tinyurl.com/termservice, we see that the developers want to determine whether an external app or its own Activity makes the incoming IPC. However, TermService tries to achieve this by checking whether the incoming Intent contains a custom action that is claimed in the <intent-filter>. Developers believe that an external app would use that custom action to launch IPC, but actually an attack app can explicitly call TermService without setting that action. Consequently, TermService's action-based checking can be bypassed. With SCLib, we can prevent such attacks and provide developers a solid mechanism to differentiate external IPC calls.

Case 5 & 6: Fixing system weaknesses with a broader platform and app coverage. Next, we introduce two cases to illustrate that SCLib can fix system weaknesses with a broader platform and app coverage than Android's system updates. In case 5, Zirco Browser (org.zirco)'s ZircoBookmarksProvider is by default exported by Android system, causing the leakage of users' bookmarks. Although Android changed this by-default policy since 4.2, the new exposure policy is not applicable to apps with a target SDK version below 4.2. In contrast, SCLib leverages the policy P1 to protect all implicitly exported Provider components even when they run on legacy phones or are compiled with target SDKs of older versions.

As another example, Signal Private Messenger (org.thoughtcrime.securesms) contains two dynamically registered Receiver components, NewKeyReceiver and ClearKeyReceiver, which are protected with a custom signature-level permission called ACCESS_SECRETS. As explained in §4.2, they are subject to the permission pre-occupy attack. Android fixes this weakness only after 5.0, whereas SCLib can eliminate its impact even on Android versions prior to 5.0.

Case 7 & 8: Fixing common developer mistakes and stopping common attack patterns. We now present case 7 and 8 to illustrate how SCLib helps fix a common developer mistake and stop a common attack pattern, respectively. In case 7, Telegram (org.telegram.messenger) defines an AppStartReceiver component to listen to the BOOT_COMPLETED broadcast, but the developers forgot to check this system-only action in its code (see http://tinyurl.com/startreceiver), making it possible that the component execution be triggered by any app. With SCLib, developers no longer need to worry about such checking because SCLib automatically performs the checking based on policy P5. We further mimic a SQL injection attack on WeaveContentProvider in case 8, which can be defended by our policy P6, as shown in http://tinyurl.com/sqlweave.

5.3 Performance Evaluation

We now evaluate the performance overhead of SCLib under different scenarios. Here we focus only on the results. Interested readers can refer to our technical report [35] for more details about evaluation methodology and experimental setup. Table 5 shows the performance results for the tested Activity and Provider, respectively. We can see that the cumulative overhead (i.e., the worst-scenario overhead) is below 5% for both components, with 4.42% for Activity

Table 5: Breakdown of SCLib's overheads.

Scenario	Category	Time cost	Overhead %
Activity			
Original scenario	Normal IPC latency: t_0	464.40ms	-
Overheads introduced by SCLib	Binder analysis: t_1	8.73ms	1.88%
	Manifest analysis: t_2	0.24ms†	0.05%†
	Policy assessment: t_3	0.05ms	0.01%
	Popping up alerts: t_4	11.53ms	2.48%
	Sum (worst-scenario)	20.55ms	4.42%
Provider			
Original scenario	Normal IPC latency: t_0'	10.82ms	-
Overheads introduced by SCLib	Getting caller identity: t_1'	0.24ms	2.22%
	SQL filtering: $t_{1.5}'$	0.001ms	0.01%
	Manifest analysis: t_2'	0.146ms†	1.35%†
	Policy assessment: t_3'	0.014ms	0.13%
	Sum (worst-scenario)	0.401ms	3.71%

† SCLib analyzes manifest only once for the entire lifecycle of the app. In the Activity context, manifest analysis takes 2.41ms in the first run and zero for the rest of runs. Similarly, the analysis of the first run on Provider takes 1.46ms. Therefore, we calculate an estimated value by assuming that there are ten IPC transactions in a lifecycle of the app.

and 3.71% for Provider. Also, the absolute cumulative timing overhead is only 20.55ms and 0.4ms, which is unnoticeable to human users. Moreover, we would like to underline that SCLib brings overheads only at the entry points of risky components, while existing defenses cause slowdown to the entire app or system.

6 CONCLUSION AND FUTURE WORKS

In this paper, we presented a practical and lightweight approach called SCLib to defend against component hijacking in Android apps. SCLib is essentially a secure component library that performs in-app mandatory access control on behalf of app components. We designed six mandatory policies for SCLib to stop attacks originated from both system weaknesses and common developer mistakes. We have implemented a proof-of-concept SCLib prototype and demonstrated its efficacy and efficiency. In the future, we will try to integrate SCLib into Boxify [11] after its code is released.

ACKNOWLEDGEMENTS

We thank all the reviewers of this paper for their valuable comments. This work is partially supported by the Singapore National Research Foundation under NCR Award Number NRF2014NCR-NCR001-012.

REFERENCES

[1] 2013. The IntentFirewall code. http://tinyurl.com/IFcode. (2013).
[2] 2015. Android Fragmentation Report. http://tinyurl.com/frag1508. (2015).
[3] 2015. A Fix to the Issue #374 in Android-Terminal-Emulator. http://tinyurl.com/fixissue374. (2015).
[4] 2015. Issue #374 in Android-Terminal-Emulator. https://tinyurl.com/pull375. (2015).
[5] 2015. The Custom Permission Problem. http://tinyurl.com/CusPerm. (2015).
[6] 2015. Works with K-9 Mail. http://tinyurl.com/WorksWithK9. (2015).
[7] 2017. IntentFirewall in SEAndroid. http://tinyurl.com/IFwall. (2017).
[8] 2017. OkHttp. http://square.github.io/okhttp/. (2017).
[9] 2017. The Protection Levels of Permissions. http://tinyurl.com/permlevel. (2017).
[10] Michael Backes, Sven Bugiel, and Sebastian Gerling. 2014. Scippa: System-Centric IPC Provenance on Android. In *Proc. ACM ACSAC*.
[11] Michael Backes, Sven Bugiel, Christian Hammer, Oliver Schranz, and Philipp Von Styp-Rekowsky. 2015. Boxify: Full-fledged App Sandboxing for Stock Android. In *Proc. USENIX Security Symposium*.
[12] Sven Bugiel, Lucas Davi, Alexandra Dmitrienko, Thomas Fischer, Ahmad Sadeghi, and Bhargava Shastry. 2012. Towards Taming Privilege-Escalation Attacks on Android. In *Proc. ISOC NDSS*.
[13] Sven Bugiel, Lucas Davi, Alexandra Dmitrienko, Stephan Heuser, Ahmad-Reza Sadeghi, and Bhargava Shastry. 2011. Practical and Lightweight Domain Isolation on Android. In *Proc. ACM SPSM*.
[14] Erika Chin, Adrienne Felt, Kate Greenwood, and David Wagner. 2011. Analyzing Inter-Application Communication in Android. In *Proc. ACM MobiSys*.
[15] Lucas Davi, Alexandra Dmitrienko, Ahmad Sadeghi, and Marcel Winandy. 2010. Privilege Escalation Attacks on Android. In *Proc. Springer ISC*.
[16] Michael Dietz, Shashi Shekhar, Yuliy Pisetsky, Anhei Shu, and Dan Wallach. 2011. QUIRE: Lightweight Provenance for Smart Phone Operating Systems. In *Proc. USENIX Security Symposium*.
[17] Adrienne Felt, Erika Chin, Steve Hanna, Dawn Song, and David Wagner. 2011. Android Permissions Demystified. In *Proc. ACM CCS*.
[18] Adrienne Felt, Elizabeth Ha, Serge Egelman, Ariel Haney, Erika Chin, and David Wagner. 2012. Android Permissions: User Attention, Comprehension, and Behavior. In *Proc. ACM SOUPS*.
[19] Adrienne Felt, Helen Wang, Alexander Moshchuk, Steven Hanna, and Erika Chin. 2011. Permission Re-Delegation: Attacks and Defenses. In *Proc. USENIX Security*.
[20] Aleksandar Gargenta. 2013. Deep Dive into Android IPC/Binder Framework. http://tinyurl.com/diveIPC. (2013).
[21] Michael Grace, Yajin Zhou, Zhi Wang, and Xuxian Jiang. 2012. Systematic Detection of Capability Leaks in Stock Android Smartphones. In *Proc. NDSS*.
[22] Norm Hardy. 1988. The Confused Deputy: (or why capabilities might have been invented). In *ACM SIGPOS Operating Systems Review*.
[23] Ahn Joonseok. 2012. Binder: Communication Mechanism of Android Processes. http://tinyurl.com/bindercomm. (2012).
[24] David Kantola, Erika Chin, Warren He, and David Wagner. 2012. Reducing Attack Surfaces for Intra-Application Communication in Android. In *Proc. ACM SPSM*.
[25] Yu Liang, Xinjie Ma, Daoyuan Wu, Xiaoxiao Tang, Debin Gao, Guojun Peng, Chunfu Jia, and Huanguo Zhang. 2015. Stack Layout Randomization with Minimal Rewriting of Android Binaries. In *Proc. Springer International Conference on Information Security and Cryptology (ICISC)*.
[26] Long Lu, Zhichun Li, Zhenyu Wu, Wenke Lee, and Guofei Jiang. 2012. CHEX: Statically Vetting Android Apps for Component Hijacking Vulnerabilities. In *Proc. ACM CCS*.
[27] Claudio Marforio, Hubert Ritzdorf, AurÃlien Francillon, and Srdjan Capkun. 2012. Analysis of the Communication between Colluding Applications on Modern Smartphones. In *Proc. ACM ACSAC*.
[28] Patrick Mutchler, Yeganeh Safaei, Adam Doupe, and John Mitchell. 2016. Target Fragmentation in Android Apps. In *Proc. IEEE SPSM*.
[29] Damien Octeau, Patrick McDaniel, Somesh Jha, Alexandre Bartel, Eric Bodden, Jacques Klein, and Yves Le Traon. 2013. Effective Inter-Component Communication Mapping in Android with Epicc: An Essential Step Towards Holistic Security Analysis. In *Proc. USENIX Security Symposium*.
[30] Machigar Ongtang, Stephen McLaughlin, William Enck, and Patrick McDaniel. 2009. Semantically Rich Application-Centric Security in Android. In *Proc. ACSAC*.
[31] Thorsten Schreiber. 2012. Android Binder: Android Interprocess Communication. http://www.nds.rub.de/media/attachments/files/2012/03/binder.pdf. (2012).
[32] Stephen Smalley and Robert Craig. 2013. Security Enhanced (SE) Android: Bringing Flexible MAC to Android. In *Proc. ISOC NDSS*.
[33] Daoyuan Wu and Rocky K. C. Chang. 2014. Analyzing Android Browser Apps for file:// Vulnerabilities. In *Proc. Springer Information Security Conference (ISC)*.
[34] Daoyuan Wu and Rocky K. C. Chang. 2015. Indirect File Leaks in Mobile Applications. In *Proc. IEEE Mobile Security Technologies (MoST)*.
[35] Daoyuan Wu, Yao Cheng, Debin Gao, Yingjiu Li, and Robert H. Deng. 2018. SCLib: A Practical and Lightweight Defense against Component Hijacking in Android Applications. *CoRR abs/1801.04372 (2018)*. https://arxiv.org/abs/1801.04372
[36] Daoyuan Wu, Ximing Liu, Jiayun Xu, David Lo, and Debin Gao. 2017. Measuring the Declared SDK Versions and Their Consistency with API Calls in Android Apps. In *Proc. Conference on Wireless Algorithms, Systems, and Applications*.
[37] Daoyuan Wu, Xiapu Luo, and Rocky K. C. Chang. 2014. A Sink-driven Approach to Detecting Exposed Component Vulnerabilities in Android Apps. *CoRR abs/1405.6282 (2014)*. http://arxiv.org/abs/1405.6282
[38] Rubin Xu, Hassen Saidi, and Ross Anderson. 2012. Aurasium: Practical Policy Enforcement for Android Applications. In *Proc. USENIX Security*.
[39] Carter Yagemann. 2016. IntentFirewall Unofficial Document. http://www.cis.syr.edu/~wedu/android/IntentFirewall/. (2016).
[40] Carter Yagemann and Wenliang Du. 2016. Intentio Ex Machina: Android Intent Access Control via an Extensible Application Hook. In *Proc. ESORICS*.
[41] Mu Zhang and Heng Yin. 2014. AppSealer: Automatic Generation of Vulnerability-Specific Patches for Preventing Component Hijacking Attacks in Android Applications. In *Proc. ISOC NDSS*.
[42] Wu Zhou, Yajin Zhou, Xuxian Jiang, and Peng Ning. 2012. Detecting Repackaged Smartphone Applications in Third-Party Android Marketplaces. In *ACM CODASPY*.
[43] Yajin Zhou and Xuxian Jiang. 2013. Detecting Passive Content Leaks and Pollution in Android Applications. In *Proc. ISOC NDSS*.

SecuPAN: A Security Scheme to Mitigate Fragmentation-Based Network Attacks in 6LoWPAN

Mahmud Hossain, Yasser Karim and Ragib Hasan
SECRETLab, Department of Computer Science
University of Alabama at Birmingham, AL, USA
{mahmud,yasser,ragib}@uab.edu

ABSTRACT

6LoWPAN is a widely used protocol for communication over IPV6 Low-power Wireless Personal Area Networks. Unfortunately, the 6LoWPAN packet fragmentation mechanism possesses vulnerabilities that adversaries can exploit to perform network attacks. Lack of fragment authentication, payload integrity verification, and sender IP address validation lead to fabrication, duplication, and impersonation attacks. Moreover, adversaries can abuse the poor reassembly buffer management technique of the 6LoWPAN layer to perform buffer exhaustion and selective forwarding attacks. In this paper, we propose SecuPAN – a security scheme for mitigating fragmentation-based network attacks in 6LoWPAN networks and devices. We propose a Message Authentication Code based per-fragment integrity and authenticity verification scheme to defend against fabrication and duplication attacks. We also present a mechanism for computing datagram-tag and IPv6 address cryptographically to mitigate impersonation attacks. Additionally, our reputation-based buffer management scheme protects 6LoWPAN devices from buffer reservation attacks. We provide an extensive security analysis of SecuPAN to demonstrate that SecuPAN is secure against strong adversarial scenarios. We also implemented a prototype of SecuPAN on Contiki enabled IoT devices and provided a performance analysis of our proposed scheme.

CCS CONCEPTS

• **Security and privacy** → **Security protocols**; *Public key (asymmetric) techniques*; • **Networks** → **Signaling protocols**;

KEYWORDS

Fragmentation; Security Service; 6LoWPAN; Threat; Attack; Adversary; Internet of Things.

ACM Reference Format:
Mahmud Hossain, Yasser Karim and Ragib Hasan. 2018. SecuPAN: A Security Scheme to Mitigate Fragmentation-Based Network Attacks in 6LoW-PAN. In *CODASPY '18: Eighth ACM Conference on Data and Application Security and Privacy, March 19–21, 2018, Tempe, AZ, USA.* , 12 pages.
https://doi.org/10.1145/3176258.3176326

1 INTRODUCTION

6LoWPAN [25] is envisioned as the main building block for a number of network scenarios in the Internet of Things (IoT) [2, 22]. The IoT-based systems are becoming ubiquitous in a wide range of application domains due to the recent advances in wireless communications and pervasive computing. A recent research anticipates that, over the next few years, on an average one million new IoT devices will be deployed to different application domains in every year [37, 42]. Therefore, IPv6 is a necessity for IoT networks. The 6LoWPAN protocol stack implements an adaptation layer between network and data link layers to support transmission of IPv6 packets over 6LoWPAN. The underlying 6LoWPAN network are required to support small-sized transmissions such as sensor data or control commands, and large transmissions such as firmware updates or security protocol handshakes [15, 18, 39]. Therefore, it provides fragmentation support at the adaptation layer. However, there are vulnerabilities in the fragment processing method that adversaries can exploit performing network attacks in the 6LoWPAN network. Such attacks can lead to havoc in IoT-based systems.

Malicious or misconfigured devices may send duplicate or overlapping fragments. Due to the lack of authentication at the 6LoWPAN layer, recipients are unable to distinguish these undesired fragments from legitimate ones for packet reassembly. Moreover, reassembling nodes have to optimistically store fragments of a packet and rely on a timeout mechanism to discard incomplete packets. This, however, may cause the scarce memory of a node to be occupied with incomplete packets due to missing fragments. Thus, lossy links as well as malicious or misconfigured nodes can block the processing of newly received fragmented packets by spuriously occupying buffer resources. The lack of verification at the 6LoWPAN layer also brings the chance of fabrication into the picture. A malicious node can intentionally fabricate the payload of one or multiple fragments of a packet and the target has to accept these because it can not verify this at the 6LoWPAN layer. Also this weak niche allows an attacker to impersonate as legitimate nodes by spoofing IPv6 addresses.

So far, some research proposed mechanisms [17, 21] to protect resource-constrained IoT devices against the fragmentation attack. However, these mechanisms do not protect the devices against network attacks, such as selective forwarding, spoofing or replay attack. In the selective forwarding attack, a malicious device selectively drops certain packets again and again. By doing so, the attacker prevents a client device from accessing resources provided by a service device or prevents a service device from publishing updates to clients. Also, the current solutions do not handle IP address spoofing attack. There is no authentication scheme present at the 6LoWPAN layer to verify the source of the fragments. An attacker can exploit this vulnerability to launch spoofing attacks targeting an IoT network.

In this paper, we present a novel approach to defend a wide range of fragmentation attacks like replaying, alteration, spoofing, duplication, buffer exhaustion, and selective forwarding. We propose SecuPAN – a security scheme addressing the short comings of the 6LoWPAN layer. In SecuPAN, we introduce a nonce field in the fragment header to defend replay attacks. Spoofing attacks are prevented by using a cryptographically generated datagram-tag and IPv6 address. SecuPAN mitigates fabrication of a fragment using a Message Authentication Code (MAC)-based scheme. SecuPAN also provide a reputation-based buffer allocation mechanism to prevent reassembly-buffer overflow.

Contribution: The contributions of this work are as follows:

(1) We propose a security mechanism based on Cryptographically Generated IPv6 Address to mitigate impersonation attacks.

(2) We provide a MAC-based fragmentation scheme to verify authenticity and integrity of packet fragments.

(3) We present a reputation-based buffer management scheme to protect resource-limited devices from buffer overflow.

(4) We evaluated performance of SecuPAN with IoT devices running the Conitki operating system.

Organization: We present background and threat model in Section 2 and 3 respectively. Section 4 and 5 describe our proposed scheme and its security analysis respectively. Experimental results are presented in Section 6. We provide a comparison of SecuPAN with prior research in Section 7. Finally, we conclude in Section 8.

2 BACKGROUND

2.1 Cryptographically Generated Address (CGA)

A CGA is an Internet Protocol Version 6 (IPv6) address that contains a host identifier computed from a cryptographic hash function [3]. The least-significant 64 bits of the 128-bit IPv6 address is replaced by the cryptographic hash of the address owner's public key. Figure 1 presents the process to compute a CGA. Let's suppose, a node operates on a network with subnet prefix SP has an Elliptic Curve Cryptography (ECC) key pair (d_n, Q_n). Then, the coordinator (e.g., Gateway or Router) of the network computes an interface identifier for the node as: $Hash\ (Q_n \| SP)$. Hence, the public key of a node is linked to its IPv6 address.

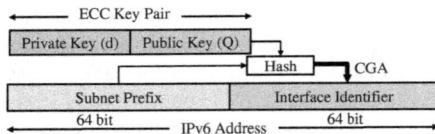

Figure 1: Secure IP Address Computation.

During two-party communications, a sender sends its public key and a signature to a receiver. The receiver computes a hash of the public key and checks if the hash value matches the interface identifier of the sender; thus, the receiver ensures that the public key is bound to the sender's IPv6 address. Next, the receiver verifies the signature by using the public key, and confirms that the sender possesses the private key.

2.2 6LoWPAN Network Topology

The 6LoWPAN nodes form a Destination Oriented Acyclic Graph (DODAG) for end-to-end communications [24] as shown in Figure 2. There are three types of nodes in a DODAG: root (gateway), parent (intermediate nodes), and leaf (has no child nodes). Each node in

a DODAG is assigned a Rank which strictly increase in the Down direction and strictly decreases in the Up direction. The DODAG root has rank zero and the rank of a child node is greater than the rank of its parent node.

6LoWPAN supports three types of traffic flows (see Figure 2): point to multipoint (P2MP), multipoint to point (MP2P), and point to point (P2P). In P2MP communications, traffic flows from a DODAG root to a subset of

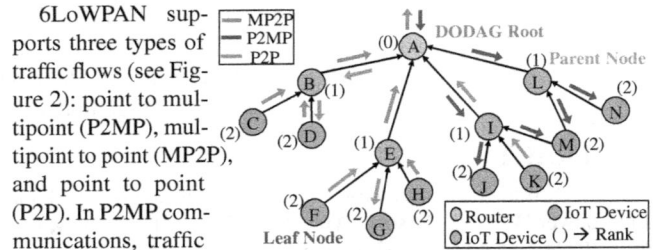

Figure 2: 6LoWPAN Traffic.

6LoWPAN devices. Traffic flows from 6LoWPAN devices to a DODAG root in MP2P communications. In P2P communications, traffic flows between two 6LoWPAN devices.

6LoWPAN devices implement the Routing Protocol for Low-Power and Lossy Networks (RPL) [41] to form a DODAG and route traffics. The RPL defines a set of control messages (ICMPv6 type 155) for DODAG formation. An RPL node that wants to join a DODAG broadcasts a DODAG Information Solicitation (DIS) message to solicit DODAG Information Object (DIO) messages from nearby RPL nodes. In the DIS message, the joining node sets its rank to INFINITY. Nearby RPL nodes reply with DIOs. The joining node uses the DIOs to select its parent(s). Finally, the node sends a Destination Advertisement Object (DAO) message to the DODAG root so that on-path nodes can update their routing tables.

2.3 Fragmentation and Reassembly

Maximum Transmission Unit of 6LoWPAN Links: The 6LoWPAN nodes communicate over an IEEE 802.15.4 radio link [1, 24]. The Maximum Transmission Unit (MTU) of an IEEE 802.15.4 link is 127 octets. However, the MTU size for IPv6 packets over an IEEE 802.15.4 medium is 1280 octets. As such, a full IPv6 packet does not fit an IEEE 802.15.4 frame. Starting from a maximum physical layer packet size of 127 octets and the maximum header overheads of 98 octets, the resultant maximum frame size at the application layer is 29 octets (see Figure 23 in Appendix). Application payloads larger than 29 bytes are sent in multiple fragments.

Fragmentation Mechanism: The 6LoWPAN adaptation layer located between the network and link layers (see Figure 24 in the Appendix) provides functionalities for packet fragmentation. Each 6LoWPAN fragment contains a fragment header that carries information for in-place reassembly. The first fragment of a packet contains the first fragment header (FRAG1). The second and subsequent fragments, up to and including the last, contain the second fragment header (FRAGN).

FRAG1 contains three fields: *dispatch*, *datagram size*, and *datagram tag* (see Figure 3). The *dispatch* field is used to distinguish between FRAG1 and FRAGN. The *datagram size* field encodes the size of an entire IP packet (IP header + payload). The *datagram tag* is unique per sender and fragmented packet, and is included in each fragment header. In contrast to the FRAG1 header, the FRAGN header contains an addition field *datagram offset* which indicates the position of the current payload within the original IPv6 packet.

Only the first fragment (FRAG1) contains end-to-end routing information (IPv6 address). However, a receiving node uses the *datagram tag* of the reaming fragments (FRAGN) to correlate them to the FRAG1, derive IP-based routing, or processing decisions for these fragments. Thus, *datagram tag* enables a receiving node to look up routing information for all the fragments belonging to a fragmented packet after the FRAG1 has been received.

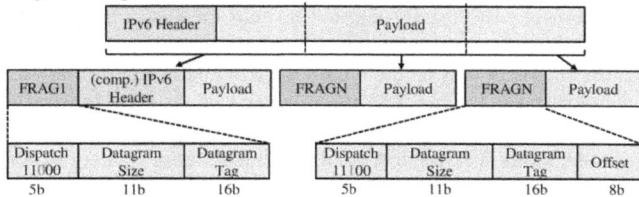

Figure 3: Packet Fragmentation.

Fragmentation Forwarding Mechanism: There are three types protocols for routing fragments in a DODAG: [5, 9, 41]: *mesh-under*, *route-over*, and *enhanced router-over*. In the *mesh-under* scheme, the routing decision is taken in the adaptation layer (see Figure 24). The 6LoWPAN layer prepends each fragment with a mesh routing header (see Figure 23c). This header contains end-to-end source and destination link layer addresses. A forwarding node uses the link layer addresses to derive a routing decision on a per-fragment basis. A destination node reassembles fragments into an IP packet only after it receives all the packet fragments successfully. The adaptation layer of the destination node preforms the reconstruction process. However, if a fragment is missing in the forwarding process, all the fragments of this IP packet are retransmitted from the source to the destination.

The *route-over* routing scheme delegates the decision to the network layer on a per-packet basis. An IP packet is fragmented by the adaptation layer and all fragments are sent to the next hop based on the information available in a routing table. The next hop reassembles them in order to reconstruct the original IP packet in the adaptation layer when all fragments are received successfully. Once reconstructed, the packet is sent to the network layer. Finally, the packet is fragmented again and these fragments are delivered to the next hop.

Enhanced route-over scheme [5] proposes an optimization of the route-over approach to achieve *mesh-under* like forwarding efficiency. *Enhanced route-over* derives routing decisions directly based on the IP header information in the FRAG1. It then stores the forwarding decision, forwards the FRAG1 to the next hop, and applies the same forwarding decision to the following fragments FRAGNs. Hence, while FRAGNs can be forwarded individually, they are transmitted along the same path, similar to route over.

3 THREAT MODEL

The design of 6LoWPAN fragmentation and routing mechanisms has some vulnerabilities, such as the lack of fragment authentication, payload integrity verification, and source IP address validation. Adversaries can exploit these vulnerabilities to perform various network attacks. Here, we identify these fragmentation-based attacks.

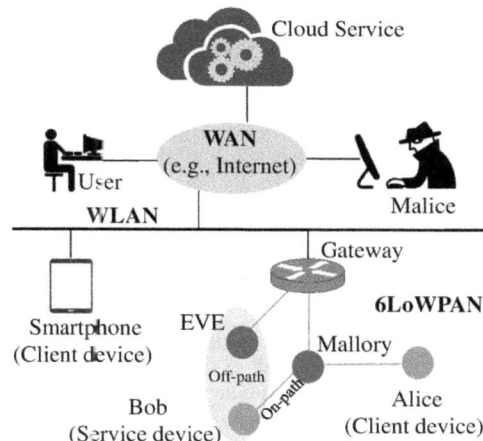

Figure 4: Network Scenario

3.1 Capability of Target and Malicious Devices

In our 6LoWPAN network scenario (see Figure 4), target devices (Alice and Bob) are resource constrained. They have very limited ability to process and store fragmented packets. They are driven by batteries most of the time and communicate over a lossy IEEE 802.15.4 link.

An adversary simply places malicious devices (Eve and Mallory) within radio range of the target network without link layer security. However, the adversary can extract key materials (e.g., pre-shared key) stored in its storage, which is known as *memory probing*, to gain unauthorized access to a protected network [4, 16]. The adversary uses these keys to install Eve and Mallory in the network.

Malice is located in the Internet and sends message to the 6LoWPAN nodes through the gateway. Eve and Mallory are located inside the network. Mallory is located in the forwarding path between Alice and Bob. She can delay, reorder, alter, or simply drop legitimate packet fragments. Eve is located beside the forwarding path. She can over hear the communication channel between Mallory and Bob, and can send forged packets in response to overheard messages.

3.2 Network External Attacks

Resource-rich attackers, such as Malice, can flood a constrained 6LoWPAN node by sending large number of packets. These packets are further broken into fragments at the gateway and forwarded to the target node. As a result, the constrained node has to process a huge amount of fragmented packets, which may cause resource exhaustion. The victim is prevented from processing legitimate fragments. The gateway can prevent such flooding-based attacks by employing an authenticated tunnel, such as IPSec [12], to external hosts. The authentication tunnel enables the gateway to exclude external nodes from communication if they behave maliciously. Additionally, the gateway can adopt secure rate limiting mechanisms [32] for large packets from authenticated sources.

3.3 Network Internal Attacks

The security mechanisms at the gateway defend against external attacks. However, they leave the 6LoWPAN network susceptible to network-internal attacks. The 6LoWPAN fragmentation mechanism lacks an authentication scheme. Hence, it becomes vulnerable to replay attack. Also, the lack of verification at 6LoWPAN layer brings the possibility of fabrication or alteration into the plate. Moreover, the timeout mechanism to discard incomplete packets could lead to scarcity of memory. Therefore, first, we identify the attacks that Eve and Malory can mount by exploiting the vulnerabilities in the 6LoWPAN fragmentation scheme. Next, we provide mitigation strategies to protect 6LoWPAN devices from the network-internal attacks. The attacks are as follows.

Replay: Alice sends a request that routes through Mallory to Bob at time t_1 (Figure 5). Mallory stores the request fragments.

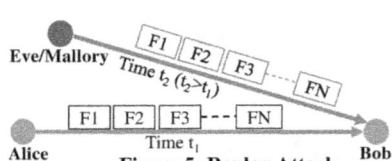

Figure 5: Replay Attack

She retransmits the request to Bob at time t_2 ($t_1 < t_2$). In the 6LoW-PAN layer, it cannot be verified whether the fragments were sent earlier. Therefore, Bob has to receive and process the fragments, which costs extra memory and computation resource of Bob.

Alteration: Mallory modifies the payload of a packet fragment sent by Alice to Bob (see Figure 6). The 6LoWPAN layer does not provide mechanisms to verify the integrity of each fragment. Therefore, Bob precesses all fragments (legitimate and modified) that appear to belong to the same IPv6 packet according to the sender's MAC address and the 6LoWPAN *datagram tag*. After that, he verifies the integrity of the packet and discards it.

Figure 6: Alteration

Address Spoofing: Mallory sends fragments of a spoofed packet to Bob (see Figure 7). Mallory uses Alice's IPv6 address as the value of the *source* field of the IP header attached to FRAG1. Bob thinks that the fragments are sent from Alice since FRAG1 contains Alice's IPv6 address. However, Bob cannot verify if the fragments are really originated from Alice. The 6LoWPAN layer lacks host IP address verification scheme while receiving FRAG1. Therefore, Bob has no choices but to process the fragments.

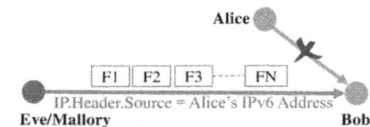

Figure 7: Address spoofing

Duplicate fragment: Mallory sends legitimate fragments F_1–F_n of a packet to Bob (see Figure 8). She also sends an additional fragment F_2'. The header information of F_2' is same as F_2. However, F_2' contains forged payload. In the 6LoWPAN layer, Bob cannot distinguish the legitimate fragment F_2 from the duplicate fragment F_2' at the time of reception. As a result, Bob has to discard the entire packet. In another attack scenario, Mallory forwards F_1 to F_n to Bob. Eve eavesdrops on the communication between Alice and Mallory and sends a duplicate fragment F_2' to Bob.

Buffer exhaustion: The buffer exhaustion attack targets the limited memory of resource constrained nodes and leverages the fact

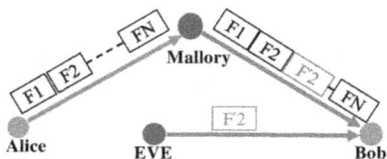

Figure 8: Duplicate fragment

that the recipient of a fragmented packet cannot determine apriori if all fragments will be received correctly (Figure 9). Hence, a receiving node must optimistically reserve buffer space for the reassembly of the complete packet as indicated in the 6LoWPAN header. In this scenario, an attacker can only send the first segment of a large packet to the victim. The victim will allocate memory as indicated in the first fragment's header and wait for the rest of the fragments. But the attacker never sends the rest of the packets. In 6LoWPAN, a reassembly timeout is defined up to 60 seconds to handle fragment loss on the communication path. But during this timeout, the attacker can send new fragments of a new packet continuously, and the victim will allocate resource according to the request until the buffer is exhausted. As a result, the victim cannot receive requests from a benign node.

Selective forwarding: Mallory selectively drops packet fragments so that Bob cannot process a request made by Alice. She also does not forward some of the fragments of a request originated from network-external client devices or cloud services. Such

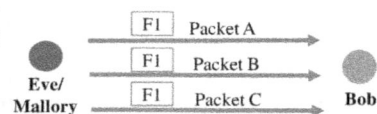

Figure 9: Buffer exhaustion

selective forwarding of fragments leads to the buffer reservation attack as described above and increases resource consumption for fragment processing.

4 SECUPAN FOR SECURE 6LOWPAN FRAGMENTATION

We propose SecuPAN to defend against fragmentation-based attacks as pointed out in Section 3. To protect replay attacks and to ensure the freshness of the fragments, we propose a Nonce field in the FRAG1 header. We use cryptographic *datagram-tag* and cryptographically generated IPV6 address (CGA-IPv6) to prevent address spoofing attacks. Moreover, we ensure fragments integrity using a MAC-based scheme. Finally, we prevent reassembly-buffer exhaustion attack by introducing a reputation-based buffer management mechanism.

4.1 Cryptographic IPv6 Address Assignment

A Border router (BR) in a 6LoWPAN network assigns a CGA-IPv6 address to a joining device (JD). In Step 1–2, the joining node selects its parent (see Figure 10). In Step 3–12, the device computes an ECC key pair by using ECQV Implicit Certificate-based cryptography [7]. The router assigns a CGA-IPv6 address to the node in Step 13–22. The details of the address assignment process are as follows.

Step 1–2: The JD broadcasts a DIS message to the network. Neighboring nodes reply with DIO messages. After analyzing the DIO messages the JD selects its parent node. The JD also selects a temporary IPv6 address to communicate with the BR. **Step 3–4:** The JD selects a random number r, computes $R = r * G$, and sends R to the BR. **Step 5–6:** The BR computes an implicit certificate P. **Step 7–9:** The BR signs the certificate P by using the private key (d_b) of its ECC pair (d_b, Q_b). Next, the BR sends the signature s, implicit certificate P, and its public key Q_b to the JD. **Step 10-12:** The JD computes its ECC pair (d_d, Q_d) by using the parameters s and P. **Step 13-14:** The JD computes a shared key k by using its private key d_b and BR's public key Q_b. Next, the JD selects a nonce N and

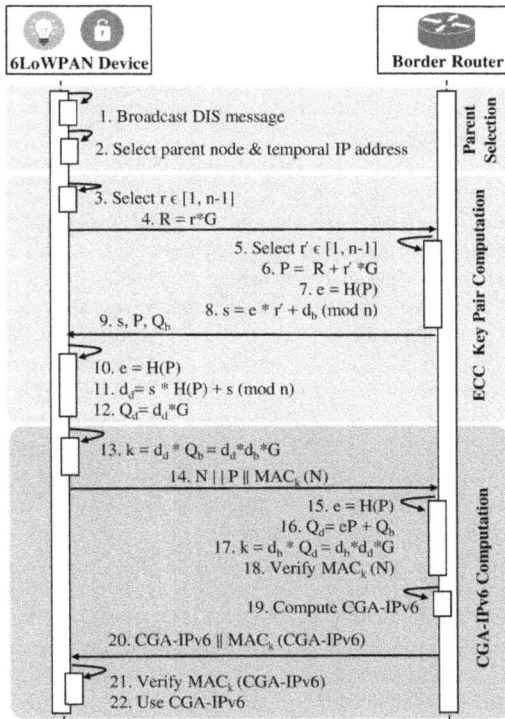

Figure 10: Secure Network Admission.

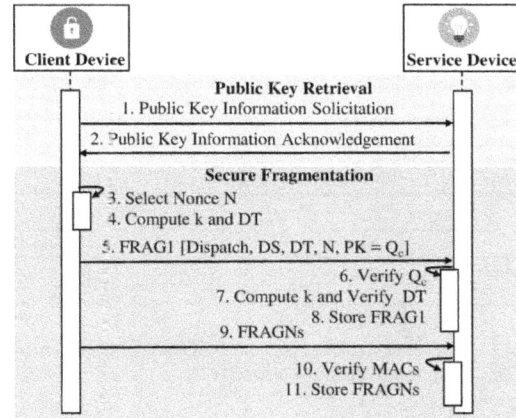

Figure 11: Secure Fragmentation. DT = Datagram Tag.

Bit Offset	0-7	8-15	16-31
0	Type = 155	Code = 0x10	Checksum
31	Target Device IPv6 Address (128 bits)		

(a) Public Key Solicitation. ICMPv6 (Type 155)

Bit Offset	0-7	8-15	16-31
0	Type = 155	Code = 0x11	Checksum
31	Target Device Public Key Q (80 bits)		

(b) Public Key Solicitation Ack. ICMPv6 (Type 155)

Figure 12: Public key solicitation message. ICMPv6 type 155.

computes a $MAC_k(N)$. Afterwards, the JD sends N, $MAC_k(N)$, and P to the BR. **Step 15-18:** The BR computes the shared key k and verifies the $MAC_k(N)$. Thus, the BR ensures that the JD used the parameters sent in *Step 9* to compute its ECC pair (d_d, Q_d). **Step 19-20:** The BR computes a *CGA-IPv6* address for the JD by using the JD's public key Q_d as shown in Figure 1. Next, the BR sends $MAC_k(CGA\text{-}IPv6)$ and *CGA-IPv6* to the JD. **Step 21-22:** The JD verifies $MAC_k(CGA\text{-}IPv6)$ by using k. Thus, the JD ensures that *CGA-IPv6* was sent by the BR. Finally, the JD configures itself using the *CGA-IPv6* address and drops the temporary IPv6 address.

4.2 Secure Transfer of Packet Fragmentations

The process of delivering packet fragments securely is shown in Figure 11. **Step 1-2:** A Client Device (CD) sends a Public Key Information Solicitation (PKS) message to a Service Device (SD). The SD replies with a Public Key Information Acknowledgment (PKS-A) message. The PSK-A contains information about the SD's public key Q_{sd} – the SD's ECC pair is (d_{sd}, Q_{sd}). The CD can start from *Step 3* if it knows the SD's public key. The details of our proposed PSK and PKS-A messages are shown in Figure 12. We use RPL control message (ICMPv6 Type 155) with code 0x10 and 0x11, that are reserved according to the RPL specification [41], for the PSK and PKS-A messages respectively. **Step 3-5:** The CD selects current timestamps N as a nonce and then computes a shared key $k = d_{cd} * Q_{sd} * N = d_{cd} * d_{sd} * N$ and a cryptographic *datagram tag* $CDT = MAC_k(N || Payload)$. Next, the CD constructs FRAG1. We propose a modified header for FRAG1 as shown in Figure 13. The proposed header contains additional fields for encoding nonce and sender's public key. The CD sets the *datagram tag* field to the *CDT*, Nonce field to N, and Public Key field to its public key Q_{sc} – the

CD's ECC pair is (d_{cd}, Q_{cd}). **Step 6-8:** The SD retrieves Q_{cd} from the FRAG1 and uses it to compute the CD's CGA-IPv6 address (see Figure 1). The SD matches the CGA-IPv6 address with the *source* field of the IPv6 header of FRAG1. Thus, the SD ensures that the Q_{sc} is bound to the CD's CGA-IPv6 address. Next, the SD computes the shared key $k = d_{sd} * Q_{cd} * N = d_{sd} * d_{cd} * N$, verifies the value of the *datagram tag* using k, and stores FRAG1. **Step 9:** The CD creates subsequent FRAGNs and sends to the SD. For each FRAGN the CD sets its *datagram tag* to *CDT* and *MAC* field to $MAC_k(payload)$. We propose to add an additional field for MAC in the FRAGN header as shown in Figure 13. **Step 10-11:** The SD verifies the MACs fields of the received FRAGNs and stores them. If the value of the *MAC* computed by the SD for a fragment F_i does not match the value present in the MAC field of that fragment, the SD sends a fragment solicitation (FRAGS) message to CD as proposed in Figure 13. The SD specifies the *datagram tag* and *offset* of F_i in the FRAGS. The CD retransmits the corrupted fragment.

4.3 Secure Management of Reassembly Buffer

We propose a reputation point based buffer management scheme. Every node maintains a reputation point $r_j \in [0.0, 1.0]$ for its peer to prevent buffer overflow attacks. The reputation point of a node indicates the probability of sending all the fragments of a packet by that node. A receiving device (RD) assigns an initial reputation point $r_j = 0.5$ to a sending device (SD) when the SD communicates to the RD for the very first time. We assigned 0.5 or 50% because at the very beginning, it is difficult for the RD to identify whether the SD is malicious or not. For this reason, 50% is a safe choice. The RD updates the reputation point of the SD upon receiving the entire

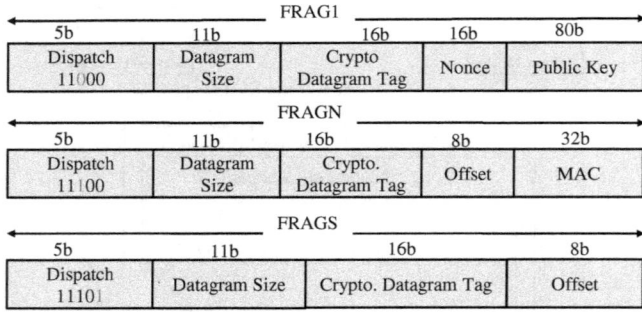

Figure 13: Proposed modification of FRAG1 and FRAGN headers. FRAGS = Fragment solicitation header.

packet, when it does not receive all the fragments, but the timer that is set for the packet expires, or when it discards fragments to free buffer for new requests. A receiver adjusts the reputation point (r_j) of a sender as follows:

$$r_j = \begin{cases} min\{\frac{r_j+1}{2}, 1\} \text{ if a sender sends all the fragments.} \\ \qquad\qquad\qquad \text{if the receiver fails receiving} \\ max\{r_j - \frac{buf_j}{r_j}(1 - \mu_j), 0.1\} \text{ all the packet fragments} \\ \qquad\qquad\qquad\qquad\qquad \text{before time expires} \end{cases}$$

Here $\mu_j \in [0.0, 1.0]$ and $buf_j \in [0.0, 1.0]$ are calculated as $\mu_j = \frac{\text{Total bytes received}}{\text{Total length of the packet}}$ and $buf_j = \frac{\text{Total Allocated Portion of the Buffer (}buf_a\text{)}}{\text{Total Size of the Buffer}}$. A receiver allocates buf_a for a fragmented packet as $buf_a = p + q$, $p = r_j * datagram\_size$, and $q = (p + 8) \bmod 8$.

The reputation point ensures the reliability of the sending device. However, during the reassembling process, there could be a scenario when most of the buffer memory is occupied with incomplete packets and the receiving device can not allocate memory to new incoming packets. To tackle this scenario we need to address the discard policy. SecuPAN waits for 60 seconds for packet fragments to get transmitted. Additionally, when 90% of total buffer is consumed, our system will start to discard fragments of incomplete packets based on the uncertainty point uc_p calculated for each packet as $uc_p = \frac{f_r * t_r * n_s}{r_s}$. Here, f_r = Number of remaining fragments of that packet, t_r = Time left to expire, n_s = Number of sessions opened by the sending device, and r_s = Reputation point of the sending device.

The system discards the fragments with highest uncertainty point. If two fragments have same uncertainty point then one of them is discarded randomly. For a certain packet, the number of remaining fragments and time left to expire plays an important role. t_r indicates how much time is left until the timer expires. Also, we consider the number of open session for a particular sending device. It impacts the uncertainty points of all the incomplete packets that are occupying the buffer.

5 SECURITY ANALYSIS OF SECUPAN

Replay: Eve or Mallory replays fragments F1 to FN (see Figure 5). Bob recognizes that F1 (FRAG1) was sent in the past by looking at its Nonce field (see Figure 13) and discards the packet fragments.
Alteration: Mallory modifies the payload (P) of the fragment F3 and sends to Bob (see Figure 6). We denote the modified payload and fragment as P′ and F3′ respectively. Mallory has to compute $MAC_k(P')$ for the MAC field of F3′. However, Mallory does not know the shared key (k), which is computed in Step 4 of Figure 11,

for the on going session between Alice and Bob. Therefore, she cannot compute $MAC_k(P')$ and creates F3′ by simply replacing P with P′. However, Bob discards the modified fragment after verifying F3′'s MAC field. Bob finds that $MAC_k(P)$ does not match $MAC_k(P')$ – Step 10 of Figure 11.

Spoofing: A malicious node cannot spoof the cryptographic IPv6 address of a victim node which is computed in Step 19–20 of Figure 10. Let's suppose, Mallory wants to send a message to Bob impersonating Alice (see Figure 7). To construct fragment FRAG1 of the message, Mallory has to compute a value for the cryptographic *datagram-tag* by using the private key (d_a) of Alice's ECC pair (d_a, Q_a) as described in Step 3–5 of Figure 11. However, Mallory does not know Alice's private key d_a. Therefore, she cannot compute the value of the *datagram-tag* field. However, Mallory can use a forged ECC pair (d_a', Q_a') to compute the *datagram-tag* to fool Bob. If Mallory does so then Bob detects such address spoofing in Step 6–8 of Figure 11. Alice's IPv6 address is computed using Q_a and cannot be verified using the forged public key Q_a'. Therefore, Bob discards the spoofed fragments.

Duplicate fragment: Mallory sends a duplicate fragment (F_2') in addition to the legitimate fragments (F_1–F_n) to Bob (see Figure 8). However, Bob can identify the duplicate fragment F_2' by verifying the MAC field. Bob computes a MAC for the received F_2''s payload. Bob finds that the value present in the MAC field of F_2' does not match the value of the MAC computed using F_2''s payload. Thus, Bob ensures that F_2 is the legitimate fragment.

Buffer exhaustion: Buffer exhaustion: If a malicious node does not send the fragments of a packet after sending the first fragment during the timeout, then the reputation point of the node will be reduced. Therefore, the victim will allocate a smaller size buffer (buf_a) for a packet that will be sent by the attacker in the future. If the attacker keep doing this then the reputation point of the attacker will gradually drop and the packets from the attacker will be discarded. The minimum reputation can be 0.1 (10%). This will allow some opportunity to benign user to recover whose reputation point is penalized because of lossy connections. In another scenario, the attacker keep sending the first fragment of some packets during the timeout period to overflow the reassembly buffer. However, when 90% of the total buffer is consumed the victim frees memory by discarding incomplete packet fragments. Thus, the victim makes room for new requests. At the same time, the victim recalculates the reputation point of the attacker, then the reputation point is lowered drastically due to the multiple unsuccessful transmission of packets. As a result, the victim allocates a very tiny portion of the reassembly buffer for the future packets from the attacker.

Selective forwarding: The reputation point of a victim node keeps decreasing as an on-path adversary selectively drops packet fragments. Eventually, the victim node's reputation point (r_v) becomes 0.1. The receiving node broadcasts a message containing the victim node's r_v to the DODAG when the r_v hits 0.1. The receiving node signs the message $sign_{d_r}(victim\text{-}IPv6 \| r_v)$ with the private key d_r of its ECC pair (d_r, Q_r) to protect it from forgery. The receiver broadcasts the message to ensure that it reaches to the victim node through multiple routes in case the adversary blocks the message. The victim node receives the message and verifies the signature using Q_r. Thus, the victim node ensures that the message was sent from the receiver and learns that the fragments of it previously sent

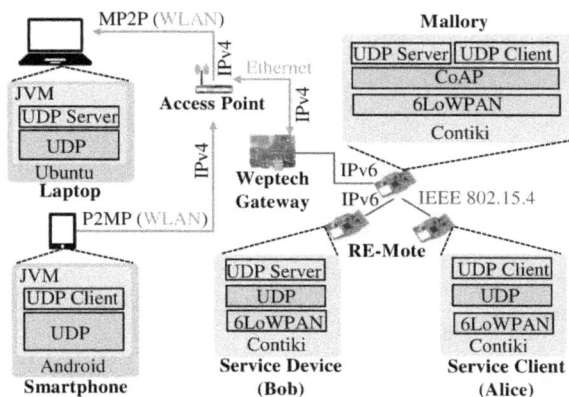

Figure 14: Experimental Setup

packets was dropped by an on-path adversary. The victim node selects a new parent node in the 6LoWPAN to avoid the route on which the attacker is present. The victim node follows the Local Repair mechanism as described in the RFC of RPL routing to select the new parent node [41]. The victim node ensures that the new parent has a lower rank than the last parent and is not located on the previous sub-network. Thus, the target avoids the on-path attacker.

Memory probing: The pre-shared key used in the 6LoWPAN link layer security is stored in the device's non-volatile memory, such as SD card or ROM. An adversary can tamper with the device's storage to extract the pre-shared key. Thus, the adversary gets unauthorized access to a 6LoWPAN network and resources. However, in SecuPAN, a device computes a new ECC key pair everytime it joins a network. Furthermore, the key pair is stored in the volatile memory (RAM). Therefore, SecuPAN is secure against memory probing attacks.

6 EXPERIMENT AND EVALUATION

6.1 Experimental Setup

We implemented a prototype of SecuPAN for the Contiki 3.0 operating system [31]. We formed a 6LoWPAN network using RE-Mote IoT devices [35] and a Weptech border router [40]. As shown in Figure 14, an RE-Mote UDP client and an RE-Mote UDP server performed as Alice and Bob respectively. The RE-Mote device running both UDP server and client was Mallory. We simulated the P2P traffic as follows. Alice sent a UDP packet to Mallory's UDP server which her UDP client forwarded to Bob's UDP server. In the P2MP traffic flow, a Smartphone sent a UDP packet to Mallory which she forwarded to Bob. To simulate MP2P traffic flow, Mallory forwarded a UDP packet sent by Alice to the Laptop's UDP server. We configured Mallory such that she could drop, modify, or duplicate packet fragments. Mallory could also replay a request. Furthermore, Mallory established multiple connections with Bob and sent incomplete packets to perform buffer reservation attack. We considered Mesh-under scheme (29 bytes application payload) and Enhanced Route-over scheme (46 bytes application payload) to route packet fragments.

6.2 Evaluation

Effective packet number (EPN): The number of packets that were successfully reassembled by Bob within the experiment time. We analyzed the performance for the duplicate fragment attack. Alice generated variable sized packets (128, 256, and 512 Bytes) and sent

to Mallory. Mallory duplicated a fragment every 500 ms, 1000 ms, or 1500 ms, and sent to Bob. The packet sending rate was 1 packet in every 300 ms. We counted the number of effective packets for SecuPAN and base Contiki separately and showed the results in Figure 15. From the graphs, we can observe that SecuPAN provides higher score on EPN than Contiki. This is because base Contiki simply drops an entire packet if it finds a duplicate fragment. However, SecuPAN identifies the duplicate fragment by verifying the fragment's MAC field. Therefore, SecuPAN drops only duplicate fragments and stores legitimate fragments.

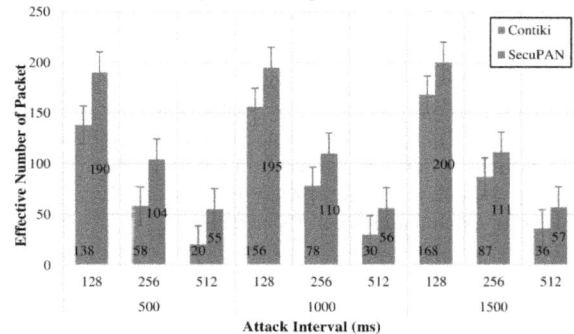

(a) Effective number of packets Vs. Attack interval (Mesh-under)

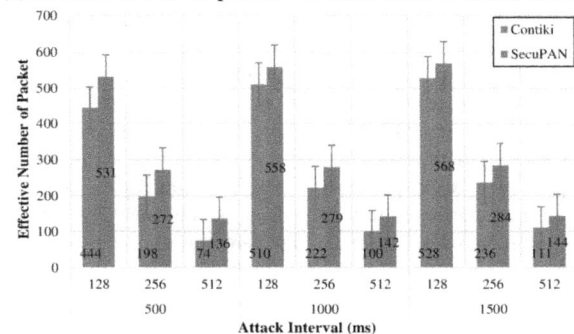

(b) Effective number of packets Vs. Attack interval (Route-over)

Figure 15: Analysis and comparison of effective number of packets.

Packet delivery ratio (fabrication): The packet delivery ratio (PDR) is defined as the ratio of the number of packets delivered to Bob to the total number of packets sent by Alice. Mallory modified a fragment every 500 ms, 1000 ms, or 1500 ms. The results for the alteration attack are shown in Figure 16 and Figure 25. From the figures, we can see that SecuPAN provides higher PDR ($> 95\%$) than Contiki. In SecuPAN, Bob identified the modified fragments by verifying their MAC fields and asked Alice to resend the modified fragments only. However, In base Conitki, Bob had to resend the entire packet. Therefore, by adopting SecuPAN, Alice delivered more messages to Bob compared to base Contiki. For the duplicate fragment attack, Alice experienced complete packet loss with a PDR 0%. In contrast, SecuPAN achieves PDR 100%. Each received fragment was verified correctly.

Packet delivery ratio (buffer reservation): We configured Mallory such that it could send packet at a rate (1 packet every 300 ms) faster than Alice's data rate (1 packet every 2 seconds). This time

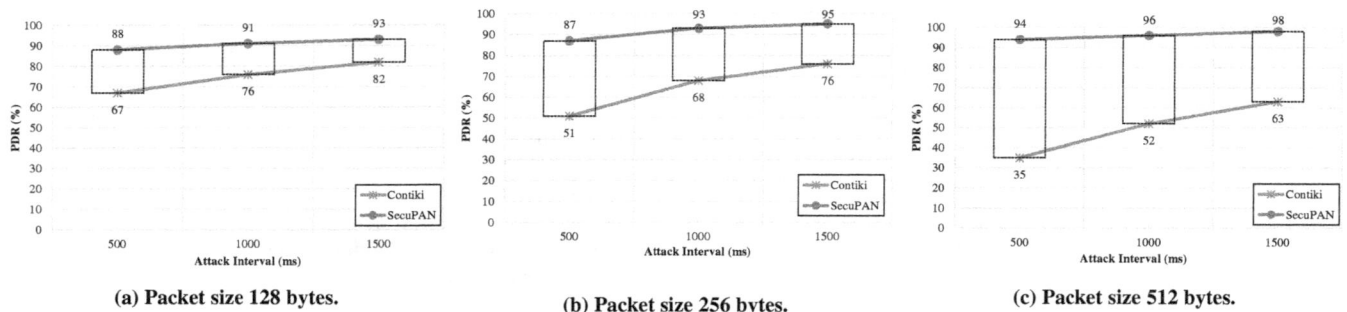

(a) Packet size 128 bytes.　　　　(b) Packet size 256 bytes.　　　　(c) Packet size 512 bytes.

Figure 16: Comparison of packet delivery ratio (Mesh-under).

packets were not routed through Mallory. Instead, Alice was configured to send packets directly to Bob. Both Mallory and Alice sent packets of size 1024 bytes. We measured the PDR at the target node every 5 seconds and plotted the result in Figure 17. From the graph 17, we can see that the buffer started overflowing after 5 seconds. The PDRs for Contiki and SecuPAN started dropping after this point. The PDR dropped as low as 7% for base Contiki. This is because base Contiki could not receive new requests when the reassembly buffer was full. Contiki waited for 60 seconds for packet fragments to be transmitted and discarded incomplete packets only after their corresponding timers were expired. In contrast, with our reputation based buffer management scheme, the PDR increased up to 97%. SecuPAN also waited 60 seconds for discarding incomplete packets. In addition to that, SecuPAN discarded incomplete packets based on senders' reputation and packets' uncertainty points as described in Section 4.3 when 90% of the reassembly buffer was full. In our buffer management, the PDR dropped at the very beginning but after the timer expiration or 90% buffer occupancy, the model recalculated reputation point for each sending devices. Therefore, the reputation point of the attacker node went down and they would get less space in buffer reservation. Hence, SecuPAN could receive and accommodate more legitimate requests compared to base Contiki and showed the higher score on PDR than Contiki.

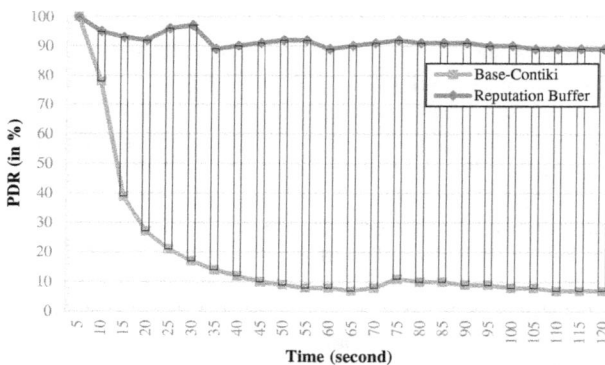

Figure 17: Packet delivery ratio (Contiki vs SecuPAN.)

Average end to end delay: The end-to-end delay (EED) is defined as the average time consumed for delivering packets under the experiment time. Average EED was calculated as Avg. EED = $\frac{\text{Total EED}}{\text{Total Packets Delivered}}$. The delivery time for a packet was calculated as *Packet Delivery Time = Time taken for sending a packet from source to destination + Time taken for retransmitting the packet or its fragments if one or more fragments of that packet are modified by*

an intermediate node. We varied the number of intermediate nodes from one to three and recorded the end-to-end delay for 128, 256, and 512 bytes packets. We used Contiki clock library [29] to measure the delays. An analysis of percentage of EED reduction by SecuPAN is shown Figure 18 and Figure 26. From the graphs, we can observe that SecuPAN reduces end-to-end delay both in the Mesh-under and Route-over routing schemes when 6LoWPAN is under the alteration and duplication attack. In SecuPAN, a sending node only sends the modified fragments of a packet SecuPAN since a receiving node can identify the modified fragments by verifying their MAC fields. However, in base Contiki, a receiver cannot determine which fragment of a packet is modified. A sender has to retransmit all the fragments of a modified packet. Therefore, retransmission in base Contiki added additional delays to the packet delivery time compared to SecuPAN's selective-fragment retransmission technique.

Throughput: To calculate the throughput, we divided the total data packets that are successfully delivered by the total time taken to deliver the packets. The total packet delivery time is the sum of the time taken to transmit and retransmit (if modified) the packets. An analysis and comparison of throughput are presented in Figure 19 and 27 for variously sized packets of 128, 256, and 512 bytes and attack intervals of 500, 1000, and 1500 ms. We can see from the Graphs 19 and 27 that the number of bytes sent per second increased in SecuPAN. The MAC-based per fragment integrity verification capability of SecuPAN reduced the total number of bytes required to retransmit for the modified packets. As a result, the number of bytes transmitted per second is significantly larger in SecuPAN than in base Contiki.

Average energy consumption: Energy consumption is defined as the average energy required for delivering packets. The energy consumption for delivering a packet is the sum of the energy required for transmitting the packet and, if modified, retransmitting all the fragments (base Contiki) or modified fragments (SecuPAN) of the packet. We recorded the total amount of energy required for delivering packets during the experiment time using Contiki Energy library [30], and then divided the total energy consumption by the number of delivered packets. We presented an analysis and comparison of average energy consumption in Figure 20a and 20b. From the Graphs 20a and 20b, we can observe that the average energy consumption in SecuPAN is significantly lower than in base Contiki. This is because SecuPAN could verify the integrity of each fragment of a packet. As a result, unlike Contiki, SecuPAN consumed energy only for retransmitting the modified fragments of a packet instead of resending all the packet fragments.

(a) Attack interval 500 ms.

(b) Attack interval 1000 ms.

(c) Attack interval 1500 ms.

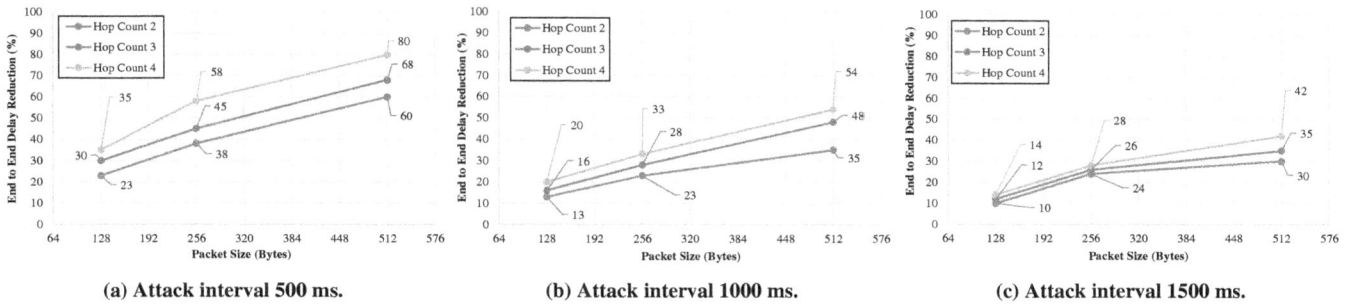

Figure 18: Percentage of end to end delay reduction by SecuPAN (Mesh-under).

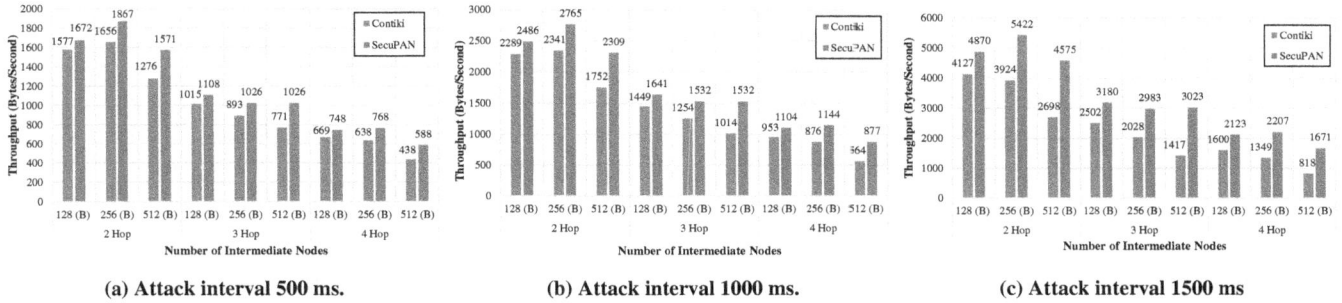

(a) Attack interval 500 ms.

(b) Attack interval 1000 ms.

(c) Attack interval 1500 ms

Figure 19: Comparison of throughput (Mesh-under).

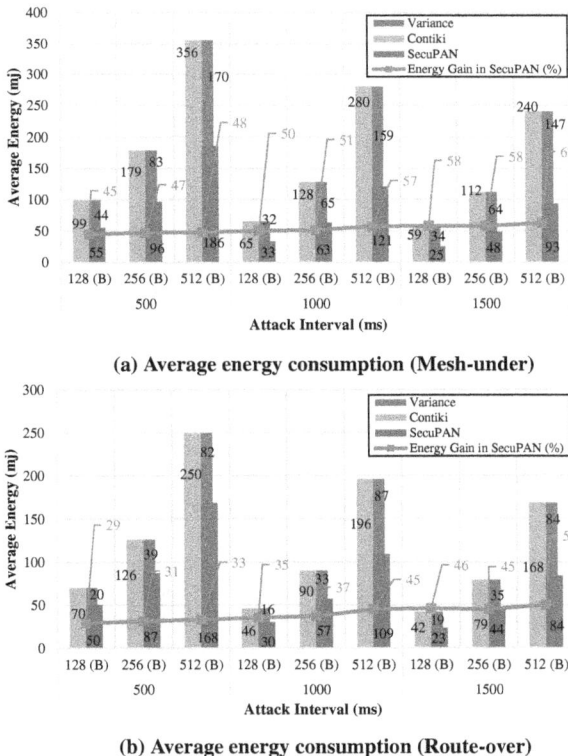

(a) Average energy consumption (Mesh-under)

(b) Average energy consumption (Route-over)

Figure 20: Analysis and comparison of energy consumption.

Runtime Performance: We recorded the time taken by a sending node and receiving node for performing packet fragmentation, re-assembly, and MAC operations, and presented the results in Figure 21 and 22. At a sending node, the run time for these operations

was computed as $T_s = Time\ to\ fragment\ a\ packet + Sum\ of\ the\ time\ required\ to\ compute\ a\ MAC\ for\ each\ fragment$. On the other hand, the computation time at a receiving node was calculated as $T_r = Time\ to\ reassemble\ a\ packet + Sum\ of\ the\ Time\ required\ to\ compute\ a\ MAC\ for\ each\ fragment + Time\ to\ update\ Reputation\ point$. We used modified Chaskey MAC [28] algorithm to verify the integrity and authenticity of a fragment. The modified Chaskey MAC is especially proposed for low-powered CPUs (16-bit MSP430 micro-controller with 16 MHz clock); therefore, it is suitable for RE-Mote IoT devices.

From the runtime analysis Figures 21 and 22, we can observe that the overall run-time for base Contiki (both at the sending and receiving nodes) is lower than for SecuPAN. This is because Contiki does not verify the integrity and authenticity (MAC operation) of a fragment and implement Reputation-based buffer management scheme. Although lack of these security features makes the fragment processing task faster in base Contiki, they make a 6LoWPAN network susceptible to the network attacks described in Section 3. We can also observe that the performance overhead at the receiving node is higher than on a the sending node due to the buffer management functionalities of the Reputation-buffer approach. Such increase in the runtime for adopting SecuPAN is acceptable since SecuPAN provides a higher degree of security for 6LoWPAN network compared to base Contiki.

7 RELATED WORK

In the IP-based communication, packet fragmentation has always been a potential threat. 6LoWPan-enabled networks are also at security risk due to packet fragmentation. In the literature, several works had explored fragmentation-based attacks [6, 43]. However, these attacks commonly focus on deficiencies of the respective IP protocol implementation, e.g., for IDS or firewall evasion, or for DoS purposes [34]. Gilad et al. [13] discovered an IP design vulnerability

(a) Run-time at sender.

(b) Run-time at receiver.

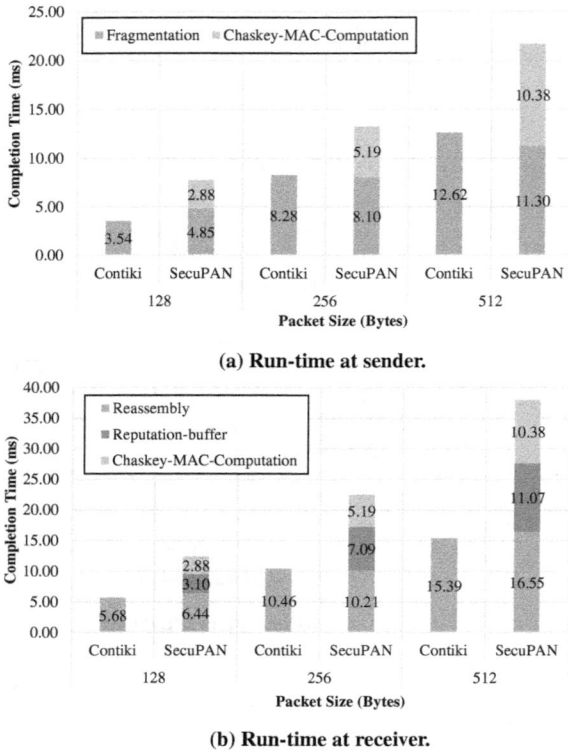

Figure 21: Comparison of runtime (Mesh-under scheme).

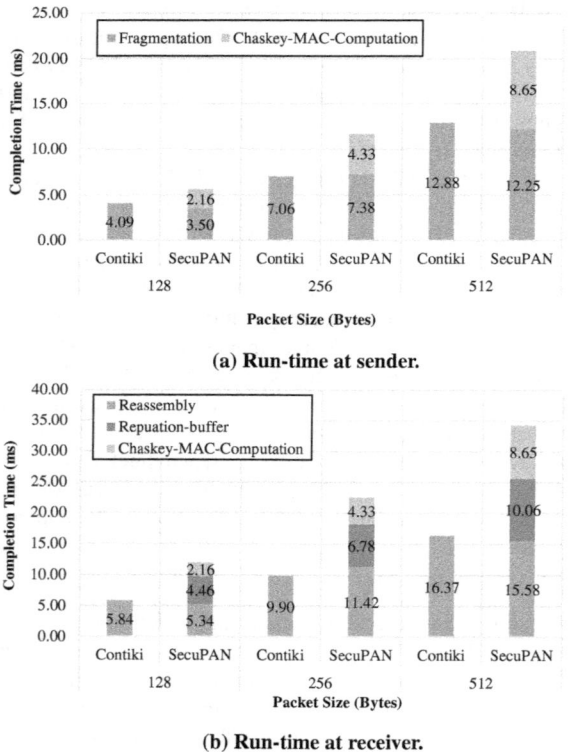

(a) Run-time at sender.

(b) Run-time at receiver.

Figure 22: Comparison of runtime (Route-over scheme).

that is based on spoofed fragments with a correctly guessed IP-ID field. Incomplete packets have been found to cause vulnerabilities in commodity operation systems and security appliances [38]. The transmission of large packets stretched over the reassembly timeout allows to maliciously occupy scarce buffer resources. Hummen et al. [17] counters such attacks with split buffer approach that was inspired by early queuing strategies for congested ATM switches in case of packet-based communication [8, 36]. With regard to 6LoW-PAN, the author in [21] claims that implementation deficiencies may enable fragmentation attacks similar to the ones found in IP implementations and that replayed fragmented packets may be a potential security risk. In [27], the authors analyze the vulnerability of the RPL routing protocol and propose IDS-based countermeasures.

Hash chain schemes based on the delayed disclosure of token information such as μTESLA [33] have been proposed for the authentication of broadcast messages in resource constrained environments. In [11, 26], the authors propose constructions similar to content chaining scheme for the purpose of secure network programming. In [10, 20] the above schemes are extended in order to handle packet reordering by employing hash tree-based constructions. Hussain et al. [19] proposed migration scheme for unmodified IoT device. Kolbe et al. [23] presented a situation aware framework for IoT with Knowledge Base and Reasoning Components.

In comparison with the prior work, SecuPAN provides protection against a wider range of fragmentation attacks. Most of the previous works only covered one or two types of fragmentation attack. However, our proposed scheme tackles six types of fragmentation attacks as shown in Table 1.

Table 1: Prior Research Vs. SecuPAN. Spf = Spoofing, BE= Buffer Exhaustion, SF = Selective Forwarding, MP = Memory Probing.

Scheme	Replay	Alteration	Spf	Dup	BE	SF	MP
Kim[21]	✓	✗	✗	✗	✗	✗	✗
Halcu et al.[14]	✓	✗	✗	✓	✗	✗	✗
Hummen et al.[17]	✗	✗	✗	✓	✓	✗	✗
SecuPAN	✓	✓	✓	✓	✓	✓	✓

8 CONCLUSION

In this paper, we proposed SecuPAN, a security scheme that provides a complete protection against 6LoWPAN fragmentation attacks. We analyzed the 6LoWPAN fragmentation mechanism and found vulnerabilities in it. We identified possible network attacks that an adversary can perform by exploiting these vulnerabilities. We also provided defense mechanisms for the identified attacks. We proposed a nonce field in the fragment header to prevent fragmentation replay attacks. We incorporated a MAC-based scheme to protect packet fragments from fabrication, modification, or duplication attacks. Our scheme includes a cryptographic IPv6 address assignment mechanism to mitigate spoofing attacks. Furthermore, we proposed a reputation-based buffer management scheme to protect 6LoWPAN devices from buffer exhaustion. We conducted a complete security analysis of SecuPAN. Our analysis shows that SecuPAN performed very well against these attacks. Through a comprehensive performance analysis, we showed that SecuPAN provides a higher score on packet delivery ratio and throughput than base Contiki. The analysis also showed that SecuPAN reduces end-to-end delay and energy consumption when a 6LoWPAN is under network attacks.

ACKNOWLEDGEMENTS

This research was supported by the National Science Foundation CAREER Award CNS-1351038, ACI-1642078, and SaTC-1723768.

APPENDIX

A ADDITIONAL FIGURES

A.1 IEEE 802.15.4 Frame Details

The details of an IEEE 802.15.4 Frame are illustrated in Figure 23.

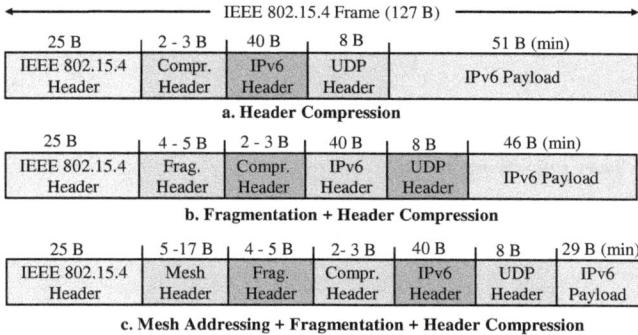

a. Header Compression

b. Fragmentation + Header Compression

c. Mesh Addressing + Fragmentation + Header Compression

Figure 23: IEEE 802.15.4 Frame. min = Minimum.

A.2 6LoWPAN Adaptation Layer

The position of the 6LoWPAN adaptation layer in the Web protocol stack is shown in Figure 24.

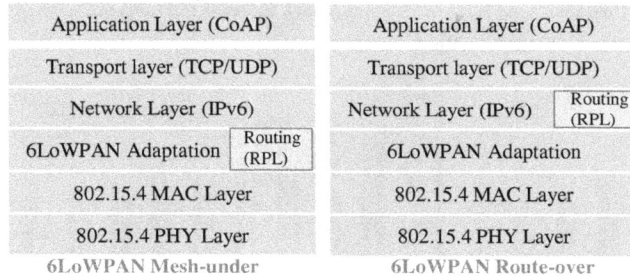

Figure 24: 6LoWPAN IP Stack.

A.3 Packet Delivery Ratio (Route-Over)

An analysis and comparison of packet delivery ratio for Route-over scheme is presented in Figure 25.

A.4 Average end to end delay (Route-over)

An analysis and comparison of percentage of end-to-end delay reduction by SecuPAN are shown in Figure 26.

A.5 Throughput (Route-over)

An analysis and comparison of number of bytes sent per second is shown in Figure 27.

REFERENCES

[1] Jon T Adams. 2006. An introduction to IEEE STD 802.15. 4. In *IEEE Aerospace Conference*. IEEE.

[2] Kazi Masudul Alam, Mukesh Saini, and Abdulmotaleb El Saddik. 2015. Toward social Internet of Vehicles: Concept, architecture, and applications. *IEEE Access* 3 (2015), 343–357.

[3] Tuomas Aura. 2005. Cryptographically generated addresses (CGA). *IETF, RFC* (2005).

[4] Alexander Becher, Zinaida Benenson, and Maximillian Dornseif. 2006. Tampering with motes: Real-world physical attacks on wireless sensor networks. In *International Conference on Security in Pervasive Computing*. Springer.

[5] Carsten Bormann. 2013. Guidance for light-weight implementations of the internet protocol suite. *IETF, RFC* (2013).

[6] CERT Coordination Center. 1997. CERT Advisory CA-1997-28 IP Denial-of-Service Attacks. (1997).

[7] Certicom. 2014. *Explaining Implicit Certificates*. Technical Report. Certicom.

[8] Sammy Chan, Eric WM Wong, and King-Tim Ko. 1997. Fair packet discarding for controlling ABR traffic in ATM networks. *IEEE Transactions on Communications* 45, 8 (1997), 913–916.

[9] Aminul Haque Chowdhury, Muhammad Ikram, Hyon-Soo Cha, Hassen Redwan, SM Shams, Ki-Hyung Kim, and Seung-Wha Yoo. 2009. Route-over vs Mesh-under Routing in 6LoWPAN. In *International conference on wireless communications and mobile computing: Connecting the world wirelessly*. ACM.

[10] Jing Deng, Richard Han, and Shivakant Mishra. 2006. Secure code distribution in dynamically programmable wireless sensor networks. In *International Conference on Information Processing in Sensor Networks*. IEEE, 292–300.

[11] Prabal K Dutta, Jonathan W Hui, David C Chu, and David E Culler. 2006. Securing the deluge network programming system. In *International Conference on Information Processing in Sensor Networks*. IEEE.

[12] Sheila Frankel and Suresh Krishnan. 2011. IP security (IPsec) and internet key exchange (IKE) document roadmap. *IETF, RFC* (2011).

[13] Yossi Gilad and Amir Herzberg. 2011. Fragmentation considered vulnerable: blindly intercepting and discarding fragments. In *Proceedings of the 5th USENIX conference on Offensive technologies*. USENIX Association, 2–2.

[14] Ionela Halcu, Grigore Stamatescu, and Valentin Sgarciu. 2016. A security framework for a 6LoWPAN based industrial wireless sensor network. *University Politehnica of Bucharest Scientific Bulletin Series* 78, 4 (2016), 57–68.

[15] Klaus Hartke and Olaf Bergmann. 2012. Datagram transport layer security in constrained environments. (2012).

[16] Carl Hartung, James Balasalle, and Richard Han. 2005. Node compromise in sensor networks: The need for secure systems. *Department of Computer Science University of Colorado at Boulder* (2005).

[17] René Hummen, Jens Hiller, Hanno Wirtz, Martin Henze, Hossein Shafagh, and Klaus Wehrle. 2013. 6LoWPAN fragmentation attacks and mitigation mechanisms. In *Proceedings of the sixth ACM conference on Security and privacy in wireless and mobile networks*. ACM, 55–66.

[18] René Hummen, Jan H Ziegeldorf, Hossein Shafagh, Shahid Raza, and Klaus Wehrle. 2013 Towards viable certificate-based authentication for the internet of things. In *Proceedings of the 2nd ACM workshop on Hot topics on wireless network security and privacy*. ACM, 37–42.

[19] Syed Rafiul Hussain, Shagufta Mehnaz, Shahriar Nirjon, and Elisa Bertino. 2017. Secure Seamless Bluetooth Low Energy Connection Migration for Unmodified IoT Devices. *IEEE Transactions on Mobile Computing* (2017).

[20] Sangwon Hyun, Peng Ning, An Liu, and Wenliang Du. 2008. Seluge: Secure and dos-resistant code dissemination in wireless sensor networks. In *International Conference on Information Processing in Sensor Networks*. IEEE, 445–456.

[21] HyunGon Kim. 2008. Protection against packet fragmentation attacks at 6lowpan adaptation layer. In *International Conference on Convergence and Hybrid Information Technology*. IEEE, 796–801.

[22] Niklas Kolbe, Sylvain Kubler, Jérémy Robert, Yves Le Traon, and Arkady Zaslavsky. 2017. Towards semantic interoperability in an open IoT ecosystem for connected vehicle services. In *Global Internet of Things Summit (GIoTS), 2017*. IEEE, 1–5.

[23] Niklas Kolbe, Arkady Zaslavsky, Sylvain Kubler, Jérémy Robert, and Yves Le Traon. 2017. Enriching a Situation Awareness Framework for IoT with Knowledge Base and Reasoning Components. In *International and Interdisciplinary Conference on Modeling and Using Context*. Springer, 41–54.

[24] Nandakishore Kushalnagar, Gabriel Montenegro, David E Culler, and Jonathan W Hui. 2007. Transmission of ipv6 packets over ieee 802.15. 4 networks. *IETF, RFC* (2007).

[25] N Kushalnagar, G Montenegro, and C Schumacher. 2007. Rfc 4919: Ipv6 over low-power wireless personal area networks (6lowpans): overview. *Assumptions, Problem Statement, and Goals* (2007).

[26] Patrick E Lanigan, Rajeev Gandhi, and Priya Narasimhan. 2006. Sluice: Secure dissemination of code updates in sensor networks. In *International Conference on Distributed Computing System*. IEEE.

[27] Anhtuan Le, Jonathan Loo, Aboubaker Lasebae, Mahdi Aiash, and Yuan Luo. 2012. 6LoWPAN: a study on QoS security threats and countermeasures using intrusion detection system approach. *International Journal of Communication Systems* 25, 9 (2012), 1189–1212.

[28] G. Lee, H. Seo, T. Park, and H. Kim. 2017. Optimized implementation of chaskey MAC on 16-bit MSP430. In *Ninth International Conference on Ubiquitous and Future Networks (ICUFN)*.

[29] Clock Library. 2017. Contiki APIs for Accessing Realtime Clock. (2017). http://www.eistec.se/docs/contiki/a02184.html

[30] Energy Library. 2017. Contiki APIs for Measuring Energy Consumption. (2017). http://contiki.sourceforge.net/docs/2.6/a00452_source.html

[31] Contiki OS. 2016. An open source operating system for the Internet of Things. (2016). http://www.contiki-os.org/

[32] R. Yogesh Patil and L. Ragha. 2011. A rate limiting mechanism for defending against flooding based distributed denial of service attack. In *World Congress on*

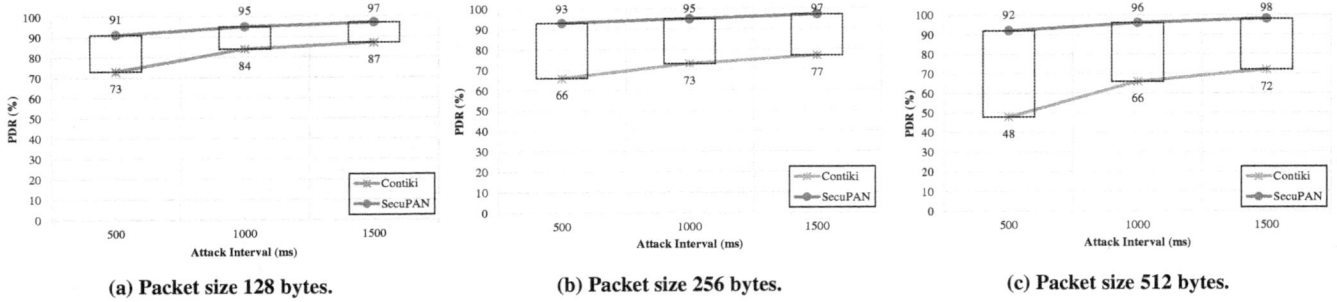

(a) Packet size 128 bytes.   (b) Packet size 256 bytes.   (c) Packet size 512 bytes.

Figure 25: Comparison of packet delivery ratio (Route-over).

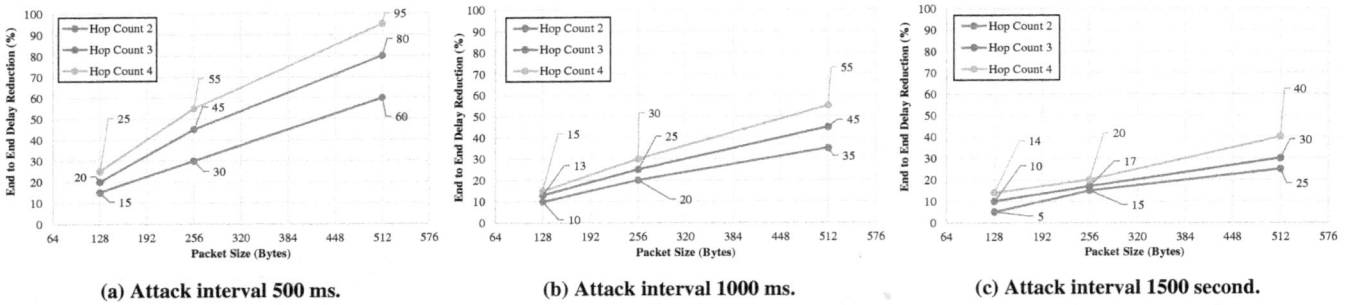

(a) Attack interval 500 ms.   (b) Attack interval 1000 ms.   (c) Attack interval 1500 second.

Figure 26: Average end to end delay reduction by SecuPAN (Route-over).

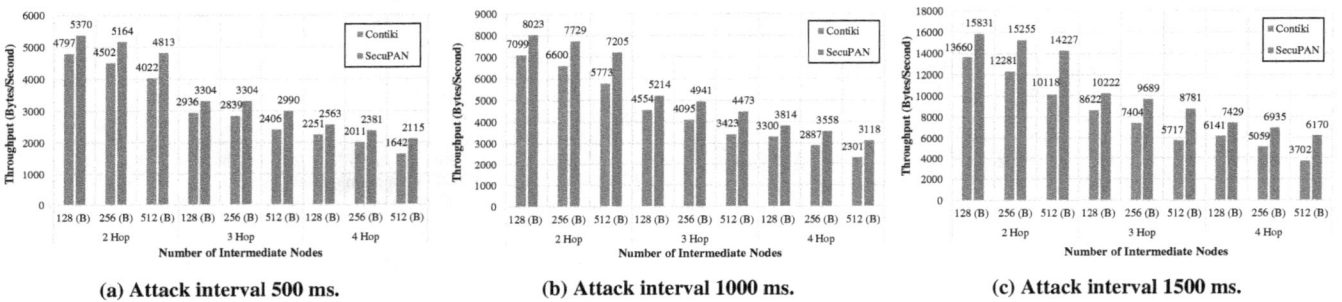

(a) Attack interval 500 ms.   (b) Attack interval 1000 ms.   (c) Attack interval 1500 ms.

Figure 27: Comparison of throughput (Route-over).

Information and Communication Technologies.

[33] Adrian Perrig, Robert Szewczyk, Justin Douglas Tygar, Victor Wen, and David E Culler. 2002. SPINS: Security protocols for sensor networks. *Wireless networks* 8, 5 (2002), 521–534.

[34] Thomas H Ptacek and Timothy N Newsham. 1998. *Insertion, evasion, and denial of service: Eluding network intrusion detection.* Technical Report. DTIC Document.

[35] ReMote. 2017. A 6LoWPAN IoT device. http://zolertia.io/z1. (2017).

[36] Allyn Romanow and Sally Floyd. 1995. Dynamics of TCP traffic over ATM networks. *IEEE Journal on selected Areas in Communications* 13, 4 (1995), 633–641.

[37] Antonino Rullo, Edoardo Serra, Elisa Bertino, and Jorge Lobo. 2017. Shortfall-Based Optimal Placement of Security Resources for Mobile IoT Scenarios. In *European Symposium on Research in Computer Security.* Springer, 419–436.

[38] SecLists. 2004. The Rose Attack. http://seclists.org/bugtraq/2004/Mar/351. (2004).

[39] P Thubert and J Hui. 2010. LoWPAN fragment Forwarding and Recovery. *Internet Draft draft-thubert-6lowpan-simple-fragment-recovery-07, work in progress* (2010).

[40] Weptech. 2017. A 6LoWPan Border Router. https://www.weptech.de/6LoWPAN_IoT_Gateway_EN.html. (2017).

[41] Tim Winter. 2012. RPL: IPv6 routing protocol for low-power and lossy networks. *IETF, RFC* (2012).

[42] www.gartner.com. 2014. The Internet of Things will transform the Data Center. (2014). http://www.gartner.com/newsroom/id/2684616

[43] G Ziemba, P Traina, and D Reed. 1995. Security considerations for IP fragment filtering. *RFC 1858* (1995).

Denial of Engineering Operations Attacks in Industrial Control Systems

Saranyan Senthivel, Shrey Dhungana, Hyunguk Yoo, Irfan Ahmed, Vassil Roussev
Department of Computer Science, University of New Orleans
(ssenthiv,sdhunga2,hyoo1)@uno.edu,(irfan,vassil)@cs.uno.edu

ABSTRACT

We present a new type of attack termed *denial of engineering operations* in which an attacker can interfere with the normal cycle of an engineering operation leading to a loss of situational awareness. Specifically, the attacker can deceive the engineering software during attempts to retrieve the ladder logic program from a *programmable logic controller* (PLC) by manipulating the ladder logic on the PLC, such that the software is unable to process it while the PLC continues to execute it successfully. This attack vector can provide sufficient cover for the attacker's actual scenario to play out while the owner tries to understand the problem and reestablish positive operational control. To enable the forensic analysis and, eventually, eliminate the threat, we have developed the first decompiler for ladder logic programs.

Ladder logic is a graphical programming language for PLCs that control physical processes such as power grid, pipelines, and chemical plants; PLCs are a common target of malicious modifications leading to the compromise of the control behavior (and potentially serious consequences). Our decompiler, *Laddis*, transforms a low-level representation to its corresponding high-level original representation comprising of graphical symbols and connections. The evaluation of the accuracy of the decompiler on the program of varying complexity demonstrates perfect reconstruction of the original program. We present three new attack scenarios on PLC-deployed ladder logic and demonstrate the effectiveness of the decompiler on these scenarios.

CCS CONCEPTS

• **Security and privacy** → **Denial-of-service attacks**;

KEYWORDS

Disassembler, Ladder logic, PLC, SCADA, Industrial Control System, Forensics, Protocol Reverse Engineering

ACM Reference Format:
Saranyan Senthivel, Shrey Dhungana, Hyunguk Yoo, Irfan Ahmed, Vassil Roussev. 2018. Denial of Engineering Operations Attacks in Industrial Control Systems. In *CODASPY '18: Eighth ACM Conference on Data and Application Security and Privacy, March 19–21, 2018, Tempe, AZ, USA.* ACM, New York, NY, USA, Article 4, 11 pages. https://doi.org/10.1145/3176258.3176319

1 INTRODUCTION

Programmable logic controllers (PLCs) are embedded devices used in industrial control systems (ICS) to automate the control and monitoring of physical industrial and infrastructure processes such as gas pipelines, nuclear plants, power grids, and wastewater treatment facilities [11]. Thus, their safety, durability, and predictable response times are the primary design concerns. Unfortunately, they are not designed to be resilient against cyberattacks [10]. If a PLC is compromised, the physical process controlled by the PLC is also compromised which could lead to a catastrophic incident.

To compromise a PLC, an attacker infiltrates into an ICS network to communicate with the PLC, or gains physical access of the PLC to communicate using local USB or serial ports. The attacker may attempt to modify either the firmware (or the operating system) of the PLC, or the control logic (typically written in the languages defined by IEC 61131-3 such as Ladder Logic). The firmware is hard to modify for the attacker because it has to be signed by the corresponding vendor's private key [19]. The attacker may find and utilize any debugging/testing ports (such as JTAG/UART) at hardware level to compromise the firmware [17]. However, this requires physical access, which makes it impractical as a remote attack.

The control logic defines how a PLC controls a physical process. Unfortunately, it is vulnerable to malicious modifications because PLCs either do not support digital signatures for control logic, or the ICS operators do not use/configure them. The adversaries target the control logic to manipulate the control behavior of the PLC. For instance, Stuxnet targets Siemens S7-300 PLCs that are specifically connected with variable frequency drives [15]. It infects the control logic of the PLCs to monitor the frequency of the attached motors, and only launches an attack if the frequency is within a certain normal range (i.e. 807 Hz and 1,210 Hz). The attack involves disrupting the normal operation of the motors by changing their motor speed periodically from 1,410 Hz to 2 Hz to 1,064 Hz and then over again.

For the purposes of our discussion, we define *engineering operations* as a continuous cycle of developing and updating the PLC control logic in response to changing operational requirements in ICS. A vendor-supplied programing software is used to create a control logic program and then to transfer it to/from a remote PLC over the network. In case of an incident, a forensic investigator (or a control operator) is likely to use the software to acquire the control logic from a suspicious PLC since the PLCs are often located at remote sites that may be difficult to get to.

We present three new attack scenarios, referred to as *denial of engineering operations* (DEO) attacks that subvert the capability of the programing software to acquire the actual control logic from an infected PLC. The first two attacks employ man-in-the-middle approach to control the network traffic during attempts to acquire the control logic from an infected PLC. In the first (and most conventional) attack, the attacker removes the infected code from the packets to hide the infection, such that the programing software shows the original (uninfected) logic to the investigator. In the second attack, the attacker replaces the selected control logic instructions in the packets with noise; in our experiments, this caused confusion and crashed the software. In the third attack, the attacker creates a well-crafted malicious control logic that runs on a PLC successfully but crashes the software when attempting to acquire the control logic from the PLC. This attack does not employ man-in the middle and allows the attacker to leave the network after transferring the malicious control logic to the PLC.

Since the firmware is intact in these attacks, the PLC sends the entire (infected) control logic to the programing software. Although the attacker intercepts the traffic and/or crashes the software, the original (infected) control logic can be captured and extracted from the network traffic for forensic analysis. However, the control logic being transferred is the compiled version, which is the binary (low-level representation of) control logic.

This paper presents a decompiler Laddis for the ladder logic, which is a widely-used programing language for PLCs. Laddis is the first decompiler developed for ladder logic programs. It supports ladder logic instructions extensively. Laddis extracts and decompiles a ladder logic program from the network traffic on both directions i.e. when a ladder logic is downloaded to and uploaded from a PLC. The programing software downloads a ladder logic program to a PLC to configure and/or update the logic in the PLC. However, it cannot show a ladder logic program from the download stream of an attacker. The only option is to let the attacker download the program completely to a target PLC, and then use the software to upload the program from the PLC, which is unacceptable since it may damage the physical process being controlled by the PLC.

For the evaluation, we use Allen-Bradley Micrologix 1400-B PLC and RSLogix 500 programing software. Laddis is currently developed and tested for RSLogix 500. We created 91 ladder logic programs of varying complexity and also downloaded 58 programs from PLCS.net [7] to evaluate the accuracy of Laddis. The downloaded programs are developed by different programmers for different physical processes such as traffic lights, an elevator, and a train crossing. We further use six versions of RSLogix 500 to generate six instances of each ladder logic program. Our evaluation results show that Laddis is compatible with all the versions of RSLogix and decompiles all the binary programs with 100% accuracy. Furthermore, Laddis was evaluated against the proposed three attacks and decompiles the infected programs successfully.

The contribution of this work is threefold: a) we identify new attack scenarios specific to the manner in which ICS are operated; b) we present a new decompiler tool that can reconstruct the attack code from network capture; and c) we show how to perform forensic analysis in response to the attacks

2   NEW ATTACK SCENARIOS

We start our discussion with an outline of the three new attack scenarios that incapacitate PLC programming software by limiting its abilities of acquiring and displaying a ladder logic program from

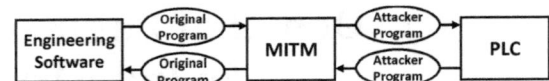

Figure 1: DEO Attack 1 – Hiding infected ladder logic (running in a target PLC) from the engineering software.

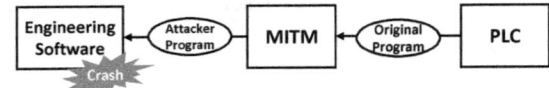

Figure 2: DEO Attack 2 – Crashing the engineering software.

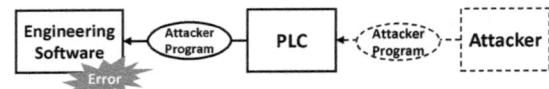

Figure 3: DEO Attack 3 – Injecting a crafted ladder logic program to a PLC that crashes the engineering software.

a PLC. We briefly introduce the three attack scenario in this section, and we will describe them in detail in section 6.4 along with the usage of Laddis.

DEO Attack 1: Hiding infected ladder logic (running in a target PLC) from the PLC programing software. In this attack scenario, an attacker performs man-in-the-middle between a PLC and an engineering workstation running a PLC programing software. When a ladder-logic program is being downloaded from the programming software to the PLC, the attacker replaces a part of an original ladder logic with an infected logic. When a control engineer tries to upload the (infected) program from the PLC to the programing software, the attacker intercepts the traffic and replaces infected part with the original logic. Hence, the software displays the normal program that clearly deceives the control engineer (Figure 1).

DEO Attack 2: Crashing the PLC Programing Software. In this attack scenario, the attacker employs the man-in-the-middle to intercept the network traffic between the programing software running on an engineering workstation and a target PLC. When a ladder logic program is being uploaded from a PLC to the programing software, the attacker intercepts the traffic and changes the original ladder logic programs into malformed programs by replacing ladder logic instructions with noise such as the sequence of 0xFF bytes. The software crashes when it tries to process the malformed ladder logic program (Figure 2).

DEO Attack 3: Injecting a crafted ladder logic program to a PLC that crashes the PLC programing software. This attack scenario is the stealthiest among the three proposed scenarios. The attacker creates a well-crafted (malicious) ladder-logic program at the binary-level that runs on a target PLC successfully. However, when the programing software tries to acquire the program from the PLC, it cannot process it and gives an error, causing the denial of service (refer to Figure 3). This scenario does not involve any man-in the middle attacks and allows the attacker to leave the ICS network after installing the malicious program to the PLC.

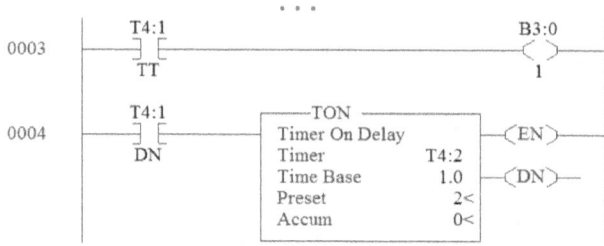

a) Ladder-logic source code snippet of a traffic-light program

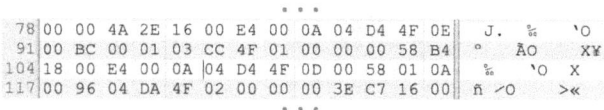

b) Binary ladder-logic snippet of a traffic-light program

```
Rung-3: (XIC/[T4:1/TT]) --> (OTE/[B3:0/1])
Rung-4: (XIC/[T4:1/DN]) --> (TON/[T4:2/1.0/2/0])
```

c) *Laddis* ASCII output of decompiling the binary ladder-logic snippet

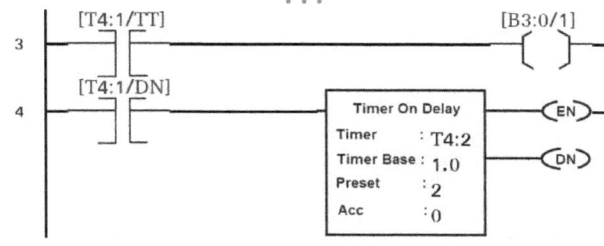

d) *Laddis* graphical output of decompiling the binary ladder-logic snippet

Figure 4: Overview of the Decompiler Laddis. **A ladder logic program is compiled to a binary ladder logic, which is then decompiled by** Laddis

3 OVERVIEW OF THE DECOMPILER - LADDIS

Figure 4 presents the three stages of a ladder logic program, beginning from the creation of the program (source code) (Figure 4(a)), which is then compiled into a binary form that is run by a PLC (Figure 4(b)). Finally, the proposed decompiler Laddis transforms the binary ladder logic back to its original form i.e. source code (Figures 4(c) and 4(d)).

Ladder-logic Program. Ladder logic is widely-used to program PLCs. It is a graphical language comprising of symbols that are placed together to form a control logic. Each symbol is an instruction such as timer, counter, input, output, move etc., and is analogous to opcode in Assembly language. It works on data to affect the current state of a physical process. The data is referenced in the symbols and is analogous to an operand.

A ladder logic program is divided into rungs (horizontal lines) placed one after another (similar to the steps of a ladder). Each rung has symbols that can be placed in series or parallel depicting AND

or OR logic respectively. The execution of the program starts from the instructions of the first rung from left to right and then moves to the next rung in the sequence.

Figure 4(a) depicts a ladder logic code snippet of a traffic-light program that controls red, orange and green lights using timers. The snippet shows the third and the fourth rungs of the program, each has two instructions (or symbols) placed in a series. When a timer runs, it turns on its respective light; after the timer completes its execution, it turns off the light.

Binary ladder logic. A PLC does not run graphical symbols of ladder logic directly. A ladder logic program is compiled into its binary (low-level representation) form that a PLC can execute. Figure 4(b) depicts the code snippet of the binary ladder logic of the traffic-light program, which contains rungs and instructions at binary-level. (The next section presents the details)

Decompiler. We develop Laddis that understands the binary ladder logic and decompiles it into its high-level representation in a human-readable form. Figures 4(c) and 4(d) present the snippet of a decompiled code generated by Laddis. It is the traffic-light program (shown in Figure 4(a)). The Laddis output clearly identifies rungs and the logic in each rung. In Figure 4(c), the output only consists of the ASCII characters that is useful for automating further forensic analysis such as via Python scripts. Laddis replaces the graphical symbols with their equivalent instruction codes derived from the abbreviations of the instructions. For instance, TON is used for the Timer-On-Delay instruction, XIC for Examine-If-Closed, and OTE for Output-Energizer. In Figure 4(d), Laddis takes its ASCII output as input and generates the graphical ladder logic.

The ladder logic instructions contain data or the addresses of the data. For instance, timer instruction has three types of data i.e. Timer Base, Preset, and Accum. The OTE has the address of the bit representing the current state of a traffic light i.e. ON or OFF. The Laddis output (Figures 4(c) and 4(d)) is complete and equivalent of the original code (in Figure 4(a)), which includes rungs, instructions and their respective data and the addresses of the data.

4 LADDIS DECOMPILATION INTERNALS

To decompile a binary ladder logic, a number of challenges are involved including understanding the anatomy of rungs and different ladder logic instructions at binary-level. Apparently, the binary ladder logic file is not self-contained for an accurate decompilation and the associated data and configurations are required.

It is worth mentioning that we use Allen-Bradley's RSLogix 500 programing software to discover the internals of a binary ladder logic. The findings may reflect RSLogix 500 internals. However, it does not hinder the goal of this work, which is to evaluate the effectiveness of this decompiler under the three proposed attacks. These attacks subvert the capability of a programming software to acquire a ladder logic program from a remote compromised PLC, restricting a forensic investigator from acquiring and analyzing an important piece of evidence.

This section further discusses the internals of a binary ladder logic and how they are used by Laddis to perform decompilation.

4.1 Identifying the Rungs

Figure 5 shows an example of a binary ladder-logic with the labels for the bytes of the first rung. A binary ladder-logic starts with a rung and may consist of multiple rungs located in a sequence. Each rung always starts with two bytes of zero values, followed by two bytes containing a signature of the rung. If a rung has multiple exact instances in the binary logic, all the instances have the same signature. The fifth and sixth bytes are the rung size. The instructions start from the sevenths bytes (discussed in the next section). The size of the rungs varies depending on the type and the number of the instructions.

Laddis uses the rung-size field to identify the rungs in a binary logic. Since the rungs are located contiguously in a sequence, Laddis starts with the first rung and then traverses the subsequent rungs; each rung always starts with 0x00 and 0x00.

4.2 Identifying the Instructions in a Rung

The instructions in a rung are located contiguously in a sequence, starting from the seventh byte of each rung. An instruction comprises of an opcode (two bytes), a file-number (one byte), an operand consisting an offset of a word-address (two bytes) and a bit address (two bytes). The *Opcode* represents the operation of the instruction such as XIC (Examine-if-closed) and RES (Reset). It typically works on data; each type of data has an assigned number that is referred to as file-number. For instance, 0x00, 0x01, 0x03 are used for output, input and status data respectively. The operand points to the data of interest. The operand size may vary in the instructions, thereby varying the length of the instructions. For instance, the instructions JMP (Jump-to-label), SUB (Subtraction) and ASC (ASCII-String-Search) are 10, 22 and 28 bytes long. Some instructions such as END do not have an operand (the last rung in the last line in Figure 5).

Branch instruction is an exception. It is used to place the symbols in parallel in a ladder logic source code. At the binary-level, branch instruction does not have the prescribed structure of an instruction and comprises of three components, 1) branch start, 2) branch continue, and 3) branch end; each component has a specific unique code at binary-level (similar to opcode) i.e. 0x0800D402, 0xD0021000, and 0x14000C00 and 0xD0020C00 respectively.

To identify each instruction in a rung, Laddis maintains the mapping between ladder logic instructions (the graphical symbols) and their binary-representation along with the size of the instructions and their short forms in ASCII characters. Table 1 lists the type of ladder logic instructions that are supported by Laddis. The total supported instructions are 120 (refer to Table 8 in appendix for the complete list).

4.3 Obtaining the Addresses in the Instructions

The instructions use addresses to point to the data of interest. Figure 8 presents an example of the addressing format i.e. 0:1/3. '0' refers to the type of file/data i.e. output. After colon, '1' and '3' are the *word* and *bit* index numbers that are pointing to a specific bit.

The instructions at the binary level contain the *bit index number* and the *file number* (pointing to the type of a file/data). However, it does not have the *word index*. Recall that a binary ladder logic is not self-contained to perform accurate decompilation. In this

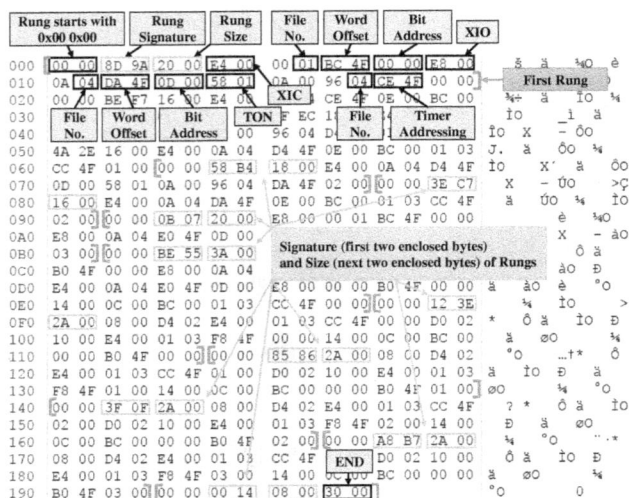

Figure 5: Binary ladder logic consisting of several rungs; each has multiple instructions. A pair of brackets encloses a rung.

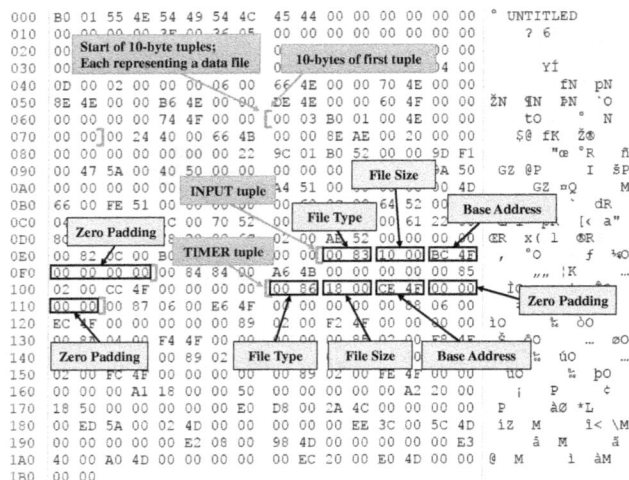

Figure 6: Configuration file for addressing in the instructions.

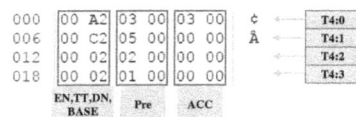

Figure 7: Timer file for the data in the timer instruction.

case, it requires the associated configuration file to determine the *word index*. Figure 6 shows the configuration data. It contains 10 byte-tuple for each type of file/data t (such as timer, input, output etc). Each tuple has a base-address (let say, B_t). In binary ladder logic, an instruction contains a *word offset* (let say, O_t). To find out the *word index* for an instruction, $O_t - B_t$ is performed. For instance, in Figure 5, the first instruction in the first rung is XIC.

Table 1: Ladder logic instructions supported by Laddis.

Instruction Type	No. of Instructions	Minimum Inst. Size	Maximum Inst. Size
Bit	9	8	16
Timer	14	2	16
Input/Output	6	2	22
Compare	8	16	22
Compute	10	16	22
Move/Logical	7	10	22
File/Misc	16	10	46
File Shift/ Sequences	9	22	28
Program Control	8	2	10
ASCII Control	8	16	28
ASCII String	6	16	28
High Speed Counter	2	16	34
Trigonometry	6	20	20
Advanced Math	11	16	40
TOTAL	120	-	-

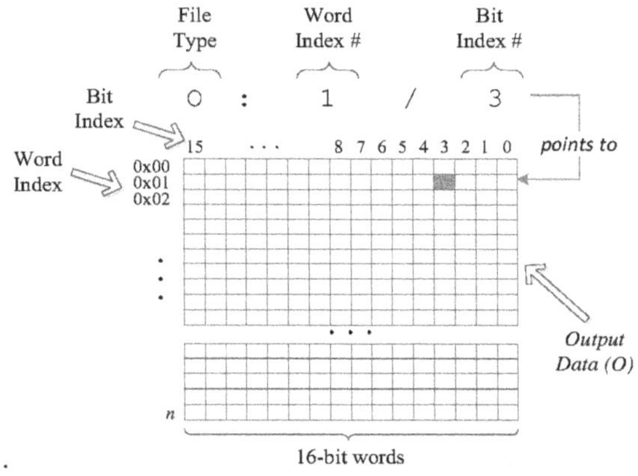

Figure 8: Addressing in the instructions. O:1/3 **address is used for illustration.**

Its word offset is 0x4FCE. In the configuration file, the base-address of the input file (pointed to by the XIC) is 0x4FBC. Hence, the *word index* of the XIC is 0x12.

Laddis parses the configuration file, obtains the relevant base addresses for the instructions in a binary ladder logic and then, resolves the addresses by subtracting the *word offsets* with the *base addresses*.

4.4 Obtaining the Data in the Instructions

Some instructions (such as timer and counter) have parametric data that is not present in binary ladder logic. For instance, a timer instruction has three parameters, Base, Preset (Pre) and Accumulated (ACC). The *Base* sets the interval of timing. When timer runs, it keeps incrementing ACC until it reaches to the *Preset* value, which resets the timer. These parameters are stored in a separate timer file (Figure 7). Each parameter is of two bytes and appears in the following sequence: Base, Pre and ACC.

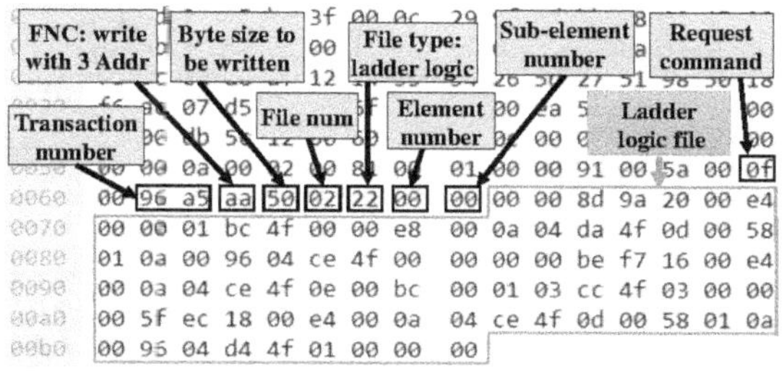

Figure 9: File extraction from downloading traffic

A ladder logic program may define and use multiple timers. To determine the correct parameters associated with a timer instruction, consider the TON timer instruction in the first rung of Figure 5. It has two bytes of timer-address *offset* (i.e. 0x4FCE), which is then subtracted from the *base address* (i.e. 0x4FCE) in the timer tuple in the configuration file (Figure 6). Hence, the TON instruction uses the first timer at 0th index in the timer file.

Laddis parses the data files associated with these instructions to obtain the relevant data for decompilation.

5 IMPLEMENTATION

Laddis is developed in Python [9] and can perform two basic functions: a) extract a binary ladder logic from a network traffic, and b) decompile the binary logic into a human-readable source code.

Extractor. The extractor component was developed using PyShark library [8], and is based on our prior experience in this area [26]. Allen Bradley Micrologix 1400-B and RSLogix 500 employ the PCCC communication protocol [1]. PCCC messages are transmitted using the EtherNet/IP protocol that adapts the *common industrial protocol* (CIP) to Ethernet. In our experiments, the PCCC message is embedded in CIP with type ID 0x91, or 0xB1 (connected data item). When it is embedded with type ID 0x91, the PCCC message comes at the start of the common packet format data section. When type ID 0xB1 is used, the PCCC message comes at byte offset 7 of the CIP data section after Requester ID length (1 byte), Vendor ID (2 bytes), and CIP Serial Number (4 bytes).

A ladder logic program developed by RSLogix is transferred in multiple files, including a configuration file, ladder logic file, and data files (output, input, status, timer, etc.). When a program is downloaded into a PLC, the extractor locates the files by parsing the message type (0x0F: request) field and function code (0xAA: write with 3 address fields) field (Figure 9). The start offset of file contents is flexible because the element field and the sub-element field can have 1 byte (number for 0-254) or 3 bytes (number for >=255) size. If the first byte is 0xFF, then next two bytes represent element/sub-element number. When a ladder logic program is uploaded from a PLC, the extractor finds PCCC reply messages that contains files for a ladder logic program by monitoring request messages with function code 0xA2 (read with 3 address fields), file number, and file type. Then a reply message that has the same transaction number contains a file corresponding to the requested file (Figure 10).

Decompiler. The decompiler builds a complete human readable representation of the ladder logic program from the binary ladder

a) Request message for a ladder logic file

b) Reply message containing a ladder logic file

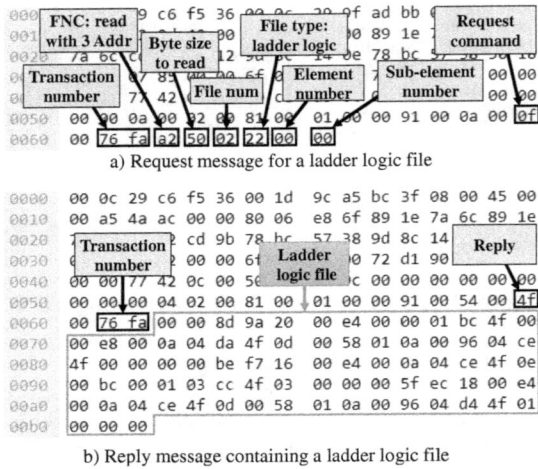

Figure 10: File extraction from uploading traffic

logic file outputs of the extractor program. The decompiler uses a configuration file which stores information like opcode, size, start and end addresses of various types of instructions. Based on that information it can identify the rungs, instructions and branchings. During the course of its development, we tested it with a variety of ladder logic programs to configure their instruction types. We used techniques of differential analysis to configure different types of the instructions [18]. With every subsequent test case, we changed one specific instruction of the program and analyzed the binary values. The tests were repeated until we obtained complete configuration mapping of the 120 types of instructions used in the ladder logic programs by RSLogix. We stress-tested our decompiler with many variations of RSLogix programs to find any configuration our program would have missed. We used GNU Diffutils [2] for this differential analysis. After creating a complete decompiler based on the information gained from various test datasets, we repeated more tests to find new types of instructions. The final part of the decompilation included drawing the images of the ladder logic program using the Python Image Library (PIL). The result of this program is easy to understand ladder logic program constructed solely from the network capture packets.

6 EVALUATION

6.1 Experimental Settings

Lab Setup. We use six versions of Allen-Bradley's RSLogix 500 programing software and Micrologix 1400 Series B controller. The RSLogix software (running on Windows 7 virtual machine (VM)) and Micrologix PLC communicate with each other over Ethernet. We also install Wireshark on the VM for capturing network packets.

Dataset. We developed 91 ladder logic programs of varying complexity for initial experiments and testing. However, for the evaluation, we use a different potentially-unbiased dataset consisting of 58 ladder logic source-code programs downloaded from various sources on the Internet (including github.com, plctalk.net, and theautomationstore.com). The programs are written for different physical processes (such as traffic-light, elevator and train-crossing)

Table 2: Dataset summary of ladder logic programs

File Info.		Rungs				Instructions			
File Size (kB)	# of Files	Min	Max	Total	Avg	Min	Max	Total	Avg
20-40	29	2	22	166	5.72	3	67	428	14.76
41-60	17	3	40	158	9.29	5	104	569	33.47
61-80	7	4	17	66	9.43	9	63	235	33.57
81-100	3	7	15	30	10.00	15	31	65	21.67
101-120	2	10	63	73	36.50	24	249	273	136.50
Total	58	-	-	493	-	-	-	1,628	-

involving various detectors, sensors, device controllers and counters. They have 493 rungs and 1628 instructions in total. These programs are particularly useful for performing unbiased evaluation since they are developed by different authors. Table 2 summarizes the dataset based on the file size, number of instructions and rungs.

Methodology for Experiments. A typical experiment involves RSLogix to transfer a ladder logic program to/from the Micrologix PLC, while capturing the network traffic. Laddis then, takes the traffic as input, extracts binary ladder logic and its associated configuration and data to separate files. It further takes the files as input and processes them to generate a decompiled ladder logic, which is then, compared with the original ladder logic program manually.

6.2 Decompilation Accuracy of Laddis

Recall that Laddis performs three main functions to decompile a binary ladder logic. It first 1) identifies the rungs and 2) the instructions in the rungs and then, 3) reconstructs the ladder logic from the binary logic. This section evaluates the accuracy of Laddis on performing these functions.

1) Identifying the Rungs. To evaluate the Laddis accuracy on the rungs, we analyze each ladder logic file in the dataset and count the total number of rungs and the number of instructions in each rung manually. At this stage, we only count the instructions without considering what are these instructions.

We further obtain the Laddis ASCII output of decompiling the files in the dataset and use a python script that processes the output of all the file and obtains the counts. Our results show that both RSLogix and Laddis reported exact number of rungs and instructions i.e. 493 and 1,628 in total, respectively. Hence, we conclude that Laddis is 100% accurate in identifying rungs.

2) Identifying the Instructions. To evaluate the Laddis accuracy on identifying exact instructions, we obtain the frequency of each instruction in the dataset files using RSLogix manually and a python script for Laddis. We found 33 unique instructions. Table 3 shows the frequency of the instructions for both RSLogix and Laddis. The comparison shows 100% accuracy concluding that the Laddis can identify instructions accurately.

3) Reconstructing the Ladder Logic. To evaluate whether Laddis ladder logic output conforms with the original ladder logic, we obtain Laddis graphical output of the ladder logic files in the dataset and compare them with the original ladder logic in RSLogix manually, using the following parameters: position of an instruction in a rung, address and configuration data in each instruction, and

Table 3: Comparison with RSLogix on decompiling

Symbols	Name	Types	RS-Logix	Laddis	Accu-racy
XIC	Examine if open		521	521	100%
XIO	Examine if closed		179	179	100%
OTE	Output Energize	Bit	183	183	100%
OTL	Output Latch		20	20	100%
OTU	Output Unlatch		41	41	100%
ONS	One Shot		44	44	100%
TON	Time On Delay		58	58	100%
TOF	Timer Off Delay	Timer and Counter	5	5	100%
RTO	Retentive Timer		3	3	100%
CTU	Count Up		7	7	100%
RES	Reset		11	11	100%
EQU	Equal		43	43	100%
GEQ	Great Than or Equal		20	20	100%
GRT	Greater Than	Comparison	6	6	100%
LEQ	Less Than or Equal		5	5	100%
LES	Less Than		8	8	100%
LIM	Limit Test		14	14	100%
MEQ	Masked Comparison for Equal		2	2	100%
NEQ	Not Equal		7	7	100%
ADD	Add		13	13	100%
SUB	Subtract		14	14	100%
MUL	Multiply	Math	1	1	100%
DIV	Divide		4	4	100%
CLR	Clear		4	4	100%
SCP	Scale with Parameters		1	1	100%
MOV	Move	Data	92	92	100%
MVM	Masked Move	Handling	2	2	100%
OR	Logical OR	Branch	202	202	100%
JSR	Jump to Subroutine	Program Control	43	43	100%
BSL	Bit Shift Left	Application Specific	5	5	100%
SQO	Sequencer Output		4	4	100%
MSG	Message	SLC Communication	8	8	100%
END	End	Unspecified	58	58	100%
	Total		1628	1628	100%

the connection of two instructions whether in series (AND logic) or parallel (OR logic). Figures 11a and 11b shows an example of RSLogix and Laddis that are used for comparison. Our comparison results show that RSLogix source code and Laddis graphical output comply with each other, concluding that Laddis can reconstruct the source code of a ladder logic from its binary representation accurately.

6.3 Laddis Compatibility with Older RSLogix

We use RSLogix 9.00.04 version to perform the experiments on Laddis accuracy in the last section. We further repeat the experiments on five older versions of RSLogix to evaluate the compatibility of Laddis with these version. Table 4 shows the overall results.

Table 4: Laddis compatibility with older RSLogix versions

RSLogix Versions	Number of Files	Laddis Accuracy(%)
8.10.00	28	100%
8.20.00	35	100%
8.30.00	40	100%
8.40.00	58	100%
9.00.00	58	100%
9.00.04	58	100%

We did not find any discrepancies in the Laddis output. Thus, we conclude that Laddis is compatible with the older versions.

6.4 Detailed Attack Scenarios

This section evaluates the effectiveness of Laddis under the three attack scenarios outlined earlier.

Assumption. In the first two scenarios, we assume that the attacker can intercept and modify the network traffic between an engineering workstation and a target PLC using man-in-the-middle (MITM) [6]. In ICS, MITM is a known threat. Kaspersky Lab reported that 91.6% of the ICS environments (that they analyzed) use insecure protocols that are prone to data interception and modification using MITM [5]. In the past, MITM was observed in the ICS operational environments such as Stuxnet [15] and IRONGATE [4]. The third attack scenario does not involve MITM.

1) DEO Attack 1: Hiding infected ladder logic (running in a target PLC) from RSLogix.

Attack Scenario: The attacker transfers an infected ladder logic to a target PLC. To hide the infection, when a control operator/engineer tries to acquire the program from the PLC using RSLogix, the attacker intercepts the traffic via MITM and replaces the infection with the original logic. Consequently, the RSLogix shows the original (uninfected) ladder logic to the operator (Figure 1).

Attack Execution: We use traffic-light ladder logic program, which consists of three timers, each controlling one of the three signal lights (green, orange, and red). The goal of the attacker is to make consistent change in the timing of green light so that the light remains on for 100 seconds, instead of original 5 seconds.

We employ infamous ARP poisoning using Ettercap [23] to achieve MITM. When a control engineer downloads the traffic-light program to a target PLC using RSLogix, the attacker intercepts the network traffic, and the *preset* value of the timer controlling the green light from 5 seconds (original value) to 100 seconds (attacker's desired value) (Figure 12). Now the PLC turns on the green light for 100 seconds Recall that a timer instruction has three parameters: base, preset, and accumulated. The *preset* sets the timing. At this stage, if RSLogix uploads the program from the PLC, it will show the attacker's change in the timer instruction. Thus, the attacker also intercepts the upload traffic and replaces the 100 seconds with 5 seconds in the timer instruction, which hides the infection from RSLogix (shown in Figure 13).

Forensic Analysis with Laddis: Strange ARP table (due to ARP poisoning) or duplicated packets (due to the MITM) may raise suspicion that can lead to a forensic investigation. If the network is captured, a forensic investigator can filter the traffic based on source

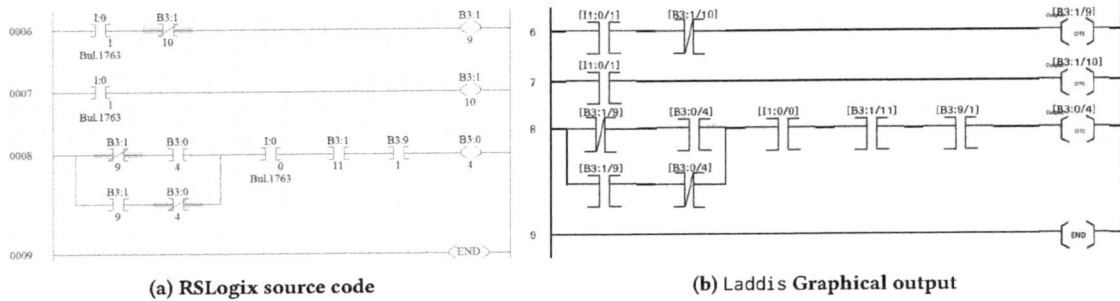

(a) RSLogix source code

(b) Laddis Graphical output

Figure 11: Comparison of RSLogix source code and Laddis Graphical output

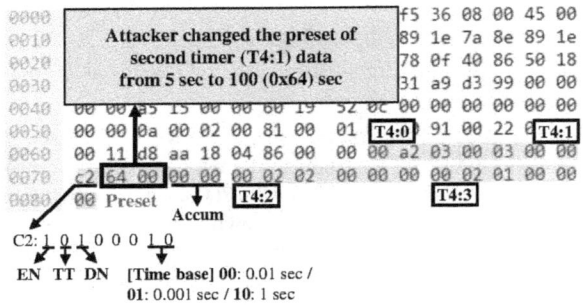

Figure 12: Modifying timer data in downloading traffic

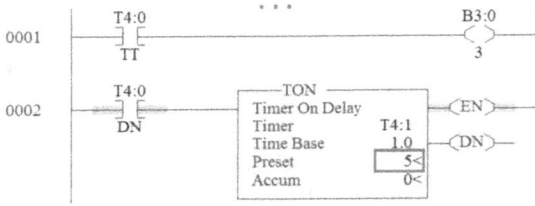

Figure 13: RSLogix cannot show the program actually running in PLC

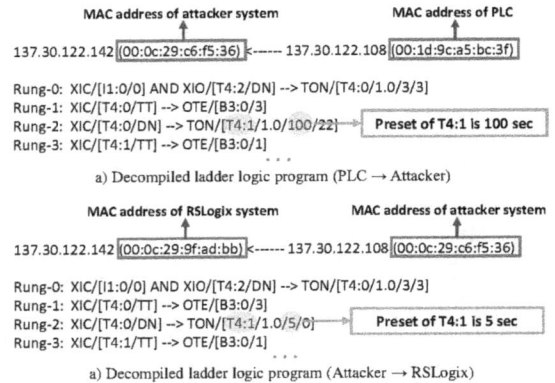

a) Decompiled ladder logic program (PLC → Attacker)

a) Decompiled ladder logic program (Attacker → RSLogix)

Figure 14: Laddis ASCII output: attack scenario #1

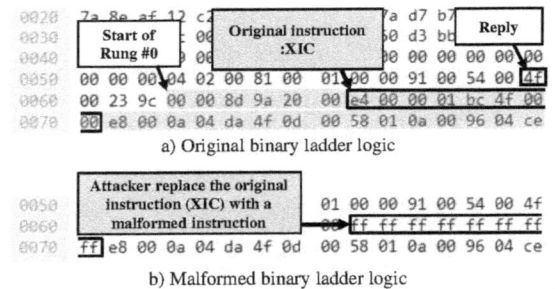

a) Original binary ladder logic

b) Malformed binary ladder logic

Figure 15: Modifying ladder logic program

and destination MAC addresses and then, use Laddis to extract two versions of the ladder logic program. First is the original that is exchanged between RSLogix and the attacker and the second is exchanged between the attacker and the PLC. Laddis further decompiles both ladder logic programs. Figure 14 shows Laddis ASCII output and points to the differences in the timer instruction.

2) DEO Attack 2: Crashing the Programing Software.

Attack Scenario: The attacker infects the ladder logic in a target PLC. The goal of this attack is to create a denial of service when the programing software tries to acquire the logic from the PLC. In particular, the attacks achieves to crash the software while uploading the ladder logic from the PLC (Figure 2).

Attack Execution: We use ARP poisoning (with Ettercap) for MITM and the traffic light program to execute this attack. To crash RSLogix, the attacker replaces an instruction with unexpected byte codes in the ladder logic program while it is being transferred to RSLogix. Figure 15(a) depicts the original piece of ladder logic code

in a network packet transferring from the PLC to RSLogix. The attacker intercepts the packet and replaces the XIC instruction in the first rung with 8 bytes of '0xFF' byte code (Figure 15(b)) and then, forwards the malformed packet to the RSLogix, which apparently crashes the software.

Forensic Analysis with Laddis: A forensic investigator can use Laddis to extract the *original* (from PLC to the attacker) and *malformed* (from the attacker to RSLogix) ladder logic programs from the network traffic. Laddis can further decompiles the programs. The malformed logic is challenging. However, Laddis is equipped to identify the ladder logic instruction while ignoring the malformed or corrupted logic. Figure 16 shows the Laddis output. Laddis ignores the first rung that has the corrupted (0xFF

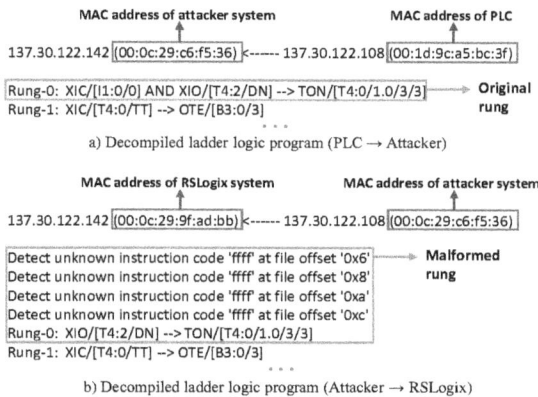

Figure 16: Laddis ASCII output: attack scenario #2

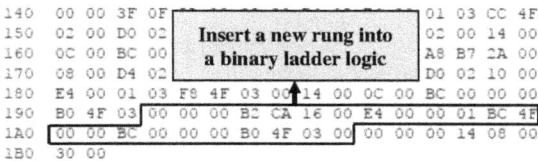

Figure 17: Inserting a new rung into the ladder logic

sequence of bytes in the) instruction and decompiles the second rung successfully.

3) DEO Attack 3: Injecting a crafted ladder logic program to a PLC that crashes the programing software.

Attack Scenario: The goal of this attack is to crash the programing software when it attempts to acquire the ladder logic from an infected PLC *without* needing to maintain a MITM posture. In this case, the attacker creates a specially crafted ladder logic program that runs successfully on a PLC, but when the programing software attempts to acquire the logic, the program crashes the software (Figure 3). This is the stealthiest attack among the three attack scenarios and only requires to update the PLC once with the manipulated program. The attacker can achieves it by infiltrating into the ICS network or obtaining local access to the PLC.

Attack Execution: To perform this attack, we first craft a ladder logic program. In particular, we insert a new (malicious) rung before the last rung (which contains only END instruction) of the traffic-light program. It is done at the binary-level, since RSLogix or any other ladder logic programming software does not allow to make certain changes due to incompatibility. Figure 17) shows a sequence of bytes that is the new rung at binary-level.

Adding a rung influences both size and contents of the ladder logic file, and we found six byte locations related to ladder logic size or ladder logic integrity in the configuration file (type:0x03) and in an unknown file (type:0x24). Figure 18(a) depicts a configuration file which has type '0x03'. In the configuration file, byte location 0x88 - 0x89, two bytes right after the file type 0x22 (ladder logic file), represents size of the ladder logic file. And we also found that the value of location 0x7a - 0x7b is unknown, but it varies as size of ladder logic file. Meanwhile, the values of location 0x36 - 0x37

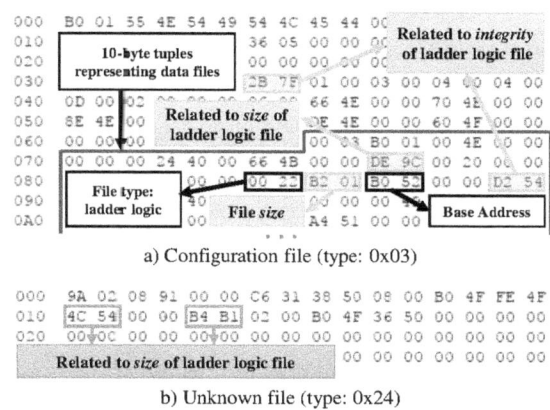

a) Configuration file (type: 0x03)

b) Unknown file (type: 0x24)

Figure 18: Byte locations related to the integrity of ladder logic

and location 0x8e - 0x8f are related to integrity of ladder logic file. They are changed according to contents of ladder logic files even if size are the same. If we do not correct these values according to changed ladder logic files, the PLC always refused to accept the program. On the other hand, Figure 18(b) depicts an unknown file which has type '0x24'. We also found two byte locations, 0x10 - 0x11 and 0x14 - 0x15, changed according to size of ladder logic files.

If we correct all these values, the modified ladder logic programs runs in PLCs and also can be acquired by RSLogix without crashing. However, if we correct the values only in the configuration file and do not change the values in the other file (type 0x24), this semi-valid programs runs successfully in PLCs but RSLogix fails with an "Unknown error" message.

Forensic Analysis with Laddis: To investigate this attack, the investigator can use RSLogix to attempt to acquire the crafted ladder logic program from the PLC. It crashes the RSLogix, but apparently, makes the PLC to send the entire ladder logic to RSLogix over the network. If the network traffic is captured, the Laddis will extract the ladder logic program from the network traffic dump and can further decompile it to show the infected code that has an additional rung in the end of the logic. Laddis is able to decompile the crafted program because it concentrates on the actual contents of the program without depending on non-essential metadata for decompiling (Figure 19).

6.5 Performance Measurement

We carried out performance tests for each extracting part and decompiling part of Laddis with 58 pcap files. We ran experiments on a Virtual machine running Ubuntu 16.04 on a single Intel 3.40 Ghz core with 4GB of RAM. Execution time for extracting files of ladder logic programs was directly proportional to pcap file size and the number of packets in a file (Table 5). On the other hand, execution time of decompiling part of Laddis is affected by the number of rungs in extracted ladder logic programs (Table 6 in Appendix) and the number of instruction in the programs (Table 7 in Appendix).

MAC address of RSLogix system   MAC address of PLC

137.30.122.142 [00:0c:29:9f:ad:bb] ◄------ 137.30.122.108 [00:1d:9c:a5:bc:3f]

```
Rung-0:  XIC/[I1:0/0] AND XIO/[T4:2/DN] --> TON/[T4:0/1.0/3/3]
Rung-1:  XIC/[T4:0/TT] --> OTE/[B3:0/3]
Rung-2:  XIC/[T4:0/DN] --> TON/[T4:1/1.0/5/0]
Rung-3:  XIC/[T4:1/TT] --> OTE/[B3:0/1]
Rung-4:  XIC/[T4:1/DN] --> TON/[T4:2/1.0/2/0]
Rung-5:  XIC/[T4:2/TT] --> OTE/[B3:0/2]
Rung-6:  XIO/[I1:0/0] AND XIO/[T4:3/DN] --> TON/[T4:3/1.0/1/0]
Rung-7:  ( ( XIC/[O0:0/0] AND XIO/[T4:3/DN] ) OR ( XIC/[T4:3/DN] AND XIO/[O0:0/0] ) )
         --> OTE/[B3:0/0]
Rung-8:  ( ( XIC/[B3:0/0] ) OR ( XIC/[B8:0/0] ) ) --> OTE/[O0:0/0]
Rung-9:  ( ( XIC/[B3:0/1] ) OR ( XIC/[B8:0/1] ) ) --> OTE/[O0:0/1]
Rung-10: ( ( XIC/[B3:0/2] ) OR ( XIC/[B8:0/2] ) ) --> OTE/[O0:0/2]
Rung-11: ( ( XIC/[B3:0/3] ) OR ( XIC/[B8:0/3] ) ) --> OTE/[O0:0/3]
Rung-12: XIC/[I1:0/0] --> OTE/[O0:0/3]            ------► Inserted rung by attacker
Rung-13: END
```

Figure 19: `Laddis` **ASCII output: attack scenario #3**

Table 5: Extractor performance vs. *pcap* size

FileSize (KB)	# of Files	Avg.#of Packets	Max # of Packets	Avg Time (sec)	Max Time (sec)
0-100	14	3,663	10,288	4.517	11.51
101-300	11	4,602	17,414	5.86	22.74
301-400	8	3,033	6,164	3.78	7.69
401-500	8	4,017	5,143	5.03	6.50
501-600	10	1,625	4,959	2.07	6.05
>=601	7	2,305	7,721	3.15	10.20

7 RELATED WORK

PLCs are built with safety and endurance as primary requirements, and very few private protocols have built-in security features [24]. Patel et al acknowledge that SCADA devices using secret proprietary protocols can be easily targeted by attackers attempting to reverse engineer those protocols. Our study is an example of reverse engineering of PCCC protocol used by many popular Allen Bradley PLCs [1]. Narayan et al mention that unspecified protocols exist in different OSI models [22]. These protocols are not immune to reverse engineering techniques and attackers can extract communication data from a SCADA network by decoding such protocols. Authors mention that task of protocol reverse engineering is "tedious" and "time consuming" manually. There are disassembly tools like IDA Pro [3] to perform the disassembly of binary executable; however, analysts [28] mention that its disassembly is prone to errors and requires further manual analysis. Our tool provides a simpler way to analyze the malicious code without the need for access to the PLC.

Fovino et al. [16] propose the SCADA protocol sensor, which is analogous to Snort [25]. The authors use the network analysis of the traffic to detect malicious code in the devices using DNP3 and Modbus protocols. They use databases to store the signature of the single packet-based attacks, maintain the status of network devices, use state validation based on another database which includes the rules that system adopts during the critical control.

Cheung et al. proposed model-based intrusion detection system for SCADA network. They construct normal model that characterize the expected behavior of SCADA network, and detect attacks that deviate from the constructed normal model [13]. Derarnan et al. emphasize the importance of network behavioral analysis and

warn that signature-based detection systems can fall short in case of zero-day attacks [14]. These authors have based their research on securing the SCADA networks from intrusions through the implementation of protocol reversing, misuse detection, anomaly detection and the successful analysis of network traffic. Our tool constructs the actual ladder logic program from the network traffic and in case of attack without reliance on the HMI to detect the changes; it also provides the extracted malicious code.

The discovery of Stuxnet attracted huge worldwide interest in the field of industrial control system security [21]. When the Iranian nuclear facilities using Siemens SIMATIC WinCC SCADA systems were compromised, it was evident that the further study in securing the critical infrastructures is crucial [12].

As discussed in Kotler et al. [20], running additional software to check the programs in a PLC has performance drawbacks. They used finite state machine to check computational tree logic and linear temporal logic to detect malicious or faulty PLC programs. They show how small changes induced by intrusions can go undetected in the ladder logic software. Their method analyzed minute malfunctions in ladder logic programs running a virtual crane, and found unnoticeable changes that could cause catastrophic outcomes [20]. Similarly, Valentine & Farkas state that an attacker can remove an instruction like a coil needed to trigger an alarm but the code will compile in the Human Machine Interface (HMI) and will be downloaded to the PLC [27]. The authors propose code validation process using a database to flag malicious code.

Cutter [26] is a parsing tool for data files exchanged between a PLC and engineering workstation. It is developed by the authors. Cutter is not a decompiler and has mainly developed for the data files.

8 CONCLUSION

In this work, we introduced a new class of attacks on industrial control systems–*denial of engineering operations*, which can severely impact the situational awareness of the operator, and can provide time and cover for a malicious control logic installed on a PLC to produce the effects in the physical world.

Fundamentally, the vulnerability stems from the fact that engineering software used to develop, test, and deploy the control logic expects any program retrieved from the PLC to be properly formatted and there are few (if any) provisions to recover from a malformed responses that fail integrity checks. At the same time, the PLC has fewer such verifications, which allows it to execute the malformed code. This dichotomy allows an adversary who has access to the PLC via the network the opportunity to deceive the operator by crafting and installing programs that function as desired but not understood by the engineering software. Although, it is possible to overcome this by reprogramming the PLC with a known-good version of the code; this would also destroy all the traces of the attack for analytical purposes.

To address the problem, we developed `Laddis`–a ladder logic decompiler that can correctly reconstruct the source of the original code from a network trace. This allows the operator to quickly analyze the attack and respond accordingly. Future extension can automate this process and allow defensive reaction in real time.

APPENDIX

Table 6: Decompiler performance vs. number of rungs

# of Rung	# of Files	Max # of Rung	Avg time (sec)	Max time (sec)
0-3	8	3	0.16	0.19
4-5	18	5	0.30	0.58
6-9	11	9	1.26	3.15
10-14	16	13	1.01	2.60
>=15	5	63	5.46	16.41

Table 7: Decompiler performance vs. number of inst.

# of Inst.	# of Files	Max # of Inst.	Avg time (sec)	Max time (sec)
0-10	8	9	0.176	0.36
11-20	16	20	0.356	1.19
21-30	9	27	0.922	1.55
31-40	14	37	0.897	2.60
41-60	5	60	1.509	3.15
>=61	6	312	4.738	16.41

Table 8: Instruction Information

Op-code	Byte code	Size (byte)	Op-code	Byte code	Size (byte)	Op-code	Byte code	Size (byte)
END	0030	2	MUL	00A4	22	LBL	00EC	8
XIC	00E4	8	DIV	00A8	22	JSR	0054	10
XIO	00E8	8	SQR	0118	16	RET	0024	2
OTE	00BC	8	NEG	0078	16	SBR	00F4	10
OTL	00C0	8	TOD	0148	16	TND	002C	2
OTU	00C4	8	FRD	014C	16	MCR	0020	2
ONS	02AC	8	GCD	02BC	16	SUS	007C	10
OSR	0278	16	MOV	0070	16	ABL	01E0	16
OSF	0274	16	MVM	0098	22	ACB	01E4	16
TON	0158	10	AND	008C	22	ARD	0200	22
TON	003C	10	OR	0090	22	ARL	0204	22
TON	029C	10	XOR	0094	22	AWT	0210	22
TOF	0154	10	NOT	006C	16	AWA	020C	22
TOF	0040	10	CLR	0050	10	AHL	01F8	28
TOF	0298	10	COP	0088	22	ACL	01F0	22
RTO	0150	10	FLL	0084	22	ACN	01EC	22
RTO	0038	10	DLG	02B0	10	ACI	01E8	16
RTO	028C	10	SCL	0114	28	AIC	01FC	16
CTU	0044	10	INT	012C	10	AEX	01F4	28
CTD	0048	10	STS	0290	10	ASC	0208	28
RES	004C	10	PID	027C	22	ASR	0214	16
RHC	035C	16	PTO	0280	10	HSL	026C	34
RTA	02B4	2	PWM	0284	10	RAC	0288	16
IIM	0174	22	UID	02A0	10	SIN	024C	20
IOM	0178	22	UIE	02A4	10	COS	0248	20
SVC	0294	10	UIF	02A8	10	TAN	0250	20
MSG	0270	16	CPW	02B8	22	ASN	0240	20
MSG	02CC	22	RCP	02C0	16	ACS	023C	20
REF	0120	2	LCD	02C8	46	ATN	0244	20
LIM	00FC	16	RPC	037C	16	LN	0234	24
MEQ	00E0	22	BSL	00B0	22	LOG	0238	24
EQU	00C8	16	BSR	00AC	22	DEG	0264	24
NEQ	00CC	16	SQC	00B8	28	RAD	025C	16
LES	00D8	16	SQL	0100	22	XPY	0230	22
GRT	00D0	16	SQO	00B4	28	ABS	0260	16
LEQ	00DC	16	FFL	0104	22	SCP	0254	40
GEQ	00D4	16	FFU	0108	22	SWP	0258	16
CPT	0228	20	LFL	010C	22	DCD	0080	16
ADD	009C	22	LFU	0110	22	ENC	0190	16
SUB	00A0	22	JMP	0058	10	TDF	0360	22

REFERENCES

[1] 1996. DF1 Protocol and Command Set Reference Manual. http://ow.ly/N61S30fsdqg. (1996). [Online; accessed 23-Sept-2017].

[2] 2017. GNU Diffutils. https://www.gnu.org/software/diffutils/. (2017). [Online; accessed 23-Sept-2017].

[3] 2017. Hex-Rays. https://www.hex-rays.com/. (2017). [Online; accessed 23-Sept-2017].

[4] 2017. IRONGATE ICS Malware. https://www.fireeye.com/blog/threat-research/2016/06/irongate_ics_malware.html. (2017). [Online; accessed 23-Sept-2017].

[5] 2017. Kaspersky. https://www.kaspersky.com/blog/industrial-vulnerabilities/12596/. (2017). [Online; accessed 23-Sept-2017].

[6] 2017. Man-in the middle attack in ICS. https://ics-cert.us-cert.gov/content/overview-cyber-vulnerabilities#man. (2017). [Online; accessed 23-Sept-2017].

[7] 2017. PLCS.net. http://www.plcs.net/downloads/index.php?&direction=0&order=&directory=Allen_Bradley. (2017). [Online; accessed 23-Sept-2017].

[8] 2017. Python Package Index Pyshark. https://pypi.python.org/pypi/pyshark. (2017). [Online; accessed 23-Sept-2017].

[9] 2017. Python Software Foundation. https://www.python.org/. (2017). [Online; accessed 23-Sept-2017].

[10] I. Ahmed, S. Obermeier, S. Sudhakaran, and V. Roussev. 2017. Programmable Logic Controller Forensics. IEEE Security Privacy 15, 6 (November 2017), 18–24. https://doi.org/10.1109/MSP.2017.4251102

[11] Irfan Ahmed, Vassil Roussev, William Johnson, Saranyan Senthivel, and Sneha Sudhakaran. 2016. A SCADA System Testbed for Cybersecurity and Forensic Research and Pedagogy. In Proceedings of the 2Nd Annual Industrial Control System Security Workshop (ICSS '16). ACM, New York, NY, USA, 1–9. https://doi.org/10.1145/3018981.3018984

[12] T. M. Chen and S. Abu-Nimeh. 2011. Lessons from Stuxnet. Computer 44, 4 (April 2011), 91–93.

[13] S. Cheung, B. Dutertre, M. Fong, U. Lindqvist, K. Skinner, and A. Valdes. 2007. Using Model-based Intrusion Detection for SCADA Networks. (jan 2007), 127–134.

[14] M. Deraman, J. M. Desa, and Z. A. Othman. 2010. Multilayer packet tagging for network behaviour analysis. In 2010 International Symposium on Information Technology, Vol. 2. 909–913.

[15] Nicolas Falliere, Liam O Murchu, , and Eric Chien. 2011). W32.Stuxnet Dossier. Technical Report. Symantec.

[16] I. N. Fovino, A. Carcano, T. D. L. Murel, A. Trombetta, and M. Masera. 2010. Modbus/DNP3 State-Based Intrusion Detection System. In 2010 24th IEEE International Conference on Advanced Information Networking and Applications. 729–736.

[17] Luis Garcia, Ferdinand Brasser, Mehmet H. Cintuglu, Ahmad-Reza Sadeghi, Osama Mohammed, and Saman A. Zonouz. 2017. Hey, My Malware Knows Physics! Attacking PLCs with Physical Model Aware Rootkit. In 24th Annual Network & Distributed System Security Symposium (NDSS).

[18] Simson Garfinkel, Alex Nelson, and Joel Young. 2012. A General Strategy for Differential Forensic Analysis. In The Digital Forensic Research Conference DFRWS. S50–S59.

[19] Naman Govil, Anand Agrawal, and Nils Ole Tippenhauer. 2017. On Ladder Logic Bombs in Industrial Control Systems. CoRR abs/1702.05241 (2017). http://arxiv.org/abs/1702.05241

[20] S. Kottler, M. Khayamy, S. R. Hasan, and O. Elkeelany. 2017. Formal verification of ladder logic programs using NuSMV. In SoutheastCon 2017. 1–5.

[21] R. Langner. 2011. Stuxnet: Dissecting a Cyberwarfare Weapon. IEEE Security Privacy 9, 3 (May 2011), 49–51.

[22] John Narayan, Sandeep K. Shukla, and T. Charles Clancy. 2015. A Survey of Automatic Protocol Reverse Engineering Tools. ACM Comput. Surv. 48, 3, Article 40 (dec 2015), 26 pages.

[23] A. Ornaghi and M. Valleri. 2017. Ettercap. https://ettercap.github.io/ettercap/. (2017). [Online; accessed 23-Sept-2017].

[24] Sandip C. Patel, Ganesh D. Bhatt, and James H. Graham. 2009. Improving the Cyber Security of SCADA Communication Networks. Commun. ACM 52, 7 (July 2009), 139–142.

[25] Martin Roesch et al. 1999. Snort: Lightweight intrusion detection for networks.. In Lisa, Vol. 99. 229–238.

[26] Saranyan Senthivel, Irfan Ahmed, and Vassil Roussev. 2017. SCADA network forensics of the PCCC protocol. Digital Investigation 22 (2017), S57–S65.

[27] S. Valentine and C. Farkas. 2011. Software security: Application-level vulnerabilities in SCADA systems. In 2011 IEEE International Conference on Information Reuse Integration. 498–499.

[28] K. Yakdan, S. Dechand, E. Gerhards-Padilla, and M. Smith. 2016. Helping Johnny to Analyze Malware: A Usability-Optimized Decompiler and Malware Analysis User Study. In 2016 IEEE Symposium on Security and Privacy (SP). 158–177.

A Domain is only as Good as its Buddies: Detecting Stealthy Malicious Domains via Graph Inference

Issa M. Khalil, Bei Guan, Mohamed Nabeel, Ting Yu

(ikhalil,bguan,mnabeel,tyu)@qf.org.qa

Qatar Computing Research Institute

ABSTRACT

Inference based techniques are one of the major approaches to analyze DNS data and detect malicious domains. The key idea of inference techniques is to first define associations between domains based on features extracted from DNS data. Then, an inference algorithm is deployed to infer potential malicious domains based on their direct/indirect associations with known malicious ones. The way associations are defined is key to the effectiveness of an inference technique. It is desirable to be both accurate (i.e., avoid falsely associating domains with no meaningful connections) and with good coverage (i.e., identify all associations between domains with meaningful connections). Due to the limited scope of information provided by DNS data, it becomes a challenge to design an association scheme that achieves both high accuracy and good coverage.

In this paper, we propose a new approach to identify domains controlled by the same entity. Our key idea is an in-depth analysis of active DNS data to accurately separate public IPs from dedicated ones, which enables us to build high-quality associations between domains. Our scheme avoids the pitfall of naive approaches that rely on weak "co-IP" relationship of domains (i.e., two domains are resolved to the same IP) that results in low detection accuracy, and, meanwhile, identifies many meaningful connections between domains that are discarded by existing state-of-the-art approaches. Our experimental results show that the proposed approach not only significantly improves the domain coverage compared to existing approaches but also achieves better detection accuracy.

Existing path-based inference algorithms are specifically designed for DNS data analysis. They are effective but computationally expensive. To further demonstrate the strength of our domain association scheme as well as improve the inference efficiency, we construct a new domain-IP graph that can work well with the generic belief propagation algorithm. Through comprehensive experiments, we show that this approach offers significant efficiency and scalability improvement with only a minor impact to detection accuracy, which suggests that such a combination could offer a good tradeoff for malicious domain detection in practice.

CODASPY '18, March 19–21, 2018, Tempe, AZ, USA
© 2018 Association for Computing Machinery.
ACM ISBN 978-1-4503-5632-9/18/03...$15.00
https://doi.org/10.1145/3176258.3176329

KEYWORDS

Malicious Domains, Graph Inference, DNS Data, Domain Association, Belief Propagation

ACM Reference Format:
Issa M. Khalil, Bei Guan, Mohamed Nabeel, Ting Yu. 2018. A Domain is only as Good as its Buddies: Detecting Stealthy Malicious Domains via Graph Inference. In *CODASPY '18: Eighth ACM Conference on Data and Application Security and Privacy, March 19–21, 2018, Tempe, AZ, USA*. ACM, New York, NY, USA, 12 pages. https://doi.org/10.1145/3176258.3176329

1 INTRODUCTION

DNS data is one of the most notable sources of information utilized to detect malicious domains [27, 43]. In general, there are two types of approaches that complement each other. In classification-based approaches, a classifier is built from local features of domains extracted from DNS data, which may be further enriched with other network and host features. A classifier is then trained using a ground truth dataset of benign and malicious domains, and used to classify new unknown domains. Inference-based approaches, which is the focus of this paper, are centered on building associations between domains from DNS data to reflect their meaningful connections (e.g., deployed and controlled by the same entity). Once such associations are defined, an inference algorithm is deployed to reason the maliciousness of a domain based on its direct/indirect associations with known malicious ones.

Inference-based approaches are based on a simple intuition: if a domain has strong associations with known malicious domains, it is likely to be malicious as well. Clearly how such associations are defined is key to the effectiveness of malicious domain detection. Ideally, it should satisfy two properties. First, it should be *accurate*, in the sense that the connections identified are indeed strongly relevant to maliciousness inferences. For example, it is reasonable to define associations when two domains are controlled and deployed by the same entity: if one domain is malicious, it is probably either directly deployed by or compromised by an attacker. In either case, it raises the probability of maliciousness of the other domain. As a contrast, it would not be reasonable to associate two domains just because they start with the same character. Associations based on irrelevant or weak connections would result in high false positives in malicious domain detection. Second, associations should be defined to have good *coverage*: it should reveal as many relevant connections between domains as possible. An overly strict association (e.g., two domains must have the same owner in their WHOIS records and the same authoritative server, be with the same subdomain names, and meanwhile have the same access pattern at all time) would overlook a large portion of relevant connections between domains, and thus could only detect a small number of malicious domains. Ideally, we would like domain associations to be both highly accurate and with high coverage. However, in practice it becomes quite challenging to do so because, depending on how they are collected, the scope of information in DNS data could be very limited.

In this paper, we investigate the design of effective domain association schemes based on *active* DNS data to enhance inference-based malicious domain detection. Active DNS data is collected by periodically querying a large pre-compiled list of domains in the Internet. One advantage of active DNS data is that it does not contain Internet activities of any real users, and could be made widely available with no privacy concerns. However, compared to other types of DNS data (e.g., passive DNS data or logs of DNS servers), the information provided by active DNS data is quite limited: only the (possibly incomplete) mapping between domains and IPs at different periods of time is available. This imposes significant challenges to reveal meaningful connections between domains.

Belief propagation (BP), as a popular inference algorithm, has been successfully applied to analyze system and network logs and infer malicious entities. It is compelling to apply BP directly to detect malicious domains by treating the active DNS data as a bipartite graph, where on one side are domains and the other are IPs, and an edge represents the resolution of a domain to an IP. This approach implicitly builds associations between domains if they are resolved to the same IP (a "co-IP" relationship). Intuitively, it seems that domains hosted at the same IPs tend to be related and could be used for maliciousness inferences. However, this is a very weak association as it fails to consider the many complicated ways that domains are deployed in the Internet. In particular, public web hosting services could cause unrelated domains to be hosted at the same pool of IPs. Malicious domain inference based on co-IP relationships thus would result in a very poor detection accuracy.

To overcome the inherent weakness of simple "co-IP" associations, Khalil et al. proposes to establish explicit association between two domains if they share common IPs that do not all come from the same Autonomous Systems (AS). The number of ASs of these common IPs further indicates the strength of the association. The intuition is reasonable: even with web hosting services, it is unlikely that two unrelated domains happen to be hosted at the same set of IPs belonging to different ASs during a short period of time (say a week). The more the number of different ASs among the shared IPs is, the more likely their deployments are coordinated, and thus the more likely these domains are related.

However, the above associations, though most of the time accurate, tend to be overly restrictive, which would result in poor coverage of malicious domains. Specifically, it largely focuses on domains that frequently change hosting environments among different ASs. Related domains that do not change hosting IPs and those that change hosting IPs within the same AS would be omitted. In fact, we notice that the majority of domains with shared IPs in active DNS data belong to this uncovered category (e.g., 82% of domain pairs with common IPs in the data of the week of Feb. 4-10 2017 belong to this category). Meanwhile, the accuracy of associations could still be affected by web hosting services whose hosting IPs span over multiple ASs (e.g., both AS16509 and AS14618 belong to Amazon). Associations could still be incorrectly established between unrelated domains if they happen to use the same web hosting service.

Our goal in this research is to construct new algorithms defining a new set of richer and stronger associations that both expand the coverage of domains as well as improve the detection accuracy. To expand the coverage of domains, we first explore the possibility of differentiating between dedicated hosting environments and the public hosting ones. Our intuition is that domains that share dedicated IPs are likely owned by the same entity, and hence are related, irrespective of the number of ASs. For this purpose, we identify a set of features of IPs in active DNS data, and build a classifier to distinguish these two types of different IPs. We then propose a new association scheme based on the classification of IPs. Specifically, two domains are associated if they either (i) share at least one dedicated IP, or (ii) share more than one public IP from different ASs. Our experiments show that, used within an existing path-based inference algorithm [25], the new associations significantly expand the coverage of related domains. More importantly, the proposed new association proves to be also stronger and more meaningful as evidenced by the improvement in detection accuracy.

The path-based inference algorithm is specifically designed for DNS data analysis. It is effective but computationally expensive. To further demonstrate the strength of our domain association scheme as well as improving inference efficiency, we further investigate the effectiveness of combining our association scheme with the generic belief propagation algorithm. Through comprehensive experiments, we show that this approach significantly improves the efficiency and scalability of malicious domain inference with only minor negative impacts on detection accuracy, which suggests that such a combination would offer a good tradeoff for malicious domain detection in practice.

Our contributions in this work is summarized as follows:

- We design and implement an IP classifier based on features extracted from DNS data. The classifier labels each IP as either dedicated or public with high accuracy of 98.2%.
- Based on this IP classification, we design a new algorithm to discover strong domain associations among the domains in the DNS data.
- We apply the path-based inference algorithm on our domain graph and perform extensive set of experiments to show that our algorithms not only significantly expands the coverage of domains, but more importantly, improves the detection accuracy.
- Direct application of BP on active DNS data to detect malicious domains result in a very poor detection accuracy. We construct a new domain-IP bipartite graph derived from the domain graph and apply BP in order to improve the performance by several order of magnitudes compared to path-based algorithms and vastly improve the detection accuracy compared to the direct application of BP on active DNS data.

The rest of the paper is organized as follows. In Section 2, we provide background material about DNS data, and the state of the art inference algorithms, namely, Belief Propagation and Path-based algorithm. Section 3.2 defines and constructs domain associations. Specifically, in this section, we first provide details about our novel IP classification scheme and then use it to construct domain graphs. Section 4 presents the experiments to show the domain coverage and detection accuracy. We discuss detection accuracy and scalability in Section 5. Section 6 critically analyzes the work closely related to ours and justifies why our approach is superior. Finally, we conclude the paper in Section 7.

2 BACKGROUND

2.1 DNS Data

DNS is a hierarchical naming system that helps locate any resource connected to the Internet. In fact, it is one of the core protocol suites of the Internet. It provides a distributed database that maps domain name to record sets, such as IP addresses. DNS consists of recursive resolvers, authoritative name servers, and root name servers. Every DNS query starts from a recursive resolver, which usually resides within the local network where the query is issued. DNS data can be obtained by deploying sensors in the DNS query process. Based on the location and the method of collection, the DNS data can be grouped into three main categories: passive DNS data [20, 43], active DNS data [27], and logs of DNS servers. Our malicious domain detection approach uses active DNS data due to its readily availability with little privacy concerns compared to passive DNS data.

2.2 Belief Propagation (BP)

BP [45] is an efficient approximation algorithm for solving inference problems on graphical models such as Bayesian networks [21] and Markov random fields [34]. The algorithm was first proposed by Judea Pearl [31] in 1982. BP was initially formulated on trees, but since then it has shown to work on poly-trees and then subsequently on general graphs [46].

In BP, each node infers a final belief distribution by listening to its neighbors. BP is an iterative message passing process. In each iteration, each node updates and passes messages to its neighbors based on the messages it received from other neighbours in the previous iteration. This process continues until all the messages converge. The final belief of each node is calculated based on the final messages. The high-level idea is that given a small set of labeled nodes, BP infers the labels of the rest of the nodes in the graph. The propagation of belief also depends on either the *homophily* ("birds of a feather flock together") or the *heterophily* ("opposites attract") property of a given network. The network graphs we are dealing with in this work are known to demonstrate certain homophily properties. That is, if a node is surrounded by many malicious nodes than benign nodes, that node is likely to be malicious as well.

BP has already been applied in the field of malicious domain detection [24, 30]. For example, Manadhata et. al [30] apply BP over host-domain bipartite graphs, which represent hosts querying domains, in order to discover new malicious domains based on known malicious and benign domains as ground truth. They collected passive DNS data from HTTP proxies deployed in a global enterprise. The intuition behind their associations is that if a host access a malicious domain, it is likely to be infected or compromised. Further, the domains queried by this infected host are likely to be malicious as well. In fact, Manadhata et. al empirically show that the belief propagation algorithm achieves high detection rates of malicious domains with low false positive rates.

2.3 Path based Algorithm

Khalil et al. [25] designed a path-based malicious domain detection algorithm over a domain graph, which is built from a domain resolution graph (which domains are being hosted at which IPs). A domain graph comprises nodes representing domains and weighted edges that represent strengths of direct associations between domains. The algorithm further computes indirect associations between pairs of domains. Specifically, the strength of a path between two nodes u and v is defined as the multiplication of the weights of the edges on the path. The association between u and v is defined as the weight of the strongest path between them. Given a set of known malicious domains, the maliciousness of a domain is then inferred as an exponentially decaying weighted sum of its associations with all known malicious ones.

3 DEFINING AND CONSTRUCTING DOMAIN ASSOCIATIONS

3.1 IP Classification

As mentioned in Section 1, we classify the IPs in domain-IP graphs into *public* and *dedicated* as a basis for defining a new set of stronger and more meaningful domain associations. We define public domain-hosting IPs, public IPs for short, as those IPs that are publicly available for domain hosting and consequently, host domains from multiple unrelated entities (e.g. Amazon Public IPs [8], Ephemeral external IPs in Google Cloud Platform [10]). In contrast, dedicated domain-hosting IPs, dedicated IPs for short, are defined as those IPs that are exclusively used to host domains of the same entity for a certain time interval (e.g. Amazon Elastic IPs [9], IPs of most universities and government institutions).

Naturally, the first option to identify public IPs is to check in publicly available APIs from hosting providers [4] or static cloud IP lists compiled by hosting providers [2] and third parties [6]. However, such APIs may have rate limits of checking or such static lists may often compiled manually and cannot keep up with domain hosting dynamics. Additionally, such tools usually have limited coverage of IPs. Most importantly, they may not capture the notions of public and dedicated IPs as we define in this study. For example, Which-Cloud [11] not only have limited coverage of cloud hosting IPs, but also do not differentiate between public and dedicated IPs. More specifically, Which-Cloud classifies Amazon Elastic IPs [9] as public. However, these IPs are usually allocated to one entity for a certain time interval, and hence, are considered dedicated according to our definition. For example, consider the IP "35.160.237.41" from the domain graph of the week of Feb. 4-10 2017. Which-Cloud classifies this IP as public since it belongs to Amazon AWS IP pool. However, we classify this IP as dedicated, even though it belongs to a public hosting organization. By consulting DNS databases as well as VirusTotal [42], we verify that this IP is used to host five domains during our study period: spoonerrisk.com, spoonerinc.net, spoonermai.com, medadmin.com and thomasproductiontraining-manuals.com, all of which belong to the same entity, Spooner Inc. and its subsidiaries.

In the following, we walk through the details of our solution to classify IPs into dedicated and public according to our definition of the two classes.

Table 1: Selected IP Attributes for IP Classification

Attributes Set	#	Attributes Name for IP
Domain based	1	# of FQDNs
	2	# of second level domains
	3	# of third level domains
IP block based	4	# of FQDNs in its /24 IP block
	5	# of second level domains in its /24 IP block
	6	# of third level domains in its /24 IP block
	7	# of IPs in its /24 IP block

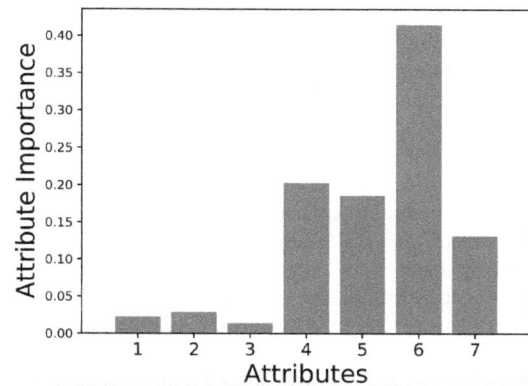

Figure 1: Attribute Importance of IP classification

Attribute Selection. The accuracy of classification depends on the selection of the right attributes of DNS resolved IPs. After anayzing many IP attributes for accuracy, we selected 7 attributes that collectively differentiate dedicated IPs from public ones. As shown in Table 1, we categorize them into two groups: (i) domain based attributes and (ii) IP block based attributes. The three attributes in the first group are: the number of fully qualified domain names (FQDNs) (e.g., www.foo.example.com is a FQDN), the number of second level domains (2LDs) (e.g., example.com), and the number of third level domains (3LDs) (e.g., foo.example.com), which an IP hosts during a certain time period (e.g., one week). Attributes 4-6 (Table 1) of the second group are similar to attributes 1-3, but computed over all the IPs, in the selected data set, which belong to the same /24-subnet of the IP under consideration. Attribute 7 is the number of IPs in the /24-subnet of the IP under consideration, that has been used to host domains in the selected data set.

Domain based attributes capture statistics about the domains that each IP is associated with. Intuitively, a public IP has many second level domains, whereas a dedicated IP has less. Web-hosting services and cloud providers host many domains under the same IP block. That is, such public hosting providers usually allocate complete blocks or large portion of the same IP block for public hosting, which results in a large number of domain resolutions within such blocks. On the other hand, dedicated hosting usually uses a fewer number of domains within their IP blocks. The attributes of the second group help to correctly classify dedicated IPs that happen to host a relatively large number of domains (e.g., a big company and its subsidiaries), which otherwise may be misclassified based on the first group of features.

Ground Truth Collection. To train any classifier, one needs to first compile a ground truth of labeled data. We use the following process to collect a ground truth consisting of both dedicated IPs and public IPs. We manually verify these IPs, by checking whether the domains hosted at each of these IPs belong to the same entity using WHOIS database [12].

Dedicated IP ground truth collection: Intuitively, it is less likely for a university or a government website to share IPs with domains from other different organizations. We compiled a set of organizations that are likely to use dedicated IP hosting for their domains including known universities from different countries (e.g.,

MIT, Purdue, Tsinghua University, Oxford university), governmental organizations (e.g., U.S. Dept. of Health and Human Services, Sandia National Laboratories), military related organizations (e.g., US Coast Guard Home, U.S. Air Force, United States Army), and private organizations (e.g., Google, Oracle, AliBaba, NJEDge.Net, Inc., Merit Network Inc.). Such communities of organizations usually use certain top level domains such as, .gov, .edu, .ml, and .com. We then compile the set of IPs that are used to host domains from these communities. We check all the ASs of the IPs in a one-week active DNS data and search for keywords such as "University" and "Government" to identify research institutes and government agencies. For other types of organizations, we simply randomly select IPs from the active DNS data. Then, we manually check if these IPs are historically only used to host domains belonging to specific organizations. For example, for purdue.edu, the AS of its IPs is indeed "PURDUE - Purdue University, US", and the IP "128.210.7.200" has been used to host only the domain purdue.edu at least since 2014. We conduct further manual verification when the AS of an IP is not directly linked to the domain. For example, the AS of the IP of tsinghua.edu.cn is "China Education and Research Network Center", which does not seem directly related to Tsinghua University. However, further investigation shows that Chinese universities indeed get their dedicated IPs from this AS to host their domains.

Public IP ground truth collection: Similar to the dedicated IP ground truth, we first select a set of second level domains of popular web-hosting and cloud provider domains, such as Amazon AWS, bulehost.com and ehost.com. Then, we identify FQDNs belonging to these 2LDs from our active DNS dataset and the resolving IPs are marked as candidate public IPs. However, some of the IPs in this list may be assigned for dedicated use. That is, some cloud IPs may be reserved and exclusively used by a single entity for a certain period of time (e.g. Amazon Elastic IPs [9]), and hence may not qualify as public IPs as defined above. Therefore, we manually check domains hosted at each candidate public IPs and verify whether they are owned by the same entity based on their WHOIS records, the length of continuous duration of domain IP mapping (e.g., using the DNS TTL of domain-IP resolution), and possibly the contents of these websites.

Classification Algorithm. We have tried different classifiers including decision trees, SVM, and random forest and found that semi-supervised random forest is the most suitable classifier for our IP classification problem [28]. Semi-supervised random forest is a machine learning technique where it uses labeled data (seed) as well as unlabeled data to do the classification. We design a random forest classifier based on the aforementioned 7 attributes extracted from the active DNS dataset. The classifier is implemented using the Python scikit-learn package [7]. Notice that random forest is an iterative algorithm. In each round, it uses the seed to classify a set of IPs from the unlabeled data set and adds it to the input seed. The new seed and the remaining unlabeled domains are then used in the second round, and so on until all the unlabeled set is labeled. We observe that random forest classifier converges in 10 to 11 rounds with a classification accuracy above 98% for the active DNS dataset we use in this study. Figure 1 shows the importance of each attribute after convergence. Out of the 7 attributes, IP block based attributes clearly have more significance in the classification compared to domain based attributes. While some dedicated IPs (e.g., IPs of big organizations) may exhibit similar domain based attributes to public IPs, dedicated IP blocks are highly unlikely to exhibit similar attributes to public IP blocks, which makes IP block based attributes more distinctive. In other words, it is more likely for IPs in public blocks to have consistent domain attributes compared to IPs in dedicated blocks, which results in different block based domain attributes.

It is important to choose the classifier with the highest accuracy as it directly affects the accuracy of the malicious domain detection described later in this paper. The /24-subnet for the IP classification is chosen based on the accuracy of the classifier. We evaluated the accuracy of the classifier for different subnet sizes from 12 to 30. It is observed that when the subnet sizes are either large, i.e. close to 12 or small, i.e. close to 30, the accuracy of the classifier falls below 98%. Based on the accuracy, we identified several candidate subset sizes including 18, 20, 22, 24 and 26. As explained later, we selected /24-subnet out of the above candidate subnets as it results in the lowest false positive rate when detecting malicious domains. Intuitively, large blocks are most likely shared by multiple entities, which leads to wrong associations between domains that are not owned by the same entity and hence results in high false positives. On the other hand, small blocks may split domains owned by the same entity, which may result in missing important associations among domains owned by the same entity.

3.2 Construction of Domain Graphs

IP classification is motivated by the need to define a new set of domain associations that strike the right balance between domain coverage and detection accuracy. As mentioned earlier, a weak or irrelevant association would result in high false positives; meanwhile, an overly restrictive/strong association will overlook many potentially malicious domains as they do not possess such a strong association with known malicious ones. In other words, many such domains would be filtered out before an inference algorithm could be applied. Our key observation is that dedicated IPs host domains that belong to the same entity, and hence are related. On the other hand, public IPs host domains from many unrelated entities, and therefore, sharing a public IP is not a conclusive evidence of a good relationship among domains. In the latter case, we utilize the traces

left by the evading behavior of malicious domains to create associations among them. More specifically, some owners of malicious domains frequently change their hosting environment to evade detection, which creates intrinsic relations among them. We use here the same heuristic that is used in [25] to capture such behavior, that is, the number of common ASs in which domains are hosted during a certain time period.

We define two types of new domain associations based on the outcome of the IP classifier:

The first association type utilizes the common dedicated IPs as well as the common ASs between domains. More specifically, two domains are associated if they: share either (i) at least one dedicated IP, which we call the *dedicated association rule*; or (ii) more than one public IP from more than one AS, which we call the *public association rule*. The dedicated association rule is motivated by the fact that sharing even a single dedicated IP is a good evidence of a relation since, by definition, dedicated IPs host domains that belong to the same entity. The public association rule is triggered by the observation that some malicious domain owners avoid using dedicated IPs as they may be easily identified and blocked. At the same time, they frequently move across different hosting environments to avoid detection and blocking of the domains themselves.

The strength of the first type of associations depends on the number of shared dedicated and public IPs. Specifically, given a pair of domains d_1 and d_2 that share a set I of resolved IPs, let IP_d denote the set of resolved dedicated IPs in I, IP_u is the set of resolved public IPs in I, while $AS(IP_u)$ denote the set of ASs that the resolved public IPs in I belong to. We define the association weight between two domains d_1 and d_2, $w(d_1, d_2)$, as

$$w(d_1, d_2) = \begin{cases} 1 - \frac{1}{n+1}; & \text{if } d_1 \neq d_2 \\ 1 & ; & \text{if } d_1 = d_2 \end{cases} \quad (1)$$

$$\text{where} \quad n = 2|IP_d| + |AS(IP_u)| - 1$$

Note that the weight is in $[0, 1]$ and the weight of the association between the domain and itself is 1. Formula 1 captures four intuitions: (1) A minimum of one dedicated IP or two common ASs are required to establish an association, (2) sharing a dedicated IP is stronger than sharing AS, (3) the more the number of ASs and dedicated IPs are, the stronger the association, and (4) the size of ASs and dedicated IPs set has a diminishing return of strength.

The second type of associations is similar to the first type with only one difference. It relaxes the dedicated association rule by using the shared /24-subnets instead of the shared dedicated IPs. More specifically, we replace the dedicated association rule with a new rule, dubbed *relaxed association rule*. In the relaxed association rule, two domains are associated if they are resolved to dedicated IPs that belong to the same /24-subnet. The strength of this type of associations follows the same intuition as that in the first type of associations with some changes in Formula 1. More specifically, we replace $2|IP_d|$ in Formula 1 with $|IP_{d1}| + |IP_{d2}|$, where IP_{d1} and IP_{d2} are the set of dedicated IPs in the shared /24-subnets to which domains d_1 and d_2 are resolved, respectively. For example, assume that d_1 is resolved to ip_1 and ip_2 in $subnet_1$, ip_3 in $subnet_2$, and ip_4 in $subnet_3$; while d_2 is resolved into ip_2 in $subnet_1$, ip_5 in $subnet_2$.

The number of shared subnets between d_1 and d_2 is 2 ($subnet_1$ and $subnet_2$), $|IP_{d1}| = 2 + 1 = 3$, and $|IP_{d2}| = 1 + 1 = 2$.

We build two domain graphs based on the aforementioned two types of associations. The first graph captures the first type of associations and is dubbed, *G-New* to differentiate it from the domain graph in [25], which we call *G-Baseline*. The second graph captures the second type of association and is dubbed, *G-Relaxed*. Figure 2 shows an example of an original domain-IP graph and the three constructed domain graphs, *G-Baseline*, *G-New*, and *G-Relaxed*.

4 DOMAIN COVERAGE VERSUS DETECTION ACCURACY

Active DNS Dataset. Our experiments are performed on the active DNS datasets made available by the system called Thales by the Georgia Institute of Technology's Active DNS project [1, 27]. Thales scans DNS using a set of seed domain list compiled from multiple sources, including public blacklists (e.g. [19, 40, 47]), the Alexa list [13], the Common Crawl dataset [3], the domain feed from an undisclosed security vendor, and the zone files for the TLDs consisting of com, net, biz and org. We observe that Thales provides a complete coverage of domains in its seed list roughly in 3 days. Cyber criminals in general make extensive use of short lived random disposable domains to carry out malicious activities. Domains with long term malicious activities are likely to be identified and blocked. In general, long-lived domains are likely to be benign. Even though sometimes such benign domains may get compromised, their administrators eventually clean and regain control of them. Therefore, we focus our analysis on new domain-IP mappings that are first observed in a certain time period. Similar to [25], we set the study period to one week, which is long enough for Thales to crawl all the domains in its seed, and meanwhile not too long, thus minimizing long-lived domains included. We conduct experiments over two time periods: (i) Feb. 4-10, 2017 (week-1), and (ii) Feb. 20-26, 2017 (week-2). Each dataset comprises a list of $< domain, IP >$ tuples of domains and the hosting IPs. Each dataset is represented by a bipartite graph with domains on one side and IPs on the other. An edge is created for each $< domain, IP >$ tuple in the dataset. The bipartite graph is dubbed domain resolution graph.

Intuitively, web-hosting services, cloud providers and content delivery network (CDN) may host many unrelated domains under one or several IP addresses. For example, two domains hosted by the same IP in Amazon Web Service (AWS) (or CloudFlare, Akamai) could belong to different owners. One domain being malicious does not imply that the other one is likely to be malicious. An efficient heuristic approach to fix this problem is to exclude the "popular" IPs, which host more than t domains in a certain period, from the domain resolved data [25].

Ground Truth Collection. Our malicious ground truth is collected through McAfee SiteAdvisor [5]. It labels each domain into one of the four categories: *safe*, *caution*, *warning* and *unknown*. The label "safe" indicates that a domain is benign, whereas "caution" is used to show that a domain may bring a minor risk. The label "unknown" means that SiteAdvisor does not have sufficient information to categorize a domain. Finally, the label "warning" indicates that a domain has a major risk of being malicious. In our experiments, we use "warning" domains as our malicious ground truth. For benign ground truth, we follow previous research in this area [25, 30], and use Alexa top 1 million domains [13], in addition to the "safe" domains from SiteAdvisor.

Empirical Evaluaton. We conduct experiments to study the impact of different types of associations on domain coverage and detection accuracy. We use the association defined in [25] as a baseline. Table 2 lists the sizes of the domain graphs generated from our two types of associations, as well as the baseline graph for the two active DNS datasets (week-1 and week-2). The table clearly shows that both of our proposed associations significantly expand the domain coverage. For example, *G-New* is almost 10 times the size of *G-Baseline* in the active DNS data of the week of Feb. 4-10, 2017. This is mainly because the associations defined in [25] are overly restrictive. Specifically, associations are established only between domains that frequently change hosting environments among different ASs. Domains that do not change hosting IPs and those that change hosting IPs within the same AS are not considered. For example, in week-1 (Table 2), more than 82% of the domains that share IPs satisfy only the dedicated association rule, and hence are completely ignored in *G-Baseline*. The table also shows that our second type of associations provides even larger domain coverage compared to the first type. For example, *G-Relaxed* is about 2.7 times the size of *G-New* in week-1. This is due to the relaxed association rule which generates a super-set of the associations generated by the corresponding dedicated association rule. Specifically, two domains that resolve to different dedicated IPs in the same /24-subnet are associated in *G-Relaxed* but are not associated in *G-New*.

Table 2: Sizes of Domain Graphs

Dataset	# of Domains in domain graph		
	G-Baseline	G-New	G-Relaxed
week-1 (Feb. 4-10, 2017)	3,980	39,604	106,222
week-2 (Feb. 20-26, 2017)	2,449	18,779	43,661

We conduct extensive set of experiments to infer malicious domains by applying the path-based algorithm over the three domain graphs (*G-Baseline*, *G-New*, and *G-Relaxed*). We implemented the path-based inference algorithm with Apache Giraph, running on a cluster with 2 nodes (each with 48 2.7-GHz cores and 256 GB aggregated memory).

When computing true positive rate (TPR) and false positive rate (FPR), we use ten-fold cross validation. We randomly divide the malicious ground truth into ten folds and perform 10 round executions of the inference algorithm. In each round, we pickup one different fold as training set and the remaining nine folds as test set. We repeat the ten-fold testing for 5 times using different random divisions of the malicious ground truth each time, which gives a total of 50 execution rounds of the inference algorithm. For each round, we compute the TPR and the FPR for various threshold values ($malicious_t$). For each $malicious_t$ value, the TPR is computed as the percentage of malicious domains in the malicious test set with scores above $malicious_t$. The FPR is computed as the percentage of domains in the benign ground truth with scores above $malicious_t$. $malicious_t$ is varied between 0 and 1 with 0.01 steps. We finally

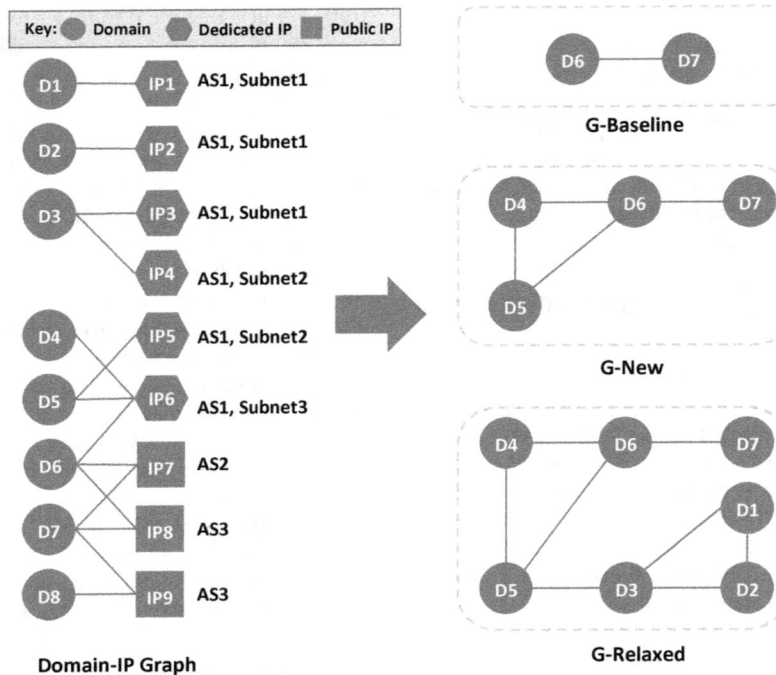

Figure 2: An example domain-IP graph and its corresponding domain graphs

report TPR and FPR for each *malicious_t* threshold value as the average over the values in the fifty rounds.

Figure 3 shows the ROC curves of the true positive rate and the false positive rate on the three domain graphs for two different weeks. The figure clearly shows that our first type of associations results in better detection accuracy than the baseline. For example, with the same 99% true positive rate, *G-New* has a 0.63% false positive rate compared to the 1.33% false positive rate in *G-Baseline* for the week of Feb. 4-10, 2017. Therefore, our first type of associations not only significantly expands domain coverage, but also proves to be stronger and more meaningful as evidenced by the improvement in detection accuracy. The degradation in detection accuracy in *G-Baseline* is mainly due to the noise introduced by the public hosting environments. In public hosting environments, domains from unrelated owners would be hosted at the same pool of IPs. Combining this with the fact that some public hosting environments span more than one AS (e.g., both AS16509 and AS14618 belong to Amazon), would result in wrong associations. That is, two unrelated domains may still be associated even if they only use services from a single provider, which degrades the quality of the associations, and consequently affects the detection accuracy.

Figure 3 also shows that, even though our second type of associations has the largest domain coverage (Table 2), the detection accuracy on *G-Relaxed* is much worse. For example, to achieve a reasonable true positive rate of 93.16%, the false positive rate soars to 2.36% in the active DNS data of the week of Feb. 4-10, 2017. This can be attributed to the relaxed association rule that obviously generates weak or irrelevant associations. Therefore, not all associations that expand domain coverage lead to acceptable detection accuracy. This clearly highlights the intricate challenge

in designing appropriate associations that can achieve the delicate balance of increasing domain coverage while improving, or at least not considerably degrading, detection accuracy.

Before we conclude this section, we would like to provide our rationale behind using /24-subnet for the construction of domain graphs. We in fact experimented with different subnet sizes from 18 to 26 to study the effect on the expansion of the domain graph and the accuracy of malicious domain detection. As can be seen from Figure 4, the domain coverage increases with increasing size of subnets. This is expected as with larger subnets, our association rules are able to find more domains that can be associated with one another. However, not all such associations are strong enough to accurately detect malicious domains. As shown in Figure 5, we get the best accuracy, i.e., the least false positive rate, when the subnet size is 24. Figure 5 shows the false positive rate for path-based and BP algorithms on $G - New$ domain graph. One possible reason for this behavior, as mentioned earlier, is that when subnet sizes are large, it may represent IPs from multiple unrelated ASs and when subnet sizes are small, IPs for the same AS may get split into different subnets resulting in weaker or incorrect associations.

5 DETECTION ACCURACY AND SCALABILITY TRADEOFF

The path-based inference algorithm has a complexity of $O(s|V|^2)$, where s is the size of the malicious seed and V is the set of vertexes in *G-New*. Even with the help of distributed computing platforms, it could still be quite expensive to handle large-scale DNS data. In this section, we investigate techniques to strike a good balance between detection accuracy and efficiency.

(a) dataset week-1

(b) dataset week-2

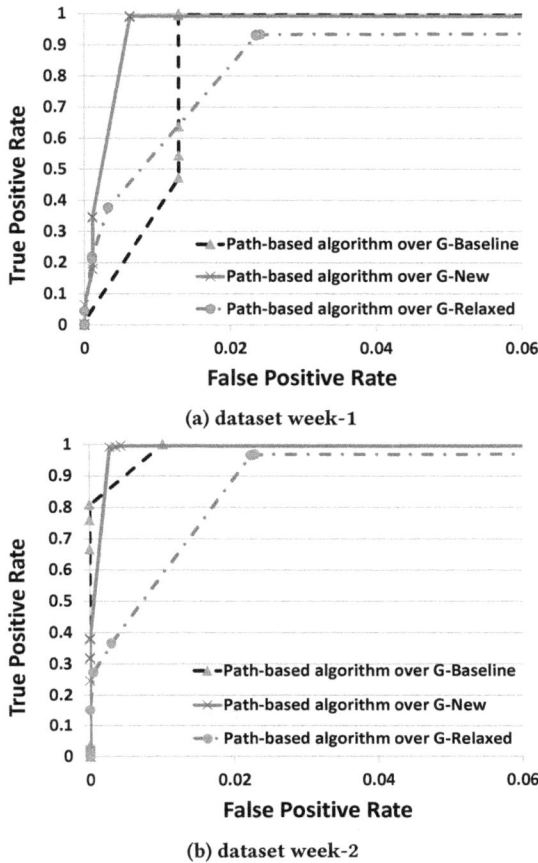

Figure 3: Path-based algorithm over three domain graphs

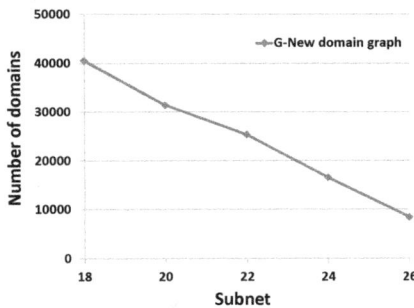

Figure 4: $G - New$ **graph expansion (week-1) under different subnets**

One natural alternative is BP. We implemented the BP algorithm in C program and ran it in a single multi-core server with 48 2.7-GHz cores and 256 GB memory. Our experiments follow the convergence rules of BP that are mentioned earlier in Section 2 with the convergence threshold and the maximum number of iterations are empirically selected as 1×10^{-10} and 15, respectively.

As shown in Figure 6, our experiments confirm what has been shown before [25] that applying BP directly on the bipartite graph corresponding to the whole DNS data yields very poor detection

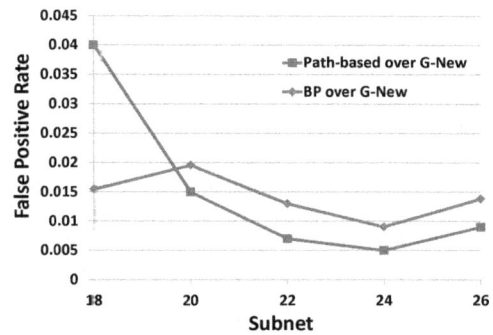

Figure 5: False positive rate of the two inference algorithms on $G - New$ **graph of week-1 under different subnets**

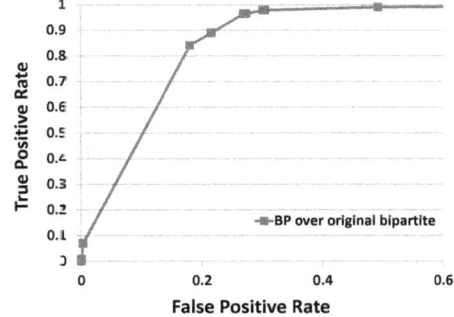

Figure 6: BP on bipartite graph of whole DNS data of week-1

accuracy. For example, applying BP on week-1 results in 49% false positive rate for a true positive rate of 99%. The reason is that we cannot conclude the maliciousness of an IP simply because a malicious domain is resolved to it. In other words, hosting relationships alone are not strong enough to reliably reason the maliciousness of unknown domains and IPs. As shown in Section 3.2, the enhanced domain graph captures much stronger relationships between domains. It would be compelling to investigate how BP on domain graphs could assist in producing results with acceptable accuracy with much less computational cost.

As in each round of BP a single message is passed along each edge, the complexity of one-round BP is simply $O(|E|)$, where E is the set of edges. In a sparse graph, $|E|$ is multi-magnitude smaller than $|V|^2$. Though in the worst case, many rounds of propagation has to be performed until convergence[1], in practice it is often sufficient to stop after a pre-determined constant number of rounds (e.g., 15 or 20). Thus, BP over the domain graph could be much more efficient than using the path-based algorithm.

Note that the path-based algorithm is specifically designed for malicious domain detection over domain graphs (e.g., the explicit decay mechanism and the particular way of combining inferences from multiple malicious seeds). BP on the other hand is a generic inference algorithm that could only implicitly reflect some of the intuitions behind the path-based approach (e.g., the influence of a

---

[1]In fact for some special graphs, BP may never converge

node is diminishing when a message is passed along a long path), which may lead to lower detection accuracy.

We also explore another possible way to apply BP over *G-New*, based on the following observation. Suppose that an entity hosts n domains on its server with a dedicated IP. Reflected in *G-New*, we will have a clique among these n domains, with $n(n-1)/2$ edges. Meanwhile, in the original bipartite domain resolution graph, there will be only n edges between these domains and the dedicated IP. In general, *G-New* would be much denser than the bipartite domain resolution graph. Since the complexity of BP is proportional to the number of edges, to further improve efficiency, another alternative is to run BP on the bipartite graph reduced by the domains in *G-New*. In detail, given the original domain resolution graph, we keep an edge between a domain d and an IP only if d is in *G-New*. The resulting bipartite graph has the same set of domains as *G-New*, but would be much sparser. Therefore, running BP over this reduced bipartite graph would also be more efficient than over *G-New*.

This approach, however, could cause further deterioration of detection accuracy, due to several reasons. First, inferences become less direct. An edge in *G-New* is now corresponding to multiple indirect paths due to intermediate IP nodes in the bipartite graph. The longer the paths, the weaker the inference. Second, probably more importantly, the induced bipartite graph could introduce unreliable associations. For instance, consider two domains d_1 and d_2 who only share a single public IP i, though they may share dedicated IPs or IPs from different ASs with other domains, and thus appear in *G-New*. In *G-New* there would be no direct edge between them. However, in the induced graph, we will have edges (d_1, i) and (d_2, i), which could cause unwanted inference with BP.

Figure 7 shows ROC curves of the three approaches: the path-based approach and BP over *G-New*, and BP over the induced bipartite graph. Our first observation is that all three approaches achieve high detection accuracy. For both datasets, they achieve more than 99% true positive rates with less than 1% false positive rates. This demonstrates the effectiveness of our proposed association scheme. Since it captures accurately the connection between domains, even with generic inference techniques, malicious domains could still be identified accurately. Second, the path-based approach indeed offers superior detection accuracy in both datasets, which is consistent with our intuition. Depending on the datasets, with the same high true positive rate (over 99%), the path-based inference algorithm's false positive rates are one-third or half of that of the approaches using BP. For the two approaches using BP, in general, the one running over *G-New* offers a little better accuracy, though it could be insignificant, depending on the datasets.

Given the seemingly rather small advantage of the path-based approach in terms of false positive rates, one may wonder whether it matters in practice. We note that, due to base-rate fallacy [17], it could indeed have a significant impact. For example, suppose 98% of all checked domains are benign (the base rate), with the same high true positive rate (99%), a 0.2% false positive rate would result in 90% precision (i.e., the percentage of the detected domains that are indeed malicious). A seemingly slight increase of the false positive rate to 0.6% would reduce the precision to 70%.

Next, we compare their efficiency and scalability when handling large-scale DNS data. For this purpose, we generate synthetic domain resolution graphs with different scales (5×, 10×, 20× and 40×

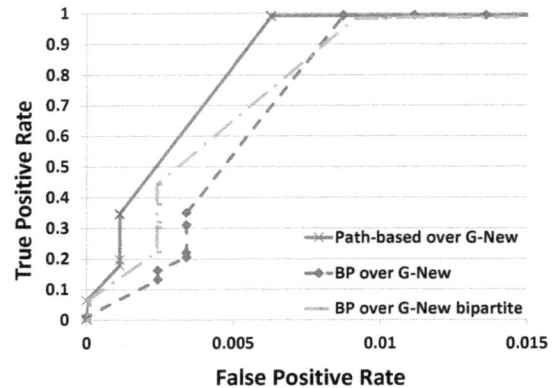

(a) dataset week-1

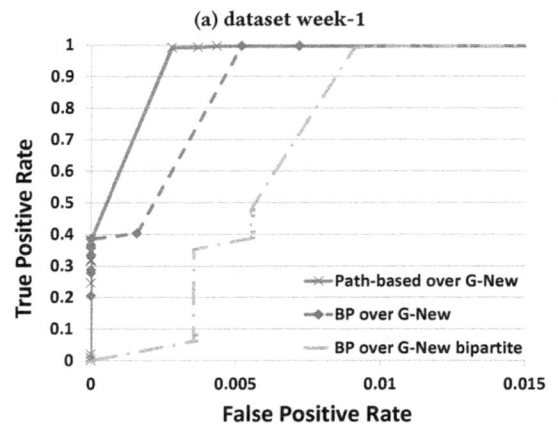

(b) dataset week-2

Figure 7: Detection accuracy of Path-based algorithm and BP algorithm

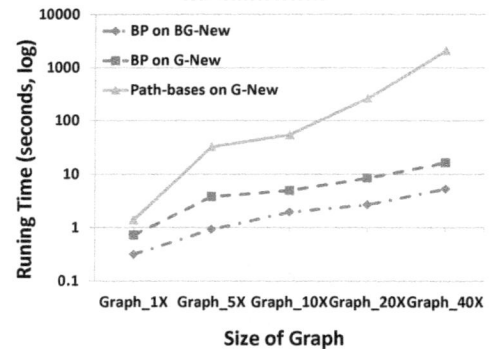

Figure 8: Running time of Path-based and BP algorithms

respectively) based on a real domain resolution graph (Feb. 20-26, 2017). The graph generation algorithm ensures that the synthetic graphs have the same degree distribution as the real one.

Figure 8 shows the running time (in log scale) of the three approaches when we scale up the DNS dataset. Note that the running time reported here excludes the time of other overheads (e.g., loading graphs to the distributed file system in Giraph) to clearly illustrate the difference of their computational costs. We see that though all three algorithms can handle the small graph (Graph_1×) efficiently, the running time of the path-based algorithm increases rapidly when we scale up the graph. For example, when handling the domain graph (with 751,160 nodes and 4,129,156 edges) derived from Graph_40×, it takes the path-based approach more than 2000 seconds to finish, while the running times of the two BP approaches are below 20 seconds. BP over the induced bipartite graph (*BG-New*) clearly offers the best performance due to the reduced number of edges.

Figures 7 and 8 suggest a clear tradeoff between the three approaches: with sufficient computational resources and when handling moderate scale data, the path-based approach would yield the best detection accuracy. When handling large-scale data, applying BP over *G-New* or the induced bipartite graphs would offer practical scalable solutions with good detection accuracy.

6 RELATED WORK

IP Address Classification: Historically, IP address classification is motivated by the need to efficiently allocate IPs to different organizations as well as to improve the efficiency of routing IP packets from one router to another [35]. Xie et al. [44] propose a technique to automatically classify IP addresses as dynamic, that is, DHCP allocated IPs, and static using Hotmail server logs in order to identify spams. Their observation is that most of the spam email servers are hosted at dynamic IP addresses. However, this observation is not reflected on the malicious domains we identified and, thus, such an IP classification does not assist us in constructing domain graphs with strong associations. Recently, Scott et al. [36] propose to capture the IP footprint of CDN (content delivery network) deployments. While this work identifies IPs of shared infrastructures, these IPs may not necessarily be public IPs as we classify in our work in order to detect malicious domains. IP ranges of Cloud computing platforms, such as Amazon AWS [8], Microsoft Azure [6] and Google Cloud [10], are usually available for everyone. However, not all these IPs are public as we define in this study. To the best of our knowledge, we are the first to accurately classify IPs in the wild as public and dedicated.

Malicious Domain Detection: There is a vast body of research devoted to detecting malicious domains via static analysis. Such research work can be classified into two techniques, host-based and network-based. Briefly, host-based approaches rely on detecting malware signatures in programs running on end hosts [26, 33], whereas network-based approaches rely on detecting specific patterns and fingerprints by monitoring the network traffic [16, 25]. Since our approach is network-based, we compare and contrast the most relevant network-based proposals which rely on DNS data for malicious domain detection. Network-based approaches can further be divided into classification based (e.g., [14, 15, 18, 22, 32, 41]) and inference based approaches (e.g., [25, 30, 39, 48]). While the classification based approaches primarily rely on local network and host information, inference based approaches exploit the global relationships among domains along with local information in order to better detect malicious domains. Our work falls in the latter category. Now we compare and contrast our work with respect to these two categories below.

Classification based approaches. Many approaches [14, 22, 32, 41], including Notos [15] and EXPOSURE [18], identify malicious domains by building a classifier using the local features extracted from passive DNS data along with other network information such as WHOIS records [29]. Such approaches are effective as long as the local features used in the classification are not manipulated. However, it has been shown [38] that many local features such as TTL based features and patterns in domain names, are easy to manipulate and thus rendering such techniques less effective. These approaches perform best when one has access to sensitive individual DNS queries which are difficult to gain access to. On the other hand, inference based approaches like ours can detect malicious domains with high accuracy using only aggregate DNS data which is relatively easier to gain access to.

Inference based approaches. Inference based approaches have been proposed to complement classification based approaches by considering not only local network features but also the associations among domains. We already discussed the related work by Manadhata et al. [30] and Khalil et al. [25] in Section 1 and Section 2.

Additionally, Gao et al. [23] propose an approach to detect malicious domains exploiting temporal correlations in DNS queries. Rahbarinia et al. [32] constructs a host-to-domain bipartite graph to efficiently detect new malicious domains by tracking the DNS query behavior using DNS data collected from within large scale ISP networks. SMASH [48] proposes an unsupervised approach to infer groups of related servers involved in malware campaigns using HTTP traffic data. Zou et al. [49] proposed a similar approach based on BP but they utilized domain-IP associations in addition to domain-host associations in order to build the graph. Stevanovic et al. [37] identify compromised hosts by analyzing DNS traffic traces from different operational ISP networks. All of these approaches rely on individual DNS queries made by users which are not readily available with aggregate data sources such as Active DNS datasets we use in this study.

7 CONCLUSION

Active DNS data is an important and easily accessible information source for malicious domain detection. However, compared to other types of DNS data, active DNS data offer limited information. Overcoming the inherent limitations, we design new algorithms for associating domains based on active DNS data to facilitate inference-based malicious domain detection. Our scheme relies on a deep analysis of dedicated and public IPs, which significantly improves over existing domain association schemes in terms of not only domain coverage but also detection accuracy. We show that our scheme could be integrated with both specific path-based inference algorithms and generic inference algorithms such as BP. We further explore ways to improve the efficiency and scalability of malicious domain detection, and carefully study the tradeoff with detection accuracy. For future work, it would be interesting to investigate means to integrate active DNS data with other pubic data sources (e.g, domain authoritative servers and WHOIS records) and further strengthen the quality of domain associations. Another possible avenue is to empirically evaluate the effectiveness of our association scheme with other types of DNS data.

REFERENCES

[1] Active DNS Project. https://activednsproject.org/. Accessed: 17-04-2017.
[2] AWS Public IP Ranges. https://ip-ranges.amazonaws.com/ip-ranges.json. Accessed: 17-04-2017.
[3] Common Crawl. https://commoncrawl.org/. Accessed: 17-04-2017.
[4] Google Public IP API. https://github.com/bcoe/gce-ips/blob/master/index.js. Accessed: 17-04-2017.
[5] McAfee SiteAdvisor. http://www.siteadvisor.com/. Accessed: 10-08-2016.
[6] Microsoft Azure Public IP Ranges. https://github.com/bcoe/which-cloud/blob/master/data/PublicIPs.xml. Accessed: 17-04-2017.
[7] scikit-learn. http://scikit-learn.org/. Accessed: 20-04-2017.
[8] Team AWS. https://docs.aws.amazon.com/AWSEC2/latest/UserGuide/using-instance-addressing.html/. Accessed: 17-04-2017.
[9] Team AWS. https://docs.aws.amazon.com/AWSEC2/latest/UserGuide/elastic-ip-addresses-eip.html. Accessed: 17-04-2017.
[10] Team Google. https://cloud.google.com/compute/docs/ip-addresses/ephemeraladdress. Accessed: 17-04-2017.
[11] Which-Cloud Tool. https://github.com/bcoe/which-cloud. Accessed: 17-04-2017.
[12] WHOIS Records. https://whois.icann.org/. Accessed: 20-04-2017.
[13] Alexa. Alexa Top Sites. http://aws.amazon.com/alexa-top-sites/. Accessed: 30-03-2016.
[14] Hyrum S. Anderson, Jonathan Woodbridge, and Bobby Filar. DeepDGA: Adversarially-Tuned Domain Generation and Detection. In *Proceedings of the 2016 ACM Workshop on Artificial Intelligence and Security*, pages 13–21, 2016.
[15] Manos Antonakakis, Roberto Perdisci, David Dagon, Wenke Lee, and Nick Feamster. Building a Dynamic Reputation System for DNS. In *Proceedings of the 19th USENIX Conference on Security*, pages 273–290, 2010.
[16] Manos Antonakakis, Roberto Perdisci, Wenke Lee, Nikolaos Vasiloglou, II, and David Dagon. Detecting malware domains at the upper dns hierarchy. In *Proceedings of the 20th USENIX Conference on Security*, pages 27–42. USENIX Association, 2011.
[17] Stefan Axelsson. The base-rate fallacy and the difficulty of intrusion detection. *ACM Trans. Inf. Syst. Secur.*, 3(3):186–205, 2000.
[18] Leyla Bilge, Sevil Sen, Davide Balzarotti, Engin Kirda, and Christopher Kruegel. Exposure: A Passive DNS Analysis Service to Detect and Report Malicious Domains. *ACM Transactions on Information and System Security*, 16(4):14:1–14:28, apr 2014.
[19] Black Hole DNS. Black hole dns list. http://www.malwaredomains.com/bhdns.html. Accessed: 17-05-2017.
[20] Farsight Security, Inc. DNS Database. https://www.dnsdb.info/. Accessed: 28-03-2016.
[21] Nir Friedman, Dan Geiger, and Moises Goldszmidt. Bayesian network classifiers. *Journal of Machine Learning*, 29(2-3):131–163, November 1997.
[22] Kensuke Fukuda and John Heidemann. Detecting Malicious Activity with DNS Backscatter. In *Proceedings of the 2015 ACM Conference on Internet Measurement Conference*, pages 197–210, 2015.
[23] H. Gao, V. Yegneswaran, J. Jiang, Y. Chen, P. Porras, S. Ghosh, and H. Duan. Reexamining DNS From a Global Recursive Resolver Perspective. *IEEE/ACM Transactions on Networking*, 24(1):43–57, Feb 2016.
[24] Nan Jiang, Jin Cao, Yu Jin, Li Erran Li, and Zhi-Li Zhang. Identifying suspicious activities through dns failure graph analysis. In *Proceedings of the The 18th IEEE International Conference on Network Protocols*, pages 144–153. IEEE Computer Society, 2010.
[25] Issa M. Khalil, Ting Yu, and Bei Guan. Discovering Malicious Domains through Passive DNS Data Graph Analysis. In *Proceedings of the 11th ACM Symposium on Information, Computer and Communications Security*, pages 663–674, 2016.
[26] Clemens Kolbitsch, Paolo Milani Comparetti, Christopher Kruegel, Engin Kirda, Xiaoyong Zhou, and XiaoFeng Wang. Effective and efficient malware detection at the end host. In *Proceedings of the 18th Conference on USENIX Security Symposium*, pages 351–366. USENIX Association, 2009.
[27] Athanasios Kountouras, Panagiotis Kintis, Charles Lever, Yizheng Chen, Yacin Nadji, David Dagon, and Manos Antonakakis. Enabling Network Security Through Active DNS Datasets. In *Proceedings of the 19th International Symposium on Research in Attacks, Intrusions, and Defenses*, pages 188–208, 2016.
[28] C. Leistner, A. Saffari, J. Santner, and H. Bischof. Semi-supervised random forests. In *Proceedings of IEEE 12th International Conference on Computer Vision*, pages 506–513, 2009.
[29] Suqi Liu, Ian Foster, Stefan Savage, Geoffrey M. Voelker, and Lawrence K. Saul. Who is .com?: Learning to parse whois records. In *Proceedings of the 2015 Internet Measurement Conference*, pages 369–380. ACM, 2015.
[30] Pratyusa Manadhata, Sandeep Yadav, Prasad Rao, and William Horne. Detecting Malicious Domains via Graph Inference. In *Proceedings of the 19th European Symposium on Research in Computer Security*, pages 1–18, 2014.
[31] Judea Pearl. Reverend Bayes on inference engines: A distributed hierarchical approach. In *Proceedings of the National Conference on Artificial Intelligence*, 1982.
[32] B. Rahbarinia, R. Perdisci, and M. Antonakakis. Segugio: Efficient Behavior-Based Tracking of Malware-Control Domains in Large ISP Networks. In *Proceedings of*

the 45th Annual IEEE/IFIP International Conference on Dependable Systems and Networks, pages 403–414, 2015.
[33] Konrad Rieck, Philipp Trinius, Carsten Willems, and Thorsten Holz. Automatic analysis of malware behavior using machine learning. *Journal of Computer Security*, 19(4):639–668, December 2011.
[34] Havard Rue and Leonhard Held. *Gaussian Markov Random Fields: Theory And Applications (Monographs on Statistics and Applied Probability)*. Chapman & Hall/CRC, 2005.
[35] M. A. Ruiz-Sanchez, E. W. Biersack, and W. Dabbous. Survey and taxonomy of ip address lookup algorithms. *Magazine of Global Internetworking*, 15(2):8–23, March 2001.
[36] Will Scott, Thomas Anderson, Tadayoshi Kohno, and Arvind Krishnamurthy. Satellite: Joint analysis of cdns and network-level interference. In *Proceedings of the 2016 USENIX Conference on Usenix Annual Technical Conference*, pages 195–208. USENIX Association, 2016.
[37] Matija Stevanovic, Jens Myrup Pedersen, Alessandro D'Alconzo, and Stefan Ruehrup. A Method for Identifying Compromised Clients Based on DNS Traffic Analysis. *International Journal of Information Security*, 16(2):115–132, 2017.
[38] Elizabeth Stinson and John C. Mitchell. Towards Systematic Evaluation of the Evadability of Bot/Botnet Detection Methods. In *Proceedings of the 2Nd Conference on USENIX Workshop on Offensive Technologies*, pages 5:1–5:9, 2008.
[39] Acar Tamersoy, Kevin Roundy, and Duen Horng Chau. Guilt by association: Large scale malware detection by mining file-relation graphs. In *Proceedings of the 20th ACM SIGKDD International Conference on Knowledge Discovery and Data Mining*, pages 1524–1533. ACM, 2014.
[40] The DNS-BH project. DNS-BH – Malware Domain Blocklist. http://www.malwaredomains.com/. Accessed: 16-05-2016.
[41] Van Tong and Giang Nguyen. A Method for Detecting DGA Botnet Based on Semantic and Cluster Analysis. In *Proceedings of the Seventh Symposium on Information and Communication Technology*, pages 272–277, 2016.
[42] VirusTotal, Subsidiary of Google. VirusTotal – Free Online Virus, Malware and URL Scanner. https://www.virustotal.com/. Accessed: 04-05-2016.
[43] Florian Weimer. Passive DNS Replication. In *FIRST Conference on Computer Security Incident*, page 98, 2005.
[44] Yinglian Xie, Fang Yu, Kannan Achan, Eliot Gillum, MoisĀĪs Goldszmidt, and Ted Wobber. How dynamic are ip addresses? In *The Proceedings of the Special Interest Group on Data Communication (SIGCOMM)*, pages 301–312, ACM, 2007.
[45] Jonathan S Yedidia, William T. Freeman, and Yair Weiss. Generalized belief propagation. In T. K. Leen, T. G. Dietterich, and V. Tresp, editors, *Proceedings of the Advances in Neural Information Processing Systems*, pages 689–695. MIT Press, 2001.
[46] Jonathan S. Yedidia, William T. Freeman, and Yair Weiss. Exploring artificial intelligence in the new millennium. chapter Understanding Belief Propagation and Its Generalizations, pages 239–269. Morgan Kaufmann Publishers Inc., 2003.
[47] Zeus Tracker. Zeus domain blocklist. https://zeustracker.abuse.ch/. Accessed: 17-05-2017.
[48] Jialong Zhang, Sabyasachi Saha, Guofei Gu, Sung-Ju Lee, and Marco Mellia. Systematic mining of associated server herds for malware campaign discovery. In *Proceedings of the 35th IEEE International Conference on Distributed Computing Systems*, pages 630–641, 2015.
[49] Futai Zou, Siyu Zhang, Weixiong Rao, and Ping Yi. Detecting Malware Based on DNS Graph Mining. *International Journal of Distributed Sensor Networks*, 2015, 2015.

Input : $IP_{p\_labeled}$, public IPs in the seed
$\qquad$ $IP_{d\_labeled}$, dedicated IPs in the seed
$\qquad$ $IP_{unlabeled}$, DNS resolved IPs to be classified
Output: IP_{public}, IPs classified as public including seed
$\qquad$ $IP_{dedicated}$, IPs classified as dedicated including
seed

$IP_{public}, IP_{dedicated} = IP_{p\_labeled}, IP_{d\_labeled}$
while *True* **do**
$\quad$ model = train_classifier_module($IP_{public}, IP_{dedicated}$)
$\quad$ S = predict_unknown_ip(model, $IP_{unlabeled}$)
$\quad$ **for** *each element in S* **do**
$\quad\quad$ # IP address
$\quad\quad$ $IP = element.ip$;
$\quad\quad$ $score_{public} = element.public\_confidence\_score$;
$\quad\quad$ # dedicated confidence score
$\quad\quad$ $score_{dedicated} = 1 - score_{public}$;
$\quad\quad$ **if** $score_{public} > confidence\_thresh_{public}$ **then**
$\quad\quad\quad$ Move IP from $IP_{unlabeled}$ to IP_{public};
$\quad\quad$ **else if** $score_{dedicated} > confidence\_thresh_{dedicated}$
$\quad\quad$ **then**
$\quad\quad\quad$ Move IP from $IP_{unlabeled}$ to $IP_{dedicated}$;
$\quad$ **end**
$\quad$ # convergence
$\quad$ **if** $|IP_{public}|$ *is not changed and* $|IP_{dedicated}|$ *is not*
$\quad$ *changed* **then**
$\quad\quad$ exit while;
$\quad$ **end**
end

for *each IP in $IP_{unlabeled}$* **do**
$\quad$ Move IP to IP_{public} ;
end
return $IP_{public}, IP_{dedicated}$

Algorithm 1: IP Classification Algorithm

APPENDIX

IP Classification Algorithm

Our Random Forrest based classification procedure is shown in Algorithm 1. After each classification round, we revise the seeds based on the two thresholds, $confidence\_thresh_{public}$ and $confidence\_thresh_{dedicated}$. We empirically set the thresholds $confidence\_thresh_{public}$ and $confidence\_thresh_{dedicated}$ to 0.5 and 0.9 respectively in order to obtain a classification accuracy above 98%. The subsequent iterations uses the manually collected seed as well as the already labeled IPs as the new seed. The algorithm converges when the two output sets, IP_{public} and $IP_{dedicated}$, remain unchanged.

Active DNS Datasets

Figure 9 shows the degree distribution of IPs in the original domain resolution graphs of the two datasets (week-1 and week-2). The $x-axis$ is the accumulation of the numbers of IPs sorted based on their degrees, while the $y-axis$ axis shows the corresponding degrees.

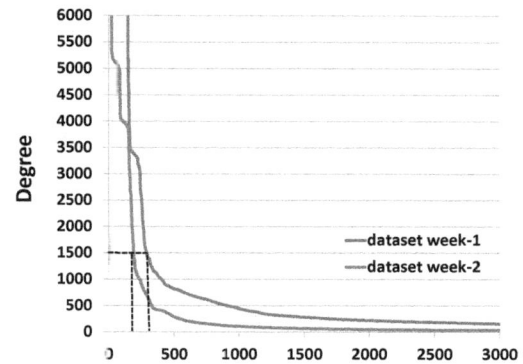

Figure 9: Degree distribution of IP nodes in domain resolution graphs. Only 3000 IPs with the highest degrees are shown in the figure

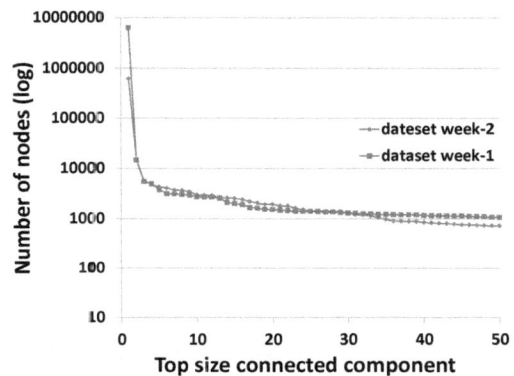

Figure 10: Distribution of connected component sizes in domain resolution graphs for the two datasets. Only 50 top size connected components are shown in this figure

For example, the point (300, 1500) in Figure 9 means that there are 300 IPs each hosts 1500 domains. The IP degree distribution shows us that a small group of IPs host most of the domains. Empirically, we set t to be 1500, where only 292 and 190 IPs respectively are excluded from the domain resolution graphs of the two datasets. It is a negligible percentage (0.05% and 0.09% respectively) of the total IPs in the original datasets.

Another important property of our datasets is the number and size of connected components in the domain resolution graph. The size of connected components in the domain resolution graphs has a significant effect on the malicious score computation time, especially for message passing approaches, such as BP algorithm. Figure 10 provides the distribution of the number of nodes (domains and IPs) of the top connected components in the domain resolution graphs of the two datasets. It roughly follows a power law distribution based on the logarithmic scale. An efficient heuristic to reduce the computation time of both domain graph generation as well as inference algorithm execution is to operate on each connected component separately instead of the whole graph.

Forgetting with Puzzles:
Using Cryptographic Puzzles to support Digital Forgetting

Ghous Amjad
Brown University & NYUAD
Providence, Rhode Island, USA
ghous_amjad@brown.edu

Muhammad Shujaat Mirza
NYUAD
Abu Dhabi, UAE
muhammad.mirza@nyu.edu

Christina Pöpper
NYUAD
Abu Dhabi, UAE
christina.poepper@nyu.edu

ABSTRACT

Digital forgetting deals with the unavailability of content uploaded to web and storage servers after the data has served its purpose. The content on the servers can be deleted manually, but this does not prevent data archival and access at different storage locations. This is problematic since then the data may be accessed for unintended or even malicious purposes long after the owners have decided to abandon the public availability of their data. Approaches which assign a lifetime value to data or use heuristics like interest in data to make it inaccessible after some time have been proposed, but digital forgetting is still in its infancy and there are a number of open problems with the proposed approaches.

In this paper, we outline a general use case of cryptographic puzzles in the context of digital forgetting which—to the best of our knowledge—has not been proposed or explored before. One problem with recent proposals for digital forgetting is that attackers could collect or even delete anyone's public data during their lifetime. In our approach, we deal with these problems by making it hard for the attacker to delete large quantities of data while making sure that the proposed solutions will not adversely deteriorate user experience in a disturbing manner. As a proof-of-concept, we propose a system with cryptographic (time-lock) puzzles that deals with malicious users while ensuring the permanent deletion of data when interest in it dies down. We have implemented a prototype and evaluate it thoroughly with promising results.

CCS CONCEPTS

• **Security and privacy** → **Privacy-preserving protocols**; **Privacy protections**;

KEYWORDS

Digital Forgetting; Cryptographic Puzzles; Time-lock Puzzles

ACM Reference Format:
Ghous Amjad, Muhammad Shujaat Mirza, and Christina Pöpper. 2018. Forgetting with Puzzles: Using Cryptographic Puzzles to support Digital Forgetting. In *CODASPY '18: Eighth ACM Conference on Data and Application*

Security and Privacy, March 19–21, 2018, Tempe, AZ, USA. ACM, New York, NY, USA, 12 pages. https://doi.org/10.1145/3176258.3176327

1 INTRODUCTION

Users share tremendous amounts of data by uploading content on social media: in 2017, users have been reported to have shared 46,000+ photos on Instagram and watched 4,000,000 videos on Youtube, they have published 75,000 pieces of content on Tumblr and have sent roughly 456,000 tweets on Twitter—all *per minute* [4]. Typically, the content uploaded to social networks and sharing platforms, such as photos, videos, and messages, has relevance only for a certain amount of time and loses importance when time passes. The data, though, often remains available, potentially open to misuse by third parties out of curiosity or with malicious intent.

Content owners and persons related to the content may not want the data to remain publicly accessible after a certain amount of time has passed since the availability of past data might be damaging for them in present or in the future. The Right to be Forgotten [15] and ephemerality [21] are concepts that are gaining momentum in digital contexts with the passage of time. However, when something is deleted from the Internet there is no guarantee that the content is indeed gone for good. The data might have been shared, duplicated, or archived elsewhere online since the time of its creation and users generally do not have control over this process.

To deal with these issues, technical proposals with the purpose of *Digital Forgetting* have been made, including Vanish [7], EphPub [3], and Neuralyzer [28]. They try to achieve their goals by uploading the content in encrypted form along with information on where and how to extract the decryption key during the data lifetime. Since trust in a central third party is not a generally applicable assumption, these approaches store the decryption key on a public distributed infrastructure, such as in distributed hash tables [7], on domain name system servers [3, 28], or using public websites [19]. The main property that is desired by such an infrastructure is that it 'forgets' the key with time and that content owners are also able to manually destroy the key when needed. The system and attacker model that these approaches deal with is one where the attacker becomes interested in the data after its expiration. Due to the deletion of the key by then, the attacker will be unable to access the unencrypted content.

In this paper, we build on these approaches and focus on impeding and preventing an attacker from interfering with the data before its expiration time. This is challenging because it concerns a time when data is meant to be publicly available. We concentrate on the part where an attacker may want to proactively collect large amounts of content or remove it by interfering with the key or deleting it on the public infrastructure. Knowing that an attacker can pretend to be a normal user that should be granted access to public data during its lifetime, our goal is to make it as difficult and costly for an attacker to interfere or access data *on a large scale* before the expiration time. The solution should affect normal users as little as possible and still be effective against a strong adversary with strong computing and storage power.

With these goals in mind, we introduce the idea of applying *cryptographic puzzles* to support distributed schemes for digital forgetting by securing them against attacks that aim to destroy or collect data on a large scale. Our basic idea is that everybody accessing the data, including future adversaries, needs to provide a proof of work before being able to access the content of an encrypted object. We achieve this without a central server for work verification but instead only use the distributed infrastructure and *implicit verification with time-lock puzzles* [20], given at the moment when a participant is able to decrypt the data. This ensures that if an attacker has access to the underlying data, he or she indeed has done some work. Time-lock puzzles also have the property of being sequential in nature, which means using more machines will not reduce the time to their solution. We show that it is hard for an attacker to successfully delete the decryption key and collect data on a large scale when addressing the system as a whole, in particular a large percentage of all objects protected by a scheme for digital forgetting.

As proof of concept, we present a system that incorporates puzzles with the recent Neuralyzer [28] and show that introducing cryptographic puzzles substantially reduces the impact of an attacker that attempts to delete or collect a lot of data. In more details, we design and evaluate a scheme in which a normal user gets to solve one easier, faster-to-solve puzzle, which takes little time. An attacker, however, will have to go through the process of solving two puzzles, the second one being more time consuming, before data can be deleted (we can have more than two puzzles of increasing difficulty as long as this does not increase setup time significantly). Our evaluation results demonstrate that our proposal can be realized and the extra time needed for creating the puzzles is minimal. The extra overhead in terms of file sizes is small and it is independent of the data type and size. The time to break the puzzle to gain data access varies smoothly with the selected difficulty of the puzzle.

In short, our main contributions are as follows:

- We revise and extend previous adversarial models that have been proposed for digital forgetting to incorporate attacks during the data lifetime.
- We propose the use of cryptographic puzzles for digital forgetting and demonstrate how they can be applied in a distributed manner without trust in one central verification party.
- We design a scheme that enables access to public data at very low cost for regular users but make it very costly (time-consuming) for an attacker to save or delete decryption keys on a large scale.
- We develop a prototype implementation based on Neuralyzer [28]. Our results show that the overhead in terms of the time needed for data object creation and the increase in

file size are minimal. The time to access data for a normal user can flexibly be adjusted with the difficulty of the puzzle.

2 MODELS AND RESEARCH GOALS

A number of proposals have been made to assign a pre-determined lifetime value to published data [3, 7, 19] or to use heuristics to make the data inaccessible [28]; heuristics may, e. g., be based on the interest in data as determined by the number of recent access operations. In the following, we introduce the considered system and attacker models, describe our research goals, and give background information on one specific system we will base our evaluations on.

2.1 System Model

The general procedure of all schemes above is as follows:

(1) The owner of the data content creates an encrypted data object and assigns a (preliminary or fixed) expiration time t_e^0 for the object. We denote the time at which the encrypted data content is published or uploaded for public access as t_c.

(2) During the lifetime of the data object, i. e., at all times t with $t_c \leq t < t_e^x$, anyone can access the object and can successfully decrypt it to access the data. x here represents the total amount of lifetime which may have been extended from the originally assigned lifetime of the object: $t_e^x \leftarrow t_e^0 + x$. If no lifetime extensions were made then $x = 0$ and $t_e^x = t_e^0$.

(3) After t_e^x, no one should be able to access the data object other than the people who already know the decryption key.

We consider systems with a distributed, dynamic, and publicly accessible infrastructure where data—in particular decryption keys—can be temporarily stored. This does not need to be an infrastructure with the primary purpose of data storage (like cloud servers) but rather comprises a secondary storage system where data is stored in ephemeral storage (such as cache entries); examples include entries in distributed hash tables (DHTs) [7], website encodings [19], and domain name server (DNS) caches [3, 28] (Sec. 2.4 & App. A.1 provide details). We do not alter the infrastructure itself, but make use of states or storage space to upload and retrieve keys during their lifetimes. The dynamics of the infrastructure lead to modifications (churn) and data loss that result in automatic deletion of the stored data (keys) after some time. The solutions we consider place no trust in a third-party server.

The encrypted data objects from a digital forgetting scheme comprise the encrypted content as well as the information required to successfully retrieve and/or build the required decryption key. The successful retrieval of the key is only possible if the object has not yet expired and is still accessible. Once keys are uploaded to the ephemeral storage, they typically cannot be modified directly (at least for DHTs and DNS cache entries).

2.2 Attacker Model

In our threat model we consider attackers whose target is not a single user but rather system-wide attacks that attempt to collect or interfere with data on a large scale for many users. In a sense these attackers are similar to perpetrators in a network-wide denial-of-service attack as they want to cause damage to millions of users

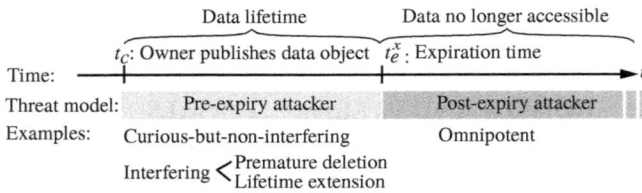

Figure 1: Considered attacker model: Before the data expiration, we consider curious-but-non-interfering attackers and interfering attackers. After the expiration time, we consider omnipotent attackers that may also attempt to attack targeted users/data objects.

indiscriminately. That means, our threat model does not focus on targeted attacks on specific users before the expiration time, but includes attackers that want to collect or delete lots of data during the data lifetime; a specific user and a data object may turn into a focused attack target only after expiration of said object.

This threat model is novel in the sense that, in previous schemes, a user could be turned into an attack target by an adversary only *after* the content of interest had expired as it was assumed that the attacker becomes interested in a specific data object after its expiry. Our new attacker may have the following malicious intents (see Fig. 1):

(1) The *curious-but-non-interfering* attacker may want to proactively collect a large amount of data indiscriminately once available in order to extract data of interest and use it for malicious purposes after its expiration. Such an attacker is looking to take a snapshot of all the publicly available data in some fixed time period and can keep repeating this regularly, e. g., daily, weekly, or monthly. Taking such snapshots is feasible for a strong adversary where its success and extent depend only on the size of the available communication bandwidth and size of the storage space. This attacker essentially defeats the essence of digital forgetting.

(2) The *interfering* attacker may want to make (large amounts of) data inaccessible during the data lifetime by launching an attack that exploits the weakness of the proposed schemes, deleting decryption keys during the lifetimes and thus making data objects inaccessible. A second instance of an interfering attacker would keep data alive by extending their lifetimes.

Curious-but-non-interfering attackers are threats to all proposals for digital forgetting [3, 7, 19], while interfering attackers are an issue mainly to schemes that allow flexible lifetime extensions (e. g., based on user interest [28]).

2.3 Goals and Challenges

Although we may not be able to prevent attacks entirely due to the intended public and unrestricted availability of the data during its lifetime, our goal is to make sure that these attacks and actions become costly enough to deter attackers. This evokes a need for making an attacker (and common users) do work before they are able to save or delete a data object. The work should be of such a nature that over time, once an attacker has gone through a certain

number of objects, it should not take less time than before to access or delete the next object.

A few additional thinkgs need to be kept in mind: Having many machines should not make the process of getting to one object faster; if that happens any proposed scheme would have very little impact for resource-rich attackers. Another important thing to consider is that we should have strong control over how much work a normal user on a normal machine (or mobile device) will need to do so that they do not face difficulty in obtaining the requested data.

With respect to our system model, we can thus formalize our goals as follows:

Functional Goal: Between data object creation time t_c and the expiration time t_e^x, anyone who has the (encrypted) data object can access its content, including curious-but-non-interfering attackers and interfering attackers.

Security Goal 1: An attacker who becomes interested in a specific data object (for whatever reason) after t_e^x (after its expiration), should not be able to access it.

Security Goal 2: A curious-but-non-interfering attacker should find itself in a situation where it is infeasible to take a snapshot of a meaningful percentage of publicly accessible content (data objects between t_c and t_e^x) in a fixed time period, e. g., a day.

Security Goal 3: An interfering attacker should find itself in a situation where a deletion attack over a meaningful percentage of accessible data is infeasible.

The first security goal concerns only specific data objects whereas the latter two security goals are concerned with large sets of publicly available data objects. Our **notion of security** is as follows: Suppose an attacker could take a snapshot or delete tens of thousands of data objects (some percentage of the total available public content) in a fixed time period with one (powerful) machine. If we can increase the number of machines required to pull off such an attack to a number which increases the costs for an attacker in terms of power or rent for the machines by a huge percentage and thereby reduces the amount of data objects captured in a snapshot or deleted in a fixed time period, we say a large-scale attack has now become infeasible for the attacker.

2.4 Background on Neuralyzer Scheme

As our proposed system is designed to support the existing distributed schemes for digital forgetting, this section serves as an overview of one such scheme: Neuralyzer [28]. We will be referring to this scheme later in the paper to evaluate the effectiveness of incorporating cryptographic puzzles against attacks that aim to destroy or collect data on a large scale.

In Neuralyzer [28], similar to EphPub [3], data is encrypted and stored along with a list of domains on DNS server (resolver) caches that encode the decryption key. This object is called Ephemeral Data Object (EDO). To encode the key in a list of resolver-domain pairs, the following steps are taken:

(1) Per key bit, a domain and a DNS resolver are chosen at random. The domain is selected from a list of domains that are used infrequently (i. e., not part of the Alexa list). To add redundancy and enable key lifetime extensions, multiple resolver-domain pairs are selected per key bit.

(2) It is checked whether that domain is in the server's cache by sending the server a *non-recursive* request.

(3) If it is uncached, the resolver-domain pair is selected to be used. If the pair is meant to represent a key bit of value 0 then it is kept the way it is, otherwise (for key bits 1) a *recursive* DNS request is sent to the resolver so that the domain is stored in the server's cache.

This allows to encode the key bits to be temporarily stored in distributed DNS resolver cache entries and the key bits to be extracted as long as they are present in the cache. The decryption process is as follows:

(1) For each key bit, several resolver-domain pairs are stored. Each resolver is sent a non-recursive request about the respective domain. If more than a threshold of domains are present in the caches of their respective servers, the key bit is interpreted as 1, otherwise as 0.

(2) Now for each key bit representing 1, one of its resolver-domain pairs is selected and a recursive request is sent if the TTLs (time-to-lives) of all these pairs fulfill a certain criteria. This is done in order to extend the lifetime of the EDO. Hence, the key only gets deleted either by manual revocation or when the interest in its underlying data dies down. The lifetime extension is called 'refreshing' the EDO.

Note that manual revocation is done in a similar fashion as lifetime extension. For each key bit 0, its resolver-domain pairs are selected and recursive requests are sent.

3 USE OF CRYPTOGRAPH. PUZZLES

Cryptographic puzzles are a well-known defense strategy against distributed denial-of-service (DDoS) attacks [10, 27]. In these attacks many machines send simultaneous requests to a particular server, which overwhelms the server and makes the service unavailable to its intended users. Cryptographic puzzles are used to prevent such attacks; they can be time-based [20], memory-based [5], or bandwidth-based [24]. When an attacker sends a request, the server replies with a question or puzzle (see Fig. 2a). To answer that question, an attacker will have to perform considerable computations or use substantial memory. The server then verifies the answer and serves the data. Now for a normal user the amount of time spent on solving the puzzle is negligible but an attacker would need to solve thousands of puzzles to make the DDoS attack successful which will cost him a lot of time and power.

We argue that a defense against the collection or deletion of large amounts of data in digital forgetting can be similar to defending against a network-based denial-of-service attack. In our case, the goal is to make it difficult for attackers to delete each data object by making them solve puzzles before they get access to the objects.

As a difference, we are forced to use *self-decrypting puzzles* in the sense that once the attacker has the data object, there will be no communication with the data uploader or any third party server for the purposes of verifying the solution of the puzzle (we stress that we are addressing data that is supposed to be publicly available at some point in time—so we cannot make use of classical access-control mechanisms to restrict the access to the data).

Our puzzles and data are contained inside a data object and the data should only be accessible after the puzzle is solved correctly.

Proposals involving cryptographic puzzles and proof of work typically involve three entities: the system that creates the puzzle, the one which solves it, and then the one that verifies it. Typically the verifier is a third party or the creator of the puzzle itself. In our setting, we can neither resort to a third party nor add more communication to the system (see Figure 2b).

3.1 The Time-Lock Puzzle

Different cryptographic puzzles are commonly used. They are, e. g., based on the factorization problem (factorizing the product of two large primes) or on finding a string such that the hash of the string begins with a certain number of zeros [1] (as used in the mining algorithm of current digital currencies). Puzzles like hashcash can be solved faster if the solvers have many machines at their disposal.

We base our proposal on the time-lock puzzle proposed by Rivest et al. [20]. Its security depends on the hardness of the factorization problem. The main idea behind the puzzle is making sure that an attacker must spend a certain amount of time on the puzzle before getting the data. The major strength of this puzzle is the fact that it is intrinsically sequential in nature and having more computers will not help in getting to the solution faster. The time-lock puzzle is based on repeated squarings which are not parallelizable. We describe it first for encrypting a general message m and then demonstrate its applicability to digital forgetting.

3.1.1 Creating the Puzzle. We want to encrypt a message M such that its decryption takes at least a period of T seconds. Choose two large random primes p and q. Let n be their product and $\Phi(n) = (p-1)(q-1)$. Let S be the squarings modulo n per second a computer can perform. Call t the product of T and S. Generate a random key K which should be big enough that brute-force searching for it is infeasible. Encrypt the message M with K to produce the ciphertext C_m. Pick a number $\alpha \bmod n$ and encrypt the key K as $C_k = K + \alpha^{2^t} \bmod (n)$. To do this efficiently, first compute $e = 2^t \bmod (\Phi(n))$ and then $b = \alpha^e \bmod (n)$. Forget everything and only keep n, α, t, C_m, and C_k.

3.1.2 Solving the Puzzle. As searching for the key K is infeasible, the fastest approach is to compute $b \bmod (n)$. Knowing $\Phi(n)$ will make computing e efficient and hence b will be computed easily too, but to get $\Phi(n)$ from n is as hard as factoring n, which is far less efficient than repeated squaring. So the fastest way of computing b is to start with α and square the result t times sequentially. To control the difficulty of the puzzle we can toggle t; the bigger t, the more time it will take to get to the solution.

3.2 Puzzles for Digital Forgetting

In digital forgetting, we deal with content available online to which we add the property of becoming forgotten. Online data needs to be accessed quickly by a normal user. When we add puzzles, it means that more time will be needed to access the object as a user will spend some time on solving the puzzle. So we need puzzles which can be solved in an acceptable time.

Our major insight is that we can add more than one puzzle to the same data object in such a way that a malicious user will need to solve all of the puzzles to be able to launch deletion attacks while a normal user only accessing the data needs to solve only as little

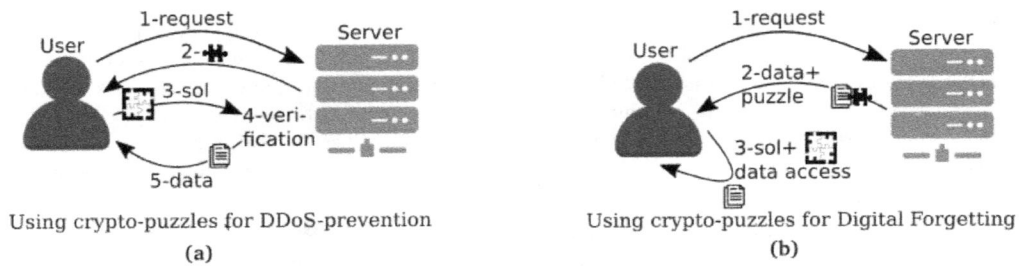

Figure 2: Use of Crypto Puzzles. (a) The parties and communication involved in DDoS prevention based on cryptographic puzzles: 1) The user requests data, 2) the server responds with a cryptographic puzzle, 3) the user solves it and returns the solution, 4) the server verifies the solution and 5)—given successful verification—transmits the requested data. (b) The setup and communication involved in our use of cryptographic puzzles for digital forgetting: 1) The user requests the data, 2) obtains a data object that contains the data protected by a cryptographic puzzle, and 3) can access the data after having successfully solved the puzzle.

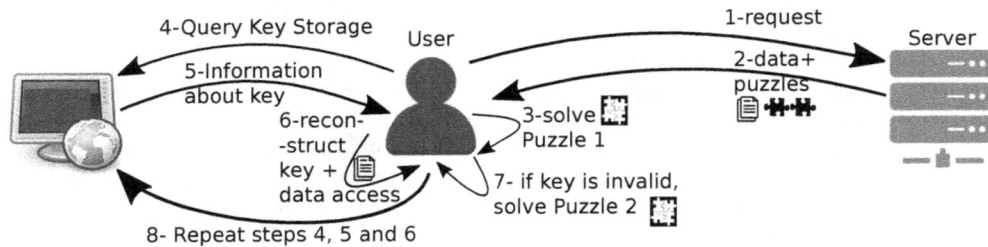

Figure 3: Our basic design: 1) The user requests data, 2) the server responds with a data object containing two timelock puzzles and encrypted data content, 3) the user solves the first puzzle and gets access to the decryption key retrieval information, 4) the user uses this information to retrieve the key by querying the distributed key storage, 5) the user gets a response from the key storage, 6) the user constructs the key and decrypts the data content. 7) If the reconstruction was not successful (e. g., due to an interfering attacker), the user solves the second puzzle, and 8) the user repeats steps 4 to 6 using the new key retrieval information.

as possible, thus introducing a form of asymmetry between regular users and active attackers. Since the puzzles can be of increasing difficulty, a framework of puzzles is being put to use; it will be explained in detail in the next section.

For a realization of our proposal we need to select parameters for the time-lock puzzle (for concrete instantiations in our implementation, see Section 5). Typically we consider a puzzle easy if can be solved by a standard PC or laptop within a few seconds. We should thus set t to a value that allows one puzzle to be so solved within this timeframe (depending on the assumed number of squarings per second that can be calculated). We give typical values when reporting our evaluation and results.

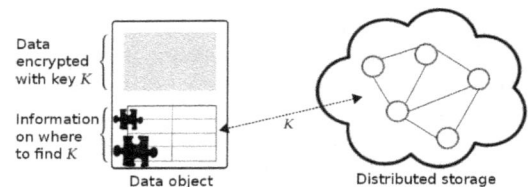

Figure 4: Idea: The public data object contains the relevant data in encrypted form. The encryption key K is stored in a dynamic distributed storage that automatically deletes the key after a while. The data object also contains information on where to find K during its lifetime; we assume it is stored in a table with (<key bits>, <address>)-tuples. Our proposal protects the table by cryptographic puzzles.

4 SYSTEM DESIGN

Our proposed system design is depicted and explained in Figure 3. Before we present details of our proposal, we shortly review the general concept of schemes proposed for digital forgetting with and without the capability to update and reset data lifetimes.

4.1 Preliminaries

We consider a public data object in which data is encrypted with an encryption key K. This data object additionally contains information on where to find the key during the data lifetime, see Figure 4. Without loss of generality, we assume that the encryption key K is split into one or more key parts (key shares or key bits) K_i that

Figure 5: Structure of a digital-forgetting data object, consisting of the data itself and two tables for key-lookup, each encrypted with a key protected by a puzzle of increasing difficulty.

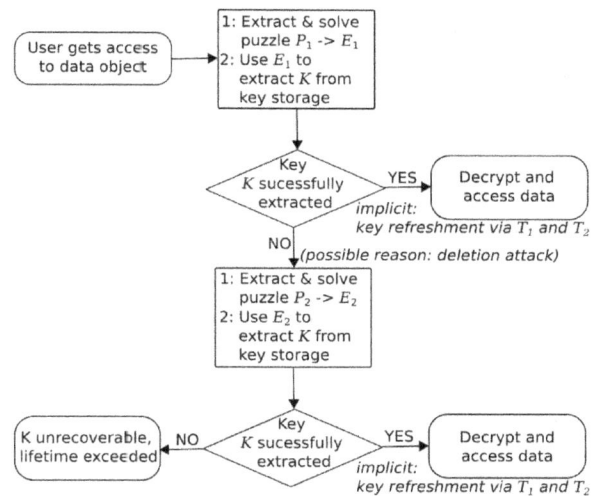

Figure 6: Process and steps in using our puzzle-based structure.

are stored by the data publisher/creator on a dynamic distributed storage that automatically and gradually deletes the K_i after a while. We assume that the information on where to find the key bits is stored in a table $\mathcal{T}$ with (<key bits>, <address>)-tuples. The key is generally recoverable as long as the key bits are available and extractable from the infrastructure. The scheme may provide support for lifetime extension, e. g., based on user interest in the data: as long as there is sufficient interest, the key will remain available in the infrastructure. These lifetime extensions can be realized in a manner that is fully transparent to the users, but they may also enable an attacker to interfere with the intended lifetimes in a malicious manner.

4.2 Our Approach

Our scheme adds cryptographic time-lock puzzles to protect the access information table $\mathcal{T}$ in the data object, thus adding a layer of difficulty for the key extraction process. The idea is to encrypt $\mathcal{T}$ using a symmetric key E, protect E by a time-lock puzzle, and make the resulting puzzle part of the data object. To access the information on where to find the key bits K_i will require the user (and any potential attacker) to solve a puzzle first, thus extracting E, which will then reveal the table $\mathcal{T}$ with the storage locations of K_i. The puzzle itself does not have an expiration time, but the table that can be accessed with the extracted key E will only contain valuable information during the lifetime of the data object.

More precisely and in order to make the premature deletion of data more difficult than data access during the data lifetime, our scheme consists of the use of *two* tables $\mathcal{T}_1$ and $\mathcal{T}_2$, each protected by a time-lock puzzle of different difficulty level, see Figure 5. The tables $\mathcal{T}_i$, $i \in \{1, 2\}$, contained in each data object have the following properties:

(1) $\mathcal{T}_1$ and $\mathcal{T}_2$ provide access information to separate storage locations of the key K. No matter which table (and puzzle) a receiver uses to access the decryption key K, (s)he will be able to get the data before its expiry date.

(2) $\mathcal{T}_1$ is protected by an easier puzzle $\mathcal{P}_1$, $\mathcal{T}_2$ by a harder puzzle $\mathcal{P}_2$ that takes more time to solve. The first puzzle $\mathcal{P}_1$ provides a hurdle against large-scale data collection attacks. The second puzzle $\mathcal{P}_2$ provides protection against data deletion attacks in which an attacker tries to remove/invalidate key bits during the data lifetime.

(3) If the key bits K_i accessible by the information in table $\mathcal{T}_1$ get inaccessible as a result from a deletion attack, the data can still be accessed by recovering the key K from table $\mathcal{T}_2$. If the key bits K_i accessible by the information in table $\mathcal{T}_1$ get inaccessible as a result of other natural reasons near the object's expiry time, a user can still try his luck with table $\mathcal{T}_2$ and if that works out, potentially be able to restore the key in the storage locations of table $\mathcal{T}_1$ as long as the underlying scheme provides this functionality and allows to reset specific entries (as, e. g., DNS-based schemes do).

We note that we can have as many tables and hence puzzles with different difficulty levels as desired. The number of puzzles should depend on how much this affects setup time of the object and the size of the final data object. If the underlying scheme takes long time in distributing a key, it might be not be desirable to have multiple puzzles. For our evaluation we chose two tables, one guarded by an easier and one by a harder puzzle. The process of interaction with the puzzles and data retrieval are demonstrated in Figure 6.

Opposed to other uses of cryptographic puzzles, there is no need to verify the solutions to our puzzles before someone gets access to the underlying data. Incorrect solutions would only mean that the required work has not been done, leading to incorrect retrieval information about the key.

Key Refreshment / Lifetime Extension: The following considerations apply to schemes that enable flexible lifetime extensions. The more difficult puzzle $\mathcal{P}_2$ will have to be solved less frequently or not at all. Thus key access and refresh operations for the key stored in $\mathcal{T}_2$ will occur rarely or not at all. So we need a mechanism that allows to refresh the key bits of table $\mathcal{T}_2$ when a refresh operation for the key of the first table $\mathcal{T}_1$ is happening—*without having to solve* $\mathcal{P}_2$.

Mechanism: The exact mechanism to enable the lifetime extension for the key encoded by table $\mathcal{T}_2$ depends on the type of representation of the key bits K_i in the distributed storage. We here provide the idea for Neuralyzer [28] (as described in Sec. 2.4): By encrypting the tables with puzzles, we are trying to hide from an interfering attacker (who wants to delete lots of data) the table rows that represent a key bit of 0. The reason is that this attacker can delete the object by picking resolver-domain pairs that represent 0 key bits and sending recursive queries to the servers for those domains. So without solving puzzle $\mathcal{P}_2$, the attacker will not know the resolver-domain pairs representing 0 bits and hence will not be able to destroy the key in the distributed storage prematurely by sending a recursive request.

However, picking pairs that represent key bit 1 and sending recursive requests to the servers about the domains would also have an opposite effect as it will essentially extend the lifetime of the object. Due to asymmetry of 0 and 1 key bits in the scheme of Neuralyzer [28] as well as EphPub [3], 1 key bits cannot be deleted prematurely but will only be removed by the natural replacements in DNS resolver caches. That means, we can make available a copy of the addresses of the resolver-domain pairs that represent key bits 1 from the table $\mathcal{T}_2$ without requiring a user to decrypt $\mathcal{T}_2$ as they cannot be used to delete the object.

Thus, our process is as follows: Whenever we refresh a DNS entry of the easier table $\mathcal{T}_1$ (using the 1 key bit addresses in $\mathcal{T}_1$) we do the same for $\mathcal{T}_2$ without ever solving the harder puzzle $\mathcal{P}_2$ (using the 1 key bit addresses in $\mathcal{T}_2$ that we are making available now by keeping them unencrypted). So in short, additional to the encrypted table $\mathcal{T}_2$, we keep a *copy* of the unencrypted information about the resolver-domain pairs in the second table representing the key bit 1 (and only bit 1!).

Resistance to attacks: As far as attacks during the lifetime of an object are concerned, we note that this does not reveal exactly which bits are 1 (and hence the key) because $\mathcal{T}_2$ that captures the ordering of the 1s and 0s is encrypted. The only information that the unencrypted pairs give away is the total number of key bits that represent 1. Arguably, it is much more efficient to solve the easier puzzle $\mathcal{P}_1$ (or even the harder one) to get the actual key than to brute force the key using a reduced key space as we now know the total number of 1s the key contains.

However, if we were to leave these resolver-domain pairs unencrypted, then after the object has expired the number of 1s the key K consists of would become common knowledge to an attacker. So the object would indeed become less secure because of the reduced key space. But actually if the attacker then solves $\mathcal{P}_2$ to get $\mathcal{T}_2$, it can map the unencrypted pairs to $\mathcal{T}_2$ and reconstruct the key without ever querying, even after the object has expired. That is why we encrypt this information along with the actual data content. Now whenever an easier puzzle is solved, the solver gets the key to decrypt the data content as long as the object still has not yet expired. He or she decrypts the data and along with it the 1 key bit information which is then used to extend the lifetime of the addresses of the second table $\mathcal{T}_2$ (and hence the key).

One final remark here is that an attacker with different intentions like extending the lifetime of a multitude of different objects would not be deterred by this too much as compared to an attacker who targets deletion. But this attacker would still have to solve all the easier puzzles.

4.3 Security Analysis

Before analyzing the security of our proposal with respect to the security goals defined in Section 2.3, we shortly discuss how it meets the functional goal defined in same section.

Functional Goal: Our timelock puzzle system is implemented on top of the underlying scheme used to provide digital forgetting. We encrypt the information required to retrieve the encryption key with a timelock puzzle. Anyone with access to the (encrypted) data object who can solve the (first) puzzle before the expiration time t_e^x, can then follow the underlying scheme to retrieve the key. If c_1 is the time used to solve the (first) puzzle, this provides access to specific data objects until $t_e^x - c_1$ for all parties, including curious-but-non-interfering attackers and interfering attackers. Our second puzzle is another way to get the same key using the same scheme. The data is retrievable as long as users can solve the second puzzle in time c_2 before $t_e^x - c_2$. We note that this reduces the data access time by a maximum of $c_1 + c_2$ (if Puzzle 2 has to be leveraged to recover the key), but argue that this time is significantly shorter than typical data lifetimes and does thus fulfill the functional requirement.

Regarding the security of our proposal, we note that it becomes harder to delete an object (specifically its key K) due to the presence of two puzzles. It is also hard to collect large amounts of data because a cryptographic puzzle will have to be solved in all cases. More specifically, we relate our proposal back to the three security goals:

Security Goal 1: After t_e^x, if the underlying scheme provides no further access to the data, we argue that Security Goal 1 is achieved since our system operates on top of the underlying digital forgetting scheme. In other words, we are only adding a delay before key retrieval and the puzzle does not contain information on the key bits, but only references to their storage locations. Hence, after expiry, successful recoverability of the encryption key and knowledge of the cryptographic puzzles cannot lead to a successful access to data content.

Security Goal 2: Before t_e^x, a curious-but-non-interfering attacker can save a data object for the purposes of malicious use in the future. The timelock puzzles essentially guarantee that given a machine of certain processing power (with capabilities for specific numbers of squarings modulo n per second), the puzzle creator can set the time needed to solve the puzzle. Since the puzzle is sequential in nature, a solver cannot break it into sub tasks and do them in parallel. So by using the puzzle we make sure that an attacker spends at least a few seconds working on a single data object before saving it or its key. We thus limit the number of successful attacks an attacker can do per day based on the number of used machines and their processing power. While it is true that we cannot make an attacker spend too much time on a data object given the nature of our data that is meant to be consumed by normal users as well, we will discuss in Sections 5 and 6 how costly we still make these attacks for an attacker. Hence, although we cannot fully prevent curious-but-non-interfering attacks, we make taking regular, complete snapshots much harder.

Security Goal 3: Before t_e^x, our first puzzle targets Security Goal 2. Given the inherent difference in attacks (unfocused data collection vs. targeted interference), we make it even more costly for an interfering attacker to delete a data object. More specifically, we decouple the time for curious-but-non-interfering attacks from interfering attacks by distributing the same encryption key twice. If an attacker manages to delete the key from the first location successfully, the data object has still not been deleted. Instead, the attacker must solve a more time-consuming second puzzle and delete the backup for an effective attack (note that solving two puzzles can be done in parallel, but the first puzzle will add only a few more seconds to the time needed by an attacker per object if done in a sequential manner). In other words, we make a single machine spend more time deleting an object than saving it. Naturally, doing this on a large scale for the interfering attacker is even harder to achieve than a curious-non-interfering attack against Security Goal 2 (discussed further in Sections 5 and 6).

5 EVALUATION

We have implemented a prototype of our scheme based on Neuralyzer [28] (for key aspects of [28] see Sec. 2.4) using DNS cache entries as its public infrastructure. It uses interest in the object as a heuristic to determine when the object should become inaccessible.

5.1 Implementation Details

We obtained Neuralyzer's source code from the authors and integrated our proposed scheme with it. All of our code was written in Python and it relies primarily on Python's Crypto library. We also used PyDNS (version 2.34) in our code which provides a module to perform DNS queries from python applications. We use 128-bit keys to encrypt our objects. Each bit is encoded in 8 resolver-domain pairs for redundancy like in the original scheme. A key bit is interpreted as '1' if at least 4 out of 8 of these servers return true on a non-recursive request about their respective domain where 'true' means that the domain is still in the server's cache.

To get the key to decrypt the data, one needs to get access to a table ($\mathcal{T}_1$) containing these $128 \cdot 8$ (1024) resolver-domain pairs and to get this information, a puzzle ($\mathcal{P}_1$) needs to be solved. Only those resolver-domain pairs are used where the time to live in the cache is at least two hours to make practical sense. We encode the same key in 1024 other different pairs ($\mathcal{T}_2$) and then restrict access to it by a harder puzzle ($\mathcal{P}_2$). When an object is decrypted, all the key bits representing one-key bit in both the tables are refreshed as the act of decryption shows that there is still some interest in the data. For each one-key bit, we check whether at least five of the pairs still respond true to a non-recursive request. If the number is less than five we take a pair at random and send a recursive request to the server about the pair's domain so that it is put inside the server's cache. We also check other criteria set by the original Neuralyzer code such as if the median of the time to live values of these pair is less than a pre-configured value, we must refresh.

As discussed in Section 4.2, we also need to store a copy of all the resolver-domain pairs that represent one key bit in $\mathcal{T}_2$ separately.

We encrypt this copy along with the data. After solving $\mathcal{P}_1$, the user is able to decrypt $\mathcal{T}_1$ and get the decryption key for the data, which means he will be able to get access to this copy as well and will be able to refresh $\mathcal{T}_2$ without even solving $\mathcal{P}_2$. Both tables are encrypted with separate keys (E_1, E_2). The keys that encrypt the tables are modified as described in Section 3.1.1 such that these modified keys together with the information required to correct them (α, number of times (t) that α needs to be squared, and n) make up the puzzles as part of the EDO (Ephemeral Data Object, App. 2.4). We set n to be a product of two 1024-bit random prime numbers and α to be a random 512-bit number.

We ran all our experiments on an Intel Core i7-6600U laptop (4M Cache, 2.60GHz). The squarings per modulo n our machine could do were 58 000. So setting t to a value of 58 000 gave us a puzzle that could be solved in 1 second, $2 \cdot 58\,000$ gave us a puzzle that could be solved in 2 seconds and so on. What we call a harder puzzle is one which is set to be solved in more than 6 seconds.

We created about 350 different random EDOs whose original sizes are either 100 kB, 500 kB, 1 MB, 5 MB, or 10 MB. In our experiments, the difficulty of the easier puzzle $\mathcal{P}_1$, i.e., the time needed to solve it, is set from minimum 1 s to maximum 6 s across these objects. The difficulty of the harder puzzle $\mathcal{P}_2$ was set to times between 8 s to 1 min. We decrypted all the objects with success multiple times over a period of 8 hours. We made sure that the harder puzzle works like it is meant to by manually making the table locked by the easier puzzle invalid.

5.2 Results

Our experiments were divided into encryption and decryption phases.

During the **encryption phase**, the important aspects worth considering were i) time taken to create an EDO and ii) size of an EDO. Figure 7 shows how creating the puzzles takes almost negligible time compared to the time spent in finding the usable resolver-domain pairs to encode a key-bit. Usable pairs are those where the domain is not yet in the server's cache and the time-to-live (TTL) field takes a value that is appropriate for the type of content we are dealing with. For example, for a blog we might want greater TTL values compared to a tweet. So the majority of the time is spent on this process, which is costly in terms of communication. But this work of finding a pair can be done in advance, i.e., there can be a precomputed list of suitable pairs that is updated by a process running in the background that adds more pairs to this list periodically and removes if any of the pairs become unusable. Given that we have this list now, we will then just need to communicate with 2048 ($2 \cdot 128 \cdot 8$) DNS servers as we have two tables, 128-bit keys, and and a redundancy of 8 for each key bit. This will reduce communication cost during EDO creation making it faster for a user to create and upload an EDO.

The results also show that the file size has no significant bearing on the amount of time spent on creating an EDO because almost all the time is spent on the DNS communication and creating the tables and this process is in fact file independent. The average time (one time cost to create an object) was approximately 70 s if we do not process resolver-domain pairs in advance. We also see how the

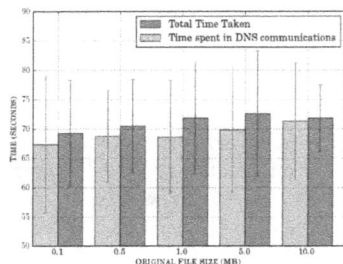

Figure 7: Total time spent in creating an EDO vs. Time spent on communicating with DNS servers

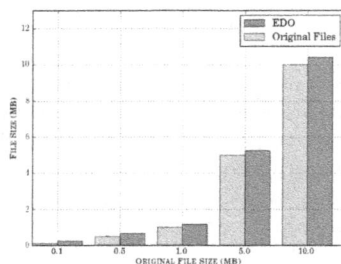

Figure 8: Original File Sizes vs. EDO Sizes

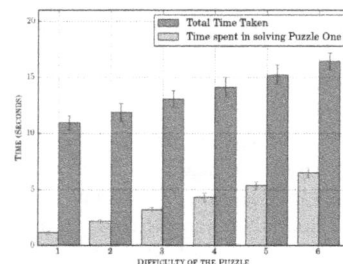

Figure 9: Time taken to decrypt an EDO. Difficulty of the puzzle represents the expected time needed to solve it.

work other than the communication just takes a few seconds on average.

Figure 8 depicts how the size of an EDO exceeds the actual file size. This increase starts to become negligible as the original file sizes increase. This makes sense because in every EDO, regardless of the original file size, we only add limited data such as variables for both puzzles, encrypted tables, and copy of the resolver-domain pairs representing the one key-bits in $\mathcal{T}_2$. This increase in file size is almost of a constant size.

For evaluating the **decryption phase**, we are interested in the following questions:

(1) Did the puzzles get solved in expected time?
(2) How much time does refreshing the one-bits take?
(3) What was the total time taken to decrypt an EDO?

Figure 9 shows how the puzzles were solved in about the time that they were meant to be solved in. We found out that refreshing a table took around 4 to 5 seconds on average. The taller bars in Figure 9 represent the total time taken that was equal to the time it took the user to solve the easier puzzle together with the time taken to refresh two tables (8 to 10 seconds). It needs to be stressed here that refreshing a table can be done using a background process and a user can get to see the content as soon as he solves the puzzle whose difficulty (time needed to solve) we directly control.

6 DISCUSSION

In this section we discuss the impact of our proposal on the success of an attacker and its performance against specialized devices. For a discussion and outline of possible integration of our proposal in online social networks (OSNs) we refer to App. A.4.

Curious-but-non-interfering Attacker: While proposals such as Vanish [7] and Neuralyzer [28] undermine attackers who aim to access the data objects after their expiration times, they do not provide resistance against attackers that are tricking the system by actively trying to take a snapshot of the data for future use. This kind of attacker's job is made extremely tough by our addition of puzzles over the underlying mechanism, since he will need access to a large number of machines to perform the extra computation overhead. An easy puzzle such as the one used in our implementation requires 174,000 squarings for decryption. In other words,

one million of such EDOs would require 174 billion squarings to be done in order to get compromised—in addition to the effort required to retrieve the data object from the underlying mechanism such as Neuralyzer. It is estimated that 300 million photos are uploaded on Facebook daily [22]. An adversary who would be interested in saving these data objects will need to do alarming 53 trillion squarings daily.

The time it takes to do the above computations to compromise the daily 300 million uploads on Facebook varies depending on the number and the processing power of the devices used. Given the large scale of computation required, the attackers might outsource the task of taking snapshot of the system to cloud computing services. To put this effort into perspective, we leverage Amazon's EC2 cloud computing service to test the resilience of our added puzzles.

Table 1 details the approximate number of required compute-optimized EC2 C4.8xlarge instances and the corresponding *daily* monetary costs for an attacker to take varied (one quarter, one half and whole) snapshots of the photos uploaded on Facebook. The numbers show that the computation costs of conducting such a vast attack will be too high to make it feasible for the attacker to save large amounts of uploaded data on regular intervals. It is important to recognize that this additional effort is required solely to solve the puzzle(s) and does not account for the time needed to retrieve the data object from the underlying key storage mechanisms. Moreover, this analysis does not take those EDOs into consideration that expire before they were saved.

Interfering Attacker: Another major contribution of our proposal is the resilience added to the underlying scheme against large-scale early deletion attacks. An adversary who wants to delete, say, at least a quarter of the 1.2 billion photos uploaded on Facebook in four days would have to spend about 12,000 days on this mission if he stays within the allowed limit of 20 Amazon EC2 C4 instances, given our easy puzzle takes 3 seconds and the harder one takes a minute. This means that he would need access to roughly two hundred fifty thousand compute-optimized Amazon C4 instances for deleting 300 million photos within one day. Even if we believe in the unlikely scenario where this massive number of instances exist in the first place and that the attacker manages to get access to those, this will cost him around 9 million dollars a day to compromise these data objects (as illustrated in Table 1). This cost can

Volume	Snapshot Attack			Deletion Attack		
	No. of Squarings	No. of Instances	Monetary Cost	No. of Squarings	No. of Instances	Monetary Cost
75 million	13 trillion	2,840	$108,440	274 trillion	59,625	$2,276,720
150 million	26 trillion	5,680	$216,880	548 trillion	119,250	$4,553,440
300 million	53 trillion	11,360	$433,770	1.1 quadrillion	238,500	$9,106,880

Table 1: The number of Amazon C4 instances required and the resulting daily costs for an attacker to perform Snapshot and Deletion attacks on 25%, 50% and 100% of the daily uploaded photos on Facebook.

increase even further if additional puzzles of harder difficulty are added to the system.

It is important to consider that if there were no puzzles in place to solve at all, only 14,500 Amazon instances or machines of similar computational abilities would help him to save and/or delete more than a billion photos in a day easily, assuming that it takes around a second to download them/send recursive queries. All of this also does not take into account the fact that this content also can expire naturally even before the adversary gets to it; either to save or delete. And with no puzzle guarding the access to these objects, the probability of an adversary getting to the object before it expires gets higher as the adversary will be going through objects on a much greater speed in this scenario.

Attacker with Specialized Hardware: While a higher clock speed will ensure that more squarings are done per unit time and the puzzles are solved faster than the intended time, the clock speeds have become static in the last decade owing to size of transistors reaching its limits [14]. Thus, the performance improvements today are achieved by the use of multi-core processors and parallel computing practices instead. These techniques do not yield significant improvement on our scheme as the repeated squaring algorithm used in our proposal is essentially sequential [20]. However, the well-funded attackers can make use of specialized hardware such as FPGAs and the latest generations of GPUs, equipped with support for integer operations, in order to achieve speed up. Some researchers have shown that off-the-shelf hardware could be used to accelerate the public key cryptosystems such as RSA scheme by roughly 4 times and this could in turn be used on these puzzles as well [9]. Referencing the above calculation, it will still take an adversary to use roughly 50,000 of these specialized hardware devices to compromise only one quarter of the billion photos uploaded on the Facebook. So, the expected time improvement for such an attacker will still be in the order of a small constant number and the added puzzles will continue to limit the scale of disruption or copying attacks.

Pre-computations: It could be said that an adversary can solve a puzzle and start saving the solution. We argue that it will be very rare that such a strategy would benefit him. Again, let us take Facebook as an example. The number of objects uploaded in a matter of days on Facebook is in order of billions but the number of values of α in the puzzle is an exponentially larger number. Not to mention α alone does not determine the solution, but it is determined by the combination of α, n and t. So saving solutions would not make a significant difference at all. And we can increase the length of these numbers as well, leading to a much bigger space from which puzzles can be generated. Creating such a storage by a single adversary with

a finite number of machines appears prohibitive. If the attacker were to decrypt these billions and billions of objects uploaded in a year across major social networks and other platforms and assuming all the puzzles on these objects are supposed to be solved in 5 seconds, for a single machine this task will take more than a million years.

7 CONCLUSION

In this paper, we outlined and investigated a general use case of cryptographic puzzles to support the concept of digital forgetting. The pervasiveness and ubiquity of digital data creates a desideratum for solutions that enable transientness and ephemerality of person-related information, data, and media. The attacker model here differs from classical attackers since we are trying to protect data from access and deletion during its lifetime when the data is supposed to be publicly available. The approach we propose introduces an asymmetry between regular users and active attackers and specifically takes into account the attacks that attempt to delete public data during their lifetime. Our proposal makes it hard for the attacker to delete large quantities of data while making sure that the proposed solutions will not adversely deteriorate user experience in a disturbing manner. Our system relies on cryptographic time-lock puzzles and deals with malicious users while ensuring the permanent deletion of data when interest in it dies down. We have implemented a prototype and evaluated it thoroughly with promising results, which makes a case for further research in this area.

8 ACKNOWLEDGEMENTS

This work was supported by the Center for Cyber Security at NYUAD and by the German BMBF under grant 16KIS0581.

REFERENCES

[1] Adam Back. 2002. Hashcash – A Denial of Service Counter-Measure. (2002). http://www.hashcash.org/papers/hashcash.pdf.

[2] Dan Boneh and Richard J. Lipton. [n. d.]. A Revocable Backup System. In *Proceedings of the 6th USENIX Security Symposium, San Jose, CA, USA, July 22-25, 1996*.

[3] C. Castelluccia, E. De Cristofaro, A. Francillon, and M.-A. Kaafar. 2011. EphPub: Toward robust Ephemeral Publishing. In *19th IEEE International Conference on Network Protocols (ICNP)*. 165–175. https://doi.org/10.1109/ICNP.2011.6089048

[4] Domo. 2017. Data never sleeps 5.0. https://www.domo.com/learn/data-never-sleeps-5 (June 2017). https://www.domo.com/learn/data-never-sleeps-5

[5] Sujata Doshi, Fabian Monrose, and Aviel D. Rubin. 2006. Efficient Memory Bound Puzzles Using Pattern Databases. In *Proceedings of the 4th International Conference on Applied Cryptography and Network Security (ACNS)*. 98–113.

[6] Roxana Geambasu, Tadayoshi Kohno, Arvind Krishnamurthy, Amit Levy, Henry Levy, Paul Gardner, and Vinnie Moscaritolo. 2011. *New Directions for Self-Destructing Data Systems*. Technical Report UW-CSE-11-08-01. University of Washington.

[7] Roxana Geambasu, Tadayoshi Kohno, Amit A. Levy, and Henry M. Levy. 2009. Vanish: Increasing Data Privacy with Self-destructing Data. In *Proceedings of the 18th Conference on USENIX Security Symposium*. USENIX Association, Berkeley, CA, USA, 299–316.

[8] Peter Gutmann. 1996. Secure deletion of data from magnetic and solid-state memory. In *Proceedings of the 6th USENIX Security Symposium, Focusing on Applications of Cryptography*. USENIX Association, Berkeley, CA, USA, 77–90.

[9] Owen Harrison and John Waldron. 2009. Efficient Acceleration of Asymmetric Cryptography on Graphics Hardware. In *Proceedings of the 2Nd International Conference on Cryptology in Africa: Progress in Cryptology (AFRICACRYPT '09)*. Springer-Verlag, Berlin, Heidelberg, 350–367.

[10] Ari Juels and John G. Brainard. 1999. Client Puzzles: A Cryptographic Countermeasure Against Connection Depletion Attacks. In *Proceedings of the Network and Distributed System Security Symposium, NDSS*.

[11] Ghassan Karame and Srdjan Capkun. 2010. Low-Cost Client Puzzles Based on Modular Exponentiation. In *Proceedings of the 15th European Symposium on Research in Computer Security (ESORICS)*. 679–697.

[12] Jaeheung Lee, Sangho Yi, Junyoung Heo, Hyungbae Park, Sung Y. Shin, and Yookun Cho. 2010. An Efficient Secure Deletion Scheme for Flash File Systems. *Journal of Information Science and Engineering* 26, 1 (2010), 27–38. http://www.iis.sinica.edu.tw/page/jise/2010/201001_03.html

[13] Frank Li, Prateek Mittal, Matthew Caesar, and Nikita Borisov. 2012. SybilControl: Practical Sybil Defense with Computational Puzzles. In *Proceedings of the Seventh ACM Workshop on Scalable Trusted Computing (STC'12)*. 67–78.

[14] Pär Persson Mattsson. 2013. Why Haven't CPU Clock Speeds Increased in the Last Few Years? (Nov 2013). https://www.comsol.com/blogs/havent-cpu-clock-speeds-increased-last-years/

[15] Viktor Mayer-Schönberger. 2011. *Delete: The Virtue of Forgetting in the Digital Age*. Princeton University Press, Princeton, NJ, USA.

[16] Mainack Mondal, Johnnatan Messias, Saptarshi Ghosh, Krishna P. Gummadi, and Aniket Kate. 2016. Forgetting in Social Media: Understanding and Controlling Longitudinal Exposure of Socially Shared Data. In *Twelfth Symposium on Usable Privacy and Security, SOUPS 2016, Denver, CO, USA, June 22-24, 2016*. 287–299.

[17] Joel Reardon, David A. Basin, and Srdjan Capkun. 2013. SoK: Secure Data Deletion. In *IEEE Symposium on Security and Privacy (SP), Berkeley, CA, USA*. 301–315.

[18] Joel Reardon, Srdjan Capkun, and David A. Basin. 2012. Data Node Encrypted File System: Efficient Secure Deletion for Flash Memory. In *Proceedings of the 21th USENIX Security Symposium*. 333–348.

[19] Sirke Reimann and Markus Dürmuth. 2012. Timed revocation of user data: long expiration times from existing infrastructure. In *WPES*. 65–74.

[20] Ronald. L. Rivest, Adi Shamir, and David A. Wagner. 1996. *Time-lock Puzzles and Timed-release Crypto*. Technical Report. Cambridge, MA, USA.

[21] Esther Shein. 2013. Ephemeral Data. *Commun. ACM* 56, 9 (Sept. 2013), 20–22.

[22] Cooper Smith. 2013. Facebook Users Are Uploading 350 Million New Photos Each Day. (Sep 2013). http://www.businessinsider.com/facebook-350-million-photos-each-day-2013-9

[23] Douglas Stebila, Lakshmi Kuppusamy, Jothi Rangasamy, Colin Boyd, and Juan Gonzalez Nieto. 2011. Stronger Difficulty Notions for Client Puzzles and Denial-of-Service-Resistant Protocols. In *Proceedings of CT-RSA 2011: The Cryptographers' Track at the RSA Conference 2011*. Springer Berlin Heidelberg, 284–301.

[24] XiaoFeng Wang and Michael K. Reiter. 2004. Mitigating Bandwidth-exhaustion Attacks Using Congestion Puzzles. In *Proceedings of the 11th ACM Conference on Computer and Communications Security (CCS '04)*. 257–267.

[25] Michael Wei, Laura M. Grupp, Frederick E. Spada, and Steven Swanson. 2011. Reliably Erasing Data from Flash-based Solid State Drives. In *Proceedings of the 9th USENIX Conference on File and Stroage Technologies (FAST)*. USENIX Association, Berkeley, CA, USA, 8–8.

[26] Scott Wolchok, Owen S. Hofmann, Nadia Heninger, Edward W. Felten, J. Alex Halderman, Christopher J. Rossbach, Brent Waters, and Emmett Witchel. 2010. Defeating Vanish with Low-Cost Sybil Attacks Against Large DHTs. In *Proc. 17th Network and Distributed System Security Symposium*.

[27] Y. Wu, Z. Zhao, F. Bao, and R. H. Deng. 2015. Software Puzzle: A Countermeasure to Resource-Inflated Denial-of-Service Attacks. *IEEE Transactions on Information Forensics and Security* 10, 1 (2015), 168–177.

[28] Apostolis Zarras, Katharina Kohls, Markus Dürmuth, and Christina Pöpper. 2016. Neuralyzer: Flexible Expiration Times for the Revocation of Online Data. In *Proceedings of the Sixth ACM Conference on Data and Application Security and Privacy (CODASPY'16)*. 14–25.

A APPENDIX

A.1 Extension of Puzzles On Vanish

An encrypted data object in Vanish [7] is essentially a tuple consisting of a random access key L which is used to generate indices where the shares of encryption key K are stored, Ciphertext (C),

Threshold (T, where T is the percentage of key shares required for the successful reconstruction of K) and N as the total number of shares K was split into.

The ideas described in this paper can be applied to Vanish. We can have a puzzle that guards L. The attacker has to solve the puzzle first to get information about how to retrieve and save K. Note that this does not defeat the successful attack on Vanish (Unvanish) [26] which basically targets weaknesses in Vuze, the distributed hashtable that stores the shares of K. Neither was this our intention in the first place as our proposal does not fix the weaknesses of the underlying schemes. Possible defenses against Unvanish are listed in [6].

A.2 Related Work

We further describe related work more broadly: *i*) general solutions for the deletion of data and *ii*) context as well as applications of cryptographic puzzles.

Deletion of Data. Approaches for secure data deletion have been investigated at multiple layers of abstraction [17]: from user-level approaches [8], to deletion in file systems [18] and hardware deletion techniques [25]. User behaviors wrt. deletion have been analyzed for the Facebook OSN [16]. Orthogonal to these approaches—and closer to our investigations—are techniques that focus on the secure deletion of data by securely deleting a key that encrypts that data in *offline* contexts. The encrypted data becomes infeasible to recover without knowledge of the encryption key, given that computational hardness assumptions hold for the encryption. Examples include the early revocable backup system [2] as well as the secure deletion in the YAFFS file system [12].

Applications of Cryptographic Puzzles. It has been suggested that computational puzzles can be used to deal with Sybil attacks [13]. Vanish was mentioned as a system that could benefit from this as it relied on a distributed hash table which could be infiltrated by sybil nodes [26]. But the suggestion was to add these puzzles to the underlying architecture, DHT in Vanish's case. In our setting, we consider a different setup where puzzles are included inside the data objects. We are not making any changes to the underlying public infrastructures and we are not trying to defend them against exploits. We are trying to solve the problem where the attackers abuse the data object itself. Also, they use a puzzle and solution verification process that is distributed in nature and do not rely on a central server or completely different third party for verification of work done. However, their scheme is still very different from ours as it deals with a system where the aim is to bar entry of dishonest nodes who will not solve puzzles. The nodes are supposed to solve puzzles periodically and send the solutions to other nodes for verification. In contrast, we propose a self-decrypting/self-verifying scheme which means that there is no communication cost.

Cryptographic puzzles have been proposed and investigated in further contexts [11, 23]. The ideas by Stebila et al. in [23] are mostly applicable to scenarios in which server and clients are communicating, which is not the case for us. They also observe that a puzzle is 'strong' if an adversary takes n amount of time to solve a puzzle, for 30 puzzles the total time should not be less than $30n$. In the spirit of this observation we argue that caching results will not help the adversary to do better as discussed in Section 6. Proposals such as [11] need a verification of the solution step as an extra round of communication, which we cannot incorporate. Their main aim was also to reduce the time for puzzle generation by exploiting a certain class of keys where the private key was much smaller than the public key, leading to less time spent on generation and verification. They did not have any control over the time spent on solving the puzzles. Our scheme on the other hand generates a puzzle fairly quickly and does not need a separate verification step.

To the best of our knowledge, the idea to use puzzles to support digital forgetting has not been investigated before. We demonstrate that they can be used for making users do work in order to access data objects that are tailor-made to be forgotten with the passage of time, which allows to solve various problems and prevent attacks for approaches that deal with digital forgetting.

A.3 Costs for Attacks on Facebook

Table 1 details the approximate number of required compute-optimized EC2 C4.8xlarge instances and the corresponding *daily* monetary costs for an attacker to take varied (one quarter, one half and whole) snapshots of the photos uploaded on Facebook.

A.4 Integration in OSNs

We wrote a Firefox extension for Neuralyzer that worked with textual content. By natural extension the proposed scheme in this paper can be also turned into an extension that works on emails and various social networks. If a social network limits the type of file that can be uploaded, for example it does not recognize EDO due to any factor or it only accepts files of a specific type that it can verify before uploading, a user can upload the EDO to a cloud storage and share the link on that social network instead.

Objects on a social network need to be accessed fast. We can run background processes that keep decrypting and caching objects before a user scrolls down to them to reduce the time delay. A normal user is not looking to access even a hundred thousand objects in a day. These background processes can, as the objects flow into social media timelines, decrypt and cache them in the users' devices for a sensible period of time. We do recognize that this will have some effect on the experience. But this might be for now the price that we have to pay for enabling digital forgetting. Specific studies can be conducted in the future as to how much this affects user experience on an online social network or given the option will people care enough to opt for it or can we make compromises with respect to user experience if we move from the domain of OSNs to emails etc.

Beyond Precision and Recall: Understanding Uses (and Misuses) of Similarity Hashes in Binary Analysis

Fabio Pagani
EURECOM
France
fabio.pagani@eurecom.fr

Matteo Dell'Amico
Symantec Research Labs
France
matteo_dellamico@symantec.com

Davide Balzarotti
EURECOM
France
davide.balzarotti@eurecom.fr

ABSTRACT

Fuzzy hashing algorithms provide a convenient way of summarizing in a compact form the content of files, and of looking for similarities between them. Because of this, they are widely used in the security and forensics communities to look for similarities between binary program files; one version of them, ssdeep, is the de facto standard to share information about known malware.

Fuzzy hashes are quite pervasive, but no study so far answers conclusively the question of which (if any) fuzzy hashing algorithms are suited to detect similarities between programs, where we consider as similar those programs that have code or libraries in common. We measure how four popular algorithms perform in different scenarios: when they are used to correlate statically-compiled files with the libraries they use, when compiled with different flags or different compilers, and when applied to programs that share a large part of their source code. Perhaps more importantly, we provide interpretations that explain the *reasons* why results vary, sometimes widely, among apparently very similar use cases.

We find that the low-level details of the compilation process, together with the technicalities of the hashing algorithms, can explain surprising results such as similarities dropping to zero with the change of a single assembly instruction. More in general, we see that ssdeep, the de facto standard for this type of analysis, performs definitely worse than alternative algorithms; we also find that the best choice of algorithm to use varies depending on the particularities of the use case scenario.

KEYWORDS

binary analysis, fuzzy hash, malware, approximate matching

ACM Reference Format:
Fabio Pagani, Matteo Dell'Amico, and Davide Balzarotti. 2018. Beyond Precision and Recall: Understanding Uses (and Misuses) of Similarity Hashes in Binary Analysis. In *CODASPY '18: Eighth ACM Conference on Data and Application Security and Privacy, March 19–21, 2018, Tempe, AZ, USA*. ACM, New York, NY, USA, 12 pages. https://doi.org/10.1145/3176258.3176306

1 INTRODUCTION

Fuzzy hashes[1] were introduced in the computer security field more than a decade ago. Unlike cryptographic hashes (e.g., MD5 or SHA512), fuzzy hashes can be compared to find *similar* pieces of data. The need for comparable hashes came mainly from two different, yet related, problems. The first one, historically speaking, is spam detection: Spamsum [29] and Nilsimsa [8] compute email signatures that are compared against known unsolicited messages to label emails accordingly. The second problem comes from the forensic community, where fuzzy hashes are used to correlate forensics artifacts. In this scenario, comparable hashes can be used to locate incomplete file fragments in disk or memory dumps, or to raise red flags if files similar to known suspicious ones are present.

Fuzzy hashing is a simple and cheap solution that can be applied to arbitrary files, requires few computational resources, and produces results in a compact text format. This convenience, combined with some early promising results in binary analysis [21], is probably the main reason why ssdeep, one of the earliest fuzzy hashing algorithms, is widely adopted in the cyber security industry.

While fuzzy hashing for binary comparison is undoubtedly widespread on the industrial side, there is no academic consensus on its merits. Some works [1, 10, 19, 21, 27, 30] measure the effectiveness of different fuzzy hashing algorithms to identify similar binaries and malicious files, often with contradictory conclusions: one study may suggest that tlsh is completely ineffective for binary comparison [30] while another finds it to be one of the best available solutions for this problem [1]; these studies generally focus on understanding *if* a given algorithm works in a certain setting, but do not investigate *why*—thus missing the opportunity to fully understand this phenomenon and generalize their findings beyond the samples used in their experiments.

Other studies [6, 16, 17, 31] have instead focused on developing alternative solutions that often provide higher accuracy in exchange for a loss in convenience in terms of generality (e.g., only being applicable to binaries for a given hardware architecture, requiring dynamic analysis of the samples, or assuming each binary can be successfully disassembled) and/or needed computational and storage resources. Maybe because of these limitations, these solutions have not yet been largely adopted by the security industry.

From the existing literature, one can understand that fuzzy hashing can *sometimes* be an easy and effective solution for binary analysis problems, and yet it is unsatisfactory in many other cases; in a malware analysis scenario, fuzzy hashes seem to identify quite consistently the similarities between samples of certain malware

---

[1]We use the "fuzzy hashing" and "approximate matching" terms interchangeably.

families, and fail to capture any similarity for other families. Unfortunately, in a given practical setting, it is difficult to understand whether fuzzy hashing would be useful, or if one should rather need to use more sophisticated approaches.

To overcome these limitations, we propose a comprehensive analysis of how the main fuzzy hash families behave in three binary analysis case studies. Our first main contribution is to go beyond simply comparing and clustering malware samples: we discuss other common problems such as identifying statically-linked libraries, recognizing the same software across various releases, or detecting the same program across recompilation (with different flags or different compilers altogether). Our second main contribution is to avoid performing yet another large scale experiment on fuzzy hashing, which could provide useful statistics but does not allow for a manual inspection and verification of the results. Instead, we focus on few selected test cases with the goal of pinpointing the *reason* behind the individual results and provide practical examples of when each algorithm succeeds or fails at a given task.

Our experiments shed light on the low-level details that can completely overturn the similarity between binary files. For example, we found that the similarity is not just a consequence of the size of the change. So, a single assembly instruction modified at the right position in the program is sufficient to reduce the similarity to zero. Similarly, and against the common belief in the security community, it can also be enough to replace a URL with one that contains few more characters to destroy the similarity as captured by current fuzzy hash algorithms.

More in general, different algorithm families are based on distinct *concepts* of file similarity, and distinct problems are better solved with algorithms of different families. We find that CTPH—the concept behind ssdeep, the de-facto industry standard—is not very well suited to binary analysis in general. Depending on the problem, approaches based on n-grams (such as tlsh) or on statistically improbable features (such as sdhash) are definitely preferable.

2 BACKGROUND

Fuzzy hashes are instances of the locality-sensitive hashes (LSH) family [12]. While for traditional hashes the only meaningful operation is checking for equality, comparing LSH hashes yields non-binary similarity values, such that similar data will have similar hashes. Fuzzy hashes apply the LSH concept to arbitrary strings or files. Depending on the particular use case in which fuzzy hashes are used, different *definitions of file similarity* may be better suited. We identify three families of fuzzy hashing algorithms, which essentially differ on the concept of similarity they apply; in our experimental section, we measure how these approaches fare when they are used in the context of different binary comparison tasks.

Context-Triggered Piecewise Hashing. Context-Triggered Piecewise Hashing (CTPH) considers two files similar if they have some *identical sub-parts*. A naïve way to apply this concept would be breaking files in fixed-size blocks, hash them, and then look for collisions. Unfortunately, this simple approach is not resilient to shifts in block boundaries: for example, prepending a single byte to a file could generate different hashes for each block, hence resulting in zero similarity. This problem was first solved in the Low-Bandwidth network File System (LBFS) [20]. To find identical file chunks (and

avoid unnecessary network traffic), LBFS computes the hash of n-bytes "context" sliding windows, and places block boundaries where the first m bits of the hash are zeroes: since block boundaries only depend on the surrounding n bytes, inserting or deleting short strings of bytes only changes the hashes of few file blocks, leaving the others unchanged. Rabin fingerprints [23] were used because they are efficient to compute on sliding windows, and m is the most important parameter to tune the expected block size.

In 2002 Spamsum [28] adapted the LBFS approach to classify spam. The Spamsum fuzzy hash chooses two consecutive values of m such that each file is split in around 64 blocks; for both values of m, Spamsum encodes via base64 the least significant 6 bits of each block hash. Therefore, two spamsum hashes can be compared only if they have compatible m values (i.e., they represent files of similar size); the similarity between the two files is a function of the edit distance between the two hashes with the same m. To avoid false positives, 0 is returned if the two hashes don't have at least a 7-character substring in common. In 2006, Kornblum proposed to apply his Spamsum implementation, **ssdeep**, to forensics applications such as altered document and partial file matching [18]. This proposal was very successful and today ssdeep is used in a wide variety of cases to discover similar files.

Over the years, various improvements to ssdeep have been proposed. For example, MRSH [26] still uses CTPH to divide files, but encodes the set of hashes in Bloom filters and evaluates similarity as a function of the number of bits in common between them; this implementation obtains a better trade-off between the hash size and the quality of comparisons. **mrsh-v2** [2], which is evaluated experimentally in this work, is an improved version of MRSH. Another approach proposes Cuckoo filters [14] to further improve on hash compression at constant quality.

In general, while technical details may change, CTPH approaches are all based on the concept of recognizing identical blocks in a file. Therefore, if even small differences are widespread through the files, CPTH-based approach often fail to identify any similarity.

Statistically Improbable Features. Based on the realization that many files have frequent sequences of bytes in common (e.g., headers, zero padding, frequent words in text documents, etc.), Roussev proposed a new approach through **sdhash**, which looks for statistically improbable sequences of 64 bytes (*features*); a file's feature set file is represented in Bloom filters as done in MRSH. Since sdhash considers as related files with peculiar 64-byte substrings in common, it is particularly effective in finding cases where some parts are copied from the same source but it is less likely to detect files that have some sort of structural similarity but no longer strings in common (e.g., text files written in the same language).

N-Grams. Another approach to fuzzy hashing is based on the frequency distribution of n-grams (substrings of n bytes in a file), based on the idea that similar files will have similar n-gram frequency distributions. A first approach in this direction is Nilsimsa [8], which was proposed, like spamsum, to identify spam. Nilsimsa takes in consideration all the 5-grams in a file, and for each of them it generates the 3-grams that are sorted subsets of it (e.g., "ace" is generated from "abcce"). Each of these 3-grams is hashed into a value between 0 and 255 and an array called *accumulator* holds the counts for each of these hashes. A Nilsimsa hash is a bitmap of 256 bits

(32 bytes) where a bit is set to 1 if the corresponding value of the accumulator is larger than the median; similarity between files is computed as the number of bits in common between their bitmaps. Oliver et al. proposed `tlsh` [22], which is specifically designed for binary analysis and which we include in our experimental analysis. The main differences with Nilsimsa are that `tlsh` uses 2 bits per hash value of the accumulator (using quartiles rather than medians), a 1-byte checksum is used to recognize completely identical files, and the file length is encoded in the hash.

Summary. The approaches to fuzzy hashing described here define file similarity at a different and decreasing granularity. CTPH hashes blocks that are relevant subsets of the whole file; two files will result as similar if and only if they have rather large parts in common (e.g., a chapter in a text file). The statistically improbable features of `sdhash` are 64-byte strings; hence, `sdhash` will recognize files having such segments in common (e.g., a phrase in a text file). Finally, the *n*-gram approach of `tlsh` looks at the frequency distribution of short byte sequences; it will for example put in relations text documents that have the same or similar words, such as files written in the same language. For a more complete overview of fuzzy hashing algorithms and their applications we point the reader to the available surveys on the topic [3, 15].

3 A HISTORICAL OVERVIEW

All major fuzzy hashing algorithms were initially tested on binary files. For instance, Kornblum [18] (ssdeep) performed two simple experiments using a mutated Microsoft Word document and the header and footer of a picture in a file carving operation. Roussev [24] (sdhash) used a more comprehensive corpus with six file types (Microsoft Word and Excel, HTML, PDF, JPEG, and TXT) taken from the NPS Corpus [11]. However, none of these experiments was performed on program binaries.

In 2007, the year after `ssdeep` was first published, ShadowServer published the first study testing the algorithm's ability to detect similarities between malicious binaries [21]. The study included experiments with goals such as identifying packers, the same binary packed with different packers, or malware samples belonging to the same family. The authors concluded that `ssdeep` is neither suitable to detect similar malicious code using different packers nor to identify different programs using the same packer. However, they noticed that `ssdeep` can identify malware binaries belonging to the same family and therefore suggested other malware researchers and companies to share `ssdeep` hashes to make this comparison possible. Maybe as a result of these initial findings, over the years the security industry adopted `ssdeep` as the de facto standard fuzzy hash algorithm used for malware similarity. For example, today *VirusTotal, VirusShare, Malwr, VirusSign, Malware.lu, Malshare.com,* and *vicheck.ca* all report `ssdeep` hashes for their malware samples. However, the ShadowServer results were extracted from a small number of samples belonging to only two malware families. Moreover, the authors noticed that while for some binaries `ssdeep` performed well (even when compared across packed versions), for others the similarity was always zero. Unfortunately, they did not investigate the reason behind this phenomenon.

In 2011, Roussev published the first systematic comparison between `ssdeep` and his own `sdhash` [25]. Roussev considered three

forensically sound scenarios: embedded object detection, single, and multiple common-blocks file correlation. His work also includes a second experiment using real world files from the GovDocs corpus [11]. While these experiments did not focus on program binaries or malware samples, `sdhash` outperformed `ssdeep` in all cases.

In the following year (2012), French and Casey [10] performed a first large scale evaluation of fuzzy hashing for malware analysis, using 10M PE files from the CERT Artifact Catalog. This study is particularly important because the authors look for the first time at the internal structure of Windows PE binaries to truly understand the results of the similarity. In particular, the authors distinguish changes to the code and to the data of an executable. For the code segment, the authors recognize that "*minor changes in the original source code may have unpredictably large changes in the resulting executable*" because the compilation process can permutate, reorder, and even remove pieces of code. On the other hand, for changes to the data segment the authors conclude that "*the expected changes to the resulting executable file are directly proportional to the amount of data changed. Since we only changed the values of data—not the way in they are referenced*". As we will see in Section 7, this conclusion is not correct, and even a 1-byte change in the data of a program can completely destroy the similarity between two files.

Based on their reasoning, French and Casey divided malware families in two groups: the ones whose samples only differ for their data (*generative malware*) and the ones where there is difference in the code (*evolutionary malware*). Using experiments on 1500 samples from 13 families, the authors concluded that `ssdeep` achieved a perfect classification for some families, but an almost negligible association for others; however, it never exhibited any false positive. On the other hand, `sdhash` was better at detecting files in the same family, at the price of a small false positive rate. Sadly, the authors did not examine the cases in which fuzzy hashing worked (or in which it did not) to understand if the reason was indeed the changes localized to the data or code part of the malware sample.

In 2013, Breitinger et al. [5] proposed a framework for testing fuzzy hashing algorithms. For the *sensitivity & robustness* tests, they adopted some of the experiments previously proposed by Roussev [25] as well as new ones like the random-noise-resistance test, which shows how many bytes of an input file have to be changed to result in a non-match file. The results strongly support `sdhash` over `ssdeep`. Following their framework guidelines, Breitinger and Roussev [4] tested `sdhash`, `ssdeep`, and `mrsh-v2` on a real dataset of 4 457 files (unfortunately again containing no program binaries) and found that `ssdeep` generated less false matches, while `sdhash` provided a better trade-off between precision and recall.

With their proposal of `tlsh` in 2013, Oliver et al. evaluated their algorithm on binary files from different malware families, as well as HTML and text documents [22]. These experiments showed that `tlsh` consistently outperformed both `ssdeep` and `sdhash`.

In 2014, Azab et al. [1] tested four fuzzy hash algorithms according to their ability to perform malware clustering. Using two variants of the Zeus malware family, the authors noticed that both `ssdeep` and `sdhash` "*barely match binaries for the same version*". However, when used in conjunction with *k*-NN, both `sdhash` and `tlsh` provided good clustering results. Again, the authors did not discuss neither investigate why the tested algorithms provided results that were acceptable in certain settings and bad in others.

2015 was again a prolific year for the debate on the use of fuzzy hash in binary analysis. Li et al. [19] conducted another study on fuzzy hashing for malware clustering. Interestingly, they found that all algorithms perform better when applied to the sole code segment of the binary, instead of the entire file. The same paper also proposes three custom fuzzy hash algorithms that provided better clustering results than ssdeep and sdhash; unfortunately, two of them are file-dependent, and for none of them a public implementation was available at the time of writing.

Again in 2015, Soman presented a study in which ssdeep and sdhash were used to successfully correlate many APT samples [27], with zero false positives. Soman also found relationships among samples with differences in the code, disproving the common belief at the time and French and Casey's conclusions [10].

Finally, Upchurch and Zhou [30], tired of the inconsistent results reported by previous studies, introduced a manually verified, reproducible *Gold Standard Set* for malware similarity testing. On this dataset, the authors measured the performance of several similarity algorithms, including three of the ones studied in this paper: ssdeep, sdhash and tlsh. The paper highlights strong inconsistencies between the performance published in previous papers and the performances of the same algorithms on this new dataset (which are tipically much worse). While the authors say that the reason for this inconsistency is unknown, they point to dataset quality as the likely cause of the wide range of results. As we discuss in Section 7, this is indeed a fundamental problem—which however cannot be solved by having a Gold Standard Test, but by looking beyond the simple precision and recall values to understand how the similarity reported by fuzzy hash algorithm is tied to the type of malware family and the change in the PE files. Upchurch and Zhou also report two interesting findings about the algorithms tested in this work. First, they find that both ssdeep and sdhash provide better results at the minimum possible threshold (i.e., similarity larger than 0)—something that our own evaluation confirms. Second, this is the first independent study to compare tlsh with other fuzzy hashing algorithms on program binaries—and the results are exactly the opposite of what was reported by Oliver and Azab [1, 22], placing tlsh far behind ssdeep and sdhash.

Summary. The security community invested a considerable effort to understand if, and to which extent, fuzzy hash algorithms can identify similarities between program binaries. However, results were often contradictory; it seems that each algorithm can provide interesting results in some tests, while failing completely in other experiments.

French and Casey [10], in a report which was sadly often ignored by other works, got closer to the root of the problem. They understood that the compilation process can introduce unexpected changes after modifying even small parts of the program code. However, they felt that changes in the application data should not have this side-effect, and thus are more suitable to be captured by fuzzy hashes. Our results show that this is not the case.

To date, it is still not clear what users can expect from fuzzy hashes for binary analysis and classification. As a consequence, even academic papers have resorted to these techniques without fully understanding the consequences of their choice [7, 9, 13]. Our

study attempts to bridge this gap through our experiments in three different case studies, as discussed in the following sections.

4 SCENARIOS AND EXPERIMENTAL SETUP

Similarity hashes are often used to identify smaller objects included in a larger one, or to detecting if two objects share a considerable part of their content. Putting these two cases in the context of binary analysis, we propose three scenarios: [I] library identification in statically linked programs, [II] comparing the same applications compiled with different toolchains and/or compiler options, and [III] comparing different versions of the same application.

Scenario I is a typical binary reverse engineering task; Scenario II is a common use case for embedded systems and firmware analysis, and Scenario III corresponds to the classic example of detecting malware evolution or samples belonging to the same malware family. We selected our scenarios and experiments with two main goals: 1) to test uses of fuzzy hashes in binary analysis beyond the traditional malware similarity problem; 2) to go beyond precision/recall and true/false positive measures, and describe for the first time the intricacies of similarity matching applied to binary files and the *reason* behind the results of the different tests.

All tests were performed on a Debian Testing box equipped with an Intel Core i7-3770, running Windows 7 in a virtual machine for the experiments on PE files. The compiler toolchains used were the most recent version available at the time of the experiments: gcc-5.4.1, gcc-6.3.0, clang-3.8.1 and icc-17.0.0. To compute fuzzy hashes we used ssdeep 2.31, sdhash 3.4, mrsh-v2 and tlsh 3.4.5, all compiled from sources.

Unlike the other algorithms, which output results between 0 (no similarity) and 100 (highest similarity), tlsh returns values that start at 0 (identical files) and grow indefinitely. To ease comparison with other algorithms, we adopt the approach of Upchurch and Zhou [30], re-normalizing tlsh scores to the [0, 100] range.[2]

No packing or obfuscation was applied to the binaries used in the experiments. These transformations heavily alter the binary destroying the similarity picked up by fuzzy hashing algorithms, and we consider them outside the scope of this work.

5 SCENARIO I: LIBRARY IDENTIFICATION

The goal of this first scenario is to understand if fuzzy hashes can be used to recognize object files embedded inside a statically linked binary. This task is an application of the *embedded object detection* test proposed and already analyzed by the forensics community [25].

Since static linking is much more common in the Linux environment than in Microsoft Windows, we evaluate five popular Linux libraries (libcapstone, libevent, libjpeg, libm and libtsan). Static libraries are ar archives of relocatable object files (22 to 453 in our case). We linked each library against a small C program, obtaining five different executables.[3]

5.1 Object-to-Program Comparison

In the first test, we compute the similarity score by comparing each executable against all the individual object files contained in the static libraries. We repeated the test twice, once using the

---

[2] We renormalize a score x to $y = \max\{0, (300 - x)/3\}$.
[3] By default, the linker only includes files required by symbols and functions imported by the program; for this test, we forced including the object files of tested libraries.

Table 1: Library identification: true/false positive rates.

Algorithm	Entire object			.text segment		
	TP%	FP%	Err%	TP%	FP%	Err%
ssdeep	0	0	-	0	0	-
mrsh-v2	11.7	0.5	-	7.7	0.2	-
sdhash	**12.8**	**0**	-	**24.4**	0.1	53.9
tlsh	0.4	0.1	-	0.2	**0.1**	41.7

entire .o ELF files, and once matching only their .text segments (which does not take into consideration other sections and file headers that are not linked in the final executable). Table 1 shows the results of the two tests. We considered a successful match if ssdeep, sdhash, or mrsh-v2 returned a similarity of at least 1 over 100 and tlsh returned a value lower than 300 (before the re-normalization described in Section 4).[4] The "Err" column reports instead cases in which the data was insufficient to even compute the fuzzy hash. The results were computed over 647 individual object files and false positives were computed using the same threshold, this time by matching the object files of libraries *not* linked in the executable.

These results show that not even the best algorithm in this case (sdhash) can link the individual object files and the corresponding statically-linked executables reliably enough. The worst performing one (ssdeep) *always* returned a score equal to zero, making it completely unsuitable for this scenario. In the next tests, we explore the factors that contribute to these negative results.

5.2 Impact of Library Fragmentation

In our experiments, statically-compiled binaries were larger than 1MB while the average non-empty library object file was smaller than 13KB: this difference makes the task of locating each fragment very difficult. CTPH solutions need files with comparable sizes; previous studies show that ssdeep works only if the embedded chunk is at least a third of the target file size [25].

Since size difference is certainly a major obstacle for this task, one may think that this problem can be mitigated by matching all object files at once, instead of one at a time. Even if the correct order is unknown, the presence of multiple fragments should improve the overall matching process - as this setup would shift the problem from the detection of a single embedded object to the easier problem of matching multiple common blocks [25].

To test if this is indeed the case, we concatenated all the library objects and all their .text sections in two different files, and then matched these files against the statically linked binaries. The experiment was repeated 100 times, each using a different random order of object concatenation. The best results were obtained by concatenating the full objects (probably due to strings stored in the data section). For example, in the case of libjpeg, fuzzy hashes were unable to match 59% of the individual object files and for the remaining sdhash (the best solution) gave an average score of 21. By concatenating all the object files and matching the resulting blob, sdhash returned 14. While this score could still be sufficient to

---

[4]We experimented with higher threshold values, but—confirming the findings of Upchurch and Zhou [30] discussed in Section 3—these values performed best.

identify the library, remember that this is a best-case scenario as all the library object files were forcefully linked to the final executable.

To confirm whether the same result can also be obtained in a more realistic setting, we downloaded and statically compiled two real world programs, one using libjpeg, which had a 14 similarity score in the concatenation approach—and the other using libevent, which did not match at all in the same experiment. In this case, the sdhash similarity score decreased to 9 for libjpeg, while it remained zero for libevent.

5.3 Impact of Relocation

Relocation is the process, applied by the linker or by the dynamic loader, of adjusting addresses and offsets inside a program to reflect the actual position of symbols in memory. Static libraries contains relocatable objects, which means that the code of those object files contains several place-holders that are later filled by the linker when the file is included in the final executable.

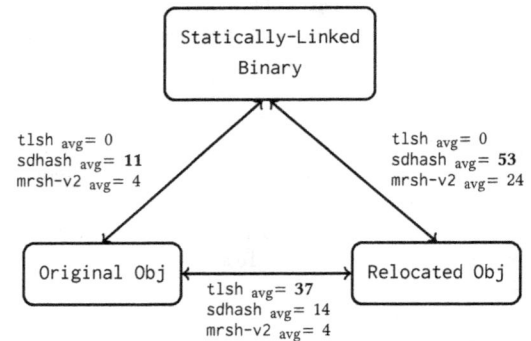

Figure 1: Average similarities after linking/relocation.

To understand the impact of relocation on similarity scores, we extracted the .text segments of library object files from the final binaries *after* relocations were applied by the linker. This version, which we call *relocated obj*, has the same size of the original object file, but in different bytes spread across its code a relocation was applied to a pointer. We used these files to perform two different comparisons, which are presented in Figure 1: the first is between the *relocated* and the *non relocated* versions of the same object, while the second is between the relocated object and the final executable.

On average, sdhash returns strong similarities between relocated objects and final binaries; this is in line with the *embedded object detection* results by Roussev [25], who showed that sdhash can detect files embedded in targets that are up to 10 times bigger than them. However, sdhash fails to recognize similarities between the relocated and not relocated versions of the same object file—thus showing that the relocation process is the main culprit for the poor results of sdhash. This confirms the *random-noise-resistance* test conducted by Breitinger and Bayer [5], who found that sdhash assigns scores greater than 10 only if less than 1% of the bytes are randomly changed. In our tests, the relocation process changes on average 10% of the object bytes, thus causing sdhash to fail.

Interestingly, for tlsh the behavior is the opposite. In fact, tlsh assigns high similarity to the two versions of the .text section (relocated and not relocated), but it is unable to match them against the final program, suggesting that in this case relocation is not the main obstacle. Figure 1 does not report results for ssdeep because it always returns a zero similarity in all tests.

Overall, we can summarize the results of the three tests we performed in this Scenario by stating that matching a static library to a statically linked binary is a difficult task, which is complicated by three main factors: 1) the fact that libraries are broken in many object files and only a subset of them is typically linked to the final executable; 2) the fact that each object file is often very small compared with the size of the statically linked binary; and 3) the fact that the content of the object files is modified (with an average byte change-rate of 10%) by the linker. Some classes of fuzzy hash algorithms are able to cope with some of these problems, but the combination of the three factors is problematic for all solutions. In fact, the *n*-gram approach of tlsh falls short when recognizing similarities between the (small) relocated object and the (large) statically-linked binary and the statistically improbable features recognized by sdhash get broken by the relocation process.

6 SCENARIO II: RE-COMPILATION

The goal of the second scenario is to recognize the same program across re-compilations—by evaluating the effect of the toolchain on the similarity scores. In particular, we look at the separate impact of the compiler and of the compilation flags used to produce the final executable. There are no previous studies about this problem, but researchers have commented that changes to the compilation process can introduce differences that hamper fuzzy hashing algorithms [10]. This scenario is also relevant to the problem of identifying vulnerable binary programs across many devices, even when libraries or software have been compiled with different options.

We test this scenario on two different sets of programs. The first one (Coreutils) contains five popular small programs (base64, cp, ls, sort, and tail) having size between 32K and 156KB each, while the second dataset (Large) contains five common larger binaries (httpd, openssl, sqlite3, ssh, and wireshark), with sizes ranging between 528KB and 7.9MB. All the experiments were repeated on four distinct versions of each program, and the results represent the average of the individual runs.

6.1 Effect of Compiler Flags

Since the number of possible flags combinations is extremely high, we limited our analysis to the sets associated to the optimization levels proposed by gcc. The first level (-O0) disables every optimization and is tipically used to ease debugging; the next three levels (-O1,-O2 and -O3) enable increasing sets of optimizations. Finally, -Os applies a subset of the -O2 flags plus other transformations to reduce the final executable size. Each test was repeated twice, once by comparing the whole binaries and once by comparing only the .text section. The first provides better results, and therefore for the sake of space we will mainly report on this case.

Results are shown in matrix plots (Figures 2 and 6–8). Histograms below the diagonal show the individual results distributions (with similarity on the X axis and percentage of the samples on the Y axis). For each algorithm, the threshold was chosen as the most conservative value that produced zero false matches. Values above the diagonal show the percentage of comparisons with a similarity

greater than the threshold value. All the similarity scores used in the figure are between true positives.

We find that neither ssdeep nor its successor mrsh-v2 can reliably correlate Coreutils programs compiled at different optimization levels. However, neither algorithm ever returned a positive score when comparing unrelated binary files: hence, any result greater than zero from these tools can be considered a true match. sdhash returned low similarity scores in average (in the range 0-10) but by setting the threshold to 4 the tool generated zero false matches and was able to detect some of the utilities across all optimization levels. Finally, tlsh deserves a separate discussion. From a first glance at the matrix plot, its performance may appear very poor; this is because the graph was generated by setting the threshold at zero FP. To better understand its behavior we increased the threshold leaving 1%, 5% and 10% FP rates. Figure 6 presents the results: tlsh matches programs compiled with -O1, -O2, -O3 and -Os but cannot match programs compiled with -O0. This is reasonable as -O0 has zero optimization flags while -O1 already uses more than 50.

The picture changes slightly when testing the Large dataset programs. In this case, sdhash clearly outperforms all the other algorithms, always returning zero to unrelated files and always giving a score greater than zero to related ones.

A closer look at the data shows that all algorithms perform better using the entire file because data sections (e.g., .rodata) can remain constant when changing compiler flags. By looking at the .text section only one program was matched: openssl, which was constantly recognized also across optimization levels. We investigated this case by comparing all functions using the radiff utility, and found that many functions were unchanged even with very different compilation flags. The reason is that openssl includes many hand-written assembly routines that the compiler has to transcribe and assemble as-is, with no room for optimization.

6.2 Different Compilers

In this test we compiled each program in the Large dataset using all five optimization flags and using four different compilers: clang-3.8, gcc-5, gcc-6 and icc-17 - the Intel C compiler. The compilation process resulted in 100 distinct binaries. We then performed an all-to-all comparison with all fuzzy hash algorithms, considering as true positives the same programs compiled with a different compiler and true negatives different programs independently to the compiler used. Figure 3 summarizes the results using the matrix plot format already introduced for the previous experiment. Thresholds are again specific for each algorithm and computed to obtain a zero false positive rate.

Even if the results are better than in the previous experiment, ssdeep still performs worst. sdhash, tlsh and mrsh-v2 successfully matched all programs between gcc-5 and gcc-6 except sqlite (this is the reason why they all have 96% detection). This is because the sqlite version used (*sqlite-amalgamation*) merges the entire sqlite codebase in one single large (136k lines long) C file. This results in a single compilation unit, which gives the compiler more room to optimize (and therefore change) the code. We again show tlsh's behavior using different false positive rates in Figure 9.

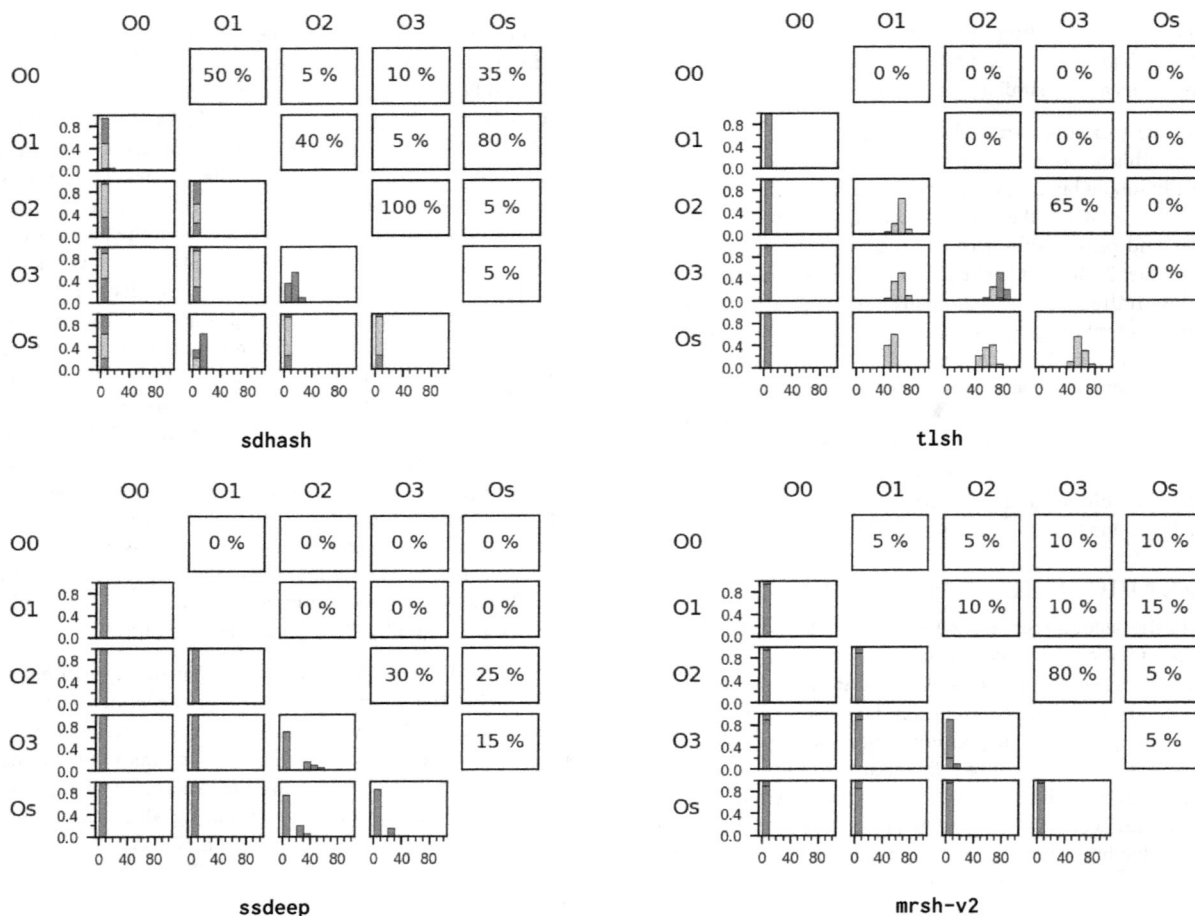

Figure 2: Coreutils compiled with different optimization levels. Red bars represent scores equal to 0, yellow bars scores below the threshold (chosen to have 0% false positive rate), green bars scores above the threshold.

7 SCENARIO III: PROGRAM SIMILARITY

Our third scenario explores one of the most interesting and common use cases for fuzzy hashing in binary analysis: the ability to correlate similar software artifacts. In our experiments we consider three types of similarity (all computed by maintaining the compilation toolchain constant): 1) binaries that originate from the same exact source code, but to whom few small changes have been applied at the assembly level; 2) binaries that originate from sources that are only different for few instructions, and 3) binaries compiled from different versions of the same software. Finally, we will compare between malware belonging to the same families to understand why fuzzy hashes work in some cases but not in others.

7.1 Small Assembly Differences

We start by assessing the impact of small-scale modifications at the assembly level, to understand their macroscopic impact on the similarity of binary programs. We apply this test to the stripped version of ssh-client, a medium-size program containing over 150K assembly instructions. We consider two very simple transformations: 1) randomly inserting NOP instructions in the binary,

and 2) randomly swapping a number of instructions in the program. These transformation were implemented as target specific LLVM Pass which run very late during the compilation process. The results, obtained by repeating the experiment 100 times and averaging the similarity, are presented in Figures 4 and 5. To ease plot readability, we smoothed the curves using a moving average.

At first, the curves may seem quite counter-intuitive. In fact, the similarity seems to drop very fast (e.g., it is enough to randomly swap 10 instructions out of over 150K to drop the sdhash score to 38 and ssdeep to zero) even when more than 99.99% of the program remains unchanged. Actually, if the plots were not averaging the results over multiple runs, the picture would look much worse. For example, we observed cases in which the similarity score went to zero when just two NOP instructions were inserted in the binary. By manually investigating these cases, we realized that this phenomenon is due to the combination of three factors: the padding introduced by the compiler between functions, the padding added by the linker at the end of the .text section, and the position in which the instruction is added. In the right conditions, just few bytes are enough to increase the overall size of the code segment.

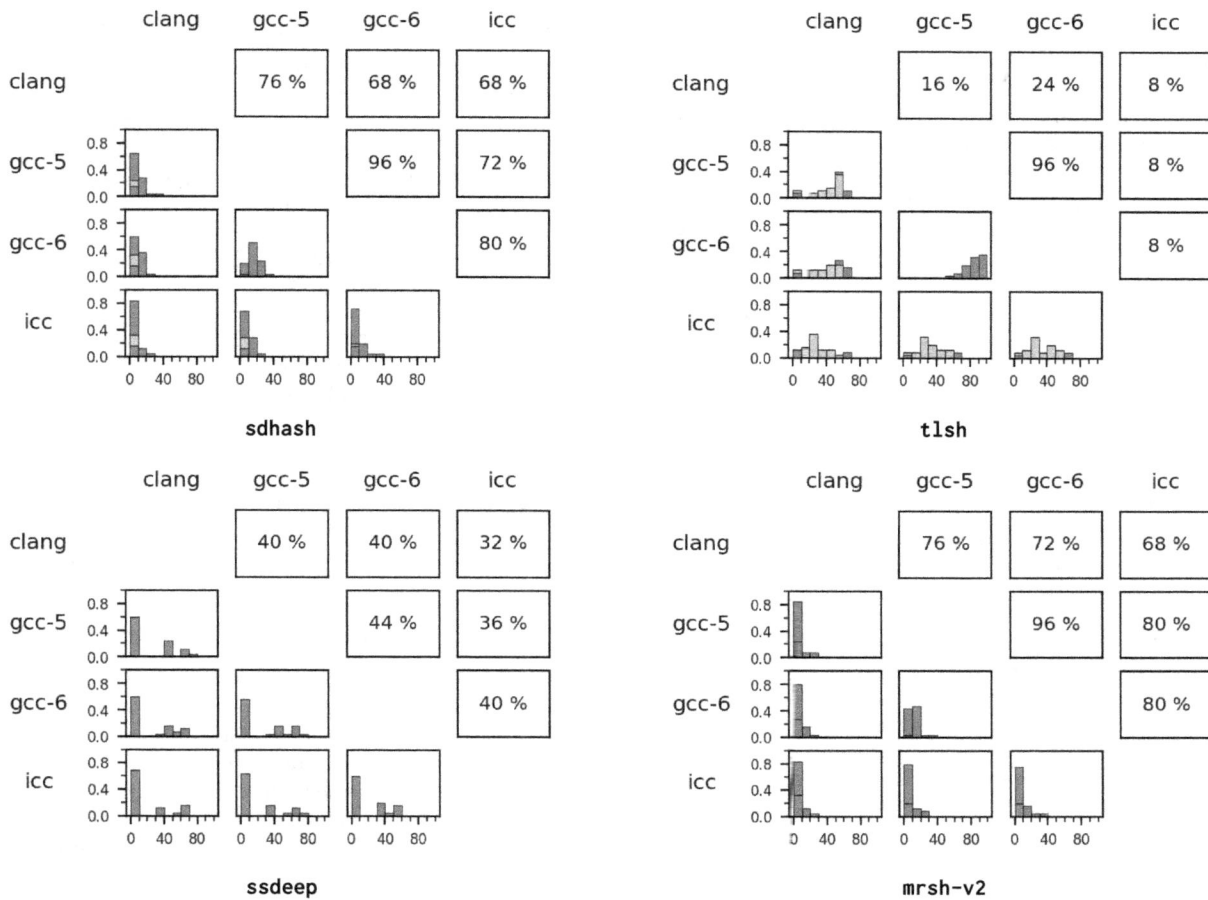

Figure 3: Large programs compiled with different compilers.

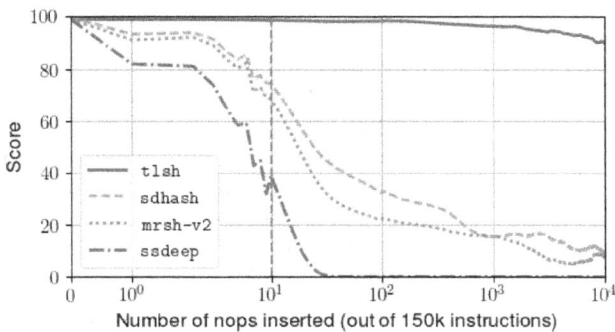

Figure 4: Inserting NOPs in random points of the program.

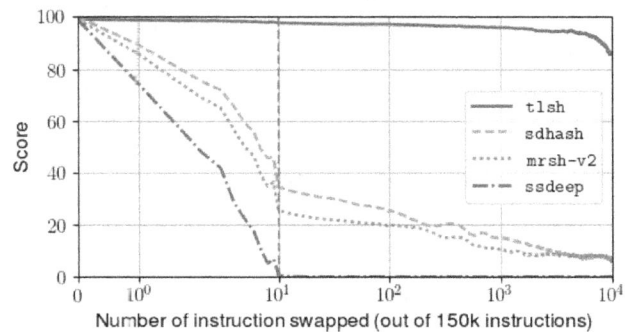

Figure 5: Swapping instructions.

As a side-effect, the successive sections are also shifted forward. The most relevant in our case is .rodata, which is located just after the .text section in memory. Shifting down this section triggers a large chain reaction in which all references in the code to global symbols are adjusted, introducing a multitude of changes spread over the .text section. Moreover, a substantial number of other sections needs to be adjusted: for example, consider the case where

the same .rodata contains a jump table with relative offset to the code. Being 16 bytes farther, all these offsets needs to be adjusted as well. Another example is .data, which contains pointers to rodata. In total, adding two NOPs generated changes over 8 distinct sections.

To confirm this phenomenon, we wrote a linker script to increase the padding between .text and .rodata. This way, increases in the .text section size don't impact the position of .rodata. With this modification, the same two NOPs have a more limited effect, and all four algorithms are able to match the two binaries.

This effect is more pronounced in Linux than in Windows binaries. In fact, in Linux the default settings for gcc align both functions and sections at 16 bytes. In Windows the picture is quite different: we analyzed PE files downloaded from Internet and part of the Windows Server 2012 R2 and Windows 7 installations. While some executables don't have padding between functions, others - similarly to Linux - align functions to 16 bytes. On the other hand, the offset inside the file of every section has the lower 9 bits cleared, which effectively aligns each Section to 512 bytes. This makes Windows binaries more 'resistant' to small instructions insertion.

The only algorithm that does not seem to be affected by these microscopic changes is tlsh, which thanks to its frequency-based nature is able to maintain a high similarity even when 10K NOPs are inserted or instructions are swapped.

7.2 Minor Source Code Modifications

We now examine more traditional changes between programs, through small modifications to the source code of ssh-client. We intentionally selected changes that do not add or remove lines of code from the program:

- *Different comparison operator.* This can modify the binary in very different ways. For example, after changing a "<" to a "≤", scores remained high since the difference between binaries was just one byte. At the other end of the spectrum, compilers can statically detect that some branches are never taken and remove them from the code; in these cases, the ssdeep score was always 0.

- *New condition.* Again, results are quite unpredictable. Compilers can generate a few additional instructions to perform the added check, and the macroscopic effect of those instructions depends on their location and on the padding of functions and sections.

- *Change a constant value.* Effects are again hard to predict. For example, setting constants to zero can change the resulting assembly instructions (to zero a variable compilers typically emit an xor rather than a mov). Size also plays a role since the Intel instruction set offers different encodings depending on it.

Table 2: Similarity ranges for manual changes to openssh.

Change	ssdeep	mrsh-v2	tlsh	sdhash
Operator	0–**100**	21–**100**	**99**–**100**	22–**100**
Condition	0–**100**	22–99	**96**–99	37–**100**
Constant	0–97	28–99	**97**–99	35–**100**

Table 2 shows the similarity score ranges for the three experiments. Again, tlsh is immune to these small changes. In fact, while a single change to the source file may result in widespread changes through the binary, it is very unlikely to modify significantly the *n*-gram histogram. Other algorithms provides inconsistent results, ranging from perfect matches to poor ones (or no match at all for ssdeep) due to the chain effects described above.

7.3 Source Code Modifications On Malware

Our final experiment uses two real-world malware programs: Grum and Mirai. We chose those two malware families because: 1) the source code for both is available online, allowing us to compile different "variants" of each, and 2) they cover both Windows (Grum) and Linux (Mirai) environments. This experiment lets us test in a real setting the insights we gained previously.

Table 3: Manual modifications applied to malware. "M" and "G" stand respectively for "Mirai" and "Grum".

Change	ssdeep		mrsh-v2		tlsh		sdhash	
	M	G	M	G	M	G	M	G
C&C domain (real)	0	0	97	10	**99**	**88**	98	24
C&C domain (long)	0	0	44	13	**94**	**84**	72	22
Evasion	0	0	17	0	**93**	**87**	16	34
Functionality	0	0	9	0	**88**	**84**	22	7

We selected again three types of changes, reflecting differences we can expect between malware samples of the same family:

- *New C&C Domain*: we changed the Command and Control (C&C) server that the bots contact to fetch commands. Since in both cases the C&C had a default value, we decided to set it to one domain associated to the real Mirai Botnet (*real domain* in Table 3) or to an 11-character longer domain name (*long domain* in Table 3). In both malware, C&Cs are defined inside the code and not read from a configuration file, so we are sure the modification affects the compiled binary.

- *Evasion*: this modification uses real anti-analysis tricks to detect the presence of a debugger or if the sample is running inside a virtual machine. The implementation of the anti-VM function is based on timing measurements, while the anti-debugging mechanism is built around the Windows API IsDebuggerPresent from Grum and ptrace from Mirai. The cumulative sizes of these two functions is 110 bytes for Grum and 80 bytes for Mirai.

- *New Functionality*: in this case we added a malicious functionality to collect and send to the C&C the list of users present on the infected system. For Grum we used the Windows API NetUserEnum to retrieve the users, while for Mirai glibc's getpwent was used. In terms of size, Grum's functionality adds 414 bytes to the bot binary, while Mirai's one added 416 bytes.

Results are presented in Table 3. As expected, the introduction of a longer domain name had a larger impact on the similarity. In particular this is the case for Mirai, which is statically compiled. In this case, the linker combined in the final .rodata both the data from Mirai itself and the glibc one. The C&C string, in both experiments, is placed towards the end of the *.rodata* part reserved for Mirai, but growth is absorbed by the padding and is not enough to move the libc .rodata. This means that the only references that needs to be adjusted are those of Mirai, while the libc blob remains the same. The longer domain was instead larger than the padding between the "two" .rodata, causing the libc's .rodata to shift down and impact all the glibc's references.

A second observation is that in this experiment Windows variants have lower similarity than their Linux counterparts. While this seems to contradict the results presented in the previous test, the reason is that the Linux binary is statically compiled and therefore—despite the changes to the botnet code—the two binaries share big chunks of glibc code. At a closer look, we confirmed that the "Evasion" binary shares exactly the same section offsets (and thus have a good similarity score), while in the "Functionality" binaries (lower similarity) the sections are shifted down by 512 bytes.

Finally, as already shown in the previous experiments, the ability of ssdeep to compare binary files is very limited.

7.4 New Insights on Previous Experiments

In this final test we take a closer look at a malware dataset used in a previous study, to test if what we learned so far allows us to better understand the results of past experiments. Intrigued by the good results scored by ssdeep in the recent work by Upchurch and Zhou [30], and thanks to the fact that the authors shared the MD5s of the 85 samples used in their dataset, we retrieved the same set of files and use it for this final test. The samples, all manually verified by the authors [30], belong to eight different families.

We manually investigated all cases in which ssdeep was able to capture the similarity between files of the same family (it was the case for five of them) and found some interesting results. In two cases, the similarity was the consequence of the fact that different *dropper* files contained exactly the same second-stage program embedded in their data. In another family, 17 out of 19 files have exactly the same .data and .text sections, and 10 of them only differ in a few padding bytes at the end of the file, in what is commonly called the *file overlay*. However, since the overlay counter was zero in the PE header, it is possible that this files just contained few additional bytes because of the way they were acquired. A similar phenomenon affected also another family, in which 3 out of 6 matches were identical files except for the very last byte.

Overall, ssdeep was indeed able to match some different malware samples, but this happened on files that either differed only for cosmetic aspects or had large common files embedded in them.

The last and most interesting case was a family in which all similar samples had the same rdata section and all the section start at the same address/file offset (and therefore have the same size). In this case, a manual analysis revealed that samples shared large chunks of their code, with the only differences in the .text section located in parts that did not contain valid instructions (so probably related to some form of packing mechanism). In this case, due to the perfect match of the remaining part and on the fact that no offset or instruction was modified among the files, ssdeep successfully captured the similar malware samples.

7.5 Scenario III Findings Summary

In this third and last scenario we studied why it can be difficult to capture program modifications through fuzzy hashing algorithms. If we assume the compilation process is maintained constant among consecutive versions (we discussed its impact in the previous scenarios) we can now distinguish two cases.

If the programmer only modifies the application data (such as strings, URLs, paths and file names, global numerical constants, domain names or IP addresses) then we can expect a high similarity if the data size is not changed (e.g., if the new URL contains the exact same characters of the previous one). Otherwise, the impact depends on the number of references from the code section to data stored after the one that has been modified. In the worst case, for CTPH-based approaches and, to a minor extent, for sdhash, it can be enough to change few bytes in a filename to completely destroy any fuzzy hash similarity between the two versions.

It is also worth mentioning that not all "data" is part of the traditional data sections. PE files can also have overlays—i.e. bytes appended at the end of the file after all sections—and malware can embed entire files inside them. In these cases fuzzy hashes shine, as they can reliably capture the similarity between different binaries.

If the programmer modifies instead the code of the application, then the factors that affect the similarity are the size of the modification, how distributed it is on the entire code section, the function alignment used by the compiler, and the segment alignment used by the linker. Again, our experiments show that it is possible to have entirely new functions that barely modify the similarity, as well as cases in which just two NOPs can bring down the similarity computed by CTPH algorithms to zero.

Unlike the previous case, which was largely dominated by sdhash, tlsh shines in this scenario. In this case, the small changes applied to the assembly or source code have a very minor impact over the statistics about *n*-gram frequencies that tlsh uses.

8 CONCLUSIONS

This study sheds light on how fuzzy hashing algorithms behave in program analysis tasks, to help practitioners understand *if* fuzzy hashing can be used in their particular context and, if so, *which* algorithm is the best choice for the task: an important problem that is not answered conclusively by the existing literature.

Unfortunately, we found that the CTPH approach adopted by ssdeep—the most widely used fuzzy hashing algorithm—falls short in most tasks. We have found that other approaches (sdhash's statistically improbable features and tlsh's *n*-gram frequency distribution) perform way better; more in particular, we have found that sdhash performs well when recognizing the same program compiled in different ways, and that tlsh is instead very reliable in recognizing variants of the same software when the code changes.

Instead of blindly applying algorithms to recognize malware families and collecting difficult to interpret results, our evaluation looked at the details of both hashing algorithms and the compilation process: this allowed us to discover why fuzzy hashing algorithms can fail, sometimes surprisingly, in recognizing the similarity between programs that have undergone only very minor changes.

In conclusion, we show that tlsh and sdhash consistently outperform ssceep and should be recommended in its place (tlsh is preferable when dealing with source code changes, and sdhash works better when changes involve the compilation toolchain); our analysis on where and why hashing algorithms are or are not effective sheds light on the impact of implementation choices, and can be used as a guideline towards the design of new algorithms.

REFERENCES

[1] Ahmad Azab, Robert Layton, Mamoun Alazab, and Jonathan Oliver. 2014. Mining malware to detect variants. In *Cybercrime and Trustworthy Computing Conference (CTC), 2014 Fifth*. IEEE, 44–53.

[2] Frank Breitinger and Harald Baier. 2012. Similarity preserving hashing: Eligible properties and a new algorithm MRSH-v2. In *International Conference on Digital Forensics and Cyber Crime*. Springer, 167–182.

[3] Frank Breitinger, Barbara Guttman, Michael McCarrin, Vassil Roussev, and Douglas White. 2014. Approximate matching: definition and terminology. *NIST Special Publication* 800 (2014), 168.

[4] Frank Breitinger and Vassil Roussev. 2014. Automated evaluation of approximate matching algorithms on real data. *Digital Investigation* 11 (2014), S10–S17.

[5] Frank Breitinger, Georgios Stivaktakis, and Harald Baier. 2013. FRASH: A framework to test algorithms of similarity hashing. In *Digital Investigation*, Vol. 10. Elsevier, S50–S58.

[6] Sagar Chaki, Cory Cohen, and Arie Gurfinkel. 2011. Supervised learning for provenance-similarity of binaries. In *Proceedings of the 17th ACM SIGKDD international conference on Knowledge discovery and data mining*. ACM, 15–23.

[7] Andrei Costin, Jonas Zaddach, Aurélien Francillon, Davide Balzarotti, and Sophia Antipolis. 2014. A Large-Scale Analysis of the Security of Embedded Firmwares.. In *USENIX Security*. 95–110.

[8] Ernesto Damiani, Sabrina De Capitani di Vimercati, Stefano Paraboschi, and Pierangela Samarati. 2004. An Open Digest-based Technique for Spam Detection. *ISCA PDCS* 2004 (2004), 559–564.

[9] Parvez Faruki, Vijay Laxmi, Ammar Bharmal, Manoj Singh Gaur, and Vijay Ganmoor. 2015. AndroSimilar: Robust signature for detecting variants of Android malware. *Journal of Information Security and Applications* 22 (2015), 66–80.

[10] David French and William Casey. 2012. Two Fuzzy Hashing Techniques in Applied Malware Analysis. *Results of SEI Line-Funded Exploratory New Starts Projects* (2012), 2.

[11] Simson Garfinkel, Paul Farrell, Vassil Roussev, and George Dinolt. 2009. Bringing science to digital forensics with standardized forensic corpora. *digital investigation* 6 (2009), S2–S11.

[12] Aristides Gionis, Piotr Indyk, Rajeev Motwani, et al. 1999. Similarity search in high dimensions via hashing. In *VLDB*. 518–529.

[13] Mariano Graziano, Davide Canali, Leyla Bilge, Andrea Lanzi, and Davide Balzarotti. 2015. Needles in a Haystack: Mining Information from Public Dynamic Analysis Sandboxes for Malware Intelligence.. In *USENIX Security*. 1057–1072.

[14] Vikas Gupta and Frank Breitinger. 2015. How cuckoo filter can improve existing approximate matching techniques. In *International Conference on Digital Forensics and Cyber Crime*. Springer, 39–52.

[15] Vikram S Harichandran, Frank Breitinger, and Ibrahim Baggili. 2016. Bytewise Approximate Matching: The Good, The Bad, and The Unknown. *The Journal of Digital Forensics, Security and Law: JDFSL* 11, 2 (2016), 59.

[16] Jiyong Jang, David Brumley, and Shobha Venkataraman. 2011. Bitshred: feature hashing malware for scalable triage and semantic analysis. In *Proceedings of the 18th ACM conference on Computer and communications security*. ACM, 309–320.

[17] Dhilung Kirat, Lakshmanan Nataraj, Giovanni Vigna, and BS Manjunath. 2013. Sigmal: A static signal processing based malware triage. In *Proceedings of the 29th Annual Computer Security Applications Conference*. ACM, 89–98.

[18] Jesse Kornblum. 2006. Identifying almost identical files using context triggered piecewise hashing. *Digital investigation* 3 (2006), 91–97.

[19] Yuping Li, Sathya Chandran Sundaramurthy, Alexandru G Bardas, Xinming Ou, Doina Caragea, Xin Hu, and Jiyong Jang. 2015. Experimental study of fuzzy hashing in malware clustering analysis. In *8th Workshop on Cyber Security Experimentation and Test (CSET 15)*.

[20] Athicha Muthitacharoen, Benjie Chen, and David Mazieres. 2001. A low-bandwidth network file system. In *ACM SIGOPS Operating Systems Review*.

[21] Digital Ninja. 2007. Fuzzy Clarity: Using Fuzzy Hashing Techniques to Identify Malicious Code. http://www.shadowserver.org/wiki/uploads/Information/FuzzyHashing.pdf. (2007).

[22] Jonathan Oliver, Chun Cheng, and Yanggui Chen. 2013. TLSH–A Locality Sensitive Hash. In *Cybercrime and Trustworthy Computing Workshop (CTC)*.

[23] Michael O Rabin et al. 1981. *Fingerprinting by random polynomials*. Center for Research in Computing Techn., Aiken Computation Laboratory, Univ.

[24] Vassil Roussev. 2010. Data fingerprinting with similarity digests. In *IFIP International Conference on Digital Forensics*. Springer, 207–226.

[25] Vassil Roussev. 2011. An evaluation of forensic similarity hashes. *digital investigation* 8 (2011), S34–S41.

[26] Vassil Roussev, Golden G Richard, and Lodovico Marziale. 2007. Multi-resolution similarity hashing. *digital investigation* 4 (2007), 105–113.

[27] Bhavna Soman. 2015. Ninja Correlation of APT Binaries. *First* (2015).

[28] Andrew Tridgell. 2002. spamsum. https://www.samba.org/ftp/unpacked/junkcode/spamsum/README. (2002).

[29] Andrew Tridgell. 2002. Spamsum readme. https://www.samba.org/ftp/unpacked/junkcode/spamsum/README. (2002).

[30] Jason Upchurch and Xiaobo Zhou. 2015. Variant: a malware similarity testing framework. In *2015 10th International Conference on Malicious and Unwanted Software (MALWARE)*. IEEE, 31–39.

[31] Georg Wicherski. 2009. peHash: A Novel Approach to Fast Malware Clustering. *LEET* 9 (2009), 8.

9 APPENDIX

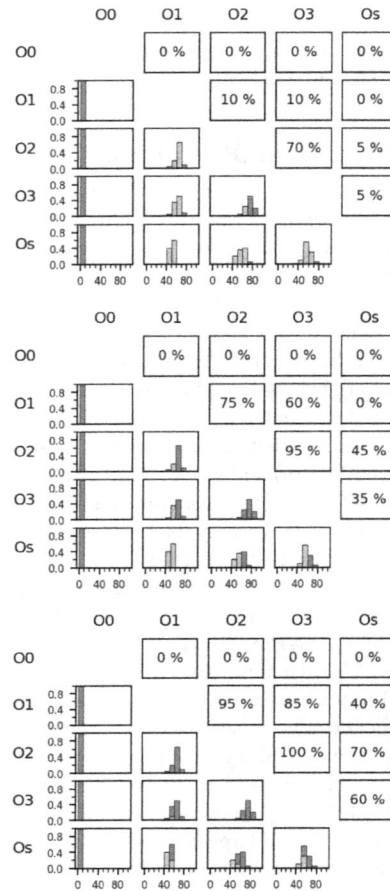

Figure 6: `tlsh` behavior on Coreutils while varying thresholds: from top to bottom, 1%, 5% and 10% false positives.

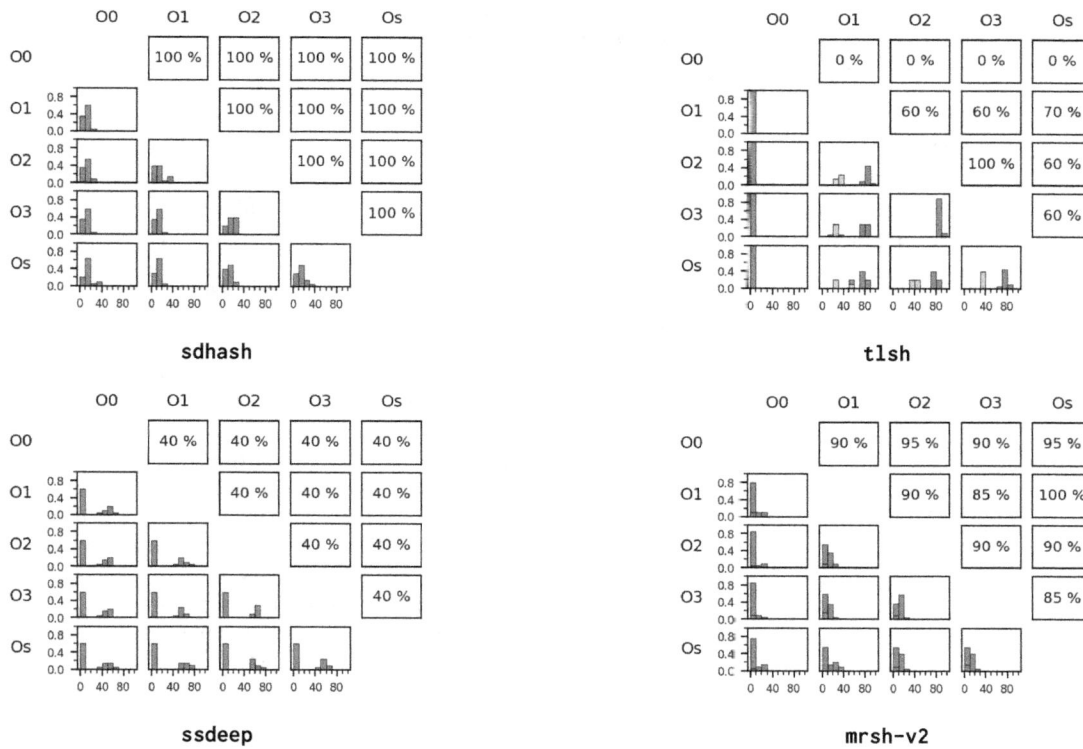

Figure 7: Programs included in the Large dataset, compiled with different optimization levels.

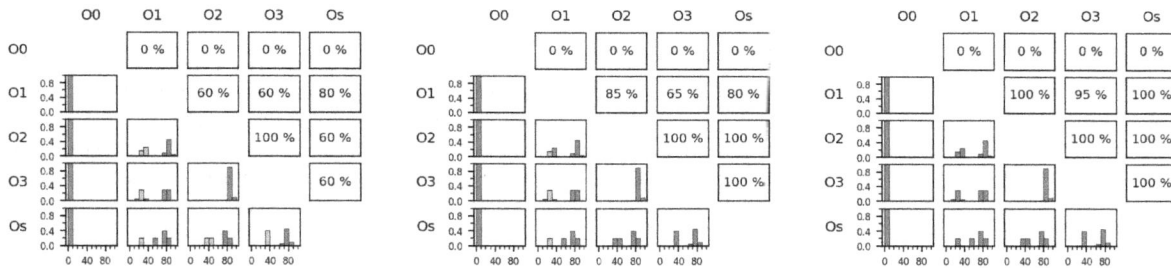

Figure 8: tlsh on the Large dataset, varying optimization levels and thresholds: from left to right, 1%, 5% and 10% false positives.

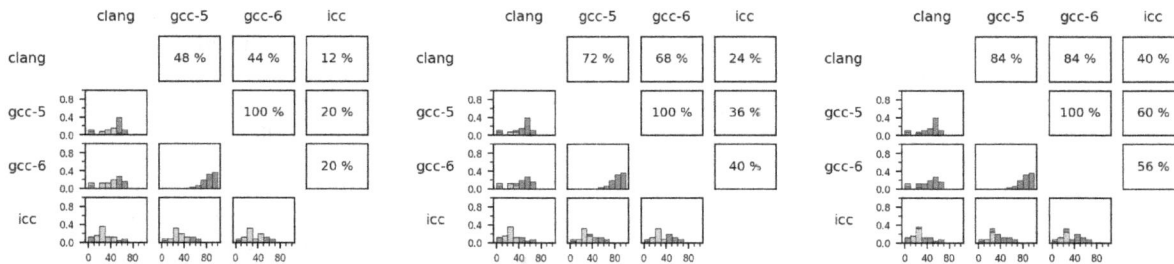

Figure 9: tlsh on the Large dataset, varying compilers and thresholds: from left to right, 1%, 5% and 10% false positives.

From Debugging-Information Based Binary-Level Type Inference to CFG Generation

Dongrui Zeng
Pennsylvania State University
State Collge, PA, USA
dongrui.zeng@gmail.com

Gang Tan
Pennsylvania State University
State Collge, PA, USA
gtan@cse.psu.edu

ABSTRACT

Binary-level Control-Flow Graph (CFG) construction is essential for applications such as control-flow integrity. There are two main approaches: the binary-analysis approach and the compiler-modification approach. The binary-analysis approach does not require source code, but it constructs low-precision CFGs. The compiler-modification approach requires source code and modifies compilers for CFG generation. We describe the design and implementation of an alternative system for high-precision CFG construction, which still assumes source code but does not modify compilers. Our approach makes use of standard compiler-generated meta-information, including symbol tables, relocation information, and debugging information. A key component in the system is a type-inference engine that infers types of low-level storage locations such as registers from types in debugging information. Inferred types enable a type-signature matching method for high-precision CFG construction.

CCS CONCEPTS

• **Security and privacy → Software reverse engineering**;

KEYWORDS

Control flow graphs; type inference; debugging information

ACM Reference Format:
Dongrui Zeng and Gang Tan. 2018. From Debugging-Information Based Binary-Level Type Inference to CFG Generation. In *CODASPY '18: Eighth ACM Conference on Data and Application Security and Privacy, March 19–21, 2018, Tempe, AZ, USA.* ACM, New York, NY, USA, 11 pages. https://doi.org/10.1145/3176258.3176309

1 INTRODUCTION

A program's Control-Flow Graph (CFG) is a representation of the program's possible control flows. Constructing CFGs for binary programs is a necessary step for many security applications. A prominent example is Control-Flow Integrity (CFI [1]), which enforces a binary-level CFG on a program to mitigate control-flow hijacking attacks such as Return-Oriented Programming [25]. Another example is binary-level program analysis (e.g., [4, 9, 24, 26, 34, 35]) including symbolic execution, taint analysis, program slicing, testing-suite

generation, and liveness analysis, which all require the CFG of a binary program to operate. Finally, binary rewriting (e.g., [1, 29, 31]) requires CFGs to rewrite code for security.

The main difficulty of constructing binary-level CFGs is to compute control-flow targets for indirect branches, which include return instructions, indirect jumps (jumps via register or memory operands), and indirect calls (function calls via register or memory operands). Since indirect-branch targets depend on values that are computed at runtime, it is challenging to predict them statically.

Researchers have explored two main approaches for binary-level CFG construction: the binary-analysis approach and the compiler-modification approach. The *binary-analysis* approach [19, 28, 36, 37] analyzes binary code and its contained information for CFG construction and has the benefit of not requiring source-code availability. However, the drawback is that its constructed CFGs are of low precision, for the reason that binary code lacks structured information that helps disassembly and compute accurately the target sets of indirect branches [2]. Consequently, its constructed CFGs contain many spurious edges and may miss edges. The precision of CFGs is critical for some security applications. In CFI, a lower-precision CFG allows the attacker greater freedom over how control flows can be manipulated. It has been shown that coarse-grained CFI (which enforces low-precision CFGs) is much easier to attack than fine-grained CFI [8, 10, 12].

Another way is to use compilers for CFG construction. Existing compilers construct CFGs of programs for the purpose of program analysis and optimization. However, CFGs constructed by compilers are at the level of Intermediate Representations (IR). After IR code is translated to assembly code (which is further optimized through architecture-specific optimizations), the IR-level CFG cannot be directly transferred to the low level. Furthermore, the IR-level CFGs by most compilers are often incomplete, especially for those interprocedural edges resulting from indirect calls and returns.

To address these problems, the *compiler-modification* approach for binary-level CFG generation[20, 23, 27, 30] modifies existing compilers to propagate information from source to binary code and then performs CFG construction directly at the binary level. For instance, while standard compilers throw away type information during compilation, MCFI [20] modifies LLVM 3.5 to preserve type information in binaries and implements a type-signature approach for binary-level CFG generation. Forward-Edge CFI [27] modifies GCC 4.9 to enforce a form of CFI that protects virtual calls in C++ applications. This approach constructs CFGs of much higher precision than the binary-analysis approach. However, it requires source code. Furthermore, the practical limitation of modifying a compiler is that the CFG-construction code has to be upgraded when the compiler is upgraded. When a compiler migrates to a newer version, its internal API often changes, meaning any passes that were added to an older version have to be changed to use the new API; this is not an easy task. Upgrading MCFI to the latest LLVM (version 5.0) and Forward-Edge CFI to the latest GCC (version 7.2) would be a major engineering undertaking. In the case when a CFI implementation (e.g., Forward-Edge CFI in LLVM) has been upstreamed to the main branch of the compiler, it does force compiler developers to migrate the CFI implementation with compiler upgrades; however, it can be laborious for compiler developers. Moreover, CFG construction in one compiler cannot easily be reused for a different compiler.

In this paper, we describe the design and implementation of an alternative approach for high-precision CFG construction, without compiler modification. The key observation is that compilers already generate a collection of standard meta-information such as debugging information that can be reused for CFG construction. Therefore, our system takes binary code with standard meta-information as input, performs the key step of type inference at the binary level, and uses the recovered types for CFG construction.

Meta-information used in our system includes symbol tables, relocation information, and debugging information; they are designed for purposes such as debugging and standard compilers generate and maintain them across upgrades. Our approach still requires source code for meta-information generation. But it has the benefit of not modifying compilers, meaning that the implementation can largely be reused across different compiler versions and even across compilers. Moreover, our experiments show that the precision of CFGs generated by our implementation is comparable to the precision of CFGs generated by those that do modify compilers. Major contributions of our system are the followings:

- As far as we are aware, our system is the first one that constructs CFGs from standard meta-information generated by compilers. Compared to the approach of modifying compilers, most of our system can be reused across compiler versions and across compilers. Compared to the binary-analysis approach, our system generates CFGs of much higher precision, comparable to those systems that modify compilers.
- The key step in our CFG construction is a general binary-level type-inference procedure. Flow-based constraints are generated from binary code together with meta information and are solved to infer types of registers and stack locations. From type-inference results, a high-precision CFG is constructed following the type-signature approach for CFG construction.
- We have performed thorough experiments to evaluate the effectiveness of type inference and the precision of generated CFGs, and validated our system with different optimization levels used by compilers, multiple compiler versions, and multiple compilers (GCC and LLVM).

2 BACKGROUND

Standard compiler-generated meta-information includes symbol tables, relocation information, and debugging information. We next briefly describe the information contained in each kind.

Symbol tables. Compilers generate information about symbols (e.g., function and variable names) from source code in the form of symbol tables and embed the tables in binaries. Tools such as linkers and debuggers consume symbol tables to locate and relocate a program's symbolic definitions for static/dynamic linking and debugging. Symbol tables contain entries for symbols and each entry stores a name, a binding address, the type of the symbol, and other information. Our system compiles source code to generate unstripped binaries, which have the full symbol tables.

Relocation information. Before linking, memory addresses of compilation units such as functions and global data are unknown. Compilers therefore generate relocation entries so that static/dynamic linkers can patch the program's code and data after memory addresses become known. The patch process is for relocating code and data in object code and is crucial for separate compilation.

Debugging information. There are several formats for debugging information including STABS [16] and DWARF [11]. We focus on DWARF since it is the standard format adopted by most compilers including GCC and LLVM and also most debuggers.

The DWARF format is well-designed for debugging and includes several kinds of debugging information: (1) information in source code such as types and scope of identifiers is included in the form of *Debugging Information Entries (DIEs)*; (2) line-number information is included for recording the correspondence between binary and source code; (3) *location descriptions* are included for describing storage locations of variables during execution; (4) the *Canonical Frame Address (CFA)* information is included for describing the stack layout; this information is used during debugging and can also be useful for producing back traces when exceptions are raised. More details about debugging information, especially types, will be discussed in Sec. 4.1.

Incomplete and inaccurate meta-information. Symbol tables and relocation information are critical to static and dynamic linkers and therefore it is reasonable to assume that they are complete and accurate. The picture is different for debugging information, however. First, while all compilers generate a basic set of debugging information, the generation of advanced debugging information is compiler dependent. For example, GCC generates call-site information, which tells whether calls are tail calls and the types of arguments, while LLVM does not produce such information.

Second, debugging information may be inaccurate, especially in optimized code. It is well known that line-number information becomes unusable in optimized code: after optimizations such as code motion, it is often not possible for the compiler to update the relationship between binary and source code in terms of line numbers. Another example is that the CFA information for describing stack layouts may become inaccurate after compiler optimizations.

Inaccurate debugging information is a concern for our system as this can lead to wrong CFGs being constructed. Our decision is to not use such information, including line-number information and stack-layout information. Our CFG construction relies on type information, scope information, and location descriptions in debugging information; these kinds of information are found to be accurate across compilers, even after optimizations. Incomplete debugging information is less of a concern in that our system uses only what is available in debugging information to refine CFGs so that incomplete information just results in less-precise CFGs.

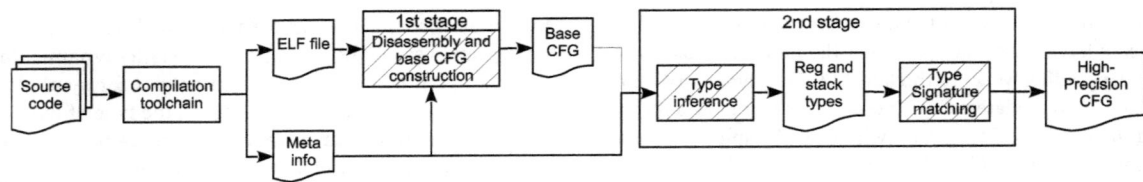

Figure 1: System architecture for high-precision CFG construction.

3 OVERVIEW

Fig. 1 presents the architecture of our CFG-construction system. The system takes source code, which is fed to an unmodified compilation toolchain (a compiler and a linker) to generate a binary program with standard meta-information. It then constructs the binary program's CFG in two stages.

In the first stage, a recursive-traversal disassembly algorithm is applied to disassemble the binary program and construct a coarse-grained CFG, which is called the base CFG in the figure. The first stage also takes as input compiler-generated meta-information, which tells the entries of all functions and makes disassembly complete. Its generated CFG is coarse grained in that many targets are allowed for indirect branches. On the other hand, control-flow edges out of direct branches (gotos, if conditionals, and direct calls) are accurate because their targets can be statically computed.

The second stage takes the base CFG and the meta information as input and refines the control-flow targets of indirect branches. Its key component is a type-inference engine that infers types of storage locations from types in debugging information. From the inferred types, the second stage follows a type-signature approach [20, 27] to narrow down the target list of an indirect branch.

Following the two-stage design, we have built a prototype system that constructs high-precision CFGs for binaries that are generated from different compilers (GCC and LLVM) and different compiler versions. The prototype is for Linux x86-32 binaries in the ELF format.[1] Further, the prototype assumes that the source code is in the C language because its type-inference engine infers C-like types for storage locations. Previous work [13, 21] has shown that the type-signature approach applies equally well on C++'s type system with the help of Class Hierarchy Analysis (CHA). This work and recent work on C++ CFG construction [22] give us confidence that our meta-information based approach can be generalized to programs in C++, with more work on type inference.

As a high-level note, our approach is compiler independent since the meta information relied on by our system (symbol tables, relocation and debugging information) all have standard formats that are independent of compilers; in particular, ELF and DWARF. As long as a compiler supports those standard formats, the parsing and use of meta information are compiler independent.

4 TYPE INFERENCE

The key component in our CFG-building framework is a generic type-inference system that infers types of storage locations (registers and stack slots) from source-level types included in debugging information. The type-inference engine works on one function at a time, starting from types in debugging information (which tell at least the entry types of parameters and local variables) and inferring the types of storage locations in the middle of the function.

It has four major components: (1) a component that collects types from debugging information; (2) a stack-layout inference algorithm that normalizes the representation of stack slots with respect to a canonical frame address; (3) a constraint-generation component that turns instructions and control flows into type constraints; (4) a constraint-solving component that solves constraints and computes a set of types for storage locations at every code address in the function. We next discuss these components in detail.

4.1 Debugging type information

Type inference starts from those types already included in debugging information. We next describe in detail what type information is there in debugging information. At a high level, types of source-code identifiers are included. What types of information are attached depends on the kinds of identifiers.

Functions. For a function, debugging information contains a debugging entry for the function, followed by entries for the function's formal parameters and local variables. From the entry of the function and the entries of its formal parameters, we can know the function's number of parameters, the parameter types, the return type, and also the range of code addresses of the function's body.

Formal parameters and local variables. These are function-local identifiers. The debugging entry for such an identifier contains the type of the identifier as well as a location description that describes where the identifier is stored.

A location description $[(st_1, rng_1), (st_2, rng_2), \ldots, (st_n, rng_n)]$ is a list of pairs, where st_i is a storage location, which is either a register (such as eax in x86-32), a stack location, or a location in global data sections (which store global variables), and rng_i is a code-address range. The above location-description list is interpreted as follows: the identifier is stored in location st_i before any instruction whose address is within address-range rng_i.

Fig. 2 presents an example. In this and other examples of the paper, for clarity we will use a pseudo-assembly syntax whose notation is described as follows. We use ":=" for an assignment (that is, a move instruction). When an operand represents a memory operand, the memory address is put into mem(-). For instance, mem(esp) is a memory operand with the address in esp, while esp itself represents a register operand. We will also use the syntax "if ... goto ..." for conditional jumps (on x86, it represents a comparison followed by a jump instruction).

The example in Fig. 2 includes the skeleton code for a function. Assume there is a local variable named i in the function and it is initially allocated on the stack; specifically, i is stored at the top of

---

[1] The prototype relies on a previous formal model of x86-32 for decoding [17]. That model lacks the decoding support for x86-64. We are in the process of extending it to cover the 64-bit.

```
// Assume variable i is initially at the top of the stack
addr1:  ...

        ...
addr2:  eax := mem(esp)

        ...
addr3:  ebx := eax

        ...
addr4:  ret
```

Debugging entry for i :
int; [(CFA-8,[addr1,addr2]), (eax,[addr2+1,addr3]),
     (ebx,[addr3+1,addr4])]

Figure 2: An example for debugging entries.

the stack. At addr2, the storage location of i is moved to register eax and at addr3 the location is moved to ebx.[2] The debugging entry for *i* is also shown in the figure (for brevity, we have omitted information irrelevant for our discussion, such as line numbers). It tells the source-code type of the variable and its location description, which means that the variable is stored in stack slot "CFA-8" between addr1 and addr2, in eax between addr2+1 and addr3, in ebx between addr3+1 and addr4.

The representation of a stack slot is normalized relative to CFA (Canonical Frame Address). The CFA address is typically defined to be the value of the stack pointer at the call site that invokes the current function. Therefore, the return address is stored at "CFA-4" since the return address is pushed by the call instruction (and the stack grows from high to low memory addresses). When local variables are allocated on the stack, their addresses are expressed relative to CFA in location descriptions. For the example, the relation between CFA and esp at the beginning is shown as follows:

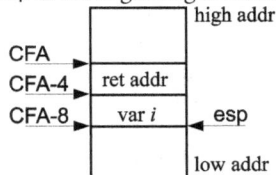

The types and location descriptions in debugging entries for local variables (and parameters) tell the types of some storage locations at specific code addresses. For the example in Fig. 2, the debugging entry for i tells that int is the type of stack slot cfa-8 between addr1 and addr2, the type of eax between addr2+1 and addr3, and the type of ebx between addr3+1 and addr4.

Global variables. Similar to local-variable entries, debugging entries for global variables tell their types and location descriptions. However, a global variable's storage location does not change over the course of program execution and therefore its location description has only one pair $[(st, rng)]$, where st encodes the memory address where the global variable is stored in global data sections, and rng is either the entire range of code addresses or a portion of it depending on whether the global variable is external or static.

---

[2]In unoptimized code, a local variable is stored in a specific stack slot for the entire function; however, code produced by higher-optimization levels can move the storage of a variable to a register to improve the efficiency of accessing the variable.

Incomplete type information. As we have shown, debugging information tells the types of some storage locations at certain code addresses. However, types in debugging information are for source-level constructs and, when source code is compiled to binary code, compilers are conservative in embedding types in debugging information, resulting in incomplete type information. As an example in Fig. 2, the location description does not tell the type of eax between addr3+1 and addr4, even though the type should remain the same before eax is modified. As another example, suppose a local variable is stored in eax initially and is then copied to ebx, and the location description states that the variable is stored in eax even after copying; then ebx's type after copying should be the same as eax, even though debugging information does not tell it directly. Sec. 6 will show that for large programs types can be missing in debugging information for over 50% of indirect-call operands.

4.2 Stack layout inference

As presented earlier, stack slots in debugging information are normalized and encoded as offsets to CFA. A binary program accesses stack slots, however, via memory addresses in the form of offsets to registers such as esp and ebp. To be able to track and infer types of stack slots, we must infer the relationship between registers and CFA. As a simple example, suppose the program reads the stack at address "esp" and debugging information tells us that the value at stack slot "CFA-8" is of type t; we cannot know the type of the value at address "esp" unless it is given that esp=CFA-8.

Some compilers generate in debugging information call-frame information that encodes the relation between CFA and register values. However, it is often incomplete and sometimes inaccurate. For instance, LLVM generates call-frame information for function prologues but such information is not generated for code after prologues. GCC's call-frame information may become inaccurate after code is optimized, for example, when code is moved after return instructions during optimization. Therefore, we have built a static analysis that infers the relation between registers and CFA; we call it stack layout inference.

The static analysis takes the assembly code of a function and its base CFG as input and at every address builds a set of equations of the following form: $\{r_1 = \text{CFA} + off_1, ..., r_n = \text{CFA} + off_n\}$. If a register does not point to the stack, then no equation for the register is included in the above set.

At the beginning of the function, the analysis assumes "{esp=CFA-4}" (the four bytes between CFA and esp are the return address). The transfer function for an instruction is built straightforwardly based on the instruction's semantics. Fig. 3 provides some examples: after "push ebp", we have "{esp=CFA-8}"; after another instruction "ebp:=esp", we get "{esp=CFA-8, ebp=CFA-8}".

At a control-flow merge point, the merge function is defined to be the intersection of the sets of equations from the paths being merged. In Fig. 3, address 7 is both a destination of the if-test at address 5 and the fall-through destination of the instruction at address 6. Therefore, we take the intersection of "{esp=CFA-20, ebp=CFA-8}" and "{esp=CFA-20, ebp=CFA-8, ebx=CFA-20}".

For a function call, the stack layout remains the same after the call; it assumes a function call preserves the stack layout. If the

```
        {esp=CFA-4}
1   push ebp
        {esp=CFA-8}
2   ebp := esp
        {esp=CFA-8, ebp=CFA-8}
3   push ebx
        {esp=CFA-12, ebp=CFA-8}
4   esp := esp - 8
        {esp=CFA-20, ebp=CFA-8}
5   if  eax==0 goto 7
        {esp=CFA-20, ebp=CFA-8}
6   ebx := esp
        {esp=CFA-20, ebp=CFA-8, ebx=CFA-20}

        {esp=CFA-20, ebp=CFA-8}
7   esp := esp + 8
        {esp=CFA-12, ebp=CFA-8}
8   pop ebx
        {esp=CFA-8, ebp=CFA-8}
9   pop ebp
        {esp=CFA-4}
10  ret
```

Figure 3: Stack layout inference for a toy function.

$$st \quad ::= \quad r \mid CFA + \mathit{off}$$
$$x,y,z \quad ::= \quad st_l^- \mid st_l^+ \mid gl$$
$$C \quad ::= \quad x \supseteq y \mid x \supseteq *(y + \mathit{off}) \mid x \supseteq \&(y + \mathit{off})$$

$$t \quad ::= \quad \top \mid void \mid int \mid char \mid float \mid double \mid t* \mid t[n] \mid$$
$$(t_1,\ldots,t_n) \to t \mid \{id_1 : t_1,\ldots,id_n : t_n\} \mid tbl\_ent$$
$$X,Y,Z \quad ::= \quad x \mid x : t$$
$$D \quad ::= \quad X \supseteq Y \mid X \supseteq *(Y + \mathit{off}) \mid X \supseteq \&(Y + \mathit{off})$$

Figure 4: Syntax of type constraints.

function has a loop, a standard worklist algorithm is used to calculate a fixed point; the worklist terminates since the underlying lattice is of finite height.

With the result of stack layout inference, accesses to the stack via registers plus constants can be normalized with respect to CFA.

4.3 Constraint generation

At a high level, constraints specify relations between types of storage locations based on how values flow in the input function. Our system tracks the types of registers, stack slots, and locations in global data sections. It does not explicitly track the types of heap locations that are dynamically allocated; however, values read from memory can still be assigned types in some cases. For instance, if eax holds a pointer to a dynamically allocated struct and debugging information tells that eax's type is a struct-pointer type, then a memory read via eax plus a constant offset returns a value whose type can be inferred from the struct type and the offset.

Fig. 4 presents the syntax of type constraints. We use st for a storage location, which is either a register or a stack slot in the form of CFA plus some offset. We use gl for the location of a global

Code	Constraints
10: eax:=ebx	$eax_{10}^+ \supseteq ebx_{10}^-$ $\forall st \neq eax,\ st_{10}^+ \supseteq st_{10}^-$
// assume ebp=CFA-8 20: eax:=mem(ebp+12)	$eax_{20}^+ \supseteq (CFA + 4)_{20}^-$ $\forall st \neq eax,\ st_{20}^+ \supseteq st_{20}^-$
// ebx unrelated to CFA 30: eax:=mem(ebx+4)	$eax_{30}^+ \supseteq *(ebx_{30}^- + 4)$ $\forall st \neq eax,\ st_{30}^+ \supseteq st_{30}^-$
// assume ebp=CFA-8 40: eax:=lea(ebp+12)	$eax_{40}^+ \supseteq \&(CFA + 4)_{40}^-$ $\forall st \neq eax,\ st_{40}^+ \supseteq st_{40}^-$
// ebx unrelated to CFA 50: eax:=lea(ebx+4)	$eax_{50}^+ \supseteq \&(ebx_{50}^- + 4)$ $\forall st \neq eax,\ st_{50}^+ \supseteq st_{50}^-$
60: i1 70: i2 80: i3	$\forall st,\ st_{80}^- \supseteq st_{60}^+$ $\forall st,\ st_{80}^- \supseteq st_{70}^+$

Figure 5: Examples for constraint generation.

variable (which resides in global data sections). We separate gl from st since the type of a global variable does not change over the course of program execution (further, debugging information tells the type); in contrast, types in registers and stack slots may change over program execution.

We use x, y, and z for type variables. They can stand for the set of types of registers or stack slots at a particular point, or the type of a global variable. In particular, we use st_l^- to stand for the type set of storage location st before the instruction at address l, and st_l^+ for the type set of storage location st after the instruction at address l. For instance, eax_{10}^- stands for the type set of eax before instruction at address 10 and eax_{10}^+ for the type set of eax afterwards. Since the type of a global variable does not change, gl is used to stand for the type of the corresponding global variable.

Type constraints are of three forms. Value-flow constraint "$x \supseteq y$" models the case when y's value flows to x; as a result, x's type set should be a superset of y's type set. A dereference-flow constraint "$x \supseteq *(y + \mathit{off})$" models the case when the value at address $y + \mathit{off}$ is read from memory and flows to x; address $y + \mathit{off}$ is assumed to not point to a stack slot, since stack slots are represented using CFA plus an offset. An address-flow constraint "$x \supseteq \&(y + \mathit{off})$" models the case when the memory address of $y + \mathit{off}$ flows to x.

Constraints are generated conservatively from instructions. Due to space limitation, we cannot enumerate all the cases. Instead, we just discuss the cases for typical instructions and illustrate them via examples in Fig. 5. For a register-to-register move instruction $r_1 := r_2$, constraints are generated to express that the type set of r_1 afterwards is a superset of r_2 beforehand (since r_2's value flows to r_1) and the type set of other storage locations afterwards is a superset of the same storage locations beforehand since their values are unchanged (for brevity, we will omit the mentioning of constraints concerning unchanged storage locations in the rest of the discussion). An example of "eax:=ebx" is in Fig. 5.

For a memory-to-register move $r_1 := \mathit{mem}(op)$, constraint generation depends on operand op. Suppose $op = r_2 + \mathit{off}$. If r_2 points to the stack before the move instruction (determined by stack layout analysis), then a constraint is generated to state that r_1's type set afterwards is a superset of the type set of the corresponding stack slot beforehand. An example of "eax:=mem(ebp+12)" is in Fig. 5. If r_2 does not point to the stack, then a dereference-flow constraint is generated to relate r_1 and r_2. An example of "eax:=mem(ebx+4)" is included in Fig. 5. When op is an immediate value, our system checks whether it is a memory address that holds a global variable. If it is, a value-flow constraint states that r_1's type set is a superset of the global variable's type. If it is not, no constraint is generated for r_1 after the move; this is an approximation, an unconstrained type variable will be assigned the $\top$ type, meaning no information is there for its type. In x86, an operand op can also use other complex addressing modes (such as a base register plus a register times a scalar and a displacement); in these cases, we approximate by not generating constraints for r_1.

x86 also has lea (load effective address) instructions, which move memory addresses but do not perform memory reads. Fig. 5 shows two examples. In example one, "eax:=lea(ebp+12)" moves the address of ebp+12 into eax. Assuming ebp=CFA-8, the instruction moves the address of stack storage location CFA+4 to eax; we use an address-flow constraint to model that. The second example is similar, except it moves a heap address; it is also modeled by an address-flow constraint.

Constraints generated for a register-to-memory move $mem(op) :=$ r_1 also depend on the shape of op. If $op = r_2 + off$, and r_2 points to the stack, then a value-flow constraint is generated to relate the type sets of r_1 and the associated stack slot. Otherwise, no constraints are generated since types of global variables do not change and we do not infer types of heap memory locations.

For a function call, constraints are generated to state that the stack slots are unchanged and values of certain register values are preserved according to the calling convention and the type signature of the callee.

Finally, constraints are also generated based on the control-flow graph. When there is a control-flow edge from instruction $i1$ to instruction $i2$, then the value of a storage location after $i1$ conceptually flows to the storage location before $i2$. The last row in Fig. 5 illustrates the generation of constraints from an example CFG.

In the next step, constraints are decorated with types that are included in debugging information. Fig. 4 shows the syntax of types. Type t can be either common base types, a function type "$(t_1, \ldots, t_n) \to t$" whose parameter types are t_1 to t_n and return type is t, a pointer type $t*$, a fixed-size array type $t[n]$, or a struct type in the form of a list of fields and field types. We augment C's type system with type tbl_ent, which is used as the type of jump-table entries and helps our system refine targets of indirect jumps. When debugging information tells that the type of x is t, we write $x : t$. For instance, "$eax_{10}^{-} : int$" means that eax before address 10 is of type int. We use capital letters X, Y, and Z for *decorated type variables*, which are either x or $x : t$; the second form is used when debugging information tells that x is of type t. A type constraint C is then turned into a *decorated type constraint D* by annotating type variables in C with types provided in debugging information.

4.4 Constraint solving

Decorated type constraints are solved in two steps: (1) constraints are turned into a graph whose nodes are decorated type variables and whose edges model value flows; (2) types are propagated on the graph and a type set for each node is produced.

From constraints to a constraint graph. In the resulting graph, nodes are decorated type variables and edges are of three kinds. For a constraint of the form $X \supseteq Y$, we add a value-flow edge from node Y to node X, written as $Y \to X$. For a constraint of the form $X \supseteq *(Y + off)$, we add a dereference-flow edge from node Y to X and label the edge with off; this is written as $Y \overset{off}{\Rightarrow} X$. For a constraint of the form $X \supseteq \&(Y + off)$, we add an address-flow edge from node Y to X and label the edge with off; this is written as $Y \overset{off}{\dashrightarrow} X$. An example is shown in Fig. 6: part (a) shows a set of constraints and part (b) shows its corresponding graph.

Constraint graph solving. Algorithm 1 presents the algorithm for solving a constraint graph. At a high level, it uses a worklist to propagate types forward along edges in the graph and computes a *typeOf* function that assigns sets of types to nodes. In more detail, $typeOf(n)$ is initialized according to n's kind: if n is $x : t$, then its type is t since we trust debugging information; if n has no incoming edges, we initialize its type as $\top$, meaning there is no information about the type; otherwise, it is initialized to be $\emptyset$. Then a while loop is used to process the nodes in the worklist. For a node, the algorithm iterates through its outgoing edges. For a value-flow edge $n \to n'$, when $n' = y$, the types for n are propagated to n'; note if "$n' = y : t$", then there is no need to perform forward propagation since the type of y is already known. For a dereference-flow edge $n \overset{off}{\Rightarrow} n'$, when $n' = y$, the type is propagated according to each type t in $typeOf(n)$. For an address-flow edge $n \overset{off}{\dashrightarrow} n'$, when $n' = y$, the types for n are transformed into correspondent pointer types and propagated to n'. In the case when t is a struct type, we use offsetTy(t, off) to compute the field type in the struct according to a static offset for both kinds of edges. Part (c) in Fig. 6 shows the solved example according to the algorithm.

5 CFG CONSTRUCTION

In this section, we present how our system constructs high-precision CFGs for binaries in two stages. The first stage produces a coarse-grained, base CFG. The second stage uses type-inference results to enhance CFG precision.

5.1 Base CFG construction

The base CFG construction relies on the classic recursive-traversal disassembly algorithm, which mixes disassembly and CFG construction. It maintains a work list, initialized with known code entries of binaries. The control flows of already disassembled instructions are followed for finding new code addresses to add to the work list for continuing disassembly. It can accommodate data embedded in code since such data should not be targets of control-transfer instructions. However, when a basic block ends with an indirect branch such as an indirect call through a memory operand, without further information it is difficult to predict what the branch may target and add appropriate addresses for further disassembly.

(a) Constraints

$$x_3 \supseteq \&(x_1 : t_1)$$
$$x_4 \supseteq *((x_2 : t_2) + 4)$$
$$y \supseteq x_3$$
$$y \supseteq x_4$$

(b) Constraint graph

(c) Solved constraint graph

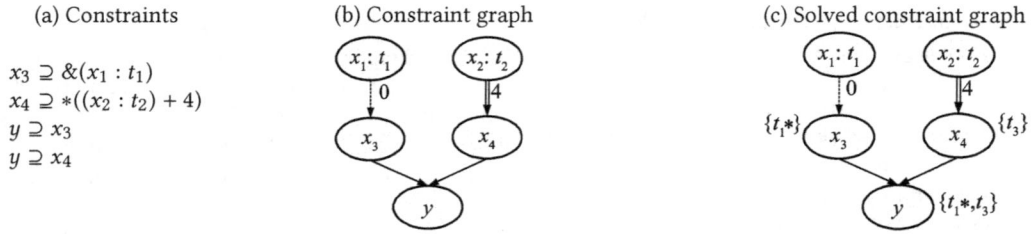

Figure 6: An example for illustrating constraint solving. Assume $t_1 = $ int, $t_2 = \{f1 : \text{int}, f2 : \text{float}*\}$, and $t_3 = $ float*.

Algorithm 1 Constraint solving

Global:
> $worklist : \mathcal{P}(N)$
> $typeOf : N \rightarrow \mathcal{P}(Type)$

> **procedure** SOLVE($G = (N, E)$)
> > $worklist \leftarrow N$
> > **for** $n \in N$ **do**
> > > **switch** n **do**
> > > > **case** $n = $ "$x : t$":
> > > > > $typeOf(n) \leftarrow \{t\}$
> > > > **case** $n = x$ and n has no incoming edges:
> > > > > $typeOf(n) \leftarrow \{\top\}$
> > > > **case** $n = x$ and n has incoming edges:
> > > > > $typeOf(n) \leftarrow \emptyset$
> > **while** $worklist$ is not empty **do**
> > > $n \leftarrow$ remove a node from $worklist$
> > > **for** $e \in$ outgoing edges of n **do**
> > > > **switch** e **do**
> > > > > **case** $e = n \rightarrow y$:
> > > > > > **for** $t \in typeOf(n)$ **do** ADD(t, y)
> > > > > **case** $e = n \overset{off}{\Rightarrow} y$:
> > > > > > **for** $t \in typeOf(n)$ **do**
> > > > > > > **switch** t **do**
> > > > > > > > **case** $t = \{id_1 : t_1, \ldots, id_n : t_n\}$:
> > > > > > > > > ADD(offsetTy(t, off), y)
> > > > > > > > **case** $t = t' *$ or $t'[k]$: ADD(t', y)
> > > > > > > > **case** others: ADD($\top, y$)
> > > > > **case** $e = n \overset{off}{\dashrightarrow} y$:
> > > > > > **for** $t \in typeOf(n)$ **do**
> > > > > > > **switch** t **do**
> > > > > > > > **case** $t = \{id_1 : t_1, \ldots, id_n : t_n\}$:
> > > > > > > > > ADD(offsetTy(t, off)*, y)
> > > > > > > > **case** others: ADD($t*, y$)

> **procedure** ADD(t, y)
> > **if** $t \notin typeOf(y)$ **then**
> > > $typeOf(y) \leftarrow typeOf(y) \cup \{t\}$
> > > $worklist \leftarrow worklist \cup \{y\}$

A tool may ignore the issue by not adding any address, but this would result in incomplete disassembly. Many tools such as IDAPro make assumptions about compilers and rely on heuristics and code patterns for remedying the situation partially, but they still cannot achieve complete disassembly in all cases since it is limited by the amount of information in binary code.

Our implementation of recursive traversal utilizes meta-information generated by compilers to determine control-flow targets of indirect branches and adds those targets to the worklist for further disassembly. Since it retrieves all possible targets for indirect branches from meta-information, it is able to achieve a complete disassembly and a sound base CFG for further refinement in the second stage of CFG construction.

How our recursive traversal algorithm determines the targets of indirect branches depends on the types of indirect branches. For both indirect calls and indirect jumps, we take advantage of relocation information to narrow down potential targets; therefore, we first explain how potential targets for indirect calls/jumps are retrieved from relocation information.

Indirect targets retrieval via relocation information. Since a function cannot be invoked indirectly unless its address is taken somewhere in code, several previous systems [1, 20, 36] refine CFGs to allow indirect calls to target only address-taken functions. This is possible because at compile time the compiler does not know the exact addresses of functions and it must generate relocation entries for places where function addresses are used so that during linking they can be patched when the exact function addresses become known. The same applies to targets of indirect jumps; relocation entries are generated at places where those targets are used.

Therefore, our system searches for relocation entries that require the linker to put in absolute addresses during linking. If the symbol name of such an entry is a function name, the function's address must be taken and it is collected into the set FSA (Function-Start Addresses), which is the set of start addresses of address-taken functions. If the symbol name of such an entry is not a function name, the corresponding address is internal to a function and possibly the target of an indirect jump; the address is then collected into ICA (Internal Code Addresses); that is, it is the set of code addresses that can be the targets of indirect jumps.

Handling indirect calls. In the base CFG, an indirect call is allowed to target any address in FSA, the set of start addresses of address-taken functions; furthermore, since functions contained in dynamically linked libraries are called through entries in the Procedure Linkage Table (PLT) in the binary, our system also adds the start addresses of PLT entries to the targets of indirect calls.

Handling indirect jumps. An indirect jump is allowed to target an address if (1) the address is in FSA, or if (2) the address is in ICA and the address falls within the code-address range of the function that contains the indirect jump. The reason for (1) is that tail calls are implemented via indirect jumps; an indirect jump for implementing a tail call is like an indirect call and is therefore allowed to target any function whose address is taken. For (2), the justification is that non-tail-call indirect jumps are for compiling switch statements and goto statements through labels that are stored in composite data structures; in these cases, targets of an indirect jump are local (within the function that contains the indirect jump).

Handling returns. When processing a basic block that ends with a direct or indirect call instruction, our recursive-traversal algorithm adds the code address immediately following the call instruction into the disassembly worklist. This is speculative disassembly since it assumes the callee function has a return instruction that will return to the address following the call instruction. The speculative disassembly can produce spurious basic blocks, because the call may target functions that never return; for example, calling the library function exit stops the program. Our system assumes that compilers do not put non-executable bytes after call instructions; consequently, spurious basic blocks are not harmful.

With speculative disassembly for return addresses, the targets of return instructions can be computed after the disassembly is complete. Specifically, after computing targets of indirect calls/jumps, our system computes a call graph to compute targets of return instructions. The call graph collects a list of functions that a call instruction can reach, either directly or indirectly through a series of tail calls. Then, return instructions in this list of functions can target the return address following the call instruction.

5.2 Enhanced CFG construction

Base CFG construction results in coarse-grained CFGs: all indirect calls share the same set of targets; indirect jumps are allowed to target either function-start addresses or some local targets or both. In this section, we discuss how to use the results of type inference described in Sec. 4 to substantially enhance the CFG precision. A previous CFI system [20] adopts a type-signature approach for CFG construction: an indirect call through an operand is allowed to invoke any function whose type is compatible with the operand's function pointer's type. This type-based method requires that source code does not contain type casts that involve function-pointer types; if this is violated, a small amount of changes can be made to the source code to respect the requirement.

The type-signature method requires knowing two pieces of knowledge: (1) the types of functions; and (2) the function-pointer types of operands used in indirect calls. As presented before, types of functions can be acquired from debugging information. However, debugging information does not always tell the types of operands in indirect calls; this is where our type inference comes into play. After type inference, an operand in an indirect call is assigned a set of types. For each function-pointer type $(t_1, \ldots, t_n \rightarrow t)*$ in the set, we allow an indirect call via the operand to invoke any function with type "$t_1, \ldots, t_n \rightarrow t$". In the worst case, the set may contain $\top$; for example, when the operand is loaded from a piece of memory for which there is no type information; in this case, the target-set of the indirect call cannot be refined.

For an indirect jump, thanks to the new type tbl_ent, the type-inference also tells whether it is a tail call or a local jump based on jump tables. If the type set of the indirect jump's operand contains

only function-pointer types, then it is treated as a tail call and its target set is refined as if it were an indirect call. If the type set of the operand contains only tbl_ent, the set of targets is refined to include only the local targets. Each PLT entry also contains an indirect jump; we allow it to target the address of the dynamic linker as well as a symbolic target that indicates that the jump is allowed to jump into a dynamically linked library. The target sets of remaining indirect jumps are not refined.

After the target sets of indirect calls and jumps are refined, a refined call graph is constructed. The refined call graph is then used to calculate the targets of return instructions.

6 IMPLEMENTATION AND EVALUATION

Our system is implemented with a decoder for x86-32, 18K lines of OCaml code for disassembly, type inference, and CFG construction, 4K lines of C code for collecting debugging information, and a few Python and Shell scripts for relocation information collection and data handling.

The disassembler is built based on the decoder. The disassembler first parses the ELF file to obtain all headers and sections. Symbol tables are already retrieved during ELF parsing. Relocation information is collected during compilation with the help of the Linux utility readelf and a custom Python script. Debugging information is collected with the help of the libdwarf library, implemented in C. Disassembly and CFG construction are implemented in OCaml and communicate with the debugging-information collection in C via the OCaml-C interface.

For evaluation, we are interested in the following questions: (1) how effective is our type inference for inferring types of operands in indirect branches? (2) How precise are the CFGs generated by our system and how does the precision compare with the binary-analysis approach and the compiler-modification approach?

To answer these questions, we conducted our experiments in a Linux box running x64 Ubuntu 14.0.4 on a PC with 16GB-memory and Intel Core i5-4590 CPU at 3.30GHz. Our evaluation was performed on SPEC2006 C benchmarks and Nginx-1.4.0. Since the type-based approach requires that source code does not contain type casts that involve function-pointer types, we used MCFI's patched SPEC2006 C benchmarks and Nginx-1.4.0 (downloaded from https://github.com/mcfi); MCFI made small changes to the benchmarks to remove type casts that involve function pointers (mostly by adding function wrappers). Our prototype system can construct CFGs for both GCC and LLVM at all optimization levels (from O0 to O3). We also tested the CFG construction on multiple versions of the two compilers (in particular, GCC 4.8.4, GCC 5.4.0, GCC 6.2.0, LLVM 3.9, LLVM 4.0). For conciseness, we will present the detailed results only for GCC 4.8.4 and results are generally similar for other GCC versions and LLVM.

6.1 Effectiveness of type inference

Tbl. 1 presents indirect-branch type-inference results for SPEC2006 C benchmarks. In the table, the benchmarks are sorted according to their sizes in the ascending order. We omitted small benchmarks including lbm, mcf and libquantum since they do not contain indirect calls/jumps. For each benchmark, column NeedInfer/Total lists the number of indirect calls whose operands do not have debugging type information versus the total number of indirect calls. The

Benchmarks	NeedInfer/ Total	ICALL-Precise	ICALL-Imprecise	Inferred Rate	TailCall	Local	PLT	IJUMP-Imprecise
bzip2	20/20	20	0	100.0%	0	2	22	0
sjeng	1/1	1	0	100.0%	0	15	38	0
milc	0/4	0	0	N.A.	0	5	40	0
sphinx3	9/9	9	0	100.0%	0	1	60	0
hmmer	0/9	0	0	N.A.	1	24	69	0
h264ref	40/352	40	0	100.0%	0	12	44	0
perlbench	55/109	52	3	94.5%	30	80	114	0
gobmk	30/44	30	0	100.0%	0	13	49	0
gcc	292/442	291	1	99.7%	20	426	72	1
Total	447/990	443	4	99.1%	51	578	508	1

Table 1: Indirect-call and Indirect-jump type-inference results (GCC 4.8.4 with O2 optimization).

numbers show that there are many indirect calls (around 50% for large benchmarks including perlbench, gobmk, and gcc) for which debugging information misses types for their operands.

Column ICALL-Precise shows the number of indirect calls whose operands type inference infers a single function-pointer type for; Column ICALL-Imprecise shows the number of indirect calls when type inference includes ⊤ or non-function-pointer types in the inferred type set; Column Inferred Rate shows the percentage of indirect calls for which type inference can give precise function-pointer types (column ICALL-Precise) over the indirect calls whose operands debugging information carries no types for. The numbers show that type inference can infer the types for a high percentage (over 99%) of indirect calls.

We also investigated those imprecise cases. Some were caused by union types. For instance, one call site in perlbench has a union type for the operand. Since the inference system does not know which case of the union type is the operand's exact type, it collects all cases from the union type for the operand's type set; and one of those is void*, a non-function-pointer type. Other cases were caused by over-approximation in our constraint generation since it does not track the types of storage locations in the heap.

The second half of Tbl. 1 presents indirect-jump type-inference results. Column TailCall presents the number of indirect jumps our system infers as tail calls (recall that the operand type of such an indirect jump should be a function-pointer type). Column Local presents the number of indirect jumps that are inferred as jumps via jump tables. A large number of indirect jumps are in PLT entries and their numbers are shown in Column PLT. Column IJUMP-Imprecise shows the number of indirect jumps whose operand types include ⊤. The data shows that there is only one indirect jump for which our system cannot infer precise information.

6.2 CFG precision and validation

For a control-flow graph, Average Indirect-Branch Targets (AIBT) introduced by Niu [18] is defined to be the number of targets averaged over all indirect branches in the graph.[3] The smaller the AIBT is, the more precise the CFG is. In Tbl. 2, we present AIBT numbers for SPEC2006 C benchmarks for GCC 4.8.4 across different

optimization levels. Each data entry shows AIBTs for the enhanced CFG (left) and the base CFG (right).

Comparison with binary-analysis approach. The precision of base CFGs is roughly the same as the precision of CFGs produced by a typical binary-analysis approach, which commonly allows all indirect calls to target the same set of functions and employs optimizations for handling indirect jumps. As the table shows, the improvement of our type-inference based CFG enhancement is small for small benchmarks; since lbm, mcf, and libquantum do not contain indirect branches, there is no improvement during CFG enhancement. However, for large benchmarks including perlbench, gobmk, and gcc, the CFG improvement is substantial: average reduction is between 60 to 90%; many spurious edges were removed during type-based CFG enhancement.

Comparison with compilter-modification approach. When compared with the compiler-modification approach, the precision of our system's enhanced CFGs is only slightly worse than MCFI. A direct comparison by the AIBT statistics is infeasible, because MCFI's implementation does not support 32-bit binaries and our current implementation supports only 32-bit binaries. However, based on the fact that both systems use the type-signature approach for matching indirect branches and targets, we can still perform an indirect comparison. MCFI propagates types inside the compiler to binaries; so an indirect call's operand has exactly one type. Our system performs type inference to infer the types of indirect-call operands. As seen in a previous table, around 99% of indirect-call operands get one type signature. Therefore, the CFG precision of our system is very close to the one of MCFI. As a previous survey paper [5] shows, MCFI enforces the highest-precision CFGs among all existing CFI enforcement tools. For instance, Forward-Edge CFI [27] enforces a less precise CFG: it uses arity matching for pairing indirect calls and functions (i.e., it matches the number of parameters) and it does not enforce CFI on return instructions.

Experiment on Nginx 1.4.0. To further evaluate our approach, we conducted an experiment on Nginx. In Tbl. 3, we present experimental results for MCFI-patched Nginx-1.4.0. As the table shows, our approach is able to generate high-precision CFGs for practical applications such as Nginx.

---

[3]We did not use the AIR (Average Indirect-target Reduction) metric because it has been criticized to not capture the ability of a CFG to withstand control-flow hijacking attacks [7].

Benchmarks	O0	O1	O2	O3	AvgRed
lbm	1.7/1.7	1.7/1.7	1.7/1.7	1.7/1.7	0%
mcf	1.6/1.6	1.6/1.6	1.5/1.5	1.4/1.4	0%
libquantum	3.0/3.0	3.2/3.2	4.0/4.0	4.8/4.8	0%
bzip2	2.6/3.0	2.7/3.0	2.5/2.7	1.9/2.2	11.1%
sjeng	5.0/9.0	4.9/4.9	6.5/6.5	6.8/6.8	11.1%
milc	3.3/3.3	3.3/3.3	3.6/3.6	3.9/3.9	0%
sphinx3	4.5/4.6	4.7/4.7	4.9/4.9	5.7/5.7	0.5%
hmmer	4.1/7.8	4.8/4.9	4.9/5.0	4.9/4.9	12.9%
h264ref	4.0/31.8	4.3/32.1	6.1/34.7	6.2/34.9	84.7%
perlbench	17.2/563.0	19.5/102.8	23.6/232.6	34.1/357.6	89.6%
gobmk	19.7/104.6	22.0/61.2	19.5/58.1	28.9/68.7	67.4%
gcc	23.2/1735.0	26.2/192.8	32.3/212.3	42.3/345.5	89.4%

Table 2: Average Indirect-Branch Targets for SPEC benchmarks (GCC 4.8.4).

Benchmarks	NeedInfer/ Total	ICALL- Precise	ICALL- Imprecise	Inferred Rate	TailCall	Local	PLT	IJUMP- Imprecise	AIBT	Red
nginx	201/289	191	10	95.0%	26	60	133	0	20.7/213.0	90.3%

Table 3: Experimental results for Nginx-1.4.0 (GCC 4.8.4 with O2 optimization).

CFG validation. We have performed testing to validate the enhanced CFGs our system generated for SPEC benchmarks and Nginx. We used PIN [15] to instrument the benchmarks' binaries to collect runtime traces for reference data sets and configurations; the reference data sets are included in the original benchmarks and provide good test coverage. The control-flow edges made by indirect branches in the runtime traces were checked to see if they were included in the CFGs generated by our system. In our experiments, CFGs generated by our system for all benchmarks passed the validation. Because the runtime overhead introduced by PIN is substantial and the trace output file is large, we had to perform optimizations for large benchmarks during validation. Since the difficulty of CFG construction lies in control transfers from indirect branches, we instrumented only indirect branches through PIN instead of all control-flow transfer instructions. One downside of resorting to testing for CFG validation is that it can find bugs but cannot show correctness. Unfortunately, the CFI field lacks a method for verifying the correctness of CFGs; addressing this problem would be an interesting research direction.

7 RELATED WORK

Previous binary-level type-inference systems assume stripped binaries (Caballero and Lin [6] provide a comprehensive survey). In contrast, our system uses debugging information for type inference. This comes with the downside of assuming source-code availability, but it enables more complete type inference since debugging information provides a wealth of source-level types. Thanks to debugging information, our flow-based type inference can infer most of the types in operands of indirect branches, while previous systems on stripped binaries had trouble of inferring function-pointer types [6], even after employing more complex techniques including heuristics (e.g., for classifying whether an immediate is an integer or a pointer), points-to analysis, and dynamic analysis.

Static disassembly of binaries and CFG construction have always been a challenge in reverse engineering binary programs. Other

than the standard linear-sweep and recursive-traversal algorithms, other attempts at better static disassembly and CFG construction have been presented in previous papers. Kruegel et al. [14] proposed to combine linear sweep with recursive traversal. The system does not follow the control flows of indirect branches and suffers from incomplete disassembly. Balakrishnan et al. proposed Value Set Analysis (VSA [3]) that can sometimes statically determine the control-flow targets of indirect branches. Wartell et al. [32, 33] described a machine-learning approach for discovering the most likely disassemblies with the help of a training corpus. TypeArmor [28] performs liveness-analysis based arity matching to refine the control-flow targets of indirect calls. All previous systems assume stripped binaries.

8 CONCLUSIONS

We have designed and implemented an alternative approach for high-precision CFG construction, without compiler modification. The approach uses compiler-generated meta-information to retrieve source-level information for CFG construction. It relies on a type-inference engine that deduces types of indirect-branch operands from source-level types in debugging information. Our experiments demonstrate that the precision of CFGs produced by our system is comparable to previous systems that modify compilers and our system is compatible with multiple compilers and multiple compiler versions, thanks to its compiler-independent design. As future work, we plan to expand the implementation to cover C++ applications by adding the support for classes.

Acknowledgments. We thank reviewers for their insightful comments. This research is based upon work supported by US NSF grants CCF-1624124 and CNS-1624126. The research was also supported in part by the Defense Advanced Research Projects Agency (DARPA) under agreement number N6600117C4052 and Office of Naval Research under agreement number N00014-17-1-2539.

REFERENCES

[1] Martín Abadi, Mihai Budiu, Úlfar Erlingsson, and Jay Ligatti. 2005. Control-flow integrity. In *12th ACM Conference on Computer and Communications Security (CCS)*. 340–353.

[2] Dennis Andriesse, Xi Chen, Victor van der Veen, Asia Slowinska, and Herbert Bos. 2016. An In-Depth Analysis of Disassembly on Full-Scale x86/x64 Binaries. In *25th Usenix Security Symposium*. 583–600.

[3] Gogul Balakrishnan and Thomas Reps. 2004. Analyzing Memory Accesses in x86 Executables. In *13th International Conference on Compiler Construction (CC)*. 5–23.

[4] David Brumley, Ivan Jager, Thanassis Avgerinos, and Edward J. Schwartz. 2011. BAP: A Binary Analysis Platform. In *Computer Aided Verification (CAV)*. 463–469.

[5] Nathan Burow, Scott A. Carr, Joseph Nash, Per Larsen, Michael Franz, Stefan Brunthaler, and Mathias Payer. 2017. Control-Flow Integrity: Precision, Security, and Performance. *Comput. Surveys* 50, 1 (2017), 16:1–16:33.

[6] Juan Caballero and Zhiqiang Lin. 2016. Type Inference on Executables. *Comput. Surveys* 48, 4 (2016), 65:1–65:35.

[7] Nicholas Carlini, Antonio Barresi, Mathias Payer, David Wagner, and Thomas R. Gross. 2015. Control-Flow Bending: On the Effectiveness of Control-Flow Integrity. In *24th Usenix Security Symposium*. 161–176.

[8] Nicholas Carlini and David Wagner. 2014. ROP is Still Dangerous: Breaking Modern Defenses. In *23rd Usenix Security Symposium*. 385–399.

[9] Mihai Christodorescu and Somesh Jha. 2003. Static Analysis of Executables to Detect Malicious Patterns. In *12th Usenix Security Symposium*. 169–186.

[10] Lucas Davi, Ahmad-Reza Sadeghi, Daniel Lehmann, and Fabian Monrose. 2014. Stitching the Gadgets: On the Ineffectiveness of Coarse-Grained Control-Flow Integrity Protection. In *23rd Usenix Security Symposium*. 401–416.

[11] DWARF Debugging Information Format Committee 2017. *DWARF Debugging Information Format Version 5*. DWARF Debugging Information Format Committee.

[12] Enes Göktas, Elias Athanasopoulos, Herbert Bos, and Georgios Portokalidis. 2014. Out of Control: Overcoming Control-Flow Integrity. In *IEEE Symposium on Security and Privacy (S&P)*. 575–589.

[13] Dongseok Jang, Zachary Tatlock, and Sorin Lerner. 2014. SafeDispatch: Securing C++ Virtual Calls from Memory Corruption Attacks. In *Network and Distributed System Security Symposium (NDSS)*.

[14] Christopher Kruegel, William Robertson, Fredrik Valeur, and Giovanni Vigna. 2004. Static Disassembly of Obfuscated Binaries. In *13th Usenix Security Symposium*. 255–270.

[15] Chi-Keung Luk, Robert Cohn, Robert Muth, Harish Patil, Artur Klauser, Geoffrey Lowney, Steven Wallace, Vijay Janapa Reddi, and Kim Hazelwood. 2005. Pin: building customized program analysis tools with dynamic instrumentation. In *ACM Conference on Programming Language Design and Implementation (PLDI)*. 190–200.

[16] Julia Menapace, Jim Kingdon, and David MacKenzie. 1999. *The "stabs" debug format*.

[17] Greg Morrisett, Gang Tan, Joseph Tassarotti, Jean-Baptiste Tristan, and Edward Gan. 2012. RockSalt: Better, Faster, Stronger SFI for the x86. In *ACM Conference on Programming Language Design and Implementation (PLDI)*. 395–404.

[18] Ben Niu. 2015. *Practical Control-Flow Integrity*. Ph.D. Dissertation. Lehigh University, Bethlehem, PA.

[19] Ben Niu and Gang Tan. 2013. Monitor Integrity Protection with Space Efficiency and Separate Compilation. In *20th ACM Conference on Computer and Communications Security (CCS)*.

[20] Ben Niu and Gang Tan. 2014. Modular Control Flow Integrity. In *ACM Conference on Programming Language Design and Implementation (PLDI)*. 577–587.

[21] Ben Niu and Gang Tan. 2014. RockJIT: Securing Just-In-Time Compilation Using Modular Control-Flow Integrity. In *21st ACM Conference on Computer and Communications Security (CCS)*. 1317–1328.

[22] Andre Pawlowski, Moritz Contag, Victor van der Veen, Chris Ouwehand, Thorsten Holz, Herbert Bos, Elias Athanasopoulos, and Cristiano Giuffrida. 2017. MARX: Uncovering class Hierarchies in C++ Programs. In *Network and Distributed System Security Symposium (NDSS)*.

[23] Jannik Pewny and Thorsten Holz. 2013. Control-Flow Restrictor: Compiler-based CFI for iOS. In *ACSAC '13: Proceedings of the 2013 Annual Computer Security Applications Conference*.

[24] Thomas Reps, Junghee Lim, Aditya Thakur, Gogul Balakrishnan, and Akash Lal. 2010. There's Plenty of Room at the Bottom: Analyzing and Verifying Machine Code. In *Computer Aided Verification (CAV)*. 41–56.

[25] Hovav Shacham. 2007. The geometry of innocent flesh on the bone: return-into-libc without function calls (on the x86). In *14th ACM Conference on Computer and Communications Security (CCS)*. 552–561.

[26] Dawn Song, David Brumley, Heng Yin, Juan Caballero, Ivan Jager, Min Gyung Kang, Zhenkai Liang, James Newsome, Pongsin Poosankam, and Prateek Saxena. 2008. BitBlaze: A New Approach to Computer Security via Binary Analysis. In *Proceedings of the 4th International Conference on Information Systems Security*.

[27] Caroline Tice, Tom Roeder, Peter Collingbourne, Stephen Checkoway, Úlfar Erlingsson, Luis Lozano, and Geoff Pike. 2014. Enforcing Forward-Edge Control-Flow Integrity in GCC & LLVM. In *23rd Usenix Security Symposium*.

[28] Victor van der Veen, Enes Göktas, Moritz Contag, Andre Pawoloski, Xi Chen, Sanjay Rawat, Herbert Bos, Thorsten Holz, Elias Athanasopoulos, and Cristiano Giuffrida. 2016. A Tough Call: Mitigating Advanced Code-Reuse Attacks at the Binary Level. In *IEEE Symposium on Security and Privacy (S&P)*. 934–953.

[29] R. Wahbe, S. Lucco, T. Anderson, and S. Graham. 1993. Efficient Software-Based Fault Isolation. In *ACM SIGOPS Symposium on Operating Systems Principles (SOSP)*. ACM Press, New York, 203–216.

[30] Zhi Wang and Xuxian Jiang. 2010. HyperSafe: A Lightweight Approach to Provide Lifetime Hypervisor Control-Flow Integrity. In *IEEE Symposium on Security and Privacy (S&P)*. 380–395.

[31] Richard Wartell, Vishwath Mohan, Kevin W. Hamlen, and Zhiqiang Lin. 2012. Securing untrusted code via compiler-agnostic binary rewriting. In *Proceedings of the 28th Annual Computer Security Applications Conference*. 299–308.

[32] Richard Wartell, Yan Zhou, Kevin W. Hamlen, and Murat Kantarcioglu. 2014. Shingled Graph Disassembly: Finding the Undecidable Path. In *Proceedings of the 18th Pacific-Asia Conference on Knowledge Discovery and Data Mining (PAKDD)*. Tainan, Taiwan, 273–285.

[33] Richard Wartell, Yan Zhou, Kevin W. Hamlen, Murat Kantarcioglu, and Bhavani Thuraisingham. 2011. Differentiating Code from Data in x86 Binaries. In *Proceedings of the European Conference on Machine Learning and Principles and Practice of Knowledge Discovery in Databases (ECML PKDD)*, Vol. 3. 522–536.

[34] Zhichen Xu, Barton Miller, and Thomas Reps. 2000. Safety checking of machine code. In *ACM Conference on Programming Language Design and Implementation (PLDI)*. 70–82.

[35] Bennet Yee, David Sehr, Gregory Dardyk, Brad Chen, Robert Muth, Tavis Ormandy, Shiki Okasaka, Neha Narula, and Nicholas Fullagar. 2009. Native Client: A Sandbox for Portable, Untrusted x86 Native Code. In *IEEE Symposium on Security and Privacy (S&P)*.

[36] Chao Zhang, Tao Wei, Zhaofeng Chen, Lei Duan, Laszlo Szekeres, Stephen Mc-Camant, Dawn Song, and Wei Zou. 2013. Practical Control Flow Integrity and Randomization for Binary Executables. In *IEEE Symposium on Security and Privacy (S&P)*. 559–573.

[37] Mingwei Zhang and R. Sekar. 2013. Control Flow Integrity for COTS Binaries. In *22nd Usenix Security Symposium*. 337–352.

MASCAT: Preventing Microarchitectural Attacks Before Distribution

Gorka Irazoqui
Worcester Polytechnic Institute
Nagravision Iberica
gorka.irazoqui@nagra.com

Thomas Eisenbarth
Worcester Polytechnic Institute
University of Lübeck
thomas.eisenbarth@uni-luebeck.de

Berk Sunar
Worcester Polytechnic Institute
sunar@wpi.edu

ABSTRACT

Microarchitectural attacks have gained popularity lately for the threat they pose and for their stealthiness. They are stealthy as they only exploit common harmless resources accessible at lowest privilege level, e.g. timed memory and cache accesses. Microarchitectural attacks have proven successful on shared cloud instances across VMs, on smartphones with sandboxing, and on numerous embedded platforms. Further they have shown to have catastrophic consequences such as critical data recovery or memory isolation bypassing. Due to the rise of malicious code, app store operators such as Microsoft, Apple and Google are already vetting apps before releasing them. Microarchitectural attacks however still bypass such detection mechanisms as they mainly utilize standard resources and look harmless. Given the rise of malicious code in app stores and in online repositories it becomes essential to scan applications for such stealthy attacks to prevent their distribution.

We present a static code analysis tool, MASCAT, capable of scanning for ever-evolving microarchitectural attacks. MASCAT can be used by app store service providers to perform large scale fully automated analysis of applications. The initial MASCAT suite is built to include cache/DRAM access attacks and rowhammer. MASCAT detects several patterns that are common and necessary to execute microarchitectural attacks. MASCAT currently has a detection rate of 96% and an average false positive rate tested in 1200 applications of 0.75%. Further, our tool can easily be extended to cover newer attack vectors as they emerge.

KEYWORDS

Microarchitectural attacks, cache attacks, static code analysis.

ACM Reference Format:

Gorka Irazoqui, Thomas Eisenbarth, and Berk Sunar. 2018. MASCAT: Preventing Microarchitectural Attacks Before Distribution. In *CODASPY '18: Eighth ACM Conference on Data and Application Security and Privacy, March 19–21, 2018, Tempe, AZ, USA.* ACM, New York, NY, USA, 12 pages. https://doi.org/10.1145/3176258.3176316

1 INTRODUCTION

In recent years the security community has witnessed the rise of microachitectural side channel attacks. New sophisticated attacks are discovered frequently, e.g. memory bus locking attacks or rowhammer attacks, raising concerns among software and hardware security developers. In fact, they already provide a wide range of threats. Cache attacks can recover cryptographic keys [8, 12, 23, 25, 47] and passwords in a TLS session [26] and infer sensitive information, e.g. the number of items in a shopping cart [51]. In addition, memory bus locking attacks are capable of acting as covert-channels and may be used for detecting hardware co-residency or for Quality of Service (QoS) degradation [22, 42]. Lastly, rowhammer attacks pushed the envelope further by introducing cryptographic faults or by breaking memory isolation techniques [10, 44]. One reason why microarchitectural attacks are so dangerous is the wide range of situations they apply. Contrary to early popular belief, microarchitectural attacks have proven to work in commercial clouds (e.g. Amazon EC2) [20], in browsers as Javascript extensions [33], in trusted execution environments or even on mobile devices, e.g. as smartphone applications [31]. In short, microarchitectural attacks are applicable and even practical in numerous security-critical scenarios.

Due to the severity of the threat, it is important to roll out protection against microarchitectural attacks before they find widespread adoption. Solutions proposed so far, can be divided into preventive and reactive (online detection) categories. However, the implementation of preventive methodologies, e.g., page coloring or Intel Cache Allocation Technology [32], requires changes to current infrastructure (hardware or OS/hypervisor), and usually incurs noticeable performance overheads, making infrastructure providers unlikely to deploy them. Similarly, reactive approaches, such as monitoring of performance counter events by the OS [49] also incur overheads and thus make widespread adoption unlikely.

A common way to execute malware-free applications is to download them from official digital app stores, e.g., Microsoft store or Android Google Play. Users can profit from a certain level of trust for the downloaded applications, mainly because a pre-analysis of the software submitted to these stores is supposed to happen. This should serve as a mechanisms to avoid common malware reach our devices easily. The analysis method of choice for binary analysis in app stores is static analysis. While dynamic analysis is also possible, it can be much more time consuming and faces the risk that malicious code parts might be hidden in inactive parts of the code, potentially only triggerable by the adversary and thus missed by dynamic analysis. As a consequence, static analysis is the method of choice to ensure early detection at no overhead and thus prevent the spread of such attacks to a large number of users.

However, unlike other kind of malware, the main problem with microarchitectural attacks is that they look harmless, as they access resources in a natural way like other harmless code and are thus harder to detect. These attacks usually bypass the detection mechanisms and are placed in the stores as if they contain benign code. Evidence of such a mis-detection was provided by [18, 31], as both attacks were placed available to public users in the android app store. A common solution is to utilize anti-virus software to detect malicious code inside binaries once they have reached our devices. Nevertheless, this does not usually prevent the execution of such attacks since, as it will be presented later in this document, antiviruses mis-detect the majority of microarchitectural attacks.

Our Contribution

We present MASCAT (Micro-Architectural Side Channel Attack Trapper), a tool to detect microarchitectural attacks through static analysis of binaries. MASCAT works by statically analyzing binary elf files, detecting implicit characteristics commonly exhibited by microarchitectural attacks. We have identified several characteristics that give strong evidence of the presence of certain attack classes. The importance factor of each characteristic is configurable to either detect all or a specific subset of microarchitectural attacks. Further, our approach is designed to easily add more characteristics to the range of attacks that MASCAT covers. The execution of our approach is fully automated and in comparison to other solutions, the outcome is easily understandable as it not only colors the location where the threat was found in the binary but also adds an explanation on the characteristics that triggered the alarm.

MASCAT can be adopted by digital application distributors (like Androids GooglePlay, Microsoft Store or Apple app store) to ensure the applications being offered do not contain microarchitectural attacks. In fact, they can use MASCAT to detect the presence of microarchitectural attack characteristics, and decide whether the application needs to be removed. More than that, if such an attack is found, the submitter can be banned from the app store.
In summary, this work

- shows for the first time that app stores can stop microarchitectural attacks prior to their execution without the collaboration of OS/software designers;
- introduces a novel static binary analysis approach looking for attributes implicit to microarchitectural attacks in apparently innocent binaries and APKs;
- performs a full analysis of 32 attack codes designed by different research groups and identifies characteristics that are common to the various classes of attacks.
- implements an easily expandable and configurable threat score based approach.
- Presents true and false positive rates of 97% and 0.75% respectively, the latter based on analysis for Ubuntu Software Center binaries and Android APks.

2 RELATED WORK

The first practical microarchitectural attacks were proposed by Bernstein [9] and Osvik et al. [34]. The first one proposed an attack based on profiling L1 cache collisions while the latter proposed two novel spy process techniques (including the well-known Prime and Probe technique) to create cache contentions. Shortly later, Acıiçmez et al. [5] demonstrated that the spy process techniques were also applicable in the L1 instruction cache. Again Acıiçmez et al. [6] showed that Branch Prediction Units give a similar leakage by inferring whether a victim branch was taken. In 2009, Ristenpart et al. [38] demonstrated that microarchitectural attacks are applicable in commercial clouds by recovering key strokes from core co-resident VMs. Shortly later, Zhang et al. [52] performed the first fine grain attack across VMs by recovering an El Gamal decryption key from a core co-resident VM. At the same time, Gullasch et al. [17] showed that an AES key can be obtained with very few microarchitectural attack traces.

It was in 2013 when Yarom et al. [47] presented the Flush and Reload attack, capable of recovering a RSA key across VMs located in different cores. Shortly later Irazoqui et al. [25] showed that the same technique can be applied to recover AES keys. The Flush and Reload attack was demonstrated to succeed in many other scenarios, like PaaS clouds [51], as a method to perform cache template attacks [16], recover TLS messages [26], work across CPU sockets [24] or even work across smartphone applications [31]. In 2015, concurrent works from Liu et al. [12] and Irazoqui et al. [23] demonstrated to bypass this requirement by implementing the Prime and Probe attack on the LLC. Later, Oren et al. [33] showed that this attack can be further executed from a javascript inside a local browser, Inci et al. [21] demonstrated its feasibility in commercial clouds and Gruss et al. presented its applicability across cores and in mobile devices [31, 35]. Pessl et al. used similar techniques to perform a cross-core DRAM access based attack [36].

In contrast, rowhammer attacks have been exploited for as little as two years. In 2014, Kim et al. [28] discovered that by constantly accessing a DRAM location bit flips can be induced in adjacent DRAM rows, and called this effect the rowhammer attack. Shortly later, Gruss et al. [14] demonstrated to implement rowhammer attacks from javascript, while Bhattacharya et al. [10] showed that faults in cryptographic implementations can be induced with the same technique. Recently, Xiao et al. [44] demonstrated that intelligent execution of rowhammer attacks from a VM to break the memory isolation provided by virtualization, while Van der veen et al. [41] showed the applicability of rowhammer in mobile platforms.

Memory bus locking attacks were presented by Varadarajan et al. [42] and Xu et al. [45] to detect performance degradations and infer co-residency. Shortly later Zhang et al. [50] and Inci et al. [22] demonstrated that the technique can be used to cause Quality of Service degradation in co-resident processes.

Microarchitectural attack defenses have also been studied at several levels. In fact, microarchitectural attacks against security critical software exploit human coding mistakes. Aiming at fixing those mistakes, code sanity verification frameworks were proposed in [7] and [48]. Further, microarchitectural attacks can also be stopped at the OS level. For instance, Taesoo et al. [27] proposed a page coloring mechanism to avoid cache attack collisions, while Liu et al. [32] utilized the Intel Cache Allocation Technology (CAT) to prevent cache attacks. Similarly Zhou et al. [53] propose new page access based countermeasures against cache side channel attacks and Basser et al. [11] proposed two software based mechanisms to prevent rowhammer attacks. Countermeasures also can be adopted at the hardware level by proposing new microarchitectural isolation techniques to avoid exploitations [43].

3 MICROARCHITECTURAL ATTACKS

This section gives a brief description on the functionality of microarchitectural attacks that have been prosposed in the last years.

3.1 Cache Attacks

Cache attacks take advantage of cache collisions occurring in some shared cache in the cache hierarchy. These collisions are detected by measuring access times, i.e., by distinguishing accesses between two levels in the same cache hierarchy or between accesses to the cache hierarchy and accesses to the DRAM. Although several attack designs have been proposed, two (and their combinations) stand out over the rest: the Flush and Reload and the Prime and Probe attacks.

```
1   int probe(char *adrs) {
2     volatile unsigned long time;
3
4     asm __volatile__ (
5       "   mfence          \n"
6       "   lfence          \n"
7       "   rdtsc           \n"
8       "   lfence          \n"
9       "   movl %%eax, %%esi \n"
10      "   movl (%1), %%eax  \n"
11      "   lfence          \n"
12      "   rdtsc           \n"
13      "   subl %%esi, %%eax \n"
14      "   clflush 0(%1)   \n"
15      : "=a" (time)
16      : "c" (adrs)
17      : "%esi", "%edx");
18    return time < threshold;
19  }
```

Figure 1: Flush and Reload code snippet from [47].

The Flush and Reload attack assumes memory sharing between victim and attacker and is performed in three major steps. In the first step, the attacker removes a shared memory block from the cache hierarchy (e.g., with the clflush instruction). In the second step, the attacker lets the victim- interact with the shared memory block by waiting a specified number of cycles. In the last step, the attacker re-accesses the removed memory block. If the memory block comes from the cache (i.e. a fast access time observed) she derives that the victim utilized the memory block during the waiting period. Flush and Reload attacks have been exploited in [16, 25, 47].

The Prime and Probe attack does not make any special assumption between victim and attacker (rather than sharing the underlying hardware) and is also performed in three major steps. In the first step, the attacker fills a portion of the cache (usually a set) with his own data. Then the attacker waits again hoping to observe activity from the victim. In the third step, he re-accesses the data he used to fill part of the cache. If all his data comes from the cache (i.e. low access times) the attacker assumes the victim did not use the portion of the cache she filled (otherwise one of her data lines would have been evicted). Prime and Probe attacks were exploited in [12, 23].

Combinations of both techniques have also shown to be successful at executing attacks. For instance, a Prime and Reload approach would be successful in those systems in which users do not have access to a clflush like instruction, while the Flush and Flush

```
loop:
    mov    (X), %eax
    mov    (Y), %ebx
    clflush (X)
    clflush (Y)
    mfence
    jmp        loop
```

Figure 2: Rowhammer code snipper from [28].

approach is designed to run in a stealthier mode than the rest [15]. We will prove that such a stealthiness does not bypass our countermeasure.

3.2 DRAM Access Attacks

The DRAM is usually divided in channels (physical links between DRAM and memory controller), Dual Inline Memory Modules (DIMMS, physical memory modules attached to each channel), ranks (bank and front of DIMMS), banks (analogous to cache sets) and rows (analogous to cache lines). If two addresses are physical adjacent they share the same channel, DIMM, rank and bank. DRAM access side channel attacks take advantage of collisions produced between addresses physically adjacent, i.e., in the same bank, rank, DIMM and channel. More precisely, retrieving a memory location from the row buffer yields faster accesses than retrieving it from the bank. In order to build a successful attack, an attacker would first have to prime the row buffer. Then he would have to evict the cache portion that the target memory location occupies, making sure that the next victim access will hit the DRAM. Finally, the attacker probes the row buffer to check whether the victim accessed memory locations within the same bank .The attack was exploited in [35].

3.3 Rowhammer Attacks:

Rowhammer attacks take advantage of disturbance errors that occur in adjacent DRAM rows within the same DRAM bank. Continuous accesses to a DRAM row can indeed influence the charge of adjacent row cells, making them leak at a higher rate. If these cells loose charge faster than the charge refreshing interval, accesses to a DRAM row induce bit flips in adjacent rows in the same bank. In order to execute a rowhammer attack, an attacker performs three essential steps. The attacker first opens a row that resides in the same bank as the row in which bit flips want to be induced. Then the attacker performs accesses to the DRAM row, trying to influence the charge leak rate of adjacent rows. In the third step, the attacker removes the accessed DRAM row from the cache hierarchy to ensure the next subsequent accesses will access the DRAM. Examples of studies in rowhammer attacks are [10, 14, 28].

3.4 Memory Bus Locking Covert Channels:

Memory Bus Locking attacks take advantage of pipeline flushes that occur when atomic operations are performed on data that occupies more than one cache line. However, if the atomic operation is performed on data that fits within a single cache line the system locks the cache line for the atomic operation to happen. The pipeline flushing operations cause pipeline flushes that incur in performance overheads that have been used as a method to establish covert channels and derive co-residency in IaaS clouds and as a mechanism to perform Quality of Service degradation (QoS) [22, 42].

4 MASCAT: A STATIC ANALYSIS TOOL FOR MICROARCHITECTURAL ATTACKS

All countermeasures proposed to detect microarchitectural attacks so far are based on dynamically detecting specific microarchitectural patterns when the binary is executed. We observe two clear problems with this approach. First, the adoption of some of those mechanisms might not be in control of online app distributors, who might be blamed if an application offered in their repository succeeds attacking an end device. Second, these attacks can be embedded into a binary to be executed only after some specific time/date or event. Thus, the system should be monitoring the microarchitectural patterns of the binary every time it is executed.

The most common approach to validate its sanity before it is executed is to utilize an antivirus software. Although antivirus tools might work well with certain kind of malware [40], their success detecting microarchitectural attacks is still an open question. Table 1 shows the outcome of such an analysis using well known antivirus software (the best in 2016, as stated in [30]). We utilized all our examples of cache, DRAM, rowhammer and memory bus locking attacks. None of the antivirus softwares were able to detect that the binaries were malicious, except for the Drammer apk [41], which was detected by 7 of 9 antivirus tools.

In order to cope with this problem, we propose MASCAT, a tool that detects intrinsic characteristics of microarchitectural attack code in potentially malicious binaries. Furthermore, it can be offered as an online scanner for microarchitectural attack code. The following section details on the methodology that our static analysis approach uses to detect malicious microarchitectural attacks.

4.1 Identifying Implicit Characteristics of Microarchitectural Attacks

In this section we review those characteristics that well known microarchitectural attacks exhibit in their design. More in particular, we put our focus in Cache/DRAM attacks, memory bus locking and rowhammer attacks.

4.1.1 Cache/DRAM Attacks.

As already explained in the background section, cache attacks are implemented by creating cache contentions in any of the caches in the cache hierarchy. Similarly, DRAM attacks work by successfully creating contentions in a DRAM row buffer. We find that both attacks have three main characteristics in common:

High Resolution Timers Cache and RAM attacks rely on the ability of distinguishing different access patterns (e.g. L1 accesses from LLC accesses or even memory accesses). As these accesses differ at most by a few hundred cycles, the attacker needs to have access to a timer accurate enough to carry out an attack. These timers can be accessed in many different ways (e.g., the common `rdtsc` function or an incremental thread).

Memory Barriers Another common factor of these attacks is the utilization of memory barriers to ensure serialization before the targeted reads are executed (i.e. making sure any load and stores have finished before the target access). These memory barriers can sometimes be embedded in timer instructions (like the popular `rdtscp` instruction) or can come in the form of different instructions.

Cache Evictions The last factor that all cache and DRAM attacks have in common is the implementation of an eviction routine that removes a target cache line from the cache hierarchy. This can be implemented with the popular flush instruction (in the case of shared memory) or with the creation of eviction sets.

4.1.2 Rowhammer Attacks.

Rowhammer attacks are perhaps the microarchitectural attack with the most dangerous implications that has been discovered in the last decade, due to the ability of flipping bits from memory locations belonging to a victim. Rowhammer attacks only have one clearly distinguishable characteristic:

Cache Bypassing Rowhammer attacks rely on continuous access to a DRAM location that shares the DRAM bank with the victims memory location. Thus, attackers need to continuously bypass the cache, otherwise the CPU will bring the accessed DRAM portion to the cache for faster access.

4.1.3 Memory Bus Locking Covert Channels.

Memory bus locking covert channels also have their own characteristics that need to be accomplished in their design:

High Resolution Timers As with cache attacks, memory bus locking mechanisms require a fine grain timer to measures the transmission of a 1 or 0 bit depending on the time to execute atomic operations.

Lock Instructions In addition to the fine grain timer, these attacks also require of specific atomic instructions capable of locking the memory bus. In x86-64 systems these instructions include, among others, the ADC, ADD, AND with the lock prefix or the XCHG instruction without it.

4.2 Attributes Analyzed by MASCAT

This section summarizes the attributes that MASCAT detects within the binary code, given the analysis done in the previous paragraphs. None of the attributes below described was designed by taking any attack code as example, but rather acquiring the knowledge from the previous section. Note that more attributes can be added to cover more sophisticated and intelligent designs of microarchitectural attacks. All the attributes below are critical only when used in a loop, with the exception of the affinity assignment.

Cache Flushing Instructions: Cache flushing instructions are included in the ISA to perform cache coherency operations often needed in parallel processing. These instructions are commonly used for both cache attacks as well as DRAM access and rowhammer attacks, as they allow the user to evict a memory block from the cache. Intel utilizes the `clflush` instruction for this purpose, while ARM utilizes the `DC CIVAC` instructions (only available from ARMv8 on).

Table 1: As of 04.28.2017, none of the major antivirus tools detects the majority of the attacks we analyzed (✗means non-detected and ✓means detected). The only exception is Drammer, which is detected by 7 out of 9 antiviruses.

Antivirus software	Output cache/ DRAM attack	Output rowhammer	Output bus locking	Output Drammer [41]
Avast	✗	✗	✗	✓
BitDefender	✗	✗	✗	✓
Emsisoft	✗	✗	✗	✗
ESET-NOD32	✗	✗	✗	✓
KasperSky	✗	✗	✗	✓
F-secure	✗	✗	✗	✓
McAfee	✗	✗	✗	✓
Symantec	✗	✗	✗	✓
TrendMicro	✗	✗	✗	✗

Non-temporal Instructions: Non-temporal instructions permit the access to a memory location bypassing the cache hierarchy, i.e., making a direct DRAM access. Obviously, these instructions can be utilized as part of a rowhammer attack, which requires several accesses to the same DRAM bank. Examples of these instructions are the `monvnti` and `movntdq` for Intel or `STNP` for ARM.

Monotonic Timers, Thread Counters, Performance Counters, Specialized Fine-grain Timer Instructions: Fine grain timers are utilized by cache and DRAM attacks and by bus locking covert channels. Such timers can be built utilizing specialized instructions like the `rdtscp` and `rdtsc` instructions on Intel or the `c9` register on ARM. In contrast to `rdtsc`, `rdtscp` further implements memory barrier instructions before reading the clock cycle counter. Similarly, performance counters can be queried to get the number of elapsed clock cycles or the number of evictions. These can be detected through the execution of those specific instructions in the ISA. If none of these natural counters are accessible, a timer can be created by using a thread continuously incrementing a counter. MASCAT tries to detect such timers by finding continuous incremental threads, e.g., small loops constantly incrementing a variable. Lastly, and by far the noisiest method, one can utilize access to monotonic timers offered by the OS. MASCAT tries to detect that mechanisms by detecting OS calls to those specific monotonic timers.

Memory Barrier Instructions: These instructions are necessary to prevent out of order execution and to obtain accurate timings from the fine grain timers. Instructions that execute memory barrier operations in x86-64 are `lfence` (to ensure all loads have finished) and `mfence` and `cpuid` loads (to ensure all loads and stores have finished). In ARM, this can be achieved by the `DSB`, `ISB` and `DMB` instructions.

Lock Instructions: Atomic instructions that can be issued to implement memory bus locking attacks. Our tool monitors for all the instruction with the lock prefix plus the `XCHG` instruction in x86-64 binaries, as well as for `LDREX` and `STREX` instructions in ARM binaries.

Jump Ocodes: L1 instruction cache attacks are commonly designed utilizing several and continuous jump opcodes to jump to set concurrent addresses. MASCAT analyzes whether those opcodes are suspiciously being assigned and utilized.

Pointer Chasing & Page Size Jump Approaches: One of the approaches that can be taken to create cache eviction sets (which can be utilized for cache, DRAM access and rowhammer attacks) is the pointer chasing approach, in which the address of the next address is stored in contents of the previous address. This is performed to avoid the introduction of additional variables, thereby minimizing noise effects. In this case we detect whether register continuous access addresses as the previous content of the register.

Selfmap Translation & Slice Mappings Although non-available from userspace since linux kernel 4.0.0, prior kernels are still vulnerable to having an attacker looking at the physical address of his memory to facilitate eviction set creations. Aiming at avoiding these attacks, our tool also identifies accesses to this particular mapping, e.g, accessing the translation file). Further, in the case of x86-64 binaries, our tool also finds whether the *known* slice selection algorithms are utilized in the binary code to guess the slice location of the memory addresses, which are usually hardcoded in the binary.

Affinity Assignment Some of the above mentioned attacks (like the L1 cache attacks or LLC attacks) only succeed when core co-residency or CPU cluster co-residency are achieved. Thus, our tool also tries to identify whether there is any affinity assignment through function calls like `sched_setaffinity` or `CPU MASK` inside the inspected binary code.

4.3 Overall Design

One of the most important challenges of the design of our tool is to determine, based on the attributes observed, whether a threat exists or not. Although we could use machine learning algorithms to design such a methodology, we believe there are several facts that have to be taken into account (e.g. location of the attributes, location of the nested functions calling the functions where the attributes were found, etc.) that can make machine learning algorithms to perform poorly. In contrast, we design MASCAT to retrieve those

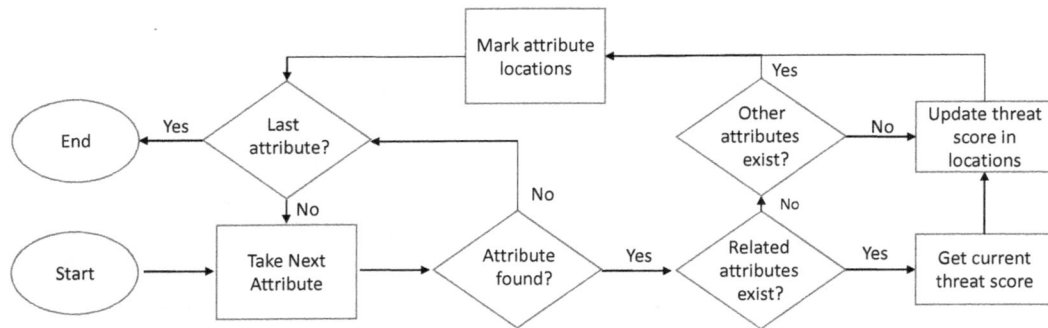

Figure 3: Attribute analysis and threat score update implemented by MASCAT.

facts, such that we do not have a necessity for utilizing an automated data analysis tool. In particular we design our tool to retrieve:

- **Location of an attribute and functions interacting with it:** Particularly useful is the knowledge of the location in which these attributes are observed. MASCAT is designed to retrieve all locations from which the code can reach the location where an attribute is observed, i.e., all possible functions that can reach the location in which the attribute was found.
- **Interaction between attributes:** A key factor of microarchitectural attacks is not only the attributes they exhibit, but also the relation between them. In that sense, MASCAT takes into account where and how attributes interact with each other to decide whether a microarchitectural attack exists.

In order to achieve the goals described above, we decide to implement a score system based on the combination of attributes observed. The main idea is represented in Figure 3. We first group the aforementioned attributes together, depending on their relation to each of the attacks. For instance, we know cache attacks utilize of timers, cache evictions and memory barriers, while rowhammer only needs of cache bypassing to perform an attack. We consider the attributes that compose an attack related attributes, i.e., the related attributes for cache attacks are timers, cache evictions and memory barriers.

To properly analyze all the segments of the binary, we design MASCAT to discover related attributes within loops, as all of them are only a threat only if executed in a loop. MASCAT considers a loop as any jump instruction to a preceding address within the same function. Further, MASCAT should not only consider marking attributes being executed in a loop within a function, as in fact, the function can be called from another code location in a loop. Thus our tool performs the following location based scanning:

(1) Upon the discovery of an attribute, MASCAT looks for the smallest loop in which the attribute is being used within the function where it was found. If a loop is found, the entire loop is marked with the appropriate threat score.

(2) If no loop is found in the function where the attribute is used, MASCAT finds the code locations where this function is being called.

(3) MASCAT again analyzes whether those code locations are executed in a loop to mark them with the appropriate threat score.

(4) if MASCAT finds that a loop is already marked by the attribute being analyzed, MASCAT does not re-mark that loop.

MASCAT therefore does consider an attribute to be found until it sees the attribute (or the functions that use the attribute) being used in loops. If those requirements are observed we call those code locations as *attribute areas*. For instance, if the *flush* is observed to be executed in a loop, we call the loop a "flush instruction area".

MASCAT analyzes, one by one, and *ordered by threat magnitude* (from maximum to minimum) all the attributes we described in Section 4.2 trying to find their attribute areas. However, MASCAT also has to define the relation between areas belonging to different attributes. As we said, an attack might not be distinguishable as long as different attributes do not interact with each other. We call these *related attributes*. To cope with that issue we designed MASCAT to make the following changes to the disassembled representation of the binary:

- If an attribute is found in the binary and no other attribute exists within the same areas, the areas are marked and assigned with the threat score of the attribute we are currently analyzing.
- If other non-related attributes exist within the same areas, the areas are marked as to contain the analyzed attribute and the areas are assigned the highest threat score between the attributes.
- If other related attributes exist within the same area, the area is marked as to contain the attribute analyzed and the threat score is updated with the addition of the threat scores of the related attributes and the attribute currently being analyzed.

Our design prevents us from raising an alarm if two attributes are found but do not interact with each other. In the following we describe the threat score assigned to each of the attributes analyzed.

4.4 Measuring the threat score:

The relations between characteristics are defined according to the description given in Section 4.1. In order to detect the set of microarchitectural attacks discussed, we designed the following score based threat classification:

- **Maximum Threat Attributes:** Attributes from this category are immediately considered a threat. Specific flushing instructions, non-temporal stores and selfmap translation attributes fall into this category. The first two because they can directly imply a rowhammer attack, the latter one because having access to the physical address space can become a threat for both cache and DRAM access rowhammer attacks. The location where these attributes (and the functions calling them) are found will be marked in red.
- **Medium Threat Attributes:** Attributes from this category are not immediately considered threats but rather warnings. The locations in which these attributes are found will only be considered a threat if the rest of the necessary attributes (as described in Section 4.1) are found within the same location of the code. Examples of these attributes are rdtscp and lock instructions, as well as pointer chasing, set-concurrent jumps and jump opcode assignments. A combination of two related medium threat attributes will immediately be considered a threat, while a combination of two non-related medium threat attributes will not change the score. For instance, rdtscp and lock instructions together would be considered a threat, while lock instructions with pointer chasing functions are not (see Section 4.1).
- **Low Threat Attributes:** Attributes from this category are not immediately considered threats but rather small warnings. Only if these attributes are observed within the same location of necessary medium or low threat attributes the code portion is considered a threat. Examples of these kind of attributes are memory barriers, timers (excluding rdtscp) and affinity assignments. Only if two low threat attributes are observed with a medium threat attribute the code location is classified as a threat.

4.5 Tool Framework

In order to implement the specified design we utilize the popular IDA PRO static binary analyzer. We chose IDA because it offers a high level programming language and several built-in functions that facilitate our attribute finding design and also permit us design MASCAT with a nicer graphical view. Note that developing our tool with another open source static binary analyzer (e.g. hooper or radare) should also be feasible with an extra amount of work.

In summary, MASCAT works by analyzing elf files *without the need for the source code*. The tool detects the attributes described above, coloring those locations where microarchitectural attack related features are found. Our tool is designed with a friendly user interface that colors area threat scores in red, warnings in orange and small warnings in magenta, depending on the attributes found within the area. Note that, as MASCAT finds new attributes in already colored locations, the colors of those locations might change. Further, the address where the attribute (or a calling function of the attribute) is found is commented to represent the threat found. Once the analysis is finished, MASCAT scans the entire binary and outputs a summary of the locations in which threats and warnings were found and their root of cause (e.g., rdtsc instruction, lock instructions, etc.). Figure 4 shows a visual example of an analysis made to one of our microarchitectural attacks. We lightened the

red color to improve the quality of the picture in this paper, but the area is marked as red (and therefore, a threat) by MASCAT. The binary is considered a threat for utilizing both flush and fine grain timer instructions, which are representative of cache attacks. Note that in this particular case, the attributes where found to be used within a loop when the function is called, and not within the function containing the attributes.

While our analysis on x86-64 binaries is performed in a single step, our analysis on Android APKs needs to be performed in a dual step. First, the attributes that we look for are scanned within the existing native code in the apk, as with x86-64 binaries. However, we find this non-sufficient, as although the necessary attributes might be found, they might only interact together in the Dalvik Executable (DEX) code. Indeed, as we do not only look for the existence but also the interaction of these parameters, checking only the native code is insufficient to conclusively categorize our attack types. For that reason, the DEX file is analyzed in a second step to check its interaction with the native code, trying to find whether the attributes interact with each other. Thus, we not only marked attributes being utilized in a loop within the native code, but also record the functions in which these have been observed. These functions are further analyzed in the DEX code to see whether again, they are being used constantly in loops. Upon an interaction being found in both steps, we categorize the APK as an attack. This approach prevents an attacker from creating microarchitectural attacks that interact and are called in the DEX file.

5 EXPERIMENT SETUP

Our analysis includes the Mastik tool (which performs all range of L1 and LLC attacks) designed by Yarom et al. [46], LLC attacks and memory bus locking attacks designed by Inci et al. [19] and Irazoqui et al. [21, 23, 25], LLC, cache prefetching, DRAM access and rowhammer attacks designed by Gruss et al. [13–16, 35], rowhammer attacks by Van der Veen et al. [41], rowhammer attacks designer Google Project Zero (which were modified to cover [37]), cache attacks from Tampere university [4], all versions of cache attacks for ARM designed by Lipp et al. [31] and DRAM access attacks designed by Abraham Fernandez, former Intel employee. Some of these codes were modified to cover additional cases (e.g. double-sided rowhammer or cache level variations). In total, we cover a total of 32 main different microarchitectural attacks (plus their variations). Note that, although this number might seem low in comparison with other kind of malware, microarchitectural attacks have not being that extensively utilized and exploited and therefore we are constrained in the range that we can consider. Although the attack sets available publicly is limited it should still be representable of the capabilities of MASCAT. Note further that MASCAT was not designed taking any of these particular attacks as an example.

Our false positive analysis covers both x86-64 binaries compiled under Linux OSs and ARM targeted Android APKs. As the x86-64 benign binary set that was included for our test framework, we chose around 750 binaries from the Ubuntu Software Center plus the Phoronix test-suite [1]. The binaries chosen were mainly the universe repository binaries, whose checksums (including the Phoronix test-suite checksum, version 5.2.1) can be obtained from [2]. The

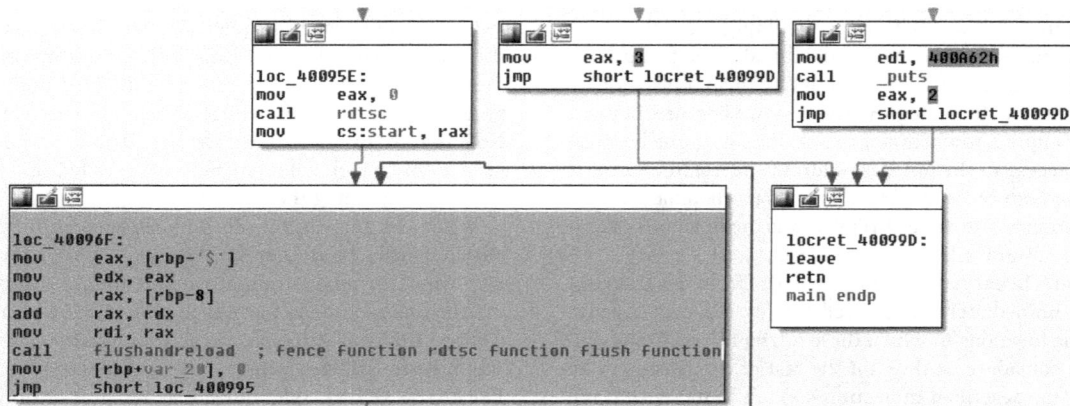

Figure 4: Example output of MASCAT, in which a flush and reload attack is detected.

Phoronix test-suite choice was not random, but was intended to maximize the number of false positives that our tool can output, as it contains performance benchmarks that might use some of the attributes that our tool looks for. In the case of android APKs we analyzed all the applications offered by www.androiddrawer.com, which contain applications with a huge variety of functionalities, e.g., media streaming or communication. We analyzed the most recent version of the apps as per 15th of February of 2017. In total we have analyzed 1268 Android applications. Note that these websites include some of the most widely used applications such as Netflix, Telegram or Whatsapp.

6 RESULTS

This section presents the results obtained both from analyzing (a priori) benign and malicious applications. The idea behind this analysis is to obtain a notion for the false negative/positive rate that MASCAT presents in real world applications. We first present an analysis on the detection rate of all the microarchitectural attack codes that we were able to obtain. Next, in order to obtain a good estimation on the false positive rate that MASCAT presents with regular-purpose binaries, we analyze over 700 and a thousand Ubuntu Software Center and Android applications respectively.

6.1 Analysis of Microarchitectural Attacks

We evaluate the full range of microarchitectural attacks that we described in Section 5, i.e., a list of 32 different microarchitectural attacks. Note that these attacks include both x86-64 binaries and Android APKs, compiled with Android NDK. The results, are presented in Table 2, which expresses the number of attacks that were correctly flagged detected by MASCAT.

We observe that the overall success rate of MASCAT was of 96.87% for the 32 malicious attacks we analyzed. In particular, MASCAT was able to correctly identify all cache attacks and bus locking covert channels, and all but one rowhammer attack codes (including their slide variations to cover additional cases). The only code that MASCAT was not able to identify was Drammer [41]. The reason behind it is that the authors utilize special DMA memory allocation that does not get loaded in the cache, and therefore no flushing, non-temporal loads nor eviction sets are necessary to

Table 2: Percentage of attacks correctly flagged by MASCAT (true positives).

Attack Type	Number of attacks	% of attacks correctly flagged
Cache attacks	25	100%
Rowhammer	5	80%
Bus Locking	2	100%
Total	**32**	**96.87%**

apply it. Therefore, it utilizes characteristics that were not considered in our initial common set characteristics MASCAT design. Although those characteristics not taken into account at design time can be added to cover the entire range of attacks, our initial MASCAT design was able to successfully detect all but one attacks without further modification. Further, as we stated in Section 4, Drammer is the *only attack that is identified by regular commercial antivirus tools*. Thus, we believe that MASCAT can also be used in conjunction with regular malware antivirus tools to catch the entire attack spectrum.

6.2 Results for Benign Binaries

As for the x86-64 benign binaries, the results are presented in Table 3, in which binaries are divided into groups as we downloaded them from the Ubuntu Software Center. We observed that even though binaries with at least one attribute of those we were looking for are rather common (30%), we only had 9 binaries in total that were categorized as threats. Particularly interesting is the case of including the Phoronix-test suite in our analysis, as 6 of the 9 binaries categorized as threats were part of it. This is not that surprising considering that Phoronix test-suite binaries are usually benchmarking applications. The overall false positive rate was 1.2%, thereby showing that most of the binaries are correctly identified as non-dangerous code.

Table 5 shows the reason why those 9 binaries flagged as threats. Nqueens, multichase, mencoder and fs_mark benchmarks flagged due to the usage of non-temporal instructions, which are indicators of a potential rowhammer attack. Aseprite, Claws mail, Fldigi, Fio

Table 3: Results for different groups of binaries from Ubuntu Software Center.

Group functionality	Number of binaries	% of binaries with at least one attribute	% of binaries considered threat
accessories	122	18	0
education	73	19.17	0
developer tools	96	23.9	0
games	116	42.2	0
graphics	84	36.9	1.2
internet	76	25.0	2.63
office	75	12	0
phoronix	100	56	6
total	742	30.05	1.2

Table 4: Results for different groups of APKs.

Group functionality	Number of APKs	% of APKs with at least one attribute	% of APKs considered threat
books	28	42	0
cars	3	0	0
comic	10	30	0
communication	130	32.3	1.53
education	49	16.3	0
entertainment	48	31.25	0
finance	35	22.8	2.86
food	1	100	0
games	130	32.3	0
health	65	24.61	1.53
libraries-demo	2	0	0
life style	30	26.6	0
media video	25	64	0
music audio	39	48.7	0
magazines	52	19.2	0
personalization	59	20.33	0
photography	64	50	0
productivity	144	22.2	0
shopping	24	29.1	0
social	59	32.2	0
sports	16	20	0
tools	175	23.4	0
transport	20	20	0
travel	38	34.2	0
video transport	1	100	0
weather	21	19	0
total	1268	28.3	0.31

and ffmpeg binaries flagged because of the usage of timers, memory barriers and pointer chasing/set congruent jump instructions within the same areas, which might indicate potential DRAM/Cache attack binaries. Lastly fs_mark and again ffmpeg flagged because of the usage of timers and atomic instructions, indicating a potential memory bus locking covert channel exploitation.

In the case of Android applications, a total of 1268 APKs were analyzed, for which table 4 presents per group threat detection statistics, including the percentage of APKs within the group that presented at least one of the attributes we look for, and the percentage of APKs that were considered a threat. Our overall results indicate that the number of APKs that might have at least one of the attributes that we look for is rather high, almost 1/3 of the APKs. However, our results also indicate that the number of APKs that we found to be flagged as threat is very low, i.e., only 4 of the total of 1268 APKs were considered threats. These applications are google

Table 5: Explanation for benign binaries classified as threats.

binary flagged	Reason
Ubuntu Software Center:	
aseprite	timers, memory barriers and pointer chasing
claws mail	timers, memory barriers and pointer chasing
ffmpeg	timers, memory barriers pointer chasing and lock
fio	timers, memory barriers and pointer chasing
fldigi	timers, memory barriers and pointer chasing
fs_mark	timers, lock and non-temporal load/store
mencoder	non-temporal load/store
multichase	non-temporal load/store
nqueens	non-temporal load/store functions
Android APKs:	
google allo	timers, memory barriers, pointer chasing
azar	timers, memory barriers, pointer chasing
eve period	timers, memory barriers, pointer chasing
spendless	timers, memory barriers, pointer chasing

allo, azar, eve period tracker and spendless. As before, Table 5 shows that the 4 APKs flagged because of the same reason: a combination of timers, fences and pointer chasing loop eviction mechanisms that can be an indicator of both cache/DRAM attacks. Thus, we observe that the combination of attributes necessary to develop an attack is rather difficult to observe in benign applications, giving a very low number of false positives.

Although the false positive percentage is low, it still yields a high number once the entire number of apps available is considered. These would have to either be further manually analyzed to make sure they are micro-architectural free or directly rejected. We understand that this is a one time process, as MASCAT could then be incorporated to the already in place manual review that takes place in online application stores, e.g., google play [3].

6.3 Varying the Threat Score

Obviously our false positive rate and our false negative rate will increase/decrease depending on the importance assigned to the attributes found. Table 6 represents the False Negatives (FN) and False Positives (FP) when the score of the attributes are changed to look only for a subset of attacks from our attack vector (rowhammer, memory bus locking, DRAM/cache attacks). We cover DRAM access and cache attacks together, as they share exploitation attributes. Our results show that, due to common characteristics between cache/DRAM access and rowhammer attacks, looking only for rowhammer also gives us zero false negatives for cache/DRAM attack binaries. If only cache/DRAM access attributes are seeked, as non-temporal loads and stores would not directly be considered a threat, nor flushes without the appropriate timers, only 40% of the rowhammer attacks are detected. On the contrary, the nature of bus locking covert channels makes our tool miss cache/DRAM and rowhammer attacks if we only look for memory bus locking characteristics. Finally, we further observe that the false positive rate drops if we only look for one of the attacks, being at most 0.67% in the case of cache attacks.

In summary covering the 4 microarchitectural attack range only lead us to 97% true positive rate in benign benchmarking code and an average of 0.75% when we analyzed a total of around two thousand regular purpose applications. Our results indicate that MASCAT can aid online application vendors to prevent the distribution of microarchitectural attack binaries through their channel,

Table 6: False Negative/Positive variation looking only for a subset of microarchitectural attacks.

Attack targeted	rowhammer	cache/DRAM	bus locking
FN rowhammer	20%	40%	100%
FN cache/DRAM	0%	0%	100%
FN bus locking	100%	100%	0%
FP benign x86-64	0.5%	0.67%	0.26%
FP benign apk	0.31%	0.31%	0%

while still correctly filter most of the benign processes. Further, the threat score presented by MASCAT can be modified to only cover a subset of the attacks we analyzed, in case a particular set of attacks raises more concern than others.

7 LIMITATIONS

As with any other static analysis approach, we need to take into account possible obfuscation techniques that an attacker can implement to bypass MASCAT. Below we include a list of actions that an attacker might try to use to bypass MASCAT:

CISC Instruction Offset Obfuscation: An attacker can take advantage of the variable instruction length in CISC ISAs by inserting arbitrary amount of junk bytes that would later be unreachable during run time. In this way, static disassemblers mistakenly interpret a large part of the binary. As our approach largely depends on a good interpretation of the instructions utilized, this approach would indeed bypass our current version of MASCAT. However, multiple de-obfuscation techniques have been proposed to cope with this issue, both for other disassemblers and for IDA Pro [29, 39]. Thus, our tool can be utilized in conjunction to these to avoid the successful usage of such obfuscation techniques.

RISC Instruction Offset Obfuscation: In this case, since the ARM architecture features a fixed length 32 byte ISA, an attacker can *only* establish four different offset obfuscations. Our defense mechanism would only have to be run with four different offsets (0, 1, 2 and 3 byte offset) to be able to cover all possibilities, thereby detecting the obfuscation.

Encrypted Executable Code: Another popular approach to bypass static analysis is to have a binary that contains, in an encrypted form, the microarchitectural attack. When the binary is executed, the microarchitectural attack is decrypted and saved into another executable binary file. Such an approach would bypass our system, but never other commercial antivirus software. In order to cope with this issue we suggest utilizing MASCAT *together with* other existing antivirus tools: not only to detect this particular malicious case, but to detect whether the binary contains further non-microarchitectural malware.

SGX to Hide Malware: Similar to the approach previously described, but harder to prevent. In fact, if an attacker decides to make use of trusted execution environments like SGX, none of the OS system prevention/detection mechanisms applied to binaries succeed. Since the binaries are encrypted and only decrypted inside the trusted execution environment (out of the control of the OS), MASCAT would not be able to analyze the attributes related to the attacks. However, although a realistic scenario, MASCAT was not designed for that purpose, as in those cases the OS is already considered a potential threat.

Alternative Microarchitectural Attacks: An attacker, knowing the parameters we are looking for, can try to bypass our approach by implementing alternative methodologies to execute an attack. One of the ways to defend against this is to hide the approach that MASCAT performs, so that the attacker does not have a motivation to change his attack patterns. With respect to new attack forms, we encourage the research community to vary their mechanisms so that we incorporate them to MASCAT. An example is [41] whose characteristics were already added to MASCAT after our analysis. However, note that attackers can only vary their implementations as long as the performance of the attack does not deteriorate. This is particularly critical in micro-architectural attacks, as they usually have limited time windows and resolution. Therefore, an attacker might still find difficult to bypass MASCAT without significantly reducing his attack efficiency.

Code Obfuscation: Certainly an attacker might attempt to obfuscate the microarchitectural attack so that it bypasses the analysis performed by MASCAT. Note that this approach is easy to take for certain parameters analyzed in this work, but harder for others. For instance, while it might become a bit easier to obfuscate the usage of a thread inside the code, it is extremely difficult to obfuscate hardware instructions like cycle counters or flushing instructions.

8 CONCLUSION

We presented the first static code analysis tool, MASCAT capable of scanning for common microarchitectural attacks. Microarchitectural attacks are particularly damaging as they are hard to detect since they use standard resources, e.g. memory accesses, made available to applications at the lowest privilege level. Given the rise of malicious code in app stores and online repositories it becomes essential to scan applications for such stealthy attacks. The proposed tool, MASCAT, is ideally suited to fill this need. MASCAT can be used by app store service providers to perform large scale fully automated analysis of applications, and prevent a malicious user from posting a microarchitectural attack in the guise of an innocent looking application to an official app store. The initial MASCAT suite includes attack vectors to cover popular cache/DRAM access attacks, rowhammer and memory bus covert channels. Nevertheless, our tool is easily extensible to include newer attack vectors as they arise.

9 ACKNOWLEDGMENTS

We would like to thank our anonymous reviewers for their valuable comments and suggestions. This work is supported by the National Science Foundation, under grant No. CNS-1618837.

REFERENCES

[1] [n. d.]. Phoronix Test Suite Tests. ([n. d.]). https://openbenchmarking.org/tests/pts.

[2] [n. d.]. Ubuntu Xenial Universe Repository. ([n. d.]). http://archive.ubuntu.com/ubuntu/ubuntu/dists/xenial/universe/binary-amd64/.

[3] 2014. Google Adds Manual Review to Android App Submission Process . (2014).

[4] Onur Aciiçmez, Billy Bob Brumley, and Philipp Grabher. 2010. New results on instruction cache attacks. In *Cryptographic Hardware and Embedded Systems, CHES 2010, 12th International Workshop, Santa Barbara, CA, USA, August 17-20, 2010. Proceedings (Lecture Notes in Computer Science)*, Stefan Mangard and François-Xavier Standaert (Eds.), Vol. 6225. Springer, 110–124.

[5] Onur Aciiçmez. [n. d.]. Yet Another MicroArchitectural Attack: Exploiting I-Cache. In *Proceedings of the 2007 ACM Workshop on Computer Security Architecture.*

[6] Onur Aciiçmez, Çetin K. Koç, and Jean-Pierre Seifert. [n. d.]. Predicting Secret Keys Via Branch Prediction. In *Topics in Cryptology CT-RSA 2007.* Vol. 4377. 225–242. https://doi.org/10.1007/11967668_15

[7] Jose Bacelar Almeida, Manuel Barbosa, Gilles Barthe, François Dupressoir, and Michael Emmi. 2016. Verifying Constant-Time Implementations. In *25th USENIX Security Symposium (USENIX Security 16)*. USENIX Association, Austin, TX, 53–70. https://www.usenix.org/conference/usenixsecurity16/technical-sessions/presentation/almeida

[8] Naomi Benger, Joop van de Pol, Nigel P. Smart, and Yuval Yarom. 2014. "Ooh Aah... Just a Little Bit": A Small Amount of Side Channel Can Go a Long Way.. In *CHES.* 75–92.

[9] Daniel J. Bernstein. 2004. Cache-timing attacks on AES. (2004). URL: http://cr.yp.to/papers.html#cachetiming.

[10] Sarani Bhattacharya and Debdeep Mukhopadhyay. [n. d.]. *Curious Case of Rowhammer: Flipping Secret Exponent Bits Using Timing Analysis.*

[11] Franz Ferdinand Brasser, Lucas Davi, David Gens, Christopher Liebchen, and Ahmad-Reza Sadeghi. 2016. CAn't Touch This: Practical and Generic Software-only Defenses Against Rowhammer Attacks. *CoRR* abs/1611.08396 (2016). http://arxiv.org/abs/1611.08396

[12] Fangfei Liu and Yuval Yarom and Qian Ge and Gernot Heiser and Ruby B. Lee. [n. d.]. Last level cache side channel attacks are practical. In *S&P 2015.*

[13] Daniel Gruss, Clémentine Maurice, Anders Fogh, Moritz Lipp, and Stefan Mangard. 2016. Prefetch Side-Channel Attacks: Bypassing SMAP and Kernel ASLR. In *Proceedings of the 2016 ACM SIGSAC Conference on Computer and Communications Security (CCS '16)*. ACM, New York, NY, USA, 368–379. https://doi.org/10.1145/2976749.2978356

[14] Daniel Gruss, Clémentine Maurice, and Stefan Mangard. 2016. Rowhammer.Js: A Remote Software-Induced Fault Attack in JavaScript. In *Proceedings of the 13th International Conference on Detection of Intrusions and Malware, and Vulnerability Assessment - Volume 9721 (DIMVA 2016)*. Springer-Verlag New York, Inc., New York, NY, USA, 300–321. https://doi.org/10.1007/978-3-319-40667-1_15

[15] Daniel Gruss, Clémentine Maurice, Klaus Wagner, and Stefan Mangard. 2016. Flush+Flush: A Fast and Stealthy Cache Attack. In *Proceedings of the 13th International Conference on Detection of Intrusions and Malware, and Vulnerability Assessment - Volume 9721 (DIMVA 2016)*. Springer-Verlag New York, Inc., New York, NY, USA, 279–299. https://doi.org/10.1007/978-3-319-40667-1_14

[16] Daniel Gruss, Raphael Spreitzer, and Stefan Mangard. 2015. Cache Template Attacks: Automating Attacks on Inclusive Last-Level Caches. In *24th USENIX Security Symposium*. USENIX Association, 897–912. https://www.usenix.org/conference/usenixsecurity15/technical-sessions/presentation/gruss

[17] David Gullasch, Endre Bangerter, and Stephan Krenn. [n. d.]. Cache Games – Bringing Access-Based Cache Attacks on AES to Practice *(SP '11)*. 490–505. https://doi.org/10.1109/SP.2011.22

[18] Mehmet Sinan Inci, Thomas Eisenbarth, and Berk Sunar. 2017. Hit by the Bus: QoS Degradation Attack on Android. In *Proceedings of the 2017 ACM on Asia Conference on Computer and Communications Security (ASIA CCS '17)*. ACM, New York, NY, USA, 716–727. https://doi.org/10.1145/3052973.3053028

[19] Mehmet Sinan İnci, Berk Gülmezoglu, Thomas Eisenbarth, and Berk Sunar. 2016. Co-location detection on the Cloud. In *COSADE.*

[20] Mehmet Sinan İnci, Berk Gulmezoglu, Gorka Irazoqui, Thomas Eisenbarth, and Berk Sunar. 2016. *Cache Attacks Enable Bulk Key Recovery on the Cloud.*

[21] Mehmet Sinan İnci, Berk Gulmezoglu, Gorka Irazoqui, Thomas Eisenbarth, and Berk Sunar. 2016. Cache Attacks Enable Bulk Key Recovery on the Cloud. In *Cryptographic Hardware and Embedded Systems–CHES 2016: 18th International Conference, Santa Barbara, CA, USA, August 17-19, 2016, Proceedings*, Vol. 9813. Springer, 368.

[22] Mehmet Sinan Inci, Gorka Irazoqui, Thomas Eisenbarth, and Berk Sunar. 2016. Efficient Adversarial Network Discovery Using Logical Channels on Microsoft Azure. In *Annual Computer Security Applications Conference.* Los Angeles, CA, US.

[23] Gorka Irazoqui, Thomas Eisenbarth, and Berk Sunar. [n. d.]. S$A: A Shared Cache Attack that Works Across Cores and Defies VM Sandboxing and its Application to AES. In *36th IEEE Symposium on Security and Privacy (S&P 2015).*

[24] Gorka Irazoqui, Thomas Eisenbarth, and Berk Sunar. 2016. Cross Processor Cache Attacks. In *Proceedings of the 11th ACM Symposium on Information, Computer and Communications Security (ASIA CCS '16)*. ACM.

[25] Gorka Irazoqui, Mehmet Sinan İnci, Thomas Eisenbarth, and Berk Sunar. 2014. Wait a Minute! A fast, Cross-VM Attack on AES. In *RAID.* 299–319.

[26] Gorka Irazoqui, Mehmet Sinan İnci, Thomas Eisenbarth, and Berk Sunar. 2015. Lucky 13 Strikes Back. In *Proceedings of the 10th ACM Symposium on Information, Computer and Communications Security (ASIA CCS '15).* 85–96.

[27] Taesoo Kim, Marcus Peinado, and Gloria Mainar-Ruiz. 2012. STEALTHMEM: System-Level Protection Against Cache-Based Side Channel Attacks in the Cloud. In *Presented as part of the 21st USENIX Security Symposium (USENIX Security 12)*. USENIX, Bellevue, WA, 189–204. https://www.usenix.org/conference/usenixsecurity12/technical-sessions/presentation/kim

[28] Yoongu Kim, Ross Daly, Jeremie Kim, Chris Fallin, Ji Hye Lee, Donghyuk Lee, Chris Wilkerson, Konrad Lai, and Onur Mutlu. 2014. Flipping Bits in Memory Without Accessing Them: An Experimental Study of DRAM Disturbance Errors. In *Proceeding of the 41st Annual International Symposium on Computer Architecture (ISCA '14)*. IEEE Press, Piscataway, NJ, USA, 361–372.

[29] Christopher Kruegel, William Robertson, Fredrik Valeur, and Giovanni Vigna. 2004. Static Disassembly of Obfuscated Binaries. In *Proceedings of the 13th Conference on USENIX Security Symposium - Volume 13 (SSYM'04)*. USENIX Association, Berkeley, CA, USA, 18–18. http://dl.acm.org/citation.cfm?id=1251375.1251393

[30] [n. d.]. Best 2016 antivirus. ([n. d.]). http://www.pcmag.com/article2/0,2817,2388652,00.asp.

[31] Moritz Lipp, Daniel Gruss, Raphael Spreitzer, Clémentine Maurice, and Stefan Mangard. 2016. ARMageddon: Cache Attacks on Mobile Devices. In *25th USENIX Security Symposium, USENIX Security 16, Austin, TX, USA, August 10-12, 2016.* 549–564. https://www.usenix.org/conference/usenixsecurity16/technical-sessions/presentation/lipp

[32] Fangfei Liu, Qian Ge, Yuval Yarom, Frank Mckeen, Carlos Rozas, Gernot Heiser, and Ruby B Lee. 2016. CATalyst: Defeating Last-Level Cache Side Channel Attacks in Cloud Computing. In *IEEE Symposium on High-Performance Computer Architecture.* Barcelona, Spain, 406–418.

[33] Yossef Oren, Vasileios P. Kemerlis, Simha Sethumadhavan, and Angelos D. Keromytis. 2015. The Spy in the Sandbox: Practical Cache Attacks in JavaScript and Their Implications. In *Proceedings of the 22Nd ACM SIGSAC Conference on Computer and Communications Security (CCS '15)*. ACM, New York, NY, USA, 1406–1418. https://doi.org/10.1145/2810103.2813708

[34] Dag Arne Osvik, Adi Shamir, and Eran Tromer. [n. d.]. Cache Attacks and Countermeasures: The Case of AES. In *Proceedings of the 2006 The Cryptographers' Track at the RSA Conference on Topics in Cryptology (CT-RSA'06).* https://doi.org/10.1007/11605805_1

[35] Peter Pessl, Daniel Gruss, Clémentine Maurice, Michael Schwarz, and Stefan Mangard. 2016. DRAMA: Exploiting DRAM Addressing for Cross-CPU Attacks. In *25th USENIX Security Symposium (USENIX Security 16)*. USENIX Association, Austin, TX, 565–581.

[36] Peter Pessl, Daniel Gruss, Clémentine Maurice, Michael Schwarz, and Stefan Mangard. 2016. Exploiting DRAM Addressing for Cross-CPU Attacks. In *25th USENIX Security Symposium, USENIX Security 16, Austin, TX, USA, August 10-12, 2016.* 565–581. https://www.usenix.org/conference/usenixsecurity16/technical-sessions/presentation/pessl

[37] Rui Qiao and Mark Seaborn. 2016. A new approach for rowhammer attacks. *2016 IEEE International Symposium on Hardware Oriented Security and Trust (HOST)* 00, undefined (2016), 161–166. https://doi.org/doi.ieeecomputersociety.org/10.1109/HST.2016.7495576

[38] Thomas Ristenpart, Eran Tromer, Hovav Shacham, and Stefan Savage. [n. d.]. Hey, You, Get off of My Cloud: Exploring Information Leakage in Third-party Compute Clouds. In *Proceedings of the 16th ACM Conference on Computer and Communications Security (CCS '09).* 199–212. https://doi.org/10.1145/1653662.1653687

[39] Rolf Rolles. 2016. TRANSPARENT DEOBFUSCATION WITH IDA PROCESSOR MODULE EXTENSIONS. (2016). http://www.msreverseengineering.com/blog/2015/6/29/transparent-deobfuscation-with-ida-processor-module-extensions

[40] Orathai Sukwong, Hyong S Kim, and James C Hoe. 2011. Commercial antivirus software effectiveness: an empirical study. *Computer* 44, 3 (2011), 0063–70.

[41] Victor van der Veen, Yanick Fratantonio, Martina Lindorfer, Daniel Gruss, Clementine Maurice, Giovanni Vigna, Herbert Bos, Kaveh Razavi, and Cristiano Giuffrida. 2016. Drammer: Deterministic Rowhammer Attacks on Mobile Platforms. In *Proceedings of the 2016 ACM SIGSAC Conference on Computer and Communications Security (CCS '16)*. ACM, New York, NY, USA, 1675–1689. https://doi.org/10.1145/2976749.2978406

[42] Venkatanathan Varadarajan, Yinqian Zhang, Thomas Ristenpart, and Michael Swift. 2015. A Placement Vulnerability Study in Multi-Tenant Public Clouds. In *24th USENIX Security Symposium (USENIX Security 15)*. USENIX Association, Washington, D.C., 913–928. https://www.usenix.org/conference/usenixsecurity15/technical-sessions/presentation/varadarajan

[43] Zhenghong Wang and Ruby B. Lee. 2007. New Cache Designs for Thwarting Software Cache-based Side Channel Attacks. In *Proceedings of the 34th Annual International Symposium on Computer Architecture.* 12. https://doi.org/10.1145/

1250662.1250723

[44] Yuan Xiao, Xiaokuan Zhang, Yinqian Zhang, and Radu Teodorescu. 2016. One Bit Flips, One Cloud Flops: Cross-VM Row Hammer Attacks and Privilege Escalation. In *25th USENIX Security Symposium (USENIX Security 16)*. USENIX Association, Austin, TX, 19–35.

[45] Zhang Xu, Haining Wang, and Zhenyu Wu. 2015. A Measurement Study on Co-residence Threat inside the Cloud. In *24th USENIX Security Symposium (USENIX Security 15)*. USENIX Association, Washington, D.C., 929–944. https://www.usenix.org/conference/usenixsecurity15/technical-sessions/presentation/xu

[46] Yuval Yarom. 2016. Mastik: A Micro-Architectural Side-Channel Toolkit. (2016).

[47] Yuval Yarom and Katrina Falkner. [n. d.]. FLUSH+RELOAD: A High Resolution, Low Noise, L3 Cache Side-Channel Attack. In *23rd USENIX Security Symposium (USENIX Security 14)*. 719–732. https://www.usenix.org/conference/usenixsecurity14/technical-sessions/presentation/yarom

[48] Andreas Zankl, Katja Miller, Johann Heyszl, and Georg Sigl. [n. d.]. Towards Efficient Evaluation of a Time-Driven Cache Attack on Modern Processors. In *ESORICS 2016*.

[49] Tianwei Zhang, Yinqian Zhang, and Ruby B. Lee. 2016. *CloudRadar: A Real-Time Side-Channel Attack Detection System in Clouds*.

[50] Tianwei Zhang, Yinqian Zhang, and Ruby B. Lee. 2016. Memory DoS Attacks in Multi-tenant Clouds: Severity and Mitigation. *CoRR* abs/1603.03404 (2016). http://arxiv.org/abs/1603.03404

[51] Yinqian Zhang, Ari Juels, Michael K. Reiter, and Thomas Ristenpart. [n. d.]. Cross-Tenant Side-Channel Attacks in PaaS Clouds. In *Proceedings of the 2014 ACM SIGSAC Conference on Computer and Communications Security*. https://doi.org/10.1145/2660267.2660356

[52] Yinqian Zhang, Ari Juels, Michael K. Reiter, and Thomas Ristenpart. [n. d.]. Cross-VM Side Channels and Their Use to Extract Private Keys. In *Proceedings of the 2012 ACM Conference on Computer and Communications Security*. https://doi.org/10.1145/2382196.2382230

[53] Ziqiao Zhou, Michael K. Reiter, and Yinqian Zhang. [n. d.]. A software approach to defeating side channels in last-level caches. In *CCS 2016*.

Author Index